If you were inclined to lose your mind, you could stay on the Internet all day.
—David Remnick, *New Yorker* Editor

Microsoft no longer has to ask, "Where do you want to go today?"
It already knows.
—Jim Sterns, American Internet-Marketing Specialist

Increasingly, the center of the marketing universe is the customer.
It is the customer who sets the rules and the marketer who responds.
—Robert Wientzen, CEO, Direct Marketing Association

The question for all of us is **are you creating value?**
The Web is a great place for companies of all kinds that are creating
genuine value for customers, and it is a terrible place for companies that are not.
—Jeff Bezos, CEO, Amazon.com

The road to success is dotted with many tempting parking places.
—Anonymous

Put it to them briefly, so they will read it;
clearly, so they will appreciate it;
picturesquely, so they will remember it;
and, above all, accurately, so they will be guided by its light.
—Joseph Pulitzer (1847–1911), American Publisher

Consumers are statistics. **Customers are people.**
—Stanley Marcus (1905–), Chairman Emeritus, Neiman Marcus Department Stores

We've certainly wanted computers to listen—every time we've shouted obscenities at them.
—Lincoln Spector, American Business Writer

**There is only one valid definition of business purpose:
to create a customer.**
—Peter Drucker (1909–), American Business Philosopher and Author

Every company's greatest assets are its customers,
because without customers there is no company.
—Michael LeBoeuf (1942–), American Business Writer

CONTEMPORARY

MARKETING

10TH EDITION

CONTEMPORARY MARKETING

10TH EDITION

LOUIS E. BOONE
Ernest G. Cleverdon Chair of Business and Management
University of South Alabama

DAVID L. KURTZ
The R.A. and Vivian Young Chair of Business Administration
University of Arkansas

SOUTH-WESTERN
————★————™
THOMSON LEARNING

Australia • Canada • Mexico • Singapore • Spain
United Kingdom • United States

SOUTH-WESTERN
★
™
THOMSON LEARNING

Contemporary Marketing, 10e

Louis E. Boone, David L. Kurtz

Publisher:
Mike Roche

Acquisitions Editor:
Bill Schoof

Developmental Editor:
Tracy L. Morse

Market Strategist:
Beverly Dunn

Project Editor:
Claudia Gravier

Art Director:
Linda Beaupré

Production Manager:
James McDonald

Compositor:
GAC/Indianapolis

Printer:
RR Donnelley & Sons
Willard, OH

Cover Designer:
Pierre-Yves Goavec

For permission to use material from
this text or product, contact us by
Tel (800) 730–2214
Fax (800) 730–2215
http://www.thomsonrights.com

Library of Congress Catalog Card
Number: 00-101060

ISBN: 0-03-031403-8

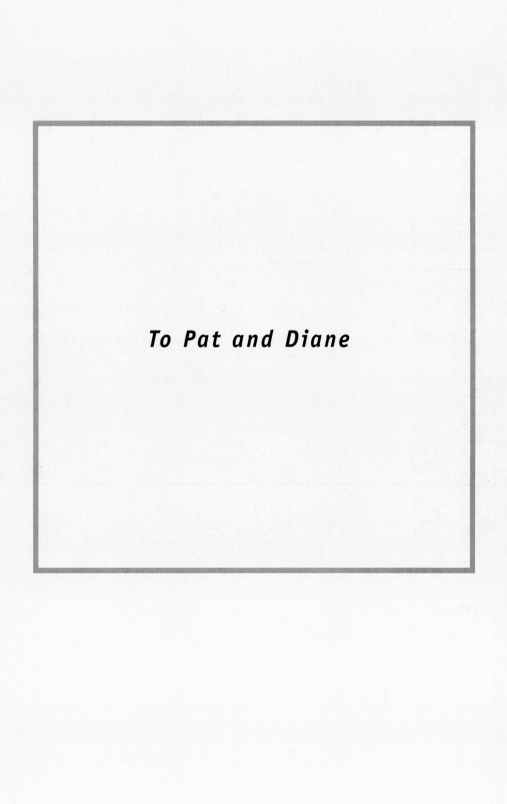

To Pat and Diane

Welcome to *Contemporary Marketing*'s new millennium. Today's marketers know that the key to success is keeping up with change. This challenge seems tougher each day. Consider that e-commerce began less than a decade ago. Today . . . well, you know the story . . . the Internet is the driving force in the economy.

Keeping pace with this technological revolution, the tenth edition of *Contemporary Marketing*, is the *first* text to devote two full chapters (an entire part) to technology issues. Part 2 "Managing Technology to Achieve Marketing Success" explores emerging e-commerce and related concepts. Another chapter considers the impact of technology and the Internet on relationship marketing. Further, greatly expanded Internet and e-commerce materials are also included in virtually every chapter.

We recently ran across a quote that is a good description of our view of the technological revolution occurring in the modern marketplace.

> **Within five years, the term "Internet Company" won't mean anything, because everyone will be an Internet company. The Internet becomes a fundamental part of your business**
>
> Kim Polese, in *So Long, Wild, Wild, Web*[1]

CONTEMPORARY MARKETING FIRSTS

vii

Previous users will recognize that our new orientation is a trend we established way back in the first edition—to lead the principles of marketing with new "firsts." We know that keeping several steps ahead of the competition is the way we became the best selling basic marketing text. We plan to keep it that way.

Consider our record of providing instructors and students with "firsts":

- The FIRST marketing text written specifically for the student—rather than the professor—featuring a clear, concise style which students readily understand and enjoy.
- The FIRST marketing text based on marketing research, written the way instructors actually teach the course.
- The FIRST marketing text to integrate computer application into each chapter.
- The FIRST marketing text to employ extensive pedagogy—such as boxed features—to breathe life into the exciting concepts and issues of marketing.
- The FIRST marketing text to introduce end-of-chapter video cases tied to professionally produced video segments.
- The FIRST marketing text to offer early services and international chapters and to thoroughly integrate those topics throughout with literally hundreds of examples.
- The FIRST marketing text to utilize multimedia technology to integrate all components of the principles of marketing ancillary program—videos, overhead transparencies, and material from the text—enabling instructors to custom create lively lecture presentations.
- The FIRST marketing text to integrate a true technology emphasis throughout the entire package, incorporating a technology theme into every facet: opening vignettes; chapter concepts; end-of-chapter assignments; boxed features; cases; such innovative learning tools as CD-ROMs, multimedia materials, a robust Web site, and much more.
- The FIRST marketing text to include an entire, separate chapter on relationship marketing.

[1]Quoted in Individual Investor.com January, 2000, p. 26

KEY FEATURES OF THE TENTH EDITION

The new edition of *Contemporary Marketing* is also packed full of new innovations. Here are some of the exciting new features of the 10th edition.

NEW! Succinct nineteen-chapter tenth edition introduces readers to the 21st century marketplace with a more streamlined approach.

NEW! End-of-Part Continuing Case on Gateway now includes a strong emphasis on strategy, which enables students to follow one company case through all the marketing functions. The case is integrated with the Boone & Kurtz Web site, which incorporates marketing planning material and activities for each part.

NEW! Eye-catching, easy-to-read, one-column format gives instructors the added margin space they requested for their notes.

NEW! "Strategic Implications" sections in each chapter spotlight the marketing strategy concepts illustrated in chapter material, helping equip readers with a solid foundation in strategic thinking.

NEW! "Ethical Implications" sections in each chapter enhance coverage of marketing ethics by providing specific focus to broader ethical issues involved in decisions affecting product, distribution, promotion, pricing, and other marketing management issues.

NEW! "Strategy Successes" and "Strategy Failures" boxes present concise illustrations of marketing strategy in action—both the good and bad highlights.

COMPLETELY REVISED! Chapter 1, "Customer-Driven Marketing," explores the role of marketing and technology in the 21st century marketplace. Setting the stage for the entire text, the chapter also examines the meaning of marketing and explores the importance of effective marketing strategy.

NEW! Part 2, "Managing Technology to Achieve Marketing Success," incorporates technology issues and the Internet into a new part focusing on interactive marketing and relationship marketing.

NEW! Chapter 4, "E-Commerce: Electronic Marketing and the Internet," takes an in-depth look at e-commerce and e-marketing. This innovative new chapter offers comprehensive coverage of online marketing, including how marketers use the Internet, effective Web designs, marketing strategies driving online campaigns, tools to measure the effectiveness of online marketing efforts, and much more.

NEW! Use of shopping bots in identifying low-price suppliers is discussed in Chapter 19 "Managing the Pricing Function."

REVISED! The Relationship Marketing chapter has been revamped and updated to reflect the latest trends from the field. Presented earlier in the text, the new Chapter 5 explores the impact of database marketing and new technology on relationship marketing.

REVISED! Part 4, "Customer Behavior," reflects the latest thinking on buyer and consumer issues.

NEW! Questions for Critical Thinking have been added to end-of-chapter materials.

UPDATED! "Careers in Marketing" Appendix answers the question "Why study marketing?" It also explores 21st century marketing career opportunities, immediately bringing a current, real world focus to the study of marketing.

New Content

As usual, the authors have updated the text's content to include the latest business practices and topics. Here are just a few examples:

- Coverage of the newly-enacted Children's Online Privacy Act in Chapter 2
- Banners, keyword ads, and insterstitials as online advertising alternatives
- Importance of bandwidth in offering high-quality interactive communication
- Use of cookies in providing personalized customer service in online marketing.
- Enhanced discussion of supply chain management.
- New coverage of enterprise resource planning.
- Expanded coverage of data mining.

- The new NAICS (North American Industrial Classification System), which replaces the SIC codes
- The sale of captive brands in modern merchandising
- The Microsoft ruling and its aftermath
- Updates to ISO 9002 (formerly ISO 9000)
- Growth of inside selling in 21st century promotional mixes
- Yield management as a pricing technique
- Using bundle pricing

Pedagogical Features

Each Chapter includes a "Solving an Ethical Controversy" box which is set up in a debate format. Examples include:

- Fighting Spam (Chapter 4)
- Questionable Advertising Aimed at Teens (Chapter 8)
- PCs for Free? (Chapter 19)

Each chapter of the new edition includes special inserts featuring marketing successes and marketing failures.

Marketing Strategy Successes include:

- International Golf Outlet: Selling Golf Clubs Online (Chapter 4)
- The Grateful Dead is Still Alive (Chapter 15)
- *The Blair Witch Project* Conjures Up Guerrilla Advertising (Chapter 16)

Marketing Strategy Failures include:

- Cigar Craze Burns Out (Chapter 9)
- Pointcast Gets Pushed Out (Chapter 15)
- Buying College Textbooks Online—Not In Line (Chapter 19)

Contemporary Marketing has long been noted for its attention-grabbing opening stories. Here are some examples from the new edition:

- Jeff Bezos Navigates the Mighty Amazon (Chapter 11)
- NBA Tries to Score Big with Its Brand (Chapter 13)
- eBay Customers Name Their Own Price (Chapter 18)

And More Features . . .

In addition to all these unique new innovations, *Contemporary Marketing*, tenth edition, also includes Boone & Kurtz's signature features—all completely updated—which have helped make our text the nation's best seller.

- The tenth edition includes traditional *Contemporary Marketing* strengths, such as early and integrated coverage of services, quality, ethics, social responsibility and international marketing.

- Examples, tables, figures, charts, and graphs have been fully revised or replaced, giving students the most up-to-the-minute insight available on marketing trends and issues as they emerge.

- Chapter opening vignettes bring real world marketing issues and dilemmas to life. These lively illustrations detail how today's technology relates to chapter concepts as they describe how actual companies apply technology to their unique marketing advantage.

- End-of-chapter 'netWork technology exercises give students hands-on experience employing the Internet in a marketing environment. These exercises include problems requiring students to locate data on different Web sites, computer exercises that can be completed on the *Contemporary Marketing* Web site, and follow up assignments, enabling students to further research in-text examples on other Web locations.

- Students like our end-of-chapter achievement oriented summaries that uniquely reinforce chapter concepts by reviewing chapter highlights with quiz like true/false and short multiple-choice questions. This question and answer format which provides a more interactive and creative method for reviewing key chapter concepts and has received rave reviews from students.

- Completely integrated with the text, chapter video case questions include exercises requiring students to apply the concepts they've learned in the chapter. Some cases require students to visit specific Web sites—related to the company or concepts covered in the video to find the solutions.

- Web addresses for companies used as in-text examples are included in the chapter margins.

- Back by student demand, the Marketing Dictionary defines key terms as they appear in the text, providing a list of definitions for each two-page spread.

MARKETING | DICTIONARY

intranet Internal corporate network that allows employees within an organization to communicate with each other and gain access to corporate information.

- New to the tenth edition, numbered chapter objective icons allow students to easily follow and find chapter content for each objective.

Unparalleled Resource Package

Like the nine editions before it, *Contemporary Marketing*, tenth edition, is filled with innovation. The result: the most powerful marketing package available.

We lead the market with precedent-setting learning materials, as well as continuing to improve on our signature package features—equipping students and instructors with the most comprehensive collection of learning tools, teaching materials, and innovative resources available. As per our traditional approach, this edition delivers the most extensive, technologically advanced, user friendly package on the market.

For the Professor

Instructor's Resource Manual

Boone & Kurtz's precedent-setting IRM has been completely revised and revamped to provide an even more innovative, more powerful teaching tool. Instructors will find copious, insightful material in this dynamic resource. The manual for the tenth edition IRM includes: changes from the previous edition; annotated learning goals; key terms; lecture outlines; expanded lecture illustration file; teaching suggestions for ethical controversy boxes; answers to review questions and questions for critical thinking; teaching suggestions/answers to 'netWork exercises; answers to video case questions; guest speaker suggestions; ideas for more than 100 term papers; and more.

NEW! *Media Instructor's Manual*

The Instructor's Media Manual, prepared by Reshma Shah of Emory University, contains comprehensive resource materials to help instructors incorporate the videos, Web resources, and the Instructor's PowerPoint Presentation into lectures and classroom presentations. For the each of the 19 videos, teaching objectives, lists of chapter concepts spotlighted in the videos, outlines of the videos, answers to in-text video case questions, and experiential exercises are included in the Media Manual. Also included are expanded descriptions and instructions on using the Instructor's PowerPoint CD-ROM and the Contemporary Marketing Web Site.

ALL NEW! *Test Bank*

Instructors will be hard pressed to find a more accurate collection of test questions. The tenth edition test bank underwent an exhaustive accuracy review.

This completely revised and updated test bank offers more than questions—the most of any principles text—including application and knowledge-based multiple-choice, true/false, and essay questions for each chapter. Questions vary in level of difficulty, giving instructors a wide variety from which to choose. Each question is keyed to specific text page numbers and level of difficulty. The Test Bank was written by Study Guide author Tom O'Connor of the University of New Orleans in an effort to ensure these two ancillaries thoroughly complement each other.

Computerized Test Bank

Harcourt's newest offering—Examaster—works with the latest version of Windows and Windows NT operating systems. The CD-ROMs include online testing capabilities, a grade book, and much more.

Available in IBM compatible format, the computerized version of the printed test bank enables instructors to preview and edit test questions, as well as add their own questions. The tests and answer keys also can be printed in "scrambled" formats.

RequesTest and Online Testing Service

Harcourt makes test planning quicker and easier than ever with this program. Instructors can order test masters by question number and criteria via a toll free telephone number. Test masters will be mailed or faxed within 48 hours. Dryden can provide instructors with software to install their own online testing program, allowing tests to be administered over network or individual terminals. This program offers instructors greater flexibility and convenience in grading and scoring test results.

Overhead Transparencies

The collection of approximately 200 full-color transparency acetates has been created from striking graphic illustrations and advertisements from the textbook and outside sources.

BRAND NEW! *Instructor's PowerPoint CD-ROM*

Created by Milton Pressley of the University of New Orleans, this is a powerful, easy-to-use multimedia presentation tool. It includes a wealth of resources that will bring your classroom lectures (and your students) to life. It includes virtually all of the illustrations, tables, and charts from the text, plus television commercials and other supplementary material like additional print ads and experiential exercises. Organized by chapter, all of the major definitions, topics, and concepts of the book are outlined along with completely new material from outside sources.

Professors can use this CD-ROM "as is" or may custom design their own multimedia classroom presentations by deleting (or hiding) unwanted slides and/or altering existing slides.

If your presentation computer is connected to the Web, you can even connect to specially selected Web sites by clicking on the WWW icon on many of the slides.

Included on the faculty member's copy of the CD-ROM is the entire instructors manual. For those who so desire, you may cut and paste from the instructors' manual to the note page of the presentation.

Even if you are a novice PowerPoint user in the classroom, you'll come across as the best pre-pared, most knowledgeable marketing instructor ever. The entire presentation is professionally done—it's studio quality. You'll *wow* the students by showing the TV and print ads from within the PowerPoint presentation itself. By using this presentation, your lectures will be as organized as the book itself.

19 BRAND NEW! Videos

This all new, completely custom video package was created especially for *Contemporary Marketing*, tenth edition. These professionally produced contemporary videos are tied directly to chapter concepts. All nineteen new videos were filmed during 1999–2000, giving instructor's exciting, relevant and current videos for the classroom. Each video highlights an attention-getting company and will give students a real world glimpse into how marketers meet the challenges of the marketplace today. The videos include the following companies:

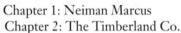

Chapter 1: Neiman Marcus	Chapter 11: Pfizer, Inc.
Chapter 2: The Timberland Co.	Chapter 12: Hasbro, Inc.
Chapter 3: ESPN	Chapter 13: RadioShack
Chapter 4: Tower Records	Chapter 14: Wine.com
Chapter 5: FedEx Corp.	Chapter 15: Polaroid
Chapter 6: Furniture.com	Chapter 16: Pizza Hut
Chapter 7: Fisher Price	Chapter 17: Concept2
Chapter 8: Fresh Samantha	Chapter 18: Cybex International
Chapter 9: Goya Foods, Inc.	Chapter 19: Learjet
Chapter 10: UPS	

Additionally, each video has a written video case with application questions to supplement the actual video case. The written video cases can be found at the end of the textbook.

The video package is further enhanced with an available Instructor's Media Manual that contains comprehensive resource materials to help instructors incorporate the videos into lectures and classroom presentations.

Telecourse Videos for *Marketing*

This telecourse, available through Coast Telecourses, part of the Coast Community College District, introduces students to the fundamentals of contemporary marketing. Basic marketing principles such as product strategy, advertising and promotion, pricing, and distribution and their interrelationships are covered. The telecourse consists of 26 video programs that focus on examples of companies that have successfully applied marketing concepts and principles. These case studies vividly illustrate many of the marketing concepts discussed in the textbook.

NEW! *Contemporary Marketing* Online Course

Delivered via the WebCT platform, this integrated Web-based learning environment combines our market leading textbook and package with the vast resources of the Internet and the convenience of anytime learning. WebCT facilitates the creation of sophisticated Web-based educational environments. It provides a set of course design tools to help you manage course content, a set of communication tools to facilitate online classroom collaboration, and a set of administrative tools for tracking and managing your students' progress.

Extremely user friendly, the powerful customization features of the WebCT framework enable instructors to customize this online course to their own unique teaching styles and their students' individual needs.

Course features include content keyed to the tenth edition, figures and graphs from the tenth edition, self tests and online exams, Internet activities and links to related resources, a suggested course syllabus, student and instructor materials, free technical support for instructors, and much more. In addition, the text's PowerPoint Presentation Software also is integrated into the WebCT course.

NEW! WebCT Testing Service

If testing is all you want, we will upload the computerized Test Bank into a course with no publisher content. If you like, we will even host it for you on our server.

EXPANDED! Boone & Kurtz Web site

Completely revised based on user feedback, this robust site delivers exactly what students and instructors have requested—and much more. This interactive Web site gives students hands-on experience using the Internet as a marketing tool, as well as helps them develop important life skills.

This easy-to-navigate site is contains a wealth of *Marketing Topics.* After following the link to each topic, users will find topic-specific publication links, trends and forecasts, data, company profiles, general articles, tools, exercises and much more. In addition, each topic site links instructors to teaching resources, bibliographies of articles related to text material, ideas on incorporating the Internet into the classroom, and more.

In addition, the *Reading Room* links users to business journals, daily newspapers, magazines, and marketing publications across the country and around the world.

Also, a *Syllabus Generator* is available to help professors quickly customize a course syllabus.

The *Contemporary Marketing* WEB site is a reservoir of marketing information. In fact, it includes so many resources for each chapter that it can be used as the foundation for a distance learning course. Our interactive site helps students sharpen their surfing skills, while driving home key marketing concepts. Located at

http://www.harcourtcollege.com/marketing/boone/

The site is updated regularly.

For Students

. . . and more on the Boone & Kurtz Web site

In addition to the many features that benefit professors and students alike (described above), students will especially find the following useful:

An *Online Quizzing* section allows students to take multiple quizzes comprised of approximately 20 questions per quiz. Quizzes include True/False and Multiple-Choice questions covering content read in each chapter.

A *Marketing Careers* section enables students learn more about marketing careers and locate currently posted business job opportunities. Also, many sites include extensive career information and guidance, such as interviewing techniques and resume writing.

A *time management* section features advice and guidelines on effectively managing your study, work, and leisure time as a college student, including how to set priorities and avoid procrastinating on your studying.

Brand New! *Student PowerPoint CD ROM*

Students will receive their own CD ROM (a condensed version of the Instructor's PowerPoint CD ROM without the extra TV and print ads—or the instructor's manual). However, they'll have all the chapter outline slides to study from. *Plus,* they'll get extra study questions for each chapter. *And,* they'll get a special marketing plan . . . a professionally designed plan they can use by answering the questions asked by the plan.

Study Guide

This comprehensive learning tool is designed to enhance student understanding and provide additional practical application of chapter content. Features include chapter objectives, key concepts, key term exercises, self quizzes featuring multiple-choice and true/false questions, exercises on applying marketing concepts that include cases and short answer questions, surf the 'net exercises, marketing planning exercises, solutions to study questions, and more. Tom O'Connor, of the University of New Orleans, who prepared the Test Bank, also prepared the study guide.

NEW! *Web CT Student Manual*

Included with the Boone & Kurtz Online course, this unique manual offers a wealth of information for Web users, from novices to the most advanced. The manual provides general instruction about the World Wide Web for Internet beginners, while more experienced users can skip to the step-by-step information on how to use WebCT's course tools.

NEW! *The Marketing Game*

This innovative, Web-based computer simulation (also available on CD-ROM), created by Robert Schaffer of California State Polytechnic–Pomona, offers a marketing simulation game with some novel twists. The underlying model is based on the digital camera industry and helps students develop their marketing skills within the framework of an evolving product life cycle.

Large classes can play *The Marketing Game* in solitaire mode, with each student competing against computer-generated opponents. The option greatly reduces classroom game management. The game's link to the Internet also allows competitive play between teams of students at different universities.

The Marketing Game is available on the Boone & Kurtz Web site or it can be shrink-wrapped with the text.

Discovering Your Marketing Career CD-ROM

An expanded version of the popular Marketing Career Design Software, this CD enables students to explore career opportunities in marketing based on their personal interests and skills. Along with the traditional software's features—self-assessment tools, resume and letter writing assistance—this newly expanded CD also adds videos, interviews with marketing professionals, and an interactive student study component integrated with chapter material. Also, a comprehensive study program and tutorial written in Windows allows students to learn key words and concepts and to test their knowledge of each chapter through matching quizzes, true/false tests, and multiple-choice tests. Students can use the glossary to reinforce terms and concepts from each chapter. Chapter outlines and summaries provide a comprehensive look at each chapter. This unique CD-ROM program reinforces text material, provides practical application of chapter concepts, and gives students a real-world taste of actual careers and career paths in today's market.

Telecourse Study Guide

A Telecourse Study Guide is available for users of the Coast Telecourse, *Marketing*. The study guide's basic function is to help students develop an organized approach to the course. The 26 lessons of the study guide parallel the 26 video lessons of the telecourse. The components include assignments, lesson notes, learning objectives, review activities, self tests and answer keys, application of marketing concepts, and additional activities to enhance students' understanding of material presented in the video lessons. This valuable guide helps facilitate students taking the telecourse.

ACKNOWLEDGMENTS

The authors would like to gratefully thank the assistance of Alice Fugate, Karen Hill, Nancy Moudry, Tammye Deimel Bandy, and Jeanne Bartimus. Their efforts on our behalf are most appreciated.

We would also like to thank our editorial team: Bill Schoof, Tracy Morse, and Claudia Gravier. We realize that we are not always the easiest authors to deal with, but we appreciate your patience and support. Thanks also to our other team members: James McDonald, production manager; Linda Beaupré, art director; Beverly Dunn, market strategist; and Lisa Kelly, manufacturing manager.

Finally, a large number of marketing colleagues made major contributions to the tenth edition. Our special thanks go out to:

Keith Absher	University of North Alabama	Anthony Miyazaki	University of Miami
Alicia T. Aldridge	Appalachian State University	Jerry W. Moorman	Mesa State College
Amardeep Assar	City University of New York	Linda Morable	Richland College
Tom F. Badgett	Angelo State University	Diane Moretz	Ashland University
Joe K. Ballenger	Stephen F. Austin State University	Eugene Moynihan	Rockland Community College
Michael Bernacchi	University of Detroit Mercy	Margaret Myers	Northern Kentucky University
David Blanchette	Rhode Island College	Nita Paden	Northern Arizona University
Barbara Brown	San Jose State University	George Palz	Erie Community College-North
Reginald E. Brown	Louisiana Tech University	George Prough	University of Akron
Marvin Burnett	St. Louis Community College-Florissant	Warren Purdy	University of Southern Maine
Scott Burton	University of Arkansas	Salim Qureshi	Bloomsburg University
Howard Cox	Fitchberg State College	Thomas Read	Sierra College
James Coyle	Baruch College	Joel Reedy	University of South Florida
William Demkey	Bakersfield College	Dominic Rella	Polk Community College
Michael Drafke	College of DuPage	Ken Ridgedell	Southeastern Louisiana University
Joanne Eckstein	Macomb Community College	Lillian Roy	McHenry County College
John Frankel	San Juan College	Arthur Saltzman	California State-San Bernardino
Robert Georgen	Trident Technical College	Elise T. Sautter	New Mexico State University
Robert Googins	Shasta College	Johnathon E. Schroeder	University of Rhode Island
Arlene Green	Indian River Community College	Farouk Shaaban	Governors State University
Joel Haynes	State University of West Georgia	John Sondey	South Dakota State University
Mabre Holder	Roane State Community College	James Spiers	Arizona State University
Andrew W. Honeycutt	Clark Atlanta University	David Starr	Shoreline Community College
Dr. H. Houston	California State University-Los Angeles	Bob Stassen	University of Arkansas
John Howe	Santa Ana College	Sue Taylor	Belleville Area College
Tom Jensen	University of Arkansas	Lars Thording	Arizona State University-West Campus
Stephen C. King	Keene State College	Rajiv Vaidyanathan	University of Minnesota
Kathleen Krentler	San Diego State University	Charles Vitaska	Metro State College of Denver
Laddie Logan	Arkansas State University	Cortez Walker	Baltimore City Community College
Kent Lundin	College of the Sequoias	Roger Waller	San Joaquin Delta College
Patricia Macro	Madison Area Tech College	Mary M. Weber	Emporia State University
Frank Markley	Arapahoe Community College	Vicki L. West	Southwest Texas State University
Tom Marshall	Owens Community College	Elizabeth White	Orange County Community College
Dennis C. Mathern	The University of Findlay	David Wiley	Anne Arundel Community College
Lee McGinnis	University of Nebraska	William Wilkinson	Governors State University
Michael McGinnis	University of South Alabama	James Williams	Richard Stockton College of New Jersey
Mohan Menon	University of South Alabama	Mary Wolfindarger	California State University-Long Beach
Norma Mendoza	University of Arkansas	Joyce Wood	North Virginia Community College

Earlier reviewers of *Contemporary Marketing* include:

Keith Absher	Robert Bielski	Grant Davis
Kerri L. Acheson	Carol C. Bienstock	Gilberto de los Santos
Zafar U. Ahmed	Roger D. Blackwell	Carol W. DeMoranville
M. Wayne Alexander	Jocelyn C. Bojack	Fran DePaul
Bruce Allen	Michele D. Bunn	Gordon Di Paolo
Linda Anglin	James Camerius	John G. Doering
Allen Appell,	Les Carlson	Jeffrey T. Doutt
Paul Arsenault	John Carmichael	Francis J. Leary, Jr.
Amardeep Assar	Robert Collins	Sid Dudley
Dub Ashton	Elizabeth Cooper-Martin	John W. Earnest
Tom F. Badgett	Deborah L. Cowles	Phillip E. Egdorf
Joe K. Ballenger	Howard B. Cox	Michael Elliot
Wayne Bascom	Jacob Chacko	Amy Enders
Richard D. Becherer	John E. Crawford	Bob Farris
Tom Becker	Michael R. Czinkota	Lori Feldman
Richard F. Beltramini	Kathy Daruty	Sandra M. Ferriter

Dale Fodness
Michael Fowler
Gary T. Ford
Edward Friese
Sam Fullerton
Ralph M. Gaedeke
G.P. Gallo
Nimish Gandhi
Sheryl A. Gatto
Robert Georgen
Don Gibson
David W. Glascoff
James Gould
Donald Granbois
John Grant
Paul E. Green
William Green
Blaine Greenfield
Matthew Gross
Robert F. Gwinner
Raymond M. Haas
John H. Hallaq
Cary Hawthorn
E. Paul Hayes
Hoyt Hayes
Betty Jean Hebel
Debbora Heflin-Bullock
John (Jack) J. Heinsius
Sanford B. Helman
Nathan Himelstein
Robert D. Hisrich
Ray S. House
George Housewright
Michael D. Hutt
Gregory P. Iwaniuk
Donald Howard,
Don L. James
James Jeck,
Candida Johnson,
David Johnson
Eugene M. Johnson
James C. Johnson
Harold H. Kassarjian
Bernard Katz
Stephen K. Keiser
Michelle Keller
J. Steven Kelly
James H. Kennedy
Charles Keuthan
Maryon King
Randall S. Kingsbury
Donald L. Knight
Linda S. Koffel
Philip Kotler
Terrence Kroeten
Russell Laczniak,
Martha Laham
L. Keith Larimore
Edwin Laube,
Ken Lawrence,

Mary Lou Lockerby
James Lollar
Paul Londrigan
David L. Loudon
Dorothy Maass
James C. Makens
Lou Mansfield
Warren Martin
James McCormick
Carl McDaniel
Michael McGinnis
James McHugh
Faye McIntyre
H. Lee Meadow
Mohan Menon
William E.(Gene) Merkle
John D. Milewicz
Robert D. Miller
Laura M. Milner
Banwari Mittal
Harry J. Moak
J. Dale Molander
John F. Monoky
James R. Moore
Thomas M. Moran
Susan Logan Nelson
Colin F. Neuhaus
Robert T. Newcomb
Jacqueline Z. Nicholson
Tom O'Connor
Robert O'Keefe
Sukgoo Pak
Eric Panitz
Dennis D. Pappas
Constantine Petrides
Barbara Piasta
Dennis D. Pitta
Barbara Pletcher
Carolyn E. Predmore
Arthur E. Prell
Bill Quain
Rosemary Ramsey
Thomas C. Reading
Gary Edward Reiman
Glen Riecken
Arnold M. Rieger
C. Richard Roberts
Patrick J. Robinson
William C. Rodgers
William H. Ronald
Bert Rosenbloom
Barbara Rosenthal
Carol Rowery
Ronald S. Rubin
Don Ryktarsyk
Rafael Santos
Duane Schecter
Dennis W. Schneider
Larry J. Schuetz
Bruce Seaton

Howard Seigelman
Jack Seitz
Steven L. Shapiro
F. Kelly Shuptrine
Ricardo Singson
Norman Smothers
Carol S. Soroos
James Spiers
Miriam B. Stamps
William Staples
David Steenstra
Bruce Stern
Robert Stevens
Kermit Swanson
G. Knude Swenson
Cathy Owens Swift
Clint B. Tankersley
Ruth Taylor
Donald L. Temple
Vern Terpstra
Ann Marie Thompson
Howard A. Thompson
John E. Timmerman
Frank Titlow
Rex Toh
Dennis H. Tootelian
Fred Trawick
Richard Lee Utecht
Rajiv Vaidyanathan
Toni Valdez
Peter Vanderhagen
Dinoo T. Vanier
Gayle D. Wasson
Donald Weinrauch
Fred Weinthal
Susan B. Wessels
John J. Whithey
Debbora Whitson
Robert J. Williams
Nicholas C. Williamson
Cecilia Wittmayer
Van R. Wood
Julian Yudelson
Robert J. Zimmer

With our best wishes!

Gene Boone

Dave Kurtz

Louis E. Boone (Ph.D.) holds the Ernest G. Cleverdon Chair in Business and Management at the University of South Alabama. He formerly chaired the Division of Management and Marketing at the University of Tulsa and has taught marketing in Australia, Greece, and the United Kingdom.

Dr. Boone is a prolific researcher and writer. In addition to authoring numerous marketing and business texts and computer simulation games, he recently published *Quotable Business,* Revised Edition (Random House, 1999). He is the current recipient of the Alumni Association Outstanding Scholar Award from his university.

His current research focuses on event and sports marketing. Dr. Boone's research has been published in such journals as the *Journal of Marketing, Journal of Business Strategy, Journal of Retailing, Business Horizons, Journal of Business Research, Journal of Business of the University of Chicago, Journal of Personal Selling & Sales Management, Journal of Marketing Education, Business,* and *Sport Marketing Quarterly*. He has served as president of the Southwestern Marketing Association and vice president of the Southern Marketing Association.

David L. Kurtz (Ph.D.) is the R.A. and Vivian Young Chair of Business Administration at the University of Arkansas. He was formerly the head of the Department of Marketing and Transportation at Arkansas.

Prior to returning to his graduate alma mater, Dr. Kurtz held the Thomas F. Cleed Chair in Business and Finance at Seattle University. Earlier, he was department head at Eastern Michigan University. Dr. Kurtz has also taught at Davis & Elkins College and Australia's Monash University.

Dr. Kurtz has authored or coauthored 39 books and more than 120 articles, cases, and papers. His work has appeared in such publications as the *Journal of Marketing, Journal of Retailing, Journal of the Academy of Marketing Science, Journal of Business Research,* and numerous other well-known journals.

Dr. Kurtz has been active in many professional organizations, including president of the Western Marketing Educators Association, and vice president of the Academy of Marketing Science and the Southwestern Marketing Association. The Western Marketing Educators' Association named him educator of the year. He is also the recipient of an honorary doctorate in pedagogy degree from Davis & Elkins College for his contributions to business education.

CONTENTS IN BRIEF

CONTENTS

CHAPTER 2

The Marketing Environment, Ethics, and Social Responsibility   38

CHAPTER 3

Global Dimensions of Marketing   76

PART 2
MANAGING TECHNOLOGY TO ACHIEVE MARKETING SUCCESS   113

CHAPTER 4

E-Commerce: Electronic Marketing and the Internet   114

CHAPTER 5

Succeeding Using Relationship and Database Marketing   150

PART 3
MARKETING PLANNING, INFORMATION, AND SEGMENTATION 179

CHAPTER 6

OPENING VIGNETTE
MicroStrategy Helps Marketers Plan Their Strategy 181

MARKETING STRATEGY SUCCESS
Oop!'s Success Is No "Oops" 196

MARKETING STRATEGY FAILURE
PRT Group's Forecasting Sinks Offshore 192

SOLVING AN ETHICAL CONTROVERSY
How Much Should Telemarketers Be Restricted? 184

PART 4
CUSTOMER BEHAVIOR   263

CHAPTER 9

CHAPTER 10

PART 5
PRODUCT STRATEGY   325

CHAPTER 11

Product Strategies   326

CHAPTER 12

Brand Management and New Product Planning   356

PART 6
DISTRIBUTION STRATEGY   387

CHAPTER 13

Marketing Channels and Logistics Management   388

CHAPTER 16

Advertising, Sales Promotion, and Public Relations   488

CHAPTER 17

**PART 8
PRICING STRATEGY   563**

CHAPTER 18

CHAPTER 19

VIDEO CASE CONTENTS

GATEWAY CONTINUING CASE CONTENTS

PART

1

THE CONTEMPORARY MARKETING ENVIRONMENT

3

Gateway Continuing Case Part 1 begins on page GC-2.

Customer-Driven Marketing

CHAPTER OBJECTIVES

1 Explain how marketing creates utility through the exchange process.

2 Contrast marketing activities during the four eras in the history of marketing.

3 Define the marketing concept and its relationship to marketing myopia.

4 Describe the five types of nontraditional marketing.

5 Identify the basic elements of a marketing strategy and the environmental characteristics that influence strategy decisions.

6 Outline the changes in the marketing environment due to technology and relationship marketing.

7 Identify the universal functions of marketing.

8 Demonstrate the relationship between ethical business practices and marketplace success.

idealab!

George Bernard Shaw, the English playwright, once remarked, "You see things, and you say, 'Why?' But I dream things that never were and say, 'Why not?'" Shaw never met Bill Gross, but his words sum up the very essence of this young Californian, for Gross is both a marketer and an entrepreneur extraordinaire.

And it didn't just happen overnight. As far back as junior high school, Gross displayed a knack for converting seemingly zany ideas into hard cash. He bought candy bars from the local drug store, then sold them out of his locker to fellow students, undercutting the prices charged by the school cafeteria. He next invented a solar energy gadget, ran small ads in *Popular Science* in hopes of selling a few, and ended up selling enough to finance his tuition to the California Institute of Technology.

At Cal Tech, Gross continued to make money by turning his ideas into reality. He designed and produced speakers in a uni-

versity workshop and started selling them on campus. As sales grew, he formalized his operations as GNP Loudspeakers. (GNP—which stands for Gross National Products—was another creative Gross touch.) Production was assigned to a group of fellow students, and Gross resumed his practice of cranking out new ideas.

Soon Bill Gross partnered with his brother Larry to form GNP Development Corp., an accounting software company. Bill was 23 at the time and a recent graduate, anxious to buy his ticket to the big world of business. And GNP Development turned out to be that ticket. As the story goes, "It was the best of times. It was the worst of times." Sales quickly topped $1 million, but spreadsheet giant Lotus 1-2-3 was just as quick to sue because GNP's packaging was almost identical to theirs. And, in retrospect, Gross had to agree. "It was a total rip-off of the Lotus box." The packaging was changed, and Lotus dropped the lawsuit.

But Gross was not done with Lotus. While Larry ran the operations, Bill came up with another refinement that drastically simplified the Lotus spreadsheet software. In 1985, Lotus paid the brothers $10 million for GNP Development, paving the way for Gross to enter into another venture.

With plenty of money now, Gross took time out and started a family. He began painting and dabbled in music. But ideas kept coming. It was 1991 when he started his third business. This time he was inspired by his 5-year-old son to develop an educational software program for children. His company, Knowledge Adventure, quickly grew to become the third largest producer of children's software in the United States. In 1997, he sold it to Cendant Corp. for $100 million.

By now, Gross had spotted an even bigger idea, one that was devised by a fellow Californian and former Disney manager named Toby Lenk. Lenk was an Internet expert and he was looking for the right product to sell online. The answer came to him in a hectic shopping trip to a toy store a few days before Christmas. Lenk recalls, "I saw long lines and screaming kids, and I figured there had to be a better way." A few months later, eToys.com was born.

Total spending on toys tops $22 billion a year, making for a very attractive market. Gross agreed to put up some of his

5

Knowledge Adventure money as seed capital and then joined Lenk as board chairman. The first full year of operations saw sales exceed $15 million and also saw industry giant Toys "Я" Us scramble to catch up by launching its own online store. By 2001, online sales of toys and hobbies were about $71 million.

Although eToys appeared to be a big cyberspace winner and Gross had no plans to leave the company, he was anxious to devote more time focusing on his true love: dreaming up new ideas and turning them into companies. The 30-something entrepreneur set up idealab!, an online idea factory that to date has created 20 cyber-startups. Among the more successful ones are CitySearch, cooking.com, tickets.com, and search engine GoTo.com. CitySearch is the leading operator of local Internet city guides, with an estimated 50 percent market share. It now outreaches America Online's Digital Cities and Microsoft's Sidewalk. Another of Gross' companies is Free-PC, which gives away computers and Internet access in exchange for personal information used to target advertising directly to these users. And retail giant Federated Stores recently bought a 20 percent share of another Gross start-up, WeddingChannel.com, geared to wedding planning.

Gross is currently working on what many consider a harebrained idea: an online record company where original songs could be sold as files and downloaded over the Internet, thereby eliminating the traditional record companies and distributors. It hasn't happened yet, but Gross has financial support from many of today's leading pioneers of the digital age. Investors in idealab! include such notables as director Steven Spielberg, Compaq Computer chairman Benjamin Rosen, and former AT&T executive Robert Kavner II. Says Spielberg of Gross, "If he's involved with it, I want to invest in it."[1]

 eToys.com

CHAPTER OVERVIEW

As more organizations such as idealab! discover the advantages of traveling on the Internet highway, a new path is being carved out in cyberspace. Every minute of each day is filled with entrepreneurs bringing their ideas and innovations to the world of electronic commerce. Advances in communications technology allow information to be exchanged between buyers and sellers faster, cheaper, and through more media channels than ever before, including broadcast media, print, telecommunications, online computer services, and the Internet. Companies can now offer consumers more product choices and more places to buy. Today's savvy shoppers can visit a brick-and-mortar shopping mall, hire a personal shopper, order from catalogs, watch television home shopping channels, and browse virtual stores accessed through online services.

The technology revolution is changing the rules of marketing as we enter the twenty-first century. The combined power of telecommunications and computer technology creates inexpensive, global networks that transfer voice messages, text, graphics, and data within seconds. These sophisticated technologies create new types of products, and they also demand new approaches to marketing existing products.

Communications technology contributes as well to the globalization of today's marketplace, where companies manufacture, buy, and sell across national borders. You can eat Kellogg's Corn Flakes or drink Coca-Cola almost anywhere in the world, while almost all consumer electronics products sold in the United States and Canada are manufactured in Japan and Korea. The slacks you are wearing today may have been fashioned by a French designer and sewn in Malaysia from cotton grown and milled in the United States; the shirt hanging in your closet may have been designed by an American firm and sewn in Brazil from Asian silk. Mercedes-Benz sport utility vehicles are assembled in Vance, Alabama, while many Volkswagens are imported from Mexico. Products and components routinely cross international borders, but global marketing also requires knowledge to tailor products to regional tastes. For example, an Asian food store in Austin, Texas, may also sell popular Hispanic foods such as tortillas to satisfy local tastes.

Rapidly changing business landscapes create new challenges for companies, whether giant multinational firms or small boutiques, profit-oriented or not-for-profit. They must react quickly to shifts in consumer tastes, competitive offerings, and other market dynamics. Fortunately, information technologies give organizations fast, new ways to interact and develop long-term relationships with their customers and suppliers. In fact, such links have become a core element of marketing today.

Every company must serve consumer needs to succeed. Marketing strategies provide the tools by which businesspeople identify and analyze customers' needs and then inform these customers about how the company can meet those needs. Tomorrow's market leaders will be companies who can effectively harness the vast amounts of customer feedback and respond with solutions to consumer needs.

This tenth edition of *Contemporary Marketing* focuses on the strategies that allow companies to succeed in today's interactive marketplace. This chapter sets the stage for the entire text, examining the meaning of marketing and its importance for all organizations. Initial sections describe the development of marketing, from early times to today's focus on relationship marketing, and its contributions to society. Later sections introduce the variables defined by a marketing strategy and discuss the impact of the technology revolution on future marketing strategies. ■

WHAT IS MARKETING?

Production and marketing of goods and services are the essence of economic life in any society. All organizations perform these two basic functions to satisfy their commitments to society, their customers, and their owners. They create a benefit that economists call **utility**—the want-satisfying power of a good or service. Table 1.1 describes the four basic kinds of utility—form, time, place, and ownership utility.

Form utility is created when the firm converts raw materials and component inputs into finished goods and services. By combining glass, plastic, metals, circuit boards, and other components, Toshiba creates a television set and Sony makes a camcorder. With fabric, thread, wood, springs, and down feathers, Ethan Allen produces a sofa. The television show *ER* starts with writers, artists, actors, scripts, a director, producers, technical crew, and a sound stage. Although the marketing function determines consumer and audience preferences, the organization's production function is responsible for the actual creation of form utility.

Marketing creates time, place, and ownership utilities. *Time* and *place utility* occur when consumers find goods and services available when and where they want to purchase them. Overnight

MARKETING DICTIONARY

utility Want-satisfying power of a good or service.

TABLE 1.1	Four Types of Utility

TYPE	DESCRIPTION	EXAMPLES	ORGANIZATIONAL FUNCTION RESPONSIBLE
Form	Conversion of raw materials and components into finished goods and services	Skippy Peanut Butter; State Farm automobile insurance policy; Boeing 767 aircraft	Production[a]
Time	Availability of goods and services when consumers want them	One-hour dry cleaning; LensCrafters eyeglass guarantee; Federal Express' guarantee of package delivery by 10:30 A.M. the next day	Marketing
Place	Availability of goods and services at convenient locations	Soda machines in school lobbies; coffee and snacks in Barnes & Noble bookstores; day cares in office complexes; ATM machines in gas stations; mailboxes outside convenience stores	Marketing
Ownership (possession)	Ability to transfer title to goods or services from marketer to buyer	Retail sales (in exchange for currency or credit-card payment); swap meets	Marketing

[a]Marketing provides inputs related to consumer preferences, but the actual creation of form utility is the responsibility of the production function.

courier services like Federal Express and DHL Worldwide Express emphasize time utility; vending machines focus on providing place utility for people buying newspapers, snacks, and soft drinks. The transfer of title to goods or services at the time of purchase creates *ownership utility*.

The promotional message shown in Figure 1.1 illustrates marketing's ability to create time, place, and ownership utility. The ad emphasizes the ability of service-provider FedEx to create time, place, and ownership utility by quickly, safely, and dependably shipping packages seven days a week.

All organizations must create utility to survive. Designing and marketing want-satisfying goods, services, and ideas is the foundation for the creation of utility. However, the importance of marketing in an organization's success has only recently been recognized. Corporate boards are elevating their top marketing executives to senior vice presidential positions. For the first time, management teams are being assigned to customer research, advertising, and new-product development.[2] Management author Peter F. Drucker emphasized the importance of marketing in his classic book, *The Practice of Management:*

> If we want to know what a business is, we have to start with its purpose. And its purpose must lie outside the business itself. In fact, it must lie in society since a business enterprise is an organ of society. There is one valid definition of business purpose: to create a customer.[3]

How does an organization create a customer? Professors Joseph Guiltinan and Gordon Paul explain it this way:

> Essentially, "creating" a customer means identifying needs in the marketplace, finding out which needs the organization can profitably serve, and developing an offering to convert potential buyers into customers. Marketing managers are responsible for most of the activities necessary to create the customers the organization wants. These activities include:

- Identifying customer needs
- Designing goods and services that meet those needs
- Communicating information about those goods and services to prospective buyers
- Making the goods or services available at times and places that meet customers' needs
- Pricing goods and services to reflect costs, competition, and customers' ability to buy
- Providing for the necessary service and follow-up to ensure customer satisfaction after the purchase.[4]

A Definition of Marketing

The word *marketing* encompasses such a broad scope of activities and ideas that settling on one definition is often difficult. Ask five people to define it, and five different definitions are likely to follow. Continuous exposure to advertising and personal selling leads most respondents to link marketing and selling or to think that marketing activities start once goods and services have been produced. But marketing also involves analyzing customer needs, securing information needed to design and produce goods or services that match buyer expectations, and creating and maintaining relationships with customers and suppliers. It applies not only to profit-oriented firms but also to thousands of not-for-profit organizations that offer goods and services.

Today's definition takes all these factors into account. **Marketing** is the process of planning and executing the conception, pricing, promotion, and distribution of ideas, goods, services, organizations, and events to create and maintain relationships that will satisfy individual and organizational objectives.

The expanded concept of marketing activities permeates all organizational functions. It assumes that the marketing effort will proceed in accordance with ethical practices and that it will effectively serve the interests of both society and the organization. The concept also identifies the marketing variables—product, price, promotion, and distribution—that combine to provide customer satisfaction. In addition, it assumes that the organization begins by identifying and analyzing the consumer segments that it will later satisfy through its production and marketing activities. In other words, the customer, client, or public determines the marketing program. The concept's emphasis on creating and maintaining relationships is consistent with the focus in business on long-term, mutually satisfying sales, purchases, and other interactions with customers and suppliers. Finally, it recognizes that marketing concepts and techniques apply to not-for-profit organizations as well as to profit-oriented businesses.

Today's Global Marketplace

Several factors have forced countries to extend their economic views to events outside their own national borders. First, international agreements are being negotiated in attempts to increase trade among nations. Second, the growth of electronic commerce and related computer technologies brings previously isolated countries into the marketplace for buyers and sellers around the globe. Third, the interdependence of the world's economies is a

FIGURE 1.1   Marketing: Creating Time, Place, and Ownership Utility

FedEx delivers another day of the week.

Introducing Sunday delivery from FedEx.

It's a brand new day for business. Now you can get the same reliable service you've come to expect from FedEx seven days a week. After all, the world doesn't stop on Sunday. Why should we?

FedEx
The Way The World Works.

MARKETING   DICTIONARY

marketing Process of planning and executing the conception, pricing, promotion, and distribution of ideas, goods, services, organizations, and events to create and maintain relationships that satisfy individual and organizational objectives.

BellSouth: Bringing the Global Marketplace Together

GLOBE

The word globe can have many meanings, depending on how you see it. It can be a simple sphere. A ball. Or a planet. To BellSouth, it's the entire world. Our expertise starts at home, then spans the globe. With cellular service on five continents. Powerful networks for long distance in Australia. Wireless systems in Latin America, Europe and beyond. We're bringing together the world's most advanced technology. So you can launch your words to places all over the world.

Because a word can have many meanings. But it means nothing until it's shared.

ⓐ BELLSOUTH®

It's All Here™

www.bellsouth.com/words

pringles.com

reality since no nation produces all of the raw materials and finished goods purchased by its citizens or consumes all of its output without some exporting to other countries. Evidence of this interdependence is illustrated by the introduction of the Euro as a common currency to facilitate trade among the nations of the European Union and the creation of trade alliances such as NAFTA.

A recession in Europe affects business strategies in North America and the Pacific Rim. To remain competitive, companies must continually search for the most efficient manufacturing sites and most lucrative markets for their products. Marketers now find tremendous opportunities serving customers not only in traditional industrialized nations but also in Latin America and emerging economies in eastern Europe and Asia, where rising standards of living create increased customer demand for the latest goods and services.

Expanding operations beyond the U.S. market gives domestic companies access to 6 billion international customers. This explains why over 80 percent of Coca-Cola sales are generated outside the United States. Japan alone accounts for nearly 20 percent of Coke's profit.[5] For Colgate-Palmolive, a whopping 70 percent of its revenue comes from abroad, and three-fourths of Exxon's revenues are from non-U.S. customers.

Service firms also play a major role in today's global marketplace. The Japanese subsidiary of Aflac, an international insurance company, recently generated sales of $5.8 billion, which represented four of every five dollars of total worldwide sales by the insurer.[6] Manpower Temporary Services, a worldwide firm that provides temporary and permanent workers in a broad range of jobs, earns almost 70 percent of its profits from foreign contracts. Technology products are also popular U.S. exports. Compaq's Digital Equipment subsidiary sells two-thirds of its computer products outside the United States, while Apple Computer generates half its revenues from non-U.S. sales. The importance of the global marketplace is clear in the BellSouth ad in Figure 1.2. The cellular service of this international telephone company spans the globe on five continents, bringing together the world's most advanced communications technology.

The United States is also an attractive market for foreign competitors because of its size and the high standard of living that American consumers enjoy. Companies like Matsushita, BMW, Benetton, and Sun Life of Canada operate production, distribution, service, and retail facilities in the United States. Foreign ownership of U.S. companies has increased as well. Pillsbury, MCA, and Firestone Tires are some well-known firms with foreign parents. Even American-dominated industries like computer software must contend with foreign competition. While U.S. firms still hold about 75 percent of the market, European companies are quickly gaining market share. They currently supply about 18 percent of the $100 billion worldwide market for packaged software.

In many cases, global marketing strategies are almost identical to those used in domestic markets. Rather than creating a different promotional campaign for each country where they sell Pringles potato chips, Procter & Gamble marketers used the same ad—with spectacular results. Nearly everything in the U.S.-made ads was the same—the rap music themes, the young people dancing, and the tag line, "Once you pop, you can't stop." As a result, P&G had to boost production to handle the global demand.[7]

In other instances, domestic marketing strategies may need significant changes to adapt to unique tastes or different cultural and legal requirements abroad. It is often difficult to standardize a brand name on a global basis. The Japanese, for example, like names of flowers or girls for their car models, such as Bluebird, Bluebonnet, Violet, and Gloria. Americans, on the other hand, prefer more sporty sounding names, such as animal names—Mustang, Cougar, Firebird—or some combination of letters and numbers—MR2, 240Z, RX7. The first sports car

ERA	APPROXIMATE TIME PERIOD[a]	PREVAILING ATTITUDE
	TABLE 1.2	**Four Eras in the History of Marketing**
Production	Prior to 1920s	"A good product will sell itself."
Sales	Prior to 1950s	"Creative advertising and selling will overcome consumers' resistance and convince them to buy."
Marketing	Since 1950s	"The consumer is king! Find a need and fill it."
Relationship	Began in 1990s	"Long-term relationships with customers and other partners lead to success."

[a]In the United States and other highly industrialized economies

Nissan sent to the United States was named Datsun Fair Lady. Marketing researchers, however, foresaw trouble in the making, and the name was changed to 240Z.[8]

FOUR ERAS IN THE HISTORY OF MARKETING

The essence of marketing is the **exchange process,** in which two or more parties give something of value to each other to satisfy felt needs. In many exchanges, people trade money for tangible goods, such as compact discs, clothes, or cars. In others, they trade for intangible services, such as child care, haircuts, or concert performances. In still others, people may donate funds or time for a cause, such as a Red Cross blood drive, a new gymnasium for a church or school, or a campaign to clean up the environment.

Although marketing has always been a part of business, its importance has varied greatly. Table 1.2 identifies four eras in the history of marketing: (1) the production era, (2) the sales era, (3) the marketing era, and (4) the relationship era.

1

Explain how marketing creates utility through the exchange process.

2

Contrast marketing activities during the four eras in the history of marketing.

The Production Era

Prior to 1925, most firms—even those operating in highly developed economies in western Europe and North America—focused narrowly on production. Manufacturers stressed production of quality products and then looked for people to purchase them. The history of Pillsbury provides an excellent example of a production-oriented company. The following passage is how the company's former chief executive officer, the late Robert J. Keith, described Pillsbury during its early years:

> We are professional flour millers. Blessed with a supply of the finest North American wheat, plenty of water power, and excellent milling machinery, we produce flour of the highest quality. Our basic function is to mill high-quality flour, and, of course, we must hire [salespeople] to sell it, just as we hire accountants to keep our books.[9]

The prevailing attitude of this era held that a good product (one with high physical quality) would sell itself. This **production orientation** dominated business philosophy for decades; indeed, business success was often defined solely in terms of production victories.

MARKETING **DICTIONARY**

exchange process Activity in which two or more parties give something of value to each other to satisfy perceived needs.

production orientation Business philosophy stressing efficiency in producing a quality product, with the attitude toward marketing that "a good product will sell itself."

The Worst "Better Mousetrap"

BACKGROUND In the early 1960s, the nation's largest mousetrap producer introduced a better mousetrap, a device the firm's marketing experts were convinced would prove a winner. The new brown plastic model featured a completely sanitary design, yet cost only a few cents more than the traditional wooden version.

THE MARKETING PROBLEM The problem centered around the mousetrap buying process. Men bought and set most of the new plastic mousetraps. But when they forgot to check the trap, the dead-mouse disposition chore fell to women. This was not a problem with wooden traps since both trap and mouse were swept into a dustpan and then thrown away. But the new trap looked too expensive to throw away, giving women the untidy tasks of ejecting the mouse and then cleaning the trap for reuse.

THE OUTCOME Sales of the new, "better" mousetrap were adequate for the first few weeks following its introduction, but repeat business was almost nonexistent as women insisted on returning to the traditional wood version. The "better mousetrap" became a footnote example of the shortcomings of the production era.

continued on next page

3

Define the marketing concept and its relationship to marketing myopia.

The production era did not reach its peak until the early part of the 20th century. Henry Ford's mass-production line exemplifies this orientation. Ford's slogan, "They [customers] can have any color they want, as long as it's black," reflected the prevalent attitude toward marketing. Production shortages and intense consumer demand ruled the day. It is easy to understand how production activities took precedence.

The essence of the production era resounds in a statement made over 100 years ago by the philosopher Ralph Waldo Emerson: "If a man writes a better book, preaches a better sermon, or makes a better mousetrap than his neighbor, though he builds his house in the woods, the world will make a beaten path to his door." However, a better mousetrap is no guarantee of success, and marketing history is full of miserable failures despite better mousetrap designs. In fact, over 80 percent of new products fail. Inventing the greatest new product is not enough. That product must also solve a perceived marketplace need. Otherwise, even the best-engineered, highest-quality product will fail.

The Sales Era

Production techniques in the United States and Europe became more sophisticated, and output grew from the 1920s into the early 1950s. Thus, manufacturers began to increase their emphasis on effective sales forces to find customers for their output. In this era, firms attempted to match their output to the potential number of customers who would want it. Companies with a **sales orientation** assume that customers will resist purchasing goods and services not deemed essential and that the task of personal selling and advertising is to convince them to buy.

Although marketing departments began to emerge from the shadows of production, finance, and engineering during the sales era, they tended to remain in subordinate positions. Many chief marketing executives held the title of sales manager. Here is how Pillsbury described itself during the sales era:

> We are a flour-milling company, manufacturing a number of products for the consumer market. We must have a first-rate sales organization which can dispose of all the products we can make at a favorable price. We must back up this sales force with consumer advertising and marketing intelligence. We want our sales representatives and our dealers to have all the tools they need for moving the output of our plants to the consumer.[10]

But selling is only one component of marketing. As Harvard University marketing professor Theodore Levitt has pointed out, "Marketing is as different from selling as chemistry is from alchemy, astronomy from astrology, chess from checkers."[11]

The Marketing Era

Personal incomes and consumer demand for goods and services dropped rapidly during the Great Depression of the early 1930s, thrusting marketing into a more important role. Organizational survival dictated that managers pay close attention to the markets for their goods and services. This trend ended with the outbreak of World War II, when rationing and shortages of consumer goods became commonplace. The war years, however, created only a pause in an emerging trend in business: a shift in the focus from products and sales to satisfying customer needs.

Emergence of the Marketing Concept

The marketing concept, a crucial change in management philosophy, can be explained best by the shift from a **seller's market**—one with a shortage of goods and services—to a **buyer's market**—one with an abundance of goods and services. When World War II ended, factories stopped manufacturing tanks and ships and started turning out consumer products again, a type of activity that had, for all practical purposes, stopped in early 1942.

The advent of a strong buyer's market created the need for **consumer orientation** in businesses. Companies had to market goods and services, not just produce and sell them. This realization has been identified as the emergence of the marketing concept. The recognition of this concept and its dominant role in business dates from 1952, when General Electric's *Annual Report* heralded a new management philosophy:

> [The concept] introduces the [marketer] at the beginning rather than at the end of the production cycle and integrates marketing into each phase of the business. Thus, marketing, through its studies and research, will establish for the engineer, the designer, and manufacturing [person], what the customer wants in a given product, what price he [or she] is willing to pay, and where and when it will be wanted. Marketing will have authority in product planning, production scheduling, and inventory control, as well as in sales, distribution, and servicing of the product.[12]

Marketing would no longer be regarded as a supplemental activity performed after completion of the production process. The marketer would play the lead role in product planning, for example. Marketing and selling would no longer be synonymous terms.

The fully developed **marketing concept** is a company-wide consumer orientation with the objective of achieving long-run success. The key words are *company-wide consumer orientation*. All facets of the organization must contribute first to assessing and then to satisfying customer wants and needs. The effort is not something to be left only to marketers. Accountants working in the credit office and engineers designing products also play important roles. The words *with the objective of achieving long-run success* differentiate the concept from policies of short-run profit maximization. Since the firm's continuity is an assumed component of the marketing concept, company-wide consumer orientation will lead to greater long-run profits than managerial philosophies geared toward reaching short-run goals.

A strong market orientation—the extent to which a company adopts the marketing concept—generally improves market success and overall performance. It also has a positive effect on new-product development and the introduction of innovative products. Companies that implement market-driven strategies are better able to understand their customers' experiences, buying habits, and needs. These companies can, therefore, design products with advantages and levels of quality compatible with customer requirements. Another benefit is that customers more quickly accept the new products.

The Relationship Era

The fourth era in the history of marketing emerged during the last decade of the 20th century. Organizations carried the marketing era's customer orientation one step further by focusing on establishing and maintaining relationships with both customers and suppliers. This effort represented a major shift from the traditional concept of marketing as a simple exchange between buyer and seller. *Relationship marketing*, by contrast, involves long-term, value-added relationships developed over time with customers and suppliers. *Strategic alliances* and partnerships with vendors and retailers play major roles in relationship marketing. Packaged-goods giant Procter & Gamble has contracts with giant retailers such as Wal-Mart and Safeway to automatically replenish their inventories of Head & Shoulders, Crest, Tide, and other personal-care and household products. Computerized systems track withdrawals from customers' warehouses, allowing P&G to ship 40 percent of its orders automatically, cutting paperwork and inventory costs and holding the line on retail prices. Participants in

LESSONS LEARNED Without effective marketing, a quality product will fail. Quality is determined by a buyer's perception of product performance—not by what company designers and engineers decide to produce. Even though Ray Kinsella in the movie *Field of Dreams* heard a voice exclaim, "If you build it, they will come," the reality is that today's mousetrap must go to market.

MARKETING DICTIONARY

sales orientation Business assumption that consumers will resist purchasing nonessential goods and services with the attitude toward marketing that only creative advertising and personal selling can overcome consumers' resistance and convince them to buy.

seller's market Marketplace characterized by a shortage of goods and/or services.

buyer's market Marketplace characterized by an abundance of goods and/or services.

consumer orientation Business philosophy incorporating the marketing concept that emphasizes first determining unmet consumer needs and then designing a system for satisfying them.

marketing concept Company-wide consumer orientation with the objective of achieving long-run success.

collaborative relationships generate an estimated 25 percent more sales than independent firms. Teaming up with potential buyers of their products also reduces the risks of new-product introductions. The concept of relationship marketing is discussed in detail later in this chapter.

Converting Needs to Wants

Every consumer must acquire goods and services on a continuing basis to fill certain needs. Everyone must satisfy the fundamental needs for food, clothing, shelter, and transportation by purchasing things or, in some instances, temporarily using rented property and hired or leased transportation. By focusing on the *benefits* resulting from these goods and services, effective marketing converts needs to wants. A need for clothing may be translated into a desire (or want) for designer clothes. The need for a vacation may become the desire to take a Caribbean cruise or to backpack in the Rocky Mountains.

As easier-to-use software has enabled millions of nontechnical consumers to operate personal computers and as falling retail prices make these computers affordable to most households, computers have become fixtures in many schools, offices, and homes. Thousands of tiny and large PC makers have pushed prices below $1,000, and this once-prestigious possession has been reduced to a commodity. Marketers at Apple Computer recently decided to change this image of the PC by introducing the iMac shown in Figure 1.3. The new computer is not superior in speed or capacity to its competitors at Compaq, Dell, Gateway, or IBM. But no one will argue with the design awards it has received. The iMac simply looks better than its competition. The attractive colors can be chosen to match a room's decor and the styling hints of the new century. Not surprisingly, by offering these differences in a product priced similar to its competitors, Apple has returned from near bankruptcy to once again being a force in the PC marketplace.

Companies that adopt the marketing concept focus on providing solutions to customer problems. They promote product benefits rather than features to show the added value that

apple.com

| FIGURE 1.3 | The Apple iMac: Converting Needs to Wants |

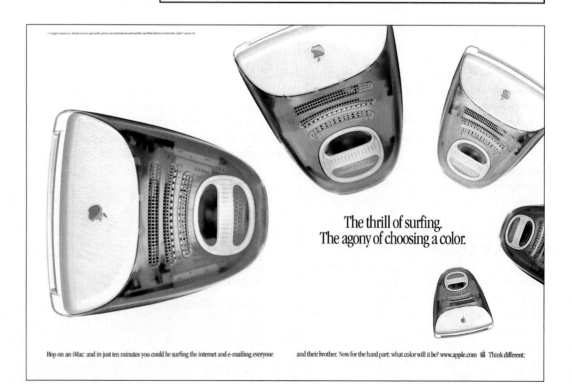

The thrill of surfing.
The agony of choosing a color.

Hop on an iMac and in just ten minutes you could be surfing the internet and e-mailing everyone   and their brother. Now for the hard part: what color will it be? www.apple.com Think different.

TABLE 1.3	Avoiding Marketing Myopia by Focusing on Benefits	
COMPANY	**MYOPIC DESCRIPTION**	**MARKETING-ORIENTED DESCRIPTION**
MCI Worldcom	"We are a telephone company."	"We are a communications company."
Northwest Airlines	"We are in the airline business."	"We are in the transportation business."
Prudential Securities	"We are in the stock brokerage business."	"We are in the financial services business."
Sony	"We are in the video game business."	"We are in the entertainment business."

customers will receive from the product. For example, car marketers emphasize powerful engines, ABS brakes, and air bags as safety benefits, while office products' dealers promote reliable, high-speed copiers and printers for the time savings and low maintenance costs they offer to companies.

AVOIDING MARKETING MYOPIA

The emergence of the marketing concept has not been devoid of setbacks. One troublesome problem led Theodore Levitt to coin the term *marketing myopia.* According to Levitt, **marketing myopia** is management's failure to recognize the scope of its business. Product-oriented rather than customer-oriented management endangers future growth. Levitt cites many service industries—dry cleaning, electric utilities, movies, and railroads—as examples of marketing myopia.

To avoid marketing myopia, companies must broadly define organizational goals oriented toward consumer needs. This approach can help a company stand out from others in highly competitive environments, such as the communications industry. The evolution of AT&T in the information age has created the largest telecommunications company in the U.S. and a world leader in communication services.

AT&T has undergone drastic changes since the demise of the regulated telephone monopoly in 1984. It began by focusing on offering long-distance service but gradually escaped the myopic view of itself as merely a telephone company. In the decades since deregulation, AT&T added Internet, wireless, cable, and local telephone service, transforming itself into a much broader role as a provider of communication services. By aggressively pursuing new emerging markets, AT&T has assumed a leading role in today's electronic communications industry.[13]

att.com

Revlon founder and president Charles Revson understood the need for a broader focus on benefits rather than on products. As Revson described it, "In our factory we make perfume; in our advertising we sell hope." Table 1.3 illustrates how firms in a number of other industries have overcome myopic thinking by developing broader marketing-oriented business ideas that focus on consumer need satisfaction.

EXTENDING THE TRADITIONAL BOUNDARIES OF MARKETING

Until fairly recently, marketing focused primarily on exchanges of goods and services between individuals and businesses. Today, both profit-oriented and not-for-profit organizations recognize universal needs for marketing and its

MARKETING DICTIONARY

marketing myopia Term coined by Theodore Levitt in his argument that executives in many industries fail to recognize the broad scope of their businesses.

importance to their success. During a television commercial break, viewers might be exposed to an advertisement for a Ford Taurus, followed by an appeal for flood relief funds, a political message by a presidential candidate, or a ticket offer for a traveling art exhibit.

Marketing in Not-for-Profit Organizations

The 1.2 million not-for-profit organizations in the United States generate an estimated $300 billion in revenues each year. One in 10 Americans already works either full time or part time for a not-for-profit organization. In addition, more than 93 million people serve as volunteers, working an average of four hours a week.[14]

Not-for-profit organizations operate in both public and private sectors. Federal, state, and local government units and agencies derive revenues from tax collection to pursue service objectives that are not keyed to profitability targets. The U.S. Department of Defense, for example, protects the nation from foreign aggression; a state's department of natural resources regulates conservation and environmental programs; the local animal-control officer enforces ordinances that protect people and animals.

The private sector has an even more diverse array of not-for-profit organizations, including art institutes, the Ohio State University football team, labor unions, hospitals, private schools, the American Cancer Society, the Rotary Club, and local youth organizations. Some, like Ohio State University's football team, may generate surplus revenues that can pay for other university activities, but the organization's primary goal is to win football games.

In some not-for-profit organizations, adopting the marketing concept means forming a partnership with a for-profit company to promote the not-for-profit's message or image. A partnership between Stride Rite and Save the Children Federation is helping children in Kosovo and other war- and poverty-ridden areas. Stride Rite contributed 4 percent of sales of a special line of children's shoes, with a guaranteed minimum donation of $82,500. Share Our Strength (SOS), a Washington-based organization that fights hunger and poverty, teamed up with the financial advisor Motley Fool on its Web site. A recent fund-raising campaign netted $196,000 from 1,400 contributors who paid to post messages on the financial Web site.

Not-for-profit organizations may form alliances with profit-seeking firms for the benefit of both. The reality of operating with multimillion-dollar budgets requires not-for-profit organizations to maintain a focused business approach. Consider some current examples:

- McDonald's Ronald McDonald House Charities work with several local and national not-for-profit organizations to help critically ill children and their families through difficult times.
- The fight against breast cancer has generated donations from many organizations, including the U.S. Postal Service, Avon, JCPenney, and Ford Motor Co., among others.
- The Children's Miracle Network, a $172 million organization that raises money for children's hospitals across the country, gets about $70 million from contributions from corporations like Wal-Mart, Toys "Я" Us, and Delta Air Lines.
- General Motors throws its charitable funding behind the United Negro College Fund.

The diversity of not-for-profit organizations suggests the presence of numerous organizational objectives other than profitability. In addition to organizational goals, not-for-profit organizations differ from profit-seeking firms in other ways.

Characteristics of Not-for-Profit Marketing

Not-for-profit organizations encounter a special set of characteristics that influence their marketing activities. Like profit-seeking firms, not-for-profit organizations may market tangible goods and/or intangible services. The Boston Museum of Fine Arts, for example, offers many gift items in its gift shop and through direct-mail catalogs (tangible goods), as well as the special exhibits and educational classes (intangible services).

mfa.org/shop

One important distinction exists between not-for-profit organizations and profit-oriented companies: Profit-seeking businesses tend to focus their marketing on just one public—their customers. Not-for-profit organizations, however, must often market to multiple publics, which complicates decision making regarding the correct markets to target. Many deal with at least two major publics—their clients and their sponsors—and often many other publics, as well. Political candidates, for example, target both voters and campaign contributors. A college targets prospective students as clients of its marketing program, but it also markets to current students, parents of students, alumni, faculty, staff, local businesses, and local government agencies.

A second distinguishing characteristic of not-for-profit marketing is that a customer or service user may wield less control over the organization's destiny than would be true for customers of a profit-seeking firm. A government employee may be far more concerned with the opinion of a member of the legislature's appropriations committee than with that of a service user. Not-for-profit organizations also often possess some degree of monopoly power in a given geographic area. An individual contributor might object to the United Fund's inclusion of a crisis center among its beneficiary agencies, but that agency still receives a portion of the person's total contribution.

In another potential problem, a resource contributor, such as a legislator or financial backer, may interfere with the marketing program. It is easy to imagine a political candidate harassed by financial supporters who want to replace an unpopular campaign manager (the primary marketing position in a political campaign).

Perhaps the most commonly noted feature of the not-for-profit organization is its lack of a *bottom line*—business jargon referring to the overall profitability measure of performance. Profit-seeking firms measure profitability in terms of sales and revenues. While not-for-profit organizations may attempt to maximize their return from specific services, they usually substitute less exact goals, such as service-level standards, for overall evaluation criteria. As a result, it is often difficult to set marketing objectives that are aligned specifically with overall organizational goals. However, in recent years, not-for-profit groups have felt increased pressure to develop more cost-effective ways to provide services. They are also being held accountable for administrative costs.

A final characteristic of a typical not-for-profit organization is the lack of a clear organizational structure. Not-for-profit organizations often respond to constituencies that they serve, but these usually are less exact than, for example, the stockholders of a profit-oriented corporation. Not-for-profit organizations often have multiple organizational structures. A hospital might have an administrative structure, a professional organization consisting of medical personnel, and a volunteer organization that dominates the board of trustees. These people may sometimes work at cross-purposes and disagree with the organization's marketing strategy.

While profit-seeking firms may share some of these characteristics, they are particularly prevalent in not-for-profit organizations. However, all organizations, both profit seekers and not-for-profit groups, must develop marketing strategies to satisfy the needs and wants of consumers.

Nontraditional Marketing

As marketing gained acceptance as a generic activity, its application broadened far beyond its traditional boundaries. In some cases, broader appeals focus on causes, events, individuals, organizations, and places in the not-for-profit sector. In other instances, they encompass diverse groups of profit-seeking individuals, activities, and organizations. Table 1.4 lists and describes five major categories of nontraditional marketing: person marketing, place marketing, cause marketing, event marketing, and organization marketing.

4

Describe the five types of nontraditional marketing.

Person Marketing

One category of nontraditional marketing, **person marketing,** refers to efforts designed to cultivate the attention, interest, and preferences of a target

M A R K E T I N G   D I C T I O N A R Y

person marketing Marketing efforts designed to cultivate the attention, interest, and preference of a target market toward a person (typically a political candidate or celebrity).

TABLE 1.4	Categories of Nontraditional Marketing	
TYPE	**BRIEF DESCRIPTION**	**EXAMPLES**
Person marketing	Marketing efforts designed to cultivate the attention, interest, and preference of a target market toward a person	Celebrities such as basketball star Shaquille O'Neal, Latin singing star Ricky Martin, comedian Chris Rock, and singer/actress Madonna; political candidates such as "Bush for President"
Place marketing	Marketing efforts designed to attract visitors to a particular area; improve consumer images of a city, state, or nation; and/or attract new business	Israel: No one belongs here more than you. Come to Jamaica and feel all right. Washington, D.C.: The American Experience
Cause marketing	Identification and marketing of a social issue, cause, or idea to selected target markets	Welfare to Work. It works. Friends don't let friends drive drunk.
Event marketing	Marketing of sporting, cultural, and charitable activities to selected target markets	NASCAR Firecracker 400; American Cancer Society Relay for Life
Organization marketing	Marketing efforts of mutual-benefit organizations, service organizations, and government organizations that seek to influence others to accept their goals, receive their services, or contribute to them in some way	Navy: Let the journey begin. United Way brings out the best in all of us. Tech Corps: America needs to know.

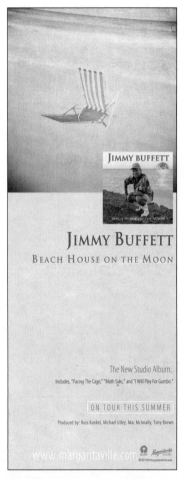

Top-grossing entertainer Jimmy Buffett practices person marketing with a combination of albums, concert tours, restaurants, and merchandise sales.

market toward a celebrity or authority figure. Celebrities can be real people (like basketball legend Michael Jordan who lends his image to such products as MCI Worldcom), fictional characters (such as Butterfinger candy bar promotions by television's Bart Simpson), or widely-recognized authority figures (like former presidential candidate Bob Dole and General Norman Schwartzkopf for prostate cancer awareness).

Campaigns for political candidates and the marketing of celebrities are examples of person marketing. In political marketing, candidates target two markets: They attempt to gain the recognition and preference of voters and the financial support of donors.

The big winners among celebrity endorsers are professional athletes. Michael Jordan earns as much as $40 million each year endorsing such products as Oakley sunglasses; Philadelphia 76ers sensation Allen Iverson has a shoe deal with Reebok; NASCAR driver Dale Earnhardt has licensed his name to Action Performance souvenir company; and Tiger Woods lends his celebrity to the Official All Star Cafe.[15]

Jimmy Buffett is the most unlikely sort of celebrity. His only top ten single hit the charts back in 1977. But here in the 21st century, he is packing in thousands of concert-goers who make his summer tours one of the top draws each year. His hard-core fans, known as Parrot Heads, often show up in full tropical attire—foam parrot hats, green and yellow grass skirts, and coconut-shell bras.

The fans are eager to participate in an illusion—those landlocked pillars of their community pretending they are finally going to cash in their chips and set sail for uncharted waters. And the man they have come to see is Jimmy Buffett. This year, they will spend over $50 million on his concert tickets, albums, books, T-shirts, trinkets, and food. The Buffett "brand" is carved from over 30 albums, eight movies, a clothing line, a series of Margaritaville Cafes, a custom record label, three best-selling novels, and hundreds of gift-shop trinkets.

Buffett works hard at perpetuating this image. He launched a Web site to sell his merchandise and was among the first stars to land a corporate sponsor —Corona Beer. His books, including *Tales from Margaritaville* and *A Pirate Looks at Fifty*, add to the carefree, beach-bum lifestyle legend. In addition, he gives freely to environmental causes, donating $1 from every concert ticket to local causes of the cities where he tours. He has served as chairman of the Save the Manatee society. Buffett's three-decades-long career is a textbook example of how to cross-market music, restaurants, and retailing.[16]

Place Marketing

Another category of nontraditional marketing is **place marketing,** which attempts to attract customers to particular areas. Cities, states, and countries publicize their tourist attractions to lure vacation travelers. They also promote themselves as good locations for businesses. Place marketing has become more important in the world economy, where localities compete for economic advantage, increased employment, trade, and investment. Organizations as varied as the San Diego Zoo, the Alamo in San Antonio, Texas, state bureaus of tourism and conventions, and the Seattle Port Authority apply place marketing techniques to attract visitors, residents, and new businesses to their areas. Their strategies include promoting positive images; marketing special attractions like The Great Wall of China, India's Taj Mahal, and Niagara Falls; highlighting efficient transportation infrastructures and communication systems; and stressing the quality of available education, low crime rates, clean air and water, and cultural and recreational opportunities. Place marketing also fills promotional messages with positive perceptions of visitors as well as people who live in the area.

Cause Marketing

A third category of nontraditional marketing, **cause marketing,** refers to the identification and marketing of a social issue, cause, or idea to selected target markets. Cause marketing covers a wide range of issues, including literacy, physical fitness, gun control, family planning, prison reform, control of overeating, environmental protection, elimination of birth defects, child-abuse prevention, and punishment of drunk drivers.

An increasingly common marketing practice is for profit-seeking firms to link their products to social causes. Recent examples include women's athletic shoe company Ryka Inc., which contributes 7 percent of its earnings to prevent violence against women; the Body Shop, which champions the environment; and Reebok International, which focuses on human rights.

Recent surveys show strong support for cause-related marketing by both consumers and company employees. Two-thirds of people surveyed said that if price and quality are equal, they were more likely to switch to a civic-minded brand or retailer. The top three issues consumers would like marketers to address are public education, crime, and the environment.[17]

Event Marketing

Event marketing refers to the marketing of sporting, cultural, and charitable activities to selected target markets. It also includes the sponsorship of such events by firms seeking to increase public awareness and bolster their images by linking themselves and their products to the events. Sports sponsorships have gained effectiveness in increasing brand recognition, enhancing image, boosting purchase volume, and increasing popularity with sports fans in demographic segments corresponding to sponsor business goals.

The premiere event in sports takes place every four years. The most recent, the 2000 Sydney Olympics, featured 10,000 athletes from 198 countries who took part in 28 sports. The games brought an extra 1.3 million visitors to Australia, including 60,000 media representatives. Over 1 billion viewers watched at least some of the globally-televised events. NBC, which bought U.S. media rights for $706 million, earned over $800 million from the sale of advertising. Marketers seeking to link their products and companies to the Olympics through ads and official sponsorships included such well-known firms as General Motors, Nike, IBM, Visa, Home Depot, McDonald's, Honda, Texaco, Toyota, and UPS.

Australia reaped a number of benefits from the Games. The Sydney Olympics added $US6 billion to the nation's gross domestic product and created 150,000 full- and part-time jobs. It also left its mark on the nation in the form of numerous world-class sports facilities paid

MARKETING | **DICTIONARY**

place marketing Marketing efforts to attract people and organizations to a particular geographic area.

cause marketing Identification and marketing of a social issue, cause, or idea to selected target markets.

event marketing Marketing of sporting, cultural, and charitable activities to selected target markets.

IBM's sponsorship of the Sydney 200 Olympics included the official provider of Internet technologies to the games. IBM participates in event marketing to increase its brand recognition and corporate image.

noma.org

for by the Games. By acquainting visitors and viewers the world over with the attractiveness of the land down under, Australia received a boost in national pride and the nation's profile in business and tourism.[18]

Organization Marketing

The category of nontraditional marketing called **organization marketing** involves attempts to influence others to accept the goals of, receive the services of, or contribute in some way to an organization. Organization marketing includes mutual-benefit organizations (churches, labor unions, and political parties), service organizations (colleges and universities, hospitals, and museums), and government organizations (military services, police and fire departments, and the U.S. Postal Service).

As cultural organizations encounter declining public funding for the arts and rising competition from other entertainment forms, they respond by actively marketing their programs. Like profit-seeking businesses, the New Orleans Museum of Art must generate funds to cover its operating expenses. Revenues come from a number of sources, including individual donations, memberships, government grants, gift-shop sales, and special fund-raising drives. The organization also has a Web site and uses such business techniques as marketing research, advertising, and publicity. Special events, such as a special exhibition of works painted in New Orleans by the French impressionist master Edgar Degas, provide added value to museum members and attract thousands of occasional and first-time visitors who may become members.

ELEMENTS OF A MARKETING STRATEGY

5

Identify the basic elements of a marketing strategy and the environmental characteristics that influence strategy decisions.

Although the product at the center of a marketing campaign may consist of a tangible good or an intangible service, cause, event, person, place, or organization, success in the marketplace always depends on an effective marketing strategy. The basic elements of a marketing strategy consist of (1) the target market and (2) the marketing mix variables of product, distribution, promotion, and price that combine to satisfy the needs of the target market. The outer circle in Figure 1.4 lists environmental characteristics that provide the framework within which marketing strategies are planned.

The Target Market

With the growing presence of computers in business today, marketing activities must focus on the consumer more than ever. Therefore, a market-driven organization begins its overall strategy with a detailed description of its **target market:** the group of people toward whom the firm decides to direct its marketing efforts.

Sears serves a target market consisting of consumers purchasing for themselves and their families. Other companies, such as Boeing, market most of their products to business buyers like United Airlines and government purchasers. Still other firms provide goods and services to retail and wholesale buyers. In every instance, however, marketers should delineate their target markets as specifically as possible. Consider the following examples:

■ Just My Size targets plus-size women (who account for over half the women in the United States) by designing casual wear, lingerie, hosiery, and jeans in sizes 16 and up.

- AT&T promotes its highly profitable 1-800-CALL-ATT collect calling service by blanketing such television programs as MTV, Buffy the Vampire Slayer, wrestling matches, and countless other programs geared to teenagers and college students. Some 70 percent of collect calls are made by people 30 and younger.[19]

- The target market for the Saab 900 convertible consists of well-educated professionals and managers aged 30 to 40 years old with household incomes over $50,000 who want a high-performance car that is fun to drive.

Although considerations about identification and satisfaction of a target market are relevant to every chapter in this text, Chapter 8 in Part 3 focuses on methods of segmenting markets. Two chapters in Part 4 discuss consumer behavior (Chapter 9) and the analysis of business-to-business marketing (Chapter 10).

Marketing Mix Variables

After marketers select a target market, they direct company activities toward profitably satisfying that segment. Although they must manipulate thousands of variables to reach this goal, marketing decision making can be divided into four strategies: product, pricing, distribution, and promotion strategies. The total package forms the **marketing mix**—the blending of the four strategy elements to fit the needs and preferences of a specific target market. Each strategy is a variable in the mix. While the fourfold classification is useful in study and analysis, a particular combination of the variables determines marketing success.

Figure 1.4 illustrates the focus of the marketing mix variables on the central choice of consumer or organizational target markets. In addition, decisions about product, price, distribution, and promotion are affected by the environmental factors in the outer circle of the figure. Unlike the controllable marketing mix elements, the environmental variables frequently lie outside the control of marketers. However, they may play a major role in the success of a marketing program, and marketers must consider their probable effects even if control remains impossible. Note also that the consumer is not a marketing mix component since marketers have little or no control over the future behavior of present and potential consumers.

Product Strategy

In marketing, the word *product* means more than a good, service, or idea. Product is a broad concept that also encompasses the satisfaction of all consumer needs in relation to a good, service, or idea. Thus, **product strategy** involves more than just deciding what goods or services the firm should offer to a group of consumers. It also includes making decisions about customer service, package design, brand names, trademarks, warranties, product life cycles, positioning, and new product development. Many of these elements are illustrated in the Champion Woman ad shown in Figure 1.5. This ad emphasizes the company's ability to provide stylish, yet sturdy, active wear designed to fit women size 14 to 28. The ad also demonstrates the product's

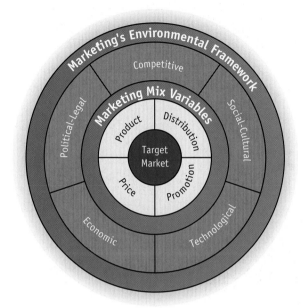

FIGURE 1.4   Elements of a Marketing Strategy and Its Environmental Framework

Elements of the Champion Product Strategy

other qualities, such as Champion's ability to make attractive, comfortable sportswear that active women will want to wear. The familiar red, white, and blue Champion label also signifies the quality for which the company is known.

The growing number of female business travelers has prompted the travel industry to modify its offerings by adding a number of services designed to increase satisfaction among women hotel guests. Based on suggestions by Wyndham Hotels & Resorts' Advisory Board of Women Business Travelers, the chain added a number of features in its product strategy:

- special amenities such as loofah mitts and skirt hangers in hotel rooms
- networking tables set aside in hotel restaurants for solo travelers who prefer to eat with others
- a warning call five minutes before room-service delivery to alert guests before a meal is delivered
- jogging partners and chilled bottled water, fresh fruit, and plush towels upon return from a run

The newly-designed product lets Wyndham and other hotel chains offer improved customer satisfaction for this growing market. As recently as 1970, women accounted for only 1 percent of all business travelers; today the number has grown to 50 percent.[20]

Two chapters in Part 5 deal with product strategy. Chapter 11 introduces the basic elements of product and service strategies, while Chapter 12 discusses product mix decisions and new-product planning.

Distribution Strategy

Marketers develop **distribution strategies** to ensure that consumers find their products in the proper quantities at the right times and places. Distribution decisions involve modes of transportation, warehousing, inventory control, order processing, and selection of marketing channels. Marketing channels are made up of institutions such as retailers and wholesalers—all those involved in a product's movement from producer to final consumer.

Technology is opening new channels of distribution in many industries. For example, software, a product made of digital data files, is ideally suited to electronic distribution. Major players like Netscape, Sun Microsystems, and Microsoft Corp. already distribute their programs and upgrades directly over the Internet. Electronic commerce holds great promise for providing quick response to purchasers while markedly reducing prices by slashing packaging and shipping costs, cutting out many intermediaries, and allowing online shoppers to look for the best prices from both domestic and international suppliers.

Distribution strategy is covered in more detail in Part 6. Topics include marketing channels and logistics management (Chapter 13) and retailing, direct marketing, and wholesaling (Chapter 14).

Promotional Strategy

Promotion is the communication link between sellers and buyers. Organizations use many different means of sending messages about their goods, services, and ideas. They may communicate messages directly through salespeople or indirectly through advertisements and sales promotions. Highly creative advertisements like the one in Figure 1.6 can even provide a form of demonstration. Pepto-Bismol marketers capitalize on their product's unique color to impart its benefits with catchy slogans like, "Gets you back in the pink of things," and this newest one,

"Lets you stomach it." The pink jalapeño tells readers that Pepto-Bismol will cool red-hot peppers to pastel pink.

In developing a **promotional strategy,** marketers blend together the various elements of promotion to communicate most effectively with their target market. Many companies use an approach called *integrated marketing communications (IMC)* to coordinate all promotional activities so that the consumer receives a unified and consistent message. Sony PlayStation Underground, for example, has built the brand and its customer base through the use of IMC programs. The subscription-driven club for video gamers who use PlayStation hardware targets consumers with a mix of direct mail, catalogs, a Web site, a computer disk magazine, television spots, package inserts, space ads, and even billboards. In just one year, PlayStation Underground members received some 47 mailings from Sony; software developers received nine; and PlayStation distributors got five mailings. Future plans include creating greater synergy between TV spots, print ads, and other marketing efforts. Sony's database has grown from 100,000 to 1.5 million names, all of whom will receive Sony's new catalog of branded merchandise. Says Peter Dille, Sony's director for product marketing, "Anything that makes the PlayStation customer relationship stronger will sell more product."[21]

Integrated marketing communications is examined further in Chapter 15 of Part 7. Chapter 16 deals with advertising, sales promotion, and public relations. Personal selling and sales management are the topics of Chapter 17.

Pricing Strategy

One of the most difficult areas of marketing decision making, **pricing strategy,** deals with the methods of setting profitable and justifiable prices. It is closely regulated and subject to considerable public scrutiny.

One of the many factors that influence a marketer's pricing strategy is competition. The computer industry has become all too familiar with price cuts by both current competitors and new market entrants. After years of steady growth, the market has become saturated with low-cost computers, driving down profit margins even farther. Big PC makers such as Dell, Compaq, and IBM are trying to compensate by focusing more on business customers. Meanwhile, start-ups like eMachines and Microworkz are the fastest growing segment of the retail computer market with a 20 percent share. In 1998, just 2 percent of computers could be bought for less than $600; today, well over 20 percent are sold at below that price.[22]

Pricing strategy is the subject of Part 8. Chapter 18 analyzes the elements involved in determining prices and Chapter 19 examines the management aspect of pricing.

The Marketing Environment

Marketers do not make decisions about target markets and marketing mix variables in a vacuum. They must take into account the dynamic nature of the five dimensions of the marketing environment shown in Figure 1.4: competitive, political-legal, economic, technological, and social-cultural factors. Environmental concerns have led to new regulations on air and water pollution. Automobile engineers, for instance,

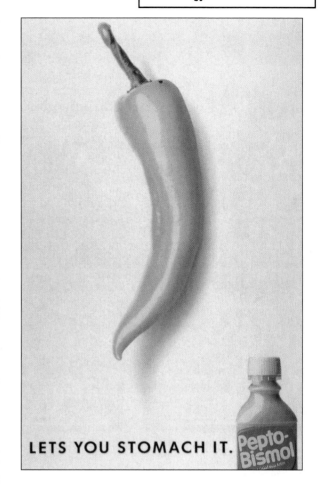

FIGURE 1.6 Advertising as Part of the Pepto-Bismol Promotional Strategy

LETS YOU STOMACH IT.

 playstation.com

MARKETING DICTIONARY

distribution strategy Element of marketing decision making concerned with activities and marketing institutions that get the right good or service to the firm's customers.

promotional strategy Element of marketing decision making that involves appropriate blending of personal selling, advertising, and sales promotion to communicate with and seek to persuade potential customers.

pricing strategy Element of marketing decision making dealing with methods of setting profitable and justifiable prices.

Does Levi's Have a Leg to Stand On?

BACKGROUND Levi's is synonymous with jeans. The brand, an American icon, is better known around the globe than Marlboro, Nike, or Microsoft. In the early 1990s, it commanded a 48 percent share of the men's jeans market. Even today, three of every four U.S. males own a pair of Levi's Dockers khakis.

THE MARKETING PROBLEM Too much success bred complacency. Levi's did not change, and competitors moved in—trendier names such as Calvin Klein, Tommy Hilfiger, Old Navy, and The GAP. Retail chains like Sears and JCPenney—major distribution channels for Levi's—began pushing their own Canyon River and Arizona brands. Also, today's teenagers and young adults, who associated Levi's with their parents, considered the brand stodgy. The company cemented this opinion with its failure to lead recent trends for cargo pants and wide-bottom slacks. By the year 2000, Levi's market share had shrunk to 25 percent.

THE OUTCOME The decline in market share has been accompanied by 29 U.S. plant closings and pink slips for over 16,000 employees. Lower-cost contract manufacturing in Mexico and South America is expected to cut production costs, but improvements are needed in undependable production and delivery schedules and lackluster advertising in the years since the "501 Blues" campaign. Do not count Levi Strauss out, but it will take years to remedy the many marketing problems.

continued on next page

have turned public concerns and legal issues into opportunities by developing hybrid cars for the new century. These new models are fueled by dual energy: a gasoline engine and an electric motor. Toyota was the first to enter the market with its Prius, which depends primarily on the electric motor, but includes a backup gasoline engine. The Prius currently sells in Japan for about $19,000. Changes in the legal environment regarding automobile emissions alerted automobile designers to make these changes. By accommodating future needs of consumers and meeting the more stringent legal requirements, they created a new market segment. It did not take long for competitors to follow Toyota's lead. Honda's new VV model runs primarily on its gasoline engine with the electric motor as its secondary energy source. Honda plans to hit the showrooms with a vehicle that offers a lower price and better gas mileage. Nissan and Fuji Heavy Industries also have models on the drawing boards for proposed debuts in 2001. European and U.S. automakers, however, have not jumped at the chance to enter the race with their version of a hybrid car. General Motors might have a so-called green car ready in 2001; Ford and DaimlerChrysler say they may be ready by 2003.[23]

Corporate giants are increasingly looking to foreign shores for new growth markets. Wal-Mart has been the star child of American business for years, although a mounting number of competitors has begun to chip away its market. When the going got tough, Wal-Mart got going—to other countries, that is. Within two years, it doubled its foreign sales to $7.5 billion. Currently only 6 percent of Wal-Mart's sales are from outside the United States, but this huge potential market is a major current focus.[24]

Two more important characteristics in the contemporary marketing environment include cultural diversity and ethical concerns. Every chapter in this book contains detailed examples that explore the impact of these factors.

Dimensions of the marketing environment are discussed in greater depth in Chapter 2. The significance of these dimensions in the global marketplace is presented in Chapter 3. Chapter 5 explains the value of relationship strategies to all organizations. The marketing environment is important because it provides a framework for all marketing activity. It influences the development of marketing plans and forecasts, which are described in Chapter 6, and the process of marketing research, the subject of Chapter 7. Marketers consider the environmental dimensions when they develop segmentation strategies (Chapter 8) and when they study consumer and organizational buying behavior, the topics of Chapters 9 and 10, respectively.

Critical Thinking and Creativity

The challenges presented by today's complex and technologically sophisticated marketing environment require critical-thinking skills and creativity from marketing professionals. *Critical thinking* refers to the process of determining the authenticity, accuracy, and worth of information, knowledge, claims, and arguments. Critical thinkers react skeptically to what they hear or see. They do not take information at face value and simply assume that it is accurate; they analyze the data themselves and develop their own opinions and conclusions.

Creative government bureaucracy might sound like an oxymoron, but it is an accurate description of the U.S. Mint since Philip N. Diehl became director. After years of fighting entrenched political resistance, Diehl was able to transform this $1 billion government agency into a close approximation of a private sector, profit-seeking business. The organization chart was reorganized, jobs were redesigned and positions added, state-of-the-art computerized information systems were installed, bureaucratic workers were trained to become customer-responsive employees, and new products were introduced. In 1998, the 50-state quarter program was launched. The Mint will release five quarters a year, each featuring a different state. It also designed the new dollar coin, first minted in January 2000, featuring the likeness of the Native American Sacajawea. The result of all these creative changes is a government agency that shines, as they say, like a brand-new penny.[25]

Creativity is an extremely valuable skill for marketers. It helps them to develop novel solutions to perceived marketing problems. Leonardo da Vinci conceived his idea for a helicopter after watching leaves twirl in the wind. Swiss engineer George de Mestral noticing that burrs stuck to his wool socks because of their tiny hooks, invented Velcro.

Creativity is particularly important in the creation of promotional messages. Figure 1.7 demonstrates the use of humor to communicate the beauty and durability of Armstrong laminate flooring.

THE TECHNOLOGY REVOLUTION IN MARKETING

As we enter the new century, we also enter into a new era in communication, considered by some as unique as the fifteenth-century invention of the printing press or the first radio and television broadcasts early in the twentieth century. **Technology** is the business application of knowledge based on scientific discoveries, inventions, and innovations. Interactive multimedia technologies such as computer networks, video conferencing, online services and the Internet, interactive kiosks, CD-ROM catalogs, and personal digital assistants have revolutionized the way people store, distribute, retrieve, and present information. Computer networks and other telecommunications technologies link employees, suppliers, and customers in different locations through the Internet or in-house Intranets.

These technological advances are revolutionizing marketing. Companies can reach specific groups of customers in a variety of ways: from hotels' in-house television channels targeting guests to toll-free telephone numbers and in-store videos with point-of-purchase product demonstrations. Now that nearly half of all U.S. households have personal computers, online services and the Internet offer a new medium over which companies can market products and offer customer service. Marketing and sales departments can quickly access vast databases with information about customers and their buying patterns. They can develop targeted marketing campaigns and zoned advertising programs for consumers located within a certain distance from a store and even within specific city blocks.

Shoppers can visit kiosks in shopping malls that feature video displays, discount coupons, and product information for a variety of merchants. They can browse through a CD-ROM product catalog on their computers or conduct specific searches to quickly find desired items. Surfing the Web or online services is another way to get product information and order merchandise from catalogs. Firms can quickly update this information at minimal costs. Online retail spending in the United States is growing at an alarming rate—from $7.8 billion in 1998 to an expected $100 billion by 2003. Consumers' willingness to spend online is growing as is the amount they spend on each visit. Says Michael West, CEO of online retailer FurniturePoint.com, "The overwhelming majority of the people [we surveyed] said that they would spend over $1,500 on the Internet."[26]

Technological developments play an important role in every phase of marketing, as you will see throughout the text. Each chapter begins with an example of a company that uses technology to develop more effective marketing strategies. We also include many examples of

6

Outline the changes in the marketing environment due to technology and relationship marketing.

FIGURE 1.7   Creative Communication of Armstrong Quality

We set out to make the most incredibly durable, beautiful floor. We think we succeeded. (knock on wood)

Armstrong
The beauty is, it stays that way.

MARKETING   DICTIONARY

technology Application to business of knowledge based on scientific discoveries, inventions, and innovations.

FurniturePoint.com

the impact of technology on marketing (www.dryden.com/mktng/boone/). Every chapter ends with a number of 'netWork assignments that let you explore the Internet and take advantage of its capabilities in solving marketing problems. The text has been expanded through the creation of the Boone & Kurtz Home Page, which contains additional case materials, up-to-date reports of recent marketing developments, and updates on people and organizations featured in the text. As an example of the effect of the technological revolution on marketing, consider two key developments: interactive marketing and the Internet.

Interactive Marketing

Interactive media technologies combine computers and telecommunications resources to create software that users can direct themselves. They allow people to digitalize reports and drawings and transmit them, quickly and inexpensively, over phone lines, coaxial cables, or fiber optic cables. People can subscribe to personalized news services that deliver article summaries on specified topics directly to their fax machines or computers. They can telecommunicate via e-mail, voice mail, fax, video conferencing, and computer networks; pay bills using online banking services; and use online resources to get information about everything from investments to a local retailer's special sale, day-care facilities, and local entertainment activities for the upcoming weekend.

Companies are now using interactivity in their marketing programs, as well. **Interactive marketing** refers to buyer-seller communications in which the customer controls the amount and type of information received from a marketer. This technique provides immediate access to key product information when the consumer wants it. Interactive techniques have been used for more than a decade; point-of-sale brochures and coupon dispensers are a simple form of interactive advertising. Today, however, the term also includes two-way electronic communication using a variety of media such as the Internet, CD-ROMs, and virtual reality kiosks.

Interactive marketing frees communications between marketers and their customers from the limits of the traditional, linear, one-way messages to passive audiences using broadcast or print ads. Now customers come to companies for information, creating opportunities for one-to-one marketing. For example, each customer who visits a Web site has a different experience, based on the pathway of links he or she chooses to follow. Interactive marketing can also allow many-to-many exchanges, where consumers can communicate with one another using e-mail or electronic bulletin boards.

Interactivity involves more than just moving from one section of a CD-ROM or Web page to another. These electronic conversations establish innovative relationships between users and the technology, providing customized information based on users' interests and levels of understanding. Interactive technologies support almost limitless exchanges of information. People gain access to chosen programs and services via their personal computers and telephones, and they can purchase products not only from stores but also via television or the Internet. For example, the Weather Channel offers extra information on local forecasts and the *Tonight Show* provides details about Jay Leno's guests on its interactive TV programs.

One of the busiest areas of interactive marketing is online auctions and name-your-own-price vendors. This sector, which is expected to draw well over 6 million buyers by 2002, includes airline tickets, hotel rooms, cruises, and rental cars. Although Budget, Avis, and Hertz all have Web reservation sites, Budget was the first to establish an interactive price bidding feature, the Bid-Budget program. Online bidders simply fill out a form indicating the desired dates and airport pickup location, preferred car type, contact information, a major credit-card number, and the price they are willing to pay. Budget notifies the bidder within 24 hours whether a bid is accepted and offers a money-back guarantee up to 48 hours before the pick up time.[27]

bid.drivebudget.com

Interactive marketing can transform and enhance customer relationships. Interactive promotions put the customer in control. They can easily get tips on product usage and answers to customer service questions, they can also tell the company what they like or dislike about a product, and they can just as easily click the exit button and move on to another area. The challenge is attracting and holding consumer attention. Marketers must devise new strategies based on interactive marketing techniques to build lasting customer relationships. Subsequent chapters will show how companies are successfully using interactive techniques in their marketing campaigns.

The Internet

Most of today's discussion of interactive marketing centers on the Internet. The **Internet** is an all-purpose global network composed of some 50,000 different networks around the globe that, within limits, lets anyone with access to a personal computer send and receive images and text anywhere.

The Internet provides an efficient way to find and share information, but until recently, most people outside universities and government agencies found it difficult to use and learn. This changed in 1993 with the advent of browser technology that provides point-and-click access to the **World Wide Web** (**WWW** or **Web**). The Web is actually an interlinked collection of graphically rich information sources within the larger Internet. Web sites provide *hypermedia* resources, a system allowing storage of and access to text, graphics, audio, and video in so-called *pages* linked to each other in a way that integrates these different media elements. When a user clicks on a highlighted word or picture (icon), the browser converts the click to computer commands and brings the requested new information—text, photograph, chart, song, or movie clip—to the user's computer.

The following statistics will give you a bird's-eye view of the electronic highway and how fast organizations are moving along it in the new millennium:

- In 1998, more than 147 million people used the Internet; 52 percent were from the United States.
- Of the 45 million Americans who shop online, 16 million buy.
- While 39 percent use the Internet for pleasure, 30 percent use it for work.
- Online transactions of $100 to $499 comprise 25 percent of all online sales.
- Convenience is the reason 60 percent of shoppers go online; 40 percent are there to save time.
- The top 100 retail sites have revenues of over $1 billion.
- Almost 7 million consumers used the Internet to make travel reservations.
- In the next 12 months, over 81 percent of consumers surveyed intend to shop or buy online.[28]

Compared to traditional media, the hypermedia resources of the Web offer a number of advantages. Data moves in seconds, without the user noticing that several computers in different locations combine to fulfill a request. Interactive control allows users to quickly access other information resources through related pages, either at the same or other sites, and easily navigate through documents. Because it is dynamic, Web site sponsors can easily keep information current. Finally, multimedia capacities increase the attractiveness of these documents.

How Marketers Use the Web

Companies are rushing to establish themselves on the World Wide Web. American Airlines' Web-based revenues grow some 22 percent each month. Dell computer reaps a 30 percent higher profit margin for each machine it sells on the Web than from any other channel. National Semiconductor uses the Web as a global communication tool for

MARKETING STRATEGY SUCCESS

Hasbro Interactive Has It All!

BACKGROUND Hasbro Interactive, a division of Hasbro toys, has launched such well-known names as Monopoly, Trivial Pursuit, Scrabble, and *Star Wars* into cyberspace. In three short years, the interactive marketer has increased sales ninefold from $35 million to over $300 million.

THE CHALLENGE After industry giant Mattel added to its marketing muscle by acquiring the Learning Company, a leader in entertainment and educational software, Hasbro Interactive president Thomas Dusenberry knew their competitive battle had intensified. "Our goal," he explains, "is to knock all of our competitors out of business. We know we need to apply technology into our business even more than we already have."

THE STRATEGY Hasbro Interactive focused on relationship marketing in a big way, partnering with

continued on next page

MARKETING DICTIONARY

interactive marketing Buyer-seller communications in which the customer controls the amount and type of information received from a marketer through such channels as the Internet, CD-ROMs, interactive toll-free telephone numbers, and virtual reality kiosks.

Internet All-purpose global communications network composed of some 50,000 different networks around the globe that, within limits, lets anyone with access to a personal computer send and receive images and data anywhere.

World Wide Web (**WWW** or **Web**) Interlinked collection of graphically rich information sources within the larger Internet.

delivering up-to-the-minute product information without any direct mail or advertising costs. The stories of new-found riches on the Web are too numerous to list. The point being that the Web offers practical strategies to everyone in business can use to increase sales and profits.[29]

The Web offers marketers a powerful, yet affordable way to reach customers across town or overseas, at almost any time, with interactive messages. The online techniques that companies use to market their businesses fall into four broad categories: interactive brochures, virtual storefronts, information clearinghouses, and customer service tools.

- *Interactive brochures* that provide company and product information are among the most popular high-tech marketing applications. These range from simple, one-page electronic flyers to multimedia presentations. When American Airlines' travelers need information, they can simply log on to AA.com to get instant access to their AAdvantage account, browse programs and services, make reservations, and check out special benefits available to them as members of American's frequent flyer programs.

- *Online newsletters* provide current news, industry information, and contacts and links for internal and external customers. *Web Commerce Today*, a monthly online newsletter, helps merchants plan, design, manage, and promote retail or business-to-business Web stores.

- The **virtual storefront** takes the interactive brochure one step further and allows customers to view and order merchandise. BuyitNow.com is one such Web site that offers one-stop shopping for people who want to avoid the crowds of a shopping mall and who want to shop from home. BuyitNow carries merchandise from name brand electronics, tools, toys, home decor items, and more. Figure 1.8, the home page for BuyitNow, gives visitors information on special sales and customer services such as gift certificates.

  Web stores can be stand-alone operations or grouped in cybermalls with links to 30 to 100 participating retailers. Some use popular national retailers to "anchor" the malls and draw traffic. Among the cyberstores at MCI Marketplace are Borders Books and Music, Day-Timers, Hammacher Schlemmer, L'Eggs, The Mac Zone, Nordstrom, and PC Zone.

- *Information clearinghouses* provide in-depth product information. Shoppers can ask questions and get online answers, and companies can hold virtual meetings (online conferences) and sponsor discussion groups. The World Wildlife Fund (WWF) maintains a Web site that provides information about the organization and its conservation activities. With 4.7 million supporters and a global network active in over 100 countries, WWF's primary mission is to protect nature. Site visitors can obtain membership information and learn about publications, fund raising campaigns, educational programs, and current conservation issues facing the world today.

- The Web can also be a *customer service tool*. Consumers can order catalogs, refer to lists of frequently asked questions with answers, place service orders online, and send questions to company representatives. For instance, they can access many Kraft Foods Web sites, such as jell-o.com, to obtain information on Kraft's many products, learn new recipes, ask questions about cooking, and even buy merchandise online.

A colorful, dynamic, user-friendly Web site is not enough to ensure cyberspace success. The online marketer must convince potential customers to visit the site. A common method of generating traffic is to advertise on heavy-traffic sites like directories and search engines such as Yahoo!, Excite, and Alta Vista. Online toy-seller eToys outperformed thousands of other Web e-tailers hawking their wares by spending $3 million for a three-year promotional space on America Online. It also pays a 25 percent promotional fee to another 5,000 Net sites like *USA Today* and Ameritech each time they steer a customer to eToys' site. Although the fee sounds high, it is similar in approach to the practice of some restaurants who offer taxi drivers cash each time they direct out-of-town diners to their establishment. The CEO of eToys defends the fee this way: "This business is all about getting customers. If we sell $40 worth of toys, $10 is a reasonable acquisition cost."[30]

Even though the Web is still in its embryonic stages, it is already being hailed as the most significant innovation affecting marketing and business in the past 50 years. Despite the hype surrounding it, few doubt the Internet's ability to transform business as we know it. Properly used, the Web should prove an indispensable tool in promoting connections, building associations, delivering information, and creating online communities.

To date, few companies have made money on the Internet. The primary beneficiaries have been firms marketing Net-related goods or services—for example, computer networking equipment; software such as access, browser, Web page authoring, and e-mail programs; consultants and Web page creators; Internet access and online service providers like PsiNet, Netcom, America Online, and CompuServe; and companies offering sites where businesses can advertise. With annual Internet service spending of $4.6 billion—over half the global total—the United States is the world leading spender on the Web. Total spending on commercial online services and access providers plus the purchase of Web-related goods and services grew from $2.2 billion in 1995 to $8 billion by 1999. By 2003, that figure is expected to top $78 billion, including $4 billion for Web advertising.[31]

As the Web evolves, marketers need to explore its capabilities and learn the best ways to use it effectively in combination with other distribution channels and communications media. Among the questions marketers need to ask are the following:

- What types of goods and services can be successfully marketed on the Web?
- What characteristics make a successful Web presentation?
- Does the Net offer a secure way to process customer orders?
- How will the Net affect traditional store-based and non-store retailing and distribution?
- What is the best use of this technology in a specific firm's marketing strategy: promotion, image building, or sales?

The importance of the Internet is reflected throughout the text. Special Internet exercises are included as student assignments at the end of each chapter. Web addresses are included throughout the text to assist the reader in contacting the firm's Web site directly to obtain more information about specific topics. A brand-new Chapter 4 discusses electronic commerce and its role in contemporary marketing in detail. Finally, as forthcoming chapters discuss specific marketing topics, we will revisit the Internet and look for answers to the questions listed above.

FIGURE 1.8   One-Stop Shopping at the BuyitNow Virtual Storefront

FROM TRANSACTION-BASED MARKETING TO RELATIONSHIP MARKETING

As marketing enters the 21st century, a significant change is taking place in the way companies interact with customers. The traditional view of marketing as a simple exchange process—a concept that might be termed *transaction-based marketing*—is being replaced by a different, longer-term approach.

Traditional marketing strategies focused on attracting customers. The goal was to identify prospects, convert them to customers, and complete sales transactions. But today's marketers realize that, although it remains important, attracting new customers is only an intermediate step in

MARKETING   DICTIONARY

virtual storefront Form of interactive media that allows customers to view and order merchandise.

Both Holiday Inn and Visa benefit from their partnership which strengthens relationships between the lodging chain and its family guests. Offers such as free kids' meals and free water bean bag animals should entice travelers with children to use their Visa cards at Holiday Inn.

the marketing process. Marketing efforts must focus on establishing and maintaining mutually beneficial relationships with existing customers. These efforts must expand to include suppliers and employees, as well.

This concept, called **relationship marketing**, refers to the development, growth, and maintenance of long-term, cost-effective exchange relationships with individual customers, suppliers, employees, and other partners for mutual benefit. It broadens the scope of external marketing relationships to include suppliers, customers, and referral sources. In relationship marketing, the term *customer* takes on a new meaning. Employees serve customers within an organization as well as outside it; individual employees and their departments are customers of and suppliers to one another. They must apply the same high standards of customer satisfaction to intradepartmental relationships as they do to external customer relationships. Relationship marketing recognizes the critical importance of *internal marketing* to the success of *external marketing* plans. Programs that improve customer service inside a company also raise productivity and staff morale, resulting in better customer relationships outside the firm.

Relationship marketing gives a company new opportunities to gain a competitive edge by moving customers up a loyalty hierarchy from *new customers* to *regular purchasers,* then to *loyal supporters* of the company and its goods and services, and finally to *advocates* who not only buy the company's products but recommend them to others. By converting indifferent customers into loyal ones, companies generate repeat sales. The cost of maintaining existing customers is far below the cost of finding new ones, and these loyal customers are profitable ones.

Programs to encourage customer loyalty are not new. Visa teams up with Holiday Inn resorts and hotels during peak vacation months. Holiday Inn advertisements target families, offering a "kids eat free, stay free" program. In addition, travelers who use their Visa cards to stay at one of over 1,000 participating hotels receive a Kids' Activity Book with valuable coupons. Visa has a similar program with Best Western; vacationers who use their Visa card to purchase a Summer Adventures Fun Plan also receive a Fujifilm QuickSnap camera with free film processing, a DC Comics activity book, and Internet software from AT&T WorldNet Service. Best Western lodgers can also enter a sweepstakes using their Visa card.

Effective relationship marketing relies heavily on information technologies such as computer databases that record customers' tastes, price preferences, and lifestyles along with the increase of electronic communications. This technology helps companies become one-to-one marketers that gather customer-specific information and provide individually customized goods and services. The firms target their marketing programs to appropriate groups, rather than relying on mass-marketing campaigns. Companies who study their customers' preferences and react accordingly gain distinct competitive advantages.

Firms in the service industry, from retailers to hotels to airlines, are among the leaders in relationship marketing. Their staff members have many opportunities to meet customers personally and build loyalty and repeat business. Rewards for frequent buyers of a firm's goods or services, such as hotel programs that reward frequent visitors with free room stays and other travel discounts, are another form of relationship marketing.

Developing Partnerships and Strategic Alliances

Relationship marketing does not apply just to individual consumers and employees, however. It also affects a wide range of other markets, including business-to-business relationships with the company's suppliers and distributors as well as other types of corporate partnerships. In the past, companies have often viewed their suppliers as adversaries against whom they must fiercely

FIGURE 1.9 MaxFactor and the Movies: Co-Marketing Cosmetics and a Shakespeare Film

negotiate prices, playing one off against the other. This attitude is much less prevalent today, however, as companies find benefits from collaborative relationships.

The formation of **strategic alliances**—partnerships that create competitive advantages—is also on the rise. These take many forms, from product development partnerships that involve shared costs for research and development and marketing to vertical alliances where one company provides a product or component to another firm who then distributes or sells it under its own brand.

One of the most popular forms of strategic alliance is the affinity credit-card program. Airline industry leaders like American, United, and Delta build brand loyalty among air travelers by offering awards for frequent travel. They have also established cooperative relationships with hotel chains, automobile-rental companies, long-distance telephone firms, and credit-card companies to jointly market their services.

Co-marketing and licensing arrangements are also popular. MaxFactor and Twentieth Century Fox Films teamed up to jointly promote their products in the ad shown in Figure 1.9. MaxFactor's new cosmetic collection, A Midsummer Night's Dream, was inspired by the movie of the same name, starring Kevin Kline and Calista Flockhart.

Clearly, relationship building begins early in the marketing process and applies to many areas. It begins with the development of quality products that meet customer needs and continues with the provision of excellent customer service during and after the purchase process. Relationship building also includes programs that encourage repeat purchases and foster customer loyalty. Chapter 5 explores the many facets of this important topic in greater depth.

MARKETING DICTIONARY

relationship marketing Development and maintenance of long-term, cost-effective exchange relationships with individual customers, suppliers, employees, and other partners for mutual benefit.

strategic alliance Partnership between organizations that creates competitive advantages.

7

Identify the universal functions of marketing.

COSTS AND FUNCTIONS OF MARKETING

Firms must spend money to create time, place, and ownership utilities. Numerous attempts have been made to measure marketing costs in relation to overall product costs, and most estimates have ranged between 40 and 60 percent of total costs. On the average, one-half of the costs involved in a product, such as a Subway sandwich, an ounce of Safari perfume, a pair of Red Line jeans, or even a European vacation, can be traced directly to marketing. These costs are not associated with fabrics, raw materials and other ingredients, baking, sewing, or any of the other production functions necessary for creating form utility. What, then, does the consumer receive in return for this 50 percent marketing cost? What functions does marketing perform?

As Table 1.5 reveals, marketing is responsible for the performance of eight universal functions: buying, selling, transporting, storing, standardizing and grading, financing, risk taking, and securing marketing information. Some functions are performed by manufacturers, others by retailers, and still others by marketing intermediaries called *wholesalers*.

Buying and selling, the first two functions shown in Table 1.5, represent *exchange functions*. *Buying* is important to marketing on several levels. Marketers must determine how and why consumers buy certain goods and services. To be successful, they must seek to understand consumer behavior. In addition, retailers and other intermediaries must seek out products that will appeal to their customers. Since they generate time, place, and ownership utilities through these purchases, they must anticipate consumer preferences for purchases to be made several months later. *Selling* is the second half of the exchange process. It involves advertising, personal selling, and sales promotion in an attempt to match the firm's goods and services to consumer needs.

Transporting and storing are *physical distribution functions*. *Transporting* involves the physical movement of goods from the seller to the purchaser. Storing involves warehousing goods until they are needed for sale. Manufacturers, wholesalers, and retailers all typically perform these functions.

The final four marketing functions—standardizing and grading, financing, risk taking, and securing marketing information—are often called *facilitating functions* because they assist the marketer in performing the exchange and physical distribution functions. Quality and quantity control *standards* and *grades*, frequently set by federal or state governments, reduce the need for purchasers to inspect each item. Specific tire sizes, for example, permit buyers to request needed sizes and to expect uniform sizes.

Financing is another marketing function because buyers often need access to funds in order to finance inventories prior to sales. Manufacturers often provide financing for their wholesale and retail customers. Some types of wholesalers perform similar functions for their retail customers. Finally, retailers frequently permit their customers to buy on credit.

The seventh function, *risk taking*, is part of most ventures. Manufacturers create goods and services based on research and their belief that consumers need them. Wholesalers and retailers

TABLE 1.5	**Eight Universal Marketing Functions**

EXCHANGE FUNCTIONS	PHYSICAL DISTRIBUTION FUNCTIONS	FACILITATING FUNCTIONS	
1. Buying Ensuring product offerings are available in sufficient quantities to meet customer demands	3. Transporting Moving products from their point of production to locations convenient for purchasers	5. Standardizing and Grading Ensuring product offerings meet quality and quantity controls of size, weight, and other variables	7. Risk Taking Dealing with uncertainty about future customer purchases
2. Selling Using advertising, personal selling, and sales promotion to match products to customer needs	4. Storing Warehousing products until needed for sale	6. Financing Providing credit for channel members (wholesalers and retailers) and consumers	8. Securing Marketing Information Collecting information about consumers, competitors, and channel members for use in making marketing decisions

SOLVING AN ETHICAL CONTROVERSY

Has the Entertainment Industry Stepped over the Line with Violence?

The tragic 1999 Columbine High School shootings in Littleton, Colorado, were followed by a search for the underlying causes behind the increase in teenage violence. Many believe that much of the problem stems from the steady barrage of violence contained in products supplied by the entertainment industry—movies, television programs, records, video games, and sites on the Internet. According to the Parents Television Council, "sexual content, foul language, and violent content combined rose by more than 30 percent" in a three-year period in the late 1990s. Video games have grown increasingly violent between the 1972 debut of Pong, the first video game, and modern offerings like the car-combat game *Carmageddon* (which carried the advertising tagline, "Easier than killing babies with axes"). When asked for a definition of obscene violence, Senator Joseph Lieberman responded, "When we see *Natural Born Killers* and video games like *Carmageddon* and listen to Marilyn Manson, I think we're there."

Entertainment industry marketers feel they already address the issue of violence through their rating systems. The G, PG, PG-13, R, and NC-17 ratings have been used for movies since the 1980s. In recent years, television networks have begun a similar system, with programs like *South Park* carrying a TV-MA warning of suitability only for mature adults. Video games carry postage-stamp-size labels categorizing titles as Adults Only, Mature, Teen, Everyone, or Early Childhood. Of 5,000 games rated in the past five years, 70 percent were considered appropriate for all ages to play. Producers of interactive games, movies, and TV shows are likely to blame parents who make these items available to children and younger teens and retailers who fail to screen purchasers. They support moves like President Clinton's request that movie theaters check identifications before selling tickets to R-rated films. The next big challenge is the Internet, which is proving to be the most elusive medium to regulate.

Should the government regulate violence in the entertainment industry?

Pro
1. Government regulations will help the industry—which currently seems to be ignoring the public interest—regulate itself.
2. Regulations make it easier to punish violators.
3. Ratings are a farce; they are voluntary for the most part and cannot be enforced without regulations.

Con
1. Government regulations will encourage witch hunts in the entertainment industry, and our culture will be poorer if films like *Saving Private Ryan* are condemned as too violent.
2. Regulations should be placed on parents, not producers.
3. It is difficult enough to regulate purchasers of products containing violence, especially on the Internet. It is impossible to regulate who will watch or read a particular production or publication after the sale.

Summary
Regulation proponents claim that the Internet, movies, video games, music, and other entertainment channels are harmfully influencing the perceptions of children and young adults toward such products as tobacco and guns and such activities as sex and violence. Critics claim regulation is not the answer; the entertainment industry is not at fault, but society as a whole—from the retail store where the goods are displayed and purchased to parents who have not taught their children right from wrong. With no clear answer in sight, the current spotlight on the media will certainly gain the attention of the entertainment industry.

Sources: Betsy Streisand, "Lawyers, Guns, Money," *U.S. News & World Report*, June 14, 1999, pp. 56–57; Dean Takahashi, "Video Games, Taking Hits, Try to Shield Kids," *Wall Street Journal*, May 25, 1999, pp. B1, B4; and Jeffrey Taylor, "How Do You Define Obscene Violence? Congress Might Try," *Wall Street Journal*, June 9, 1999, pp. A1, A10.

---

acquire inventory based on similar expectations of future consumer demand. Entrepreneurial risk takers accommodate these uncertainties about future consumer behavior when they market goods and services.

The final marketing function involves *securing marketing information*. Marketers gather information to meet the need for decision-oriented input about customers—who they are, what they buy, where they buy, and how they buy. By collecting and analyzing marketing information, marketers also seek to understand why consumers purchase some goods and services and reject others.

ETHICS AND SOCIAL RESPONSIBILITY: DOING WELL BY DOING GOOD

In recent years, headlines have publicized unethical conduct by several well-known businesses. In 1999, Microsoft Corp., which owns more than 90 percent of the PC operating-systems

8

Demonstrate the relationship between ethical business practices and marketplace success.

FIGURE 1.10

Shell Oil Promotional Message Recruiting Mentors for Inner-City Youth

software market, was convicted of violating antitrust laws by abusing its monopoly to stifle competition and harm consumers. Magazine subscription offers from such direct-marketing giants as American Family Publishers and Publishers Clearing House containing announcements like "You're our newest winner!" confused a number of recipients, prompting a series of lawsuits and investigations by government agencies, and led to more stringent regulations of such sweepstakes. The U.S. Department of Justice investigated allegations of global price fixing and other illegal activities by agribusiness giant Archer-Daniels-Midland.[32]

Despite these and other alleged breaches of ethical standards, most businesspeople do follow ethical practices. Over half of all major corporations now offer ethics training to employees, and most corporate mission statements include pledges to protect the environment, contribute to communities, and improve workers' lives. In some cases, only media attention and pressure from consumers motivate companies to implement social responsibility programs.

Such programs often produce such benefits as improved customer relationships, increased employee loyalty, marketplace success, and improved financial performance. Technology is also playing a role in helping companies like Ford Motor Co. do the right thing. Every Ford vehicle is made from 75 percent recycled materials, ranging from old soda bottles and beer cans to telephones and tires—even old personal computers. They are melted down into brand-new parts like splash shields, lamp bodies, and battery housings. The steel Ford recycles would build 200 Eiffel towers a year, and the 2-liter bottles it converts would fill a 400 acre lake. Ford believes it makes good business sense, but saving money is secondary to saving the planet.

Many companies of all types and sizes sponsor community-based programs. Shell Oil's commitment to community involvement goes back many years and includes a variety of programs, including the Youth Training Academy shown in Figure 1.10. As General Colin Powell has pointed out, the caring individuals at Shell and other companies have "given a major shot in the arm to youth-service organizations that depend on volunteers to do their work." Shell's initiative and support provides opportunities for children to lead productive lives.[33]

Because ethics and social responsibility are important topics to marketers, each chapter in this book includes an experiential exercise called "Solving an Ethical Controversy." For example, this chapter's feature presents pro and con arguments about whether government should regulate violence in the media. Chapter 2 will discuss ethics and social issues in greater detail.

STRATEGIC IMPLICATIONS OF MARKETING IN THE TWENTY-FIRST CENTURY

Unprecedented opportunities have emerged out of electronic commerce and computer technologies in business today. These advances and innovations have allowed organizations to reach new markets, reduce selling and marketing costs, and enhance their relationships with customers and suppliers. Business-to-business e-commerce has grown into a global market thanks to the Internet.

As a new universe for consumers and organizations is created, it demands new marketing approaches to meet changing environments and avoid being left behind in a desolate business world. Profit-seeking and not-for-profit organizations must broaden the scope of their activities to prevent myopic results in their enterprises.

As we begin the rapid journey on a course paved by information technology that leads to a global economy, many aspects of business will become extinct while others will be born. It seems everything is electronic these days: marketing, communications, entertainment, the economy, commerce, and business in general. While some have predicted the demise of traditional marketing and brick-and-mortar retailing, the majority feel that the world of electronic commerce will not eliminate but enhance the systems that exist today.

Marketers must be aware of today's customer-oriented environment and employ computer technologies to satisfy individual needs. One outcropping of this new electronic era is mass customization. Five key trends that will influence consumer behavior include an environment ranging from do-it-yourself, no-service to full-service organizations; a strong emphasis on healthy, better-for-you purchases; more leisure activities with less effort and physical exertion; a shift to entrepreneurialism; and a search for goods and services that save time in a multitasking society.

Marketers must understand that although consumers are empowered with unlimited accessibility to information, they still require quality and satisfaction in the products they purchase. Marketers must overcome barriers on the cyber highway, be faster than the competition, and be able to adapt to changes when necessary. The future is in the Internet, using data, voice, optical, and wireless communications to help bring buyers and sellers together. After all, this is the basis of all marketing activities.

ACHIEVEMENT CHECK SUMMARY

Read the learning objectives that follow, and consider the questions for each one. Answering these questions will reinforce your grasp of the most important concepts in the chapter and will allow you to check how well you have achieved these learning goals. Where a blank appears before a question, answer with *T* or *F* for true/false questions; for multiple-choice questions, choose the letter of the correct answer.

Objective 1.1: Explain how marketing creates utility through the exchange process.
1. _____ Utility is the want-satisfying power of a good or service.
2. _____ The marketing function creates form utility when it assembles a product, such as a television, from component parts.
3. _____ Marketing is defined as a series of activities that create exchanges of value to satisfy perceived needs.

Objective 1.2: Contrast marketing activities during the four eras in the history of marketing.
1. _____ Product marketing was a major activity during the production era.
2. _____ Which of the following strategies did not form part of the sales era? (a) Companies rely on sales forces and advertising to convince customers to buy. (b) Marketing activities begin after the completion of the production process. (c) Product benefits are a primary focus of the marketing strategy.
3. _____ The relationship era emphasizes the importance of acquiring new customers.

Objective 1.3: Define the marketing concept and its relationship to marketing myopia.
1. _____ In a buyer's market, supply exceeds demand.
2. _____ The marketing concept requires an organization to focus its activities toward the consumer.
3. _____ Focusing narrowly on a product rather than customer needs helps a company to grow.

Objective 1.4: Describe the five types of nontraditional marketing.

1. _____ A campaign by Disneyland to attract new visitors is an example of organization marketing.
2. _____ Only not-for-profit organizations use person, place, cause, event, and organization marketing.
3. _____ The Mormon Church, Metropolitan Museum of Art, U.S. Air Force, and Cedars-Sinai Hospital would be most likely to use: (a) person marketing, (b) place marketing, (c) cause marketing, (d) event marketing, or (e) organization marketing.

Objective 1.5: Identify the basic elements of a marketing strategy and the environmental characteristics that influence strategy decisions.
1. _____ The first step in developing a marketing strategy is to: (a) create a product to sell; (b) select a target market; (c) develop a pricing strategy; or (d) design a promotional campaign.
2. _____ Product strategy, pricing strategy, distribution strategy, and promotional strategy are components of the marketing environment.
3. _____ Toyota's decision to add the Prius to its product line was a response to changes in the competitive environment.

Objective 1.6: Outline the changes in the marketing environment due to technology and relationship marketing.
1. _____ Companies should replace traditional marketing communications channels with new technologies like CD-ROM and the World Wide Web.
2. _____ A television advertising campaign is an example of interactive marketing.
3. _____ The main reason companies use the World Wide Web is to provide customer service.

Objective 1.7: Identify the universal functions of marketing.
1. _____ Buying and selling are categorized as facilitating functions.
2. _____ Quality control is an example of the marketing function of: (a) risk taking; (b) storing; (c) securing market information; or (d) standardizing and grading.
3. _____ Some wholesalers perform the financing function for their retail customers.

Objective 1.8: Demonstrate the relationship between ethical business practices and marketplace success.

1. _____ The cost of social responsibility and ethical conduct generally exceeds the business value they create.

2. _____ Environmental protection measures like pollution control and recycling are the responsibility of government, not business.

Students: See solutions section located on page S-1 to check your responses to the Achievement Check Summary.

Key Terms

utility	organization marketing
marketing	target market
exchange process	marketing mix
production orientation	product strategy
sales orientation	distribution strategy
seller's market	promotional strategy
buyer's market	pricing strategy
consumer orientation	technology
marketing concept	interactive marketing
marketing myopia	Internet
person marketing	World Wide Web
place marketing	virtual storefront
cause marketing	relationship marketing
event marketing	strategic alliance

Review Questions

1. Identify the types of utility created by marketing. What types are created in each example?
   a. weekend canoe rental outlet
   b. one-hour dry cleaners
   c. Six Flags over Texas amusement park
   d. annual ice fishing tournament in Minnesota
   e. factory outlet shopping mall
2. Relate the definition of *marketing* to the concept of the exchange process.
3. Discuss the production and sales eras. How does the marketing era differ from the previous eras?
4. How does relationship marketing expand the marketing concept?
5. Explain the concept of marketing myopia. Why is this problem likely to occur? What steps can reduce the likelihood of its occurrence?
6. Explain the concepts of person marketing and event marketing. Contrast them with marketing of a consumer product such as magazines. Why is cause marketing more difficult than place, event, or organization marketing?
7. What type of not-for-profit marketing does each of the following examples represent?
   a. National Rifle Association advertisement
   b. "Don't mess with Texas" slogan
   c. "California. It's where you should be." magazine ad
   d. "Clinton for Senator" campaign
   e. March of Dimes appeal
   f. Chicago Art Institute catalog
   g. University of South Florida
   h. United Way banquet
8. Identify the major variables of the marketing mix. Briefly contrast the mix variables in not-for-profit marketing with those involved in profit-oriented marketing.
9. What are the components of the marketing environment? Why are these characteristics separate from the marketing mix? Is the target market a component of the marketing mix? Briefly describe some technological innovations that are changing the marketing environment.
10. Categorize the following marketing functions as exchange functions, physical distribution functions, or facilitating functions. Choose a local retail store and give an example of how it performs each of these eight functions:
    a. buying
    b. financing
    c. securing marketing information
    d. standardizing and grading
    e. selling
    f. risk taking
    g. storing
    h. transporting

Questions for Critical Thinking

1. Identify two firms that you feel reflect the philosophies of each of the following marketing eras. Defend your answers.
   a. production era
   b. sales era
   c. marketing era
   d. relationship era
2. How would you explain marketing and its importance in the economy to someone not familiar with the subject? Identify the product and the consumer market for each of the following:
   a. local public radio station
   b. American Cancer Society
   c. fat-free snack foods
   d. Cleveland Indians baseball team
3. Describe an experience you had as a customer in which a company used relationship marketing techniques to build customer loyalty.
4. Do you think the World Wide Web is an effective marketing tool? Why or why not? How will the Web and other technological advances affect the way you select and purchase goods in the future?
5. Can a profit-seeking company realistically expect to "do well by doing good"? Explain your answer, using examples.

1. **Today's Global Marketplace.** Ford Motor Company (*www.ford.com*) is an excellent example of a global marketer. In 2000, its seven brands (Aston Martin, Ford, Jaguar, Lincoln, Mazda, Mercury, and Volvo) were brought together with the debut of a new global anthem, "Just Wave Hello," broadcast on major television networks and cable stations on six continents. Go to Ford's Web site and complete the following assignments:

    a. Watch the online presentation of "Just Wave Hello," then download the screensaver and check out the "Sneak Behind the Scenes" link. Prepare a brief report summarizing the creation of the global anthem

    b. Go to the "Worldwide Links" option on the Ford Web site. Visit five or six different countries to learn more about Ford's products and dealers in other parts of the world. Write a 2- to 3-paragraph paper summarizing your findings.

ford.com

2. **Cause Marketing.** Locate a Web site for a company that supports a social cause in which you are interested. For example, *www.bodyshop.com* includes detailed descriptions of Body Shop's concerns about animal testing, a sustainable environment, human rights, as well as the firm's commitment to aid developing economies through trade. Write a 2- to 3-paragraph paper in which you identify the company, the social cause you researched, the effectiveness of the information presented, and your assessment of the fit between the marketer and the social cause being addressed.

bodyshop.com

3. **How Marketers Use the Web.** CommerceNet promotes itself as "the premier global industry consortium for companies using, promoting, and building electronic commerce solutions on the Internet." Review the Web site at *www.commerce.net* then prepare a list of five specific pieces of information to use in a class discussion on the topic, "How Marketers Use the Web."

commerce.net

Video Case 1 on Neiman Marcus begins on page VC-2.

The Marketing Environment, Ethics, and Social Responsibility

CHAPTER

2

1 Identify the five components of the marketing environment.

2 Explain the types of competition marketers face and the steps necessary for developing a competitive strategy.

3 Describe how government and other groups regulate marketing activities and how marketers can influence the political-legal environment.

4 Outline the economic factors that affect marketing decisions and consumer buying power.

5 Discuss the impact of the technological environment on a firm's marketing activities.

6 Explain how the social-cultural environment influences marketing.

7 Describe the role of marketing in society and identify the two major social issues in marketing.

8 Identify each of the four levels of the social responsibility pyramid.

Cleaning Up by Cleaning Up the Environment

Marketers, producers, and the world's consumers co-exist in a symbiotic relationship with their environment. Our decisions and our actions often produce great benefits but occasionally cause great harm. Witness the following:

- Over a decade has passed since the disastrous Exxon *Valdez* tanker spill poured 10 million gallons of crude oil onto Alaska's shores. But this year Americans will dump 200 million gallons of oil when they change their own auto engine oil.
- Every second another acre of the world's rain forest disappears. Environmental champions like the World Wildlife Fund and the Nature Conservancy protect more than 70 million acres worldwide.
- An estimated 2,000 Chinese die each day from smoking-related illnesses.
- The specter of slavery still exists. A 4th-grade class in Denver raised $45,000 to buy freedom for 600 Sudanese slaves.

Ray Anderson realized that he could add another frightening statistic to this list: America's floor-covering industry discards 4 billion pounds of solid waste every year.

What is interesting about Anderson is that he is no outsider railing against industry abuses. In fact, he is founder and CEO of Interface, a billion-dollar international manufacturer of carpet tile, raised flooring, adhesives, and other petrochemical compounds used in flooring. The company, which celebrates its 30th birthday in 2003, markets its output in 110 countries and operates manufacturing facilities on four continents.

Since 1987, the United Nations (UN) has championed support of sustainable businesses—companies that "meet the needs of the present without compromising the ability of future generations to meet their own needs." For example, the UN has persuaded 160 nations to pursue the goal of cutting greenhouse-gas emissions by more than 5 percent. Among the firms that have embraced sustainable growth are some of the world's largest multinationals. Petroleum giants Royal Dutch/Shell and BP Amoco, for example, have promised to cut emissions by 10 percent below 1990 levels. Royal Dutch/Shell expects to accomplish this by 2002, BP by 2010, and General Motors has pledged to cut total energy use by 20 percent by 2002. Although a member of the petrochemical products industry, Anderson regularly attacks the big oil companies of the world. He is well known for his statement, "In the future, people like me will go to jail."

Taking his cue from the physician's oath, "First, do no harm," Anderson's goal is to turn Interface into an ecologically sustainable company. But such a firm must also generate profits to survive. In the early years, Interface management's attention was centered on growth and earnings. In Anderson's words, "For the first 21 years of the company's existence, I never gave one thought to what we were taking from the earth or doing to it, except to be sure we were in compliance and keeping ourselves 'clean' in a regulatory sense." The issue struck home when a group of environmental activists pelted him with a number of questions about what Interface was doing for the environment. Anderson could not dismiss the questions; they lingered in his thoughts for months; eventually they prompted him to begin to change the way his company did business. To reach the goal of becoming a completely sustainable enterprise, Interface uses a number of technological innovations, including solar energy to run its California factory, recycling carpet and other petrochemical products, and eliminating harmful emissions from its operations. Scrap has been cut by more than 60 percent, translating into a $67 million savings.

Another Interface innovation is its emphasis on peel-and-stick carpet tiles as an environmentally superior alternative to traditional carpet rolls. Some 70 percent of all new carpet purchases are intended to replace existing carpet; resorting to carpet tiles cuts waste since only damaged and worn areas have to be replaced. In addition, the Interface self-adhesive tiles eliminate toxins used in traditional carpet adhesives and require less energy to produce. As yet, no one has invented a safe, non-petrochemical adhesive to hold nylon strands together as a carpet backing. Nor is there a technology that produces a recyclable nylon. But Anderson is working on it.[1]

CHAPTER OVERVIEW

As the successful transformation of Interface to a sustainable marketer illustrates, businesses can attain sustainable growth and still make a profit. The key for marketers is to adapt to the changing environment in which the firm operates. Consider the changes in business establishments that occurred during the last quarter century. Not a video rental outlet could be found in America in 1975, but by 2000, over 21,000 were open for business. Computer outlets exploded in number, increasing their numbers twelvefold. By contrast, male-only barbershops dropped by 80 percent as they were replaced by unisex beauty salons. Fashion changes coupled with animal rights' protests caused six of every seven fur retailers to leave the industry. The prosperity of recent years led consumers to outsource their domestic drudgery. This contributed to growth in industries ranging from restaurants and hotels to amusement parks and carpet cleaning services.[2]

In addition to making plans that reflect the changing environment, marketers must also set goals to meet concerns of customers, employees, shareholders, and members of the general public. Industry competition, legal constraints, the impacts of technology on product designs, and social concerns are some of the many important factors that shape the business environment. This chapter examines the forces that define marketing's external environment. It also discusses the social role of marketing and looks at the nature of marketers' responsibilities, both to business and to society at large.

Members of every organization need to think seriously about the environments in which they operate and the roles that they play in society. Every firm must identify, analyze, and monitor external forces and assess their potential impacts on the firm's goods and services. Although external forces frequently are outside the marketing manager's control, decision makers must still consider those influences together with the variables of the marketing mix in developing the firm's marketing plans and strategies.

1

Identify the five components of the marketing environment.

This chapter begins by describing five forces in marketing's external environment. Figure 2.1 identifies the forces—competitive, political-legal, economic, technological, and social-cultural—and illustrates them as the foundation for making marketing decisions involving the four marketing mix elements and the target market. In other words, these forces provide the frame of reference within which marketing decisions are made. The second major focus of this chapter involves social responsibility and marketing ethics. This section describes marketers' responses to people in general through socially responsible actions and ethical behavior. ■

ENVIRONMENTAL SCANNING AND ENVIRONMENTAL MANAGEMENT

Marketers must carefully and continually monitor crucial trends and developments in the business environment. **Environmental scanning** is the process of collecting information about the external marketing environment to identify and interpret potential trends. The goal is to analyze the information and determine whether these trends represent opportunities or threats to the company. These decisions allow a firm to determine the best response to a particular environmental change.

One of the most lucrative commerce strategies on the Web involves online auctions. In restaurants, corporate coffee lounges, and hair salons across America, people are comparing notes about fabulous deals on airline tickets, Beanie Babies, sports memorabilia, and other treasures. Last year, over one-third of all U.S. online retail customers made at least one online auction purchase. With over 2 million registered users, eBay is by far the industry giant among the approximately 1,000 auction Web sites. There is a problem, however. Online auction fraud is one of the leading cyber-marketing complaints received by the Federal Trade Commission. Counterfeit items, failure to deliver (or pay for) products sold at auction, and manipulation of bids by sellers are common complaints.

Recognizing this growing concern, eBay offers free insurance coverage for transactions up to $200. Rival Amazon offers similar coverage up to $250. Still another competitor, Auction Universe, provides up to $3,000 of insurance for

$19.95. Even though eBay claims that reported cases of fraud account for a minuscule one in every 3,000 transactions, company executives decided to respond to this marketplace issue.[3]

Environmental scanning is a vital component of effective environmental management. **Environmental management** involves marketers' efforts toward achieving organizational objectives by predicting and influencing the competitive, political-legal, economic, technological, and social-cultural environments. This influence can result from a number of activities by the firm's management. For example, management may exercise political power as a means of achieving desired modifications of regulations, laws, or tariff restrictions by joining political action committees (PACs) to lobby legislators and contribute to the campaigns of sympathetic politicians.

sothebys.com

For many domestic and international competitors, competing with established industry leaders frequently involves *strategic alliances*—partnerships with other firms in which the partners combine resources and capital to create competitive advantages in a new market. Amazon marketers decided to jump-start their firm's move into online auctions through a strategic alliance with the international auction house Sotheby's. The alliance gave Amazon a number of advantages: instant credibility in Sotheby's name, access to Sotheby's clients, and consumer protection in the form of guarantees of authenticity and condition. Sotheby's benefits from its use of the world's largest e-commerce site and its ability to use online auctions for lower-end collectibles, while continuing to rely on its traditional onsite auctions for most of its high-end categories of fine art, furniture, and jewelry.[4]

Strategic alliances are especially common in international marketing, where partnerships with local firms provide local expertise for a company expanding its operations abroad. Members of such alliances share risks and profits. These alliances are essential in countries such as China and Mexico, where local laws require foreign firms doing business there to work with local companies.

Through successful research and development efforts, firms may influence changes in their own technological environments. A research breakthrough may lead to reduced production costs or a technologically superior new product. While the marketing environment may exceed the confines of the firm and its marketing mix components, effective marketers continually seek to predict its impact on marketing decisions and to modify operations whenever possible.

In addition to its effect on current marketing decisions, the dynamic marketing environment demands that managers at every level continually reevaluate marketing decisions in response to changing conditions. Even modest environmental shifts can alter the results of marketing decisions.

THE COMPETITIVE ENVIRONMENT

As organizations vie with one another to satisfy customers, the interactive exchange creates the **competitive environment.** Marketing decisions by each individual firm influence consumer responses in the marketplace. They also affect the marketing strategies of competitors. As a consequence, decision makers must continually monitor competitors' marketing activities—their products, channels, prices, and promotional efforts.

Few organizations enjoy monopoly positions in the marketplace. Utilities, such as natural gas, electricity, water, and cable television service, have traditionally accepted considerable regulation from local authorities who control such marketing-related factors as rates, service levels, and geographic coverage. In exchange, the utilities gained exclusive rights to serve a particular group of consumers. The deregulation movement of the past two decades has ended total monopoly protection within their territories for most utilities. Today's shoppers can choose from alternative cable TV providers, cell phone and long-distance telephone carriers, and can even decide which natural gas and electric utilities will supply their heating and

LET THE ONLINE BIDDING BEGIN.

SOTHEBYS.COM
Browse, bid or buy

The Amazon-Sotheby's partnership combines the auction company's centuries-old reputation for quality and integrity with Amazon's unequalled access to the online market.

electrical needs. The constant stream of solicitations from long-distance telephone companies provides almost daily evidence of the increased competition in this formerly monopolized industry.

Some marketers, such as pharmaceutical firms like Merck and Pfizer, are able to achieve temporary monopolies from patents on drugs they develop. When they receive approval from the federal Food and Drug Administration to market a new antiarthritis drug, improved blood pressure medicine, or even a pill to stimulate hair growth, the firms are rewarded for the millions they invested by having the exclusive right to produce and market the product during the life of the patent.

Types of Competition

Marketers actually face three types of competition. The most direct form of competition occurs among marketers of similar products, as when a Walgreen's drugstore opens a few blocks from a RiteAid or CVC. *ESPN the Magazine* has succeeded in a crowded sports magazine field against entrenched competitors like *The Sporting News*, *Sport*, and *Sports Illustrated*. Within 24 months following its 1998 launch, the new magazine was attracting one million readers. It also prompted both *Sport* and *The Sporting News* to modernize their design and led *Sports Illustrated* to drop its cover price from $3.50 to $2.95.[5]

Enterprise Rent-A-Car takes the checkered flag when it comes to the race with industry rivals. Founded in 1957, the St. Louis–based company is now the largest in the United States with more than 3,350 offices nationwide. Enterprise has taken first place by serving the needs of everyday families who need cars when theirs are being serviced for mechanical reasons or are out of commission from accidents. The car-rental company avoids congested airport markets—which are populated largely by tourists and business travelers—and operates offices in low-rent areas located within 15 minutes of 90 percent of the population. Enterprise is also one of the top college recruiters for management positions—a strategy that has helped drive the company to become a $4 billion international company. Instead of sitting behind an airport counter, these new college hires go to local repair shops in hopes of building relationships with the shops' employees. Through these relationships, Enterprise managers end up getting car rental referrals. In 1999, Enterprise tied with Hertz for first place for the J. D. Power Award for customer satisfaction.

A second type of competition involves products that can be substituted for one another. In the business documents' delivery service industry, overnight express mail services, messenger services, and facsimile (fax) machines compete with e-mail and voice mail. In the fast-food industry, pizza competes with chicken, hamburgers, and tacos. In the transportation industry, Greyhound bus lines compete with auto rental services, airlines, and train services. Amtrak marketers realized that competing with substitute transportation services was a difficult task. Instead, they decided to team up with their cruise ship and airline competitors by offering custom designed vacation packages. With a single phone call, Amtrak can make travel arrangements to get vacationers where they want to go by air, land, and sea.

Six Flags and Universal Studios amusement parks—the traditional hot spots for family vacation destinations—now compete with outdoor adventure trips. During the past five years, one of every two U.S. adults has chosen to substitute a tranquil week at the beach, a

Give your dog relief from arthritis pain, and give your children back their favorite companion.

Rimadyl, developed by Pfizer's animal health division, offers dogs relief from arthritis pain. Pfizer's patent gives it exclusive rights to produce and market the medication.

2

Explain the types of competition marketers face and the steps necessary for developing a competitive strategy.

enterprise.com

FIGURE 2.2 **Vacation Dive Packages: Substitutes for Holiday Predictability**

cruise, or a trip to Disney World for something much more adventurous—thrill-filled experiences such as skydiving, mountain climbing, cave exploring, white-water rafting, and scuba diving. Instead of a package tour to Europe, vacationers may opt for an African safari or a two-week excursion in a tented-campsite in the wilderness. Vacation and travel marketers target these fun-seekers in ads such as the one shown in Figure 2.2.

A change such as a price increase or an improvement in a product's attributes can also directly affect demand for substitute products. A major drop in the cost of solar energy would not only increase the demand for solar power, but would also adversely affect the demand for such energy sources as heating oil, electricity, and natural gas.

The final type of competition occurs among all organizations that compete for consumers' purchases. Traditional economic analysis views competition as a battle among companies in the same industry (direct competition) or among substitutable goods and services (indirect competition). Marketers, however, accept the argument that all firms compete for a limited amount of discretionary buying power. *Competition* in this sense means that a Volkswagen Beetle competes with a Colorado ski vacation and a Korn compact disc competes with two tickets to a San Antonio Spurs' game for the buyer's entertainment dollar.

Because the competitive environment often determines the success or failure of a product, marketers must continually assess competitors' marketing strategies. New product offerings with technological advances, price reductions, special promotions, or other competitive variations must be monitored, and the firm's marketing mix may require adjustments to counter these changes.

Among the first purchasers of any new product are the firm's competitors. Careful analysis of its elements—physical components, performance attributes, packaging, retail price, service requirements, and estimated production and marketing costs—allows marketers to forecast the new product's likely competitive impact. They may need to adjust one or more marketing mix components in order to compete with the new market entry.

Developing a Competitive Strategy

Every firm's marketers must develop an effective strategy for dealing with the competitive environment. One company may compete in a broad range of markets in many areas of the world. Another may specialize in particular market segments, such as those determined by customers' geographical location, age, or income characteristics. Determining a competitive strategy involves answering the following three questions:

1. Should we compete?
2. If so, in what markets should we compete?
3. How should we compete?

The answer to the first question depends on the firm's resources, objectives, and expected profit potential. A firm may decide not to pursue or continue operating a potentially successful venture that does not mesh with its resources, objectives, or profit expectations. In recent years, Monsanto has sold its traditional textiles- and chemicals-oriented businesses to focus on its high-growth, high-profitability agricultural and biotechnology divisions. Semiconductor manufacturer Texas Instruments auctioned off its defense electronics business unit, which makes missile sensors and radar and night-vision systems, to an aircraft company where this unit was a better fit.

Answering the second question—In what markets should we compete?—requires marketers to acknowledge their firm's limited resources (sales personnel, advertising budgets, product development capability, and the like). They must accept responsibility for allocating these resources to the areas of greatest opportunity.

Some companies gain access to markets through acquisitions and mergers. A new force emerged in the automobile industry in 1999 when German automaker Daimler Benz merged with U.S. giant Chrysler. The marriage of two international giants will boost Chrysler's 1 percent market share in Europe while upgrading the Detroit carmaker's quality and technology with Mercedes' gold-plated engineering. While preserving distinct brand identities, the combination is expected to cut production costs dramatically. In addition, DaimlerChrysler marketers are out to conquer emerging markets in Asia by jointly developing a low-cost car in the near future.[6]

daimlerchrysler.com

Answering the third question—How should we compete?—requires marketers to make product, pricing, distribution, and promotional decisions that give the firm a competitive advantage in the marketplace. Firms can compete on a variety of bases, including product quality, price, and customer service. For example, retailer Neiman Marcus has gained a competitive advantage by providing superior customer service, while retailer Target competes by providing low prices.

Few events strike greater fear among retailers in small and medium-sized cities than word that Wal-Mart has decided to build a supercenter nearby. These giant buildings house up to 200,000 square feet of space for groceries, general merchandise, vision centers, tire and oil change services, photography studios, and even banks for customers seeking one-stop shopping. The shelves are well-stocked and the prices are almost impossible to beat. And, as Figure 2.3 illustrates, Wal-Mart has its own online shopping Web site for stay-at-home customers.[7]

Small-town retailers hurt most by Wal-Mart include men's and boy's apparel, hardware, lawn and garden stores, variety stores, groceries (especially sales of nonfood items), and auto parts. So how can a small retailer survive? The choices include:

■ Finding a niche by not handling identical merchandise or by offering a more complete selection of such products as hardware and building materials.

■ Handling more upscale merchandise than discount competitors.

■ Offering superior customer service in such forms as expert technical advice from well-trained employees, extended operating hours, liberal return policies, delivery service, and on-site repair service.[8]

Time-Based Competition

With increased international competition and rapid changes in technology, a steadily growing number of firms are using time as a strategic competitive weapon. **Time-based competition** is a strategy of developing and distributing goods and services more quickly than competitors. The flexibility and responsiveness of

MARKETING | **DICTIONARY**

time-based competition Strategy of developing and distributing goods and services more quickly than competitors.

FIGURE 2.3   The Internet: Sales Component of Wal-Mart's Competitive Strategy

time-based competitors enables a firm to improve product quality, reduce costs, and expand its product offering to satisfy new market segments and enhance customer satisfaction.

In an effort to stem surging imports, U.S. beer marketers tout the freshness of their products compared with imported beers. Anheuser-Busch and Boston Beer are challenging the supposed lack of freshness of imports like Heineken, Bass, and Corona through restaurant taste tests and TV ads that show skunky green-bottle imports knocking out a customs dog or reviving an unconscious man. European beer imports sit on shelves an average of 90 days versus 38 days for Budweiser.[9]

No industry relies more heavily on time-based competition than the high-tech fields of computer hardware and software and the Internet. As users demand more power and speed, the time required to develop new-generation chips has dropped dramatically. Researchers now work on several generations of their firm's technology simultaneously as opposed to starting a new product upon completion of another. The speed at which changes occur in the Internet arena is so great that marketers count time in "Internet years," actually time periods of only several weeks or months.

For major health and beauty care competitors like Procter & Gamble (P&G) and Unilever, the first to get its products on retail shelves typically reaps the most profits. Unilever's recent victories include a close race with P&G to win Food and Drug Administration approval to market its cholesterol-lowering margarine, Take Control. Its Thermasilk heat-activated, hair-care products, shown in Figure 2.4, also broke new ground and rang up sales of more than $100 million in their first year on the market. But P&G marketers are winners, as well. For example, Febreze, which removes odors from all types of fabrics, beat its Unilever competitor to store shelves and produced first-year sales of $200 million. Among other new products rolling out of P&G factories are Jif Sensations flavored peanut butter, Dryel home dry-cleaning kits, and Swiffer electrostatic dust mops. In fact, a special P&G team is responsible for finding ways to reduce the time involved in getting products off the test floor and onto retail shelves.[10]

THE POLITICAL-LEGAL ENVIRONMENT

Before you play the game, learn the rules! It is absurd to start playing a new game without first understanding the rules, yet some businesspeople exhibit a remarkable lack of knowledge about marketing's **political-legal environment**—the laws and their interpretations that require firms to operate under certain competitive conditions and to protect consumer rights. Ignorance of laws, ordinances, and regulations or noncompliance with them can result in fines, embarrassing negative publicity, and possibly expensive civil damage suits.

Businesspeople need considerable diligence to understand the legal framework for their marketing decisions. Numerous laws and regulations affect those decisions, many of them vaguely stated and inconsistently enforced by a multitude of different authorities. The existing U.S. legal framework was constructed on a piecemeal basis, often in response to concerns over important issues of the time.

Regulations enacted at the federal, state, and local levels affect marketing practices, as do the actions of independent regulatory agencies. These requirements and prohibitions touch on all aspects of marketing decision making—designing, labeling, packaging, distribution, advertising, and promotion of goods and services. To cope with the vast, complex, and changing political-legal environment, many large firms maintain in-house legal departments; small firms often seek professional advice from outside attorneys. All marketers, however, should be aware of the major regulations that affect their activities.

Government Regulation

The history of government regulation in the United States can be divided into four phases. The first phase was the antimonopoly period of the late 19th and early 20th centuries. During this era, major laws such as the Sherman Antitrust Act, Clayton Act, and Federal Trade Commission Act were passed to maintain a competitive environment by reducing the trend toward increasing concentration of industry power in the hands of a small number of competitors. Laws enacted more than 100 years ago still impact business in the 21st century.

The recent Microsoft case is a good example of antitrust legislation at work. The U.S. Justice Department accused the software powerhouse of predatory practices designed to crush competition. By bundling its own Internet Explorer Browser with its Windows operating system (that runs 90 percent of the world's personal computers), Microsoft grabbed significant market share from rival Netscape. It also bullied firms as large as America Online to drop Netscape Navigator in favor of the Microsoft browser. Microsoft countered that its bundling decisions were simply efforts to offer customer satisfaction through added value. But as a recent joke reported, "In the U.S. government's fight with Bill Gates, I'm for the federal government. I always like to root for the little guy."[11]

The second phase, aimed at protecting competitors, emerged during the Depression Era of the 1930s, when independent merchants felt the need for legal protection against competition from larger chain stores. Among the federal legislation enacted during this period was the Robinson-Patman Act. The third regulatory phase focused on consumer protection. Although the objective of consumer protection underlies most laws—with good examples including the Sherman Act, FTC Act, and Federal Food and Drug Act—many of the major

FIGURE 2.4 | **Thermasilk by Unilever: Winning the New-Product Introduction Race over Rival Procter & Gamble**

When you're hot, you're hot.
The readers of GLAMOUR just voted ThermaSilk one of the best new beauty breakthroughs of 1998. It's no surprise because ThermaSilk Shampoos and Conditioners actually improve your hair's condition as you heat style. What can we say... Where there's heat, there's healthy hair.

3

Describe how government and other groups regulate marketing activities and how marketers can influence the political-legal environment.

MARKETING | **DICTIONARY**

political-legal environment Component of the marketing environment consisting of laws and interpretations of laws that require firms to operate under competitive conditions and to protect consumer rights.

consumer-oriented laws have been enacted during the past 40 years. The fourth phase, industry deregulation, began in the late 1970s and has continued to the present. During this phase, government has sought to increase competition in such industries as telecommunications, utilities, transportation, and financial services by discontinuing many regulations and permitting firms to expand their service offerings to new markets.

The newest regulatory frontier is cyberspace. The Federal Trade Commission (FTC) is investigating ways to police the Internet and online services. The immediate goal is to protect consumers who buy goods and services online from fraud and deceptive advertising. Although the federal government has been slow to regulate *spam*—junk e-mail—many states have enacted legislation and many more have introduced bills to protect consumers. Lawmakers in California, Washington, and Virginia have made it a criminal offense to send spam with false or misleading headlines, enforcing penalties ranging from fines to incarceration. But as one anti-spam activist has pointed out, "The Internet is global and laws in any one jurisdiction are not going to stop it."[12]

The FTC and state regulators search out fraudulent schemes, like own-your-own business scams and sales promotions that, at first glance, appear to be casual chat rooms. Meta-tags are the newest shell game in town. When creating a site, a firm inserts the name of bigger competitors in a code called "meta-tags" that is read by search engines but remains invisible to casual viewers. When consumers look for a big company, they are taken to a roadside stop owned by the little company, as well. In 1999, California courts banned the use of meta-tags to lure traffic to a site because the practice breeds confusion among consumers.[13] Now that the Internet is an established medium, laws to control fraud and misrepresentation in cyberspace are inevitable.

Privacy and child protection issues may present the most difficult enforcement challenge of the Internet. With the passage of the Children's Online Privacy Protection Act, Congress took the first step in regulating what children are exposed to on the Internet. The primary focus is a set of rules regarding how and when marketers need to get parental permission before obtaining marketing research information from children over the Web.[14] Many Internet marketing decision makers are taking proactive steps to protect the consumer. For example, IBM's Web sites post a clear privacy policy; America Online promises never to disclose information about members to outside companies; and Microsoft is developing technology that lets people automatically skip sites that do not meet their privacy standards.[15]

Table 2.1 lists and briefly describes the major federal laws affecting marketing. Legislation affecting specific marketing practices, such as product development, packaging, labeling, product warranties, and franchise agreements, is discussed in later chapters.

Marketers must also monitor state and local laws that affect their industries. Many states, for instance, allow hard liquor to be sold only in liquor stores; such laws limit the distribution of low-alcohol cocktails made with rum, vodka, whiskey, and bourbon. California's stringent regulations for automobile emissions require special pollution control equipment on cars sold in the state.

Government Regulatory Agencies

Federal, state, and local governments have established regulatory agencies to enforce laws. At the federal level, the Federal Trade Commission (FTC) wields the broadest powers of any agency to influence marketing activities. It has the authority to enforce laws regulating unfair business practices and can take action to stop false and deceptive advertising. The Federal Communications Commission regulates communication by wire, radio, and television. Other federal regulatory agencies include the Food and Drug Administration, the Consumer Products Safety Commission, the Federal Power Commission, and the Environmental Protection Agency.

The FTC uses several procedures to enforce laws. It may issue a consent order through which a business accused of violating a law can agree to voluntary compliance without admitting guilt. If a business refuses to comply with an FTC request, the agency can issue a cease-and-desist order, which gives a final demand to stop an illegal practice. Firms often challenge cease-and-desist orders in court. The FTC can require advertisers to provide additional information about products in their advertisements, and it can force firms using deceptive advertising to correct

TABLE 2.1	Major Federal Laws Affecting Marketing

DATE	LAW	DESCRIPTION
A. Laws Maintaining a Competitive Environment		
1890	Sherman Antitrust Act	Prohibits restraint of trade and monopolization; identifies a competitive marketing system as national policy goal
1914	Clayton Act	Strengthens the Sherman Act by restricting such practices as price discrimination, exclusive dealing, tying contracts, and interlocking boards of directors where the effect "may be to substantially lessen competition or tend to create a monopoly"
1914	Federal Trade Commission Act (FTC)	Prohibits unfair methods of competition; establishes the Federal Trade Commission, an administrative agency that investigates business practices and enforces the FTC Act
1938	Wheeler-Lea Act	Amends the FTC Act to outlaw additional unfair practices; gives the FTC jurisdiction over false and misleading advertising
1950	Celler-Kefauver Antimerger Act	Amends the Clayton Act to include major asset purchases that will decrease competition in an industry
B. Laws Regulating Competition		
1936	Robinson-Patman Act	Prohibits price discrimination in sales to wholesalers, retailers, or other producers; prohibits selling at unreasonably low prices to eliminate competition
1993	North American Free Trade Agreement (NAFTA)	International trade agreement between Canada, Mexico, and the United States designed to facilitate trade by removing tariffs and other trade barriers among the three nations
C. Laws Protecting Consumers		
1906	Federal Food and Drug Act	Prohibits adulteration and misbranding of foods and drugs involved in interstate commerce; strengthened by the Food, Drug, and Cosmetic Act (1938) and the Kefauver-Harris Drug Amendment (1962)
1968	Consumer Credit Protection Act	Truth-in-lending law requiring disclosure of annual interest rates on loans and credit purchases
1970	National Environmental Policy Act	Establishes the Environmental Protection Agency to deal with various types of pollution and organizations that create pollution
1971	Public Health Cigarette Smoking Act	Prohibits tobacco advertising on radio and television
1972	Consumer Product Safety Act	Created the Consumer Product Safety Commission, which has authority to specify safety standards for most products
1990	Nutrition Labeling and Education Act	Requires foods manufacturers and processors to provide detailed information on the labeling of most foods
1991	Americans with Disabilities Act	Protects the rights of people with disabilities; makes discrimination against the disabled illegal in public accommodations, transportation, and telecommunications
1993	Brady Law	Imposes a five-day waiting period and a background check before a gun purchaser can take possession of the gun
1998	Children's Online Privacy Protection Act	Empowers FTC to set rules regarding how and when marketers must obtain parental permission before asking children marketing research questions
D. Laws Deregulating Specific Industries		
1978	Airline Deregulation Act	Grants considerable freedom to commercial airlines in setting fares and choosing new routes
1980	Motor Carrier Act and Staggers Rail Act	Significantly deregulates trucking and railroad industries by permitting them to negotiate rates and services
1996	Telecommunications Act	Significantly deregulates the telecommunications industry by removing barriers to competition in local and long-distance phone and cable and television markets

earlier claims with new promotional messages. In some cases, the FTC can require a firm to give refunds to consumers misled by deceptive advertising.

The FTC and U.S. Justice Department can stop mergers if they believe the proposed acquisition will reduce competition by making it harder for new companies to enter the field. In recent years, these agencies have taken a harder line on proposed mergers, especially in the computer, telecommunications, financial services, and health-care sectors.

FIGURE 2.5 **Utility Deregulation: Converting Monopolies into More Competitive Industries**

Removing regulation also affects the marketing environment. Deregulation of the telecommunications and utilities industries has changed the competitive picture considerably. No longer do utilities have the exclusive right to operate within a territory. As Figure 2.5 reveals, natural gas utilities like Mobile Gas compete with the local electric company in supplying homeowners and businesses with energy needs for heating, cooling, and preparing meals. Because of deregulation, they also compete with other gas companies. Since 1993, natural gas distributors have been able to send gas through local pipelines, similar to the way long-distance phone companies use local lines and compete with other companies around the country. The Archdiocese of Chicago saved $8 million by purchasing gas from Houston's Enron Corp. rather than its local utilities. Customers of KN Energy in southeastern Wyoming can choose from among 12 competing gas companies.

This kind of restructuring in the utility industry after 90 years of monopoly will affect many different sectors. If power costs drop the expected 20 percent due to deregulation of the generation process, businesses and individuals will have more money to spend on other things. Competition will improve efficiency in what had become a complex and inefficient market. Consolidation of the industry will increase due to mergers between utility companies.

The latest round of deregulation brought the passage of the Telecommunications Act of 1996. This law removed barriers between local and long-distance phone companies and cable companies. It allowed the seven regional Bell operating companies and GTE Corp. to offer long-distance service; at the same time, long-distance companies—such as AT&T, MCI Worldcom, and Sprint that control over 90 percent of this market—gained authority to offer local service. Cable companies can offer phone service, and phone companies can get into the cable business. The change promises huge rewards for competitive winners. Just capturing 20 percent of the local calling market, for example, is worth $15 billion to $20 billion per year to AT&T.

Other Regulatory Forces

Marketing activities also feel the effects of activities by public and private consumer interest groups and self-regulatory organizations. Consumer interest groups have mushroomed in the past 25 years. Today, hundreds of these organizations operate at the national, state, and local levels. Groups such as the National Coalition Against Misuse of Pesticides seek to protect the environment. People for Ethical Treatment of Animals (PETA) is an activist group opposing use of animals for product testing. Other groups attempt to advance the rights of minorities, elderly Americans, and other special-interest causes. The power of these groups has also grown. Pressure from antialcohol groups has resulted in proposed legislation requiring health warnings on all alcohol ads and stricter regulations of alcoholic beverage advertising.

bbb.org

Self-regulatory groups represent industries' attempts to set guidelines for responsible business conduct. The Council of Better Business Bureaus is a national organization devoted to consumer service and business self-regulation. The Council's National Advertising Division (NAD) is designed to promote truth and accuracy in advertising. It reviews and advocates voluntary resolution of advertising-related complaints between consumers and businesses. If NAD fails to resolve a complaint, an appeal can be made to the National Advertising Review Board, which is composed of advertisers, ad agency representatives, and public members. In addition, many individual trade associations set business guidelines and codes of conduct and encourage members' voluntary compliance.

In an effort to protect consumer privacy, the Direct Marketing Association (DMA) recently approved new rules requiring customers to be notified if information about them—including

SOLVING AN ETHICAL CONTROVERSY

Corporate Villain or Third-World Philanthropist?

Meet 12-year-old Pablo. He could be from Guatemala or Indonesia or several other third-world countries where unemployment is rampant, education is poor, and poverty is high. One day, a big foreign company moves into town, hires Pablo and other kids like him, and pays them a wage standard for that country. The poor get work and the company gets low-cost labor. Everyone should be happy right? Wrong!

For years now, the news media has trumpeted the battle between international corporations' labor practices and human rights activities. Nike, the $9.6 billion athletic shoe maker, has fought to justify its overseas labor practices. CEO Phil Knight has promised to raise the minimum age of workers to 18, improve factory air quality, and provide free education for workers. But it will continue to pay standard wage rates of $1.60 a day in Asia and China and a paltry $1 a day in Indonesia. Says one human rights activist, "These factories are sweatshops. They're clean, well-lighted sweatshops, but they're still sweatshops."

The Gap, Wal-Mart, and Tommy Hilfiger have also taken harsh criticism for their foreign labor practices. In fact, in 1999, activist groups filed suit against them for mistreating workers. Suddenly, khakis have become a symbol of Asian sweatshops and it is no longer cool to wave Old Glory over racks of clothes made by children in overseas sweatshops.

 Should U.S. marketers be allowed to operate overseas' sweatshops that pay the lowest wages possible?

Pro

1. Any business operating in a foreign country should be able to operate under the same regulations as domestic businesses.
2. These so-called sweatshops are some of the best working conditions in the countries in which they operate. They provide safe working conditions and sometimes offer additional benefits, such as health care and education programs.
3. U.S. businesses are not doing anything new or different from other international firms operating in third-world nations.
4. It is virtually impossible to monitor all the subcontractors' facilities used by a huge international company like The Gap.

Con

1. By paying the "standard" wage of a third-world country, huge international companies are sustaining the level of poverty by not improving living standards.
2. Too often, the end consumer pays an artificially high price for goods produced in these third-world nations. The worker gets low wages, the consumer pays high prices, and the corporation gets huge profits.
3. Thousands of U.S. suppliers of energy and component parts as well as workers are hurt when American companies move production facilities overseas.

Summary

As long as large corporations continue to operate third-world sweatshops, human rights activists and consumers will continue pressuring them to stop. With the accessibility of information as a result of the Internet, events large and small will become known to more and more people. It is probable that issues—social, political, and economic—will no longer be regional but become universal concerns. More and more regulations will become world laws rather than laws of one country or another.

SOURCES: Kelly Barron, "Gaplash," *Forbes*, June 14, 1999, pp. 110–112; and William McCall, "Nike Battles Backlash from Overseas Sweatshops," *Marketing News*, November 9, 1998, p. 14.

their name and address—was being shared with other marketers. Companies must also tell consumers that they have the option to not have their information shared. The new rules are intended to prevent unwanted mail or phone solicitations from reaching consumers and to protect consumers' privacy. These new rules apply to nearly 4,500 DMA member firms and include 2,600 Internet companies, catalogs, banks, financial institutions, publishers, not-for-profits, and book and music clubs.[16]

As mentioned earlier, regulating the online world poses a challenge. Favoring self-regulation as the best starting point, the FTC sponsored a Privacy Initiative for consumers, advertisers, online companies, and others as a way to develop voluntary industry privacy guidelines. The Interactive Services Association is also working on its own privacy standards.

Controlling the Political-Legal Environment

Most marketers comply with laws and regulations. However, noncompliance can scar a firm's reputation and hurt profits. Most companies fight regulations they consider unjust. The regional Bell operating companies filed lawsuits to protect their turf against competition from long-distance carriers and cable companies, while GTE claimed the deregulation of local phone service was unconstitutional.

Other companies have jumped in to take advantage of new opportunities. For example, Furst Group is a long-distance phone company with no lines or equipment. It buys blocks of long-distance time from major carriers at greatly reduced rates and then resells this service by the minute at a discount, becoming a distributor, or *switchless reseller*. Now the regional Bells and long-distance carriers are competing aggressively to keep their customers. They are also working with resellers to help retain small business customers that they would otherwise lose.

Consumer groups and political action committees may try to influence the outcome of the proposed legislation or change existing laws by engaging in political lobbying or boycotts. Many industry groups, trade associations, and corporations also apply pressure to legislators and regulators through political lobbying and political action committees. Lobbying groups frequently enlist the support of customers, employees, and suppliers to assist their efforts.

4

Outline the economic factors that affect marketing decisions and consumer buying power.

THE ECONOMIC ENVIRONMENT

The overall health of the economy influences how much consumers spend and what they buy. This relationship also works the other way. Consumer buying plays an important role in the economy's health; indeed, consumer outlays perennially make up some two-thirds of overall economic activity. Since all marketing activity is directed toward satisfying consumer wants and needs, marketers must understand how economic conditions influence consumer purchasing behavior.

Marketing's **economic environment** consists of forces that influence consumer buying power and marketing strategies. They include the stage of the business cycle, inflation, unemployment, resource availability, and income.

FIGURE 2.6 | **Increased Spending for Luxury Products during Periods of Prosperity**

GIVENCHY

ORGANZA

SLIP INTO LUXURY

FAMOUS • BARR   HECHT'S   KAUFMANN'S

Business Cycles

Historically, the economy has tended to follow a cyclical pattern consisting of four stages: prosperity, recession, depression, and recovery. No depressions have occurred in the United States since the 1930s, and many economists argue that society is capable of preventing future depressions through intelligent use of various economic policies. Good decision making should ensure that a recession would give way to a period of recovery, rather than sinking further into depression.

Consumer buying differs in each stage of the business cycle, and marketers must adjust their strategies accordingly. In times of prosperity, consumer spending maintains a brisk pace. Marketers respond by expanding product lines, increasing promotional efforts and expanding distribution in order to raise market share, and raising prices to widen their profit margins. During periods of prosperity, buyers often are willing to spend more for premium versions of well-known brands. Figure 2.6 illustrates how marketers appeal to the desires of shoppers to purchase more prestigious luxury items, like Givenchy's Organza fragrance, during prosperous times.

During recessions, however, consumers frequently shift their buying patterns to emphasize basic, functional products that carry low price tags. They spend more at hardware stores, auto-parts stores, and do-it-yourself centers, and they spend less on restaurant meals and nonessential products such as convenience foods. Sales of low-priced, black-and-white–label generic grocery products and private-label goods rise. In recessionary periods, marketers consider lowering prices, eliminating marginal products, improving customer service, and increasing promotional outlays to stimulate demand. They may also launch value-priced products likely to appeal to cost-conscious buyers.

Consumer spending sinks to its lowest level during a depression. The last true depression in the United States occurred during the 1930s. Although the possibility of a return to depression always persists, experts see only a slim likelihood of another severe depression. Through its monetary and fiscal policies, the federal government attempts to control such extreme fluctuations in the business cycle.

In the recovery stage, the economy emerges from a recession and consumer purchasing power increases. But while consumers' *ability* to buy increases, caution often restrains their *willingness* to buy. Remembering the tough times of recession, consumers are more likely to save than spend or buy on credit. During the recovery of the early 1990s, for instance, U.S. consumers paid down their debts for car and bank loans and borrowed less on their credit cards. With lower principal and interest payments, they actually had higher levels of disposable income to spend; however, they continued to spend cautiously. Usually, as a recovery strengthens, consumers become more indulgent, buying convenience-type products and higher-priced goods and services such as housecleaning and lawn care.

Over the course of the last 10 years, the U.S. economy has surpassed the performance of the previous quarter-century. The nation is experiencing strong productivity growth, as measured by the gross domestic product (GDP), low inflation, a strong labor market, and profits that have more than doubled.[17] As economic activity increases, businesses are investing more capital in equipment and construction. Sales of new single-family homes and cars are up reflecting an increasing confidence in the economy. These types of consumer purchases have a ripple effect in related sectors. For example, the demand for housing leads to higher sales of wallpaper, carpet, furniture, appliances, and similar home-related items.

However, consumers not only spent more, but they also charged many purchases. Once again, the level of credit-card debt climbed, due in part to the flood of attractive card offers stuffing consumers' mailboxes. Consumer debt rose faster than income, delinquent credit-card payments reached new highs, and personal bankruptcy filings showed sharp increases. Credit-card issuers that had courted new borrowers with tempting offers of low introductory interest rates and various reward programs found themselves suffering from consumers' inability to keep spending within reasonable—and repayable—limits when handed still more plastic cards. In response, these firms reduced their unsolicited mailings and adopted stricter approval guidelines.

Recovery remains a difficult stage for businesses just climbing out of a recession, since it requires them to earn profits while trying to gauge uncertain consumer demand. Many cope by holding down administrative costs as much as possible. Some trim payrolls and close down branch offices. Others cut back on employees' business travel budgets or explore the least expensive travel options. Some industries struggle more than others during recovery periods; travel and casual dining often remain weak since consumers view these services as unnecessary luxuries.

The prosperity enjoyed in 2000 is predicted to grow annually at a phenomenal rate of 3 percent over the next decade. Inflation should continue to level off, and the standard of living will rise. During the first decade of this century, established industries such as finance, media, wholesale, and retail will change dramatically and new industries will be created at an astounding pace.

Business cycles, like other aspects of the economy, are complex phenomena that seem to defy the control of marketers. Success depends on flexible plans that can be adjusted to satisfy consumer demands during the various business cycle stages.

Inflation

A major constraint on consumer spending, which can occur during any stage of the business cycle, is inflation. *Inflation* devalues money by reducing the products it can buy through persistent price increases. Inflation would restrict purchases less severely if income were to keep pace with rising prices; but often it does not. Inflation increases marketers' costs, such as expenditures for wages and raw materials, and the resultant higher prices may, therefore, negatively affect sales.

Inflation makes consumers conscious of prices, especially during periods of high inflation. This influence can lead to three possible outcomes, all important to marketers: (1) consumers can elect to buy now, in the belief that prices will be higher later (an argument that automobile dealers often cite in their commercial messages); (2) they can decide to alter their purchasing patterns; or (3) they can postpone certain purchases.

Over the past 20 years, the United States' rate of inflation has slid from 13.6 percent in 1980 to below 3 percent in 1999. Many economists predict that similarly low levels will continue throughout this decade. At these low levels, inflation may not affect the economy as strongly in the future as it has in the past.

Unemployment

Unemployment is defined as the proportion of people in the economy who do not have jobs and are actively looking for work. Unemployment rises during recessions and declines in the recovery and prosperity stages of the business cycle. Like inflation, unemployment affects marketing by modifying consumer behavior. Unless unemployment insurance, personal savings, and union benefits effectively offset lost earnings, unemployed people have relatively little income to spend. Even if these protections completely compensate people for lost earnings, their buying behavior is still likely to change. Instead of buying, they may choose to build their savings.

Unemployment rose during the 1991 recession and continued to climb during the early stages of the recovery. After peaking near 8 percent in 1992, it declined steadily, reaching about 4 percent today. This low level of unemployment contributed to the increase in spending and economic prosperity. While price increases have been modest overall in the economy, the information sector has seen dramatic drops. Personal computer systems that once cost consumers $3,000 and up, can now be bought for as little as $600.

monster.com

Internet job boards play a growing role in reducing unemployment by providing many of the matchmaking services formerly done by brick-and-mortar agencies. Although the Internet currently accounts for only 2 percent of employment advertising, experts predict the Web to be the future of recruiting. Monster.com, the first big success story in online recruiting, maintains a database of 1.5 million résumés. More than 7 million job seekers visit the site each month to search through 227,000 listings. The Web site's latest offering is Monster Talent Market, where job hunters auction their talents to the companies with the highest bids.[18]

Income

Income is another important determinant of marketing's economic environment because it influences consumer buying power. By studying income statistics and trends, marketers can estimate market potential and develop plans for targeting specific market segments. For example, U.S. household incomes have grown in recent years; coupled with a low rate of inflation, this increase has boosted purchasing power for millions of American households. For marketers, a rise in income represents a potential for increasing overall sales. However, marketers are most interested in *discretionary income*, the amount of money that people have to spend after they have paid for necessities such as food, clothing, and housing.

Changes in average earnings powerfully affect discretionary income. Historically, periods of major innovation have been accompanied with dramatic increases in living standards and rising incomes. During the first half of the 20th century—a period of unprecedented innovations in transportation from the railroads to supersonic jets—real per capita incomes tripled and even quadrupled, fueled by rising productivity. The 21st century could see similar income gains with the growth of electronic technologies. Some predictions indicate a 9 percent rise in real wages, a more than 50 percent rise in corporate earnings, and interest rates below 4 percent. These rapidly climbing income rates could lead to a 25 percent growth in the overall economy.

Signs of explosive growth rates in the U.S. economy are already evident in consumer-spending behavior. American consumers already have gone beyond conspicuous consumption; they are now more sophisticated, more complex, and have increased ability to interact directly with distant cultures. The economic growth has contributed to a new awakening in the arts. Take a look at the following surprising statistics:

- Nearly 27 million people attended theatrical stage shows (60 percent of them outside New York), generating $1.3 billion in ticket sales.
- Opera attendance is up 34 percent from 1980, which accounts for the growth in opera houses to 110 nationwide.
- Public radio stations have tripled to nearly 700.
- Book sales are at unprecedented levels, with about 430 million more purchased in 2002 than in 1982.[19]

Figure 2.7 shows the growing popularity of buying art masterpieces since income levels have risen to new heights. Once relegated to only the most prestigious art auction houses in the world, including Sotheby's and Christie's, fine works of art can now be bought at auction online.

Resource Availability

Resources are not unlimited. Shortages—temporary or permanent—can result from several causes. Brisk demand may bring in orders that exceed manufacturing capacity or outpace the response time required to gear up a production line. A shortage may also reflect a lack of raw materials, component parts, energy, or labor. Regardless of the cause, shortages require marketers to reorient their thinking.

One reaction is **demarketing,** the process of reducing consumer demand for a product to a level that the firm can reasonably supply. Oil companies, for example, publicize tips on how to cut gasoline consumption, and utility companies encourage homeowners to install more insulation to reduce heating costs. Many cities discourage central business-district traffic by raising parking fees and violation penalties and promoting mass transit and car pooling.

A shortage presents marketers with a unique set of challenges. They may have to allocate limited supplies, a sharply different activity from marketing's traditional objective of expanding sales volume. Shortages may require marketers to decide whether to spread limited supplies over all customers or limit purchases by some customers so that the firm can completely satisfy others.

By 2000, the building construction boom that accompanied the period of U.S. prosperity caught up with materials suppliers, and shortages of wallboard, lumber, and bricks slowed plans for expanding construction. The low unemployment rate produced a human resource shortage. To compete, employers had to increase wages and improve their benefits packages. Other companies turned to automated equipment to counter the employee shortage. Still others "imported" workers from regions with higher unemployment rates with promises of higher hourly wages, job security, and relocation allowances.

Marketers today have also devised ways to deal with increased demand for fixed amounts of resources. Reynolds Metal Company addresses the

Some jobs don't really need to be advertised.

The best way to fill the others is The Monster Board.

Thousands of hiring professionals know that the most successful recruiting site on the Internet is The Monster Board. We work closely with you every step of the way to ensure your success. First, we help you create your job posting to make it as effective as possible and to make sure it attracts candidates who are really qualified. We'll forward their resumes to you via fax, e-mail or regular mail — whatever is easiest for you.

Service like this is why The Monster Board really works. In fact, one in four job seekers receives at least one job offer through The Monster Board. Contact us at 1-800-MONSTER or hire@monster.com to put The Monster Board to work for you.

Call us today, and get our FREE Guide to Online Recruiting. To receive this complete guide to recruiting on the Internet, call us right away.

The Monster Board
WWW.MONSTER.COM
1-800-MONSTER

Write 255 on Reader Service Card.

Monster.com helps job seekers and employers find each other online.

FIGURE 2.7

Online Service Designed to Meet the Needs of Increasingly Wealthy Consumers

rmc.com

dwindling supply of aluminum through its recycling programs, including cash-paying vending machines. Such "reverse" vending machines allow people to insert empty cans into the machines and receive money, stamps, and/or discount coupons for merchandise or services.

The International Economic Environment

In today's global economy, marketers must also monitor the economic environment of other nations. Just as in the United States, a recession in Europe or Japan changes buying habits. Changes in foreign currency rates compared to the U.S. dollar also affect marketing decisions. The strong dollar and the problems in Asia hurt companies such as BP/Mobil, whose foreign sales fell nearly 20 percent in just two years, and international insurance provider Aflac, whose U.S. sales increased 29 percent while foreign revenues fell 7 percent.[20]

For the most part, however, U.S. companies have posted higher revenue gains in overseas operations. Technology companies are the biggest beneficiaries of U.S. expansion into the international arena. Combined, Lucent Technologies, Dell Computer, and Seagate Technology accounted for well over $12 billion in sales from outside the United States.

In 1990, when Beijing opened the huge China market to foreign business, direct selling took off rapidly, growing to over $2 billion annually. Amway revenues soared to almost $200 million a year. Mary Kay waited until the mid-1990s to enter this market and quickly hit the $25 million mark. And Avon generates about $75 million each year. Combined, these three companies alone have $180 million invested in this single foreign market. But the Chinese government was not as happy as the foreign companies were with this rapid and enormous success. In 1998, the Chinese State Counsel ordered all direct-sales operations to cease immediately. Companies from North America and Europe were understandably shaken by the news. Losing their investments and being locked out of such a promising market was more than disappointing. It also meant that 20,000 Chinese working for these firms would be unemployed—immediately! Several months later, the order was rescinded after pressure from diplomats and corporate representatives convinced Chinese authorities of the benefits of allowing direct marketing activities to continue there.[21]

THE TECHNOLOGICAL ENVIRONMENT

5

Discuss the impact of the technological environment on a firm's marketing activities.

The **technological environment** represents the application to marketing of knowledge in science, inventions, and innovations. New technology results in new goods and services for consumers; it also improves existing products, offers better customer service, and often reduces prices through new, cost-efficient production and distribution methods. Technology can quickly make products obsolete—calculators, for example, wiped out the market for slide rules—but it can just as quickly open new marketing opportunities.

As we discussed in Chapter 1, technology is revolutionizing the marketing environment. Technological innovations create not just new products but also entirely new industries. The Internet is transforming the way companies promote and distribute products. Among the new businesses developing as a result of the Net's success are Web-page designers, new types of software firms, interactive advertising agencies, and companies like CyberCash and First Virtual that allow customers to make secure financial transactions over the Web. Industrial and medical use of lasers, superconductor transmission of electricity, wireless communications products, seeds and plants enhanced by biotechnology, and genetically-engineered proteins that fight disease are just a few more examples of technological advances.

VF Corp., the $5.5 billion apparel maker, has revamped its manufacturing operations with new software applications. The 100-year-old company's product line includes four brands of jeans, (Lee, Britannia, Wrangler, and Rustler), HealthTex children's clothes, and Jantzen swimwear and backpacks. VF apparel is sold through mass-market retail chains like Wal-Mart, Target, and Macy's. Its 17 brands operated independently of one another until 1997, when integrated information systems brought the family of brands together. Marketers finally had access to company-wide data. Armed with information on customer demographics, such as popular colors and common sizes, marketers are able to identify the right mix of products for individual stores. Dubbed the micromarketing system, it allows marketers to predict how many white Wrangler jeans with a 34-inch waist would sell at a particular store in a certain city during the middle of summer. The new software was the key to growth in revenues of over $7 billion.[22]

Technology can sometimes address social concerns. Texaco marketers, for example, are acutely aware of the need to obtain sustainable growth in the petroleum industry. After 100 years of pumping oil out of California's Kern River oil field, the reservoir was finally drying up. The company slogan "A World of Energy" was certainly true—there was oil in Kern River, but Texaco could not get it out of the ground. The oil was locked in layers of rock and sand, but using modern technology, Texaco was able to heat the oil and separate it from the earth so it could be pumped to the surface. Marketers now emphasize Texaco's commitment to meeting future energy needs by bringing new life to dying oil fields. As the ad in Figure 2.8 explains, "Not even a plastic surgeon could work that kind of magic."

Industry, government, colleges and universities, and other not-for-profit institutions all play roles in the development of new technology. In the United States, research and development efforts by private industry represent a major source of technological innovation. Pfizer, a U.S.-based global pharmaceutical company, discovers, develops, manufactures, and markets innovative medicines for humans and animals. The 150-year-old company is known for developing cures of the future, spending billions each year on research that may defeat cancer, eliminate heart disease, and eradicate Alzheimer's. In 1998, Pfizer introduced Viagra, a revolutionary treatment for erectile dysfunction, and Trovan, which has become one of the most prescribed antibiotics in the United States. In addition, Pfizer Animal Health continues to provide goods and services that keep animals well, including vaccines, feed additives, and the first arthritis medication in the U.S. specifically for dogs. To maximize the strength of its product lines, Pfizer invested nearly $3 billion in research and development in 1999. Pfizer has also forged ahead in sales and marketing. The firm's pharmaceutical U.S. sales force, which doubled in just three years, has ranked number one in overall quality for the last four years. The drug giant's commitment to defeating cardiovascular disease, a leading cause of premature deaths, is described in Figure 2.9.

Another major source of technology is the federal government, including the military. In fact, many consumer products that people take for granted today originated as military projects. Examples include air bags (originally Air

FIGURE 2.8 Applying Technology to Meet the Energy Needs of Tomorrow

pfizer.com

MARKETING   DICTIONARY

technological environment Applications to marketing of knowledge based on discoveries in science, inventions, and innovations.

FIGURE 2.9   **Applying Technology to Address a Major Health Concern**

Force ejection seats), scratch-resistant sunglasses (developed first as visors for space helmets), digital computers (first designed to calculate artillery trajectories), and the microwave oven (a derivative of radar systems).

Although the United States has long been the world leader in research, competition from rivals in Japan and Europe has intensified in recent years. For the past quarter century, the United States led the way with personal computers, networking systems, and Internet technology. Japanese firms focused on industries where they could capitalize on their ability to transfer technologies into commercial products. For instance, American firms developed the technology for videocassette recorders, but two Japanese companies, Sony and JVC, commercialized the invention into one of the most successful new products of the past two decades. To remain at the leading edge, American firms have taken steps to improve technology transfers from university and military researchers as well as private companies.

Applying Technology

 xerox.com

The technological environment must be closely monitored for a number of reasons. For one, creative applications of new technologies give a firm a definite competitive edge. Marketers for Xerox's new digital color copier target the business market with the ad shown in Figure 2.10. "The Document Company" gives decision makers statistics on the benefits of using its state-of-the-art copier, including a 80 percent improvement in customer recall—a primary objective of promotional or informative messages.

Marketers who monitor new technology and successfully apply it may also enhance customer service. Breakthroughs in electronic communications have brought consumers the convenience of in-home shopping and 24-hour banking at automated teller machines. Some restaurants

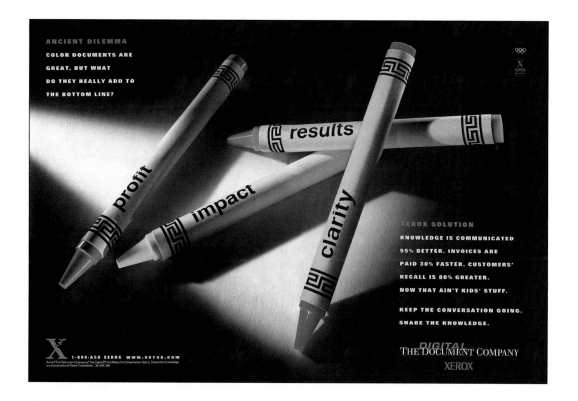
provide faster service by equipping serving staff with palmtop computers that transmit patrons' orders to the kitchen staff.

The wide range of software packages and innovative technologies offers many rewards for financial service providers. Merrill Lynch & Co., Wall Street's largest brokerage firm, recently embraced the power of online financial services. Facing the threat posed by online brokerages like E*Trade Group, Merrill entered the online stock trading business in 1999. The firm has a reputation for superior personal financial service and for relatively high transaction fees—up to several hundred dollars per transaction. With its new online capabilities, fees start at $29.95, matching discount rival Charles Schwab Corp. Future plans will permit unlimited free trading, either with a broker, online, or by phone for a flat fee of up to 2 percent of the account's assets.[23] As its current ads explain, Merrill Lynch is helping to shape the future, not just observe it.

Implementing technology is a huge expense marketers face today, and there is no guarantee that will result in instant success. For the past quarter century, automakers have spent billions of dollars on research and development of an electric car. But when GM first hit the market in 1996, a paltry $10 million was spent on advertising, less than half the typical amount spent to launch a new gasoline model. Four years later, GM had barely 500 of its lease-only EV1 electric car models on the road, and most of those were fleet sales—few were sold to individuals. Honda, Ford, and Toyota have also invested heavily in electric-car development, but all are far from showing a profit. Electric cars have not been successful; in fact, Honda stopped production of its EV Plus electric vehicle in 1999. However, car makers have started to produce and market hybrid cars fueled on both gasoline and electricity. Toyota's Prius model hit the American market in 2000, with a $2 million promotional campaign. Honda is also pushing its Insight hybrid car over the Internet.[24]

Subsequent chapters discuss in more detail how companies apply technologies—such as databases, electronic data interchange, and interactive promotional techniques—to create a competitive advantage.

The new hybrid vehicle from Honda.
What's next, perpetual motion?

By combining an ultra-low emission engine with an electric motor, the Honda hybrid vehicle has brought the future of automotive transportation a little closer. Sooner than you might imagine. And before anyone else. You see, the Honda hybrid vehicle will be available later this year. At Honda, we're committed to developing environmentally responsible vehicles that reduce emissions and improve fuel economy. The future is, well, here.

HONDA
Thinking.

Being the first on the market with the most technologically advanced product has helped position Honda as a leader in the global automobile industry.

THE SOCIAL-CULTURAL ENVIRONMENT

6

Explain how the social-cultural environment influences marketing.

As a nation, the United States is becoming older and more affluent. The birthrate is falling, and subculture populations are rising. People express concerns about the environment, buying ecologically friendly products that reduce pollution. They value the time at home with family and friends, watching videos and eating microwavable snacks. These types of events help to shape marketings' **social-cultural environment**—the relationship between marketing and society and its culture.

Marketers must cultivate sensitivity to society's changing values and demographic shifts such as population growth and age distribution changes. These changing variables affect consumers' reactions to different products and marketing practices. For example, people are more health conscious today than they were a generation ago. They watch their diets, eating more fruits and vegetables and limiting fat consumption. As a result, both food companies and restaurants have added low-fat or fat-free versions of many items. In fact, an entirely new line of frozen, meatless sandwiches and dinner entrees emerged to meet the demands of vegetarians and nutrition-conscious consumers. Gardenburgers, the first entrant in the meatless sandwich line, was launched with the support of a $12 million TV and print advertising campaign. BocaBurgers and Harvest Burgers now compete aggressively with Gardenburgers in their marketing efforts. Staying abreast of changing consumer tastes is a necessary task of new-product marketers. Says BocaBurger's vice president of marketing Kate Torres, "Years ago, it was enough to just be on the shelves, and people who didn't eat meat would come and find you. Today, that's changing. More and more consumers are aware of healthy alternatives, but they need to be informed about brands."[25]

 bocaburger.net

Another social-cultural trend has raised the importance of cultural diversity. The United States is a mixed society composed of various submarkets, each with its unique values, cultural characteristics, consumer preferences, purchasing behaviors, and differences in age and place of residence. Some companies find it highly profitable to target these submarkets. Many firms have found success selling many different products, from ethnic foods to music, to small, well-defined groups of customers. Ford Motor Co., for example, recently spent $1 million on its first advertising campaign specifically targeting Hispanic consumers. The new campaign theme, which carries the headline, "I am not a stereotype," appeared in popular Spanish-language magazines. Each version in the campaign features average Hispanic consumers talking about their collective identity and concerns, and what it means to be Hispanic. Ford marketers hope to connect with the heart of the Hispanic community by recognizing their unique heritage.[26]

Creative marketers of products for the U.S. population of the 21st century must take into consideration all the segments of their market. G+J USA Publishing targets not just women, but women in various life stages with magazines such as those shown in Figure 2.11 that are edited specifically for teens, active women, expecting and new moms, home enthusiasts, and household decision makers.

Importance in International Marketing Decisions

The social-cultural context often exerts a more pronounced influence on marketing decision making in the international sphere than in the domestic arena. Learning about cultural and societal differences among countries is paramount to a firm's success abroad. Marketing strategies that work in the United States often fail when directly applied in other countries. In many cases, marketers must redesign packages and modify products and advertising messages to suit the tastes and preferences of different cultures.

Even a seemingly simple marketing strategy, like that for Ben & Jerry's Homemade, Inc. in the United Kingdom may yield surprising results. In the U.S. market, the premium ice-cream company implemented an unconventional, limited-marketing strategy and a business philosophy of "caring capitalism." Its genuine image; all-natural, high-quality product; playful attitude; social consciousness; and low-key founders appealed to the American public. This approach, however, did not travel well across the Atlantic. Haagen-Dazs preceded Ben & Jerry's by five years in the U.K. market, effectively using high-profile advertising to promote the brand as the ultimate super-premium ice cream. Although Ben & Jerry's marketers hoped to capitalize on their U.S. counterculture image, they discovered that British consumers were largely unaware of their existence. This problem was compounded by their late arrival in the British Isles. The firm originally had planned an inexpensive product launch, but it found itself funding a high-priced venture based on product sampling to improve brand awareness. Costs increased further when the company had to expand the number of "scoop shops" and "scoop carts" dispensing Ben & Jerry's ice cream to British buyers.[27] Chapter 3 continues the discussion of the social-cultural aspects of international marketing.

Fresh from the burger garden.

In our garden, burgers are healthy, delight grows wild, flavor dances, life tastes good. Stop and pick a Gardenburger®.

Look for delicious Gardenburgers® and other meatless GardenProducts™ at natural food stores everywhere.

Gardenburgers is a leader in marketing meatless products that satisfy demands of vegetarians and health-conscious consumers.

Consumerism

Changing societal values have led to the consumerism movement. Today everyone—marketers, industry, government, and the public—is acutely aware of the impact of consumerism on the nation's economy and general well-being.

Consumerism has been defined as a social force within the environment designed to aid and protect the buyer by exerting legal, moral, and economic pressures on business. This definition sums up society's demand that organizations apply the marketing concept.

MARKETING   DICTIONARY

social-cultural environment Component of the marketing environment consisting of the relationship between the marketer and society and its culture.

consumerism Social force within the environment designed to aid and protect the consumer by exerting legal, moral, and economic pressures on business and government.

FIGURE 2.11   **Magazines Designed to Appeal to Different Segments of a Diverse Marketplace**

In recent years, marketers have witnessed increasing consumer activism. Animal-rights activists have demonstrated against furriers and firms that test their products on animals. Marketers of canned tuna have been criticized for promoting sales of tuna caught by nets that also trap and kill dolphins.

No organization or industry is immune to this activism. Almost every winter brings television news coverage of stranded travelers in airports across the nation. Anyone who has ever flown on a commercial airline in the past ten years can probably remember at least one snafu—delayed or canceled flights, confusing rules about carry-on luggage and check-in times, and lost luggage. Complaints in 1999 rose 87 percent over the same period the year before, and it seems to continue to get worse. But consumers have begun to fight back by petitioning Congress to enact a bill of rights for airline passengers. Says Oregon Senator Ron Wyden, one of several members of Congress supporting such a bill, "When people are treated like so many pieces of cargo, it's not surprising that some of them lash out." Bills pending in both houses of Congress would require airlines to inform passengers of the reasons for all flight delays and to compensate passengers held aboard stationary aircraft for more than two hours.[28]

Boycotts are another effective consumerist approach. The number of boycotts against various corporations has risen in recent years to include companies from almost every industry: Nike, McDonald's, Disney, Monsanto, and British Airways have all been targeted in recent years. Even the threat of a boycott can bring results.

Firms, however, do not fulfill all consumer demands. A competitive marketing system emerges from the individual actions of competing firms. The U.S. economic system requires that firms achieve reasonable profit objectives. Businesses cannot meet all consumer demands

FIGURE 2.12	**Addressing Consumers' Right to Be Safe**

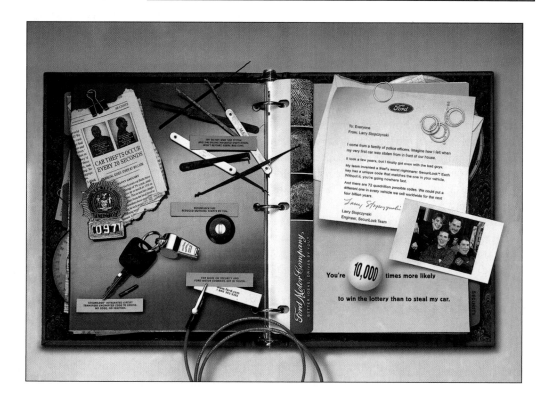

and still generate enough profits to remain viable. This choice defines one of the most difficult dilemmas facing society today. Given these constraints, what should buyers have the right to expect from the competitive marketing system?

The most frequently quoted statement of **consumer rights** was made by President John F. Kennedy in 1962. While this list does not amount to a definitive statement, it offers good rules of thumb that explain basic consumer rights:

1. *The right to choose freely.* Consumers should be able to choose from among a range of goods and services.

2. *The right to be informed.* Consumers should be provided with enough education and product information to enable them to be responsible buyers.

3. *The right to be heard.* Consumers should be able to express their legitimate displeasure to appropriate parties—that is, sellers, consumer assistance groups, and city or state consumer affairs offices.

4. *The right to be safe.* Consumers should be assured that the goods and services they purchase are not injurious with normal use. Goods and services should be designed in such a way that the average consumer can use them safely.

These rights have formed the conceptual framework of much of the consumer legislation passed in the first 40 years of the movement. However, the question of how best to guarantee these rights remains unanswered. The ad shown in Figure 2.12 explains Ford's response to customer safety by installing Securilock systems on its vehicles.

Consumer concern for the nutritional value of the food they purchase

MARKETING STRATEGY FAILURE

Giving It All Away

BACKGROUND Ben & Jerry's Homemade ice cream cofounder Ben Cohen has made a career out of protecting the environment and supporting third-world economies while continuing to run a profitable enterprise. In 1989, he founded Community Products Inc. (CPI), a for-profit company with a primary goal of saving the rain forest. CPI imported nuts from native cooperatives in the Amazon rain forest, made candy and ice-cream flavors such as Rainforest Crunch, and marketed them through partnerships with Ben & Jerry's and specialty retail stores. Sixty percent of all profits were donated to progressive causes and another 10 percent went to employees.

THE MARKETING PROBLEM The first year was a smashing success with $3 million in revenues. But danger lay on the horizon. CPI's local supplier was unable to supply nuts at the agreed-to price, and costs shot up. Then quality matters, such as bacteria- and insect-infested cashews and Brazilian nuts, produced so many customer complaints that CPI had to turn to commercial suppliers—which ended its claim of buying nuts from indigenous sources to help preserve local economies.

continued on next page

7

Describe the role of marketing in society and identify the two major social issues in marketing.

---

has led to labeling regulations. Marketers of packaged food must ensure that product label designs provide information such as weight, date of packaging or expiration, ingredients, and nutritional values. Although the laws do not include prepared foods, some restaurants and fast-food chains like Subway now include nutritional information on their menus. Recently, the FDA gave cereal-maker General Mills permission to advertise on packages of its whole-grain cereals, such as Cheerios, Total, Wheaties, and other qualifying foods, that eating these whole-grain foods is beneficial to their health. Cereal marketers want to let consumers know that eating a diet high in whole-grain foods and are also low in fat may reduce the risk of heart disease and certain cancers. To qualify, a food must contain 51 percent or more whole grain ingredients by weight. Earlier, the FDA had allowed marketers to emphasize the disease-fighting benefits of foods rich in dietary fiber, but not whole-grain foods.[29]

The social-cultural environment for marketing decisions at home and abroad is expanding in scope and importance. Today, no marketer can initiate a strategic decision without taking into account the society's norms, values, culture, and demographics. Marketers must understand how these variables affect their decisions. The constant influx of social issues requires that marketing managers focus on addressing these questions instead of concerning themselves only with the standard marketing tools. Some firms have created a new position—typically, manager of public policy research—to study the changing societal environment's future impact on their organizations.

MARKETING'S ROLE IN SOCIETY

The five environments described so far in the chapter do not completely capture the role that marketing plays in society itself and the consequent effects and responsibilities of marketing activities. Marketing's activities within society in general and in connection with various public issues invite constant scrutiny by the public. In fact, marketing may come to mirror changes in the entire business environment. Because marketing determines the final interface between an organization and the society in which it operates, marketers often carry much of the responsibility for dealing with various social issues affecting their firms.

Marketing operates in an environment external to the firm. It reacts to that environment and, in turn, is acted upon by environmental influences. Relationships with customers, employees, the government, vendors, and society as a whole form the basis of the social issues that confront contemporary marketers. While these concerns often grow out of the exchange process, they produce effects coincidental to the primary sales and distribution functions of marketing. Marketing's relationship to its external environment has a significant effect on the firm's eventual success. Marketing must continually find new ways to deal with the social issues facing the competitive system.

The competitive marketing system is a product of our drive for materialism. However, it is important to note that materialism developed from society itself. Culture in the United States is characterized by an acceptance of work ethic and a positive attitude toward the acquisition of wealth. The motto of this philosophy seems to be "more equals better." A better life has been defined in terms of more physical possessions, although that definition seems to be changing.

Evaluating the Quality of Life

One recurring theme runs through the arguments of marketing's critics: Materialism, as exemplified by the competitive marketing system, leads people to concern themselves only with the quantities of life and to ignore its quality. Traditionally, a firm was considered socially responsible in the community if it provided employment for its residents and contributed to its economic base. Employment, wages, bank deposits, and profits—the traditional measures of social contributions—are quantity indicators. But what about air, water, and cultural pollution? Should workers tolerate the boredom and isolation of mass assembly lines? Should future generations accept the depletion of natural resources? Charges of organizational neglect in these areas go largely unanswered simply because businesspeople have not developed reliable indicators with which to measure a firm's contribution to the quality of life.

Criticisms of the Competitive Marketing System

A critic's indictment of the competitive marketing system would contain at least the following complaints:

1. Marketing costs are too high.
2. The marketing system is inefficient.
3. Marketers and the business system commit collusion and price fixing.
4. Firms deliver poor product quality and service.
5. Consumers receive incomplete, false, and/or misleading information.
6. The marketing system produces health and safety hazards.
7. Marketers persuasively promote unwanted and unnecessary products to those who least need them.

Almost anyone could cite specific examples that confirm these charges. Because each person applies a somewhat different set of values, a fair judgment should recognize that each one evaluates the performance of the marketing system according to personal experience within an individual frame of reference.

Bearing this in mind and taking the system as a whole, individuals can form their own evaluation of the success or failure of the competitive marketing system in serving consumers' needs. Most people will likely arrive at the uncomfortable and somewhat unsatisfying conclusion that the system usually works quite adequately, although some aspects would improve with changes.

ETHICAL ISSUES IN MARKETING

Marketers face many diverse social issues. The current issues in marketing can be divided into two major subjects: marketing ethics and social responsibility. While the overlap and classification problems are obvious, the framework provides a foundation for systematically studying these issues.

Environmental influences have directed increased attention toward **marketing ethics**—marketer's standards of conduct and moral values. Ethics concern matters of right and wrong: the decision of individuals and firms to do what is morally right. A discussion of marketing ethics highlights the types of problems individuals face in their roles as marketers. As Figure 2.13 shows, each element of the marketing mix has its own set of ethical questions that must be answered.

Considerations of such issues should precede any suggestions for improvements in the marketing system. Increased recognition of the importance of marketing ethics is evident from the more than 600 full-time corporate ethics officers in firms as varied as Dun & Bradstreet, Dow Corning, Texas Instruments, and even the Internal Revenue Service. Ensuring ethical practices means promising customers and business partners not to sacrifice quality and fairness for profit, and in exchange it hopes that customers and partners increase their sense of loyalty toward the company.[30]

Some issues involving marketing ethics are not always clear-cut. The

MARKETING DICTIONARY

marketing ethics Marketers' standards of conduct and moral values.

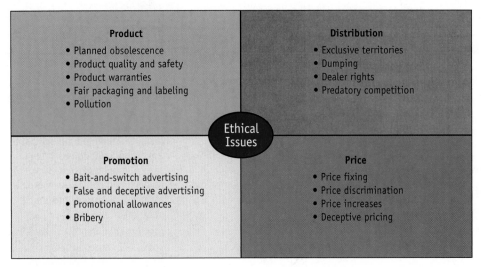

FIGURE 2.13   Ethical Questions in Marketing

issue of cigarette advertising, for example, has divided the ranks of advertising executives. Is it right for advertisers to promote a product that, while legal, has known health hazards and to make a huge profit from that promotion? Should the industry self-regulate its advertising to prevent encouraging kids to smoke?

In recent years, charges of unethical conduct have plagued the tobacco industry. But advertising executives are divided on where the lines should be drawn. In the largest civil settlement in U.S. history, the tobacco industry agreed to pay $206 billion to 46 states. Four other states—Florida, Minnesota, Mississippi, and Texas—had separate settlements totaling another $40 billion. The settlement frees tobacco companies from state claims for the cost of treating sick smokers. In addition to the monetary settlement, cigarette makers can no longer advertise on billboards or use cartoon characters in ads, nor can they sell branded merchandise. The downside to all this litigation is that it has not discouraged smoking. Harvard School of Public Health researchers reported a 28 percent rise in smoking among college students over a recent 5-year period. They also pointed their fingers at cigarette marketers. But teen smoking is rising even in California, a state considered aggressive in its antismoking advertising programs. Joe Camel may be dead, but the Marlboro man is still riding high and NASCAR still runs the Winston Racing series. Says one analyst, "Tobacco is still a highly profitable business and companies are going to remain competitive with each other. You may not be able to put up a 50-foot sign on the street, but you can still send it in the mail to smokers. I would expect to see more emphasis on direct-to-consumer marketing."[31]

People develop standards of ethical behavior based on their own systems of values. Their individual beliefs help them to deal with ethical questions in their personal lives. However, a work situation may generate serious conflicts with those beliefs. Individual ethics may differ from an employer's organizational ethics. An individual may strongly favor industry participation in developing a recycling program for industrial waste, but his or her firm may dismiss the venture as an unprofitable expense.

How can these conflicts be resolved? In addition to individual and organizational ethics, individuals may also be influenced by a third basis of ethical authority—a professional code of ethics. These standards should derive from a concept of professionalism that transcends both organizational and individual ethics. A professional peer association can exercise collective oversight to limit a marketer's individual behavior.

Any code of ethics must anticipate a variety of ethical problems that marketers will likely encounter. While promotional matters tend to receive the greatest attention, ethical issues also relate to marketing research, product strategy, distribution strategy, and pricing.

Ethical Problems in Marketing Research

Marketing research has received criticism for alleged invasions of personal privacy. People today value their individual identities more strongly than ever before. Personal privacy is important to most consumers, so it has become a public issue. As databases have proliferated and marketers have more freely rented address lists and other information, public concern about threats to personal privacy has increased. Chapter 4 will return to the issue of privacy.

Gathering marketing information in exchange for money or free offers creates another ethical concern for market researchers. Recently, California-based marketing research company Free-PC.com offered consumers a new desktop PC in exchange for their agreeing to reveal personal information, such as age, income, and spending habits. In just the first four days, over 500,000 people responded. Critics, however, feel that consumers' privacy is being compromised and that some companies will inevitably sell this information to direct marketers and others interested in gathering demographic data.[32]

Privacy issues have grown as rapidly as companies on the Web, and consumers are fighting back. In a recent move by banks to collect information about customers' individual bank transactions, more than 250,000 consumers e-mailed the Federal Deposit Insurance Corporation demanding that this practice be outlawed.[33] However, Internet consumers can find some assistance in protecting their privacy through several agencies. The Federal Trade Commission's Web page at www.ftc.gov/privacy is a good place to find information on how to stop junk mail and telemarketing calls.[34] The Direct Marketing Association also offers services, such as the Mail, Telephone, and E-Mail Preference Services, to help consumers get their names removed from marketers' targeted lists. UnlistMe.com and Junkbusters are free Web services that also help consumers remove their names from direct mail and telemarketing mailing lists.[35]

Ethical Problems in Product Strategy

Product quality, planned obsolescence, brand similarity, and packaging questions are significant concerns of consumers, managers, and governments. Competitive pressures have forced some marketers into packaging practices that may be considered misleading, deceptive, and/or unethical. Some firms make packages larger than necessary to gain shelf space and consumer exposure in the supermarket. Odd-sized packages make price comparisons difficult. Bottles with concave bottoms give the impression that they contain more liquid than they actually do. The real question seems to be whether these practices can be justified in the name of competition. Growing regulatory mandates appear to be narrowing the range of discretion in this area.

Product testing is another area that raises ethical concerns. To help assure consumers of product quality, many companies use seals of approval for their goods and services, such as the Good Housekeeping Seal of Approval and seals of the American Cancer Society and American Heart Association. Recently, however, consumers have begun to question whether the use of these seals is ethical, since they have to be purchased at fees ranging from $10,000 to $1 million. The seals also do not promise that the product is the best one on the market. Many of the organizations that offer seals of approval do not conduct product testing themselves or even compare brands.[36]

Ethical Problems in Distribution Strategy

A firm's channel strategy is required to deal with two kinds of ethical questions:

1. What is the appropriate degree of control over the channel?
2. Should a company distribute its products in marginally profitable outlets that have no alternative source of supply?

The question of control typically arises in relationships between manufacturers and franchise dealers. Should an automobile dealership, a gas station, or a fast-food outlet be coerced to purchase parts, materials, and supplementary services from the parent organization? What is the proper degree of control in the channel of distribution?

The second question concerns marketers' responsibility to serve unsatisfied market segments even if the profit potential is slight. Should marketers serve retail stores in low-income areas, serve users of limited amounts of the firm's product, or serve a declining rural market? These problems are difficult to resolve because they often involve individuals rather than broad segments of the general public. An important first step is to ensure that the firm consistently enforces its channel policies.

Wolverine marketers target the growing number of women employed in the construction industry by offering special lines of narrower, smaller-sized work shoes and boots.

Ethical Problems in Promotional Strategy

Promotion is the component of the marketing mix that gives rise to the majority of ethical questions. Personal selling has always been the target of ethically based criticism. Early traders, pack peddlers, greeters, drummers, and today's used-car salespeople, for example, have all been accused of marketing malpractice, ranging from exaggerating product merits to outright deceit. Gifts and bribes are common ethical abuses. Advertisers now show women in varied situations, especially in nontraditional work roles such as bus driver, bank officer, and heavy-equipment operator.

Since the early 1970s, the auto industry has advertised air bags as a breakthrough safety device. For years, air bags have been mandatory safety equipment on all new cars sold in the United States. Auto companies promoting safety as a distinguishing characteristic have even begun to install side air bags in door panels. But in recent years, some have called the devices child killers. As data on deaths of children and short adults caused by the pressure of inflated air bags accumulates, questions arise about the responsibility automakers have to inform the public of the danger and to take steps to solve the problems.[37]

Providing consumer information in promotional strategies also presents ethical dilemmas for Internet marketers. Because the Web is still in its infancy, deciding on how to regulate Internet transactions must involve careful consideration of the outcomes of any such rules. Marketers agree that the most important benefit in Web advertising is the staggering number of consumers that can be reached, and the greatest challenge is holding their interest. Any restraints placed on Internet marketers should not hinder these two fundamental activities. One of the more recent issues concerns full and fair disclosures in Web advertising. The question is whether disclosures must be placed at the very top of the Web page—a small area that marketers do not want to relegate to an official notice—rather than an interest-grabbing promotional message. So far, the Federal Trade Commission has not made any hard rules but, instead, has offered guidelines on how to make disclosures easy for consumers to find.[38]

Ethical Problems in Pricing

Pricing is probably the most regulated aspect of a firm's marketing strategy. As a result, most unethical price behavior is also illegal. Some areas of pricing ethics, however, are unique unto themselves. For example, should some customers pay more for merchandise if distribution costs are higher in their areas? Do marketers have an obligation to warn customers of impending price, discount, or return policy changes? All these queries must be dealt with in developing a professional ethic for marketing. The ethical issues surrounding pricing in today's highly competitive and increasingly computerized markets are discussed in greater detail in chapters 18 and 19.

SOCIAL RESPONSIBILITY IN MARKETING

8

Identify each of the four levels of the social responsibility pyramid.

As the chapter's opening vignette shows, companies like Interface can maximize the benefits of their contributions to society and at the same time minimize the negative impact on the natural and social environment. In a general sense, **social responsibility** demands that marketers accept an obligation to give equal weight to profits, consumer satisfaction, and social well-being in

The Four-Step Pyramid of Corporate Social Responsibility

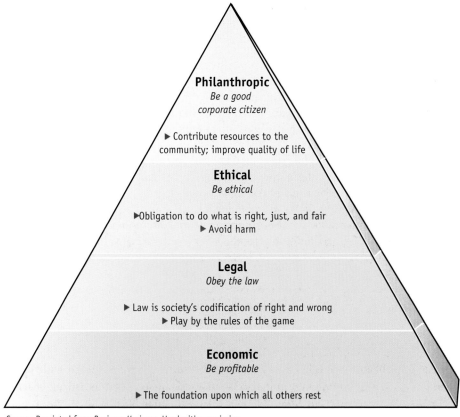

Philanthropic
Be a good corporate citizen

▶ Contribute resources to the community; improve quality of life

Ethical
Be ethical

▶Obligation to do what is right, just, and fair
▶ Avoid harm

Legal
Obey the law

▶ Law is society's codification of right and wrong
▶ Play by the rules of the game

Economic
Be profitable

▶ The foundation upon which all others rest

Source: Reprinted from *Business Horizons.* Used with permission.

evaluating their firms' performances. They must recognize the importance of relatively qualitative consumer and social benefits as well as the quantitative measures of sales, revenue, and profits by which firms have traditionally measured marketing performance.

Social responsibility allows for easier measurement than marketing ethics. Government legislation can mandate socially responsible actions. Consumer activism can also promote social responsibility by business.

Actions alone determine social responsibility, and a firm can behave responsibly, even under coercion. For example, government requirements may *force* firms to take socially responsible actions in matters of environmental policy, deceptive product claims, and so forth. Also, consumers, through their power to repeat or withhold purchases, may *force* marketers to provide honest and relevant information, fair prices, and so forth. Ethically responsible behavior, on the other hand, requires more than appropriate actions; ethical intentions must also motivate those actions. The four dimensions of social responsibility—economic, legal, ethical, and philanthropic—are shown in Figure 2.14. The first two dimensions have long been recognized, but ethical obligations and the need for marketers to be good corporate citizens have gained importance in recent years.

The locus for socially responsible decisions in organizations has always been an important issue. Who should accept specific accountability for the social effects of marketing decisions? Responses range from the district sales manager to the marketing vice president, the firm's CEO, and even the board of directors.

MARKETING | **DICTIONARY**

social responsibility Marketing philosophies, policies, procedures, and actions that have the enhancement of society's welfare as a primary objective.

Probably the most valid assessment holds that *all marketers*, regardless of their stations in the organization, remain accountable for the social aspects of their decisions.

Marketing's Responsibilities

The concept of business's social responsibility traditionally has concerned managers' relationships with customers, employees, and stockholders. Management felt responsibility for providing quality products at reasonable prices for customers, adequate wages and decent working environments for employees, and acceptable profits for stockholders. Only occasionally did the concept extend to relations with the government and rarely with the general public.

Today, the responsibility concept extends to cover the entire societal framework. A decision to temporarily delay the installation of a pollution-control device may satisfy the traditional sense of responsibility. Customers would continue to receive an uninterrupted supply of the plant's products, employees would not face layoffs, and stockholders would still receive reasonable returns on their investments in the company. Contemporary business ethics, however, would not accept this choice as a socially responsible decision.

Similarly, a firm that markets foods with low nutritional value may satisfy the traditional concept of responsibility, but such behavior is questionable in contemporary perspective. This is not to say that all firms should distribute only foods of high nutritional value; it means merely that the previous framework for evaluation is no longer considered comprehensive in terms of either scope or time.

Contemporary marketing decisions must consider the entire societal framework, not only in the United States, but throughout the world. Marketing decisions must also account for eventual, long-term effects and for future as well as existing generations. Consumer groups have criticized some companies for buying from foreign suppliers that employ children or prison convicts as laborers, damage the environment, or force employees to work in dangerous conditions. Inputs produced by cheap foreign labor in developing countries have attracted wide publicity as consumers have learned about poor conditions in overseas apparel-manufacturing factories. The subject of the Ethical Controversy box on page 51 further discusses this global issue.

Marketers can apply many methods to help their companies behave in socially responsible ways. Chapter 1 discussed cause marketing as one channel through which companies promote social causes by sponsoring programs that persuade people to support particular activities or priorities. Socially responsible marketing involves campaigns that encourage people to adopt socially beneficial behaviors, like driving more safely and eating more nutritious food. Such campaigns can help society and the firm's bottom line, as well.

Marketing and Ecology

Ecology—the relationship between organisms and their natural environments—has become one of the most important aspects of marketing in the 1990s and in the early part of this century. Many industry and government leaders rank the environment as the biggest challenge facing business. Environmental concerns of garbage disposal, acid rain, depletion of the ozone layer, global warming, and contamination of the air and water span the globe. They influence all areas of marketing decision making for product planning to public relations. Marketers must address several ecological aspects of their businesses: planned obsolescence, pollution, recycling waste materials, and resource conservation.

The initial ecological problem facing marketing was *planned obsolescence*—intentional manufacturing of products with limited durability. Some products become obsolete when technological improvements allow better alternatives. Others, however, reach physical obsolescence due to intentional design features that make them wear out within short periods of time. Marketers have responded to consumer demand for convenience by offering extremely short-lived products, such as disposable diapers, ball-point pens, razors, and cameras. In other products, such as those in the computer software industry, rapid changes in design produce obsolescence. It seems that as soon as one software package becomes standard in business, programmers come up with a revision or upgrade. Software companies argue that upgrades are inevitable and that technology changes so rapidly and the demands of users expand so much that more functions must be added. The problem is that new versions of software are often polished versions, not actually revisions of the existing software.[39]

Planned obsolescence has always represented a significant ethical question for marketers. On one side, firms need to turn over products to maintain sales and employment; on the other, they need to ensure product quality and durability. In the process, they must wrestle with the practical question of whether consumers really want or can afford increased durability. Many buyers prefer to change styles often and knowingly accept products that will quickly age. This is especially true in the computer industry. Unfortunately, increased durability has an implicit cost that may prevent some people from affording a product.

Pollution is a broad term that covers a number of circumstances. It usually implies something unclean. Public concern about polluting such natural resources as water and air has reached critical proportions in some areas. The marketing system annually generates billions of tons of packaging materials, such as glass, metal, paper, and plastics, that add to the world's growing piles of trash and waste.

Recycling—processing used materials for reuse—is another important aspect of ecology. The underlying rationale of recycling is that reprocessed materials can benefit society by saving natural resources and energy as well as by alleviating a major factor in environmental pollution. The ad in Figure 2.15 explains the efforts to encourage recycling by the Environmental Defense Fund. Municipal curbside recycling programs— a major focus of the organization—have increased 900 percent during the past decade.

As the saying goes, one person's trash is another's treasure. This is certainly true in the case of Metech International. The Swedish-owned company turns discarded computer hardware into gold—literally. In just one year, the firm recovered 120,000 ounces of gold worth $35 million, as well as other precious metals including silver, platinum, and palladium. Metech molds 24-karat gold bars and sells them on the open market. From there, the gold turns up in everything from jewelry to another computer circuit board.[40]

Many companies respond to consumers' growing concern about ecological issues through **green marketing**—production, promotion, and reclamation of environmentally sensitive products. Since the green marketing revolution began in the early 1990s, marketers have been quick to tie their companies and products to ecological themes. Television ads feature mothers holding babies saying, "We're worried about the environment. That's why . . ." Corporate CEOs talk about their firm's eco-friendly operations. And, more recently, a barrage of promotions has appeared urging Americans to buy "natural," "organic," and "herbal" products.

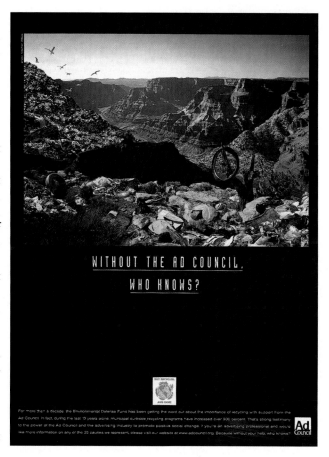

FIGURE 2.15 Promoting Recycling as a Social Responsibility Issue

WITHOUT THE AD COUNCIL, WHO KNOWS?

CONTROLLING THE MARKETING SYSTEM

When the marketing-economic system does not perform as well as we would like, we attempt to change it. We hope to make it serve us better by producing and distributing goods and services in a fairer way. Most people believe that the system is working sufficiently well and requires no changes and that relatively minor adjustments can achieve a fair distribution.

Four ways in which we control or influence the direction of the marketing system and try to rid it of imperfections

MARKETING DICTIONARY

green marketing Production, promotion, and reclamation of environmentally sensitive products.

Sears

BACKGROUND Sears, an American retailing icon, serves over 50 million households through 833 full-line stores and more than 2,600 "off-the-mall" stores. It has competed successfully by offering customer service and product guarantees that have set standards for quality in the industry. William Giffin, vice president of ethics and business practices of Sears Merchandise Group, explains the company's philosophy this way, "People believe in Craftsman and DieHard batteries. Why? Because if you buy a Craftsman tool and it breaks in your lifetime, we give you a new one."

THE CHALLENGE With a mosaic of products and customers, Sears gets its fair share of complaints. However, by acting ethically, Sears has created a competitive advantage through its strong relationships with loyal customers. In the highly competitive world of brick-and-mortar department stores, Sears' employees must understand the importance of their interactions with customers.

continued on next page

are by (1) helping the competitive market system to operate in a self-correcting manner; (2) educating the consumer; (3) increasing regulation; and (4) encouraging political action. The competitive market system operates to allocate resources and to provide most of the products we purchase to satisfy felt needs. While we may hear many complaints about the system, most of the goods and services we purchase or use flow through it with little difficulty. Competition works if the conditions of many buyers and sellers and other technical requirements of the free-market economic model allow it. We have attempted—sometimes with limited success—to restore competition where monopolies have reduced it.

Combined with the free-market system, consumer education can lead to wise choices. As products become more complex, diverse, and plentiful, the consumer's ability to make wise decisions must also expand. Educational programs and efforts by parents, schools, businesses, government, and consumer organizations all contribute to a better system. A responsible marketing philosophy should also encourage consumers to voice their opinions. Such comments can result in significant improvements in the seller's goods and services.

The marketing concept must include social responsibility as a primary function of the marketing organization. Social and profit goals are compatible, but they require the aggressive implementation of an expanded marketing concept. Explicit criteria for responsible decision making must be adopted in all companies. This is truly marketing's greatest challenge.

STRATEGIC IMPLICATIONS OF THE MARKETING ENVIRONMENT, ETHICS, AND SOCIAL RESPONSIBILITY

The leadership of corporate America is responding to a large number of important trends shaping business in the 21st century. Their decisions will influence and be influenced by changes in the competitive, political-legal, economic, technological, and social-cultural environments. Marketing ethics and social responsibility will continue to play important roles in business transactions in your hometown and around the globe.

The competitive environment will heat up in the next decade as more companies become veterans of the Web battle. Respondents to a recent survey report that competitive forces will come from every sector of business. A full third of these respondents believe the most serious competition will come from U.S. companies who are not yet a *Fortune* 500 company. Thirty percent expect foreign marketers to pose the most formidable competitive threat. By a larger than four-to-one majority, most CEOs believe that expanding their markets is a more important priority than increasing their share of current markets.[41]

Much of the competition will result from innovations in technology and scientific discoveries. Business in the 21st century will be propelled by information technologies and sustained by creativity and entrepreneurial activity. Biotechnology is an industry in its infancy that is expected to explode in the economy in the next decade. Scientists will be able to create materials atom by atom, replicating much that nature can do and more.

Indeed, the surge of innovation is fueling an expected 3 percent annual growth in the economy that experts predict will last for years to come. This age of prosperity is benefiting more people than just the established elite. By 2010, e-commerce could revolutionize all kinds of industries and account for 6 percent of the gross domestic product.[42]

In the 20th-century economy, industrial sectors included retail, financial services, and manufacturing. But today, those old sectors do not fit the networked economy. The idea of what it means to be a retail company will change in five years when a billion people are logged on to the Internet. The bundling of services on the Internet will bypass many of the financial services we take for granted today. For example, when a 14-year-old buys a digital CD off the Internet, digital cash is transferred from her hard drive to that of the recording artist, thereby eliminating the need for a bank or credit-card company. Money will eventually be relegated to encrypted numbers on disk drives and digital wallets.[43]

Dynamic growth cannot be left entirely to self-regulation. Simultaneously, as the information age builds a wealth of information, it has the ability to rob individuals of their privacy. The next decade will produce a plethora of rules and regulations to control the marketing environments. Understandably, businesses are disturbed at having limitations placed on their operations. For example, a broad federal privacy protection law that forces data gatherers to inform consumers that they have collected information on them and explain how the information is being used could cost marketing researchers and businesses billions of dollars in redesigning database configurations to be in compliance with new standards.[44]

Consumers will feel the impact of environmental changes in every aspect of their lives. The new century is ushering in new generations of consumers who expect high-quality, low-cost products readily available on demand. Every company will be forced to build relationships to attract and retain loyal customers in order to succeed.

Underlying all the changes in the business environments and marketing mix elements is a requirement for companies to act ethically and in socially responsible ways. Marketers will have to go beyond what is legally right and wrong by integrating ethical behavior in all of their actions. Forward-looking companies will reap the benefits tomorrow of socially responsible behavior today.

ACHIEVEMENT CHECK SUMMARY

Read the learning objectives that follow, and consider the questions for each one. Answering these questions will reinforce your grasp of the most important concepts in the chapter and will allow you to check how well you have achieved these learning goals. Where a blank appears before a question, answer with T or F for true/false questions; for multiple-choice questions, choose the letter of the correct answer.

Objective 2.1: Identify the components of the marketing environment.

1. _____ The process by which organizations marketing goods or services seek to satisfy markets is called (a) environmental management, (b) scanning the environment, (c) the competitive environment, (d) demarketing.

2. _____ Laws to determine competitive conditions and protect consumer rights are part of the political-legal environment.

3. _____ The social-cultural environment refers to the relationship between the marketer, society, and technology.

Objective 2.2: Explain the types of competition marketers face and the steps in developing a competitive strategy.

1. _____ The competition between cable television movie channels, rental videos, and movie theaters is an example of (a) direct competition, (b) competition among goods or services that can be substituted for one another, (c) competition among all organizations that compete for the consumer's dollars.

2. _____ When a firm decides if it should compete, it evaluates its resources, objectives, and profit potential.

3. _____ Decisions about the "four Ps" help the marketer choose the markets in which the firm will compete.

Objective 2.3: Describe how government and other groups regulate marketing activities and how marketers can influence the political-legal environment.

1. _____ Government regulation of marketing activities is a recent development that began with laws passed around 1950.

2. _____ The FTC uses consent orders and cease-and-desist orders to enforce laws regarding unfair business practices and false or misleading advertising.

3. _____ A consumer boycott is an example of self-regulation.

Objective 2.4: Outline the economic factors that affect marketing decisions and consumer buying power.

1. _____ Consumers' buying habits remain the same regardless of the stage of the business cycle.

2. _____ During periods of high inflation, consumers are likely to buy more luxury goods.

3. _____ Discretionary income is more important to marketers than total income.

Objective 2.5: Discuss the impact of the technological environment on a firm's marketing activities.

1. _____ Technological advances tend to raise product prices.

2. _____ Technology transfer from the military to the private sector is one source of new product development.

3. _____ Marketers who apply technology creatively gain a competitive advantage.

MARKETING STRATEGY SUCCESS

THE STRATEGY In 1994, Sears initiated an internal ethics and business practice control team to help employees with situations that could potentially hurt the customers, the company, or the employees themselves. All managers receive ethics literature, take training courses at Sears University, and sign a new contract each year signifying their commitment to the company's code of conduct. Sears' personnel are urged to use an internal hot line that now receives 15,000 calls a year from employees seeking guidance and clarification of ethical issues.

THE OUTCOME Having a formal conflict resolution mechanism in-house has yielded an estimated 4-to-1 return by avoiding scandals and drawn-out conflicts. Says Giffin, "It's simply less expensive for us to deal with problems swiftly and efficiently internally than to go through the Equal Employment Opportunities Commission, courts, and *Wall Street Journal*. It's not only the right thing to do, it's the practical thing to do."

Objective 2.6: Explain how the social-cultural environment influences marketing.

1. _____ Shifts in societal values influence consumer attitudes toward products.

2. _____ The consumerist movement brings legal, moral, and economic pressures on businesses to act in socially responsible ways.

3. _____ President Kennedy's statement of consumer rights includes all but one of the following: (a) the right to choose freely, (b) the right to be informed, (c) the right to the lowest price for a product, and (d) the right to be safe.

Objective 2.7: Describe the role of marketing in society and identify the two major social issues in marketing.

1. _____ Marketers are often responsible for developing strategies that shape a firm's position on social issues.

2. _____ Marketing ethics refer to standards of conduct and moral values that govern decisions regarding products, research, distribution, promotion, and pricing.

3. _____ A company that focuses on boosting sales and increasing profits meets today's definition of corporate social responsibility.

Objective 2.8: Identify each of the four levels of the social responsibility pyramid.

1. _____ The philanthropic dimension, the second highest level of the pyramid, focuses on being a good corporate citizen.

2. _____ The economic dimension focuses on profitability and is the foundation upon which all other dimensions rest.

3. _____ The obligation to do what is right, just, and fair sums up the ethical dimension.

Students: See the solutions section located on page S-1 to check your responses to the Achievement Check Summary.

Key Terms

environmental scanning	technological environment
environmental management	social-cultural environment
competitive environment	consumerism
time-based competition	consumer rights
political-legal environment	marketing ethics
economic environment	social responsibility
demarketing	green marketing

Review Questions

1. Briefly describe each of the five components of the marketing environment. Give an example of each.

2. Explain the types of competition marketers face. What steps must they complete to develop a competitive strategy?

3. Government regulation in the United States has evolved in four general phases. Identify each phase and give an example of laws enacted during that time.

4. Give an example of a federal law affecting:
   a. product strategy
   b. pricing strategy

   c. distribution strategy
   d. promotional strategy

5. Explain the methods the Federal Trade Commission uses to protect consumers. Which of these methods seems the most effective to you?

6. What major economic factors affect marketing decisions? How does each of these forces produce its effect?

7. Identify the ways in which the technological environment and the social-cultural environment affect marketing activities. Cite examples of both.

8. What arguments do consumerism assert to indict the competitive marketing system? Critically evaluate these arguments.

9. Describe the ethical problems related to:
   a. marketing research
   b. product strategy
   c. distribution strategy
   d. promotional strategy
   e. pricing strategy

10. Identify and briefly explain the major avenues through which people can resolve contemporary issues facing the marketing system. Cite relevant examples.

Questions for Critical Thinking

1. Give an example of how a marketer might meet each of the following responsibilities:
   a. economic
   b. legal
   c. ethical
   d. philanthropic

2. Classify the following laws as (1) assisting in maintaining a competitive environment, (2) assisting in regulating competitors, (3) regulating specific marketing activities, or (4) deregulating industries. Justify your classifications and identify the marketing mix variable(s) most affected by each law.
   a. Children's Online Privacy Protection Act
   b. Staggers Rail Act
   c. Clayton Act
   d. Robinson-Patman Act

3. Cite two examples of instances in which the technological environment has produced positive benefits for marketers. Give two instances of the harmful impact of the technological environment on a firm's marketing operations.

4. Should the United States impose regulations on advertising of alcoholic beverages? Explain.

5. Identify a critical social issue confronting your local community. How does this issue affect marketers in your area? Discuss.

'netWork

1. Government Regulation. Familiarize yourself with the content of the Federal Trade Commission (FTC) Web site at *www.ftc.gov.* Use the search feature at the FTC site to learn more about topics affecting this agency, as well as specific Internet-related issues. Possible topics include "spam," "scams," "Children's Online Privacy Protection Act," or others as specified by your instructor. Locate an article of interest, such as a recent publication entitled, "FTC Names Its Dirty Dozen: 12 Scams Most Likely to Arrive via Bulk E-Mail." Prepare an outline summarizing the major points of the article you select and use this outline as the basis for a brief class presentation on the topic.

ftc.gov

2. Consumerism. Use your favorite search engine (*www.google.com* is your authors' favorite) to locate Web sites on "boycotts." As you visit numerous Web sites such as *www.coopamerica/org/boycotts/bantargetchart. htm,* identify information you will use to complete a minimum of three entries in each column of a two-column chart. Column one will be titled "Boycotts I Could Support" and column two will be labeled "Boycotts I Could Not Support." Include justifications for your support (or opposition) to a particular boycott proposal under each entry.

coopamerica/org/boycotts/ bantargetchart.htm

3. Marketing and Ecology. Locate several green marketing Web sites, such as *www.ecomail.com/ greenshopping/grencorner.htm.* You and your partner should prepare a series of three to five questions and answers that provide provocative information about green marketing. To convey your findings to the rest of your class, one of you will role-play the part of a new show interviewer and the other will be a green marketing expert.

ecomail/com/ greenshopping/ greencorner.htm

One Q&A example taken from the Web site listed above is as follows:
Question: Can we develop new products that address compelling environmental issues?
Answer: One of the hottest appliances these days is Maytag's Neptune washer. Developed in response to energy-saving regulations, it saves consumers approximately $100 per year in energy and water bills and claims to wash clothes better than top-loading washers. Consumers are willing to pay a super premium price for this unique washer that has recharged its company's sales.

Video Case 2 on The Timberland Co. begins on page VC-3.

Global Dimensions
of Marketing

Taco Bell Leaves the Dog at Home

In 1998, top management at PepsiCo decided it was time for the firm's fast-food operations to leave the corporate nest. The soft drink bottler would team up with Frito-Lay, its powerhouse subsidiary in the salty-snack market, and a new company, Tricon Global Restaurants, was formed. Its purpose was to build a dominant fast-food presence with PepsiCo's Kentucky Fried Chicken (KFC), Pizza Hut, and Taco Bell divisions.

During the past quarter-century, both KFC and Pizza Hut broadened their focus beyond the United States, and by 2001, retail outlets could be found on every continent but Antarctica. The restaurants proved particularly successful in Japan and throughout Asia. Residents of the tiny island nation of Singapore have 28 Pizza Hut and 74 KFC restaurants to choose from—all within a few square miles of one another.

The big exception to this globalization of Tricon fast-food outlets was Taco Bell, which had stayed home. Of the world's 10,000 Taco Bells, only 200 are located outside the United States, and most of them are concentrated in the nearby Caribbean and Latin America.

But as Tricon marketers sought out methods for stimulating further sales growth and improving overall profits, the recent domestic success of Taco Bell could not be ignored. A phenomenally successful promotion featuring a celebrity spokes-chihuahua named Gidget saying *"Yo quiero Taco Bell"* had taught millions of Americans how to speak a few more words of Spanish. Combine this with an improved menu featuring the popular chalupas, and you have record numbers of diners hurrying in to get tacos, burritos, and talking toy replicas of Gidget. Last year, Taco Bell sales hit a record $6.8 billion. It was time to take the show on the road, and the show was about to become an international one.

The starting gate for the new international push was Australia, where many consumers were already familiar with Mexican food from their travels to North America and where fast-food dining was a popular component of Australian lifestyles. Six Taco Bells were opened in Sydney in time for the 2000 Olympics. The next stops on the international expansion involved Singapore and Hong Kong. As a Tricon marketer explained, "We hope to have 50 sites in Asia within a couple of years. It depends on how quickly people get acquainted with the concepts of Taco Bell."

If you thought Taco Bell's international marketing strategy was a no-brainer, that they would simply export their award-winning U.S. marketing program with a few minor adjustments like language translations, you would be dead wrong. Previous Asian experiences with KFC and Pizza Hut gave Taco Bell marketers insights into the unique characteristics that define the different market segments of the Pacific region. It also convinced Taco Bell marketers that attempting to export the domestic strategy was to court disaster.

Both Indonesia and Singapore have large Muslim populations, which precludes using Gidget in any promotions. Muslims consider it taboo to even touch a dog. In some other Asian countries, dogs are considered a culinary delicacy.

At the same time, Taco Bell marketers were able to take advantage of the similarities between Mexican and Asian foods. Many Asian dishes, for example, include various ingredients mixed together and placed in some sort of wrap, much like Taco Bell's burritos and gorditas. Asians also enjoy spicy foods and, in fact, frequently use chili as an ingredient in local cuisine. The culture and lifestyles of the Philippines, another Asian target market, has been influenced by U.S. culture since World War II and is receptive to accepting American foods and lifestyles.

Taco Bell promotions have also been adapted to attract the local 15-to-29-year-old Asian youth market. Instead of stuffed animal toys, Taco Bell's Singapore promotions include contests and drawings for such prizes as Ricky Martin concert tickets. Even the Taco Bell restaurants have traded in their traditional American Southwestern adobe style for modern architecture, cool colors, and modern steel furniture. And Taco Bell's Asian jingle—"Nothing ordinary about it"—is not spoken in Spanish.[1]

CHAPTER OVERVIEW

Like Taco Bell, U.S. and foreign companies are crossing national boundaries in unprecedented numbers in search of new markets and profits. International trade now accounts for 25 percent of the U.S. gross domestic product (GDP), compared to 5 percent 30 years ago. Exports of U.S. manufactured goods exceed $660 billion, more than double the amount in 1990.

International trade can be divided into two categories: **exporting,** marketing domestically produced goods and services abroad, and **importing,** purchasing foreign goods and services. International trade is vital to a nation and its marketers for several reasons. It expands markets, makes production and distribution economies feasible, allows companies to explore growth opportunities in other nations, and makes them less dependent on economic conditions in their home nations. Many also find that global marketing and international trade can help them meet customer demand, reduce costs, and provide valuable information on potential markets around the world.

For North American marketers, international trade is especially important because the U.S. and Canadian economies represent a mature market for many products. Outside North America, however, it is a different story. Economies in many parts of sub-Saharan Africa, Asia, Latin America, Europe, and the Middle East are growing rapidly. This opens up new markets for U.S. products as consumers in these areas have more money to spend and as the need for American goods and services by foreign companies expands. Exports of high-tech products accounted for 30 percent of U.S. GDP growth since 1985. And in some categories—computer equipment, semiconductors, aircraft, software, and entertainment—exports represent almost half of total sales. Hong Kong, the financial capital of Asia, invites foreign investment. The country's official transfer back to China has launched a new era of evolution and growth in commerce. Figure 3.1 shows how marketers are promoting the area as a global mecca for the 21st century.

International trade also builds employment. The world's 50 largest businesses keep 7.3 million people gainfully employed.[2] Your next job, in fact, might involve global marketing, since export-related jobs play an important role in the U.S. economy. Over 11 million U.S. workers—about 10 percent of

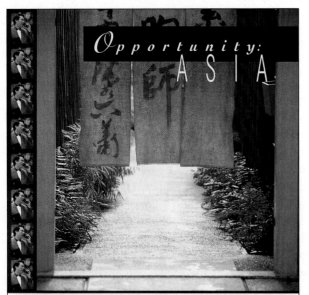

the total workforce—produce goods or provide services for export, a 75 percent increase in the last decade. In addition to representing a growing source of employment, careers in this sector often involve lucrative pay and benefits. Wages and benefits in firms producing goods for export average 13 percent to 16 percent more than the national average.

International marketers carefully evaluate the marketing concepts described in earlier chapters. However, transactions that cross national borders involve additional considerations. For example, different laws, varying levels of technological capability, economic conditions, cultural and business norms, and consumer preferences often require new strategies. Companies that want to market their products worldwide must reconsider each of the marketing variables (product, promotion, price, and distribution) in terms of the global marketplace. To succeed in global marketing, managers should answer some basic questions:

- How will our idea/good/service fit into the international market?
- What adjustments will we have to make?
- What threats will we face from global competition?
- How can we turn these threats into opportunities?
- What strategic alternatives will work in global markets?[3]

Many of the answers to these questions can be found by studying techniques used by successful international marketers. This chapter first considers the importance and characteristics of the global marketplace. It then examines the international marketing environment, the trend toward multinational economic integration, and the steps that most firms take to enter the global marketplace. Next, the importance of developing an international marketing mix is discussed. The chapter closes with a look at the United States as a target market for foreign marketers. ■

THE IMPORTANCE OF GLOBAL MARKETING

Seven of the top ten largest companies in the world are headquartered in the United States. For most U.S. companies—both large and small—global marketing is rapidly becoming a necessity. The demand for foreign products in the fast-growing economies of Asia and other Pacific Rim nations offers one example of the benefits of thinking globally. In a recent year, U.S. exports to Asia rose 37 percent to about $200 billion—almost twice its exports to Europe. A survey by South China Marketing Research revealed that 85 percent of respondents believe that Western products are higher quality; 75 percent think they last longer; and 70 percent consider them a better value than those made locally.[4] International marketers recognize how the slogan "Made in the USA" yields tremendous selling power throughout the world. As a result, overseas sales are important revenue sources for many U.S. firms.

Over the last 15 years, U.S. exports have grown an average of 10.5 percent each year. Considering the nation's reputation as a global leader in such high-tech industries as computers, pharmaceuticals, and telecommunications equipment, the answer to the question, "What is the top U.S. export?" will usually stump even the best-informed contestant. After all, agricultural products—the number one export—are typically associated with a

MARKETING DICTIONARY

exporting Marketing domestically produced goods and services in foreign countries.

importing Purchasing foreign goods and services and raw materials.

FIGURE 3.2   AT&T: The World's Leading Telecommunications Company

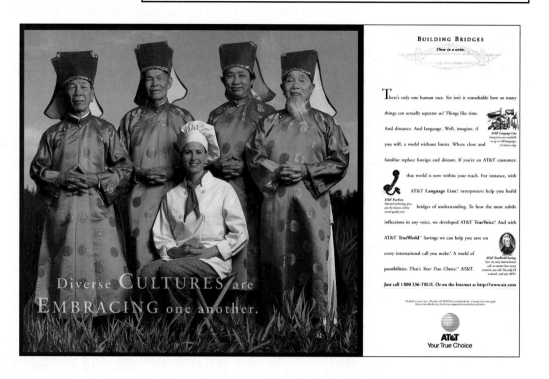

pastoral nation like Argentina or Australia rather than the United States. But the natural resources that bless America include fertile and abundant land, adequate rainfall, and the application of high-tech equipment designed to improve crop yields and enhance productivity. Surplus crops of corn, soybeans, and wheat are major U.S. agricultural exports.

Other products included among the top five U.S. exports are electrical machinery, computers and office equipment, general industrial machinery, and motor vehicle parts. Among the leading U.S. firms in terms of the portion of their revenues generated from exports are Boeing, Intel, Motorola, Caterpillar, and Sun Microsystems.

With over 80 million business, government, and individual customers, AT&T is a major global marketer. It operates the world's largest long-distance network, the largest wireless network in North America, and is a leading supplier of data and Internet services around the globe. Its Global Venture operations are headquartered in Atlanta, but it also has offices in such globally-dispersed locations as Australia, France, Germany, Hong Kong, Japan, and Singapore. In addition, it has joined forces with such global business partners as British Telephone, KDD of Japan, and Telecom New Zealand to provide seamless global capabilities. As Figure 3.2 states, AT&T serves its diverse cultural markets with its Language Line, which provides interpreters for up to 140 languages, 24 hours a day.[5]

The rapid globalization of business and the boundless nature of the Internet have made it possible for every marketer to become an international marketer. While larger corporations enjoy advantages of stronger distribution systems, financial resources, and political clout, small businesses are also making inroads into the international arena. Professional Web site designs, which only a few years ago meant a major investment, can now be accomplished by cyberstore specialists for around $300 to $700. Advances in computer and telecommunication technologies also aid smaller firms in marketing their products abroad. Le Travel Store, a small San Diego retailer that specializes in wheeled luggage that can be turned into backpacks, reached customers far beyond Southern California when it embraced e-commerce. It currently generates about 45 percent of its revenues online.[6]

Just as some firms depend on foreign sales, others rely on purchasing raw materials abroad as input for their domestic manufacturing operations. A furniture company's purchase of South

American mahogany is an example. The top five U.S. imports are computers and office equipment, crude oil, clothing, telecommunications equipment, and agricultural products.

One communications innovation that consumers quickly embraced was the cell phone. Today, seven of every ten U.S. households own at least one cell phone, a larger percentage than households with cable TV. While the widespread acceptance of wireless phones has produced an entirely new industry of both established and start-up firms, it also represents a huge market for foreign marketers. European firms like Ericsson and Nokia have proven formidable competitors to such domestic marketers as Motorola.

Over the past 15 years, U.S. imports have grown about 7 percent annually. While it is extremely rare to find a nation with which no U.S. trade exists, the United States' top ten leading trade partners shown in Figure 3.3 include nearby Canada and Mexico as well as distant China, Japan, Korea, Singapore, and Taiwan. Total exports and imports between the United States and Canada, its northern neighbor with whom it shares a 2,000-mile border, are almost one-third *trillion* dollars a year, nearly twice as much as second-place Japan.

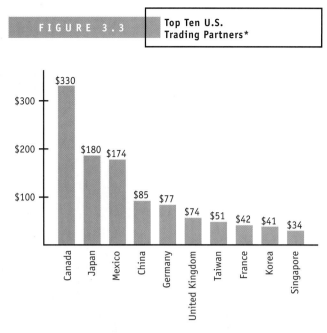

FIGURE 3.3 — Top Ten U.S. Trading Partners*

*Total imports and exports in billions.

Service and Retail Exports

In addition to agricultural products and manufactured goods, the United States is also a big exporter of services and retailing. In fact, it leads the world in services exports. Of the approximately $210 billion in annual service exports, over half comes from travel and tourism—money spent by foreign nationals visiting the United States. Tourism is the third largest industry in the United States, contributing $430 billion to its economy each year, and is responsible for creating more than $6 billion in travel and tourism-related jobs. With 102 million tourists per year, the United States ranks second only to China in visitors. By 2020, tourists will spend $2 trillion during their international travels.

Vacation marketers, intensifying their efforts to give tourists the largest variety of activities within the shortest time, have created a boom in theme parks and cruises. Over 40 new cruise vessels were put on the high seas in 2000, with the largest one capable of carrying 6,200 passengers. Theme parks under construction range from a replica of ancient Rome to central Florida's Jungle Crocs of the World. Over 500 airline alliances have been created to make it easier for globetrotters seeking undiscovered faraway destinations to reach them from the local airport. National tourism offices around the world are competing aggressively to capture shares of this growing industry.[7]

The most profitable U.S. service exports are business and technical services, such as engineering, financial, computing, legal services, and entertainment. In a recent year, worldwide Internet services revenues grew an enormous 71 percent to almost $8 billion. Even more surprising is that the growth is expected to continue at a 60 percent annual rate, passing $78 billion by 2003. The United States is the largest market for Internet service providers.[8]

The financial services industry is also going global via the cyberhighway. The rapid emergence of cross-border securities trading exemplifies how quickly the Internet is gaining acceptance among investors. Charles Schwab Europe has some 14,500 British clients who trade U.S. shares over the Internet. Ameritrade's online system allows German and French investors to buy and sell U.S. equities. E*Trade has expanded services to Australia, France, and Sweden.[9] A glance at the increasing number of foreign companies listed on the New York Stock Exchange illustrates the importance of global financial services. Figure 3.4 explains how companies listed on the exchange are changing our world, from drug companies' research to find a cure for river blindness in Central and West Africa to the launch of a new space telescope for viewing distant galaxies.

Some service exporters are household names: American Express, AT&T, Citigroup, Walt Disney, Wal-Mart, Allstate Insurance, and Federal Express. Many earn a substantial percentage of their revenues from international sales. For instance, U.S. airlines earn 25 percent of their

nyse.com

revenues from their international routes. Other service exporters are smaller companies, such as the many software firms that have found overseas markets receptive to their products. Hyperion Software, a Stamford, Connecticut, designer of financial reporting software for large business applications generates half its revenues from overseas sales. While Hyperion uses a direct sales force in North America, it sells through independent local distributors in foreign markets. San Diego–based StarGuide Digital Networks exports both goods (satellite communications equipment) and services (air time on satellites) to major Japanese corporations.

The movie industry is another major service exporter. Europe and Australia have always been receptive to American films, partly due to the similarities in language and lifestyles. British actor Hugh Grant is as famous in Los Angeles or New York as American actor Robert Redford is in Paris or Sydney. But films traveling to Asia typically have little connection with Eastern culture. The language is different and the music is different. As a result, U.S. movie marketers attempt to develop ties with Asian audiences, a relatively untapped market that currently generates only 18 cents of every dollar spent abroad on movie tickets or video sales and rentals. So when Warner Bros. released *Lethal Weapon 4* in Hong Kong, it hired local heavy-metal band Beyond to create a music video to be used for promotional purposes only. The band is highly popular in Asia, and the video received heavy airplay in Hong Kong and Taiwan. Even though the song was never a part of the movie itself, it served as a commercial for the movie each time it was played.[10]

Retailers ranging from Victoria's Secret, Foot Locker, and The Gap to Office Depot, Toys "Я" Us, and PriceCostco warehouse clubs are opening stores around the world at rapid paces. U.S. retailers do especially well in Asia, where consumers like the convenience and wide selection of American-made products. They are also attracted to products associated with American lifestyles.

During the last three decades, U.S. fast-food franchises have been opening outlets at a phenomenal rate, as the opening story on Taco Bell demonstrates. McDonald's currently operates over 6,000 outlets in 91 countries. Domino's Pizza now serves its pies to customers in 1,200 outlets in 46 countries. Arby's parent company, Florida-based Triarc Restaurant Group, operates over 3,000 outlets in the United States and has recently signed an agreement with Sybra Restaurants UK to take the roast-beef-sandwich chain to London. Over 100 Arby's restaurants are expected to open during the next 10 years.[11]

Benefits of Going Global

Besides generating additional revenue, firms are expanding their operations outside their home country to gain other benefits, including new insights into consumer behavior, alternative distribution strategies, and advance notice of new products. By setting up foreign offices and production facilities, marketers may learn new marketing techniques and gain invaluable experience.

Global marketers are typically well-positioned to compete effectively with foreign competitors. With the fall of Soviet Russia came the rise of a new economy. Although Russia has a well-deserved reputation for being a difficult market to enter, Western companies flocked to the 150 million, product-starved consumers, and many have found the effort worthwhile. A major key to achieving success in foreign markets is a firm's ability to adapt its products to local preferences. For decades, Bestfoods, makers of Hellmann's mayonnaise, has marketed different mayonnaise recipes around the world. The special recipe for Russia, for example, is a near-liquid version that is much blander than the U.S. version. Unlike Americans, who spread mayonnaise on bread, Russians pour it over vegetables.[12] Hellman's has been one of the few foreign companies that has been successful in its marketing efforts to Russia. Its greatest competitive threat comes from state-owned leader Moszhircom mayonnaise.

Another method used by international marketers before entering foreign markets is to conduct transcontinental product testing. Procter & Gamble is a veteran of global marketing but only recently began to develop truly global products. Swiffer, a lightweight mop with disposable cleaning cloths that use static electricity to pick up dust, hair, and other dirt, was test marketed in Cedar Rapids, Iowa, and in Sens, France, before its global launch. It was found to be successful in both markets. The name Swiffer is meant to convey speed and ease of use and is used in promotions as both a noun and a verb, as in "Let's Swiffer the floor." As one P&G spokesperson explained, "The more that we truly explore consumers on a global basis, the more we find that they're really more alike than they are dissimilar." Global testing was also used for P&G's Dryel home dry-cleaning products. Test sites for Dryel were in Ohio and Ireland.[13]

Since firms must perform the marketing functions of buying, selling, transporting, storing, standardizing and grading, financing, risk taking, and obtaining market information in both domestic and global markets, some may question the wisdom of treating international marketing as a distinct subject. After all, international marketing is marketing; a firm performs the same functions and works toward the same objectives in domestic or international marketing. As the chapter will explain, however, both similarities and differences influence strategies for international and domestic marketing.

THE INTERNATIONAL MARKETPLACE

Today, it is rare to find a U.S. firm that never ventures outside its domestic market. Even if it deals primarily with the U.S. market, which is huge in its own right, it may look overseas for raw materials or component parts or it may face foreign competition in its home market. Those who venture abroad may find the international marketplace far different than the domestic one they are accustomed to. Market sizes, buyer behavior, and marketing practices all vary. To be successful, international marketers must do their homework, capitalize on similarities, and carefully evaluate all market segments in which they expect to compete.

Market Size

From the dawn of civilization until the 1800s, world population grew to about 1 billion people. It almost doubled by 1900, and today over 6 billion people inhabit the planet. According to Census Bureau projections, world population will increase to nearly 8 billion in the next 25 years.

@ **triarc.com**

@ **bestfoods.com**

1

Describe the importance of international marketing from the perspectives of the individual firm and the nation.

Ninety-six percent of the increase in world population occurs in less-developed regions such as Africa, Asia, and Latin America. Population growth rates in affluent countries, however, have slowed to 0.4 percent annually—one fifth the annual growth of less-developed countries. What this all means is that, over the next quarter-century, firms will have to adapt their goods and services to meet the needs and wants of consumers in developing countries

One-fifth of the world's population—1.2 billion people—lives in China, for example, but less than one in 20 resides in the United States. Africa is growing fastest at 2.8 percent a year, followed by Latin America at 1.9 percent and Asia at 1.7 percent. Average birth rates are dropping around the world due to family planning efforts, but death rates are declining even more rapidly. However, in Africa the birth rates are still high (6 children per woman), and Indian women average 3.4 children. European birth rates have fallen considerably, and couples average only 1.5 children. This could present economic challenges as the age distribution shifts due to the low birth rate.[14]

The world marketplace is increasingly an urban marketplace. Today, almost 50 percent of its people live in large cities. As a result, city populations are swelling: 39 cities currently have a population of 5 million or more. Mexico City, whose population of 18 million ranks it as the world's largest city, is expected to grow to 31 million by 2010. Increased urbanization will expand the need for transportation, housing, machinery, and services.

The growing size and urbanization of the international marketplace does not necessarily mean all foreign markets offer the same potential. Another important influence on market potential is a nation's economic development stage. A subsistence economy offers a different environment than that of a newly industrialized country or an industrial nation. In a *subsistence economy*, most people engage in agriculture and earn low per-capita incomes, supporting few opportunities for international trade. In a *newly industrialized country*, such as Brazil or South Korea, growth in manufacturing creates demand for consumer products and industrial goods such as high-tech equipment. The *industrial nations*, including the United States, Japan, and western Europe, trade manufactured goods and services among themselves and export to less-developed countries. Although these wealthy countries account for just a small percentage of the world's population, they produce over half of its output.

As a nation develops, an increasingly affluent, educated, and cosmopolitan middle class emerges. India's middle class includes nearly 300 million people, a number larger than the entire population of the United States. India's processed food producers and marketers are now facing global competition as a result of economic reforms and market liberalization. The greatest concerns for foreign companies seeking new markets in India is overcoming inadequate and restricted marketing channels. However, significant opportunities can be found through joint ventures and strategic alliances.[15]

International marketers see similar growth in middle-income households occurring in the booming East Asian economies like China, Thailand, Singapore, South Korea, and Hong Kong, as well as in Mexico, South America, and sub-Saharan Africa. These new middle-class consumers have both the desire for consumer goods, including luxury and leisure goods and services, and money to pay for them.

Buyer Behavior

Buyer behavior differs among nations and often among market segments within a country. Marketers must carefully match their marketing strategies to local customs, tastes, and living conditions. Even McDonald's decided to tweak its standard hamburger fare to cater to diverse international tastes. The world's largest fast-food marketer offers vegetarian burgers in parts of India; some Australian outlets include beets as a condiment; beer can be purchased in German outlets; and wine is on the menu in French McDonald's restaurants.

The Coca-Cola Company, which generates 63 percent of sales and 75 percent of total profits from international markets, varies its product emphasis in different parts of the world. In Japan, it heavily promotes Leaf, a new canned-tea product that has become a hot seller there. The reason for the shift: Soft drinks make up only 20 percent of nonalcoholic beverage sales in Japan.[16]

TelePizza is another international venture that adapted its products to local preferences and customs. Founder Leopoldo Fernandez Pujals exemplifies today's international entrepreneurial ventures. Pujals is Cuban-born, American reared and educated, a Vietnam veteran, and now a businessman based in Madrid, Spain. Ten years ago, Pujals invested $100,000 in savings to launch his new business, TelePizza. Using local teenagers to test his pies, he determined the best combination of ingredients for his market before opening the doors for business. TelePizza now controls 60 percent of Spain's pizza market and has grown to more than 600 outlets in Europe and South America. Many of his strategies have been based on previous winners in the international fast-food industry—cleanliness from McDonald's, speedy home delivery from Domino's, and sit-down comforts from Pizza Hut. Using a centralized delivery service and computerized ordering systems, customers can call one number to order anything from shrimp curry to pizza topped with trout flakes and have it delivered by bicycle to their door.[17]

In some instances, international marketers succeed in changing local buyer behavior by introducing new marketing strategies that have been well-received in other countries. Johnson & Johnson (J&J) recently debuted RoC, a 40-year-old French line of skincare products, in an attempt to leverage its strong European brand. J&J marketers are targeting both the mass-market brand of L'Oréal and prestige department-store brands such as Clinique.[18]

Failure to adapt to local preferences can create costly problems, as Kellogg cereal marketers can attest. Kellogg had enjoyed success in both the United States and England and was eager to expand into other European markets. Lured by expected higher prices and profit margins, cheaper television advertising time, and fewer competitors, Kellogg opened a manufacturing plant in Italy to supply what appeared to be a market with high growth potential. But Italians do not eat corn flakes; they consider corn a product more likely to be fed to livestock; and those few cereal fanciers typically buy from health-food stores. Had Kellogg marketers bothered to check consumption data, they would have known the task they faced. On average, Italians consume 1.1 pounds of cereal annually—hardly a drop in the bucket compared to 11.7 pounds in the United States and 14.5 pounds in Britain. The U.S. firm began making inroads in the land of *la Dolce Vita* and then began linking its products to Italian food habits. For example, an ad for Crunchy Nut Corn Flakes features an Italian farm family eating breakfast outside their old stone house while their child is talking on a cell phone—an essential part of 21st-century Italian life. Eventually, Kellogg's market share floated up to 60 percent of Italy's total dry-cereal sales.[19]

Differences in buying patterns require marketing executives to complete considerable research before entering a foreign market. Sometimes the marketer's own organization or a U.S.-based research firm can provide needed information. In other cases, only a foreign-based marketing research organization can tell marketers what they need to know. Whoever conducts the research, investigators must focus on six different areas before advising a company to enter a foreign market:

1. *Demand.* Do foreign consumers need the company's good or service?
2. *Competitive environment.* How do supplies currently reach the market?
3. *Economic environment.* What is the state of the nation's economic health?
4. *Social-cultural environment.* How do cultural factors affect business opportunities?
5. *Political-legal environment.* Do any legal restrictions complicate entering the market?
6. *Technological environment.* To what degree are technological innovations used by consumers in the market?

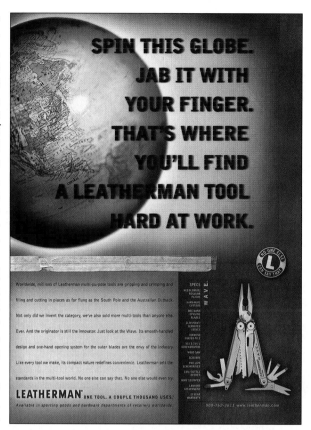

From the South Pole to the Australian Outback, Leatherman marketers fill customer needs around the globe with their unique product.

kelloggs.com

2

Identify the major components of the environment for international marketing.

THE INTERNATIONAL MARKETING ENVIRONMENT

As in domestic markets, the environmental factors discussed in Chapter 2 have a powerful influence on the development of international marketing strategies. Marketers must pay close attention to economic, social-cultural, political-legal, and technological influences as they venture abroad.

International Economic Environment

A nation's size, per-capita income, and stage of economic development determine its prospects as a host for international business expansion. Nations with low per-capita incomes may be poor markets for expensive industrial machinery but good ones for agricultural hand tools. These nations cannot afford the technical equipment that powers an industrialized society. Wealthier countries may offer prime markets for many U.S. industries, particularly those producing consumer goods and services and advanced industrial products.

In India, for example, the median annual household income is only $480. Economic reforms have improved the country's standard of living somewhat, but most Indians have very few Western conveniences. Only 2 percent own cars, 4 percent have running hot water, and 7 percent have phones. Color television and refrigerator ownership run a bit higher at 12 percent.

Successful marketing in India requires an understanding of how the economy affects Indian consumers. Both rich and poor Indians practice frugal buying habits and spend as little as possible at one time. They prefer small packages with low prices, even though larger packages may offer more economical purchases. Even the wealthy are price-conscious consumers. Nestlé S.A. improved its market penetration in India by reducing package sizes and then pricing more than half of its food products under 25 rupees (about 70 cents). For example, sales of Maggi instant noodles tripled after Nestlé reduced the price from 19 cents to 14 cents a package. Recycling, a way of life for many Indians, is another issue U.S. marketers must keep in mind before entering the Indian marketplace. Although that country is the world's largest market for razor blades, disposable razors sell very poorly because the idea of throwing them away mystifies typical Indians.[20]

Another important economic factor to consider when planning to enter a foreign market is a country's **infrastructure.** Infrastructure refers to a nation's communication systems (television, radio, print media, telecommunications), transportation networks (paved roads, railroads, airports), and energy facilities (power plants, gas and electric utilities). An inadequate infrastructure may constrain marketers' plans to manufacture, promote, and distribute goods and services in a particular country.

People living in countries blessed by navigable waters often rely on them as inexpensive, relatively efficient alternatives to highways, rail lines, and air transportation. As Figure 3.5 shows, Thai farmers use their nation's myriad rivers to transport their crops. Their boats even become retail outlets in so-called *floating markets* like this one located outside Bangkok.

Marketers expect developing economies to have substandard utility and communications networks. China encountered numerous problems in establishing a 21st-century communications industry infrastructure. The Chinese government's answer was a huge investment in wireless technology. By 2001, over 60 million Chinese had their own cell phones, and the number will grow to 200 million subscribers by 2010. Unlike the high phone rates paid by their Japanese neighbors, Chinese consumers pay only a nickel a minute, one of the cheapest rates in the world.[21]

Changes in exchange rates can also complicate international marketing. An **exchange rate** is the price of one nation's currency in terms of another country's currency. Fluctuations in exchange rates can make a nation's currency more valuable or less valuable compared to those of other nations. In Europe, a new currency was introduced—the euro—to eliminate problems associated with exchange rates. Before the euro, prices for the same goods and services varied between 30 percent and 100 percent among European nations. In the first year of the euro, price

MARKETING STRATEGY SUCCESS

Blue-Light Specials in Guam

BACKGROUND For the past decade, Kmart has fought a fierce battle with rival discounter Wal-Mart. But today on the tiny 210-square-mile island of Guam, Kmart rules supreme.

CHALLENGE No one questioned the need for a general-merchandise retailer on Guam, the U.S. protectorate made up of 150,000 retail-starved residents. The existing retailers charged sky-high prices for everything from toothpaste to crockpots. But Guam is halfway to China, and that is a long way to ship laundry detergent for a single store. Kmart could pick up sales, but could they make any money?

STRATEGY Kmart created its own version of the Mall of America on the South Pacific island. Affluent Japanese shoppers, who pay relatively high prices for the products they buy, were fascinated by this store, its huge inventory, and (to them) eye-popping low prices. And heading for Guam to shop became a featured stop on most Japanese tour packages. The average Japanese visitor to Guam makes two trips to Kmart per visit: the first to buy vacation and beach supplies upon arrival and the second to buy souvenirs to take

continued on next page

FIGURE 3.5	Transportation Systems: Important Components of a Nation's Infrastructure

home. Local shoppers are attracted by favorite food items like Spam and beef jerky as well as low prices on clothing and household supplies.

OUTCOME Guam is Kmart's island treasure chest, raking in annual sales of nearly $100 million—six to seven times the average sales of each of the other 2,100 stores in the discounter's chain. It has become a retail paradise for Pacific-island shoppers.

differences fell to only 28 percent and continue to drop as the euro becomes the dominant currency in Europe. By July 1, 2002, national currencies will no longer be legal tender for countries in the European Monetary Union.

Russian and many eastern European currencies are considered *soft* currencies that cannot be readily converted into such *hard* currencies as the dollar, euro, or Japanese yen. Rather than taking payment in soft currencies, international marketers doing business there may resort to barter, accepting such commodities as oil, timber, or even alcoholic beverages as payment for exports. Needless to say, U.S. currency is a hot commodity; in fact, demand for American dollars is higher than ever. About 60 percent of the new $100 bills printed last year were sent directly overseas. When the Berlin Wall fell in 1989, signifying the end of the cold war, U.S. dollars flooded former Soviet-bloc countries. In response, many regions, including much of Africa, Asia, and the Middle East, have placed restrictions on currency trading.[22]

International Social-Cultural Environment

Before entering a foreign market, marketers should study all aspects of that nation's culture, including language, education, religious attitudes, and social values. Advertisers in the European Union, for example, must create messages that work as effectively in Germany and Portugal as they do in Norway and France. Marketers for products as diverse as Häagen-Dazs ice cream, Nike Air Jordans, the movie *Titanic*, and McDonald's Egg McMuffins have been successful in reaching global consumers by positioning the right product in the right market. The American movie

MARKETING   DICTIONARY

infrastructure A nation's basic system of transportation networks, communication systems, and energy facilities.

exchange rate Price of one nation's currency in terms of other countries' currencies.

Targeting Latin American Travelers with Spanish and Portuguese In-Flight Magazines

industry has been particularly successful in adapting its films to diverse audiences. Increasingly, marketers are looking for similarities among markets and segments of markets they are targeting.[23]

International travelers are an inherent part of most major airlines' customer base. A major task of air travel marketers is to attract and satisfy this diverse target market. Northwest Airlines recently created a loyalty program for the Asian segment of its international market. Taking many cues from Japan Airlines' successful loyalty program, Northwest wants to attract Asian Americans and their average annual household incomes of $47,000. Northwest marketers developed a promotional campaign that reflects several Japanese core values, such as family and gift giving. Provisions of its WorldPerks frequent-flyer program include flexible use of accrued miles, allowing the traveler to share them with extended family members—even the wife of a grandson. The program also offers tailored gifts, such as hospitality tents at golf tournaments in Los Angeles or a night on the town at a famous New York City cabaret.[24]

Language also plays an important role in international marketing. Marketers must make sure not only to use the right language for a country but also ensure that the message is translated and conveys the intended meaning. Abbreviations and slang words and phrases may also cause misunderstandings when marketing abroad. A Chinese or Saudi Arabian consumer may not understand American ads with references to *Catch-22* situations or abbreviations like ASAP. American Airlines provides copies of *Nexos*, an in-flight magazine written in Spanish and Portuguese, to travelers on all flights to Latin America and the Spanish-speaking Caribbean. As Figure 3.6 illustrates, the editorial quality of the articles and the striking graphics convey American Airlines' recognition of the importance of its customers. Potential translation problems are avoided since the magazine is written and edited by professionals whose first language is Spanish or Portuguese.

nwa.com

International Technological Environment

More than any event since the telephone, Internet technology has made it possible for both large and small firms to be connected to the entire world. The Internet transcends political, economic, and cultural barriers, reaching to every corner of the globe. Consider the following facts regarding the Internet:

- Fewer than 40 million people around the world were connected to the Internet in 1996; by 2004, more than 1.5 billion will be online.
- Business-to-consumer e-commerce is expected to grow to $120 billion by 2004.
- By 2002, business-to-business Internet transactions will exceed $300 billion.
- Advertising on the Web already surpasses $4 billion.[25]

The Internet is truly a global medium that allows seamless communications and business transactions between individual consumers and multinational companies. It is critical that 21st-century marketers understand how the Web is reshaping social and cultural values. Differences between national identities are being softened as people become accustomed to the even greater similarities of a global society. Marketers must be careful not to hold on to preconceptions of foreign markets since they may no longer hold true.[26]

Technology presents challenges for international marketers that extend beyond the Internet. A major issue involving food marketers competing in Europe is genetic reengineering. Although

U.S. grocery shelves are filled with foods grown with genetically modified organisms (GMOs), most Americans do not know they are eating GMO foods, since no labeling disclosures are required. In Britain and other European countries, the story is quite different. Referred to in these countries as "Franken Foods," activists are pushing for labeling laws to inform shoppers that these foods are "not naturally grown" or to ban them altogether. Marketers of agricultural commodities and packaged goods are already taking actions in response to these concerns. Gerber recently reformulated its baby foods to remove all ingredients containing GMOs.[27]

International Political-Legal Environment

Global marketers must continually stay abreast of laws and trade regulations in each country in which they compete. Some laws, such as *Les Soldes* (The Sales) in France, are uncommon to U.S. marketers. By law, retail sales can be held only twice a year—in January or February and again during autumn. At least 30 percent of French clothing sales occur during these two sales seasons.[28]

Political conditions often influence international marketing, as well. Consider the effects of recent political turmoil in Kosovo, Indonesia, and Kenya. Such political unrest sometimes results in acts of violence, such as destruction of a firm's property. Middle Eastern terrorists have targeted U.S. companies' offices abroad. IBM and American Express have been subject to terrorist threats and attacks. As a result, many Western firms have set up internal *political risk assessment* (PRA) units or turned to outside consulting services to evaluate the political risks of the marketplaces in which they operate.

The fall of communism and the transformation of state-dominated industries into privately-owned and managed profit-seeking enterprises has been accompanied by a trend toward freer trade among nations. The movement toward capitalism is emphasized by the recent launch of *Forbes Global*, a new international business periodical, published by the well-known business magazine *Forbes*.

The legal environment for U.S. firms operating abroad results from three forces: (1) international law, (2) U.S. law, and (3) legal requirements of host nations. International law emerges from the treaties, conventions, and agreements that exist among nations. The United States has many **friendship, commerce, and navigation (FCN) treaties** with other governments. These agreements set terms for various aspects of commercial relations with other countries, such as the right to conduct business in the treaty partner's domestic market. Other international business agreements concern worldwide standards for various products, patents, trademarks, reciprocal tax treaties, export control, international air travel, and international communication.

Since the 1990s, Europe has pushed for mandatory *ISO (International Standards Organization) 9000 certification*—an internationally recognized standard that ensures a company's goods and services meet established quality levels. A decade later, the standards have crossed the Atlantic Ocean to include a growing number of U.S. businesses. Large multinational corporations were the first to undertake the costly and time-consuming ISO certification process. However, marketers in small businesses have come to realize the advantages of being ISO certified, such as access to more international markets, promotional prestige, and customer confidence of quality—all of which can lead to increased sales.[29] The International Monetary Fund, another major player in the international legal environment, lends foreign exchange to nations that require it in order to conduct international

CIAO, MAO.

Little red book? What little red book?
Today, capitalism is calling the shots all over Asia. And the world. It's calling for new ideas. New technologies. And a new magazine.
Introducing Forbes Global. With coverage of international business and finance found nowhere else, it's the first magazine completely dedicated to the global executive.
Call David Forgione at (212) 620-2309 to join the revolution.

Forbes GLOBAL

Forbes Global offers coverage of international business and finance news as it sends the message of capitalism around the globe.

trade. These agreements facilitate the whole process of world marketing. However, there are no international laws for corporations, only for governments. Therefore, marketers include special provisions in contracts, such as which country's courts have jurisdiction.

The second dimension of the international legal environment, U.S. law, includes various trade regulations, tax laws, and import/export requirements that affect international marketing. One important law, the *Export Trading Company Act of 1982*, exempts companies from antitrust regulations so they can form export groups that offer a variety of products to foreign buyers. The law seeks to make it easier for foreign buyers to connect with U.S. exporters. It also allows banks to participate directly in such ventures by financing trading activities. Although export trading companies offer many benefits to U.S. companies, relatively few firms have joined forces in these cooperative ventures.

A controversial 1996 law, the *Helms-Burton Act*, tried to impose trade sanctions against Cuba. Under this law, U.S. corporations and citizens can sue foreign companies and their executives for using expropriated U.S. assets to do business in Cuba. However, this law has not hindered other countries such as Canada from conducting trade with Cuba. Ireland's U.N. Ambassador John Campbell criticizes the Cuban government but adds, "We cannot accept that the United States may unilaterally determine or restrict the European Union's economic and commercial relations with any other state. Measures of this type violate the general principles of international law and the sovereignty of independent states." The U.S. government is listening more closely these days to what the international community has to say about its relations with Cuba, and in 1999 the Baltimore Orioles received permission to play an exhibition baseball game in Cuba—a country wild about the game. The condition was that all profits from the game go to charity and not to the Cuban government. U.S. residents are also allowed to send money to any Cuban resident, not just family members, and food can be sold to nongovernmental groups such as farmers and restaurant owners.[30]

The *Foreign Corrupt Practices Act of 1977*, which makes it illegal to bribe a foreign official in an attempt to solicit new or repeat sales abroad, has had a major impact on international marketing. The act also mandates that adequate accounting controls be installed to monitor internal compliance. Violations can result in a $1 million fine for the firm and a $10,000 fine and five year imprisonment for the individuals involved. This law has been controversial, mainly because it fails to clearly define what constitutes bribery. The 1988 Trade Act amended the law to include more specific statements of prohibited practices.

Finally, legal requirements of host nations affect foreign marketers. International marketers generally recognize the importance of obeying legal requirements since even the slightest violation could set back the future of international trade.

The Coca-Cola Company, one of the world's premier international marketers, often finds its plans for further expansion halted by legal requirements. In 1999, French regulators blocked its attempt to buy Orangina, France's second most popular soft drink. That same year, a product contamination scare led Belgian authorities to require all Coke soft drinks be pulled off retail shelves temporarily. And in Italy, where Coke products account for 46 percent of that nation's soft-drink market, the Atlanta-based marketer was accused of unfair trade practices designed to exclude Pepsi and other competitors from the market.[31]

Many types of legal requirements can affect the actions of foreign marketers. Producers and marketers of global products not only must maintain required minimum quality levels of all the countries in which they operate, but they must also comply with numerous, specific local regulations. For example, when multinational marketers in the Czech Republic were recently forced to ban promotional contests, they immediately revised marketing campaigns to comply with the new regulations. Specifically, the law forbids companies with foreign capital from holding contests that require prior purchases and feature randomly drawn winners. Well-known corporations, including Ford, McDonald's, The Coca Cola Company, Procter & Gamble, Gillette, and Eastman Kodak, were seriously affected by this law. PepsiCo ran the promotion shown in Figure 3.7, offering small prizes to everyone, rather than a few contest winners. As one PepsiCo advertising executive complained, "We can't have dream prizes, and interest and participation is down. Our last promotion only yielded 570 entrants. It's less exciting for the customer to hold these kinds of promotions, as we're forced to do."[32]

Legal requirements of host countries can create unexpected hurdles. Out of the Indian political reforms of the 1970s came volumes of new laws and regulations aimed at protecting India's commercial investments. Rather than conform, hundreds of foreign multinationals fled the country, including The Coca-Cola Company in 1977. PepsiCo, on the other hand, remained in India, swallowing huge amounts of Coke's market share in a relatively competition-free, soft-drink market. Coke returned in 1993 and has been fighting ever since to regain its first-place position. Last year, the Indian government approved the use of artificial sweeteners in carbonated drinks. Two days later, the Pepsi–Coke, one-calorie war began. Within a week, the Indian Health Ministry announced a new regulation: Any fizzy drink—even a diet drink meant to be sugar-free—must contain at least 5 percent sucrose. That meant adding 99 calories to beverages advertised as having only one. The ministry also required companies to print a warning on every can and bottle of diet cola saying, "Not recommended for children." The two soft-drink giants not only had each other to contend with but the Indian government as well. To top it all off, introducing a diet soda in a country that has long fought overpopulation and hunger meant convincing Indian consumers that not everything labeled *diet* is meant for a sick person.[33]

Pepsi: Obeying Foreign Advertising Restrictions

Trade Barriers

Assorted trade barriers also affect global marketing. These barriers fall into two major categories: **tariffs**—taxes levied on imported products—and *administrative*, or *nontariff barriers*. Some tariffs impose set taxes per pound, gallon, or unit; others are calculated according to the value of the imported item. Administrative barriers are more subtle than tariffs and take a variety of forms such as customs barriers, quotas on imports, unnecessarily restrictive standards for imports, and export subsidies. Because the GATT and WTO agreements (discussed later in the chapter) eliminated tariffs on many products, countries frequently use nontariff barriers to boost exports and control the flows of imported products.

Tariffs. The United States has long been the champion of free trade throughout the world, but recently with shrinking economies of industrialized foreign nations and a growing number of developing countries that are struggling to stabilize their economies, U.S. legislators have been pressured to protect domestic industries from troubles abroad. But protecting business at home typically penalizes consumers since prices typically rise under protectionist regulations. For example, the United States recently slapped a 30 percent import tax on frozen orange juice concentrate; duties on imported glassware, porcelain, and china as high as 38 percent; rubber boots and shoes, 20 percent; luggage, 16 percent; and canned tuna, 12.5 percent. While this may or may not create a competitive environment for domestic producers, it seldom reduces product prices for the consumer.

Tariffs can be classified as either revenue or protective tariffs. Revenue tariffs are designed to raise funds for the importing government. Most early U.S. government revenue came from this source. *Protective tariffs*, which are usually higher than revenue tariffs, are designed to raise the retail price of an imported product to match or exceed that of a similar domestic product. Some countries use tariffs in a selective manner to discourage certain consumption practices and thereby reduce access to their local markets. For example, the United States has tariffs on luxury items like Rolex watches and Russian caviar.

In the past, it was believed that a country should protect its infant industries by using tariffs to keep out foreign-made products. Some foreign goods did

MARKETING **DICTIONARY**

tariff Tax levied against imported goods.

Playing the Name Game—and Losing

BACKGROUND Every year, rapidly growing populations and rising incomes among households around the world entice hundreds of marketers to become international marketers. All too often, they simply translate their product labels, advertising, and sales displays to the local language, assuming that the attributes that led to domestic success will also work in international markets.

THE MARKETING PROBLEM The differences in language in international markets frequently add up to drastically different meanings for marketing messages.

THE OUTCOME Entire books have been written about international marketing miscommunications. Here are just a few examples of messages that met failure when translated into foreign languages:

WHAT THE MESSAGE SAID	HOW THE MESSAGE WAS INTERPRETED
Body by Fisher	Corpse by Fisher (Flemish)
Schweppes tonic water	Schweppes toilet water (Italian)
Missair Airlines (Egyptian)	Misery Airlines (French)
Come Alive with Pepsi	Come Alive out of the Grave (German)
Rendezvous lounges	Rooms for lovemaking (Portuguese)

continued on next page

enter, but high tariffs made domestic products competitive in price. Recently, it has been argued that tariffs should be raised to protect employment and profits in domestic U.S. industries. For example, the U.S. steel industry has been unsuccessful in lobbying the government to protect domestic steel producers by imposing tariffs on the rising number of imports of low-quality steel into the United States. Weak currencies in Japan, Brazil, South Korea, and Russia have stifled demand for steel in these countries, while the strong dollar in the United States has increased demand for construction materials of all kinds, especially steel. When foreign steel started arriving in the U.S. market at $50 a ton less than domestic steel, the U.S. steel industry cried for protection. But U.S. policy makers have backed away—at least temporarily—as they consider the impact of such tariffs on the current global recession.[34]

In 1988, the United States passed the Omnibus Trade and Competitiveness Act to remedy what it perceived as unfair international trade conditions. Under the so-called *Super 301* provisions of the law, the United States can now single out countries that unfairly impede trade with U.S. domestic businesses. If these countries do not open their markets within 18 months, the law requires retaliation in the form of U.S. tariffs or quotas on the offenders' imports into this country.

Some nations limit foreign ownership in the business sectors. In the United States, for example, non-U.S. citizens cannot own more than 25 percent of the voting stock in a U.S.-based airline; they cannot hold controlling interest in a U.S. television station or network; nor can they fish for mackerel—the only fish in surplus in U.S. waters.[35]

Tariffs also can be used to gain bargaining clout with other countries, but they risk adversely affecting the fortunes of domestic companies. For example, Australia and New Zealand, two of the world's largest producers of lamb exports (primarily wool), were outraged when the U.S. International Trade Commission (ITC) placed tariffs up to 40 percent on lamb imports to protect U.S. sheep producers. The ITC ruled that lamb imports were "a substantial cause of threat of serious injury" to the domestic sheep industry. The decision did not make prices any more competitive; instead, it merely reduced the amount of lamb products the United States imports. Even more serious is that the decision undercut the Clinton administration's efforts to get other countries to open their markets. Although some import relief had been expected, it was never expected to be so severely protectionist.[36]

In recent years, scores of trading nations have agreed to abolish tariffs on 500 high technology products such as computers, software, calculators, fax machines, and related goods. Elimination of such tariffs means as much as $100 million in annual savings to communication giants like IBM.

Administrative Barriers. In addition to direct taxes on imported products, governments may erect a number of other barriers ranging from special permits and detailed inspection requirements to quotas on foreign-made items to stem the flow of imported goods—or halt them altogether. Consider the case of bananas, a fruit for which European shoppers pay about twice the prices paid by their North American cousins. The reason for these high prices: Through a series of import license controls, Europe allows fewer bananas to be imported than people want to buy. Even worse, the European countries set up a system of quotas designed to support banana growing in former colonies in Africa and Asia. Imports from Latin American countries were highly restricted—to the detriment of the world's three largest banana companies, Chiquita, Dole, and Del Monte. All three firms are based in the United States and they all want a share of the lucrative European market. After years of trade tensions and threats of retaliatory tariffs against French cheeses, cashmere sweaters, and other European imports, the World Trade Organization outlawed these restrictions as violations of global trade laws.[37]

Other forms of trade restrictions include import quotas and embargoes. **Import quotas** limit the number of units of products in certain categories that can cross a country's border. The quota acts to protect domestic industry and employment and to preserve foreign exchange. For example, the United States puts limits on imports of sugar, peanuts, and dairy products. As another example, once foreign tobacco producers earn their quotas, additional shipments face 350 percent tariffs.[38]

The ultimate quota is the **embargo**—a complete ban on the import of a product. Since 1960, the United States has maintained an embargo against Cuba in protest of Fidel Castro's dictatorship and policies such as expropriation of property and disregard for human rights. Not only do the sanctions prohibit Cuban exports (cigars and sugar are the island's best-known products) to enter the country, but also apply to companies that profit from property that Cuba's communist government expropriated from Americans following the Cuban revolution.[39] However, many leading U.S. executives oppose the embargo. They are losing the opportunity to develop the Cuban market while foreign rivals establish production and marketing facilities there.

Other administrative barriers include subsidies. Airbus, the French, German, British, and Spanish aircraft consortium, often comes under attack from U.S. trade officials because it is so heavily subsidized. The Europeans, on the other hand, argue that Boeing and Lockheed Martin benefit from research done by NASA, the Pentagon, and other U.S. agencies. And still another way to block international trade is to simply create so many regulatory barriers that it is almost impossible to reach target markets. The European Union, for example, enforces more than 2,700 different sets of trade requirements by states, counties, cities, and insurance providers. Indian law contains even more complex requirements.

Foreign trade can also be regulated by exchange control through a central bank or government agency. **Exchange control** means that firms that gain foreign exchange by exporting must sell foreign currencies to the central bank or other foreign agency and importers must buy foreign currencies from the same organization. The exchange control authority can then allocate, expand, or restrict foreign exchange according to existing national policy.

Dumping

The practice of selling a product in a foreign market at a price lower than what it commands in the producer's domestic market is called **dumping.** Critics of free trade often argue that foreign governments give substantial support to their own exporting companies. Government support may permit these firms to extend their export markets by offering lower prices abroad. In retaliation for this kind of interference with free trade, the United States adds import tariffs to products that foreign firms dump on U.S. markets to bring their prices in line with those of domestically produced products. That is the current situation in the U.S. steel industry. However, businesses often complain that charges of dumping must undergo a lengthy investigative and bureaucratic procedure before the government assesses import duties.

Some 9,000 U.S. apple growers in 30 states recently asked the U.S. Commerce Department to impose a penalty tariff of up to 90 percent on apple juice concentrate from China. They hoped to stop the unfair Chinese practice of selling concentrate in the U.S. market at prices below the cost of production or the home market price. Not only did the number of shipments of concentrate rise from 1 percent to 18 percent of the total U.S. market, the price of the imported concentrate fell more than half. U.S. marketers were forced to cut their prices by 50 percent to meet competition. With the U.S. economy growing and so many foreign countries in recessionary periods, many domestic industries will continue to see increased foreign competition and a decline in domestic market share.[40]

U.S. firms that claim dumping threatens to hurt their business can file a complaint with the U.S. International Trade Commission (ITC). Between 1990 and 1995, nearly 300 cases were filed. If the ITC agrees, it can assess fines that, in theory, equalize the price for the goods in question. The ITC rejected about half of the claims filed.

MARKETING STRATEGY FAILURE

LESSONS LEARNED Marketers seeking international success should never assume that a domestic marketing program is guaranteed success abroad. Cultural differences can convert such programs from success to failure. Subtle differences in how the same word or phrase is interpreted in different regions can quickly make brand names or promotional slogans the object of ridicule. The marketer's imperative continues to be "Know your market." Translations should be made by trained specialists steeped in the language and culture of the region—people who will detect such communication mistakes before they occur and make needed changes in advance of the product's introduction.

MULTINATIONAL ECONOMIC INTEGRATION

A noticeable trend toward multinational economic integration has developed since the end of World War II. Multinational economic integration can be set up in several ways. The simplest approach is to establish a

SOLVING AN ETHICAL CONTROVERSY

Tobacco: The Smoking Gun of U.S. Exports

The U.S. tobacco industry is a pressure cooker of controversy. Antismoking activists have made great strides in regulating package labeling and advertising in American and Canadian markets. Outside U.S. borders, antismoking groups such as INFACT are also pushing for more restrictions on packaging and advertising in their home countries. All of their efforts, however, have not reduced the number of smokers. Instead, over the past decade, smoking increased among U.S. teens. Globally, teenage smokers are increasing at a rate of almost 5 percent in Europe and 8 percent in Asia. Still, the antismoking movement is building steam in nations around the world. In the United Kingdom, all print and outdoor tobacco advertising was banned in 1999; the following year, the Lithuanian Parliament imposed a similar ban; and the European Union ban on tobacco advertising takes effect in July 2001.

Big tobacco companies have adhered to the barrage of new U.S. laws and regulations. After all, Americans account for only 4 percent of smokers worldwide. Now cigarette marketers reallocate promotional funds from the United States to foreign markets, where industry profits are expected to rise about 10 percent annually for several years to come.

Should U.S. tobacco companies be required to follow U.S. laws when marketing products abroad?

Pro
1. U.S. tobacco companies should voluntarily abide by U.S. laws in foreign operations. If it was not a practical regulation of business, it would not have been made a law.

2. The objective of recent U.S. tobacco laws is to prevent illness and death in smokers, no matter where they live. Tobacco marketers should feel an ethical obligation to warn consumers about the dangers inherent in their product.

Con
1. U.S. companies are obligated to follow the laws of the country in which they operate.
2. The U.S. tobacco industry must be allowed to compete fairly against other tobacco companies throughout the world. They should not be restricted by domestic laws that competitors do not have to follow.

Summary
According to the World Health Organization, tobacco-related illnesses will be the world's leading cause of death by the year 2020, surpassing deaths from AIDS, car accidents, tuberculosis, homicide, and suicide *combined*. Most of those deaths will occur in developing Asian countries, such as China, where 40 percent of the population over the age of 15 (about 350 million people) smoke. In Vietnam, more than 70 percent of men smoke. Currently, there are no international laws to govern the tobacco industry. However, antismoking activists around the world have garnered enough support to pass new regulations on global cigarette advertising.

Sources: "EuroNews: London," *Ad Age International,* July 1999, p. 7; and Susan Headden, "The Marlboro Man Lives!" *U.S. News & World Report,* September 21, 1998, pp. 58–59.

---

free-trade area in which participating nations agree to the free trade of goods among themselves, abolishing all tariffs and trade restrictions. A *customs union* establishes a free-trade area plus a uniform tariff for trade with nonmember nations. A *common market* extends a customs union by seeking to reconcile all government regulations affecting trade.

GATT and the World Trade Organization

Outline the basic functions of WTO, NAFTA, and the European Union.

The **General Agreement on Tariffs and Trade (GATT),** a 117-nation trade accord that has sponsored several rounds of major tariff negotiations, substantially reducing worldwide tariff levels, celebrated its 50th birthday in 1997. In 1994, a seven-year series of GATT conferences, called the *Uruguay Round,* culminated in one of the biggest victories for free trade in decades. The new accord's partial opening of trade helped the U.S. economy grow by $1 trillion and created some 2 million new jobs.

The Uruguay Round cut average tariffs by one-third, or more than $700 billion. Among its major victories are the following:

■ Reduction of farm subsidies, which opened new markets for U.S. exports

■ Increased protection for patents, copyrights, and trademarks

■ Inclusion of services under international trading rules, creating opportunities for U.S. financial, legal, and accounting firms

- Phasing out import quotas on textiles and clothing from developing nations, a move that benefits U.S. retailers and consumers because quotas increase clothing prices by $15 billion

A key outcome of the GATT talks was establishment of the **World Trade Organization (WTO),** a 134-member organization that succeeds GATT. The WTO oversees GATT agreements, mediates disputes, and continues the effort to reduce trade barriers throughout the world. Unlike GATT, WTO decisions are binding.

@ **wto.org**

To date, however, the WTO has made only slow progress toward its major policy initiatives—liberalizing world financial services, telecommunications, and maritime markets. Trade officials have not agreed on the direction for the WTO. Its activities have focused more on complaint resolution than on removing global trade barriers. The United States has been the most active user of WTO dispute courts, filing 49 of the 169 complaints. During one week of 1999, the Clinton administration filed seven cases, alleging unfair trade practices against the European Union, India, South Korea, Canada, and Argentina involving aircraft manufacturing, farm goods, automobiles, beef production, construction, and patent protection. One complaint charges South Korea with restricting the ability of U.S. construction companies to bid on work at the $6 billion Inchon International Airport.[41]

Big differences between developed and developing areas create a major roadblock to WTO progress. These conflicts became apparent at the first WTO meeting in Singapore in the late 1990s. Asian nations want trade barriers lifted on their manufactured goods, but they also want to protect their own telecommunications companies. In addition, they oppose monitoring of corruption and labor practices by outsiders. The United States wants free trade for telecommunications, more controls on corruption, and establishment of international labor standards. Europe wants standard rules on foreign investments and removal of profit repatriation restrictions but is not as concerned with worker rights.

China is the world's largest nation with an economy that has grown 10 percent annually for the last two decades. It is the market of all markets and holds the promise of enormous potential for exporters. But China's exports show less than a 2 percent annual growth as a result of the multitude of barriers and red tape that make it extremely difficult for foreign firms to operate there. Recently, the release of trade rights has allowed new enterprises to engage in importing and exporting. Negotiations are still being held on China's admission to the WTO. Such entrance would bring trade relations more into balance and spur foreign investment in China. However, until China controls the production and export of counterfeit and pirated goods, it is doubtful it will join the ranks of WTO global trading partners. The illegal reproduction of U.S. goods in China costs American firms an estimated $1 billion annually in lost sales and licensing fees.[42]

The NAFTA Accord

A heated controversy continues almost a decade after the passage of the **North American Free-Trade Agreement (NAFTA),** an agreement between the United States, Canada, and Mexico that removes trade restrictions among the three nations over a 14-year period. Proponents claim that NAFTA has been good for the American economy; critics charge that U.S. and Canadian workers have lost their jobs to cheap Mexican labor. The NAFTA accord brings together 390 million people and a combined gross domestic product of $7.9 trillion, making it by far the world's largest free-trade zone. It marked the first step in the creation of a free-trade zone covering the entire Western Hemisphere—850 million people, representing an expected $12 trillion annual market by 2005.

The NAFTA accord was approved despite serious concerns about job losses from the relatively high-wage industries in the United States and Canada as

MARKETING DICTIONARY

General Agreement on Tariffs and Trade (GATT) International trade accord that has helped reduce world tariffs.

World Trade Organization (WTO) A 134-member organization that succeeds GATT to oversee agreements, mediate disputes, and reduce trade barriers; unlike GATT, WTO decisions are binding.

North American Free-Trade Agreement (NAFTA) Accord removing trade barriers among Canada, Mexico, and the United States.

manufacturers relocated their production facilities in lower-wage Mexico. However, NAFTA supporters point out that imports of components and intermediate goods that require further refinements before becoming part of products "Made in the USA" actually hold down the cost of U.S.-made output and support local jobs. And even though imports of such products as autos assembled in Mexico have risen, these vehicles now include a high percentage of components manufactured in the United States.[43]

NAFTA is not the only Western Hemisphere trade bloc. Canada and Chile have a free-trade agreement. The MERCOSUR customs union, comprised of Brazil, Argentina, Paraguay, Uruguay, Chile, and Bolivia, is another group with whom the United States may have to negotiate.

NAFTA, referred to by its supporters as the Win-Win-Win accord, was supposed to bring the three partners closer. In theory, reduced trade barriers should boost market efficiency over time. While the three governments consider it a success, the industries under attack continue to complain. Florida produce growers, for example, recently petitioned the U.S. administration to stop cheaper Mexican vegetable imports.

The European Union

europa.eu.int

The best known example of a multinational economic community is the *European Union (EU)*, a customs union that is moving in the direction of an economic union. Involving the 15 countries shown in Figure 3.8, 350 million people, and a combined gross domestic product of $5 trillion, the EU forms a huge common market. In addition to the 15-member nations from Western Europe, several former Soviet republics and other Eastern European countries have applied for admission to the EU.

The goal of the EU is to eventually remove all barriers to free trade among its members, making it as simple and painless to ship products between England and Spain as it is between New Jersey and Pennsylvania. Also involved is the standardization of regulations and requirements that businesses must meet. Instead of having to comply with 15 sets of standards and 15 different currencies, companies will have to deal with just one. This should lower the costs of doing business in Europe by allowing firms to take advantage of economies of scale.

In some ways, the EU is making definite progress toward its economic goals. We have already seen that it is drafting standardized eco-labels to certify that products are manufactured according to certain environmental standards, as well as creating guidelines governing marketers' uses of customer information. Marketers can also protect trademarks throughout the entire EU with a single application and registration process through the Community Trademark (CTM), which simplifies doing business and eliminates having to register with each member country. It is, however, sometimes difficult to obtain approval for trademark protection.

Yet marketers still face challenges when selling their products in the EU. Customs taxes differ, the euro has not been adopted as the official currency by all EU members, and there is no uniform postal system. Mail between countries is extremely slow. In fact, the Federation of European Direct Marketing is pushing for modernization and integration of postal systems. Using one toll-free number for several countries will not work, either, because each country has its own telephone system for codes and numbers.

GOING GLOBAL

4

Compare the alternative strategies for entering international markets.

As we move further into the 21st century, globalization will affect almost every industry and every individual throughout the world. Traditional marketers who decide to take their firms global may do so because they already have strong domestic market shares and/or their target market is too saturated to offer any substantial growth. Sometimes, by evaluating key indicators of the marketing environment, marketers can move toward globalization at an optimal time. A critical task facing international marketers is developing strategies for successfully entering new

FIGURE 3.8   The Fifteen Nations of the European Union

foreign markets.[44] Most large firms already participate in global commerce, and many small businesses recognize the need to investigate whether to market their products overseas. It is not an easy step to take, requiring careful evaluation and preparation.

First Steps in Deciding to Market Globally

The first step toward successful global marketing is to secure top management's support. Without the enthusiasm and support of senior executives, export efforts are likely to fail. The advocate for going global must explain and promote the potential of foreign markets and facilitate the global marketing process.

The next important step is to research the export process and potential markets. Burt Cabanas, CEO of Texas-based Benchmark Hospitality, which develops and manages conference centers, hotels, and resorts, explains the consequences of failing to research a market when going global: "We went into Thailand initially without doing research and that was a mistake. We made many assumptions about how we would do marketing in ways that were a few degrees off

benchmark-hospitality.com

Taiwan. Lighting the Way to Business in Asia.

The opportunities for success in Asia expand everyday. Yet the road to profit remains obscure, especially when you're just starting out. The *Taipei World Trade Center* is your start-up solution, a lantern that lights the way to a vast network of manufacturers spread from Japan to Java. And with world-class trade shows, and more than 300,000 product samples at your fingertips,

CONNECTING THE WORLD

CONNECTING WITH ASIA

CONNECTING THROUGH TAIWAN

you'll never be left in the dark. So come to Taiwan and see the *Taipei World Trade Center*. We're illuminating Asian business.

International marketers benefit from trade shows such as those held at the Taiwan World Trade Center. Thousands of companies display more than 300,000 product samples that represent the vast network of manufacturers in the Pacific region, from Japan to Java.

target. We were told by U.S. companies that if we were going to do business in Thailand, we should be in Bangkok, and we spent a tremendous amount of time getting a presence there. We then found out we could have been just as successful outside the city. Taking someone else's word for it rather than doing the research set us back a year and a half."[45] Benchmark Hospitality has since expanded to Japan and the Philippines and is now researching six additional markets in foreign countries.

The U.S. Department of Commerce sponsors a toll-free hot line (800-872-8723) that describes the various federal export programs. Trade counselors at 68 district offices offer export advice, computerized market data, and names of contacts in over 60 countries. Some services are free, while others are available at a reasonable cost. These services include the following:

■ *National Trade Data Bank.* Large database, updated monthly, with market reports on foreign demand for specific products. Available at Commerce Department district offices or by subscription.

■ *Catalog and Video Shows.* Service that displays companies' catalogs or demonstration videos at catalog shows held at U.S. consulates and embassies. Shows are oriented toward particular industries, such as medical supplies or marine equipment.

■ *Trade Shows.* Commerce Department–sponsored trade shows in other countries; they are effective ways of getting market information and meeting customers.

Another good information source in helping companies analyze foreign markets is TradePoint USA, a Columbus, Ohio, not-for-profit service with print and online resources. Its Internet service, I-Trade, provides country data, international news, the National Trade Data Bank, and trade and country reports from several sources. Still other sources include the following:

■ *The Green Book*, published by the American Management Association, lists all market research firms and those with international capabilities.

■ Esomar, the European Society of Opinion and Market Research, has a worldwide listing by company.

■ The U.S. State Department's Web site offers commercial guides, compiled by local embassies, to almost every country in the world.

Strategies for Entering International Markets

Once marketers have completed their research, they may choose from among three basic strategies for entering international markets: importing and exporting; contractual agreements like franchising, licensing, and subcontracting; and international direct investment. As Figure 3.9 shows, the level of risk and the firm's degree of control over international marketing increase with greater involvement. Firms often use more than one of these entry strategies. L. L. Bean subcontracts with a Japanese company to handle its product returns, and it also maintains a direct investment in several Japanese retail outlets in partnership with Matsushita.

A firm that brings in goods produced abroad to sell domestically or to be used as components in its products is an *importer*. In making import decisions, the marketer must assess local demand for the product, taking into consideration such factors as the following:

■ ability of the supplier to maintain agreed-to quality levels

■ capability of filling orders that might vary considerably from one order to the next

■ response time in filling orders

■ total costs—including import fees, packaging, and transportation—in comparison with costs of domestic suppliers.

FIGURE 3.9   Levels of Involvement in International Marketing

Degree of Risk

Low · · · · · · · · · · · · · · · Moderate · · · · · · · · · · · · · · · High

Exporting and Importing	Contractual Agreements Franchising Foreign Licensing Subcontracting	International Direct Investment Acquisitions Joint Ventures Overseas Divisions

Low · · · · · · · · · · · · · · · Moderate · · · · · · · · · · · · · · · High

Degree of Control

Exporting, another basic form of international marketing, involves a continuous effort in marketing a firm's merchandise to customers abroad. Many firms export their products as the first step in reaching foreign markets. Success in exporting often encourages them to try other entry strategies.

First-time exporters can reach foreign customers through one or more of three alternatives: export-trading companies, export-management companies, or offset agreements. An *export-trading company (ETC)* buys products from domestic producers and resells them abroad. While manufacturers lose control over marketing and distribution to the ETC, it helps them export through a relatively simple and inexpensive channel, in the process providing feedback about the overseas market potential of their products.

The second option, an *export-management company (EMC)*, provides the first-time exporter with expertise in locating foreign buyers, handling necessary paperwork, and ensuring that its goods meet local labeling and testing laws. However, the manufacturer retains more control over the export process when it deals with an EMC than if it were to sell the goods outright to an export-trading company. Smaller firms can get assistance with administrative needs such as financing and preparation of proposals and contracts from large EMC contractors.

The final option, entering a foreign market under an *offset agreement*, teams a small firm with a major international company. The smaller firm essentially serves as a subcontractor on a large foreign project. This entry strategy provides new exporters with international experience, supported by the assistance of the primary contractor in such areas as international transaction documentation and financing.

Contractual Agreements

As a firm gains sophistication in international marketing, it may enter contractual agreements that provide several flexible alternatives to exporting. Both large and small firms can benefit from these methods. Franchising and foreign licensing, for example, are good ways to take services abroad. Subcontracting may set up either production facilities or services. Sponsorships are another form of international contractual marketing agreements. For example, in the 1999 Tour de France, the United States Postal Service (USPS) was the primary sponsor of the 4-year-old American team, headed by cancer survivor Lance Armstrong. The Tour de France is the most prestigious and most challenging bicycle event in the world, covering severe terrain through France and the Swiss Alps. The USPS slogan that, in spite of rain, sleet, or snow, the mail must go through, is enhanced by an association with Armstrong and his incredible two-year recovery to become the winner of the Tour de France and the best comeback story of the decade. Nike and Credit Lyonnais were also among sponsors of the U.S. team, and other organizations incorporated Armstrong's image and the ideals he symbolizes in their promotional campaigns.[46]

@ **uspsprocycling.com**

Franchising. A **franchise** is a contractual arrangement where a wholesaler or retailer (the franchisee) agrees to meet

MARKETING   DICTIONARY

franchise Contractual arrangement where a wholesaler or retailer (the franchisee) agrees to make some payment and to meet the operating requirements of a manufacturer or other franchiser in exchange for the right to use the firm's name and to market its goods or services.

FIGURE 3.10 **Franchising: A Global Strategy for Ruth's Chris Steak House**

"IT'S THE SIZZLE HEARD 'ROUND THE WORLD."

There's no other flavor and aroma like a sizzling Ruth's Chris steak. You'll taste the difference the first time you cut into that thick Midwestern beef. It's USDA Prime, the top two percent of all American beef. We broil it to order in special ovens I personally designed, and we always serve it sizzling. Fans around the world say that's what makes my steak a cut above. I say it's what makes my restaurants sizzle!

RUTH'S CHRIS STEAK HOUSE

FOR WORLDWIDE LOCATIONS CALL 1-800-544-0808
WWW.RUTHSCHRIS.COM

@ **ruthschris.com**

the operating requirements of a manufacturer or other franchiser. The franchisee receives the right to sell the products and use the franchiser's name, as well as a variety of marketing, management, and other services. As mentioned earlier, fast-food companies have been active franchisers around the world.

One advantage of franchising is risk reduction by offering a proven concept. Standardized operations typically reduce costs, increase operating efficiencies, and provide greater international recognizability. However, the success of an international franchise depends on its willingness to balance standard practices with local customer preferences. McDonald's, Pizza Hut, and Domino's are all expanding into India with special menus that feature lamb, chicken, and vegetarian items, in deference to Hindu and Muslim customers who do not eat beef and pork.

Ruth's Chris Steak House is internationally famous for two things: first, its top quality USDA prime beef, and second, its most unusual name. The restaurant, founded in 1965 by Ruth Fertel, granted its first franchise in 1977. Today, 29 restaurants are company-owned, and another 38 are franchised in locations from Puerto Rico to Canada and Hong Kong to Taiwan. Each restaurant design is an individual expression in keeping with local tastes and preferences, as are the menu selections. Variations in side dishes not only meet local preferences but also take advantage of fresh ingredients. Serving Ruth's Chris steaks (about 12,000 daily) cooks up an annual sales figure of over $250 million. As Figure 3.10 explains, serving only the top two percent of all American beef produced makes Ruth's Chris "the sizzle heard 'round the world."

Foreign Licensing. A second method of going global through the use of contractual agreements is **foreign licensing.** Such an agreement grants foreign marketers the right to distribute a firm's merchandise or use its trademark, patent, or process in a specified geographic area. These arrangements usually set certain time limits, after which agreements are revised or renewed.

Licensing offers several advantages over exporting, including access to local partners' marketing information and distribution channels and protection from various legal barriers. Because licensing does not require capital outlays, many firms, both small and large, regard it as an attractive entry strategy. Like franchising, licensing allows a firm to quickly enter a foreign market with a known product or concept. The arrangement also may provide entry into a market that government restrictions close to imports or international direct investment.

Subcontracting. A third strategy for going global through contractual agreements is *subcontracting*, the production of goods or services to local companies. Using local subcontractors can prevent mistakes involving local culture and regulations. Manufacturers might subcontract with a local company to produce their goods or use a foreign distributor to handle their products abroad or provide customer service. Manufacturing within the country can avoid import duties and may be a lower-cost alternative that makes it possible for the product to compete with local offerings. Sears subcontracts with local manufacturers in Mexico and Spain to produce many of the products—especially clothing—sold in its department stores.

In the services sector, Hilton Hotels Corp. uses a subcontracting approach to its international chain of over 450 hotels and resorts in over 50 countries. One of the newest locations opened at the Lagos Airport in Nigeria. With over 300 rooms, several conference and banquet facilities, and an adjoining casino/cabaret, the hotel is expected to attract both international business travelers and local residents. While Hilton provides management expertise, AIC, a leading African engineering and project management company, supplies the structural facilities.[47]

International Direct Investment

Another strategy for entering global markets is international direct investment in foreign firms, production, and marketing facilities. By the beginning of the 21st century, U.S. direct investment abroad was nearly $2.2 trillion, with a high number of acquisitions in the United Kingdom, the Netherlands, and Canada. On the other hand, foreign direct investment in the United States had grown to over $2.1 trillion. Three-fourths of all foreign investment in the United States came from Europe and Canada.[48]

Although high levels of involvement and high-risk potential are characteristics of investments in foreign countries, firms choosing this method often have a competitive advantage. Direct investment can take several forms. For example, an American company can acquire an existing firm in a country where it wants to do business, or it can set up an independent division outside U.S. borders with responsibility for production and marketing in a country or geographic region.

Foreign sales offices, overseas marketing subsidiaries, and foreign offices of U.S. firms all involve direct investment. For example, Michigan-based Amway Corp. employs 3 million independent distributors in over 49 countries and in 21 different languages around the globe. The 40-year-old company has gained a stronghold throughout the world by integrating regional operations, such as computer systems, warehousing and shipping, and marketing activities. Amway Scandinavia, its most recent expansion that includes Finland, Norway, Sweden, and Denmark, enhances the firm's European presence and represents the ninth largest economy in the world.

amway.com

Companies may also engage in international marketing by forming **joint ventures,** in which they share the risks, costs, and management of the foreign operation with one or more partners. These partnerships join the investing companies with nationals of the host countries. While some companies choose to open their own facilities overseas, others share with their partners. Service companies often find that joint ventures provide the most efficient way to penetrate a market. As Figure 3.11 shows, Delta Air Lines' marketers are sharpening their focus on serving the highly profitable transatlantic routes. To expand its route, Delta recently joined an alliance that added the 102 European cities served by Air France to its existing transportation network. The result is the creation of an extensive new network that rivals the coverage of competing airlines. The formation of this transatlantic team combines hubs in Atlanta—the world's busiest airport—and Paris' Charles de Gaulle—Europe's largest hub. The two carriers also share aviation-industry technology and electronic-commerce systems, quality standards, frequent-flyer programs, and reciprocal-airport lounge access. Air France marketers expect the alliance to generate an additional $150 million in net profits the first year.[49]

Although joint ventures offer many advantages, foreign investors have encountered problems in several areas throughout the world, especially in developing economies. Lower trade barriers, new technologies, lower transport costs, and vastly improved access to information means that many more partnerships will be involved in international trade.

From Multinational Corporation to Global Marketer

A **multinational corporation** is a firm with significant operations and marketing activities outside its home country. Examples of multinationals include General Electric, Siemens, and Mitsubishi in the heavy electrical equipment; and Timex, Seiko, and Citizen in watches. Table 3.1 lists the ten largest U.S. multinationals and shows not only the percentage of revenues derived from foreign operations but also the percentage of net profits and assets from these operations. Note that six of the ten receive more than half of their net profits from overseas sales.

MARKETING DICTIONARY

foreign licensing Agreement that grants foreign marketers the right to distribute a firm's merchandise or to use its trademark, patent, or process in a specified geographic area.

joint venture Agreement in which a firm shares the risks, costs, and management of a foreign operation with one or more partners who are usually citizens of the host country.

multinational corporation Firm with significant operations and marketing activities outside its home country.

| FIGURE 3.11 | Conquering the European Air Travel Market through Joint Ventures |

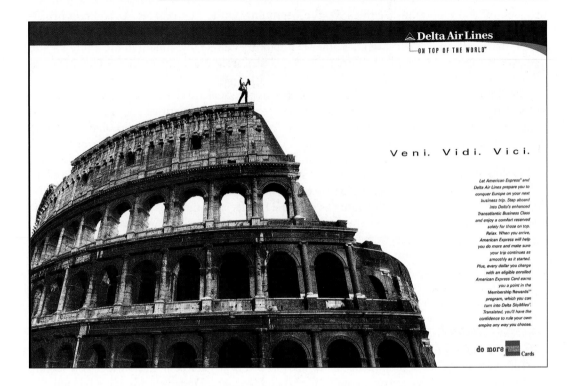

Since they first became a force in international business in the 1960s, multinationals have evolved in some important ways. First, these companies are no longer exclusively U.S. based. Today it is as likely for a multinational to be based in Japan, Germany, or Great Britain as in the United States. Second, multinationals no longer think of their foreign operations as mere outsourcing appendages that carry out the design, production, and engineering ideas conceived at home. Instead, they encourage constant exchanges of ideas, capital, and technologies among all the multinational operations.

Multinationals often employ huge foreign workforces relative to their American staffs. Over half of Ford and IBM workers are located outside the United States, for instance. These workforces are no longer seen merely as sources of cheap labor. On the contrary, many multinationals center technically complex activities in locations throughout the world. Texas Instruments, for example, does much of its research, development, design, and manufacturing in East Asia. In fact, it is increasingly common for U.S. multinationals to bring product innovations back to the United States from their foreign facilities.

Multinationals have become global corporations that reflect the interdependence of world economies, the growth of international competition, and the globalization of world markets. An increasing number of acquisitions includes U.S. multinationals as targets for takeover. In one 12-month period, the following occurred:

- Bankers Trust, with over $5 billion in foreign revenues, was acquired by Germany's Deutsche Bank.

- Amoco reported over $8 billion in overseas revenues when it became part of British Petroleum.

- Chrysler, with over $9 billion in revenues from abroad, was bought by Germany's Daimler-Benz.

TABLE 3.1	Ten Largest U.S.-Based Multinationals		
	FOREIGN REVENUE (PERCENTAGE OF TOTAL)	FOREIGN NET PROFITS (PERCENTAGE OF TOTAL)	FOREIGN ASSETS (PERCENTAGE OF TOTAL)
Exxon	80%	65%	62%
IBM	57	69	47
Ford Motor	30	14	42
General Motors	31	68	41
Texaco	79	45	58
General Electric	31	24	36
Mobil	59	69	65
Citigroup	34	58	46
Hewlett-Packard	54	77	59
Philip Morris	34	44	29

Source: Data reported in "The 100 Largest U.S. Multinationals," *Forbes,* July 26, 1999, p. 202. Mobil, Ford Motor, and Citigroup foreign net profit data is from the most recent company releases.

Mergers have also been a major part of multinational growth in the last decade. Two U.S. giants, Travelers Group and Citicorp, joined forces in 1999, creating the world's largest financial services company, Citigroup, with more than $26 billion in revenues from outside the United States.

Several computer and communications companies are rapidly moving up the multinational list. Compaq Computer, Lucent Technologies, and Electronic Data Systems all posted non-U.S. revenue gains of at least 24 percent in 1999. A full three-fourths of Hewlett-Packard profits come from overseas.

DEVELOPING AN INTERNATIONAL MARKETING STRATEGY

Like domestic firms, international marketers must follow the steps in the marketing planning process (described in Chapter 6). They should assess organizational strengths and weaknesses, study environmental factors, set marketing objectives, select target markets, and develop marketing mixes that will satisfy their chosen targets.

In developing a marketing mix, an international competitor's marketers may choose between two alternative approaches: a global marketing strategy or a multi-domestic marketing strategy. A **global marketing strategy** defines a standard marketing mix and implements it with minimal modifications in all foreign markets. This approach brings the advantage of economies of scale to production and marketing activities. Energizer battery marketers chose the image of a rocket ship blasting off to reach its target markets in Latin America. With the campaign running in many different countries, marketers were able to convey a universally recognized message of power. The campaign was evidently a success—consumers took the point-of-sale posters home as souvenirs.

Procter & Gamble (P&G) marketers follow a global marketing strategy for Pringles potato chips, their leading export brand. P&G sells one product with a consistent formulation in every country. Unlike Frito-Lay's Cheetos

5
Differentiate between a global marketing strategy and a multi-domestic marketing strategy.

6
Describe the alternative marketing mix strategies used in international marketing.

MARKETING   DICTIONARY

global marketing strategy Standardized marketing mix with minimal modifications that a firm uses in all of its domestic and foreign markets.

The universal image of long-lasting power in an Energizer battery is communicated in Latin America with this poster, part of Energizer's global marketing strategy.

snacks, which come in flavors geared to local tastes, P&G meets 80 percent of worldwide demand with only six flavors of Pringles. The brand relies on one package design throughout the world. This standardized approach saves money since it allows large-scale production runs and reinforces the brand's image. Also, similar advertising around the world builds brand awareness by featuring the slogan, "Once you pop, you can't stop." P&G intends all of these tactics to build strong global brand equity for Pringles.

A global marketing perspective can effectively market some goods and services to segments in many nations that share cultures and languages. This approach works especially well for products with strong, universal appeal, such as Pepsi and Coca-Cola, luxury items like Louis Vuitton luggage, business air travel, and many fast-food franchises. Global advertising outlets, such as international editions of popular consumer and business magazines, international transmissions of such TV programs as CNN, MTV, and the CNBC financial network, help marketers deliver a single message to millions of global viewers. International satellite television channels such as StarTV reach 260 million Asian viewers through a host of sports, news, movie, music, and entertainment channels programmed in eight languages.

A global marketing strategy can be highly effective for luxury products that target upscale consumers everywhere. DeBeers diamond marketers, for instance, typically use advertising with little or no copy—just a picture of a beautiful diamond with the name DeBeers discreetly displayed at the bottom. Seagram uses a global billboard advertising campaign to market its Chivas Regal scotch.

A major benefit of a global marketing strategy is its low cost to implement. Most firms, however, find it necessary to practice market segmentation outside their home markets and tailor their marketing mixes to fit the unique needs of customers in specific countries. This **multi-domestic marketing strategy** assumes that differences between market characteristics and competitive situations in certain nations require firms to customize their marketing decisions to effectively reach individual marketplaces. (This strategy is sometimes mistakenly called *multinational* marketing. In fact, a multinational corporation may combine both strategies in its international marketing plans.)

Many marketing experts feel that most products demand multi-domestic marketing strategies to give them realistic global marketing appeals. They cite differences among societies that prevent successful widespread globalization of marketing strategies. Marketers should base this decision on their own products and the countries they want to serve. Specific situations may allow them to standardize some parts of the marketing process while they must customize others. For example, they may market standard products, but promotions or packages may change.

Companies practice multi-domestic marketing for a variety of reasons—both bad and good. Many carry over regional strategies from old, decentralized international marketing organizations. Clearly, continuity with the past is not the best standard for marketing decisions. Because a multi-domestic strategy raises costs as compared with a global strategy, marketers should vary their strategies between markets only when the incremental revenues that the changes generate exceed their incremental expenses. This principle is particularly important for marketers of consumer nondurable goods. A company's strategy choices can determine its success in international markets, as the following sections will illustrate.

International Product and Promotional Strategies

International marketers can choose from among five strategies for selecting the most appropriate product and promotion strategy for a specific foreign market—straight extension, promotion adaptation, product adaptation, dual adaptation, and product invention. As Figure 3.12 indicates,

FIGURE 3.12   Alternative International Product and Promotional Strategies

Product Strategy		
Same Product	**Product Adaptation**	**New Product**

(1)
Straight Extension
Wrigley's gum
Coca-Cola
Eastman Kodak
  cameras and film
	(3)
	Product Adaptation
	Campbell's soup
	Exxon gasoline
		(5)
		Product Invention
		Nonelectric sewing
		  machines
		Manually operated
		  washing machines

(2) **Promotion Adaptation** Bicycles/motorcycles Outboard motors	**(4)** **Dual Adaptation** Coffee Some clothing	

(Promotion Strategy: Same Promotion — rows 1 and 3; Different Promotion — rows 2 and 4)

the strategies center on whether to extend a domestic product and promotional strategy into international markets or adapt one or both to meet the target market's unique requirements.

A firm typically follows a one-product, one-message **straight extension** strategy as part of a global marketing strategy, like Pepsi Cola's. This strategy permits economies of scale in production and marketing. Also, successful implementation creates universal recognition of a product for consumers from country to country.

Other strategies call for **product adaptation, promotion adaptation,** or both. While bicycles, motorcycles, and outboard motors primarily form part of the market for recreational vehicles in the United States, they may represent important basic transportation modes in other nations. Consequently, producers of these products may adapt their promotional messages even if they sell the product without changes.

Coca-Cola's Canadian marketing efforts are similar to those used in the United States, with only minor promotional adaptations to accommodate language differences. As Figure 3.13 illustrates, Coca-Cola marketers targeting French-speaking consumers in Quebec created bus-stop posters with an international message, "It tastes real. As real as my thirst for freedom."

In contrast, marketers for Esso Latin America avoided typical petroleum advertising messages of performance and technology in their latest promotional campaign for that region. The new ads focus on customer lifestyles and emotions, showing a baby's first steps and old friends meeting by chance at a gas pump.[50] Sometimes, international marketers must change both the product and the promotional message in a **dual adaptation** strategy to meet the unique needs of specific international markets.

As discussed earlier in the chapter, cultural forces affect promotional

MARKETING   DICTIONARY

multi-domestic marketing strategy Application of market segmentation to foreign markets by tailoring the firm's marketing mix to match specific target markets in each nation.

straight extension International product and promotional strategy whereby the same product marketed in the home market is introduced in the foreign market using the same promotional strategy.

product adaptation International product and promotional strategy wherein product modifications are made for the foreign market, but the same promotional strategy is used.

promotion adaptation International product and promotional strategy in which the same product is introduced in a foreign market with a unique promotional strategy for the new market.

dual adaptation International product and promotional strategy in which modifications of both product and promotional strategies are employed in the foreign market.

FIGURE 3.13

Promotion Adaptation Strategy in International Marketing

strategies. For example, Kia Motors attracted worldwide criticism for planning a TV commercial in which a Princess Diana look-alike survives a car chase with paparazzi. In response, Kia marketers changed actresses for the ad before airing it in South Korea.[51]

The final strategy alternative is **product invention.** In this case, the firm may decide to develop an entirely different product to take advantage of unique foreign market opportunities. For example, to match user needs in developing nations, an appliance manufacturer might introduce a hand-powered washing machine even though such products became obsolete in industrialized countries many years ago.

International Distribution Strategy

Distribution is a vital aspect of overseas marketing. Marketers must set up proper channels and anticipate extensive physical distribution problems. Foreign markets may offer poor transportation systems and warehousing facilities or none at all. International marketers must adapt promptly and efficiently to these situations in order to profit from overseas sales.

A distribution decision involves two steps. First, the firm must decide on a method of entering the foreign market. Second, it must determine how to distribute the product within the foreign market through that entry channel.

Distribution decisions balance many factors, including the nature of the firm's products, consumer tastes and buying habits, market competition, and transportation options. Even though music may be considered a universal language, U.S.-based global Internet music company Sonic-Net believes that the MTV one-world-sound approach turns off as many viewers as it serves. After all, young people do not share the same lifestyles and cultures. SonicNet's strategy involves working with foreign partners who supply rock, pop, rap, and other music video clips, live concerts, and breaking news to local cyberspace surfers. For example, it turned to telecommunications provider Swisscom to create German, French, and Italian editions of its Web-based music entertainment programming. By developing local language editions that reflect that area's taste in music, SonicNet is growing a local audience all around the world for advertisers.[52]

Pricing Strategy

Pricing can critically affect the success of an overall marketing strategy for foreign markets. Considerable competitive, economic, political, and legal constraints often limit pricing decisions. Global marketers can succeed only if they thoroughly understand these requirements.

Companies must adapt their pricing strategies to local markets and change them when conditions change. Until recently, foreign shipments carried premium prices without assurance that the package would be delivered on time in good condition—or even delivered at all. After the air-freight and overnight-delivery services boomed in the 1980s, delivery became more reliable but costs were exorbitant to many areas. To compete in this crowded market without losing market share, the United States Postal Service (USPS) began advertising International Express Mail services to over 175 countries at set delivery rates. Global Priority Mail, for example, provides prompt delivery to over 30 key business countries for as little as $3.75. USPS marketers promoted the new international services in print ads such as the one shown in Figure 3.14.

An important development in pricing strategy for international marketing has been the emergence of commodity marketing organizations that seek to control prices through collective action. The Organization of Petroleum Exporting Countries (OPEC) is the best example of this kind of collective export organization, but many others exist.

Countertrade

In a growing number of nations, the only way a marketer can gain access to foreign markets is through **countertrade**—a form of exporting in which a firm barters products rather than selling them for cash. Less-developed nations sometimes impose countertrade requirements when they lack sufficient foreign currency to attain goods and services they want or need from exporting countries. These countries allow sellers to exchange their products only for domestic products as a way to control their balance-of-trade problems.

Countertrade became popular two decades ago, when companies wanted to conduct business in eastern European countries and the former USSR. Those governments did not allow exchanges of hard currency, so this form of barter facilitated trade. PepsiCo made one of the largest countertrades ever when it exchanged $3 billion worth of Pepsi Cola for Russian Stolichnaya vodka, a cargo ship, and tankers from the former Soviet Union.

Estimating the actual volume of countertrade as percentage of world trade is difficult, but the American Countertrade Association puts the figure at about 25 percent. Countertraders include large multinational firms like General Electric and PepsiCo. Almost half of the *Fortune* 500 companies now practice countertrade in response to increasing global competition. Although countertrade is still growing at about 10 percent a year, its rate of increase has slowed.

THE UNITED STATES AS A TARGET FOR INTERNATIONAL MARKETERS

Foreign marketers regard America as an inviting target. It offers a large population, high levels of discretionary income, political stability, a generally favorable attitude toward foreign investment, and relatively well-controlled economic ills.

Among the best-known industries where foreign manufacturers have established U.S. production facilities is automobiles. Most of the world's leading auto companies have built assembly facilities in the United States: BMW in South Carolina, Toyota in Kentucky, Nissan in Tennessee, Honda in Ohio, and Mercedes-Benz in Alabama.

Many foreign executives are transforming their companies' mission statements to reflect their move toward globalization. As the French petroleum company Elf Aquitaine CEO put it, "We used to be a French company. Now we are a European company. Our goal is to be a global company—among the world's top 50 in terms of market value." Elf is currently one of the world's top ten oil companies with revenues over $36 billion.[53]

Small entrepreneurial businesses find Americans willing to accept their latest innovations and inventions. One such company is the Itsy Bitsy Entertainment Company, a British firm best known for Thomas the Tank Engine, a line of toys and products featuring a talking train. Its newest exports to the United States are called Teletubbies, talking baby aliens with televisions on their tummies. Itsy Bitsy teamed up with Microsoft to make interactive Teletubbies that help children learn letters, shapes, patterns, colors, and even songs. In another tie-in with Burger King, kids' meals include Tubby custard from Jell-O. In spite of a brief scandal that charged Tinky Winky as being homosexual, the Teletubbies have continued to be a great success with young toddlers.[54]

7

Explain the attractiveness of the United States as a target market for foreign marketers.

MARKETING | DICTIONARY

product invention In international marketing, the development of a new product combined with a new promotional strategy to take advantage of unique foreign opportunities.

countertrade Form of exporting whereby goods and services are bartered rather than sold for cash.

Time for Teletubbies.™ Time for Teletubbies.™
Tubby custard™* from Jell-O® is now at Burger King.®

Great news for kids. Now you can get delicious tubby custard.™ Made by JELL-O with wholesome skim milk,

it's only at BURGER KING. But hurry. After June 20, the tubby custard™ will go "bye-bye."

©1999 Kraft Foods, Inc.

*JELL-O Brand pudding snack

Available at participating Burger King locations through June 20, 1999, or while supplies last. Burger King Corporation is the exclusive licensee of the registered Burger King Trademarks and the registered Bun Halves Logo. ©1999 Burger King Corporation. Teletubbies™ and the distinctive likenesses thereof are trademarks of Ragdoll Productions (UK) Limited and are used with permission. ©1999 Ragdoll Productions (UK) Limited. All rights reserved. Licensed by The itsy bitsy Entertainment Company.

The popularity of British import Teletubbies among U.S. preschoolers is exploited in a promotion for Jell-O custard sold at Burger King restaurants.

As the chapter explained earlier, foreign investment continues to grow in the United States. Foreign multinationals will probably continue to invest in U.S. assets as they seek to produce goods locally and control distribution channels. Major U.S. companies owned by foreign firms include Columbia Pictures and Universal Studios, owned by Sony Corp. (Japan); Pillsbury, Burger King, Heublein, Pearle Vision, and Pet Inc., owned by Grand Metropolitan (United Kingdom); and Maybelline and Cosmair cosmetics, owned by L'Oréal (a French subsidiary of the Swiss conglomerate Nestlé SA); and Citgo Petroleum, owned by Petróleos de Venezuela (Venezuela).

The Bureau of Economic Analysis reports that the United Kingdom and Germany invest the most in the United States—$77 billion and $40 billion, respectively. The dominant theme of foreign investment in America continues to be the acquisition of big U.S. companies. Examples include Daimler-Benz's $40 billion acquisition of Chrysler and British Petroleum's $48 billion purchase of Amoco. Germany's 39 U.S. investments during 1998 generated $197 billion in revenues, while the United Kingdom's 31 investments accounted for $170 billion in revenues.[55]

STRATEGIC IMPLICATIONS OF INTERNATIONAL MARKETING

This first decade of the new century is truly the birth of global marketing, where nearly every marketer can become a global marketer. The era of domestic markets is largely being relegated to niche marketing. The Internet has played a major role in these changes in the traditional marketing practices of the last century. Marketers in both small, localized firms and giant businesses need to reevaluate the strengths and weaknesses of current marketing practices and realign their plans to meet the new demands of the information age.

Marketers are the pioneers in bringing new technologies to developing nations. Their successes and failures will determine the direction global marketing will take and the speed with which they will be embraced. Actions of international marketers will influence every component of the marketing environments: competitive, economic, social-cultural, political-legal, and technological.

The greatest competitive advantages will belong to those marketers who capitalize on the similarities of their target markets and adapt to the differences. In some instances, the actions of marketers today help determine the rules and regulations of tomorrow. PepsiCo and Coca-Cola marketers are doing that now in India, as was discussed earlier.

Marketers need flexible and broad views of an increasingly complex customer. Goods and services will become more customized as they are introduced in foreign markets. New and better products in developing markets will create and maintain relationships for the future. Specialization will once again be a viable business concept.

Marketing has just entered a new frontier of limitless opportunities. Much like the first voyages into space, the world looks more different than anyone could have ever imagined—and it looks pretty good! The impact of the Web and other new computer and communications technologies will be discussed in greater detail in the next chapter.

ACHIEVEMENT CHECK SUMMARY

Read the learning objectives that follow, and consider the questions for each one. Answering these questions will reinforce your grasp of the most important concepts in the chapter and will allow you to check how well you have achieved these learning goals. Where a blank appears before a question, answer with *T* or *F* for true/false questions; for multiple-choice questions, choose the letter of the correct answer.

Objective 3.1: Describe the importance of international marketing from the perspectives of the individual firm and the nation.

1. _____ When companies import, they purchase goods and services from overseas companies.

2. _____ International trade has a minimal effect on the growth of GDP and employment in the United States.

3. _____ Because buyer behavior is similar in most industrialized countries, firms can use the same strategies for international and domestic marketing.

Objective 3.2: Identify the major components of environment for international marketing.

1. _____ The exchange rate in a foreign country can influence a firm's pricing strategy.

2. _____ Unless exceptions have been enacted, U.S.-based international marketers are subject to both American laws and the laws of the foreign countries in which they operate.

3. _____ A quota on the number of cars the United States can sell in Brazil is an example of (a) a revenue tariff, (b) a protective tariff, (c) an administrative barrier, (d) an embargo.

Objective 3.3: Outline the basic functions of WTO, NAFTA, and the European Union.

1. _____ The World Trade Organization oversees international trade to prevent monopolies that hinder competition among countries.

2. _____ NAFTA is a free-trade area made up of the five countries identified by the NAFTA acronym: Nicaragua, Argentina, France, Trinidad, and America.

3. _____ The European Union (a) standardizes all laws among its members, (b) performs the same functions of NAFTA and the WTO, (c) has removed tariff barriers among its 15 member nations.

Objective 3.4: Compare the alternative strategies for entering international markets.

1. _____ Contractual agreements are the way most companies first enter international markets.

2. _____ When Compaq Computer arranges with a Taiwanese firm to produce components used in its computers, it engages in (a) exporting, (b) foreign licensing, (c) direct investment, (d) subcontracting.

3. _____ The rate of foreign direct investment by U.S. multinational corporations is decreasing.

Objective 3.5: Differentiate between a global marketing strategy and a multi-domestic marketing strategy.

1. _____ Because The Coca-Cola Company believes that tastes around the world are sufficiently homogeneous to allow the effective use of its existing marketing strategies everywhere, it uses a global marketing strategy.

2. _____ By selling different sized packages and different flavors for Chee-tos in Asia and in the United States, PepsiCo is taking a multi-domestic marketing approach.

3. _____ Companies should choose multi-domestic marketing strategies because (a) they already have a regional decentralized international marketing organization, (b) they produce consumer goods, (c) considerable variations in product, pricing, and distribution expectations exist among different market segments, (d) it is less costly than a global marketing strategy.

Objective 3.6: Describe the alternative marketing mix strategies used in international marketing.

1. _____ Pringle's global marketing strategy, using the standard slogan, "Once you pop, you can't stop," is an example of promotion adaptation.

2. _____ When U.S. automakers produce cars, trucks, and sports utility vehicles with the steering wheel on the right side for sale in the United Kingdom and Japan, they are (a) using a straight extension strategy, (b) introducing a new product, (c) adapting the product to meet local needs.

3. _____ Countertrade refers to pricing negotiations that involve paying for goods in currency other than that of the purchasing country.

Objective 3.7: Explain the attractiveness of the United States as a target market for foreign marketers.

1. _____ Because the United States is considered a mature market for many goods, foreign investors are less likely to acquire businesses in the United States.

2. _____ One reason foreign companies like to invest in the United States is to improve international distribution channels.

3. _____ In general, the business environment could be categorized as hostile to foreign investment in the United States.

Students: See the solutions section located on page S-1 to check your responses to the Achievement Check Summary.

Key Terms

exporting	franchise
importing	foreign licensing
infrastructure	joint venture
exchange rate	multinational corporation
friendship, commerce, and	global marketing strategy
navigation (FCN) treaties	multi-domestic marketing
tariff	strategy
import quota	straight extension
embargo	product adaptation
exchange control	promotion adaptation
dumping	dual adaptation
General Agreement on Tariffs	product invention
and Trade (GATT)	countertrade
World Trade Organization (WTO)	
North American Free-Trade	
Agreement (NAFTA)	

Review Questions

1. Why is the global marketplace so important to international marketers? Cite examples of firms that are highly successful in the global market. Why do you think these firms are successful?

2. How does the international marketplace differ from the domestic marketplace? In your answer, specifically examine market size and buyer behavior differences.

3. Name the major variables in the global marketing environment. Explain how each influences marketing decision making.

4. List the components of the legal environment for U.S. firms operating abroad. Specifically discuss friendship, commerce, and navigation (FCN) treaties, the Export Trade Act of 1982, and the Foreign Corrupt Practices Act.

5. What are the major barriers to international trade? Explain how trade restrictions may be used to either restrict or stimulate international marketing activities. Also explain the role of the WTO.

6. Explain the practice of dumping. Why does dumping sometimes occur?

7. Describe the world's growing economic interdependence. Relate this trend to the emergence of free-trade pacts in North America and the European Union.

8. Identify the basic entry strategies in international business. What factors should be considered in selecting an entry strategy?

9. Outline the basic premises behind the operation of a multinational corporation. Why have many of these organizations become global firms?

10. Differentiate between a global marketing strategy and a multidomestic marketing strategy. In what ways is the international marketing mix most likely to differ from a marketing mix used in the domestic market?

Questions for Critical Thinking

1. As marketers develop strategies to sell their goods and services in Cuba, they must decide which product and promotional strategies to use. Give examples of products that you would market using (a) straight extension, (b) product adaptation, and (c) promotion adaptation. Explain why you chose that strategy for each example.

2. Relate specific environmental considerations to each of the following aspects of a firm's international marketing mix:
   a. brands and warranties
   b. advertising
   c. distribution channels
   d. discounts to intermediaries
   e. use of comparative advertising

3. The European Union created a free-market among member nations that reduces economic barriers. Describe the benefits to EU marketers that result from this unification, and discuss the impact to foreign marketers targeting Europe. Do you predict the growth of such centralized free-trade organizations in this century? Defend your answer.

4. The WTO met with opposition in the latter half of the 1990s. Detail the reasons for this opposition. Include in your discussion the meeting in Singapore and the riots in Seattle. Were the opponents justified? Defend your answer.

5. Give a hypothetical or actual example of a firm operating at each of the following levels of international marketing:
   a. exporting
   b. franchising
   c. foreign licensing
   d. joint venture
   e. acquisition

6. Some people argue that foreign investment in the United States should be limited. Would you agree with a plan that would limit such investment to some specified amount by foreign firms or individuals in a particular firm? Do other nations have a right to limit American investment in their countries? Explain your answers.

1. Importance of Global Marketing. To learn more about the world's largest global marketers, use the link "Global 500" located at *www.ceoexpress.com*. Choose three companies listed among the top 50 that you would like to know more about and provide the following information:

- Name of company
- Global rank
- Industry
- Location of headquarters (country only)
- Number of employees
- Web address
- Brief description of how the firm showcases its global presence on its home page

ceoexpress.com

2. World Trade Organization. Visit the WTO's official Web site at *www.wto.org* and review the link "About the WTO" to learn more about the organization. Read through several of the links in this section and identify the single page you found most interesting. Download this page and prepare a brief summary to bring to class.

wto.org

3. International Product and Promotional Strategies. Go to *www.coke.com*. Review this site carefully and use your findings to create two lists. The first list should consist of 5 to 10 differences in the product or promotional strategies you found between the Coke products sold in your country and those sold in other countries. In the second list, record 5 to 10 similarities among product and promotional strategies used in different countries. Be prepared to submit your lists to your instructor or to discuss your findings in class.

coke.com

Video Case 3 on ESPN begins on page VC-4.

Gateway Continuing Case Part 1 begins on page GC-2.

PART

2

MANAGING TECHNOLOGY TO ACHIEVE MARKETING SUCCESS

113

Gateway Continuing Case Part 2 begins on page GC-3.

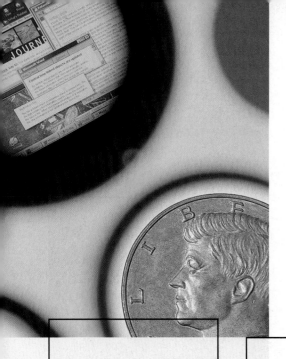

E-Commerce: Electronic Marketing and the Internet

CHAPTER

4

PaintingsDirect.com: A Virtual Art Gallery

A decade ago, Tunde Afolayan, a contemporary African artist, came to America and settled in the little Mississippi River town of Natchez. His vibrantly colored paintings that depict life in his native Nigeria quickly became popular among U.S. art lovers—at least those fortunate enough to have traveled to Mississippi to see them. But Afolayan yearned for a bigger audience, so two years ago he signed up with online gallery PaintingsDirect.com and found his desired audience. "Can you imagine bringing a whole gallery wall into your room, and you can walk through it piece by piece?" he asks. Well, that is what the Web is doing for artists and collectors in the multibillion-dollar art world.

Over half the earth's inhabitants have never set foot in an art museum or gallery. Fewer still have ever bought an original work of art. High prices—real or imagined—are a major barrier to art sales. The intimidation factor of being placed in an embarrassing environment filled with art experts—each of them able to quickly discern how little you know of the subject—turns off many would-be shoppers. Finally, there is the matter of inconvenience, unless you happen to live in major cities like New York City, Boston, Chicago, or Los Angeles. But this is where cyber-shopping comes in.

Millions of Web shoppers have reached a comfort zone after experiencing the speed, reliability, competitive prices, and convenience of Internet purchases of books, music, toys, prescrip-

tion drugs, and even cars. Now they are beginning to dabble in art. During the past five years, hundreds of artists have gone online, forming partnerships with such Web sites as Art.com, Artnet.com, icollector.com, collect.com, NextMonet.com, and PaintingsDirect.com. Even Internet bookseller Amazon.com has entered the market through an alliance with the international art auction house Sotheby's.

Each art site differs in product selection and level of interactive marketing. Some feature original art masterpieces; others offer posters, books, and art reproductions. Some market using an auction format, while still others operate as cyberspace alternatives to big-city retail art galleries. Some sites specialize in modern art; others offer impressionist works. Many online galleries also include sculpture and designer furniture as components of their product offerings.

PaintingsDirect provides original art by contemporary artists located throughout the world. Art lovers and patrons can view digital photographs of artwork posted on the Web. In an art museum, a viewer might take a magnifying glass to closely inspect each line of a Rembrandt etching. On the Web, a click of the mouse lets you zoom in on images for close-up views of individual brush strokes or the sparkle in a flower girl's eye.

Such detail was essential to PaintingsDirect founder Christine Bourron. Her online venture began with a disappointing search for a floral painting by an American artist for her mother's collection. "What really struck me was that I was a customer who knew what I wanted and couldn't find it. There was not an efficient distribution channel to bring the artists and the customer together, and that was what the Internet was going to enable me to do."

From this experience was born PaintingsDirect. A site visitor has only to click on "find painting" and select from a list of criteria, such as abstract, primitive, collage, or watercolor styles and themes involving dancers or workers or landscapes. The visitor can also select works by a particular artist, such as Tunde Afolayan, from among the 9,000 paintings posted there.

PaintingsDirect is testimony to the fact that online marketing can be a highly effective way to reach customers and build strong relationships through superior customer service.

115

Cybermarketing not only makes it easier for customers to find exactly what they want; it can also ease their worries about credit-card security and authenticity of their purchases. Such services as iEscrow and TradeSafe let PaintingsDirect hold the buyer's credit-card payments until the artwork is delivered, appraised, and approved. In addition, many virtual galleries provide detailed information to help potential buyers expand their knowledge of art. A visitor may want to know when and where an artist was born, dates and locations of major exhibitions, museums that include the artist's work in their permanent collections, and critiques of specific artworks.

Like so many individuals and organizations today, PaintingsDirect has discovered that e-commerce is a win–win situation. Artists reap the benefits of greater exposure, dealers generate revenues by serving as marketing intermediaries, and customers can find that unique work of art that enriches their lives.[1]

CHAPTER OVERVIEW

Dramatic changes in global economies and societies of the last decade have grabbed the attention of almost every person in every business in every industry, from banking and air travel to communications. Marketing now holds the key to creating a competitive advantage. Demographic and lifestyle changes have transformed homogeneous mass markets into personalized, one-to-one interactions. Deregulation, rapid technological changes, and the stability of its economy have made the United States the world leader in e-commerce.

During the final decade of the 20th century, marketing became the cutting-edge tool for success on the Internet. Profit-seeking organizations are not the only benefactors of the Internet; social organizations of all kinds are beginning to emphasize marketing's role in achieving set goals. Colleges and universities, charities, museums, symphony orchestras, and hospitals are beginning to employ the marketing concept discussed in Chapter 1—providing customers the goods and services they want to buy when they want to buy them. Marketing continues to perform its function of bringing buyers and sellers together; it just does it faster and more efficiently than ever before.

With just a few ticks of the clock and a few clicks of a mouse, the Internet revolutionizes every aspect of life. New words have emerged, such as software, Internet, extranet, and intranet; and old words have new meanings never imagined a few years ago—Web, Net, surfer and server, banner and browsers, online and offline. E-commerce has turned virtual reality into reality. With a computer and a telephone, a virtual marketplace is open twenty-four hours, seven days a week to provide almost anything anywhere to anyone, including art, clothes, food, information, entertainment, medicine, and furniture. You can do your banking, make travel reservations, send out a résumé online, or even buy a car—perhaps at a lower price than you could in person. When one shopper from New York decided to buy a new Volvo recently, she started her quest the usual way by visiting local car dealers. However, when she could not find the color she wanted, she turned to her computer. She accessed autobytel.com, an online association of car dealers. After describing her requirements, she received detailed bids from three Volvo dealers. Their best deal was $1,000 less than the lowest price she had been quoted in person at the car dealer.[2]

Internet marketers can reach individual consumers or target organizations worldwide through a vast array of computer and communications technologies. In just a few short years, more than

400,000 companies—large and small—have been connected to electronic marketing channels. Goods and services sold to American and European consumers alone now top more than $5 billion a year.[3]

This chapter examines the nature of electronic commerce and explores the many ways it is transforming marketing. Beginning with a definition of e-commerce and e-marketing, the chapter proceeds with a discussion of the Internet and the World Wide Web. It further explains the transition of industrial economies to electronic economies, the benefits online marketing provides, and the challenges it presents. The chapter then looks at the buyers and sellers who populate the Web and how marketers build online relationships with customers. Next, the chapter discusses the various digital marketing tools and how marketers use Web sites to achieve organizational goals. Finally, it examines the promises and challenges associated with online marketing. ▪

WHAT IS ELECTRONIC COMMERCE?

A number of terms have been used to describe marketing activities occurring on the Internet or through such electronic tools as computer modems, telephones, fax machines, and CD-ROMs. Among the most popular is **electronic commerce (e-commerce)**—targeting customers by collecting and analyzing business information, conducting customer transactions, and maintaining online relationships with customers by means of telecommunications networks.[4] E-commerce provides a foundation for launching new businesses, extending the reach of existing companies, and building and retaining customer relationships.

The component of e-commerce of particular interest to marketers is **electronic marketing (e-marketing)**—the strategic process of creating, distributing, promoting, and pricing goods and services to a target market over the Internet or through such **digital tools** as fax machines, computer modems, telephones, and CD-ROMs. E-marketing is the means by which e-commerce is achieved. It encompasses such activities as:

- placing a bid for a Buffalo–Los Angeles flight on Price.com
- ordering building materials from the Home Depot Web site with a guaranteed one-hour delivery
- purchasing downloaded copies of *The New York Times'* articles on European retailing to use as source materials for a research paper

The application of these electronic tools to 21st-century marketing has the potential to greatly reduce costs and increase customer satisfaction by increasing the speed and efficiency of marketing interactions. Just as e-commerce is a major function of the Internet, e-marketing is an integral component of e-commerce.

A closely related but somewhat narrower term than e-marketing is online marketing. While electronic marketing can involve noncomputer digital technologies ranging from fax machines to telephones, **online marketing** refers to marketing activities that connect buyers and sellers electronically through interactive computer systems.

Regardless of what you are selling or buying, what kind of business you are in, or whether your company has hundreds of employees or just you, e-commerce offers limitless opportunities.

1

Define e-commerce and give examples of each function of the Internet.

MARKETING | **DICTIONARY**

electronic commerce (e-commerce) Targeting customers by collecting and analyzing business information, conducting customer transactions, and maintaining online relationships with customers by means of telecommunications networks.

electronic marketing (e-marketing) Strategic process of creating, distributing, promoting, and pricing goods and services to a target market over the Internet or through digital tools.

digital tools Electronic technologies used in e-commerce including fax machines, computer modems, telephones, and CD-ROMs.

online marketing Marketing activities that connect buyers and sellers electronically through interactive computer systems.

TABLE 4.1	E-Commerce Capabilities	
CAPABILITY	**DESCRIPTION**	**EXAMPLE**
Global reach	The ability to reach anyone connected to a PC anywhere in the world.	Major car makers, such as Ford, Nissan, and Volvo, use the Web to reach car buyers around the world.
One-to-one marketing	Creating products to meet customer specifications; also called personalization.	Customers can order customized clothing—from jeans to shirts to shoes—online.
Interactive marketing	Buyer-seller communications through such channels as the Internet, CD-ROMs, toll-free telephone numbers, and virtual reality kiosks.	Intouch Group's iStations are interactive kiosks placed in retail music stores that allow customers to listen to thirty-second music clips before they purchase compact discs.
Right-time marketing	The ability to provide a good or service at the exact time needed.	FedEx customers can place service orders online and track shipments twenty-four hours a day.
Integrated marketing	Coordination of all promotional activities to produce a unified, customer-focused promotional message.	Nike marketers use the familiar Swoosh logo and "Just Do It" slogan in both online and offline promotions.

However, many of the traditional marketing issues must still be dealt with, such as pricing and distribution, inventory, advertising and promotion, and customer service. Each organization needs to develop new business models that adapt to the large volumes of traffic inherent with on-line transactions. New communities of buyers and sellers are created through e-commerce. In ways not thought of just 5 years ago, organizations are utilizing Internet technology to set up businesses and successfully conduct trade over the Internet.[5]

E-commerce offers unlimited opportunities for marketers to reach consumers. This radical departure from traditional bricks-and-mortar operations provides the following five benefits to contemporary marketers, as shown in Table 4.1.

■ Global reach. The Net eliminates the geographic protections of local businesses. Car dealers selling online, for example, have attracted buyers from hundreds of miles away.

■ One-to-one marketing (personalization). There are no Dell computers waiting for customers at the firm's Austin factory. The production process begins when an order is received and ends 36 hours later when the PC is loaded onto a delivery truck.

■ *Interactive marketing.* Customers and suppliers negotiate prices online in much the same manner as they do at a local flea market or car dealership. The result is the creation of an ideal product at the right price that satisfies both parties.

■ *Right-time marketing.* Web companies, such as bookseller Amazon.com and custom-music compiler CDNow, can provide products when and where customers want them.

■ *Integrated marketing.* The Internet enables the coordination of all promotional activities and communication to create a unified, customer-oriented promotional message.

Interactivity and E-Commerce

The e-commerce approach to buying and selling has been embraced by millions worldwide because it offers substantial benefits over traditional marketing practices. The two-way, back-and-forth communications enable marketers to supply the precise items desired by their customers. At the same time, purchasers can continue to refine their product specifications to create an optimal match that fills their precise needs.

Gap.com

One of the most successful retail chains established during the past decade is The Gap. In hundreds of Gap, GapKids, babyGap, and Old Navy retail stores, the firm's marketers succeed by offering moderately priced, fashionable casual wear for men, women, and children. Baby clothing sold by babyGap, the newest unit of the retail chain, is featured in Figure 4.1.

Recently, The Gap has added a concept called **interactive marketing** to its marketing strategies. The approach, which consists of buyer-seller communications in which the customer

FIGURE 4.1 BabyGap: Supplying Products for the Children's Apparel Market

controls the amount and type of information received from a marketer, has been used by marketers for over a decade. Point-of-sale brochures and coupon dispensers located in supermarkets are simple forms of interactive marketing. However, when digital tools such as the Internet are included in interactive marketing efforts, the results are infinitely improved for the seller and buyer alike.

Say, for example, you need a new pair of khaki pants. If you have a computer, The Gap has you covered. You do not have to get in the car and drive to the mall. Just visit The Gap's interactive Web site, answer a few questions including what style of pants you want to buy, your size, color preference, and quantity; and, with a click of the mouse, your order is placed and shipped directly to you. But The Gap marketers have not stopped there. You can sign in with The Gap, permanently registering your shipping information, and send e-mail messages directly to company marketers. The Gap marketers want you to feel that your shopping experience is just as personal as if you had spoken with a salesperson on the phone or in a store. That is interactive marketing.[6]

The Internet

Although two-way communications between buyers and sellers describe most personal selling and have been taking place electronically since the invention of the telephone, the Golden Age of interactivity began a few decades ago. Its beginnings can be traced to the creation of the **Internet (Net)**, a global collection of computer networks linked together for the purpose of exchanging

MARKETING DICTIONARY

interactive marketing Buyer-seller communications in which the customer controls the amount and type of information received from a marketer through such channels as the Internet, CD-ROMs, interactive toll-free telephone numbers, and virtual reality kiosks.

Internet (Net) All-purpose global communications network composed of some 50,000 different networks around the globe that, within limits, lets anyone with access to a personal computer send and receive images and data anywhere.

data and information. The Net originally served scientists and government researchers, but it has since evolved into a multifaceted and popular medium of communication for individual households and business users. Users can exchange data with other computer users around the world in such formats as text, graphic images, audio, and video.

Even in small, niche markets, the Internet helps build e-commerce capabilities. For example, Neoforma, a California-based medical supplies distributor, markets its products globally through its Web site. Among its best customers is the government of Oman—a market the company could never have served had it depended on traditional marketing efforts. While Neoforma relies on the Internet as a means of contacting geographically dispersed buyers, other marketers rely on it to maintain links with suppliers. A good example of this kind of communication link is exhibited by Ocean Spray, which maintains regular communication with its suppliers over the Net. Independent growers, who supply Ocean Spray with berries, receive fast, reliable information about the firm's supply needs and pricing policies.[7]

@ neoforma.com

@ oceanspray.com

Growth of the Internet

In less than a decade, the Internet has grown from a mere 18 million American users to over 70 million today, opening more channels for consumers to find a wide array of information. Over half of all U.S. households now have a PC in the home, 41 percent have CD-ROMs, and a full third are online; and all of these numbers are growing faster than surveys can count.[8] The appeal of this exciting new approach to shopping is obvious. E-commerce shifts the balance of power to the buyer. The online shopper knows that an alternative supplier is just a click away. Want to make sure a price is the best one available? CompareNet offers detailed information and price quotes on more than 100,000 consumer products. Want to avoid having to deal with a local supplier? As was discussed in Chapter 3, the Net is global. Today's online marketers are automatically global marketers.

In addition to the Internet, a number of other digital tools facilitate electronic marketing. Two of these tools are voice mail and fax machines—techniques for sending and recording messages via the telephone. Similarly, **electronic mail (e-mail)** is an Internet application for sending and receiving written messages between computers.

Intranets and Extranets

Internet technologies provide a platform for **intranets,** internal corporate networks that allow employees within a firm to communicate with each other and gain access to corporate information. **Extranets,** on the other hand, are corporate networks that allow communication between a firm and selected customers, suppliers, and business partners outside the firm. Companies that use both extranets and intranets benefit even further from online communication. For example, Prudential HealthCare links its intranet through an extranet to the intranets of its large corporate subscribers. Thus, health benefit managers at these companies are able to enroll new employees themselves rather than completing lengthy paperwork or having to contact Prudential's call center to complete this task. Employees can also check their eligibility or claim status or change primary-care doctors any time of the day or night. Prudential customers love the convenience of having their intranet connected directly to Prudential's, and the extranet saves time and money for both Prudential and its clients.[9]

@ prudential.com

Robert Mondavi Corp. has come up with an ingenious way to use its extranet to improve its products. The California-based winery already buys satellite images from NASA to identify problems in its huge vineyards. It now, however, also sends the satellite images to its independent grape growers so they can correct or avoid problems in their vineyards. Mondavi benefits in the long run by helping its suppliers produce a better crop.[10]

The World Wide Web

The Internet provides an efficient way to find and share information, but, until recently, most people outside universities and government agencies found it difficult to use. This changed in the mid-1990s, when Tim Berners-Lee at the European Center for Nuclear Research in Geneva, Switzerland, developed the *World Wide Web*. Originally thought of as an internal document-

FIGURE 4.2 A Typical Day on the Web

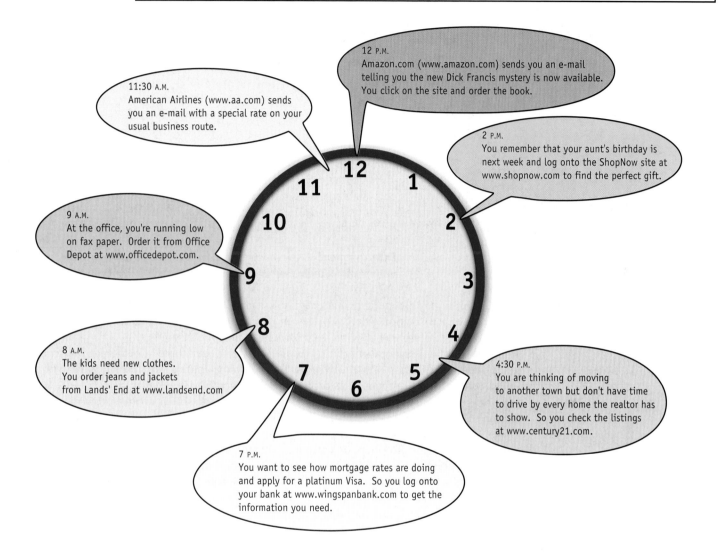

management system, the Web quickly grew to become a collection of tens of thousands of inter-linked computers, called Web servers, that function together within the Internet. These computers are located all over the world and rely on high-speed Internet circuits and software to allow users to hop from server to server, providing the illusion that the Web is one big computer. The Web can handle so much information in so many different media that it has become the premier means for marketers to reach consumers in their target markets. Currently, at least 6,000 new servers become a part of the Web each month.[11] Over a third of all online households make a purchase through the Web. Millions of other visitors, though not actually buying online, use the Web to help them make purchase decisions.

How do people use the Web? Figure 4.2 illustrates how a typical consumer might spend time online during a day. Most of these interactions occur as a means of gathering information—about airfares, gifts for friends or family members, a new home, a mortgage, or a credit card. Still other interactions—such as Lands' End clothing purchases

MARKETING **DICTIONARY**

electronic mail (e-mail) Internet application for sending written messages between computers.

intranet Internal corporate network that allows employees within an organization to communicate with each other and gain access to corporate information.

extranets Corporate network that allows communication between an organization and selected customers, suppliers, and business partners outside the firm.

FIGURE 4.3 | Three Web Functions

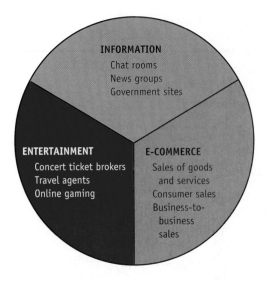

INFORMATION
Chat rooms
News groups
Government sites

ENTERTAINMENT
Concert ticket brokers
Travel agents
Online gaming

E-COMMERCE
Sales of goods
and services
Consumer sales
Business-to-business sales

resrocket.com

or an order for fax paper from Office Depot—would be considered electronic commerce. The Web's entertainment function might be performed by checking availability of seats for a Sarah McLaughlin concert through Ticketmaster or reading brief synopses of best-selling books on Amazon.com.

Three Web Functions

As Figure 4.3 shows, one or more of three primary functions are performed on the Web: providing information, entertainment, and conducting e-commerce transactions. Many Web users are not looking to buy or sell anything; they are simply looking for information. This need is served through commercial sites such as AskJeeves, as well as chat rooms, newsgroups, and government sites. A recent survey of online users revealed that 60 percent searched for information (including 46 percent who checked the news), 36 percent took courses, and 29 percent conducted job-related tasks.[12] Many information-oriented Web sites can be identified by the domain names *.org* and *.gov*.

Entertainment A growing number of people are looking for entertainment online, including everything from travel to concerts to online gaming. The travel industry, for example, has been nearly revamped by the Web. In this highly competitive market, time is a critical element. The Web provides instant access to ticket information, such as prices and available seating. Ticketmaster, one of the best-known online ticket brokers, provides information on concerts and other entertainment events around the globe. Brick-and-mortar travel agencies have been forced to embrace this technology to stay competitive with online offerings. Before going online, Pacific Express Travel, for instance, lost nearly 15 percent of its revenues to Internet sales in just one year.[13]

For entertainment marketers, the Web is a marketing tool that creates value for customers. Online marketers can offer competitive prices, speed, and boundless services. Geography no longer limits the size of the marketplace. Take, for example, Res Rocket, a Web-based music studio. Musicians living anywhere on earth can log on and find other musicians with whom to perform. They plug in their instruments, hook up microphones, connect through their computers to the Res Rocket site, and start jamming. Their impromptu performances can be just for fun. However, if they feel like doing business, Res Rocket can record their jam session in full digital sound and place it on a disk or video soundtrack.[14]

Online gaming is one of the fastest growing segments of entertainment in cyberspace. While free games generate online traffic, pay-for-play games are the real money makers. Well-known marketers like Sony, Sega, Microsoft, and Electronic Arts are just a few of the hundreds that are betting on online gaming to be the "biggest thing since Monopoly." Ultima Online, created for Electronic Arts, has proven that people—125,000 so far—will pay for online entertainment. The average Ultima player logs 17 hours a week participating in a medieval role-playing game that unfolds in a two-dimensional fictional world called Britannia. Ultima software prices range from $40 to $70 retail, not including a monthly play-fee of $10 or any Internet-access fees. "We were profitable within a month," says Kelly Flock, president of 989 Studios—the unit that created Sony's online game Everquest.[15]

As video and PC gaming invades the mainstream, a huge opportunity for marketers of all levels is created. Estimates count 34 million game-playing households in the United States alone. Marketers are targeting this market of 16- to 34-year-old males with goods and services for players' real lives and real activities. Online gamers are active, adventurous, highly competitive, and plugged in to the latest trends in such things as technology, fashion, cars, personal care products, and home furnishings. As the ad in Figure 4.4 explains, gamers are turning their televisions on not to watch, but to plug in to PlayStation, Nintendo, or Dreamcast.

E-Commerce The primary function of the Internet is undoubtedly e-commerce. Almost every organization is establishing a Web presence, from multinational corporations to individual

FIGURE 4.4 | *incite PC Games* and *Video Games:* Targeting Online Game Player Retailers

entrepreneurial ventures and from sellers of goods to service providers. Organizations ranging from not-for-profit Save-the-Whales to world famous Tiffany's are vying for space on the Web and for consumers' attention. Fashion retailer Nordstrom added online shopping to its array of buying opportunities. Its online store is stocked with 53,000 enticing items.[16]

The Web facilitates marketing activities, including buying and selling goods and services, building relationships, increasing market size, and reducing the costs of intermediaries. This chapter focuses on the e-commerce function of the Internet since it fuels the growth of electronic marketing. The Web is the most popular area of the Internet, with a predicted 320 million users by 2002. As the Web becomes even easier to use and attracts more participants, researchers predict that it soon will be a pervasive part of modern life.[17]

Most people generally think of the Web as a giant cybermall of retail stores selling millions of goods online. However, service providers are also important participants in e-commerce. Providers of financial services, for example, have become major players in the cybermarket. Traditional brokerages, such as Schwab and Fidelity, as well as many new online financial service providers, are rapidly attracting customers who want to do more of their own investment trading at a smaller trading cost, on whatever time and day that suits them. E*Trade Group, the world's second largest online brokerage, compares its Internet services to traditional brokers in ads that predict, "Someday, everyone will trade this way." Online trading allows E*Trade to offer real-time quotes—free to anyone for the asking. Fees start at a low $14.95 per stock trade, and total revenues exceeded $525 million last year, enabling E*Trade to expand the scope of investment services it offers its clients.[18] Figure 4.5 invites investors to visit its E*Offering subsidiary to find out more about the process of raising capital.

etrade.com

The Web also provides tremendous opportunities for business-to-business e-commerce. After international aircraft manufacturer Boeing spent seven months building a Web site, the firm received over $100 million from online orders for spare parts from airlines around the globe. Similarly, Cisco Systems, the world's largest server provider, takes in about $11 million in orders *each*

aol.com

day through its Web site—that adds up to $4 billion in annual revenues. In just one year, Cisco saved $363 million in technical support, marketing, and distribution costs by using the Web.[19]

Accessing the Internet

In the same way an explorer relies on a compass and map to seek out a desired destination, marketers and their customers must depend on navigation instruments to locate Web sites and find information in a database. The basic pathway for going online is through an **Internet service provider (ISP).** An ISP, such as AT&T or one of the dozens of competitors, provides individuals with organizations with direct access to the Internet. ISP giants such as America Online (AOL) let the user add the Internet through their own specially designed online sites. Such sites can be thought of as doors opening to a giant shopping mall called the Internet.

The early gateways for Internet access were called *search engines*. Over time, these Internet entrances became **portals** by adding to their sites content, shopping services, and software applications like e-mail, calendaring, and banking. In addition to AOL and Yahoo! major portals include Excite@Home and Lycos. A more recent trend is the creation of portals built around specific services or communities. These include such sites as Women.com, ESPN.com, and Broadcast.com. Their aim is to draw in Web surfers and keep their interest with specific types of content or transactions.

In addition to serving as gateways for Internet access, portals are pushing to become the grand entrance for consumer business. At present, most portal revenue comes from advertising. Portal sites produce only 18 percent of revenue generated from online shopping. But all of this is changing, and most major portals have launched vast shopping sites as a means of capturing the online shopper and a share of e-commerce revenues.

With over 20 million paid subscribers, AOL is the world's largest commercial online service. Its virtual shopping mall consists of almost 400 merchant partners who pay rent for "real estate" on AOL's shopping pages. Preview Travel shelled out $32 million to become AOL's online travel agent; CUC International spent $50 million for AOL to carry its online discount-shopping service; and 1-800-Flowers became the exclusive AOL florist for a cool $25 million.[20] Rather than charging rent, Lycos gets a cut of all transactions on its site.[21]

E-COMMERCE AND THE ECONOMY

2

Describe how marketers use the Internet and World Wide Web to achieve their firm's objectives.

The dawn of the 21st century witnessed the change from a century-old industrial economy to its electronic successor—an economy based on the Internet and other related online technologies. Many people see e-commerce as the fuel of the 21st century. Since the Web first opened for commercial activity in 1993, e-commerce has become the leading force in changing the way the world lives and breathes. In 2002, e-commerce in the United States alone totaled $3 billion or about 2 percent of the gross domestic product (GDP); by 2005, it is expected to jump past 6 percent of GDP. Industry analysts predict that up to 60 percent of entire industries will be committed to e-commerce within 10 years. So rapid are the economic changes that even the predictions must be updated almost daily.

The impact of the Internet on the economy translates to an increase estimated at between $10 billion and $20 billion in GDP.[22] The wonderful world of the Web is being explored by small, previously unheard of companies as well as large, multinational corporations. Consider the following successes:

- Ohio-based Dolphin Whale & Shark Gift Store sells more than $7 million worth of marine-themed jewelry, books, and gifts each year through its Web site, www.dolphinws.com.

- Archie McPhee, a Seattle-based cataloger that carries offbeat merchandise such as voodoo dolls and rubber chickens, created an online database of 50,000 names that records online frequency and purchase amounts.

- Leif Technologies of Lebanon, Ohio, builds computerized grave markers that function as interactive burial sites and sell for around $5,000 each.

- After learning that 35 percent of the nation's 3 million farmers use the Internet, Ben Zaitz created Farms.com, an online cattle auction that relies on digital video feeds and still images. Last year's sales topped $2 million.

- Two major catalog clothiers, Lands' End and L. L. Bean, established a presence on the Web to supplement their catalog sales, enhance customer service, and increase their million-dollar revenues.[23]

But conducting business on the Net is more than just creating a Web site. State-of-the-art graphics and pages of information do not spell success any more than fancy business cards or company brochures do. A Web site must provide a platform for communication between organizations, customers, and suppliers. A new universe is being created in which businesses now hold auctions for utilities, such as gas and electricity, banks partner with computer companies, and musicians sell directly to their fans. New businesses and new ways of conducting business on the Web are sending the economy to new heights. The following sections in this chapter illustrate the explosion of business-to-business transactions. In just a few years, more than $100 billion worth of transactions occurred over the Net—most of which are businesses selling to other businesses—and by 2005, business-to-business transactions are expected to account for 80 percent of e-commerce.[24]

Business-to-Business Online Marketing

Gordon Sinkez's Web site is nothing flashy. No fancy graphics, catchy songs, or state-of-the-art video clips—just lots of practical information, and that is the way his customers like it. Sinkez runs the Web site for CSX Corp., the Jacksonville, Florida-based operator of one of America's largest freight railroad companies. The site enables customers to obtain price quotes, schedule shipments, and examine a map of the railroad's 18,000-mile network to see where their shipments are at any given moment. This information is vital to CSX's business customers, who access the site 400,000 times every month.[25]

 csx.com

Unlike the business-to-consumer segment of the online market, business-to-business interactions involve professional buyers and sellers—people whose performances are evaluated by their purchasing and selling decisions. Consequently, business-to-business online marketing usually does not need the same glitz and glamour as the business-to-consumer segment.

Although most people are familiar with such business-to-consumer online marketers as eBay and Amazon, these transactions are dwarfed by their business-to-business counterparts who are buying and selling both business services and commodities like paper, plastics, and chemicals. For example, Chemdex.com has eliminated intermediaries and a sea of paperwork to bring together suppliers and buyers in the pharmaceutical and biotech industries. In so doing, it reduced sales and distribution costs industry-wide by 20 percent—more than $4 billion of the total $20 billion global life-sciences market. As one analyst described it, "These guys have not seen their cost structures improved like this ever. It's a tectonic shift."[26]

Figure 4.6 illustrates the growth of business-to-business e-commerce as a share of U.S. gross domestic product. By 2003, it is expected to explode to $1.3 trillion, or about 9.4 percent of total U.S. business sales. Durable goods manufacturers alone account for almost half of all business-to-business sales.

FIGURE 4.6

E-Commerce as a Percentage of GDP

E-Commerce Begins to Take Hold

U.S. Business-to-Business Internet Commerce As a Share of GDP

Data: Forrester Research Inc.   Est.

hp.com/e-services

ibm.com/e-business

Wholesalers of business products such as office supplies, electronic goods, and scientific equipment are a close second in business-to-business market share. Even though they still provide many of their services in person, professionals such as doctors, attorneys, and accountants are finding new ways to use the Internet to reach existing and potential clients as well as communicate with others in their fields.

MCI Worldcom, IBM, General Electric Information Services, and others—both large and small—are busily developing the systems and software necessary to make business-to-business online marketing a reality. Many companies already established in the computer industry have created new business units to serve the needs of customers and suppliers online. Hewlett-Packard targets business owners who are unsure of how to travel on the Internet. Through its Web site, customers can obtain everything from accounting and payroll to security needs. IBM has been highly successful with its site, as well. The ad in Figure 4.7 illustrates a few of the companies IBM's e-business unit has helped: major companies such as Gulfstream Aerospace, emerging firms such as eseeds.com, and small enterprises like hawaii-gifts.com.

Many firms are also finding entirely new markets for their goods and services—markets that either did not exist or were inaccessible without the benefit of the Internet. Network Associates, for instance, limited the marketing of its antivirus software to the United States for years because marketers believed their product was too expensive for foreign consumers. Recently, however, the Santa Clara, California-based company made its first Internet sale of a new help-desk software package to a bank in Spain that downloaded it from the firm's Web site. No additional marketing expenses were involved, and the message reached the right customers halfway around the world.[27]

An important objective of both online and offline marketing is to distinguish a firm and its products from competitive offerings. For instance, the purchasing manager for Comdisco, an Illinois-based, $4-billion technology services company, spends several million dollars of her company's budget buying office equipment and supplies each year. A global procurement manager at American Express of New York runs 25 to 30 Internet searches each month looking for new suppliers and comparing market offerings. Both of these managers like the advantages of purchasing over the Internet, and both like the freedom of selecting from hundreds of vendors. But what about the vendors themselves? How do they position themselves on the Web so that corporate buyers notice them, let alone make a purchase? A first step is to list themselves with the major search engines, such as HotBot, Lycos, Yahoo!, and Excite. But that is not enough. A single search for an item—say, an office desk or a paper shredder—could yield thousands of sites, some of which might not even be relevant. Marketers also need to list their firms with Internet yellow pages such as BigBook and BigYellow, which operate just like their printed counterparts. A purchasing manager can look up "office furniture" in one of these directories and get listings of relevant sites. Many industries have their own online references, such as the *Thomas Register of American Manufacturers.*

Successful online business-to-business marketers serve their customers by thinking like a buyer. They interview their regular customers to find out how these customers use the Internet and where they find information they need in making purchase decisions. This information can be used to devise strategies to attract new customers and improve relationships with existing ones.

Benefits of Business-to-Business Online Marketing

The advantages of business-to-business online marketing strategies over traditional methods are only beginning to be realized. Online marketers can find new markets and customers who could not have been served adequately using 20th-century techniques. They also produce cost savings in every area of the marketing mix—product, promotion, price, and distribution—as electronic marketing replaces the traditional bricks-and-mortar approach. Finally, online marketing greatly reduces the time involved in reaching target markets. Many business writers label e-commerce

3

Explain how online marketing benefits organizations, marketers, and consumers.

FIGURE 4.7 **IBM E-Business: Providing E-Commerce Solutions**

as *easy commerce*, since online marketing tools allow the direct exchange of information, such as order fulfillment and customer service, in a seamless fashion without involvement of marketing intermediaries. Communicating with suppliers, customers, and distributors over the Web is much more cost-effective and time-efficient than the letters, phone calls, faxes, and personal sales calls that were the conventional methods of the last century.

Currently, the number of Web sites is more than doubling every two months, with the most common growth being corporate sites. A home page creates a company's online storefront where consumers go for product and corporate information. A Web site should capture the personality of the company and serve as an effective public relations tool. The Web enhances an organization's operations by reducing distances and removing time zones. Both not-for-profit and profit-seeking organizations are enjoying these benefits. For example, with automatic approval built into the software system, employees for Los Angeles County now make routine purchases online. Orders and payments are handled electronically, reducing labor and paperwork costs. Employees now comparison shop online, saving the county some 5 percent—a figure that adds up to tens of millions of dollars every year. Online inventory management will also allow the county to accumulate $38 million in windfall savings over five years. Needless to say, Los Angeles county officials are sold on the Internet.[28]

Establishing a business-to-business Web site or advertising on another organization's site can be very expensive. The cost of launching a Web site can range from a few thousand dollars to several million dollars, and advertising on another site can quickly run into the tens of thousands of dollars. But marketers testify that the expense is small compared with traditional marketing costs. For Plastics Technology Group, the reward of online marketing is tremendous. The $16-million manufacturer of flexible plastic tubing paid $7,000 for links to its site under 100 different categories. By selecting a key search word that matches one of Plastics' product categories, customers will automatically be given a link site to the firm.[29]

safetyonline.com

Online Consumer Marketing

Just as e-commerce is a major function of the Internet, online marketing is an integral component of e-commerce. Lands' End, the catalog apparel company, generates 85 percent of its orders by

landsend.com

FIGURE 4.8 | Lands' End: Tailoring Products for Online Consumers

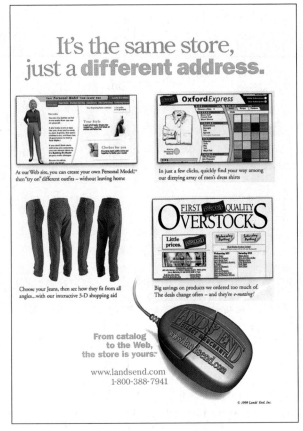

telephone (about 14 million calls a year). The Wisconsin-based company, however, recently turned to online marketing to boost its sales. With ads such as the one shown in Figure 4.8, Lands' End marketers alert consumers to this new service offering. Online customers can select an Oxford cotton shirt by simply typing in the size, color, and collar type they want, and with a few mouse-clicks, arrange for payment and delivery of their order.[30] As the following sections explain, both consumers and marketers alike enjoy the benefits of online marketing.

Online marketing is inherently interactive marketing. While it obviously expands the reach of marketers in connecting with customers, to be effective it must be part of an overall marketing strategy before it can create value for customers. A point to remember is that just as quickly as a firm can rise to become a star in cyberspace, if not launched properly and operated efficiently, it can just as quickly burn out.

Consumers who shop online can point to a number of advantages to online marketing. Figure 4.9 shows the results of a recent survey of why consumers buy online and why they avoid online transactions.

The benefits online shoppers obtain from Web purchases fall into three categories: lower prices, convenience, and personalization. Marketers should ensure their Web sites offer consumers these basic advantages over traditional shopping in retail stores, by telephone, and by mail. In addition, Web sites should be easy to navigate, offer security and privacy, and provide information that consumers can use in making product comparisons and purchase decisions.

Lower Prices

Many goods and services actually cost less online. Visitors to the Books-A-Million Web site discover that they can purchase book titles from *The New York Times* best-seller list at a 55 percent discount—even lower than the 50 percent off price of the industry's leading e-tailer,

Amazon.com. It comes as no surprise to anyone who has ever searched the Web for the best price for an airline ticket, software, or a newly-released CD that three Web shoppers in four listed lower prices as a primary motivation for venturing online.

The Web is an ideal method for savvy shoppers to compare prices from dozens—even hundreds—of sellers. The car shopper at the beginning of the chapter who turned to autobytel.com to locate a particular color was also able to find a lower price. Online shoppers can compare features and prices at their leisure, without being pressured by a salesperson or having to conform to the company's hours of operation. Those who shop online auction sites such as eBay often find even better deals.

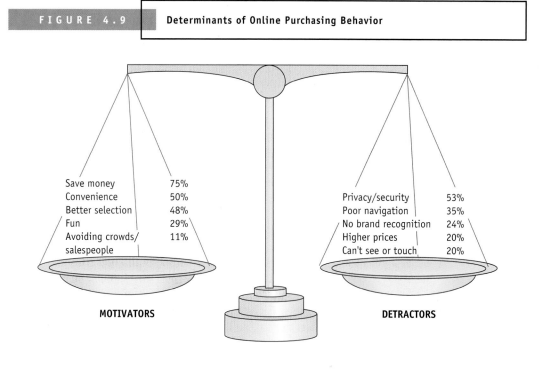

FIGURE 4.9   Determinants of Online Purchasing Behavior

MOTIVATORS	
Save money	75%
Convenience	50%
Better selection	48%
Fun	29%
Avoiding crowds/ salespeople	11%

DETRACTORS	
Privacy/security	53%
Poor navigation	35%
No brand recognition	24%
Higher prices	20%
Can't see or touch	20%

The newest e-commerce tools, **bots,** aid consumers in comparison shopping. Bots—short for robots—are search programs that check hundreds of sites, gather and assemble information, and bring it back to the sender. New software packages and even some Web sites offer automatic price and product comparison searches. Chapter 19 covers the benefits bots offer customers and their impact on e-marketing.

Convenience

A second important factor in prompting online purchases is shopper convenience. Cybershoppers can order goods and services from around the world at any hour of the day or night. Many online sellers allow customers to register their credit-card and shipping information for quick use in making additional purchases. Online retailers of products like books and CDs simply ask their regular customers to type in a password to place their order. The buyer then receives an e-mail message confirming the order, its shipping date, and the amount charged to the credit-card number on file.

Many Web sites offer custom-fitted products to match individual customer requirements. Levi Strauss' customers, for instance, can order guaranteed-to-fit jeans on the company Web site at prices slightly higher than those charged in retail stores for standard Levi sizes and off-the-rack versions. Fashion retailer Nordstrom spent $30 million on its state-of-the-art site, which can store information on customer sizes as well as color, style, and brand preferences to add to the convenience of ordering custom purchases. Customers can also receive e-mails on special notices, including sales, new product lines, and special promotions in Nordstrom's 70 retail locations.

@ **nordstrom.com**

Personalization

Citing personalized service as an important component of online shopping sounds like an oxymoron, since electronic marketing operates with little or no human interaction. But cyberspace marketers know how important personalization is to the quality of the shopping experience. Customer satisfaction is greatly affected by

MARKETING **DICTIONARY**

bot Search program that checks hundreds of sites, gathers and assembles information, and brings it back to the sender.

the marketer's ability to offer service tailored to many customers. But each person expects a certain level of customer service. According to a recent survey of 25 top online retailers, 40 percent of them currently offer personalized features on their Web sites and 93 percent have plans to offer customized products within the next 12 months.

The early years of e-commerce saw Web marketers casting their nets broadly in an effort to land as many of the world's customers as possible. Today, the emphasis has turned toward one-to-one marketing as marketers recognize the key role customer satisfaction plays in creating loyal customers who are likely to make repeat purchases.

How does personalized marketing work online? Say you buy a book at Amazon.com, for example. The site will welcome you back for your next purchase by name. Using special software that analyzes your previous purchases, it will also suggest several other books you might like. Whereas music lovers used to sift through bins of CDs at large chain stores to find their music selections and typically had to buy several to get all the songs and artists they wanted, today they can log on to CDNow's Web site and create a customized CD. If you visit CDNow's new personalized site, you will find a virtual music store that stocks titles and types of music suited to your own taste. You can create a customized CD featuring only the tracks of artists you like. "Every single home page will be built [one-to-one]," claims CEO and founder Jason Olim. "It really is a music store for each of our 600,000 customers."[31]

Personalization is an online bonus for marketers. A recent survey of 25 highly customized e-commerce sites reported that the move to customization attracted 47 percent more new customers during the first year and increased revenues by 52 percent. Even though personalization software costs ranged between $50,000 and $3 million, these costs were recovered within 12 months from additional online sales.[32]

cdnow.com

Benefits of Online Consumer Marketing

Many of the same benefits achieved by business-to-business online marketers are also realized by marketers of consumer products who rely on the Web in their businesses. As Figure 4.10 indicates, marketers can use their Web sites to build strong relationships, reduce costs, increase efficiency, and achieve a global presence.

Relationship Building   Building relationships with consumers is crucial to the success of both offline and online marketing. As an earlier section explained, personalization is an important component of online relationship building. If a shopper visits a Web site that sells accessories and buys a dress and a purse, the next time she visits the site, she may be greeted with an attractive ad showing a belt or shoes that can be coordinated with her previous purchase. In this way, marketers create a one-on-one shopping experience that often leads to customer satisfaction and repeat purchases. Brand loyalty forms a part of many offline relationships that can be transferred to online sites. In fact, customers expect Web sites to emulate the traditional brick-and-mortar retail world. They like being greeted when they enter a store or a Web site.[33]

Internet marketers like CDNow use shopper input to design customized products and produce customer satisfaction.

FIGURE 4.10   Benefits of Business-to-Consumer Online Marketing

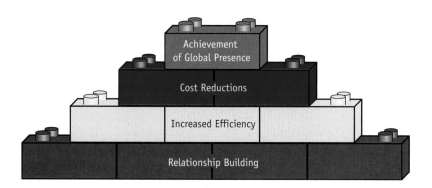

Small businesses, with even smaller budgets, can use the Internet to find customers in unexpected places and build relationships with them. Rick Brown, president of Newspaper Collectors Society of America, holds online auctions to sell historic papers to collectors. Recently, he sold a 19th century receipt from an old drugstore in Canton, Maine. Ordinarily, this would not be a big seller, but it proved highly desirable to residents of Canton who were establishing a local historical society. Another antiques dealer had difficulty at first selling a 1903 bicycle-parts catalog from France, but it sold quickly after French collectors discovered Brown's Web site.[34] Once these customers have received quick and efficient service from online dealers, they often return in search of other oddities and rare objects for which they might be looking.

Customer service is the key to building strong customer relationships, in both traditional and online marketing. Because the Web has the power to create two-way communications between companies and their customers instantly, many people get a good feeling about shopping online, believing that someone is on the other end with immediate answers to their questions and solutions to their problems. Unfortunately, that is often not the case. Many consumers report waiting hours and even days for a reply; others get no reply at all. In fact, less than 5 percent of retail Web sites offer immediate customer service assistance. Recently, some Web firms have established preformatted answers that appear to be personalized. A few Web upstarts, including Acuity, Icontact.com, E-Share Technologies, and LivePerson, now serve as links between the customer and Web businesses in providing customer service assistance. These services are being taken advantage of by such companies as CarFinance.com and igogolf.com, featured in this chapter's Marketing Strategy Success.[35]

Cost Reductions   Marketers have found that e-commerce can markedly reduce the costs of starting and operating a business. This, in turn, reduces marketing costs and leaves more dollars free for new marketing efforts. When a college professor wanted to create a business called Cyberstudy 101, she envisioned it as a traditional business. She wanted to create study aids for high school and college students, place them on computer disks, and distribute them throughout the United States. But one barrier had to be overcome: Going that route would mean preparing and shipping 217,000 packages to 58 universities each year—at a cost of $2.2 million. Instead, to eliminate the shipping costs, the professor started Cyberstudy 101 online, where customers can download study materials directly from the Web site. Most of her operating costs now result from marketing and managing the Web site—a modest $65,000 a year.[36]

Increased Efficiency   Cyberstudy 101 is a small business, but even for large corporations, sales made entirely through a Web site have a much greater profit margin than sales from traditional channels such as catalogs, retail outlets, or phone centers. However, even if the sale does not close online, marketers who educate their customers online ultimately save money because salespeople are then freed from spending their time answering routine questions.

International Golf Outlet

BACKGROUND David Schofman decided to take his golf equipment discount store online in 1995. With just $5,000 he jumped from being a tiny, local player to an international marketer when he launched International Golf Outlet. His Web domain name: igogolf.com.

CHALLENGE Rather than take on established catalogers like GolfSmith and Edwin Watts in the domestic market, Schofman focused on international customers who loved golf, were willing to spend hundreds of dollars on individual clubs, and were annoyed at having to wait for several months after clubs had been introduced in the United States before they could buy them in their local markets. His plan hinged on the fact that the domestic competitors were not online and that international customers would pay more for rapid order fulfillment.

STRATEGY The Web site igogolf.com went online as a multilingual site understood in the 140 countries in which igogolf.com sells its golf products. Web pages can be read in English, Chinese, French, German, Japanese, and Spanish. The promise to online buyers is speedy delivery. Right-time marketing allows customers in Japan or Spain to order a new Callaway driver as soon as it is introduced—not the traditional six-month delay of catalog orders.

continued on next page

cyberstudy101.com

AACBG.com

Minority business owners believe that the anonymity provided them by the Internet has allowed them to succeed on their own merits in a world where discrimination still exists. Betty A. Ford, former owner of Mailbox Haven, a Seattle package-delivery service, remembers how customers would approach her white, male employee assuming he was the boss. Today, as owner of City Boxers, an online retailer of hand-tailored boxer shorts, Ford enjoys the opportunity to compete without preconceptions of prejudice. Similarly, Roosevelt Gist, an African-American car dealership owner, often had white customers who would ask for another salesperson when he would approach them. Today, Gist is still in the car business—but in cyberspace. He runs AutoNetwork, an online forum for researching, buying, and selling cars. The site hosts 40,000 visitors a month, none of whom have had the chance to prejudge Gist on the basis of race.[37]

Online Marketing Is International Marketing

Another advantage to both online consumer and business-to-business marketers is the Internet's global reach, enabling inexpensive communication with consumers in faraway places. An American marketer who wants to contact consumers in Australia, for example, may find express mail or long distance telephone rates prohibitive, but the low cost and speed of such online marketing tools as fax machines and e-mail make global marketing a reality. Thirty percent of Australian households have computers, and the typical Australian spends more time accessing Web pages than anyone except Americans.

Culture can prove to be a barrier that hampers online marketing overseas, as Chapters 2 and 3 pointed out. Marketers, particularly those in Asia, face such barriers. Today, most e-commerce sites are in English—which automatically restricts access by Asian consumers. Although Asia contains a significant portion of the world's population and the number of Internet users there is increasing, the region still only accounts for 12 percent of Internet users worldwide. (The United States and Canada make up 62 percent.) Finally, many Asian consumers are less familiar and comfortable with catalog or telephone purchases than are U.S. and Canadian shoppers. Consequently, they are more reluctant to accept online shopping as a safe and secure way of purchasing products. Even Asian bankers worry about risks online. Most Hong Kong banks prohibit online banking and will not open accounts for online retailers unless they also have a traditional store.[38]

Even though an estimated 50 million Europeans are online, they rarely use the Internet for shopping. The European wired set is much more likely to value the Internet as a way to work from home, catch up on local politics, choose vacation destinations, and take courses. Even in Sweden and Denmark, where Net penetration is Europe's highest—at 20 percent of all households—e-commerce takes a back seat to such uses as e-mail and information services.[39]

As Chapter 3 explained, marketplaces and economies as well as competition are becoming increasingly global. E-commerce allows companies like Pacific Internet and Europe Online to create a regional framework for business transactions. Pacific Internet joined with Internet Initiative and Sumitomo (both based in Japan) and the Hong Kong Supernet, using Hong Kong and Singapore as hubs.[40] Figure 4.11 lists a sampling of international Web sites that call the world their domestic market. Marketers must not forget that although the Internet has no geographical boundaries, countries do. Issues of infrastructure, economy, and politics all come into play when marketers try to enter international markets. While astute marketers think globally, they should also remember that e-commerce is a local experience in each country.

Even though e-commerce is growing rapidly, global online commerce still lags behind the pace of cybermarketing in the United States. Web advertising revenues in Europe will not reach current U.S. levels for at least another five years. Currently, most European e-commerce revenue is generated from the sale of U.S. goods and services.[41] Some countries have infrastructure problems or other barriers. For instance, most telephone calls in Europe, including local calls, are metered and charged based on the length of the call, which makes it much more expensive for European consumers to spend time on the Internet. In addition, the waiting time to get online is much longer than it is in the United States.

Contemporary marketers recognize the tremendous potential of international Internet markets, and many are scrambling to be first online. Some experts think that the early bird marketers will grab the worm. "The timeline of [European Internet] savviness is closing faster than some may have expected," notes a business development manager for Lycos Bertelsmann GMBH. This U.S.–German joint venture media giant already operates Web sites in fourteen countries and eight languages. However, it still is not the biggest online company in Europe; America Online is. In fact, AOL created its own joint venture with Bertelsmann and now has almost 25 percent of the European online service market.[42]

Security and Privacy Issues of E-Commerce

FIGURE 4.11	Examples of Companies with Global Web Sites
www.starmedia.com	Spanish- and Portuguese-language StarMedia Network; launched in November 1998 in the United States.
www.uol.com.br	Universo Online, the largest portal serving Brazilians.
www.sina.com.tw	Sinanet.com, which targets the approximately 60 million Chinese living outside China and Taiwan.
www.khoj.com	IndiaWorld; English-language site that promotes itself as "all the India you want to know."

Security and privacy concerns are also critical factors in building a relationship online. Many consumers worry about giving their credit-card numbers to virtual businesses. A recent study by the U.S. Department of Commerce found that 40 percent of Americans are very concerned about the confidentiality of the Net, and another quarter of the population are somewhat concerned.[43] Marketers can calm these consumer fears by including information on their Web sites about what precautions have been taken to secure personal and financial information. In fact, businesses such as IBM, Hewlett-Packard, and GTE are now providing security services for their online customers.

Online art marketers, such as PaintingsDirect.com in the opening vignette, hire appraisers to verify the authenticity of a piece for their cybercustomers, and iEscrow guarantees payment between buyers and sellers. Antiques dealer Rick Brown learned the importance of online guarantees the hard way. After receiving a rare document he had purchased online for $400, he discovered that he had purchased a photocopy.[44] As the number of Internet users rises, the incidents of online fraud do as well. Last year, consumer complaints rose sixfold from 1,280 to 7,752. The Federal Trade Commission (FTC) has notified online auction houses that they need to take more precautions to protect consumers. Among the FTC's recommendations to reduce the incidence of online fraud are adding extra online security measures and handing out stiffer penalties for sellers and buyers who do not follow through on promises.[45]

Auction sites, such as eBay, are particularly complex and difficult to monitor for fraud due to the large number of vendors involved. Fortunately, most online marketers have fewer suppliers than online auctioneers, which gives them more control over their Web-site transactions. Web merchant losses due to fraudulent sales currently account for 1 percent of online revenues, making it important for marketers to do everything they can to maintain online security. By doing so, they create a relationship of trust with each customer.[46]

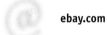

ebay.com

Online marketers are taking a variety of steps to address buyers' security and privacy concerns. Many online shopping malls now post explicit policies that make store owners responsible for the quality of the products they sell. Online book seller Amazon.com allows wary customers to order online with only the first eight digits of their credit-card number and then supply the rest of the number over a toll-free phone line.[47] Online auctioneer eBay provides $200 in free insurance per transaction to cover problems with less-expensive merchandise. Big-ticket items require the purchaser to set payments aside in escrow until they have had a chance to receive and examine the products.[48]

E-commerce marketers obtain a great deal of personal data on their customers more rapidly than was ever possible in offline transactions. Thanks to the instantaneous nature of online communication, they can quickly share information with an unprecedented number of people. According to the Federal Trade Commission, an investigation of 674 commercial Web sites showed that 92 percent of them collected personal information on visitors, but only 14 percent disclosed what they did with this data.[49]

Although marketers are increasingly targeting children as consumers, they must keep several things in mind if they are to build positive relationships with parents and future generations. As Chapter 2 explained, the Children's Online Privacy Protection Act requires all Web sites to obtain permission from parents, by e-mail or fax, before collecting personal data from children under the age of 13. However, many commercial sites surveyed have yet to comply.[50]

 **SOLVING AN ETHICAL CONTROVERSY**

Fighting Spam

It is apparent that some marketers distribute customers' e-mail addresses to other merchants, judging from the amount of *spam* (Internet junk mail) that chokes the Internet. America Online estimates that 1 million pieces of spam travel over its network every day. Sometimes spam is simply an annoying distraction. However, some mass e-mailings are so enormous they cause Internet service providers to crash. As consumers open their electronic mailboxes, they can be inundated by unwanted e-mail advertisements or solicitations that may actually cost them money to retrieve, depending on the type of payment program they have with their online service. Needless to say, many consumers are not happy about spam, so marketers might be wise to weigh the benefits against the dangers of losing current and future relationships with customers before sending out volumes of junk e-mail.

 Should the government regulate mass online mailings to prevent spam?

PRO

1. Obviously, online marketers are not regulating themselves, or this would not be an issue. Government regulation is required to stop invasion of personal privacy by corporate America.
2. No matter how many new software programs and e-mail filters are developed to seek and destroy spam before it reaches a consumer's PC, companies will find ways to break through, unless they are threatened with some type of penalty resulting from government regulation.

Con

1. Government regulation is just another way of controlling people's lives. It is another step toward the big brother syndrome.
2. Government regulation will be obtrusive and ineffective, since many junk mailers go out of business and reappear a day later with different corporate names and different e-mail addresses.

Summary

Although government regulation has helped control other media, such as television, it is a much larger task to try and regulate the Internet. Its reach goes beyond one country's laws and regulations, and the amount of information it receives, stores, and sends is astronomical. It will be hard to distinguish spam from desirable e-mail for a mass audience. However, as Internet technologies continue to be developed, there lies hope in creating an environment where Internet users can individually select what they want to see on their PC screens and fax machines.

SOURCES: Ira Teinowitz, "Privacy Regulation Grows as Legislation Passes," *Advertising Age*, October 26, 1998, pp. S16, S30; David Doran, "Hit List: The Senate Cracks Down on Spam," *Entrepreneur*, September 1998, p. 24; and William Baldwin, "Spam Killers," *Forbes*, September 21, 1998, pp. 254–255.

The Direct Marketing Association disagrees with the new legislation, asserting that parents prefer education over legislation. Often, children do not even know that data about them is being collected. Games, contests, and free merchandise offers coax children into volunteering information about themselves and their families. It makes sense for marketers to act in good faith and comply with the new regulation because doing so will build trust with adult consumers as well as youngsters in the long run. However, a recent FTC survey of 1,400 Web sites found only 2 percent provided full privacy policies.[51]

RECIPROCAL EFFECTS OF MARKETING AND THE INTERNET

In industry after industry, the Internet's impact on marketing has been revolutionary. However, marketing has also played a major role in how effective an organization becomes once it goes online. This section examines issues that have evolved out of the interactions of traditional marketing efforts and the Internet.

The Internet's Impact on Marketing

The impact of the Internet on marketing is easily observed in the growth rate of e-commerce sites—some 25,000 per month. Even more mind-boggling is that by 2005, total revenues will hit $1 trillion.[52] With numbers like these, there is little doubt that e-commerce is an unstoppable force that requires innovative marketing plans and strategies. For those who still are not convinced that change is good, here are some benefits of e-commerce that marketers have already seen. An effective Web site builds customer loyalty, saves organizations and customers money, quickens the sales process, lowers costs, and boosts profits.

Traditional marketing channels have been among the first to experience changes brought about through e-commerce. Some customers and marketers readily accept this; others do not. Online marketing bypasses many traditional outlets or substitutes more efficient intermediaries. For example, in the travel industry, the agents are the intermediaries. These travel agents typically collect a commission of about 8 percent on tickets, tours, and other services they sell to travelers. Today, however, online services like Microsoft's Expedia bypass travel agents by selling tickets directly to consumers. Customers get low prices, Expedia collects $10 from every ticket sold, and airlines see tremendous savings.[53] Travel agents and marketers must engage in e-commerce to survive in this extremely competitive industry.

expedia.com

Distributors are also being forced to adjust their strategies to include online transactions. Traditionally, the medical products unit of Hewlett-Packard (HP), which generates sales of over $1 billion annually, has employed an international sales staff and used dozens of distributors worldwide. But HP's hospital customers now want the convenience of one-stop, online shopping that allows equipment to be ordered directly from the company. HP marketers, recognizing they had to satisfy customers without alienating distributors and laying off salespeople, established a Web presence for online ordering. While HP still relies on traditional marketing methods, marketers are carefully integrating e-commerce into plans and strategies to accomplish objectives. For example, prices are the same online and offline, and sales representatives still receive commissions on their accounts, whether the order is placed online or offline.[54]

corporate.com

Recently, news headlines have offered a glimpse of what the future will hold for e-commerce. Certainly, the roles of intermediaries in marketing channels have already been drastically altered, but, contrary to what many fear, the Internet does not mean the death of traditional sales activities or the end to bricks-and-mortar retailing. Instead, the Internet should be viewed as the most recent stage in the evolution of marketing, one that enhances every aspect of contemporary business. E-commerce changes the marketing environment by creating entirely new companies and imaginative goods and services and by giving birth to more efficient and effective marketing techniques.

The Company Corp. ad shown in Figure 4.12 recognizes that no two companies will adapt to the e-commerce environment in the same way. Many organizations are outsourcing e-commerce activities to firms such as The Company Corp. for services such as domain name registration, Web site creation, and credit-card processing services. Hewlett-Packard, for example, uses its Internet capabilities somewhat differently than Dell Computer. Similar to HP, Dell offers customers the option of ordering products online through its Premiere Page Web sites. However, Dell customizes each customer's page to match previous ordering practices. Where once it took an hour to complete the paperwork to place one order for a computer, today it takes only four minutes. Also like HP, the online system has not replaced Dell representatives. Instead, it reduces their paperwork and frees them to concentrate on interacting with customers, providing superior service, and finding new business. In fact, Dell has found the online system to be a big selling point in attracting new customers.[55]

Traditional marketers realize the importance of technology in remaining competitive in an e-commerce world, but they also realize the need to keep customers coming into their offline retailing establishments. "In order to get someone to come into the store, retailers really need to create a compelling environment; a combination of product, value, and experience," notes one marketing consultant. Thus, marketers are finding ways to turn shopping into a pleasurable experience rather than a dreaded task. Barnes & Noble went online a few years back, but it still continues

FIGURE 4.12 | The Company Corporation: Providing Services for E-Commerce

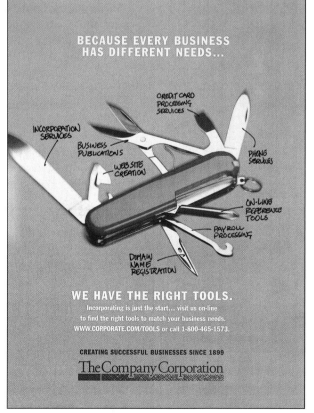

operating individual book stores in malls and shopping centers. To create an environment that surpasses anything found online or at competing book stores, marketers are creating in-store recreational activities that enhance the customer's shopping experience. For instance, shoppers who visit the stores can enjoy a lecture series, children's areas where stories are read and games are played, and attractive coffee shops and cafes.

Marketers are also finding new ways to combine tradition with technology to enhance their brick-and-mortar operations. Hollywood Entertainment, a competitor to Blockbuster Entertainment, has caught the first wave of Net surfers by acquiring online retailer Reel.com. Hollywood uses this Web site to sell as well as to draw customers into its traditional stores. Customers can review movies in stock at local outlets, reserve tapes, and then pick them up. Inside the stores, computer terminals allow customers to log on to Reel.com's database to help them select movies. Meanwhile, Blockbuster may turn out to be the last on the block to adopt e-commerce. Blockbuster marketers still focus on the company's lucrative rental business, which generally has a higher profit margin than video sales. Currently, Blockbuster's efforts at drawing customers into its stores have relied on e-mail messages when new movies are released on video.[56]

Pricing strategies have also been affected by e-commerce. Because the Web provides quick and easy access to comparative information, prices have become more standardized. Traditionally, a price often depended on where it was purchased; a luxury boutique might charge $1,000 for the same dress that a department store might sell for $500, and a catalog retailer might be even lower, say $300. With e-commerce, these price variations are likely to cost the same no matter where it is purchased due to the availability of pricing information over the Internet. This is similar to the price of a company's stock, which is the same worldwide because that information is accessible to stock traders using online global networks. Scott Blum, founder and CEO of online computer store Buy.com, understands the pressures of e-commerce all too well. Each day, Buy.com's 300,000 item inventory is price checked to ensure customers are quoted the lowest price on the market.[57] Chapters 18 and 19 discuss online pricing tools and strategies in further detail.

Marketing's Impact on the Internet

While most of the discussions on e-commerce focus on the impact the Internet has on marketing, this section is devoted to the effect marketing has on the Internet. A few years ago, marketers promoted the Internet as a new product, using many of the traditional channels to do their advertising. Ads placed in newspapers across the nation and in magazines from *Rolling Stone* to *Fortune* to *Family Circle* brought the Internet concept into American households and businesses. Free disks with necessary software to connect to the Net were sent in direct mailings from companies including America Online and Microsoft. Other disks provided samples of innovative software packages with accounting, inventory, and personal finance applications. Some of the top-rated television commercials were created by marketers of computer software companies and Internet service providers.

All of these traditional marketing techniques proved highly effective in stimulating demand for Internet access. Marketers still rely on basic marketing principles to develop online plans and strategies for interactive marketing channels. (The various alternative online marketing channels are discussed in depth in a later section of this chapter.) Marketers are adapting their advertising messages to these new channels through such tools as Internet links and banner ads. Chapters 15, 16, and 17 will further describe integrated marketing communications, advertising, personal selling, and other promotional efforts that have been adapted to the Web.

WHO ARE THE ONLINE BUYERS AND SELLERS?

4

Identify the most frequent Internet buyers and sellers and the goods and services marketed most often on the Internet.

As the growth of e-commerce continues to exceed even the most optimistic forecasts, it becomes easier to use and much broader in its appeal to online shoppers. Over the past year, online spending grew by almost 200 percent. Leading the charge were two primary groups of consumers:

people who had never bought online before and consumers over the age of 50. These shoppers spent an average of over $600 each, compared with only $97 the previous year. Figure 4.13 indicates this rapid growth in consumer spending on the Internet.

Another indication of the growth of e-commerce (i.e., an increase in online buyers and sellers) is the number of new small businesses with Web sites. Today, over 2 million small businesses are online, four times as many as in 1997. One recent report reveals that about 20 percent of small businesses with 10 or fewer employees now have Web sites. As one small business expert warns, "If you own a small company and you're not online or planning to be online [in the near future], you're heading toward obsolescence and you'll ultimately go out of business."[58] Time-strapped shoppers are searching the Web for 24/7 online sellers of goods and services they want and need.

FIGURE 4.13   Growth in Consumer Online Spending*

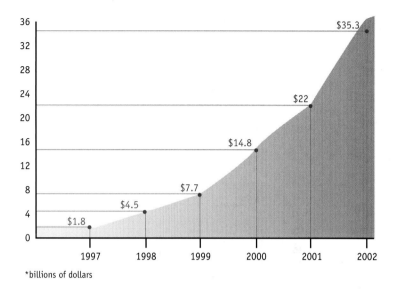

*billions of dollars

Online Buyers

A recent study by the U.S. Department of Commerce sheds considerable light on the demographics of Internet users—the target market for e-commerce marketers. The heaviest Internet users, at 62 percent, make $75,000 or more a year and live in urban areas; conversely, low-income, rural dwellers, at least 10 percent of whom do not even have telephones, account for only 3 percent of Internet users. On the other hand, the top 5 states for cumulative use are Alaska (44 percent), New Hampshire and Washington (both at 37 percent), Utah (36 percent) and Colorado (35 percent). Americans of Asian and Pacific Island origin are the racial group most likely to use the Internet. In fact, they are twice as likely as African-Americans and Hispanics to own PCs and three times more likely to be online. About 75 percent of all employed people use the Internet at work, and more than 87 percent of college graduates do so. Over half of all unemployed people now go online to send out résumés and look for jobs.[59]

ZDNet, a conglomerate of diverse businesses from cable TV stations to Web publications to consulting services, offers marketers a way to target messages based on geography and demographics. The online research site has always offered the ability to target ads based on editorial content, but now targeted segments can be defined by state, zip code, country, designated market area, or company type and size. ZDNet draws on a database of 2.5 million registered users to create another option for marketers to "ensure that they're reaching the prospects that are most important to them," says ZDNet's vice president of sales and marketing, Barry Briggs.[60]

zdnet.com

Marketers must continually be aware of the ways in which e-commerce is actually changing customers. For one thing, online marketing reaches people who do not normally watch television or read magazines. For another, online marketing is educating consumers in ways that traditional marketing cannot—by offering more information (often personalized) more rapidly than a retail salesperson, product brochure, or 30-second television commercial. Customers are more knowledgeable—and sometimes more demanding—than they used to be. Once consumers learn about wines at Virtual Vineyards' Web site, they may be disappointed with their wine-shopping experience in a supermarket.

Online Sellers

Realizing that their customers would have little or no opportunity to rely on many of the sense modes—smelling the freshness of direct-from-the-oven rolls, touching the soft fabric of a new sweater, or squeezing the fruit to assess its ripeness—early online sellers focused on offering

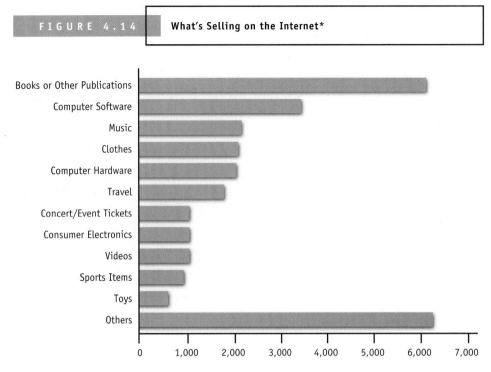

What's Selling on the Internet*

*number of household transactions by product type

ibeauty.com

streamline.com

products that consumers were familiar with and tended to buy frequently, such as books and music, computer hardware and software, and travel and concert tickets. Figure 4.14 shows the most popular goods and services sold on the Internet.

Until recently, Web sellers tried to avoid unique items that consumers preferred to experience personally. It was widely believed that buyers would be reluctant to purchase items like fresh food, fragrances, and many services online because they could not touch, smell, try on, or sample the product before buying it. But a quick glance at the thousands of Web offerings in categories ranging from prescription drugs and toys to home delivery of groceries and dry cleaning reveals a mind-boggling array of diverse products that are now offered to cybershoppers.

For example, many people would say selling fragrances online is almost impossible. But not Eli Katz, the CEO of Fragrance Counter. Katz came up with the idea to sell perfume online after learning that 70 percent of perfume sales represent repeat business—people already loyal to a particular fragrance. Many of the remaining 30 percent actually become familiar with various fragrances outside stores, such as through friends, scented strips in magazines, and gifts they have received. The company first began selling fragrances through America Online in 1995, when e-commerce was still a novelty. Two years later, Fragrance Counter launched its own site on the Web. The first day Katz opened his electronic store with perfumes, he received 26 orders; the second day, 65; and on the third day, 76. Since then, Fragrance Counter has grown to become the world's most successful online fragrance retailer.[61]

Until the early part of the 20th century, many urban dwellers had many goods and services, such as milk, ice, coal for fuel, and even doctors' care, delivered to their doors. However, as automobiles and supermarkets began to focus on providing mass market goods, personalized goods and services were not cost effective or time efficient. Now, however, the Internet is enabling companies to return to mass customization and personalization. And, having traveled full-circle, groceries are now being ordered online and once again being delivered door-to-door. Across the United States, more and more households—double income, technologically savvy, and time pressed—are buying groceries over the Internet. ShopLink, HomeGrocer, Streamline, Peapod, and Whole Foods Market are a few of the growing number of virtual grocery delivery services on the Web today. Timothy DeMello, founder and CEO of Streamline, believes that his company will be successful because of the value people place on their free time. The last place they want to spend that time is in a supermarket, particularly if they have children. Streamline creates extra value for its customers by offering unattended delivery to a special refrigerator-shelf installed at no extra charge in each customers' garage. While some online groceries strive to make three deliveries per hour, Streamline maps its routes for efficiency and claims it can make 10 deliveries an hour, thus increasing the speed with which customers receive their orders. ShopLink, on the other hand, delivers groceries in yellow plastic bins for dry goods and green "chill" bins for meat, fruit, vegetables, milk, and other perishable foods. The base cost for online grocery services ranges from $10 to $30, although many firms offer additional services including dry cleaning, film processing, video rental, shoe repair, and stamps. Industry experts predict that online groceries will generate $11 billion in sales by 2003.[62]

INTERACTIVE ONLINE MARKETING CHANNELS

Both manufacturers and marketing intermediaries frequently turn to online channels to market their goods and services. Want Gateway to build a PC that meets all your computing needs? Click www.Gateway.com. Need toys for all those nieces and nephews? Click www.eToys.com. Need money to pay for all those toys? Click www.e-loan.com. Looking for a better textbook price than the campus bookstore offers? Click www.Varsity.com.

Each of these marketers—and thousands more like them—has turned to online marketing as a faster, less expensive, more efficient alternative to the traditional approach of setting up retail stores and waiting for customers to drop by. As Figure 4.15 shows, businesses deciding to market their goods and services online do so through one or a combination of three primary online alternatives: company Web sites, online advertisements on other sites, and online communities. Other interactive marketing links include Web kiosks, smart cards, and virtual coupons and samples.

FIGURE 4.15	Online Marketing Channels

Company Web Sites	**Online Communities**
- corporate Web sites	- online forums
- marketing Web sites	- newsgroups
- virtual storefronts	- electronic
- cybermalls	bulletin boards

Advertisements on Other Web Sites	**Other Interactive Marketing Links**
- banner ads	- interactive kiosks
- pop-up windows	- smart cards
	- virtual coupons
	and samples

5

Identify the primary online marketing channels.

Company Web Sites

Most online marketers have their own Web sites that offer general information, electronic shopping, and promotions such as games and contests. Click in the firm's Internet address (typically beginning with *http://www.* and ending with *.com* for commercial sites), and the Web site's main or central page—its "home page"—will appear on your computer screen.

Two types of company Web sites exist. Many firms have established **corporate Web sites** designed to increase their visibility, promote their goods and services, and provide information for potential investors, employees, and the general public. Rather than selling the firm's products directly, these sites attempt to build customer goodwill and assist channel members in their marketing efforts. For example, Claritin, a prescription drug for allergies, sponsors an OnHealth Network site. Visitors to the site are offered customized information about allergies and remedies.[63]

Although **marketing Web sites** often include information about company history, its products, locations, and financial information, their goal is to increase the likelihood of purchases by site visitors. The marketing Web site tries to engage consumers in interactions that will move them closer to a demonstration, trial visit, purchase, or other marketing outcome. Some marketing Web sites—such as Sony Online Entertainment—are quite complex. The Sony Web site offers games, film content distributed by Sony Pictures, and links to sites sponsored by other advertisers such as AT&T, IBM, and Citigroup. A popular component of the Sony site is College Jeopardy! Online, an annual 10-week tournament with about 100,000 registered players.[64]

 **sony.com**

Electronic Storefronts and Cybermalls

Click www.jcpenney.com and you are transported on a virtual visit to the mall. This **electronic storefront** is just what its name implies—an online store where customers can view and order merchandise much like window shopping at brick-and-mortar retail establishments. The JCPenney online shopper is offered links to coupons, the JCP Grandparents club, savings for frequent customers, gift registry, thousands of

MARKETING	DICTIONARY

corporate Web site Web site that seeks to build customer goodwill and supplement other sales channels rather than to sell goods and services.

marketing Web site Web site designed to engage consumers in an interaction that increases their desire to make a purchase.

electronic storefront Online store where customers can view and order merchandise much like window shopping at traditional retail establishments.

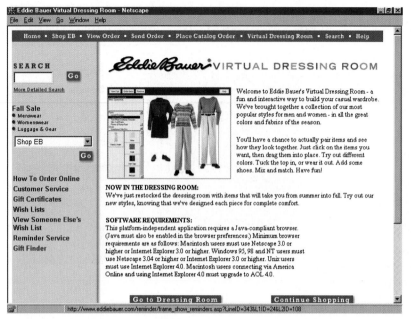

Consumers can mix and match outfits on cyber-mannequins included on the Eddie Bauer Web site.

inventory items, and Secure Shopping Online, an electronic order form.

Whether a supplement to existing bricks-and-mortar retail outlets or as a virtual replacement, electronic storefronts can offer marketers a number of advantages. These include the ability to expand operations in different cities, states, or countries without the major capital investments typically required for such growth. In addition, virtual stores provide great flexibility since the business is open 24 hours a day and time-zone barriers are removed. Inventory locations can be centralized and orders can be filled from them. In addition, the image of the electronic storefront is controlled by the quality, creativity, and originality of the Web site and the ability of the Web marketers to offer customer satisfaction. As the success of eToys and Amazon.com in competing with industry giants Toys "Я" Us and Barnes & Noble demonstrates, offline market dominance does not guarantee industry leadership in cyberspace.

Web stores such as Godiva chocolates and Virtual Vineyards can operate as stand-alone operations. However, a common approach is for them to be grouped into **cybermalls** that link as many as 400 participating online retailers. Like concrete shopping malls, cybermalls typically feature a popular national retailer with high customer traffic as an anchor tenant. Other stores included in the mall are selected to produce a good match of merchandise offerings for the shopper. The MCI Marketplace cybermall hosts stores such as Borders Books and Music, Day-Timers, Hammacher Schlemmer, L'Eggs, The Mac Zone, Nordstrom, and PC Zone. The operators of cybermalls charge each individual storefront operator a fee—either a flat monthly charge or a sliding scale depending on the number of visits to the storefront.

Advertisements on Other Web Sites

Rather than relying completely on their Web sites to attract buyers, online marketers frequently expand their reach in the marketplace by placing ads on sites where their prospective customers are likely to visit. *Banner ads*, the most common form of Internet advertising, are typically small, strip messages placed in high-visibility areas of frequently visited Web sites. Pop-up windows may be added to the banner for variety as an attention grabber, and the ad may include a click-on question to encourage surfers to interact with the advertiser. A recent banner by the online game show Uproar presented readers with the question, "Where does Homer Simpson work?" It then offered four choices to select from: a bar, a bank, a nuclear plant, or a sewer. Over 2.5 million persons viewed this ad during a single week.

Many online marketers advocate using a variety of online and offline advertising combined with other forms of interactive promotion for better results. To familiarize Web shoppers with the virtual dressing room included on its award-winning e-commerce site, apparel marketer Eddie Bauer gives away virtual reality software that lets shoppers "click and drag" items across the screen to assemble a complete outfit. In addition to traditional print and broadcast advertising, the firm's marketers use banners and links with other sites to target its customer base of baby boomers and young adults.[65]

Online Communities

In addition to such direct channels as marketing goods and services through a firm's Web site, many firms are turning to Internet forums, newsgroups, electronic bulletin boards, and Web communities that appeal to people who share common interests. Members congregate online and exchange views and information on topics of interest. These communities may be organized for commercial or noncommercial purposes.

Online communities can take several forms, but all offer specific advantages to members and marketers alike. **Online forums**, for example, are Internet discussion groups located on commercial online services. Users log on, type in a password, and participate by sending comments and questions or receiving information from other forum members. Forums may operate as "chat rooms," as libraries for storing input, or even as a form of classified ad directory. Marketers often use forums to ask questions and exchange information with customers. Adobe, which designs such software as Pagemaker, Photoshop, and Illustrator, operates a "user-to-user" forum on its Web site as a support community for its customers. Customers who share common personal and professional interests can congregate, exchange industry news and practical product tips, share ideas, and—equally important—create publicity for Adobe products. [66]

Newsgroups are noncommercial Internet versions of forums. Here people post and read messages on specific topics. More than 22,000 newsgroups are on the Internet today, and their numbers continue to rise. **Electronic bulletin boards** are specialized online services that center on a specific topic or area of interest. For instance, white-water rafters might check online bulletin boards to find out about the latest equipment, new places to raft, or current rafting conditions on a particular waterway. While newsgroups resemble two-way conversations, electronic bulletin boards are more like announcements.

The five largest online communities are GeoCities, Angelfire, Tripod, Zoom, and FortuneCity. The largest community, GeoCities, is inhabited by more than 700,000 individuals, each of whom receives a free home page and e-mail account upon signing up. In making purchase decisions, members rely less on advertisements and more on fellow members who can discuss their experiences in buying and using specific goods and services. They also solidify attitudes of community members, such as a product's likely impact on the environment. And community members return to the site again and again. In a typical month, nearly 15 million people will log on.

Some Web communities are created and maintained with business in mind. One community called CyberSites surveys its members before exposing them to ads, negotiates group discounts for products marketed on-site, and allows each member to participate in some offerings. Figure 4.16 shows how CyberSites' customers and companies can benefit from one another in a community where they can also be partners.[67]

As the CyberSites' community demonstrates, online communities are not limited to consumers. They also facilitate business-to-business marketing. For instance, they help small businesses develop relationships that transcend the former limits of their real-world, local communities. Using the Internet to build communities helps companies find other organizations to benchmark against, including suppliers, distributors, and competitors that may be interested in forming an alliance. Business owners who want to expand internationally frequently seek advice from other members in their online community.

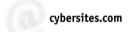

cybersites.com

6

Explain how marketers use Web kiosks, smart cards, and virtual coupons and samples as part of their online marketing strategies.

Other Interactive Marketing Links

A variety of high-tech interactive tools are used by today's marketers to reach targeted segments of their markets. These buyerseller links include interactive kiosks, smart cards, and virtual coupons and samples. **Web kiosks** are freestanding computers, often located in retail showrooms or shopping centers. They are versatile, multimedia devices that deliver information on demand.

MARKETING   DICTIONARY

cybermalls Group of virtual stores planned, coordinated, and operated as a unit for online shoppers.

online forum Discussion groups located on commercial online services.

newsgroup Noncommercial Internet version of online forum that are limited to people posting and reading messages on a specified topic.

electronic bulletin board Specialized online service that provides information on a specific topic or area of interest.

Web kiosk Small, free-standing structure with one or more sides that provides consumers with Internet connections to a firm and its goods and services.

FIGURE 4.16   How CyberSites Transforms Members into Marketers

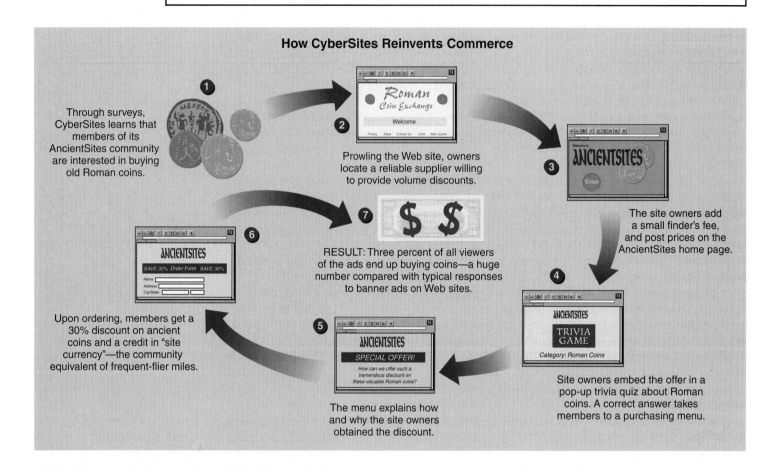

How CyberSites Reinvents Commerce

1 Through surveys, CyberSites learns that members of its AncientSites community are interested in buying old Roman coins.

2 Prowling the Web site, owners locate a reliable supplier willing to provide volume discounts.

3 The site owners add a small finder's fee, and post prices on the AncientSites home page.

4 Site owners embed the offer in a pop-up trivia quiz about Roman coins. A correct answer takes members to a purchasing menu.

5 The menu explains how and why the site owners obtained the discount.

6 Upon ordering, members get a 30% discount on ancient coins and a credit in "site currency"—the community equivalent of frequent-flier miles.

7 RESULT: Three percent of all viewers of the ads end up buying coins—a huge number compared with typical responses to banner ads on Web sites.

Kmart shoppers can go online with a Kmart Solutions Web kiosk located inside the store to buy nonstocked items, such as Omaha Steaks.

Shoppers can stop by a kiosk and get discount coupons or product information for stores located in the mall. Web kiosks are a marriage of traditional kiosks and Internet connections. Officially dubbed "in-store, Web-assisted selling," the goal of these kiosks is to keep customers from leaving empty-handed and provide new levels of selection, especially for customers who may not otherwise have Internet access.

Shoppers at many Kmart stores have a vastly expanded assortment of items available for purchase through the chain's Kmart Solutions kiosks. These Web kiosks, located at service desks and at electronics and sporting-goods counters in 625 Kmart stores, allow customers to buy items and brands that the retailer does not ordinarily stock. Among the approximately 2,000 kiosk items are Callaway golf clubs, Coleman camp tents, and Indian River fruit baskets. "We carry cameras in our stores, for example, but it may not be an $800 digital camera, which would be available through Kmart Solutions," says a Kmart spokesperson.[68]

Another e-commerce innovation involves **smart cards**—plastic cards similar to credit cards that are embedded with computer chips that store personal and financial information. To buy an item, the card is inserted into a card scanner or reader, which electronically debits the purchase amount. The card can be "reloaded" periodically with cash from a checking or savings account. Smart cards were the first step toward **electronic currency**—a system of exchange in which a consumer can set up accounts at Web sites and place credits based on a monetary amount in those accounts. Although smart cards have been popular for years in Europe and Asia, where they are commonly used to store medical information and security clearances, they have been slower to catch on in the United States, as the Marketing Strategy Failure explains.

International examples, however, provide numerous success stories on the use of smart cards. Take petroleum giant Shell Oil, for example. Its Shell Smart card allows customers to accumulate and redeem points through more than 25 participants. The cards are purely storage and tracking cards, not payment cards. Rewards include free movie tickets, British Airways frequent flyer points, and mail-order gifts ranging from watches to television sets. Points can also be transferred to charities. Participating companies now include Avis Rent-a-Car, British Gas, Virgin Net, and UCI cinemas. Shell marketers get access to an exclusive database of more than 4 million consumers, while Shell customers get rewards.[69]

Recently, many traditional direct marketing companies are going online with *virtual coupon* and *online sample* offerings. Customers can find virtual coupons on their PCs by such criteria as business name, location, and keyword and can download them on a home computer. Online consumers can also register to have coupons e-mailed directly to them. Val-Pak Direct Marketing Systems, a longtime leader in the paper coupon industry, now offers the online equivalent at its Web site, Val-Pak Coupons Online.[70]

Other Web sites offer free product samples. Members of FreeSampleClub.com complete interactive profiles that include information such as age, family data, and pet ownership. Based on the profiles, the system creates a personal sample menu from merchants who are targeting that profile. Members click on their choices and receive the products within a week. In its first three months, FreeSampleClub.com had 15,000 visits from consumers and processed 10,000 requests for samples.[71]

What's on *your* NextCard?

Get it online. Use it anywhere. NextCard, the First True Internet Visa, lets you personalize by picture. Customize by feature. And shop online with absolutely no risk.

nextcard.com

NextCard, an Internet-only credit-card company, posts about 70 million ad banners each day across thousands of Web sites and grants credit to some 10,000 applicants each day.

CREATING AN EFFECTIVE WEB PRESENCE

One of the preliminary tasks of starting a business or entering a new market is performing market research. Marketers evaluate every proposed e-commerce venture to ensure it benefits the firm by cutting costs, improving customer satisfaction, and increasing revenues. To have a successful e-commerce business,

7

Describe how an effective Web site can enhance customer relationships.

MARKETING DICTIONARY

smart card Multipurpose card embedded with computer chips that store personal and financial information, such as credit-card data, health records, and driver's license number.

electronic currency System of exchange in which consumers can set up accounts at Web sites and place credits in those accounts based on a monetary amount.

MARKETING
STRATEGY

vans.com

cdkayak.com

it is also essential that marketing activities remain customer-oriented. Other areas that must be assessed include the competitive environment and the costs of updating the firm's technological infrastructure. An effective Internet strategy should create sustainable shareholder value by increasing profits, accelerating growth, reducing time-to-market for goods and services, improving customer service, and improving the public perception of the organization.

Building an Effective Web Site

To be effective, a firm's strategies must focus on building relationships through the use of company Web sites. Because of the high costs associated with going online, marketers must get the highest possible return on their Web site investments. Building an effective Web site follows three primary steps: establish a mission for the company's site, identify the purpose of the site, and satisfy customer needs and wants through a clear site design.

The first step is to establish a mission for the site. A *site mission* involves the creation of a statement that explains the organization's overall goals. Without a mission to guide decision makers, the technology will be aimless. Dell Computer describes its mission in three clicks: to make it easier for customers to do business with them, to reduce the cost of business for Dell and its customers, and to enhance Dell's relationship with its customers.[72]

Next, marketers must identify the purpose of the site. Is it primarily to provide information or entertainment, or is it intended solely to connect buyers and sellers? Priceline.com, which auctions such things as cars and airline tickets, posts the phrase, "Name your price," prominently on the first page of its site. This lets visitors know exactly what they are supposed to do. In addition, marketers should educate themselves—not so much about the details of technology but about how Web sites enhance customer communications and how those communications can benefit the company.

Marketers should also be clear about how the purpose of the site fits in with the company's overall marketing strategy. For example, shoe manufacturer Vans recently established a Web site to supplement its sales by carrying merchandise not offered in traditional stores. In the past, Vans let shoppers order customized shoes in their school colors. Retailers have discontinued this practice, but Vans has revived it on the Web, thus boosting its brand and offering customers a distinctive service.[73]

Finally, identifying customer needs and wants is critical to marketers both online and offline. However, online marketers must consider how their strategies will need to be adjusted to continue satisfying customers through online transactions. Well-designed Web sites are straightforward, provide security and privacy, and, most important, are easy to navigate. Successful sites follow accepted Internet conventions and familiar screen layouts so customers will not get lost on the site. Figure 4.17 is an example of a clear, attractive Web site that is easy for kayakers (and nonkayakers) to paddle through. Current Designs is not a big company, so it does not have a large marketing budget. The site, however, is informative, friendly, and easy to use.

Web surfers look at online text briefly and do not usually read it in detail. They skim or scan the material, looking for visual cues to stop them. As for visual cues, surprisingly, one researcher has found that black-and-white ads get the best response. Perhaps this is because in the United States, black is perceived as sophisticated. But customers from around the world may have very different feelings about certain colors, so experts recommend a color with positive connotations globally.[74] Many organizations outsource their Internet services entirely, from building Web sites to designing intranets and extranets.

Managing a Web Site

Once a site is up and running, it has to be managed. Marketers must update the site frequently, flagging new merchandise and services and eliminating items that did not sell well and references to past events. Some marketers recommend avoiding dates on site pages, so the site always appears to be current. Web site management involves constant attention not only to content but to technical presentation as well. Frequent software updates may be necessary to take advantage of new technologies that permit increasing levels of customer interaction. Marketers should keep track of costs associated with Web sites. Because the Web is still in its infancy, profits have been slow in coming. When costs surpass sales revenues, as they did for 1-800-Flowers in its first five years online, marketers need to reevaluate whether the site is meeting expected goals or whether changes need to be implemented to boost the site's effectiveness.

Jeffrey Bezos, founder and CEO of Amazon.com, the world's largest online bookseller, manages a wildly successful Web site that generates an average of $260 million in annual book sales. But it is still operating in the red. Bezos understands that when the profits do come, they will be huge. Amazon.com now offers its customers access to over 3 million titles—15 times more than any bookstore on earth—along with technology that personalizes customer relationships. The online giant is now expanding its product line to include CD and video sales, toys, gifts, and art.

Amazon was the first commercial site to use software technology that could analyze a customer's purchases and suggest other related items—a terrific way of targeting a market. In order to keep up with future technology needs, Amazon has recently acquired Junglee Corp., a developer of comparison-shopping technologies, and PlanetAll, a computerized registry of customer information from addresses to birthdays. Amazon marketers use this personalized marketing tool to send e-mail reminders to customers.[75]

FIGURE 4.17   Kayakers' Web Site Is Effective

Dedicated to designing and building exceptional touring kayaks and accessories. Current Designs is an industry leader in quality, value, innovation and service.

What's new for '99
NEW 1999 kayak catalogue now available!
Choosing the right kayak

{Products} {Features} {Dealers} {About Current Designs} {Resources} {Development}

Head Office:	U.S.A.:	Japan:
Current Designs,	We-No-Nah,	A&F Corporation,
10124 McDonald Park Rd.,	P.O. Box 247,	1-1-9 Okubo,
Sidney, B.C.	Winona, Mn.,	Shinjuko-Ku,
Canada V8L 3X9	USA 55987	Tokyo, Japan
Ph: (250) 655-1822	Ph: (507) 454-5430	Ph: 81-03-3209-7575

Measuring Effectiveness of Online Marketing

Measuring the effectiveness of a Web site is an elusive task in these early days of the Internet. However, some generalizations have already been made concerning e-commerce that allow marketers to refine their strategies to improve effectiveness. For instance, the online learn-shop-buy cycle favors products that are planned purchases as opposed to impulse buys. That is why cars, books, and customized music marketers have been so successful. But marketers are warned not to gauge success by looking only at sales figures. Says one expert, "The benefits of communication, information, entertainment, and the creation of community are enormously important but harder than sales to quantify."[76]

More than a decade since the Internet went commercial, measuring online effectiveness still presents major challenges for marketers. Part of the reason is due to the huge number of Internet users who go online while they are at work. Understandably, companies do not want researchers monitoring their internal operations. As Richard LeFurgy, head of the Internet Advertising Bureau, points out, "What company wants to acknowledge that most of its employees surf the Internet for things not related to their work?"

Measurement tools and techniques for e-commerce are being developed to utilize the burgeoning amount of information being poured into data banks. Some of the first steps online marketers took to measure the effectiveness of their Web efforts included counting *hits* and *page views*. Many sites today contain monitors that record the number of visits to the site. These may be recorded as **hits**—the number of times a visitor goes to a home page—or **page views**—the number of times a page is actually accessed by each visitor. Not surprisingly, home pages get more page views than the pages within a site. Page views give marketers a more

8

Explain how marketers measure the effectiveness of their online marketing efforts.

Amazon.com

accurate assessment of how often the site is actually visited, along with which pages seem to be most popular.[77]

Recently, Nielsen Media Research began monitoring Internet users. The famed New York-based, television ratings company provides data used in setting advertising prices and often has the power to make or break a network TV program. Working with California-based NetRatings, Nielsen is tracking consumer behavior on Web sites and selling that research to clients. It has equipped 9,000 consumers with software that tracks their every move on the Internet—the sites they visit, the ads they look at, and what they do when they see those ads. Another New York-based firm, Media Metrix, has been measuring Internet audiences since 1996. Media Metrix is considered the most reliable Internet researcher, but it still has a rather high margin of error among its sample of 40,000 Internet users.[78]

Several guiding principles for measuring Web effectiveness have been offered by Bob Wehling, vice president of advertising for Procter & Gamble:

- Audience measurement of interactive media should be directly comparable to the measures used for other media. This is fundamental to the reliability of audience research.

- Audience measurements should be taken by objective third-party research suppliers and not by the medium being measured. What little measurement there is today rarely follows this principle.

- Interactive media research standards must be set by a broad representation of the advertising industry.[79]

STRATEGIC IMPLICATIONS OF E-COMMERCE

The future is bright for marketers who take advantage of the tremendous potential of e-commerce. Online channels that seem cutting-edge today will be eclipsed within the next decade by integrated computer-based media. E-commerce will first and foremost empower consumers. Business writers Gary Hamel and Jeff Sampler present the following bird's-eye view of a rising sun in cyberspace—e-commerce:

> Think about this. Already 16 percent of car buyers shop online before showing up at a dealership, and they aren't comparing paint jobs—they're arming themselves with information on dealer costs. So forget all the patronizing nonsense about being market-led or customer-focused. The new reality is consumer control, and it's as ominous as it sounds if you're not prepared for this radically different future. Indeed, the Internet represents the ultimate triumph of consumerism. . . .
>
> . . . Main Street in the 1950s, malls in the 1970s, superstores in the 1990s—since World War II we've seen a fundamental shift in the retailing paradigm with each new generation, and now we're on the verge of another revolution. It's worth noting that each time the business model changed, a new group of leaders emerged. Woolworth's never really escaped Main Street. Sears, for the most part, remains stuck in the mall. Again and again, incumbents missed the early warning signs because they were easy to ignore. Who was really paying attention when Sam and James "Bud" Walton opened their first Wal-Mart in 1962? Who really understood the impact that superstores and category killers would ultimately have on the supply chain? Are you convinced that you really understand the potential impact of the Web?[80]

Many experts fear the death of traditional retailing, but many more predict a marketing evolution for organizations that embrace Internet technologies as essential parts of their marketing strategies. E-commerce is fueled by information; marketers who effectively use the wealth of data available will not only survive, but thrive in cyberspace. Amazon's CEO Jeff Bezos sees the future of e-commerce with optimism. "People will know about thousands of Web sites that are important parts of their lives. Some will be important only once every three years. Some will be important every day. In any of these niches, there may be only a few significant leaders. But there will be thousands of those areas."[81]

ACHIEVEMENT CHECK SUMMARY

Read the learning objectives that follow, and consider the questions for each one. Answering these questions will reinforce your grasp of the most important concepts in the chapter and will allow you to check how well you have achieved these learning goals. Where a blank appears before a question, answer with *T* or *F* for true/false questions; for multiple-choice questions, choose the letter of the correct answer.

Objective 4.1: Define e-commerce and give examples of each function of the Internet.

1. _____ Providing a fast and convenient shopping experience for the consumer is one of the three primary functions of the Internet.

2. _____ The Internet can serve as a channel for information, entertainment, and e-commerce.

3. _____ E-commerce (a) relies on digital tools such as typewriters, calculators, and computers; (b) is a one-way sales channel controlled by the consumer; (c) is a valuable marketing tool for building customer relationships.

Objective 4.2: Describe how marketers use the Internet and World Wide Web to achieve their firm's objectives.

1. _____ Interactive and integrated marketing enable open communications between marketers and consumers and coordination of all promotional activities.

2. _____ The Web serves as a mass marketing channel and eliminates the possibility of one-to-one marketing.

3. _____ The Internet offers marketers a global reach in providing goods and services when and where customers want them.

Objective 4.3: Explain how online marketing benefits organizations, marketers, and consumers.

1. _____ Online marketing helps organizations reduce costs in every area of the marketing mix—product, distribution, promotion, and price.

2. _____ Consumers benefit from the convenience, lower prices, and personalization of online transactions.

3. _____ Because intense competition on the Web presents tremendous challenges and creates numerous problems for marketers, they typically prefer offline transactions.

Objective 4.4: Identify the most frequent Internet buyers and sellers and the goods and services marketed most often on the Internet.

1. _____ Internet sales have declined over the past five years as buyers have turned into passive shoppers instead of active online purchasers.

2. _____ Internet marketers recognize that online shoppers will not purchase unique items that are traditionally experienced personally, such as perfume and clothing.

3. _____ Online sellers must create information-intensive Web sites to meet competition and attract and retain cybershoppers.

Objective 4.5: Identify the primary online marketing channels.

1. _____ Electronic magazines represent a popular channel for online marketers.

2. _____ Three primary online channels include (a) marketing Web sites, electronic storefronts, and corporate Web sites; (b) commercial Web sites, online advertising, and online communities; (c) newsgroups, forums, and smart cards.

3. _____ Company Web sites offer general information, electronic shopping, and promotions such as games and contests.

Objective 4.6: Explain how marketers use Web kiosks, smart cards, and virtual coupons and samples as part of their online marketing strategies.

1. _____ Samples are not feasible with the mass-market capabilities of the Internet.

2. _____ Marketers use Web kiosks for promotional strategies to reach customers in undeveloped countries who do not have access to personal computers.

3. _____ Smart cards, which allow personal and financial information to be stored and accessed on a card similar to a credit card, are popular in European and Asian markets and are growing in acceptance among U.S. consumers.

Objective 4.7: Describe how an effective Web site can enhance customer relationships.

1. _____ Effective Web sites enable marketers to gather information on what consumers are buying and allows them to suggest other related purchases that increase customer satisfaction.

2. _____ An effective Web site builds customer relationships by (a) providing information; (b) delivering entertainment; (c) bringing buyers and sellers together; (d) all of the above; (e) none of the above.

3. _____ Building and maintaining customer relationships is facilitated through interactive capabilities and personalized online marketing strategies.

Objective 4.8: Explain how marketers measure the effectiveness of their online marketing efforts.

1. _____ Market research helps to evaluate the effectiveness of a Web site in reaching targeted segments, reducing costs, and increasing revenues.

2. _____ Marketers frequently use Web site monitors to count the number of times Internet users visit an organization's home page.

3. _____ Audience measurement of interactive media should be comparable to traditional industry standards.

Students: See the solutions section located on page S-1 to check your responses to the Achievement Check Summary.

Key Terms

electronic commerce (e-commerce)	bot
	corporate Web site
electronic marketing (e-marketing)	marketing Web site
	electronic storefront
digital tools	cybermalls
online marketing	online forum
interactive marketing	newsgroup
Internet (Net)	electronic bulletin board
electronic mail (e-mail)	Web kiosk
intranet	smart card
extranet	electronic currency
Internet service provider (ISP)	hits
portal	page views

Review Questions

1. What is e-commerce? Explain the advantages electronic technologies offer to marketers.
2. Identify the three primary functions of the Internet.
3. Explain the importance of interactive marketing in e-commerce.
4. Explain how online marketing benefits the following organizations:
   a. American Cancer Society

    b. Voodoo dolls designed by the Voodoo Cultural Center in New Orleans

    c. Ford Motor Company

    d. local chapter of the National Chess Federation

5. Which products are best suited for Web selling? Which products present challenges in online selling? Which products do consumers frequently buy online?

6. Give some examples of how organizations, marketers, and consumers benefit from online marketing. What are some of the disadvantages?

7. Explain how marketers use the three primary online alternatives of company Web sites, online advertisements on other sites, and communities to further their firms' objectives.

8. How do marketers use Web kiosks, smart cards, and virtual coupons and samples in their online marketing strategies?

9. Describe the process of establishing an online presence and explain the importance of Web site design.

10. How can marketers measure the effectiveness of their online marketing efforts?

Questions for Critical Thinking

1. How can marketers use the concept of community to add value to their products? Give an example of each of the types of communities discussed in the chapter.

2. Define interactive marketing and explain how it helps build relationships among suppliers, organizations, and their customers.

3. Assume you are a Web site designer. Identify a local company that operates without an online presence, and outline a proposal that explains the benefits to the firm of going online.

4. Suggest ways in which a Web marketer might reduce consumer reluctance to purchase products that are perishable or that consumers typically like to touch, feel, or smell before buying.

5. Compare the similarities and differences of traditional and online marketing strategies and the emphasis on the marketing mix components.

'netWork

1. Three Web Functions. Locate a Web site that you consider to be an outstanding example for each of the three Web functions—information, entertainment, and e-commerce. For example, an information Web site is *www.admedia.org;* an entertainment site is *www.shockwave.com;* and an e-commerce site is *www.dell.com.* Write a brief review of the Web site you selected for each function and include its Web address.

2. Lower Prices. Shopping bots are software tools that aid in comparison shopping across the Web. They find products you're looking for and supply descriptions, prices, and other related information. Over 200 shopping bots are available, including such popular sites as:

www.dealtime.com
www.bottomdollar.com
www.mysimon.com
www.ichoose.com
www.shoppinglist.com
www.storerunner.com

Select an item you need or would like to purchase and use three different shopping bots to help you find the best price. Report your results by identifying which bots you used to conduct your research and the results that each bot returned for you.

3. Advertisements on Other Web Sites. Go to *www.hoovers.com/* Select the "Companies & Industries" link, then the "Companies" link, and finally "The List of Lists" link. Scroll down to "Brands/Products" and select "Top 15 Internet Banner Ads" updated weekly from listings in *Advertising Age.* Review the banners and list the top five together with the number of persons viewing each ad during the week. Identify the banner ad that is most appealing to you. Explain your choice.

shockwave.com

admedia.org

dell.com

dealtime.com

mysimon.com

hoovers.com

Video Case 4 on Tower Records begins on page VC-5.

Succeeding Using Relationship and Database Marketing

CHAPTER OBJECTIVES

1 Contrast relationship marketing with transaction-based marketing.

2 List the goals of internal marketing.

3 Identify and explain each of the core elements of relationship marketing.

4 Outline the steps in the development of a marketing relationship and the different levels of relationship marketing.

5 Explain the primary methods used to measure customer satisfaction.

6 Explain the role of databases in relationship marketing.

7 Compare the different types of partnerships and explain how they contribute to relationship marketing.

8 Relate the concepts of co-marketing and co-branding to relationship marketing.

9 Describe how relationship marketing incorporates electronic data interchange, vendor-managed inventories, and national account selling.

10 Discuss the value of strategic alliances to a company's relationship marketing strategy.

11 Identify and evaluate the most common measurement and evaluation techniques within a relationship marketing program.

On Air Digital Audio Forges Relationships with Technology

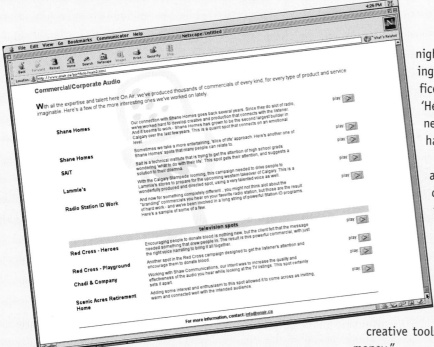

When a real estate company wants to record a radio ad featuring retirees searching for the perfect home, the recording requires professional actors with voices from the right age group and maybe a few children's voices to pose as the grandchildren and perhaps a soothing voice to portray the real-estate broker. Suppose a travel agency wants to develop an ad aimed at Midwesterners who want a break from winter—promoting trips to the Caribbean or to Florida during February and March. The agency wants the voice actors to sound "relaxed" and "sunny."

Studios that produce these recordings have been around for a long time. Until now, they have had to rely on voice actors who lived nearby or who could record tapes at other locations and ship them to the studio. Customers frequently had to sift through tape after tape at a studio before settling on the right voice. The whole process was time consuming and costly for both sides.

Greg Habstritt, founder of On Air Digital Audio, recently decided he could transform the process. He had the technology to offer convenience to customers and, in using it, began to forge a relationship that would keep these customers coming back. What was his strategic weapon? He posted his company's voice samples on a Web site in RealAudio, which customers could access any time, anywhere. Now, "customers can sit at home at

night or on the weekend [and review sample recordings]," explains Habstritt. "When they're in the office, they can call the boss or a client in and say, 'Here's the voice I was considering.' They don't need a tape. They don't need a CD player. All they have to do is log on."

Building on that change, Habstritt has found all kinds of ways to make doing business with his company easier for existing and potential customers. "We approached our site from the perspective of our client," explains Habstritt. "We asked ourselves what we could add to our site that would enhance their experience, and ultimately make their job easier. Our site isn't just a brochure online—it's designed to be a resource to our client, and we've built some creative tools into the site that help clients save time and money."

Potential advertisers discover voice samples divided into categories, such as gender or age, and short descriptions of the character of specific recordings, such as "rich and mellow." In addition, On Air has an online portfolio of finished recordings made for other customers so that new customers can get an idea of what the finished product would be like. Habstritt has not stopped there. Currently he is working on an online forum that allows customers to share questions about audio and is working on a real-time system as well that will let them check the status of their ongoing projects. On Air also plans to set up home pages for its voice actors so that customers can get a personal feel for who these actors are. "Those customers would visit the talents' Web sites to find out more about them and see the link to On Air and click on that," explains Habstritt. "Then after a bit of reading, they might decide to get On Air to do the project using this particular voice talent." In this case, the marketing relationship would begin with the voice talent—in effect, On Air's supplier—and move through the supply chain to On Air, instead of the other way around.

Habstritt also wants to court more sophisticated clients—news-media companies that already expect a strong Web presence. "I think the Web site confirms people's thoughts about us," he notes. "If we're going to be delivering our services to news-media clients, we need to prove that we know what we're

151

talking about." Thus, the Web site helps establish trust up front in On Air's capabilities.

Finally, Habstritt has developed relationships with other organizations, such as Media Dog Productions and Cybersurg Corp.—partnerships designed to enhance each participant's business. Upon receiving *Inc.* magazine's first annual "Best of the Small Business Web" award, Habstritt acknowledged the importance of these relationships: "This award not only recognizes On Air's vision of where our company is going, but also that we've got some talented partners that are helping put that vision onto the screen."[1]

CHAPTER OVERVIEW

As Chapter 1 discussed, marketing revolves around exchange relationships. The shift away from transaction-based marketing, which focuses on short-term, single exchanges, to customer-focused relationship marketing is one of the most important trends in marketing today. Companies recognize that they cannot prosper simply by identifying and attracting new customers; to succeed, they must build loyal, mutually beneficial relationships with existing customers, suppliers, distributors, and employees, as well. This strategy also benefits the bottom line, because retaining customers costs much less than acquiring new ones.

Building and managing long-term relationships between buyers and sellers is the hallmark of relationship marketing. **Relationship marketing** is the development, growth, and maintenance of long-term, cost-effective relationships with individual customers, suppliers, employees, and other partners for mutual benefit. It expands the scope of a company's relationships to integrate these stakeholders, who also include distributors and retailers, into a company's product design and development, manufacturing, and sales processes.

Building long-term relationships with consumers and other businesses involves three basic steps. First, database technology helps a company to identify current and potential customers with selected demographic, purchase, and lifestyle characteristics. Second, by analyzing this information, the firm can modify its marketing mix to deliver differentiated messages and customized marketing programs to individual consumers. Finally, monitoring each relationship provides a way to measure the success of marketing programs. The company can calculate the cost of attracting one new customer and how much profit that customer will generate during the relationship.[2]

As Figure 5.1 illustrates, relationship marketing emphasizes cooperation rather than conflict between all of the parties involved. This ongoing collaborative exchange creates value for both parties and builds customer loyalty.[3] Partnerships, co-marketing, co-branding, and strategic alliances all play major roles in relationship-marketing programs. This chapter begins by examining the reasons organizations are moving to relationship marketing and the impact this move has on producers of goods and services and their customers. ■

FIGURE 5.1 **Forms of Buyer-Seller Interaction**

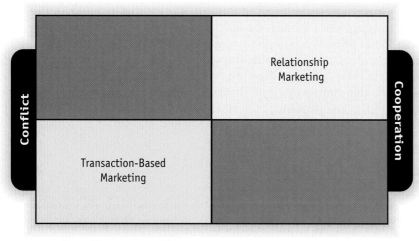

Ongoing Relationship

Relationship Marketing

Conflict

Cooperation

Transaction-Based Marketing

One-Time Transaction

Source: Based on Joseph P. Cannon and Jag N. Sheth, "Developing a Curriculum to Enhance Teaching of Relationship Marketing," *Journal of Marketing Education,* p. 5.

THE SHIFT FROM TRANSACTION-BASED MARKETING TO RELATIONSHIP MARKETING

Since the Industrial Revolution, most manufacturers have run production-oriented operations. They have traditionally focused their energies on making products and then promoting those products to customers in hopes of selling enough of them to cover costs and earn profits.

The emphasis for production-led companies is to focus on individual sales or *transactions.* **Transaction-based marketing** involves buyer and seller exchanges characterized by limited communications and little or no ongoing relationship between the parties. In transaction-based marketing, the primary goal is to entice a buyer to make a purchase based on such reasons as low price, convenience, packaging, or similar inducements. This activity serves a short-term goal: Create a sale—now.

Transaction-based marketing still characterizes some marketing exchanges. For example, residential real estate sales are primarily transaction-based. Real estate agents attempt to maintain the appearance of an ongoing, buyer-seller relationship, but in most cases, the best an agent can hope for is to get the property listing of a past customer that now needs to sell his property due to a job transfer, for instance, and positive referrals from past customers to other potential customers and sellers. For customers that remain in their homes for long periods, the exchange is purely transaction-based. To a lesser extent, automobile purchases are transaction-based for customers who shop around for each new car and typically do not purchase from one dealer only.

While transaction-based marketing is still widespread, many organizations are trying a new approach—one that looks at customers in a different light. Indeed, organizations have found that creating long-term *relationships* with customers pays off through better sales and lower marketing costs.[4]

1

Contrast relationship marketing with transaction-based marketing.

MARKETING DICTIONARY

relationship marketing The development and maintenance of long-term, cost-effective relationships with individual customers, suppliers, employees, and other partners for mutual benefit.

transaction-based marketing Involves buyer and seller exchanges characterized by limited communications and little or no ongoing relationship between the parties.

The move from transactions to relationships is reflected in the changing nature of the interactions between customers and sellers themselves. Transaction-based marketing relationships are generally sporadic in nature, often disrupted by conflict. As marketing interactions shift toward a relationship focus, however, conflict changes to cooperation, and infrequent contacts between buyers and sellers become ongoing interactions. Businesses now understand they must do more than simply create products and then sell these products. With so many goods and services to choose from, customers look for added value from their marketing relationships.

 wal-mart.com

Wal-Mart and its primary vendors have forged important marketing relationships. Wal-Mart gets good prices and attention to its specific merchandising needs from its vendors, while these vendors get a significant portion of their sales volume through the nation's largest retailer. This relationship marketing effort is illustrated by the fact that roughly half of the nation's 500 largest firms maintain offices and personnel in northwestern Arkansas near Wal-Mart's home office in Bentonville.

Internal Marketing

2

List the goals of internal marketing.

The concept of customer satisfaction is usually discussed in terms of **external customers**—people or organizations that buy or use another firm's goods or services. However, as noted in Chapter 1, marketing in organizations concerned with quality must also address **internal customers**—employees or departments within an organization whose jobs depend on the work of other employees or departments. For example, a person processing an order for a new piece of equipment is the internal customer of the salesperson who completed the sale, just as the person who bought the product is the salesperson's external customer. Although the order processor might never directly encounter an external customer, his or her performance can have direct impact on the overall value the firm is able to deliver to the marketplace.

Internal marketing involves managerial actions that help all members of the organization understand, accept, and fulfill their respective roles in implementing the organization's marketing strategy. Applying concepts of internal customer satisfaction helps organizations to attract, select, and retain outstanding employees who appreciate and value their role in the delivery of superior service to external customers. Employees are crucial to the achievement of a firm's objectives.[5]

ibm.com

Computer giant IBM recently reorganized its sales force to maximize customer focus. Each sales executive is assigned responsibility for a certain number of accounts. They also manage product rep teams, engineers, and consultants. They even complete a 9-month course at Harvard Business School to learn all the aspects of financial analysis. By working across numerous functions at different levels in the organization, they are better able to serve key accounts and develop relationships with customers, both internal and external to the firm.[6] An internal marketing program shows employees how their work aids the firm's marketing strategy and also promotes customer satisfaction. Employees must also view coworkers as internal customers. In this way, they are motivated to deliver high quality goods and services to their coworkers and add further value to the marketing process.

Employee knowledge and involvement are important goals of internal marketing. Companies that excel at satisfying customers typically place a priority on keeping employees informed about corporate goals, strategies, and customer needs. Employees must also have the tools necessary to address customer requests and problems in a timely manner. Often, marketers are part of the conduit disbursing this information throughout the organization. To this end, some companies are introducing intranets to aid the flow of communications between departments and functions within the organization. An *intranet* is an internal network that conforms to Internet standards in order to support two-way corporate communications. Businesses can send information, distribute technical data, and support team processes through intranets.

Intranets are crucial strategic elements that aim to create quality customer service through employee involvement, teamwork, and training. The need for firms to be connected electronically to all their units and employees is evident in the recent increase in the number of intranets. Each organization modifies its internal communications to suit the operations and objectives of

TABLE 5.1	Comparing Transaction-Based Marketing and Relationship Marketing Strategies	

CHARACTERISTIC	TRANSACTION MARKETING	RELATIONSHIP MARKETING
Time orientation	Short-term	Long-term
Organizational goal	Make the sale	Emphasis on retaining customers
Customer service priority	Relatively low	Key component
Customer contact	Low to moderate	Frequent
Degree of customer commitment	Low	High
Basis for seller-customer interactions	Conflict manipulation	Cooperation; trust
Source of quality	Primarily from production	Companywide commitment

Source: Adapted from Martin Christopher, Adrian Payne, and David Ballantyne, *Relationship Marketing*, p. 4.

MARKETING STRATEGY FAILURE

RealNetworks Violates Listeners' Trust

BACKGROUND RealNetworks' marketers wanted to learn more about the consumers who were listening to its free version of RealJukebox, an online software program that allows users to download and listen to music. The site was incredibly popular, with 13.5 million registered users. But in order to grow, the company reasoned, it needed to know more about what consumers liked and wanted.

THE MARKETING PROBLEM To obtain the consumer information it wanted, RealNetworks required its users to give their names and e-mail addresses prior to being assigned an identity number. The company was then able to track and store data about what types of music consumers preferred, a list of the CDs played on their computers, and even indications of their level of computer knowledge. RealNetworks, however, did not tell users it was collecting and storing this information.

continued on next page

the firm. Cisco Systems has an open intranet. Cicso does not restrict the amount or type of information that employees send through the intranet. On the other hand, Motorola restricts employee intranet access and what is said on it. As the company intranet name—the CEO Townhall—implies, its primary function is to disseminate information from the top down.[7]

Employee satisfaction is another critical objective of internal marketing. Employees can seldom, if ever, satisfy customers if they themselves are unhappy. Dissatisfied employees are likely to spread negative word-of-mouth messages to relatives, friends, and acquaintances, and these reports can affect purchasing behavior. Satisfied employees often buy their employer's goods and services, sending a powerful message to potential customers.[8] For this reason, some companies set up internal promotion programs to complement their external advertising and marketing campaigns.

What Is Relationship Marketing?

In rapidly increasing numbers, producers of goods and services have shifted away from transaction-based systems of marketing to longer-term, more customer-focused relationship systems. Table 5.1 summarizes the differences between the narrow focus of transaction marketing and the much broader view that relationship marketing takes.

Every marketing transaction involves a relationship between the buyer and seller. In a transaction-based situation, the relationship may be quite short in duration and narrow in scope. Few if any social relationships may develop between buyer and seller.

For example, a traveler who is running dangerously low on gas in an unfamiliar town will likely stop at the first gas station she encounters, whether or not this station carries Exxon, the customer's preferred brand. When the driver gets back home, however, she is likely to return to her previous practice of buying her preferred brand. In short, the single emergency transaction is unlikely to affect future gasoline purchase patterns by this customer.

The customer-seller bonds developed in a relationship marketing situation, on the other hand, last longer and cover a much broader scope than those

 3

Identify and explain each of the core elements of relationship marketing.

MARKETING | DICTIONARY

external customer People or organizations that buy or use another firm's goods or services.

internal customer Employee or department within an organization that depends on the work of another employee or department to perform a job.

internal marketing Managerial actions that help all members of the organization understand and accept their respective roles in implementing the organization's marketing strategy.

THE OUTCOME When news of RealNetworks' practices was made public by *The New York Times*, the company's CEO, Rob Glaser, quickly issued a statement saying, "After reviewing the situation carefully, we reached the conclusion that we screwed up. . . We made a mistake in not being clear enough to our users what kinds of data [were] being generated and transmitted by the use of Real-Jukebox." Indeed, the company had broken its customers' trust. This was a huge mistake in a fledgling industry that has already struggled with privacy issues.

LESSONS LEARNED RealNetworks learned that regardless of its reasons for collecting information about users—even if it was simply to find out what types of music they wanted to hear—to collect it without their consent was not only wrong but damaging to the company's relationship with the very people it wanted to attract. So the company instituted changes. First, it offered blocking software that could be downloaded by current users. Second, it added a new consumer software privacy statement to its Web site privacy statement, notifying consumers that they could elect not to participate in any information gathering. Third, the company released a new version of its downloadable audio and video player, with the new statements incorporated and a mechanism that consumers must turn on themselves to participate in information gathering. Finally, RealNetworks formed a privacy advisory board to investigate ongoing Internet privacy issues.

| FIGURE 5.2 | Relationship Marketing Orientation |

developed in transaction marketing. Customer contacts are generally more frequent. A companywide emphasis on customer service contributes to customer satisfaction. Figure 5.2 shows the need to blend quality and customer service with traditional elements of the marketing mix. When a company integrates customer service and quality with marketing, the result is a relationship marketing orientation.[9]

Relationship marketing creates a new level of interaction between buyers and sellers. Rather than focusing exclusively on attracting new customers, marketers have discovered that it pays to retain current customers. Consider the success of SWF3, Germany's most popular radio station, which retains its daily 2.3 million listeners with an active relationship marketing program, SWF3 THE CLUB. Club members receive regular newsletters that offer comics, music journalism, concert ticket and merchandise discounts, and previews of upcoming events. SWF3 sponsors more than 100 events every year, from intimate recitals to giant outdoor festivals. At every event there is a special lounge for club members only that features catered food and impromptu interviews and jam sessions with performers. Every year, they can attend a weekend-long party with their favorite on-air personalities. The station has opened its own music-related theme restaurant and bar, the SWF3 Rock Cafe, and has even started its own record label, which has released 29 compact discs so far.[10]

BASIC FOUNDATIONS OF MODERN BUYER-SELLER RELATIONSHIPS

Relationship marketing depends on the development of close ties between the buyer, whether an individual or a company, and seller. This section considers the core elements of the buyer-seller relationship: the three promises that form the basis of relationship marketing and the four dimensions of the relationship marketing model.

Promises in Relationship Marketing

Relationship marketing is based on promises from organizations that go beyond obvious assurances that potential customers expect. A network of promises—outside the organization, within the organization, and between buyer and seller interactions—determine whether a marketing encounter will be positive or negative and will either enhance or detract from an ongoing buyer-seller relationship.[11]

Making Promises

Most firms make promises to potential customers through *external marketing*. As discussed earlier in the book, this term refers to the marketing efforts that a company directs toward customers, suppliers, and other parties outside the organization. These promises communicate what a customer can expect from the firm's good or service.

For example, the NBC television network might run an advertisement for its upcoming coverage of the National Basketball Association finals, touting the great games, great coverage, and great entertainment viewers will experience if they tune in. In this ad, the network would make a promise to its potential viewers and advertisers about what to expect and what the network would deliver. In the ad in Figure 5.3, W. L. Gore & Associates promises customers that its Gore-Tex outerwear is "Guaranteed to Keep You Dry."

External marketing goes beyond advertising, however. Special sales promotions, the physical design of a business facility, its cleanliness, and the service process all provide other ways that companies make promises to potential customers. For example, at Disneyland in California and Walt Disney World in Florida, management makes special efforts to ensure that the amusement parks remain spotless at all times. If a visitor drops a box of popcorn or spills a soda, a cast member—Disney's term for their employees—will soon clean it up. This obsession with cleanliness fulfills Disney's implicit promise to its customers to expect a wholesome, family experience when they visit one of its parks.

The promises that companies communicate to potential customers must be both realistic and consistent with one another. A firm that makes unrealistic promises can create a disappointed customer who may not buy the good or service again. For example, an infomercial for a new psychic hot line promises to improve your love life. If after six months and numerous expensive 900 calls, however, your love life is still in the dumps, you are likely to be very disappointed.

Enabling Promises

A company can follow through on its promises to potential customers through external marketing only if it enables these promises through *internal* marketing. Internal marketing includes recruiting talented employees and providing them with the tools, training, and motivation they need to do their jobs effectively. The company structure itself must facilitate rather than hinder the provision of quality offerings. Efficient systems and processes, empowered front-line workers, and flat organizational hierarchies all contribute to a company's ability to provide quality goods and services.

Unless a company meets these needs, employees can face serious difficulties keeping their employers' promises through external marketing. Ritz-Carlton Hotels' Customer Loyalty Anticipation Satisfaction System (CLASS) empowers its staff to take the initiative in meeting customers' needs. Any employee who notices something about a guest—perhaps the person requests a hypoallergenic pillow—notes the fact in a special "guest-preference" notepad. At the end of each day, the notes are removed from the pads and entered into the hotel's computer system. From then on, whenever that guest checks into any Ritz-Carlton anywhere in the world, staff members are prompted to offer a hypoallergenic pillow.[12]

FIGURE 5.4 **The Dimensions of Marketing Relationships**

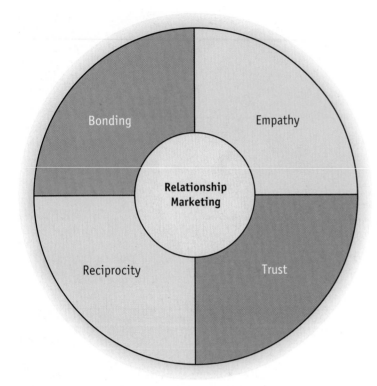

4

Outline the steps in the development of a marketing relationship and the different levels of relationship marketing.

kinkos.com

blimpie.com

Keeping Promises

Every customer interaction with a business reaches the moment of truth when a good or service is provided to the customer. This action was defined in Chapter 1 as the exchange process. This exchange, the third stage in the buyer-seller relationship following external and internal marketing, defines the point at which a company keeps its promises.

The exchange also provides the place where long-term relationships develop between buyers and sellers. Positive encounters help to build long-term relationships, with the added benefit of possible positive word-of-mouth recommendations from satisfied customers to other potential customers. On the other hand, a company that fails to keep its promises at the exchange point in the marketing process may destroy any hope of continuing buyer-seller relationships. Even a single negative encounter can have a devastating effect.

The Four Dimensions of Relationship Marketing

Clearly, making, enabling, and keeping promises are crucial parts of the relationship marketing process, but developing relationships requires more than promises. All relationships depend on the development of *emotional links* between the parties. Figure 5.4 identifies the four key dimensions of relationship marketing: bonding, empathy, reciprocity, and trust.[13]

Bonding

Two parties must *bond* to one another in order to develop a long-term relationship. In other words, mutual interests or dependencies between the parties must be strong enough to tie them together. If the bonds are weak, then the relationship is in imminent danger of falling apart at any time. Stronger bonds increase each party's commitment to the relationship.

FedEx has an interest in minimizing its costs. Kinko's wants to increase business traffic in its stores. That is why FedEx locates drop boxes in most Kinko's stores. FedEx customers drop their shipments in the boxes, limiting the number of individual pickups the company must make. As individual pickups decrease, FedEx needs fewer trucks and drivers. Kinko's also gains because business customers who drop packages into the FedEx boxes may also use Kinko's business services, such as copying documents or printing business cards.

FedEx and Kinko's share common interests, and they cooperate with one another to reach their goals. As a result, bonds have developed between the two firms. As time goes on and the relationship matures, both firms hope that the bonds will become progressively stronger.

Empathy

Empathy—the ability to see situations from the perspective of the other party—is another key emotional link in the development of relationships. More than 100 Blimpie Subs and Salads shops have created ongoing relationships with Pasta Central restaurants, a venture that has expanded Blimpie's menus by adding macaroni and cheese, lasagna, and other pasta dishes. The move has been profitable for both restaurant chains because it has increased dinner traffic and enabled the expanded shops to compete for better locations.

The combo restaurants are also successful because the partners show empathy—they are careful to complement, not compete against, each other. Employees are trained to learn the expanded menu to avoid steering customers away from unfamiliar meals. Restaurant owners must also agree to purchase and display new signs and equipment that give equal time to both companies.[14]

Reciprocity

Every long-term relationship includes some give-and-take between the parties; one makes allowances and grants favors to the other in exchange for the same treatment when its own need arises. This give-and-take process, termed *reciprocity*, becomes a web of commitments among the parties in the relationship, binding them ever closer together.

For example, a sales representative might offer additional supplies for new equipment to a buyer who is willing to accelerate payment of the invoice. Similarly, the buyer may be willing to interrupt a production schedule and install the new equipment immediately, enabling the salesperson to exceed his sales quota and earn a Caribbean cruise as a bonus, if the seller will extend the warranty for an additional 90 days.

Trust

Trust is ultimately the glue that holds a relationship together over the long haul. *Trust* reflects the extent of one party's confidence in another party's integrity. When parties follow through on commitments, they enhance trust and strengthen relationships. When they do not fulfill commitments, however, trust suffers.

Stronger trust leads to more cooperation between parties in a relationship. A customer's level of trust and satisfaction with salespeople affects the quality of the organizational relationship. Manufacturers and dealers who trust each other can cooperate much more effectively in producing, distributing, and selling products.[15]

THE RELATIONSHIP MARKETING CONTINUUM

Like all other interpersonal relationships, buyer-seller relationships function at a variety of levels. As an individual or firm progresses from the lowest level to the highest level on the continuum of relationship marketing, shown in Table 5.2, the strength of commitment between the parties grows. The likelihood of a continuing, long-term relationship, as well, grows. Whenever possible, marketers want to move their customers along this continuum, converting them from Level 1 purchasers, who focus mainly on price, to Level 3 customers, who receive specialized services and value-added benefits that may not be available from another firm.[16]

The First Level of Relationship Marketing

Interactions at the first level of relationship marketing are the most superficial and the least likely to lead to a long-term relationship. In the most prevalent examples of this first level,

TABLE 5.2	**Three Levels of Relationship Marketing**		
CHARACTERISTIC	LEVEL 1	LEVEL 2	LEVEL 3
Primary bond	Financial	Social	Structural
Degree of customization	Low	Medium	Medium to high
Potential for sustained competitive advantage	Low	Moderate	High
Examples	American Airlines' AAdvantage program	Harley-Davidson's Harley Owners Group (HOG)	Federal Express' PowerShip program

Source: Adapted from information in Leonard L. Berry, "Relationship Marketing of Services Growing Internet, Emerging Perspectives," *Journal of the Academy of Marketing Science,* p. 240.

Garden.com

BACKGROUND Cliff Sharples, his wife Lisa, and their good friend Jamie O'Neill are three young MBAs who are savvy about the potential of the Internet in changing the way marketing channels are managed. Several years ago, they decided to put their business talents to work, building what one writer calls "the perfect Internet business." Lisa Sharples recalls, "The idea was to find an industry where no one company had channel power." They honed in on America's most popular hobby—gardening—which happens to be a nearly $50 billion per-year industry. But the gardening industry had neither updated the way it managed its supply and marketing channels nor figured out how to use the Internet to do so. So the Sharples and O'Neill launched Garden.com.

THE CHALLENGE The Sharples and O'Neill had to find a way to attract consumers to a virtual garden, luring them away from traditional ways of buying flowers, seeds, and other gardening products. They also had to establish key relationships with growers and distributors. They needed to focus not only on the products themselves but on how their customers wanted to shop for those products.

THE STRATEGY Garden.com dug up the best suppliers they could find and signed them to exclusive deals. Under the agreement, all of a supplier's online sales would channel through Garden.com, and in return Garden.com would not sign any

continued on next page

MARKETING STRATEGY SUCCESS

agreements with direct competitors of that supplier. Suppliers thus enjoy security in a somewhat risky environment, but they must live up to the bargain. "We have a high level of customer service the supplier has to adhere to," notes Lisa Sharples. Building on success, the group later launched Fresh Stems by Garden.com, a fresh-cut flower line that offers consumers a convenient way to order fresh and unique flowers from more than 250 growers around the world. "The power is in the idea of tying all these niche growers together into a virtual store," explains Jamie O'Neill.

THE OUTCOME Garden.com is virtually blooming, with more than half a million members, increasing sales by 300 percent a year. By signing the best growers they could find and by charging reasonable prices for their products, they have begun to build brand-name recognition as Garden.com, which in turn reflects back to the suppliers themselves, continuing to solidify the relationship. Garden.com continues to grow its relationship with consumers, as well, offering how-to information, replying to individual e-mails, and even getting out in the sun and dirt with some customers in their own gardens. Finally, the company has begun to forge relationships with other organizations, such as iVillage.com, a Web site targeted to women. The group is passionate in its strategy for the future. "Companies that focus on the Internet channel will dominate—not traditional companies with Internet divisions," claims Lisa Sharples.

relationship marketing efforts rely on pricing and other financial incentives to motivate customers to enter into buying relationships with a seller. Examples include offers for two Big Macs for the price of one at McDonald's, American Airlines' AAdvantage frequent-flyer program, and the General Motors MasterCard that rewards cardholders with credits for every dollar charged toward purchases of GM products.

Although these programs can be attractive to users, they may not create long-term buyer relationships. Because the programs are not customized to the needs of individual buyers, they are easily duplicated by competitors. For example, when McDonald's runs its two-for-one special on Big Macs, there is a chance that Burger King will respond with a similar offer on its Whopper sandwiches. Within three years after American Airlines introduced its AAdvantage frequent-flyer program, some 23 other airlines enacted similar programs. The lesson here is that it takes more than a low price or other financial incentive to create a long-term relationship between buyer and seller.

The Second Level of Relationship Marketing

As buyers and sellers reach the second level of relationship marketing, their interactions develop on a *social* level—one that features deeper and less superficial links than the financially motivated first level. Sellers have begun to learn that social relationships with buyers can be very effective marketing tools. Customer service and communication are key factors at this stage. Many firms publish custom magazines to communicate with their customers. Examples include Chevrolet's *Corvette Quarterly*, Northwestern Mutual Life's *Creative Living* for policyholders, and American Airlines' *American Way* for in-flight passengers, which is shown in Figure 5.5.

College and university alumni associations are masters of the second level of relationship marketing. They inundate graduates with all sorts of alumni newspapers; magazines; and invitations for football game tailgate parties, holiday parties, and any number of other social activities. The institution wants to develop and maintain a long-term social relationship with its graduates—one that goes beyond the few years that they actually spend in school.

Harley-Davidson also uses social relationships to strengthen customer bonds. Local dealers sponsor Harley Owners' Groups (HOGs), and the company includes a one year free membership to HOG with the purchase of a motorcycle. In addition to member newsletters and magazines, club members can participate in road rallies, training sessions, and similar activities to increase their motorcycle driving pleasure.[17]

| FIGURE 5.5 | Developing a Social Relationship with Customers |

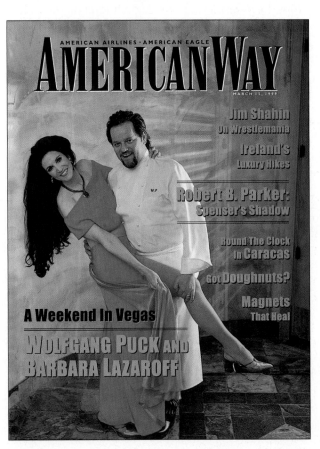

The Third Level of Relationship Marketing

At the third level of relationship marketing, relationships are transformed into structural changes that ensure buyer and seller are true business partners. As buyer and seller work more closely together, they develop a dependence on one another that continues to grow over time.

These partnerships occur for both industrial and service companies. Office products manufacturer Canon has worked hard to nurture third level relationships with its dealers. All new Canon dealers receive free CD-ROMs containing extensive training programs on sales and negotiation skills. The company hosts an annual three-day meeting for all dealers that includes more training sessions on sales techniques and on new Canon products. Part of one day of this meeting is reserved for dealers to meet with regional Canon managers to discuss their local markets and to develop ideas for new products and marketing programs.[18]

Harley-Davidson uses relationship marketing in consumer markets, and Canon uses it to strengthen relationships in business-to-business markets. The next section looks at the nature of buyer-seller relationships in both of these markets.

MEASURING CUSTOMER SATISFACTION

Marketing research can also be used to monitor customer satisfaction. Companies that commit themselves to satisfying customers must institute a system to continually measure how well they perform the task. Figure 5.6 shows the three main steps involved in this process: understanding customer needs, obtaining customer feedback, and instituting an ongoing program to ensure customer satisfaction.

Understanding Customer Needs

When they try to measure customer satisfaction, marketers must keep in mind that gaps, or differences, between expected and perceived quality of the firm's goods and services may occur. Such gaps can produce favorable or unfavorable impressions. A product may be better than expected or worse than expected. To avoid unfavorable gaps, marketers need to keep in touch with current and potential customers. Companies must look beyond traditional performance measures and explore the factors that determine purchasing behavior in order to formulate customer-based missions, goals, and performance standards.

Knowledge of what customers need, want, and expect is a central concern of companies focused on customer satisfaction. This information is also a vital first step in setting up a system to measure customer satisfaction. Marketers must carefully monitor the characteristics that really matter to customers. They also must remain constantly alert to new elements that might affect customer satisfaction.

Obtaining Customer Feedback

The second step in measuring customer satisfaction is to compile feedback from customers regarding present performance. In a sense, this action captures a snapshot of how well the firm currently meets customer expectations. This information can be gathered in two ways using either reactive or proactive methods.

To monitor customer feedback, most firms rely on reactive methods that include using toll-free, customer-service telephone lines or systems to track customer complaints. Increasingly,

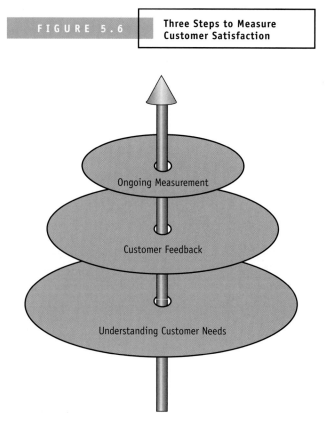

FIGURE 5.6 | Three Steps to Measure Customer Satisfaction

Ongoing Measurement

Customer Feedback

Understanding Customer Needs

5

Explain the primary methods used to measure customer satisfaction.

firms are monitoring Usenet and other online discussion groups as a means of tracking customer comments and attitudes about the value received. Some companies hire *mystery shoppers*, who visit or call businesses posing as customers, to evaluate the service they receive. A mystery shopper is typically a disinterested party with no prior experience with the company. These unbiased appraisals are usually conducted on a biannual or quarterly basis to monitor employees, diagnose problem areas in customer service, and measure the impact of employee training.

@ **wyndham.com**

Wyndham Hotels and Resorts' commitment to customer service involves everyone in the company. The international lodging chain boasts of comfortable rooms, delicious meals, and superior service. Perhaps more important is the attention Wyndham's staff gives to guests to make their visit perfect in every way. Marketers promote the excellent service in ads that state, "Where there's a Wyndham, there's a person waiting to take care of you." For instance, one guest began to panic when he discovered that he had forgotten to pack dress shoes for his big presentation. No worry. The Wyndham concierge did not panic. Instead, he immediately recognizes what his guest needs, removes his black, size 10 wing tips, wipes them down, hands them over to the guest, and carries on the rest of his morning duties in stocking feet. This is the type of service that the hotel calls "The Right Way. The Wyndham Way."

Any method that makes it easier for customers to complain benefits a firm. As the chief marketer at one of the nation's largest car-rental agencies put it, "We view a customer who is complaining as a real blessing in disguise. He or she is someone we can resell."[19] Customer complaints offer organizations the opportunity to overcome problems and prove their commitment to service. Customers often have greater loyalty to a company after a conflict has been resolved than if they had never complained at all.

Many firms also use proactive methods to assess customer satisfaction. These include visiting, calling, or mailing out written surveys to clients to find out how satisfied they really are. Xerox gathers information by mailing approximately 60,000 customer satisfaction surveys per month to its customers, and AT&T's Universal Credit Card division calls 2,500 customers every month to measure quality in the company's nine most important areas of service performance. Pizza Hut calls 50,000 customers each week to ask about their experiences at the restaurant chain's units. Many car dealers call or send surveys to customers asking them to rate the service they received, either in a purchase situation or service visit.

BUYER-SELLER RELATIONSHIPS IN CONSUMER GOODS AND SERVICES MARKETS

Marketers of consumer goods and services have discovered that they must do more than simply create products and then sell them. With a dizzying array of products to choose from, many customers are seeking ways to simplify both their business and personal lives, and relationships provide a way to do this.

One reason many consumers form continuing relationships is their desire to reduce choices. Through relationships, they can simplify information gathering and the entire buying process as well as decrease the risk of dissatisfaction. They find comfort in brands that have become familiar through their ongoing relationships with companies. In fact, studies show that consumers patronize their habitual brands, stores, and malls about 90 percent of the time.[20] Such relationships may lead to more efficient decision making by customers and higher levels of customer satisfaction.

A key benefit to consumers of long-term, buyer-seller relationships is the perceived positive value they receive. Relationships add value through increased opportunities for frequent customers to save money through discounts, rebates, and similar offers, through special recognition from the relationship programs, and through convenience in shopping. Figure 5.7 points out the benefits of exclusive discounts that Sears offers customers that are members of its Pulse Card program.

Marketers should also understand why consumers end relationships. If these customers become dissatisfied or bored with their current providers, they are likely to sample the competition. Many consumers also dislike feeling that they are locked into a relationship with one company. Computerized technologies and the Internet have made consumers better informed than ever before by giving them unprecedented abilities to compare prices, products, and customer service.[21]

Consumer marketers use relationship-marketing techniques like affinity and frequency programs to attract new customers and retain existing ones. Databases also play important roles in developing good relationships with consumers.

The Rewards of Retaining Customers

One of the major forces driving the push from transaction-based marketing to relationship marketing is the realization that retaining customers is far more profitable than losing them. Customers usually allow a firm to generate more profits with each additional year of the relationship. Indeed, marketing consultant Frederick Reichheld notes that a 5 percent gain in customer retention can pay off with an 80 percent increase in profits.[22]

A good example of this is the Marriott Rewards program, which now boasts 10 million members. Members spend an average of 2.5 times more at Marriott hotels than nonmembers and account for 20 percent of Marriott's total sales.[23] This underscores the importance of customer satisfaction and quality in relationship marketing programs.

Affinity Programs

Each of us holds certain things near and dear to our hearts. Some may feel strongly about Eastern Michigan State University, while others admire the New York Yankees or singer Shania Twain. These symbols, along with an almost unending variety of others, are subjects of affinity programs. An **affinity program** is a marketing effort sponsored by an organization that solicits involvement by individuals who share common interests and activities. With affinity programs, organizations create extra value for members and encourage stronger relationships.

Affinity credit cards are a popular form of this marketing technique. The sponsor's name appears prominently in promotional materials, on the card itself, and on monthly statements. For example, the National Association for Female Executives, a professional networking organization, offers qualified members a Gold Visa or MasterCard with no first-year fee and with low interest rates. A not-for-profit organization such as a charity or educational institution may sponsor such a card if the issuer donates a percentage of user purchases to the group. For example, the Smithsonian Institution invites members to apply for the museum's affinity credit card in the ad shown in Figure 5.8. Not all affinity programs involve credit cards. KETC, the St. Louis public television station, thanks members who contribute more than $50 annually with a diners card that entitles them to discounts at participating restaurants.

Frequent Buyer and Frequent User Programs

Perhaps the most popular means of practicing relationship marketing are frequent-buyer and frequent-user programs. Commonly known as **frequency marketing**, these programs reward customers with cash, rebates, merchandise, or other premiums. Buyers who

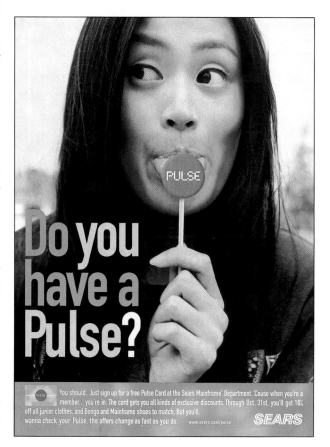

marriott.com

FIGURE 5.8 **Example of an Affinity Credit Card**

EARN $50 U.S. SAVINGS BONDS.

Shop 'til you bebop.

"Dizzy" Gillespie's trumpet
National Museum of American History

This is guaranteed to make your shopping trip swing.
Not only do your Smithsonian Card purchases earn you
points towards $50 U.S. Savings Bonds, they also help the Smithsonian.   All without an annual fee.
Apply today for the only credit card that lets you save for your future while you support the Smithsonian.
To apply, call toll-free 1-888-33-CASTLE or visit us at www.smithsoniancard.com

SMITHSONIAN

Accepted
where you see

DicksSupermarket.com

6

Explain the role of databases in
relationship marketing.

purchase an item more often earn higher rewards. Frequency marketing focuses on a company's best customers with the goal of increasing their motivation to buy even more of the same or other products from the seller.

Many different types of companies use frequency programs, from fast food restaurants to retail stores, telecommunications companies, and travel firms.[24] Popular programs include airline frequent-flyer programs, such as United Airlines' Mileage Plus, and retail programs, such as Hallmark's Gold Crown Card.

The Internet is proving a fertile medium for frequency-marketing initiatives. Dick's Supermarkets, an eight-store chain based in Illinois, rewards loyal customers with online coupons. Customers register at Dick's home page, click on the coupons that interest them, and receive the discounts electronically at checkout time. Internet marketer Webstakes rewards frequent visitors to its Web site by offering weekly prizes; the more often they visit, the better their chances of winning. Prizes are offered in several interest areas and range in value from $200 to $400.[25]

Database Marketing

When marketing centers on a one-to-one interaction between a salesperson and an individual customer, buyer-seller relationships are fairly easy to track and manage. A few notes jotted in an appointment book often supply enough information to salespeople in carrying out such relationships. However, large-scale marketers like Talbot's, Lexus, and Nordstrom require database technology to maintain their customer relationships.

Database marketing refers to the use of computers to analyze data then identify and target specific groups of potential customers. Database marketing is a particularly effective tool for building relationships because it allows sellers to sort through huge quantities of buyer information to fine-tune marketing efforts. This activity helps create long-term relationships with customers and improve sales.

Modern information technology provides essential support for a first-rate customer relationship. Companies can track buying patterns, develop customer relationship profiles, customize their product offerings and sales promotions, reduce errors, and personalize customer service. Properly used, databases can help companies in several ways:

- Selecting their best customers
- Calculating the lifetime values of their business
- Creating a meaningful dialogue that builds genuine loyalty

Effective database marketing improves customer retention and referral rates, boosts sales volume, and reduces direct costs and marketing outlays.

Databases can precisely identify the potential customers in crowds of less qualified prospects. They also allow sellers to focus on their best current customers, measured both by the quantity these customers purchase and by the profitability of those sales. Each buyer is unique with individual priorities about important features of a product—price, service, product quality, and other factors. Databases gather and analyze this information, revealing characteristics and requirements of specific customers. Companies can then use this knowledge to identify potential customers who share a similar profile.[26]

Where do organizations find all the data that fill these vast marketing databases? Everywhere! If you have a credit card, you probably filled out a questionnaire as a part of the application

---

| FIGURE 5.9 | Using a Database to Personalize Service |

process. The information on that questionnaire was entered into a computer system that tracks every purchase you make with the credit card. Likewise, filling out and returning the registration card for a new piece of software also puts your name and other vital statistics into a computer database along with those of the other people who returned their registration cards. Other sources of database information include warranty cards, cash register scanners in supermarkets and other retail stores, customer opinion surveys, and sweepstakes entry forms. By combining personal demographic data with records of buyers' spending habits, a company creates an incredibly helpful source of marketing information.

Because databases contain such valuable information, database marketers frequently sell their mailing lists to interested parties. Consumers who subscribe to a magazine, such as *Wired*, soon begin receiving unsolicited marketing offers from a variety of related sellers—in this case, computer hardware and software manufacturers and retailers.

In a way, the world of marketing is returning to the old days of one-to-one marketing, where sellers got to know their customers and could tailor each product offering and sales presentation to the specific needs of the individual prospect. Databases have played a major role in the switch from mass marketing to precisely targeted marketing.[27] As American Express explains in its ad in Figure 5.9, the company gathers information from customers' credit card usage to design award programs suited to individual tastes and preferences.

The Internet can help companies develop even better customer information databases and to also apply this information to improving customer service. Internet connections bring instant feedback from customers. This speed helps marketers respond quickly to market changes.

Web sites provide real value to visitors and the sponsoring company by allowing information processing and presentations, both based on information likely to be in databases. Gathering such information from the Web is

MARKETING   DICTIONARY

database marketing Software that analyzes marketing information, then identifies and targets messages toward specific groups of potential customers.

becoming easier thanks to new software that allows companies to link Internet sites to their databases while preventing unauthorized access to the databases. For example, visitors to the Metropolitan Museum of Art's Web site can order items from the museum shop through an online catalog. Clicking on a desired item puts these items into the customer's "shopping bag," actually a database on a museum computer. The customer can even save a bag and come back later to finish the order. The completed order goes to the museum's distribution center, reducing the chance for errors while speeding up delivery. This popular service provides a high level of customer satisfaction and convenience while helping the museum learn more about customer preferences.[28]

BUYER-SELLER RELATIONSHIPS IN BUSINESS-TO-BUSINESS MARKETS

Relationship marketing is not limited to consumer goods and services. Building strong buyer-seller relationships is a critical component of business-to-business marketing as well.

Business-to-business marketing involves an organization's purchase of goods and services to support company operations or the production of other products. Buyer-seller relationships between companies involve working together to provide advantages that benefit both parties.[29] These advantages might include lower prices for supplies, quicker delivery of inventory, improved quality and reliability, customized product features, and more favorable financing terms.

7

Compare the different types of partnerships and explain how they contribute to relationship marketing.

Chapter 10 will discuss business-to-business marketing in more detail. This chapter will instead focus on business-partner relationships, including comarketing and co-branding programs.

| FIGURE 5.10 | A Partnership Based on Common Goals |

Building and Maintaining Business Partnerships

A **partnership** is an affiliation of two or more companies that assist each other in the achievement of common goals. Partnerships cover a wide spectrum of relationships from informal cooperative purchasing arrangements to formal production and marketing agreements. Such a link can involve a single function or activity of production and marketing—for example, distribution—or all functions, such as the research and development, manufacturing, and marketing of a new product. In business-to-business markets, partnerships form the basis of relationship marketing.

Businesses form partnerships with one another for many reasons. In some cases, choosing a supplier may lead to cost savings. Partnering can provide a small firm with an added measure of stability in volatile markets. In addition, marketing goods and services through partners offers many advantages to both large and small firms.

A variety of common goals motivate organizations in forming partnerships. Companies may want to protect or improve their positions in existing markets, gain access to new domestic or international markets, or quickly enter into new markets. Expansion of a product line—to fill in gaps, broaden the product line, or differentiate the product—is another key reason for joining forces. Other motives include sharing resources, reducing costs, warding off threats of future competition, raising or creating barriers to entry, and learning new skills. As the ad in Figure 5.10 explains, Aramark, a managed service provider, formed a partnership with the Colorado Rockies baseball team based on a shared vision of building a great family experience at the ball park. By providing food courts, a microbrewery, and a concession area for children, Aramark helped the park boost overall sales.

Choosing Business Partners

How does an organization decide which companies to select as partners? The first priority is to locate firms that can add value to the relationship—whether through financial resources, contacts, extra manufacturing capacity, technical know-how, or distribution capabilities. The greater the value added, the greater the desirability of the partnership. In many cases, the attributes of each partner complement those of the other; each firm brings something to the relationship that the other party needs but cannot provide on its own. Some partnerships join firms with similar skills and resources, however, perhaps motivated to reduce costs.

Organizations must share similar values and goals for a partnership to succeed in the long run. Sears and Walt Disney World joined forces to promote Disney's Animal Kingdom because managers for both realized they both sought the same group of customers—married women, aged 25 to 54, with children. Sears wanted to capitalize on the excitement of the theme park's opening by publicizing its stores to families; Disney wanted to extend this excitement into an ongoing marketing program that would continue to make customers aware of the park.

Like the Sears-Disney partnership, many business relationships are designed to achieve a specific purpose. In this case, the result was the highly successful Win and Be Wild Sweepstakes, which awarded a lucky high-school student the chance to take his or her family as well as his or her entire high school class to Walt Disney World. Registration forms for the sweepstakes were available only in Sears stores.[30]

FIGURE 5.11 Example of a Buyer Relationship

Types of Partnerships

Companies form four key types of partnerships in business-to-business markets: buyer, seller, internal, and lateral partnerships. The following section briefly examines each type.

In a *buyer* partnership, a firm purchases goods and services from one or more providers. For example, a company may contract with a certified public accountant (CPA) to conduct annual audits of its accounting system and to file federal and state income tax returns. Another company might purchase pens, pencils, and other office supplies exclusively from Office Depot. To improve passengers' dining experience, United Airlines purchased the services of award-winning chefs and premium brand products. The airline formed partnerships with Starbucks, Ben & Jerry's Ice Cream, Mrs. Field's Cookies, and Eli's Cheesecake, as shown in Figure 5.11.

When a company assumes the buyer position in a relationship, it has a unique set of needs and requirements that vendors must meet in order to make the relationship successful over a long period of time. While buyers want sellers to provide fair prices, quick delivery, and good quality, a lasting relationship often requires more effort. To induce a buyer to form a long-term partnership, a supplier must also be responsive to the purchaser's unique needs. For example, if the buyer has a rush job that must be done in one hour, a vendor will score highly if it can perform. Similarly, buyers want reliable partners.

Suppose a caterer contracts with a new food supplier to provide ingredients for a major charity fund-raising dinner. The supplier, however, fails to perform satisfactorily. The caterer is not likely to use the supplier again, and no relationship results.

Seller partnerships set up long-term exchanges of goods and services in return for cash or other valuable consideration. Sellers, too, have specific needs

MARKETING DICTIONARY

partnership An affiliation of two or more companies that assist each other in the achievement of common goals.

SOLVING AN ETHICAL CONTROVERSY

Should You Think before You Click?

Suppose you decide to do a little shopping online during your lunch hour or you want to e-mail a silly joke to a coworker in another office. Can your boss "see" what you are doing? Yes, and with increasing frequency employers are checking their employees' computer habits. According to the American Management Association, the electronic monitoring of employees' online communications and computer use has increased to 45 percent, and the share of major American firms that monitor employee e-mail has nearly doubled, from 15 percent to 27 percent, in just two years.

Although some organizations use software programs to keep close tabs on nearly every keystroke an employee makes, others simply use them to ferret out obscene language or signs of industrial espionage. Some organizations, such as the New York Times Co., have cracked down to the point of firing employees who were caught sending "inappropriate and offensive" e-mails. Others, such as Certicom, allow employees to use downtime to conduct personal business such as online shopping. The problem is, although companies may have the technology and legal right to monitor employees this way, critics warn that it may undermine relationships among internal partners in the organization and, in the end, hinder productivity.

Should employers monitor their employees' online communications?

Pro

1. Employers have a right to know what their employees are doing on company time. If they inform employees that it is company policy to monitor electronic communications, workers who remain on the job should accept the policy.

2. Companies need to be watchful for any communications that create a hostile workplace, such as obscene jokes, racial slurs, and the like. Monitoring electronic activities is one way to ensure a safe, nonprejudicial environment for all workers.

3. Companies must be alert to the loss of trade secrets through e-mail. Catching this type of activity shows a commitment to preserving the work of honest employees.

Con

1. Employers should trust their employees, and monitoring shows a lack of trust, thereby undermining the relationship with internal partners.

2. Employees spend so much time at work nowadays, including evenings and weekends, that they should be allowed to take care of some personal business at the office without worrying about privacy. An employer who allows this freedom shows confidence in the integrity of its employees and shows an understanding of their need to balance work and life.

3. Monitoring could reveal personal information that an employer should not—or does not want to—know, such as an employee who seeks help from an employer-sponsored assistance program for mental or physical problems. The information could adversely affect the employer's perception of the employee.

Summary

The Internet has created boundless communication, in which employees can quickly and easily send information to each other, either within the company or outside it. Organizations are trying to curb the transmission of information that may damage the company or other employees in some way. Although it is important for workers to be able to express themselves and for companies to have some control over information flow, both must be achieved in a manner that enhances the partnership between employee and employer.

SOURCE: Nick Wingfield, "More Companies Monitor Employees' E-mail," *Wall Street Journal*, December 2, 1999, p. B8; Chris Oakes, "23 Fired for E-mail Violations," www.wired.com, December 1, 1999; Jennifer Beauprez, "Privacy under Attack on 'Net," www.denverpost.com, November 29, 1999; and James Lardner, "Every Click You Make," *U.S. News & World Report*, November 8, 1999, p. 69.

---

as partners in ongoing relationships. Most prefer to develop long-term relationships with their partners. Sellers also want prompt payment.

The importance of *internal* partnerships is widely recognized in business today. The classic definition of the word *customer* as the buyer of a good or service is now more carefully defined in terms of *external* customers. However, customers within an organization also have their own needs. For example, in a company that manufactures cellular phones, the unit that assembles the phones is a customer of the company's purchasing department. In essence, the manufacturing plant "buys" cellular phone parts from the purchasing department, and the purchasing department supplies these parts to the plant. In this partnership, the purchasing department must continue to fulfill the needs of manufacturing by selecting vendors that can provide the parts needed with the price, quality, and time-frame characteristics specified by manufacturing. Similarly, the payroll department is a customer of all company employees; data processing is a customer of the accounting department; and a supervisor may be considered the customer of her employees.

Internal partnerships are the foundation of an organization and its ability to meet its commitments to external entities. For example, if the purchasing department selects a parts vendor that fails to ship on the dates required by manufacturing, production will halt, and phones will not be delivered to customers as promised. As a net result, external customers will likely seek other, more reliable suppliers. Without building and maintaining internal partnerships, it will be difficult for an organization to meet the needs of its external partnerships.

Lateral partnerships include strategic relationships such as co-marketing and co-branding alliances, global strategic alliances, alliances with not-for-profit organizations, and research alliances with universities and colleges. In each of these cases, the relationship reaches external entities, and it involves no buyer or seller interactions.

A later section of this chapter will examine the role of strategic alliances in relationship marketing, but two kinds of lateral partnerships—co-marketing and co-branding—are becoming increasingly important in the marketing efforts of companies today. The next section takes a closer look at these forms of relationship marketing.

Co-Marketing and Co-Branding

Co-marketing and co-branding have been around for some time. Today, however, these types of business-to-business relationships have become especially popular as marketers rediscover their benefits.

Co-marketing describes formal links between two or more businesses to jointly market each other's products. Computer manufacturers practice co-marketing. For example, when they put "Intel Inside" labels on their machines based on the Pentium microprocessor, they are practicing co-marketing. They also prominently feature the Pentium chip and the "Intel Inside" logo in print advertising. The PC makers benefit through their associations with the high-quality, cutting-edge reputation of Intel Corp. Intel benefits because its name appears in more places and more often than it could achieve on its own.

Co-branding occurs when two or more companies team up to closely link their names together for a single good or service. By creating an essentially new product bearing the name of both firms, co-branding reflects a much deeper commitment than co-marketing involves and a potentially longer-term relationship between businesses.

MBE Business Express Centers represent a co-branding arrangement between three companies. First, Mail Boxes Etc. teamed with USA Technologies to develop business equipment centers that feature personal computers, printers, fax machines, and photocopiers. Then, AmeriSuites hotels agreed to place MBE centers in 100 hotels and make them available on a 24-hour basis to guests.[31]

8

Relate the concepts of co-marketing and co-branding to relationship marketing.

LINKS BETWEEN BUYERS AND SELLERS IN BUSINESS-TO-BUSINESS MARKETS

Partnerships between buyers and sellers are facts of life in today's competitive business environment. Organizations that know how to find and nurture partner relationships, whether through informal deals or contractual co-marketing and co-branding agreements, can enhance revenues and increase profits. Partnering often leads to lower prices, better products, and improved distribution, resulting in higher levels of customer satisfaction. Closer relationships also improve communications between partners. This change can be particularly helpful at a time when many firms are dealing with fewer suppliers and are requiring adherence to high quality and delivery standards. Partners

MARKETING   DICTIONARY

co-marketing Formal links between two or more businesses to jointly market each other's products.

co-branding Partnership between two or more companies that closely links their brand names together for a single product.

who know each other's needs and expectations are more likely to satisfy them and forge stronger long-term bonds.

In the past, business relationships were conducted primarily in person, over the phone, or by mail. Today, businesses are using the latest electronic, computer, and communications technology to link up. E-mail, fax machines, the Internet, and other telecommunications services allow businesses to communicate any time and any place. Chapter 4 discussed the business role of the Internet in detail. The following sections explore other ways that buyers and sellers cooperate in business-to-business markets.

The Use of Databases

As an earlier section noted, databases are indispensable tools in relationship marketing. While that discussion explained the use of databases to target specific kinds of consumers, databases are also used in business-to-business situations.

Using information generated from sales reports, register scanners, and many other sources, sellers can create databases that help to guide their own efforts and those of buyers who resell products to final users. Quaker Oats Company teamed with San Francisco–based ThirdAge Media Inc., which operates an Internet site geared to older adults, to build a database of health information. The Heart Smart Challenge offered 1,500 ThirdAge members a free bowl of oatmeal every day for a month in exchange for information on their cholesterol levels. Quaker tracked and tabulated the responses and used these responses in a promotional campaign documenting the link between good nutrition and cardiovascular health. At the same time, ThirdAge acquired valuable data about the health and interests of its members.[32]

Electronic Data Interchange

9

Describe how relationship marketing incorporates electronic data interchange, vendor-managed inventories, and national account selling.

Some years ago, when a store ran a big sale on athletic shoes and then ran out of the product, the store's buyer might have had to phone their local sales representative to place a rush order. The shoe company's sales rep, assuming he was not out visiting other customers, checked the price and availability of the item and then placed an order for more shoes. To officially formalize the transaction, the buyer mailed a copy of the purchase order to the sales rep.

While this system worked fine for decades, it just does not meet the needs of today's competitive environment. A large retailer such as the Sports Authority or Wal-Mart would scoff at the unbelievable inefficiency and cost of employing a huge staff of buyers to call vendors to check on prices and availability of the thousands of items stocked at each store. These retailers would also object to the tremendous volume of paper-based purchase orders that the old system would generate each day. Fortunately, computers have automated the buying process. At the same time, they have opened new channels for gathering marketing information and creating business-to-business links and long-term relationships.

Electronic data interchange is one such computer-based technology. **Electronic data interchange (EDI)** involves computer-to-computer exchanges of invoices, orders, and other business documents. EDI is rapidly gaining popularity because it allows firms to reduce their costs and improve their efficiency and competitiveness. Retailers using EDI can implement so-called **quick-response** strategies that reduce the time merchandise is held in inventory, resulting in substantial cost savings. Quick response is essentially the just-in-time process used in merchandising.

The advantages of electronic data interchange are so compelling that many large retailers—Wal-Mart, Dillard's, and Lowe's—now require all their vendors to possess and use EDI. In fact, EDI is now considered essential for long-term relationships with major retailers and others.

National Account Selling

Some relationships due to the large investments at stake are more important than others. A large manufacturer such as Procter & Gamble pays special attention to the needs of large retailers such as Kmart ,Wal-Mart, and others, which sell many millions of dollars of P&G products each

Utilizing the quick-response systems, Calvin Klein monitors its merchandise and is able to replenish stores with its cK suits.

year. Manufacturers use a technique called *national account selling* to serve their largest, most profitable customers. The cluster of vendor offices in northwestern Arkansas—near Wal-Mart's home office—suggests how national account selling might be implemented.

The advantages of national account selling are many. By assembling a team of individuals to service just one account, the seller demonstrates the depth of its commitment to the buyer. The buyer-seller relationship is strengthened. Rather than engaging in the kind of adversarial relationship common in many business settings, buyers and seller work together to find solutions that benefit *both* parties. Finally, cooperative buyer-seller efforts can bring about dramatic improvements in both efficiency and effectiveness for both firms. These improvements find their way to the bottom line in the form of decreased costs and increased profits.[33]

Vendor-Managed Inventory

The proliferation of electronic data interchange and the constant pressure on suppliers to improve response time has led to a new way for buyers and sellers to do business. Vendor-managed inventory has replaced buyer-managed inventory in many instances. **Vendor-managed inventory (VMI)** is an inventory management system in which the *seller*—based on an existing agreement with the buyer—determines how much of a product a buyer needs and automatically ships new supplies to that buyer.[34]

Consider Fruit of the Loom's Activewear Online, an Internet-based, inventory-management system for its suppliers and dealers. Fruit of the Loom distributors receive computer software that helps them develop electronic catalogs of merchandise. Customized Web site software lets them track orders, manage stock, and process orders around the clock.

In the past Fruit of the Loom took almost five days to fill a retailer's order for more merchandise. Now retailers can

fruit.com

MARKETING | DICTIONARY

electronic data interchange (EDI) Computer-to-computer exchanges of invoices, orders, and other business documents.

quick response EDI strategy that reduces the time a retailer must hold merchandise in inventory, resulting in substantial cost savings.

vendor-managed inventory (VMI) Inventory management system in which the seller—based on an existing agreement with a buyer—determines how much of a product is needed.

| FIGURE 5.12 | Dell Computer's Supply Chain |

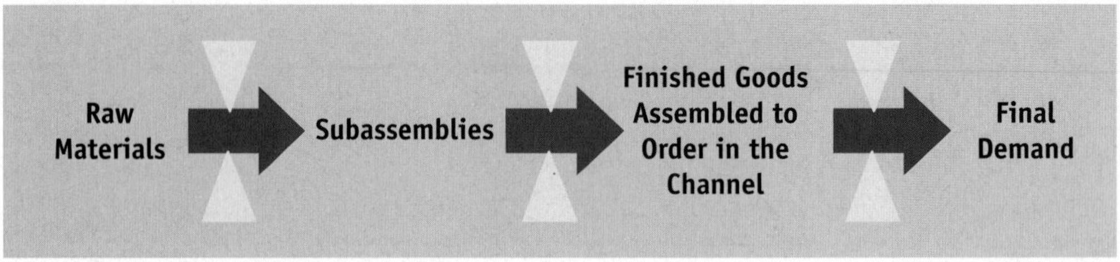

Source: Charles H. Fine, "The Primary of Chains," *Supply Chain Management Review,* Spring 1999, p. 80. Excerpt from Charles H. Fine, *Clockspeed. Winning Industry Control in the Age of Temporary Advantage.* (Perseus Books, 1998).

search Activewear Online and place an order in five minutes; as an added benefit, a VMI order costs approximately $10 to $20 less to process than a paper-based order. EDI systems exchange retailers' daily sales figures, inventory balances, sales forecasts, and other marketing data with the vendor, allowing the vendor to manage production more efficiently. Fruit of the Loom managers report that some participating retailers have seen their sales rise by as much as 25 percent.[35]

Managing the Supply Chain

Good relationships between businesses require careful management of the **supply chain** (sometimes called the *value chain),* which is the entire sequence of suppliers that contribute to the creation and delivery of a product. This process affects both *upstream* relationships between the company and its suppliers and *downstream* relationships with the product's end users. Figure 5.12 illustrates the supply chain for Dell Computer. Raw materials go into making subassemblies. When Dell receives an order, these subassemblies are put together into a finished computer that is then shipped to the buyer. The first steps shown in Figure 5.12 are Dell's upstream relationships, while the final two steps are its downstream relationship with its customers.

Effective supply-chain management can provide an important competitive advantage for a business marketer that results in the following:

- Increased innovation
- Decreased costs
- Improved conflict resolution within the chain
- Improved communication and involvement among members of the chain

By coordinating operations with the other companies in the chain, boosting quality, and improving its operating systems, a firm can improve speed and efficiency. Because companies spend considerable resources on goods and services from outside suppliers, cooperative relationships can pay off in many ways.[36]

Strategic Alliances

10

Discuss the value of strategic alliances to a company's relationship marketing strategy.

Strategic alliances are the ultimate expression of relationship marketing. Recall from Chapter 1 that a *strategic alliance* is a partnership formed to create a competitive advantage. These more formal long-term partnership arrangements improve each partner's supply-chain relationships and enhance flexibility in operating in today's complex and rapidly changing marketplace. The size and location of strategic partners is not important. Strategic alliances include businesses of all sizes, all kinds, and in many locations; it is what each partner can offer the other that is important.

TABLE 5.3	Resources and Skills That Partners Contribute to Strategic Alliances

RESOURCES		SKILLS
Patents	Customer base	Marketing Skills
Product lines	Marketing resources	• Innovation and product development
Brand equity	• Marketing infrastructure	• Positioning and segmentation
Reputation	• Sales force size	• Advertising and sales promotion
• For product quality	Established relationship with:	Manufacturing Skills
• For customer service	• Suppliers	• Miniaturization
• For product innovation	• Marketing intermediaries	• Low-cost manufacturing
Image	• End-use customers	• Flexible manufacturing
• Companywide	Manufacturing resources	Planning and implementation skills
• Business unit	• Location	R&D skills
• Product line/brand	• Size, scale economies, scope economies, excess capacity, newness of plan and equipment	Organizational expertise, producer learning, and experience effects
Knowledge of product-market	Information technology and systems	

Source: Adapted from P. Rajan Varadarajan and Margaret H. Cunningham, "Strategic Alliances: A Synthesis of Conceptual Foundations," *Journal of the Academy of Marketing Science,* p. 292.

Companies can structure strategic alliances in two ways. Alliance partners can establish a new business unit in which each takes an ownership position. In such a joint venture, one partner might own 40 percent, while the other owns 60 percent. Alternatively, the partners may decide to form a cooperative relationship that is less formal and does not involve ownership—for example, a joint new-product design team. The cooperative alliance can operate more flexibly and can change more easily as market forces or other conditions dictate. In either arrangement, the partners agree in advance on the skills and resources, such as those listed in Table 5.3, that each will bring into the alliance to achieve their mutual objectives and gain a competitive advantage.

Companies form many types of strategic alliances today. Some create *horizontal* alliances between firms at the same level in the supply chain; others define *vertical* links between firms at adjacent stages. The firms may serve the same or different industries. Alliances can involve cooperation among rivals who are market leaders or between a market leader and a follower.

Strategic alliances can also be domestic or international. The Star Alliance is an international airline network that began as a partnership between U.S.-based United Airlines and German airline Lufthansa and has since expanded to include Thai, Ansett Australia, Air New Zealand, Air Canada, SAS, and Brazilian airline Varig as shown in Figure 5.13. Today, Star Alliance planes service 578 cities around the world. Star's competitors, meanwhile, have formed their own strategic alliances. One is Delta, which has created partnerships with Swissair, Austrian, Sabena, Air France, and other carriers.[37]

MANAGING RELATIONSHIPS FOR SUPERIOR PERFORMANCE

Clearly, relationship marketing techniques help companies create better ways to communicate with customers and to develop long-term relationships. A company's relationship marketing efforts challenge managers to develop

MARKETING DICTIONARY

supply (value) chain Sequence of suppliers that contribute to the creation and delivery of a good or service.

FIGURE 5.13 **An International Strategic Alliance**

Star Alliance Gold members get priority check-in on all eight airlines. And these days, it seems we all want more ways to reduce the stress in our lives.

STAR ALLIANCE
The airline network for Earth.
www.star-alliance.com

strategies that closely integrate customer service, quality, and marketing functions. This goal may require changes in organizational philosophy, structure, and procedures. For example, companies must begin to think of customers as assets and to use techniques designed to calculate these customers' value. By analyzing customer databases, marketers can match the costs of acquiring and maintaining customer relationships with the profits received from these customers. This information allows managers to evaluate the return on a proposed relationship marketing program before making the investment.

Assessing the Costs and Benefits

How can organizations determine whether relationship marketing strategies pay off? Some companies hesitate to commit to large investments in database systems because customized programs cost much more per customer than mass marketing. The first step in evaluating this investment is to identify and compare its costs and benefits, both tangible and intangible. Because customers are assets, a company can analyze its marketing and communication investments in much the same way as it evaluates capital equipment investments.

Before Sony teamed up with Citibank to issue the Sony Visa credit card, Sony managers compared the estimated costs of the program against its potential benefits. They studied the credit-card market and analyzed the history of other co-branded cards, both profitable and unprofitable, to learn why some partnerships succeeded while others failed. Managers assessed this information against the advantages that Sony was likely to gain from the partnership, such as increased sales and greater control over its marketing message, and decided that these advantages justified the cost of the program.[38]

Without a thorough cost-benefit analysis, companies may waste money on such programs. If Nabisco distributes 50 million cents-off coupons, but less than about 2 percent are redeemed, it must consider the cost of the mass distribution in relation to the benefits—increased sales to both new and repeat buyers and improved customer relationships. If the actual costs from a prior program or estimated costs for a proposed mailing exceed the benefits, the company should not proceed.

Structuring Relationships: Strategic Implications

Partners can structure relationships in many different ways to improve performance, and these choices will vary for consumer and business markets. First, these partners should examine existing company systems involved in delivering customer service. The points at which customer interaction occurs are the most risky. By identifying the processes, people, and materials required to deliver the product, potential problem areas can be determined. If the customer has a good experience, the relationship is enhanced. Setting standards for these interaction points gives employees guidelines for action and increases the likelihood of achieving the company's goals.

In developing consumer relationships, marketers must recognize the inefficiency and high cost of trying to reach all consumers. Instead, they should use databases to identify prospects with the best profit potential. Programs that promote high levels of customer involvement—in design, development, and marketing phases—increase loyalty. The earlier this involvement begins in the process, the more feedback the company receives. Through communications from customers— warranty cards, contacts with customer service reps, contests—companies learn about consumer priorities. Listening to customer responses can help them eliminate unnecessary activities and focus on ones that customers value. A marketer should ask and answer the following key question: "Would the customer pay for this activity if the firm were to offer it as an option?"

In business-to-business relationships such as vendor/retailer partnerships, it is especially important to build shared trust. This goal may require both parties to provide detailed financial information—data some may prefer to keep confidential, for fear of partners possibly using this data to push for unfair pricing concessions. However, successful partnerships start with the premise that both parties need to make reasonable profits, and cooperation can pay off in lower costs and better sales for all concerned.[39]

Measurement and Evaluation Techniques

One of the most important measures of relationship marketing programs is the **lifetime value of a customer:** the revenues and intangible benefits (referrals, customer feedback, etc.) that a customer brings to the seller over an average lifetime, less the amount the company must spend to acquire, market to, and service the customer. Long-term customers are usually more valuable assets than new ones, because they buy more, cost less to service, refer other customers, and provide valuable feedback. The "average lifetime" of a customer relationship depends on industry and product characteristics. Customer lifetime for a consumer product like breakfast cereal or laundry detergent may be very short, while that for a computer system will last longer.

For a simple example of a lifetime value calculation, assume that a Chinese takeout restaurant determines that its average customer buys dinner twice a month at an average cost of $25 per order over a lifetime of five years. That business translates this calculation to revenues of $600 per year and $3,000 for five years. The restaurant can calculate and subtract its average costs for food, labor, and overhead to arrive at the per-customer profit. This figure serves as a baseline against which to measure strategies to increase the restaurant's sales volume, customer retention, or customer referral rate.

Another approach is to calculate the payback from a customer relationship, or how long it takes to break even on customer acquisition costs. For example, assume that an Internet-service provider spends $40 per new customer on direct mail and enrollment incentives. Based on average revenues per subscriber, the company takes about three months to recover that $40. If an average customer stays with the service 32 months and generates $500 in revenues, the rate of return is 11.5 times the original investment. Once the customer stays past the payback period, the provider should make a profit on that business.

In addition to lifetime value analysis and payback, companies use other techniques to evaluate relationship programs:

- Tracking rebate requests, coupon redemption, credit-card purchases, and product registrations
- Monitoring complaints and returned products and analyzing why customers leave
- Reviewing reply cards, comment forms, and surveys

These tools give the organization information about customer priorities so that managers can make changes to their systems, if necessary, and set appropriate, measurable goals for relationship programs.

A hotel chain may set a goal of improving the rate of repeat visits from 44 percent to 52 percent. A mail-order company may want to reduce time from 48 to 24 hours to process and mail orders. If a customer survey reveals late flight arrivals as the number one complaint of an airline's passengers, the airline might set an objective of increasing the number of on-time arrivals from 87 percent to 93 percent.

11

Identify and evaluate the most common measurement and evaluation techniques within a relationship marketing program.

MARKETING   DICTIONARY

lifetime value of a customer The revenues and intangible benefits, such as referrals and customer feedback, that a customer brings to the seller over an average lifetime, less the amount the company must spend to acquire, market to, and service the customer.

ACHIEVEMENT CHECK SUMMARY

Read the learning objectives that follow, and consider the questions for each one. Answering these questions will reinforce your grasp of the most important concepts in the chapter and will allow you to check how well you have achieved these learning goals. Where a blank appears before a question, answer with *T* or *F* for true/false questions; for multiple-choice questions, choose the letter of the correct answer.

Objective 5.1: Contrast relationship marketing with transaction-based marketing.

1. _____ Transaction-based marketing emphasizes long-term customer satisfaction.

2. _____ Which of the following is not part of relationship marketing? (a) high level of communication with customers; (b) quality programs; (c) emphasis on product features; (d) customer service orientation.

3. _____ Relationship marketing strategies make extensive use of mass market advertising.

Objective 5.2: List the goals of internal marketing.

1. _____ Only employees who interact directly with customers can influence customer satisfaction.

2. _____ Internal marketing efforts help employees support each other.

3. _____ Communicating with employees about customer needs helps a business reach its objectives.

Objective 5.3: Identify and explain each of the core elements of relationship marketing.

1. _____ Mothers against Drunk Driving (MADD) enables promises with its direct-mail campaign for donations.

2. _____ Understanding a situation from the perspective of the other party is called (a) trust; (b) reciprocity; (c) bonding; (d) empathy.

3. _____ An Apple computer users group would occupy a position at the high end of the relationship continuum.

Objective 5.4: Outline the steps in the development of a marketing relationship and the different levels of relationship marketing.

1. _____ Of the following benefits, which is not a reason that consumers form relationships? (a) simplify decisions; (b) reduce boredom; (c) decrease risk; (d) save money.

2. _____ Costs are typically three times higher to keep a customer than to acquire a new one.

3. _____ AT&T's True Rewards program, which gives customers points based on long-distance charges that they can redeem for gifts, is an affinity program.

Objective 5.5: Explain the primary methods used to measure customer satisfaction.

1. _____ Businesses must be sure they are measuring the right things when they track customer satisfaction.

2. _____ The only way to measure customer satisfaction is to conduct regular customer surveys.

3. _____ Studying the reasons behind customer defections can help improve customer satisfaction.

4. _____ Measurement must be combined with action in order to fully meet customer expectations.

Objective 5.6: Explain the role of databases in relationship marketing.

1. _____ Database marketing is useful only in marketing programs for existing customers.

2. _____ With the information in databases, companies can design programs tailored to specific customer segments, rather than to their "typical" customers.

Objective 5.7: Compare the different types of partnerships and explain how they contribute to relationship marketing.

1. _____ Companies choose partners based primarily on the financial assets they bring to the relationships.

2. _____ A restaurant supply company and the Olive Garden restaurant chain can form an internal relationship.

3. _____ A partnership between a company and a not-for-profit agency to sponsor a golf tournament is an example of (a) supplier partnership; (b) internal partnership; (c) lateral partnership; (d) buyer partnership.

Objective 5.8: Relate the concepts of co-marketing and co-branding to relationship marketing.

1. _____ Companies in a co-marketing agreement gain additional exposure for their products.

2. _____ Co-marketing programs require stronger commitments and longer-term relationships than co-branding programs.

3. _____ Nike ads featuring baseball outfielder Ken Griffey, Jr. are part of the shoemaker's co-branding strategy.

Objective 5.9: Describe how relationship marketing incorporates electronic data interchange, vendor-managed inventories, and national account selling.

1. _____ Electronic data interchange refers to the use of databases to forecast inventory levels.

2. _____ The customer determines the timing and quantities of product orders in a vendor-managed inventory system.

3 _____ Cooperative buyer-seller teams increase the commitment between companies, thereby strengthening their relationship.

Objective 5.10: Discuss the value of strategic alliances to a company's relationship marketing strategy.

1. _____ Coordinating operations with suppliers tends to improve quality and provide other competitive advantages.

2. _____ Strategic alliances bring together the skills and resources of partners to achieve common goals, such as entry into new markets and reducing manufacturing costs.

3. _____ To make a strategic alliance effective, each partner must take an ownership position.

Objective 5.11: Identify and evaluate the most common measurement and evaluation techniques within a relationship marketing program.

1. _____ A company's customers are an asset, and calculating their value provides a way to measure the return on investment of a relationship marketing program.

2. _____ Cost-benefit analysis deals primarily with the financial impact of a relationship marketing program.

3. _____ Customer communication materials are a valuable resource for evaluating relationship marketing programs.

Students: See the solutions section located on page S-1 to check your responses to the Achievement Check Summary.

Key Terms

relationship marketing	partnership
transaction-based marketing	co-marketing
external customers	co-branding
internal customers	electronic data interchange (EDI)
internal marketing	quick response
affinity program	vendor-managed inventory (VMI)
frequency marketing	supply (value) chain
database marketing	lifetime value of a customer

Review Questions

1. Trace the evolution from transaction-based to relationship marketing, and explain why relationship marketing suits today's marketing environment.
2. Distinguish between external customers and internal customers.
3. Briefly describe the three types of promises that form the basis of relationship marketing, and give an example of each.
4. Identify and explain the four dimensions of relationship marketing.
5. Describe the characteristics of relationships at the low, medium, and high points on the relationship marketing continuum.
6. Explain the role of customer feedback in achieving customer satisfaction. What are the primary methods of securing such feedback?
7. How can companies use affinity programs and frequent buyer programs to build relationships with consumers?
8. Discuss the benefits of database marketing in both consumer and business-to-business buyer-seller relationships.
9. Summarize the reasons why businesses form partnerships, and identify the four types of business partnerships.
10. Differentiate between co-marketing and co-branding programs.
11. Explain how effective supply-chain management and strategic alliances build relationships and provide competitive advantages.
12. What are the major techniques by which companies can measure and evaluate the effectiveness of their relationship marketing programs?

Questions for Critical Thinking

1. Select an organization in your area and describe a relationship marketing strategy that could help it build better customer relationships. How could this organization use relationship marketing to increase customer-retention rates and find new customers?
2. A hotel chain's database has information on guests that includes demographics, number of visits, and lifestyle preferences. Describe how the company can use this information to develop several relationship marketing programs. How can it use a more general database to identify potential customers and to personalize its communications with them?
3. Find an example of a strategic alliance in a current business magazine. Analyze the partners' motives for forming the alliance, their level(s) in the supply chain, and the benefits to each member.
4. Find an example of an operational supply chain. Draw, label, and explain this supply chain.
5. Why should a company calculate the lifetime value of a customer? How can managers use this information to improve the firm's relationship marketing programs?

1. **Frequency Marketing.** Locate Web sites that offer coupons and rewards to frequent visitors. If you need help getting started, go to *www.quickcoupons.net* or *www.couponsdirectory.com*. Write a 2- to 3-paragraph summary in which you identify two Web addresses you selected and the frequency marketing strategies used at the site. Explain whether you thought the frequency marketing strategies were effective or ineffective, the reasons for your opinion, and offer at least one way your chosen sites could improve the chances of repeat visits to their Web sites.

2. **Co-marketing.** Co-marketing involves not only companies but institutions as well. Go to Compaq Computer's site at *www.coursepaq.com*. Here Compaq provides an online course for those interested in developing *distance-* or *distributed-learning programs*. (Definition: Information is exchanged between an instructor and students who are not in the same location. Examples include connecting to the campus server from a dorm room and accessing video materials from the campus video server and taking a course via the Web.) At *www.coursepaq.com* choose "Express to Syllabus" and "Virtual Campus Solution Providers." Check out several links to the companies that Compaq promotes on its Web site. If the Web site you visit has a search option, type "co-marketing" to see how common co-marketing is among companies involved in providing some aspect of distance learning.

3. **Database Marketing.** Go to *www.ecomworld.com* where you will find *Faulkner & Gray's ECOM-WORLD, The Online Magazine for EC Professionals*. Choose the link for "Database Marketing," and find five facts about database marketing that you can contribute during a classroom discussion on the topic.

quickcoupons.com

couponsdirectory.com

coursepaq.com

ecomworld.com

Video Case 5 on FedEx Corp. begins on page VC-6.

Gateway Continuing Case Part 2 begins on page GC-3.

PART

3

MARKETING PLANNING, INFORMATION, AND SEGMENTATION

179

Gateway Continuing Case Part 3 begins on page GC-5.

Marketing Planning and Forecasting

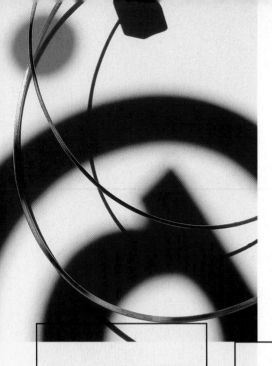

CHAPTER

6

1. Distinguish between strategic planning and tactical planning.

2. Explain how marketing plans differ at various levels in an organization.

3. Identify the steps in the marketing planning process.

4. Describe the concept of SWOT analysis and its major elements.

5. Explain how the strategic business unit concept, the market share/market growth matrix, the market attractiveness/business strength matrix, and spreadsheet analysis can be used in marketing planning.

6. Identify the major types of forecasting methods.

7. Explain the steps in the forecasting process.

MicroStrategy Helps Marketers Plan Their Strategy

Michael Saylor has a mission: "We think we've found the next great market—the ability to provide information to everybody, everywhere, anytime, and to automate sales and marketing services. We have multidecades of growth ahead of us. . . We will have finished when we employ 20,000 or 30,000 or 40,000 people, and we're a $10 billion company, and everybody on the planet lives every hour of every day dependent upon our technology." Not every marketer has such a grandiose mission, but every organization needs a mission, and every organization needs a marketing plan. Saylor's company, MicroStrategy Inc., helps an organization establish a mission and a marketing plan.

MicroStrategy creates software that enables customers to query huge database "warehouses" to sort and extract pertinent information. With one of MicroStrategy's programs, retailer Best Buy was able to analyze which of its products customers bought together—for instance, CDs and videos. With this information, Best Buy redesigned its store layout for better customer convenience—and for more sales. PetsMart uses MicroStrategy software to analyze inventory in individual markets, such as cat or

dog products. While Sabre Group, which sells $66 billion in travel reservations annually, uses MicroStrategy software to analyze airline, hotel, and rental car bookings. Eventually, the travel group plans to sell e-mailed reports to organizations that want to track the travel costs of their employees. Each of these organizations is using MicroStrategy's software to aid its own marketing planning.

In addition to aiding marketing planning, MicroStrategy's products now give more employees access to more customer information. For instance, 1,000 Sabre employees have access to the data, and roughly 800 Marks & Spencer department store employees in Britain have access to pertinent customer and product information. By improving employee knowledge, these organizations also increase their planning power.

Saylor's own strategic plans for MicroStrategy, which, like the company's mission, are aggressive. He intends to offer data warehouse information to consumers in the near future. For instance, a bank customer could ask to be alerted via computer if his or her checking account balance dropped below a certain amount. "We're going to use our technology to obliterate entire supply chains, to move the way people shop," he says.

In addition, Saylor has begun to form alliances with other organizations, such as Sybase, another high-tech firm. The Sybase agreement combines MicroStrategy's ability to analyze, personalize, and transmit information with Sybase's templates for customer-relationship management. "This solution will offer businesses a complete answer to their customer relationship management needs," claims Eric Miles, senior vice president and general manager of Sybase's Business Intelligence Division. Thus, MicroStrategy's newest strategic plan will assist other companies in their marketing planning with regard to customer relationships.

Saylor and his vision do have their detractors. His aggressive style rubs some the wrong way, and his grand plan seems to others more like a dream than a true corporate mission. Indeed, one expert in the field cautions that if too many queries come through the database system at once, the MicroStrategy warehouse slows down. But others believe that MicroStrategy is definitely headed in the right direction, particularly as it continues to develop new and better products. "He's a visionary [who has] learned how to run a business," says Robert Moran of the Aberdeen Group. "And he markets what he's got."[1]

181

CHAPTER OVERVIEW

- Will a change in the time and date of a musical performance affect concert attendance?

- Should a company assign its own sales personnel or independent agents to serve a new territory?

- Should a company offer discounts to cash customers? How would credit customers react to this policy?

These questions illustrate the decisions that a marketing manager regularly faces. The marketplace changes continually in response to emerging consumer expectations, technological developments, competitors' actions, economic trends, and political-legal events, as well as product innovations and pressures from channel members. Although the causes of these changes often lie outside the marketer's control, effective planning can anticipate many of these changes. Indeed, effective planning often means the difference between success and failure.

This chapter as well as Chapter 7 provide a foundation for all subsequent chapters by demonstrating the necessity for effective planning and gathering reliable information. These activities provide a structure within which a firm can take advantage of its unique strengths. Marketing planning specifies both the specific target markets that the firm will serve and the most appropriate marketing mix to satisfy those markets. This chapter examines marketing planning. Chapter 7 discusses marketing research and marketers' applications of decision-oriented information to plan and implement marketing strategies. ■

WHAT IS MARKETING PLANNING?

Planning is the process of anticipating future events and conditions and of determining courses of action for achieving organizational objectives. As the definition indicates, planning is a continuous process that includes specifying objectives and then determining the actions through which a firm can attain these objectives. The planning process creates a blueprint that specifies the means for achieving organizational objectives. It also defines checkpoints at which comparisons of actual performance with expectations indicate whether current activities are moving the organization toward its objectives.

Marketing planning—implementing planning activities devoted to achieving marketing objectives—establishes the basis for any marketing strategy. Product lines, pricing decisions, selection of appropriate distribution channels, and decisions relating to promotional campaigns all depend on plans formulated within the marketing organization.

An important trend in marketing planning centers on *relationship marketing*. You will recall from Chapter 5 that this term refers to a firm's attempt to develop long-term, cost-effective links

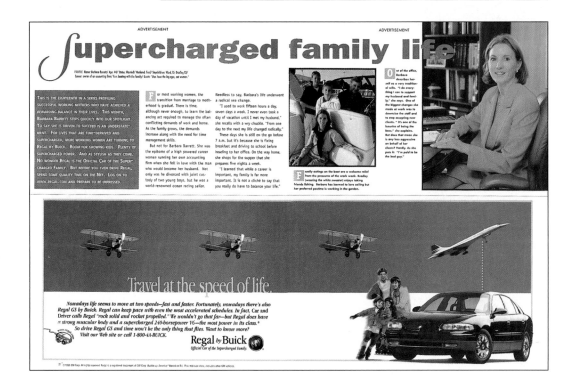

with individual customers and suppliers for mutual benefit. Good relationships with customers can arm a firm with vital strategic weapons. Many companies now include relationship-building goals and strategies in their plans.

For example, General Motors (GM) is working to strengthen its relationships with women, who have increasing clout in vehicle purchases. Chrysler and Ford sell larger percentages of their cars to women than GM does. GM research showed that women expressed neutral attitudes toward the GM brand, while men had stronger positive or negative opinions. To develop relationships with potential female buyers, GM has sponsored fashion shows, conventions for female business owners, and other women-oriented events. GM also created an advertising campaign targeting women. The ads, such as the one in Figure 6.1, give profiles of working mothers who succeed in balancing their work and family obligations and promote GM's Regal by Buick as a car designed for busy families.

Relationship marketers frequently maintain databases to track customer preferences. These marketers may also manipulate spreadsheets, which is discussed later in the chapter, to answer what-if questions related to prices and marketing performance.

 gm.com

Strategic Planning versus Tactical Planning

Planning is often classified on the basis of its scope or breadth. Some extremely broad plans focus on long-range organizational objectives that will significantly affect the firm for a time period of five or more years. Other, more targeted plans cover the objectives of individual units over shorter periods of time.

1

Distinguish between strategic planning and tactical planning.

| MARKETING | DICTIONARY |

planning The process of anticipating future events and conditions and determining the courses of action necessary to achieve organizational objectives.

marketing planning The process of anticipating future events and conditions and determining the courses of action necessary to achieve marketing objectives.

SOLVING AN ETHICAL CONTROVERSY

How Much Should Telemarketers Be Restricted?

Most marketers would agree that the best way to find out what consumers want is to go directly to the source. In many cases, this is true. Customer surveys, focus groups, and test marketing can all help firms determine what types of goods and services their customers prefer to buy. But telemarketing, which involves calling people in their homes either to ask for information on buying habits or to actually ask them to buy products, has crossed the line for many consumers and may actually backfire as a strategy.

The major issues concerning telemarketing tactics are privacy and fraud. People perceive telemarketing calls as an intrusion into their homes. Some consumers, such as senior citizens, may be susceptible to fraudulent calls that request credit-card numbers or other personal data. Federal and state legislators tend to side with consumers. The Telephone Consumer Protection Act of 1991 (TCPA) provides federal guidelines regarding telemarketing practices, but each state has its own laws, including the hours and days during which calls can be made, an obligation to adhere to "no-call" lists, and requests from consumers to not call them again. State laws usually include exemptions for charities, political candidates, and companies that consumers have already done business with, such as credit-card companies and utility companies. It is difficult, however, for telemarketers from outside a calling area to keep track of the separate regulations of each state.

  Should telemarketers be subject to stricter regulations in their practices?

Pro
1. Consumers have rights to privacy in their own homes, and the government should help restrict marketers who call in spite of a customer's wish to avoid these calls.

2. The only way to protect senior citizens and others who are most susceptible to telemarketing fraud is through stricter legislation.

Con
1. Telemarketing is a terrific opportunity for consumers to directly inform marketers what they want in terms of goods and services. Personal feedback is too valuable to lose.
2. Stricter regulations reduce the opportunities for marketers to engage in free enterprise, keeping markets and prices competitive and having a better offering of goods and services to customers.

Summary
Restricting telemarketing continues to be a hot consumer issue. Colorado state representative Steve Johnson, who developed a tough telemarketing bill, notes, "I don't understand why [telemarketers] are insisting on bugging those people who don't want to be called. They refuse to respect the wishes of those people, and that's what really irritates me." But those who support the intelligent use of telemarketing look for moderation. Tyler Prochnow, an attorney who specializes in telemarketing law, observes, "I think that empirical data and common sense will show that most of the new laws enacted in the name of reducing fraud have done nothing but place a greater regulatory burden and more shackles on the legitimate part of the industry that is the fastest-growing and largest direct marketing medium in the world."

SOURCES: Meredith Oakley, "Real Consumer Protection Is Lacking," *Arkansas Democrat-Gazette*, www.ardemgz.com, December 8, 1999; Laura Shin, "Hanging Up on Hucksters," *Newsweek*, www.newsweek.com, November 18, 1999; Michael Booth, "Bill Aims to Tame Telemarketing," *Denver Post*, www.denverpost.com, November 1, 1999; and Kelly J. Andrews, "Privacy Issues Hit Telemarketers First, Harder and With Two Fists," *Target Marketing*, www.targetonline.com, April 1999.

Strategic planning can be defined as the process of determining an organization's primary objectives and then adopting courses of action that will eventually achieve these objectives. This process includes, of course, allocation of necessary resources. The word *strategy* is derived from a Greek term meaning "the general's art." Strategic planning has a critical impact on a firm's destiny because it provides long-term direction for its decision makers.

Strategic planning is complemented by **tactical planning,** which guides the implementation of activities specified in the strategic plan. Unlike strategic plans, tactical plans typically address shorter-term actions that focus on current and near-future activities which a firm must complete to implement its larger strategies.

Mistakes in strategic decisions and in tactical planning are usually costly. For example, Tyson Foods has built a $7.4 billion-a-year business on its efficient system for processing, distributing, and selling chicken. However, when the company tried to duplicate its success with seafood, it lost millions of dollars. Tyson marketers expected to encounter challenges similar to the ones they had already conquered in the poultry industry, but they soon discovered the seafood industry operates by different rules. Some of these rules are dictated by nature—unlike chickens, fish can move where they want. Other rules are dictated by governments, such as regulations limiting the number of fish that can be caught. To implement its seafood strategy, Tyson Foods

 **tyson.com**

	TYPES OF PLANNING	
TABLE 6.1	Planning at Different Management Levels	

MANAGEMENT LEVEL	TYPES OF PLANNING EMPHASIZED AT THIS LEVEL	EXAMPLES
Top Management		
Board of directors Chief executive officer (CEO) Chief operating officer (COO) Divisional vice presidents	Strategic planning	Organization-wide objectives; fundamental strategies; long-term plans; total budget
Middle Management		
General sales manager Marketing research manager Advertising director	Tactical planning	Quarterly and semi-annual plans; divisional budgets; divisional policies and procedures
Supervisory Management		
District sales manager Supervisors in staff Marketing departments	Operational planning	Daily and weekly plans; unit budgets; departmental rules and procedures

purchased a large fishery, Arctic Alaska. Tyson managers—who have had great success with marketing chicken in stir-fry kits, frozen nuggets, hamburger-like patties, and other forms—developed similar tactical plans to process and package fish. Tyson ended up shouldering legal responsibility for fishing and safety violations that had been committed by Arctic Alaska. The company was forced to pay more than $4 million in fines for using the wrong type of fishing equipment in restricted areas. Eventually Tyson sold its fishing fleet and fishing rights to Trident Seafoods and announced plans to refocus on its poultry business.[2]

PLANNING AT DIFFERENT ORGANIZATIONAL LEVELS

Planning is a major responsibility for every manager, and managers at all organizational levels should devote portions of their work days to planning. However, the relative proportions of time spent planning activities and the types of planning typically vary.

Top management—the board of directors, chief executive officers (CEO), chief operating officers (COO), and functional vice presidents, such as chief marketing officers—spend greater proportions of their time engaged in planning than do middle-level and supervisory-level managers. Also, top managers usually focus their planning activities on long-range strategic issues. In contrast, middle-level managers—such as advertising directors, regional sales managers, and marketing research managers—tend to focus on operational planning, which includes creating and implementing tactical plans for their own departments. Supervisors often engage in developing specific programs to meet goals in their areas of responsibility. Table 6.1 summarizes the types of planning undertaken at various organizational levels.

To be most effective, the planning process should include input from a wide range of sources—employees, suppliers, and even customers. For instance, Microsoft operates computer-testing labs where marketers observe more than 30 people per day through one-way mirrors to identify which software features they find difficult to use. Input can also be obtained informally: Microsoft marketer Shawn Sanford meets regularly with his parents' retirement community computer club to

2

Explain how marketing plans differ at various levels in an organization.

MARKETING   DICTIONARY

strategic planning Process of determining an organization's primary objectives, allocating funds, and then initiating actions designed to achieve those objectives.

tactical planning Process of defining implementation activities that the firm must carry out to achieve its objectives.

solicit suggestions for improving the company's Windows operating system. (A frequent comment: Translate software error messages into everyday language.)[3]

STEPS IN THE MARKETING PLANNING PROCESS

3

Identify the steps in the marketing planning process.

The marketing planning process begins at the corporate level with the development of objectives. It then moves to develop procedures for accomplishing those objectives. Figure 6.2 shows the basic steps in the process. First, a company must define its mission. It then determines its objectives, assesses its resources, and evaluates environmental risks and opportunities. Guided by this information, marketers then formulate a marketing strategy, implement the strategy through marketing plans, and gather feedback to monitor and adapt strategies when necessary.

Defining the Organization's Mission

The planning process begins with activities to define the firm's **mission,** the essential purpose that differentiates the company from others. The mission statement specifies the organization's overall goals and operational scope and provides general guidelines for future management actions. Adjustments in this statement reflect changing business environments and management philosophies.

One example of a mission statement is the one posted by Globalstar, a satellite-based digital telecommunications system, on its Web site:

> Our philosophy is uncomplicated: to provide wireless satellite telephones—mobile and fixed—that are easy to use and inexpensive to operate and maintain; to apply advanced technology that delivers clear and reliable service at low cost throughout the world; to work in cooperation with existing telephone infrastructure around the world; to allow our Partners and service providers—major international telecommunications companies—to share in the growth of this new system by expanding their customer base into new, untapped markets.[4]

@ **globalstar.com**

Clearly, Globalstar's mission is to make wireless communication services available around the world. Other mission-related information on its Web site discusses the organization's business partners, technical architecture, research and development initiatives, technological capabilities, and potential markets.[5]

FIGURE 6.2   **The Marketing Planning Process**

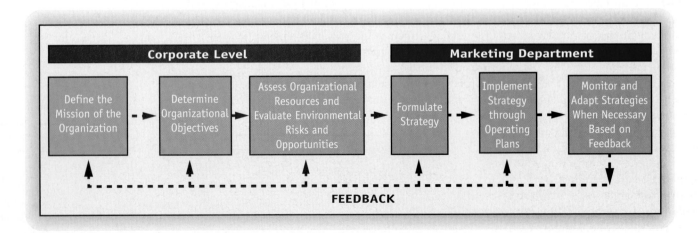

Determining Organizational Objectives

An organization lays out its basic objectives, or goals, in its mission statement. These objectives in turn guide development of supporting marketing objectives and plans. Soundly conceived objectives should state specific intentions (for example, generate a 12 percent increase in profits over last year, attain a 20 percent share of the market by 2008, or increase sales 15 percent over last year). In addition, these objectives should specify the time periods for specific achievements. For example, Globalstar's mission statement includes a schedule describing when it will roll out its commercial service.[6]

Assessing Organizational Resources and Evaluating Environmental Risks and Opportunities

The third step of the marketing-planning process involves a back-and-forth assessment of strengths, risks, and available opportunities. As Figure 6.1 illustrated, organizational resources and environmental factors affect marketing opportunities. Both are important considerations in the planning process.

Organizational resources include the capabilities of the firm's production, marketing, finance, technology, and employees. An organization's planners should pinpoint its strengths and weaknesses. Strengths help them to set objectives, develop plans for meeting those objectives, and take advantage of marketing opportunities. For example, in its assessment, Microsoft can identify several strengths: a globally-known and recognized brand name, software installed on a majority of computers around the world, financial soundness, marketing and advertising efficiency, technical expertise, and a dedicated team of managers and employees.[7]

The environmental components discussed in Chapter 2—the competitive, political-legal, economic, technological, and social-cultural environments—also influence marketing opportunities. Environmental effects can emerge both from within the organization and from the external environment. For example, the World Wide Web has transformed the way people communicate and do business.

SWOT Analysis

An important strategic planning tool, **SWOT analysis,** helps planners to compare internal organizational strengths and weaknesses with external opportunities and threats. (*SWOT* is an acronym for **s**trengths and **w**eaknesses, **o**pportunities, and **t**hreats.) This form of analysis provides managers with a critical view of the organization's internal and external environments and helps them to evaluate the firm's fulfillment of its basic mission.

A company's strengths reflect its *core competencies*—that which it does well. Core competencies are capabilities that customers value and competitors find difficult to duplicate.[8] As Figure 6.3 shows, matching an internal strength with an external opportunity produces for the organization a situation known as *leverage*. Managers face a *problem* when environmental threats attack their organization's weaknesses.

Planners anticipate *constraints* when internal weaknesses or limitations prevent their organization from taking advantage of opportunities. These internal weaknesses can create *vulnerabilities* for a company—environmental threats to its organizational strength.

Take, for example, General Motors (GM). Its strengths are its financial resources; as shown in Table 6.2, the giant automaker sells billions of dollars worth of vehicles every year. On the other hand, lack of responsiveness to changing consumer preferences is one of GM's weaknesses. As an example, consider four-door pickup trucks: Even after they became big sellers for Ford and Dodge, GM continued to produce three-door trucks instead. Auto industry analysts detect various other constraints at GM.

4

Describe the concept of SWOT analysis and its major elements.

MARKETING   DICTIONARY

mission A general, enduring statement of the overall organizational purpose.

SWOT analysis A method of studying organizational resources and capabilities to assess the firm's strengths and weaknesses and scanning its external environment to identify opportunities and threats.

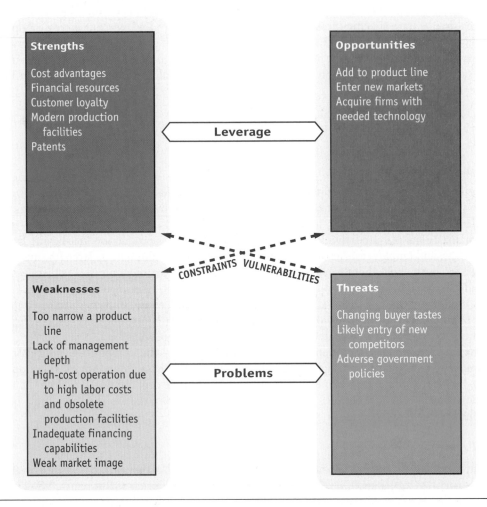

| FIGURE 6.3 | SWOT Analysis |

Strengths

Cost advantages
Financial resources
Customer loyalty
Modern production
    facilities
Patents

Opportunities

Add to product line
Enter new markets
Acquire firms with
    needed technology

Leverage

CONSTRAINTS VULNERABILITIES

Weaknesses

Too narrow a product
    line
Lack of management
    depth
High-cost operation due
    to high labor costs
    and obsolete
    production facilities
Inadequate financing
    capabilities
Weak market image

Threats

Changing buyer tastes
Likely entry of new
    competitors
Adverse government
    policies

Problems

Source: Adapted from a discussion in Ramon J. Aldag and Timothy M. Stearns, *Management* .

Note in Table 6.2 that, while GM's revenue is higher than Ford's, GM also has higher overhead costs per vehicle. Employee productivity is lower, more labor hours go into producing each vehicle, and the company deploys a larger network of dealers even though individual dealerships are less profitable than Ford's.

With such constraints, GM is definitely vulnerable to rivals such as Ford, which aggressively continues to cut costs by $1 billion or more a year. Thirty years ago, GM enjoyed 50 percent of the U.S. market; these days, its market share is closer to 28 percent.[9]

The Strategic Window

Professor Derek Abell has suggested the term **strategic window** to define the limited periods during which the key requirements of a market and the particular competencies of a firm best fit together.[10] The view through a strategic window shows planners a way to relate potential opportunities to company capabilities. Such a view requires a thorough analysis of (1) current and projected external environmental conditions, (2) current and projected internal company capabilities, and (3) how, whether, and when the firm can feasibly reconcile environmental conditions and company capabilities by implementing one or more marketing strategies.

The explosive growth in Internet services and in the users is creating a strategic window that allows computer and chip-maker manufacturers to compete more effectively against industry

TABLE 6.2	SWOT Analysis: GM Versus Ford	
	GENERAL MOTORS	**FORD**
Annual Revenue	$178 billion	$154 billion
Vehicles sold annually, worldwide	8.78 million	6.94 million
Labor hours spent per vehicle	46.5	34.7
Selling, general, and administrative expenses as percentage of sales	8.2%	5.6%
Productivity: Revenue per senior manager	$2.12 billion	$2.67 billion
Productivity: Units produced per hourly worker	27.3 units	45.6 units
Number of dealers	8,000	5,000
Vehicles sold per dealership	552	761

Source: Adapted from chart: "*GM* vs. *Ford:* Who's No. 1?" In Kathleen Kerwin, "GM: It's Time to Face the Future," *Business Week,* July 27, 1998, p. 28.

giants Microsoft and Intel. Compaq Computer, for instance, has developed computer keyboards with four buttons that bypass Microsoft's Windows desktop and take consumers immediately to Internet sites such as electronic mail, search engines, and online stores. Meanwhile, Packard Bell-NEC has introduced PCs with screen icons—also outside the Windows desktop—that link users quickly to various Internet sites.[11] The rise in Internet users created a window of opportunity for chip-maker Cyrix. In its ad in Figure 6.4, Cyrix explains how it developed a processor for entry-level PC users, enabling them to access the Internet and run multimedia applications.

FORMULATING A MARKETING STRATEGY

Opportunity analysis culminates in the formulation of marketing objectives designed to achieve overall organizational objectives and help planners develop a marketing plan. The marketing plan revolves around a resource-efficient, flexible, and adaptable marketing strategy.

A **marketing strategy** is an overall, companywide program for selecting a particular target market and then satisfying consumers in that market through a careful balance of the elements of the marketing mix—product, price, distribution, and promotion—each of which represents a subset of the overall marketing strategy.

Strategic Implications: Implementing a Strategy through Marketing Plans

The two final steps of the marketing-planning process consist of using operating plans to implement the previously developed marketing strategy and then monitoring performance to ensure that objectives are being achieved. In some cases, strategies may require some modifications if actual performance is not in line with expected results.

Consider what happened at Blockbuster. Customers complained that the videotapes they wanted were never in stock, and one in five shoppers went home empty-handed. New memberships fell and earnings declined by 20 percent. Parent company Viacom hired a new CEO, John Antioco, to help turn

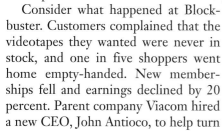

MARKETING **DICTIONARY**

strategic window A limited period of optimal fit between the key requirements of a market and the particular competencies of a firm.

marketing strategy A firm's overall program for selecting and satisfying a target market.

FIGURE 6.4   Taking Advantage of a Strategic Window

the company around. Antioco's marketing strategy seemed deceptively simple: Carry the products that customers want. While this may sound obvious, it required a major change in Blockbuster's business model. The company had always purchased tapes from the movie studios for about $65 per tape. With an average inventory of 10,000 tapes at each outlet, the expense limited managers' willingness to stock up on the more popular titles.

To help alleviate this expense, Antioco developed revenue-sharing arrangements with major movie studios that lowered Blockbuster's per-tape costs dramatically, to about $6 per tape. This allowed individual stores to keep multiple copies in stock and ensured that customers could always find the tapes they wanted.

So far Antioco's new strategy is succeeding. Worldwide, rental revenues at stores that have been open a year or more have soared by 13.3 percent, and active memberships have risen 7 percent. Blockbuster's share of the video-rental market rose from 25 percent to 30 percent, and Antioco expects to achieve his goal—40 percent market share—well ahead of his five-year schedule.[12]

As Blockbuster's experience shows, the overall strategic marketing plan serves as the basis for a series of operating plans necessary to move the organization toward accomplishing its objectives. Marketing planning affects activities discussed throughout this text, including analysis and selection of a target market and development of a marketing mix designed to satisfy that market.

blockbuster.com

5

Explain how the strategic business unit concept, the market share/market growth matrix, the market attractiveness/business strength matrix, and spreadsheet analysis can be used in marketing planning.

TOOLS FOR MARKETING PLANNING

As growing numbers of firms have discovered the benefits of effective marketing planning, they have developed a number of planning tools to assist in this important function. This section discusses four specific tools: the strategic business unit concept, the market share/market growth matrix, the market attractiveness/business strength matrix, and spreadsheet analysis.

Strategic Business Units (SBUs)

Although a relatively small firm may offer only a few items to its customers, a larger organization frequently produces and markets numerous offerings to widely diverse markets. Top managers at these larger firms need some method for identifying promising product lines that warrant investments of additional resources, as well as those lines that they should weed out from the firm's product portfolio. The concept of an SBU supports this analysis.

Strategic business units (SBUs) are key business units within diversified firms. Each SBU has its own managers, resources, objectives, and competitors. A division, product line, or single product may define the boundaries of an SBU. Each SBU pursues its own distinct mission, and each develops its own plans independently of other units in the organization.

Strategic business units focus the attention of company managers so they can respond effectively to changing consumer demand within limited markets. Companies redefine their SBUs as market conditions dictate. An example of this redefinition is Maine-based outfitter L. L. Bean, a longtime family-run enterprise. Indeed, its current president, Leon Gorman, is a grandson of L. L. himself and has run the company since 1967. To counter recent sagging sales, Gorman reorganized the company's hierarchical management structure to create SBUs that focus on specific merchandise areas, such as sporting goods and clothing. A new SBU, Freeport Studio, offers jewelry and casual clothing for baby-boomer women and promotes the merchandise through ads like the one in Figure 6.5.[13]

FIGURE 6.5   An SBU Focused on Merchandise for Women

TO DO: *Throw out to do list.*

llbean.com

Market Share/Market Growth Matrix

To evaluate their organization's strategic business units, marketers need some type of portfolio performance framework. The most widely used framework was developed by the Boston Consulting Group. This **market share/market growth matrix** places SBUs in a four-quadrant chart that plots market share—the percentage of a market that a firm controls—against market growth potential. The position of an SBU along the horizontal axis indicates its market share relative to those of competitors in the industry. Its position along the vertical axis indicates the annual growth rate of the market. After plotting all of a firm's business units, planners divide them according to the matrix's four quadrants. Figure 6.6 illustrates this matrix by labeling the four quadrants *cash cows, stars, dogs,* and *question marks.* Firms in each quadrant require a unique marketing strategy.

Stars represent units with high market shares in high-growth markets. These products or businesses are high-growth market leaders. While they generate considerable income, they need inflows of even more cash to finance further growth. Microsoft's Windows operating system requires ongoing expenditures on research and development in order to stay current, but the outlay pays off by maintaining the company's dominant position in the global personal computer market.[14]

MARKETING   DICTIONARY

strategic business unit (SBU) Business unit built around related product groupings or business activities with its own managers, resources, objectives, competitors, and structure for optimal, independent planning.

market share/market growth matrix Marketing planning tool that classifies a firm's products according to industry growth rates and market shares relative to competing products.

MARKETING STRATEGY FAILURE

PRT Group's Forecasting Sinks Offshore

BACKGROUND Doug Mellinger had a dream. Mellinger wanted to start a custom-software-programming business, but he could not hire enough software engineers in the United States. He also could not recruit enough foreign programmers because of immigration restrictions. So Mellinger investigated other countries as possible sites for his new operation, such as Australia, Ireland, and China, but each location had serious limitations, whether it was distance, unskilled labor, or lack of technological development. So Mellinger decided that if he could not find a country, he would "create" one. He chose Barbados for his new company, PRT Group Inc. For awhile, the strategy appeared successful; the company did so well that Mellinger took it public in an initial public stock offer that made him and his family worth over $100 million. But then sales began to drift.

THE MARKETING PROBLEM Mellinger chose Barbados to house his programmers based on qualitative forecasting techniques, or subjective data. The island had all the attributes that he and his investors were looking for, but customers had a hard time accepting the location as a viable one. "The uniqueness of the idea made it a tougher sell, with a longer sales cycle," notes Tarun Chandra, a senior analyst at Punk Ziegel & Co. Once the company went public, its managers made wildly

continued on next page

FIGURE 6.6   Market Share/Market Growth Matrix

Relative Market Share

	High	**Low**
Industry Growth Rate — High	**Stars** Generate considerable income **Strategy:** Invest more funds for future growth	**Question Marks** Have potential to become stars or cash cows **Strategy:** Either invest more funds for growth or consider disinvesting
Industry Growth Rate — Low	**Cash Cows** Generate strong cash flow **Strategy:** Milk profits to finance growth of stars and question marks	**Dogs** Generate little profits **Strategy:** Consider withdrawing

Cash cows command high market shares in low-growth markets. Marketers for such an SBU want to maintain this status for as long as possible. The business produces strong cash flows, but instead of investing heavily in the unit's own promotions and production capacity, the firm can use this cash to finance the growth of other SBUs with higher growth potentials. Gillette Company, for instance, treats the Sensor Excel razor as a cash cow; the product continues to generate huge profits without the need for large, new investments, so the company can invest instead in developing new generations of razors like the Mach3.[15]

Question marks achieve low market shares in high-growth markets. Marketers must decide whether or not to continue supporting these products or businesses since question marks typically require considerably more cash than they generate. If a question mark cannot become a star, the firm should pull out of the market and target other markets with greater potential. For example, several pharmaceutical companies have introduced herbal products in an effort to tap the $4-billion-a-year U.S. market for herbal medicines. Giant drug-makers such as Bayer and American Home Products spent an estimated $100 million last year to market their herbal remedies, but sales have been disappointing. These products remain definite question marks for these companies.[16]

Dogs manage only low market shares in low-growth markets. SBUs in this category promise poor future prospects, and marketers should withdraw from these businesses or product lines as quickly as possible. For example, after Stroh beer sales had languished for several years, managers finally decided to sell the company to Miller and Pabst.[17]

Market Attractiveness/Business Strength Matrix

Another model that can aid marketing planning is the **market attractiveness/business strength matrix,** a portfolio analysis technique that rates SBUs according to the attractiveness of their markets and their organizational strengths, as illustrated in Figure 6.7. Market

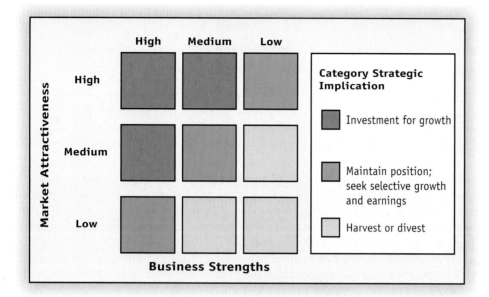

FIGURE 6.7 Market Attractiveness/Business Strength Matrix

inaccurate quantitative forecasts, projecting a doubling of revenues in one year, and they began expanding its programming capabilities based on those projections. But several major projects fell through, and PRT suddenly had high overhead expenses, maintaining a full-time skilled workforce offshore.

THE OUTCOME As the news of PRT's troubles became public, its stock—and its sales—began to plummet. Eventually, Mellinger was replaced as CEO by Dan Woodward, a former EDS executive, who quickly employed SWOT analysis and employed other planning and forecasting techniques. "I was amazed at [Dan's] speed, how fast he saw strengths and weaknesses in people and in areas of our business, and how decisive he was," notes Mellinger.

LESSONS LEARNED PRT founders learned how crucial it was to choose a location for business that customers could readily accept; and in hindsight, perhaps taking the company public was not a healthy solution for a small company. Pressured to meet shareholders' expectations, PRT was less free to make the planning and forecasting mistakes of a growing company. "[Securities] analysts are unforgiving," notes Mark Prieto, a vice president at J. P. Morgan. Rita Terdiman, a Gartner Group research director concurs. "You're a totally different company after going public; nothing remains the same."

attractiveness criteria include market share, growth, size, and stability; potential profitability; extent of government regulation; potential environmental and social impacts; and competitive conditions.[18] Managers must also take into account the organization's specific strengths and areas of competence, including its financial resources, image, relative cost advantages, customer base, and technological capabilities, along with the skills of its personnel.

Based on these criteria, managers create composite evaluations of SBUs. The most promising units in the upper-left area of the matrix offer strong business positions in attractive markets. These initiatives should receive the most company support. Those in the lower-right corner, on the other hand, offer little potential since they hold weak business positions in unattractive markets. Managers may choose to reduce funding for these operations or discontinue them altogether. In between, other SBUs rank from low to medium on market attractiveness and business strength. Decisions about allocating resources to these borderline SBUs depend on the strengths and weaknesses of the firm's entire portfolio.

Planners apply this matrix in the course of analyzing both their core competencies and their industry environments. This cautious planning prevents wasting investments on resources with potentially low returns.

Evaluating the Matrix Approach to Planning

The market share/market growth matrix emphasizes the importance of creating market offerings that will position the firm to its best advantage. It also acknowledges changes in successful SBUs as they move through their life cycles. A successful product or business typically begins as a question mark, then becomes a star, and eventually drops into the cash-cow category, generating surplus funds that finance its owner's new stars. Ultimately, it becomes a dog at the end of its life cycle, and the firm drops it from future plans.

The market attractiveness/business strength matrix is a useful diagnostic tool for identifying SBUs with the greatest and least potential. It can also help managers identify a firm's need for new sources of growth while indicating its most and least attractive markets.

MARKETING | DICTIONARY

market attractiveness/business strength matrix Portfolio analysis technique that rates SBUs according to the attractiveness of their markets and their organizational strengths.

TABLE 6.3		Example of Spreadsheet Analysis					
	FIXED COSTS				PER-UNIT VARIABLE	SALES	BREAK-EVEN
MANUFACTURING	MARKETING	R & D	TOTAL		COST	PRICE	POINT
$100,000	$120,000	$90,000	$310,000		$5	$10	62,000
$100,000	$230,000	$90,000	$420,000		$5	$10	84,000
$100,000	$120,000	$90,000	$310,000		$4	$9	62,000

Spreadsheet Analysis

Spreadsheet programs make up a class of computer software that helps planners to answer what-if questions. Electronic spreadsheets are the computerized equivalent of an accountant's hand-prepared worksheet. The electronic spreadsheet, like its manual counterpart, lays out a rigid grid of columns and rows that organizes numerical information in a standardized, easily understandable format. Microsoft's Excel is a popular example.

Spreadsheet analysis helps planners anticipate marketing performance given specified sets of circumstances. For example, a spreadsheet might project the outcomes of different pricing decisions for a new product, as shown in Table 6.3.

In this example, the item will be marketed at $10 per unit and can be produced for $5 in variable costs. The total fixed costs of $310,000 include $100,000 for manufacturing-overhead outlays, such as salaries, general office expenses, rent, utilities, and interest charges; $120,000 for marketing expenditures; and $90,000 for research and development to design the product. The spreadsheet calculation, using the basic model on line 1, reveals that the product would have to achieve sales of 62,000 units in order to break even.

What if a marketing manager, however, convinces other members of the group to increase marketing expenditures to $230,000? In line 2 of Table 6.3 the $120,000 marketing expenditure changes to $230,000, and the newly calculated break-even point is 84,000 units. As soon as an amount in one or more cells changes, the software automatically recalculates all affected amounts.

Line 3 of Table 6.3 demonstrates the impact of a reduction in variable costs to $4 (perhaps the result of switching to lower-cost materials) coupled with a $1 reduction in the product's selling price. The new break-even point is 62,000 units.

This figure demonstrates the ease with which a marketing manager can use a microcomputer spreadsheet program to determine the potential results of alternative decisions. More complex spreadsheets may include 50 or more columns of data and formulas but can complete new calculations as quickly as the manager changes the variables.

SALES FORECASTING

6

Identify the major types of forecasting methods.

A basic building block of a marketing plan is a **sales forecast,** an estimate of a firm's sales or income for a specified future period. In addition to marketing planning, sales forecasts play major roles in new-product decisions, production scheduling, financial planning, inventory planning and procurement, product distribution, and human-resource planning. An inaccurate forecast leads to incorrect decisions in each of these areas. A sales forecast is also an important tool for marketing control because it sets standards against which to measure actual performance. Without such standards, no comparisons can be made. Without a criterion for success, a firm cannot define failure.

Planners rely on short-run, intermediate, and long-run sales forecasts. A short-run forecast usually covers a period of up to one year, an intermediate forecast covers one to five years, and a

TABLE 6.4	**Benefits and Limitations of Various Forecasting Techniques**

TECHNIQUES	BENEFITS	LIMITATIONS
Qualitative Methods		
Jury of executive opinion	Opinions come from executives in many different departments; quick; inexpensive	Managers may lack sufficient knowledge and experience to make meaningful predictions
Delphi technique	Group of experts can accurately predict long-term events such as technological breakthroughs	Time-consuming; expensive
Sales force composite	Salespeople have expert customer, product, and competitor knowledge; quick; inexpensive	Inaccurate forecasts may result from low estimates of salespeople concerned about their influence on quotas
Survey of buyer intentions	Useful in predicting short-term and intermediate sales for firms that serve only a few customers	Intentions to buy may not result in actual purchases; time-consuming; expensive
Quantitative Methods		
Market test	Provides realistic information on actual purchases rather than on intent to buy	Alerts competition to new product plans; time-consuming; expensive
Trend analysis	Quick; inexpensive; effective with stable customer demand and environment	Assumes the future will continue the past; ignores environmental changes
Exponential smoothing	Same benefits as trend analysis, but emphasizes more recent data	Same limitations as trend analysis, but not as severe due to emphasis on recent data

long-run forecast extends beyond five years. The time frame of a forecast depends on many factors, including available resources, environmental forces, and the intended uses of the forecast.

Although sales forecasters practice dozens of techniques to divine the future—ranging from computer simulations to studying trends identified by futurists—their methods fall into two broad categories: qualitative and quantitative forecasting. *Qualitative* forecasting techniques supply rather subjective data that reports opinions rather than exact historical data. *Quantitative* forecasting methods, by contrast, develop numerical data through statistical computations such as trend extensions based on past data, computer simulations, and econometric models. As Table 6.4 shows, each method has benefits and limitations. Consequently, most organizations combine techniques.

Qualitative Forecasting Techniques

Planners apply qualitative forecasting methods when they want judgmental or subjective indicators. Qualitative forecasting techniques include the jury of executive opinion, Delphi technique, sales force composite, and survey of buyer intentions.

Jury of Executive Opinion

The technique called the **jury of executive opinion** combines and averages the outlooks of top executives from such areas as finance, production, marketing, and purchasing. It provides particularly

MARKETING   DICTIONARY

spreadsheet analysis Marketing planning tool that uses a decision-oriented computer program to answer what-if questions posed by marketing managers.

sales forecast Estimate of company sales for a specified future period.

jury of executive opinion Qualitative sales forecasting method that combines and averages the sales expectations of various executives.

Oop!'s Success Is No "Oops"

BACKGROUND Entrepreneurs Jennifer Neuguth and her husband David Riordan believe that shopping should be fun—even dazzling. The owners of a trendy, high-end gift shop called Oop! Contemporary Gift Gallery, located in Providence, Rhode Island had a decade of steady revenue growth, from $200,000 to $1.3 million.

THE CHALLENGE For their idea to succeed, Riordan and Neuguth had to plan carefully in choosing the right location, the right atmosphere, and the right products to attract customers. Once the shop opened, they continued with careful planning and forecasting to keep their business on the right track and attracting customers in a fiercely competitive industry.

THE STRATEGY Riordan and Neuguth decided that their best strategy was to communicate directly with customers to find out what people wanted and needed. They began with customer surveys. After a decade in business, they still hand out a 30-question customer survey in the store. "We do tons and tons of surveys," says Neuguth. Then they take the process a step further by offering $5 gift certificates as a thank you to customers who take the time to complete the survey and return it to the office. As soon as a customer's name is added to the database, the store communicates with the person. Instead of sending out a form letter, Neuguth encloses a handwritten note, a newsletter about Oop!

continued on next page

effective input when top managers bring the following important capabilities to the process: experience and knowledge about situations that influence sales, open-minded attitudes toward the future, and awareness of the bases for their judgments. This quick and inexpensive method generates effective forecasts for sales and new-product development. It works best for short-run forecasting.

Delphi Technique

Like the jury of executive opinion, the **Delphi technique** solicits opinions from several people, but it also gathers input from experts outside the firm, such as university researchers and scientists, rather than relying completely on company executives. It is most appropriately used to predict long-run issues, such as technological breakthroughs, that could affect future company sales and the market potential for new products.

The Delphi technique works as follows: A firm selects a panel of experts and sends each a questionnaire relating to a future event. After combining and averaging the answers, the firm develops another questionnaire based on these results and sends it to the experts. The process continues until it identifies a consensus of opinion. Although firms have successfully used Delphi to predict future technological breakthroughs, the method is both expensive and time-consuming.

Sales Force Composite

The **sales force composite** technique develops forecasts based on the belief that organization members closest to the marketplace—those with specialized product, customer, and competitor knowledge—offer the best insights concerning short-term future sales. It typically works from the bottom up: Forecasters consolidate salespeople's estimates first at the district level, then at the regional level, and finally nationwide to obtain an aggregate forecast of sales that reflects all three levels.

Few firms rely solely on the sales force composite for their forecasts, however. Since salespeople recognize the role of their sales forecasts in determining sales quotas for their territories, they are likely to make conservative estimates. Moreover, their narrow perspectives from within their limited geographic territories may prevent them from considering the impact on sales of trends developing in other territories, the forthcoming technological innovations, or the major changes in marketing strategies. Consequently, the sales force composite gives the best forecasts in combination with other techniques.

Survey of Buyer Intentions

A **survey of buyer intentions** gathers input through mail-in questionnaires, online feedback, telephone polls, and personal interviews to determine the purchasing intentions of a representative group of present and potential customers. This method suits firms that serve limited numbers of customers. This method often proves impractical for those with millions of customers. Also, buyer surveys gather useful information only when customers willingly reveal their buying intentions. Moreover, customer intentions do not necessarily translate into actual purchases. These surveys may help a firm to predict short-run or intermediate sales, but they employ time-consuming and expensive methods.

Quantitative Forecasting Techniques

Quantitative techniques apply math-based methods to forecast sales. They attempt to eliminate the guesswork of the qualitative methods. Quantitative techniques include such methods as market tests, trend analysis, and exponential smoothing.

Market Tests

One quantitative technique, the **market test,** frequently helps planners in assessing consumer responses to new-product offerings. The procedure typically begins by establishing a small number of test markets to gauge consumer responses to a new product under actual marketplace conditions. Market tests also permit experimenters to evaluate the effects of different prices,

alternative promotional strategies, and other marketing mix variations by comparing results among different test markets.

Based on consumer responses in test markets, a firm can predict sales for larger market areas. Goodyear, for example, test marketed its new run-flat tires by placing them as spare tires in only two brands of cars, the Chevrolet Corvette and the Plymouth Prowler. Consumer response was so favorable that the company began offering the tires to more automobile manufacturers.[19] Goodyear also introduced its run-flat technology in the replacement tire market and promotes the new tire directly to consumers in ads like the one in Figure 6.8.

The primary advantage of market tests is the realism that they provide for the marketer. On the other hand, these expensive and time-consuming experiments may also communicate marketing plans to competitors before a firm introduces a product to the total market. Test marketing is discussed in further detail in Chapter 12.

Trend Analysis

The technique of **trend analysis** develops forecasts for future sales by analyzing the historical relationship between sales and time. It implicitly assumes that the collective causes of past sales will continue to exert similar influence in the future. When historical data are available, planners can quickly and inexpensively complete trend analysis. Software programs can calculate the average annual increment of change for the available sales data. This average increment of change is then projected into the future to come up with the sales forecast. So, if the sales of a firm has been growing $15.3 million on average per year, this amount of sales could be added to last year's sales total to arrive at next year's forecast.

Of course, trend analysis cannot be used if historical data are not available, as in new-product forecasting. Also, trend analysis makes the dangerous assumption that future events will continue in the same manner as the past. Any variations in the determinants of future sales will cause deviations from the forecast. In other words, this method gives reliable forecasts only during periods of steady growth and stable demand. If conditions change, predictions based on trend analysis may become worthless. For this reason, forecasters have applied increasingly sophisticated techniques and complex, new forecasting models to anticipate the effects of various possible changes in the future.

Exponential Smoothing

A more sophisticated method of trend analysis, the **exponential smoothing** technique, weighs each year's sales data, giving the greatest weight to results from the most recent years. Since causes that have contributed to the most recent revenue changes are most likely to continue to interact similarly for the next time period, exponential smoothing assigns greater weights to these data than to those for earlier years. Otherwise, the statistical approach used in trend analysis is applied here. For example, last year's sales might receive a 1.5 weight, while sales data from two years could get a 1.4 weighting. Exponential smoothing is considered the most commonly used quantitative forecasting technique.

Steps in Sales Forecasting

Sales forecasting methods vary widely. However, typically they begin with an environmental forecast of general economic conditions.[20] This background information helps marketers project industry sales and then forecast company and product sales. This method is referred to as *top-down forecasting*.

Explain the steps in the forecasting process.

MARKETING DICTIONARY

Delphi technique A qualitative sales forecasting method that gathers and redistributes several rounds of anonymous forecasts until the participants reach a consensus.

sales force composite A qualitative sales forecasting method that develops sales estimates based on the combined estimates of the firm's salespeople.

survey of buyer intentions A qualitative sales forecasting method that samples opinions among groups of present and potential customers concerning their purchase intentions.

market test A quantitative forecasting method that introduces a new product, price, promotional campaign, or other marketing variable in a relatively small test-market location in order to assess consumer reactions.

trend analysis A quantitative sales forecasting method that estimates future sales through statistical analyses of historical sales patterns.

exponential smoothing A quantitative forecasting technique that assigns weights to historical sales data, giving the greatest weight to the most recent data.

Environmental Forecasting

The broad-based **environmental forecast** focuses on events and influences external to the firm that affect its markets, such as consumer spending and saving patterns, balance-of-trade surpluses and deficits, government expenditures, and business investments. By accumulating these projections, planners develop an overall economic forecast.

The most common measure of economic output is the country's gross domestic product (GDP), the sum of all goods and services produced within its borders in a given year. Trend analysis is the most popular method of forecasting increases in the GDP. Since many federal agencies and other organizations develop regular GDP forecasts, a firm may adopt their estimates, which are regularly reported in popular business publications.

Industry Sales Forecasting

The general economic forecast combines with other relevant environmental conditions to guide development of an industry sales forecast. Since industry sales often maintain stable relationships with GDP or some other measure of national economic activity, an industry forecast may begin by measuring the degree of this relationship and then applying the trend analysis method. Trade associations and publications for most industries provide short-term, intermediate, and long-term forecasts. These forecasts provide valuable input because they adjust an overall economic outlook for trends and environmental effects that influence specific industries.

Company and Product Sales Forecasting

After completing their industry forecast, marketing planners develop company and product forecasts. This process begins with a detailed analysis of performance in previous years. Planners review the firm's past and present market share and invite input from product managers, as well as regional and district sales managers, regarding expected sales. Since an accelerated promotional budget or introduction of a new product may stimulate additional sales, the forecast should also reflect marketing plans for the coming year.

Product and company forecasts must evaluate such factors as sales of each product; future sales trends; sales by customer, territory, salesperson, and order size; and financial resources. After planners develop the preliminary sales forecast, they ask for reviews of its content by the sales force and by district, regional, and national sales managers. Quaker Oats forecasts product sale in future planning for its Gatorade thirst quencher, shown in the ad in Figure 6.9. Worldwide sales of Gatorade exceed $1.7 billion, up from $100 million in 1984. This change represents an average annual growth rate in sales of 20 percent since Quaker acquired Gatorade in 1983. Because Gatorade is relatively new to most foreign markets, Quaker expects substantial sales growth in international markets based on consumer trends of expanded sports competition worldwide and a growing and younger population in Asian and Latin American countries.

doverdowns.com

Service enterprises also benefit from sales forecasting. Dover Downs, a Delaware-based horse track and casino, used sales forecasting methods to predict customer interest in slot machines. Dover Downs' prediction was right on target. Today, each of its 1,554 slot machines rings up $240 daily in gross revenue. Casino activity has outstripped track betting and now accounts for 80 percent of Dover's earnings.[21]

Grass-Roots Forecasting

An alternative approach to top-down forecasting is *grass-roots* or *bottom-up forecasting*. This method begins with sales estimates provided by each salesperson for his or her sales territory.

Later analysis by sales and marketing managers combines and refines these estimates at the divisional, regional, and national levels. The results reach the national sales manager who then combines these results into one sales estimate for the forthcoming time period. Proponents of bottom-up forecasting stress the benefits to employee morale and the motivation that results when each member of the sales force participates in developing the forecasts that helps to establish sales quotas. In addition, the approach ensures inputs from each individual territory and personal inputs from the salespeople who maintain direct and continuing contact with the firm's customers.

One shortcoming of grass-roots forecasts is that individual salespeople lack perspective on the organization as a whole. Sales estimates for individual territories may not reflect major trends, such as forthcoming new product entries, new items set for introduction by the company, planned price changes, new promotional campaigns, packaging changes, and other variables likely to affect results throughout the marketplace. In addition, since salespeople recognize the relationships between their sales forecasts and sales quotas, they may feel tempted to make relatively low forecasts that they can easily exceed. Consequently, firms that practice bottom-up planning depend heavily upon the compromises and final estimates that result from discussions at the divisional, regional, and national levels.

Since both top-down and grass-roots sales forecasting offer strengths and weaknesses, many marketers combine the two approaches to obtain the most realistic forecasts possible.

New-Product Sales Forecasting

Forecasting sales for a new product is an especially hazardous undertaking because no historical data is available. Companies typically employ consumer panels to obtain reactions to the products and to gauge probable purchase behavior. Test market data may also guide forecasts.

Since few products introduce totally new features to the market, forecasters can gain insight by carefully analyzing the sales of competing products that the new entry may displace. A new type of fishing reel, for example, will compete in an established market with other kinds of reels. This substitution method provides the forecaster with an estimate of market size and potential demand.

FIGURE 6.9 — Using Product Sales Forecasting

ACHIEVEMENT CHECK SUMMARY

Read the learning objectives that follow, and consider the questions for each one. Answering these questions will reinforce your grasp of the most important concepts in the chapter and will allow you to check how well you have achieved these learning goals. Where a blank appears before a question, answer with *T* or *F* for true/false questions; for multiple-choice questions, choose the letter of the correct answer.

Objective 6.1: Distinguish between strategic planning and tactical planning.

1. _____ When PepsiCo spun off its Taco Bell, Pizza Hut, and KFC fast-food operations into a separate company, it (a) formulated tactical plans; (b) changed its strategic plan; (c) applied relationship marketing concepts; (d) violated the tenets of its mission statement.

2. _____ Tactical planning involves allocating resources to implement actions designed to achieve a firm's strategic objectives.

3. _____ A firm's decision to spend $4 million on an advertising campaign is an example of strategic planning.

Objective 6.2: Explain how marketing plans differ at various levels in an organization.

1. _____ Top managers devote more time than middle managers to tactical planning.

MARKETING   DICTIONARY

environmental forecast Broad-based projection of economic activity that focuses on the impact of external events and influences on the firm's markets.

2. _____ Developing an operational plan such as a departmental budget is typically the responsibility of a supervisory manager.

3. _____ Strategic and tactical planning should reflect input only from employees.

Objective 6.3: Identify the steps in the marketing planning process.

1. _____ A company's first task is to (a) develop a strategic plan; (b) assess its objectives; (c) monitor plans; (d) define its mission.

2. _____ The statement, "Introduce three new products over the next two years," is an example of (a) a vision statement; (b) an organizational objective; (c) risk assessment; (d) SWOT analysis.

3. _____ A marketing strategy presents a comprehensive plan that balances the marketing mix and helps the company to reach its marketing goals.

Objective 6.4: Describe the concept of SWOT analysis and its four major elements.

1. _____ *SWOT* is an acronym for *strengths, weaknesses, opportunities,* and *timing*.

2. _____ Companies that evaluate their strengths and pursue opportunities that take advantage of those capabilities (a) are vulnerable to environmental threats; (b) focus mainly on external factors; (c) create leverage; (d) pay too much attention to problems.

3. _____ Constraints arise when an organization lacks sufficient internal resources to take advantage of opportunities.

Objective 6.5: Explain how the strategic business unit concept, the market share/market growth matrix, the market attractiveness/business strength matrix, and spreadsheet analysis can be used in marketing planning.

1. _____ By grouping company operating divisions into SBUs, a firm can focus on customer needs and set up distinct strategies for individual SBUs.

2. _____ The Gillette Company's Cricket disposable lighter failed to overtake the rival Bic product, so the company withdrew from the market. According to the market share/market growth matrix, the Cricket would be categorized as a (a) star; (b) question mark; (c) cash cow; (d) dog.

3. _____ The market attractiveness/business strength matrix for analyzing a portfolio of products helps companies weed out weak products and identify promising candidates for further investment.

Objective 6.6: Identify the major types of forecasting methods.

1. _____ A technique that is not used in quantitative sales forecasting is (a) sales force composite; (b) trend analysis; (c) least-squares analysis; (d) market testing.

2. _____ The Delphi technique solicits forecasts from persons outside the firm.

3. _____ Trend analysis is most useful for new-product sales forecasts.

Objective 6.7: Explain the steps in the forecasting process.

1. _____ Top-down sales forecasting starts by projecting the effects of external market events and industry trends on the firm.

2. _____ Grass-roots forecasting is the last step in top-down forecasting.

3. _____ The sales force composite method provides a broad view of the company's market situation.

Students: See the solutions section located on page S-1 to check your responses to the Achievement Check Summary.

Key Terms

planning	mission
marketing planning	SWOT analysis
strategic planning	strategic window
tactical planning	marketing strategy

strategic business unit (SBU)	Delphi technique
market share/market growth matrix	sales force composite
market attractiveness/business strength matrix	survey of buyer intentions
	market test
spreadsheet analysis	trend analysis
sales forecast	exponential smoothing
jury of executive opinion	environmental forecast

Review Questions

1. List three differences that distinguish strategic planning from tactical planning.

2. What are the basic steps in the marketing planning process? Give an example of a decision that planners might make at each step.

3. Discuss how analysis of an organization's external environment and assessment of internal strengths and weaknesses can identify strategic opportunities and threats. Examine in your answer the concepts of leverage, problems, constraints, and vulnerabilities.

4. Explain the concept of a strategic window. Provide one example for a not-for-profit organization and one for a profit-seeking business.

5. Identify the two major components of a firm's marketing strategy. Why must planners consider them in a specific order?

6. What characteristics differentiate stars, cash cows, question marks, and dogs in the market share/market growth matrix? Give examples of products in each of the four quadrants of the matrix, and suggest a marketing strategy for each product.

7. What dangers might result from rigid application of SBU portfolio models such as the market share/market growth matrix or the market attractiveness/business strength matrix?

8. Explain how spreadsheet analysis can assist a marketing manager in planning and implementing marketing strategies.

9. Compare the major types of forecasting methods. Explain the steps for the most typical method.

10. Discuss the advantages and risks of basing sales forecasts exclusively on estimates developed by the firm's sales force.

Questions for Critical Thinking

1. Find three corporate mission statements not found in Chapter 6 or the accompanying appendix. What is the key point in each of the mission statements? How do these mission statements differ? How are they similar?

2. Prepare a case history of the strategic plans for a *Fortune* 500 company. Leading business magazines often report information of this nature.

3. Describe an application of SWOT analysis to the following marketing situations:

   a. A pharmaceutical company's patent for a market-leading drug is about to expire.

   b. A large construction company is located in a state that just passed a road-construction bond issue.

   c. A large commercial bank is known for its relationships with mid-sized businesses, supplying loans and mortgages as well as a range of business accounts and services. The bank's executives begin to worry when two smaller commercial banks in the region merge.

   d. Royal Crown Cola was the first to develop a low-calorie, diet soft drink, but financial, distribution, and size constraints prevented the firm from exploiting its early opportunity to capture and hold the market.

4. A major film studio is about to release a new adventure movie starring George Clooney. How might the strategic window concept be used in picking a release date for the new movie?

5. Which forecasting technique(s) are most appropriate for each product? Defend your answer.

a. Post Shredded Wheat breakfast cereal
b. Hootie and the Blowfish rock group
c. Kinko's copy shops
d. *Rolling Stone* magazine

1. Defining the Organization's Mission. Locate and print out two mission statements, such as the one found at Lockheed Martin's Web site (*www.lmco.com/mission/index.htm*). Bring your printouts to class to contribute during the discussion of the first step of the planning process.

2. Strategic Business Units (SBUs). Broaden your understanding of SBUs by locating information for Dana Corporation's SBU at *www.dana.com/corporate/sbu.htm*. In addition, examine Dana's Key Strategic Objectives, Key Financial Data, and Main Brands. Explain how all four areas support and relate to one another.

lmco.com

3. Sales Forecasting. Visit any two of the following sites that provide information about sales forecasting software products: *www.forecastx.com, www.greatlakessoftware.com, www.forecastpro.com, http://wml-marketing.com/sales.htm*. Based on what you've learned about sales forecasting in reading the chapter and in the classroom, which product would you purchase if you were in a job where you needed to forecast sales? State your reasons for choosing the product you choose.

dana.com

forecastx.com

Video Case 6 on Furniture.com begins on page VC-7.

Developing a Marketing Plan

The natural outgrowth of the planning process is a *marketing plan*—a detailed description of resources and actions a firm needs to achieve its stated marketing objectives. A marketing plan is an important part of an organization's overall business plan.

A marketing plan is necessary to any organization, for several reasons:

- It is needed to obtain financing since banks and most private investors require a detailed business plan before they will even consider a loan application or venture capital investment.

- It provides direction for the firm's overall business and marketing strategies.

- It supports the development of long-term and short-term organizational objectives.

- It guides employees in achieving these objectives.

- It serves as a standard against which the firm's progress can be measured and evaluated.

After creating and implementing this plan, marketers should reevaluate it periodically to gauge its success in moving the organization toward its goals. If necessary, changes should be implemented promptly.

COMPONENTS OF A MARKETING PLAN

Marketing plans may vary in length and format. However, most contain the following components:

- Mission statement that summarizes the organization's purpose, vision, and overall goals. (As noted in Chapter 6, the mission statement provides the foundation upon which further planning is based.) Component plans that present goals and strategies for each functional area of the enterprise include:
  - Marketing plan: Describes strategies for informing potential customers about goods and services that are offered, and describes strategies for winning repeat business.
  - Financing plan: Lays out a realistic approach in obtaining financing and managing cash flow and debt.
  - Production plan: Describes how the organization will go about producing its products in the most efficient, cost-effective manner possible.

- Facilities plan: Describes the physical environment and equipment necessary to implement the production plan.

- Human-resources plan: Estimates employment needs and staff skills necessary to achieve organizational goals.

This basic format applies whether a company operates in the manufacturing, wholesaling, retailing, or service industry. It is also important to remember that the marketing plan must be developed in conjunction with other functional plans.

Creating the Mission Statement and Determining Organizational Objectives

The mission statement presents the organization's broad objectives—its overall purpose and reason for existing. Consider the following mission statement of Unilever:

Our purpose in Unilever is to meet the everyday needs of people everywhere—to anticipate the aspirations of our consumers and customers and to respond creatively and competitively with branded products and services which raise the quality of life. Our deep roots in local cultures and markets around the world are our unparalleled inheritance and the foundation for our future growth. We will bring our wealth of knowledge and international expertise to the service of local consumers—a truly multi-local multinational.[1]

These broad mission statements can then be used to develop more specific objectives that state a course of action to be followed. These objectives should be both quantifiable and measurable so they can be evaluated objectively and adjusted as necessary.

Based on the preceding mission statement, Unilever's foods division developed a number of organizational objectives, such as the following:

- Establish four main "innovation centers" that focus on research and development related to margarine. For example, the company's Vlaardingen innovation center developed two new products, Rama margarine and Calvé mayonnaise, to cater to the growing market in Russia.

- Produce different types of tea bags tailored to consumer preferences in different areas of the world, such as pyramid tea bags in the United Kingdom and squeezable bags in Australia.

- Build a new sales information network, using encrypted personal computers, to serve facilities around the world.[2]

Clearly, Unilever's marketing plan guides it in achieving goals on a global scale. However, smaller organizations also benefit from the discipline and guidance of a well thought-out marketing plan.

When Roberta Lamb, a former professional opera singer, decided to start her own opera company in Boston, her mission statement consisted of two goals: (1) Provide a showcase for local musical talent and (2) sell enough tickets to fill every seat in whatever facility she booked. Realizing she needed a specific plan to help her achieve her ambitious mission, Lamb developed the following organizational objectives:

- Offer performances during the summer, when other Boston-area opera theaters are closed

- Reserve a small theater of fewer than 1,000 seats, since it will be easier to fill

- Limit performances to a two-week run, to leave audiences wanting more

- Recruit local celebrities for non-singing roles, to attract a broader audience

Lamb signed up singers from other opera companies, who readily agreed to accept lower fees for the chance to perform during the summer. A popular local broadcaster, eager to broaden his skills, was happy to take a speaking role. Lamb booked a 500-seat theater at Boston University for two weeks and sold out every performance. Ticket sales generated a profit of $16,000—an impressive achievement for a fledgling opera company and a tribute to Lamb's well-conceived marketing plan.[3]

Formulating a Marketing Strategy

As discussed in earlier chapters, a marketing strategy starts with the selection of a target market. For example, the typical patron of Wisconsin-based Kohl's department stores is a working woman aged 30 to 49 who has a family and a household income of up to $70,000 a year.[4] By contrast, the target market for the $40,000 Dodge Prowler is a married man, average age 53, and who can afford a third car.[5] After selecting the target market, the marketer develops a marketing mix to reach the chosen consumer segments:

- Product strategy. Which goods and services should the firm offer to meet customers' needs? For instance, Unilever's foods division groups its products into five key categories—culinary, frozen foods, ice cream, tea-based beverages, and spreads and cooking products—and concentrates on developing new consumer items in each category.[6]

- Distribution strategy. Through which channel(s) and physical facilities will the firm distribute its products? Sherwin-Williams, as an example, bases its distribution strategy on company-owned stores. By contrast, Avon uses a direct channel based on its network of independent contractors.

- Promotional strategy. What mix of personal selling, advertising, and sales promotion activities should the firm pursue? Safeco, the Seattle-based insurance company, decided that naming the Seattle Mariners' new ballpark, Safeco Field should be part of its promotional strategy.

- Pricing strategy. At what general level should the firm set prices? Everyday low prices is the foundation of Wal-Mart's pricing strategy. By contrast, the expensive gifts in Neiman Marcus's annual Christmas catalog suggest that this upscale retailer is using a different pricing strategy to reach its intended market—primarily women age 35 to 55 with household incomes of $150,000 or more.

ASSIGNMENT

Follow the format described in this appendix to develop a marketing plan for one of the following organizations:

a. a WNBA franchise such as the Charlotte Sting, New York Liberty, or Detroit Shock

b. a local Best Western franchise motel

c. a start-up software firm located near Boston

d. Florida State University

Marketing Research and Decision-Support Systems

CHAPTER

7

1 Describe the development of the marketing research function and its major activities.

2 List and explain the steps in the marketing research process.

3 Differentiate between the types and sources of primary and secondary data.

4 Explain the different sampling techniques used by marketing researchers.

5 Identify the methods by which marketing researchers collect primary data.

6 Discuss the challenges of conducting marketing research in global markets.

7 Outline important uses of computer technology in marketing research.

Wal-Mart Wants to Know What You Buy

An Angel for our Angel

"From the minute we brought the Christmas angel home, our daughter Raven seemed to instantly connect with her, as if she was a new-found friend. It was the first time Raven had ever seen an angel that reflected her heritage, and the bond was magical! That's why the angel's up all year long – even after all the other decorations have been put away.

When you see the smile this angel brings to our angel, it's easy to understand why Wal-Mart is our store."

– Kathy (Raven's mother)
Wal-Mart Customer

WAL★MART
ALWAYS LOW PRICES.
Always.

RAVEN, WAL-MART CUSTOMER

You might think all Wal-Marts are the same: The smiling greeter as you walk through the door, the stacks of toys and snacks on the shelves near the entrance, the fast-food restaurant tucked into a corner, those ubiquitous smiling yellow faces that sometimes wear hats. Wal-Mart generally does have a look and feel that travels from store to store, but all stores are *not* alike in the merchandise they carry. One Wal-Mart in Decatur, Georgia, for instance, carries African-American Barbies and CDs by Snoop Doggy Dogg; another in Dunwoody, Georgia, features music by Garth Brooks and an expensive porcelain doll called Soft Expressions. A Wal-Mart in Mountain View, California, offers mountain bikes and health supplements, while another in Union City, California, showcases big-screen televisions. None of this takes place by chance. Rather, it is the result of careful research on the part of Wal-Mart marketers that informs decision makers. Wal-Mart's managers want to know which goods and services

their customers will buy, and they do everything they can to find out.

Technology has played a large part in Wal-Mart's recent efforts to collect information about consumers. Individual store computers feed bits of data to a huge data warehouse at the company headquarters in Bentonville, Arkansas. Before 1999 the company's data warehouse contained so much consumer data that if the data were printed out on standard sheets of paper and those sheets were laid end to end, they would reach to the moon and back six times. But Wal-Mart doubled its size in 1999 and, hence, increased the amount of its data. At over 100 terabytes, it is the largest commercial data warehouse in the nation, perhaps the world. "Our NCR Teradata-based data warehouse enables us to better serve consumers with each transaction in each store, helping Wal-Mart build stronger relationships with every shopper," comments Randy Mott, Wal-Mart's chief information officer.

Wal-Mart's computers analyze data to find trends that can help the company's marketers to determine which products will move quickly and at which stores. "They can look at Christmases over the past five years and make a judgment about what will move and what won't," observes Andrew Filipowski, chief executive of Platinum Technology, which sells sophisticated 3-D visualization software that helps marketers view data and predict shoppers' behavior based not only on consumer demographics but also on geographical location, weather and climate patterns, and even local sports teams.

In addition, Wal-Mart is connected to about 5,000 manufacturers through its Retail Link software program, which allows organizations like Disney or Mattel to check on their inventory at each store. "They can look at how things are selling in individual areas and make decisions about categories where there may be an opportunity to expand," explains Mott.

Predicting the future is every marketer's goal, and Wal-Mart has proved itself to be a champion at the game. The company not only uses data about current and past consumer practices and purchases but also factors in other information such as changing weather conditions in order to predict both long- and short-term future outcomes. For instance, during one unseasonably warm winter, other retailers suffered because they had stocked too many winter clothes that were not selling.

Wal-Mart's information system, however, is so fast that marketers were able to make changes in orders for winter items through the supply chain.

It is one thing to collect large amounts of data yet quite another to be able to analyze it and convert it into useful information. Some retailers obtain information about their customers by issuing credit cards or special affinity cards. But Wal-Mart computers scan and analyze everything that goes into the shopping cart.

"We carry over 100,000 items in stock at a Supercenter," notes Randy Mott. "The combination of [the cart's contents] gives you a good indication of the age of that consumer and the preferences in terms of ethnic background." That is why marketing research is truly about people. If marketers can learn more about the people they want to reach and serve, they will be more successful at selling their products.[1]

CHAPTER OVERVIEW

Marketers must not only solve problems as they arise, but they must also anticipate and prevent those that may occur in the future. To avoid surprises and to make the best decisions possible, the right information in sufficient quantities is required in choosing effective solutions.

Marketing research is the process of collecting and using information for marketing decision making. This decision-oriented marketing information comes from a variety of sources that provide *data* to the researcher. Some data comes from well-planned studies designed to elicit specific information. Researchers may obtain other valuable information from sales force reports, accounting data, and published reports. Still other data may emerge from controlled experiments and computer simulations. Marketing research, by presenting pertinent *information* in a useful format, aids decision makers in analyzing data and in suggesting possible actions.

This chapter deals with the marketing research function, which is closely linked with the other elements of the marketing planning process. Indeed, all marketing research should fit within the framework of the organization's strategic plan.

Information collected through marketing research underlies much of the material on marketing planning and forecasting in Chapter 6 and on market segmentation in Chapter 8. Clearly, the marketing research function is the primary source of the information needed in making effective marketing decisions. ■

THE MARKETING RESEARCH FUNCTION

1

Describe the development of the marketing research function and its major activities.

Before looking at how marketing research is conducted, its historical development, the people and organizations it involves, and the activities it entails must first be examined. New media technologies such as the World Wide Web and virtual reality are opening up new channels through which researchers can tap into data and information. A key focus of this chapter will be the relationship between technology and marketing research.

Development of the Marketing Research Function

More than 100 years has passed since N. W. Ayer conducted the first organized marketing research project in 1879. A second important milestone in the development of marketing research occurred just 32 years later, when Charles C. Parlin organized and became manager of the nation's first commercial research department at Curtis Publishing Company.

Parlin got his start as a marketing researcher by counting soup cans in Philadelphia's garbage. Parlin was employed selling advertising space in the *Saturday Evening Post*, but the Campbell Soup Company resisted his offers believing that it reached primarily working-class readers who preferred to make their own soup rather than spend 10 cents for a can of prepared soup. Campbell was targeting its product at higher-income people who could afford to pay for convenience. In response, Parlin began counting soup cans in the garbage collected from different neighborhoods. To Campbell's surprise, Parlin's research revealed that more soup was bought by working-class families than wealthy ones, who had servants to make soup for them. Campbell Soup quickly became a *Saturday Evening Post* client. It is interesting to note that garbage remains a good source of information for marketing researchers. Some airlines, for example, have studied the leftovers from onboard meals to determine what to serve passengers.

Most early research gathered little more than written testimonials from purchasers of firms' products. Research methods became more sophisticated during the 1930s as the development of statistical techniques led to refinements in sampling procedures and greater accuracy in research findings.

In recent years, advances in computer technology have significantly changed the complexion of marketing research. Besides accelerating the pace and broadening the base of data collection, computers have aided marketers in making informed decisions about problems and opportunities. Computer simulations, for example, allow marketers to evaluate alternatives by posing what-if questions. Marketing researchers at many consumer goods firms simulate product introductions through computer programs to determine whether to risk real-world product launches or even to subject products to test marketing.

Who Conducts Marketing Research?

In a recent survey of *Fortune* 200 firms the majority of them reported an average budget of $11 million each for in-house marketing research departments. This amount represents a 38 percent increase over the previous year, indicating that the marketing research industry is growing rapidly and that the demand for good research continues to rise.[2]

The size and organizational form of the marketing research function is usually tied to the structure of the company. Some firms organize research units to support different product lines, brands, or geographic areas. Others organize their research functions according to the types of research they need performed, such as sales analysis, new-product development, or advertising evaluation.

Many firms depend on independent marketing research firms.[3] These independent organizations might handle one part of a larger study, such as conducting consumer interviews. Firms can also contract out entire research studies.

Marketers usually decide whether to conduct a study internally or through an outside organization based on cost. Another major consideration in the decision to hire an outside organization is the reliability and accuracy of the information collected by this organization. Because collecting marketing data is what these outside organizations do full time, oftentimes this information is more thorough and accurate than if collected by an inexperienced in-house staff. A marketing research firm can provide technical assistance and expertise not available within the contracting firm. Interaction with

MARKETING **DICTIONARY**

marketing research Process of collecting and using information for marketing decision making.

outside suppliers also helps to ensure that a researcher does not conduct a study only to validate a favorite personal theory or preferred option.

Marketing research companies range in size from sole proprietorships to national and international firms such as A. C. Nielsen, Information Resources Inc., and Arbitron. Recently, the 25 largest marketing research firms earned total revenues of $6.643 billion—a 9 percent increase from the year before. Almost 45 percent of these revenues were generated outside the firms' home countries.[4]

Marketing research suppliers can be classified as syndicated services, full-service suppliers, or limited-service suppliers, depending on the primary thrust of their methods. Some full-service organizations are also willing to take on limited-service activities.

Syndicated Services

An organization that regularly provides a standardized set of data to all customers is called a *syndicated service*. Mediamark Research Inc., for example, operates a syndicated product research service based on personal interviews with adults regarding their exposure to advertising media. Clients include advertisers, advertising agencies, magazines, newspapers, broadcasters, and cable TV networks.

Full-Service Research Suppliers

jdpower.com

An organization that contracts with clients to conduct complete marketing research projects is called a *full-service research supplier*. J. D. Power and Associates is a full-service firm that specializes in the domestic and international automobile markets. Questar is a full-service research firm specializing in linking management practices to long-term customer satisfaction, loyalty, and retention, as shown in Figure 7.1. A full-service supplier becomes the client's marketing research arm, performing all of the steps in the marketing research process (as discussed later in this chapter).

FIGURE 7.1   **A Full-Service Marketing Research Firm**

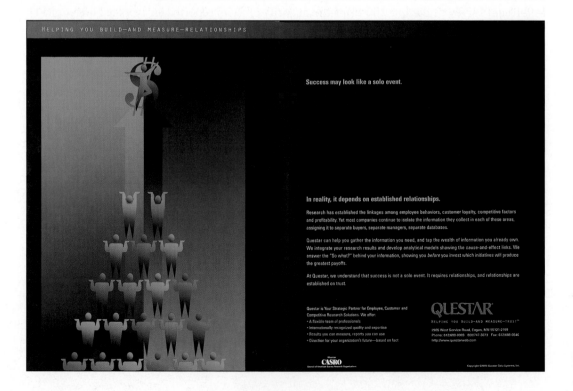

Limited-Service Research Suppliers

A marketing research firm that specializes in a limited number of activities, such as conducting field interviews or performing data processing, is called a *limited-service research supplier*. Working almost exclusively for clients in the movie industry, The National Research Group specializes in rating entertainment facilities through input from moviegoers. The firm also prepares studies to help clients develop advertising strategies and to track awareness and interest. Syndicated services can be considered a type of limited-service research supplier.

STRATEGIC IMPLICATIONS OF MARKETING RESEARCH

Marketing research can help an organization develop effective marketing strategies. Approximately 75 percent of new products eventually fail to attract enough buyers to remain viable. Why? A major reason is the seller's failure to understand market needs.

Consider Unilever's embarrassment when it introduced a new laundry powder called Persil that was supposed to contain extra scrubbing ingredients to get clothes cleaner. The laundry powder contained so much scrubbing ingredients, it actually shredded clothing. Niall Fitz-Gerald, chief of Unilever's soap division, quickly yanked Persil off store shelves and called an emergency meeting of 30 executives to find out what went wrong. When he asked how many of the executives did their own laundry, not one raised their hands. FitzGerald wryly noted the irony of trying to understand why customers were not using Unilever's soap when Unilever managers had never used it themselves.[5]

Marketing research ideally matches new products to potential customers to improve those products' performances and chances of success. Marketers also conduct research to analyze sales of their own and competitors' products, to gauge the performance of existing products, to guide the development of promotional campaigns and product enhancements, and to develop and refine goods and services. All of these activities enable marketers to fine-tune their marketing strategies and reach customers more effectively and efficiently.

Marketing research can even reveal new insights into why products are not selling. One cheese manufacturer, frustrated by low sales despite glowing feedback from tasters in focus groups, hired marketing researchers to discover why it was experiencing low sales. Exploratory research showed that the cheese was more difficult to slice than other brands. As a result, to make their own jobs easier, deli-counter clerks were steering customers to other cheeses.[6]

MARKETING RESEARCH ACTIVITIES

Marketing research activities can be divided into three main categories: scanning, risk assessment, and monitoring.[7] Figure 7.2 illustrates the types of questions that each activity can help answer.

Scanning activities search for opportunities and challenges in the firm's environment. As Chapter 2 indicated, a firm's environment can change rapidly. The marketing research function should play a key role in marketers' efforts to track and identify any changes in technology, markets, and cultural and economic conditions that will affect the firm. Scanning activities involve primarily future-oriented research.

After identifying potential opportunities and challenges, marketing research helps businesses to develop effective strategies and tactics. These decisions often carry considerable risk: The firm has no guarantee that its chosen programs will succeed. Therefore, marketing researchers direct their *risk assessment* activities toward evaluating the likelihood of commercial success by linking proposed actions to feedback from customers in real or simulated conditions. Risk assessment activities also help the firm to measure the costs and benefits of a particular course of action, such as introducing a new product or implementing a new promotional technique.

| FIGURE 7.2 | Types of Questions Marketing Research Can Help Answer |

---

❶ Scanning

   a. What kinds of people buy our products? Where do they live? How much do they earn? How many of them can we identify?

   b. Are the markets for our products increasing or decreasing? Can research indicate promising markets that we have not yet reached?

   c. What economic, social, political, and technological trends are likely to affect our markets? How?

❷ Risk Assessment

   a. Which of several product designs is most likely to generate the most success?

   b. What price should we charge for our products? How will profits change under various pricing strategies?

   c. Where and by whom should our products be sold?

   d. How much should we spend on promotion? How should we allocate this amount among products and geographic areas? What type of media will most effectively distribute our message?

   e. What costs and benefits can we expect with certain planned marketing strategies?

❸ Monitoring

   a. What is our overall market share? What is our share in each geographic area? What is our share for each customer type?

   b. Who are our competitors? What are their strengths and weaknesses? How do our strengths and weaknesses compare?

   c. Are customers satisfied with our products? How well have we served them?

   d. How does the public perceive our company? What is our reputation with the trade?

Scanning and risk assessment activities focus on the future. Monitoring activities, however, assesses current events. This part of marketing research seeks to discover how well past decisions are working out in the present. *Monitoring* activities includes analyzing sales and profit data, customer satisfaction levels, and results from advertising and promotion programs. In a sense, monitoring activities can be defined as diagnostic tools. These activities aim the marketing research efforts toward identifying problems and suggesting ways for correcting these problems.

While marketing research can provide insight into marketers' questions, not every marketing research effort yields valuable results. When marketing research is poorly designed or implemented, companies can face unpleasant surprises. The next section will explain the steps of an effective marketing research process.

Customer Satisfaction Measurement Programs

Once a company identifies priorities that determine customer satisfaction components and gathers feedback on present performance, its next step is to initiate an ongoing **customer satisfaction measurement (CSM) program**. CSM systems provide a procedure for tracking customer satisfaction over time. Rather than just a snapshot of how the firm is doing at a particular moment, ongoing measurement allows the firm to identify changes in customer attitudes and satisfaction and to develop action plans for improvement. Such programs can become quite sophisticated, sometimes requiring the aid of outside consultants.

While most customer satisfaction measurement programs focus on tracking the satisfaction levels of current customers, some companies have gained valuable insights by tracking the dissatisfaction that leads customers to abandon certain products for those of competitors. Some customer defections are only partial; customers may remain somewhat satisfied with a business but not completely satisfied. Such attitudes could lead them to take their business elsewhere. Studying the underlying causes of customer defections, even partial defections, can be useful for identifying problem areas which need attention.

THE MARKETING RESEARCH PROCESS

As discussed earlier, businesspeople rely on marketing research to provide the information they need to make effective decisions regarding their firm's current and future activities. The chances of making a successful decision improve when the right information is provided at the right time in the decision-making process. To achieve this goal, marketing researchers often follow the six-step process shown in Figure 7.3. In the initial stages, researchers define the problem, conduct exploratory research, and formulate a hypothesis to be tested. Next, they create a design for the research study, followed by the collection of data. Finally, researchers interpret and present the information in decision making. The following sections take a closer look at each step of the marketing research process.

2

List and explain the steps in the marketing research process.

Define the Problem

Someone once said that well-defined problems are half-solved. A well-defined problem permits the researcher to focus on securing the exact information needed for the solution. Clearly defining the question that research needs to answer increases the speed and accuracy of the research process.

Researchers must carefully avoid confusing symptoms of a problem with the problem itself. A symptom merely alerts marketers that they have a problem. For example, suppose that a maker of frozen pizzas sees its market share drop from 8 percent to 5 percent in six months. The loss of market share is a symptom of the problem the company must solve. To define the problem, the firm must look for the underlying causes of its market share loss.

A logical starting point in identifying the problem might be to evaluate the firm's marketing mix elements and target market. Suppose, for example, a firm has recently changed its promotional strategies. Research might then seek to answer the question, "What must we do to improve the effectiveness of our marketing mix?" The firm might also look at possible environmental changes. Perhaps a new competitor entered the firm's market. Decision makers will need information to help answer the question, "What must we do to distinguish our company from the new competitor?"

Tom Stemberg, chief executive officer and chairman of office-supply retailer Staples, values marketing research so highly that he often does his own. Stemberg makes a habit of secretly visiting a different competitor's store at least once a week. During these visits, he pushes himself to answer what he views as the most important question: In what ways are they doing a better job than Staples? Stemberg views every shopping visit as an opportunity to learn from his competition.[8] The goal in the first stage of the marketing research process is, therefore, to pinpoint the main question that decision makers need to answer to make successful choices.

staples.com

MARKETING   DICTIONARY

customer satisfaction measurement (CSM) program Procedure for measuring customer feedback against customer satisfaction goals and developing a plan of action for improvement.

FIGURE 7.3   The Marketing Research Process

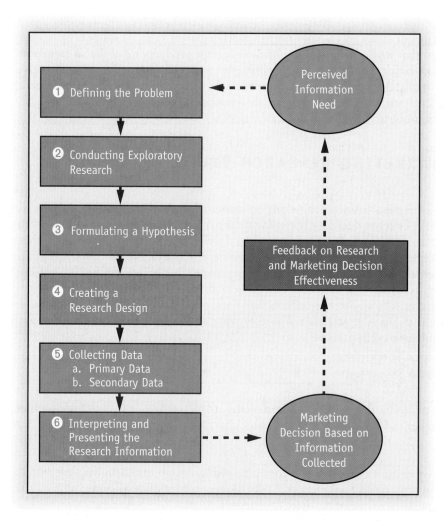

Conduct Exploratory Research

Once a firm has defined the question they want to answer, researchers can begin exploratory research. **Exploratory research** seeks to discover the cause of a specific problem by discussing the problem with informed sources both within and outside the firm and by examining data from other information sources. The pizza firm, for example, might talk with its wholesalers, retailers, and customers. Executives might also ask for input from the sales force or look for overall market clues.

Staples chairman Stemberg even enlists family members as undercover researchers. When a new Office Depot store opened in south Florida, for example, Stemberg asked his mother-in-law to investigate its competitive potential by buying items, noting how long they took to be delivered, and then reporting on the easiness of returning these items. His mother-in-law, clearly a talented researcher in her own right, quickly obtained even more valuable insights into the efficiency of the new store's delivery operations by talking to the experts—the delivery truck drivers.[9]

Before creating ads for its first global campaign, Saab conducted exploratory research by surveying Saab owners around the world. Researchers asked owners what the Saab brand meant to them. They learned that owners viewed their cars as dynamic, distinctively styled, high performance, and exceptionally safe. These findings helped Saab create ads such as the one in Figure 7.4 that promotes the car's safety features.

In addition to talking with employees, exploratory research can include evaluation of company records, such as sales and profit analyses, and data about the sales and profits of competitors' products. Marketing researchers often refer to internal data collection as *situation analysis.* The term *informal investigation* is often used for exploratory interviews with informed persons outside the researchers' firms.

Using Internal Data

Marketers can find valuable data in their firm's own internal records. Three commonly available sources of valuable internal data are sales records, financial statements, and marketing cost analyses. Marketers analyze sales performance records to gain an overall view of company efficiency and to find clues to potential problems. Easily prepared from company invoices or a computer database system, this **sales analysis** can give quite revealing results for the marketing executive. The study typically compares actual and expected sales based on a detailed sales forecast by territory, product, customer, and salesperson. Once the *sales quota*—the level of expected sales to which actual results are compared—has been established, it is a simple process to compare actual results with expected performance.

Other possible breakdowns for sales analysis separate transactions by customer type, product, method of sale (mail, telephone, or personal contact), type of order (cash or credit), and size of order. Sales analysis is one of the least expensive and most important sources of marketing information available to a firm.

Accounting data, as summarized in the firm's financial statements, can be another good tool for identifying financial issues that influence marketing. Financial statements, which report nondescript accounts, contribute mainly by helping analysts raise more specific questions. Using ratio analysis, researchers can compare performance in current and previous years against industry benchmarks. These exercises may hint at possible problems, but only more detailed analysis would reveal specific causes of indicated variations.

A third source of internal information is **marketing cost analysis**—evaluation of expenses for tasks like selling, warehousing, advertising, and delivery in order to determine the profitability of particular customers, territories, or product lines. Firms most commonly examine the allocation of costs to products, customers, and territories or districts. Marketing decision makers then evaluate the profitability of particular customers and districts on the basis of the sales produced and the costs incurred in generating those sales.

Like sales performance and financial research, marketing cost analysis is most useful when it provides information linked to other forms of marketing research. Later in this chapter, the issue of how computer technologies can accomplish these linkages and move information between a firm's units will be addressed.

Formulate a Hypothesis

After defining the problem and conducting an exploratory investigation, the marketer should be able to formulate a **hypothesis**—a tentative explanation for some specific event. A hypothesis is a statement about the relationship among variables that carries

| FIGURE 7.4 | Advertising Guided by Exploratory Research |

Saab vs. Parenthood

A child is born. And there is a new center of your universe. You begin to consider a new car to satisfy the needs of your family. You assume you must sacrifice the pure pleasure of driving for safety and space. But what if the car is a Saab 9-5 Wagon? It has antisubmarining seats designed to prevent your child from sliding under the seat belt. It has sixteen separate storage compartments for all your child's playthings. And, what's this? A turbocharged engine. Yes, one car can accommodate both your family and you.

www.saabusa.com
1 800 SAAB USA

MARKETING DICTIONARY

exploratory research Process of discussing a marketing problem with informed sources both within and outside the firm and examining information from secondary sources.

sales analysis In-depth evaluation of a firm's sales.

marketing cost analysis Evaluation of expenses for tasks like selling, billing, and advertising to determine the profitability of particular customers, territories, or product lines.

hypothesis Tentative explanation for some specific event.

@ **galileesplendor.com**

clear implications for testing this relationship. It sets the stage for more in-depth research by further clarifying what researchers need to test.

Peter Shamir, vice president of marketing for Israeli cracker company Galilee Splendor, came to the United States to launch Galilee's U.S. subsidiary. At first Shamir planned to distribute his crackers the usual way, through supermarkets, so he met with grocery retailers and distributors to explore the industry.

Soon, however, Shamir realized he lacked a crucial piece of information: the reason why the average American chooses one cracker over another. He conducted his own informal marketing research by hanging out in supermarkets and observing customers. He quickly realized that the average consumer takes all of 10 seconds to select a box of crackers and then quickly moves on. Shamir concluded that Bible Bread, Galilee's entry in the cracker wars, would probably be overlooked in the cracker aisle of a typical supermarket. Instead, he hypothesized that Bible Bread would sell more successfully in the deli section, where customers tended to linger and look for new products.

Shamir swiftly put his hypothesis into action, and sales immediately began to increase. The number of stores carrying Bible Bread rose rapidly, by 50 percent in one year. U.S. revenues are now approaching $1 million. He notes that Galilee already knew it had a good cracker, but research informed the company about the best way to sell it.[10]

Not all marketing research studies test specific hypotheses. However, a carefully designed study can benefit from the rigor introduced by developing a hypothesis before beginning data collection and analysis.

Create a Research Design

To test hypotheses and find solutions to marketing problems, a marketer creates a **research design,** a series of decisions that, taken together, comprise a master plan or model for conducting marketing research. In designing a research project, marketers must be sure that the study will measure what they intend to measure. When Seattle-based health information marketer Lexant decided to develop a Web site to address weight management, user-research manager Kelly Franznick quickly noticed a large hurdle to researching this issue. "It's very hard to get people to talk about their weight," comments Franznick. "You need to use methods that allow them to reveal what they want on their own terms." Franznick mailed disposable cameras and logbooks to 30 potential customers, who were asked to photograph themselves whenever they "became conscious of a weight-management issue" and quickly jot a caption for each photo in the logbook. The resulting information proved valuable in helping Lexant create its new Web site, and many of the concerns revealed by the captions became popular online discussion topics.[11]

A second important research design consideration is the selection of respondents. Marketing researchers use sampling techniques, discussed later in the chapter, to determine which consumers to include in their studies.

Collect Data

3

Differentiate between the types and sources of primary and secondary data.

Marketing researchers gather two kinds of data: secondary data and primary data. **Secondary data** is data from previously published or compiled sources. Census data is one example. **Primary data** refers to data collected for the first time specifically for a marketing research study. An example of primary data are statistics collected from a survey that asks current customers about their preferences for product improvements.

Secondary data offers two important advantages: (1) It is almost always less expensive to gather than primary data, and (2) researchers usually must spend less time to locate and use secondary data. A research study that requires primary data may take three to four months to complete, while a researcher can often gather secondary data in a matter of days.

Secondary data does have limitations that primary data does not. First, published information can quickly become obsolete. A marketer analyzing population statistics for various areas may discover that the most recent census figures are already out of date because of continued growth and changing demographics. Second, published data collected for an unrelated purpose may not be completely relevant to the marketer's specific needs. For example, census data does not reveal the brand preferences of consumers in a particular region.

Although research to gather primary data can cost more and take longer, the results can provide richer, more detailed information than secondary data offers. The choice between secondary and primary data is tied to cost, validity, and effectiveness. In reality, many marketing research projects combine secondary and primary data to fully answer marketing questions. This chapter will examine specific methods for collecting both secondary and primary data in later sections.

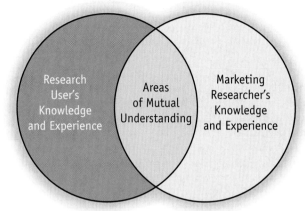

FIGURE 7.5 The Research Report and Presentation: Linking the Study and the Research User

Interpreting and Presenting Research Information

The final step in the marketing research process is to interpret the findings and present the research information to decision makers in a format that allows them to make effective judgments. Figure 7.5 illustrates possible differences between marketing researchers and their audiences in interpretations of research results due to differing backgrounds, levels of knowledge, and experience. Marketing researchers should target presentations at the areas of mutual understanding. The cardinal rule of presenting marketing research requires that it assist decision making rather than being an end in itself.

Marketing researchers and research users must cooperate at every stage in the research process. Too many marketing studies go unused because management fears restrictions on the results after hearing lengthy discussions of research limitations or unfamiliar terminology. Marketing researchers must remember to direct their reports toward management and not to other research specialists. They should spell out their conclusions in clear, concise, and actionable terms. Their reports should outline technical details of the research methods in an appendix, if at all. These precautions will increase the likelihood that management will utilize the research findings.

MARKETING RESEARCH METHODS

Clearly, data collection is an integral part of the marketing research process. One of the most time-consuming parts of collecting data is determining what method the marketer should use to obtain the data. This section will discuss the most commonly used methods by which marketing researchers find both secondary and primary data.

Secondary Data Collection

Secondary data comes from many sources. The overwhelming quantity of secondary data available at little or no cost challenges researchers to select data that is pertinent.

Secondary data consists of two types: internal and external data. Internal data, as discussed earlier, includes sales records, product performance reviews, sales force activity reports, and marketing cost reports. External data comes from a variety of sources, including government records, syndicated research services, and industry publications.

MARKETING **DICTIONARY**

research design Series of decisions that, taken together, comprise a master plan for conducting marketing research.

secondary data Previously published data.

primary data Data collected for the first time.

SOLVING AN ETHICAL CONTROVERSY

Who Owns Your Driver's License Data?

We all hate our driver's license photo. But consumers might hate them even more if they knew that at least one company, Image Data of Nashua, New Hampshire, wants to buy their photos to include in a national database that could be made available to marketers. Although the company insists that it wants to build the database to help stop retail fraud, reduce airport terrorism, and verify the identity of immigrants, privacy activists and legislators fear that the database could be used for unethical purposes. Until the Drivers' Privacy Protection Act was proposed, state agencies routinely sold their motor vehicle records, including personal information, to direct marketing firms, charities, and companies who were searching for secondary data about potential customers. In fact, New York collected $17 million in one year from the sale of New Yorkers' license data. Now, some states—including New Hampshire, where Image Data is located—give drivers the option to decline the sale of this information. But the warehousing of photos and the potential for marketers and others to obtain this information creates a whole new picture.

Robert Houvener, founder of Image Data, claims that his company's database could "save consumers, businesses, and governments billions of dollars in identity theft." When it was revealed, however, that the Secret Service planned to assist Image Data in evaluating the technology, privacy activists and legislators sought to block the sale of photographs. Meanwhile, the U.S. Supreme Court decided to hear arguments about whether Congress can actually compel states to offer the no-sale option to drivers or allow the choice to remain with each state. In other words, the debate rages about who owns the data.

Should the sale of driver's license records be restricted by law?

Pro

1. Since anyone wishing to obtain a driver's license must furnish certain personal information to a state, the applicant does not have a choice about whether to provide the information. Thus, he or she is not freely agreeing to the sale of this data and may not be aware that it is being distributed to others.

2. The state is not engaged in commerce with a driving applicant and thus is not just collecting information about buying habits. States should not sell personal data or photos obtained from the applicant.

3. The state does not own the data and should not profit from information that its citizens must provide. Instead, the driver should have a say in who can have access to personal information.

Con

1. Department of Motor Vehicle records have always been considered public information and should remain so.

2. The distribution of photographic and print data could actually benefit the consumer by reducing fraud and preventing or detecting other crimes.

3. Because detecting fraud would be more difficult with tighter restrictions, insurance rates would increase, which is not in consumers' best interests.

Summary

Selling driver's license records can be beneficial to states, marketers, and even consumers in the long run. However, this practice should be done with each driver's knowledge and permission. At the beginning of 2000, the U.S. Supreme Court unanimously agreed and sided with Congress in protecting drivers' privacy.

Sources: "On the Docket," Northwestern University: Reno vs. Condon, 98–1464, Opinion issued January 12, 2000, accessed at www.medill.nwu.edu/docket; "Supreme Court to Study States' Right to Sell Driver's License Data," CNN online, accessed at www.cnn.com, November 10, 1999; Declan McCullagh, "Your Driver License, For Sale?" *Wired News*, accessed at www.wired.com, June 25, 1999; and Robert O'Harrow Jr., and Liz Leyden, "Driver's-License Photo Database Got Federal Funds, Secret Service Help," *The Washington Post News Service*, accessed at www.seattletimes.com, February 18, 1999.

Computerized databases can give access to data from both inside and outside an organization. A *database* is any collection of data retrievable through a computer. A great deal of information is available in this form. The following paragraphs on government data, private data, and online sources will focus on some databases and other external data sources available to marketing researchers.

Government Data

The U.S. government is the nation's most important source of marketing data. Census data provides the most frequently used government statistics. The U.S. government spends more than $2.5 billion to conduct a census of population every ten years, but it makes census information available at no charge in local libraries, on computer disks, and through the Internet. Through ads like the one in Figure 7.6, the government encouraged citizens to fill out and mail in their Census 2000 forms by explaining how the information they provide can benefit their communities. The

Bureau of the Census also conducts a periodic census of housing, population, business, manufacturers, agriculture, minerals, and governments.

The census of population breaks down U.S. population characteristics by very small geographic areas. The census determines population traits by city block or census tract in large cities. It divides the populations of nonmetropolitan areas into block-numbering areas (BNAs). The BNAs and census tracts are important for marketing analysis because they highlight populations with similar traits, avoiding diversity within political boundaries such as county lines. This data helps marketers such as local retailers and shopping center developers to gather specific information about customers in an immediate neighborhood without spending time or money to conduct comprehensive surveys.

To improve its ability to collect demographic data from U.S. residents, the Census Bureau has proposed supplementing its traditional counting techniques with statistical sampling, on the grounds that this would reduce historical undercounting of minority and indigent residents.[12] The Supreme Court has upheld laws prohibiting the Census Bureau from using statistical sampling to determine the population count for congressional apportionment purposes. Instead, the Bureau will use a sampling ratio of about one long form (sample) questionnaire for every six households to obtain sample data on content, as it has in previous censuses.[13]

Marketing researchers find even more valuable resources in the government's computerized mapping database called the *TIGER system*, for Topographically Integrated Geographic Encoding and Referencing system. This system combines topographic features such as railroads, highways, and rivers with census data such as household income figures. Marketers can buy digital tapes of TIGER data from the Census Bureau.

Marketers often purchase other information from the federal government, such as the following:

FIGURE 7.6 Persuading People to Participate in Census 2000

- *Monthly Catalog of the United States Government Publications* and *Statistical Abstract of the United States*, published annually
- *Survey of Current Business*, updated monthly
- *County and City Data Book*, typically published every three years, providing data on each county and city of over 25,000 residents

State and city governments serve as additional important sources of information on employment, production, and sales activities. In addition, university bureaus of business and economic research frequently collect and disseminate such information.

Private Data

Many private organizations provide information for marketing decision makers. A trade association may be an excellent source of data on activities in a particular industry. Gale Publishing's *Encyclopedia of Associations*, available in most libraries, can help marketers to track down trade associations that may have useful data pertinent to their company. Also, advertising agencies continuously collect data on audiences reached by various media.

Business and trade magazines also publish a wide range of valuable data. Ulrich's *Guide to International Periodicals*, another common library reference, can point researchers in the direction of trade publications that conduct and publish industry-specific research. General business magazines can also be good sources. *Sales & Marketing Management*, for instance, publishes an annual Survey of Media Markets that combines statistics for population, effective buying income (EBI), and retail sales into buying power indexes that indicate each market's ability to buy.

While most general business publications are available at public libraries, few libraries carry specialized trade journals. The best way to gather data from these sources may be to contact the publications directly or to use an online periodical database like Dialog's ABI/Inform, available at many libraries and on CompuServe's Knowledge Index. Some trade publications may also maintain Web home pages that allow archival searches. Larger libraries can often provide directories and other publications that can help researchers find secondary data. For instance, Find/SVP's *FindEx, the Directory of Market Research Reports, Studies, and Surveys* lists a tremendous variety of completed research studies that are available for purchase.

Several national firms offer information to businesses by subscription. For example, in the ad in Figure 7.7, Roper Starch Worldwide describes its *Roper Reports Worldwide*, a global database service with consumer attitudes, lifestage, and behavior information for 30 countries. Roper also provides *Starch Readership Reports* that measure more than 20,000 ads in 400 magazines.

Electronic systems that scan UPC bar codes speed purchase transactions, and they also provide data for inventory control, ordering, and delivery. Scanning technology is widely used by grocers and other retailers, and marketing research companies, such as A. C. Nielsen and Information Resources Inc., store this data in commercially available databases. These scanner-based information services track consumer purchases of a wide variety of UPC-coded products. Retailers can use this information to retain customers with the right products at the right time.

A. C. Nielsen SalesNet uses the Internet to deliver scanner data quickly to clients. A. C. Nielsen processes the data as soon as it is received from supermarkets and forwards a copy of the data to market researchers so they can perform more in-depth analysis. At the same time, however, A. C. Nielsen representatives summarize the data in both graphic and spreadsheet form and post it on the Internet for immediate access by clients. As a result, the clients receive the data within a few days, rather than having to wait weeks for it to first be analyzed. They also appreciate receiving it in a format that can easily be edited and used for sales presentations.[14]

Online Sources of Secondary Data

The tools of cyberspace sometimes simplify the hunt for secondary data. Hundreds of databases and other sources of information are available online, both through the Internet and through commercial services such as America Online. A well-designed, Internet-based marketing research project can cost less, yet yield faster results than offline research.[15]

Today, industry experts estimate that about half of all marketing research could easily be done online. Internet research is projected to comprise at least 10 percent of all research by the year 2000.[16]

The *Directory of Online Databases*, published quarterly by Cuadra Associates, lists many sources of online information. Figure 7.8 lists some of the most important online sources. Government information, private data, and other databases can offer marketers a wide range of data on specific companies, industries, and geographic areas, as well as business-oriented news and reports.

Internet search tools such as Infoseek and Yahoo! can help researchers to track down specific sites that are rich with information. Discussion groups may also provide information and insights that can help answer some marketing questions. Additionally, a post to a chat room or newsgroup may draw a response that uncovers previously unknown sources of secondary data.[17]

Researchers must, however, carefully evaluate the validity of information they find on the Internet. People without in-depth knowledge of the subject matter may post information in a newsgroup. Similarly, Web pages might contain information that has been gathered using

FIGURE 7.8   Online Sources of Secondary Data

FIGURE 7.8   Online Sources of Secondary Data

Government Data Sources

U.S. Census Bureau (http://www.census.gov/)—This site provides free access to many census data reports and tables. Also available are international census data from many countries.

U.S. Bureau of Economic Analysis (http://www.bea.doc.gov/)—This site provides national and regional economic information, including gross domestic product by industry.

U.S. Bureau of Labor Statistics (http://stats.bls.gov/)—This site gives access to the BLS survey of consumer expenditures, a report on how U.S. consumers spend their money.

Department of Commerce/STAT-USA (http://www.stat-usa.gov/)—This subscription-based site provides access to hundreds of government-sponsored marketing research studies and other statistical information.

FedWorld (http://www.fedworld.gov/)—This site provides a central access point for locating government information. If you need data from the government but don't know where to find it, start here.

Private Data Sources

Knight-Ridder (http://www.dialog.com/)—This extensive database provides access to thousands of marketing research reports, industry and competitor information, and trade publications. Although it proves itself an excellent source for secondary data of all types, a typical search can be expensive. Knowledge Index, available on CompuServe, provides access to many of the Knight-Ridder databases for an hourly fee.

Lexis-Nexis (http://www.lexis-nexis.com/)—This is another extensive—and expensive—database of directories, trade publications, and legal information.

Search Engines

These search engines can help track down online information on a variety of topics:

Search.com (http://www.search.com/)—This site gives access to over 300 specialized indexes and search engines.

Metacrawler (http://www.metacrawler.com/)—This tool submits your query to nine of the top search engines at once.

Altavista (http://altavista.digital.com/)—This service provides one of the largest search indexes on the Web.

Infoseek Guide (http://www.infoseek.com/)—This search index includes millions of listings.

Yahoo! (http://www.yahoo.com/)—This useful search index divides reference sites into logical groups.

Source: Compiled and developed by Marlene G. Bellamy and Carolyn Z. Lawrence.

questionable research methods. The saying *caveat emptor* (buyer beware) should guide Internet searches for secondary data.

Sampling Techniques

4

Explain the different sampling techniques used by marketing researchers.

Before undertaking a study to gather primary data, researchers must first identify which participants to include in the study. **Sampling** is the process of selecting survey respondents or research participants. It is one of the most important aspects of marketing research design because if a study fails to involve consumers who accurately reflect the target market, the research will likely yield misleading conclusions.

MARKETING   DICTIONARY

sampling Process of selecting survey respondents or other research participants.

The total group of people that the researcher wants to study is called the **population** (or **universe**). For a political campaign study, the population would be all eligible voters. For research about a new cosmetics line, it might be all women in a certain age bracket. The *sample* is a representative group from this population. Researchers rarely gather information from a study's total population. If they do, the results are known as a **census.** Unless the total population is small, the costs of a census are very high and generally only the federal government can afford to conduct a census (and it uses this method only once every ten years).

Samples can be classified as either probability samples or nonprobability samples. A **probability sample** is one that gives every member of the population a known chance of being selected. Types of probability samples include simple random samples, stratified samples, and cluster samples.

In a **simple random sample,** every member of the relevant universe has an equal opportunity of selection. The draft lottery of the Vietnam era was an example. Each day of the year, draft-age males born on that day had the same chance of being placed on a conscription list. In a **stratified sample,** randomly selected subsamples of different groups are represented in the total sample. Stratified samples provide efficient, representative groups for such studies as opinion polls, in which groups of individuals share various divergent viewpoints. In a **cluster sample,** researchers select areas (or clusters) from which they draw respondents. This cost-efficient type of probability sample may be the best option where the population cannot be listed or enumerated. A good example is a marketing researcher identifying various U.S. cities and then randomly selecting supermarkets within those cities to study.

In contrast, a **nonprobability sample** is an arbitrary grouping that does not permit the use of standard statistical tests. Types of nonprobability samples are convenience samples and quota samples. A **convenience sample** is a nonprobability sample selected from among readily available respondents. Broadcasters' "on-the-street" interviews are a good example. Marketing researchers sometimes use convenience samples in exploratory research but not in definitive studies. A **quota sample** is a nonprobability sample that is divided to maintain representation for different segments or groups. It differs from a stratified sample, in which researchers select subsamples by some random process; in a quota sample, they hand-pick participants. An example would be a survey of owners of imported autos that includes two Hyundai owners, ten Honda owners, four Volvo owners, and so on.

Primary Research Methods

5

Identify the methods by which marketing researchers collect primary data.

Marketers use a variety of methods for conducting primary research. The three methods for collecting primary data include observation, surveys, and controlled experiments. The choice among these methods depends on the research questions under study and the marketing decisions that researchers hope to support. In some cases, researchers may decide to combine techniques during the research process.

Observation Method

In observational studies, researchers actually view, or watch, the overt actions of the subjects. Marketers trying to understand how consumers actually behave in certain situations find observation to be a useful technique. Observation tactics may be as simple as counting the number of cars passing by a potential site for a fast-food restaurant or checking the license plates at a shopping center to determine where shoppers live. Rubbermaid, Inc. conducts observational research by visiting consumers in their homes. By observing the ways consumers store items, Rubbermaid researchers get ideas for new storage products, such as the deck box shown in Figure 7.9.

Technological advances provide increasingly sophisticated ways for observing consumer behavior. The television industry, for example, relies on data from people meters, which are electronic remote-control devices that record the TV-viewing habits of individual household members to measure the popularity of TV shows. Traditional people meters require each viewer to punch a button each time he or she turns on the TV, changes channels, or leaves the room.

Marketers have long worried that some viewers do not bother to push people meter buttons at appropriate times, which could skew the research findings. In response, other companies have introduced simplified remote controls that allow even young children to record their TV viewing by choosing familiar onscreen icons.[18]

Another approach in observing the TV viewing and radio listening habits of people, a passive people meter, uses a computer chip to measure both. The passive people meter has two important advantages for marketers. One is its small size—it can be worn as a pin or beeper—which lets marketers measure media usage in the car, office, or other places away from home. The other plus is the ability to measure both TV watching and radio listening, allowing researchers to combine data for more than one medium. Up to now, researchers have been able to measure radio usage only through listeners' handwritten diaries.

Videotaping consumers in action is also gaining acceptance as a viable marketing research technique. Cookware manufacturers may videotape consumers cooking in their own kitchens to evaluate how they really use their pots and pans. A toothbrush manufacturer asked marketing research firm E-Lab to videotape consumers brushing their teeth and using mouthwash in its quest to develop products that would leave behind the sensation of a freshly-brushed mouth.

When French electronics maker Thomson developed a new, digital technology for storing, accessing, and playing music, the company also hired E-Lab to study how, when, and where people listen to music. To get the information, E-Lab researchers issued beepers to consumers. At certain times of the day, E-Lab researchers beeped study participants and asked them to make a note of the music they were listening to, who chose it, and their mood. Researchers also followed people as they moved around their homes, recording where they kept their stereos and how they organized their music collections.[19]

In an effort to understand what makes teenagers tick, advertising agency Bates USA mailed disposable cameras to 36 teens around the United States and asked them to document their favorite possessions, locations, and people. Back came snapshots of everything imaginable, including (literally) a kitchen sink. One ninth-grader, Amy, photographed her hockey stick and enclosed a note explaining that making the hockey team was her way of showing she was as good an athlete as her brothers. Bates senior vice president Janice Figueroa notes that information like this is valuable because it goes beyond mere statistics, which document that more girls are participating in sports, and reveals these girls' underlying motivations. Athletics may actually relate to self-confidence— a powerful motivator that marketers can use.[20]

Marketers have implemented another new technology to observe consumer behavior—virtual reality. Virtual reality allows marketers to simulate real-world situations and experiences.

FIGURE 7.9 | Observation Research Results in New Products

If deck cushions were meant to be stored in the house, they'd call them house cushions.

Our easy-to-assemble deck box is specifically sized for lounge chair cushions. But use it for charcoal, citronella candles or anything else you don't feel like lugging inside. **Rubbermaid**

MARKETING | DICTIONARY

population (universe) Total group that researchers want to study.

census Collection of data on all possible members of a population or universe.

probability sample Sample that gives every member of the population a known chance of being selected.

simple random sample Basic type of probability sample in which every individual in the relevant universe has an equal opportunity of selection.

stratified sample Probability sample constructed to represent randomly selected subsamples of different groups within the total sample.

cluster sample Probability sample in which researchers select geographic areas or clusters, and all of the chosen individuals within this area become respondents.

nonprobability sample Arbitrary grouping that produces data unsuited for most standard statistical tests.

convenience sample Nonprobability sample selected from among readily available respondents.

quota sample Nonprobability sample divided to ensure representation of different segments or groups in the total sample.

Focus Groups Help a Hospital Find a Promising New Name

BACKGROUND Merging two hospitals can be a giant headache for executives and managers, caregivers, and patients. One of the issues of the merger is deciding on a new name—one that will convey to everyone involved the new organization's identity, including its mission and its services. That was the hurdle faced by officials at two merging hospitals in Saginaw, Michigan: St. Luke's and Saginaw General Hospital. When the merger was completed, however, the 709-bed hospital system had a new name.

THE CHALLENGE Hospital officials needed the right market research to find a name that reflected the characteristics of both hospitals.

THE STRATEGY Deb Babcock, president of PTM Research, recommended the use of focus groups. Babcock gathered groups of employees from both hospitals, as well as a sample of the general public. For the public sample, she chose women ages 18 to 40 with children, as well as women in the same age group without children at home, because, according to Babcock, women tend to make the household decisions on health care.

"The most important information we got from the research was that we were going to have to do a good job of explaining what the name meant," explains Tom Dorle, director of business development.

continued on next page

They can then observe consumer reactions and behavior to identify priorities for potential marketing strategies and tactics.[21]

Survey Method

Observation alone cannot supply all of the desired information. The researcher must ask questions to get information on attitudes, motives, and opinions. It is also difficult to get exact demographic information—such as income levels—from observation. To discover this information, researchers can use either interviews or questionnaires.

Telephone Interviews   A telephone interview provides an inexpensive and quick method for obtaining a small quantity of relatively impersonal information. Telephone surveys have relatively high response rates, especially with repeated calls; calling a number once yields a response rate of 50 to 60 percent, but calling the same number five times raises the response rate to 85 percent.

Telephone interviews do have some limitations, however. Only simple, clearly worded questions draw appropriate responses, and respondents cannot view pictures to illustrate those questions. Also, respondents are hesitant to give personal characteristics about themselves over the telephone. Finally, the results of the survey may be biased by the omission of households without phones or with unlisted numbers. Certain market segments, such as single women and physicians, are more likely than most people to have unlisted numbers. To help remedy this, some telephone interviewers have tried to reach unlisted numbers by matching digits selected at random to chosen telephone prefixes, perhaps through computerized dialers. However, several states have restricted random dialing, and others propose to do so. The ultimate technological step in telephone interviewing links computerized dialing with a digitally synthesized voice to do the interviewing.

Two obstacles to telephone surveys in the United States and other developed countries are answering machines and caller-ID systems. Answering machines cause a growing problem for marketing researchers because many people use them to screen incoming calls. A related obstacle, the caller-ID system, displays the telephone numbers from which incoming calls originate, giving receivers the option of ignoring unfamiliar, unwelcome, or unidentified callers. Many consumers favor this option, and caller ID is one of the telephone industry's fastest-growing services. However, some legal experts believe that it violates the caller's right to privacy; in one case, the Pennsylvania state courts ruled it unconstitutional. State laws on caller ID vary. Some require vendors to offer a blocking service to callers who wish to evade the system.

Other obstacles may restrict the usefulness of telephone surveys abroad. In areas where telephone ownership is rare, survey results will be highly biased. Telephone interviewing is also difficult in countries that lack directories or where call volumes congest limited phone line capacity.

In the United States, the most desirable market for phone survey research is Topeka, Kansas, followed by four towns in Wisconsin: Kenosha, Sheboygan, Racine, and Milwaukee-Waukesha. Phone researchers prefer smaller cities like these to large urban centers because they better reflect average U.S. demographics, and residents are less likely to screen calls.[22]

Personal Interviews   The best means for obtaining detailed information about consumers is usually the personal interview since the interviewer can establish rapport with respondents and explain confusing or vague questions. Although careful wording, and often pretesting, helps to eliminate potential misunderstandings from mail questionnaires, the forms still cannot answer unanticipated questions.

Personal interviews, although slow and expensive to conduct, offer a flexibility and a return of detailed information that often offsets the limitations of mail questionnaires. Marketing research firms can conduct interviews in rented space in shopping centers, where they gain wide access to potential buyers of the products they are studying. These locations sometimes feature private interviewing compartments, videotape equipment, and food-preparation facilities for taste tests. Interviews conducted in shopping centers are typically called *mall intercepts*. Downtown retail districts and airports provide other valuable locations for marketing researchers.

Focus Groups Marketers also gather research information through the popular technique of focus groups. A **focus group** brings together 8 to 12 individuals in one location to discuss a subject of interest. Unlike other interview techniques that elicit information through a question-and-answer format, focus groups usually encourage a general discussion of a predetermined topic. Focus groups can provide quick and relatively inexpensive insight into consumer attitudes and motivations.

The focus group leader, called a *moderator*, typically explains the purpose of the meeting and suggests an opening topic. The moderator's main purpose, however, is to stimulate interaction among group members in order to encourage their discussion of numerous points. The moderator may occasionally interject questions as catalysts to direct the group's discussion. The moderator's job is a difficult one, requiring preparation and group facilitation skills.

Focus group sessions often last one or two hours. Researchers usually record the discussion on tape,

| FIGURE 7.10 | Using Focus Groups to Develop Advertising |

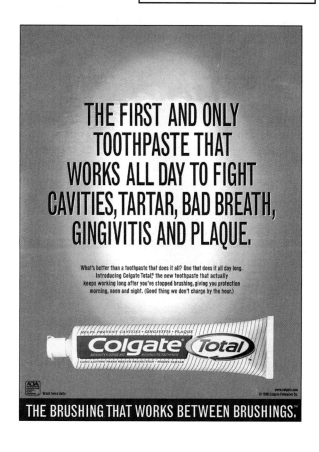

Out of the focus groups came the right name: Covenant Healthcare, connoting promise and commitment. But the focus group work did not end there. Babcock continues, "We had our ad agency develop three image concept campaigns, and we also took those to focus groups in which we showed them creative concepts and asked for feedback." Based on responses from the focus groups, a corporate logo was developed, and an image campaign followed.

THE OUTCOME Dorle believes that the use of focus groups was the best method of marketing research for the problem. "As long as you have a visual type of issue, you're better off with a focus group. You also have a chance, by the way focus groups are designed, to probe on comments or suggestions," he explains.

and observers frequently watch through a one-way mirror. Some research firms also allow clients to view focus groups in action through video-conferencing systems.

Marketers use focus groups for a variety of purposes. Colgate-Palmolive used focus groups to design ads that emphasize the benefits of its new Colgate Total toothpaste shown in Figure 7.10. Teenage Research Unlimited conducts focus groups for a variety of clients to explore aspects of U.S. adolescent life. The research firm has found that indirect questions can be the best way to elicit information from teens. For instance, the moderator may display a cartoon drawing of a young woman and ask focus group participants to describe her clothes, accessories, and favorite magazines and music. Rather than inquiring into fast-food preferences directly, the moderator might ask participants to match a list of restaurants with the celebrities most likely to eat at each one. Another favorite ploy, especially for gaining insight into modern teen fashion trends, is to ask teens to pretend they are costume designers for a hit TV show, such as *Dawson's Creek*, and describe how they would dress the show's characters.[23]

Focus groups make a particularly valuable tool for exploratory research, developing new product ideas, and preliminary testing of alternative marketing strategies.[24] They can also aid in the development of well-structured questionnaires for larger-scale research.[25]

Focus groups do have some drawbacks, however; some researchers fear that the focus group setting is sterile and unnatural and may not produce completely honest responses to questions. Focus groups generate less than the entire truth, according to anthropologist Ilsa Schumacher of Cultural Dynamics. She

MARKETING DICTIONARY

focus group Information-gathering procedure in marketing research that typically brings together 8 to 12 individuals to discuss a given subject.

believes that participants feel they have an image to maintain and need to identify with the other members of the group.[26]

Mail Surveys   Although personal interviews can sometimes provide very detailed information, cost considerations usually prevent an organization from using personal interviews in a national study. A mail survey can be a cost-effective alternative. Mail surveys also provide anonymity that may encourage respondents to give candid answers.

Mail surveys help marketers track consumer attitudes through ongoing research. Corning, for example, conducts a semiannual survey of consumers to measure customer awareness and satisfaction and to provide its marketers with information for new-product development. Mail surveys can also bring back demographic data on customers to support effective market segmentation.

Mail questionnaires do, however, have several limitations. First, response rates are typically much lower for mail surveys than for personal interviews. Because researchers must wait for respondents to complete and return questionnaires, mail surveys also usually take a long time to conduct. For a third limitation, questionnaires cannot answer unanticipated questions that occur to respondents as they complete the forms. Complex questions may not be suitable for a mail questionnaire. Finally, unless they gather additional information from nonrespondents, researchers must worry about bias in the results of mail surveys since important differences may distinguish respondents from nonrespondents.

Researchers try to minimize these limitations by paying careful attention in developing and in pretesting effective questionnaires before distributing the final version. Researchers can boost response rates by keeping questionnaires short and by offering incentives to respondents who complete and return the survey documents.

Fax Surveys   The low response rates and long follow-up times associated with mail surveys have spurred interest in the alternative of faxing survey documents. In some cases, faxing provisions may supplement mail surveys; in others, it may be the primary method for contacting respondents and obtaining their answers.

Online Surveys and Focus Groups   The growing population of Internet users has sparked interest among researchers in going online to conduct surveys and even focus groups. Online research can speed the survey process and dramatically reduce the costs of other, more traditional survey techniques.

For example, a standard research project can take up to eight weeks to complete, while a thorough online project may take two weeks or less. The traditional study has to work around participants' schedules, while online subjects can participate at their own convenience. Additional questions and longer responses have only a slight effect, if any, on an online study's cost, allowing researchers the luxury of gathering more detailed information. Furthermore, since online research is already in digital form, it generally requires less preparation before analysis.[27]

Some firms include questionnaires on their Web pages to solicit information about consumer demographics, attitudes, and other issues. Others convene online focus groups and panels. Research firm Greenfield Online used an online focus group to test reactions to a redesigned Web site for Captain Morgan Original Spiced Rum. Participants "gathered" in Greenfield's private chat room. A moderator posed questions and responded to answers on one side of a split screen, while participants typed their comments on the other side.

greenfieldonline.com

How can researchers tell if online participants are being truthful? Greenfield staff members cross-checked participants' answers to screening questionnaires against the information they entered to register for the database. The company then cross-checked a second time before the focus group began and found substitutes for respondents whose answers appeared inconsistent.

Benefits of online surveys and groups include the lack of geographic restrictions, faster turnaround time on responses, and dramatically lower costs, perhaps 50 percent of what person-to-person study would cost. Some researchers also feel that online respondents are more likely to give frank and truthful answers. Others point out that the novelty and ease of answering online encourages higher response rates. In any case, as more consumers around the world gain access to the Internet, it becomes possible to perform any type of traditional marketing research online as well as offline.[28]

Researchers should remember, however, that certain approaches to online research may be unreliable. Examples of less-than-optimal research include the following:

- Site-specific studies. Surveys that are restricted to a few Web sites tend to be questionable. Very little research has been done to analyze consumers' buying habits in terms of their on-line navigation habits, which makes it difficult to choose appropriate sites.

- Self-selected samples. Sites that invite visitors to volunteer their opinions encourage those who feel most strongly to express their views. This may not yield a representative sample.

- Community-based samples. Research that is limited to subscribers of a specific online community or newsgroup will reflect a particular viewpoint. The sample will lack diversity.

- Mass mailings disguised as research. Some marketers send huge amounts of "spam" (junk e-mail) and base their results on the small percentage of responses they receive. These mass mailings may not be targeted or may be targeted to poorly chosen samples and, thus, do not provide reliable results.[29]

Certain groups—such as females, seniors, and minority groups—are currently underrepresented on the Internet, and this imbalance may limit the effectiveness of Web-based research seeking input from those groups.

The growth of the Internet is creating a need for new research techniques to measure and capture information about Web-site visitors. At present, no industry-wide standards define techniques for measuring Web use. In an effort to gather data about visitors to their pages, some business sites ask users to register before accessing the pages. Others merely keep track of the number of "hits" or number of times a visitor downloads a page. Many researchers value stickiness (longer-lasting site visits) over number of hits as a measure of effectiveness.[30] As will be discussed in Chapter 16, some sites use cookies to track visitors' paths as they move through the site.[31]

Most tracking techniques are limited to collecting such data as the type of network browser a visitor uses and her country of residence. Some software can monitor the overall content that a person is viewing and display related advertisements. For example, if someone is doing a search using the keyword "car," ads for General Motors or Ford might appear onscreen. CMG Information Services offers a service called Engage.Knowledge, which collects profiles of Web users from numerous sites and organizes the data into 800 categories, including sports and hobbies. Advertisers and Web site operators can use this information to get a better idea of how to attract potential customers.[32]

The Experimental Method

The least-used method for collecting primary data is the controlled experiment. A marketing research **experiment** is a scientific investigation in which a researcher controls or manipulates a test group or groups and compares the results with those of a control group that did not receive the experimental controls or manipulations. Although researchers can conduct such experiments in the field or in laboratory settings, most have been performed in the field.

To date, the most common use of this method by marketers has been in test marketing, that is, introducing a new product or marketing strategy in an area and then observing its degree of success. After learning that its consulting and technology services has a low awareness, IBM Global Services designed a new advertising campaign to increase brand awareness. Ads like the one in Figure 7.11 were tested in Canada and the United Kingdom before the company ran them worldwide. Marketers usually

continued on next page

engagetech.com

MARKETING | **DICTIONARY**

experiment Scientific investigation in which a researcher manipulates a test group(s) and compares the results with those of a control group that did not receive the experimental controls or manipulations.

MARKETING STRATEGY FAILURE

THE OUTCOME Huge volumes of real-time data poured in from Digital Dashboard, swamping the Web masters operating the individual Turner sites. In addition, technical problems hampered use of the program by site visitors. In many cases, the program was far more sophisticated than either the hardware or the software that site visitors were using. Finally, Digital Dashboard was simply too expensive for the individual Web units to use continuously.

LESSONS LEARNED Both Turner Entertainment and Burke Interactive learned that a marketing information system needs to be practical for it to be a useful marketing tool. "One of our outcomes from this project was, just because you can incorporate all of this stuff and create one large online report that encompasses everything, doesn't mean that you should," observes Coates.

6

Discuss the challenges of conducting marketing research in global markets.

esomar.nl

FIGURE 7.11 | Testing a Global Advertisement

pick geographic areas that reflect the markets they envision for their products. For instance, Seattle and Milwaukee might serve as test markets for a new diet soft drink because these cities share the lead for the highest per-capita consumption in this product category. Chapter 12 will take a closer look at how marketers test market new products.

The major problem with controlled experiments comes from failure to take into account all the variables in a real-life situation. How can a marketing manager determine the effect of, say, reducing a product's retail price through refundable coupons when competitors simultaneously issue such coupons? Experimentation may become more common as firms develop sophisticated competitive models.

Conducting International Marketing Research

As corporations expand globally, they need to gather correspondingly more knowledge about consumers in other countries. Although marketing researchers follow the same basic steps for international studies as for domestic ones, they do face some different challenges.

U.S. organizations can tap many secondary resources as they research global markets. One major information source is the U.S. government, particularly the Department of Commerce. The Commerce Department regularly publishes two useful reports, *Foreign Economic Trends and Their Implications for the United States* (semiannual) and *Overseas Business Reports* (annual), that discuss marketing activities in more than 100 countries. The Department of State offers commercial guides to almost every country in the world, compiled by the local embassies. Other government sources include state trade offices, small business development centers, and U.S. embassies in various nations. Esomar, the European Society of Opinion and Market Research, offers a worldwide listing companies on its Web site.

When conducting international research, companies have to be prepared to deal with both language issues—communicating their message in the most effective way—and cultural issues—capturing local citizens' interests while avoiding missteps that could unintentionally offend them. Companies also need to take a good look at a country's business environment, including political and economic conditions, local tariffs and trade regulations, and the potential for short- and long-term growth.

When Benchmark Hospitality Inc., which develops and manages conference centers and resorts, entered the Thailand market, Burt Cabanas, chief executive officer, was careful to do his research first. Benchmark first established a Bangkok office and hired an expert on Thai culture to explore the feasibility of expanding in that country. The company also formed a corporation with Thai citizens on its board of directors, including Thailand's supreme commander of the Armed Forces. Although General Somchai Dhanarajata was not familiar with the hotel business,

Cabanas felt that government and military personnel were key to helping Benchmark understand Thailand's business climate.[33]

Many managers recommend tapping local researchers to investigate foreign markets. Greg Brophy, president of shredding-machine manufacturer Shred-It in Mississauga, Ontario, hired a German graduate student to research the European business landscape. The student, whom Brophy found by calling the top universities in Germany, was eager to supplement his academic experience with an on-the-job research project. Brophy had him put together binders with competitive analyses of other firms in Shred-It's industry. The student also totaled the number of companies with more than 15 employees in various cities, since Brophy reasoned that firms of that size would be good prospective customers. To date, Shred-It has successfully opened more than 54 offices in the United States, Canada, Argentina, Belgium, Luxembourg, and Hong Kong.[34]

Businesses may need to adjust their data collection methods for primary research in other countries because some methods do not easily transfer across national frontiers. Face-to-face interviewing, for instance, remains the most common method for conducting primary research outside the United States.

These days, having learned from its negative experience with Persil laundry powder, as you will recall, Unilever does extensive in-person research. Chairman FitzGerald is known for making "house calls" on foreign consumers to quiz them about their use of soaps and other items. "I usually ask them to show me how they clean their clothes," says FitzGerald. "One woman in Thailand was kind enough to show me how she washed her hair. I always ask to look in the fridge—not so much looking for my products, but just to get a sense of what people are buying." New employees at Hindustan Lever, the company's India subsidiary, are asked to live for six weeks with a family in a remote Indian town to help them better understand their customers.[35]

While mail surveys are a common data collection method in developed countries, they are less useful in many other nations due to low literacy rates, unreliable mail service, and a lack of address lists. Telephone interviews may also not be suitable in other countries, especially those where many people do not have phones.

Marketers need to consider all of these factors when conducting research abroad. In some cases, businesses may decide to contract with marketing research firms based in the countries they want to study. Also, a number of international research firms offer experienced assistance in conducting global studies. For example, Hispanic & Asian Marketing Communication Research, Inc. promotes its multicultural service in the ad in Figure 7.12. The company specializes in markets in the United States, Latin America, and Asia. It conducts custom research in English, Spanish, Portuguese, and most Asian languages by native-speaking researchers.

COMPUTER TECHNOLOGY IN MARKETING RESEARCH

In a world of rapid change, the ability to quickly gather and analyze business intelligence can create a substantial strategic advantage. A growing number of businesses are attempting to meet this challenge by harnessing the power of computers. As noted earlier, computer databases provide a wealth of data for marketing research, whether they are maintained outside the company or designed specifically to gather important facts about its customers. As you will recall, Chapter 5 explores how companies use internal databases in further detail. This section will address three important uses of computer technology related to marketing research—the marketing information system (MIS), marketing decision support system (MDSS), and data mining.

7

Outline important uses of computer technology in marketing research.

The Marketing Information System (MIS)

Many marketing managers discover that their information problems result from too much rather than too little information. They may feel pressured to sort through reams of data pertaining to scores of products, hundreds of locations, and thousands of customers. Such data may be

difficult to use; even if some of the information is relevant, it may be almost impossible to find.

A marketing information system can help decision makers obtain relevant information. A **marketing information system (MIS)** is a planned, computer-based system designed to provide managers with a continuous flow of information relevant to their specific decisions and areas of responsibility. The marketing information system is a component of an organization's overall management information system (also often called an MIS) that deals specifically with marketing data and issues.

Properly constructed, a marketing information system can serve as a company's nerve center, continually monitoring the marketplace and providing instantaneous information. An MIS gathers data from both inside and outside the organization and processes it to produce relevant marketing information. Processing steps could involve storing data for later use, classifying and analyzing that data, and retrieving the data easily when needed.

The Marketing Decision Support System (MDSS)

A **marketing decision support system (MDSS)** consists of computer software that helps users quickly obtain information and apply that information in a way that supports marketing decisions. An MDSS takes the MIS one step further by allowing managers to explore and make connections between such varying information as the state of the market, consumer behavior, sales forecasts, competitors' actions, and environmental changes. An MDSS can create simulations or models to illustrate the likely results of changes in marketing strategies or market conditions. Figure 7.13 shows the components of a typical MDSS, often including databases, graphics functions, electronic spreadsheets, and modeling software. Decision makers access such a system through interactive instructions and on-screen displays.

In general, while an MIS provides raw data, an MDSS develops this data into business intelligence—information useful for decision making. For example, an MIS might provide a list of product sales from the previous day. The manager could use an MDSS to transform this raw data into graphs illustrating sales trends or reports estimating the impacts of specific decisions, such as raising prices or expanding into new regions.

Data Mining

Data mining is the process of searching through customer files to detect patterns. The data is stored in a huge database called a *data warehouse*. Software for the marketing decision support system is often associated with the data warehouse and can be used to mine the data. Once marketers identify patterns and connections, they use this intelligence to increase the accuracy of their predictions about the likely effectiveness of strategy options.[36]

Data mining can be an efficient way to sort through huge amounts of data and to make sense of that data. It can help marketers create customer profiles, pinpoint reasons for customer loyalty or the lack thereof, analyze the potential returns on changes in pricing or promotion, and forecast sales. Some companies invest as much as 19 percent of their total technology budgets on data warehouses and associated software. Data warehousing is especially common in the telecommunications, health-care, petrochemicals, and banking industries.[37]

Health insurer Empire Blue Cross and Blue Shield estimates it saves $4 million a year by mining its data. For instance, Empire staffers grew suspicious when one physician seemed to be sending an unusually large number of bills for reimbursement. By comparing the cost of his cases against the cost of all physicians' cases billed to the company, they discovered that he had submitted more than $500,000 in falsified invoices.[38]

Sometimes the associations revealed by data mining can be unexpected as well as enlightening. Camelot Music Holdings identified a group of customers ages 65-plus who tended to buy lots of classical music, jazz tunes, and movies. Surprisingly, though, Camelot found that a large percentage of them were also buying rap and alternative music. Further analysis of the data revealed that they were buying gifts for their grandchildren.[39]

Unfortunately, not all data mining projects prove this helpful. A survey of European companies by British consulting firm Organisation & Technology Research shows that most of them received almost no financial benefit from their data warehouses. Meanwhile, U.S. consultants estimate that almost 70 percent of American warehouse projects fail to meet expectations regarding costs, time, or return on investment.[40]

Why do so many data mining projects stumble? Often companies underestimate the amount of money and effort necessary to integrate different computer systems and create common data definitions and formats. Organizational politics can also be a barrier; typically it takes two years to create a comprehensive data warehouse that cuts across a wide variety of functional areas, and it can be difficult to get all divisions to agree on how it should be done. Unrealistic expectations are a third problem with data mining. "You can't dump data into a massive computer and expect marketing insights to jump up and bite you on the nose," says Herbert Edelstein, president of the consulting firm Two Crows Corp. "You have to understand the data, massage it, build and test models and be prepared for many failures before you get a success."[41]

As computer technology continues to develop, businesses are likely to improve data mining and find new ways to use customer data as a tool for marketing decision making.

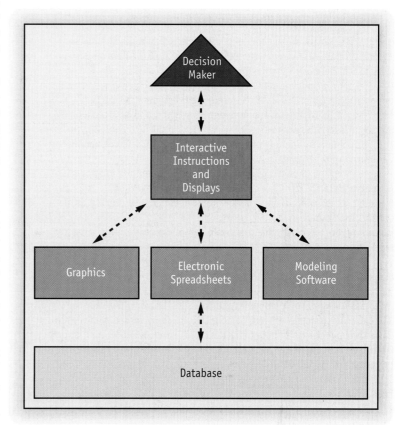

FIGURE 7.13   Functions of an MDSS

twec.com

ACHIEVEMENT CHECK SUMMARY

Read the learning objectives that follow, and consider the questions for each one. Answering these questions will reinforce your grasp of the most important concepts in the chapter and will allow you to check how well you have achieved these learning goals. Where a blank appears before a question, answer with *T* or *F* for true/false questions; for multiple-choice questions, choose the letter of the correct answer.

Objective 7.1: Describe the development of the marketing research function and its major activities.
1. _____ The marketing research function is organized the same way in most firms.
2. _____ If a company wanted to hire an outside firm to conduct all stages of a marketing research study, it would probably contract with (a) a syndicated service; (b) a full-service supplier; (c) a limited-service supplier.
3. _____ Marketing researchers seldom care about financial performance.

MARKETING   DICTIONARY

marketing information system (MIS) Planned, computer-based system designed to provide managers with a continuous flow of information relevant to their specific decisions and areas of responsibility.

marketing decision support system (MDSS) Marketing information system component that links a decision maker with relevant databases and analysis tools.

data mining Process of searching through customer information files to detect patterns that guide marketing decision making.

Objective 7.2: List and explain the steps in the marketing research process.

1. _____ The goal of exploratory research is to discover possible causes of a specific problem.

2. _____ A hypothesis is a (a) research technique used to identify hypothetical customer needs; (b) tentative explanation for some specific event; (c) scientific format for conducting marketing research studies.

3. _____ Research design determines which type of data collection method will be most effective for a particular study.

4. _____ Marketing researchers and their audiences sometimes reach different interpretations of data collected in the course of a study.

Objective 7.3: Differentiate between the types and sources of primary and secondary data.

1. _____ Secondary data is often less expensive and time-consuming to gather than primary data.

2. _____ Primary data can provide richer, more detailed information than secondary data.

3. _____ Cost is not an issue in deciding whether to use primary or secondary data sources.

Objective 7.4: Explain the different sampling techniques used by marketing researchers.

1. _____ Sampling is the process of choosing the questions to be included in a marketing research survey.

2. _____ The population is (a) the total group to be studied; (b) a representative group; (c) a probability sample.

3. _____ In a simple random sample, all members of the total group have an equal chance of being included in the study.

Objective 7.5: Identify the methods by which marketing researchers collect primary data.

1. _____ Observation is a useful method for gathering primary data to help researchers understand customer behavior.

2. _____ Survey methods provide the most effective help for researchers who want to understand consumer attitudes and motives.

3. _____ An example of a commonly used experimental method is (a) conducting a focus group; (b) videotaping customer's shopping behavior; (c) evaluating a marketing strategy's effectiveness in a test market location.

Objective 7.6: Discuss the challenges of conducting marketing research in global markets.

1. _____ Data collection methods transfer easily to other countries.

2. _____ Cultural beliefs may complicate global marketing research.

3. _____ A business may lack the necessary capabilities to conduct its own international marketing research study.

Objective 7.7: Outline important uses of computer technology in marketing research.

1. _____ A planned, computer-based system designed to provide a continuous flow of relevant information related to marketing issues is a (a) marketing information system; (b) marketing decision support system; (c) data warehouse.

2. _____ A marketing decision support system allows managers to explore and link information from various sources.

3. _____ Data mining is the process of searching through customer files to detect behavior patterns relevant to marketing decisions.

Students: See the solutions section located on page S-1 to check your responses to the Achievement Check Summary.

Key Terms

marketing research	simple random sample
customer satisfaction measurement (CSM) program	stratified sample
	cluster sample
exploratory research	nonprobability sample
sales analysis	convenience sample
marketing cost analysis	quota sample
hypothesis	focus group
research design	experiment
secondary data	marketing information system (MIS)
primary data	
sampling	marketing decision support system (MDSS)
population (universe)	
census	data mining
probability sample	

Review Questions

1. Outline the development and current status of the marketing research function. What role did Charles Parlin play in the development of marketing research?

2. List and explain the various steps in the marketing research process. Trace a hypothetical study through the various stages of this process.

3. Distinguish between primary and secondary data. When should researchers collect each type of data?

4. Compare and contrast sales analysis and marketing cost analysis.

5. What are the major sources of secondary data? What are the advantages and limitations of secondary data?

6. Explain the differences between probability and nonprobability samples. Identify the various types of each.

7. Distinguish among surveys, experiments, and observational methods of primary data collection. Cite examples of each method.

8. Define and give an example of each of the four methods of gathering survey data. Under what circumstances should researchers choose each?

9. How might a company that has never exported its products obtain information about international markets? How does this process compare to domestic marketing research?

10. Distinguish among marketing information systems, marketing decision support systems, and data mining.

Questions for Critical Thinking

1. A. C. Nielsen offers data collected by optical scanners from the United Kingdom, France, Germany, Belgium, the Netherlands, Austria, Italy, and Finland. This scanner data tracks sales of UPC-coded products in those nations. If you were a Nielsen client in the United States, what types of marketing questions might this data help you answer?

2. Some politicians criticize the U.S. census for undercounting minorities and the homeless. This alleged undercounting becomes a political and financial issue. In New York, for example, each person counted is worth $150 in federal funds, which are distributed on the basis of census counts. The Census Bureau has proposed statistical sampling to minimize the problem, but this approach was blocked by the Supreme Court.[42] Suggest other ways in which the Census Bureau might address the undercount problem.

3. Burt Cabanas, chief executive officer for conference center developer Benchmark Hospitality Inc., always hires a local firm to research a new market. "You want the research to be in-country, because there's a uniqueness to how the economy of the culture runs," says Cabanas. "It's also easier to get information quicker if we have someone there with contacts in that country. The Internet is a great source for data, but we're more interested in knowing how open the door is for us to do business and how deep the market is."[43] Do you agree with Cabanas' viewpoint? Discuss the advantages and disadvantages of using the Internet to research foreign markets.

4. Are you looking for a new home? Today, one in three of the new homes sold in America is likely to be a manufactured home. Today's manufactured homes are better built using higher-quality materials than those of the past. As a result, the market for manufactured homes has grown to include ever more affluent buyers. Alabama-based Southern Energy Homes tries to appeal to upscale buyers by custom-building its homes according to customer specifications. What type of data and information should Southern Energy gather through its ongoing marketing intelligence functions in order to predict demand for its products? Would secondary or primary methods work best? Name some specific secondary sources of data that Southern Energy might study to find useful business intelligence.

5. Discuss some of the challenges McDonald's Corp. might face in conducting marketing research in potential new international markets. What types of research would you recommend the company use in choosing new countries for expansion?

'netWork

1. **Secondary Data Collection—Government Data.** Go to the U.S. Department of Commerce's Census Bureau Web site at *www.census.gov* and complete the following:

   a. Using the population clock, identify the most recent U.S. population and world population statistics.

   b. Choose three links on the front page of the Web site that you wish to learn more about. Identify for each of the three links the link name, what information is available, and how the information at the link might be helpful to someone conducting marketing research for a company.

census.gov

2. **Secondary Data Collection—Private Data.** Go to *www.nielsen-netratings.com* and answer as many of the following questions as you can:

   a. According to the most recent *daily* statistics, how many people were on the Internet? What was the average time spent per person? How many sites did each person visit?

   b. According to the most recent *weekly* statistics, what were the top three advertisers for the most recent week? What were the top three Web properties for the most recent week?

nielsen-netratings.com

3. **Focus Groups.** Like other marketing research methods, focus groups are going high tech.

   a. Use your search engine to find a Web site or use the Web address provided here to find information on how video-conferencing technology is being used to facilitate the focus group process.

   b. Use your search engine or the Web address below to find information on how computer software is being used by focus group members.

   Be prepared to report your findings during a class discussion.

cosmos.ot.buffalo.edu/html/focus_groups.html

facilitate.com/product.com/product/Brief02.shmtl

Video Case 7 on Fisher Price begins on page VC-9.

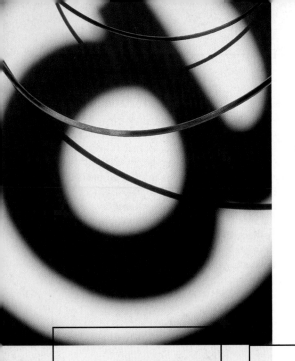

Market Segmentation, Targeting, and Positioning

CHAPTER OBJECTIVES

1. Identify the essential components of a market.

2. Outline the role of market segmentation in developing a marketing strategy.

3. Describe the criteria necessary for effective segmentation.

4. Explain each of the four bases for segmenting consumer markets.

5. Identify the steps in the market segmentation process.

6. Discuss four alternative strategies for reaching target markets.

7. Summarize the types of positioning strategies and the purposes of positioning and repositioning products.

Powell's Finds Its Niche Online and Off

All bookworms are not created equal. Some thrive on thriller novels, while others crave cookbooks. Some like the hottest bestsellers, and others cool off with the classics. Powell's Books, founded nearly thirty years ago in Portland, Oregon, by Walter and Michael Powell, has been adept at identifying who its customers are—or will be. The bookseller has been successful at finding and offering its customers the books they want. Powell's has even gone a step farther: successfully combining its seven brick-and-mortar bookstores with a growing online business.

Powell's has managed to survive the onslaught of large bookselling chains like Waldenbooks because it offers something the chains do not: rare and used books. Powell's stocks books that collectors and bargain hunters want. Customers can find the latest John Grisham novel at any chain store, but if someone is looking for a set of children's books by Walt Morey, a signed first edition of one of Salman Rushdie's novels, or any out-of-print book, Powell's is the place to look. Powell's identifies the specific group of readers who are most likely to want something a

bit different and stocks its shelves with over one million titles for them.

If you want to buy a book at Powell's, you can visit any of its stores, including its 43,000-square-foot flagship store in Portland. In fact, 3,000 people a day do this. There you receive service, and you have a chance to browse among the stacks. If you do not have the time to visit the store or live too far away to do so, you can log on to Powell's Web site and let your mouse do the browsing. Powell's targets two major market segments—it sells directly to consumers and also to other online booksellers, including Amazon.com. With its huge inventory of used books, Powell's was a natural for fulfilling Amazon.com's orders; the Seattle-based company is now Powell's largest business customer, accounting for nearly a quarter of Powell's annual revenue. Powell's also markets to other business customers through its institutional sales division, fulfilling orders for companies like Yahoo! Shopping and Bookfinder.com.

Powell's has identified retail customers as the other important segment of its online market. The company buys 2,000 to 3,000 titles a day from estate sales, bankrupt book dealers, wholesalers, and consumers. These books are then resold to customers online. "Before this year, the Net was a hedge," admits Kanath Gopalpur, Powell's Internet marketing and business development manager. "But now this is where the growth is coming from, and we're really focusing on it." Delving deeper into this market, Powell's has tried auctions of used books on Egghead.com, which prompted the two firms to discuss further alliances. The intellectually oriented *Utne Reader* has arranged for Powell's to serve as its online bookstore, and Powell's is now involved in moderating the online book discussion groups for the *Reader*.

A visitor to Powell's Web site will find it tailored to just about every need, yet identifying specific interests is simple. You can create your own "wish list" of books through WishClick, Powell's gift registry service. The Recommendation Center highlights staff picks in certain categories, such as humor, biography, and science. You can try the Other Voices program, which offers online alternative reviews and viewpoints on a variety of book-related topics. You can also wander into Powell's cybercafe and ponder what book may become your next favorite. Finally, you can pop into the Rare Books room and browse for treasures. Powell's seems to have something for everyone, and tailoring to personal needs is what a friendly bookstore should do.[1]

233

CHAPTER OVERVIEW

Development of a successful marketing strategy begins with an understanding of the market for the good or service. A **market** is composed of people or institutions with sufficient purchasing power, authority, and willingness to buy.

Products seldom succeed by appealing to single, homogeneous markets. Most markets likely include consumers with different lifestyles, backgrounds, and income levels. It is improbable that a single marketing mix strategy will attract all sectors of a market. By identifying, evaluating, and selecting a target market to pursue, marketers are able to develop more efficient and effective marketing strategies. The **target market** for a product is the specific segment of consumers most likely to purchase a particular product.

Internet users provide a good example of how diverse a population can be. As the number of people navigating the Internet has grown, so has the diversity of this population. Once the domain of researchers and government workers, the World Wide Web's audience now includes students, families, workers in a wide variety of professions, and retirees. As a result, the number of Web sites targeted to specific demographic and special-interest groups has shown a corresponding increase.

This chapter will discuss useful ways for segmenting markets, explain the steps of the market segmentation process, and survey strategies for reaching target markets. Finally, it will look at the role of positioning in developing a marketing strategy. ■

TYPES OF MARKETS

1

Identify the essential components of a market.

Products are often classified as either consumer products or business products. **Consumer products** are those bought by ultimate consumers for personal use. **Business products** are goods and services purchased for use either directly or indirectly in the production of other goods and services for resale. Most goods and services purchased by individual consumers—books, cleaning services, and clothes, for example—are considered consumer products. Rubber and raw cotton are examples of items generally purchased by manufacturers and are, therefore, classified as business products. For example, Goodyear buys rubber to manufacture tires; textile manufacturers such as Burlington Industries convert raw cotton into cloth.

Sometimes a single product can serve different uses. Tires purchased for the family car constitute consumer products; tires purchased by Ford to be mounted during production of its Explorer are business products because they become part of another product destined for resale. (Some marketers add another term, *commercial products*, for business products like legal services that do not contribute directly to the production of other goods.) The key to proper classification of goods and services is determining who will buy the product and why it was bought. Chapters 8 and 9 focus on segmentation and buying behavior in the consumer markets. Chapter 10 will cover business-to-business markets.

THE ROLE OF MARKET SEGMENTATION

Attempts to attract all consumers with a single marketing mix would probably fail since the diversification of people causes too many variables in consumer needs, preferences, and purchasing abilities. Instead, marketers attempt to identify the factors that affect purchase decisions and then group consumers according to the presence or absence of these factors. Finally, they adjust marketing strategies to meet the needs of each group.

Consider toothpaste, for instance. Everyone uses it, yet toothpaste manufacturers have found that consumers have different preferences regarding the varying qualities possessed by each toothpaste. As a result, Crest focuses on preventing tooth decay, Close Up hints at enhanced sex appeal, Gleem emphasizes whiter teeth, Topol promises removal of smoking stains, and Colgate Junior is designed to appeal to kids while satisfying parents' concerns for fluoride protection. As the ad in Figure 8.1 shows, Tom's of Maine markets an all-natural fluoride toothpaste without the artificial preservatives and sweeteners included in other toothpaste.

The division of the total market into smaller, relatively homogeneous groups is called **market segmentation.** Both profit-oriented and not-for-profit organizations practice market segmentation to reach both business and consumer markets.

The popular story of Henry Ford's resistance to market segmentation is worth repeating here. Ford's continued reliance on the Model T cost his firm the leading position in the developing automobile industry. While Ford insisted that his Model T was all that car buyers needed, Alfred P. Sloan Jr. of General Motors developed specific models to suit different groups of customers. Sloan's segmentation strategy worked, and General Motors replaced Ford as the leading U.S. automaker.[2]

FIGURE 8.1 Targeting a Specific Market Segment

Criteria for Effective Segmentation

Segmentation does not promote marketing success in all cases. Effectiveness depends on the following basic requirements:

1. The market segment must present measurable purchasing power and size. For example, after research disclosed that U.S. health professionals spend about $1 billion a year on medical books, Sundeep Bhan, founder of online medical book retailer MedBookStore.com, decided to target health professionals. This research also found that health professionals in other countries account for another $1 billion annually. Twenty percent of MedBookStore.com's business now comes from 60 nations outside the United States.[3]

2. Marketers must find a way to effectively promote to and serve the market segment. MedBook-Store.com, for example, reaches medical students by operating on-line bookstores for five American medical schools and by forming partnerships with professional groups such as the American

Outline the role of market segmentation in developing a marketing strategy

Describe the criteria necessary for effective segmentation.

MARKETING   DICTIONARY

market People or institutions with sufficient purchasing power, authority, and willingness to buy.

target market Specific segment of consumers most likely to purchase a particular product.

consumer product Good or service purchased by an ultimate consumer for personal use.

business product Good or service purchased for use either directly or indirectly in the production of other goods and services for resale.

market segmentation Division of the total market into smaller, relatively homogeneous groups.

Medical Association. The retailer's organizational partners receive a 5 percent cut of sales made to their members.[4]

3. Marketers must identify segments that are sufficiently large enough to give them good profit potential. Ads from the Wine Market Council target "marginal wine consumers," Americans who like wine but only drink a few glasses per month. The Council estimates that these consumers number about 21 million, are in their thirties, and have annual incomes of $60,000 or higher.[5]

4. The firm must target segments that match its marketing capabilities. Targeting a large number of niche markets can produce an expensive, complex, and inefficient strategy. This is why Chattahoochee National Bank, located in an Atlanta suburb, focuses on a specialized market: white-collar service companies with annual revenues of $3 million to $30 million. To save time for its busy clients, the bank offers a courier service for check deposits and equips loan officers with laptop computers, enabling them to make "house calls" to customers' offices. Chattahoochee's loan rate averages 1/8 of a point higher than that of many banks, but customers are willing to pay more for what they view as superior service.[6]

SEGMENTING CONSUMER MARKETS

4

Explain each of the four bases for segmenting consumer markets.

Market segmentation attempts to isolate the traits that distinguish a certain group of consumers from the overall market. An understanding of the group's characteristics—such as age, sex, geographical location, income, and expenditure patterns—plays a vital role in developing a successful marketing strategy. In most cases, marketers seek to pinpoint a number of factors affecting buying behavior in the target segment. For example, toy manufacturers such as Ideal, Hasbro, Mattel, and Kenner look not only at birthrate trends but also at changes in income levels and expenditure patterns to successfully market their products. In trying to attract new students, colleges and universities are affected not only by the number of graduating high-school seniors but also by changing attitudes toward the value of a college education and trends in enrollment of older adults. Also, few, if any, marketers identify totally homogeneous segments; they always encounter some differences among members of a target group.

The four common bases for segmenting consumer markets are geographic segmentation, demographic segmentation, psychographic segmentation, and product-related segmentation. These segmentation techniques can give important guidance for marketing strategies, provided they identify significant differences in buying behavior.

Geographic Segmentation

A logical starting point in market segmentation is an examination of population characteristics. Marketers have practiced **geographic segmentation**—dividing an overall market into homogeneous groups on the basis of their locations—for hundreds of years. While geographic location does not ensure homogeneity of consumer buying decisions, this segmentation approach is useful in identifying product-specific patterns as well as generalized purchase tendencies.

The U.S. population of roughly 280 million is not distributed evenly within the country; rather, people are concentrated in major metropolitan areas. New York City is the largest city in the United States, with over 7 million residents, and Los Angeles ranks second with about 3.5 million. However, the biggest metropolitan areas are not necessarily the fastest growing; in a recent six-year period New York City's population grew by only 0.8 percent and Los Angeles' by 2 percent. In contrast, Phoenix experienced population growth of 17.7 percent and El Paso was close behind with 16.4 percent.[7]

A look at the worldwide population distribution illustrates why so many firms are pursuing customers around the globe. As in the United States, many of these people live in urban environments. The two metropolitan areas with the world's largest populations, Tokyo and Mexico City, dwarf New York City. Crunch Fitness, a health-club chain that targets young professionals in urban markets, opened a club in Tokyo as well as in the major U.S. cities listed in its ad in Figure 8.2.

Population size alone, however, may not be reason enough for a business to expand into a specific country. Businesses also need to look at a wide variety of microeconomic variables. Some businesses may decide to cluster together countries that share similar population and product-use patterns instead of treating each country as an independent segment.

While population numbers indicate the overall size of a market, other geographic indicators, such as job growth, can also give useful guidance to marketers, depending on the type of products they sell. Food companies might look for geographic segments with large populations because food is an essential product used by everyone. Automobile manufacturers, on the other hand, might segment geographic regions by household income because it is an important factor in the purchase of a new car.

Geographic areas also vary in population-migration patterns. The United States, for example, has traditionally been a mobile society. About one of every six Americans moves each year. However, this figure is down from one out of five a few decades ago. The slowdown has resulted from changes such as increased home ownership due to increased home ownership.

U.S. census data also indicates two major population shifts: migration toward the Sunbelt states of the Southeast and Southwest and toward the West. Researchers expect this trend to continue. Between now and 2020, the states expected to experience the fastest population growth are Nevada, Hawaii, California, and Washington.[8]

As people migrate from one geographic area to another, regional consumer tastes often change. Catfish, a longtime staple in the diet of the southern United States, is now popular in all parts of the country. By contrast, cornbread and other popular southern recipes using cornmeal are considered exotic in Great Britain, where cornmeal is available mainly through health-food stores.

The move from urban to suburban areas after World War II created a need to redefine the urban marketplace. This trend radically changed cities' traditional patterns of retailing and led to disintegration in many downtown shopping areas. It also rendered traditional city boundaries almost meaningless for marketing purposes.

In an effort to respond to these changes, the government now classifies urban data using three categories outlined below. Other representative examples of these categories are shown in Table 8.1.

- A **Metropolitan Statistical Area (MSA)** is a freestanding urban area with a population in the urban center of at least 50,000 and a total MSA population of 100,000 or more. Buyers in MSAs exhibit social and economic homogeneity. They usually border on nonurbanized counties. Examples include Rochester, New York; Odessa-Midland, Texas; and Visalia-Tulane-Porterville, California.

- The category of **Consolidated Metropolitan Statistical Area (CMSA)** includes the country's 25 or so urban giants such as Chicago, Illinois-Gary, Indiana-Kenosha, Wisconsin, and Detroit-Ann Arbor-Flint, Michigan. A CMSA must include two or more Primary Metropolitan Statistical Areas, discussed below.

FIGURE 8.2 Using Geographic Segmentation

MARKETING DICTIONARY

geographic segmentation Dividing an overall market into homogeneous groups on the basis of population.

Metropolitan Statistical Area (MSA) Freestanding urban population center.

Consolidated Metropolitan Statistical Area (CMSA) Major population concentration, including the country's 25 or so urban giants.

TABLE 8.1	Representative CMSAs, PMSAs, and MSAs

Consolidated Metropolitan Statistical Area (CMSA)	Primary Metropolitan Statistical Area (PMSA)	Metropolitan Statistical Area (MSA)
• Boston-Worchester-Laurence	• Fitchburg-Leominister, Massachusetts	• Bakersfield, California
• Philadelphia-Wilmington-Atlantic City	• Ventura, California	• Charlotte-Gastonia-Rock Hill, North Carolina
• Los Angeles-Riverside-Orange County	• Middlesex-Somerset-Hunterdon, New Jersey	• Kalamazoo-Battle Creek, Michigan
• New York City-Northern New Jersey-Long Island	• Vineland-Millville-Bridgeton, New Jersey	• Salt Lake City-Ogden, Utah
• San Francisco-Oakland-San Jose	• Santa Rosa, California	• Wichita, Kansas

■ A **Primary Metropolitan Statistical Area (PMSA)** is an urbanized county or set of counties with social and economic ties to nearby areas. PMSAs are identified within areas of 1-million-plus populations. Olympia, Washington, is part of the Seattle-Tacoma-Bremerton PMSA. Bridgeport, Connecticut, is part of the New York-Northern New Jersey-Long Island PMSA and Riverside-San Bernardino, California, is a PMSA within the Los Angeles-Riverside-Orange County PMSA.

Using Geographic Segmentation

Demand for some categories of goods and services can vary according to geographic region, and marketers need to be aware of how these regions differ. Most major brands get 40 to 80 percent of their sales from what are called *core regions;* elsewhere in the national marketplace, such a good or service is essentially a specialty brand.

FIGURE 8.3	Segmentation by Residence Location

Residence location within a geographic area is an important segmentation variable. Urban dwellers may have less pressing needs for automobiles than their suburban and rural counterparts have, and suburbanites spend proportionately more on lawn and garden care than rural and urban residents. Rural and suburban dwellers may spend more of their household incomes than urban households on gasoline and automobile needs and are more likely to purchase riding lawn mowers, like the Kubota mower in the ad in Figure 8.3.

Climate is another important segmentation factor. Consumers in chilly, northern states, for example, eat more soup than residents in warmer, southern markets.

Geographic segmentation provides useful distinctions only when regional preferences exist. Even then, geographic subdivisions of the overall market tend to be rather large and often too heterogeneous for effective segmentation without the careful consideration of additional factors. In such cases, more than one segmentation variable may be used to target a specific market.

Geographic Information System (GIS)

At Domino's Pizza, Super Bowl Sunday is more than a sporting event—it is also the company's single biggest sales day of the year. As the football teams face off, Domino's tackles its own challenge: planning and executing timely delivery of more than 900,000 pizzas to residences throughout the country.

Traditionally, companies like Domino's obtained much of their geographic data for deliveries from statistical databases and reports. While these sources provide valuable information, they do not always present it in a format that makes it easy to analyze and use.

Domino's uses information from a new resource, a geographic information system. Once used mainly by the military, a **geographic information system (GIS)** simplifies the job of analyzing marketing information by placing data in a spatial format. The result is a geographic map overlaid with digital data about consumers in a particular area.

@ **dominos.com**

Thanks to its GIS, Domino's delivery drivers can map in advance the best route to reaching each customer's address. Managers use the GIS to pinpoint the best locations for stores, based on purchase data and driving distances, and identify areas that are promising candidates for new stores. The system also helps them to allocate inventory more efficiently.[9]

The earliest geographic information systems were prohibitively expensive for all but the largest companies. Recent technological advances, however, have made GIS software available at a much lower cost, increasing usage among smaller firms. Like Domino's, a growing number of companies benefit from using a GIS to locate new outlets, assign sales territories, and plan distribution centers and delivery routes.[10] Marketing researchers agree, however, that firms have not yet realized the full potential of GIS technology.

Demographic Segmentation

The most common method of market segmentation—**demographic segmentation**—defines consumer groups according to demographic variables such as gender, age, income, occupation, education, household size, and stage in the family life cycle. This approach is also sometimes called *socioeconomic segmentation*. Marketers review vast quantities of available data to complete a plan for demographic segmentation. One of the primary sources for demographic data in the United States is the Bureau of the Census. Many of the Census Bureau's statistics can be accessed online. The following discussion considers the most commonly used demographic variables.

@ **census.gov**

Segmenting by Gender

Gender is an obvious variable that helps to define the markets for certain products. When segmenting by gender, marketers need to be sure they are targeting consumers correctly. Take consumer electronics, for instance; they are traditionally assumed to be a male-dominated purchase. The Consumer Electronics Marketing Association (CEMA), however, reports that women influence 50 percent of these sales. Furthermore, during a recent holiday season, a significant percentage of women indicated that computers topped their gift wish list. The CEMA survey also revealed that the marketing of most technical products leaves women cold. Female consumers look to electronics to serve a practical purpose, as tools and sources of entertainment, but many ads overemphasize technical jargon.

Microsoft woos female customers by focusing on what computers can do for them. Ads feature headlines such as "What the heck is a hand-held PC? For people on the go it's convenient computing." Microsoft ends with the tag line "Where do YOU want to go today?"[11] Similarly, Philips markets its home cinema videotape collection as an aid to entertainment and socializing. In the ad in Figure 8.4, a young woman boasts, "None of my friends go to the movies anymore. They come over to my place instead."[12]

Some companies market successfully to both genders. Clothing retailer Banana Republic, for example, offers men's and women's apparel in distinct areas of its stores. The company's research shows that male customers feel uncomfortable walking through the women's department, so the men's clothing section is located near the entrance. Based on the same principle, the company is considering printing separate catalogs for men and women.[13]

Other marketers may start by targeting one gender and then later switch to both. An example is *The Highlander* catalog, a direct-mail piece based on the

MARKETING | **DICTIONARY**

Primary Metropolitan Statistical Area (PMSA) An urbanized county or set of counties with social and economic ties to nearby areas.

geographic information system (GIS) Computer technology that records several layers of data on a single map.

demographic segmentation Dividing consumer groups according to characteristics such as gender, age, income, occupation, education, household size, and stage in the family life cycle.

FIGURE 8.4 Segmenting by Gender

syndicated television series of the same name. Originally the catalog's market was 80 percent young adult men, a frequent audience for action shows. However, marketing research by catalog consultant Carol Worthington Levy revealed that the show also had a loyal female following. She redesigned the catalog to make it look more romantic, added photos of the series' male stars, and broadened the product line to include jewelry inspired by *Highlander* characters. Today, the catalog's mailing list is 50 percent female.[14]

Segmenting by Age

Many firms identify market segments on the basis of consumers' ages. Indeed, they develop some products specifically to meet the needs of people in certain age groups. Gerber Food focuses on food for infants and toddlers. Del Webb Corp. creates Sun Cities retirement communities. Warner-Lambert developed Halls Juniors cough drops for children 5 years and over. Age distribution and projected changes in each age group are important to marketers because consumer needs and wants differ notably among age groups.

Sociologists attribute these differences to the **cohort effect**—the tendency of members of a generation to be influenced and bound together by significant events occurring during their key formative years, roughly 17 to 22 years of age. These events help to define the core values of the age group that eventually shape consumer preferences and behavior.[15] The following sections outline four main generations of today, and describe specific characteristics of each.

Generation Y. Born primarily between 1979 and 1994, often to baby boomers, members of this cohort are sometimes called *Generation Y* or *echo boomers*. Numbering perhaps 60 million, this large group is already making an impact on the way items are marketed.

Generation Y is more racially diverse than older generations; one-third of them are not Caucasian. One in four lives in a single-parent household, and three out of four have mothers who work outside the home. They are highly computer-literate, looking to the Internet for much of their entertainment and information about goods and services. Members of Generation Y tend to be practical in their outlook and cynical about standard sales pitches.

Clothing cataloger Delia's, for example, targets the 12- to 17-year-old age bracket by modeling its fashions on actual teenagers rather than professional models. The company's order form includes advice on how to order pants that fit properly—in other words, loose and baggy, with drooping hems and waistlines that sag below the hips. Like many other successful Generation Y marketers, Delia's has an active presence with its own Web site and online shopping capability. It also sponsors gURL.com, a popular Web fashion game and chat site.[16] Through ads in teen magazines, like the one in Figure 8.5, Delia's previews the content of its Web site and other interesting links on the Internet.

Generation X. People born between 1965 to the late 1970s, dubbed *Generation X* by some marketers, were the first large group to experience day care and the effects of widespread parental divorce. Currently, this age group accounts for 21 percent of the U.S. population. Overall, Xers tend to have more egalitarian views of gender roles than the general population holds, and they react strongly to influences from their peers. As a group, they delay marriage and careers, accept cultural diversity, and value the quality of personal life above work life.[17]

Beyond these basic statements, researchers have encountered difficulties trying to categorize the Generation X age group. Many Xers know what they want in a product and are turned off by marketing ploys that come across as patronizing or self-serving. Differences between generation subgroups can also complicate marketing.

AT&T focused on a specific Generation X subgroup—college students—by creating its Student Advantage membership program. The Student Advantage card combined discounted long distance telephone rates with 10 to 15 percent discounts on hundreds of products from pizza to movie tickets. Another telephone service offered to students through this membership—call organizer—which sorts calls according to person.

AT&T publicized the program with irreverent ads—proclaiming "It's So Money"—via radio, TV, and print and Internet publications. On campus, AT&T representatives hosted tables and posted placards informing students about the card, with messages such as "Rave when you save." Charts helpfully compared AT&T's rates with those of arch-competitor Sprint. Other AT&T initiatives included a campus tour in a van decorated with a football theme, which offered new customers the chance to win free bowl tickets. It also cosponsored, with *Rolling Stone* magazine, a tour of 20 campuses that featured a multimedia retrospective of *Rolling Stone* covers.[18]

Baby Boomers. Baby boomers—people born from 1946 until 1965—are a popular segment to target because of their numbers. Nearly 42 percent of U.S. adults were born in this period. The values of this age group were influenced both by the counterculture movement of the Vietnam War era and the materialistic, career-oriented drive of the 1970s and 1980s.

There is no doubt that baby boomers are a lucrative market. Marketing research and consulting company FIND/SVP Inc. estimates that boomers over the age of 50 have a total disposable income of $930 billion, and this amount could rise to $1 trillion by 2003.[19]

Many members of the group, however, are not behaving as expected, complicating segmentation and targeting

FIGURE 8.5 Marketing to Generation Y

delias.com

att.com/college/

MARKETING DICTIONARY

cohort effect Tendency for members of a generation to be influenced by events occurring during their key formative years.

continued on next page

Vans Targets Generation Y

BACKGROUND Baby boomers grew up with Keds and P. F. Flyers, which made the wearer "run faster and jump higher." Now *their* kids have their own hot brand of sneakers: Vans. The shoe company has actually been around for 30 years, and by the mid-1990s had become a family shoe manufacturer, diluting its focus by producing shoes for several markets. When Jeff Schoenfeld took over as CEO in 1995, he recognized immediately that to retain its competitive edge, the company needed to refocus on one market: teens and preteens.

THE CHALLENGE Schoenfeld wanted to "get everyone inside the company thinking about Vans as a global brand aimed at consumers aged 10 to 24. Vans really thought of itself to be much more product and customer driven." Generation Y is a tricky market to satisfy—racially and ethnically diverse, computer literate, and savvy about marketing tactics. "Kids don't relate to direct hard-sell advertising," Schoenfeld notes. "They see through a company that's just spending money to attract their attention."

THE STRATEGY To target Vans marketing efforts, Schoenfeld approached his customers through their lifestyle. In addition to designing shoes that this group wanted, Vans began to affiliate itself with sports and activities that teens and preteens like. "Rather than pour money into advertising, we invest in sports and music and entertainment, sponsoring music festivals

strategies. For instance, although pundits have predicted the demise of movie theaters, boomers are flocking to the cinema in record numbers. Over the past decade, the number of people over the age of 40 who go to the movies regularly has risen by 35 percent, more than any other age group.[20]

Like their Xer counterparts, different subgroups within this generation are also complicating segmentation and targeting strategies. Some boomers put off starting families until their 40s, while others of their age have already become grandparents. Boomer grandparents are healthier and more physically active than their own grandparents were, and they expect to take an active role in their grandchildren's lives. When buying toys, for instance, they tend to purchase items that focus on a shared experience—games they can play with their grandchildren or craft sets they can assemble together.

Nostalgic references that remind baby boomers of their own childhood and adolescence are a popular way to target this segment. Retro toys such as Sock Monkey, a stuffed-sock simian, are big sellers at home-furnishings retailer Restoration Hardware. The William Carter Company markets a successful line of children's clothing decorated with drawings by boomer icon John Lennon. Burger King uses top-40 songs from the 1960s and 1970s in the soundtracks for its TV commercials.[21]

Seniors. Marketers also recognize a trend dubbed *the graying of America*. By 2025, Americans over 65 will comprise 18.5 percent of the population.[22] As Americans continue to live longer, the median age of the U.S. population has dramatically increased. The current median age is now 35.2 years, up from 32.8 years a decade ago.[23] Most major industrialized nations are seeing a similar demographic trend. Since 1972, the average worldwide life span has lengthened by more than 13 years.[24]

Seniors are a powerful economic force. In the United States, heads of households aged 55-plus control about three-quarters of the country's total financial assets. Their discretionary incomes and rates of home ownership are higher than those of any other age group. These statistics show why many marketers are targeting this group. Some refer to these prosperous consumers as *WOOFS*—Well-Off Older Folks.

Lifestage Matrix Marketing, a California-based consulting firm, designed a marketing campaign for a cable TV station that targeted this generation. The ads showed photos of President Eisenhower and played to viewers' memories of Eisenhower's campaign slogan: "If you remember 'I like Ike,' we've got something you're going to love." Paid subscription response rates for the station soon rose from 1.7 percent to over 10 percent.[25]

Marketing experts caution about the importance of avoiding stereotypes when targeting older consumers. Although they will respond to promotions and advertising that appeal to the changing interests, needs, and wants of their later years, they often reject appeals that use terms such as *senior citizens*, *golden years*, and *retirees*. The GE Financial Assurance ad in Figure 8.6 appeals to older consumers because the message focuses on satisfying their needs for long-term care insurance so they can preserve their independence and protect their life savings.

Segmenting by Ethnic Group

The Census Bureau classifies the U.S. population into the following list of racial categories: white, African American, American Indian or Alaskan Native, Asian Indian, Chinese, Filipino, Korean, Vietnamese, Japanese, other Asian, Native Hawaiian, Guamanian or Chamorro, Samoan, other Pacific Islander, and other race. ("Hispanic" is considered an ethnic, rather than racial, classification.)[26]

According to the Census Bureau, America's racial and ethnic makeup is changing. Because of comparatively high immigration and birthrates among some minority groups, the Census Bureau projects that by 2050, nearly half of the population will belong to nonwhite minority groups.

The three largest and fastest-growing racial/ethnic groups are African Americans, Hispanics, and Asian Americans. From a marketer's perspective, it is important to note that spending by these groups is rising at a faster pace than it is for U.S. households in general.[27]

African Americans are currently the largest racial/ethnic minority group in the United States—some 13 percent of the U.S. population. Their numbers are projected to grow to 45 million by 2020.[28]

Hispanics, the nation's second-largest subculture, account for about 10 percent of the population. The Hispanic population's growth rate is four times that of the African-American population and nine times the growth rate for whites. Census projections predict that by 2020, more Hispanics than African Americans will be living in the United States.[29]

Although Asian Americans and Pacific Islanders represent a smaller segment than either the African-American or Hispanic populations, they are the fastest-growing segment of the U.S. population. The Census Bureau estimates that this group will grow to 23 million by 2020. Asian Americans are an attractive target for marketers because they also have the fastest-growing income. Their average income per household is considerably higher than that of any other ethnic group, including whites.[30]

The Asian-American population is concentrated in fewer geographic areas than are other ethnic markets. For instance, a particularly high concentration of Asian Americans live in California. Companies can lower their costs of reaching Asian-American consumers by advertising in appropriate local markets rather than on a national scale.

Researchers have identified differences in consumer preferences, motivations, and buying habits among different ethnic and racial segments. Increasingly, businesses are targeting their marketing strategies to more closely match those differences. For example, all three of the major greeting-card manufacturers have launched ethnically oriented card lines. Chapter 9 will take a closer look at how ethnic and racial culture affects consumer behavior.

Beginning with the 2000 census, U.S. residents have the option of identifying themselves as more than one category. Marketers need to be aware of this change. In some ways, it benefits marketers by making racial statistics more accurate—respondents are no longer forced to place themselves in arbitrary categories. On the other hand, marketers may find it difficult to compare the new statistics with data from earlier censuses. For example, families that were previously reported as African-American or white could now be classified as both, causing them to be tabulated separately from the exclusively African-American or white totals. It remains to be seen how the new approach will affect market segmentation by ethnic groups.[31]

FIGURE 8.6 | Targeting Older Consumers

and events in our core sports—surfing, skateboarding, BMX biking, and snowboarding—all closely related to the Southern California lifestyle," explains Schoenfeld. The company's original brand image was based on the California surfer culture, and Schoenfeld has decided to return to this strength. Vans has opened several skateparks in California and sponsors the Vans Triple Crown Series involving snowboarding, wakeboarding, surfing, freestyle motorcross, and BMX racing. Vans has also entered into a sponsorship and licensing partnership with Sony Computer Entertainment, in which Sony will have the rights to use leading Vans athletes for development of PlayStation video games.

THE OUTCOME Generation Y consumers seem to like the new Vans approach: Within two years of Schoenfeld's revamping of the company, Vans was doing $205 million a year in sales. Schoenfeld plans to keep close watch over what his customers like and want. Perhaps wisely, he has decided not to try to chase his teenagers into adulthood. "You have to be comfortable with not retaining a customer for his or her entire life," he notes. "Our focus will be on a new batch of young consumers. That's where we've been successful. If you really want to reach the teen market, you have to focus on them specifically."

Segmenting by Family Life Cycle

Still another form of demographic segmentation employs the stages of the **family life cycle**—the process of family formation and dissolution. The

MARKETING | **DICTIONARY**

family life cycle Process of family formation and dissolution, which affects market segmentation because life stage, not age, is the primary determinant of many consumer purchases.

underlying theme of this segmentation approach is that life stage, not age per se, is the primary determinant of many consumer purchases. As people move from one life stage to another, they become potential consumers for different types of goods and services.

For example, an unmarried person setting up an apartment for the first time is likely to be a good prospect for inexpensive furniture and small home appliances. This consumer probably must budget carefully, ruling out expenditures on luxury items. On the other hand, a young, single person who is still living at home will probably have more money to spend on goods such as sporting and entertainment equipment, personal-care items, and clothing.

As couples marry, their consumer profiles change. Couples without children are frequent buyers of personalized gifts, power tools, furniture, and homes. Eating out and travel may also be part of their lifestyles.

The birth of a first child changes any couple's consumer profile considerably; parents must buy cribs, changing tables, baby clothes, baby food, car seats, and similar products. Parents usually spend less on the children who follow the first because they have already bought many essential items for the first child.

In the United States, the divorce rate averages 4.5 married couples per 1,000 people.[32] Divorce can dramatically alter an individual's consumer profile. As the household breaks up, the partners may need new household items at the same time that their income levels drop.

"Empty nesters"—married couples whose children have grown up and moved away from home—are an attractive life-cycle segment for marketers. Empty nesters may also have the disposable incomes necessary to purchase premium products. Such a household may struggle to maintain a four-bedroom home and a half-acre lawn, making them customers for lawn-care and home-care services, as well as townhouses or condominiums. Later, these people may become customers for retirement centers, supplemental medical insurance, and hearing aids. This is also a prime target market for travel and leisure products.

One trend noted by researchers in the past decade is an increase in the number of grown children who have returned home to live with their parents. Some of these grown children bring along families of their own.

Segmenting by Household Type

The first U.S. census in 1790 found an average household size of 5.8 persons. By 1960, this number had fallen to 3.4 persons, and today that number is below 3.0. The U.S. Department of Commerce cites several reasons for the trend toward smaller households: lower fertility rates, young people's tendency to postpone marriage or to never marry, the increasing tendency among younger couples to limit the number of children or to have no children at all, the ease and frequency of divorce, and the ability and desire of many young singles and the elderly to live alone.

Population data around the world show a similar pattern. On a global average, women are bearing only half the number of children they had in 1972. While American women bear a lifetime average of two children each, women in many other countries have even fewer, further shrinking household size.[33]

An important U.S. trend over the past 20 years has been the decline of the so-called traditional family, consisting of two parents and their children living in one household. Thirty years ago this segment included 40 percent of all American households; currently it comprises 26 percent.[34]

Meanwhile, three other segments—single-parent families, single-person households, and nonfamily group households—have each more than doubled in size during the same time period. These nontraditional households make likely consumers for single-serving and convenience foods, such as Campbell's Soup for One and Budget Gourmet and Weight Watchers' single-serve casseroles, as well as Stouffer's homestyle meals for two shown in Figure 8.7.

While the percentage of married-couple families has fallen, the number of unmarried individuals living together has risen. Consequently, the Bureau of the Census created another category, POSSLQ, which stands for unmarried *people of the opposite sex in the same living quarters.*

Finally, one of the most actively pursued market segments are DINKs—dual-income couples with no kids. With high levels of spendable income, such couples are big buyers of gourmet foods, luxury items, and travel.

campbellkitchen.com

FIGURE 8.7   Targeting Smaller Households

Segmenting by Income and Expenditure Patterns

The earlier definition of *market* described people or institutions with purchasing power. Not surprisingly, then, a common basis for segmenting the consumer market is income.

Mass-marketers aim their appeals at middle-income groups. Makers of Rutt kitchen cabinets, on the other hand, target more affluent segments with ads that feature "Cabinetry for those who have no patience with standard or run-of-the-mill." Potential customers must pay $15 just to receive a catalog of Rutt designs.[35]

Marketers often target geographic areas known for the high incomes of their residents. *Sales & Marketing Management* magazine conducts a periodic *Survey of Buying Power*, which lists metropolitan markets by income. According to recent surveys, the Connecticut metropolitan area of Bridgeport-Stamford-Norwalk-Danbury ranks first, with a median household Effective Buying Income (disposable income) of $57,941.[36]

Metropolitan markets that rise dramatically in the Effective Buying Income often make promising targets for income-related segmentation. Cities that have enjoyed recent increases include Des Moines, Iowa; Boulder, Colorado; Sioux Falls, South Dakota; and Salt Lake City, Utah. Leading the country with the largest increase, 46 percent, is Austin, Texas.[37]

rutt1.com/company.htm

Engel's Laws.   How do expenditure patterns vary with income? Over a century ago, Ernst Engel, a German statistician, published what became known as **Engel's laws**—three general statements based on his studies of the impact of household income changes on consumer spending behavior. According to Engel, as family income increases, the following will take place:

1. A smaller percentage of expenditures go for food.
2. The percentage spent on housing and household operations and clothing remains constant.
3. The percentage spent on other items (such as recreation and education) increases.

Are Engel's laws still valid? Newer studies say essentially *yes*, with a few exceptions. Researchers note a steady decline

MARKETING   DICTIONARY

Engel's laws Three general statements based on Ernst Engel's studies of the impact of household income changes on consumer spending behavior. As family income increases, (1) a smaller percentage of expenditures go for food, (2) the percentage spent on housing and household operations and clothing remains constant; and (3) the percentage spent on other items (such as recreation and education) increases.

Segmenting by Income and Expenditure Patterns

AN AROMATIC MASSAGE.

FOLLOWED BY A SEAWEED WRAP.

FOLLOWED BY A BOWL OF FRESH FRUIT POOLSIDE.

FOLLOWED BY A RENDEZVOUS IN A LITTLE BISTRO WITH A HANDSOME MAN-THE ONE I MARRIED.

THIS IS NOT A NORMAL DAY.
This is a Norwegian Day.

*As far from the everyday as a ship can take you.
That's The Norwegian Way.*

Talk to your travel agent or contact NCL at 1-800-327-7030 or www.ncl.com
©1999 Norwegian Cruise Line. Ship's Registry: Bahamas and Panama.

NORWEGIAN
CRUISE LINE

@ **Euromonitor.com**

in the percentage of total income spent on food, beverages, and tobacco as income increases. Although high-income families spend greater absolute amounts on food items, their purchases represent declining percentages of their total expenditures as compared with low-income families. The second law remains partly accurate since the percentage of expenditures for housing and household operations remains relatively unchanged in all but the very lowest income groups. The percentage spent on clothing, however, rises with increased income. The third law is also true, with the exception of medical and personal-care costs, which appear to decline as a percentage of increased income. The Norwegian Cruise Line ad in Figure 8.8 is targeted at higher income households that spend higher percentages of their incomes (relative to less affluent families) on such recreational services as luxury travel.

Engel's laws provide the marketing manager with useful rules about the types of consumer demand that evolve with increased income. These laws can also help marketers to evaluate a foreign country as a potential target market.

Demographic Segmentation Abroad

Marketers often face a difficult task in obtaining the data necessary for global demographic segmentation. Many countries do not operate regularly scheduled census programs. For instance, the most recent count of the Dutch population is now over two decades old. Germany skipped counting from 1970 to 1987, and France conducts a census about every seven years. By contrast, Japan and Canada conduct censuses every five years; however, the mid-decade assessments are not as complete as the end-of-decade counts.

Also, some foreign data includes demographic divisions not found in the U.S. census. Canada collects information on religious affiliation, for instance. On the other hand, some of the standard segmentation data for U.S. markets is not available abroad. Many nations do not collect income data. Great Britain, Japan, Spain, France, and Italy are examples. Similarly, family life cycle data is difficult to apply in global demographic segmentation efforts. Ireland acknowledges only three marital statuses—single, married, and widowed—while Latin American nations and Sweden count their cohabitants.

One source of global demographic information is the International Programs Center (IPC) at the U.S. Bureau of the Census. The IPC provides a searchable online database of population statistics for many countries on the Census Bureau's Web page.

Another source is the United Nations, which sponsors national statistical offices that collect demographic data on a variety of countries. In addition, private marketing research firms can supplement government data. For example, Euromonitor, based in London, specializes in demographic information on European residents.[38]

Psychographic Segmentation

Marketers have traditionally referred to geographic and demographic characteristics as the primary bases for dividing consumers into homogeneous market segments. Still, they have long recognized the need for fuller, more lifelike portraits of consumers in developing their marketing programs. As a result, psychographic segmentation can be a useful tool for gaining sharper insight into consumer purchasing behavior.

What Is Psychographic Segmentation?

Psychographic segmentation divides a population into groups that have similar psychological characteristics, values, and lifestyles. **Lifestyle** refers to a person's mode of living; it describes how an individual operates on a daily basis. Consumers' lifestyles are composites of their individual psychological profiles, including their needs, motives, perceptions, and attitudes. A lifestyle also bears the mark of many other influences, such as family, job, social activities, and culture.

The most common method for developing psychographic profiles of a population is to conduct a large-scale survey that asks consumers to agree or disagree with a collection of several hundred *AIO statements*. **AIO statements** describe various activities, interests, and opinions. Data from respondents' choices between these statements allows researchers to develop lifestyle profiles. Marketers can then develop a separate marketing strategy that closely fits the psychographic makeup for each lifestyle segment.

Marketing researchers have conducted psychographic studies on hundreds of goods and services, ranging from beer to air travel. Hospitals and other health-care providers use such studies to assess consumer behavior and attitudes toward health care in general, to learn the needs of consumers in particular marketplaces, and to determine how consumers perceive individual institutions. Many businesses turn to psychographic research in an effort to learn what consumers in various demographic and geographic segments want and need.

VALS 2

In 1978, the research and consulting firm SRI International developed a psychographic segmentation system called *VALS*. The name stands for "values and lifestyles," and the original VALS scheme categorized consumers by their opinions regarding social issues. A decade later, SRI revised the system to link it more closely with consumer-buying behavior. The revised system, VALS 2, is based on two key concepts: resources and self-motivation. **VALS 2** divides consumers into eight psychographic categories. Figure 8.9 details the profiles for these categories and their relationships.

SRI.com

The VALS network chart in the figure displays differences in resources as vertical distances, while self-orientation is represented horizontally. The resource dimension measures income, education, self-confidence, health, eagerness to buy, and energy level. Self-orientations divide consumers into three groups: principle-oriented consumers who have a set of ideas and morals—principles—that they live their lives by; status-oriented consumers that are influenced by what others think; and action-oriented consumers that seek physical activity, variety, and adventure.

SRI has created several specialized segmentation systems based on this approach. GeoVALS, for instance, estimates the percentage of each VALS type in each U.S. residential zip code. JapanVALS was developed to help companies understand Japanese consumers, and iVALS focuses on Internet sites and users.[39]

SRI uses the VALS 2 segmentation information in conjunction with marketers in consulting projects and on a subscriber basis. Product, service, and media data are available by VALS-type from companies' databases.

Curious about which psychographic segment claims you? See the 'netWork exercises at the end of this chapter for directions on how to find your VALS 2 type.

Several other commercially available psychographic profile systems offer their own insights to marketers. One is MONITOR, available from Yankelovich Partners.[40] A newer syndicated psychographic service, from marketing research firm Odyssey, focuses on the psychographics of people who use new technologies, such as the Internet.

Psychographic Segmentation of Global Markets

Psychographic profiles can cross national boundaries. Roper Starch Worldwide, a marketing research firm, recently surveyed 7,000 people in 35

MARKETING   DICTIONARY

psychographic segmentation Dividing a population into homogeneous groups on the basis of psychological and lifestyle profiles.

lifestyle Activities that reflect a person's needs, motives, perceptions, and attitudes.

AIO statements Statements in a psychographic survey that reflect a respondent's activities, interests, and opinions.

VALS 2 Commercially available system for psychographic segmentation of consumers.

FIGURE 8.9   VALS Network

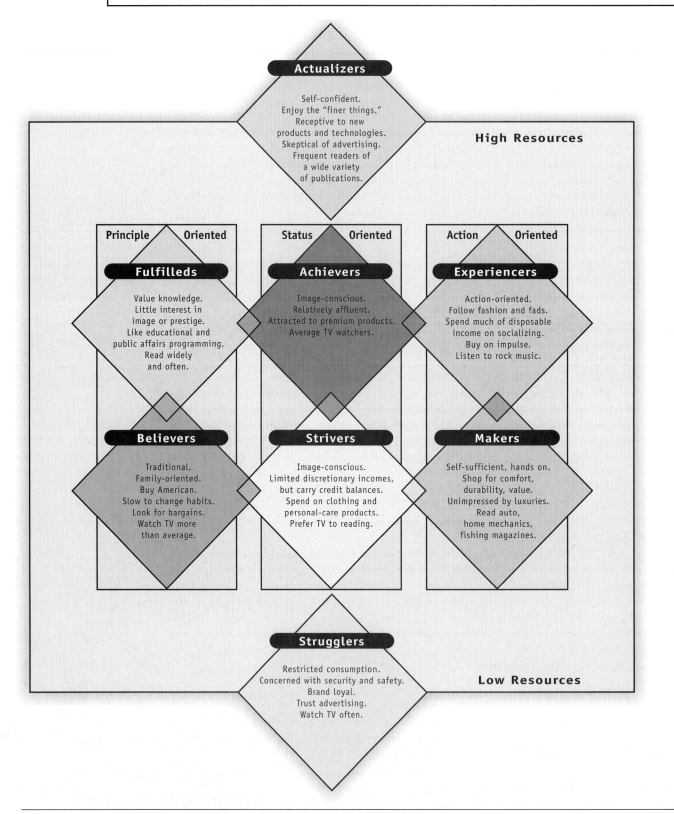

countries. From the resulting data, Roper identified six psychographic consumer segments that exist in all 35 nations, although to varying degrees:

- *Strivers*, the largest segment, value professional and material goals more than the other groups. One-third of the Asian population and one-fourth of Russians are Strivers. They are slightly more likely to be men than women.

- *Devouts* value duty and tradition. While this segment comprises 22 percent of all adults, they are most common in Africa, the Middle East, and developing Asia. They are least common in Western Europe and developed Asian countries. Worldwide, they are more likely to be female.

- *Altruists* emphasize social issues and societal well-being. Comprising 18 percent of all adults, this group shows a median age of 44 and a slightly higher percentage of women. Altruists are most common in Latin America and Russia.

- *Intimates* value family and personal relationships. They are almost equally divided between males and females. One-fourth of people in America and Europe are intimates, but only 7 percent of consumers in developing Asia fall into this category.

- *Fun seekers*, as you might guess from their name, focus on personal enjoyment and pleasurable experiences. They comprise 12 percent of the world's population, with a male-female ratio of 54 to 46. Many live in developed Asia.

- *Creatives*, the smallest segment, account for just 10 percent of the global population. This group seeks education, technology, and knowledge, and their male-female ratio is roughly equal. Many creatives live in Western Europe and Latin America.

@ **roper.com**

Roper researchers note that some principles and core beliefs apply to more than one psychographic segment. For example, consumers in all 35 countries cite "family" as one of their five most important values, and "protecting the family" ranks as one of the top 10.[41]

FIGURE 8.10 Using Psychographic Segmentation

Using Psychographic Segmentation

Psychographic profile systems like those of Roper Starch and SRI can paint useful pictures of the overall psychological motivations of consumers. These profiles produce much richer descriptions of potential target markets than other techniques can achieve. The enhanced detail aids in matching a company's image and product offerings with the types of consumers who use its products.

Learning which psychographic segments are most prevalent in a country helps marketers plan and promote more effectively. For example, fun seekers enjoy going to movie theaters and restaurants, making them good targets for related goods and services. The Outward Bound ad in Figure 8.10 may appeal to people who enjoy action-oriented experiences. Intimates, on the other hand, enjoy gardening and cooking at home, so they are promising customers for makers of cookware and garden tools.[42]

Psychographic segmentation is a good supplement to segmentation by demographic or geographic variables. For example, marketers may have access to each consumer type's media preferences in network television, cable television, radio format, magazines, and newspapers. Intimates, for example, spend a great deal of time watching television and listening to the radio, so these media are effective channels for reaching them.[43] Psychographic studies may then refine the picture of segment characteristics to give a more elaborate lifestyle profile of the consumers in the firm's target market.

Product-Related Segmentation

Product-related segmentation involves dividing a consumer population into homogeneous groups based on characteristics of their relationships to the product. This segmentation approach can take several forms:

1. Segmenting based on the benefits that people seek when they buy a product
2. Segmenting based on usage rates for a product
3. Segmenting according to consumers' brand loyalty toward a product

Segmenting by Benefits Sought

This approach focuses on the attributes that people seek in a good or service and the benefits they expect to receive from that good or service. It groups consumers into segments based on what they want a product to do for them.

starbucks.com

Consumers who quaff Starbucks' premium coffees, for example, are not just looking for a dose of caffeine. They are willing to pay extra to savor a pleasant experience, one that makes them feel pampered and appreciated. Kellogg is attempting to provide similar benefits for consumers wishing to reproduce the relaxation and self-indulgence of a vacation getaway with Country Inn, a new premium cereal.[44] The Celestial Seasonings ad in Figure 8.11 promotes a caffeine-free herbal tea as a soothing drink that relieves tension.

Even if a business offers only one product line, however, marketers must remember to consider product benefits. Two people may buy the same product for very different reasons. A box of Arm & Hammer baking soda could end up serving as a refrigerator freshener, a toothpaste substitute, an antacid, or a deodorizer for a cat's litter box.

FIGURE 8.11   **Segmenting by Benefits Sought**

Segmenting by Usage Rates

Marketers may also segment a total market by grouping people according to the amounts of a product that they buy and use. Markets can be divided into heavy-user, moderate-user, and light-user segments. The **80/20 principle** holds that a big percentage of a product's revenues—roughly 80 percent—comes from a relatively small, loyal percentage of total customers—perhaps 20 percent. The 80/20 principle is sometimes referred to as "Praedo's Law."

While the percentages need not exactly equal these figures, the general principle often holds true: Relatively few heavy users of a product can account for much of its consumption. Consider the case of Internet users. One study shows that only a tiny fraction—5 percent—of visitors to a commercial Web site account for nearly 70 percent of clicks and over 50 percent of page views.[45]

Depending on their goals, marketers may target heavy, moderate, or light users as well as nonusers. A company may attempt to lure heavy users of another product away from their regular brands to try a new brand. Nonusers and light users may be attractive prospects because other companies are ignoring them. Usage rates can also be linked to other segmentation methods such as demographic and psychographic segmentation.

Segmenting by Brand Loyalty

A third product-related segmentation method groups consumers according to the strength of the brand loyalty they feel toward a product. For example, in addition to selling exotic coffee beans through its catalog, Starbucks sells coffee mugs, scoops, espresso makers, and other items

CELESTIAL SEASONINGS
Caffeine Free   Natural Herb Tea
Tension Tamer

Works approximately six years faster than psychotherapy.

Tension Tamer® has the subtle sweetness of peppermint and cinnamon. A soothing blend of ginger root and chamomile. And it's even more comfortable than the couch.

emblazoned with the Starbucks logo. Its marketers have found that consumers who enjoy the company's coffees are likely to also purchase related products.[46]

A classic example of brand loyalty segmentation is airline frequent-flyer programs. Originally targeted at heavy users—business travelers—frequent-flyer programs now help to bind even occasional travelers to specific airlines. The success of these programs has resulted in similar efforts in the hotel industry and elsewhere.

THE MARKET SEGMENTATION PROCESS

To this point, the chapter has discussed various bases on which companies segment markets. How does a marketer decide which segmentation base to use? As Figure 8.12 shows, marketers follow a five-step decision process.

5

Identify the steps in the market segmentation process.

Stage I: Identify Market Segmentation Process

Segmentation begins when marketers determine the bases on which to identify markets. They follow two methods for achieving this goal. In the first, management-driven method, segments are predefined by managers based on their observation of the behavioral and demographic characteristics of likely users. The market-driven method defines segments by asking customers which attributes are important to them and then clusters responses to identify potential segments. Both methods try to develop segments that group customers who respond similarly to specific marketing-mix alternatives. For example, Procter & Gamble cannot simply target Crest toothpaste to large families. Management must first confirm that most large families are interested in preventing tooth decay and will be receptive to the Crest marketing offer.

Sometimes marketers have trouble isolating a preferred segment. Many toy and clothing manufacturers would like to target grandparents, but this group can be difficult to identify and reach. Age-related segmentation strategies do not always work because people become grandparents at different ages and not all seniors have grandchildren. One successful initiative is Grandparents "Я" Us, a joint venture between retailer Toys "Я" Us and Third Age, an online community for older adults. This Web site offers grandparents helpful tips on selecting and purchasing toys.[47]

thirdage.com

Stage II: Develop a Relevant Profile for Each Segment

After identifying promising segments, marketers should seek further understanding of the customers in each one. This in-depth analysis of customers helps managers to accurately match customers' needs with the firm's marketing offers. The process must identify characteristics that both explain the similarities among customers within each segment and account for differences among segments.

The task at this stage is to develop a profile of the typical customer in each segment. Such a profile might include information about lifestyle patterns, attitudes toward product attributes and brands, product-use habits, geographic locations, and demographic characteristics.

Stage III: Forecast Market Potential

In the third stage, market segmentation and market opportunity analysis combine to produce a forecast of market potential within each segment. Market potential sets the upper limit on the demand that competing firms can expect

MARKETING | **DICTIONARY**

product-related segmentation Dividing a consumer population into homogeneous groups based on characteristics of their relationships to a product.

80/20 principle (also known as Praedo's Law) General belief that a big percentage of a product's revenues—roughly 80 percent—comes from a relatively small percentage of total customers—around 20 percent.

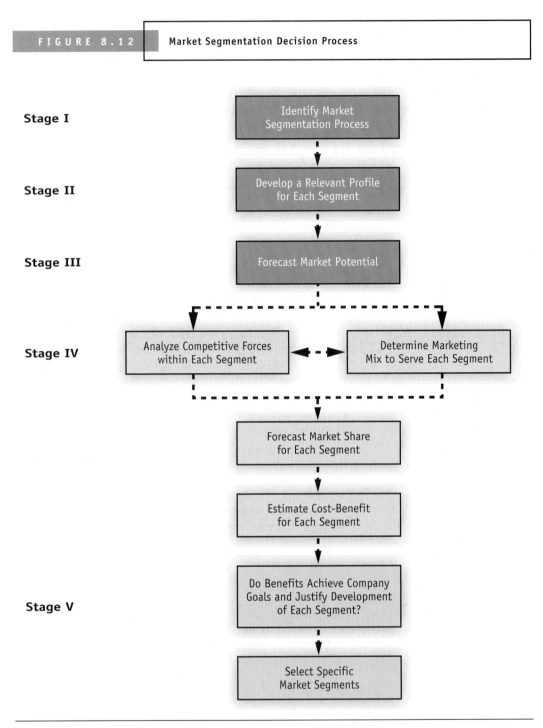

FIGURE 8.12 | Market Segmentation Decision Process

Source: M. Dale Beckman, Louis E. Boone, David L. Kurtz, Foundations of Marketing, Sixth Edition.

from a segment. Multiplying by market share determines a single firm's maximum sales potential. This step should define a preliminary go or no-go decision from management since the total sales potential in each segment must justify resources devoted to further analysis.

An example of a segment that shows tremendous market potential is U.S. children ages 4 to 12. Aggregate spending by consumers in this age group or on their behalf doubled every decade between the 1960s and 1980s and tripled during the 1990s to reach its current level of $24 billion a year. Thirty years ago children spent most of their money on candy. Today, only one-third is spent on food and beverages; the rest goes toward clothing, movies, games, and toys.

SOLVING AN ETHICAL CONTROVERSY

Questionable Advertising Aimed at Teens

One hundred years ago—long before seniors, baby boomers, generation X and Y, not to mention today's teens, were born—Abercrombie & Fitch began selling outdoor equipment to a few rugged Americans who liked to camp and fish. Today, the company has refocused on entirely different market segments and products. Recognizing the enormous market potential among teenagers and college-age young adults, the company now produces casual clothing for these two groups.

Recently, Abercrombie & Fitch has been the subject of quite a controversy. The controversy does not pertain to the clothing, however. What has many parents and legislators upset is the company's catalog, which features scantily dressed male and female models in suggestive poses. The clothes the models do wear, of course, are Abercrombie fashions. Abercrombie claims that the catalog is intended for young adults ages 18 to 22, not the younger set of teens and preteens. "We've always said this is adult stuff, not for anyone under eighteen," insists company spokesperson Hampton Carney. But teenagers love the clothing and the catalog and, until recently, have had no difficulty obtaining either. When Michigan's attorney general wrote to the company warning that the catalog contained sexual material that was illegal under state law to distribute to minors, Abercrombie responded by agreeing to require age identification of all young people attempting to purchase the catalog—it sells for $6—in all of its stores nationwide.

Even if the catalog is restricted to those over age eighteen, there is another ethical issue: In the past, the catalog has featured stories that contain recipes for alcoholic beverages and descriptions of drinking games. In most states, drinking under the age of 21 is illegal. Groups such as Mothers Against Drunk Drivers consider this content to be irresponsible.

Teens, however, love Abercrombie's clothes and gear. In one survey, teens ranked the brand as "sixth-coolest" on a list that included Coca-Cola and Levi's. And the company stands its ground with regard to its market segmentation and its catalog content. Hampton Carney remarks, "Everything we do is about a youthful and spirited, responsible life. We never do anything to let our customers down in any way."

 Should a company like Abercrombie & Fitch restrict its use of adult content in advertising that may reach younger consumers?

Pro
1. The company should acknowledge the fact that younger consumers have access to its catalog and revise its advertising accordingly.
2. If the company does not establish some boundaries in its advertising, it will create a negative image among parents and other adults whose money is being spent in Abercrombie's stores.
3. If the company does not establish its own boundaries, angered legislators may introduce tighter restrictions on catalog advertising.

Con
1. Parents should decide whether or not to allow teens access to advertising that contains adult content.
2. Restricting advertising content is like restricting freedom of speech, which is protected under the Constitution.
3. Marketers have been using varying degrees of sexual content to sell products for years; Abercrombie & Fitch's catalog is no different than others.

Summary
Once marketers have determined the market potential of a segment, it makes sense to design advertising geared to that group's interests. But if that advertising conflicts with the best interests of another segment, then perhaps marketers need to reconsider their approach. Even though the complaints against Abercrombie have drawn attention to the company, the question remains of whether its marketing practices are ethical. "There's no question that Abercrombie appeals to teenagers because it's the whole forbidden fruit syndrome," notes Peter Zollo, president of Teenage Research Unlimited. Indeed, immediately after Abercrombie recalled the catalog containing drinking recipes, circulation of its next catalog jumped from 75,000 to 100,000, and clothing sales are soaring.

SOURCES: Susan Chandler, "Sexy Catalog Draws Fire," *Chicago Tribune*, December 9, 1999, www.cnews.tribune.com; Marguerite Nugent, "Complaints Over Abercrombie Catalog Mount," *Reuters*, December 8, 1999, www.news.excite.com; and Chris Stallman, "Abercrombie & Fitch," July 26, 1999, www.companyethics.com.

Clothing retailers, noting this trend, have opened new stores that specialize in fashions for this age segment. An example is the Limited Too, which now has 311 stores nationwide. Competitors Abercrombie & Fitch and Gymboree have also opened separate outlets for preteens.[48]

 **limited.com**

Stage IV: Forecast Probable Market Share

Once market potential has been estimated, a firm must forecast its probable market share. Competitors' positions in targeted segments must be analyzed and a specific marketing strategy must be designed to serve these segments. These two activities may be performed simultaneously. Moreover, by settling on a marketing strategy and tactics, a firm determines the expected level

Pocketalk Falls Silent

BACKGROUND Forecasting market potential and probable market share can mean the difference between life and death for a new product. Cecil Duffie and Bill deKay learned this the hard way. In the mid-1990s, wireless telecommunications technology was advancing at top speed toward commercial development. The big companies were pouring millions—even billions—into new products designed ultimately for consumer use. When the Federal Communications Commission (FCC) began to auction about $2 billion worth of untapped airwaves, deKay and Duffie, founders of Conxus Communications, put in their bid.

THE MARKETING PROBLEM The product that deKay and Duffie planned to launch was called Pocketalk. Touted as an "answering machine in your pocket," the hand-held device would beep its owners and deliver voice messages. Duffie and deKay envisioned traveling businesspeople, busy moms, even kids carrying Pocketalks. But they needed to launch the product out ahead of competitors, and they needed enough subscribers to make it a hit. They also needed the technological infrastructure to make the product work. All of these variables made forecasting tricky.

continued on next page

6

Discuss four alternative strategies for reaching target markets.

of resources it must commit, that is, the costs that it will incur to tap the potential demand in each segment.

As part of its marketing strategy, Limited Too seeks to convince girls ages 6 to 14 that its retail outlets are geared to serve them, not their parents or older siblings. The stores are designed as comfortable places to hang out, with popular music in the background, flower-shaped chairs to lounge in, and psychedelic light designs flashing on the walls. They carry apparel that resembles clothing for teenagers but is sized for younger bodies; miniskirts are not as short and hip-hugging pants do not hang as low. The trendy styling pleases young customers, but the less-extreme cut pleases their parents.[49]

Stage V: Select Specific Market Segments

The information, analysis, and forecasts accumulated throughout the entire market segmentation decision process allows management to assess the potential for achieving company goals and to justify committing resources in developing one or more segments. For example, demand forecasts together with cost projections determine the profits and the return on investment (ROI) that the company can expect from each segment. Marketing strategy and tactics must be designed to reinforce the firm's image, yet keep within its unique organizational capabilities.

At this point in the analysis, marketers weigh more than monetary costs and benefits; they also consider many difficult-to-measure but critical organizational and environmental factors. For example, the firm may lack experienced personnel to launch a successful attack on an attractive market segment. Similarly, a firm with 60 percent of the market faces legal problems with the Federal Trade Commission if it increases its market concentration. This assessment of both financial and nonfinancial factors is a difficult but vital step in the decision process.

A useful tool in helping marketers choose specific markets is **target market decision analysis.** This procedure evaluates potential market segments on the basis of their relevant characteristics and their potential for satisfying business objectives.

Fleetwood Enterprises Inc., a California-based manufacturer of recreational vehicles (RVs), used target market decision analysis before deciding to focus their advertising efforts on baby boomers. Fleetwood's research showed that 13 percent of RV owners are in the 45-to-54 age bracket, and 17 percent fall into the 55-to-64 group. However, by 2010 those percentages are projected to swell to 32 percent and 64 percent respectively. Currently, about 9 million U.S. households own an RV; by 2010, this number is expected to rise to 10.4 million. Fleetwood also learned that a significant number of baby boomers already possessed the discretionary income necessary to purchase an RV. Clearly, the financial data looked promising. In addition, Fleetwood researchers considered psychographic characteristics of the market, such as baby boomers' belief in the importance of recreation and their desire to make the most of their leisure time.

As a result of its marketing research, the company decided to target baby boomers by emphasizing that recreational vehicles offer both flexibility and comfort—the ability to travel on one's own terms.[50]

STRATEGIES FOR REACHING TARGET MARKETS

Considerable marketing efforts are dedicated to developing strategies that will best match the firm's product offerings to the needs of particular target markets. An appropriate match is vital to the firm's marketing success. Marketers have identified four basic strategies for achieving consumer satisfaction: undifferentiated marketing, differentiated marketing, concentrated marketing, and micromarketing.

Undifferentiated Marketing

A firm may produce only one product or product line and promote it to all customers with a single marketing mix; such a firm is said to practice **undifferentiated marketing,** sometimes called *mass marketing.* Undifferentiated marketing was much more common in the past than it is today.

As noted earlier, Henry Ford built the Model T and sold it for one price. He agreed to paint his cars any color that consumers wanted, "as long as it is black." Ford's only concession to more specific customer needs was to add a truck body for Model T purchasers who needed more hauling capacity.

While undifferentiated marketing is efficient from a production viewpoint, the strategy also brings inherent dangers. A firm that attempts to satisfy everyone in the market with one standard product may suffer if competitors offer specialized units to smaller segments of the total market and better satisfy individual segments. Indeed, firms that implement strategies of differentiated marketing, concentrated marketing, or micromarketing may capture enough small segments of the market to defeat another competitor's strategy of undifferentiated marketing.

Differentiated Marketing

Firms that promote numerous products with differing marketing mixes designed to satisfy smaller segments are said to practice **differentiated marketing.** By providing increased satisfaction for each of many target markets, a company can produce more sales by following a differentiated marketing strategy than undifferentiated marketing would generate. Oscar Mayer, a marketer of a variety of meat products, practices differentiated marketing. They introduced a new product—Lunchables—aimed at children and increased their sales. In general, however, differentiated marketing also raises costs. Production costs usually rise because additional products and variations require shorter production runs and increased setup times. Inventory costs rise because more products require added storage space and more efforts for record keeping. Promotional costs also increase because each segment demands a unique promotional mix.

Despite higher marketing costs, however, an organization may be forced to practice differentiated marketing in order to remain competitive. For example, the travel industry now recognizes the need to target small groups of travelers with specialized interests. One such program is Culture's Edge, sponsored by the California Division of Tourism, which offers a wide range of trips exploring ethnic, cultural, and lifestyle-based issues. Each tour lasts 9 to 15 days and focuses on a specialized topic such as African-American heritage, performance art, or Pacific Rim cultures.[51]

American Airlines also conducts differentiated marketing to attract segments as diverse as college students and wedding party members. The carrier's College Saavers program offers U.S. student travelers discounts of up to 45 percent, depending on their destination. American primarily markets College

| FIGURE 8.13 | Using a Differentiated Marketing Strategy |

Lunchables

MARKETING STRATEGY FAILURE

THE OUTCOME With Motorola's help, Conxus built the product, along with the necessary infrastructure and support technology, but it took three years to do so. By that time, the market had changed. Cell phones had already hit the market with lower prices and more services than Pocketalk could offer. While the demand for Pocketalk existed in 1994—when Conxus began—by 1997, the market was no longer there. Although Conxus managed to attract 87,000 subscribers, the company needed one million just to break even; those FCC licenses alone had cost $90 million. Although Motorola helped keep the company alive with interim financing, eventually Conxus was forced to shut down.

LESSONS LEARNED "We were very disappointed that the market didn't embrace the technology as we had anticipated it would," says a Motorola spokesperson.

continued on next page

aa.com

MARKETING DICTIONARY

target market decision analysis Procedure for evaluating the relevant characteristics and the prospects for satisfying business objectives of potential market segments.

undifferentiated marketing Marketing strategy to produce only one product and market it to all customers using a single marketing mix.

differentiated marketing Marketing strategy to produce numerous products and promote them with different marketing mixes designed to satisfy smaller segments.

As Conxus developed its new product, perhaps it failed to continue monitoring its forecasts, or perhaps it was already so committed to the project that deKay and Duffie could not turn back. Fierce competitors, with lower-priced products offering a wider array of services, pounced on Pocketalk before it ever reached the marketplace. Accurate forecasting should be able to determine whether demand within a market segment will still exist when a new product hits the shelves. But with rapid changes in technology, even experienced marketers—Duffie and deKay already had successful careers in telecommunications—can make fatal mistakes.

7

Summarize the types of positioning strategies and the purposes of positioning and repositioning products.

Saavers through its Web site since its research shows college students are more likely to obtain information from the Internet than from mail or telephone promotions. Meanwhile, the airline also targets wedding party travelers through its First Call program, which provides airfare, car rental, and other discounts for groups of 10 or more people who are journeying to the same locale.[52]

Concentrated Marketing

Rather than trying to market its products separately to several segments, a firm may opt for a concentrated marketing strategy. With **concentrated marketing** (also known as *niche marketing*), a firm focuses its efforts on profitably satisfying only one market segment. This approach can appeal to a small firm that lacks the financial resources of its competitors and to a company that offers highly specialized goods and services.

Honolulu-based Magneato sells nothing but refrigerator magnets—600 different styles at prices ranging from $5 to $10. Concentrated marketing that successfully addresses market demand can be highly profitable; Magneato's Guam store sold $17,600 worth of magnets on one New Year's Day alone.[53]

Along with its benefits, concentrated marketing has its dangers. Since the strategy ties a firm's growth to a specific segment, sales can suffer if new competitors appeal successfully to the same segment. Furthermore, errors in forecasting market potential or customer buying habits lead to severe problems. Susan Kezios, president of the nonprofit American Franchisee Association, recalls one ambitious entrepreneur who decided to open a chain of pet stores. There was just one problem: He insisted on selling only one species of pet, the colorful Siamese betta fish well-known for its aggressive attacks on other fish. Notes Kezios wryly, "He's not in business anymore."[54]

Micromarketing

The fourth targeting strategy, still more narrowly focused than concentrated marketing, is **micromarketing,** which involves targeting potential customers at a very basic level, such as by zip code, specific occupation, lifestyle, or individual household. Hyseq, Inc., for example, introduced an occupation-specific online service for pharmaceutical and biological researchers. The ad in Figure 8.14 promotes GeneSolutions.com as the world's largest catalog of genes and related analytical data. Ultimately, micromarketing may even target individuals themselves.

William Sinclair, president of the Bank of Lakewood near Long Beach, California, practices micromarketing. Every week he faxes information to 355 small companies within a five-mile radius of the bank and mails promotional materials to affluent households in the same zip code.[55]

The Internet may allow marketers to make micromarketing even more effective. By tracking specific demographic and personal information, marketers can send e-mail directly to individual consumers who are most likely to buy their products.

Selecting and Executing a Strategy

Although most organizations adopt some form of differentiated marketing, no single, best choice suits all firms. Any of the alternatives may prove most effective in a particular situation. The basic determinants of a market-specific strategy are (1) company resources, (2) product homogeneity, (3) stage in the product life cycle, and (4) competitors' strategies.

A firm with limited resources may have to choose a concentrated marketing strategy. Small firms, for example, may be forced to select small target markets because of limitations in their financing, sales force, and promotional budgets. On the other hand, an undifferentiated marketing strategy suits a firm selling items perceived by consumers as relatively homogeneous. Marketers of grain, for example, sell standardized grades of generic products rather than individual brand names. Some petroleum companies implement undifferentiated marketing to distribute their gasoline to the mass market.

The firm's strategy may also change as its product progresses through the stages of the life cycle. During the early stages, undifferentiated marketing might effectively support the firm's attempt to develop initial demand for the product. In the later stages, however, competitive pressures may force modifications in products and in the development of marketing strategies aimed at segments of the total market.

The strategies of competitors also affect the choice of a segmentation strategy. A firm may encounter obstacles to undifferentiated marketing if its competitors actively cultivate smaller segments. In such instances, competition usually forces each firm to adopt a differentiated marketing strategy.

Having chosen a strategy for reaching their firm's target market, marketers must then decide how best to position the product. The concept of **positioning** seeks to place a product in a certain "position" in the minds of prospective buyers. Marketers use a positioning strategy to distinguish their firm's offerings from those of competitors and to create promotions that communicate the desired position.

To achieve this goal, marketers follow a number of positioning strategies. Possible approaches include positioning a good or service according to the following areas:

1. *Attributes*—Chevy Suburban is strong "Like a Rock."
2. *Price/quality*—Saks Fifth Avenue is a quality store.
3. *Competitors*—Visa's ads point out that some establishments do not accept American Express.
4. *Application*—Xerox is "The Document Company."
5. *Product user*—Southwest Airlines targets the budget-oriented traveler.
6. *Product class*—Tony Roma's is "Famous for Ribs."

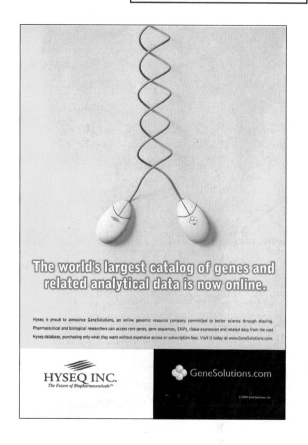

Whatever the strategy they choose, marketers want to emphasize a product's unique advantages and to differentiate it from competitors' options. Companies may even promote similar products by stressing different advantages. Managers at Sprint, for instance, feel that the long-distance carrier's prices offer a competitive advantage against AT&T. Sprint ads, therefore, tend to stress price and value. Meanwhile, marketers for AT&T feel that the company has a positive image with customers based on its longevity and experience in telecommunications. AT&T ads, therefore, often emphasize reliability and the high quality of its overall service.

 **sprint.com**

A **positioning map** provides a valuable tool in helping managers position products by graphically illustrating consumers' perceptions of competing products within an industry. Marketers can create a competitive positioning map from information solicited from consumers or from their accumulated knowledge about a market. For instance, a positioning map might present two different characteristics—price and perceived quality—and show how consumers view a product and its major competitors based on these traits. The hypothetical positioning map in Figure 8.15 compares selected retailers based on possible perceptions of their prices and quality of their offerings.

Sometimes, changes in the competitive environment force marketers to **reposition** a product—changing the position it holds in the minds of prospective buyers relative to the

MARKETING DICTIONARY

concentrated marketing Marketing strategy that commits all of a firm's marketing resources to serve a single market segment.

micromarketing Marketing strategy to target potential customers at basic levels such as by zip codes.

positioning Marketing strategy that emphasizes serving a specific market segment by achieving a certain position in buyers' minds.

positioning map Graphic illustration that shows differences in consumers' perceptions of competing products.

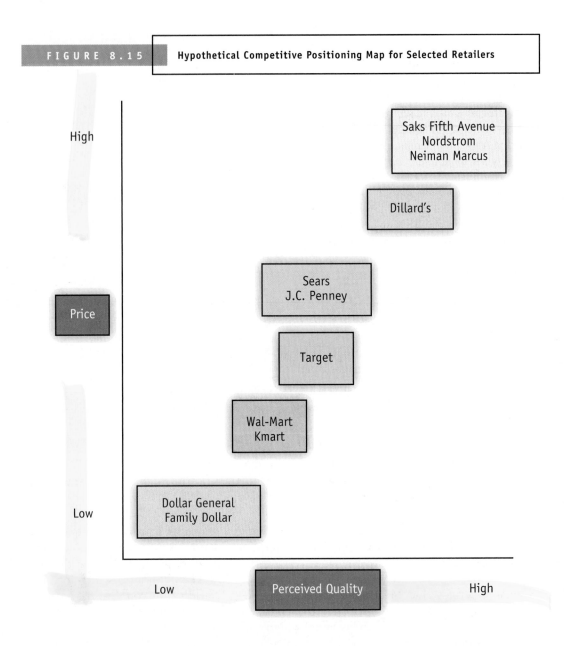

FIGURE 8.15 | Hypothetical Competitive Positioning Map for Selected Retailers

positions of competing products. Repositioning may become necessary even for highly successful products. For example, Campbell Soup Company has seen soup consumption drop in recent years. Why the decline? Consumers' eating habits have changed: They are cooking less and eating in restaurants more. Campbell's condensed soups, which require adding water or milk, have lost market share to products that are perceived as ready-to-serve and more convenient.

Campbell is fighting back by repositioning its soups as quick, easy-to-prepare, one-dish meals. Several strategies have been used in this effort:

- Redesigning its packaging to include reusable plastic bottles and microwaveable single-serving sizes

- Introducing new products, such as gourmet soup-in-a-pouch that can be stored in the refrigerator

- Expanding distribution to sell more soup through convenience stores, college cafeterias, and restaurants

Campbell marketers are also testing vending machines that would dispense hot soup in 7-11 stores. They vow to continue introducing at least two new products every year.

Will Campbell's repositioning strategy work? It remains to be seen. However, food industry analysts praise the company's new products as significantly better targeted than before.[56]

MARKET SEGMENTATION: STRATEGIC IMPLICATIONS

Looking for a business challenge? How about entering a foreign market in which the government censors all communication with your customers and the population is officially barred from purchasing your service at all?

This is the situation that faces Phoenix Satellite Television Company, an affiliate of News Corp.'s Star TV, in its continuing effort to become profitable in China. It is succeeding with a three-pronged strategy that targets China's expanding middle class, the government, and advertisers.

Phoenix's key to attracting consumers is to offer better programs than the competition. Eighty-five percent of Chinese households now have TVs, and many tune into Phoenix rather than state-owned stations. While official channels offer less-than-riveting reports on government speeches, factory openings, and other predictable events, Phoenix provides lively talk shows, interviews, and even a dating-game show that embarrasses participants with personal questions. While Chinese citizens are not supposed to watch foreign satellite broadcasts, the government cannot stop Phoenix from broadcasting its signal from Hong Kong.

Phoenix networking also appeals to the Chinese because of such shows that feature native talent and are actually filmed in Chinese. Other media companies targeting China, such as Time Warner and Walt Disney Company, produce programs in their home markets and dub or subtitle them in Chinese.

Phoenix's news costs offer China's growing middle class a look at controversial topics that government networks rarely touch. One recent talk show, "Behind the Headlines with Wen Tao," discussed the legal issue of police listening in on mobile phone conversations. On another show, "Good Morning China," an anchor reads aloud articles from Hong Kong and Taiwan newspapers, sometimes broaching subjects never discussed in mainland publications.

Even as it targets consumers, Phoenix lures government officials. While its shows may explore uncharted territory on occasion, Phoenix executives acknowledge that they do not want to alienate the Chinese government. They are careful to avoid airing negative publicity on the country or those who run it. "If a particular issue is taboo, there's no point in knocking someone over the head with it," comments N. K. Leung, Phoenix's deputy chief executive. At a Phoenix-sponsored music-awards ceremony in Shanghai, for instance, managers allowed the government to mandate what performers could and could not wear. (It banned baseball caps and sunglasses, on the grounds that they showed disrespect for authority.)

Phoenix also targets advertisers by offering attractive discounts for broadcast time. Its advertising prices average 10 percent of those at government-owned stations, and big advertisers get a volume discount.

Despite its success so far, Phoenix still faces hurdles. The government periodically enforces its thumbs-down policy on foreign broadcasts, and the network's inability to count actual viewers discourages some advertisers. However, its Chinese audience is already estimated to be equal to half the U.S. population and continues to increase, even as ad sales rise more than 40 percent annually.[57]

ACHIEVEMENT CHECK SUMMARY

Read the learning objectives that follow, and consider the questions for each one. Answering these questions will reinforce your grasp of the most important concepts in the chapter and will allow you to check how well you have achieved these learning goals. Where a blank appears before a question, answer with *T* or *F* for true/false questions; for multiple-choice questions, choose the letter of the correct answer.

Objective 8.1: Identify the essential components of a market.

1. _____ A market consists of people and organizations with the necessary purchasing power, willingness, and authority to buy.

2. _____ The overall market for a product always includes a homogeneous group of individuals.

3. _____ The target market for a product is the specific segment of prospective customers who are most likely to buy.

4. _____ Products purchased for use directly or indirectly in the production of other goods are classified as (a) consumer products or (b) business products.

Objective 8.2: Outline the role of market segmentation in developing a marketing strategy.

1. _____ *Market segmentation* refers to the process of dividing a total market into several heterogeneous groups.

2. _____ A market segmentation strategy attempts to identify the criteria that affect purchase decisions for various groups.

3. _____ Market segmentation benefits only profit-oriented firms.

Objective 8.3: Describe the criteria necessary for effective segmentation.

1. _____ The firm's ability to effectively promote to and serve a segment is an important consideration in market segmentation.

2. _____ Firms can serve even very small segments if their purchases create potentially profitable opportunities.

3. _____ A firm's marketing capabilities do not limit the number of segments in which it chooses to compete.

Objective 8.4: Explain each of the four bases for segmenting consumer markets.

1. _____ Marketers have identified four bases for segmenting consumer markets.

2. _____ The most common form of segmentation is (a) geographic; (b) demographic; (c) psychographic; (d) product-related; (e) none of these; (f) marketers rely equally heavily on all four.

3. _____ Segmenting ethnic groups as markets is an example of (a) geographic segmentation; (b) demographic segmentation; (c) psychographic segmentation.

4. _____ Psychographic segmentation divides a population into groups by looking at consumer lifestyles.

5. _____ Product-related segmentation focuses on consumers' relationships to goods or services.

Objective 8.5: Identify the steps in the market segmentation process.

1. _____ The first step in the market segmentation process is to develop a profile of relevant characteristics for each segment.

2. _____ Target market decision analysis involves identifying the specific characteristics of market segments.

3. _____ Projecting profit and return on investment is not part of the market segmentation decision process.

Objective 8.6: Discuss four alternative strategies for reaching target markets.

1. _____ A marketing strategy should match the firm's products to the needs of particular target markets.

2. _____ Henry Ford's strategy for the Model T is an example of (a) undifferentiated marketing; (b) differentiated marketing; (c) concentrated marketing.

3. _____ Marketing a number of products designed to appeal to individual parts of the total market is called (a) differentiated marketing; (b) concentrated marketing; (c) micromarketing.

4. _____ Focusing on satisfying the needs of only one market segment is called (a) differentiated marketing; (b) concentrated marketing; (c) micromarketing.

Objective 8.7: Summarize the types of positioning strategies and the purposes of positioning and repositioning products.

1. _____ Developing a marketing strategy aimed at a particular market segment to distinguish a good or service from those of competitors is called (a) marketing mix; (b) positioning; (c) concentrated segmentation.

2. _____ Marketers use a positioning map to (a) determine geographic segments; (b) track changes in sales figures; (c) illustrate how a product compares to its competitors in the minds of consumers.

3. _____ Repositioning is not necessary if the firm's competitive environment changes.

Students: See the solutions section located on pages S-1–S-2 to check your responses to the Achievement Check Summary.

Key Terms

market	family life cycle
target market	Engel's laws
consumer product	psychographic segmentation
business product	lifestyle
market segmentation	AIO statements
geographic segmentation	VALS 2
Metropolitan Statistical Area (MSA)	product-related segmentation
	80/20 principle
Consolidated Metropolitan Statistical Area (CMSA)	target market decision analysis
	undifferentiated marketing
Primary Metropolitan Statistical Area (PMSA)	differentiated marketing
	concentrated marketing
geographic information system (GIS)	micromarketing
	positioning
demographic segmentation	positioning map
cohort effect	reposition

Review Questions

1. What is a market? Explain the components needed to create a market.

2. Bicycles are consumer goods; iron ore is a business good. Are trucks consumer goods or business goods? Support your answer.

3. Identify and briefly explain the bases for segmenting consumer markets. Which approach is the oldest? Which one is used most frequently?

4. Distinguish among MSAs, PMSAs, and CMSAs. How can marketers use these concepts?

5. How can lifestyles affect market segmentation?

6. Explain the use of benefits sought, usage rates, and brand loyalty as segmentation variables.

7. What market segmentation basis would you recommend for each of the following products, and why?

a. Dallas Stars hockey team
b. Canon copiers
c. Bumble Bee Fat-Free Tuna Salad

8. What is target market decision analysis? Relate this activity to the concept of market segmentation.

9. Outline the basic features of undifferentiated marketing. Contrast differentiated marketing with micromarketing.

10. Name six positioning strategies and give an example of each.

Questions for Critical Thinking

1. Match the following bases for market segmentation with the appropriate examples. Explain your choices.
   a. geographic segmentation
   b. demographic segmentation
   c. psychographic segmentation
   d. product-related segmentation

   _____ Regional broadcasting system for the St. Louis Cardinals baseball team

   _____ Microsoft's slogan, "Where do you want to go today?"

   _____ Pfizer advertisements in which former Senator Robert Dole discusses impotency (Pfizer is the maker of Viagra, a popular drug used to address impotency problems.)

   _____ Aleve's slogan, "All Day Strong: All Day Long"

2. Utah has the youngest state population in the United States, and West Virginia is the oldest. The median age for Utah is 26.7 years, while West Virginia's median age is 38.6.[58] How would you explain the median age differences? Discuss how these median ages could be used in market segmentation strategies?

3. Eighty-three percent of Diet Coke's sales are produced by just 13 percent of Diet Coke drinkers.[59] Relate this information to the concepts covered in Chapter 8.

4. Frito-Lay markets Cheetos snacks without cheese flavoring in Asia because consumers there prefer steak-flavored and cuttlefish-flavored snacks. What type of segmentation strategy is Frito-Lay employing in its Asian markets?

5. Canyon Ranch is an exclusive fitness resort with locations in Tucson, Arizona, and the Berkshire Mountains of Massachusetts. Peak season weekly rates can top over $5,000 per person. The fee covers use of the fitness facility, programs, and meals. Canyon Ranch has also opened a Day Spa in Las Vegas. Discuss possible segmentation and positioning strategies for Canyon Ranch's regular programs, as well as the day spa.

1. **Segmenting Consumer Markets.** Go to www.williams-sonoma.com and find one example of how Williams-Sonoma has segmented its market on its Web site for at least two of the four common bases for segmenting consumer markets: geographic, demographic, psychographic, and product-related.

2. After studying Figure 8.9, you may already have an idea which of the eight psychographic categories you fall into. Either to confirm your guess or to find out which type you are, go to www.future.sri.com and choose the VAL and Go to Survey links. Complete the survey and submit it. Then read the various links of information concerning your type and submit 2 to 3 paragraphs to your instructor in which you summarize the following:

• Your type.
• Characteristics described in your type that were true of you.
• Characteristics described that were untrue.
• Concluding comments stating whether you agree with the results. If you think you should have been categorized as a different type, include the type and why it is more like you are than the one the survey results identified.

3. **Segmenting by Age.** A recent Nielsen/Net Ratings report listed the following sites among the post popular teen Web hangouts:

www.react.com   www.audiofind.com   www.blot.com
www.ubl.com   www.way-too-cool.com   www.artistdirect.com

Visit three of the sites and describe features that you think make these sites appealing to 12- to 17-year-olds.

williams-sonoma.com

future.sri.com

react.com

way-too-cool.com

audiofind.com

blot.com

ubl.com

artistdirect.com

Video Case 8 on Fresh Samantha begins on page VC-10.

Gateway Continuing Case Part 3 begins on page GC-5.

PART

4

CUSTOMER BEHAVIOR

263

Gateway Continuing Case Part 4 begins on page GC-6.

Consumer Behavior

CHAPTER OBJECTIVES

1. Differentiate between customer behavior and consumer behavior.

2. Identify the interpersonal determinants of consumer behavior.

3. Explain each of the personal determinants of consumer behavior.

4. Explain how marketers classify behavioral influences on consumer decisions.

5. Outline the steps in the consumer decision process.

6. Differentiate among routinized response behavior, limited problem solving, and extended problem solving.

Who Shops Online?

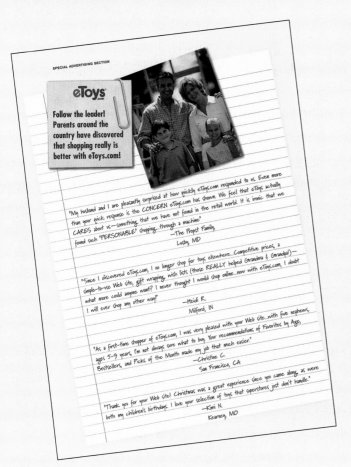

What does an Internet shopper look like? Would you find one in your own mirror? That is what marketers want to know, and various research groups are doing studies to find out. Learning who shops online, what they buy, and why will help Internet marketers attract and keep customers for their goods and services.

According to Scarborough Research, 60 percent of online shoppers are men, 70 percent attended college, and 65 percent have white-collar jobs. Thirty-six percent have a household income of at least $75,000. These statistics only begin to make up a profile of a "typical" Internet shopper. Scarborough says that the e-shopper may belong to a health club and is likely to enjoy swimming, biking, and other sports. He also likes photography and attends roughly three movies a month. He is also very busy and active. "E-shoppers clearly evidence a rich, active, and diverse lifestyle," notes Bob Cohen, president of Scarborough Research. "Given their predisposition and time constraints, it is not surprising that the choice and convenience provided by e-commerce offers attractive benefits for this segment."

If this description of an online shopper does not sound like you or anyone you know, do not worry. More than 75 percent of Internet users still do not shop regularly online, although that percentage is steadily decreasing. "Out of all online activities, making purchases shot up the most this year," notes Bob Pittman, president and co-chief operating officer of AOL–Time Warner, pertaining to 1999. Many new shoppers are women. "One third more Internet consumers say they are shopping on-line," continues Pittman, "with women shoppers increasing by over 50 percent. We are seeing the online population become more like the mass market, with women again coming online faster than men."

Perhaps even more important than the rate at which women are going online is the fact that they now make the majority of household purchasing decisions, a bit of information not lost on marketers. "Women make the majority of online health-care decisions, retail purchases, and financial choices for the household," claims Gina Carrubbo, executive vice president of Women.com, which recently conducted a survey of women online. The study showed that women make 80 percent of household purchasing decisions; 73 percent of women access online product information regularly; and women, like men, value the speed and convenience of online shopping. They also use the Internet to research products bought through more traditional channels, such as cars, computers, and appliances. The "typical" female Internet shopper is usually married, in her thirties, with an upscale household income.

Nearly 90 percent of college students are online, the most active single demographic group on the Internet. Giving the picture a bit more detail, senior citizens have increased their Internet spending dramatically, accounting for roughly 20 percent of total consumer online spending in the United States; Hispanics represent the largest online ethnic group, with African Americans and Asians close behind. Teenagers spend the most time online, but they do not yet represent actual purchasing

265

power over the Net because they do not generally have their own credit cards.

All of this information creates a portrait of the Internet consumer. And although the online population is diverse, it is important for marketers to try to learn what makes the online shopper tick, so they may be able to turn those consumers into loyal customers.[1]

women.com

1

Differentiate between customer behavior and consumer behavior.

> ### Briefly Speaking
>
> *"It's the first company to build the mental position that has the upper hand, not the first company to make the product. IBM didn't invent the computer; Sperry Rand did. But IBM was the first to build the computer position in the prospect's mind."*
>
> *Al Ries (1929–)*
> *Chairman, Trout & Ries, Inc., advertising agency*

CHAPTER OVERVIEW

Why do people buy one product over another competing product? Answering this question is the basic task of every marketer. The answer directly affects every aspect of the marketing strategy, from product development to pricing and promotion. Discovering that answer requires an understanding of customer behavior, the process by which consumers and business-to-business buyers make purchase decisions. **Customer behavior** is a broad term that covers both individual consumers who buy goods and services for their own use and organizational buyers who purchase business products.[2]

A variety of influences affect both individuals buying products for themselves and professional buyers purchasing products for their firms. This chapter will focus on individual purchasing behavior. **Consumer behavior** is the process through which the ultimate buyer makes purchase decisions. Chapter 10 will focus on additional organizational influences affecting business buying decisions.

The study of consumer behavior builds upon an understanding of human behavior in general. In their efforts to understand why and how consumers make buying decisions, marketers borrow extensively from the sciences of psychology and sociology. The work of psychologist Kurt Lewin, for example, provides a useful classification scheme for influences on buying behavior. (The same concept also sheds light on motivation theory discussed in your management courses.) Lewin's proposition is:

$$B = f(P,E)$$

This statement means that behavior (B) is a function (f) of the interactions of personal influences (P) and pressures exerted by outside environmental forces (E).

This statement is usually rewritten to apply to consumer behavior as follows:

$$B = f(I,P)$$

Consumer behavior (B) is a function (f) of the interactions of interpersonal influences (I)—such as culture, friends, and relatives—and personal factors (P)—such as attitudes, learning, and perception. In other words, inputs from others and an individual's psychological makeup both affect his or her purchasing behavior. Before looking at how consumers make purchase decisions, the chapter will first consider how both interpersonal and personal factors affect consumers. ◼

INTERPERSONAL DETERMINANTS OF CONSUMER BEHAVIOR

Consumers do not make purchase decisions in a vacuum; rather, they respond to a number of external, interpersonal influences. Consumers often decide to buy goods and services based on what they believe others expect of them. They may want to project positive images to peers or to satisfy the unspoken desires of family members. Marketers recognize three broad categories of interpersonal influences on consumer behavior: cultural, group, and family influences.

2

Identify the interpersonal determinants of consumer behavior.

Cultural Influences

Culture can be defined as the values, beliefs, preferences, and tastes handed down from one generation to the next. Culture is the broadest environmental determinant of consumer behavior. Therefore, marketers need to understand its role in consumer decision making, both in the United States and abroad. They must also monitor trends in cultural values as well as spot changes in these values.

Marketing strategies and business practices that work in one country may be offensive or ineffective in another. Marketers in Thailand offended many U.S. consumers when they included a dancing figure of Adolf Hitler in an American commercial for potato chips. British consumers complained about a Kia Motors automobile ad that featured a Princess Diana look-alike after a car chase by camera-wielding paparazzi in which she survived. In both cases the companies were forced to apologize and replace their ads with less controversial entries.[3]

Core Values in U.S. Culture

While some cultural values change over time, basic core values do not. The work ethic and the desire to accumulate wealth are two such core values in American society. Even though the typical family structure and family members' roles have changed in recent years, American culture still emphasizes the importance of family and home life. Nestlé appeals to the importance of family by developing convenient family-size entrees such as its Stouffer's Family Style Favorites promoted in the ad in Figure 9.1. Other core values include individualism, freedom, youthfulness, activity, humanitarianism, efficiency, and practicality. Each of these values influences consumer behavior.

The personal services industry thrives because it addresses many of the following core values: freeing busy consumers to use their time more efficiently and focus on work and family rather than household chores. Tidy Lawn, based in Omaha, Nebraska, prospers by offering "professional scooping"—cleaning dog owners' yards of what their pets left behind. The response has been so enthusiastic that Tidy Lawn is planning to go nationwide and sell franchises. A more appetizing service involves personal chefs, who handle grocery shopping, prepare meals, and even do the dishes for people who want a home-cooked meal but are too busy to make it. Until recently, only about 5,000 customers per year hired personal chefs; today, more than 30,000 people annually enjoy their services.[4]

Values that change over time also have their effects. American children's increasing exposure to the Internet has created a generation of sophisticated,

| FIGURE 9.1 | Core Value: The Importance of Family |

Tavolo Taps into American Family Life

BACKGROUND The American work ethic is alive and well: Americans now work more hours than anyone else in the world, including the Japanese. But the 50-hour work week clashes with another core value of American culture: family life. It also pushes aside the basic need for food, though not for long. Several online companies have recognized an opportunity to serve consumers what they want: home-cooked meals during which they can spend time with family without having to sacrifice work hours. Tavolo, based in San Rafael, California, is one of these companies.

THE CHALLENGE Tavolo, formerly known as Digital Chef, needed to find a way to convince consumers that they could combine their work ethic and desire for family time by purchasing gourmet-quality, time-saving foods and kitchen products. Although many consumers already buy luxury food items as gifts, the ultimate challenge, according to an e-commerce analyst with Jupiter Communications, is to get consumers to buy these items for themselves.

continued on next page

univision.com

globally-aware teens. "There are no rules for this group," says one researcher. "With all the media stimulus, things like the Internet, there's no one authority for them. Every voice has equal power and you see more fusion and hybrids." The result is an explosion in products and an ever wider range of product choices: new technologies, new colors (such as blue Gatorade and M&Ms), and new combinations (Snapple beverages that mix fruit juice and tea). The purchasing power of these young but savvy consumers gives them impressive clout in the marketplace: Although teenagers represent less than 29 percent of all American consumers, they account for 46 percent of the money spent on audio equipment and 48 percent of what is spent on athletic shoes.[5]

An International Perspective on Cultural Influences

Cultural differences are particularly important for international marketers. Marketing strategies that prove successful in one country often cannot extend to other international markets because of cultural variations.

Europe is a good example, with nine different languages and a wide range of lifestyles and product preferences. Even though the continent is becoming a single economic unit, cultural divisions continue to define multiple markets. Cultural preferences can even affect a product as widely popular as chocolate candy. The British want their chocolate mellow and caramelized, while the Swiss like it milky, and the Italians prefer it dark and creamy. However, all European consumers agree on one thing: They dislike American milk chocolate, which they consider sour and waxy.[6]

Sometimes cultural differences can work to a marketer's advantage; consider the poultry industry. American consumers mostly prefer white meat such as chicken breasts, which sell for around 90 cents per pound wholesale. Fatty dark chicken meat is much less popular in the United States, where it fetches only 20 to 30 cents per pound. The reverse is true in Russia, where most consumers prefer dark meat and are more than willing to pay for it. This is a bonus for poultry farmers, who can sell white meat at home and dark meat overseas. Russian consumers often buy 25 percent of all the chicken legs produced in the United States. Indeed, American chicken is so popular in Russia that drumsticks are nicknamed *Bushskie nozhki*, "Bush's legs," in honor of former president George Bush, who okayed the first poultry imports.[7]

Subcultures

Cultures are not homogenous entities with universal values. Each culture includes numerous **subcultures**—groups with their own distinct modes of behavior. Understanding the differences among subcultures can help marketers develop more effective marketing strategies.

The United States, like many nations, is composed of significant subcultures that differ by race, nationality, age, rural versus urban location, religion, and geographic distribution. The lifestyle in the southwestern United States emphasizes casual dress, outdoor entertaining, and active recreation. Mormons refrain from buying or using tobacco and liquor. Orthodox Jews purchase and consume only kosher foods. Understanding these and other differences among subcultures contributes to successful marketing of goods and services.

As Chapter 8 indicated, America's racial mix is changing. In the next century, marketers will no longer easily spot the "typical" American. Ethnic and racial minority groups will compose much larger percentages of the population. Marketers will need to be sensitive to these changes and to the differences in shopping patterns and buying habits among ethnic segments of the population. Businesses will no longer succeed by selling one-size-fits-all products; they will need to consider consumer needs, interests, and concerns when developing their marketing strategies.

For example, Univision, the leading Spanish-language broadcaster in the United States, prospers by targeting the interests of Hispanic households. Soccer is a popular sport in Central and South America, so Univision competed for and won the rights to broadcast all 64 soccer games of a recent World Cup. Millions of Latin American viewers tuned in, earning the company a staggering $50 million in advertising revenue. Not coincidentally, Univision is trouncing its English-speaking competitors. Over the past five years, network broadcasters CBS and ABC have each lost more than 2 million viewers, while Univision has gained half a million.[8]

Marketing concepts may not always cross cultural boundaries without changes. For example, new immigrants may not be familiar with cents-off coupons and contests. Marketers may need to provide specific instructions when targeting such promotions to these groups.

According to the U.S. Census Bureau, the three largest and fastest-growing ethnic subcultures in the United States are African Americans, Hispanics, and Asians. While no ethnic or racial subculture is entirely homogeneous, researchers have found that each of these three ethnic segments have identifiable consumer behavior profiles.

Profile of African-American Consumers.   A recent study shows African-American buying power rose 73 percent over the past decade, compared to 57 percent for U.S. consumers in general. The growing African-American market offers great potential success for marketers who understand its buying patterns. For example, NationsBank Corp.'s marketing efforts to target African-American customers earned the company $620 million of new business in just three years.[9]

Family structures may differ for African-American consumers. The median age of the typical African-American family is about five years younger than that of the average white family. This creates differences in preferences for clothing, music, cars, and many other products. Through ads like the one in Figure 9.2, McDonald's targets the younger African-American family. Further, African-American households are twice as likely as non-African-American households to be headed by women who make the majority of the purchase decisions.

Successful firms try to reach African-American consumers through different approaches than they employ for other groups. For example, a survey by financial services company Charles Schwab revealed that many African-American investors feel insecure about their investment knowledge and do not fully trust financial advisers. Adding to the credibility issue is a perceived lack of African-American financial professionals. Perhaps as a result, African-Americans tend to invest more conservatively than other groups. They are more likely to choose real estate and life insurance as investments and are less likely to put their money in the stock market. Says marketing consultant Michael DeFlorimonte, "In a lot of cases African Americans view the stock market like going to Vegas, and that it's like a roll of the dice." Schwab used this information to design programs specifically for African-Americans. The company teamed up with the Coalition of Black Investors to sponsor nationwide investment seminars at beginner, intermediate, and advanced levels. Schwab is also actively recruiting new stockbrokers at conferences hosted by professional groups, such as the National

THE STRATEGY Tavolo began offering free recipes, menu planners, and culinary advice from experts on its Web site at www.tavolo.com. The Tavolo site offers a large selection of specialty products from herbal teas and exotic honeys to top-name appliances. Consumers can write their own online "cookbook," create menus, and generate grocery lists.

THE OUTCOME Harried consumers are buying what Tavolo has to sell, which is not only kitchen and food products but precious time. So Tavolo has expanded, entering into an agreement to become the exclusive retailer for gourmet food and cooking products on "Shopping Solutions," which is part of the iVillage.com site for women. Tavolo has also teamed up with wine.com, which selects products to accompany special meals. Finally, Tavolo has not overlooked the importance of gifts: with everything from specialty chocolates to hickory-smoked Virginia ham to the perfect wine. Those are delicious words for any shopper.

FIGURE 9.2	Advertising Aimed at Young African-American Families

"So when can he have a Happy Meal?"

She's ready to teach her little brother all about happiness! The McDonald's Hamburger Happy Meal for just $1.99 each, gives kids the food they love at a price you'll love. And they get a toy with that!

did somebody say 🅜 ?

@ schwab.com

@ cobinvest.com

Association of Black Accountants, National Association of Black MBAs, and Blacks in Government. To date, more than 1,400 people have attended Schwab's seminars, which are now so popular the company has expanded its original schedule.[10]

Successful promotions targeted to African Americans present marketing messages in credible, culturally sensitive ways. For instance, African-American writers find that word-of-mouth marketing often works better for their books than more traditional tactics such as book signings and talk shows. Authors Denene Miller and Nick Chiles launched their book *What Brothers Think, What Sistahs Know* with a series of parties across the United States, where African-American singles and couples could mingle and discuss relationships. To publicize her book *Just Between Girlfriends*, author Chrisena Coleman obtained corporate backing to organize a getaway weekend in the Bahamas for 200 African-American women. Cheryl Woodruff, associate publisher of One World Books, the African-American division of Ballantine, distributed sample chapters from new romance novels to more than 1,000 African-American-owned beauty parlors nationwide. Sales promptly soared.[11]

Consultant DeFlorimonte cautions against approaching all African-American consumers in the same way; demographic factors such as age, language, and educational level must be considered as well. Some African Americans are recent immigrants, while others are descended from families who have lived in the United States for generations. "You can't just lump them all together," he says. "That's a mistake a lot of marketing firms make in terms of marketing to ethnic groups."[12]

Profile of Hispanic Consumers. Marketers face several challenges in appealing to Hispanic consumers. The 30 million Hispanics in the United States are not a homogeneous group. They come from a wide range of countries, each with its cultural differences. Some 64 percent come from Mexico, about 15 percent from Central and South America, 10.5 percent from Puerto Rico, and approximately 4.7 percent from Cuba. Cultural differences between these segments often affect consumer preferences.

The term "Hispanic" is a complex concept that includes a wide spectrum of national identities. "There are white, black, and brown Hispanics," says Esteban Torres, a former Congressman from California. "You are what you think you are." Even the word *Hispanic* is not universal; Puerto Ricans and Dominicans in New York and Cubans in Florida refer to themselves as Hispanic, but many Mexican and Central Americans in the southwest United States prefer to be called Latino.

More important than differences in national origin are differences in *acculturation*, or the degree to which newcomers have adapted to U.S. culture. Acculturation plays a vital role in consumer behavior. For instance, marketers should not assume that all Hispanics understand Spanish; by the third generation after immigration, most Hispanic Americans speak only English. Furthermore, some recent immigrants are actually ethnic Indians who have never learned Spanish, and immigrants from Brazil speak Portuguese.

Researchers divide Hispanics into three major acculturation groups:

- Largely unacculturated Hispanics (about 28 percent of the U.S. Hispanic population) often were born outside the United States and have lived in the country for less than 10 years. They tend to have the lowest income of the three groups and depend almost exclusively on Spanish-language media.

- Partially unacculturated Hispanics (approximately 59 percent) were born in the United States or have lived there for more than 11 years. Most are bilingual, speaking English at work and Spanish at home. Many are middle-income, and marketers can reach them through both Spanish- and English-language media. For example, Procter & Gamble promotes its Sunny Delight drink shown in Figure 9.3 in *Latina* magazine, which includes ads both in English and Spanish.

- Highly acculturated Hispanics (13 percent) enjoy the highest income of the three groups. Usually born and raised in the United States, they are English-speaking but retain many Hispanic cultural values and traditions.

Research indicates several other important points:

- The Hispanic market is large and fast-growing. Already the United States is home to the fifth-largest Hispanic population in the world; only the populations of Mexico, Spain, Argentina, and Colombia are bigger. Researchers estimate that by 2005 Hispanics will outnumber African Americans to become America's largest minority group.

- Hispanics tend to be young with a median age of 25. (34 is the median age for the general U.S. population.)

- Hispanic consumers are geographically concentrated. More than 70 percent of them live in only four states: California, Florida, New York, and Texas. More than 45 percent reside in just five cities: New York, Los Angeles, Miami, San Francisco, and Chicago.

Hispanics tend to have larger households than non-Hispanics, making them good customers for products sold in large sizes. They spend more on their children than parents in other subcultures, especially on clothing. Hispanics also place great importance on keeping in touch with relatives in other countries, making them excellent customers for long-distance phone service, air travel, and wire transfers of money.[13]

FIGURE 9.3   Spanish-Language Ad Targets Partially Unacculturated Hispanics

Profile of Asian-American Consumers.   Marketing to Asian Americans presents many of the same challenges as reaching Hispanics. Like Hispanics, Asian Americans are spread among culturally diverse groups, many retaining their own languages. The Asian-American subculture actually consists of more than two dozen ethnic groups, including Chinese, Japanese, Indians, Koreans, Filipinos, and Vietnamese. Each group brings its own language, religion, and value system to purchasing decisions.

When Ford marketed its Windstar minivan and Explorer and Expedition sport-utility vehicles to California's Asian residents, it created commercials in three languages—Chinese, Korean, and Filipino—and hired a separate set of actors for each commercial because the three subgroups are recognizably different in appearance. Ford also established a toll-free telephone number consumers could call with questions and employed operators fluent in the three languages. The ads appeared in Asian-language cable TV programs and Asian-language newspapers.[14]

Approximately 90 percent of Vietnamese, Chinese, and Korean Americans prefer television shows and print media in their native languages. However, many people from India and Japan studied English in their home countries, so they are comfortable reading and listening to it. In fact, many Japanese Americans are second- or third-generation Americans who speak no Japanese at all. One study found that, while most new Asian immigrants prefer to use their native tongue, after five to ten years many become comfortable with English-language media.[15]

Car dealers find that brands are important to Asian Americans, who are willing to pay more for a respected brand name such as Cadillac. To many immigrants, a car is an important symbol of success. Some Asian Americans live in extended families comprising several generations, so they tend to prefer minivans and other roomy vehicles that can accommodate several people.[16]

No matter which Asian subgroup they target, companies should take care to avoid sounding patronizing. Eliot Kang, president of Kang & Lee Advertising in New York City, tells of an AT&T commercial featuring an elderly Korean woman who complained of being deceived by a competitor's claims. While well-intentioned, the ad implied she was ignorant of American business practices. "It showed her as weak and foolish," explains Kang, whose firm redesigned the ad. "We said, 'Let's make her smart and aggressive, and let's throw in a Korean idiom: To really see which one is longer you have to put them side by side.' " The new commercial depicted an intelligent, bilingual Korean American who was fully capable of selecting the best value for her money.[17]

Group Membership: Influencing Behavior and Purchase Decisions

He made a statement by passing the bar.

Not entering one.

Social Influences

Every consumer belongs to a number of social groups. A child's earliest group experience comes from membership in a family. As children grow older, they join other groups such as friendship groups, neighborhood groups, school groups, and organizations such as Girl Scouts and Little League. Adults are also members of various groups—at work and in the community.

Group membership influences an individual's purchase decisions and behavior in both overt and subtle ways. Every group establishes certain norms of behavior. **Norms** are the values, attitudes, and behaviors that a group deems appropriate for its members. Group members are expected to comply with these norms. For example, Bacchus & Gamma Peer Education Network is an international organization of college students that promotes positive lifestyles and responsible decision making. Group members focus on alcohol abuse prevention and other health issues such as tobacco prevention by planning campus programs like National Collegiate Alcohol Awareness Week. The group's values, which are promoted in ads such as the one in Figure 9.4, influence students' decisions in purchasing tobacco and alcohol products. Norms can even affect nonmembers. Individuals who aspire to membership in a group may adopt its standards of behavior and values.

Differences in group status and roles can also affect buying behavior. **Status** is the relative position of any individual member in a group; **roles** define behavior that members of a group expect of individuals who hold specific positions within that group. Some groups (such as Rotary Club or Lion's Club) define formal roles, and others (such as friendship groups) impose informal expectations. Both types of groups supply each member with both status and roles; in doing so, they influence that person's activities—including his or her purchase behavior.

The Internet provides an opportunity for individuals to form and be influenced by new types of groups. Usenet mailing lists and chat rooms allow groups to form around common interests. Some of these online "virtual communities" can develop norms and membership roles similar to those found in real world groups. For example, to avoid criticism, members must observe rules for proper protocol in posting messages and participating in chats.

The Asch Phenomenon

Groups often influence an individual's purchase decisions more than is realized. Most people tend to adhere in varying degrees to the general expectations of any group that they consider important, often without conscious awareness of this motivation. The surprising impact of groups and group norms on individual behavior has been called the **Asch phenomenon,** named after S. E. Asch who through his research first documented characteristics of individual behavior.

Asch found that individuals would conform to majority rule, even if that majority rule went against their beliefs. The Asch phenomenon can be a big factor in many purchase decisions, from major choices such as buying a house or car to deciding whether to buy an item at a Tupperware party.[18]

Reference Groups

Discussion of the Asch phenomenon raises the subject of **reference groups**—groups whose value structures and standards influence a person's behavior. Consumers usually try to coordinate their purchase behavior with their perceptions of the values of their reference groups. The extent of reference-group influence varies widely among individuals. Strong influence by a group on a member's purchase requires two conditions:

1. The purchased product must be one that others can see and identify.
2. The purchased item must be conspicuous; it must stand out as something unusual, a brand or product that not everyone owns.

Reference-group influence would significantly affect the decision to buy a Jaguar, for example, but it would have little or no impact on the decision to purchase a loaf of bread. The status of the individual within a group produces three subcategories of reference groups: a membership group to which the person actually belongs, such as a country club; an aspirational group with which the person desires to associate; and a dissociative group with which the individual does not want to be identified.

Children are especially vulnerable to the influence of reference groups. They often base their buying decisions on outside forces—what they see on television, popular choices among friends, fashionable products among adults. Advertising, especially endorsements by admired people, can have much bigger impacts on children than on adults, in part because children want so badly to belong to aspirational groups.

Reference-group influences appear in other countries, as well. Many young people in Japan aspire to represent American culture and values. Buying products decorated with English words and phrases—even if inaccurate—helps them to achieve this feeling.

Social Classes

Research initiated a number of years ago by W. Lloyd Warner identified six classes within the social structures of both small and large cities in the United States: the upper-upper, lower-upper, upper-middle, and lower-middle classes, followed by the working class and lower class.

Class rankings are determined by occupation, income, education, family background, and residence location. Note, however, that income is not always a primary determinant; pipe fitters paid at union scale earn more than many college professors, but their purchase behavior may be quite different. Thus, marketers frequently disagree with the old adage that "a rich man is a poor man with money."

Traditionally, family characteristics—the father's occupation in particular—have been the primary influences on social class. This relationship is likely to change as women's careers assume more prominent roles in their families. And social classes are in transition due to other changes, as well. This makes it more difficult to market to these members.

People in one social class may aspire to a higher class and therefore exhibit buying behavior common to that class rather than to their own. For example, middle-class consumers often buy items they associate with the upper classes. Although the upper classes themselves account for a very small percentage of the population, many more consumers treat themselves to prestigious products, such as designer clothing or luxury cars. For this reason, even though Ford owns British car-maker Jaguar, Ford marketers are careful to distinguish the two product lines from each other. "Jaguar has a very specific appeal with the customers and is known for being beautiful, having wonderful performance and handling and a high degree of luxury," says Judy Sturrup, regional public affairs manager for Jaguar North America. "We needed to maintain that image and those qualities because that's what customers want in Jaguar."[19]

Opinion Leaders

In nearly every reference group, a few members act as **opinion leaders.** These trendsetters are likely to purchase new products before others in the group and then share their experiences and opinions via word of mouth. As others in the

Cigar Craze Burns Out

BACKGROUND Everyone wants to be cool, to belong to the "in crowd." So, regardless of how dubious the distinction was, when celebrities such as Madonna, Sylvester Stallone, and Matt Dillon were seen sporting cigars, average folks decided to try stogies, too. "When Demi Moore went on that magazine cover, everyone wanted to smoke cigars," explains Richard Galdieri, owner of the Las Vegas Cigar Co. Consumers raced to buy premium cigars, along with all the paraphernalia, including cutters and ashtrays. They then puffed them at popular cigar "pubs" such as Miami's Cuba Club and Washington's Grand Havana Room. At the height of the craze, Abraham Shafir and Ian Markofsky thought they had hit on a sure thing when they decided to manufacture their own brand of fancy cigars.

continued on next page

ford.com

MARKETING | DICTIONARY

norm Value, attitude, or behavior that a group deems appropriate for its members.

status Relative prominence of any individual in a group.

role Behavior that members of a group expect of an individual who holds a specific position within that group.

Asch phenomenon Effect of a reference group on individual decision making.

reference group Group with which an individual identifies strongly enough that it dictates a standard of behavior.

opinion leader Trendsetter likely to purchase new products before others and then share the resulting experiences and opinions via word of mouth.

MARKETING STRATEGY FAILURE

THE MARKETING PROBLEM Initially, Shafir and Markofsky's hand-rolled cigars, manufactured in the Dominican Republic and sold under the name of Tamboril Cigar Co., were praised by connoisseurs as "creamy" with "herbal character." Sales topped $6.4 million during Tamboril's first year of business. But Tamboril and other companies like it could not keep the public puffing long enough to achieve long-term success, even though the cigar industry has somehow managed to stay disconnected in people's minds from the cigarette industry.

THE OUTCOME Cigar prices soared during peak demand, then plummeted, and never quite recovered. Consumers, along with celebrities, had moved on to something else. Only the die-hard cigar aficionados were left. "The boom was an illusion," says the president of Pro-Cigar, an association of cigar manufacturers in the Dominican Republic, where Tamboril was located. Caught in the tumbling market, Tamboril was forced to shut down.

LESSONS LEARNED The cigar craze of the 1990s was a fad based on consumers' desires to identify with those who have wealth, beauty, and live the "good life." In fact, the craze was not about smoking at all, it was about entertainment. Since then, people have gone on to other forms of entertainment. Cashing in on a craze may be pure luck. But savvy marketers understand how people want to see themselves and offer up merchandise to enhance that image over the long run.

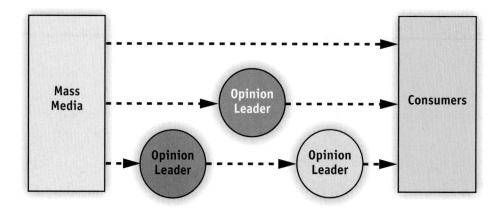

FIGURE 9.5 **Alternative Channels for Communications Flow**

group decide whether to try the same product, they are influenced by the reports of opinion leaders.

Generalized opinion leaders are rare; instead, individuals tend to act as opinion leaders for specific goods or services based on their knowledge of and interest in those products. Their interest motivates them to seek out information from mass media, manufacturers, and other sources and, in turn, transmit this information to associates through interpersonal communications. Opinion leaders are found within all segments of the population.

Information about goods and services sometimes flows from the Internet, radio, television, and other mass media to opinion leaders and then from opinion leaders to others. In other instances, information flows directly from media sources to all consumers. In still other instances, a multistep flow carries information from mass media to opinion leaders and then on to other opinion leaders before dissemination to the general public. Figure 9.5 illustrates these three types of communication flows.

Some opinion leaders influence purchases by others merely through their own actions. Hello Kitty, a cartoon cat, has long been popular with Japanese schoolgirls, who eagerly buy notebooks, barrettes, and book bags emblazoned with the logo. But when the cat's Tokyo-based creator, Sanrio Co., tried to market the concept to adult women by placing the image on lingerie, candles, and cell-phone covers, initial sales were disappointing. Then Tomomi Kahara, a popular 24-year-old singer, revealed on television that she was a devoted collector of Hello Kitty memorabilia. Almost overnight, Japanese women in their 20s and 30s bought out retailers' supplies of Hello Kitty merchandise. Today, Kitty's image is available on a wide range of adult-oriented products, including ties, electronic mail software, and golf bags.[20]

Family Influences

Most people are members of at least two families during their lifetimes—the ones they are born into and those they eventually form as they marry and have children. The family group is perhaps the most important determinant of consumer behavior because of the close, continuing interactions among family members. Like other groups, each family typically has norms of expected behavior and different roles and status relationships for its members.

The traditional family structure consists of a husband and wife. Although these and other members can play an infinite variety of roles in household decision making, marketers have created four categories to describe the role of each spouse:[21]

1. *Autonomic* role is when the partners independently make equal numbers of decisions. Personal-care items would fall into the kinds of purchase decisions each would make for themselves.

2. *Husband-dominant* role is when the husband makes most of the decisions. Insurance is typically a husband-dominant purchase.

3. *Wife-dominant* role is when the wife makes most of the decisions. Children's clothing is typically a wife-dominant decision.

4. *Syncratic* role is when both partners jointly make most decisions. The purchase of a house follows a syncratic pattern.

The emergence of the two-income family has changed the role of women in family purchasing behavior. In 1950, only one-fourth of married women were employed outside the home; now over 60 percent have paid jobs. In the 1950s and early 1960s, women exercised only limited control of family purchasing decisions. A woman might make buying decisions about household items, but she was likely to defer to her husband on larger expenditures. Today, however, women are likely to have more say in large ticket family purchases such as automobiles and computers. Studies of family decision making have also shown that households with two wage earners are more likely than others to make joint purchasing decisions.

While women are becoming more involved in decision making for large family purchases, men's roles are also changing. More and more men are now major food purchasers, shopping either alone or with their partners. Members of two-income households often do their shopping in the evening and on weekends.

Shifting family roles has created new markets for time-saving goods and services. The desire to save time is not new—as early as 1879, Heinz advertised its ready-made ketchup "for the blessed relief of mother and other women of the household"—but it has taken on new urgency as growing numbers of parents juggle multiple roles: raising families, building careers, and managing households. This explains the growing market for home-meal replacement, as more and more grocery stores prepare and sell complete meals to go. In 1987, 43 percent of all meals in the United States included at least one item made from scratch; today only 38 percent do. In a recent year, Americans paid $691 billion for food, and 46 percent of the money spent for food went for meals bought outside the home.[22] The Kellogg Company created the slogan "Good Food To Go" and the Nutri-Grain Cereal Bar promoted in Figure 9.6 for parents juggling multiple roles.

 kelloggs.com

Children and Teenagers in Family Purchases

As parents have become busier, they have delegated some family purchase decisions to children, specifically teenagers. Children learn about the latest products and trends because they watch so much television and cruise the Internet, often becoming the family experts on what to buy. As a result, children have gained sophistication and assumed new roles in family purchasing behavior.

A growing number of children and teenagers are assuming responsibility for family shopping. Parents give them more than $48.8 billion annually to purchase household groceries. Both alone and with parents, children average more than 200 store visits per year. Food manufacturers such as Mazola Oil, recognizing this trend, have started advertising in media aimed specifically at young people, such as *Seventeen* magazine.

Children also influence what their parents buy. They determine as much as $500 billion of annual household spending in the United States, either directly or indirectly, and take a role in selecting numerous products. Consider car selection; once a parental decision, it is now more likely to be a joint family decision. Kids' growing impact at the car dealership reflects several trends, such as increasing family travel, parents' unwillingness to leave them home alone, and parents' concern about kids' sedentary lifestyles. Several automakers now advertise in issues of *Crayola Kids*.

 **crayola.com**

Children and teenagers represent a huge market—over 50 million strong—in their own right. Both their numbers and their income are growing. Growing up in single-parent or dual-career

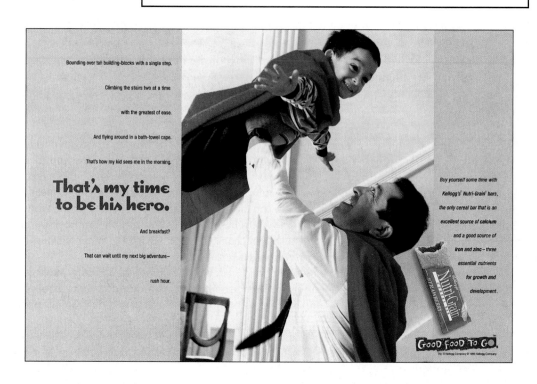

FIGURE 9.6   A Time-Saving Product

households, they are more independent and more likely to help around the house. These children accept responsibilities that were not common until recently. A decade ago, the average 10 year old's weekly income was $7.90; more recently it was $13.93, a 76 percent increase. The difference is largely due to additional income earned from doing household chores. One-third of this money is spent on food and beverages, while the rest goes for clothing, movies, toys, pay-for-play games, and toiletries. Candy-maker Mars, Inc. attempts to reach the youth market by placing ads like the one in Figure 9.7 in childrens' and teens' magazines. Electronics are also popular purchases; 17 percent of teenagers have their own telephone number, 18 percent own their own pager, and 66 percent watch their own TV in their bedroom.

Even after they are grown, children continue to play roles in family consumer behavior, often by recommending products to their parents. Advertisers try to influence these relationships by showing adult children interacting with their parents.[23]

mars.com

PERSONAL DETERMINANTS OF CONSUMER BEHAVIOR

3

Explain each of the personal determinants of consumer behavior.

Consumer behavior is affected by many internal, personal factors, as well as interpersonal ones. Each individual brings unique needs, motives, perceptions, attitudes, values, and self-concepts to buying decisions. This section will look at how these factors influence consumer behavior.

Needs and Motives

Individual purchase behavior is driven by the motivation to fill a need. A **need** is an imbalance between the consumer's actual and desired states. Someone who recognizes or feels a significant or urgent need then seeks to correct the imbalance. Marketers attempt to arouse this sense of urgency, that is making a need "felt," and then influence consumers' motivation to satisfy their needs by purchasing specific products.

Motives are inner states that direct a person toward the goal of satisfying a felt need. The individual takes action to reduce the state of tension and return to a condition of equilibrium.

Maslow's Hierarchy of Needs

A. H. Maslow developed a theory that characterized needs and arranged them in a hierarchy to reflect their importance. Maslow identified five levels of needs, beginning with physiological needs and progressing to the need for self-actualization. A person must at least partially satisfy lower-level needs, according to his theory, before higher needs can affect behavior. In developed countries, where relatively large per-capita incomes allow most people to satisfy the basic needs on the hierarchy, higher-order needs may be more important to consumer behavior. Table 9.1 illustrates products and marketing themes designed to satisfy needs at each level.

Physiological Needs. Needs at the most basic level concern essential requirements for survival, such as food, water, shelter, and clothing. Ads for Post cereals appeal to physiological needs by stating the following, "Breakfast is supposed to be the most important meal of the day."

Safety Needs. The second-level needs include security, protection from physical harm, and avoidance of the unexpected. To gratify these needs, consumers may buy mutual fund shares, disability insurance, or security devices. Lysol addresses the safety concerns of mothers with its ad for Basin Tub & Tile Cleaner. The ad shows a baby in a bathtub under the headline, "This is no place for germs." It ends with the tagline, "Deep down you know it's clean."

Social/Belongingness Needs. Satisfaction of physiological and safety needs leads a person to attend to third-level needs—the desire to be accepted by people and groups important to that individual. To satisfy this need, individuals may conform to certain standards of behavior in order to feel that they belong. Marketers for Broderbund Software and Nickelodeon target children's social/belongingness needs when they organize "kid's clubs" with entertainment and group events that promote products.

Esteem Needs. The desire to feel a sense of accomplishment and achievement, to gain the respect of others, and even to exceed the performance of others is a universal human trait that emerges after lower-order needs are satisfied. Virgin Atlantic Airlines marketers appeal to this need with the firm's "Upper Class" service that offers chauffeured transportation to and from the airport.

Self-Actualization Needs. At the top rung of Maslow's ladder of human needs is people's desire to realize their full potential and to find fulfillment by fully expressing their talents and capabilities. Self-help books, spiritually oriented "New Age" products, and exotic adventure vacations are aimed at satisfying consumers' needs for self-actualization. Some travel providers, such as Smithsonian Study Tours, offer specialized educational trips that appeal to consumers' desires for a meaningful experience as well as a vacation. Participants in Smithsonian Tours can go behind the scenes into kitchens of renowned French restaurants, study music at Oxford University, or attend an international symposium on world peace.[24]

FIGURE 9.7 Ad Targeted at Children and Teens

 **kraftfoods.com**

 **virginatlantic.com**

MARKETING DICTIONARY

need Lack of something useful; an imbalance between a desired state and an actual state.

motive Inner state that directs a person toward the goal of satisfying a felt need.

TABLE 9.1		Marketing Strategies Based on Maslow's Needs Hierarchy
Physiological Needs	Products	Vitamins, herbal supplements, medicines, food, exercise equipment, fitness clubs
	Marketing themes	Church's Fried Chicken—"Gotta love it."; Campbell's Soups—"M'm! M'm! Good!"; Campbell's Healthy Request Soups—"M'm! M'm! Good! . . . and Healthy!"; Post Cereals—"Commitment to Quality."
Safety Needs	Products	Cars and auto accessories, burglar alarm systems, retirement investments, insurance, smoke and carbon-monoxide detectors, medicines
	Marketing themes	Fireman's Fund insurance—"License to get on with it."; American General Financial Group—"Live the life you've imagined."; Shell Oil—"Count on Shell."; Bayer—"Changing the world with great care."; Volvo—"Protect the body. Ignite the soul."
Belongingness	Products	Beauty aids, entertainment, clothing, cars
	Marketing themes	Cadillac Seville—"It's what's next."; Blue Ridge Knives—"Follow the leader."; Lawson Software—"Leading-edge technology without the attitude."; Egift online retailer—"Great gifts for everyone . . . starting with you."
Esteem Needs	Products	Clothing, cars, jewelry, liquors, hobbies, beauty spa services
	Marketing themes	Saks Fifth Avenue—"Defining Style."; Van Cleef & Arpels—"The pleasure of perfection."; Serta—"We make the world's best mattress."; Jenn-Air kitchen appliances—"The sign of a great cook."
Self-Actualization	Products	Education, cultural events, sports, hobbies, luxury goods
	Marketing themes	Microsoft—"Where do you want to go today?"; Baccarat Crystal—"Beauty has its reasons."; Grand Lido Resorts—"Lost and found for the soul."; Gauthier jewelry—"Wear art."

Maslow noted that a satisfied need no longer motivates a person to act. Once the physiological needs are met, the individual moves on to pursue satisfaction of higher-order needs. Consumers are periodically motivated by the need to relieve thirst and hunger, but their interests soon return to focus on satisfaction of safety, social, and other needs in the hierarchy.

Critics have pointed out a variety of flaws in Maslow's reasoning. For example, some needs can be related to more than one level. However, the hierarchy of needs continues to occupy a secure place in the study of consumer behavior.

Perceptions

Perception is the meaning that a person attributes to incoming stimuli gathered through the five senses—sight, hearing, touch, taste, and smell. Certainly a buyer's behavior is influenced by his or her perceptions of a good or service. Only recently have researchers come to recognize that people's perceptions depend as much on what they want to perceive as on the actual stimuli. It is for this reason that Talbot's and Godiva chocolates are perceived so differently from Kmart and Hershey, respectively.

A person's perception of an object or event results from the interaction of two types of factors:

1. *Stimulus factors*—characteristics of the physical object such as size, color, weight, and shape
2. *Individual factors*—unique characteristics of the individual, including not only sensory processes but also experiences with similar inputs and basic motivations and expectations

Perceptual Screens

The average American today is constantly bombarded by marketing messages. According to the Food Marketing Institute, for example, a typical supermarket now carries 30,000 different packages, each serving as a miniature billboard vying to attract consumers' attention. Over 6,000 commercials a week are aired on network TV. Prime-time TV shows carry more than

SOLVING AN ETHICAL CONTROVERSY

Do Computers Solve Needs or Stunt Social Growth?

Mitch Maddox wants to prove that his computer can fulfill every daily need. He has rented an empty house in Dallas and moved in with nothing but a laptop computer, declaring that he will not leave his new abode for a year. He has even changed his name to DotComGuy and set up a company with the same name to go along with what looks to many observers like a giant publicity stunt. "Our vision is that new online shoppers will go to our site to learn how to utilize e-commerce," said Maddox when he began his marketing experiment. He then added, "I'm going to come out being a loon."

Maddox's last comment might be closer to the truth than he realizes. Psychologists and consumer groups are beginning to question whether computers and the Internet are simply tools for satisfying many of the needs on Maslow's hierarchy, from the physiological need for groceries to the esteem need for fine jewelry, or whether our reliance on high technology actually stunts social growth. "Digital technologies encourage us to abandon whatever vestiges of community are left to us," warns Stephen Talbott, a former software programmer and founder of an online newsletter, NetFuture. "This is a disastrous loss, since our encounters with others and with the world are the primary matrix for all human growth and development." Now consumers can order everything from groceries to automobiles online, can conduct banking transactions, and communicate with each other by e-mail, some experts fear that in fulfilling some needs, we are actually denying other needs, namely, those that are social. These experts fear that denying these needs may actually be harmful in the long run.

The impact on children is of particular concern. Author Kay S. Hymowitz notes, "Kids are living much more isolated lives than ever before. They just disappear into their rooms and spend all of their time with [these] media." Even Len Critcher, a friend of Mitch Maddox and president of DotComGuy Inc. admits, "We certainly don't recommend that people lock themselves away from the world, but we will prove that it can be done."

Some people, however, feel that the anonymity created by computer communication is positive. Writer Maia Szalavitz believes that when she socializes with others via the Internet, people respond to her words, not her looks. "My style online is conveyed by my sentences and syntax, not my fashion sense or physical appearance."

 Should consumers limit their reliance on computers and other high-technology media because it may stunt social growth?

Pro
1. The Internet fulfills some consumer needs, but we do not yet know the negative impact it may have on society.
2. Computers do not give children the amount of interpersonal contact with others that they need to develop socially.
3. Computers can create virtual communities but may destroy actual communities.

Con
1. The Internet can fulfill so many needs that marketers and consumers should seize the opportunity to use it.
2. With computer technology, people can communicate better than ever before, even with people around the globe.
3. Computer technology allows marketers and consumers to communicate more quickly and more freely, developing better relationships.

Summary
Years will probably pass before we see the lasting social impact of computer technology. "The benefits are personally experienced while the downside is more diffused," observes a member of the Loka Institute, a nonprofit group dedicated to public involvement in technology decisions. For instance, although the automobile has given us greater personal mobility, it has also generated pollution and changed patterns of geographic and economic development nationwide. Meanwhile, the Internet offers an explosion of information, products, and services to any consumer who knows how to click a mouse. And Mitch Maddox is determined to prove that he can live within the Web.

SOURCES: Troy Goodman, "Man Plans to Live Year Online," January 19, 2000, www.dailynews.yahoo.com; "In the Web Without a Net," *Christian Science Monitor*, January 3, 2000, www.csmonitor.com; Maia Szalavitz, "Can We Become Caught in the Web?" *Newsweek*, December 6, 1999, www.newsweek.com; and Katy Kelly, "Get That TV Out of Your Children's Bedroom," *U.S. News & World Report*, November 29, 1999, p. 79.

---

15 minutes of advertising every hour. Thousands of businesses have set up World Wide Web sites to tout their offerings. Marketers have also stamped their messages on everything from popcorn bags in movie theaters to airsickness bags on planes.

This unceasing marketing clutter has caused consumers to ignore many promotional messages. People respond selectively to attend only to messages that manage to break through their **perceptual screens**—the filtering processes through which all inputs must pass.

MARKETING **DICTIONARY**

perception Meaning that an individual creates by interpreting a stimulus.

perceptual screen Consumers' mental filtering processes through which all marketing messages must pass to gain attention.

FIGURE 9.8

Breaking Through Perceptual Screens

"Mind doing that again? I was changing my battery." Only Sony Handycam camcorders allow you to record with a 12-hour battery. And along with this added stamina, you'll also get up-to-the-minute battery life readings. So you'll always know exactly how much recording time you have left. Because no moment is going to repeat itself. No matter how politely you ask.

SONY
www.sony.com/handycam

crazybones.com

All marketers struggle to determine which stimuli evoke responses from consumers. They must learn how to capture a customer's attention long enough to read an advertisement, listen to a sales representative, or react to a point-of-purchase display. In general, marketers seek to make a message stand out and to gain the attention of prospective customers.

To break through the perceptual screens of Generation X consumers (Americans aged 23 to 36), Atcall, a Virginia-based, long-distance phone company, sponsors the popular Jenni Show on the Web. Jenni, 21 years old, resides in Washington but lives on the Internet: A camera in her apartment records every event in her daily life, from making humus to getting ready for a date. About 5,000 people from around the world tune in to the Jenni Show daily. There they have the option of clicking on Atcall's ad, which links them to the company's Web page where they can sign up for service. The click-through rates are 10 times higher for the Jenni site than for a standard Internet ad.[25]

Another way to break through clutter is to run large ads. Doubling the size of an ad in printed media increases its attention value by about 50 percent. Advertisers use color to make newspaper ads contrast with the usual black-and-white graphics, providing another effective way to penetrate the reader's perceptual screen. Other methods for enhancing contrast include arranging a large amount of white space around a printed area or placing white type on a dark background. Vivid illustrations and photos can also help to break through clutter in print ads. The Sony Electronic ad in Figure 9.8 uses an attention-getting photo to promote the 12-hour battery feature of its camcorder.

The psychological concept of closure also helps marketers create a message that stands out. *Closure* refers to the human tendency to perceive a complete picture from an incomplete stimulus. Advertisements that allow consumers to do this often succeed in breaking through perceptual screens. During a Kellogg campaign promoting consumption of fruit with cereal, the company emphasized the point by replacing the letters *ll* in *Kellogg* with bananas. In a campaign featuring a 25-cent coupon offer, Kellogg reinforced the promotional idea by replacing the letter *o* in the brand name with the image of a quarter.

Word-of-mouth marketing can be a highly effective way of breaking through consumers' perceptual screens. Take, for instance, the surprising success of Crazy Bones, popcorn-sized plastic figures with names like Bone Jour and James Bone. Spanish inventor Jose Maria Bella created Crazy Bones after his children raved about a museum exhibit of ancient toys made from animal knuckles. Spanish toy company Magic Box International introduced the concept in Europe, where, unable to afford a big advertising campaign, it hired vendors who peddled Crazy Bones to kids on school grounds. The tiny plastic figures quickly became a success in Europe.

The school yard strategy did not work in the United States, however, because officials chased salespeople off school property. Cleveland-based Toy Craze, the U.S. distributor, therefore, has adapted the word-of-mouth approach by marketing Crazy Bones at Boy Scout meetings, church youth groups, and after-school programs. Toy Craze representatives meet with school and youth group leaders to describe Crazy Bones, which are positioned as an inexpensive and educational alternative to TV and video games. After obtaining the leaders' permission, they meet with groups of kids to demonstrate the toys.

As a result, Crazy Bones have caught on in the United States without any sort of national promotion. Recently, a Zany Brainy toy store in Newtown, Pennsylvania, hosted an afternoon event for Crazy Bones' collectors; more than 7,000 boys showed up to watch game demonstrations and buy and trade figures.

A new tool that marketers are exploring is the use of virtual reality. Some companies have created presentations based on virtual reality that display marketing messages and information in a three-dimensional format. Eventually, experts predict, consumers will be able to tour resort areas via virtual reality before booking their trips or to walk through the interiors of homes they are considering buying via virtual reality . Virtual reality technology may allow marketers to penetrate consumer perceptual filters in a way not currently possible with other forms of media.

With selective perception at work screening competing messages, it is easy to see the importance of marketers' efforts in developing brand loyalty. Satisfied customers are less likely to seek information about competing products. Even when advertising by competitors is forced on them, they are less apt than others to look beyond their perceptual filters at those appeals. Loyal customers simply tune out information that does not agree with their existing beliefs and expectations.

Subliminal Perception

In 1956, a New Jersey movie theater tried to boost concession sales by flashing the words *Eat Popcorn* and *Drink Coca-Cola* between frames of Kim Novak's image in the movie *Picnic.* The messages flashed on the screen every five seconds for a duration of one three-hundredth of a second each time. Researchers reported that these messages, though too short to be recognizable at the conscious level, resulted in a 58 percent increase in popcorn sales and an 18 percent increase in Coca-Cola sales. After the findings were published, advertising agencies and consumer protection groups became intensely interested in **subliminal perception**—the subconscious receipt of incoming information.

Subliminal advertising is aimed at the subconscious level of awareness to circumvent the audience's perceptual screens. The goal of the original research was to induce consumer purchases while keeping consumers unaware of the source of the motivation to buy. All later attempts to duplicate the test findings, however, have been unsuccessful.

Although subliminal advertising has been universally condemned as manipulative, it is exceedingly unlikely that it can induce purchasing except by people already inclined to buy. Three reasons assure that this fact will remain true:

1. Strong stimulus factors are required just to get a prospective customer's attention.

2. Only a very short message can be transmitted.

3. Individuals vary greatly in their thresholds of consciousness. Messages transmitted at the threshold of consciousness for one person will not be perceived at all by some people and will be all too apparent to others. The subliminally exposed message, "Drink Coca-Cola," may go unseen by some viewers, while others may read it as "Drink Pepsi-Cola," "Drink Cocoa," or even "Drive Slowly."

Despite early fears, research has shown that subliminal messages cannot force receivers to purchase goods that they would not consciously want without the messages.

In recent years, subliminal communication has spread to programming for self-help tapes. These tapes play sounds that listeners hear consciously as relaxing music or ocean waves; subconsciously, imperceptibly among the other sounds, they hear thousands of subliminal messages. Americans spend millions of dollars a year on subliminal tapes that are supposed to help them stop smoking, lose weight, or achieve a host of other goals. Unfortunately, the National Research Council recently concluded that the subliminal messages do little to influence personal behavior.

Attitudes

Perception of incoming stimuli is greatly affected by attitudes. In fact, the decision to purchase an item is strongly based on currently held attitudes about the product, store, or salesperson.

Attitudes are a person's enduring favorable or unfavorable evaluations, emotional feelings, or action tendencies

4

Differentiate between customer behavior and consumer behavior.

MARKETING DICTIONARY

subliminal perception Subconscious receipt of information.

attitude A person's enduring favorable or unfavorable evaluation, emotional feeling, or action tendency toward a product.

toward some object or data. As they form over time through individual experiences and group contacts, attitudes become highly resistant to change.

Because favorable attitudes likely affect brand preferences, marketers are interested in determining consumer attitudes toward their offerings. Numerous attitude-scaling devices have been developed for this purpose.

Attitude Components

An attitude has cognitive, affective, and behavioral components. The *cognitive* component refers to the individual's information and knowledge about an object or concept. The *affective* component deals with feelings or emotional reactions. The *behavioral* component involves tendencies to act in a certain manner. For example, in deciding whether to shop at a warehouse-type food store, a consumer might obtain information about what the store offers from advertising, trial visits, and input from family, friends, and associates (cognitive component). The consumer might also receive affective input by listening to others about their shopping experiences at this type of store. Other affective information might lead the person to make a judgment about the type of people who seem to shop there—whether they represent a group with which he or she would like to be associated. The consumer may ultimately decide to buy some canned goods, cereal, and bakery products there but continue to rely on his regular supermarket for major food purchases (behavioral component).

All three components maintain a relatively stable and balanced relationship to one another. Together they form an overall attitude about an object or idea.

Changing Consumer Attitudes

Since a favorable consumer attitude provides a vital condition for marketing success, how can a firm lead prospective buyers to adopt such an attitude toward its products? Marketers have two choices: (1) attempt to produce consumer attitudes that will motivate purchase of a particular product or (2) evaluate existing consumer attitudes and then make the product characteristics appeal to them.

If consumers view an existing good or service unfavorably, the seller may choose to redesign it or offer new options. Cruise ships are a good example. After 25 years of continuous growth, passenger bookings began to drop in reaction to media reports of problems encountered on cruises such as hurricanes, ship fires, and disease outbreaks. Cruise lines also generally focused on attracting experienced passengers rather than new, younger customers who believed that only rich people took cruises and that most shipboard activities were geared toward older people.

To change these attitudes, the cruise-ship industry opened new markets and developed onboard programs designed to serve the needs of families with children. These marketers also added attractions such as adventure excursions ashore and a variety of onboard classes. Their advertising conveyed to consumers the message that cruises had changed.

renaissancecruises.com   Renaissance Cruise Lines targeted younger consumers by cosponsoring a virtual reality exhibit with online provider America Online. The exhibit, which simulated a cruise experience, traveled to shopping malls across the United States. Renaissance also sponsors AOL's Cruise Center, a Web site that allows would-be cruisers to book their trips online and obtain discounts.[26]

Modifying the Components of Attitude

Attitudes frequently change in response to inconsistencies among the three components. The most common inconsistencies result when new information changes the cognitive or affective components of an attitude. Marketers can work to modify attitudes by providing evidence of product benefits and by correcting misconceptions. The Bayer Corporation tries to correct misconceptions some consumers have that taking aspirin is not safe by developing ads stating the benefits of aspirin, like the one shown in Figure 9.9. They may also attempt to change attitudes by getting buyers to engage in new behavior. Free samples, for instance, can change attitudes by getting consumers to try a product.

Sometimes new technologies can encourage consumers to change their attitudes. Many people, for example, are reluctant to purchase clothing by mail-order mainly because they are afraid it will not fit properly. To address these concerns, retailer Lands' End has introduced a "personal model" feature on its Web site. Women who visit the site answer a series of questions about height, body proportions, and hair color, and the software creates a three-dimensional figure reflecting their responses. Consumers can then adorn the electronic model with Lands' End garments to get an idea of how various outfits might look on them.[27]

Learning

Marketing is concerned as seriously with the process by which consumer decisions change over time as with the current status of those decisions. **Learning,** in a marketing context, refers to immediate or expected changes in consumer behavior as a result of experience. The learning process includes the component of **drive,** which is any strong stimulus that impels action. Fear, pride, desire for money, thirst, pain avoidance, and rivalry are examples of drives. Learning also relies on a **cue,** that is any object in the environment that determines the nature of the consumer's response to a drive. Examples of cues are a newspaper advertisement for a new French restaurant (a cue for a hungry person) and a Shell sign near an interstate highway (a cue for a motorist who needs gasoline).

A *response* is an individual's reaction to a set of cues and drives. Responses might include such reactions as purchasing a package of Gillette Mach 3 razor blades, dining at Pizza Hut, or deciding to enroll at a particular community college or university.

Reinforcement is the reduction in drive that results from a proper response. As a response becomes more rewarding, it creates a stronger bond between the drive and the purchase of the product. Should the purchase of Mach 3 razor blades result in better shaves through repeated use, increased future purchases by the consumer are likely. Reinforcement is the rationale that underlies frequent-buyer programs, which reward repeat purchasers for their loyalty. Such programs give consumers points for buying particular brands; they can redeem these points for premiums like electric can openers or barbecue grills. Another example is an airline's frequent-flyer program, which rewards travelers who use that airline regularly with free airline tickets. Citibank reinforces repeated use of its Driver's Edge credit card by rewarding card owners with rebates they can use to buy a car or a cash-back option, as shown in Figure 9.10.

Applying Learning Theory to Marketing Decisions

Learning theory has some important implications for marketing strategists, particularly those involved with consumer packaged goods.[28] They must develop a desired outcome such as repeat purchase behavior gradually over time. *Shaping* is the process of applying a series of rewards and reinforcements to permit more complex behavior to evolve over time.

Both promotional strategy and the product itself play a role in the shaping process. Assume that marketers are attempting to motivate customers to become regular buyers of a certain product. Their first step is to induce an initial product trial by offering a free-sample package that includes a substantial

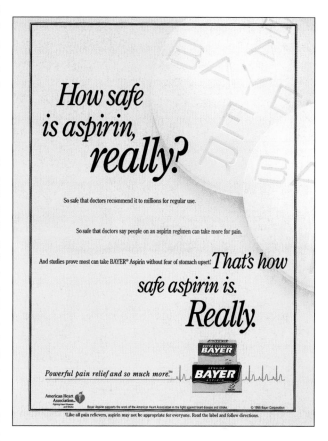

@ landsend.com

discount coupon for a subsequent purchase. This example illustrates the use of a cue as a shaping procedure. The purchase response is reinforced by satisfactory product performance and yet another, less substantial inducement (the coupon) for another purchase.

The second step is to entice the consumer to buy the item with little financial risk. The large discount offered by the coupon enclosed with the free sample prompts this action. The package that the consumer purchases has still another, smaller discount coupon enclosed. Again, satisfactory product performance and the second coupon provide reinforcement.

The third step is to motivate the person to buy the item again at a moderate cost. A discount coupon accomplishes this objective, but this time the purchased package includes no additional coupon. The only reinforcement comes from satisfactory product performance.

The final test comes when the consumer decides whether to buy the item at its true price without a discount coupon. Satisfaction with product performance provides the only continuing reinforcement. Repeat purchase behavior is literally shaped by effective application of learning theory within a marketing strategy context.

Self-Concept Theory

The consumer's **self-concept**—a person's multifaceted picture of himself or herself—plays an important role in consumer behavior. One young man, for example, may view himself as an intellectual, self-assured, talented, and rising young business executive. He will be disposed to buy products that agree with this conception of himself, such as elegant suits, unique ties, and a fine watch. A woman who views herself as a fashionable and upwardly mobile corporate or community leader may purchase designer clothes to reinforce her perceptions.

The concept of self emerges from an interaction of many of the influences—both personal and interpersonal—that affect buying behavior. The individual's needs, motives, perceptions, attitudes, and learning lie at the core of his or her conception of self. In addition, family, social, and cultural influences affect self-concept.

The self-concept has four components: real self, self-image, looking-glass self, and ideal self. The *real self* is an objective view of the total person. The *self-image*—the way an individual views himself or herself—may distort the objective view. The *looking-glass self*—the way an individual thinks others see him or her—may also differ substantially from the self-image because people often choose to project different images to others than their perceptions of their real selves. The *ideal self* serves as a personal set of objectives, since it is the image to which the individual aspires. In purchasing goods and services, people are likely to choose products that move them closer to their ideal self-images.

THE CONSUMER DECISION PROCESS

5

Outline the steps in the consumer decision process.

Consumers complete a step-by-step process in making purchasing decisions. The length of time and the amount of effort they devote to a particular purchasing decision depends on the importance of the desired good or service to the consumer.

Purchases with high levels of potential social or economic consequences are said to be *high-involvement* purchase decisions. Buying a new car or deciding where to go to college are two examples of high-involvement decisions. Routine purchases that pose little risk to the consumer are *low-involvement* decisions. Purchasing a candy bar from a vending machine is a good example.

Consumers generally invest more time and effort in buying decisions for high-involvement products than in those for low-involvement products. A car buyer, for example, will probably compare prices, spend time visiting dealer showrooms, and ask for advice from friends before making the final decision. Few buyers invest that much effort in choosing between Nestlé's and Hershey's candy bars. They will still go through the steps of the consumer decision process but on a more compressed scale.

Figure 9.11 shows the six steps in the consumer decision process. First, the consumer recognizes a problem or unmet need and then searches for goods or services that will fill that need and evaluates the alternatives before making a purchase decision. The next step is the actual purchase act. After completing the purchase, the consumer evaluates whether he or she made the right choice. Much of marketing involves steering consumers through the decision process in the direction of a specific item.

Consumers apply the decision process in solving problems and taking advantage of opportunities. Such decisions permit them to correct differences between their actual and desired states. Feedback from each decision serves as additional experience in helping guide subsequent decisions.

Problem or Opportunity Recognition

During the first stage in the decision process, the consumer becomes aware of a significant discrepancy between the existing situation and a desired situation. After recognizing the problem, the consumer must define it as preparation for seeking out methods for its solution. Problem recognition motivates the individual to achieve the desired state of affairs.

Perhaps the most common cause of problem or opportunity recognition is routine depletion of the individual's stock of an item. A large number of purchases simply replenish products ranging from gasoline to groceries. In other instances, the consumer may possess an inadequate assortment of products. The gardening hobbyist may make regular purchases of different fertilizers, seeds, or gardening tools as the season progresses.

A third cause of problem or opportunity recognition is dissatisfaction with a present brand or product type. This situation is common in purchases of new automobiles, furniture, or Fall clothing. Consumers often become bored with current products; nothing more than a desire for change may be the underlying rationale for the decision process that leads to a new product purchase.

Another important effect on problem or opportunity recognition results from changed financial status. Additional financial resources from such sources as salary increases or inheritances may permit some consumers to make purchases that they had previously postponed.

The marketer's main task during this phase of consumer decision making is to help prospective buyers identify and recognize potential problems or needs. For instance, sales personnel in an upscale department store may point out accessories to complete an outfit that a customer has already decided to buy.

Search

During the second step in the decision process, the consumer gathers information related to the attainment of a desired state of affairs. This search identifies alternative means of problem solution. High-involvement purchases may elicit extensive information searches, while low-involvement purchases require little search activity.

The search may cover internal or external sources of information. Internal search is a mental review of stored information relevant to the problem situation. This sequence includes both actual experiences or observations and memories of personal communications or exposures to persuasive marketing messages. An external

MARKETING | **DICTIONARY**

self-concept Person's conception of himself or herself, composed of the real self, self-image, looking glass self, and ideal self.

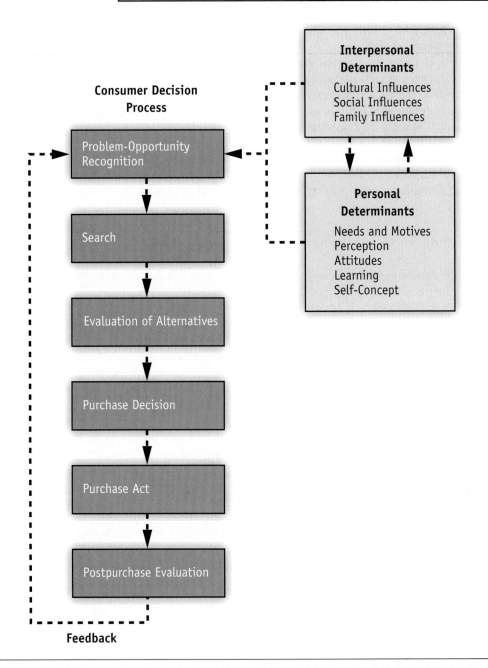

FIGURE 9.11   An Integrated Model of the Consumer Decision Process

Source: Roger D. Blackwell, Paul W. Miniard, and James F. Engel, *Consumer Behavior,* Eighth Edition (Fort Worth, TX: Dryden Press, 1998), pp. 747–750.

search gathers information from outside sources, which may include family members, friends, associates, store displays, sales representatives, brochures, and product-testing publications such as *Consumer Reports.* For some purchases, the Internet may be another source of information. Consumers can search for information directly at corporate Web sites or ask for recommendations from others through online newsgroups.

Consumers often solve problems through an internal search—that is, by relying on mentally stored information to make purchase decisions. Achieving favorable results using a certain car polish may motivate a consumer to repurchase this brand rather than to consider other options.

Since external search involves both time and effort, consumers will complete it only when memory cannot supply adequate information.

The search identifies alternative brands for consideration and possible purchase. The number of alternatives that a consumer actually considers in making a purchase decision is known in marketing as the **evoked set.** In some searches, consumers already know of the brands that merit further consideration; in others, their external searches develop such information. The actual number of brands included in the evoked set will vary depending on both the situation and the person. For example, an immediate need might limit the evoked set, while someone who has more time to make a decision might expand the evoked set to choose from a broader range of options.

Consumers now choose among more alternative products than ever before. This can confuse and complicate the analysis necessary to narrow the range of choices for consumers. Instead of comparing one or two brands, a consumer often faces a dizzying array of brands and sub-brands. Products that once included only one or two categories—regular coffee versus decaffeinated—are now available in many different forms—cappuccino, latte, double latte, flavored coffee, and iced coffee, just to name a few possibilities. Similarly, formats and features of consumer electronics have multiplied to offer so many options that even salespeople cannot keep up; a recent survey of 10 electronics stores in *Wall Street Journal* found only one sales representative who could accurately explain the difference between digital and high-definition TV.[29]

Marketers try to influence buying decisions during the search process by providing persuasive information about their goods or services in a format useful to consumers. As discussed earlier, marketers encounter a difficult challenge in breaking through the clutter that distracts customers. To achieve success and be included in a consumer's evoked set of alternatives, the marketer must find creative ways to meet this challenge.

Evaluation of Alternatives

The third step in the consumer decision process is to evaluate the evoked set of options identified during the search step. Actually, it is difficult to completely separate the second and third steps since some evaluation takes place as the search progresses; consumers accept, discount, distort, or reject incoming information as they receive it.

The outcome of the evaluation stage is the choice of a brand or product in the evoked set or possibly a decision to renew the search for additional alternatives, should all those identified during the initial search prove unsatisfactory. To complete this analysis, the consumer must develop a set of evaluative criteria to guide the selection. **Evaluative criteria** may be defined as features that a consumer considers in choosing among alternatives. These criteria can either be objective facts (government tests of an automobile's miles-per-gallon rating) or subjective impression (a favorable view of DKNY clothing). Common evaluative criteria include price, brand name, and country of origin. Evaluative criteria can also vary with the consumer's age, income level, social class, and culture.

Marketers attempt to influence the outcome of this stage in three ways. First, they can try to educate consumers about attributes that they view as important in evaluating a particular class of goods. They also identify which evaluative criteria are important to an individual and attempt to show why a specific brand fulfills those criteria. For example, TPC tries to influence consumers to purchase its Progresso brand of soup by asking them to consider taste rather than tradition as an evaluation criterion, as shown in Figure 9.12. Finally, they try to induce a customer to expand the evoked set to include the product being marketed. A travel agent, for example, might ask a client about the family's budget and recreational preferences. The agent might also explain the differences between two destinations that the client had not considered, pointing out important considerations, such as weather and activities. Finally, the agent might suggest other destinations or resorts, increasing the client's range of choices.

MARKETING DICTIONARY

evoked set Number of alternative brands that a consumer considers buying before making a purchasing decision.

evaluative criteria Features considered in a consumer's choice of alternatives.

Purchase Decision and Purchase Act

The search and alternative evaluation stages of the decision process result in the eventual purchase decision and the act of making the purchase. At this stage, the consumer has evaluated each alternative in the evoked set based on his personal set of evaluative criteria and narrowed the alternatives down to one.

The consumer then decides the purchase location. Consumers tend to choose stores by considering such characteristics as location, price, assortment, personnel, store image, physical design, and services. In addition, store selection is influenced by the product category. Some consumers choose the convenience of in-home shopping via telephone or mail order rather than traveling to retail stores to complete transactions. Marketers can smooth the purchase decision and purchase act phases by helping customers arrange for financing or delivery.

Postpurchase Evaluation

The purchase act produces one of two results. The buyer feels either satisfaction at the removal of the discrepancy between the existing and desired states or dissatisfaction with the purchase. Consumers are generally satisfied if purchases meet their expectations.

Sometimes, however, consumers experience some postpurchase anxieties, called **cognitive dissonance.** This psychologically unpleasant state results from an imbalance among a person's knowledge, beliefs, and attitudes. For example, a consumer may experience dissonance after choosing a particular automobile over several other models when some of the rejected models have desired features that the chosen one does not provide.

Dissonance is likely to increase (1) as the dollar values of purchases increase, (2) when the rejected alternatives have desirable features that the chosen alternatives do not provide, and (3) when the purchase decision has a major effect on the buyer. In other words, dissonance is more likely with high-involvement purchases than with those that require low involvement. The consumer may attempt to reduce dissonance by looking for advertisements or other information to support the chosen alternative or by seeking reassurance from acquaintances who are satisfied purchasers of the product. The individual may also avoid information that favors a rejected alternative. Someone who buys a Toyota is likely to read Toyota advertisements and avoid Nissan and Honda ads.

Marketers can help buyers to reduce cognitive dissonance by providing information that supports the chosen alternative. Automobile dealers recognize the possibility of "buyer's remorse" and often follow up purchases with letters or telephone calls from dealership personnel offering personal attention to any customer problems. Advertisements that stress customer satisfaction also help to reduce cognitive dissonance. With ads stressing customer satisfaction like the one in Figure 9.13, Michelin reduces cognitive dissonance by assuring customers they've made a good choice.

A final method of dealing with cognitive dissonance is to change product options, thereby restoring the cognitive balance. The consumer may ultimately decide that one of the rejected alternatives would have been the best choice and vow to purchase it in the future.

Classifying Consumer Problem Solving Processes

6

Differentiate among routinized response behavior, limited problem solving, and extended problem solving.

As mentioned earlier, the consumer decision processes for different products require varying amounts of problem-solving efforts. Marketers recognize three categories of problem-solving behavior: routinized response, limited problem solving, and extended problem solving.[30] The classification of a particular purchase within this framework clearly influences the consumer decision process.

Routinized Response Behavior

Consumers make many purchases routinely by choosing a preferred brand or one of a limited group of acceptable brands. This type of rapid consumer problem solving is referred to as *routinized response behavior*. A routine purchase of a regular brand of soft drink is an example. The consumer has already set evaluative criteria and identified available options. External search is limited in such cases, which characterize extremely low-involvement products.

Limited Problem Solving

Consider the situation in which the consumer has previously set evaluative criteria for a particular kind of purchase but then encounters a new, unknown brand. The introduction of a new shampoo is an example of a limited problem-solving situation. The consumer knows the evaluative criteria for the product, but she has not applied these criteria to assess the new brand. Such situations demand moderate amounts of time and effort for external searches. Limited problem solving is affected by the number of evaluative criteria and brands, the extent of external search, and the process for determining preferences. Consumers making purchase decisions in this product category are likely to feel involvement in the middle of the range.

Extended Problem Solving

Extended problem solving results when brands are difficult to categorize or evaluate. The first step is to compare one item with similar ones. The consumer needs to understand the product features before evaluating alternatives. Most extended problem-solving efforts involve lengthy external searches. High involvement purchase decisions usually require extended problem solving.

FIGURE 9.13 Reducing Cognitive Dissonance

More awards for customer satisfaction than any other tire brand.

{ And to think, no babies were asked their opinion. }

After surveying hundreds of thousands of vehicle owners, J.D. Power and Associates ranked Michelin as the Best Replacement Tire in Customer Satisfaction ten times from 1992–1999 for either passenger or light-truck vehicles. So if you need tires for your car, truck or SUV, we suggest you choose the brand that's appreciated by those who sit in the driver's seat. Not to mention the baby seat. To find the dealer nearest you, call 1-888-MICHELIN or visit michelin.com.

MICHELIN

Because so much is riding on your tires.

CONSUMER BEHAVIOR: STRATEGIC IMPLICATIONS

STRATEGY

Marketers who understand the consumer decision process use this knowledge to design an effective marketing strategy. As an example, consider the rapidly growing market in cosmetics for preteen girls.

Of the more than 15 million American girls ages 5 to 12, an estimated two-thirds of them use cosmetics. While they are enthusiastic consumers, persuading them to retain a brand in their evoked set can be a challenge for marketers. "The one thing you have to know about this market is they're very, very fast," says Abe Safdieh, chief executive officer of Townley Inc., a producer of cosmetics. Companies that market nail polish to adults introduce new colors twice a year; Townley comes out with new shades every month in order to penetrate this market of young girls. While traditional makeup marketers get many of their ideas from Hollywood and the fashion industry, Townley marketers get theirs from toy stores. The toy store strategy inspired Yo-Yo lip gloss, a fruit-flavored tint packaged in a clear plastic yo-yo. Townley also developed a Disney-licensed line of cosmetics, such as Cinderella lip gloss, aimed at 3- to 5-year-olds.

In addition to capturing the girls' interests, marketers of preteen cosmetics must understand another consumer decision process: that of their customers' parents. While the girls love bright colors and lots of glitter, their mothers frown on products that look too much like actual makeup. Comments Kimberly Turiano, mother of 8-year-old Jennifer and 7-year-old Christina, "They're really into it, but I don't want

townleycosmetics.com

MARKETING **DICTIONARY**

cognitive dissonance Postpurchase anxiety that results from an imbalance among an individual's knowledge, beliefs, and attitudes.

them to grow up faster than they should. Kids should be kids." Mothers often control the purchase process, so marketers must remain sensitive to their concerns.

Marketers can appeal to both preteens and their parents by creating products that seem real to the girls, but different enough from adult cosmetics to reassure mothers. For example, the Tinkerbell Glamour Compact, sold by Connecticut-based Renaissance Cosmetics, features colors that look bright in the compact but are almost transparent on the skin. Intimate Brands markets lipsticks and lip glosses that are heavily flavored and scented with aromas like grape and fudge but go on lightly to give just a hint of color.

Companies must also address mothers' concerns about product safety. Tinkerbell nail polishes are sold in spill-proof bottles, and the colors peel off easily without nail polish remover, which contains harsh ingredients such as acetone. While adult cosmetics contain fragrance and alcohol, preteen products are made with water- and flavor-based ingredients similar to those used in foods.

Do these strategies work? Apparently, because U.S. preteens now spend $200 million each year on cosmetics, and sales continue to rise. Says one mother of her daughter's sparkling purple eye shadow. "It's definitely marketed for the kids. No adult would wear this stuff."[31]

ACHIEVEMENT CHECK SUMMARY

Read the learning objectives that follow, and consider the questions for each one. Answering these questions will reinforce your grasp of the most important concepts in the chapter and will allow you to check how well you have achieved these learning goals. Where a blank appears before a question, answer with *T* or *F* for true/false questions; for multiple-choice questions, choose the letter of the correct answer.

Objective 9.1: Differentiate between customer behavior and consumer behavior.

1. _____ Customer behavior is the process by which consumers and business buyers make purchase decisions.

2. _____ The process by which the ultimate buyers of a product make a purchase decision is called *consumer behavior*.

Objective 9.2: Identify the interpersonal determinants of consumer behavior.

1. _____ The interpersonal determinants of consumer behavior are cultural influences, social influences, and family influences.

2. _____ Cultural values never change.

3. _____ African-Americans, Hispanics, and Asian Americans are subcultures with similar consumer profiles.

4. _____ The values, attitudes, and behavior that a group deems appropriate for its members are called (a) group roles; (b) group norms; (c) group determinants.

Objective 9.3: Identify the personal determinants of consumer behavior.

1. _____ An individual's needs and motives, perceptions, attitudes, learning, and self-concept all affect his consumer behavior.

2. _____ A. H. Maslow theorized that (a) needs can be categorized in a hierarchy of importance; (b) consumer behavior is influenced by a number of factors; (c) consumers are not motivated by external influences.

3. _____ By including humorous messages, advertising can effectively break through consumers' perceptual screens.

4. _____ A customer who is dissatisfied with a product says he or she will never use it again. This is an example of (a) perceptual screening; (b) learning; (c) need fulfillment.

Objective 9.4: Explain how marketers classify behavioral influences on consumer decisions.

1. _____ Kurt Lewin's model of human behavior states that behavior is influenced by (a) personal influences; (b) social influences; (c) both personal and social influences.

2. _____ Consumer behavior differs substantially from Lewin's model of human behavior.

Objective 9.5: Outline the steps in the consumer decision process.

1. _____ Buying chewing gum is an example of a high involvement purchase.

2. _____ Recognizing a need is the first phase of the consumer decision process.

3. _____ Marketers try to influence consumers during the search phase by (a) helping them identify needs; (b) providing persuasive information; (c) helping to arrange financing.

4. _____ Cognitive dissonance is likely to increase (a) when the cost of a purchase rises; (b) when the purchase requires high involvement; (c) when the consumer sees other products with better features; (d) all of the above.

Objective 9.6: Differentiate among routinized response behavior, limited problem solving, and extended problem solving.

1. _____ Buying your regular toothpaste is a routinized response.

2. _____ Deciding to try a new brand of breakfast cereal most likely involves (a) routinized response behavior; (b) limited problem solving; (c) extended problem solving.

3. _____ Buying a new car usually requires extended problem solving.

Students: See the solutions section located on page S-2 to check your responses to the Achievement Check Summary.

Key Terms

customer behavior	perception
consumer behavior	perceptual screen
culture	subliminal perception
subculture	attitude
norm	learning
status	drive
role	cue
Asch phenomenon	reinforcement
reference group	self-concept
opinion leader	evoked set
need	evaluative criteria
motive	cognitive dissonance

Review Questions

1. What are the primary determinants of consumer behavior? What sub-classifications further characterize these determinants?
2. What is culture? How does it affect buying patterns? Identify the subcultures that are most important to marketers in the United States today.
3. Explain the social influences on consumer behavior. Examine the specific roles of the Asch phenomenon, reference groups, social class, and opinion leaders.
4. For which of the following products is reference group influence likely to have a strong effect on consumer behavior?
   a. Sharp's nonalcoholic brew
   b. Rollerblade in-line skates
   c. Pantene Pro-V shampoo
   d. Trek mountain bikes
   e. Lady Fitness health clubs
   f. Nicotrol stop-smoking patches
5. Outline Maslow's hierarchy of needs. Cite examples of needs at each level.
6. Explain the concept of perception. Detail the effects of perceptual screens, selective perception, and subliminal perception in your explanation.
7. How do attitudes influence consumer behavior? How can marketers change negative attitudes toward a product?
8. Differentiate among the four components of the self-concept: ideal self, looking glass self, self-image, and real self. Which is the most important to marketers?
9. List the steps in the consumer decision process. Detail your application of this process in a recent purchase.
10. Explain how marketers can use their knowledge of consumer behavior to develop a marketing strategy.

Questions for Critical Thinking

1. U.S. marketers doing business in Spain are sometimes shocked when they are invited to dinner at 10:30 or 11:00 at night. However, most Spanish restaurants do not open until 9:00 P.M. Furthermore, many businesses are closed for a couple of hours in the afternoon, but they stay open later than comparable U.S. establishments. Relate this situation to the chapter materials.
2. Consider the following advertising line from Cyrix, which manufactures microprocessors for personal computers: "The liberation of information." Does this advertising copy suggest an emerging American core value? Explain your answer.
3. Poll your friends about subliminal perception. How many believe that marketers can control consumers at a subconscious level? Report the results of this survey to your marketing class.
4. Many consumers are switching from traditional soft drinks to alternative beverages like Snapple, Arizona Iced Tea, Koala, and Evian Natural Spring Water. What attitude is reflected in this trend? How are soft-drink bottlers trying to counter this trend?
5. Video rentals include previews of movies not yet shown in theaters. How does this information relate to the chapter's discussion of learning theory?

1. **Maslow's Hierarchy of Needs.** Notice in Table 9.1 that cars are listed as product examples on three levels: safety, belongingness, and esteem needs. Go to several car company Web sites and find examples of features at the sites that focus on meeting each of these three needs.

2. **Virtual Reality.** Go to "The Largest Virtual Reality Shopping Mall on the Web" at *www.vr-mall.com*. At this site you can do basic shopping that is available at many e-commerce sites. Spend some time browsing at this site, and identify at least three features that qualify this site to be called a "virtual reality" shopping mall.

3. **Consumer Decision Process.** In this exercise you will evaluate how effectively the Internet allows you to complete the "Search," "Alternative Evaluation," and "Purchase Decision" steps of the Consumer Decision Process (Figure 9.11). If you're in the market for a particular good or service, you may use this assignment to conduct your own search and may also complete the "Purchase Act" and "Postpurchase Evaluation" steps if you wish. If you'd rather use the search problem here, you may do so.

Assume you need an airline ticket for a flight from Boston to Denver on the 21st of next month. You will return to Boston on the 28th. Go to a Web site, such as *www.travelocity.com*, where you can purchase airline tickets online. After specifying your travel requirements and initiating the search for your options, print out the search results. Write the following on a separate piece of paper:

(a) List the evaluative criteria that are important to you when choosing among the alternatives.

(b) Identify the option you would choose if you, in fact, needed this airline ticket.

(c) Summarize your opinion about using this method to help you make a purchase decision.

gm.com

ford.com

chrysler.com

toyota.com

mazda.com

vr-mall.com

travelocity.com

Video Case 9 on Goya Foods, Inc. begins on page VC-11.

B2B: Business-to-Business Marketing

CHAPTER

10

Sight & Sound Software Has Plenty of Reservations

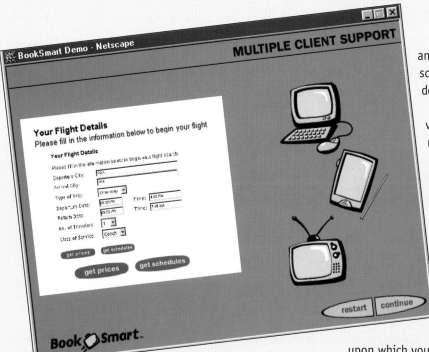

Jeff Kennedy and Mark Tilden were doing pretty well with their Portland-based company, Sight & Sound Software. The small multimedia s293oftware development firm brought in enough revenue for its two founders to put dinner on the table, which is an entrepreneurial achievement. But with one phone call, all that changed: American Airlines asked Sight & Sound to help with its e-commerce site, www.aa.com, so that travelers could more easily plan their own trips. Sight & Sound was to build the booking engine for the site.

This new venture with American Airlines, and later Wal-Mart, meant Kennedy and Tilden needed a better understanding of the purchasing process of large organizations. Kennedy and Tilden developed a strong relationship with John Samuel, managing director of interactive marketing and leader of the project at American Airlines. Samuel explained American's needs and expectations of the software. One major issue for American was speed. "We noticed that every increase in speed had a corresponding increase in revenue," says Samuel. Personalization for the consumer was also important. "People love to see their name

and [earned frequent-flyer] miles on the welcoming screen," says Terri Falconer, interactive marketing development manager at American.

With these issues in mind, Sight & Sound developed a program called BookSmart. BookSmart not only satisfied American Airline's needs, it also answered the needs of the ultimate users of the program, the consumers. The program was a hit. The site now provides travel information and services to roughly 350,000 potential travelers a day, generating $500 million a year in revenues.

Wal-Mart soon decided to enter the online travel business, and it chose BookSmart as its booking engine. David White, Sight & Sound's vice president of marketing, believes that Wal-Mart made the choice "because our semi-custom software gives you the framework upon which you can build a travel site using a set of tools, close to a turnkey approach." In other words, the BookSmart software program offers organizational customers flexibility in the way it operates, allowing them to tailor it to certain market segments, adjust it according to their own business goals, and remain flexible with inventory sources. BookSmart is also easy to customize and easy to use—something that organizational buyers like.

Originally focused solely on marketing to businesses (B2B), Sight & Sound now intends to include the consumer market (B2C) as well. "Sight & Sound's business model is to release a tool set with a lot of flexibility to serve a number of markets," notes White. "We still have a lot of work in the business and consumer space to make online travel bookings easier and more powerful, closer to the service you get from a good travel agent." Using BookSmart, a large corporation could save millions by handling travel arrangements in-house instead of outsourcing them to travel agencies. "The payback is immediate and sustained," claims White. Those are words that every CEO would love to hear.[1]

293

CHAPTER OVERVIEW

Although an average person sees more evidence of the consumer market, the business-to-business marketplace is, in fact, significantly larger than sales to ultimate consumers. U.S. companies pay more than $300 billion each year just for office and maintenance supplies. Government agencies inflate the business-to-business market even further; the Department of Defense alone has an annual purchase budget of about $270 billion.[2] Whether conducted through face-to-face transactions or via telephone, fax machines, or the Internet, these organizations must deal with complex purchasing decisions, buying situations that range from local to global exchanges, and differences between multiple decision makers.

Some firms focus entirely on business markets. For instance, Hoechst sells chemicals to manufacturers, who use them in a variety of products. Advanced Micro Devices makes flash memory chips for the cellular phone and Internet-provider markets. Manpower Inc., provides temporary personnel services to firms that need extra workers. Computer Associates, Oracle, and Sybase are software vendors specializing in corporate business applications. StorageTek provides network computing goods and services, such as shown in Figure 10.1, to help organizations store, transport, and secure information.

| FIGURE 10.1 | Firm Specializing in the Business-to-Business Market |

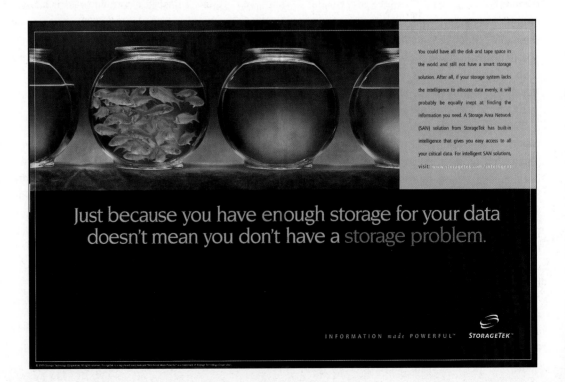

netscape.com

Other firms sell to both consumer and business markets. Netscape, best-known for selling its Navigator Web browser to consumers, actually gets about 80 percent of its revenues from corporate customers. It offers a complete line of sophisticated networking software for companies like 3M and Chrysler. Similarly, Eastman Kodak sells film to consumers, and it also sells photofinishing paper, chemicals, and services to wholesale photofinishing companies.

As you will recall from Chapter 9, attitudes, perceptions, family and social influences, and other factors affect consumer buying behavior. This chapter will discuss buying behavior in the business market, also known as the *organizational market*. **Business-to-business marketing** deals with organizational purchases of goods and services to support production of other goods and services, to facilitate daily company operations or for resale. The term **B2B** is now a widely accepted acronym for business-to-business marketing.   ▪

NATURE OF THE BUSINESS MARKET

Like final consumers, an organization purchases products to fill needs. However, its primary need—meeting the demands of its own customers—is similar from organization to organization. A manufacturer buys raw materials to create the company's product, while a wholesaler or retailer buys products to resell. Companies also buy services from other businesses. Institutional purchasers such as government agencies and nonprofit organizations buy things to meet the needs of their constituents.

Business buying decisions, while handled by individuals, occur in the context of formal organizations. Environmental, organizational, and interpersonal factors are among the many influences in B2B markets. Budget, cost, and profit considerations all play parts in business buying decisions. In addition, the organizational buying process typically involves complex interactions among many people. An organization's goals must also be considered in the organizational buying process.[3] Later sections of the chapter will explore these topics in greater detail.

The B2B market is diverse. Transactions can range from orders as small as a box of paper clips or copy-machine toner for a home-based business to deals as large as thousands of parts for an automobile manufacturer or massive turbine generators for an electric power plant. Businesses are also big purchasers of services, such as telecommunications, computer consulting, and transportation services. Four major categories define the business market: (1) the commercial market, (2) trade industries, (3) government organizations, and (4) institutions.

Components of the Business Market

The **commercial market** is the largest segment of the business market. It includes all individuals and firms that acquire goods and services to support, directly or indirectly, the production of other goods and services. When Lufthansa buys aircraft built by the European consortium Airbus Industrie, when Sara Lee purchases wheat to mill into flour for an ingredient in its cakes, and when a plant manager orders light bulbs and cleaning supplies for a factory, these transactions

1

Explain each of the components of the business market.

MARKETING   DICTIONARY

business-to-business marketing Organizational purchase of goods and services to support production of other goods and services for daily company operations or for resale.

B2B A popular acronym for the business-to-business market.

commercial market Individuals and firms that acquire goods and services to support, directly or indirectly, production of other goods and services.

SOLVING AN ETHICAL CONTROVERSY

Should Internet Alliances Be Regulated?

"The Internet is the first limitless medium, and by its very nature, no single company or group can hope to control it," says Scott Miller, communications director at Time Warner. But with the merger of two media giants—Time Warner and AOL—some experts worry that a deal such as this will not only limit consumer choice but also the independence of news organizations. "What this merger invites is the possibility of a new era in American communications that sees the end of an independent press," warns Tom Rosenstiel, director of the Project for Excellence in Journalism. Through its purchase of Time Warner, AOL will own its own cable systems, which may mean that AOL will back down from its traditional fight for open cable access. AOL may now be more apt to channel users toward CNN and Time sites that are owned by Time Warner instead of MSNBC or Newsweek sites.

In other Internet business-to-business transactions, agreements such as the one between Priceline and NextCard could result in noncompetitive services. Priceline, which is well known for its innovative name-your-own-price system of selling items such as airline tickets online, has expanded to offer credit cards online. According to critics, the problem is that Priceline only offers these services through NextCard, who then has no incentive to provide competitive rates and services.

Business-to-business e-commerce has reached nearly $700 billion annually. "By 2003, the transaction value of B2B e-commerce over the Internet will be $2 trillion, and an additional $780 billion in purchases will be made over private networks using EDI [electronic data interchange]," predicts David Pecaut, senior vice president of The Boston Consulting Group. Thus, it is important to study the effects of Internet business alliances on competition, availability of information, and product selection.

Should business-to-business alliances on the Internet be regulated?

Pro

1. Such alliances will inhibit competition in e-commerce.
2. Mergers creating huge media companies will limit or influence the amount and type of news information available to customers. The freedom of journalists could be hampered if they are employed by and reporting on the same company.
3. With such huge corporate mergers, smaller companies will have a harder time establishing a presence on the Internet.

Con

1. We have only begun to see the potential of the Internet. The Net is, as noted previously, a "limitless medium," so there is room for everyone to compete.
2. The Internet provides smaller companies greater opportunities to make alliances with other companies, which can ultimately give them more exposure.
3. The Internet offers smaller companies unlimited opportunities to locate business customers anywhere in the world.

Summary

Siding with the benefits of business alliances, Richard Epstein, a law professor at the University of Chicago, notes that the Internet actually provides a global medium for competition, dissent, and choice. As for competition among media giants, he quips, "If there are just two newspapers in town, one will happily dump on the other" if favoritism is shown in news reporting. But others do worry that smaller businesses will be swallowed up by larger ones. "The rise of the Internet was supposed to be the rise of the independent voice," notes Matthew Felling, media director of the Center for Media and Public Affairs. "With the auditorium being filled with large bands, the guy playing his clarinet is really going to get outshouted and is going to get completely crowded out of the concert."

SOURCES: Robin Estrin, "Critics Fear Dilution of News," Associated Press, January 12, 2000, www.dailynews.yahoo.com; Lisa M. Bowman, "Will Merger Shut Lid On Open Access?" *ZDNet News*, January 12, 2000, www.dailynews.yahoo.com; Jim Romeo, "U.S. B2B to Reach $2.8 Trillion by 2003," *E-commerce Times*, January 12, 2000, www.EcommerceTimes.com; "Priceline and NextCard Unveil Name-Your-Terms Credit Card," *E-commerce Times*, January 11, 2000, www.EcommerceTimes.com; Saul Hansell, "Credit-Card Issuers Wary of Name-a-Price System," *The New York Times*, January 10, 2000, www.nytimes.com.

---

all take place in the commercial market. Some products aid in the production of other items (the new airplane). Others are physically used up in the production of a good or service (the wheat). Still others contribute to the firm's day-to-day operations (the maintenance supplies). The commercial market includes manufacturers, farmers, and other members of resource-producing industries; construction contractors; and providers of such services as transportation, public utilities, financing, insurance, and real-estate brokerage.[4]

The second segment of the organizational market, **trade industries,** includes retailers and wholesalers that purchase goods for resale to others. The term **reseller** is often used to describe the wholesalers and retailers that operate in the trade sector.

Most of these resale products, such as clothing, appliances, sports equipment, and automobile parts, are finished goods that the buyers sell to final consumers. In other cases, the buyers may complete some processing or repackaging before reselling the products. For example, retail meat markets may carry out bulk purchases of sides of beef and then cut individual pieces for their

TABLE 10.1	Examples of E-Commerce Sites Engaged in B2B Marketing

E-EXCHANGES	WHAT THEY DO
PAPEREXCHANGE	Helps businesses trade pulp and paper
Universal Access	Allows businesses to trade datacom services
Arebinet Communications	Allows business to trade bandwidth
Autovia	Helps mechanics procure auto parts
Bidcom	Brings together builders and their suppliers
Collabria	Allows businesses to trade printing equipment
Commerx	A trading post for the plastics industry
E-chemicals	A place for businesses to procure bulk chemicals
iParts	Allows businesses to trade electronic parts

Source: Adapted from Erick Schonfeld, "A One Stock Way to Play the Net," *Fortune*, September 27, 1999, p. 154.

customers. Lumber dealers and carpet retailers may purchase in bulk and then provide quantities and sizes to meet customers' specifications. In addition to resale products, trade industries buy such things as computers, display shelves, and other products they need to operate their businesses. These goods, as well as maintenance items, and specialized services such as marketing research, accounting, and management consulting all represent organizational purchases. Chapter 16 provides detailed discussions of the trade industries.

Government organizations, the third category of the business market, include domestic units of government—federal, state, and local—as well as foreign governments. This important market segment purchases a wide variety of products, ranging from highways to social services. The primary motivation of government purchasing is to provide some form of public benefit, such as national defense or pollution control.

Institutions, both public and private, are the fourth component of the business market. This category includes a wide range of organizations, such as hospitals, churches, skilled care centers, colleges and universities, museums, and not-for-profit agencies. Some institutions—state universities, for instance—must rigidly follow standardized purchasing procedures, while others may employ less formal buying practices. Business-to-business marketers often benefit by setting up separate divisions to sell to institutional buyers.

B2B Markets—The Internet Connection

Like other areas of e-commerce, the Internet is now playing an important role in B2B marketing. For example, many business-to-business marketers have set up Web sites allowing their customers to buy needed items. Service and customized pages are accessed through a password provided by B2B marketers. Other examples of business-to-business e-commerce includes online auctions and virtual marketplaces where buyers and vendors negotiate exchanges. Table 10.1 lists some of the B2B e-commerce firms and briefly explains what each of them does.

While consumers' use of the Internet markets receive the bulk of public attention, in fact, about 70 percent of all Internet sales are B2B transactions. It has been estimated that the Internet will account for approximately 9 percent of all B2B sales in 2003.[5]

Differences in Foreign Business Markets

Business markets in other countries may differ due to variations in government regulations and cultural practices. Some

MARKETING DICTIONARY

trade industry Retailers or wholesalers that purchase products for resale to others.

reseller Marketing intermediaries that operate in the trade sector.

business products need modifications to succeed in foreign markets. In Australia, Japan, and Great Britain, for instance, motorists drive on the left side of the road. Modifications need to be made to automobiles to accommodate such differences. As another example, the electrical wiring of a European building differs from that of a building in the United States. Again, modifications are necessary.

Business marketers must be willing to adapt to local customs and business practices when operating in foreign markets. Factors as deceptively simple as the time of a meeting and methods of address for associates can make a difference. A company even needs to consider what ink colors to use for documents because colors can have different meanings in different countries. Marketers should research cultural preferences carefully before conducting business in other countries.

SEGMENTING BUSINESS-TO-BUSINESS MARKETS

2

Describe the major approaches to segmenting business-to-business markets.

Like consumer markets, business-to-business markets include wide varieties of customers. By applying market segmentation concepts to groups of business customers, a firm's marketers can develop a strategy that best suits a particular segment's needs. The overall process of segmenting business markets resembles consumer market segmentation, but it divides markets based on different criteria, usually organizational characteristics and product applications. Among the major ways to segment business markets are demographics (size, geographic location), customer type, end-use application, and purchasing situation.[6]

Demographic Segmentation

As with consumer markets, demographic characteristics define useful segmentation criteria for business markets. For example, firms can be grouped by *size*, based on sales revenues or number of employees. Marketers may develop one strategy to reach *Fortune* 500 corporations with complex purchasing procedures and another strategy for small firms where decisions are made by one or two people. Small businesses—especially companies with under 100 employees—have caught the eye of business-to-business marketers. This fast-growing segment of about 20 million firms offers tremendous potential.[7] For example, American Express created a Small Business Services unit to assist entrepreneurs and small business owners. Through ads like the one in Figure 10.2, American Express informs this segment how it can organize its financial data and how it can purchase equipment.

Segmentation by Customer Type

Another useful segmentation approach groups prospects according to *type of customer*. Marketers can apply this principle in several ways. They can group customers by broad categories—manufacturer, service provider, government agency, nonprofit organization, wholesaler, or retailer—and also by industry. These groups may be further divided using other segmentation approaches discussed in this section. The North American Industrial Classification System (NAICS), for instance, provides a useful tool for segmenting business-to-business markets by customer type.

Customer-based segmentation is a related approach often used in the business-to-business marketplace. Organizational buyers tend to detail much more precise product specifications than ultimate consumers do. As a result, business products often fit narrow market segments as compared to consumer products. This fact leads some firms to design business goods and services to meet specific buyer requirements, creating a form of market segmentation.

North American Industrial Classification System (NAICS)

Back in the 1930s, the U.S. government set up a uniform system for subdividing the business marketplace into detailed market segments. The Standard Industrial Classification (SIC) system standardized efforts to collect and report information on U.S. industrial activity.

The SIC codes divided firms into broad industry categories: agriculture, forestry, and fishing; mining and construction; manufacturing; transportation, communication, electric, gas, and sanitary services; wholesale trade; retail trade; finance, insurance, and real-estate services; public administration; and nonclassifiable establishments. The scheme then assigned each major category within these classifications its own two-digit number. Three-digit and four-digit numbers further subdivided each industry into smaller segments.

For some 60 years, B2B marketers used SIC codes as a tool for segmenting markets and identifying new customers. The system, however, became outdated with implementation of the North American Free Trade Agreement (NAFTA). Each of NAFTA's three participants—the United States, Canada, and Mexico—had its own system for measuring business activity. The new North American Free Trade Area required a joint classification system that would allow marketers to compare business sectors among the member nations.

As a result of this statistical need, the **North American Industrial Classification System** (NAICS) was created. This new uniform reporting system provided more detail than was available with SIC. NAICS created new service sectors to better reflect the economy of the year 2000 and beyond. The new NAICS sectors are information; health care and social assistance; and professional, scientific, and technical services.

Table 10.2 demonstrates the more detailed NAICS system for software. NAICS uses six digits, compared to the four digits used in the SIC. The first five digits are fixed among the members of NAFTA. The sixth digit can vary among U.S., Canadian, and Mexican data. In short, the sixth digit accounts for specific data needs of the member nation.

The NAFTA nations agreed to update NAICS every five years. The first NAICS statistics were released in 1999. Business marketers now have a segmentation tool that can cross national borders.[8]

FIGURE 10.2 Using Demographic Segmentation in Business Markets

Segmentation by End-Use Application

A third basis for segmentation, **end-use application segmentation,** focuses on the precise way in which a business purchaser will use a product. For example, a printing equipment manufacturer may serve markets ranging from a local utility to a bicycle manufacturer to the U.S. Department of Defense. Each end use of the equipment may dictate unique specifications for performance, design, and price. Praxair, a supplier of industrial gases, for example, might segment its markets according to user. Steel and glass manufacturers might buy hydrogen and oxygen, while food and beverage manufacturers need carbon dioxide. Praxair also sells krypton, a rare gas, to companies that produce lasers, lighting, and thermal windows. Many small- and medium-sized companies also segment markets according to end-use application. Instead of competing in markets dominated by large firms, they concentrate on specific end-use market segments.

praxair.com

Segmentation by Purchasing Situation

Yet another approach to dividing business markets centers on the *purchasing*

MARKETING DICTIONARY

customer-based segmentation Dividing a business-to-business market into homogeneous groups based on buyers' product specifications.

North American Industrial Classification System (NAICS) A classification used by NAFTA countries to categorize the business marketplace into detailed market segments. NAICS replaced the Standard Industrial Classification (SIC).

end-use application segmentation Segmenting a business-to-business market based on how industrial purchasers will use the product.

TABLE 10.2		An Example of the NAICS Hierarchy

NAICS LEVEL	NAICS CODE	DESCRIPTION
Sector	31-33	Manufacturing
Subsector	334	Computer and electronic product manufacturing
Industry group	3346	Manufacturing and reproduction of magnetic and optical media
Industry	33461	Manufacturing and reproduction of magnetic and optical media
U.S. Industry	334611	Reproduction of software

Source: Reprinted from www.census.gov/eped/www.naics, downloaded September 22, 1999.

ibm.com

situation. As a later section of the chapter explains, organizations use purchasing procedures more complicated than those of consumers. Firms also structure their purchasing functions in specific ways, and for some business marketers, this may be the best way to segment the market. Some companies designate centralized purchasing departments to serve the entire firm, while others allow each unit to handle its own buying. A supplier may deal with one purchasing agent or several decision makers at various levels. Each of these structures results in different buying behavior.

When the buying situation is important to marketers, they typically consider whether the customer has made previous purchases or if this is the customer's first order. For example, IBM's Integrated Systems Solutions Corp. subsidiary might use a different marketing approach to sell to Lucent Technologies, an existing customer of its computer support services, than to a potential new customer who is unfamiliar with its offerings.

CHARACTERISTICS OF THE B2B MARKET

3

Identify the major characteristics of the business market and its demand.

Businesses that serve both B2B and consumer markets must understand the needs of their customers. However, several characteristics distinguish the business market from the consumer market: (1) geographic concentration, (2) the sizes and numbers of buyers, (3) purchase decision procedures, and (4) buyer-seller relationships. The next few sections will consider how these traits influence business-to-business marketing.

Geographic Market Concentration

As noted in the previous section, the U.S. business market is more geographically concentrated than the consumer market. Manufacturers concentrate in certain regions of the country, making these areas prime targets for business marketers. For example, the Midwestern states that make up the East North Central region—Illinois, Ohio, Wisconsin, Indiana, and Michigan—lead the nation in industrial concentration, followed by the Middle Atlantic and the South Atlantic regions.

Certain industries locate in particular areas to be close to customers. In the automobile industry, for example, suppliers of components and assemblies frequently build plants close to their customers. As the Dana Corp. ad in Figure 10.3 states, being close to customers can help them to reduce inventory and investment costs and can help them bring products to market more quickly. Others establish facilities near power sources (chemical plants near Niagara Falls), populations of skilled workers (high-tech firms in California's Silicon Valley), or concentrations of lower-paid labor (factories along the U.S.-Mexican border that employ Mexican workers).

FIGURE 10.3	Locating Close to Customers

As Internet-based technology continues to improve, allowing companies to transact business even with distant suppliers, business markets may become less geographically concentrated. However, at present, identifying geographical concentrations of customers enables business marketers to allocate resources effectively. Firms may choose to locate sales offices and distribution centers in these areas to provide more attentive service.[9]

Sizes and Numbers of Buyers

In addition to geographic concentration, the business market features a limited number of buyers. Marketers can draw on a wealth of statistical information to estimate the sizes and characteristics of business markets. The federal government is the largest single source of such statistics. Every five years it conducts both a Census of Manufacturers and a Census of Retailing and Wholesaling, which provide detailed information on business establishments, output, and employment. Many government units and trade organizations also operate Web sites that contain helpful information.

Many buyers in limited-buyer markets are large organizations. The international market for jet engines is dominated by three manufacturers: United Technology's Pratt & Whitney unit, General Electric, and Rolls-Royce. These firms sell engines to Boeing and the European consortium, Airbus Industrie. These aircraft manufacturers compete for business from passenger airlines like American Airlines, British Airways, KLM, and Singapore Airlines, along with cargo carriers such as Federal Express and United Parcel Service.

Trade associations and business publications provide additional information on the business market. Private firms such as Dun & Bradstreet publish detailed reports on individual companies. This data serves as a useful starting point for analyzing a business market. Finding data in such a source requires an understanding of the NAICS, which identifies much of the available statistical information.

dnb.com

The Purchase Decision Process

To market effectively to other organizations, businesses must understand the dynamics of the organizational purchase process. Suppliers who serve business-to-business markets must work with multiple buyers, especially when selling to larger customers. Decision makers at several levels may influence final orders, and the overall process is more formal and professional than the consumer purchasing process. Purchases typically require a longer time frame because B2B involves more complex decisions. Suppliers must evaluate customer needs and develop proposals that

Intergram Fails to Connect Overseas

BACKGROUND Differences in pricing and regulations in foreign markets can spell doom to companies trying to establish themselves in business-to-business markets overseas. Intergram Corp., a new Internet telecommunications company, was counting on making major connections in Europe and South America by hooking up corporate communicators like Lufthansa and Disney Argentina with its system.

THE MARKETING PROBLEM Intergram executives, including CEO George Schad and CFO Philip Varley, thought they could nab a share of the foreign telecommunications market by offering low prices. Historically, prices on both continents had run very high. So engineers were dispatched around the world to set up the system while marketers approached firms to sign them up for cheap, fast communications. One way Intergram promised to save organizations money was through its paperless fax system, a program that customers could download for free, then use the Internet and Intergram's global network to send digital-quality paperless faxes. But success of the entire system depended on foreign phone rates remaining high.

THE OUTCOME Before Intergram could even open for business overseas, European phone rates began to plunge. Europe's previously tightly regulated telephone industry started to relax, and prices dropped even farther.

continued on next page

meet technical requirements and specifications. Also, buyers need time to analyze competing proposals. Often, decisions require more than one round of bidding and negotiation, especially for complicated purchases.

The prize for the most complex purchase decision process may belong to the U.S. Pentagon, which has been known to take 13 years to analyze proposals from suppliers and to reach a decision. The Department of Defense often creates new specifications for every purchase, no matter how minor. During the Persian Gulf War, for example, military engineers drafted pages of specifications that instructed suppliers on the correct ways to mow lawns at Army bases (grass no taller than one-quarter inch) and ways to bake chocolate chip cookies for the troops (at least two chips per cookie).[10]

Buyer-Seller Relationships

An especially important characteristic of B2B marketing is the relationship between buyers and sellers. Such relationships are more intense than consumer relationships, and they require better communication among the organizations' personnel.

As Chapter 5 explains, *relationship marketing* involves developing long-term, value-added customer relationships. A primary goal of business-to-business relationships is to provide advantages that no other seller can provide—for instance, lower price, quicker delivery, better quality and reliability, customized product features, or more favorable financing terms. For the business marketer, providing these advantages means expanding the company's external relationships to include suppliers, distributors, and other organizational partners. For example, John Deere has built strong relationships with its worldwide network of 5,000 dealerships that sell the company's agricultural products to farmers. Deere recently created a new distribution system that electronically connects the dealers' sales reports to a centralized warehouse that replenishes products as the dealers need them. Deere emphasizes the importance of relationships with its business partners and their customers in ads like the one in Figure 10.4.

Close cooperation, whether through informal contacts or under terms specified in contractual partnerships and strategic alliances, enables companies to meet buyers' needs for quality products and customer service. This holds true both during and after the purchase process.[11]

Evaluating International Business Markets

Business purchasing patterns differ from one country to the next. Researching these markets poses a particular problem for B2B marketers. Of course, as explained earlier, NAICS is correcting this problem in the NAFTA countries.

In addition to quantitative data such as the size of the potential market, companies must also carefully weigh its qualitative features. This involves considering cultural values, work styles, and generally the best ways to enter overseas markets. For example, Dell Computer Corp. sells its computers to U.S. companies through telemarketing, mail order, and the Internet, since American purchasers are comfortable buying computers without looking at them first. However, when Dell entered the Chinese market, it found that Chinese businesspeople were reluctant to buy computers sight unseen. Dell decided to supplement its telemarketing operations by opening sales centers in nine metropolitan areas in China, where Chinese customers could examine the merchandise before placing orders. Dell also organized a factory in Xiamen, employed a Chinese-speaking technical support staff for its toll-free phone lines, and created a Web sales site in both the Chinese and English languages.[12]

In today's international marketplace, companies often practice **global sourcing,** which involves contracting to purchase goods and services from suppliers worldwide. This practice can result in substantial cost savings. FedEx, for example, estimates that it saves over 30 percent on the prices of computer hardware and software by soliciting bids worldwide.

However, global sourcing requires companies to adopt a new mind-set; some must actually reorganize their operations. Customers with multiple multinational locations should streamline

FIGURE 10.4 Stressing the Importance of Business Relationships

"We were trying to squeeze through a closing window," recalls George Schad. Within six months, Intergram was forced to shut down its European offices. Although rates remained high in Buenos Aires, they were not high enough to keep Intergram afloat, and the company was forced to file for bankruptcy.

LESSONS LEARNED "Everyone knew prices were going to come down," claims Keith Mallinson, managing director of the Yankee Group Europe, a telecommunications consulting firm. "But it would have been hard to know by just how much." Intergram took a huge risk by counting on marketing its services based solely on price in an environment that could shift based on government regulations. Even when it became apparent that the project was in trouble, local managers continued to chew up more than $2.5 million in operating expenses a month. Varley admits, "We had not done a good enough job policing" operations on a local level. So Intergram found itself dug deep into a hole that it couldn't climb out of, no matter how good the connections could have been.

the purchase process and minimize price differences due to labor costs, tariffs, taxes, and currency fluctuations.[13]

BUSINESS MARKET DEMAND

The previous section's discussion of business market characteristics demonstrated considerable differences between marketing techniques for consumer and business products. Demand characteristics also differ in these markets. In business markets, the major categories of demand include derived demand, volatile demand, joint demand, and demand created by inventory adjustments.

Derived Demand

The term **derived demand** refers to the linkage between consumer demand for a company's output and its purchases of business products such as machinery, components, supplies, and raw materials. For example, demand for microprocessor chips within a computer's central processing unit is derived from the demand for personal computers from both business and individual consumers. Slowdowns in sales of personal computers have reduced demand for these chips.[14] Intel, for example, which makes microprocessors for several different market segments, is affected by derived demand.

FIGURE 10.5 Microprocessors: An Example of Derived Demand

intel.com

While the demand for Intel's microprocessor for entry-level PCs has weakened, the demand for its Pentium II brand, promoted in the ad in Figure 10.5, has increased because it is the chip used in the growing market segment of servers and workstations. At the same time, demand for so-called embedded chips—microprocessors built into other consumer devices ranging from rice cookers to automobiles—has risen dramatically. For every personal computer shipped, companies ship approximately 30 toasters, pagers, watches, and other items that rely on built-in chips. So, while derived demand for computer chips is falling, derived demand for embedded chips is at an all-time high.[15]

Organizational buyers purchase two general categories of business products: capital items and expense items. Derived demand ultimately affects both. *Capital items* are long-lived business assets that must be depreciated over time. (Depreciation is the accounting act of charging a portion of a capital item's cost as a deduction against the company's annual revenue for purposes of determining its net income.) Examples of capital items include major installations such as new plants, office buildings, and computer systems.

Expense items, in contrast, are inputs consumed by the production process within short time periods. Accounting procedures usually charge the cost of such products against income in the year of purchase. Examples of expense items include the supplies necessary to operate the business, ranging from paper clips to machine lubricants.

Joint Demand

Another important influence on business market demand is **joint demand,** which results when the demand for one business product is related to the demand for another business product that is necessary for the use of the first item. For example, both coke and iron ore are required to make pig iron. If the coke supply falls, the drop in pig iron production will immediately affect the demand for iron ore.

Another example is the joint demand for electrical power and large turbine engines. If consumers decide to conserve power, demand for new power plants drops, as does the demand for components and replacement parts for turbines.

Volatile Demand

Derived demand creates immense volatility in business market demand. As an example, assume that gas stations derive demand for a certain type of gasoline pump from consumers' demand for a brand whose gallon volume has been growing at an annual rate of 5 percent. Now suppose that the demand for this gasoline brand slows to a 3 percent annual increase. While not a dramatic drop, this slowdown might convince the gasoline retailers to keep its current gasoline pumps and replace them only when market conditions improve. In this way, even modest shifts in consumer demand for gasoline would greatly affect the pump manufacturer. This disproportionate impact of changes in consumer demand on business market demand is referred to as the *accelerator principle*.

Inventory Adjustments

Adjustments in inventory and inventory policies can also affect business demand. Assume that manufacturers in a particular industry consider a 60-day supply of raw materials to be the optimal inventory level. Now suppose that economic conditions or other factors induce these firms to increase their inventories to a 90-day supply. The change will bombard the raw-materials supplier with new orders.

Further, innovative *just-in-time (JIT)* inventory policies seek to boost efficiency by cutting inventories to absolute minimum levels and by requiring vendors to deliver inputs as the production process needs them. JIT allows companies to better predict which supplies they will require and the timing for when they will need them, markedly reducing their costs for production and storage.[16] Widespread JIT practices have produced a substantial impact on organizations' purchasing behavior. Firms that practice JIT tend to order from relatively few suppliers. In some cases, JIT may lead to **sole sourcing** for some inputs—that is, the practice of buying a firm's entire stock of a product from just one supplier. *Electronic data interchange (EDI)* and quick-response inventory policies have produced similar results in the trade industries.

The latest inventory trend, *JIT II*, leads suppliers to place representatives at the customer's facility to work as part of an integrated, on-site customer-supplier team. Suppliers plan and order in consultation with the customer. This streamlining of the inventory process improves control of the flow of goods.

THE MAKE, BUY, OR LEASE DECISION

Before a company can decide what to buy, it should decide whether to buy at all. The first step in organizational buying requires purchasers to figure out the best way to acquire needed products. In fact, a firm considering the acquisition of a finished good, component part, or service has three basic options:

1. Make the good or provide the service in-house.
2. Purchase it from another organization.
3. Lease it from another organization.

Manufacturing the product itself, if the company has the capability to do so,

4

Describe the major influences on business buying behavior.

MARKETING   DICTIONARY

joint demand Demand for a business product that depends on the demand for another business product that is necessary for the use of the first.

sole sourcing Purchasing a firm's entire stock of a product from just one vendor.

may be the best route. It may save a great deal of money if its own manufacturing division does not incur costs for overhead that an outside buyer would otherwise charge.

On the other hand, most firms cannot make all of the business goods they need. Often, they would simply have to spend too much to maintain the necessary equipment, staff, and supplies. Therefore, purchasing from an outside vendor is the most common choice. Companies can also look outside their own plants for goods and services that they formerly produced in-house, a practice called *outsourcing* that the next section will describe in more detail.

In some cases, however, a company may choose to lease inputs. This option spreads out costs as compared to lump-sum costs for up-front purchases. The company pays for the use of equipment for a certain time period. For example, a small business may lease a copy machine for a few years, making monthly payments. At the end of the lease term, the firm can buy the machine at a prearranged cost or replace it with a different model under a new lease. This option can provide useful flexibility for a growing business, allowing it to easily upgrade as its needs change.

Companies can also lease sophisticated computer systems and heavy equipment. For example, some airlines prefer to lease airplanes rather than buy them outright because short-term leases allow them to adapt quickly to changes in passenger demand.

The Rise of Outsourcing

Citibank depends on a huge, sophisticated computer network to help service corporate clients around the world. However, Citibank does not manage the network itself. Instead, it hires AT&T Solutions to integrate hardware, software, and regional networks into a global system that functions around the clock. This arrangement frees Citibank to concentrate on what it does best—providing banking services—as it subcontracts technology management to an outside company with expertise in that area.[17]

Welcome to the world of **outsourcing,** the practice of turning to outside vendors for goods and services formerly produced in-house. In their rush to improve efficiency, firms look outside for just about everything from mailroom management, customer service, human resources, and accounting, to information technology, manufacturing, and distribution.

About 60 percent of all outsourcing is done by North American–based companies. However, the practice is rapidly becoming more popular in Asia and Europe; European firms' expenditures for outsourcing are growing by an impressive 34 percent annually.

Why Outsource?

Why do firms outsource? Businesspeople once considered outside purchases of component parts or technology services to be signs of weakness—particularly for a major corporation. Now, they look favorably on opportunities to deal with cost-effective outside suppliers. Other reasons go beyond cost control. Outsourcing allows companies to obtain specialized technological expertise. Like Citibank, many organizations decide to outsource their information technology functions.[18] Dun & Bradstreet is one such company that offers services for other organizations, including a credit and collection outsourcing service. In the ad in Figure 10.6, the company describes how customers benefit from Dun & Bradstreet's database of nearly 50 million companies worldwide in increasing productivity and lowering risk.

Outsourcing can be a smart strategy if a company chooses a vendor that can provide high-quality products and perhaps at a lower cost than could be achieved on the company's own. This priority allows the outsourcer to focus on its core competencies. Successful outsourcing

FIGURE 10.6 | **An Outsourcing Service for Reducing Risk and Increasing Productivity**

requires that companies carefully oversee contracts and manage relationships. Some vendor companies now provide performance guarantees to assure their customers that they will receive high-quality service that meet their needs.

Problems with Outsourcing

Outsourcing is not without its downside, however. Many companies discover that their cost savings average closer to 10 percent than the 20 to 40 percent that vendors promise. Also, companies may sign multiyear contracts that no longer compare well with market conditions after a year or two. Another problem with outsourcing production of proprietary technology concerns internal security.

Suppliers who fail to deliver goods promptly or provide required services can adversely affect a company's reputation with its customers. General Electric had to delay the introduction of a new washing machine because of a contractor's production problems. Southern Pacific Rail had problems with an outsourced computer network.

Outsourcing is a controversial topic with unions, especially in the auto industry, as the percentage of component parts made in-house has steadily dropped. Outsourcing can create conflicts between nonunion outside workers and in-house union employees, who fear job loss from outsourcing. Management initiatives to outsource jobs can lead to strikes and plant shutdowns.

A major danger of outsourcing is the risk of losing touch with customers. Outsourcing can reduce a company's ability to respond quickly to the marketplace or slow efforts in bringing new products to market. Some consultants believe that firms can take outsourcing too far; they advise keeping such important departments as customer service in-house. Another concern is the possible decline in work culture and company pride because outsourcing fragments responsibilities.

THE BUSINESS BUYING PROCESS

Suppose that CableBox Inc., a hypothetical manufacturer of cable television decoder boxes, decides to upgrade its manufacturing facility with $1 million in new automated assembly equipment. Before approaching equipment suppliers, the company must analyze its needs, determine goals that the project should accomplish, develop technical specifications for the equipment, and set a budget. Once it receives vendors' proposals, it must evaluate them and select the best one. But what does *best* mean in this context? The lowest price or the best warranty and service contract? Who in the company is responsible for such decisions?

Clearly, the business buying process is more complex than the consumer decision process described in Chapter 9. Business buying takes place within a formal organization's budget, cost, and profit considerations. Furthermore, B2B and institutional buying decisions usually involve many people with complex interactions among individuals and organizational goals. To understand organizational buying behavior, business marketers require knowledge of influences on the purchase decision process, the stages in the organizational buying model, types of business buying situations, and techniques for purchase decision analysis.

Influences on Purchase Decisions

Organizational buying decisions react to various influences, some external to the firm and others related to internal structure and personnel. In addition to product specific factors such as purchase price, installation, operating and maintenance costs, and vendor service, companies must also consider broader environmental, organizational, and interpersonal influences.

FreeMarkets Captures Companies' Buying Centers

BACKGROUND Glen Meakem understands the way Internet buying and selling works. He also understands the importance of buying centers in business purchasing decisions. His company, FreeMarkets Online, helps businesses make complex buying decisions by prescreening suppliers and then conducting an online "reverse" auction, in which suppliers make successively lower bids until the auction ends at the lowest bid, resulting in a contract. When the deal is closed, FreeMarkets collects service fees from the buyer and a sales commission from the seller.

THE CHALLENGE To make the reverse auctions work, Meakem and his partner, Sam Kinney, needed to be able to identify the participants within each customer's buying center. Meakem noted that the buyers and deciders didn't always necessarily know enough about potential vendors to make complex purchasing decisions, so he looked for ways to help them. If he did his job well, everyone would make money—customers, suppliers, and FreeMarkets.

continued on next page

grainger.com

Environmental Factors

Environmental conditions such as economic, political, regulatory, competitive, and technological considerations influence B2B buying decisions. For example, CableBox may wish to defer purchases of the new equipment in times of slowing economic activity. During a recession, sales to cable companies might drop because households hesitate to spend money on cable service. The company would look at the derived demand for its products, possible changes in its sources of materials, employment trends, and similar factors before committing to such a large capital expenditure.

Political, regulatory, and competitive factors also come into play in influencing purchase decisions. For example, passage of a law freezing cable rates would affect demand, as would an introduction of a less expensive decoder box by a competitor. Finally, technology plays a role in purchase decisions. For example, cable-ready televisions decreased demand for set-top boxes, and smaller, more powerful satellite dishes have cut into the market for cable TV, reducing derived demand. CableBox can benefit from technological advances, too. As more homes want fast Internet connections, adding cable modems to its product line may present a growth opportunity.

Organizational Factors

Successful business-to-business marketers understand their customers' organizational structures, policies, and purchasing systems. A company with a centralized procurement function operates differently than one that delegates purchasing decisions to divisional or geographic units. Trying to sell to the local store when head office personnel make all the decisions would clearly waste salespeople's time. Buying behavior also differs between firms. For example, centralized buyers tend to emphasize long-term relationships, while decentralized buyers often focus more on short-term results. Personal selling skills and user preferences carry more weight in decentralized purchasing situations than in centralized buying.

How many suppliers should a company patronize? Because purchasing operations spend over half of each dollar their companies earn, consolidating vendor relationships can lead to large cost savings. Grainger, for example, encourages organizations to use the company's catalog and new online service to purchase maintenance, repair, and operating supplies. Grainger's ad in Figure 10.7 promotes the company as a single source that gives customers fast service in purchasing thousands of brand-name products. However, a fine line separates maximizing buying power from relying too heavily on a few suppliers.

Some organizations engage in **multiple sourcing**—purchasing from several vendors. Spreading orders ensures against shortages if one vendor cannot deliver on schedule. However, dealing with many vendors can be counterproductive and take too much time. Each company sets its own criteria for this decision.

Interpersonal Influences

Many people may influence B2B purchases, and considerable time may be spent obtaining the input and approval of various other organization members. Both group and individual forces are at work here. When committees handle buying, they must spend time to gain majority or unanimous approval. Also, each individual buyer brings to the decision process her individual preferences, experiences, and particular needs.

Business marketers should know who will influence buying decisions in an organization for their products and should know each of their priorities. To choose a supplier for an industrial press, for example, a purchasing manager and representatives of the company's production, engineering, and quality control departments may jointly decide on a supplier. Each of these principals may have a different point of view that the vendor's marketers must understand.

As a result, sales representatives must be well-versed in the technical features of their products, and they must interact effectively with employees of the various departments involved in the purchase decision. Sales representatives for medical products, for example, are frequent visitors to hospitals and surgery centers, where they discuss their product line with clinical staff and demonstrate new devices.

The Role of the Professional Buyer. Most organizations attempt to make their purchases through systematic procedures employing professional buyers. These technically qualified employees are responsible for securing needed products at the best possible prices. Unlike ultimate consumers, who incorporate periodic buying decisions with other activities, a firm's purchasing department devotes all of its time and effort in determining needs, locating and evaluating alternative suppliers, and making purchase decisions.

Purchase decisions for capital items vary significantly from those for expense items. Firms often buy expense items routinely with little delay. Capital items, however, involve major fund commitments and usually undergo considerable review.

One way in which a firm may attempt to streamline the buying process is through **systems integration,** centralization of the procurement function. One company may designate a lead division to handle all purchasing. Another firm may choose to designate a major supplier as the systems integrator. This vendor then assumes responsibility for dealing with all of the suppliers for a project and for presenting the entire package to the buyer.

A business marketer may set up a sales organization to serve national accounts that deals solely with buyers at geographically concentrated corporate headquarters. A separate field sales organization may serve buyers at regional production facilities.

As noted earlier in the chapter, many corporate buyers now use the Internet to identify supplier sources. They view online catalogs and Web sites to compare vendors' offerings and to obtain product information.

FreeMarkets Online, an Internet-based electronic marketplace, saves business clients both money and time by locating appropriate vendors. CEO Glen Meakem promises customers that his company can improve the quality of

MARKETING DICTIONARY

multiple sourcing Spreading purchases among several vendors.

systems integration Centralization of the procurement function within an internal division or as a service of an external supplier.

FIGURE 10.8   **Online Auction Service for Buyers of Industrial Supplies**

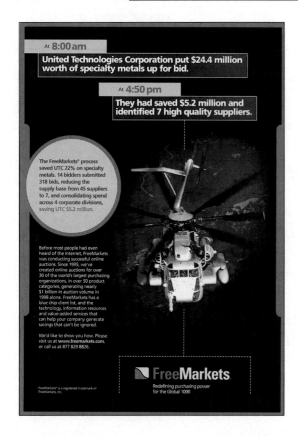

At **8:00am**

United Technologies Corporation put $24.4 million worth of specialty metals up for bid.

At **4:50pm**

They had saved $5.2 million and identified 7 high quality suppliers.

The FreeMarkets® process saved UTC 22% on specialty metals. 14 bidders submitted 318 bids, reducing the supply base from 45 suppliers to 7, and consolidating spend across 4 corporate divisions, saving UTC $5.2 million.

Before most people had even heard of the Internet, FreeMarkets was conducting successful online auctions. Since 1995, we've created online auctions for over 30 of the world's largest purchasing organizations, in over 50 product categories, generating nearly $1 billion in auction volume in 1998 alone. FreeMarkets has a blue chip client list, and the technology, information resources and value-added services that can help your company generate savings that can't be ignored.

We'd like to show you how. Please visit us at www.freemarkets.com, or call us at 877 829 8826.

FreeMarkets
Redefining purchasing power for the Global 1000

FreeMarkets® is a registered trademark of FreeMarkets, Inc.

hunterdirect.com

5

Outline the steps in the organizational buying process.

the goods and services they purchase, while cutting the purchase price by 15 to 20 percent. FreeMarkets works closely with a customer's procurement staff to formulate detailed specifications for industrial parts. Then it researches potential suppliers, assembles a list of qualified applicants, screens their references, and invites them to bid on the contract. Vendors compete for the job in a real-time online auction.[19] The ad in Figure 10.8 describes how FreeMarkets' service saved a customer money as well as finding it quality suppliers.

Model of the Organizational Buying Process

An organizational buying situation requires a sequence of activities similar to the six-step consumer decision model presented in Chapter 9. Figure 10.9 illustrates an eight-stage model of a complex organizational buying process. The additional steps arise because business purchasing introduces new complexities that do not affect consumers. Not every buying situation will follow these precise steps, but this model presents a useful overview of the general process.[20]

Stage 1: Anticipate or Recognize a Problem/Need/Opportunity and a General Solution

Both consumer and business purchase decisions begin when the recognition of problems, needs, or opportunities triggers the buying process. Perhaps a firm's computer system has become outdated or a sales representative demonstrates a new good or service that could improve the company's performance.

Companies may decide to hire an outside marketing specialist when their sales stagnate. This was the case for a large building-products manufacturer, which had traditionally sold its products through a catalog mailed to approximately 45,000 building contractors. When its mail-order business stalled, the purchasing manager interviewed several marketing firms, including Milwaukee-based Hunter Business Direct, to create new ways for the company to increase sales.[21]

Stage 2: Determine the Characteristics and Quantity of a Needed Good or Service

The problem described in Stage 1 translated into a service opportunity for Hunter Business Direct. To stimulate the manufacturer's sales, Hunter executive vice president Mark Peck suggested a database marketing strategy.

Peck quickly assembled a marketing team, consisting of employees from both Hunter and the manufacturer's marketing department, to determine what was needed. The team ranked the manufacturer's customers into 10 groups according to total sales. Peck decided to focus on the top three groups, a total of approximately 1,000 contracting businesses. Customers in the top 10 percent of this group placed an average of 18 orders per year, approximately $20,000 per order; the other 90 percent averaged about six orders per year at $5,500 each.

Stage 3: Describe Characteristics and the Quantity of a Needed Good or Service

After determining the characteristics and quantity of needed products, B2B buyers must translate these ideas into detailed specifications. For his manufacturer client, Peck prepared a detailed proposal that described how Hunter would implement a database marketing program for his client. His goals were to increase the frequency of target customers' orders, the amount they ordered, and the number of repeat purchases they made.

Depending on the type of purchase, a company's technical personnel can play an important role in this early stage of the B2B buying process. For instance, a quality control engineer might establish certain specifications for a product that only a few suppliers could meet. This type of decision could have a big impact on the ultimate evaluation and selection of vendors.

Stages 2 and 3 apply mostly to organizations rather than individual consumers. While consumers may perform these steps, they would use a much more superficial analysis.

Stage 4: Search for and Qualify Potential Sources

Both consumers and businesses search for good suppliers of desired products. The choice of a supplier may be relatively straightforward; the manufacturer's purchasing manager decided within a few days to hire Hunter Business Direct.

Other searches may involve more complex decision making. A company that wants to buy a group life and health insurance policy, for example, must weigh the varying provisions and programs of many different vendors.

Stage 5: Acquire and Analyze Proposals

The next step is to acquire and analyze suppliers' proposals, which are generally submitted in writing. If the buyer is a government or public agency, this stage of the purchase process may involve competitive bidding. During this process, each marketer must develop an appropriate bid, including a price, that will satisfy the criteria determined by the customer's problem, need, or opportunity.[22] While competitive bidding is less common in the business sector, a company may follow the practice to purchase nonstandard materials, complex products, or products that are made to its own specifications.

Stage 6: Evaluate Proposals and Select Suppliers

Next in the buying process, buyers must compare vendors' proposals and choose the one that seems best suited to their needs. Proposals for sophisticated equipment, such as a large computer networking system, can include considerable differences between product offerings, and the final choice may involve tradeoffs.

Price is not the only criterion for the selection of a vendor. Relationship factors like communication and trust may also be important to the buyer. Other issues include reliability, delivery record, time from order to delivery, quality, and order accuracy. As the ad in Figure 10.10 explains, nutritional value was the reason Whole Foods Market selected Bell & Evans as a poultry supplier for its stores in the Southwest. Bell & Evans' chickens do not contain animal by-products or preservatives, which is in keeping with Whole Foods' philosophy of selling natural products.

When The Coca-Cola Company and Pepsi competed to become the exclusive soft drink vendor to Wendy's restaurants, relationship factors tipped the balance in The Coca-Cola Company's favor. As part of the deal, Coca-Cola offered to create a cross-functional team of 50 employees around the country who would work exclusively with the Wendy's account; The Coca-Cola Company also allocated a generous budget to share joint marketing campaigns with its client. Even more valuable was Coca-Cola's willingness to share its marketing research. The soft-drink company has analyzed the demographics and preferences of residents in every zip code in the United States, creating a gold mine of consumer research. It has also done extensive research to measure the effectiveness of

| FIGURE 10.9 | Stages in the B2B Buying Process |

Obtain Feedback and Evaluate Performance	8
Select Order Routine	7
Evaluate Proposals and Select Suppliers	6
Acquire and Analyze Proposals	5
Search for and Qualify Sources	4
Describe Characteristics and Quantity	3
Determine Characteristics and Quantity	2
Recognize Problem and General Solution	1

Source: Based on Michael P. Hutt and Thomas W. Speh, *Business Marketing Management,* Sixth Edition (Fort Worth, TX: The Dryden Press, 1998), pp. 4–71.

| FIGURE 10.10 | Selecting a Supplier |

various marketing materials, such as how different menu board designs influence customers' orders and even shared with Wendy's its expertise on human resource challenges, such as hiring and retaining workers.[23]

Stage 7: Select an Order Routine

Once a supplier has been chosen, buyer and vendor must work out the best way to process future purchases. Ordering routines can vary considerably. Most orders will, however, include product descriptions, quantities, prices, delivery terms, and payment terms. Today, companies have many new order options for submitting order requests through written documents, phone calls, faxes, or electronic messages.

Stage 8: Obtain Feedback and Evaluate Performance

At the final stage, buyers measure vendors' performances. Sometimes this judgment may involve a formal evaluation of each supplier's product quality, delivery performance, prices, technical knowledge, and overall responsiveness to customer needs. At other times, vendors may be measured according to whether they have lowered the customer's costs or reduced its employees' workloads.

In general, large firms are more likely to use formal evaluation procedures, while smaller companies lean toward informal evaluations. Regardless of the method used, buyers should tell suppliers how they are evaluated.

Returning to the example of Hunter Business Direct, evaluation of the database marketing program showed it was highly successful. During the first six months of the program, 380 of the targeted customers purchased supplies from the manufacturer. The number of orders they placed rose by an impressive 112 percent, and the average size of individual orders also increased. Hunter's client spent approximately $50,000 to implement the program but increased its revenues by nearly $3 million.[24]

Classifying Business Buying Situations

6

Classify organizational buying situations.

As discussed earlier in the chapter, business buying behavior responds to many purchasing influences such as environmental, organizational, and interpersonal factors. This buying behavior also involves the degree of effort that the purchase decision demands and the levels within the organization where it is made. Like consumer behavior, marketers can classify organizational buying situations into three general categories, ranging from least to most complex: (1) straight rebuying, (2) modified rebuying, and (3) new-task buying. Business buying situations may also involve reciprocity. The following sections look at each type of purchase by a company like CableBox.

Straight Rebuying

The simplest buying situation is a **straight rebuy,** a recurring purchase decision in which an existing customer places a new order for a familiar product that has performed satisfactorily in the past. This organizational buying situation occurs when a purchaser likes the product and the terms of the sale. Therefore, the purchase requires no new information. The buyer sees little reason to assess other options and so follows a routine repurchase format. A straight rebuy is the business market equivalent of routinized response behavior in the consumer market.

Purchases of low cost items such as paper clips and pencils for an office are typical examples of straight rebuys. If the products and their prices and terms satisfy the organization, it will treat future purchases as straight rebuys from the current vendor. For instance, CableBox probably has an account with an office supply firm that provides prompt service.

A marketer who wants to ensure continuing straight rebuys should concentrate on maintaining a good relationship with the buyer by providing excellent service and delivery performance. Competitors will then find it difficult to present unique sales proposals that would break this chain of repurchases. OfficeMax, for example, encourages straight rebuying by enabling customers to order some 20,000 business supplies from its Web site. Easy ordering and excellent service are promoted in company ads like the one in Figure 10.11.

Modified Rebuying

In a **modified rebuy,** a purchaser is willing to reevaluate available options. The decision makers see some advantage in looking at alternative offerings using established purchasing guidelines. They might take this step if a marketer allows a straight rebuy situation to deteriorate because of poor service or delivery performance. Perceived quality and cost differences can also provoke modified rebuys. Modified rebuys resemble limited problem solving in consumer markets.

Business marketers want to induce current customers to make straight rebuys by responding to all of their needs. Competitors, on the other hand, try to induce buyers to make modified rebuys by raising issues that will convince these buyers to reconsider their decisions. Suppose that CableBox wants to upgrade its computer equipment. In addition to requesting proposals from its current supplier, IBM, the firm will probably investigate competing proposals from other computer manufacturers like Compaq, Dell, and Hewlett-Packard. Each vendor will promote its computers' technological advantages and other unique features.

New-Task Buying

The most complex category of business buying is **new-task buying**—first-time or unique purchase situations that require considerable effort by the decision makers. The consumer market equivalent of new-task buying is extended problem solving. Frito-Lay faced a new-task buying situation in building a plant to produce its new Wow! snack line. Frito-Lay decision makers chose The Haskell Company as a single-source supplier to design and develop the facility, as described in Figure 10.12.

A new-task buy often requires a purchaser to carefully consider alternative offerings and vendors. For example, a company entering a new field must seek suppliers of component parts that it has never before purchased. If CableBox was to decide to manufacture cable modems, it would have to buy new equipment and component parts. This new-task buying would require several stages, each yielding a decision of some sort. These decisions would include developing product requirements, searching out potential suppliers, and evaluating proposals. Information requirements and decision makers can complete the entire buying process, or they may change from stage to stage.

Reciprocity

Reciprocity—a policy to extend purchasing preference to suppliers that are also customers—is a controversial practice in a number of organizational buying situations. For example, an office equipment manufacturer may favor a particular supplier of component parts if the supplier has recently made a major purchase of the manufacturer's products. Reciprocal arrangements traditionally have been common in industries featuring homogeneous products with similar prices, such as the chemical, paint, petroleum, rubber, and steel industries.

Reverse reciprocity is the practice of extending supply privileges to firms that

FIGURE 10.11   Promoting a Straight Rebuy

Get office supplies without getting off your rear

Just reach for your keyboard and enter OfficeMax.com. You'll find over 20,000 business supplies just a few clicks away. And orders over $50 include free next business day delivery.* But, best of all, with OfficeMax.com, we guarantee you get everyday low prices. See website for details. So, you can get the best deal, quickly. And, instead of running your tail off, you can sit on it.

OfficeMax.com
Your link to getting more done.

*Within trading areas, see website for details.

MARKETING   DICTIONARY

straight rebuy Recurring purchase decision in which a customer repurchases a good or service that has performed satisfactorily in the past.

modified rebuy Purchase decision in which a purchaser is willing to reevaluate available options for repurchasing a good or service.

new-task buying First-time or unique purchase situation that requires considerable effort by the decision makers.

reciprocity Policy to extend purchasing preference to suppliers that are also customers.

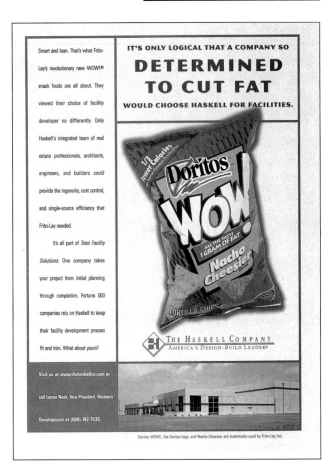
provide needed supplies. In times of shortages, firms occasionally practice reverse reciprocity as they attempt to obtain raw materials and parts to support continuing operations.

Reciprocity suggests close links among participants in the organizational marketplace. It can add to the complexity of organizational buying behavior for new suppliers who are trying to compete with preferred vendors. Although buyers and sellers enter into reciprocal agreements in the United States, both the Justice Department and the Federal Trade Commission view them as attempts to reduce competition.

Outside the United States, however, governments may take more favorable views of reciprocity. Business-to-business buyers in Canada, for instance, see it as a positive, widespread practice. In Japan, close ties between suppliers and customers are common.

Analysis Tools

Two tools that help professional buyers in improving purchase decisions are value analysis and vendor analysis. **Value analysis** examines each component of a purchase in an attempt to either delete the item or replace it with a more cost-effective substitute. For example, airplane designers have long recognized the need to make planes as light as possible. Value analysis supports using DuPont's synthetic material Kevlar in airplane construction because it weighs less than the metals it replaced. The resulting fuel savings are significant for the buyers in this marketplace.

Vendor analysis carries out an ongoing evaluation of a supplier's performance in categories such as price, EDI capability, back orders, delivery times, liability insurance, and attention to special requests. In some cases, vendor analysis is a formal process. Some buyers use a checklist to assess a vendor's performance. A checklist quickly highlights vendors and potential vendors that do not satisfy the purchaser's buying requirements.

THE BUYING CENTER CONCEPT

7

Explain the buying center concept.

dupont.com

The buying center concept provides a vital model for understanding organizational buying behavior. A company's **buying center** encompasses everyone who is involved in all aspects of its buying action. For example, a buying center may include the architect who designs a new research laboratory, the scientist who works in the facility, the purchasing manager who screens contractor proposals, the chief executive officer who makes the final decision, and the vice president for research who signs the formal contracts for the project. Buying center participants in any purchase seek to satisfy personal needs, such as participation or status, as well as organizational needs.

A buying center is not part of a firm's formal organizational structure. It is an informal group whose composition and size varies among purchase situations and firms.

Buying Center Roles

Buying center participants play different roles in the purchasing decision process. *Users* are the people who will actually use the purchased good or service. Their influence on the purchase decision may range from negligible to extremely important. Users sometimes initiate purchase actions by requesting products, and they may also help to develop product specifications. Users, for example, often influence the purchase of office equipment. Steelcase promotes its Turnstone brand of affordable office furniture by featuring different users and by matching these users to different chairs and desks, as shown in the ad in Figure 10.13.

Gatekeepers control the information that all buying center members will review. They may exert this control by distributing printed product data or advertisements or by deciding which salespeople will speak to which individuals in the buying center. For example, a purchasing agent might allow some salespeople to see the engineers responsible for developing specifications but deny others the same privilege.

Influencers affect the buying decision by supplying information to guide evaluation of alternatives or by setting buying specifications. Influencers are typically technical staff such as engineers, quality control specialists, and research-and-development personnel. Sometimes a buying organization hires outside consultants, such as engineers and architects, who influence its buying decisions.

The *decider* actually chooses a good or service, although another person may have the formal authority to do so. The identity of the decider is the most difficult role for salespeople to pinpoint. For example, a firm's buyer may have the formal authority to buy, but the firm's chief executive officer may actually make the buying decision. A decider might be a design engineer who develops specifications that only one vendor can meet.

The *buyer* actually has the formal authority to select a supplier and to implement the procedures for securing the good or service. The buyer often surrenders this power to more influential members of the organization, though. The purchasing manager often fills the buyer's role and executes the administrative functions associated with a purchase order.[25]

B2B marketers face a critical task of determining the specific role and the relative decision-making influence of each buying-center participant. Salespeople can then tailor their presentations and information to the precise role that an individual plays at each step of the purchase process. Business marketers have found that their initial—and, in many cases, most extensive—contacts with a firm's purchasing department often fail to reach the buying-center participants who have the greatest influence, since these people may not work in that department at all.

Consider the selection of meeting and convention sites for trade or professional associations, for example. The primary decision maker could be an association board or an executive committee, usually with input from the executive director or a meeting planner; the meeting planner or association executive might choose meeting locations, sometimes with input from members; finally, the association's annual-meeting committee or program committee might make the meeting location selection. Because officers change annually, centers of control may change from year to year. Therefore, in the example above, destination marketers and hotel operators are constantly assessing how an association makes its decisions on conferences.

FIGURE 10.13 Users: A Buying Center Participant

Marketing to Buying Centers: Strategic Implications

To develop a marketing strategy for a particular buying center, B2B marketers must identify people who play the various roles in a buying center. They must also understand how these members interact with each other, other members of their own organizations, and outside

AGAnet.com

vendors. Marketers must be careful to direct their marketing efforts to their organization, to broader environmental influences, and to *individuals*, who operate within the constraints of the buying center.

Many suppliers find effective support from **team selling**—introducing other associates in addition to salespeople into selling situations—to reach all members of a customer's buying center. Team selling is why AGA Catalog Marketing & Design sends potential customers an extensive questionnaire in which these customers can request follow-up by a senior AGA manager. Thomas Taubes, a direct marketing planner at Avon Products, checked this follow-up box and received a prompt phone call from AGA senior vice president Andy Russell. Taubes was so impressed that he hired AGA to create Avon's holiday catalog.[26]

Team selling may also involve various members of their own supply networks in the sales process. For example, small resellers of specialized computer applications have developed alliances with distributors and major resellers. To sell these technical products to demanding clients, these small resellers need to expand the traditional sales and technical support teams. Clients require higher levels of product knowledge and training in the use of the programs. Because many small resellers cannot handle this component, they form alliances with distributors to provide training. In this way, the vendors get the training they need, and they can then offer it to their clients.

International Buying Centers

Two distinct characteristics differentiate international buying centers from domestic ones. First, marketers may have trouble identifying members of foreign buying centers. In addition to cultural differences in decision-making methods, some foreign companies lack staff personnel. For example, in less developed countries, line managers may make most purchase decisions.

For a second distinction, a buying center in a foreign company may include more participants than U.S. companies involve. International buying centers employ from one to 50 people, with 15 to 20 participants being commonplace. Global B2B marketers must recognize and accommodate this greater diversity of decision makers.

International buying centers can change in response to political and economic trends. Many European firms, for instance, once maintained separate facilities in each European nation where they operated in order to avoid tariffs and customs delays. As the European Community lowered trade barriers between member nations, however, many companies closed distant branches and consolidated their buying centers. The Netherlands has been one of the beneficiaries of this trend.

DEVELOPING EFFECTIVE BUSINESS-TO-BUSINESS MARKETING STRATEGIES

8

Discuss the challenges of marketing to government, institutional, and international buyers.

A business marketer must develop a marketing strategy based on a particular organization's buying behavior and on the buying situation. Clearly, many variables affect organizational purchasing decisions. This section will examine three market segments whose decisions present unique challenges to B2B marketers: units of government, institutions, and international markets. Finally, it will summarize key differences between consumer and business marketing strategies.

Challenges of Government Markets

Government agencies—federal, state, and local—together make up the largest customer in the United States. Over 85,000 government units buy a wide variety of products, including office supplies, furniture, concrete, vehicles, grease, military aircraft, fuel, and lumber, to name just a few.

To compete effectively for these sales, business marketers must understand the unique challenges of selling to government units. One challenge results because government purchases typically involve dozens of interested parties who specify, evaluate, or use the purchased goods and services. These parties may or may not work within the government agency that officially handles a purchase.

For another challenge, government purchases are influenced by social goals, such as minority subcontracting programs. Government entities such as the U.S. Postal Service strive to maintain diversity in their suppliers, often making a special effort to purchase goods and services from small firms and companies owned by minorities and women.[27]

Contractual guidelines create a third important influence in selling to government markets. The government buys products under two basic types of contracts: fixed-price contracts, in which seller and buyer agree to a firm price before finalizing the contract, and cost-reimbursement contracts, in which the government pays the vendor for allowable costs, including profits, incurred during performance of the contract. Each type of contract has advantages and disadvantages for B2B marketers. While the fixed-price contract offers more profit potential than the alternative, it also carries greater risks from unforeseen expenses, price hikes, and changing political and economic conditions.

Government Purchasing Procedures

Many U.S. government purchases go through the General Services Administration (GSA), a central management agency that sets federal policy in such areas as procurement, property management, and information resources management. The GSA buys goods and services for its own use and for use by other government agencies. In its role as, essentially, the federal government's business manager, it purchases billions of dollars worth of goods and services. The Defense Logistics Agency (DLA) serves the same function for the Department of Defense.

By law, most U.S. government purchases must be awarded on the basis of **bids**, or written sales proposals, from vendors. As part of this process, government buyers develop **specifications**—detailed descriptions of needed items—for prospective bidders. Some purchases demand highly complicated specifications; government specifications for athletic supporters, for example, run 22 pages, while the Defense Department imposes 18 pages of specifications for the fruitcakes it buys. Federal purchases must comply with the Federal Acquisition Regulation (FAR), a 30,000-page set of standards originally designed to cut red tape in government purchasing. FAR standards have been further complicated by numerous exceptions issued by various government agencies. Numerous additional restrictions are designed to prevent overspending, corruption, and favoritism.[28]

State and local government purchasing procedures resemble federal procedures. Most states and many large cities have created buying offices similar to the GSA. Detailed specifications and open bidding are common at this level, as well. Many state purchasing regulations typically give preference to in-state bidders. For example, the state of Ohio allows a 5 percent preference to businesses with a presence in that state. The preference increases the price upon which the out-of-state bid is evaluated by 5 percent. (This does not apply to bordering states.)

Government spending patterns may differ from those in private industry. Because the federal government's fiscal year runs from October 1 through September 30, many agencies spend much of their procurement budgets in the fourth quarter (July 1 to September 30). They hoard their funds to cover unexpected expenditures, and if they encounter no such problems, they find themselves with money to spend in late summer. Companies understand this system and keep their eyes on government bulletins, so they can bid on the listed agency purchases, which often involve large amounts of money.

Online with the Federal Government

Like their colleagues in the private sector, government procurement professionals are streamlining purchasing procedures with new technology. Rather than paging through piles of paper catalogs and submitting handwritten purchase orders, government buyers now prefer online catalogs that help them to compare competing product offerings. In fact, vendors find business with the government almost impossible unless they embrace electronic commerce.

gsa.gov

Vendors can sell products to the federal government through three electronic options. Web sites provide a convenient method of exchanging information for both parties. Government buyers locate and order products, paying by a federally issued credit card, and the vendors deliver the items within about a week. Another route is through government-sponsored electronic ordering systems, which help to standardize the buying process. GSA Advantage, shown in Figure 10.14, and the National Institutes of Health Computer Store are two of the largest such systems. Agencies can search through thousands of products from hundreds of vendors to find the items that meet their needs. The third alternative, *value-added networks (VANs)*, amount to a type of electronic data interchange. However, VANs are losing ground to the Internet, which is becoming the preferred medium for electronic government commerce.

To help businesses and other government agencies benefit from online technologies, the Department of Commerce works with the National Institute of Standards and Technology to establish standards for electronic purchasing programs. These initiatives promote electronic commerce and related technologies in helping companies improve their competitive positions in global markets.[29]

defenselink.mil

Despite these advances, many government agencies remain less sophisticated than private-sector businesses. The Pentagon, for instance, is still coping with procurement procedures that were developed over the last fifty years. However, it is introducing a streamlined approach to defense contracting that reduces the time necessary to develop specifications and select suppliers. The Department of Defense is spearheading 63 new weapons programs under the new procurement system and plans to spend up to $60 billion annually over the next five years to upgrade its current technology and to purchase new products.[30]

FIGURE 10.14   Government Purchasing Online

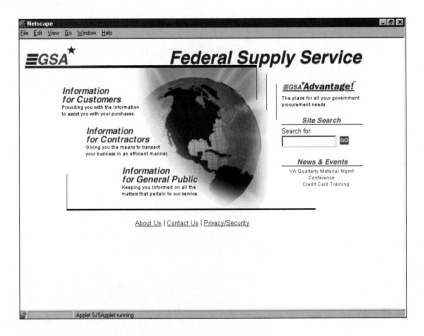

Challenges of Institutional Markets

Institutions constitute another important market. Institutional buyers include a wide variety of organizations, such as schools, hospitals, libraries, foundations, clinics, churches, and not-for-profit agencies.

This variety is reflected in widely diverse buying practices. Some institutional purchasers behave like government purchasers because laws and political considerations determine their buying procedures. Many of these institutions, such as schools and prisons, may even be managed by government units. Other, privately managed institutions may, however, implement buying procedures that resemble those of private companies.

Buying practices can differ even between institutions of the same type. For instance, in a small hospital, the chief dietitian may approve all food purchases, while in a larger hospital, food purchases may go through a committee consisting of the dietitian and a business manager, purchasing agent, and cook. Other hospitals may belong to buying groups, perhaps health maintenance organizations or local hospital cooperatives. Still others may contract with outside firms to prepare and serve all meals.

Within a single institution, multiple-buying influences may affect decisions. Many institutions, staffed by professionals such as physicians, nurses, researchers, and professors, may also employ purchasing managers or even entire purchasing departments. Conflicts may arise among these decision makers. Professional employees may prefer to make their own purchase decisions and resent giving up control to purchasing staff. This conflict can force a business marketer to cultivate both professionals and purchasers. For instance, a sales representative for a pharmaceuticals firm must convince physicians and nurses of the value to patients of a certain drug while simultaneously convincing the hospital's purchasing department that the vendor offers superior prices, delivery schedules, and service.

Group purchasing is an important factor in institutional markets since many institutions join cooperative associations to pool purchases for quantity discounts. Universities may join the Education and Institutional Purchasing Cooperative; hospitals may belong to regional associations; profit-oriented hospitals may obtain inputs through large chains, such as Columbia/HCA Healthcare. Central headquarters staff usually handles purchasing for all members of such a chain.

columbia.net

Diverse practices in institutional markets pose special challenges for B2B marketers. They must maintain flexibility in developing strategies for dealing with a range of customers, from large cooperative associations and chains to medium-sized purchasing departments and institutions to individuals. Buying centers can work with varying members, priorities, and levels of expertise. Discounts and effective distribution functions play important roles in obtaining—and keeping—institutions as customers.

Challenges of International Markets

To sell successfully in international markets, business marketers must consider buyers' attitudes and cultural patterns within areas where they operate. In Asian markets, for example, a firm must maintain a local presence to sell products. Personal relationships are also important to business deals in Asia. Companies that want to expand globally often need to establish joint ventures with local partners.

International marketers must be poised to respond to shifts in cultural values. Consider the island of Taiwan, which has long viewed itself as part of mainland China. Government laws even mandated that advertisers had to use the official language of Beijing, Mandarin, instead of Taiwan's native dialect. However, a recent surge in patriotism among the Taiwanese has made their native culture fashionable. In response, advertisers such as Japan's Kirin Brewery Company quickly developed new ads with Taiwanese songs and dialog. Book sellers are asking their suppliers to locate works on Taiwanese history; music stores are seeking recordings by native artists; and art stores are ordering record numbers of posters featuring Taiwan's former world champion Little League baseball players.[31]

Local industries, economic conditions, geographic characteristics, and legal restrictions must also be considered in international marketing. For instance, many local industries in Spain specialize in food and wine; therefore, a maker of forklift trucks might market smaller vehicles to Spanish companies than to German firms, which require bigger, heavier trucks to serve the needs of that nation's large automobile industry.

Remanufacturing—production to restore worn-out products to like-new condition—can be an important marketing strategy in a nation that cannot afford to buy new products. Developing countries often purchase remanufactured factory machinery, which costs 35 to 60 percent less than new equipment.

Foreign governments represent another important business market. In many countries, the government, government agencies, or state-owned companies dominate certain industries, such as construction and other infrastructure sales. Additional examples include airport and highway construction, telephone system equipment, and computer networking equipment. Sales to a foreign government can involve an array of regulations. For example, many governments, like that of the United States, limit foreign participation in their defense programs. Joint ventures and countertrade are common, as are local-content laws, which mandate local production of a certain percentage of a business product's components.

Strategies for Marketing to Both Business Purchasers and Final Users

Some firms market their goods and services to both consumer and business markets. One example, the J. M. Smucker Company, sells jellies and preserves to consumers and also sells filling mixes to companies that manufacture yogurt and dessert products.

Table 10.3 shows significant differences between B2B and consumer-goods marketing. Firms generally sell less standardized products to organizational buyers than to ultimate consumers, and customer service is extremely important to buying organizations. Advertising plays a much smaller role in the business market than in the consumer market. Business marketers advertise primarily to enhance their company images and the images of their products and to attract new prospects, who are then contacted directly by salespeople. Personal selling plays a much bigger role in business markets than in consumer markets; distribution channels are shorter; customer relations tend to last longer; and purchase decisions can involve multiple decision makers.

In marketing its fruit spreads to consumers, Smucker uses a varied promotional program that includes TV and print advertising, special offers, grocery-store displays, and coupons. The

9

Summarize key differences between consumer and business-to-business marketing.

smucker.com

TABLE 10.3	**Comparing Business-to-Business Marketing and Consumer Marketing**	
	BUSINESS-TO-BUSINESS MARKETING	**CONSUMER MARKETING**
Product	Relatively technical in nature, exact form often variable, accompanying services very important	Standardized form, service important but less than for business products
Price	Competitive bidding for unique items, list prices for standard items	List prices
Promotion	Emphasis on personal selling	Emphasis on advertising
Distribution	Relatively short, direct channels to market	Product passes through a number of intermediate links en route to consumer
Customer relations	Relatively enduring and complex	Comparatively infrequent contact, relationship of relatively short duration
Decision-making process	Diverse group of organization members makes decision	Individual or household unit makes decision

distribution chain includes several intermediaries, leading to infrequent contacts between Smucker employees and retailers.

In contrast, Smucker's marketing to business customers focuses on frequent personal contact. Suppose, for example, that a food company is creating a new dessert with a fruit filling. A Smucker salesperson spends a lot of time with the company's research and product development personnel to determine their preferences and to create detailed specifications for the filling—its taste, color, consistency, and calorie content. The salesperson forwards this information to Smucker's research-and-development department, which then prepares samples.

Meanwhile, the salesperson negotiates a price with the customer's purchasing department. Since the order would specify large quantities, even a few cents per pound can make a big difference. Once these representatives finalize the transaction, the Smucker facility ships the filling directly to the customer's factory. After delivery, the salesperson follows up frequently with the customer's purchasing agent and plant manager to build repeat business.[32]

ACHIEVEMENT CHECK SUMMARY

Read the learning objectives that follow, and consider the questions for each one. Answering these questions will reinforce your grasp of the most important concepts in the chapter and will allow you to check how well you have achieved these learning goals. Where a blank appears before a question, answer with *T* or *F* for true/false questions; for multiple-choice questions, choose the letter of the correct answer.

Objective 10.1: Explain each of the components of the business market.

1. _____ B2B transactions involve large purchases by firms.

2. _____ A purchase by Marriott Corp. of linens for its hotels is an example of a trade industry transaction.

3. _____ Resellers are usually considered part of the commercial market.

Objective 10.2: Describe the major approaches to segmenting business-to-business markets.

1. _____ Size is a way to segment business-to-business markets.

2. _____ NAICS codes help European business marketers to target potential customers in a particular geographic area.

3. _____ Companies that assign different sales forces for existing customers and new customers are segmenting their markets by (a) demographics; (b) end-use application; (c) purchasing situation; (d) customer base.

Objective 10.3: Identify the major characteristics of the business market and its demand.

1. _____ Like the consumer market, business markets are geographically spread out with many small buyers.

2. _____ Business purchasing is typically not characterized by (a) multiple decision makers; (b) use of several vendors for the same product; (c) greater complexity than consumer buying; (d) short purchase time frames.

3. _____ Derived demand refers to the relationship between the demand for jointly used business products.

Objective 10.4: Describe the major influences on business buying behavior.

1. _____ A change in pollution control laws is an example of an organizational influence on buying behavior.

2. _____ Purchasing strategies have a major impact on a company's financial performance because purchased goods and services represent 50 cents of every dollar of its revenue.

Objective 10.5: Outline the steps in the organizational buying process.

1. _____ The organizational buying process starts with a description of the characteristics and quantity of the needed product.

2. _____ Competitive bidding occurs only in government markets.

3. _____ Vendor analysis looks at each component of a purchase to see if the item can be deleted or replaced with a more cost-effective substitute.

Objective 10.6: Classify organizational buying situations.

1. _____ Excellent customer service and product quality are keys to maintaining straight rebuy relationships.

2. _____ A modified rebuy is the equivalent of routinized response behavior in consumer markets.

3. _____ A company that wishes to install its first database system faces a modified rebuy situation.

Objective 10.7: Explain the buying center concept.

1. _____ A buying center is a formal group of people that handles purchasing for a particular department or division.

2. _____ An engineer who provides technical requirements for a new automated manufacturing system is an example of (a) a gatekeeper; (b) an influencer; (c) a user; (d) a buyer.

3. _____ Team selling is a common sales strategy used in dealing with B2B buying center roles.

Objective 10.8: Discuss the challenges of marketing to government, institutional, and international buyers.

1. _____ Businesses that sell to government agencies can limit their dealings to the particular agencies that need their products.

2. _____ Group purchasing is not important in institutional markets.

3. _____ Attitudes and cultural patterns influence global consumer marketing, but they are not critical in international business-to-business markets.

Objective 10.9: Summarize key differences between consumer and business-to-business marketing.

1. _____ B2B markets require stronger customer service than consumer markets demand.

MARKETING | DICTIONARY

remanufacturing Production to restore worn out products to like new condition.

2. _____ Business products move through fewer channels than consumer products.

3. _____ Of the following statements, which does not apply to business marketing? (a) Customer relationships last longer in business markets than in consumer markets. (b) Prices of business products are open to negotiation. (c) Business buyers tend to purchase less standardized products than consumers buy. (d) Advertising is more important than personal selling to business marketing.

Students: See the solutions section located on page S-2 to check your responses to the Achievement Check Summary.

Key Terms

business-to-business marketing	outsourcing
B2B	multiple sourcing
commercial market	systems integration
trade industry	straight rebuy
resellers	modified rebuy
customer-based segmentation	new-task buying
North American Industrial	reciprocity
Classification System (NAICS)	value analysis
end-use application	vendor analysis
segmentation	buying center
global sourcing	team selling
derived demand	bid
joint demand	specifications
sole sourcing	remanufacturing

Review Questions

1. Outline the four components of the business market. Cite examples of each.
2. What are the characteristics of the commercial market? Show how each characteristic affects the marketing strategies of firms serving that market.

3. What are NAICS codes? How do they differ from the former SIC codes?
4. Contrast organizational buying behavior and consumer purchasing behavior. What are the primary differences and similarities?
5. Give examples of the effects on B2B markets of derived demand, volatile demand, joint demand, inventory adjustments, and the accelerator principle.
6. What is outsourcing? Explain the advantages and disadvantages of this practice.
7. Discuss the major influences on organizational purchasing with examples of each.
8. Describe the roles in a buying center. Identify the person in an organization who would most likely play each role. How is team selling used in buying center situations?
9. In what ways is the government market similar to other organizational markets? How does it differ?
10. Describe major characteristics of institutional and international markets. How might these characteristics affect marketing strategy?

Questions for Critical Thinking

1. Research the buying process through which your school purchases needed products. Compare this process to the chapter's discussion of institutional markets.
2. Choose a commercial product and analyze its foreign market potential. Report your findings to the class.
3. Investigate the qualifications needed to be a purchasing manager in an industry located in your area. Discuss these qualifications in class. What general statements can you make?
4. How has the federal government market changed in recent years? How should business marketers deal with these developments?
5. Investigate Canada's Department of Supply and Services. What function does the department perform? What is the comparable agency in the U.S. government?

'net**W**ork

1. **Outsourcing.** Visit one or more of the following Web sites, where you can learn more about outsourcing. Record three facts from your research that you can contribute during a class discussion on this topic.

www.outsourcing-journal.com
www.outsourcing.com
www.outsourcing-suppliers.com
www.outsourcing-jobs.com

2. **Stages in the B2B Buying Process.** In this exercise, you will visit a widely-used Web site that helps organizations at several stages of the B2B buying process outlined in Figure 10.9. Go to www.thomasregister.com. If you're involved in some aspect of purchasing at an organization where you work, you can sign up for free membership at this site. If you're unable to register, you'll be denied access to submit search requests but will still be able to complete this exercise. Find answers to the following questions:

- How many companies are in the Thomas Register database?
- Does the Thomas Register include only U.S.–based companies?
- How many brand names are in the Thomas Register database?
- Do users have to pay to become a member or to access information?
- How many online catalogs and Web links are available on the Thomas Register?

3. **E-commerce Sites Engaged in B2B Marketing.** Your assignment is to add five new e-commerce sites to Table 10.1 and describe what the companies do. On a separate sheet of paper, list the following five Company Web sites, along with a brief description of what they do.

- Chemdex
- VerticalNet
- Altra Energy Technologies
- Instill
- Commerce One Marketsite.net

chemdex.com

verticalnet.com

altranet.com

instill.com

marketsite.net

thomasregister.com

outsourcing.com

Video Case 10 on UPS begins on page VC-12.

Gateway Continuing Case Part 4 begins on page GC-6.

PART

5

PRODUCT
STRATEGY

325

Gateway Continuing Case Part 5 begins on page GC-8.

Product Strategies

CHAPTER

11

Jeff Bezos Navigates the Mighty Amazon

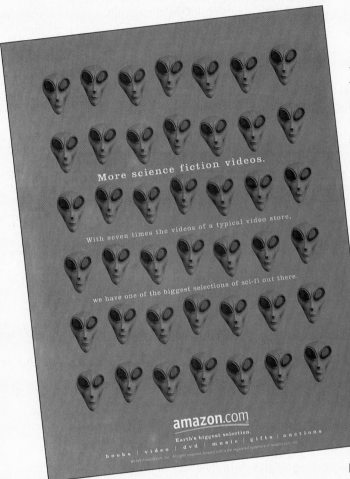

More science fiction videos.

With seven times the videos of a typical video store,

we have one of the biggest selections of sci-fi out there.

amazon.com
Earth's biggest selection.
books | video | dvd | music | gifts | auctions

Just a few years ago, Jeff Bezos had an idea for a new product: selling books online. So he started a company in Seattle that he named Amazon.com, which turned out to be the perfect name for his adventure. Amazon now has nearly as many product lines as the river it is named after has tributaries. Amazon has also become a marketing phenomenon, literally changing the way America shops.

Selling books isn't a new idea, but selling them via the Internet is. Bezos chose books because, he says, he could "create the most value for customers . . . Unless you could create something with a huge value proposition for the customer, it would be easier for them to do it the old way." In other words, consumers could just as easily visit the local bookstore or order books by mail. So Bezos couldn't think of himself simply as a bookseller. He had to sell service, convenience, low prices, selection, and reliable delivery.

To Bezos's advantage, books are comparatively small-ticket items that are bought either on impulse or as small luxuries. They are easy to ship, don't break down or go stale, and won't be returned because they don't fit. The same thing holds true for music and videos, which he soon added to the mix of products, because they complemented the book product line so well. Amazon continually expanded its idea of service, including book searches and customized recommended reading lists for customers. Bezos doesn't like to think of Amazon as an online store. He thinks of the company more broadly, as being engaged in satisfying the wants of customers: "helping people make purchase decisions. It's a new way of looking at retailing," he boasts.

Amazon's success is huge, making Bezos a billionaire in stock holdings and many of his employees millionaires. Amazon has yet to show a profit because earnings are plowed back into expanding the company. So far, stockholders have been content to support its efforts. Amazon claims more than 13 million customers and "has become the default name when you think of buying on the Net," says Keith Benjamin, an Internet analyst with BancAmerica. Because of its reputation for customer service and reliability, consumers recently rated Amazon the 16th most-trusted brand in the United States. Time magazine even named Bezos Person of the Year for 1999. One reason for Amazon's success is that Bezos was the first to sell books online. Another reason is the way he approached marketing his products. "A lot of companies just throw a catalog online and hope people buy stuff in cyberspace," explains Stan Dolberg, software strategies director at Forrester Research. "Amazon really understood the elements that make buying a book rewarding and then tried to address those elements on the Web."

With books, music, and video product lines selling steadily, Bezos decided it was time to expand to include toys, home improvement products, consumer electronics, and software. In addition, Amazon now has equity stakes in other online start-ups, including pets.com, drugstore.com, and Gear.com. Not content to stop there, Bezos expanded even further, setting up zShops, a group of independent vendors who can sell whatever they want—except for pornography, firearms, and certain live animals—at Amazon's site. Some experts worry that this rapid expansion of product lines may be too much, too fast. "No one's

327

sure where all this is going," observes Carrie Johnson, an analyst with Forrester Research. "Initiatives like zShops and Auctions are distracting to the brand." However, even Johnson agrees with Bezos's strategy of reinvesting in new markets, rather than banking profits prematurely. It seems that Bezos wants to grab every online consumer, in every online market, early on the Internet game and turn them into loyal Amazon customers. Industry analysts agree that Amazon has executed its strategy particularly well.

In spite of Amazon's expansion, Bezos continues to think about ways to market his original product line—books. He talks about "customizing the store for the individual, so that the site reconfigures to reflect the things that interest you most. The book finding the reader rather than the reader finding the book." He has plenty of other ideas, as well. In fact, he wants his site to be the place that consumers go to buy anything at all. "Anything," he insists, "with a capital A."[1]

CHAPTER OVERVIEW

Previous chapters have dealt with topics such as marketing research and customer behavior and have covered activities aimed at identifying the firm's target market. Now the attention shifts to the firm's marketing mix.

The next part of this book focuses on the first element of the marketing mix—the products the firm offers to its target market. Planning efforts begin with the choice of goods or services to offer. The other variables of the marketing mix—distribution channels, promotional plans, and pricing discussions—must accommodate the product strategy selected.

Marketers develop programs to promote both goods and services in the same manner. Any such program begins with investigation, analysis, and selection of a particular target market and it continues with the creation of a marketing mix designed to satisfy that segment. But while the designs of tangible goods and intangible services both work to satisfy consumer wants and needs, their marketing efforts diverge significantly in some ways.

This chapter examines both the similarities and the differences in marketing goods and services. It then presents basic concepts—classifications of products, development of product lines, and the product life cycle—that marketers apply in developing successful products. Finally, the chapter discusses product deletion and product mix decisions. ■

WHAT IS A PRODUCT?

1

Explain the broader marketing view of products, and differentiate service offerings from other products.

A narrow definition of the word *product* focuses on the physical or functional characteristics of a good or service. For example, a VCR is a rectangular container of metal and plastic connected via wires to a television set with equipment for recording and replaying video signals on special tapes. But the purchaser has a much broader view of the VCR. Some buyers may want it so they can view soap operas they recorded during their work hours; others may be interested in recording home movies from their camcorders for viewing later; still others may want to rent movies for home viewing.

Marketers must acknowledge this broader conception of product; they must realize that people buy *want satisfaction* rather than objects. For example, most buyers know little about the

FIGURE 11.1 Goods-Services Continuum

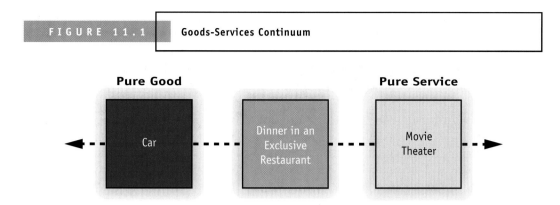

FIGURE 11.1 Goods-Services Continuum

gasoline they buy. In fact, many view it not as a product but as a price they must pay for the privilege of driving their cars.

A broader view of product extends beyond physical or functional attributes. This total product concept includes package design and labeling, symbols such as trademarks and brand names, warranties, and customer-service activities that add value for the customer. Consequently, a **product** is a bundle of physical, service, and symbolic attributes designed to enhance a consumer's want satisfaction.

WHAT IS A SERVICE?

The term *service* covers a wide range of products. A general definition identifies **services** as intangible tasks that satisfy the needs of consumer and business users. Most service providers cannot transport or store their products; customers simultaneously buy and consume these products.

One way to distinguish services from goods employs a product spectrum, or a **goods-services continuum** like that shown in Figure 11.1. This device helps marketers to visualize the differences and similarities between goods and services.[2] A car is a pure good, but the dealer may also offer repair and maintenance services or include the services in the price of a lease. Movie theaters provide pure services, but they also sell goods such as soft drinks and popcorn. The car falls at the pure-good extreme of the continuum because the customer values the repair service less than the car itself, just as movie patrons consider refreshments less important than the entertainment that the theater provides. In the middle range of the continuum, dinner at an exclusive restaurant has equally important good and service components. Customers derive satisfaction not only from the food and beverages but also from services rendered by the establishment's staff.

The discussion so far hints at a diverse market for services. This diversity, which exceeds the diversity of the goods market, results from several characteristics that distinguish services from goods:

1. Services are intangible. Unlike goods, they lack physical features that buyers can see, hear, smell, taste, or touch prior to purchase. Service firms essentially ask their customers to buy a promise.

2. Services are inseparable from the service providers. Consumer perceptions of a service provider become their perceptions of the service itself.

3. Services are perishable. Providers cannot maintain inventories of their services. During times of

peak demand, prices may rise, only to fall drastically when demand declines. For instance, hotels often raise room rates during special events and lower them to normal levels after the end of the events.

4. Companies cannot easily standardize services. For example, Atlanta-based concierge service 2 Places at 1 Time assists busy clients by handling a variety of errands. These tasks range from the standard—picking up dry cleaning—to the specialized—timely delivery of chilled fertility injections from doctors' offices to patients at their jobs.[3]

5. Buyers often play roles in the development and distribution of services. Service transactions frequently require interaction between buyer and seller at the production and distribution stages. For instance, a hair stylist's customer may describe the desired look and make suggestions before, during, and after the styling process.

6. Service quality shows wide variations. Posh Le Cirque in New York and your local Pizza Hut are both restaurants. Their customers, however, experience considerably different cuisine, physical surroundings, service standards, and prices.

Keep in mind that sometimes a product blurs the distinction between services and goods, as when a service provides a good. Consider the retail sector, for example. While all retailers provide services, a further distinction divides them into services retailers and goods retailers. Aaron Rents Furniture offers rentals with options to purchase. It provides both services (rental agreements) and goods (sofas and other furniture) when the buyer eventually takes ownership. Similarly, independent optometrists work in conjunction with Pearle Vision Centers to provide eye examinations (services), while Pearle sells eyeglasses and contact lenses (goods).

Importance of the Service Sector

People would probably live very different lives without service firms to fill many needs. You could not place a telephone call, plug into the Internet, flip a switch for electricity, or even take a college course if organizations did not provide such services. During an average day, you probably use many services without much thought, but these products play an integral role in your life.

The service sector makes a crucial contribution to the U.S. economy. Consider that there are more than one million retail trade establishments in the United States, and they produce almost $2.5 billion annually in sales receipts. While there are fewer finance and insurance service firms—approximately 400,000—their annual sales of over $2.2 billion come close to the retail figure.

Services represent nearly 80 percent of all jobs in the United States. While manufacturing firms employ a total of 17 million Americans, many more work for a service provider. The biggest service employers are retail (14.1 million employees) and health care (13.6 million employees).[4]

Services also play a crucial role in the international competitiveness of U.S. firms. While the United States runs a continuing trade deficit in goods, it has maintained a trade surplus in services for every year since 1970. This trade surplus continues to rise from its current total of roughly $70 billion. Some economists think that more precise measurements of service exports would reveal an even larger surplus.

Observers cite several reasons for the growing economic importance of services, including consumer desire for speed and convenience and technological advances that allow firms to fulfill this demand. For example, online banking services simplify paying bills and balancing your checkbook. NetBank, which exists only on the Internet, allows its customers to pay bills electronically and to check their accounts for free from any computer that offers online access.[5] The E-LOAN ad in Figure 11.2 promotes a convenient online service that allows consumers to quickly compare mortgage loan rates offered by many different lenders.

Most service firms emphasize marketing as a significant activity for two reasons. First, the growth potential of service transactions represents a vast marketing opportunity. Second, increased competition is forcing traditional service industries to emphasize marketing in order to compete in the marketplace.

netbank.com

IMPORTANCE OF QUALITY

Few aspects of product strategy have attracted as much attention during the past two decades as the quality of the firm's output. The result of these efforts to create and market goods and services equal to any in the world has been a movement referred to as **total quality management (TQM)**. It requires all employees in a firm to continually improve products and work processes with the goal of achieving customer satisfaction and world-class performance. In a total quality organization, marketers develop products that people want to buy; engineers design items to work the way customers want to use them; production workers build quality into everything they produce; salespeople deliver what they promise customers; information systems' experts apply technology to ensure that customer orders are filled correctly and on time; financial specialists help to determine prices that give customers value.

The quality movement started in the United States during the 1920s as an attempt to improve product quality by improving the manufacturing process itself. Walter Shewhart, a physicist at AT&T Bell Laboratories, pioneered an innovative approach called *statistical quality control*, which employed statistical techniques to locate and measure quality problems on production lines. Using the principles of statistics and probability, Shewhart developed control charts for detecting variations in the manufacturing process that could generate defective products. By controlling these variations, this innovative method built quality into the production process rather than relying on inspectors to remove defective output at the end of the production line.

W. Edwards Deming, a statistician who worked with Shewhart, helped to popularize Shewhart's quality control methods in the United States and abroad. Deming's 14 Points for Quality Improvement, one of the best-known descriptions of total quality management, offers special advice to marketers seeking to include quality as a key ingredient throughout the organization. Deming encouraged managers to view their organizations as systems that direct the knowledge and skills of all employees toward improving quality. Managers are responsible for communicating the goals of total quality management to all staff members and for encouraging workers to improve themselves and take pride in their work.

Research identifies customer needs and wants. Based on this information, the company designs and redesigns functional, dependable goods and services. It removes defects by steadily reducing process variations. Organizations build relationships of loyalty and trust with suppliers to improve incoming materials and decrease costs. As Deming said, "Better quality and lower prices with a little ingenuity in marketing will create a market."[6] Figure 11.3 shows how quality improvements affect an organization, both internally and externally. To show their appreciation for Deming, the Japanese government created the Deming Prize, which recognizes companies that produce high-quality goods and services. Today it remains Japan's most coveted industrial award.

Worldwide Quality Programs.   During the 1980s, the quality revolution picked up speed in U.S. corporations. The campaign to improve quality found leadership in large manufacturing firms like Ford, Xerox, and Motorola that had lost market share to Japanese competitors. Smaller companies that supplied parts to large firms then began to recognize quality as a requirement for success. Today, a commitment to quality has spread to service industries, not-for-profit organizations, government agencies, and educational institutions.

As part of the national quality improvement campaign, Congress

FIGURE 11.2   Service Technology Satisfies Demand for Speed and Convenience

2

Discuss the roles of top management and employees in implementing total quality management (TQM).

MARKETING   DICTIONARY

total quality management (TQM) Approach that involves all employees in continually improving products and work processes to achieve customer satisfaction and world-class performance.

MARKETING STRATEGY FAILURE

Office Depot Forgets the Staples

BACKGROUND A decade ago, Office Depot was the largest office-supply chain in the world. Most of its sales involved convenience products—staples, both literally and figuratively—to small businesses. Customers could drop into an Office Depot and pick up tape, envelopes, pens, staplers, and staples. But then-president Mark Begelman was worried that if the company didn't grow, by diversifying its product lines and customer base, it would be overtaken by competitors.

THE MARKETING PROBLEM Begelman decided that Office Depot should grow by pursuing large corporations as customers. But he did so by acquiring established companies. He acquired eight independent office-product dealers that were already serving corporate customers in twenty states. He thought this would bring the company instant growth in the new markets: "I figured, how hard could it be?"

continued on next page

europa.eu.net

3

Explain the role benchmarking plays in achieving continuous improvement.

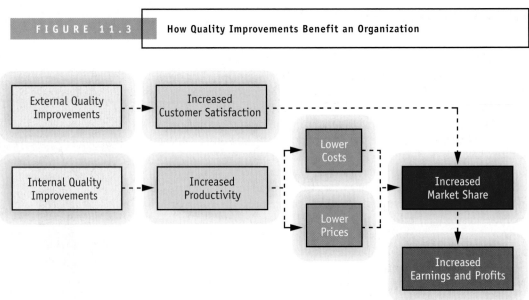

FIGURE 11.3 How Quality Improvements Benefit an Organization

established the Malcolm Baldrige National Quality Award in 1987 to recognize excellence in quality management. Named after late Secretary of Commerce Malcolm Baldrige, the award is the highest national recognition for quality that a U.S. company can receive. The award works toward promoting quality awareness, recognizing quality achievements of U.S. companies, and publicizing successful quality strategies. No more than two awards can be given in each of five categories: manufacturing, service, small business, education, and health care. Thirty-five companies (including one company that has won twice) have earned the award in a wide variety of industries. Applicants for the award must show achievements and improvements in seven areas: leadership, strategic planning, customer and market focus, information and analysis, human resource focus, process management, and results.[7] Recently, Ritz Carlton won in the service category. It was the first time a firm had won a second Baldrige Award in the service category (the first was in 1992)[8].

The quality movement has also spread to European countries. The European Union's **ISO 9002** (formerly ISO 9000), standards define international criteria for quality management and quality assurance. These standards were developed by the International Standards Organization in Switzerland to ensure consistent quality among products manufactured and sold throughout the nations of the European Union (EU).

Many European companies now require suppliers to complete ISO certification as a condition of doing business with them. To become ISO certified, a company must undergo an on-site audit that includes an inspection of the firm's facilities to ensure that documented quality procedures are in place and that all employees understand and follow those procedures. Meeting ISO requirements is an ongoing process, typically covering a 14-month period, during which periodic audits verify conformance. Once granted certification, the firm must frequently ensure that its suppliers are also ISO certified. Clearly, ISO 9002 will soon be a minimum requirement for firms doing business in Europe. Competitors in non-EU countries, concerned over the threats of exclusion from this huge market, have moved quickly to implement ISO 9002 standards.

The Role of Benchmarking

Most quality-conscious marketers rely on an important tool called **benchmarking** to set performance standards. This method for creating a world-class marketing operation seeks to identify how business leaders achieve superior marketing performance levels in their industries and to develop a system for continuously comparing and measuring performance against outstanding performers. The technique involves learning how the world's best goods and services are designed,

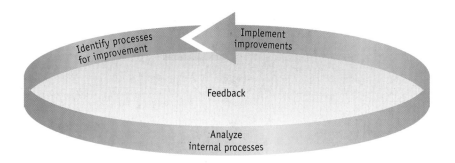

FIGURE 11.4 The Benchmarking Process

Identify processes for improvement

Implement improvements

Feedback

Analyze internal processes

produced, and marketed. The purpose of benchmarking is to achieve superior performance that results in a competitive advantage in the marketplace.

A typical benchmarking process involves three main activities: identifying processes that need improvement, comparing internal processes against similar activities of industry leaders, and implementing changes for better quality. As Figure 11.4 shows, the process continuously repeats itself since vigilant companies continue to search for and identify areas that need improvement, even after implementing changes. This ongoing devotion helps these firms to ensure that they remain market leaders.

Benchmarking requires two types of analyses: internal and external. Before a company can compare itself with another, it must first analyze its own activities to determine strengths and weaknesses. This establishes a baseline for comparison. External analysis involves gathering information about the benchmark partner to find out why the partner is perceived as the best. A comparison of the results of the analysis provides an objective basis for making improvements.

CLASSIFYING GOODS AND SERVICES FOR CONSUMER AND BUSINESS MARKETS

A firm's choices for marketing a good or service depend largely on the offering itself and on the nature of the target market. Product strategies differ for consumer and business markets. As defined in Chapter 9, *consumer products* are those destined for use by ultimate consumers, while *business* or *B2B products* (also called *industrial* or *organizational products*) contribute directly or indirectly to the output of other products for resale. Marketers further subdivide these two major categories into more specific categories.

Types of Consumer Products

Several classification systems divide consumer goods and services in different ways. One basic distinction focuses on the buyer's perception of a need for the product. So-called *unsought products* are marketed to consumers who may not yet recognize any need for them. Examples of unsought products are life insurance and funeral services.

In contrast, most consumers recognize their own needs for various types of consumer purchases. The most common classification scheme divides

MARKETING DICTIONARY

ISO 9002 Set of standards for quality management and quality assurance developed by the International Standards Organization in Switzerland for countries in the European Union

benchmarking Process in which an organization improves performance by continuously comparing and measuring itself against the leading firms in an industry.

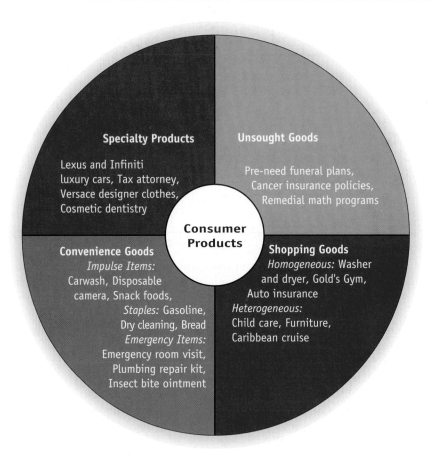

FIGURE 11.5 | Classification of Consumer Products

Specialty Products

Lexus and Infiniti
luxury cars, Tax attorney,
Versace designer clothes,
Cosmetic dentistry

Unsought Goods

Pre-need funeral plans,
Cancer insurance policies,
Remedial math programs

Consumer Products

Convenience Goods
Impulse Items:
Carwash, Disposable
camera, Snack foods,
Staples: Gasoline,
Dry cleaning, Bread
Emergency Items:
Emergency room visit,
Plumbing repair kit,
Insect bite ointment

Shopping Goods
Homogeneous: Washer
and dryer, Gold's Gym,
Auto insurance
Heterogeneous:
Child care, Furniture,
Caribbean cruise

consumer goods and services into three groups: convenience, shopping, and specialty. These categories are based on customers' buying behavior. Figure 11.5 illustrates samples of these three categories, together with the unsought classification.

Convenience Products

4

List the classifications of consumer goods and services, and briefly describe each category.

Convenience products refer to goods and services that consumers want to purchase frequently, immediately, and with minimal effort. Milk, bread, and soft drinks are examples of these products, as are chewing gum, candy, and most vending machine items. Convenience services include 24-hour quick-stop stores, many hair-styling salons, quick-print shops, and dry cleaners.

Marketers further subdivide the convenience category into impulse items, staples, or emergency items:

■ *Impulse items and services* are purchased on the spur of the moment, such as a visit to a car wash or a pack of gum tossed in at the register.

■ *Staples* are convenience goods and services that consumers constantly replenish to maintain a steady stock—for instance, gasoline and dry cleaning.

■ *Emergency items and services* are bought in response to unexpected and urgent needs. An ice scraper purchased during a snowstorm and a visit to a hospital emergency room to treat a sprained ankle are examples.

Since consumers devote little effort to these purchase decisions, marketers must strive to make these exchanges as convenient as possible. Store location can boost a convenience product's visibility. Marketers compete vigorously for prime locations, which can make all the difference between a consumer choosing one gas station, vending machine, or dry cleaner over another.

Shopping Products

In contrast to their purchases of convenience items, consumers buy **shopping products** only after comparing competing offerings on such characteristics as price, quality, style, and color. Shopping products typically cost more than convenience purchases. This category includes tangible items such as clothing, furniture, and appliances and services such as child care, home remodeling, auto repairs, and insurance. The purchaser of a shopping product lacks complete information prior to the buying trip and gathers information during the buying process.

Several important features distinguish shopping products: physical attributes, service attributes (warranties and after-sale service terms), prices, styling, and places of purchase. A store's name and reputation have considerable influence on people's buying behavior. The personal selling efforts of salespeople provide important promotional support.

Buyers and marketers treat some shopping products, such as refrigerators and washing machines, as *homogeneous* products. To the consumer, one brand seems largely the same as another. Marketers may try to differentiate homogeneous products from competing products in several ways. They may emphasize price and value, or they may attempt to educate buyers about less obvious features that contribute to a product's quality, appeal, and uniqueness. To differentiate its refrigerators from those of its competitors, Amana designed a special compartment inside of its refrigerators that keeps milk colder. Amana's ad in Figure 11.6 promotes the new feature by appealing to a household's "designated milk smeller."

Other shopping products seem *heterogeneous* due to essential differences between them. Examples include furniture, physical-fitness training, vacations, and clothing. Differences in features often separate competing heterogeneous shopping products in the minds of consumers. Perceptions of style, color, and fit can all affect consumer choices.

Specialty Products

Specialty products offer unique characteristics that cause buyers to prize those particular brands. They typically carry high prices, and many represent well-known brands. Examples of specialty goods include Gucci handbags, Ritz-Carlton resorts, Tiffany jewelry, and Rolls-Royce automobiles. Specialty services include professional services such as financial, legal, and medical services.

Purchasers of specialty goods and services know just what they want—and they are willing to pay accordingly. These buyers begin shopping with complete information, and they refuse to accept substitutes. Because consumers are willing to exert considerable effort to obtain specialty products, producers can promote them through relatively few retail outlets. Indeed, some intentionally limit the range of outlets that carry their

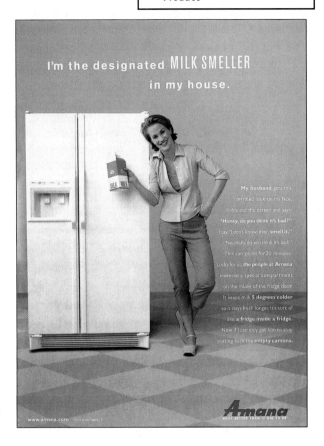

FIGURE 11.6 Differentiating a Homogeneous Shopping Product

I'm the designated MILK SMELLER in my house.

My husband gets this terrified look on his face, holds out the carton and says: "Honey, do you think it's bad?" I say, "I don't know, dear, smell it." "No, really, do you think it's bad?" This can go on for 20 minutes. Lucky for us, the people at Amana invented a special compartment on the inside of the fridge door. It keeps milk 5 degrees colder so it stays fresh longer. It's sort of like a fridge inside a fridge. Now if I can only get him to stop putting back the empty cartons.

www.amana.com

Amana
BUILT BETTER THAN IT HAS TO BE

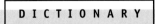

gucci.com

MARKETING DICTIONARY

convenience product Good or service that consumers want to purchase frequently, immediately, and with minimal effort.

shopping product Good or service purchased only after the consumer compares competing offerings from competing vendors on such characteristics as price, quality, style, and color.

specialty product Good or service with unique characteristics that cause the buyer to value it and make a special effort to obtain it.

continued on next page

Big Blue Focuses on Business Customers

BACKGROUND IBM has had its ups and downs. But the company once known exclusively for big mainframe computer installations has not only managed to survive, it has been introducing new innovations designed to help others do business. Currently, Big Blue, as the company is often called, is focused on diversifying its product line, particularly in the area of e-commerce and communications. So, IBM now offers installations as well as accessory equipment and services.

THE CHALLENGE Many of IBM's business customers held off making major computer installation purchases until the new millenium began. Still, the company had to find ways to move ahead with innovative goods and services which businesses were ready to embrace.

THE STRATEGY In addition to developing its own products, IBM entered into alliances with other companies. Big Blue joined forces with Sprint PCS to develop and test wireless business applications for a traveling workforce.

On the e-commerce front, IBM reorganized its software business to serve business customers better. John Thompson, senior vice president and group executive of IBM software explains that his customers "not only need [electronic] commerce systems, but they need to link them to the systems that support people and their applications." Finally, IBM unveiled

products to add to their cachet. For example, Gucci Group sells its $295 loafers, $600 handbags, and $1,600 sport coats through its own exclusive boutiques.[9]

Both highly personalized service by sales associates and image advertising help marketers to promote specialty items. Because these products are available in so few outlets, advertisements frequently list the locations or give toll-free telephone numbers that provide customers with this information.

Applying the Consumer Products Classification System

The three-way classification system of convenience, shopping, and specialty goods and services helps to guide marketers in developing a marketing strategy. Consumer behavior patterns differ for the three types of purchases. For example, classifying a new food item as a convenience product leads to insights about marketing needs in branding, promotion, pricing, and distribution decisions. Table 11.1 summarizes the impact of this classification system on the development of an effective marketing mix.

The classification system, however, also poses problems. The major obstacle in implementing this system results from the suggestion that all goods and services must fit within one of the three categories. Some fit neatly into one category, but others share characteristics of more than one category.

For example, how would you classify the purchase of a new automobile? Before classifying the expensive good, which is sold by brand and handled by a few exclusive dealers in each city as a specialty product, consider other characteristics. Most new car buyers shop extensively among competing models and dealers before deciding on the best deal. Consider a continuum representing degrees of effort expended by consumers. At one end of the continuum, they casually pick up convenience items; at the other end, they search extensively for specialty products. Shopping products fall between these extremes. In addition, car dealers may offer services, both during and after the sale, that play a big role in the purchase decision. On this continuum, the new car purchase might appear between the categories of shopping and specialty products but closer to specialty products.

A second problem with the classification system emerges because consumers differ in their buying patterns. One person may make an emergency visit to the dentist because of a toothache, while another may extensively compare prices and services before selecting a dentist. But one

TABLE 11.1	Marketing Impact of the Consumer Products Classification System

	CONVENIENCE PRODUCTS	SHOPPING PRODUCTS	SPECIALTY PRODUCTS
Consumer Factors			
Planning time involved in purchase	Very little	Considerable	Extensive
Purchase frequency	Frequent	Less frequent	Infrequent
Importance of convenient location	Critical	Important	Unimportant
Comparison of price and quality	Very little	Considerable	Very little
Marketing Mix Factors			
Price	Low	Relatively high	High
Promotion	Advertising and promotion by producer	Personal selling and advertising by both producer and retailer	Personal selling and advertising by both producer and retailer
Distribution channel length	Long	Relatively short	Very short
Number of sales outlets	Many	Few	Very few; often one per market area
Importance of seller's image	Unimportant	Very important	Important

FIGURE 11.7   **Classification of Business Products**

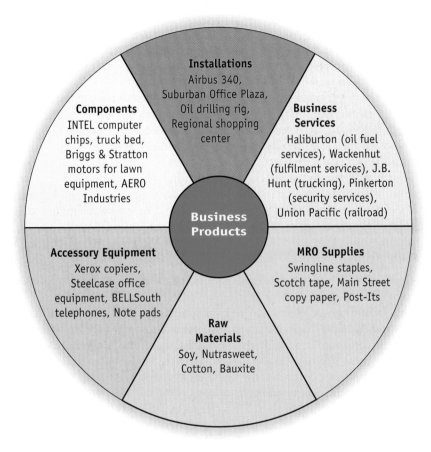

buyer's impulse purchase does not make dental services a convenience item. Marketers classify goods and services by considering the purchase patterns of the majority of buyers.

Types of Business Products

Business buyers are professional customers; their job duties require rational, cost-effective purchase decisions. For instance, General Mills applies much of the same purchase decision process to buy flour that Pillsbury does.

The classification system for business products emphasizes product uses rather than customer buying behavior. Business products generally fall into one of six categories for product uses: installations, accessory equipment, component parts and materials, raw materials, supplies, and business services.[10] Figure 11.7 illustrates the six types of business products.

Installations

The specialty products of the business market are called **installations.** This classification includes major capital investments for new factories and heavy machinery and for telecommunications systems. Purchases of Boeing 737s for Air New Zealand and locomotives for Burlington Northern are considered installations.

Since installations last for long periods of time and their purchases involve

5

Describe each of the types of business goods and services.

MARKETING   DICTIONARY

installation Major capital investment by a business buyer that typically involves expensive and relatively long-lived products, such as a new factory or piece of heavy machinery.

large sums of money, they represent major decisions for organizations. Negotiations often extend over several months and involve numerous decision makers. Vendors often provide technical expertise along with tangible goods. Representatives who sell custom-made equipment work closely with buying firms' engineers and production personnel to design the most satisfactory products possible.

Price typically does not dominate purchase decisions for installations. A purchasing firm buys such a product for its efficiency and performance over its useful life. The firm also wants to minimize breakdowns. Downtime is expensive because the firm must pay employees while they wait for repairs on the machine.

Installations are major investments often designed specifically for the purchasers. Effective operation may also require considerable training of the buyer's workforce along with significant after-sale service. As a result, marketers of these systems typically emphasize highly trained sales representatives, often with technical backgrounds. Advertising, if the firm employs it at all, emphasizes company reputation and directs potential buyers to contact local sales representatives.

Most installations are marketed directly from manufacturers to users. Even a one-time sale may require continuing contacts for regular product servicing. Some manufacturers prefer to lease extremely expensive installations to customers rather than selling the items outright and assign personnel directly to the lessees' sites to operate or maintain the equipment.

Accessory Equipment

Only a few decision makers may participate in a purchase of **accessory equipment**—capital items that typically cost less and last for shorter periods than installations.

Although quality and service exert important influences on purchases of accessory equipment, price may significantly affect these decisions. Accessory equipment includes products such as hand tools, portable drills, small lathes, and laptop computers. Although these products are considered capital investments and buyers depreciate their costs over several years, their useful lives generally are much shorter than those of installations.

FIGURE 11.8   Promoting Accessory Equipment

Marketing these products requires continuous representation and dealing with the widespread geographic dispersion of purchasers. To cope with these market characteristics, a wholesaler—often called an **industrial distributor**—contacts potential customers in its own geographic area. Customers usually do not need technical assistance, and a manufacturer of accessory equipment often can sell its products effectively through wholesalers.

Advertising is an important component in the marketing mix for accessory equipment. Hyster Company's ad in Figure 11.8, as an example, promotes forklifts, an accessory product used in manufacturing and in the warehouse facilities. Hyster markets its products through a worldwide network of dealers.

Component Parts and Materials

Whereas business buyers use installations and accessory equipment in the process of producing their own final products, **component parts and materials** represent finished business products of one producer that actually became part of the final products of another producer. Spark plugs complete new Chevrolets; Harley-Davidson motorcycles carry batteries; buyers receive tires with their Dodge pickup trucks. Some fabricated materials, such as flour, undergo further processing before becoming part of finished products. Textiles, paper pulp, and chemicals are also examples of component parts and materials.

Purchasers of component parts and materials need regular, continuous supplies of uniform-quality products. They generally contract to purchase these items for set periods of time. Marketers commonly emphasize direct sales, and satisfied customers often become regular buyers. Wholesalers sometimes supply fill-in purchases and handle sales to smaller purchasers.

Raw Materials

Farm products, such as beef, cotton, eggs, milk, poultry, and soybeans, and *natural products*, such as coal, copper, iron ore, and lumber, constitute **raw materials.** These products resemble component parts and materials in that they actually become part of the buyers' final products.

Most raw materials carry grades determined according to set criteria, assuring purchasers of the receipt of standardized products of uniform quality. As with component parts and materials, vendors commonly market raw materials directly to buying organizations, typically according to contractual terms. Wholesalers are increasingly involved in purchasing raw materials from foreign suppliers.

Price is seldom a deciding factor in a raw materials purchase since terms are often set at central markets, determining virtually identical exchanges among competing sellers. Purchasers buy raw materials from the firms they consider best able to deliver the required quantities and qualities.

Supplies

If installations represent the specialty products of the business market, operating supplies are its convenience products. **Supplies** constitute the regular expenses that a firm incurs in its daily operations. These expenses do not become part of the buyer's final products.

Supplies are sometimes called **MRO items** because they fall into three categories: (1) *maintenance items*, such as brooms, filters, and light bulbs; (2) *repair items*, such as nuts and bolts used in repairing equipment; and (3) *operating supplies*, such as fax paper, Post-it notes, and pencils.

A purchasing manager regularly purchases operating supplies as a routine job duty. Wholesalers often facilitate sales of supplies due to the low unit prices, the small order size, and the large number of potential buyers. Since supplies are relatively standardized, heavy price competition frequently keeps costs under control. However, a business buyer spends little time making decisions about these products. Exchanges of products frequently demand simple telephone or EDI orders or regular purchases from a sales representative of the local wholesaler.

Business Services

The **business services** category includes the intangible products that firms buy to facilitate their production and operating processes. Examples of business services are financial services, leasing and rental services that supply equipment and vehicles, insurance, security, legal advice, and consulting. Many service providers sell the same services—telephone, gas, and electric, for example—to both consumers and organizational buyers, although service firms may maintain separate marketing groups for the two customer segments.

Organizations also purchase many *adjunct services* that assist their operations but are not essentially a part of the final product. Andersen Consulting, for example, provides consulting services to help businesses improve the effectiveness of their management, finance, and technology programs.

Price often strongly influences purchase decisions for business services. The buying firm must decide whether to purchase a service or provide that service internally. For example, a firm may purchase the services of a public relations agency rather than assume the costs of maintaining an in-house public relations department. This decision may depend on how frequently the firm needs the service and the specialized knowledge required to provide it.

MARKETING | DICTIONARY

accessory equipment Capital product, usually less expensive and shorter-lived than an installation, such as a laptop computer.

industrial distributor Wholesaling marketing intermediary that handles purchases of small accessory equipment and operating supplies.

component parts and materials Finished business products that become parts of buying firms' final products..

raw material Business product, such as a farm product (wheat, cotton, soybeans) or natural product (coal, lumber, iron ore) that becomes part of a final product.

supplies Products that represent regular expenses necessary to carry out a firm's daily operations but not part of the final product.

MRO item Part of business supplies categorized as maintenance items, repair items, or operating supplies.

business service Intangible product purchased to facilitate a firm's production and operating processes.

TABLE 11.2	Marketing Impact of the Business Products Classification System					
FACTOR	**INSTALLATIONS**	**ACCESSORY EQUIPMENT**	**COMPONENT PARTS AND MATERIALS**	**RAW MATERIALS**	**SUPPLIES**	**BUSINESS SERVICES**
Organizational Factors						
Planning time	Extensive	Less extensive	Less extensive	Varies	Very little	Varies
Purchase frequency	Infrequent	More frequent	Frequent	Infrequent	Frequent	Varies
Comparison of price and quality	Quality very important	Quality and price important	Quality important	Quality important	Price important	Varies
Marketing Mix Factors						
Price	High	Relatively high	Low to high	Low to high	Low	Varies
Promotion method	Personal selling by producer	Advertising	Personal selling	Personal selling	Advertising by producer	Varies
Distribution channel length	Very short	Relatively short	Short	Short	Long	Varies

Purchase decision processes vary considerably for different types of business services. For example, a firm may purchase window-cleaning services through a routine and straightforward process similar to that for buying operating supplies. By contrast, a purchase decision for highly specialized environmental engineering advice requires complex analysis and perhaps lengthy negotiations similar to those for purchases of installations. This variability of the marketing mix for business services and other business products is outlined in Table 11.2.

MARKETING ENVIRONMENT FOR SERVICE FIRMS

6

Explain how environmental factors affect services.

Economic, social-cultural, political-legal, technological, and competitive forces vary as much for service firms as for goods producers, and they can affect the strategies for service providers as well. For example, Internet and Web technology has created a host of opportunities for service companies. Online services and Internet service providers like America Online and Netcom connect consumers to the many offerings promoted via the new media. Other companies develop the content for specialty areas on these services, like the Motley Fool investment area or CNET's News.Com technology news area. Systems consultants set up company networks, and site developers and computer graphics specialists design Web pages for firms. Other consultants train people to use the technology.

Economic Environment for Services

Consumer expenditures for services have grown in parallel with an expansion of business and government services to keep pace with the increasing complexity of the U.S. economy. The resulting sharp increase in spending for services and in the development of service industries as a major employer rank among the most significant trends in the post World War II economy. Most explanations of these trends highlight changes associated with a maturing economy and byproducts of rapid economic growth.

A theory developed by economist Colin Clark describes the growth of service industries in the following way. In the first, most primitive stage of economic development, the vast majority of a population work in farming, hunting, fishing, and forestry. As the society becomes more advanced, the economic emphasis shifts from agrarian pursuits to manufacturing. The third, most advanced stage of development occurs when most of a society's labor pool works in **tertiary industries**—those involved in the production of services. While some people associate service

FIGURE 11.9 Servicing the Needs of Business Customers

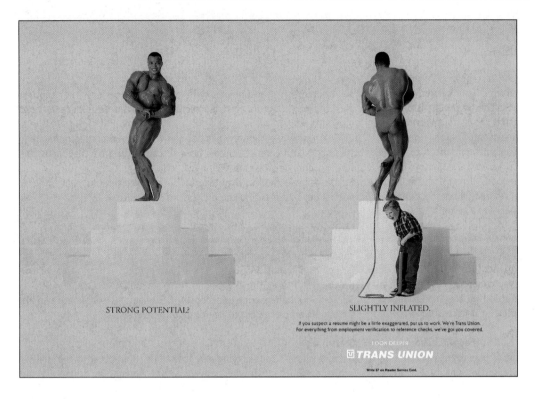

industries with minimal job skills and low pay, many service-sector jobs, such as those in communications and computer software, command high salaries and require complex skills.

As much as consumer expenditures for services have grown, business expenditures for services have shown even more remarkable increases. Servicing the needs of business customers has become a very profitable endeavor that has expanded into many areas. Two causes have primarily driven the rapid growth of business services. First, service firms frequently can perform specialized functions for their customers at lower costs than the customers could do the same jobs themselves. Enterprises that provide maintenance, cleaning, and protection services for office buildings and industrial plants are common examples. Second, many companies lack the equipment or expertise they need to perform certain specialized services themselves.

For organizations that do not have the personnel or expertise in background screening, Trans Union offers the specialized service of conducting reference checks on employee candidates. Trans Union targets ads like the one in Figure 11.9 to human resource managers.

Social-Cultural Environment for Services

The social-cultural environment changes over time, causing corresponding changes in consumer preferences for services. An important factor is the expansion of the U.S. work week. Americans now spend an average of 163 more hours a year on the job than they did thirty years ago—the equivalent of one extra month every year.

Tight schedules boost demand for many different types of services as consumers seek ways to become more efficient and to maximize their leisure hours. For instance, a trend toward reliance on counselors, coaches, and consultants has affected many aspects of modern people's personal, family, and work lives. Some people even

MARKETING   DICTIONARY

tertiary industry Industry that rises to dominance in the third stage of an economy's development; service firms are considered components of tertiary industries.

SOLVING AN ETHICAL CONTROVERSY

The Troubled Business of Healing

Suppose you need minor surgery or medication to relieve skin problems. Your doctor requests approval for the treatment from your insurer, a health maintenance organization (HMO). And suppose the treatment is denied. So your doctor embellishes your symptoms and the seriousness of your condition to get the HMO to approve the treatment. There's a name for this practice—gaming the system—and it happens more often than you might suppose. Pressure from HMOs to contain costs puts doctors in the uncomfortable position of doing wrong to do good. "I feel that I'm doing something that is not purely right and good," admits Georgetown ethicist and physician, Daniel P. Sulmasy. "I feel that I'm also doing right and good on behalf of patients."

In a survey conducted by the American Medical Association's Institute for Ethics, one fourth of the physicians surveyed said that they had exaggerated patients' conditions to keep those patients from being discharged from the hospital too early. In another survey conducted by the Kaiser Family Foundation, five hundred doctors reported that they had exaggerated at least one patient's condition "out of medical necessity." According to the study, most doctors feel that it is their highest priority to obtain the correct treatment for their patients, and they will advocate for their patients whenever possible. "The finding is consistent with the hypothesis that, as managed care brings more restrictions to a market, physicians practicing in that market become more willing to support deception as a means of circumventing those restrictions," write the study authors.

Although managed-care firms agree that physicians have a right to advocate for their patients, they stress that there is an appropriate appeals process. And not every physician sanctions the practice of gaming. "There is an obligation to advocate and make every effort to get the preferred treatment paid for under the plan," says Dr. Jonathan D. Moreno, director of the University of Virginia Center for Biomedical Ethics and columnist for ABCNEWS.com. "But I don't think anybody can advocate lying to achieve those ends."

Pro
1. A doctor's first responsibility is to his or her patients, not the insurance industry. Doctors must represent patients' interests because no one else will.
2. The health care industry has become completely focused on money instead of health care, so doctors need to counterbalance that focus to ensure patients get the care they need.
3. The appeals process may take too long; some patients may suffer and possibly even die during the process.

Con
1. Doctors should not try to get around the system. They should use the appeals process when necessary to obtain approval for treatments.
2. Lying is fraud, and doctors are professionals who should be trustworthy.
3. Doctors who prescribe unnecessary treatments or exaggerate symptoms simply drive up the cost of health care for everyone.

Summary
Doctors who are caught lying may lose their contracts with the HMOs. "It is a criminal act, it's fraud," notes Jonathan Moreno. But surveys continue to indicate that the restrictions and financial pressures exerted on doctors by managed-care companies point to an industry that is in trouble. "If the health care delivery system is heading in a direction that requires physicians to misrepresent their patients' needs in order to be able to get services for a patient, then I think that we need to look hard at what we're evolving here as a mechanism of taking care of patients," observes Larry Oates, associate medical director of the physicians group of Kaiser Permanente HMO in the mid-Atlantic region.

SOURCES: Joseph P. Shapiro, "Giving Doctors the Final Word," *U.S. News & World Report*, November 22, 1999, pp. 20–24; Avery Comarow, "Is Your Doctor Lying for You?" *U.S. News & World Report*, October 25, 1999, pp. 66–67; Giselle Smith, "Truth or Care? White-Coat Lies," ABCNEWS.com, October 18, 1999; David S. Hilzenrath, "Healing or Honesty? For Doctors, Managed Care's Cost Controls Pose Moral Dilemma," *Washington Post*, March 15, 1998, www.washingtonpost.com.

Do economic pressures in the health services industry force people to lie?

---

hire leisure consultants to advise them on what to do in their spare time. A few years ago, some of these services were not even available, let alone in demand.

Political-Legal Environment for Services

Many service businesses operate under closer government regulation than other enterprises. Some service industries must comply with regulations of national government agencies such as the Federal Power Commission, the Federal Trade Commission (FTC), the Federal Communications Commission (FCC), and the Securities and Exchange Commission (SEC). The industries subject to federal regulations include banking, electric utilities, television, and telecommunications.

Other service industries answer to state and local regulators. Doctors, attorneys, and dentists must meet state licensing requirements before they can practice. Hair stylists, auto mechanics, restaurants, and funeral homes also comply with state and local requirements for fees, taxes, certification, and licensing.

Service firms seeking to expand globally must also consider the political-legal environments abroad. Several European countries have eliminated government monopolies in telecommunications, allowing U.S. phone companies to compete there. Deregulation of financial services in Latin America has opened up new opportunities for accounting firms, insurance companies, and banks. Movie studios anticipate great opportunities in China, the world's most populous country, but they must deal with strict government controls and bureaucratic procedures in the process. For instance, the China Film Ministry, a government agency, decides how many foreign films will appear in the country, and it limits both the timing and duration of the engagements. It stocks the country's theaters with 200 Chinese films and only 60 foreign films.

Technological Environment for Services

The technological environment may emerge as the primary determinant of future growth in the service sector. Technological advances can improve the productivity of service workers, open new distribution methods, and even create opportunities for business expansion. **Productivity**—output as measured by the production of each worker—is especially important to service firms. Service marketers hunt constantly for technologically generated opportunities that open new strategic windows for their firms.

Major shipping companies, including United Parcel Service (UPS) and FedEx, have also applied technology to improve productivity and customer service. The UPS ad in Figure 11.10 introduces the company's new online service that promises customers a faster and easier shipping experience. FedEx uses bar-coded labels to track the status of packages as they move through the company's distribution system. By logging onto FedEx's Web site, customers can download free software that helps them prepare packages and print bar-coded shipping documents. They can also follow the progress of their packages around the world and obtain information about all the company's services. FedEx regards the expanded contacts as a win-win situation; it benefits by reducing errors on the customer's end, and customers benefit by speeding up their shipping process.[11]

fedex.com

Competitive Environment for Services

Service marketers face several challenges when assessing the competitive environment. In many service industries, especially those regulated by the government, competition may come from government services rather than other service firms. Also, price competition is limited in certain service fields, such as communication, legal, and medical services. In other service industries, not-for-profit organizations such as hospitals, educational institutions, and religious agencies regard competition from a noncommercial point of view. Many service industries feature substantial barriers to entry, requiring a new competitor to make a major financial investment or to bring special education or training to the business.

Service marketers often need to look beyond obvious direct competitors and evaluate the effects of indirect competitors. For example, a movie complex

MARKETING | **DICTIONARY**

productivity Ratio of output to input of goods and services for a nation, industry, firm, or individual worker.

competes not only with other theaters but also with a host of other entertainment and recreation options. Consumers may decide to spend their time and money watching a play, attending a ball game, or even staying home and watching television. Theater owners must find ways to position their service to attract consumers away from these competing activities.

Competition from Government

Only government agencies can provide some services, but some official service providers compete with privately produced products. For example, the U.S. Postal Service's Express Mail competes with FedEx, Airborne, UPS, and other delivery services. Similarly, the research and training efforts of more public academic institutions often compete with similar newer efforts by the private sector.

Outsourcing in the Service Sector

Many goods manufacturers practice outsourcing, or moving company operations and production outside the organization, typically to inexpensive facilities overseas. Outsourcing has also found ready supporters in service industries such as telephone answering systems, customer service, and technical support. Several companies are also outsourcing computer programming tasks, sometimes to foreign suppliers. Workers in India, Ireland, the Philippines, Russia, and Singapore, for example, handle programming duties for U.S. firms.

7

Explain why most firms develop lines of related products rather than marketing individual items.

DEVELOPMENT OF PRODUCT LINES

Few firms today market only one product. A typical firm offers its customers a **product line,** that is, a series of related products. For example, Sara Lee Hosiery's L'eggs division does not sell just one line of pantyhose; it offers consumers a range of styles, colors, and sizes. Sheer Energy stockings provide light support, Just My Size includes larger sizes, and Smooth Silhouettes seek to eliminate the "panty line" problem. Recently L'eggs introduced Silken Mist, a line of pantyhose aimed at African-American women. Silken Mist stockings are sheer, which many African-American women prefer, and come in shades suited to darker skin tones.[12] Kimberly-Clark, manufacturers of Huggies disposable diapers, continues to add related products to its line for infants and toddlers. Its newest offering is Little Swimmers disposable swim pants shown in Figure 11.11.

By developing complete product lines as opposed to concentrating *solely* on individual products, firms benefit primarily in four ways. These motivations for marketing full product lines include the desire to grow, optimal use of company resources, enhancing the company's position in the market, and exploiting the product life cycle. The following paragraphs look at the first three reasons, and the next section of the chapter deals with the product life cycle.

FIGURE 11.11   Developing a Product Line

Desire to Grow

A company limits its growth potential when it concentrates on a single product. Consider International Home Foods' Pam cooking spray. While Pam dominates the nonstick cooking spray market with a hefty 52.2 percent market share, sales have stagnated. The company is attempting to grow by developing new products that enhance flavor while aiding clean-up. Examples include a new lemon butter spray, to be used with fish, and a garlic-flavored spray for pasta dishes.

Sometimes firms may introduce new items to offset seasonal variations in sales of their current products. Another Pam spray, sold only during the summer, tolerates higher cooking temperatures and is meant to be used with barbecues.[13]

pam4you.com

Optimal Use of Company Resources

By spreading the costs of its operations over a series of products, a firm may reduce the average production and marketing costs of each product. Hospitals have taken advantage of idle facilities by adding a variety of outreach services. Many now operate health and fitness centers that, besides generating profits themselves, also feed customers into other hospital services. For example, a blood pressure check at the fitness center might result in a referral to a staff physician.

Enhancing the Company's Position in the Market

A company with a line of products often makes itself more important to both consumers and marketing intermediaries than a firm with only one product. A shopper who purchases a tent often buys related camping items. Recognizing this tendency, Coleman Co. has developed a complete line of camping products that includes canoes, ice chests, sleeping bags, cots, tents, cookers, and trailers. Few would know of the firm if it sold only lanterns. Business buyers often expect a firm that manufactures a particular product to offer related items as well.

THE PRODUCT LIFE CYCLE

Products, like people, pass through stages as they age. Successful products progress through four basic stages: introduction, growth, maturity, and decline. This progression, known as the **product life cycle,** is depicted in Figure 11.12 along with examples of products that currently fit into each stage. Notice that the product life cycle concept applies to products or product categories within an industry, not to individual brands. Also, some products may move rapidly through the product life cycle, while others pass through those stages over long time periods.

8

Explain the concept of the product life cycle and how a firm can extend a product's life cycle.

Introductory Stage

During the early stages of the product life cycle, a firm works to stimulate demand for the new market entry. Products in the introductory stage often bring new technical features to a product category. Since the product is unknown to the public, promotional campaigns stress information about its features. Additional promotions directed toward distribution channel members try to induce these members to carry the product. In this phase, the public becomes acquainted with the item's merits and begins to accept it.

Technical problems are common during the introductory stage as companies fine-tune product design. This is especially true of new technologies, such as electronic books. Compared to traditional books, e-books are heavy, software is temperamental, prices are high, and the print is fuzzy and hard to read. On the other hand, e-books offer advantages that paper books cannot, such as rapid text-searching and the ability to read text aloud. Despite their undeniable glitches, several companies are convinced that electronic books are only at the beginning of their product life cycle. The Electronic Book Consortium, a Japan-based group of more than 100 firms, is spending $90 million to develop marketable products.[14]

Financial losses are common during the introductory stage as the firm incurs considerable costs associated with heavy

MARKETING **DICTIONARY**

product line Series of related products.

product life cycle Progression of products through introduction, growth, maturity, and decline stages.

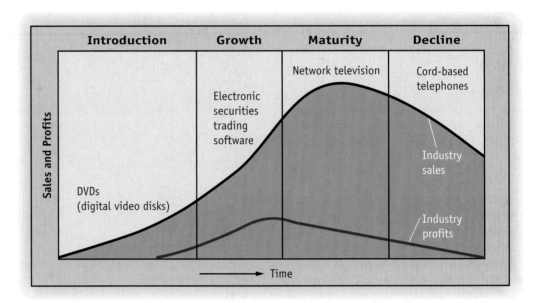

FIGURE 11.12   Stages in the Product Life Cycle

promotion and extensive research-and-development costs. However, by finding the correct formula for consumer trial and acceptance during the introductory stage, a business lays the groundwork for future profits. Firms can then focus on recovering their costs and on beginning to earn profits as the new product moves into the second phase of its life cycle—the growth stage.

Growth Stage

Sales volume rises rapidly during the growth stage as new customers make initial purchases and early buyers repurchase the product. Word-of-mouth reports and mass advertising encourage hesitant buyers to make trial purchases. The growth stage usually begins when a firm starts to realize substantial profits from its investment.

However, the growth stage may also bring new challenges for marketers. Inevitably, success attracts competitors, who rush into the market with similar offerings. In fact, most firms enter the market with its product during the product's growth stage. An item that built enviable market share during the introductory stage may suddenly lose sales to competitive products. To compete effectively, a firm may need to make improvements and changes to a product during this stage. Additional spending on promotion and distribution may also be necessary.

Maturity Stage

Industry sales continue to grow during the early part of the maturity stage, but eventually they reach a plateau as the backlog of potential customers dwindles. By this time, many competitors have entered the market, and the firm's profits begin to decline as competition intensifies.

At this stage in the product life cycle, differences between competing products diminish as competitors discover the product and promotional characteristics most desired by customers. Available supplies exceed industry demand for the first time. Companies can increase their sales and market shares only at the expense of competitors.

In the maturity stage, heavy promotional outlays emphasize any differences that still separate competing products, and brand competition intensifies. Some firms try to differentiate their products by focusing on attributes such as quality, reliability, and service. Compaq Computer, for example, competes against other hardware manufacturers by offering business customers a package of computer-related services, such as Internet systems and software, with its machines.[15]

As competition intensifies, competitors tend to cut prices to attract new buyers. Although a price cut may seem like the easiest method for boosting purchases, it is also one of the simplest moves for competitors to duplicate. Reduced prices decrease revenues for all firms in the industry, unless the lower prices stimulate enough new purchases to offset the loss in revenue on each unit sold.

Decline Stage

In the final stage of a product's life, innovations or shifts in consumer preferences bring about an absolute decline in industry sales. The safety razor replaced the straight razor years ago, and the electric shaver has taken customers from the safety razor. Later, consumers replaced CB radios with cellular telephones. As Figure 11.13 indicates, the decline stage of an old product often coincides with the growth stage for a new entry.

As sales fall, industry profits decline, sometimes actually becoming negative. This change forces firms to cut prices further in a bid for the dwindling market. Manufacturers gradually drop the declining items from their product lines and search for alternatives.

The emergence of new technologies can help push mature technologies into decline. Ford Motor Co. and General Motors Corp. are equipping new vehicles with radios that can receive satellite transmissions. The new systems will beam digital programs from orbiting satellites directly to vehicles; special on-ground antennas will enhance the reception to compensate for buildings that could interfere with satellite signals. This move represents a growth opportunity for CD Radio Inc. and XM Satellite Radio Inc., the two biggest players in the young industry of satellite radio. At the same time, it represents a threat to the mature industry of broadcast radio, for which automobile drivers are an important market segment.[16]

The traditional product life cycle differs from fad cycles. Fashions and fads profoundly influence marketing strategies. *Fashions* are currently popular products that tend to follow recurring life cycles. Women's apparel and accessories provide the best examples. After more than a decade out of fashion, the miniskirt became stylish again during the 1990s. Small, wire-rimmed

compaq.com

cdradio.com

xmsatelliteradio.com

FIGURE 11.13   **Overlapping Life Cycles for Two Products**

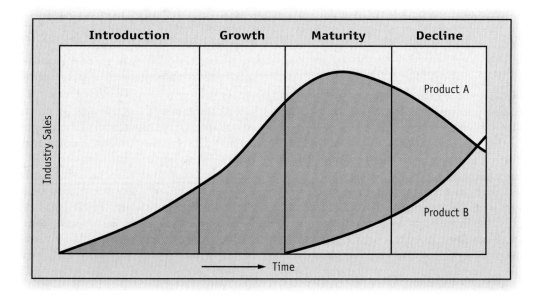

sunglasses, popular during the late 1960s, became fashionable again more than 20 years later. Convertible cars are another example. Popular in the 1950s, they disappeared from the market in the 1970s but have become stylish again in recent years.

In contrast, *fads* are fashions with abbreviated life cycles. Most fads experience short-lived popularity and then quickly fade, although some maintain residual markets among certain segments. The average clothing fad is popular for only six to 12 weeks, after which customers abandon it for the next fad.[17]

STRATEGIC IMPLICATIONS OF THE PRODUCT LIFE CYCLE CONCEPT

The product life cycle provides useful guidance for marketing strategy decisions. Marketers can anticipate that sales and profits will assume a predictable pattern throughout the life cycle stages, so they can shift promotional emphasis from product information in the early stages to brand promotion in the later ones. This kind of insight helps marketers to focus on maximizing sales and profits at each stage through appropriate promotional efforts.

At the introductory stage, a firm's marketing efforts should emphasize the goal of stimulating demand. The focus then shifts to cultivating selective demand in the growth period. Extensive market segmentation helps to maintain momentum in the maturity period. During the decline stage, the emphasis returns to increasing primary demand. Chapter 12 will cover new product strategies in more detail.

Extending the Product Life Cycle

Marketers usually try to extend each stage of the life cycles for their products as long as possible. They can often accomplish this goal if they take action early in the maturity stage. Product life cycles can stretch indefinitely as a result of decisions designed to increase the frequency of use by current customers, increase the number of users for the product, find new uses, or change package sizes, labels, or product quality.

Increasing Frequency of Use

During the maturity stage, the industry sales curve for a product reaches a maximum point as the competitors exhaust the supply of potential customers who previously had not made purchases. However, if current customers buy more frequently than they formerly did, total industry sales will rise even though no new buyers enter the market.

For instance, consumers buy some products in certain seasons of the year. Marketers can boost purchase frequency by persuading these people to try the product year-round. Marketers may try to connect the use of holiday products to additional occasions throughout the year. Kraft Foods has done this for its Jell-O brand by offering free molds with holiday themes.

Increasing the Number of Users

A second strategy for extending the product life cycle seeks to increase the overall market size by attracting new customers who previously have not used the product. Marketers may find their products in different stages of the life cycle in different countries. This difference can help firms to extend product growth. Items that have reached the maturity stage in the United States may still be in the introductory stage somewhere else.

For example, in North America and Europe, bottled water is a mature product. However, in developing countries, bottled water is scarce and perceived as a luxury. Consumers there consider it a healthy alternative to local water supplies, which may be contaminated. Swiss-based Nestlé, which markets the upscale Perrier and San Pellegrino brands of bottled water in industrialized countries, has introduced a lower-priced line of bottled water, called Pure Life, for consumers in Asia and South America. Nestlé is spending $100 million to launch Pure Life in 20 countries, starting with Pakistan and Brazil.[18]

nestle.com

Finding New Uses

Still another strategy for extending a product's life cycle is to identify new uses for it. New applications for mature products include oatmeal as a cholesterol-reducer, waxed paper to cover food in microwave cooking, and mouthwash as an aid in treating and preventing plaque and gum disease. Figure 11.14 shows one of a series of ads that Quaker Oats created to promote oatmeal as a heart-healthy product that may reduce cholesterol.

Arm & Hammer has done an effective job of identifying and publicizing new ways to use its venerable baking soda. Once promoted solely as a cooking ingredient, today baking soda is also touted as a deodorizer, wintergreen-flavored toothpaste, laundry freshener, cat litter, stomach antacid, household cleaner, and teeth whitener. Arm & Hammer even recommends adding 1/2 cup to bath water as a skin conditioner.[19]

Changing Package Sizes, Labels, or Product Quality

Many firms try to extend their product life cycles by introducing physical changes in their offerings. Food marketers have brought out small packages designed to appeal to one-person households and extra large containers for customers who want to buy in bulk. Other firms offer their products in convenient packages for use away from home or for use at the office.

Changes in packaging can make products much more affordable in developing countries. In the United States, Unilever packages its Close-Up toothpaste in the familiar laminated tube. However, its Indian subsidiary, Hindustan Lever, packages Close-Up in small packets fitted with a nozzle. Indian consumers can buy a 15-gram packet, enough for 20 brushings, for 3.5 rupees, a much less daunting expenditure than spending 14.5 rupees for a 50-gram tube.[20]

FIGURE 11.14 | A New Application for a Mature Product

Product Deletion Decisions

To avoid wasting resources promoting unpromising products, marketers must sometimes prune product lines and eliminate marginal products. Marketers typically face this decision during the late maturity and early decline stages of the product life cycle. Periodic reviews of weak products should justify either eliminating or retaining them.

A firm may continue to carry an unprofitable item in order to provide a complete line for its customers. For example, while most grocery stores lose money on bulky, low-unit-value items such as salt, they continue to carry these items to meet shopper demand.

Shortages of raw materials sometimes prompt companies to discontinue production and marketing of previously profitable items. Due to such a shortage, Alcoa discontinued making its brand of aluminum foil. A firm may even drop a profitable item that fails to fit into its existing product line. Some of these products return to the market carrying the names of other firms that purchase the brands from the original manufacturers.

9

Identify the major product mix decisions that marketers must make.

THE PRODUCT MIX

A company's **product mix** is the assortment of product lines and individual product offerings that the company sells. The right blend of product lines and products allows a firm to maximize

MARKETING | DICTIONARY

product mix Company's assortment of product lines and individual offerings.

TABLE 11.3	Clorox's Mix of U.S. Retail Consumer Products

Laundry Additives	Automotive Care	Bags, Wraps, and Containers	Dressings and Sauces
Clorox	*Armor All*	*Glad*	*Hidden Valley*
Clorox 2	*No. 7*	*Glad-Lock*	*K.C. Masterpiece*
Stain Out	*Rain Dance*	*Gladware*	*Kitchen Bouquet*
Household Cleaners	*Rally*	**Cat Litter**	**Water Filtration**
Clorox toilet bowl	**Charcoal**	*EverClean*	*Brita*
Clorox Clean-Up	*Kingsford*	*EverFresh*	**Home Fireplace**
Formula 409	*BBQ Bag*	*Jonny Cat*	*Crackling HearthLogg*
Formula 409 carpet cleaner	*Match Light*	*Scoop Away*	*HearthLogg*
Liquid-Plumr	**Insecticides**	*Fresh Step*	*StarterLogg*
Lestoil	*Black Flag*	*Fresh Step Scoop*	
Pine Sol	*Roach Motel*	*Perfomax*	
Soft Scrub	*Combat*		
S.O.S.			

Source: Clorox Web page, www.clorox.com/products, downloaded March 22, 2000.

sales opportunities within the limitations of its resources. Marketers typically measure product mixes according to width, length, and depth.

clorox.com

The *width* of a product mix refers to the number of product lines the firm offers. As Table 11.3 shows, Clorox offers a broad line of retail consumer products in the U.S. market. (Clorox also has products designed for professional users.) Some ten different product lines are offered: laundry additives; household cleaners; automotive care; charcoal; insecticides; bags, wraps, and containers; cat litter; dressings and sauces; water filtration; and home fireplaces. Contrast this width with that of Colgate-Palmolive: oral care, personal care, household surface cleaners, fabric care, and pet food.

The *length* of a product mix refers to the number of different products a firm sells. Table 11.3 shows 42 separate Clorox products ranging from Clorox and Formula 409 to Armor All, Black Flag, and Hidden Valley dressings. By comparison, Colgate-Palmolive offers only nine major brands in the U.S. market. Some of Colgate's leading brands are Colgate, Palmolive, Mennen, Ajax, and Fab. The firm has other brands targeted at selected foreign markets.

Depth refers to variations in each product that the firm markets in its mix. For instance, Clorox sells Glad, Glad-Lock, and Gladware in its bags, wraps, and containers line. Formula 409 and Formula 409 carpet cleaner are included among its household-cleaners line. Similarly, Colgate-Palmolive offers Hill's Prescription Diet and Hill's Science Diet in its pet food line.

To evaluate a firm's product mix, marketers look at the effectiveness of all three elements—width, length, and depth. Has the firm so far failed to serve a viable consumer segment? It may improve performance by increasing product line depth to offer a product variation that will attract the new segment. Can the firm achieve economies of scale in its sales and distribution efforts by adding complementary product lines to the mix? If so, a wider product mix may seem appropriate. Does the firm gain equal contributions from all products in its portfolio? If not, it may decide to lengthen or shorten the product mix to increase revenues.

Product Mix Decisions

As products and product lines move through their life cycles, marketers face some characteristic product mix decisions. To recap, in the growth stage, a firm may lengthen or widen its product mix to take advantage of sales opportunities. As a product matures, the company may decide to add variations that will attract new users. A product near the end of its life cycle may be pruned or altered, and new products may extend the product life cycle.

Managing the product mix has become an increasingly important marketing task. In the 1980s, many large firms added depth, length, and width to their product mixes without fully considering the consequences of expansion. Recently many of these same firms contended with unprofitable product lines and products. Retailers could not carry the full range of this merchandise, and consumers felt overwhelmed by their choices. A number of companies decided to eliminate poor sellers and focus on a few key products.

Other firms, however, seek to expand their product mixes. This is especially true for newer and smaller firms seeking to grow. Often, firms purchase product lines from other companies that want to narrow their product mixes. Other firms expand their offerings by acquiring entire companies through mergers or acquisitions.

A firm should assess its current product mix for another important reason: to determine the feasibility of a line extension. A **line extension** develops individual offerings that appeal to different market segments while remaining closely related to the existing product line. Since introducing its Jell-O gelatin snacks, Kraft has extended the product line shown in Figure 11.15 by adding pudding and cheesecake snacks. A line extension provides a relatively inexpensive way to increase sales with minimal risk. For example, both Hershey and Mars have introduced lowfat versions of their candy bars. Both companies hope to attract consumers whose health and weight concerns might otherwise prevent them from buying candy.

Careful evaluation of a firm's current product mix can also help marketers in making decisions about brand management and new-product introductions. Chapter 12 will examine the importance of branding, brand management, and the development and introduction of new products.

FIGURE 11.15 | Kraft Extends Its Snack Line

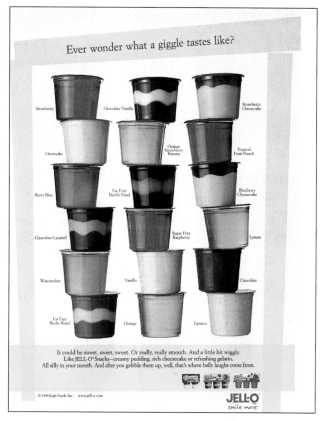

MARKETING MIX STRATEGIES FOR SERVICES

Service marketers can also segment markets according to geographic, demographic, psychographic, or product-related criteria. As with goods markets, demographic segmentation is the most common segmentation variable for services marketing.

Along with careful segmentation, satisfying buyers' service needs also requires an effective marketing mix. Service policies, pricing, distribution, and promotion strategies must combine to produce an integrated marketing program. The following sections briefly describe marketing mix considerations for service firms.

10

Discuss segmentation strategies and the marketing mix for services.

Service Strategy

Just as goods manufacturers struggle to find the best product mixes, service firms must also identify the service mixes that will successfully attract consumers. The target market picked for a service influences the elements of the service mix.

Service firms often look for ways to extend their service mixes by offering new services. For example, telephone companies have added a variety of new

MARKETING | **DICTIONARY**

line extension Introduction of a new product that is closely related to other products in the firm's existing line.

functions to basic telephone access. Customers can now identify callers before answering their phones and can even block calls from all but previously specified numbers. Phone companies have also added services geared toward the needs of business. Customers who dial a single toll-free number for a firm may be automatically routed to the sales outlet closest to the customer's location.

Service businesses must continually adapt their service mixes as environmental conditions change. Travel agents, for instance, have faced a variety of environmental challenges in recent years. Airlines have reduced the commission fees traditionally paid to travel agents for booking customers. Online travel services such as Travelocity and Expedia encourage consumers to make their own flight reservations. Other online services allow travelers to book hotel rooms, rent cars, and purchase rail passes directly. Want to find lodgings in Frankfurt, Germany? The Internet's Hotel Reservation Service displays hotel ratings, prices, amenities, locations, and distances from major attractions and lets you reserve rooms online.[21]

The intangible nature of their products prevents service providers from duplicating some tangible goods marketing strategies. For example, packaging and labeling decisions are limited. Service marketers rarely use packages as promotional tools. In addition, they cannot usually introduce new services to the market by distributing samples, although some have tried the tactic. Health clubs and cable television channels frequently offer trial periods without charge or at greatly reduced rates to move potential customers through the stages of the adoption process and to convert them to regular patrons.

Pricing Strategy for Services

Pricing decisions pose major problems for service firms. In developing a pricing strategy, service marketers must consider the demand for the service; production, marketing, and administrative costs; and the influence of competition. Another key consideration is perceived value: the relationship between a customer's perception of the service's quality and its cost. Customers may happily pay higher prices for unique or extremely high quality services. However, many service providers face only limited price competition. For instance, the prices charged by most utilities are closely regulated by federal, state, and local government agencies.

Price negotiation is an integral part of many professional service transactions. Examples of consumer services that sometimes involve price negotiations include personal trainers, financial services, and lawn care. Direct negotiations may also set prices for specialized business services, such as equipment rental, marketing research, insurance, maintenance, and protection services, as well.

Distribution Strategy for Services

Figure 11.16 shows the distribution channels for services. Service providers often distribute their products through simpler and more direct channels than those for goods. This difference results largely from the intangibility of services. Service marketers worry less than goods manufacturers about storage, transportation, and inventory control, and they typically employ shorter channels of distribution. For another consideration, many kinds of service marketers must maintain continuing, personal relationships with their customers. Consumers will remain clients of the same insurance agents, banks, or travel agents if those service providers keep them reasonably satisfied. Similarly, organizations often retain public accounting firms and lawyers over lengthy periods of time.

Two major exceptions contradict the principle of direct distribution of services: consolidators and franchises. *Consolidators* are commonplace in the air travel business, particularly for international flights. These intermediaries purchase seats from airlines at substantial discounts and then resell them to travel agents, to other consolidators, and directly to individual consumers. *Franchises* provide distribution channels for services that do not allow geographic separation of production from consumption. Mail Boxes Etc., Super Cuts, and Minit-Lube are examples.

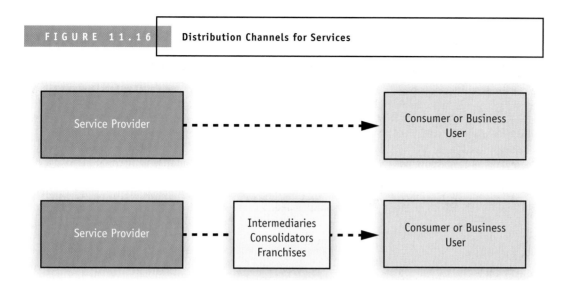

FIGURE 11.16   **Distribution Channels for Services**

Promotional Strategy for Services

Marketers face several challenges as they develop promotional strategies for services. They must find a way to fill out the intangible images of most services and successfully convey the benefits that consumers receive.

Advertising portrayals of insurance services, for example, must overcome problems of perception since the end benefit of the service is often, in a sense, a negative event. Insurance also brings extremely intangible benefits. Most people have difficulty even explaining what an insurance company does.

The need to differentiate a service defines a particular goal for promotional strategy. Service marketers must work carefully to identify specific features and benefits that set their firm apart from the competition. Since service purchase decisions often require consumers to buy on trust, service providers also need to clearly portray a strong company image. Finally, service marketers must avoid overselling the service since inflated expectations can result in customer dissatisfaction.

Charles Schwab's promotional strategy involves developing its Web site as a one-stop source for investment information. In addition to allowing clients to buy stocks online, the site allows them to search for financial news and data, look up current stock prices, and identify top-performing mutual funds. Schwab is also exploring joint ventures with other Internet services, such as Intuit's Quicken.com and search engine Excite, to provide online information about insurance, taxes, mortgages, and retirement planning.[22]

ACHIEVEMENT CHECK SUMMARY

Read the learning objectives that follow, and consider the questions for each one. Answering these questions will reinforce your grasp of the most important concepts in the chapter and will allow you to check how well you have achieved these learning goals. Where a blank appears before a question, answer with *T* or *F* for true/false questions; for multiple-choice questions, choose the letter of the correct answer.

Objective 11.1: Explain the broader marketing view of products, and differentiate service offerings from other products.

1. _____ Marketers concern themselves only with the physical characteristics of a good.

2. _____ A product is a bundle of physical, service, and symbolic attributes that enhance consumer satisfaction.

3. _____ Services are intangible tasks that satisfy consumers' and business users' needs.

4. _____ Many products have both goods and services components.

Objective 11.2: Discuss the roles of top management and employees in implementing total quality management (TQM).

1. _____ Senior managers must take an active role in the quality process.

2. _____ Empowerment involves providing additional financial resources to a department so that employees can improve productivity.

3. _____ A quality circle is a method of organizing the workspace in an office so employees can interact more effectively.

Objective 11.3: Explain the role benchmarking plays in achieving continuous improvement.

1. _____ The factors that are most important in gaining competitive advantage are called (a) critical success factors, (b) benchmarking factors, (c) marketing mix factors.

2. _____ Firms usually choose to benchmark against other firms in the same industry.

3. _____ A firm can inspect finished products for defects more cost effectively than it can change a plant's operating processes.

4. _____ Eliminating waste is important to customer satisfaction because (a) customers are worried about environmental concerns, (b) waste can contribute to higher prices, (c) cycle times fall dramatically when a firm eliminates waste.

Objective 11.4: List the classifications of consumer goods and services, and briefly describe each category.

1. _____ Consumers purchase convenience goods or services after extensive comparisons of price, quality, and style.

2. _____ Dry cleaning, gasoline, and quick print shops fall into the category of shopping goods and services.

3. _____ Specialty products offer unique features that induce buyers to seek them out.

Objective 11.5: Describe each of the types of business goods and services.

1. _____ Business products are classified based on their uses rather than on customers' buying behavior.

2. _____ Installations represent major purchase decisions, often requiring months of negotiations.

3. _____ Ink cartridges for a new copy machine are an example of (a) component parts and materials; (b) supplies; (c) accessory equipment; (d) raw materials.

4. _____ Examples of business services include equipment suppliers, group insurance plans, financial consulting, and patent and trademark litigation.

Objective 11.6: Explain how environmental factors affect services.

1. _____ Recent conditions in the economic environment have allowed only slow growth for the service sector.

2. _____ Changes in consumer demographics usually do not influence the demand for services.

3. _____ The technological environment produces innovations that lead to increased productivity in the service sector.

4. _____ The competitive environment for services sometimes includes threats from goods producers or the government rather than other service providers.

Objective 11.7: Explain why most firms develop lines of related products rather than marketing individual items.

1. _____ A firm usually can achieve consistent growth by marketing only one product.

2. _____ A product line is several unrelated products marketed by the same firm.

3. _____ One reason for producing a line of products rather than a group of individual offerings is to optimize company resources.

Objective 11.8: Explain the concept of the product life cycle and how a firm can expand a product's life cycle.

1. _____ In the introductory stage of the product life cycle, marketers focus on (a) enticing consumers to try a product; (b) raising prices; or (c) stealing market share from competitors.

2. _____ During the growth stage, marketers often face reduced competition.

3. _____ The decline stage of an old product often coincides with the growth stage for a new market entry.

4. _____ Marketers cannot extend a product's life cycle indefinitely.

5. _____ If a product has reached mturity in the U.S. market, a firm might manage to increase market potential by entering other countries.

Objective 11.9: Identify the major product mix decisions that marketers must make.

1. _____ A product mix is a group of related products.

2. _____ The length of a firm's product mix refers to the number of product lines it offers.

3. _____ The number of variations of each product in a firm's product mix determines the depth of the mix.

4. _____ Line extensions add individual products that appeal to different market segments while remaining closely related to the existing product line.

5. _____ A firm can expand its product mix by buying an established brand.

Objective 11.10: Discuss segmentation strategies and the marketing mix for services.

1. _____ Most service marketers rely primarily on demographic segmentation.

2. _____ Pricing strategy is usually not an important element of the marketing mix for services.

3. _____ The most important goal of a service provider's promotional strategy is to (a) get the service firm's name in front of customers; (b) criticize competing services; (c) demonstrate tangible benefits.

Students: See the solutions section located on page S-2 to check your responses to the Achievement Check Summary.

Key Terms

product	component parts and materials
service	raw material
goods-services continuum	supplies
total quality management	MRO item
ISO 9002	business service
benchmarking	tertiary industry
convenience product	productivity
shopping products	product line
specialty products	product life cycle
installation	product mix
accessory equipment	line extension
industrial distributor	

Review Questions

1. Compare and contrast the narrow and broader views of a *product*.
2. Explain the difficulties in defining the term *services*. How does the goods-services continuum help marketers define *services?*
3. Identify the key characteristics of services. What is the current status of the service sector in the U.S. economy?
4. Compare a typical marketing mix for a convenience product with one for a specialty product. What are the primary differences in these mixes?

5. Outline the categories of business products. What kind of marketing mix suits each category?

6. How does total quality management help an organization compete more effectively?

7. Explain the product life cycle concept. Include a drawing of the progressive stages in the product life cycle.

8. How can the product life cycle concept influence marketing strategy? Explain how marketers can extend a product's life cycle.

9. What is a product mix? How does the concept help businesspeople make effective marketing decisions?

10. How do service providers segment markets? Which is the most commonly used approach?

Questions for Critical Thinking

1. Classify the following consumer products and discuss how these classification decisions might affect marketing strategy.
   a. Alltel (cellular service)
   b. Baltimore Ravens (NFL team)
   c. Andrew Jankowski, CPA
   d. Ethan Allen (furniture)
   e. Play It Again Sports
   f. Mary Kay Cosmetics
   g. *Newsweek*

2. Classify the following business goods and services and explain how these classification decisions could guide development of a marketing strategy.
   a. land for an apartment complex
   b. orthodontics center
   c. cotton
   d. cooking oil
   e. light bulbs
   f. paper clips
   g. tax accounting service

3. Cite a product that serves as an example for each stage of the product life cycle (other than those mentioned in the text). Explain how marketing strategy varies by life cycle stage for each product.

4. Outline a marketing mix for each of the following service firms:
   a. local television station
   b. residential real-estate brokerage firm
   c. bed and breakfast inn
   d. law firm specializing in family law

5. As discussed in the chapter, Ford Motor Company and General Motors Corporation are outfitting new vehicles with satellite radios.[23] Currently, commuters and other drivers are an important market segment for broadcast radio stations. How are satellite radios likely to affect the broadcast radio industry? Based on your knowledge of the product life cycle and product mix management, what advice would you give to broadcast station executives? Could they expand—or revive—the life cycle for broadcast radio? What product mix decisions should they consider?

1. **Service.** This exercise is designed to help you identify several service issues related to an organization's Web site. Visit *www.servicemetrics.com* and answer these two questions:
   - How can Service Metrics help an organization improve its Web site performance?
   - How can Service Metrics help an organization understand its customers' experience at the organization's Web site?

servicemetrics.com

2. **Shopping Products.** At *www.webcriteria.com* you will find free samples of various industry benchmark reports. Find one example of an e-commerce industry for goods (apparel, for example) and another e-commerce industry for a service (telecommunications, for example). You will need the Adobe Acrobat Reader to access the benchmark reports (information at the site will help you download and install the Acrobat Reader on your computer if you need to do so). Print out both reports, read them, and be prepared to contribute your thoughts during classroom discussion.

webcriteria.com

3. **Pricing Strategy for Services.** After browsing the Professional Pricing Society's Web site at *www.pricing-advisor.com,* list three ways this organization could help a service provider in pricing its services.

pricing-advisor.com

Video Case 11 on Pfizer, Inc. begins on page VC-13.

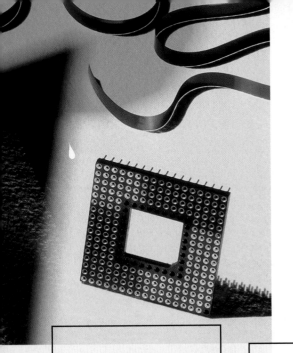

Brand Management and
New Product Planning

CHAPTER

12

CHAPTER OBJECTIVES

1. Explain the benefits of branding and brand management.

2. Describe the different types of brands.

3. Explain the strategic value of brand equity.

4. Describe how firms develop strong identities for their products and brands.

5. Identify alternative new product development strategies and the determinants of each strategy's success.

6. Identify the determinants of a new product's rate of adoption and the methods for accelerating the speed of adoption.

7. Explain the various organizational structures for new product development.

8. List the stages in the new product development process.

9. Outline the functions of the Consumer Product Safety Commission, and summarize the concept of product liability.

NBA Tries to Score Big with Its Brand

Dribble.
Pass.
Shoot.
Shop.

NBA STORE
THE ULTIMATE BASKETBALL SHOPPING EXPERIENCE.
Fifth Avenue and 52nd Street
New York, NY
212-515-NBA1
NBA.com

What do you think of when you see or hear the letters NBA? Reggie Miller? Kobe Bryant? The Utah Jazz? The Milwaukee Bucks? Jackets and caps with team logos? Screaming fans? The National Basketball Association (NBA) wants you to think of all these things and much, much more. The NBA isn't just about basketball. It's about marketing and managing a very successful brand.

The NBA is, in fact, a brand. The name identifies professional basketball in consumers' minds, distinguishing it from professional football, baseball, and hockey. The name identifies member teams and players, as well as officially sanctioned retail products—from clothing to sports gear. If all of this makes sense, what about adding restaurants and exclusive sports clubs to the mix? What about an Internet site? What about sports entertainment TV shows? What about an entire entertainment division within the NBA organization to oversee all of these activities?

In fact, all of these things exist. Some of the new sports arenas aren't about the game at all; they are about luxury. The Grand Reserve Club at Los Angeles's new Staples Center arena features oysters on the half shell and single malt scotches. Patrons can relax in front of a roaring fire or out on a private patio. Membership to the club costs $10,500, and that's on top of $12,800 to $14,800 for premium season seating. "These kinds of facilities are necessary for teams to compete in the business of sports today," explains National Basketball Association Commissioner David Stern. If these clubs seem a bit expensive for most consumers, there is the NBA City restaurant in Orlando, which is a joint venture with Hard Rock Café International, where fans can get "official" burgers and fries. Another restaurant is opening in New York, with several more scheduled for overseas markets, where people love the NBA. If consumers want to buy more stuff, they can visit the NBA Store in New York, with more on the way in other cities. "We're looking for ways fans can directly experience what the NBA is about," says Adam Silver, president and chief operating officer of NBA Entertainment.

But there's more. The NBA isn't content just to broadcast basketball games to diehard fans. In addition to traditional sports entertainment and commentary shows, the organization is working on extending into high-tech outlets. These include an animated show that viewers can receive in several different languages; a sitcom based on real NBA members, featuring a real game; and All-Star 2000 ballot kiosks, which will be set up in movie theaters. Of course, prominent NBA players will be featured in trailers at the theaters, asking people to vote at the kiosks.

Finally, there is NBA.com and NBA.com TV, the organization's official Web site and new 24-hour network. For the cable TV network, executives have signed up top-name broadcasters, including Ahmad Rashad. The channel will pepper viewers with statistics, scores, and news from NBA.com, live studio-based programming with cuts to ongoing games, highlights, and classics from NBA archives. "NBA.com TV represents the convergence of the Internet, television, and basketball," boasts David Stern. This is the first full-time television network created by a professional sports league. "We see this as an opportunity to tap into the rich array of information available on NBA.com and the vast television programming from our video and film library," notes Adam Silver.

At the Internet site, fans who can't attend games can still get good seats by clicking on one of three camera vantage points and taking a digital snapshot of a pivotal play. The cameras were so popular during one game between the Chicago Bulls and Utah Jazz that 90,000 pictures were taken. "We've always linked the brand with what I'd broadly call technology," notes Silver. "Being on the Internet is critical for how we define ourselves."

In sum, the NBA wants consumers to think of it as more than the game of basketball, more than the players and teams. The NBA brand name allows the organization to expand into new markets with credibility—because consumers already know and trust the name, they are willing to try new products. However, NBA executives need to plan carefully the directions in which the organization will expand. If they don't, they could dilute the name or lose credibility because of poorly planned or inappropriate new projects. The goal is to get consumers to follow the bouncing orange ball without falling out of bounds.[1]

1

Explain the benefits of branding and brand management.

 quakeroats.com

CHAPTER OVERVIEW

This chapter reviews the requirements for effective product decisions and these decisions' crucial roles in determining a firm's success. Developing and marketing a product are costly propositions. To protect its investment and maximize the return on this investment, a business must carefully nurture both existing and new products.

This chapter focuses on two critical elements of product planning and strategy. First, it looks at how firms build and maintain identity and competitive advantage for their products through branding. Second, it focuses on the new product planning and introduction process. Effective new product planning requires vital preparation. The needs of consumers change constantly; most firms manage to grow only if they provide innovative and useful solutions to fill those needs. ■

MANAGING BRANDS FOR COMPETITIVE ADVANTAGE

Think of the last time you went shopping for groceries. As you moved through the store, chances are your recognition of various brand names influenced many of your purchasing decisions. Perhaps you chose Colgate toothpaste over competitive offerings or loaded Heinz ketchup into your cart instead of the store brand. Walking through the soft drink aisle, you might have reached for Coca-Cola or Pepsi without much thought.

Marketers recognize the potentially powerful influence on customer behavior that creating and protecting a strong identity for products and product lines has. Branding is the process of creating that identity. A **brand** is a name, term, sign, symbol, design, or some combination that identifies the products of one firm while differentiating these products from competitors' offerings. For example, the brand name Toasted Oatmeal Squares, the slogan "Quaker Oatmeal Goodness in Every Box," and the familiar drawing of a white-haired gentleman in a broad-brimmed black hat all serve to identify a cereal made by the Quaker Oats Co. Table 12.1 shows some selected brands, brand names, and brand marks.

Buyers respond to branding by making repeat purchases of the same product because they identify the item with the name of its producer. The purchaser can associate the satisfaction derived from an ice cream bar, for example, with the brand name Häagen-Dazs.

Brand Loyalty

Brands achieve widely varying consumer familiarity and acceptance. While a boating enthusiast may insist on a Johnson outboard motor, the same consumer might show little loyalty to

T A B L E 1 2 . 1	Selected Brands, Brand Names, and Brand Marks
Brand type	Dr Pepper or IBC Root Beer
Private brand	Sam's Choice beverage (Wal-Mart) or ACE brand tools
Family brand	Heinz 57 or the RAID insect sprays, or Campbell
Individual brand	Tide or Purex
Brand name	Special K or Oops!
Brand mark	Colonel Sanders for KFC or Mr. Peanut for Planters

particular brands in another product category such as chocolate. Marketers measure brand loyalty in three stages: brand recognition, brand preference, and brand insistence.

Brand recognition is a company's first objective for newly introduced products. Marketers begin the promotion of new items by trying to make these items familiar to the public. Advertising offers one effective way for increasing consumer awareness of a brand. Kellogg's, for example, introduced its new Smart Start cereal with ads that prominently display the brand name, as shown in Figure 12.1. Other strategies for creating brand recognition include offering free samples or discount coupons for purchases. Once consumers have used a product, seen it advertised, or noticed it in stores, it moves from the unknown to the known category, which increases the probability that those consumers will purchase it.

 kelloggs.com

At the second level of brand loyalty, **brand preference,** consumers rely on previous experiences with the product when choosing that product, if available, over competitors' products. For example, Kellogg's new Raisin Bran Crunch cereal was quick to reach this stage. After only six months on the market, it reached 1 percent of total breakfast cereal sales—an impressive achievement for a new entry on already crowded cereal shelves. Kellogg's, however, hopes that Raisin Bran Crunch will ultimately achieve brand insistence, the level enjoyed by its top-selling cereal, Frosted Flakes, which has been popular for close to half a century.[2]

Brand insistence, the ultimate stage in brand loyalty, leads consumers to refuse alternatives and to search extensively for the desired merchandise. A product at this stage has achieved a monopoly position with its consumers. Although many firms try to establish brand insistence with all consumers, few achieve this ambitious goal.

Types of Brands

Companies that practice branding classify brands in several ways: private, manufacturer's (national), family, and individual brands. In making branding decisions, firms must weigh the benefits and disadvantages of each type of brand.

Some firms, however, sell their goods without any efforts at branding. These items are called **generic products.** They are characterized by plain labels, little or no advertising, and no brand names.

Common categories of generic products include food and household staples. These no-name products were first sold in Europe at prices as much as 30 percent below those of brand name products. This marketing strategy was introduced in the United States in 1977. The market shares for generic products

2

Describe the different types of brands.

M A R K E T I N G   D I C T I O N A R Y

brand Name, term, sign, symbol, design, or some combination that identifies the products of a firm.

brand recognition Stage of brand acceptance at which the consumer knows of a brand but does not prefer it to competing brands.

brand preference Stage of brand acceptance at which the consumer selects one brand over competing offerings based on previous experiences with that brand.

brand insistence Stage of brand acceptance at which the consumer refuses to accept alternatives and searches extensively for the desired good or service.

generic product Item characterized by a plain label, with no advertising and no brand name.

Building Consumer Awareness for a New Brand

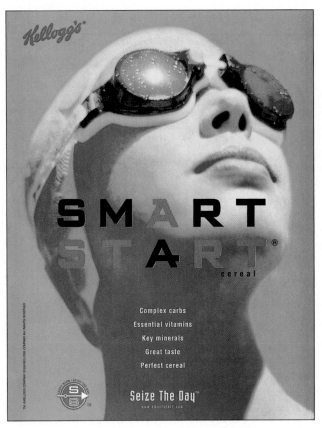

increase during economic downturns but subside when the economy improves.

Manufacturers' Brands versus Private Brands

Manufacturers' brands, also called *national brands*, define the image that most people form when they think of a brand. A **manufacturer's brand** refers to a brand name owned by a manufacturer or other producer. Well-known manufacturers' brands include Kodak, Whirlpool, and Heinz.

In contrast, many large wholesalers and retailers place their own brands on the merchandise they market. The brands offered by wholesalers and retailers are usually called **private brands** (or private labels). Although some manufacturers refuse to produce private label goods, most regard such production as a way to reach additional market segments. Every year, for example, cereal maker Ralston Purina has steadily increased its budget for its 17 private-label cereals, such as Corn Flakes and Crispy Rice, to compete with such cereals as Kellogg's Corn Flakes and Rice Krispies.

Private brands and generic products expand the number of alternatives available to consumers. As Figure 12.2 illustrates Sears sells its own brands under the names of Craftsman, Kenmore, DieHard, and Harmony House. Sears also launched a private label line of jeans, Canyon River Blues. Safeway stocks its shelves with such private brands as Bel Air, Canterbury, Cragmont, Party Pride, Manor House, and Scotch Buy. McDonald's Corp. even introduced its own private brand of bottled water.[3]

The growth of private brands has paralleled that of chain stores in the United States, most of the growth occurring since the 1930s. Manufacturers not only sell their well-known brands to stores, they also put the store's own label on these products. Such leading manufacturers as Westinghouse, Armstrong Rubber, and Heinz generate ever-increasing percentages of their total incomes by producing goods for sale under retailers' private labels. Not only is this popular in the United States, but the practice is gaining strength in European countries, as well.

Although some manufacturers refuse to produce private-label goods, some experts are predicting that private brands could still end up with about 45 percent of the U.S. packaged goods market. The growth of private brands results largely from the desire of retailers and wholesalers to maintain control over the images, quality levels, and prices of the products they sell. Moreover, private brands usually carry lower prices, sometimes up to 35 percent less, than manufacturers' brands. Private labels can also be more profitable to retailers. Safeway offers 850 items under its "select" label. Safeway's private label merchandise margins are 10 percentage points above the national brands.[4]

As noted above, private brands are also selling well abroad. Consumers in Germany, the United Kingdom, and France welcome private-label goods and most regard such production as a way to reach additional segments of their total markets.

Captive Brands

The nation's major discounters—Wal-Mart, Kmart, and Target—have come up with a spin-off of the private-label idea. So-called **captive brands** are national brands that are sold exclusively by a retail chain. Captive brands typically provide better profit margins than private labels. Kmart's captive brands include women's clothing with the Jaclyn Smith label. (Smith is a celebrity most famous for her starring role in the 1970s hit TV series *Charlie's Angels*.) Kmart also carries such captive brands as Martha Stewart's home décor merchandise and White-Westinghouse appliances.

The following scenario, regarding Wal-Mart's decision to sell General Electric (GE) small appliances and related items, provides an excellent illustration of how a captive branding strategy is implemented. General Electric had exited the small appliance business back in 1984. Then a decade and a half later, Wal-Mart reached an agreement with General Electric to bring the once popular brand back. Wal-Mart provided the retailing clout, while General Electric used its engineering prowess to design a line of quality products.

Actual production of the GE-branded merchandise was not handled by GE or Wal-Mart, however. Instead, Hamilton Beach/Proctor Silex and The Rival Co. make the small appliances; Conair produces the hair dryers and curling irons for Wal-Mart's captive brand; and Holmes Products and Lasko Metal Products manufacture the electric fans.[5]

Family and Individual Brands

A **family brand** is a single brand name that identifies several related products. For example, KitchenAid markets a complete line of appliances under the KitchenAid name, and Johnson & Johnson offers a line of baby powder, lotions, plastic pants, and baby shampoo under one name. All Ocean Spray products, from its fresh cranberries to its line of juices shown in Figure 12.3, carry the Ocean Spray family brand name.

A manufacturer may instead choose to market a product under an **individual brand,** which uniquely identifies a product itself, rather than promoting it under the name of the company or under an umbrella name covering similar items. Lever Brothers, for example, markets Aim, Close Up, and Pepsodent toothpastes; All and Wisk laundry detergents; Imperial margarine; Caress, Dove, Lifebuoy, and Lux bath soaps; and Shield and Lever 2000 deodorant soaps. Quaker Oats markets Aunt Jemima breakfast products, Gatorade beverages, and Celeste Pizza. Individual brands cost more than family brands to market because the firm must develop a new promotional campaign to introduce each new product to its target market. Distinctive brands are extremely effective aids, however, in implementing market segmentation strategies.

On the other hand, a promotional outlay for a family brand benefits all items in the line. For example, a new addition to the Heinz line gains immediate recognition as part of the well-known family brand. Family brands also help marketers to introduce new products to

FIGURE 12.2 **Craftsman: A Private Brand for Sears**

© 1998 Sears, Roebuck and Co.

EATS TACKS AND WASHES THEM DOWN WITH A COUPLE GALLONS OF DIRTY WATER.

Take on the elements with the Craftsman portable two-gallon Wet/Dry Vac. At six-and-a-half pounds, this tough little machine is a compact version of our big vacs. So cleaning up the workshop, or any other dirty job, is easily within your grasp.

CRAFTSMAN

MAKES ANYTHING POSSIBLE

www.sears.com/craftsman

MARKETING DICTIONARY

✓**manufacturer's brand** Brand name owned by a manufacturer or other producer.

✓**private brand** Brand name placed on products marketed by wholesalers and retailers.

captive brands National brands that are sold exclusively by a retail chain.

✓**family brand** Brand name that identifies several related products.

individual brand Unique brand name that identifies a specific offering within a firm's product line and that is not grouped under a family brand.

brainstormed about the middle-income market. So Old Navy decided to go for fun on a budget. Designers created a casual, young-looking line of clothing that was less expensive than Gap clothing, sold in separate Old Navy stores with a warehouse feeling—exposed pipes, cement floors, chrome fixtures. The hippest music would be piped in while shoppers browsed for bargains.

THE OUTCOME Some observers worried about cannibalization—the Old Navy and Gap brands gobbling each other up by competing with each other—but so far, it hasn't happened. Old Navy has been an astounding success with consumers. Old Navy now operates over 480 stores, compared with 2,600 Gap stores. Perhaps surprisingly, Old Navy shoppers are not always lower income consumers. Research by one group shows that 72 percent of Old Navy sales go to households with incomes of $50,000 per year. Gap sales have drifted off the mark somewhat, but Gap officials blame this on "fashion missteps," not Old Navy's success. Either way, the brand is strong and growing stronger. Perhaps casual Friday will be spreading around the workplaces of the world.

3

Explain the strategic value of brand equity.

| FIGURE 12.3 | Example of a Family Brand Name |

both customers and retailers. Since supermarkets stock thousands of items, they hesitate to add new products unless they confidently expect active demand.

Family brands should identify products of similar quality, or the firm risks harming its overall product image. If Rolls Royce marketers were to place the Rolls name on a low-end car or a line of discounted clothing, they might severely tarnish the image of the luxury car line. Conversely, Lexus, Infiniti, and Mercedes-Benz put their names on luxury sport-utility vehicles to capitalize on their reputations and to enhance the acceptance of the new models in a competitive market.

Individual brand names should, however, distinguish dissimilar products. Quaker Oats markets its dog food line under the Ken-L Ration brand name and its cat food line under the Puss 'n' Boots brand name. Marketers of grocery products, such as Procter & Gamble, General Foods, and Lever Brothers, develop individual brands to appeal to unique market segments. These brands also enable the firms to stimulate competition within their own organizations and to increase total company sales. Consumers who do not want Tide can choose from Cheer, Dash, or Oxydol—all Procter & Gamble products—rather than choose a competitor's brand.

STRATEGIC IMPLICATIONS OF BRAND EQUITY

A strong brand identity has important strategic advantages for a firm. First, it increases the likelihood that consumers will recognize the firm's product or product line when they make purchase decisions. Second, a strong brand identity can contribute to buyers' perceptions of product quality. Branding can also reinforce customer loyalty and repeat purchases. A consumer who tries a brand and likes it will likely look for that brand on future store visits. All of these benefits contribute to a valuable form of competitive advantage called *brand equity*.

Brand equity refers to the added value that a certain brand name gives to a product in the marketplace. Brands with high equity confer financial advantages on a firm because they often command comparatively large market shares and consumers may give little attention to differences in prices. Studies have also linked brand equity to high profits and stock returns.[6]

In global operations, high brand equity often facilitates expansion into new markets. Coca-Cola is a high-equity brand recognized around the world. Similarly, Disney successfully markets products under its brand in Europe, Japan, and even China.

How can a business evaluate brand equity? The global advertising agency Young & Rubicam (Y&R) developed one measurement system called the *Brand Asset Valuator*. Y&R interviewed more than 90,000 consumers in 30 countries and collected information on over 13,000 brands to help create this measurement system. According to Y&R, a firm builds brand equity sequentially on four dimensions of brand personality. As shown in Figure 12.4, these four dimensions are differentiation, relevance, esteem, and knowledge.

Differentiation refers to a brand's ability to stand apart from competitors. Brands like Disney, Porsche, Rolls Royce, and Victoria's Secret stand out in consumers' minds as symbols of unique product characteristics. According to the Y&R model, marketers who want to develop a strong brand must start with a feature that no competitor can match in consumers' minds.

The second dimension in the Y&R model, *relevance*, refers to the real and perceived appropriateness of the brand to a large consumer segment. A large number of consumers must feel a need for the benefits offered by the brand. According to Y&R, brands with high relevance include AT&T, Hallmark, Kodak, and Campbell Soup.

Esteem is a combination of perceived quality and consumer perceptions about the growing or declining popularity of a brand. A rise in perceived quality enhances consumer admiration for the brand. Positive public opinion about a brand also promotes the brand's esteem. On the other hand, negative impressions about a brand's popularity reduce esteem. Brands with high esteem include Microsoft, Hershey, and Rubbermaid.

The final brand equity dimension is knowledge. *Knowledge* refers to the extent of customers' awareness of the brand and understanding of what a good or service stands for. Knowledge implies that customers feel an intimate relationship with a brand. Y&R lists Coca-Cola, Jell-O, Kodak, Campbell, and Crest as brands with high knowledge with customers.[7]

Unfortunately, even brands with high equity can lose their luster. This may be especially true of technology dependent goods and services, such as Internet search engines. AltaVista was once a leading brand name on the Internet, with state-of-the-art search capabilities that made it one of the ten most popular Web sites. Today, it attracts less than a third of the traffic enjoyed by its leading competitor, Yahoo! Inc. While Yahoo! and other sites evolved to meet burgeoning consumer demand for online shopping, gaming, e-mail, and stock market information, AltaVista stagnated.

However, AltaVista's current owner, Internet investment company CMGI Inc., feels the brand has the potential to regain its equity. AltaVista's search engine is still considered the fastest available, so it remains popular with engineers, professionals, and other research-oriented Internet users. AltaVista's secret to regaining a commanding presence in the market is its newly developed software called "spider"—software that scans the World Wide Web for new information and retrieves thousands of pages at a time. AltaVista's computer chips enable the system to index pages quickly, making them rapidly accessible.

CMGI plans to capitalize on AltaVista's technology and brand equity by transforming it into a major Internet portal. This will involve adding new content to the site, such as genealogy searches, automobile information, on-line shopping, Web broadcasting, and financial messages. Services on the site will be expanded to include instant messaging and home-page building.

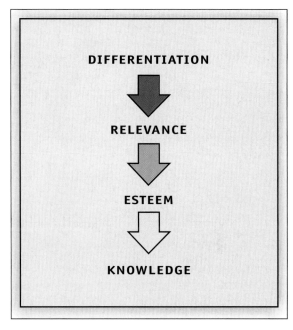

FIGURE 12.4 — Dimension of Brand Equity: The Young & Rubicam Model

DIFFERENTIATION

RELEVANCE

ESTEEM

KNOWLEDGE

Source: David A. Aaker, *Building Strong Brands,* p. 306

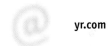

yr.com

altavista.com

MARKETING | **DICTIONARY**

brand equity Added value that a certain brand gives to a product.

FIGURE 12.5 **Investing in Brand Equity**

Compaq Computer, an investor in AltaVista, has added a button to its computer keyboards that connects users immediately to the search engine.

Investments in brand equity are not cheap; CMGI spent $100 million to improve and promote AltaVista, but the potential payoff is tremendous. CMGI views this as an investment in its strategy to become a dominant player on the Internet.[8] Figure 12.5 shows one of the ads in AltaVista's new print campaign, which is designed to inform readers about the search engine's new features.

The Role of Brand Managers

Because of the tangible and intangible value associated with strong brand equity, marketing organizations invest considerable resources and effort in developing and maintaining these dimensions of brand personality. Many large companies assign the task of managing a brand's marketing strategies to a **brand manager.** This marketing professional plans and implements the balance of promotional, pricing, distribution, and product arrangements that lead to strong brand equity. The next section looks at some of the tactics by which brand managers and other marketers create strong brand and product identities.

PRODUCT IDENTIFICATION

4

Describe how firms develop strong identities for their products and brands.

Organizations identify their products in the marketplace with brand names, symbols, and distinctive packaging. Almost every product that is distinguishable from another gives buyers some means of identifying it. Sunkist Growers, for instance, stamps its oranges with the name Sunkist. For nearly 100 years, Prudential Insurance Co. has used the Rock of Gibraltar as its organization-wide symbol. Choosing how to identify the firm's output represents a major strategic decision for marketers.

Brand Names and Brand Marks

What is in a name? According to researchers, a name plays a central role in establishing brand and product identity. The American Marketing Association has defined a **brand name** as the part of the brand consisting of words or letters that form a name that identifies and distinguishes the firm's offerings from those of its competitors. The brand name is, therefore, the part of the brand that people can vocalize. Firms can also identify their brands by brand marks. A **brand mark** is a symbol or pictorial design that distinguishes a product. The green giant in the ad shown in Figure 12.6 is the brand mark of the Green Giant Co., which uses the symbol to differentiate its brand from other food marketers.

Effective brand names are easy to pronounce, recognize, and remember. Short names, such as Nike, Geo, Crest, and Tide, meet these requirements. Marketers try to overcome problems with easily mispronounced brand names by teaching consumers the correct pronunciations. For example, early advertisements for the Korean car maker Hyundai explained that the name rhymes with *Sunday.*

A brand name should also give buyers the correct connotation of the product's image. The Tru-Test name for True Value Hardware's line of paints suggests reliable performance. Visa suggests a credit card that provides global acceptance. Zebco, a manufacturer of fishing equipment, chose Rhino as the brand name for a fishing rod to convey the product's strength.

A brand name must also qualify for legal protection. The Lanham Act of 1946 states that registered trademarks must not contain words or phrases in general use, such as *automobile* or *suntan lotion.* These generic words actually describe particular types of products, and no company can claim exclusive rights to them.

Marketers feel increasingly hard-pressed to coin effective brand names, as multitudes of competitors rush to stake out brand names for their own products. Some companies register names before they have products to fit the names in order to stop competitors from using them.

When a class of products becomes generally known by the original brand name of a specific offering, the brand name may become a descriptive **generic name.** If this occurs, the original owner loses exclusive claim to the brand name. The generic names nylon, aspirin, escalator, kerosene, and zipper started as brand names. Other generic names that were once brand names include cola, yo-yo, linoleum, and shredded wheat.

Marketers must distinguish between brand names that have become legally generic terms and those that seem generic only in many consumers' eyes. Consumers often adopt legal brand names as descriptive names. Jell-O, for instance, is a brand name owned exclusively by General Foods, but many consumers casually apply it as a descriptive name for gelatin desserts. Many English and Australian consumers use the brand name Hoover as a verb for vacuuming. Similarly, Xerox is such a well-known brand name that people frequently—though incorrectly—use it as a verb. To protect its valuable trademark, Xerox Corp. has created advertisements explaining that Xerox is a brand name and registered trademark and should not be used as a verb.

Trademarks

Businesses invest considerable resources in developing and promoting brands

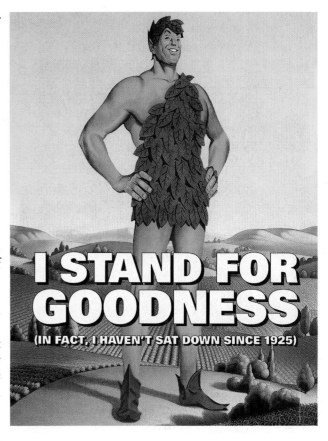

I STAND FOR GOODNESS

(IN FACT, I HAVEN'T SAT DOWN SINCE 1925)

MARKETING DICTIONARY

brand manager Marketing professional charged with planning and implementing marketing strategies and tactics for a brand.

brand name Part of a brand consisting of words or letters that forms a name to identify and distinguish a firm's offerings.

brand mark Symbol or pictorial design that identifies a product.

generic name Brand name that has become a generally descriptive term for a class of products.

FIGURE 12.7 | **Registered Trademarks of The Coca-Cola Company**

and brand identities. The high value of brand equity encourages firms to take steps in protecting the expenditures they invest in their brands.

A **trademark** is a brand for which the owner claims exclusive legal protection. A trademark should not be confused with a trade name, which identifies a company. The Coca-Cola Company is a trade name, but Coke is a trademark of the company. Some trade names duplicate companies' brand names. For example, Rubbermaid is the brand name of Rubbermaid, Inc.

Protecting Trademarks

Trademark protection confers the exclusive legal right to use a brand name, brand mark, and any slogan or product name abbreviation. It designates the origin or source of a good or service. Registered trademarks of The Coca-Cola Company, shown in Figure 12.7, include the red disk icon, the brand name Coca-Cola Classic, and the contour bottle design. Frequently, trademark protection is applied to words or phrases, such as Bud for Budweiser or the Met for the New York Metropolitan Opera.[9] For example, the courts upheld Budweiser's trademark in one case, ruling that an exterminating company's slogan "This Bug's for You" infringed on Budweiser's rights.

Firms can also receive trademark protection for packaging elements and product features such as shape, design, and typeface. Even a date can qualify. Retail designer Ken Walker, for example, obtained trademark protection for the numeric sequence "01-01-00," which he placed on clothes and household items to commemorate the dawning of the 21st century.[10]

U.S. law has fortified trademark protection in recent years. The Federal Trademark Dilution Act of 1995 gives a trademark holder the right to sue for trademark infringement even if other products using its brand are not particularly similar or easily confused in the minds of consumers. The infringing company does not even have to know that it is diluting another's trademark. The act also gives a trademark holder the right to sue if another party imitates its trademark.

The Internet may be the next battlefield for trademark infringement cases. Some companies are attempting to protect their trademarks by filing infringement cases against companies using similar Internet addresses.

Trade Dress

Visual cues used in branding create an overall look sometimes referred to as **trade dress**. These visual components may be related to color selections, sizes, package and label shapes, and similar factors. For example, McDonald's golden arches, Merrill Lynch's bull, Coca-Cola's unique bottle shape, and the yellow of Shell's seashell are all part of these products' trade dress. A combination of visual cues may also constitute trade dress. Consider a Mexican food product that uses the colors of the Mexican flag: green, white, and red.

@ cadillac.com

When Le Sieur Antoine de la Mothe Cadillac founded Detroit hundreds of years ago, he had no idea that his name would be used for a domestic luxury car and that his coat of arms would become the basis of the model's trade dress. Cadillac's logo is used on its trunks, steering wheels, car seats, and hoods. But times change: Cadillac has recently replaced its 36-year-old wreath and crest logo with an abstract design that retains the traditional wreath.

Cadillac is clearly targeting a more youthful customer segment. The new trade dress is part of its strategy. John F. Smith, Cadillac's general manager comments: "The new wreath and crest depicts a forward-looking and youthful image while maintaining distinctiveness and a sense of prestige." Cadillac's redesign of its trade dress suggests the importance General Motors assigns to their aspect of the marketing strategy.[11]

SOLVING AN ETHICAL CONTROVERSY

When Big Companies Act Small

Everyone loves a David and Goliath story, in which a smaller, weaker character battles a larger, stronger one. Several such stories have surfaced lately, in which large organizations claim they are protecting their trademarks by ordering smaller companies to stop conducting business under certain names. Take the *Small Street Journal,* a tiny newspaper published in Maine and distributed free to children in hospitals, schools, and libraries. The children's journal, produced by a middle-aged couple who earn roughly $6,000 a year, is filled with poems, stories, and drawings by Maine kids. No one would confuse this publication with the *Wall Street Journal,* which has annual revenues of $2 billion, yet attorneys for WSJ sent a letter to Small Journal publishers Noreen Reed and Chris Yountz stating, "Your registration and use of *Small Street Journal* constitutes trademark infringement, trademark dilution and unfair competition under federal and state law." The letter ordered Reed and Yountz to stop publishing their paper and destroy all copies.

Across the Atlantic Ocean, McDonald's sent a similar letter to Scottish sandwich shop owner Mary Blair, informing her that she could no longer use the name McMunchies because McDonald's is the registered user of the Mc prefix. Blair's shop doesn't even sell burgers or fries; she chose the name because she simply wanted to add Scottish flavor to the shop.

Should large organizations such as McDonald's and the *Wall Street Journal* go to extremes to protect their trademarks?

Pro
1. Trademarks are valuable property. Under the Federal Trademark Dilution Act of 1995, organizations have the right to protect their trademarks from use by any other organization.
2. Brand equity is extremely important to both McDonald's and WSJ, and both organizations should protect it at all costs.
3. Organizations need to protect their trademarks from infringement by all other companies, regardless of whether they are large or small.

Con
1. No consumer would confuse either of these businesses with the products of their larger counterparts. Corporate lawyers should save their lawsuits for serious business threats.
2. The smaller organizations do not present any competitive threat to the larger corporations. They are in completely different markets.
3. Prosecuting these smaller organizations will only generate bad publicity for the larger organizations, who seem to be bullies.

Summary
"This isn't David vs. Goliath," insists Richard Tofel, vice president of corporate communications for Dow Jones, which owns the *Wall Street Journal.* "We're not trying to put little children out of business. We're just trying to preserve a 110-year-old brand name. They filed for trademark registration; by doing that, they're saying they want to own the name. That presents a problem for us." Richard Yountz argues that none of his readers will confuse the *Small Street Journal* with WSJ, and in no way does his paper compete with the Dow Jones publication. "In my opinion, if a guy picks up my paper and thinks he's got the *Wall Street Journal,* he shouldn't be reading any of them."

In Scotland, McDonald's is claiming that Mary Blair's "unauthorized" use of Mc will confuse the public. But where did the prefix Mc actually originate? In Scotland, of course, says Lord Godfrey McDonald, chief of the clan.

SOURCES: Allyson Lieberman, "Kids Paper Bullied by WSJ," *New York Post Online Edition,* accessed January 25, 2000; Stephen Sawicki, "Showdown on Small Street," *U.S. News & World Report,* November 8, 1999, p. 23; Sydney Schanber, "Wall Street Journal vs. Small Street Journal," November 2, 1999, www.apbnews.com; "Scots Chief to Defend His Clan," *The Herald* (UK), October 7, 1996.

Trade dress disputes have led to numerous courtroom battles. In one widely publicized case, Kendall-Jackson Vineyards and Winery sued Ernest & Julio Gallo Winery Inc., claiming that the bottle design used for Gallo's Turning Leaf Chardonnay was too similar to its Kendall's Vintner's Reserve chardonnay bottle. Kendall-Jackson lost in court, but this case suggests the importance that firms assign to trade dress.[12]

gallo.com

kendall-jackson.com

Developing Global Brand Names and Trademarks

International marketers face a particularly acute problem in selecting brand names and trademarks; an excellent brand name or symbol in one country may prove disastrous in another. A firm marketing a product in multiple countries must decide whether to define a

MARKETING   DICTIONARY

trademark Brand to which the owner legally claims exclusive access.

trade dress Visual cues used in branding to create an overall look.

single brand name for universal promotions or tailor names to individual countries. Most languages contain *o* and *k* sounds, so *okay* has become an international word. Most languages also have a short *a*; so Coca-Cola, Kodak, and Texaco work as effective brands in any country.

Trademarks that are effective in their home countries may do less well in other cultures. Consider Charlie, the 103-year-old rooster that symbolizes the output of French film company Pathé SA. Early ads featured Charlie (named for company cofounder Charles Pathé) with his head held high and his beak pointing jauntily upward, boasting "I crow loud and clear," a reference to the films' excellent sound qualities. However, while French audiences liked the proud bird, moviegoers in other countries perceived him as haughty and arrogant. "The rooster is very Gallic and doesn't necessarily represent the best qualities of the French," admits Pathé chairman Jerome Seydoux.

The company hired Landor Associates, a San Francisco-based consulting firm, to give Charlie a makeover. The new rooster is a whimsical creature portrayed in unexpected settings, like, for instance, in the back seat of a limousine or in the cockpit of a 1910-era biplane, from which he crows "Pathé" in a large cartoon-like bubble. The company uses the new Charlie on everything from corporate stationery to cinema marquees, movie tickets, and popcorn containers, to reinforce its brand name around the world. Charlie's new look may even make him a movie star; Pathé plans to feature him in animated introductions to its films.[13]

Packaging

A firm's product strategy must address questions about packaging. Like its brand name, a product's package can powerfully influence buyers' purchase decisions.

Firms are applying increasingly scientific methods to their packaging decisions. Rather than experimenting with physical models or drawings, more and more package designers work on special computer graphics that create three-dimensional images of packages in thousands of colors, shapes, and typefaces. Another computer system helps firms design effective packaging by simulating the displays shoppers see when they walk down supermarket aisles. Companies conduct marketing research to evaluate current packages and to test alternative package designs. Kellogg, for example, tested its Nutri-Grain cereal's package, as well as the product itself before launching the product into the market.

A package serves three major objectives: (1) protection against damage, spoilage, and pilferage; (2) assistance in marketing the product; and (3) cost effectiveness.

Protection against Damage, Spoilage, and Pilferage

The original objective of packaging was to offer physical protection for the merchandise. Products typically pass through several stages of handling between manufacturing and customer purchases, and a package must protect the contents from damage. Furthermore, packages of perishable products must protect the contents against spoilage in transit and in storage until purchased by the consumer. The American Plastics Council had developed an advertising campaign to promote the benefits of using plastics in food packaging. The ad in Figure 12.8 informs consumers that plastic bottles, wraps, and containers reduce the chance of food contamination and that tamper evidence plastic seals provide product safety assurance.

Fears of product tampering have forced many firms to improve package designs. Over-the-counter medicines are sold in tamper resistant packages covered with warnings informing consumers to not purchase merchandise without protective seals intact. Many grocery items and light-sensitive products are packaged in tamper-resistant containers as well. For example, products in glass jars, like spaghetti sauce and jams, often come with depressed buttons in the lids that pop up the first time the lids are opened.

Likewise, many packages offer important safeguards for retailers against pilferage. Shoplifting and employee theft cost retailers several billion dollars each year. To limit this activity, many packages feature oversized cardboard backings too large to fit into a shoplifter's pocket or purse. Efficient packaging that protects against damage, spoilage, and theft is especially important for international marketers, who must contend with varying climatic conditions and the added time and stress involved in overseas shipping.

Assistance in Marketing the Product

The proliferation of new products, changes in consumer lifestyles and buying habits, and marketers' emphasis on targeting smaller market segments have increased the importance of packaging as a promotional tool. Many firms are addressing consumer concerns about protecting the environment by designing packages with minimal amounts of biodegradable and recyclable materials. To demonstrate serious concern regarding environmental protection, Procter & Gamble, Coors, McDonald's, Amoco Chemical, and other firms have created ads that describe their efforts in developing environmentally sound packaging.

In a grocery store where thousands of different items compete for notice, a product must capture the shopper's attention. Marketers combine colors, sizes, shapes, graphics, and typefaces to establish distinctive trade dress that set their products apart from the products of their competitors. Packaging can help to establish a common identity for a group of items sold under the same brand name.

Like the brand name, a package should evoke the product's image and communicate its value. Some companies patent their package designs, which may play crucial roles in consumers' brand insistence. As noted earlier, people around the world recognize Coca-Cola's curved bottle, for example.

Packages can also enhance convenience for the buyers. Pump dispenser cans, for example, facilitate the use of products ranging from mustard to insect repellent. Squeezable bottles of honey and ketchup make the products easier to use and store. Packaging provides key benefits for convenience foods such as meals and snacks packaged in microwavable containers, juice drinks in aseptic packages, and frozen entrees and vegetables packaged in single-serving portions.

Some firms increase consumer utility with packages designed for reuse. Empty peanut butter jars and jelly jars have long doubled as drinking glasses. Parents can buy bubble bath in animal-shaped plastic bottles suitable for bathtub play. Packaging is a major component in Avon's overall marketing strategy. The firm's decorative, reusable bottles have even become collectibles.

avon.com

Cost-Effective Packaging

Although packaging must perform a number of functions for the producer, marketers, and consumers, it must do so at a reasonable cost. Sometimes changes in the packaging can make packages both cheaper and better for the environment. Compact disk manufacturers, for instance, once packaged CDs in two containers, a disk-sized plastic box inside a long, cardboard box that fit into the record bins in the stores. Consumers protested against the waste of the long boxes, and the recording industry finally agreed to eliminate the cardboard outer packaging altogether. Now CDs come in just the plastic cases, and stores display them in reusable plastic holders to discourage theft.

Labeling

Labels were once a separate element that was applied to a package; today, it is an integral part of a typical package. Labels perform both promotional and informational functions. A **label** carries an item's brand name or symbol, the name and address of the manufacturer or distributor, information about the product's composition

MARKETING DICTIONARY

label Descriptive part of a product's package that lists the brand name or symbol, name and address of manufacturer or distributor, product composition and size, and recommended uses.

and size, and recommended uses. The right label can play an important role in attracting consumer attention and encouraging purchase.

Consumer confusion and dissatisfaction over such incomprehensible descriptions as *giant economy size*, *king size*, and *family size* led to the passage of the Fair Packaging and Labeling Act in 1966. The act requires that a label offer adequate information concerning the package contents and that a package design facilitate value comparisons among competing products.

The Nutrition Labeling and Education Act of 1990 imposes a uniform format in which food manufacturers must disclose nutritional information about their products. In addition, the Food and Drug Administration (FDA) has mandated design standards for nutritional labels that provide clear guidelines to consumers about food products. The FDA has also tightened definitions for loosely used terms like *light*, *fat free*, *lean*, and *extra lean*, and it mandates that labels list the amounts of fat, sodium, dietary fiber, calcium, vitamins, and other components in typical servings.

Labeling requirements differ elsewhere in the world. In Canada, for example, labels must give information in both French and English. The type and amount of information required on labels also varies among nations. International marketers must carefully design labels to conform to the regulations of each country in which they operate and market their merchandise.

Green Labeling.   Green labeling is a product-related extension of green marketing discussed in Chapter 2. Green labeling practices place product seals and environmental claims on packages to designate environmentally safe products. For instance, package labels may describe the packages as recyclable or biodegradable or assert that a product causes less waste than its competitors.

The U.S. government has started to regulate these and other environmental claims. The Federal Trade Commission (FTC) has issued *Guides for the Use of Environmental Marketing Claims*, a booklet that gives standards for frequently misused terms. Firms that make unsubstantiated or misleading claims on product labels risk fines from the FTC or lawsuits by states whose laws ban deceptive environmental labeling.

Several nations in Europe have developed their own standards for green product labels. The European Union's ecolabel program specifies a standard symbol for products that are manufactured with reduced energy, water, and detergent consumption.

Universal Product Code.   The **Universal Product Code (UPC)** designation is another very important aspect of a label or package. Introduced in 1974 as a method for cutting expenses in the supermarket industry, UPCs are numerical bar codes printed on packages. Optical scanner systems read these codes, and computer systems recognize items and print their prices on cash register receipts. Virtually all packaged grocery items carry the UPC bars. While UPC scanners are costly, they permit both considerable labor savings over manual pricing and improved inventory control. The Universal Product Code is also a major asset for marketing research.

BRAND EXTENSIONS, BRAND LICENSING, AND CO-BRANDING

Some brands become so popular that companies carry these products over to unrelated products in pursuit of marketing advantages. The strategy of attaching a popular brand name to a new product in an unrelated product category is known as **brand extension.** Marketers should not confuse this practice with *line extensions*, which refers to new sizes, styles, or related products. A brand extension, in contrast, carries over from one product nothing but the brand name. In establishing brand extensions, companies hope to gain access to new customers and markets by building on the equity already established in their existing brands.

jello.com

Consider the case of Jell-O. In certain markets, this popular brand has been extended to Jell-O Pudding Pops, Jell-O Slice Crème, and Jell-O Gelatin Pops. Similarly, the Bic brand made popular with ballpoints was later used for a line of disposable razors and the utility lighter shown in Figure 12.9.[14]

Brand extensions run considerable risk of brand dilution. *Brand dilution* occurs when a firm introduces too many brand extensions, some of which might not succeed. Scattered marketing programs may then erode the firm's brand equity.

Brand Licensing

A growing number of firms have authorized other companies to use its brand names. This practice, known as **brand licensing,** expands a firm's exposure in the marketplace, much as a brand extension does. The brand name's owner also receives an extra source of income in the form of royalties from licensees, typically from 4 to 8 percent of wholesale revenues.

Hasbro Inc., for example, has successfully licensed its Monopoly brand to cover a wide array of products. WMS Industries has licensed the venerable board game concept to produce Monopoly slot machines for casinos. The game's Rich Uncle Pennybags figure, complete with top hat and luxuriant white mustache, appeared on drink cups at McDonald's restaurants as part of a Monopoly game promotion. Other companies have purchased the right to create geographic variations of the board game—St. Louis Monopoly, for example— while others are cooking up Monopoly chocolate and cookie dough. At last count, Hasbro had 36 licensing agreements related to the brand.[15]

Brand experts note several potential problems with licensing, however. Brand names do not transfer well to all products. If a licensee produces a poor quality product or an item ethically incompatible with the original brand, the arrangement could change the reputation of the brand.

Co-branding, a practice closely related to brand licensing, joins together two strong brand names, perhaps owned by two different companies, to sell a product. In addition to its licensing agreements, Hasbro has negotiated a number of co-branding ventures. It has teamed up with semiconductor maker Intel Corp. to craft digital cameras for kids, with IS Robotics to design robotic toys, and with Converse to produce a line of Koosh-ball footwear.[16]

NEW PRODUCT PLANNING

As its offerings enter the maturity and decline stages of the product life cycle, a firm must add new items to continue to prosper. Regular additions of new products to the firm's line helps to protect it from product obsolescence.

New products are the lifeblood of any business, and survival depends on a steady flow of new entries. Some new products may implement major technological breakthroughs. Other new products simply extend existing product lines. In other words, a new product is

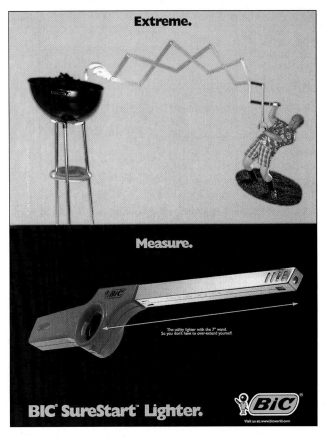

| FIGURE 12.9 | Utility Lighter: A Bic Brand Extension |

Extreme.

Measure.

The utility lighter with the 7" wand.
So you don't have to over-extend yourself.

BIC® SureStart™ Lighter. **BIC®**

Visit us at www.bicworld.com

hasbro.com

5

Identify alternative new product development strategies and the determinants of each strategy's success.

MARKETING DICTIONARY

Universal Product Code (UPC) Bar code on a product's package that provides information read by optical scanners.

brand extension Application of a popular brand name to a new product in an unrelated product category.

brand licensing Practice of allowing other companies to use a brand name in exchange for a payment.

co-branding Practice of combining two strong brands, perhaps owned by different companies, to sell a product.

Fruit of the Loom

BACKGROUND No one can forget those crazy underwear ads, with human fruit bumping into each other. But the owner of one of America's oldest brands has filed for bankruptcy after years of slumping sales. In 1856, a company founded in Rhode Island adopted one of the first brand names—Fruit of the Loom—for bolts of fabric produced in its textile mills. In 1871, Fruit of the Loom became one of the first registered trademarks. And in 1875, the unforgettable image of three fruits—an apple, a pear, and a cluster of grapes—became the brand mark for the Fruit of the Loom label. From there, Fruit of the Loom products became household basics.

THE MARKETING PROBLEM By the turn of a second century, however, Fruit of the Loom was in trouble. Sales of its laundry list of branded products had fallen steadily for a decade. In a huge cost-cutting effort, the company decided to close many of its U.S. plants and move manufacturing operations overseas.

THE OUTCOME The overseas move failed because untrained workers began turning out lower quality products, causing the company to hire more expensive contractors and pay overtime to fix the problem. Eventually, Fruit of the Loom filed for Chapter 11 reorganization. But executives were counting on the venerable reputation of the Fruit of the Loom brand ultimately to save the organization.

continued on next page

FIGURE 12.10 Alternative Product Development Strategies

	Old Product	**New Product**
Old Market	Market Penetration	Product Development
New Market	Market Development	Product Diversification

one that either the company or the customer has not handled before. Only about 10 percent of new product introductions bring truly new capabilities to people who are completely unfamiliar with them.

Product Development Strategies

A firm's strategy for new product development varies according to its existing product mix and the match between current offerings and the firm's overall marketing objectives. The current market positions of products also affect product development strategy. Figure 12.10 identifies four alternative development strategies: market penetration, market development, product development, and product diversification.

A *market penetration strategy* seeks to increase sales of existing products in existing markets. Firms can attempt to extend their penetration of markets in several ways. They may modify products, improve product quality, or promote new and different ways to use products. Packaged goods marketers often pursue this strategy to boost market share for mature products in mature markets. Product positioning often plays a major role in such a strategy.

Product positioning refers to consumers' perceptions of a product's attributes, uses, quality, and advantages and disadvantages relative to competing brands. Marketers often conduct marketing research studies to analyze consumer preferences and to construct product positioning maps that plot their products' positions in relation to those of competitors' offerings.

A *market development strategy* concentrates on finding new markets for existing products. Market segmentation, discussed in Chapter 8, provides useful support for such an effort. For example, cigarette makers have adopted a market development strategy by targeting bartenders. Tobacco companies shower the bartenders with gifts, such as exclusive parties, all-expenses-paid vacations, gift certificates, and concert and movie tickets; some firms simply write these bartenders checks ranging from $2,000 to $50,000 a year. With the gifts come free bar supplies emblazoned with the companies' brand names. In exchange, the bartenders are asked to stock the companies' cigarettes—and none of the competing brands—in their establishments and to recommend the cigarettes to customers who light up. One bartender in New York's East Village is under no illusions: "They give me all this stuff because they want me to like their products and push their products," he admits.[17]

The strategy of *product development* refers to the introduction of new products into identifiable or established markets. For instance, about 10 percent of the 90 million prescription eyeglasses sold each year in the United States are photochromic—chemicals in the lenses darken when exposed to sunlight. While this may sound like a great idea in theory, in practice the lenses can take an annoyingly long time to respond to sudden changes in light, such as when driving through a series of tunnels. To gain a larger share of the prescription eyeglasses market, Pittsburgh–based

PPG Inc. is developing battery-powered lenses that darken when the wearer flips a tiny switch in the frame. Preliminary tests show its lenses can go from clear to dark in about 25 seconds, compared to several minutes for conventional lenses.[18]

Firms may choose to introduce new products into markets in which they have already established positions to try to increase overall market share. These new offerings are called *flanker brands*. Toy company Hedstrom Corp., based in Mount Prospect, Illinois, flanks established products such as its battery-operated Power Riders car with additional products for the children's leisure market. An example of a new additional product is the company's new multiplayer game table, equipped with an electronic scorekeeper for Ping-Pong and other pastimes.[19]

Finally, a *product diversification* strategy focuses on developing entirely new products for new markets. Some firms look for new target markets that complement their existing markets; others look in completely new directions.

Several companies, for example, are working to develop innovative ovens that combine the speed of a microwave oven with the superior cooking results of a conventional oven. General Electric's Advantium supplements microwave heat with super-hot halogen light bulbs that brown foods while leaving them appetizingly crispy. Amana Appliances' Wave oven cooks with halogen bulbs only. Maytag Corp. is exploring a different technology altogether in its TurboChef model, which bombards food with high-velocity jets of hot air.[20]

Marketers need to consider **cannibalization** in picking a new product strategy. Any firm wants to avoid investing resources in a new product introduction that will adversely affect sales of existing products. A product that takes sales from another offering in the same product line is said to *cannibalize* that line. While a firm can accept some sacrifice when a promising new product takes some sales from existing, products, marketing research should ensure that the new offering will guarantee sufficient additional sales to warrant the firm's investment in its development and market introduction.

The Consumer Adoption Process

Consumer purchases also influence decisions regarding a new product offering. In the **adoption process,** potential consumers go through a series of stages from learning about the new product to trying it and deciding whether to purchase it regularly or to reject it. These stages in the consumer adoption process can be classified as the following:

1. *Awareness.* Individuals first learn of the new product, but they lack full information about it.
2. *Interest.* Potential buyers begin to seek information about it.
3. *Evaluation.* They consider the likely benefits of the product.
4. *Trial.* They make trial purchases to determine its usefulness.
5. *Adoption/Rejection.* If the trial purchase produces satisfactory results, they decide to use the product regularly.[21]

Marketers must understand the adoption process in order to move potential consumers to the adoption stage. Once marketers recognize a large number of consumers at the interest stage, they can take steps to stimulate sales by moving these buyers through the evaluation and trial stages. For example, Johnson & Johnson enhanced the evaluation and trial of its disposable contact lenses by offering free trial pairs to consumers. America Online mails its Internet-access software and offers a free one-month membership to computer owners who are not AOL members. From time to time you may receive

MARKETING STRATEGY FAILURE

LESSONS LEARNED Brand equity itself may not be enough to save a company that is in trouble. Although it is difficult to pinpoint exactly what went wrong in the decade before Fruit of the Loom's potentially fatal move overseas, it's possible that the company simply had too many brands in too many markets—from infants to senior citizens—to manage them effectively. By the year 2000, the company was managing products under the brand names Fruit of the Loom, BVD, Underoos, Gitano, Best, Cumberland Bay, and Screen Star. So perhaps the company had begun to lose control of its once-profitable image: a bunch of goofy guys in fruit costumes, bumping into each other, making us all laugh.

ppg.com

maytag.com

MARKETING **DICTIONARY**

product positioning Consumers' perceptions of a product's attributes, uses, quality, and advantages and disadvantages in relation to those of competing brands.

cannibalization Loss of sales of a current product due to competition from a new product in the same line.

adoption process Series of stages through which consumers decide whether or not to become regular users of a new product, including awareness, interest, evaluation, trial, and rejection or adoption.

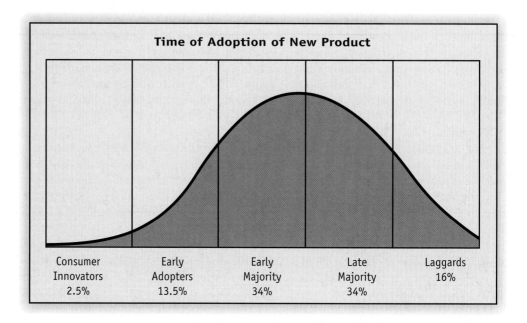

FIGURE 12.11 Categories of Adopters Based on Relative Times of Adoption

free samples of breakfast cereals, snack foods, cosmetics, or shampoos in the mail. These companies are encouraging you to try their products in the hopes that you will adopt these products.

Adopter Categories

Consumer innovators are people who purchase new products almost as soon as these products reach the market. Other adopters wait for additional information and rely on the experiences of initial buyers before making trial purchases. Consumer innovators welcome innovations in each product area. Some computer users, for instance, rush to install new software immediately after each updated version becomes available. Some physicians, as well, pioneered the uses of new pharmaceutical products for their AIDS patients. Some fans bought season tickets before the NFL Browns came back to Cleveland.

A number of studies about the adoption of new products have identified five categories of purchasers based on relative times of adoption. These categories, shown in Figure 12.11, are consumer innovators, early adopters, early majority, late majority, and laggards.

The **diffusion process** brings acceptance of new goods and services by the members of the community or social system. Figure 12.11 shows a normal distribution over the course of this process. A few people adopt at first, then the number of adopters increases rapidly as the value of the innovation becomes apparent. The adoption rate finally diminishes as the number of potential consumers who have not adopted, or purchased, the product diminishes.

Since the categories are based on a normal distribution, marketers can apply standard deviations to quantify the adopters. Innovators make up the first 2.5 percent of buyers who adopt the new product; laggards are the last 16 percent to do so. Figure 12.12 excludes those who never adopt the innovation.

Identifying Early Adopters

Marketers foresee substantial benefits in locating the likely first buyers of new products (those in the consumer innovator and early adopter categories). By reaching these buyers early in the

FIGURE 12.12   **An Innovation for Surfing the Internet**

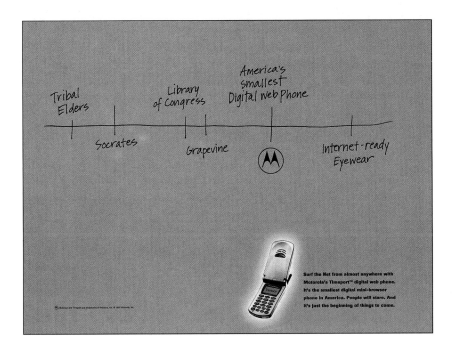

FIGURE 12.12   **An Innovation for Surfing the Internet**

product's development or introduction, marketers can treat these adopters as a test market, evaluating the product and discovering suggestions for modifications. Since early purchasers often act as opinion leaders from whom others seek advice, their attitudes toward new products quickly spread to others. Acceptance or rejection of the innovation by these purchasers can help forecast its expected success.

When Honda Motor Co. built its new S2000 sports car, it used extensive research to identify early adopters. After studying the buyers of popular competing sports cars, Honda concluded that 70 percent of S2000 customers would be college-educated men between the ages of 40 to 55 and with a median annual income of $100,000. The principal quality these customers seek in a car is one that is "fun to drive." Honda advertised the S2000 to this demographic section through its Web site, direct mail, TV commercials, and ads in consumer and automobile-oriented magazines.[22]

A large number of studies have established the general characteristics of first adopters. These pioneers tend to be younger, have higher social status, are better educated, and enjoy higher incomes than other consumers. They are more mobile than later adopters and change both their jobs and home addresses more often. They also rely more heavily than later adopters on impersonal information sources; more hesitant buyers depend primarily on company generated promotional information and word-of-mouth communications.

Rate of Adoption Determinants

Frisbees progressed from the product introduction stage to the market maturity stage in a period of six months. By contrast, the U.S. Department of Agriculture tried for 13 years to convince corn farmers to use hybrid seed corn, an innovation capable of doubling crop yields. Five characteristics of a product innovation influence its adoption rate:

6
Identify the determinants of a new product's rate of adoption and the methods for accelerating the speed of adoption.

MARKETING   DICTIONARY

consumer innovator Initial purchaser of a new product.

diffusion process Sequence of acceptance of new products by the members of a community or social system.

1. *Relative advantage.* An innovation that appears far superior to previous ideas offers a greater relative advantage—reflected in terms of lower price, physical improvements, or ease of use—and increases the product's adoption rate. For instance, some early adopters are installing digital subscriber lines to their home computers. Although expensive, the lines offer immediate Internet access when a computer is turned on and enable users to transmit and download information more rapidly than a conventional telephone modem.[23]

2. *Compatibility.* An innovation consistent with the values and experiences of potential adopters attracts new buyers at a relatively rapid rate. People who already enjoy surfing the Internet, for example, are more likely to spend money for a digital subscriber line. This same group of people may be early adopters of Motorola's Timeport digital Web phone shown in Figure 12.12, an innovation that allows people to surf the Internet from almost anywhere.

3. *Complexity.* The relative difficulty of understanding the innovation influences the speed of acceptance. In most cases, consumers move slowly in adopting new products that they find difficult to understand or use. Farmers' cautious acceptance of hybrid seed corn illustrates how long an adoption can take.

4. *Possibility of trial use.* An innovation that allows limited initial use may meet with early approval. First, adopters face two types of risk—financial loss and ridicule from others—if they rush to welcome a new product that provides unsatisfactory service in full. The option of limited sampling reduces these risks and generally accelerates the rate of an innovation's adoption.

5. *Observability.* If potential buyers can observe an innovation's superiority in a tangible form, the adoption rate increases. Recognizing this, General Electric sells its new Advantium speed cooking oven only through appliance dealers who agree to offer in-store demonstrations of its technology.[24]

Marketers who want to accelerate the rate of adoption can manipulate these five characteristics to some extent. Informative promotional messages help to overcome consumer hesitation in adopting a complex product. Effective product design emphasizes relative advantages. Whenever possible, marketers sell or give away small samples of innovative new products, offering these products in low-risk trials. If marketers cannot offer the product on a trial basis, in-home demonstrations or trial home placements can achieve similar results. Marketers must also make positive attempts in ensuring the innovation's compatibility with adopters' value systems.

These suggestions for action have grown out of extensive research studies of innovators in agriculture, medicine, and consumer products. These suggestions, if applied correctly, should pay off in increased sales by accelerating a new product's adoption rate in each adopter category.

Organizing for New Product Development

7

Explain the various organizational structures for new product development.

A firm needs an effective organizational structure to stimulate and coordinate new product development. Some companies contract with independent design firms to develop new products.[25] However, most assign product-innovation functions to one or more of the following entities: new product committees, new product departments, product managers, and venture teams.

New Product Committees

The most common organizational arrangement for activities in developing a new product is to center these functions in a new product committee. This group typically brings together experts in such areas as marketing, finance, manufacturing, engineering, research, and accounting. Committee members spend less time conceiving and developing their own new product ideas than reviewing and approving new product plans that arise elsewhere in the organization. Publishing houses, for instance, often pass ideas for new book projects through editorial review committees that must approve of these ideas before editors can begin working with authors.

Since members of a new product committee hold key posts in the firm's functional areas, their support for any new product plan likely foreshadows approval for further development. However, new product committees tend to reach decisions slowly and maintain conservative views. Sometimes members may compromise so they can return to their regular responsibilities.

New Product Departments

Many companies establish separate, formally organized departments to generate and refine new product ideas. The departmental structure overcomes the limitations of the new product committee system and encourages innovation as a permanent, full-time activity. The new product department is responsible for all phases of a development project within the firm, including screening decisions, developing product specifications, and coordinating product testing. The head of the department wields substantial authority and typically reports to the chief executive officer, chief operating officer, or a top marketing executive.

Product Managers

A **product manager** is another term for a brand manager, a function mentioned earlier in the chapter. This marketing professional determines the objectives and marketing strategies for an individual product or product line. Procter & Gamble, for instance, assigned its first product manager in 1927, when it made one person responsible for Camay soap. The product manager concept is widely used by such marketers as General Foods, Pillsbury, Bristol-Myers, Gillette, and Quaker Oats.

Product managers set prices, develop advertising and sales promotion programs, and work with sales representatives in the field. In a company that markets multiple products, product managers fulfill key functions in the marketing department. They provide individual attention for each product and support and coordinate efforts of the firm's sales force, marketing research department, and advertising department. Product managers often lead new product development programs, including creation of new product ideas and recommendations for improving existing products.

In recent years, advocates of the product management system have modified it to deal with environmental changes. The system was developed to mass market leading brands to large segments of consumers with similar tastes, but the increasing fragmentation of the mass market into smaller segments has forced firms to rethink product management. Several firms, including Procter & Gamble, have assigned product managers to work in teams made up of research, manufacturing, and sales managers.

Venture Teams

A **venture team** gathers a group of specialists from different areas of an organization to work together in developing new products. The venture team must meet criteria for return on investment, uniqueness of product, serving a well-defined need, compatibility of the product with existing technology, and strength of patent protection. Although the organization sets up the venture team as a temporary entity, its flexible life span may extend over a number of years. When purchases confirm the commercial potential of a new product, an existing division may take responsibility for that product, or it may serve as the nucleus of a new division within the company or of an entirely new company.

Some marketing organizations differentiate between venture teams and task forces. A new product **task force** assembles an interdisciplinary group working on temporary assignment through their functional departments. Its basic activities center on coordinating and integrating the work of the firm's functional departments on a specific project.

MARKETING DICTIONARY

product manager Marketing professional who determines the objectives and marketing strategies for an individual product or product line.

venture team New product development organization that brings together specialists from different functional areas.

task force Interdisciplinary group on temporary assignment that works through functional departments in examining new product issues.

Unlike a new product committee, a venture team does not disband after every meeting. Team members accept project assignments as major responsibilities, and the team exercises the authority it needs to both plan and implement a course of action. To stimulate product innovation, the venture team typically communicates directly with top management, but it functions as an entity separate from the basic organization. For example, IBM formed a venture team to develop the company's first personal computer. Other firms that have created venture teams include Monsanto, Xerox, Exxon, and Motorola. Procter & Gamble (P&G) partnered with Institutional Venture Partners to form a new venture team to launch Reflect.com, a Web-based venture for marketing custom-designed beauty products, as shown in the ad in Figure 12.13. The 25-person team included marketing specialists from different P&G functional disciplines. Procter & Gamble also formed a corporate new venture group to develop projects that did not fit into P&G's other existing businesses.

THE NEW PRODUCT DEVELOPMENT PROCESS

Once a firm has defined its organization for new product development, it can establish procedures for moving new product ideas to the marketplace. Developing a new product requires a time-consuming, risky, and expensive project. Firms must generate dozens of new product ideas to produce even one successful product. But most new products do not achieve success in the market. The alarmingly high failure rate of new products averages 80 percent. Firms invest nearly half of the total resources devoted to product innovation on products that become commercial failures. Products fail for a number of reasons, including inadequate market assessments, lack of market orientation, poor screening and project evaluation, product defects, and inadequate launch efforts.

8

List the stages in the new product development process.

Effective management of the development process increases the likelihood of a new product's success. An essential contribution to new product success comes from a six-step development process: (1) idea generation, (2) screening, (3) business analysis, (4) development, (5) test marketing, and (6) commercialization. At each step, management faces a continuing choice between abandoning the project, continuing to the next step, or seeking additional information before proceeding further. In most cases, each stage of the process costs more than the previous one, and constant evaluation is necessary to avoid investing in what could be a financial disaster for a firm.

Traditionally, most companies have developed new products through *phased development*, which follows the six step process in an orderly sequence. Responsibility for each phase passes first from product planners to designers and engineers, to manufacturers, and finally to marketers. The phased development method can work well for firms that dominate mature markets and can develop variations on existing products.

However, firms in many markets feel pressured to speed up the development process of a new product to keep pace with rapidly changing technologies, shifts in consumer preferences, or competitive pressures. In the electronics industry, for example, a new product that reaches its market just nine months later than originally planned can sacrifice half of its potential revenue.

This time pressure has encouraged many firms to implement *parallel product development* programs. These programs generally consist of teams with representatives from design, manufacturing, marketing, sales, and service that carry out development projects from idea generation to commercialization. Venture teams, discussed earlier, follow this parallel development model. This method can reduce the time needed to develop products because team members work on the six steps concurrently rather than in sequence.

Whether a firm pursues phased development or parallel product development, all phases can benefit from planning tools and scheduling methods such as the program evaluation and review technique (PERT) and the critical path method (CPM). These techniques, originally developed by the U.S. Navy in connection with construction of the Polaris missile and submarine, map out the sequence of each step in a process and show the time allotments for each activity. Detailed PERT and CPM flowcharts help marketers to coordinate all activities entailed in the development and introduction of new products.

Idea Generation

New product development begins with ideas from many sources: the sales force, suggestions from customers, employees, research-and-development specialists, competing products, suppliers, retailers, and independent inventors. Consumer feedback is an important source of many new product ideas.

Some innovations arise as a solution to a practical problem. Computer-maintenance personnel at Digital Equipment Corporation, for example, asked for a portable computer that would allow them to communicate with colleagues while leaving their hands free to deal with repair work. Designers came up with the MOCCA (Mobile Computing and Communication Appliance), a hands-off, 4-inch-by-4-inch device with an attached neck strap and a screen that tilts upward for easy viewing. The tiny MOCCA is operated entirely by voice commands and packs enough power for users to create reports, cruise the Internet, and exchange diagrams and other graphics.[26]

Screening

The critical stage of screening separates ideas with commercial potential from those that cannot meet company objectives. Some organizations maintain checklists of development standards in determining whether a project should be abandoned or considered further. These checklists typically include such factors as product uniqueness, availability of raw materials, and the proposed product's compatibility with current product offerings, existing facilities, and present capabilities. The screening stage may also allow for open discussions of new product ideas among different parts of the organization.

Entrepreneur Dean Kamen wanted to develop a better wheelchair that would give disabled people greater mobility. The challenge was to find a commercially viable way to do develop this wheelchair. Kamen experimented with several designs, including collapsible wheels and tank-like treads, but none of them seemed practical.

Then one day, Kamen slipped as he stepped out of the shower, and regained his balance only by moving his arms rapidly. This experience inspired him to try a new approach: design a self-balancing wheelchair that uses sensors and gyroscopes to adjust continually to uneven surfaces. He built a prototype chair and sold the concept to Johnson & Johnson (J&J). Although J&J is new to the wheelchair industry, Kamen's chair successfully passed its screening process. J&J managers believe this product will allow them to develop a new business in four-wheel-drive wheelchairs.[27]

jnj.com

Business Analysis

A product idea that survives the initial screening must then pass a thorough business analysis. This stage consists of assessing the new product's potential market, growth rate, and likely competitive strengths. Marketers must evaluate the compatibility of the proposed product with organizational resources.

Before deciding to enter the wheelchair market, for example, Johnson & Johnson marketers analyzed its profit potential. They found that wheelchair sales bring in $1 billion each year in the United States and more than $2 billion worldwide. Annual unit sales in North America, Europe, and Japan top one million chairs.

Concept testing subjects the product idea to additional study prior to its actual development. This important aspect of a new product's business analysis represents a marketing research project that attempts to measure consumer attitudes and perceptions about the new product idea. Focus groups and in-store polling can contribute effectively to concept testing.

The screening and business analysis stages generate extremely important information for new product development because they (1) define the proposed product's target market and customers' needs and wants and (2) determine the product's financial and technical requirements. Firms that are willing to invest money and time during these stages tend to be more successful at generating viable ideas and at creating successful products.

Development

Financial outlays increase substantially as a firm converts an idea into a physical product. The conversion process is the joint responsibility of the firm's development engineers, who turn the original concept into a product, and of its marketers, who provide feedback on consumer reactions to the product design, package, color, and other physical features. Many firms implement computer-aided design systems to streamline the development stage.

Prototypes may go through numerous changes before the original mock-up reaches the stage of a final product. To improve on microwave ovens' mediocre cooking performance, General Electric engineers started by creating hamburger-shaped sensors and "baking" them repeatedly in prototype Advantium ovens. From the resulting data, they designed patterns of heat conduction that would cook food evenly and produce more consistent results.[28]

Designers of Honda's S2000 sports car measured a variety of performance factors, both in their prototypes and in competing vehicles: shift strokes, braking forces, decibel levels, G-forces, and yaw rates. They designed the S2000's frame and transmission to be stiffer than those of other cars. Engineers developed a four-cylinder, 2.0-liter, 240-horsepower engine that cranks up to 9,000 revolutions per minute, approximately 50 percent more than conventional motors. Fortunately, they also installed stronger brakes and built special mufflers to compensate for engine noise.[29]

Test Marketing

To gauge consumer reactions to a product under normal conditions, many firms test market their new offerings. Up to this point, a product development team has obtained consumer information by submitting free products to consumers, who then give their reactions to the products. Other information may come from shoppers' evaluations of competing products. Test marketing is the first stage at which the product must perform in a real-life business environment.

Test marketing introduces a trial version of a new product supported by a complete marketing campaign to a selected city or television coverage area with a population representative of targeted market segments. A carefully designed and controlled test induces consumers in the test-market city to respond naturally to the new offering without knowledge of the test. After the test has been under way for a few months and sales and market share in the test market city have been calculated, marketers can estimate the product's likely performance in a full-scale introduction.

Many new movies, for instance, undergo test marketing: They first appear in a few selected theaters and are then released more widely in response to positive reviews and box-office receipts.[30]

In selecting a test market location, marketers look for an area with a manageable size. In addition, its residents should share with the chosen consumer segment such characteristics as age, education, and income. Finally, self-contained media in the location allow marketers to direct promotional efforts to people who represent the target market of the test-marketed product. Procter & Gamble test marketed its new line of Oil of Olay cosmetics for four years in Evansville, Indiana, because residents in the city fit the profile of the line's target market. After

FIGURE 12.14 Test Marketing a New Line of Cosmetics

indicating that the new line could be successful, P&G launched it nationally through ads like the one in Figure 12.14.

Some firms omit test marketing and move directly from product development to full-scale production. These companies cite four problems with test marketing:

1. Test marketing is expensive. A firm can spend more than $1 million to complete the 12- to 18-month process, depending on the size of the test market city and the cost of buying media to advertise the product.

2. Competitors who learn about the test marketing project may disrupt its findings. They can skew results by reducing the prices of their own products in the area, distributing cents-off coupons, installing better in-store displays, or boosting discounts to retailers to induce them to display more of the competitors' products.

3. Few firms test market long-lived, durable goods due to the major financial investments required for their development, the need to establish networks of dealers to distribute the products, and requirements for parts and servicing.

4. Test marketing a new product communicates company plans to competitors prior to full-scale introduction.

Companies that decide to skip the test marketing process can choose several other options. A firm may simulate a test marketing campaign through computer-modeling software. By plugging in data on similar products, it can turn small amounts of information into a

MARKETING   DICTIONARY

concept testing Initiative to measure consumer attitudes and perceptions of a product idea prior to actual development.

test marketing Introduction of a trial version of a new product supported by a complete marketing campaign to a selected city or television coverage area.

sales projection for a new product. Another firm may offer an item in just one region of the United States or in another country, adjusting promotions and advertising based on local results before going to other geographical regions. Another option may be to limit a product's introduction to just one retail chain to help the producing company's marketers carefully control and evaluate promotions and results.

Commercialization

The few product ideas that survive all the steps in the development process emerge ready for full-scale marketing. Commercialization of a major new product can expose the firm to substantial expenses. It must establish marketing strategies, fund outlays for production facilities, and acquaint the sales force, marketing intermediaries, and potential customers with the new product.

To commercialize its all-terrain wheelchair, called the IBOT, Johnson & Johnson enlisted 100 disabled consumers to test and refine early models on a private obstacle course at company headquarters. J&J then signed up more people to use the IBOT in their own homes and neighborhoods. These testers included potential customers and early adopters, such as paraplegic John Hockenberry, an NBC correspondent who presented a favorable TV report on the device on *Dateline*. The company submitted the test results to the Food and Drug Administration and applied for approval to market the IBOT. Johnson & Johnson has established a separate division, Independence Technology, to market the wheelchair and develop other new products for the disabled.[31]

PRODUCT SAFETY AND LIABILITY

9

Outline the functions of the Consumer Product Safety Commission, and summarize the concept of product liability.

A product can fulfill its mission of satisfying consumer needs only if it ensures safe operation. Manufacturers must design their products to protect users from harm. Products that lead to injuries, either directly or indirectly, can have disastrous consequences for their makers. **Product liability** refers to the responsibility of manufacturers and marketers for injuries and damages caused by their products. Chapter 2 discussed some of the major consumer protection laws that affect product safety. These laws include the Flammable Fabrics Act of 1953, the Fair Packaging and Labeling Act of 1966, the Poison Prevention Packaging Act of 1970, and the Consumer Product Safety Act of 1972.

Federal and state legislation plays a major role in regulating product safety. The Poison Prevention Packaging Act requires drug manufacturers to place their products in packaging that is child resistant yet accessible to all adults, even ones who have trouble opening containers. The Consumer Product Safety Act created a powerful regulatory agency—the Consumer Product Safety Commission (CPSC). This agency has assumed jurisdiction over every consumer product category except food, automobiles, and a few other products already regulated by other agencies. The CPSC has the authority to ban products without court hearings, order recalls or redesigns of products, and inspect production facilities. It can charge managers of negligent companies with criminal offenses. In addition, many states have instituted their own product safety statutes.

The federal Food and Drug Administration (FDA) must approve food, medications, and health-related devices such as Johnson & Johnson's IBOT wheelchair before they can be marketed. The FDA can also take products off the market if concerns arise about the safety of these products. An example of such a recall is the diet drug fenfluramine ("fen-phen"), which the FDA pulled after examining reports that claimed this drug may have caused dangerous scarring in patients' heart valves.[32]

The number of product liability lawsuits filed against manufacturers has skyrocketed in recent years. Although many such claims reach settlements out of court, juries have decided on many claims, sometimes awarding multimillion-dollar settlements. This threat has led most companies to step up efforts to ensure product safety. Safety warnings appear prominently on the labels of such potentially hazardous products as cleaning fluids and drain cleaners to inform users of the dangers of these products out of the reach of children. Changes in product design have reduced the hazards posed by such products as lawn mowers, hedge trimmers, and toys. Product liability insurance has become an essential element for any new or existing product strategy. Premiums for this insurance have risen alarmingly, however, and insurers have almost entirely abandoned some kinds of coverage.

Regulatory activities and the increased number of liability claims have prompted companies to sponsor voluntary improvements in safety standards. Safety planning is now a vital element of product strategy.

ACHIEVEMENT CHECK SUMMARY

Read the learning objectives that follow, and consider the questions for each one. Answering these questions will reinforce your grasp of the most important concepts in the chapter and will allow you to check how well you have achieved these learning goals. Where a blank appears before a question, answer with *T* or *F* for true/false questions; for multiple-choice questions, choose the letter of the correct answer.

Objective 12.1: Explain the benefits of branding and brand management.

1. _____ One of the main goals of branding is to create an identity for a product that will differentiate it from competing offerings.

2. _____ Consumers are said to be *brand loyal* when (a) they tell their friends about a brand; (b) they recognize a brand name; (c) they choose a brand over competing products.

3. _____ Most firms achieve brand insistence with their products.

Objective 12.2: Describe the different types of brands.

1. _____ Private brands identify products available only to wealthy consumers.

2. _____ When a single brand name spans several related products, it is called (a) a manufacturer's brand; (b) a family brand; (c) an individual brand.

3. _____ A firm should market very dissimilar products under a single family brand name.

Objective 12.3: Explain the strategic value of brand equity.

1. _____ *Brand equity* refers to (a) how much a company has invested in a brand; (b) the added value that a brand name confers on a product; (c) the dividend a stockholder receives from a branded product's manufacturer.

2. _____ High brand equity helps a firm to expand into global markets.

3. _____ Brand equity reflects the ability of a product to stand apart from competitors.

Objective 12.4: Describe how firms develop strong identities for their products and brands.

1. _____ An effective brand name should give buyers an idea of the product's image.

2. _____ If a brand name becomes a descriptive, generic name, (a) the original owner can sue others for using the name; (b) the original owner has no exclusive claim to the name; (c) the name will help sell the brand in international markets.

3. _____ Firms can establish trademarks for (a) brand names only; (b) brand names, slogans, and packaging elements; (c) pictorial designs in ads only.

4. _____ Properly designed labels can encourage consumer purchases.

5. _____ A brand extension allows a firm to carry brand equity over to unrelated products.

Objective 12.5: Identify alternative new product development strategies and the determinants of each strategy's success.

1. _____ A market penetration strategy involves (a) finding a new market for an established product; (b) modifying an existing product in an existing market; (c) introducing a new product into an established market.

2. _____ The strategy of creating a new product for a new market is (a) market development; (b) market penetration; (c) product diversification.

3. _____ Cannibalization occurs when a newly introduced product steals sales from a firm's existing product.

4. _____ A flanker brand is a product that a firm introduces to serve a new market.

Objective 12.6: Identify the determinants of a new product's rate of adoption and the methods for accelerating the speed of adoption.

1. _____ A new product department is a temporary group set up to develop a specific product or product line.

2. _____ A new product committee is a review committee with authority over new product decisions.

3. _____ Marketing professionals with responsibility for developing marketing strategies for products, brands, or product lines are called product managers.

Objective 12.7: Explain the various organizational structures for new product development.

1. _____ First adopters are usually the same people for any product.

2. _____ A product is more likely to achieve consumer adoption if (a) the product is compatible with the values of consumers; (b) it costs a lot of money; (c) it offers more complex features than currently available rivals include.

3. _____ Businesses can seldom influence first adopters.

4. _____ A product design increases the likelihood of adoption if it provides an advantage over existing products.

5. _____ Marketers usually need not supply informative promotional messages to get first adopters to try a new product.

Objective 12.8: List the stages in the new product development process.

1. _____ In an important part of the screening process, marketers determine how well a product idea fits with the capabilities of the firm.

M A R K E T I N G   D I C T I O N A R Y

product liability Responsibility of manufacturers and marketers for injuries and damages caused by their products.

2. _____ During the business analysis stage, firms evaluate a product's potential acceptance by consumers.

3. _____ Development usually takes less time than other parts of new product development.

Objective 12.9: Outline the functions of the Consumer Product Safety Commission, and summarize the concept of product liability.

1. _____ The Consumer Product Safety Commission exercises jurisdiction over all consumer products, including food and automobiles.

2. _____ Product safety is an integral feature of a design to satisfy customers.

3. _____ The Consumer Product Safety Commission cannot ban a product without a court hearing.

Students: See the solutions section located on pages S-2 to check your responses to the Achievement Check Summary.

Key Terms

brand	label
brand recognition	Universal Product Code (UPC)
brand preference	brand extension
brand insistence	brand licensing
generic product	co-branding
manufacturer's brand	product positioning
private brand	cannibalization
captive brands	adoption process
family brand	consumer innovator
individual brand	diffusion process
brand equity	product manager
brand manager	venture team
brand name	task force
brand mark	concept testing
generic name	test marketing
trademark	product liability
trade dress	

Review Questions

1. Identify and briefly explain each of the three stages of brand loyalty. How does brand loyalty differ among product categories?
2. Explain the differences among manufacturer's, private, and family brands. Provide examples of each.
3. Describe the advantages of brand equity.
4. Differentiate among the terms *brand, brand name, brand mark, trademark,* and *trade name.* Specify examples of each.
5. List the characteristics of an effective brand name. What differences distinguish brand extensions, brand licensing, and co-branding? Cite examples of each.
6. Outline the different product development strategies. Cite an example of each strategy.

7. What happens during the consumer adoption process? Outline and explain the stages in this process.
8. Outline alternative organizational structures for new product development. Identify the steps in the new product development process.
9. What purpose does test marketing serve? What potential problems may complicate test marketing?
10. Explain the primary activities of the Consumer Product Safety Commission. What steps can this agency take to protect consumers from defective and hazardous products?

Questions for Critical Thinking

1. Using Young & Rubicam's dimensions of brand equity, evaluate the brand equity levels of the following products. Which brands have the greatest brand equity? Explain.
   a. Merit cigarettes
   b. Musselman's apple sauce
   c. Snackwell's cookies
   d. Allstate insurance
   e. Rolex watches
2. Smart Balance and Benecol spreads are targeted at cholesterol sensitive consumers. What product development strategies are evident in these alternative products? Identify the likely consumer innovators for these products? Do you like the brand names that were picked? Explain your opinions.
3. Starbucks, the Seattle-based gourmet coffee retailer, has launched e-commerce Web sites that will sell coffee, gourmet food, and even furniture. Starbucks employs a so-called "Canopy site" that will link an array of Internet addresses starting with a Starbucks coffee Web page.[33] Check out the Starbucks Web site at www.starbucks.com. Do you think Starbucks will be successful with their version of brand extension via the Internet?
4. M&M candies were introduced in 1940. The new candy took a long time to melt, a real virtue in the days before air conditioning. M&Ms were soon part of World War II soldiers' rations, and as the saying goes, "The rest is history." Relate the success of M&Ms to this chapter's discussion of the diffusion process and the determinants of a product's rate of adoption.
5. In electronics, consumer products are hot. One popular new product combines a TV and VCR in one unit. According to industry analysts, consumers like the sets because they take up less space than conventional combinations of equipment and are more convenient to use. What other new products might electronics manufacturers combine with a basic TV? Choose one and evaluate its commercial potential. What advantages would it offer consumers? What other products would make up its competition? Would you test market the new product? Why or why not?

1. Brand Management. Use your search engine to find a marketing research and consulting firm that specializes in branding. One such site is at *www.cheskin.com*. Locate, read, and print out recent research conducted in the area of branding. Be prepared to share your findings during a class discussion on the topic.

2. Brand Equity. Go to Young & Rubicam's Web site at *www.yr.com* to find out more about the Brand Asset Valuator (BAV). After reading the basic BAV information, look through several of the links that provide BAV applications, such as the "Four Basic Pillars" under "Interpreting Brand Patterns," the "Brand Development Cycle," or the "Sample Brands" grid. Print out the one item that interested you most. Submit the printout as an attachment to a 2- to 3-paragraph paper addressing any aspect of what you've learned about BAV.

3. Product Safety and Liability. Go to the Web sites of each of the following regulatory agencies: U.S. Consumer Product Safety Commission *(www.cpsc.gov)*, U.S. Food and Drug Administration *(www.fda.gov)*, National Highway Traffic Safety Administration *(www.nhtsa.dot.gov)*. Find an example of a recent product recall by each of these agencies.

cheskin.com

yr.com

cpsc.gov

fda.gov

nhtsa.dot.gov

Video Case 12 on Hasbro, Inc. begins on page VC-14.

Gateway Continuing Case Part 5 begins on page GC-8.

PART

6

DISTRIBUTION STRATEGY

387

Gateway Continuing Case Part 6 begins on page GC-10.

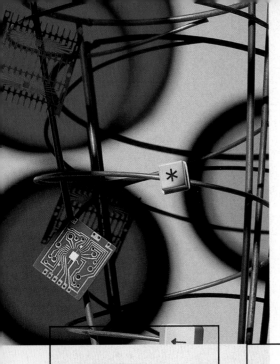

Marketing Channels and Logistics Management

The Fast-Moving World of Air Express International

AEI Home Page - Netscape
File Edit View Go Window Help

AEI. Quality Worldwide Logistics

Customs Clearance

What's New
Company Information
Logistics Services
Global Resource Guide
AEI's World
  North America
  Latin America
  Europe
  Middle East & India
  Africa
  South Pacific
  Asia
Search AEI

Our View

Languages German

AEI in Europe

Thousands of businesses around the world depend on shipping companies to move their goods from one place to another—whether it's Florida grapefruit or palm-size computers. Thus, an entire industry has grown up around manufacturers' transportation needs. These needs are much more complicated than loading a few boxes on a truck and trundling them down the highway. They include a constant flow of information, warehousing services, and assistance with documentation for customs and other international agencies. Air Express International is a type of company in the freight industry, called a freight forwarder, that works with shippers themselves to move goods around the world. Founded in 1935 as the first freight partner for brand new Pan American World Airways, AEI is now the top U.S.-based international airfreight forwarder. AEI also provides customers with international ocean freight services, customs brokerage services, and global logistics management for its cus-

tomers—which means that it offers warehousing, distribution, and freight tracking and tracing services. AEI doesn't own any shipping vehicles, but it arranges for transportation of customers' cargo via commercial carriers. The 2 million individual airfreight shipments to 3,000 cities in 200 countries that AEI handles each year seem mind boggling.

As in so many other areas of commerce, computers have revolutionized the freight industry. As a freight forwarder's customers increase their technological capabilities, the freight forwarder must keep up. "Many larger customers seek unique [infotech] development," notes Reg Kenney, vice president of North American sales and marketing for AEI. "Often, work done to meet these specific requirements results in technology that proves to have a much broader usefulness" for his company. In fact, technological improvements that AEI makes to accommodate its larger customers often benefit its smaller customers as well. "Medium to small customers piggyback on a lot of excellent technology and systems solutions we have developed for our largest customers," says Kenney. So AEI can provide value to both its large and small customers at the same time. When AEI instituted its web-based shipment tracking system, through which a shipment could be tracked either by part number or order number, everyone benefited.

AEI constantly seeks to create value for its shipping customers. "At AEI, logistics is much more than just the movement of goods," says the company's Web site. "We analyze available resources and identify the optimum critical path that results in the ultimate satisfaction of our customers." In other words, AEI does its best to get its customers' shipments from here to there, as the fastest, smartest crow flies.[1]

389

CHAPTER OVERVIEW

Distribution—moving goods and services from producers to customers—is an important marketing concern. Although good design and creative promotion may motivate consumers to purchase a product, these things are useless if consumers cannot actually buy the product. Businesses, by managing their distribution strategy, must carefully choose how and where their goods reach consumers. Distribution strategy has two critical components: marketing channels and logistics.

A **marketing channel** (sometimes called a *distribution channel*) can be defined as an organized system of marketing institutions and their interrelationships that promote the physical flow and ownership of goods and services from producer to consumer or business user. The choice of marketing channels should support the firm's overall marketing strategy.

Logistics refers to the process of coordinating the flow of information, goods, and services among members of the marketing channel. Efficient logistical systems support attentive customer service—an important goal of any organization's marketing strategy.

A key aspect of logistics is **physical distribution,** which covers a broad range of activities aimed at efficient movement of finished goods from the end of the production line to the consumer. Although some marketers use the terms *transportation* and *physical distribution* interchangeably, these terms do not carry the same meaning. Physical distribution extends beyond transportation to include such important decision areas as customer service, inventory control, materials handling, protective packaging, order processing, transportation, warehouse site selection, and warehousing.

Well-planned marketing channels and effective logistics provide ultimate users with convenient ways for obtaining the goods and services they desire. This chapter discusses the activities, decisions, and marketing intermediaries involved in managing marketing channels and logistics. Chapter 14 looks at other players in the marketing channel: retailers, direct marketers, and wholesalers. ■

1

Describe the role that marketing channels and logistics play in marketing strategy.

STRATEGIC IMPLICATIONS: THE ROLE OF MARKETING CHANNELS IN MARKETING STRATEGY

A firm's distribution channels play a key role in its marketing strategy because these channels provide the means by which the firm moves the goods and services it produces to ultimate users. Channels perform four important functions. First, they facilitate the exchange process by cutting the number of marketplace contacts necessary to make a sale. Suppose you want to buy a new motorcycle. You see a Harley-Davidson ad like the one in Figure 13.1 and read that the company sells its motorcycles through a network of dealers. You can call the toll-free number listed in the ad or visit Harley-Davidson's Web site to find a dealer in your area. A local dealer forms part of the channel that brings you, a potential buyer, and Harley-Davidson, the seller, together to complete the exchange process.

Distributors also adjust for discrepancies in the market's assortment of goods and services via a process known as *sorting*, the second channeling function. A single producer tends to maximize the quantity it makes of a limited line of goods, while a single buyer needs a limited quantity of a wide selection of merchandise. Sorting alleviates such discrepancies by channeling products to suit both the buyer's and the producer's needs.

The third function of marketing channels involves standardizing exchange transactions by setting expectations for products, and it involves the transfer process itself. Channel members tend to standardize payment terms, delivery schedules, prices, and purchase lots among other conditions.

Finally, marketing channels facilitate searches by both buyers and sellers. Buyers search for specific goods and services to fill their needs, while sellers attempt to learn what buyers want. Channels bring buyers and sellers together to complete the exchange process.

Literally hundreds of marketing channels carry products today, and no single channel best serves the needs of every company. Instead of searching for the best channel for all products, a marketing manager must analyze alternative channels in light of consumer needs to determine the most appropriate channel or channels for the firm's goods and services.[2]

Marketers must remain flexible, however, since channels, like so many marketing variables, may change. Today's ideal channel may prove inappropriate in a few years. As an example, for many years flowers were sold exclusively through independent specialty shops. During the past decade, however, consumer shopping habits have changed as customers started to look for convenience and one-stop shopping. Increasingly, consumers decided to buy flowers in supermarkets, over the telephone, or through the Internet. Consequently, florist services are now available via a variety of marketing channels.

The following sections examine the diverse types of channels available to marketers. The chapter then focuses on the decisions marketers must make in order to develop an effective distribution strategy that supports their firm's marketing objectives.

FIGURE 13.1 Marketing Channels: Bringing Buyers and Sellers Together

TYPES OF MARKETING CHANNELS

The first step in selecting a marketing channel is determining which type of channel will best meet both the seller's objectives and the distribution needs of customers. Figure 13.2 depicts the major channels available to marketers of consumer and business goods and services.

Some channel options involve several different **marketing intermediaries.** A marketing intermediary (or *middleman*) is an organization that operates between producers and consumers or business users. Retailers and wholesalers are both marketing intermediaries. A retail store owned and operated by someone other than the manufacturer of the products it sells is one type of marketing intermediary. A **wholesaler** is an intermediary

MARKETING DICTIONARY

marketing channel System of marketing institutions that promotes the physical flow of goods and services, along with ownership title, from producer to consumer or business user; also called a *distribution channel.*

logistics Process of coordinating the flow of information, goods, and services among members of the distribution channel.

physical distribution Activities to achieve efficient movement of finished goods from the end of the production line to the consumer.

marketing intermediary Wholesaler or retailer that operates between producers and consumers or business users; also called a *middleman.*

wholesaler Marketing intermediary that takes title to goods and then distributes these goods further; also called a *jobber* or *distributor.*

FIGURE 13.2   Alternative Marketing Channels

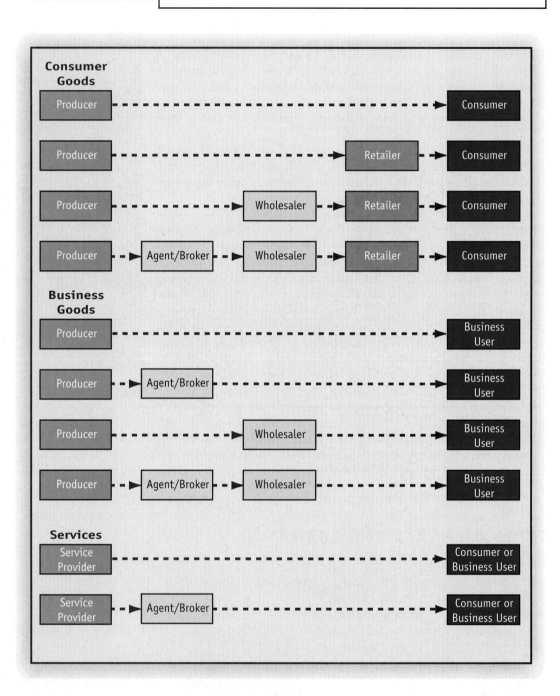

that takes title to the goods it handles and then distributes these goods to retailers, other distributors, or sometimes end consumers.

A *short marketing channel* involves few intermediaries. By contrast, the term *long marketing channel* refers to many intermediaries working in succession to move goods from producers to consumers. In general, business products tend to move through shorter channels than consumer products due to geographical concentrations and comparatively few business purchasers. Service firms market primarily through short channels because they sell intangible products and need to maintain personal relationships within their channels.

Not-for-profit organizations also tend to work with short, simple, and direct channels. Any marketing intermediaries in such a channel usually act as agents, such as independent ticket agencies or fund-raising specialists. In a major distribution decision, both service firms and not-for-profit organizations must designate the specific locations of where the services will be delivered.

The following section deals with direct selling, which is the shortest channel. Other channel options involving marketing intermediaries are then examined.

Direct Selling

The simplest, most direct marketing channel is a direct channel. A **direct channel** carries goods directly from a producer to an ultimate user. This channel forms part of **direct selling,** a marketing strategy in which a producer establishes direct sales contact with its product's final users. Direct selling is an important option for goods that require extensive demonstrations in convincing customers to buy.

Direct selling plays a significant role in business-to-business marketing. Most major installations, accessory equipment, and even component parts and raw materials are sold through direct contacts between producing firms and final buyers. Firms that market products to other businesses often develop and maintain large sales forces to call on potential customers.

Direct selling is also important in consumer goods markets. Direct sellers, like Mary Kay, Amway, and Avon, sidestep competition in store aisles by developing networks of independent dealers that sell their products direct to consumers. Avon promotes its cosmetics through ads like the one in Figure 13.3 as well as its direct sales representatives by listing them as one of the top 10 reasons consumers should buy Avon products.

One direct selling strategy is the so-called party plan. The seller recruits someone to invite friends to her home, where the seller demonstrates goods and encourages guests to make purchases. One of the best-known firms using party-plan selling is Tupperware. A Tupperware party takes place somewhere in the world every 2.2 seconds; 85 percent of party sales now occur outside the United States.[3] Other direct sellers have used the method to sell everything from lingerie to popcorn.

tupperware.com

Dell Computer Corp. sells computers and computer parts directly to companies, government agencies, and consumers. Dell builds computers based on customer specifications for performance characteristics such as processor speed, hard drive size, and monitor type. Michael Dell founded the company when he was a 19-year-old college student and found it difficult to track down parts for his own computer system. His experience convinced him that he could buy computer parts from manufacturers, assemble them, and sell them directly, thus reducing overhead costs and saving customers money at the same time. Dell sold his first products by placing small ads in trade magazines, handling orders via mail. Next, he set up a toll-free sales and support telephone number so customers could order over the phone. Today, Dell sells more than $18.2 billion worth of computers each year, and it continues to grow rapidly. [4]

dell.com

Channels Using Marketing Intermediaries

Although direct channels allow simple and straightforward marketing, they do not always move goods from producers to consumers in the most efficient way. Some products serve geographically dispersed markets or large numbers of potential end users. Other categories of goods rely heavily on repeat purchases. The producers of these goods may find more efficient, less expensive, and less time-consuming alternatives to direct channels by using marketing intermediaries. This section considers five channels that involve marketing intermediaries.

MARKETING DICTIONARY

direct channel Marketing channel that moves goods directly from a producer to an ultimate user.

direct selling Strategy designed to establish direct sales contact between producer and final user.

Avon: Using Direct Selling as a Marketing Strategy

Producer to Wholesaler to Retailer to Consumer

The traditional channel for consumer goods proceeds from producer to wholesaler to retailer to user. This method carries goods between small retailers and literally thousands of small producers with limited lines. Small producers with limited financial resources rely on the services of wholesalers as immediate sources of funds and as conduits to hundreds of retailers that will stock their output. Small retailers draw on wholesalers' specialized buying skills, which ensure balanced inventories of goods produced in various regions of the world. The wholesaler's sales force promotes the producer's output to its market. In addition, many manufacturers employ field sales representatives to contact retail accounts. These representatives serve as sources of marketing information, but they do not actually sell products.

Producer to Wholesaler to Business User

Similar characteristics in the organizational market often attract marketing intermediaries to operate between producers and business purchasers. The term *industrial distributor* commonly refers to intermediaries in the business market that take title to the goods.

Producer to Agent to Wholesaler to Retailer to Consumer

When many small companies serve a market, a unique intermediary—the agent—performs the basic function of bringing buyer and seller together. An *agent* may or may not take possession of goods but never takes title to these goods. The agent merely represents a producer by seeking a market for its output or a wholesaler (which does take title to the goods) by locating a source of supply.

Producer to Agent to Wholesaler to Business User

Like agents, *brokers* are independent intermediaries who may or may not take possession of goods but never take title to these goods. Agents and brokers also serve the business market when small producers attempt to market their offerings through large wholesalers. Such an intermediary, often called a *manufacturer's representative*, provides an independent sales force to contact wholesale buyers.

Producer to Agent to Business User

For products sold in small units, only merchant wholesalers can economically cover the markets. A *merchant wholesaler* is an independently owned wholesaler that takes title to the goods. By maintaining regional inventories, this wholesaler achieves transportation economies, stockpiling goods and making small shipments over short distances. For a product with large unit sales, however, and for which transportation accounts for a small percentage of the total cost, the producer-agent-business user channel is usually employed. The agent in effect becomes the producer's sales force, but bulk shipments of the product reduce the intermediary's inventory management function.

DUAL DISTRIBUTION

Dual distribution refers to movement of products through more than one channel to reach the same target market. Marketers usually adopt this distribution strategy either to maximize their firm's coverage in the marketplace or to increase the cost effectiveness of the firm's marketing effort. In an example of the first objective, automobile parts manufacturers promote products through both direct sales forces and independent jobbers. The cost-effectiveness goal, on the other hand, might lead a manufacturer to assign its own sales force to sell in high potential areas while relying on manufacturers' representatives (independent, commissioned salespeople) in lower volume areas.

2

Describe the various types of distribution channels available to marketers.

REVERSE CHANNELS

While the traditional concept of marketing channels involves movement of goods and services from producer to consumer or business user, marketers should not ignore **reverse channels**—channels designed to return goods to their producers. Reverse channels have gained increased importance with rising prices for raw materials, spreading availability of recycling facilities, and passage of additional conservation laws. For instance, consumers pay refundable deposits for bottled products in states like Maine, Michigan, and Oregon. New Jersey requires businesses and households to separate their trash to aid recycling.

Some reverse channels move through the facilities of traditional marketing intermediaries. In states that require bottle deposits, retailers and local bottlers perform these functions in the soft-drink industry. For other products, manufacturers establish redemption centers, develop systems for rechanneling products for recycling, and create specialized organizations to handle disposal and recycling. Other reverse channel participants include community groups that organize cleanup days and develop recycling and waste disposal systems.

Reverse channels also handle product recalls and repairs. Registration of car owners allows manufacturers to send proper notification in the event of recalls. For example, an automobile recall notice might advise owners of potential problems that may need correcting at their dealerships. Similarly, reverse channels have carried some items to manufacturers' repair centers. The warranty for a small appliance might direct the owner to return a defective unit to the dealer for repairs within 90 days after the sale and to the factory after that period. Such reverse channels are a vital element of product recall and repair procedures.

MARKETING   DICTIONARY

dual distribution Network that moves products to a firm's target market through more than one marketing channel.

reverse channels Channels designed to return goods to their producers.

SOLVING AN ETHICAL CONTROVERSY

What Do We Do With That Pile of Used Computers?

Think about it: For every new computer unwrapped at Christmas, one is toted up to the attic or down to the basement. Because of the rapid advance of technology, computers become obsolete faster and faster. According to one study, over 315 million computers will become obsolete by the year 2004. By the year 2005, one computer will become obsolete for every new one that comes to market. Whereas the average lifespan of a computer is now approximately five years, that will decrease to two years by 2005. What is happening to all these used computers?

Many are sitting in people's basements and garages. A precious few can be donated to schools or other nonprofit organizations, but many of these entities now refuse to accept old computers because they are outdated. Many are already sitting in landfills. To complicate matters further, computers contain toxic materials, including lead and cadmium, that may be harmful to the environment if disposed of improperly. So the EPA has stepped in with regulations prohibiting the disposal of computers in landfills by organizations. Thus, institutions like Cornell University offer free removal and recycling of computers.

Should computer manufacturers work more closely with consumers, regulatory agencies, and recycling industries to participate in reverse channels for computers?

Pro
1. Since manufacturers are responsible for bringing the products to the marketplace in the first place, they should participate in finding ways to use reverse channels to reduce pollution from old computers.
2. By making the most of reverse channels, such as entering into alliances with recycling companies, computer manufacturers may discover financial and other benefits.

3. Recycling may actually cause computer manufacturers to come up with better designs for their products that reduce waste and encourage reuse.

Con
1. Computer manufacturers actually profit from planned obsolescence in computers, so they have little incentive to participate in recycling.
2. It is dangerous and complicated to get involved with toxic or hazardous waste; computer manufacturers should leave that to someone else.
3. Getting involved with reverse channels could be very costly to computer manufacturers. They should concentrate on what they do best—providing cutting-edge technology.

Summary
Some companies, like United Recycling Industries, have begun to build their business on a reverse marketing channel: recycling used computers. United Recycling, located outside Chicago, hopes to become "the leading full-service recycling center for recovering and maximizing value from the environmentally safe processing and recycling of excess, obsolete, or end of life commercial, industrial, military, and electronic equipment." So a new industry may be part of the solution. In the meantime, the public needs to become aware of and raise the issue to get people thinking about the problem of techno-junk.

SOURCES: Steve Wyatt, "Recycle Your Old Computer," *ZDTV*, www.zdnet.com, accessed February 3, 2000; "United Recycling Industries," www.unitedrecycling.com, accessed February 3, 2000; "Solid Waste Management," Cornell University, www.fm.cornell.edu, accessed February 3, 2000; Vincent J. Schodolski, "Computer Throwaways Swamping Us Bit by Bit," *Chicago Tribune*, December 19, 1999, pp. 1, 16; "Stop the WTO Attack on Computer Recycling," *Econet Alerts*, November 10, 1999, www.igc.apc.org; "Silicon Valley Toxics Coalition," June 15, 1999, www.svtc.org.

CHANNEL STRATEGY DECISIONS

3

Outline the major channel strategy decisions.

Marketers face several strategic decisions in choosing channels and marketing intermediaries for their products. Selecting a specific channel is the most basic of these decisions. Marketers must also resolve questions about the level of distribution intensity, the desirability of vertical marketing systems, and the performance of current intermediaries.

Selection of a Marketing Channel

Consider, for example, the following questions: What characteristics of a franchised dealer network make it the best channel option for a company? Why do operating supplies often go through both agents and merchant wholesalers before reaching their actual users? Why would a firm market a single product through multiple channels? Marketers must answer many such questions in choosing marketing channels.

A variety of factors impact the selection of a marketing channel. Some channel decisions are dictated by the marketplace in which the company operates. In other cases, the product itself may be a key variable in picking a marketing channel. Finally, the marketing organization may set limits or offer opportunities related to specific distribution channels.

Market Factors

Channel structure reflects a product's intended markets—either for consumers or business users. Business purchasers usually prefer to deal directly with manufacturers (except for routine supplies or small accessory items), but most consumers make their purchases from retailers. Marketers often sell products that serve both business users and consumers through more than one channel.

Other market factors also affect channel choice, including the market's needs, its geographical location, and its average order size. To serve a concentrated potential market with a small number of buyers, a direct channel offers a feasible alternative. To serve a geographically dispersed potential market in which customers purchase small amounts in individual transactions—the conditions in the consumer goods market—distribution through marketing intermediaries makes sense.

Product Factors

Product characteristics also guide the choice of an optimal marketing channel strategy. Perishable goods, such as fresh produce, beverages, and fashion products with short life cycles, typically move through short channels.

The Coca-Cola Company already sells its beverages through vending machines, a relatively short channel. Now the firm wants to make it possible for consumers to purchase through this channel even if they lack the correct change. Coca-Cola is testing a new machine in Helsinki, Finland, that dispenses cold drinks when a thirsty customer simply dials a phone number displayed near the coin slot. The sale is posted to the customer's cellular telephone account.[5]

Complex products, producers of custom-made installations, and computer equipment are often sold directly to ultimate buyers. In general, relatively standardized items pass through comparatively long channels. For another generalization, low product unit values, such as a pack of Wrigley's gum shown in Figure 13.4, call for long channels.

Organizational Factors

Companies with adequate financial, management, and marketing resources feel little need for help from intermediaries. A financially strong manufacturer can hire its own sales force, warehouse its own goods, and grant credit to retailers or consumers. A weaker firm must rely on marketing intermediaries for these services. (In one exception, a large retail chain may purchase all of a manufacturer's output, bypassing independent wholesalers.) A production-oriented firm may need the marketing expertise of intermediaries to offset its own lack of those skills.

A firm with a broad product line can usually market its products directly to retailers or business users since its own sales force can offer a variety of products. High sales volume spreads selling costs over a large number of items, allowing good returns from direct sales. Single product firms often regard direct selling as an unaffordable luxury.

The manufacturer's desire for control over marketing of its product also influences channel selection. To ensure aggressive promotion by retailers, producers often choose the shortest available channels. To

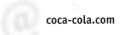
coca-cola.com

FIGURE 13.4 | Distribution Channel Influenced by Product Factors

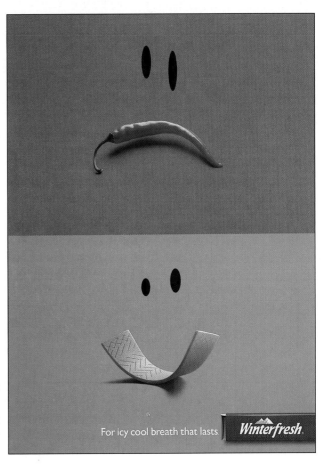

For icy cool breath that lasts. *Winterfresh*.

TABLE 13.1	Factors Influencing Marketing Channel Strategies	

	CHARACTERISTICS OF SHORT CHANNELS	CHARACTERISTICS OF LONG CHANNELS
Market factors	Business users	Consumers
	Geographically concentrated	Geographically disbursed
	Extensive technical knowledge and regular servicing required	Little technical knowledge and regular servicing not required
	Large orders	Small orders
Product factors	Perishable	Durable
	Complex	Standardized
	Expensive	Inexpensive
Producer factors	Manufacturer has adequate resources to perform channel functions	Manufacturer lacks adequate resources to perform channel functions
	Broad product line	Limited product line
	Channel control important	Channel control not important
Competitive factors	Manufacturing feels satisfied with marketing intermediaries' performance in promoting products	Manufacturer feels dissatisfied with marketing intermediaries' performance in promoting products

distribute a new product, the producer may have to implement an informative advertising campaign before independent wholesalers will agree to handle the campaign.

Businesses that explore new marketing channels must be careful to avoid antagonizing their marketing intermediaries. Consider Hewlett-Packard (HP), which has long sold its personal computers through retailers. While HP sells directly to consumers through its Web site, regional dealers are responsible for installation and service after the sale. This strategy helps the company stay on good terms with its intermediaries, who still provide 80 percent of its sales.[6]

hewlett-packard.com

Competitive Factors

Some firms feel compelled to develop new marketing channels to remedy inadequate promotion of their products by independent marketing intermediaries. In one popular alternative, a manufacturer might add a direct sales force or set up its own retail distribution network (a move discussed later in the chapter). Table 13.1 summarizes the factors that affect the selection of a marketing channel and examines the effect of each on the channel's overall length.

Determining Distribution Intensity

Another key channel strategy decision is the intensity of distribution. **Distribution intensity** refers to the number of intermediaries through which a manufacturer distributes its goods. The decision about distribution intensity should ensure adequate market coverage for a product. Adequate market coverage varies depending on the goals of the individual firm, the type of product, and the consumer segments in its target market. In general, however, distribution intensity varies along a continuum with three general categories: intensive distribution, selective distribution, and exclusive distribution.

Intensive Distribution

An **intensive distribution** strategy seeks to distribute a product through all available channels in a trade area. M&M Mars, Inc., for example, implements an intensive distribution strategy, placing its products in supermarkets, chain stores, vending machines, and drugstores. Producers

FIGURE 13.5   **Using a Selective Distribution Strategy**

of convenience goods try to saturate their markets, enabling purchasers to buy their products with minimum efforts. Usually, an intensive distribution strategy suits items with wide appeal across broad groups of consumers.[7] Examples of goods distributed through this strategy include soft drinks, candy, gum, and cigarettes.

Selective Distribution

In another market coverage strategy, **selective distribution,** a firm chooses only a limited number of retailers in a market area to handle its line. This arrangement helps to control price cutting since relatively few dealers handle the firm's line. By limiting the number of retailers, marketers can reduce total marketing costs while establishing strong working relationships within the channel. Cooperative advertising, in which the manufacturer pays a percentage of the retailer's advertising expenditures and the retailer prominently displays the firm's products, can be utilized for mutual benefit, and marginal retailers can be avoided. Where service is important, the manufacturer usually provides training and assistance to dealers it chooses.

Ermenegildo Zegna, a high-end maker of men's clothing, has chosen a selective distribution strategy for its products. Its $130 ties, $1,700 suits and sportswear shown in Figure 13.5 are available through upscale retailers such

ezegna.com

MARKETING   DICTIONARY

distribution intensity Number of intermediaries through which a manufacturer distributes its goods.

intensive distribution Channel policy in which a manufacturer of a convenience product attempts to saturate the market.

selective distribution Channel policy in which a firm chooses only a limited number of retailers to handle its product line.

as Neiman Marcus and Saks Fifth Avenue. To qualify as a Zegna dealer, retailers must comply with the company's strict rules for advertising, pricing, and displaying its products.[8]

Exclusive Distribution

When a producer grants exclusive rights to a wholesaler or retailer to sell its products in a specific geographic region, it practices **exclusive distribution,** an extreme form of selective distribution. The automobile industry provides the best example of exclusive distribution. A city with a population of 40,000 may have a single Mazda or Ford dealer. Exclusive distribution agreements also govern marketing for some major appliance and apparel brands.

Marketers may sacrifice some market coverage by implementing a policy of exclusive distribution. As compensation, however, they often develop and maintain an image of quality and prestige for the product. In addition, exclusive distribution limits marketing costs since the firm deals with a smaller number of accounts. In exclusive distribution, producers and retailers cooperate closely in decisions concerning advertising and promotion, inventory carried by the retailers, and prices.

Legal Problems of Exclusive Distribution Exclusive distribution presents a number of potential legal problems mainly in three areas: exclusive dealing agreements, closed sales territories, and tying agreements. While none of these practices is illegal per se, all may break the law if they reduce competition or tend to create monopolies.

As part of an exclusive distribution strategy, marketers may try to enforce an **exclusive-dealing agreement,** which prohibits a marketing intermediary (a wholesaler or, more typically, a retailer) from handling competing products. Producers of high-priced shopping goods, specialty goods, and accessory equipment often require such agreements to assure total concentration on their own product lines. Such a contract violates the Clayton Act if the producer's or dealer's sales volumes represent a substantial percentage of total sales in the market area. The courts have ruled that a seller can use an exclusive-dealing agreement to strengthen its competitive position when initially entering a market. However, the same agreement would violate the Clayton Act if used by a firm with a sizable market share since it could help the seller to bar competitors from the market.

Producers may also try to set up **closed sales territories** to restrict their distributors to certain geographic regions. Although the distributors gain protection from rival dealers in their exclusive territories, they sacrifice any opportunities in opening new facilities or marketing the manufacturers' products outside their assigned territories. The legality of a system of closed sales territories depends on whether the restriction decreases competition. If it does, the closed sales territories violate the Federal Trade Commission Act and provisions of the Sherman Act and the Clayton Act.

The legality of closed sales territories also depends on whether the system imposes horizontal or vertical restrictions. Horizontal territorial restrictions result from agreements between retailers or wholesalers to avoid competition among sellers of products from the same producer. Such agreements consistently have been declared illegal. However, the U.S. Supreme Court has ruled that vertical territorial restrictions—those between producers and wholesalers or retailers—may meet legal criteria. While the ruling gives no clear-cut rules, such agreements likely satisfy the law in cases where manufacturers occupy relatively small parts of their markets. In such instances, the restrictions may actually increase competition among competing brands; the wholesaler or retailer faces no competition from other dealers carrying the manufacturer's brand, so it can concentrate on effectively competing with other brands.

The third legal question of exclusive dealing involves **tying agreements,** which allow channel members to become exclusive dealers only if they also carry products other than those that they want to sell. In the apparel industry, for example, such an agreement may require a dealer to carry a comparatively unpopular line of clothing in addition to desirable, fast-moving items.

Tying agreements violate the Sherman Act and the Clayton Act when they reduce competition or create monopolies that keep competitors out of major markets. For this reason, the courts prohibited International Salt Company from selling salt as a tying product with leases of its patented salt-dispensing machines for snow and ice removal. The Supreme Court ruled that such an agreement unreasonably reduced competition among sellers of salt.

Who Should Perform Channel Functions?

A fundamental marketing principle governs channel decisions: *Some member of the channel must perform certain marketing functions; channel members can shift responsibility, but they cannot eliminate central functions.* While wholesalers perform many of these functions for manufacturers, retailers, and other wholesaler clients, other channel members could fulfill these roles instead. Manufacturers may bypass independent wholesalers by establishing networks of regional warehouses, maintaining field sales forces to provide market coverage, serving as sources of information for retail customers, and arranging details of financing. Alternatively, manufacturers might push responsibility for some of these functions through the channel to retailers or ultimate purchasers. Large retailers face the same choices, but the principle remains the same: Channel members can eliminate an intermediary only when someone else performs its channel functions.

An independent intermediary earns a profit in exchange for providing services to manufacturers and retailers. This profit margin is low, however, ranging from 1 percent for food wholesalers to 5 percent for durable goods wholesalers. Manufacturers and retailers could reap these profits, or they could market directly and reduce retail prices—but only if they could perform the channel functions and match the efficiency of the independent intermediaries.

To grow profitably in a competitive environment, an intermediary must provide better service at lower costs than manufacturers or retailers can provide for themselves. In this case, consolidation of channel functions can represent a strategic opportunity for a company.

CHANNEL MANAGEMENT AND LEADERSHIP

Distribution strategy does not end with the choice of a channel. Manufacturers must also focus on channel management by developing and maintaining relationships with the intermediaries in their marketing channels. Positive channel relationships encourage channel members to pay attention to and to market a particular good. Manufacturers also must carefully manage the incentives offered to induce channel members to promote their products. This effort includes weighing decisions about pricing, promotion, and other support efforts that the manufacturer performs.

Increasingly, marketers are managing channels in partnership with other channel members. Effective cooperation allows all channel members to achieve goals that they could not achieve on their own. Keys to successful management of channel relationships include the development of high levels of coordination, commitment, and trust between channel members.[9]

Not all channel members wield equal power in the distribution chain, however. The dominant and controlling member of a marketing channel is called the **channel captain.** This firm's power to control a channel may result from its control over some type of reward or punishment to other channel members, such as granting an exclusive sales territory or taking away a dealership. Power might also result from contractual arrangements, specialized expert knowledge, or agreement among channel members about their mutual best interests. For example, Central Wire & Steel controls the distribution of its products through its Performance Assured service system described in the ad in Figure 13.6. The company

4

Describe the concepts of management, conflict, and cooperation within the marketing channel.

MARKETING DICTIONARY

exclusive distribution Channel policy in which a firm grants exclusive rights to a single wholesaler or retailer to sell its products in a particular geographic area.

exclusive-dealing agreement Arrangement between a manufacturer and a marketing intermediary that prohibits the intermediary from handling competing product lines.

closed sales territory Exclusive geographic selling region of a distributor.

tying agreement Arrangement that requires a marketing intermediary to carry items other than those they want to sell.

channel captain Dominant and controlling member of a marketing channel.

provides on-time delivery by operating its own fleet of delivery trucks and helps customers reduce their inventory costs by offering just-in-time and distributor managed inventory programs.

Channel Conflict

Channel captains often must work to resolve channel conflicts. Marketing channels work smoothly only when members cooperate in well-organized efforts to achieve maximum operating efficiencies, yet channel members often perform as separate, independent, and even competing forces. Too often marketing institutions see only one step forward or backward along a channel. They think about their own suppliers and customers rather than about vital links throughout the channel. Two types of conflict, horizontal and vertical conflict, may hinder the normal functioning of a marketing channel.

Horizontal Conflict

Horizontal conflict sometimes results from disagreements among channel members at the same level, such as two or more wholesalers or two or more retailers, or among marketing intermediaries of the same type, such as two competing discount stores or several retail florists. More often, however, horizontal conflict causes sparks between different types of marketing intermediaries that handle similar products. A retail druggist competes with discount houses, department stores, convenience stores, and mail-order houses, all of which may buy identical branded products from a single producer. Varied consumer preferences have drawn products into multiple channels and numerous, rival outlets.

Vertical Conflict

Vertical relationships also cause frequent and often severe conflict. Channel members at different levels find many reasons for disputes, as when retailers develop private brands to compete with producers' brands or when producers establish their own retail stores or create mail-order operations that compete with retailers. Producers may annoy wholesalers and retailers when they attempt to bypass these intermediaries and sell directly to consumers. For example, men's clothier Ermenegildo Zegna angered retailers when it launched its own Web site from which consumers could purchase suits directly. During its first two weeks of operation, the site attracted 25,000 visitors.[10]

In other instances, retailers may anger suppliers by requesting concessions the suppliers feel are unfair. Bayer AG and other suppliers have criticized some drug store chains, such as Rite Aid Corporation and Eckerd, for making unexpected deductions from payments for products. The retailers allege these deductions are necessary for covering the cost of defective or damaged goods; the suppliers claim the retailers are using their power as channel captains to reduce their bills.[11]

The Grey Market

Another type of channel conflict results from activities in the grey market. As U.S. manufacturers license their technology and brands abroad, they sometimes find themselves in competition in the U.S. market against versions of their own brands produced by overseas affiliates. These **grey goods,** sometimes called *parallel goods*, enter U.S. channels through the actions of foreign distributors. While licensing agreements usually prohibit foreign licensees from selling in the United States, no such rules inhibit their distributors.

A decade ago, the grey market became a problem for U.S. firms in the electronics field. It then spread to such products as flashlight batteries, photographic film, packaged goods, and the apparel industry. While some manufacturers have protested against this practice, retailers can still legally buy goods through the grey market because the Supreme Court has ruled that products made under legitimate licenses can legally enter the market regardless of their countries of origin.

Achieving Channel Cooperation

The basic antidote to channel conflict is effective cooperation among channel members. Most channels function harmoniously more often than they erupt in conflict; if they did not operate like this, they would cease to operate at all. Cooperation is best achieved when all channel members regard themselves as components of the same organization. Achieving this kind of cooperation is the primary responsibility of the dominant member—the channel captain, which must provide the leadership necessary to ensure the channel's efficient functioning.[12]

VERTICAL MARKETING SYSTEMS

Efforts to reduce channel conflict and to improve the effectiveness of distribution have led to the development of vertical marketing systems. A **vertical marketing system (VMS)** is a planned channel system designed to improve distribution efficiency and cost effectiveness by integrating various functions throughout the distribution chain.

A vertical marketing system can achieve this goal through either forward or backward integration. In *forward integration*, a firm attempts to control downstream distribution. For example, a manufacturer might buy a retail chain that sells its products. *Backward integration* occurs when a manufacturer attempts to gain greater control over inputs in its production process. For example, a manufacturer might buy the supplier of a raw material the manufacturer uses in the production of its products. Backward integration can also extend the control of retailers and wholesalers over producers that supply them.

A VMS offers several benefits. First, it improves chances for controlling and coordinating the steps in the distribution or production process. It may lead to the development of economies of scale that ultimately saves money. A VMS may also let a manufacturer expand into profitable new businesses. However, a VMS also involves some costs. A manufacturer assumes increased risk when it takes over control of an entire distribution chain. Manufacturers may also discover that they lose some flexibility in responding to market changes.[13]

Marketers have developed three categories of VMSs: corporate systems, administered systems, and contractual systems. These categories are outlined in the sections that follow.

Corporate Systems

Where a single owner runs organizations at each stage of the marketing channel, it operates a **corporate marketing system.** Hartmarx Corp., for example, markets its Hart Schaffner & Marx suits through company-owned stores and some independent retailers. At one time, Holiday Corp. owned a furniture manufacturer and a carpet mill that supplied its Holiday Inns. Other well-known corporate systems include Firestone and Sherwin-Williams. The paints advertised in Figure 13.7 are produced by Sherwin-Williams and distributed exclusively through thousands of company-operated stores.

down. Twice a year, Home Depot conducts product line reviews.

Home Depot establishes vertical marketing systems whenever possible to maximize control in both forward and backward integration. When the company began selling large appliances, it announced that it would personally stock about 60 percent of its full appliance line. The other 40 percent, supplied by General Electric, would be shipped by GE directly to consumers' homes.

If conflict crops up, Home Depot squashes it. When it looked like some suppliers might sell their products directly to consumers via the Internet Home Depot sent strong letters to the suppliers, asking them to stop or risk having their merchandise dropped altogether.

THE OUTCOME Home Depot's strong stance as channel captain has earned grudging respect from suppliers, who grumble but seem willing to do what it takes to maintain a good relationship with its giant customer. CEO Arthur Blank was recently named one of Business Week's top twenty-five managers of the year. "We spend 80 percent of our time talking about things we could do better," he says, and that includes enhancing channel cooperation.

FIGURE 13.7 — A Corporate Vertical Marketing System

Administered Systems

An **administered marketing system** achieves channel coordination when a dominant channel member exercises its power. Even though Goodyear sells its tires through independently owned and operated dealerships, Goodyear controls the stock that these dealerships carry. Other examples of powerful channel captains leading administered channels include McKesson, Sears, and Wal-Mart.

Contractual Systems

Instead of common ownership of intermediaries within a corporate VMS or the exercising of power within an administered system, a **contractual marketing system** coordinates distribution through formal agreements among channel members. In practice, three types of agreements set up these systems: wholesaler-sponsored voluntary chains, retail cooperatives, and franchises.

Wholesaler-Sponsored Voluntary Chain

A wholesaler-sponsored voluntary chain represents an attempt by an independent wholesaler to preserve a market by strengthening its retail customers. To enable independent retailers to compete with outlets of rival chains, the wholesaler enters into a formal agreement with retailers to use a common name, maintain standardized facilities, and purchase the wholesaler's products. Often, the wholesaler develops a line of private brands to be stocked by the members of the voluntary chain.

IGA (Independent Grocers' Alliance) Food Stores is a good example of a voluntary chain. Other wholesaler-sponsored chains include Associated Druggists, Sentry Hardware, and Western Auto. Since a single advertisement promotes all the retailers in the trading area, a common store name and similar inventories allow the retailers to save on advertising costs.

Retail Cooperative

In a second type of contractual VMS, a group of retailers establish a shared wholesaling operation to help them compete with chains. This is known as a retail cooperative. The retailers purchase ownership shares in the wholesaling operation and agree to buy a minimum percentage of their inventories from this operation. The members typically adopt a common store name and develop common private brands. Ace Hardware is an example of a retail cooperative.

Franchise

A third type of contractual vertical marketing system is the franchise, in which a wholesaler or dealer (the franchisee) agrees to meet the operating requirements of a manufacturer or other franchiser. Franchising is a huge and growing industry. Twenty years ago, Subway had 134 franchises and McDonald's had 5,749; today, Subway has almost 13,400 franchises and McDonald's boasts more than 16,000 outlets worldwide. Over 3,000 U.S. companies distribute goods and services through systems of franchised dealers, and numerous firms also offer franchises in international markets. The total number of franchise units tops 250,000, and it continues to rise. The five fastest-growing franchise categories are photo processing, human resource training, children's businesses, computer services, and maintenance companies. Duraclean, the oldest cleaning and maintenance franchise in the United States, has expanded its services worldwide. Through ads like the one in Figure 13.8, Duraclean seeks new franchises for countries outside the United States.

Franchise owners pay anywhere from several thousand dollars to hundreds of thousands of dollars to purchase their franchises. Typically, they also pay a royalty on sales to the franchising company. In exchange for these initial and ongoing fees, the franchise owner receives the right to use the company's brand name, as well as services such as training, marketing, advertising, and volume discounts.[14]

FIGURE 13.8 — Duraclean: A Franchised Cleaning and Maintenance Service

THE ROLE OF LOGISTICS IN DISTRIBUTION STRATEGY

Herman Miller Inc., one of the largest makers of office furniture and accessories, processes more than 3,000 orders every week. Most of these orders involve products from several of the company's five plants. If only one piece of an order is late, it can delay the entire shipment—and endanger Herman Miller's relationship with its customers.

This illustrates the importance of logistics. Careful coordination of Miller's manufacturing and shipping processes is the key to its continuing success. To ensure that all components of an order are completed simultaneously, the company installed a computerized system to track the movements of all parts and to ship them according to customer specifications. The system has reduced manufacturing time from six weeks to four weeks and improved the rate of on-time delivery from 76 percent to 99 percent. As an added bonus, Herman Miller's logistical planning has decreased the cost of goods sold by $56 million. The company passes on these savings to customers by offering discounts, ensuring even greater customer loyalty.[15]

Effective logistics requires proper management of the **supply chain** (also known as the value chain). As discussed in Chapter 5, the supply chain is the complete sequence of suppliers that contribute to the creation and delivery of a good or service. The supply chain begins with the raw-material inputs for the manufacturing process of a product and then proceeds to the actual production activities. The final link in the supply chain is the movement of finished goods through the marketing channel to end customers. Each link of the chain benefits the consumers as goods move from raw materials through manufacturing to distribution. The value chain encompasses all activities that enhance the value of the finished goods, including design, quality manufacturing, customer service, and delivery. Customer satisfaction results directly from the perceived value of a purchase to its buyer. To manage the supply chain, businesses must look for ways to add and maximize customer value in each activity they perform.

MARKETING DICTIONARY

administered marketing system VMS that achieves channel coordination when a dominant channel member exercises its power.

contractual marketing system VMS that coordinates channel activities through formal agreements among channel members.

supply (value) chain Sequence of suppliers that contributes to the creation and delivery of a good or service.

As Herman Miller's experience makes clear, logistical management plays a major role in giving customers what they need when they need it. Therefore, logistical management plays a central role in the supply chain. Another important component of this chain, **value-added service,** adds some improved or supplemental service that customers do not normally receive or expect.

Enterprise Resource Planning

Software is an important aspect of logistics management and the supply chain. Consider the case of Mott's, the applesauce people. Their ideal production plan is developed from software sold by SAP—the largest German software producer. Then Mott's Enterprise Resource Planning (ERP) kicks in. **Enterprise resource planning** is an integrated software system that moves data among the firm's units. Roughly two-thirds of ERP users are manufacturers that are concerned with production issues like sequencing and scheduling.

As valuable as it is, ERP and its related software aren't always perfect. For example, ERP failures were blamed for Hershey's inability to fulfill all of its candy orders during a recent Halloween period. The nation's major retailers were forced to shift their purchases to other candy vendors. [16]

Logistical Cost Control

In addition to enhancing their products by providing value-added services to customers, many firms are focusing on logistics for another important reason: to cut costs. Distribution functions currently represent almost half of a typical firm's total marketing costs.

Historically, cost-cutting efforts have focused on economies in production. These attempts began with the Industrial Revolution, when the emerging science of management emphasized efficient production and a continual drive to decrease production costs and improve the output levels of factories and production workers. Managers, however, now recognize that production efficiency leaves few easy opportunities for further cost savings. Increasingly, managers are looking for possible cost savings in their logistical functions. [17]

To reduce logistical costs, businesses are reexamining each link of their supply chains to identify activities that do not add value for customers. By eliminating, reducing, or redesigning these activities, they can often cut costs and boost efficiency. Some companies try to cut costs and offer value-added services by outsourcing some or all of their logistics functions to specialist firms. The **third party (contract) logistics firms** specialize in handling logistical activities for their clients. One highly-successful third party logistics firm is Pinacor, which distributes 300 tons of high-tech products on a daily basis. Its shipments include 30,000 products, from more than 200 manufacturers, that Pinacor ships to more than 25,000 computer resellers. [18] Penske, one of the world's largest logistics firms, handles customer's order delivery, warehousing, facilities management, inventory control, and transportation systems. Penske's ad in Figure 13.9 promotes the benefits of outsourcing logistics, including reducing customers' costs and improving customer satisfaction.

Through such outsourcing alliances, producers and logistical service suppliers cooperate in developing innovative, customized systems that speed goods through carefully constructed manufacturing and distribution pipelines. Although many companies have long outsourced transportation and warehousing functions, today's alliance partners use similar methods to combine their operations.

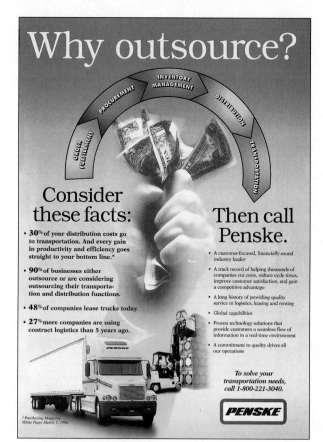

PHYSICAL DISTRIBUTION

A **system,** formally defined, is an organized group of components linked according to a plan for achieving specific objectives. A company's physical distribution system contains the following elements:

Identify and compare the major components of a physical distribution system.

1. *Customer service.* The level of customer service that the distribution activities should support.
2. *Transportation.* How the firm should ship its products.
3. *Inventory control.* How much inventory the firm should maintain at each location.
4. *Protective packaging and materials handling.* How the firm can efficiently handle goods in the factory, warehouse, and transport terminals.
5. *Order processing.* How the firm should handle orders.
6. *Warehousing.* Where the distribution system will locate stocks of goods. The number of warehouses the firm should maintain.

All of these components function in interrelated ways. Decisions made in one area affect relative efficiency in others. The physical distribution manager must balance each component so that the system avoids stressing any single aspect to the detriment of overall functioning. For example, a firm might decide to reduce transportation costs by shipping its products by inexpensive—but slow—water transportation. However, slow deliveries would likely force the firm to maintain high inventory levels and to raise inventory holding costs, such as warehousing expenses. This kind of mismatch between system elements often leads to increased production costs.

The Problem of Suboptimization

A logistics manager seeks to establish a specified level of customer service while minimizing the costs of physically moving and storing goods from their production point to their ultimate purchasers. Marketers must first agree on their customer service priorities and then seek to minimize the total costs of moving goods to buyers, all while meeting customer service goals. In order to meet customer service levels at minimum costs, marketers must mesh all physical distribution elements together rather than setting up independent arrangements. Marketers do not always achieve this goal, however.

Suboptimization results when the managers of individual physical distribution functions attempt to minimize costs, but the impact of one task on the others leads to less than optimal results. A frequently used analogy describes a football team composed of numerous, talented players who hold individual records in different aspects of the game. Unfortunately, however, these personal accomplishments fail to result in winning games if the players do cooperate in a larger endeavor—scoring more points than their opponents.

Suboptimization may cause problems in physical distribution when marketers judge each logistics activity by its ability to achieve its own objectives, some of which may work at cross-purposes with other goals. Suboptimization becomes particularly likely when a firm introduces a new product that may not fit

6
Outline the suboptimization problem in logistics.

MARKETING DICTIONARY

value-added service Improved or supplemental service that customers do not normally receive or expect.

enterprise resource planning Software system that moves data among a firm's units.

third party (contract) logistics firm Company that specializes in handling logistics activities for other firms.

system Organized group of components linked according to a plan for achieving specific objectives.

suboptimization Condition that results when individual operations achieve their objectives but interfere with progress toward broader organizational goals.

continued on next page

Hershey's Suffers a Halloween Nightmare

BACKGROUND Marketers for Hershey Foods Corp. wanted to upgrade their distribution system so that all of its sweets—Kisses, Reese's Peanut Butter Cups, Twizzlers, Milk Duds, and more—would get to the right store shelves more efficiently. For decades, store owners have relied on Hershey's to provide favorite holiday sweets, and the company decided it was time to invest in a $112 million enterprise resource planning computer system designed to unify and upgrade its customer-service, warehousing, and order-fulfillment capabilities.

THE MARKETING PROBLEM The design of the new system went smoothly, but Hershey's needed to find the right time to bring it online. Initially, the company targeted April, traditionally a slower time for candy sales. But delays meant that the system didn't come online until July. In addition, managers decided to use what some writers call the "Big Bang" approach, implementing the entire system at once, rather than phasing it in one component at a time.

THE OUTCOME By opting out of the phase-in approach, Hershey's was hit with glitches throughout the system that it could not correct in time for the autumn candy rush. In late October, retailers became disgruntled when they didn't receive promised deliveries. Candy shelves had gaping holes where Hershey's candies should have

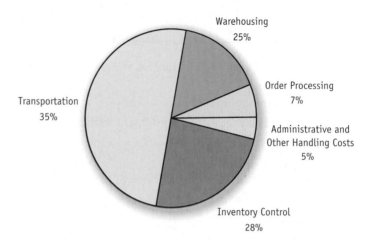

FIGURE 13.10 Allocation of Physical Distribution Expenditures, 2000–2003

Source: These estimates were provided by Dr. Julie Gentry, Logistics Faculty, University of Arkansas–Fayetteville, October 25, 1999.

easily into its current physical distribution system. Businesspeople often focus on certain adjustments to their systems without anticipating related problems that eventually arise.

Effective management of the physical distribution function requires some cost trade-offs. By accepting relatively high costs in some functional areas in order to cut costs in others, managers can minimize their firm's total physical distribution costs. Of course, any reduction in logistical costs should support progress toward the goal of maintaining customer service standards.

Customer Service Standards

Customer service standards state goals and define acceptable performance for the quality of service that a firm expects to deliver to its customers. For example, one firm might set a customer service standard that calls for the shipment of 95 percent of all orders within 48 hours after the receipt of the orders and the shipment of all orders within 72 hours after the receipt of the orders.

Designers of a physical distribution system begin by establishing acceptable levels of customer service. These designers then assemble physical distribution components in a way that will achieve this standard at the lowest possible total cost. As shown in Figure 13.10 this overall cost breaks down into five components: (1) transportation, (2) warehousing, (3) inventory, (4) order processing, and (5) administrative and other handling costs.

Transportation

Transportation costs represent the largest category of logistics-related expenses for most firms. Moreover, for many products—particularly perishable ones—transportation makes a central contribution to satisfactory customer service. When Pepsico and Starbucks launched Frappucino, a new milk-and-coffee beverage, they allotted a generous budget for refrigerated transport in getting the product to store shelves as quickly as possible. Pepsi's proprietary logistical software enabled the companies to coordinate manufacturing and transportation efficiently.[20] Many logistics managers have found the key to controlling their shipping costs is careful management of relationships with shipping firms. Freight carriers set two basic types of rates: class and commodity rates. A **class rate** is a standard rate for a specific commodity moving between any pair of destinations. A carrier may charge a lower **commodity rate,** sometimes called a *special rate*, to a favored shipper as a reward for either regular business or a large-quantity shipment. Railroads and inland water carriers frequently reward customers in this way.

In addition, the railroad and motor carrier industries sometimes supplement this rate structure with *negotiated* or *contract* rates. In other words, the two parties finalize terms of rates, services, and other variables in a contract.

Transportation Deregulation

The deregulation of the U.S. transportation industry began in 1977 with the removal of regulations governing cargo air carriers not engaged in passenger transportation. The following year, the Airline Deregulation Act granted passenger airlines considerable freedom in establishing fares and in choosing new routes.

In 1980, the Motor Carrier Act and the Staggers Rail Act deregulated the trucking and railroad industries. These laws enabled transportation carriers to negotiate rates and services with shippers. Before deregulation, no truck carrier served all 48 contiguous U.S. states. Today, more than 4,000 carriers have that authority. In addition, the trucking industry now operates far more efficiently than it did under government regulation; many carriers have reduced empty mileage by two-thirds.

Classes of Carriers

Freight carriers are classified as common, contract, and private carriers. Common carriers, often considered the backbone of the transportation industry, provide transportation services as for-hire carriers to the general public. The government still regulates their rates and services, and they cannot conduct their operations without permission from the appropriate regulatory authority. Common carriers move freight via all modes of transport.

Contract carriers are for-hire transporters that do not offer their services to the general public. Instead, they establish contracts with individual customers and operate exclusively for particular industries (most commonly the motor freight industry). These carriers operate under much looser regulations than common carriers.

Private carriers do not offer services for hire. These carriers provide transportation services solely for internally generated freight. As a result, they observe no rate or service regulation. The Interstate Commerce Commission (ICC), a federal regulatory agency, permits private carriers to operate as common or contract carriers, as well. Many private carriers have taken advantage of this rule by operating their trucks fully loaded at all times.

Major Transportation Modes

Logistics managers choose among five major transportation alternatives: railroads, motor carriers, water carriers, pipelines, and air freight. Each mode has its own unique characteristics. Logistics managers select the best options for their situations by matching the situation features to their specific transportation needs.

Railroads—The Nation's Leading Transporter

Railroads continue to control the largest share of the freight business, as measured by ton-miles. The term *ton-mile* indicates shipping activity required to move 1 ton of freight 1 mile. Thus, a 3-ton shipment moving 8 miles equals 24 ton-miles. Rail shipments quickly rack up ton-miles because this mode provides the most efficient way for moving bulky commodities over long distances. For instance, rail carriers generally transport huge quantities of coal, chemicals,

7

Explain the impact of transportation deregulation on logistics activities.

MARKETING   DICTIONARY

customer service standard Statement of goals and acceptable performance for the quality of service that a firm expects to deliver to its customers.

class rate Standard transportation rate established for shipments of a specific commodity between any pair of destinations.

commodity rate Special, favorable transportation rate granted by a carrier to a selected shipper as a reward for either regular business or a large quantity shipment.

FIGURE 13.11 | Railroads: Efficient Transportation for Commodities

8

Compare the major transportation alternatives on the basis of speed, dependability, cost, frequency of shipments, availability in different locations, and flexibility in handling products.

grain, nonmetallic minerals, lumber and wood products, and automobiles. The Norfolk Southern ad shown in Figure 13.11 emphasizes the importance of railroads for transporting commodities such as grain for food producers, steel for automobile makers, and coal for electric utilities.

The railroads have improved their service standards through a number of innovative concepts, such as unit trains, run-through trains, intermodal (piggyback) operations, and double-stack container trains. Unit trains carry much of the coal, grain, and other high volume commodities shipped, running back and forth between single loading points (such as a mine) and single destinations (such as a power plant) to deliver a single commodity. Run-through trains bypass intermediate terminals to speed up schedules. They work similar to unit trains, but a run-through train may carry a variety of commodities.

In piggyback operations, highway trailers and containers ride on railroad flatcars, thus combining the long haul capacity of the train with the door-to-door flexibility of the truck. A double-stack container train pulls special rail cars equipped with bathtub-shaped wells so they can carry two containers stacked on top of one another. By nearly doubling train capacity and slashing costs, this system offers enormous advantages to rail customers.

Motor Carriers—Flexible and Growing   The trucking industry has grown dramatically over recent decades. It offers some important advantages over the other transportation modes, including relatively fast shipments and consistent service for both large and small shipments. Motor carriers concentrate on shipping manufactured products, while railroads typically haul bulk shipments of raw materials. Motor carriers, therefore, receive greater revenue per ton shipped, since the cost for shipping raw materials is higher than for shipping manufactured products.

Technology has also improved the efficiency of trucking. Many trucking firms now track their fleets via satellite communications systems, and in-truck computer systems allow drivers and dispatchers to make last-minute changes in scheduling and delivery. The Internet is also adding new features to motor carrier services.

Some private fleets function as rolling assembly plants that pick up semi-finished products from manufacturers, assemble them en route, and deliver the finished goods to customers, increasing overall service and customer satisfaction. Arizona-based distributor Pinacor, for example, partners with New Jersey–based Lucent Technologies to perform final testing and configuration of Lucent's telecommunications systems. Pinacor's ability to assume these final manufacturing steps reduces product lead time dramatically, from an average of 30 to 45 days to about 10 days.[21]

Water Carriers—Slow but Inexpensive   Two basic types of transport methods move products over water: inland or barge lines and oceangoing, deep-water ships. Barge lines efficiently transport bulky, low unit value commodities such as grain, gravel, lumber, sand, and steel. A typical lower Mississippi River barge line may stretch more than a quarter-mile across.

Oceangoing ships carry a growing stream of containerized freight between ports around the world. Large ships also operate on the Great Lakes. Shippers that transport goods via water carriers incur very low costs compared to the rates for other transportation modes. Standardized, modular shipping containers maximize savings by limiting loading, unloading, and other handling.

Pipelines—Specialized Transporters   Although the pipeline industry ranks third after railroads and motor carriers in ton-miles transported, many people scarcely recognize its existence. More than 214,000 miles of pipelines crisscross the United States in an extremely efficient network for transporting natural gas and oil products. Oil pipelines carry two types of commodities: crude (unprocessed) oil and refined products, such as gasoline, jet fuel, and kerosene. In addition, one so-called *slurry pipeline* carries coal in suspension after it has been ground up into a powder and mixed with water. The Black Mesa Pipeline, owned by Union Pacific moves the coal 290 miles from northern Arizona into southern Nevada.

Although pipelines offer low maintenance and dependable methods of transportation, a number of characteristics limit their applications. They have fewer locations than water carriers, and they can accommodate shipments of only a small number of products. Finally, pipelines represent a relatively slow method of transportation; liquids travel through this method at an average speed of only 3 to 4 miles per hour.

Air Freight—Fast but Expensive   International water carriers still transport many low value products or heavy mass-market goods such as automobiles, but more and more international shipments travel by air. The significant growth in shipping volume handled by air carriers will probably continue as freight carriers seek to satisfy increased customer demand for fast delivery. While 80 percent of the world's overnight air deliveries take place in the United States, international demand for overnight air-freight service is soaring by 18 percent every year. Already more than 1.3 million 24-hour deliveries are made daily outside the United States.[22]

Table 13.2 compares the five transport modes on several operating characteristics. Although all shippers judge reliability, speed, and cost in choosing the most appropriate transportation methods, they assign varying importance to specific criteria when shipping different goods. For example, while motor carriers rank highest in availability in different locations, shippers of petroleum products frequently choose the lowest ranked alternative, pipelines, for their low cost. Examples of the types of goods most often handled by the various transport modes include the following:

- *Railroads.* Lumber, iron and steel, coal, automobiles, grain, chemicals
- *Motor carriers.* Clothing, furniture and fixtures, lumber and plastic products, food products, leather and leather products, machinery
- *Water carriers.* Fuel, oil, coal, chemicals, minerals, petroleum products

		DEPENDABILITY IN MEETING	FREQUENCY OF	AVAILABILITY IN DIFFERENT	FLEXIBILITY	
MODE	SPEED	SCHEDULES	SHIPMENTS	LOCATIONS	IN HANDLING	COST
Rail	Average	Average	Low	Low	High	Average
Water	Very slow	Average	Very low	Limited	Very high	Very low
Truck	Fast	High	High	Very extensive	Average	High
Pipeline	Slow	High	High	Very limited	Very low	Low
Air	Very fast	High	Average	Average	Low	Very high

TABLE 13.2 Comparison of Transport Modes

- *Pipelines.* Oil, diesel fuel, jet fuel, kerosene, natural gas
- *Air carriers.* Flowers, technical instruments and machinery, high priced specialty products

Freight Forwarders and Supplemental Carriers

Freight forwarders act as transportation intermediaries, consolidating shipments to gain lower rates for their customers. The transport rates on less-than-truckload (LTL) and less-than-carload (LCL) shipments often double the per-unit rates on truckload (TL) and carload (CL) shipments. Freight forwarders charge less than the higher rates but more than the lower rates. They profit by consolidating shipments from multiple customers until they can ship at TL and CL rates. The customers gain two advantages from these services: lower costs on small shipments and faster delivery service than they could achieve with their own LTL and LCL shipments.

In addition to the transportation options reviewed so far, a logistics manager can also ship products via a number of auxiliary, or supplemental, carriers that specialize in small shipments. These carriers include bus freight services, United Parcel Service, FedEx, DHL International, and the U.S. Postal Service.[23]

Intermodal Coordination

9

Discuss how transportation intermediaries and combined transportation modes can improve physical distribution.

Transportation companies emphasize specific modes and, therefore, serve certain kinds of customers, but they sometimes combine their services to give shippers the service and cost advantages of each. Piggyback service, mentioned in the section on rail transport, is the most widely used form of intermodal coordination. *Birdyback* service, another form of intermodal coordination, sends motor carriers to pick up a shipment locally and deliver that shipment to local destinations, while an air carrier takes it between airports near those locations. *Fishyback* service sets up a similar intermodal coordination system between motor carriers and water carriers.

Intermodal transportation generally gives shippers faster service and lower rates than either mode could match individually since each method carries freight in its most efficient way. However, intermodal arrangements require close coordination between all transportation providers.

Recognizing this need, multimodal transportation companies have formed to offer combined activities within single operations. Piggyback service generally joins two separate companies—a railroad and a trucking company. A multimodal firm provides intermodal service through its own internal transportation resources. Shippers benefit because the single service assumes responsibility from origin to destination. This unification prevents arguments over which carrier delayed or damaged a shipment.

In addition, major U.S. carriers are increasingly looking toward vertical integration for providing coordinated door-to-door service. A good example is FedEx's ShipAPI system, which serves business clients such as florist Proflower.com. When a customer orders from Proflower's Web site, the transaction generates a FedEx label and an order form, which are then faxed to a grower. The grower fills the order, prints a paper copy of the label, and attaches it to the package for FedEx pickup. The system automatically confirms pickup, shipment, and delivery of the order.[24]

FIGURE 13.12 Goods Moving Through a Break-Bulk Distribution Center

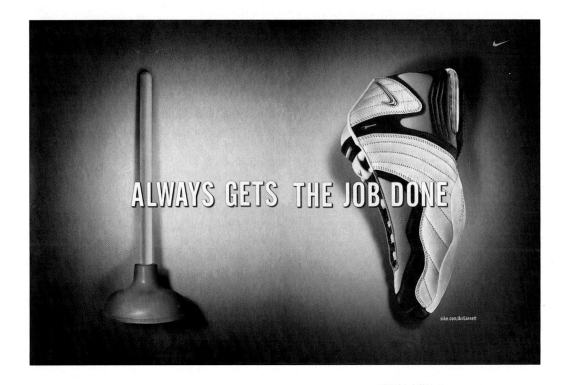

ALWAYS GETS THE JOB DONE

nike.com/AirGarnett

Warehousing

Products flow through two types of warehouses: storage and distribution warehouses. A **storage warehouse** holds goods for moderate to long periods in an attempt to balance supply and demand for producers and purchasers. For example, controlled atmosphere—also called cold storage—warehouses in Yakima and Wenatchee, Washington serve nearby apple orchards. By contrast, a **distribution warehouse** assembles and redistributes goods, keeping them moving as much as possible. Many distribution warehouses or centers physically store goods for less than 24 hours before shipping them on to customers.

Logistics managers have attempted to save on transportation costs by developing central distribution centers. A manufacturer located in Philadelphia, for example, could send direct shipments to customers in the Illinois-Wisconsin-Indiana area, but if each customer placed small orders, the shipper would pay high transportation charges. Instead, it might send a single, large, consolidated shipment to a *break-bulk center*—a central distribution center that breaks down large shipments into several smaller ones and delivers them to individual customers in the area. Many Internet retailers, for example, use break-bulk distribution centers. In handling the logistics for the Nike.com shoes in Figure 13.12, United Parcel Service breaks down large shipments of shoes it stocks at a UPS warehouse and sends them to individual customers. Conversely, a *make-bulk center* consolidates several small orders into one large shipment and delivers the entire shipment to a single destination.[25]

Automated Warehouse Technology

Logistics managers can cut distribution costs and improve customer service dramatically by automating their warehouse systems. Although automation technology represents an expensive investment, it can provide major labor savings for high volume distributors such as grocery chains. A computerized system might store orders, choose the correct number of cases, and move these cases in the desired sequence to loading docks. This kind of warehouse system reduces labor costs, worker injuries, pilferage, fires, and breakage.

Warehouse Locations

Every company must make a major logistics decision when it determines the number and locations of its storage facilities. Two categories of costs influence this choice: (1) warehousing and materials-handling costs and (2) delivery costs from warehouses to customers. Large facilities offer economies of scale in facilities and materials-handling systems; per-unit costs for these systems decrease as volume increases. Delivery costs, on the other hand, rise as the distance from warehouse to customer increases.

Warehouse location also affects customer service. Businesses must place their storage and distribution facilities in locations from which they can meet customer demands for product availability and delivery times. They must also consider population and employment trends. For example, the growth of metropolitan areas throughout the southern and western United States has caused some firms to relocate distribution centers to these areas.

Inventory Control Systems

Inventory control captures a large share of a logistics manager's attention because companies need to maintain enough inventory to meet customer demand without incurring unneeded costs for carrying excess inventory. Some firms attempt to keep inventory levels under control by implementing just-in-time (JIT) production, discussed in Chapter 10.

@ **wal-mart.com**

Wal-Mart has been a pioneer in using JIT to keep its costs down. The giant retailer's supply chain consists of a hub-and-spoke network of distribution centers surrounded by several stores, each within one day's journey by truck. This arrangement allows Wal-Mart to warehouse inventory at distribution centers until needed, then deliver products quickly to selected stores.

Like other logistics tasks, inventory control can help a firm build a competitive advantage. At Wal-Mart, JIT results in fresher products and fewer markdowns. It also reduces labor costs because individual stores require fewer employees to unload merchandise and to stock shelves.[26]

Order Processing

Like inventory control, order processing directly affects the firm's ability to meet its customer service standards. A company may have to compensate for inefficiencies in its order processing system by shipping products via costly transportation modes or by maintaining large inventories at many expensive field warehouses.

Order processing typically consists of four major activities: (1) a credit check; (2) keeping a record of the sale, which involves record-keeping tasks such as crediting a sales representative's commission account; (3) making appropriate accounting entries; and (4) locating ordered products, shipping them, and adjusting inventory records. A **stockout** occurs when an order for an item is not available for shipment. A firm's order processing system must advise affected customers of a stockout and offer a choice of alternative actions.

As in other areas of physical distribution, technological innovations improve efficiency in order processing. Many firms are streamlining their order processing procedures by using e-mail.[27]

Protective Packaging and Materials Handling

Logistics managers arrange and control activities for moving products within plants, warehouses, and transportation terminals, which together comprise the **materials handling** system. Two important concepts influence many materials handling choices: unitizing and containerization.

Unitizing combines as many packages as possible into each load that moves within or outside a facility. Logistics managers prefer to handle materials on *pallets* (platforms, generally made of wood, on which goods are transported). Unitizing systems often lash materials in place with steel bands or *shrink packaging*. A shrink package surrounds a batch of materials with a sheet of plastic that shrinks after heating, securely holding individual pieces together. Unitizing promotes efficient materials handling because each package requires minimal labor to move. Securing the materials together also minimizes damage and pilferage.

Logistics managers extend the same concept through **containerization**—combining several unitized loads. A container of oil rig parts, for example, can be loaded in Tulsa and trucked to Kansas City, where rail facilities place the shipment on a high-speed, run-through train to New York City. There, the parts are loaded on a ship headed to Saudi Arabia.

In addition to the benefits outlined for unitizing, containerization also markedly reduces the time required to load and unload ships. Containers limit in-transit damage to freight because individual packages pass through few handling systems en route to purchasers.

ACHIEVEMENT CHECK SUMMARY

Read the learning objectives that follow, and consider the questions for each one. Answering these questions will reinforce your grasp of the most important concepts in the chapter and will allow you to check how well you have achieved these learning goals. Where a blank appears before a question, answer with *T* or *F* for true/false questions; for multiple-choice questions, choose the letter of the correct answer.

Objective 13.1: Describe the role that marketing channels and logistics play in marketing strategy.

1. _____ A marketing channel is (a) a method of allocating products to end users; (b) a system for managing the flow of goods to users; (c) a transportation term.
2. _____ Marketing channels bring buyers and sellers together.
3. _____ Businesses work hard to reduce logistics costs because these expenses represent nearly half of overall marketing expenses.
4. _____ Once a marketing channel is established, it probably will never change.

Objective 13.2: Describe the various types of distribution channels available to marketers.

1. _____ The simplest marketing channel is (a) to sell through retail stores; (b) to use wholesalers; (c) to use direct sales or direct marketing; (d) to hire an agent.
2. _____ A Tupperware party is an example of (a) direct selling; (b) wholesaling; (c) retailing; (d) dual distribution.
3. _____ Firms usually practice dual distribution (a) to maximize distribution coverage; (b) to reduce the number of channels; (c) to move goods back from users to producers.

Objective 13.3: Outline the major channel strategy decisions.

1. _____ *Distribution intensity* refers to (a) the amount of inventory on store shelves; (b) the number of intermediaries through which a firm distributes goods; (c) the number of geographical areas covered by a distribution strategy.
2. _____ Intensive distribution is most often used by manufacturers of (a) convenience goods; (b) specialty goods; (c) luxury goods; (d) parts for other manufacturers.

3. _____ One benefit of selective distribution is (a) goods are widely available; (b) improvement in working relationships within the channel; (c) reduction in advertising costs.
4. _____ Exclusive distribution can lead to legal problems if it inhibits competition or creates a monopoly situation.

Objective 13.4: Describe the concepts of management, conflict, and cooperation within the marketing channel.

1. _____ All channel members are relatively equal in the distribution chain.
2. _____ The term *channel captain* refers to the dominant and controlling member of a marketing channel.
3. _____ Which of the following situations is an example of horizontal conflict?
(a) Wal-Mart and Kroger Supermarkets both promote and sell Bayer aspirin; (b) Kmart has developed its own brand of aspirin, which it sells on the shelf next to Bayer aspirin; (c) Microchips manufactured in China are sold in the United States as grey goods that compete against Intel microchips.
4. _____ Which of the following situations is an example of vertical conflict?
(a) Wal-Mart and Kroger supermarkets both promote and sell Bayer aspirin; (b) Kmart has developed its own brand of aspirin, which it sells on the shelf next to Bayer aspirin; (c) Microchips manufactured in China are sold in the United States as grey goods that compete against Intel microchips.
5. _____ Cooperation between channel members is best achieved by (a) making sure all members are paid adequately; (b) considering all channel

MARKETING DICTIONARY

stockout Order for a product that is unavailable for shipment or sale.

materials handling Set of activities that move production inputs and other goods within plants, warehouses, and transportation terminals.

unitizing Process of combining individual materials into large loads for easy handling.

containerization Process of combining several unitized loads into a single, well-protected load.

members as part of the same organization; (c) focusing on operating efficiencies.

Objective 13.5: Identify and compare the major components of a physical distribution system.

1. _____ A physical distribution system seldom influences customer satisfaction.

2. _____ Businesses must carefully manage their relationships with shipping firms.

3. _____ A physical distribution system can function effectively only through an organized relationship among the firm's production, finance, and marketing functions.

4. _____ A business should set the same customer service standards for all customers.

Objective 13.6: Outline the suboptimization problem in logistics.

1. _____ Logistics managers seek to provide a high level of customer service regardless of cost.

2. _____ Suboptimization is a condition in which the manager of each logistics function attempts to maximize customer service regardless of cost.

3. _____ Suboptimization describes a firm's inability to provide good customer service while keeping costs at a minimum.

Objective 13.7: Explain the impact of transportation deregulation on logistics activities.

1. _____ Deregulation has freed transportation companies to provide more flexible services than they could manage under tight regulatory control.

2. _____ Deregulated transportation firms can match their prices to customers' needs.

3. _____ The deregulated transportation environment has complicated physical distribution management.

Objective 13.8: Compare the major transportation alternatives on the basis of speed, dependability, cost, frequency of shipments, availability in different locations, and flexibility in handling products.

1. _____ Railroads offer the most suitable transportation services for (a) small package shipments; (b) bulk shipments of raw materials; (c) shipments that need to travel only short distances.

2. _____ Motor carriers generally move goods slowly.

3. _____ A cargo ship represents a very expensive option for transporting goods.

4. _____ Air freight carriers can help shippers meet their needs for rapid delivery times.

Objective 13.9: Discuss how transportation intermediaries and combined transportation modes can improve physical distribution.

1. _____ A freight forwarder is (a) a transportation firm that specializes in moving heavy materials; (b) a transportation intermediary that consolidates shipments to earn lower rates than those that individual shippers would pay; (c) a third-party firm that handles logistics management for another firm.

2. _____ Two or more transport modes often combine their capabilities to give shippers the service and cost advantages of each in a process called (a) contract logistics; (b) intermodal coordination; (c) suboptimization.

Students: See the solutions section located on page S-2 to check your responses to the Achievement Check Summary.

Key Terms

marketing channel	marketing intermediary
logistics	wholesaler
physical distribution	direct channel

direct selling	supply (value) chain
dual distribution	value-added service
reverse channels	enterprise resource planning
distribution intensity	third party (contract) logistics
intensive distribution	firm
selective distribution	system
exclusive distribution	suboptimization
exclusive-dealing agreement	customer service standard
closed sales territory	class rate
tying agreement	commodity rate
channel captain	storage warehouse
grey good	distribution warehouse
vertical marketing system (VMS)	stockout
corporate marketing system	materials handling
administered marketing system	unitizing
contractual marketing system	containerization

Review Questions

1. Outline the major categories of marketing channels. Cite an example for each type of channel a firm that uses that channel.

2. Discuss the basic reasons for the increased attention to logistics management. How has this been influenced by the emergence of a global marketplace?

3. How do marketing channels create utility? What specific functions do marketing channels perform?

4. Outline the major categories of channel decisions. How might the grey market affect a firm's channel decision?

5. Who should perform the various marketing channel functions? How have these arrangements changed over time?

6. Explain the concept of power in the marketing channel. Under what conditions do producers, wholesalers, and retailers act as channel captains?

7. Outline the basic strengths and weaknesses of each transportation mode. What types of shipments suit the strengths of each mode?

8. Identify the major forms of intermodal coordination, and give an example of a good for which each offers special advantages. Why have piggyback rail cars become so popular?

9. What considerations should influence the location decision for a new distribution warehouse? What cost trade-offs must a company consider in its location decision?

10. Explain the advantages and potential problems of the just-in-time system of inventory control. Relate your answer to the need to control inventory carrying costs.

Questions for Critical Thinking

1. Imagine a vending machine that would charge more for soft drinks during hot weather. The Coca-Cola Company has tested such a device. What is your opinion of a temperature-sensitive vending machine? How do you think customers would react? Is this a logical distribution strategy for The Coca-Cola Company to pursue?

2. Outline the marketing channel used by a firm in your area. Why did the company select this particular channel?

3. How might e-commerce lead to channel conflict? What type of channel conflict could result from e-commerce? Suggest a resolution to this conflict.

4. Many children were disappointed at Halloween 1999. Hershey was unable to stock retailer's shelves with the required supplies of chocolate candy. Research this distribution and logistics failure. What went wrong? What lessons does this offer for future distribution strategies?

5. Suggest the most appropriate method for transporting the products listed below. Defend your choices.

a. iron ore
b. oil field equipment
c. crude oil
d. cherries
e. lumber

Note: For all three exercises, you will be using the same Web site: Arthur Andersen's KnowledgeSpace—"a knowledge service designed to help improve business performance. It integrates Arthur Andersen's business resources with daily news and insights to help business professionals find answers to their key business issues."

If your business school does not already subscribe to this service, then you will need to do the following. Go to *www.knowledgespace.com* and

- Select "Subscribe Today."
- Scroll down on the left bar and select the "30 Days Free" option.
- Select "KnowledgeSpace Business Professional Community" as the community you'd like to try.
- Go through the registration process (no credit card is required, and you're not obligated to purchase anything after the trial).
- Write down your login and password information so you may gain access to the site later during the 30-day trial should you need to do so.
- Go to "Resources" and choose "Global Best Practices."
- Go to "Universal Process Classification Scheme."

knowledgespace.com

1. Marketing Channels. Go to "4.0 Market & Sell" and then to "4.1.2 Select Channels of Distribution." Using the "Executive Summary" link, find and list the six global best practices being followed by the leading companies that are high performers in the process of selecting channels of distribution (referred to as marketing channels in the text).

2. Types of Marketing Channels. Continuing at the location in the first exercise, read the article about the featured company (choose "Performer Profile" in the left sidebar), and identify the types of marketing channels used by the company.

3. Inventory Control Systems. Return to the "Universal Process Classification Scheme" and select "5.0 Produce & Deliver Products and Services." Go to "5.4.2 Manage Inventories" and choose "Interactive Tool." This feature allows you to compare your organization's current business practices with the best practices identified in the Global Best Practices knowledge base. Once you've answered the 30 questions, the tool tabulates your results and generates a report with insights into where to begin improving the effectiveness of your organization. For purposes of this exercise, you will not be completing the entire interactive tool. Instead, list the questions under "E. Streamline inventory procurement and delivery operations according to just-in-time (JIT) principles" and indicate the ideal answer with your reason for choosing each answer.

Video Case 13 on RadioShack begins on page VC-15.

Retailing, Wholesaling, and Direct Marketing

Can Buy.com Keep Its Promise?

Imagine a store that advertised "The Lowest Prices on Earth" in its window. Would you visit the store to see if the claim were true? Scott Blum, founder and CEO of Buy.com is betting that consumers will visit his site for the best prices on computers and accessories, as well as a wide variety of other products in the future. How can he guarantee the lowest price? By selling his merchandise below cost and making up the difference through advertising revenues.

Blum initially founded his company under the name Buy-Comp.com in 1996 and focused on selling computer products at discount prices. He did not want to obtain and hold inventory himself, so he arranged to have wholesalers ship items directly to his customers. Then Blum purchased SpeedServ, a smaller on-line retailer of books and videos and changed the name of his company to Buy.com. He plans to expand well beyond the sale of computers—in fact, he wants to knock Amazon.com out of its spot as the largest general Internet retailer. "We're going to be

the largest provider of e-commerce," predicts Blum. "Our target is Amazon.com." To accomplish this, he has already bought more than 2,000 Internet domain names that begin with B-U-Y. By doing this, he ensures that a consumer who types in the word "buy" will hit one of his sites. Eventually, Buy.com will be set up to handle everything from "buy clothes" to "buy potato chips."

Experts agree that if Buy.com succeeds in building its business solely on price, the Internet company will change the way marketing intermediaries relate to each other. For instance, wholesalers and distributors might have to smooth the ruffled feathers of other customers when Buy.com undercuts their prices dramatically. But these intermediaries won't be taking the loss on products, Buy.com will. If Buy.com proves that it can move ahead of its competitors simply by selling directly to consumers at the lowest price, someone new is bound to enter the market with even lower prices. And as more and more virtual stores like Buy.com gain solid positions in the marketplace, they will probably pressure manufacturers to ship products directly to consumers rather than going through standard channels like wholesalers and distributors.

Right now, when a consumer places an order for a computer at Buy.com, the order goes straight from Buy.com to distributor Ingram Micro, who ships the computer to the consumer. This way, Buy.com saves time and money by taking ownership of, but not taking possession of, the computer. Buy.com officially buys the computer from Ingram, then resells it to the consumer. But no Buy.com employee touches the product, because Buy.com doesn't warehouse or ship it.

Buy.com has its critics, the loudest of whom are its potential competitors and those who are strongly attached to traditional marketing channels. "I'm rather skeptical of the long-term prospects of a business full of loss leaders," says Ken Cassar, an analyst with Internet research firm Jupiter Communications. "It's one thing to drive people into a store like Wal-Mart by selling toilet paper for 79 cents and then also selling them a barbecue grill at a profit. But how can any business in the long run be profitable when all its products are loss leaders?" Loss leaders are products that actually lose money for the seller. Blum argues that not all of Buy.com's products lose money, and so far, his investors have bought into his ideas, despite the fact that the firm has yet to turn a profit. Blum expects to raise more money by making a public offering of stock, and of course, there's always the advertising revenue that he promises will help keep the company afloat.

Perhaps there is no way to predict how a company that relies on such a radical business model will survive, succeed, or even change the way retailers and marketing intermediaries conduct business. But a Buy.com board member with a familiar name—John Sculley, former Apple Computer CEO—sees it this way: "It's a brilliant con-cept. The way to look at it is not as selling below cost, but as building a branded franchise as the low-price leader." And Blum asserts that his business model is sound, even better than that of Amazon.com, because Buy.com has far fewer employees—85 to Amazon's 2,000—and because Buy.com holds no inventory, whereas Amazon.com continues to build huge warehouses around the country. He insists that selling for less will eventually mean greater profits.[1]

CHAPTER OVERVIEW

As we saw in Chapter 13, wholesaling and retailing are integral components of the marketing channel. A **wholesaler** is an intermediary that takes title to the goods it handles and then distributes these goods to retailers, other distributors, or sometimes end consumers. **Retailing** may be defined as all activities involved in selling goods and services to ultimate consumers.

Another important part of the marketing channel is **direct marketing,** a distribution channel consisting of direct communication to a consumer or business user. Direct marketing is designed to generate a response in the form of an order, a request for further information, or a visit to a business/store to purchase specific goods or services. In effect, it is a broad-based definition of nonstore retailing. While many people equate direct marketing with direct mail, this marketing channel also includes telemarketing, direct-response advertising and television and radio infomercials, direct-response print advertising, and electronic media. ∎

WHOLESALING INTERMEDIARIES

Recall from Chapter 13 that many channels involve marketing intermediaries called *wholesalers.* These firms sell products primarily to retailers or to other wholesalers or business users and only in insignificant amounts to ultimate consumers. **Wholesaling intermediaries,** a broader category, includes not only wholesalers, who assume title to the goods they handle, but also agents and brokers, who perform important wholesaling activities without taking title to the goods.

Functions of Wholesaling Intermediaries

1

Identify the functions performed by wholesaling intermediaries.

As specialists in certain marketing functions, as opposed to production or manufacturing functions, wholesaling intermediaries can perform these functions more efficiently than producers or consumers. The importance of these functions results from the utility they create, the services they provide, and the cost reductions they allow.

Creating Utility

Wholesaling intermediaries create three types of utility for consumers. They enhance *time utility* by making products available for sale when consumers want to purchase them. They create

TABLE 14.1	Wholesaling Services for Consumers and Producer-Suppliers		

		BENEFICIARIES OF SERVICE	
SERVICE		CUSTOMERS	PRODUCER-SUPPLIERS
Buying			
Anticipates customer demands and applies knowledge of alternative sources of supply; acts as purchasing agent for customers.		✓	
Selling			
Provides a sales force to call on customers, creating a low-cost method for servicing smaller retailers and business users.			✓
Storing			
Maintains warehouse facilities at lower costs than most individual producers or retailers could achieve. Reduces risk and cost of maintaining inventory for producers.		✓	✓
Transporting			
Customers receive prompt delivery in response to their demands, reducing their inventory investments. Wholesalers also break bulk by purchasing in economical carload or truckload lots, then reselling in smaller quantities, thereby reducing overall transportation costs.		✓	✓
Providing Marketing Information			
Offers important marketing research input for producers through regular contacts with retail and business buyers. Provides customers with information about new products, technical information about product lines, reports on competitors' activities and industry trends, and advisory information concerning pricing changes, legal changes, and so forth.		✓	✓
Financing			
Grants credit that might be unavailable for purchases directly from manufacturers. Provides financing assistance to producers by purchasing products in advance of sale and by promptly paying bills.		✓	✓
Risk Taking			
Evaluates credit risks of numerous, distant retail customers and small business users. Extends credit to customers that qualify. By transporting and stocking products in inventory, the wholesaler assumes risk of spoilage, theft, or obsolescence.		✓	✓

place utility by helping to deliver goods and services for purchase at convenient locations. They create *ownership* (or *possession*) *utility* when a smooth exchange of title to the products from producers or intermediaries to final purchasers is complete. Possession utility can also result from transactions in which actual title does not pass to purchasers, as in rental-car services.

Providing Services

Table 14.1 lists a number of services provided by wholesaling intermediaries. The list clearly indicates the marketing utilities—time, place, and possession utility—that wholesaling intermediaries create or enhance. These services also reflect the basic marketing functions of buying, selling, storing, transporting, providing market information, financing, and risk taking.

Of course, many types of wholesaling intermediaries provide varying services, and not all of them perform every service listed in the table. Producer-suppliers rely on wholesaling intermediaries for distribution, which also entails the selection of firms that offer the

M A R K E T I N G   D I C T I O N A R Y

wholesaler Intermediary that takes title to goods it handles and then distributes these goods to retailers, other distributors, or sometimes end users.

retailing Activities involved in selling goods and services to ultimate consumers.

direct marketing Distribution channel consisting of direct communication to a consumer or business user.

wholesaling intermediary Comprehensive term that describes wholesalers as well as agents and brokers.

desired combinations of services. In general, however, the critical marketing functions listed in the table form the basis for any evaluation of a marketing intermediary's efficiency. The risk-taking function affects each service of the intermediary.

Consider, for example, the ways in which SYSCO Corp., which supplies nearly 325,000 restaurants, hotels, and other food-service operations with food and related services, assists its customers. SYSCO has been known to track down exotic ingredients, develop new recipes, track consumers' food preferences, and handle time-consuming preparations, such as chopping vegetables. [2]

Lowering Costs by Limiting Contacts

When an intermediary represents numerous producers, it often cuts the costs of buying and selling. The transaction economies are illustrated in Figure 14.1, which shows five manufacturers marketing their outputs to four different retail outlets. Without an intermediary, these exchanges create a total of 20 transactions. Adding a wholesaling intermediary reduces the number of transactions to nine.

For example, Handleman Company is a wholesaler of music recordings, videos, books, and computer software to approximately 4,100 retailers throughout the United States, Canada, Brazil, and Mexico. Its retail customers avoid ordering these products directly from large numbers of different manufacturers; instead, they simply call Handleman. The savings in transaction costs is particularly important for these high-volume items that need frequent restocking. Handleman ensures that the products reach retailers' shelves, and they also track which titles are selling best.[3]

@ **syscosmart.com**

@ **handleman.com**

| FIGURE 14.1 | Transaction Economies through Wholesaling Intermediaries |

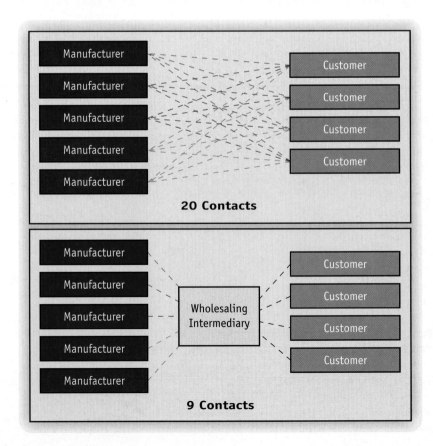

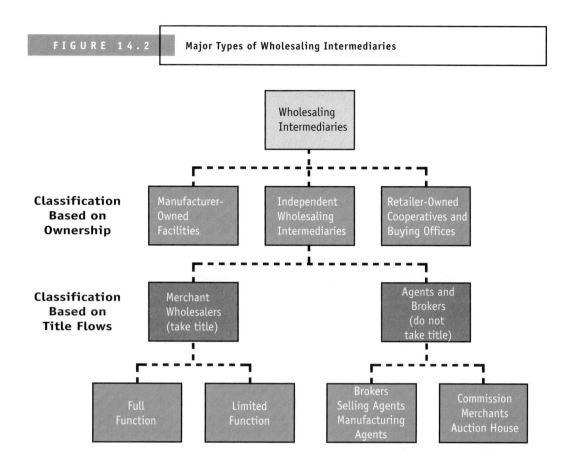

FIGURE 14.2 Major Types of Wholesaling Intermediaries

Types of Wholesaling Intermediaries

Various types of wholesaling intermediaries operate in different distribution channels. Some provide wide ranges of services or handle broad lines of goods, while others specialize in individual services, goods, or industries. Figure 14.2 classifies wholesaling intermediaries by two characteristics: *ownership* and *title flows* (whether title passes from manufacturer to wholesaling intermediary). The three basic ownership structures are as follows: (1) manufacturer-owned facilities, (2) independent wholesaling intermediaries, and (3) retailer-owned cooperatives and buying offices. The two types of independent wholesaling intermediaries are merchant wholesalers, which take title of the goods, and agents and brokers, which do not.

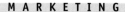

Identify the major types of independent wholesaling intermediaries and the situations appropriate for each.

Manufacturer-Owned Facilities

Several reasons may lead manufacturers to distribute their goods directly through company-owned facilities. Some perishable goods need rigid control of distribution to avoid spoilage; other goods require complex installation or servicing. Some goods need aggressive promotion. Goods with high-unit values allow profitable sales by manufacturers directly to ultimate purchasers. Manufacturer-owned facilities include sales branches, sales offices, trade fairs, and merchandise marts.

A **sales branch** carries inventory and processes orders for customers from available stock. Branches provide a storage function like independent wholesalers and serve as offices for sales representatives in their territories. They are prevalent in marketing channels for chemicals, commercial machinery and equipment, motor vehicles, and petroleum products.

MARKETING DICTIONARY

sales branch Manufacturer-owned facility that carries inventory and processes orders for customers from available stock.

A **sales office,** in contrast, does not carry inventory, but it does serve as a regional office for a manufacturer's sales personnel. Locations close to the firm's customers help limit selling costs and support active customer service. For example, numerous sales offices in the Detroit suburbs serve the area's automobile industry.

A **trade fair** (or *trade exhibition*) is a periodic show at which manufacturers in a particular industry display their wares for visiting retail and wholesale buyers. For example, the Internet World Conference sponsors an enormous trade exhibition that brings together over 600 companies to demonstrate their latest Internet technology.

A **merchandise mart** provides space for permanent showrooms and exhibits, which manufacturers rent to market their goods. One of the world's largest merchandise marts is Chicago's Mart Center, a 7-million-square-foot complex that hosts more than 30 seasonal buying markets each year.

Independent Wholesaling Intermediaries

Creating independent wholesaling intermediaries is another ownership structure. These firms fall into two categories: merchant wholesalers and agents and brokers.

Merchant Wholesalers.   A **merchant wholesaler** takes title to the goods it handles. Merchant wholesalers account for roughly 60 percent of all sales at the wholesale level. Further classifications divide these wholesalers into full-function or limited-function wholesalers, as indicated in Figure 14.2. Both SYSCO and Handleman, mentioned in the previous section, are merchant wholesalers.

A full-function merchant wholesaler provides a complete assortment of services for retailers and business purchasers. Such a wholesaler stores merchandise in a convenient location, allowing its customers to make purchases on short notice and minimizing its inventory requirements. The firm typically maintains a sales force that calls on retailers, makes deliveries, and extends credit to qualified buyers. Full-function wholesalers are common in the drug, grocery, and hardware industries. In the business-goods market, full-function merchant wholesalers (often called *industrial distributors*) sell machinery, inexpensive accessory equipment, and supplies.

A **rack jobber** is a full-function merchant wholesaler who markets specialized lines of merchandise to retailers. A rack jobber supplies the racks, stocks the merchandise, prices the goods, and makes regular visits to refill shelves.

Limited-function merchant wholesalers fit into four categories: cash-and-carry wholesalers, truck wholesalers, drop shippers, and mail-order wholesalers. Limited-function wholesalers serve the food, coal, lumber, cosmetics, jewelry, sporting goods, and general merchandise industries.

A **cash-and-carry wholesaler** performs most wholesaling functions except for financing and delivery. Although feasible for small stores, this kind of wholesaling generally is unworkable for large-scale grocery stores. Today, cash-and-carry operations typically function as departments within regular, full-service wholesale operations. Cash-and-carry wholesalers are commonplace outside the United States, such as in the United Kingdom.

A **truck wholesaler,** or *truck jobber,* markets perishable food items such as bread, tobacco, potato chips, candy, and dairy products. Truck wholesalers make regular deliveries to retailers, perform sales and collection functions, and promote product lines.

A **drop shipper** accepts orders from customers and forwards these orders to producers, which then ship the desired products directly to the customers. Although drop shippers take title to these goods, they never physically handle or even see the merchandise. These intermediaries operate in industries selling bulky goods that customers buy in carload lots, such as coal and lumber.

A **mail order wholesaler** is a limited-function merchant wholesaler who distributes catalogs as opposed to sending sales representatives to contact retail, business, and institutional customers. Customers then make purchases by mail or phone. Such a wholesaler often serves relatively small customers in outlying areas. Mail order operations mainly exist in the hardware, cosmetics, jewelry, sporting goods, and specialty food lines as well as in general merchandise.

TABLE 14.2 Comparison of the Types of Merchant Wholesalers and Their Services

SERVICE	FULL-FUNCTION	LIMITED-FUNCTION WHOLESALER			
		CASH-AND-CARRY	TRUCK	DROP SHIPPER	MAIL ORDER
Anticipates customer needs	✓	✓	✓	—	✓
Carries inventory	✓	✓	✓	—	✓
Delivers	✓	—	✓	—	—
Provides market information	✓	Rarely	✓	✓	—
Provides credit	✓	—	—	✓	Sometimes
Assumes ownership risk by taking title	✓	✓	✓	✓	✓

Table 14.2 compares the various types of merchant wholesalers and the services they provide. Full-function merchant wholesalers and truck wholesalers rank as relatively high-cost intermediaries due to the number of services they perform, while cash-and-carry wholesalers, drop shippers, and mail order wholesalers provide fewer services and set lower prices since they incur lower operating costs.

Agents and Brokers. A second group of independent wholesaling intermediaries, **agents and brokers,** may or may not take possession of the goods they handle, but they never take title. They normally perform fewer services than merchant wholesalers, typically working mainly to bring together buyers and sellers. Agents and brokers fall into five categories: commission merchants, auction houses, brokers, selling agents, and manufacturers' agents.

Commission merchants, who predominate in the markets for agricultural products, take possession when producers ship goods such as grain, produce, and livestock to central markets for sale. Commission merchants act as producers' agents and receive agreed-upon fees when they make sales. Since customers inspect the products and prices fluctuate, commission merchants receive considerable latitude in marketing decisions. The owners of the goods may specify minimum prices, but the commission merchants sell these goods at the best possible prices. The commission merchants then deduct their fees from the sales proceeds.

An **auction house** gathers buyers and sellers in one location and allows

MARKETING DICTIONARY

sales office Manufacturer's facility that serves as a regional office for salespeople but does not carry inventory.

trade fair Periodic show at which manufacturers in a particular industry display their wares for visiting retail and wholesale buyers.

merchandise mart Permanent exhibition facility in which manufacturers display products for visiting retail and wholesale buyers.

merchant wholesaler Independently owned wholesaling intermediary who takes title to the goods that it handles.

rack jobber Full-function merchant wholesaler who markets specialized lines of merchandise to retail stores.

cash-and-carry wholesaler Limited-function merchant wholesaler who performs most wholesaling functions except financing and delivery.

truck wholesaler Lmited-function merchant wholesaler who markets perishable food items; also called a *truck jobber.*

drop shipper Limited-function merchant wholesaler who accepts orders from customers and forwards these orders to producers, which then ship directly to the customers who place the orders.

mail order wholesaler Limited-function merchant wholesaler who distributes catalogs instead of sending sales representatives to contact customers.

agents and brokers Independent wholesaling intermediaries who may or may not take possession of goods but never take title to these goods.

commission merchant Agent wholesaling intermediary who takes possession of goods shipped to a central market for sale, acts as the producer's agent, and collects an agreed-upon fee at the time of the sale.

auction house Establishment that gathers buyers and sellers in one location where buyers can examine merchandise before submitting competing purchase offers.

Mile High Comics Goes Online

BACKGROUND Comic book aficionados know that 150,000 comic books have been published in the United States. Mile High Comics, founded and owned by Chuck Rozanski, already stocks 63,000 of them. The comic book business, founded by Rozanski in 1969 when he was just 14 years old, is now the largest in the United States. Mile High has six retail stores and the largest mail order subscription service for comic books. But Rozanski has set his sights even higher: he wants to develop an Internet database of all 150,000 titles, making as many available to collectors as possible via online auctions.

THE CHALLENGE So far, there has been no comprehensive database of comic book titles. And although Rozanski has conducted live auctions at his retail stores in California and Colorado, they haven't been huge money makers. So Rozanski needs to find the best methods for drawing consumers to his own site, www.milehigh-comics.com, as well as to other sites at which he conducts business, including Amazon.com.

continued on next page

ebay.com

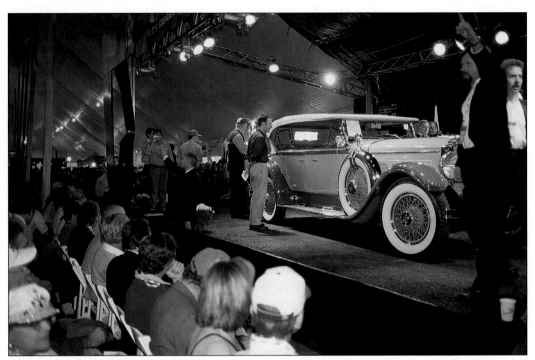

Thousands of car collectors attend the annual Barrett-Jackson classic car auction in Scottsdale, Arizona, where potential buyers inspect the cars before submitting their bids.

potential buyers to inspect merchandise before submitting competing purchase offers. Auction house commissions typically reflect specified percentages of the sales prices of the auctioned items. Auctions are common in the distribution of tobacco, used cars, artworks, livestock, furs, and fruit.

The Internet has led to a new type of auction house that connects customers and sellers in the online world. A well-known example is eBay, which auctions a wide variety of products in all price ranges.[4]

Brokers work mainly to bring together buyers and sellers. A broker represents either the buyer or the seller, but not both, in a given transaction, and the broker receives a fee from the client when the transaction is completed. Intermediaries that specialize in arranging buying and selling transactions between domestic producers and foreign buyers are called *export brokers*. Brokers operate in industries characterized by large numbers of small suppliers and purchasers, such as real estate, frozen foods, and used machinery. Since they provide one-time services for sellers or buyers, they cannot serve as effective channels for manufacturers seeking regular, continuing service. A firm that seeks to develop a more permanent channel might choose instead to use a selling agent or manufacturer's agent.

A **selling agent** typically exerts full authority over pricing decisions and promotional outlays, and it often provides financial assistance for the manufacturer. Selling agents act as independent marketing departments because they can assume responsibility for the total marketing programs of client firms' product lines. Selling agents mainly operate in the coal, lumber, and textiles industries. For a small, poorly financed, production-oriented firm, such an intermediary might prove the ideal marketing channel.

While a manufacturer may deal with only one selling agent, a firm that hires **manufacturers' agents,** commonly known as *manufacturers' reps*, often delegates marketing tasks to many of these agents. Such an independent salesperson may work for a number of firms that produce related, noncompeting products. Manufacturer's reps are paid on a commission basis, such as 6 percent of sales. Unlike selling agents, who may contract for exclusive rights to market a product, manufacturer's agents operate in specific territories. They may develop new sales territories or represent relatively small firms and those firms with unrelated lines.

TABLE 14.3	Services Provided by Agents and Brokers				
SERVICE	COMMISSION MERCHANT	AUCTION HOUSE	BROKER	MANUFACTURERS' AGENT	SELLING AGENT
Anticipates customer needs	✓	Sometimes	Sometimes	✓	✓
Carries inventory	✓	✓	—	—	—
Delivers	✓	—	—	Sometimes	—
Provides market information	✓	✓	✓	✓	✓
Provides credit	Sometimes	—	—	—	Sometimes
Assumes ownership risk by taking title	—	—	—	—	—

The importance of selling agents in many markets has declined because manufacturers want better control of their marketing programs than these intermediaries allow. In contrast, the volume of sales by manufacturer's agents has more than doubled and now accounts for 37 percent of all sales by agents and brokers. Table 14.3 compares the major types of agents and brokers on the basis of the services they perform.

Retailer-Owned Cooperatives and Buying Offices

Retailers may assume numerous wholesaling functions in an attempt to reduce costs or provide special services. Independent retailers sometimes band together to form buying groups that can achieve cost savings through quantity purchases. Other groups of retailers establish retailer-owned wholesale facilities by forming cooperative chains. Large chain retailers often establish centralized buying offices to negotiate large-scale purchases directly with manufacturers.

RETAILING

Retailing is the second level of marketing intermediaries. *Retailing* refers to the activities involved in selling services and goods to ultimate consumers. Retail outlets serve as contact points between channel members and ultimate consumers. In a very real sense, retailers represent the distribution channel to most consumers since a typical shopper has little contact with manufacturers and virtually no contact with wholesaling intermediaries. Retailers determine locations, store hours, quality and quantity of salespeople, store layouts, merchandise selections, and return policies—factors that often influence the consumers' images of the offerings more strongly than consumers' images of the products themselves. Both large and small retailers perform the major channel activities: creating time, place, and ownership utilities.

Retailers act as both customers and marketers in their channels. They sell products to ultimate consumers, and at the same time they buy from wholesalers and manufacturers. Because of their critical location in their channels, retailers often perform a vital feedback role. They obtain information from customers and transmit that information to manufacturers and other channel members.

THE STRATEGY Hooking up with Amazon.com and eBay to gain presence in a broader market has been an important strategy for Rozanski. Rozanski has stocked his own site as well as his sites at Amazon and eBay with action figures, cards, toys, Disney collectibles, movie posters, and other items that relate to his comic books.

THE OUTCOME Rozanski learned how demanding and savvy online consumers seemed to be. He also learned how important good feedback—and how devastating bad feedback—can be to a business. But e-commerce has been a huge success for Mile High Comics. E-commerce sales jumped from $800,000 to $5 million between the first and second years that the company was online. Rozanski continues to work on that database. If he doesn't have a rare title, he can use some of his contacts.

People might ask why Rozanski is going to all this trouble. "This is my way of paying back and making a contribution," he comments. When Rozanski moved to the United States from Germany at age five, he learned English by reading comic books.

MARKETING DICTIONARY

broker Agent wholesaling intermediary that does not take title to or possession of goods in the course of its primary function, which is to bring together buyers and sellers.

selling agent Agent wholesaling intermediary responsible for the entire marketing program of a firm's product line.

manufacturers' agent Agent wholesaling intermediary who represents a number of manufacturers of related but noncompeting products and who receives a commission on each sale.

Evolution of Retailing

The development of retailing illustrates the marketing concept in operation. Retailing continues to satisfy changing consumer wants and needs.

Early retailing can be traced to the establishment of trading posts, such as the Hudson Bay Company, and to pack peddlers who carried their wares to outlying settlements. The first type of retail institution in the United States, the general store, stocked a wide range of merchandise that met the needs of an isolated community or rural area. Supermarkets appeared in the early 1930s in response to consumers' desire for lower prices. In the 1950s, discount stores delivered lower prices in exchange for reduced services. The emergence of convenience food stores in the 1960s satisfied consumer demand for fast service, convenient locations, and expanded hours of operation. The development of off-price retailers in the 1980s and 1990s reflected consumer demand for brand-name merchandise at prices considerably lower than those of traditional retailers.

Retailing innovations continue into the 21st century as some retailers, like Wal-Mart, have expanded, and others, including once-dominant department stores like Frederick and Nelson in Seattle and Hornes in Pittsburgh, have disappeared.[5] An important concept, known as wheel of retailing, drives this evolutionary change.

Wheel of Retailing

The **wheel of retailing** attempts to explain the patterns of change in retailing. According to this hypothesis, a new type of retailer gains a competitive foothold by offering customers lower prices than current outlets charge, maintaining profits by reducing or eliminating services. Once established, however, the innovator adds more services, and its prices gradually rise. It then becomes vulnerable to new, low-price retailers that enter with minimum services—and so the wheel turns.

Many major developments in the history of retailing appear to fit the wheel's pattern. Early department stores, chain stores, supermarkets, discount stores, hypermarkets, and catalog retailers all emphasized limited service and low prices. Most of these retailers gradually increased prices as they added services.

Some exceptions disrupt this pattern, however. Suburban shopping centers, convenience food stores, and vending machines never built their appeals around low prices. However, the wheel pattern has been a good indicator enough times in the past to make it an accurate indicator of future retailing developments.

STRATEGIC IMPLICATIONS: RETAILING STRATEGY

Like manufacturers and wholesalers, a retailer develops a marketing strategy based on the firm's goals and strategic plans. The organization monitors environmental influences and assesses its own strengths and weaknesses in identifying marketing opportunities and constraints. A retailer bases its key decisions on two fundamental steps in the marketing strategy process: (1) picking a target market and (2) developing a retailing mix to satisfy the chosen market. The retailing mix specifies merchandise strategy, customer service standards, pricing guidelines, target market analysis, promotion goals, location/distribution decisions, and store atmosphere choices. The combination of these elements projects a desired **retail image**—consumers' perceptions of the store and the shopping experience it provides. Retail image communicates the store's identity to consumers as, say, an economical, prestigious, or contemporary outlet. All components of retailing strategy must work together to create an image that appeals to the store's target market.

Retail analysts cite compression of the retail cycle in recent years. New retail concepts appear to move through the cycle faster than previous concepts. For example, Internet-based retailers may open for business quickly but close down just as rapidly. Wedding-guide publisher Alan Fields notes that 50 percent of Web sites selling bridal apparel vanish within three years.[6]

Picking a Target Market

A retailer starts to define its strategy by selecting a target market. The size and profit potential of a target and the level of competition for its business influence this decision. Retailers pore over demographic, geographic, and psychographic profiles to segment markets. In the end, most retailers identify their target markets in terms of certain demographics.

The importance of identifying and targeting the right market is dramatically illustrated by recent events in the hardware retailing. Home Depot has dramatically changed the industry by targeting price-conscious, do-it-yourself homeowners with its large warehouse-style stores. With more than 800 stores across the United States, Canada, Chile, and Puerto Rico, the chain's popularity has compelled other hardware retailers to redefine their target marketing strategies.[7]

Lowe's, another hardware retailer, has found a different target market. The chain's research shows that women instigate most home-improvement projects. Lowe's has responded by redesigning stores to appeal to women shoppers. In addition to large selections of hardware goods, Lowe's stores also stock home appliances and home-decorating items, such as the lighting fixtures shown in Figure 14.3. This alternative strategy has worked well for Lowe's.[8]

Even retailers that traditionally sought to serve the mass market have shifted their strategies to target more narrowly defined segments. For example, F. W. Woolworth used to be a general merchandiser. Today, Woolworth has become a specialty store retailer. This format provides higher sales per square foot and thus higher profit margins and returns on investment than general merchandise stores achieve. Woolworth includes an array of shoe stores, including Foot Locker, Kids Foot Locker, Lady Foot Locker, and World Foot Locker. The firm also targeted the female market by starting Northern Reflections, a chain of women's clothing stores, and Northern Traditions, a chain of formal apparel for women.

After identifying a target market, a retailer must then develop marketing strategies to attract these chosen customers to its stores. The following sections discuss tactics for implementing different strategies.

FIGURE 14.3 Targeting Women Shoppers

3

Explain how retailers select target markets.

homedepot.com

lowes.com

4

Show how the elements of the marketing mix apply to retailing strategy.

Merchandising Strategy

A retailer's merchandising strategy guides decisions regarding the items that the retailer will offer. A retailer must decide on general merchandise categories, product lines, specific items within lines, and the depth and width of its assortment. Target stores, for example, offer customers a wide variety of merchandise, from apparel to personal care, home décor, and automotive products. But, to compete as a lifestyle trend merchandiser, Target commissioned architect/designer Michael Graves to create the special line of houseware products, shown in Figure 14.4, that are sold exclusively at its stores.

To help them organize merchandise most effectively, retailers develop **planograms**, or diagrams of how to exhibit selections of merchandise within a store. Planograms may be created using computer software and then sent electronically to branch stores where they can be downloaded.[9]

MARKETING | **DICTIONARY**

wheel of retailing Hypothesis that each new type of retailer gains a competitive foothold by offering lower prices than current suppliers charge, maintaining profits by reducing or eliminating services.

retail image Consumers' perceptions of a store and the shopping experience it provides.

planogram Diagram of how to exhibit selections of merchandise within a store.

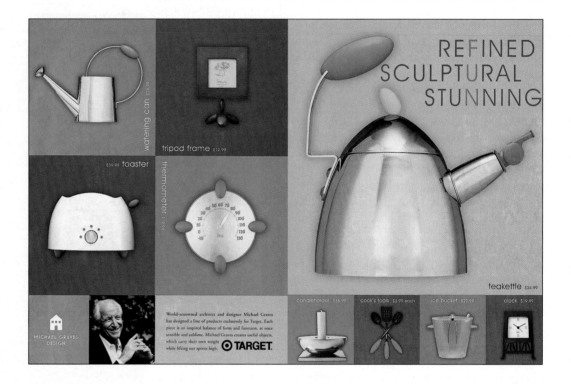

FIGURE 14.4   **Exclusively Designed Products Are Part of Target's Merchandising Strategy**

To develop a successful merchandise mix, a retailer must weigh several priorities. First, it must consider the preferences and needs of its previously defined target market, keeping in mind that the competitive environment influences these choices. The retailer must also consider the overall profitability of each product line and category.

A popular approach in merchandising strategy is **category management**, which integrates the buying and merchandising functions. In category management, each product category of a retailer's merchandise is viewed as an individual profit center, and the marketer manages the performance and growth of the entire category.[10] Department stores, for example, have suffered from weak sales in recent years as competition from specialty and discount stores has increased. To improve their profitability, some department stores have narrowed their traditionally broad product lines to eliminate high-overhead, low-profit categories such as toys, appliances, and furniture.

Sometimes a retailer's merchandise strategy must evolve in response to competitive developments. When Spencer Newman started Adventurous Traveler Bookstore (ATB) in 1994, he envisioned it as a mail-order catalog business offering books about unusual journeys. After a few years, Newman added an Internet site, and online orders flourished. The emergence of giant online bookseller Amazon.com, however, forced Newman to reconsider his merchandising strategy. Today, ATB successfully competes against Amazon.com by functioning as more than a bookstore; it is a broad information resource. Staff members spend hours every day answering customers' e-mail and phone questions on everything from traveling in Alaska to packing tips. In conjunction with the University of Vermont, ATB also sponsors a lecture series on the outdoors featuring respected speakers. Merchandise has been diversified to include videos, maps, posters, and gifts as well as books; indeed, one of its biggest sellers is the National Parks Monopoly game.[11]

www.gorp.com/atb/

The Battle for Shelf Space

Historically, producers or wholesalers have served as channel captains, with power over small, localized retailers. Since producers and service providers typically create offerings and enjoy the benefits of large-scale operations, they still fill the role of channel captain in many distribution networks. However, retailers are increasingly acting as channel captains. Many large retail chains have assumed traditional wholesaling functions. The widespread use of scanner-based research also means that retailers now provide and share the information that supports crucial marketing decisions. Some major retailers can dictate product design specifications to manufacturers. The result is a heightening battle for space on store shelves.

Adding to the pressure is the increase in the number of new products and variations on existing products. To identify the varying items within a product line, retailers refer to a specific product offering as a **stockkeeping unit (SKU)**. For example, within the skin-care line, the same manufacturer might produce a number of items, such as facial creams, body moisturizers, and sunscreens. Each of these items might also be available in a variety of sizes and formulations, such as alcohol-free moisturizers and sunscreens of varying SPFs. Each variation would be considered a SKU on a retailer's shelf. The proliferation of new SKUs is a major factor in manufacturers' battles for obtaining more shelf space.

Major retailers, such as Wal-Mart, Sears, Kmart, and JCPenney, often act as channel captains. These retailers seek promotional and pricing concessions from manufacturers as conditions for selling their products. Retailers also routinely require that manufacturers participate in their electronic data interchange (EDI) and quick-response systems. Manufacturers that cannot comply with the demands of large retailers may find themselves unable to penetrate the marketplace.

Some retailers ask producers to pay slotting allowances before they will agree to carry products. **Slotting allowances** are fees that retailers receive from manufacturers to secure shelf space for new products. A manufacturer can pay a retailer as much as $200,000 to get its new products displayed on store shelves at eye level.

Retailers are also imposing a variety of other fees on manufacturers that seek shelf space. The most common, a failure fee, imposes a charge if a new product does not meet sales projections. This fee covers the cost of removing the item from inventory as well as lost revenue. Other retailer fees include annual renewal fees for inducing retailers to continue carrying lines, trade allowances, discounts on high-volume purchases, survey fees for research done by the retailers, and even fees to allow salespeople to present new items.

Customer Service Strategy

A retailer may provide a variety of customer services for shoppers. Examples are gift wrapping, alterations, return privileges, bridal registries, consultants, interior design services, delivery and installation, and perhaps even electronic shopping via gift-ordering machines in airports for instance. A retailer's customer service strategy must specify which services the firm will offer and whether it will charge customers for these services. Those decisions depend on several conditions: store size, type, and location; merchandise assortment; services offered by competitors; customer expectations; and financial resources.

The basic objective of all customer services focuses on attracting and retaining target customers, thus increasing sales and profits. Some services, such as convenient rest rooms, lounges, complimentary coffee, and drinking fountains, enhance shoppers' comfort. Other services are intended to attract customers by making shopping easier and faster than it would be without the services. Some retailers, for example, offer child-care services for customers to ease the burden of shopping. The Sears online shopping service promoted in the ad in Figure 14.5 is intended to make it easy for customers to shop for appliances. The service lets customers research the top six appliance brands, buy products online, and arrange for delivery and installation as well as the removal of their old appliances.

A customer service strategy can also support efforts in building demand for a line of merchandise. St. Louis–based Dierbergs supermarkets, for instance,

MARKETING DICTIONARY

category management Retailing strategy in which each product category is viewed as an individual profit center.

stockkeeping unit (SKU) Specific product offering within a product line that is used to identify the varying items within the line.

slotting allowance Fee that retailers receive from manufacturers to secure shelf space for new products.

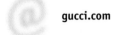
gucci.com

entices its customers to purchase their upscale food offerings and gourmet cooking tools by offering a regular schedule of cooking classes utilizing these products. Restaurant chefs and cookbook authors present informal demonstrations that give participants hands-on experience in whipping up delicacies and in choosing appropriate wines.[12]

Pricing Strategy

Prices reflect a retailer's marketing objectives and policies. These prices also play a major role in consumers' perceptions of a retailer. Consumers realize, for example, that when they enter a Gucci boutique in Milan, New York, or Tokyo, they will find such expensive products as $275 suede pumps and $1,500 boar-hide briefcases. Customers of the retail chain Everything's $1.00 expect a totally different line of merchandise; true to the name, every product in the store bears the same low price.

Markups

The amount that a retailer adds to a product's cost to set the final selling price is the **markup.** The amount of the markup typically results from two marketing decisions:

1. *The services performed by the retailer.* Other things being equal, stores that offer more services charge larger markups to cover their costs.

2. *The inventory turnover rate.* Other things being equal, a store with a higher turnover rate can cover its costs and earn a profit while charging a smaller markup.

A retailer's markup exerts an important influence on its image among present and potential customers. In addition, the markup affects the retailer's ability to attract shoppers. An excessive markup may drive away customers; an inadequate markup may not generate sufficient income to cover costs and return a profit.

Retailers typically state markups as percentages of either the selling prices or the costs of the products. The formulas for calculating markups are as follows:

$$\text{Markup Percentage on Selling Price} = \frac{\text{Amount Added to Cost (Markup)}}{\text{Selling Price}}$$

$$\text{Markup Percentage on Cost} = \frac{\text{Amount Added to Cost (Markup)}}{\text{Cost}}$$

Consider a product with an invoice cost of $0.60 and a selling price of $1.00. The total markup (selling price less cost) is $0.40. The two markup percentages are calculated as follows:

$$\text{Markup Percentage on Selling Price} = \frac{\$0.40}{\$1.00} = 40\%$$

$$\text{Markup Percentage on Cost} = \frac{\$0.40}{\$0.60} = 66.7\%$$

To determine the selling price knowing only the cost and markup percentage on selling price, a retailer applies the following formula:

$$\text{Price} = \frac{\text{Cost in Dollars}}{100\% - \text{Markup Percentage on Selling Price}}$$

In the previous example, to determine the correct selling price of $1.00, the retailer would calculate as follows:

$$\text{Price} = \frac{\$0.60}{100\% - 40\%} = \frac{\$0.60}{60\%} = \$1.00$$

Similarly, you can convert the markup percentage from one item based on the selling price to one based on cost and the reverse using the following formulas:

$$\text{Markup Percentage on Selling Price} = \frac{\text{Markup Percentage on Cost}}{100\% + \text{Markup Percentage on Cost}}$$

$$\text{Markup Percentage on Cost} = \frac{\text{Markup Percentage on Selling Price}}{100\% - \text{Markup Percentage on Selling Price}}$$

Again, data from the previous example give the following conversions:

$$\text{Markup Percentage on Selling Price} = \frac{66.7\%}{100\% + 66.7\%} = \frac{66.7\%}{166.7\%} = 40\%$$

$$\text{Markup Percentage on Cost} = \frac{40\%}{100\% - 40\%} = \frac{40\%}{60\%} = 66.7\%$$

Marketers determine markups based partly on their judgments of the amounts that consumers will pay for a given product. When buyers refuse to pay a product's stated price, however, or when improvements in other products or fashion changes reduce the appeal of current merchandise, a retailer must take a markdown.

Markdowns

The amount by which a retailer reduces the original selling price of a product is the **markdown.** The following formula gives the markdown percentage—the discount amount typically advertised for a sale item:

$$\text{Markup Percentage} = \frac{\text{Dollar Amount of Markdown}}{\text{Original Price}}$$

Returning to the previous example, suppose that no one seems willing to pay $1.00 for the product. The retailer has, therefore, decided to reduce the selling price to $0.80. Signs for the sale might emphasize the product's 20 percent markdown:

$$\text{Markup Percentage} = \frac{\$0.20}{\$1.00} = 20\%$$

Markdowns are sometimes used to evaluate merchandisers. For example, a department store might base its evaluations of buyers partly on the average markdown percentages for the product lines for which they are responsible.

Location-Distribution Strategy

Retail experts often cite location as a potentially determining factor in the success or failure of a retail business. A retailer may choose to locate at an isolated site, in a central business district, or in a planned shopping center. The location decision depends on many conditions, including the type of merchandise, the retailer's financial resources, characteristics of the target market, and site availability.

MARKETING DICTIONARY

markup Amount that a retailer adds to the cost of a product to determine its selling price.

markdown Amount by which a retailer reduces the original selling price of a product.

Rx for Shopping Malls

BACKGROUND Ask some teenagers where they like to shop, and chances are the answer will be "the mall." In fact, the teenager's parents probably shop at the mall as well. But despite their popularity with teens as a place to hang out, malls are suffering. Competition from e-commerce and "big-box" stores is taking its toll. Much to the surprise of demographers, baby boomers are shifting their shopping back to downtowns. And teenagers themselves are demanding more pizzazz from their shopping experience.

THE MARKETING PROBLEM Mall developers and retailers alike want to save their malls. According to some experts, the problem is that there are just too many of them. How can these shopping centers regain their strength as shopping destinations?

THE OUTCOME Mark London, a Chicago retail consultant, is known in the industry as the "mall doctor." He visits malls, takes note of their faults, and recommends changes—everything from trendier stores to cozy eateries to posh restrooms to rock-climbing walls and carousels. These additional frills are called "shoppertainment" in the industry. Taking note of the trend toward shopping at smaller, individual stores, London and other consultants have begun to restructure malls so that they look like downtowns, with storefronts facing outward.

continued on next page

In recent years, many retail markets have become saturated with stores. As a result, some retailers have reevaluated their location strategies. A chain may close individual stores that do not meet sales and profit goals. As an example, Toys "Я" Us once closed 59 stores worldwide because of low sales.[13]

Other retailers have experimented with nontraditional location strategies. McDonald's, for example, now has stores in hospitals, military bases, amusement parks, train stations, and gasoline stations.[14] Similarly, airports have become attractive locations for retailers such as The Walt Disney Co. and The Body Shop. Pittsburgh's modern airport, for example, features an extensive shopping concourse similar to those found in European airports.

Locations in Planned Shopping Centers

Over the past several decades, retail trade has shifted away from traditional downtown retailing districts and toward suburban shopping centers. A **planned shopping center** is a group of retail stores planned, coordinated, and marketed as a unit to shoppers in a geographic trade area. Together, the stores provide a single, convenient location for shoppers as well as free parking facilities. These stores facilitate shopping by maintaining uniform hours of operation, including evening and weekend hours.

Table 14.4 outlines the characteristics of the three main types of planned shopping centers. The smallest, the *neighborhood shopping center*, most often consists of a supermarket and a group of smaller stores, such as a drugstore, a dry cleaner, a small appliance store, and perhaps a hairstyling salon. This kind of center provides convenient shopping for 5,000 to 50,000 shoppers who live within a few minutes' commute. This kind of center typically contains 5 to 15 stores, and the product mix is usually confined to convenience goods and some shopping goods.

A *community shopping center* serves 20,000 to 100,000 people in a trade area extending a few miles from its location. Such a center contains anywhere from 10 to 30 retail stores, with a branch of a local department store or a large variety store as the primary tenant. In addition to the stores found in a neighborhood center, a community center probably encompasses more stores featuring shopping goods, some professional offices, and a branch bank.

A *regional shopping center* is a large facility with at least 400,000 square feet of shopping space. Its marketing appeal usually emphasizes one or more major department stores supplemented by as many as 200 smaller stores. A successful regional center needs a location within 30 minutes' driving time of at least 250,000 people. A regional center provides a wide assortment of convenience, shopping, and specialty goods, plus many professional and personal service facilities.

In recent years, the growth of planned shopping centers in the United States has slowed as competition from online shopping and discount chains continues to increase. Retail analysts believe that the United States, with approximately 1,800 enclosed shopping areas, is "over-malled," and they predict a continuing trend toward closing and consolidating large shopping centers.[15] However, American-style malls remain popular in foreign markets.

Shopping centers are now pursuing new retailing strategies. One approach combines shopping with entertainment; malls are adding carousels, rock-climbing walls, movie theaters, and large food courts. For example, the Mall of America in Bloomington, Minnesota, promotes its shopping center as a "shopping and fun destination." Its ad in Figure 14.6 shows some of the mall's entertainment—an amusement park, a spa, an aquarium, and nightclubs and restaurants. Others, such as the Market Place Mall in Champaign-Urbana, Illinois, emphasize customer service: well-padded playgrounds for toddlers, comfortable lounges for their parents, and luxurious bathrooms equipped with infant changing rooms and nursing rooms with rocking chairs.[16] Some malls hire concierges to help customers locate hard-to-find gifts and to order theater tickets; others may offer valet parking, gift-wrap services, and parking-lot shuttle buses.

Promotional Strategy

To entice more consumers, retailers use a variety of promotional techniques to establish store images that are attractive to consumers. Through promotional efforts, retailers communicate

| TABLE 14.4 | Comparing the Types of Shopping Centers |

TYPE	DESCRIPTION	STRENGTHS	WEAKNESSES
Neighborhood shopping center	Usually contains a supermarket and a group of smaller stores, such as a drugstore, laundry, small-appliance store, and a beauty/barber shop	Low rent and operating costs	Few tenants
	Products: Primarily convenience goods and a few shopping goods	Close proximity to customers	Susceptible to competition
	Size: Typically 50,000 square feet on four acres with a trade area population of 5,000 to 50,000 within a few minutes' driving time		
Community shopping center	Usually contains a department store or large variety store, plus some professional offices and a bank	Moderate rent and operating costs	Limited shopping variety
	Products: Primarily shopping goods, with some convenience and possibly specialty stores	Shared promotions	
		Parking availability	
	Size: Typically 150,000 square feet on ten acres with a trade area population of 20,000 to 100,000 within a few miles		
Regional shopping center	Usually built around one or more department stores with as many as 200 smaller shops	Large number of stores	High rent and operating costs
	Products: Primarily shopping and specialty goods, possibly supplemented by a convenience store	Drawing power of major retailers	Strict operating requirements (such as store hours and merchandise sold)
		Ample parking	
	Size: Typically 400,000 square feet on thirty acres with a trade area population of more than 250,000 within thirty minutes' driving time		

MARKETING STRATEGY FAILURE

LESSONS LEARNED Those who worry about the fate of the American shopping center can rest assured that it is not dead yet. In fact, some 40 million Americans visited Minnesota's Mall of America every year, a greater number than those who visited Disney World, Graceland, and the Grand Canyon combined. But developers and retailers have learned that they must change with the times; they can no longer follow what London calls "this build-it-and-they-will-come mentality" of previous decades. One mall in California is getting a facelift that reflects the new age of shopping centers. The old El Cerrito Plaza mall will be reopened as a trendy retail center called East Bay. That sounds about right for the next generation of teenaged shoppers—and their parents.

to consumers information about their stores—locations, merchandise selections, hours of operation, and prices. If a retailer's merchandise selection changes frequently to follow fashion trends, it can effectively promote current styles through advertising. In addition, promotions help retailers to attract shoppers and to build customer loyalty.

Innovative promotions can pay off in unexpected ways. Consider the advertising campaign for Target stores, for example, which featured young models wearing funky apparel emblazoned with the discounter's red-and-white target logo. While the ads were intended to be ironic—Target did not actually sell any clothes carrying its logo—stores were quickly flooded with phone calls from people who wanted to buy the items shown in the ads. Undaunted, Target managers promptly designed and produced a line of target underwear, T-shirts, and pajamas.[17]

National retail chains often purchase advertising space in newspapers, on radio, and on television. Many retail chains promote their stores through advertising circulars inserted in local and regional Sunday newspapers.

 target.com

MARKETING | DICTIONARY

planned shopping center Group of retail stores planned, coordinated, and marketed as a unit.

Other retailers are experimenting with promoting over the Internet. Coles Myer, Australia's largest retailer, supports its 2,000-plus stores in Australia and New Zealand with online grocery and mail-order promotions.[18] Several supermarket chains distribute coupons for special sale items through their Internet sites, and some music retailers sponsor Internet sites that let consumers download songs as MP3 audio files.[19]

Sometimes a well-chosen store location aids promotion; this is why Dollar General locates its retail stores on major streets leading to a large competitor, such as a Wal-Mart. Some people opt for the Dollar General's convenient location to avoid dealing with the larger store's daunting parking lot and cavernous aisles. This strategy has enabled Dollar General to eliminate most of its advertising circulars, reducing the company's promotional and administrative expenses.[20]

Retailers also try to combine advertising with in-store merchandising techniques that influence decisions at the point of purchase. Managers at Cost Plus housewares stores, for example, arrange merchandise to capture the ambiance of a bustling overseas marketplace. Mexican baskets hang from the ceiling, Oriental furniture and home decorations cover the floor, and ethnic music floats from speakers throughout the building. The unexpected juxtaposition of exotic items—Indonesian headdresses stacked next to African wooden sculptures and Japanese snacks—encourages customers to browse and buy on impulse.[21] Blockbuster Video promotes the sale of videos through ads like the one in Figure 14.7 and point-of-purchase in-store displays that encourage customers to buy the featured videos.

A retail salesperson plays a vital role in conveying a store image to consumers and in persuading shoppers to buy. Sales staff in music stores, for example, are major influences on customers shopping for new CDs.[22] To serve as a source of information, a salesperson must possess extensive knowledge regarding credit policies, discounts, special sales, delivery terms, layaways, and returns. To increase store sales, the salesperson must persuade customers that the store sells what those customers need. To this end, salespeople should receive training in *selling up* and *suggestion selling*.

Selling up involves salespeople trying to persuade customers to buy higher-priced items than originally intended. For example, an automobile salesperson might convince a customer to buy a more expensive model than the car that the buyer had originally considered. Of course, the practice of selling up must always respect the constraints of a customer's real needs. If a salesperson sells someone something that he really does not need, the potential for repeat sales dramatically diminishes.

Another technique, **suggestion selling,** seeks to broaden a customer's original purchase by adding related items, special promotional products, or holiday or seasonal merchandise. Here, too, the salesperson tries to help a customer recognize true needs rather than unwanted merchandise. Suggestion selling is one of the best methods for increasing retail sales, and all sales personnel should apply the practice.

The impressions left by sales personnel influence customers' attitudes toward a retailer. Increasing customer complaints about unfriendly, inattentive, and uninformed salespeople have prompted many retailers to intensify their attention to training and to motivating salespeople.

Helpful sales personnel can set retailers apart from competitors. Consider, for example, Girl Heaven, an Australian-owned clothing store in England's Bluewater shopping center. Its sales personnel do not just provide advice about apparel; they also staff training counters where teenagers can try out the latest hairstyles and cosmetics. There is even a hot-pink dance floor where staff personnel can teach customers the latest nightclub moves.[23]

Store Atmospherics

While store location, merchandise selection, customer service, pricing, and promotional activities all contribute to a store's consumer awareness, stores also project their personalities through **atmospherics**—physical characteristics and amenities that attract customers and satisfy their shopping needs. Atmospherics include both a store's exterior and interior decor.

A store's exterior appearance, including architectural design, window displays, signs, and entryways, helps to identify the retailer and to attract its target market. The Saks Fifth Avenue script logo on a storefront and McDonald's golden arches are exterior elements that readily identify these retailers. Other retailers design eye-catching exterior elements aimed at getting customers' attentions. Life-sized cartoon figures seem poised in mid-flight over the entrance to the Warner Brothers outlet in the Horton Plaza Shopping Center in San Diego, drawing customer interest.

The interior decor of a store should also complement the retailer's image, respond to customers' interests, and, most importantly, induce shoppers to buy. Interior atmospheric elements include store layout, merchandise presentation, lighting, color, sounds, scents, and cleanliness. The products in Costco stores, for instance, are stacked high on pallets to emphasize the chain's low-cost, no-frills premise and to encourage customers to buy in bulk. Unrelated items, such as Waterford crystal and Revlon face cream, are deliberately stacked next to each other. "We want to surprise people at every turn," explains Joseph Portera, Costco's vice president for operations. "Even if you don't buy the Waterford crystal, it makes an impact on you. Maybe you'll get a little irritated, knowing you could've [picked it up] last time but didn't, and now it's gone. So this time you'll stay awhile, and walk the entire building, to make sure you don't miss a thing."[24]

When designing the interior and exterior of a store, the fact that many people shop for reasons other than just purchasing needed products must be taken into account. Other common reasons for shopping include escaping the routine of daily life, avoiding weather extremes, fulfilling fantasies, and socializing with family and friends. Retailers expand beyond interior design to create welcoming and entertaining environments that draw shoppers. The Costa Coffee Internet Cafes, a chain of British coffee bars, for example, offer a quiet relaxed setting where customers can linger and surf the Web while sipping the beverage of their choice. A Costa interior is quite different from that of Girl Heaven, mentioned earlier, or the factory outlet shopping center in Livingston, Scotland, which features the world's largest indoor Ferris wheel.[25]

FIGURE 14.7 Combining Advertising and In-Store Displays

The Original Prize-Winning Pig

$14.99 or less

Buy It Today On Videocassette.

www.paramount.com/homevideo

costco.com

TYPES OF RETAILERS

Since new types of retailers continue to evolve in response to changes in consumer demand, a universal classification system for retailers has yet to be devised. Certain differences do, however, define several categories of retailers: (1) forms of ownership, (2) shopping effort

Atmospherics of Recreational Equipment Inc.'s flagship store in Seattle complement the retailer's image as an outdoor equipment retailer. Customers can try out mountaineering gear on a 65-foot-high climbing pinnacle and hiking gear on a simulated hiking trail as well as test water proof clothing in the retailer's Rain Room.

expended by customers, (3) services provided to customers, (4) product lines, and (5) locations of retail transactions.

Any retailing operation fits in different categories according to each of the classification schemes. A 7-Eleven outlet may be classified as a convenience store (category 2) with self-service (category 3) and a relatively broad product line (category 4). It is both a store-type retailer (category 5) and a member of a chain (category 1).

CLASSIFICATION OF RETAILERS BY FORM OF OWNERSHIP

Perhaps the easiest method for categorizing retailers divides retailers by ownership structure, distinguishing between chain stores and independent retailers. In addition, independent retailers may join wholesaler-sponsored voluntary chains, band together to form retail cooperatives, or enter into franchise agreements with manufacturers, wholesalers, or service-provider organizations. Each type of ownership has its own unique advantages and strategies.

Chain Stores

Chain stores are groups of retail outlets that operate under central ownership and management and handle the same product lines. Chains have a major advantage over independent retailers in economies of scale. Volume purchases allow chains to pay lower prices than their independent rivals must pay. Since a chain may encompass hundreds of retail stores, it can afford advertising layout specialists, sales training, and sophisticated computerized systems for merchandise ordering, inventory management, forecasting, and accounting. Also, the large sales volume and wide geographic reach of a chain may enable it to advertise in a variety of media, including television and national magazines.

Independent Retailers

The U.S. retailing structure supports a large number of small stores, many medium-sized stores, and a small number of large stores. Even though only 12 percent of the almost 2.7 million retail establishments earn annual sales of $1 million or more, those large operators account for almost three-quarters of all retail sales in the United States. On the other hand, over half of all stores generate yearly sales below $500,000. According to the Department of Commerce, independent retailers account for about 43 percent of all retail sales.

Independent retailers compete with chains in a number of ways. The traditional advantage of independent stores is friendly, personalized service. Cooperatives offer another strategy for independents. For instance, cooperatives like Ace Hardware and Valu-Rite Pharmacies help independents compete with chains by providing volume buying power as well as advertising and marketing programs. For example, independent owners of Ace Hardware stores benefit from the exposure of national advertising campaigns like the ad in Figure 14.8.

SCRAMBLED MERCHANDISING

Many traditional differences no longer distinguish familiar types of retailers, blurring any set of classifications. When you get a physician's prescription filled, you encounter the concept of **scrambled merchandising,** in which a retailer combines dissimilar product lines in an attempt to boost sales volume. The drugstore you visit after leaving the doctor's office may carry not only prescription and over-the-counter drugs but also garden supplies, gift items, groceries, hardware,

5

Explain the concept of scrambled merchandising.

housewares, magazines, and even small appliances. Another familiar example is a gas station that features a convenience store and a car wash.

Scrambled merchandising complicates manufacturers' channel decisions. As they struggle to maintain or increase market share, most have to develop multiple channels in order to reach the diverse array of retailers handling their products.

CLASSIFICATION BY SHOPPING EFFORT

Another classification system is based on the reasons why consumers shop at particular retail outlets. This approach categorizes stores as convenience, shopping, or specialty retailers.

Convenience retailers focus their marketing appeals on accessible locations, long store hours, rapid check-out service, and adequate parking facilities. Local food stores, gasoline stations, and dry cleaners fit in this category.

Shopping stores typically include furniture stores, appliance retailers, clothing outlets, and sporting goods stores. Consumers usually compare prices, assortments, and quality levels at competing outlets before making purchase decisions. Consequently, managers of shopping stores attempt to differentiate their outlets through advertising, window displays, in-store layouts, well-trained and knowledgeable salespeople, and appropriate merchandise assortments.

Specialty retailers combine carefully defined product lines, services, and reputations in attempts to convince consumers to expend considerable effort to shopping at their stores. For example, consider the Shanghai Tang Department Store in Manhattan, which sells only high-quality Oriental products such as velvet Mandarin jackets, silver-plated chopsticks, and antique Chinese furniture.[26] Other more general examples include Neiman-Marcus, Lord & Taylor, and Saks Fifth Avenue.

FIGURE 14.8 Cooperatives Help Independent Retailers Compete with Chains

CLASSIFICATION BY SERVICES PROVIDED

Another category differentiates retailers by the services they provide to customers. This classification system consists of three retailer types: self-service, self-selection, or full-service retailers.

Kmart illustrates a *self-service* store, while Kroger grocery stores and A&P Future Stores are examples of *self-selection* stores. Both categories sell convenience goods that people can purchase frequently with little assistance. By contrast *full-service retailers*, like Dillard's, focus on fashion-oriented shopping goods and specialty products, offering an array of customer services.

CLASSIFICATION BY PRODUCT LINES

Product lines also define a set of retail categories and the marketing strategies appropriate for firms within those categories. Grouping retailers by product lines produces three major categories: specialty stores, limited-line retailers, and general merchandise retailers.

MARKETING DICTIONARY

chain store Group of stores that operate under central ownership and management to sell essentially the same product lines.

scrambled merchandising Retailing practice of combining dissimilar product lines to boost sales volume.

Specialty Stores

A **specialty store** typically handles only part of a single product line. However, it stocks this portion in considerable depth or variety. Specialty stores include a wide range of retail outlets: Examples include fish markets, grocery stores, men's and women's shoe stores, and bakeries. Although some specialty stores are chain outlets, most are independent, small-scale operations. They represent perhaps the greatest concentration of independent retailers who develop expertise in one product area and provide narrow lines of products for their local markets.

Specialty stores should not be confused with specialty products. Specialty stores typically carry convenience and shopping goods. The label *specialty* reflects the practice of handling a specific, narrow line of merchandise. For example, Lady Foot Locker is a specialty store that offers a wide selection of name-brand athletic footwear, apparel, and accessories made specifically for women, such as the Nike Air Rapidup promoted in the ad in Figure 14.9.

Customers find a large assortment of products within one product line or a few related lines in a **limited-line store.** This type of retail operation typically develops in areas with a large enough population to sufficiently support it. Examples of limited-line stores are IKEA (home furnishings and housewares) and Levitz (furniture). These retailers cater to the needs of people who want to select from complete lines in purchasing particular products.

A unique type of limited-line retailer is called **category killers.** Stores combine huge selections and low prices in single product lines. Stores within this category—for example, Borders Books; Bed, Bath, and Beyond; and Home Depot—are among the most successful retailers in the nation. Category killers have taken business away from general merchandise discounters, which cannot compete in selection or price.[27] The "category killer" concept is also being seen in e-commerce. Nordstrom's, for example, is promoting its Web site as the "world's biggest shoe store." Nordstrom's, which actually began as a shoe store, offers 20 million pairs of shoes via its Web site. The new "category killer" has 60 separate vendors supplying it. [28]

@ **nordstrom.com**

FIGURE 14.9   **Lady Foot Locker: A Specialty Store**

General Merchandise Retailers

General merchandise retailers, which carry a wide variety of product lines that are all stocked in some depth, distinguish themselves from limited-line and specialty retailers by the large number of product lines they carry. The general store described earlier in this chapter is a primitive form of a general merchandise retailer. This category includes variety stores, department stores, and mass merchandisers such as catalog retailers, discount stores, hypermarkets, and off-price retailers.

Variety Stores

A retail outlet that offers an extensive range and assortment of low priced merchandise is called a **variety store.** Less popular today than they once were, many of these stores have evolved into or given way to other types of retailers such as discount stores. The nation's variety stores now account for less than 1 percent of all retail sales. However, variety stores remain popular in other parts of the world. Many retail outlets in Spain and Mexico are family-owned variety stores.

Department Stores

A **department store** gathers a series of limited-line and specialty stores under one roof. By definition, this large retailer handles a variety of merchandise, including men's, women's, and children's clothing and accessories; household linens and dry goods; home furnishings; and furniture. It serves as a one-stop shopping destination for almost all personal and household products. Chicago's Marshall Field's is a classic example.

Department stores built their reputations by offering wide varieties of services, such as charge accounts, delivery, gift wrapping, and liberal return privileges. As a result, they incur relatively high operating costs, averaging about 45 to 60 percent of sales.

Department stores have faced intense new competition over the past several years. Relatively high operating costs have left them vulnerable to retailing innovations such as discount stores, catalog merchandisers, and hypermarkets. In addition, department stores' traditional locations in downtown business districts suffered from problems associated with limited parking, traffic congestion, and population migration to the suburbs.

Department stores have fought back in a variety of ways. Many have closed certain sections, such as electronics, in which high costs kept them from competing with discount houses and category killers. They have added bargain outlets, expanded parking facilities, and opened major branches in regional shopping centers. They have attempted to revitalize downtown retailing in many cities by modernizing their stores, expanding store hours, making special efforts to attract the tourist and convention trade, and serving the needs of urban residents.[29]

Mass Merchandisers

Mass merchandising has made major inroads into department stores' sales by emphasizing lower prices for well-known, brand-name products; high product turnover; and limited services. A **mass merchandiser** often stocks a wider line of items than a department store but usually without the same depth of assortment within each line. Discount houses, off-price retailers, hypermarkets, and catalog retailers are all examples of mass merchandisers.

Discount Houses. A **discount house** charges low prices and offers fewer

MARKETING DICTIONARY

specialty store Retailer that typically handles only part of a single product line.

limited-line store Retailer that offers a large assortment within a single product line or within a few related product lines.

category killer Retailer that combines huge selection and low prices within a single product line.

general merchandise retailer Store that carries a wide variety of product lines, stocking all of them in some depth.

variety store Retailer that offers an extensive range and assortment of low-priced merchandise.

department store Large store that handles a variety of merchandise, including clothing, household goods, appliances, and furniture.

mass merchandiser Store that stocks a wider line of goods than a department store, usually without the same depth of assortment within each line.

discount house Store that charges low prices but may not offer services such as credit.

FIGURE 14.10

Discount Mass Merchandiser Selling Prestigious Brand Names

services. Early discount stores sold mostly appliances. Today, they offer furniture, soft goods, drugs, and food.

By eliminating many of the "free" services provided by traditional retailers, these operations can keep their markups 10 to 25 percent below those of their competitors. Some of the early discounters have since added services, stocked increasingly prestigious name brands, and boosted their prices; in fact, many now resemble department stores. Advertising by Kmart, for example, often features brand-name merchandise. In its ad in Figure 14.10, Kmart promotes "one of the biggest names in fashion today"—the Sesame Street collection of clothing for newborns, infants, and toddlers.

One of the newest kinds of true discounter is the *warehouse club*. These no-frills, cash-and-carry outlets offer consumers access to name-brand products at deeply discounted prices. Their selections include fax machines, peanut butter, luggage, and sunglasses in settings that look like warehouses. Customers must buy club memberships in order to shop at warehouse clubs. Costco and Wal-Mart's Sam's Wholesale Club are the largest warehouse clubs in the United States.[30]

Off-Price Retailers.   Another version of a discount house is an **off-price retailer.** This kind of store stocks only designer labels or well-known, brand-name clothing at prices equal to or below regular wholesale prices and then passes the cost savings along to consumers. While many off-price retailers are located in outlets in downtown areas or in freestanding buildings, a growing number are concentrating in **outlet malls**—shopping centers that house only off-price merchandise by many retailers.

Inventory at off-price retailers changes frequently as buyers take advantage of special price offers from manufacturers selling excess merchandise. Off-price retailers such as Loehmann's, Marshall's, Steinmart, and T. J. Maxx also keep their prices below those of traditional retailers by offering fewer services. Off-price retailing has been well received by today's shoppers.

Hypermarkets and Supercenters.   Another innovation in discount retailing is the creation of **hypermarkets**—giant, one-stop shopping facilities that offer wide selections of grocery and general merchandise products at discount prices. Store size determines the major difference between hypermarkets and supermarkets. Hypermarkets typically fill up 200,000 or more square feet of selling space, compared to about 44,000 for the average new supermarket. At Meijer stores, for example, Michigan, Ohio, and Indiana consumers can buy food, hardware, soft goods, building materials, auto supplies, appliances, and prescription drugs in locations averaging 245,000 square feet. When consumers finish shopping, Meijer customers can visit a restaurant, beauty salon, barber shop, bank branch, or bakery within the facility.

The hypermarket concept originated in France with retailer Carrefour, which has successfully transplanted the approach to Italy, Latin America, and Taiwan. The response has been less enthusiastic in the United States, where some customers complained about having to walk too far for limited brand selections. U.S. retailers have scaled down the true hypermarket concept in favor of **supercenters,** which house many of the same elements but in somewhat smaller facilities. Wal-Mart, Kmart, Target, Costco, and Sam's Club operate a total of 539 stores in California alone, each covering more than 100,000 square feet.[31]

Showroom and Warehouse Retailers.   Showroom retailers mail catalogs to their customers and sell the advertised goods from showrooms that display samples. Back-room warehouses fill orders for the displayed products. Low prices are important to catalog store customers. To keep prices low, these retailers offer few services, store most inventory in inexpensive warehouse space, limit shoplifting losses, and handle long-lived products such as luggage, small appliances, gift items, sporting equipment, toys, and jewelry. Best Products and Service Merchandise are examples of this retail format.

DIRECT MARKETING AND OTHER NON-STORE RETAILING

Although most retail transactions occur in stores, non-store retailing serves as an important marketing channel for many products. In addition, both consumer and business-to-business marketers rely on non-store retailing to generate orders or requests for more information that may result in future orders.

6

Compare the basic types of direct marketing and non-store retailing.

Direct marketing is a broad concept that includes direct mail, direct selling, direct-response retailing, telemarketing, Internet retailing, and automatic merchandising. The last sections of this chapter will consider each type of non-store retailing.

Direct Mail

Direct mail is a major component of direct marketing. It comes in many forms, ranging from sales letters, postcards, brochures, booklets, catalogs, and house organs (periodicals issued by organizations) to video and audio cassettes. Both not-for-profit and profit-seeking organizations make extensive use of this distribution channel.

Direct mail offers several advantages such as the ability to select a narrow target market, achieve intensive coverage, send messages quickly, choose from various formats, provide complete information, and personalize each mailing piece. Response rates are measurable and higher than other types of advertising. In addition, direct mailings stand alone and do not compete for attention with magazine articles and television programs. On the other hand, the per-reader cost of direct mail is high, effectiveness depends on the quality of the mailing list, and some consumers object strongly to direct mail, considering it to be "junk mail."

Direct mail marketing relies heavily on database technology in managing lists of names and in segmenting these lists according to the objectives of the campaign. Recipients get targeted materials, often personalized with their names within the ad's content.

Catalogs are a popular form of direct mail, with more than 10,000 different consumer specialty mail-order catalogs—and thousands more for business-to-business sales—finding their way to almost every mailbox in the United States. Catalogs can be a company's only or primary sales method; Spiegel, L. L. Bean, Lands' End, Eddie Bauer, and Patagonia are well-known examples. Even well-known so-called "bricks-and-mortar" retailers like Bloomingdale's and Macy's distribute catalogs. In a typical year, mail-order catalogs generate almost $40 billion in consumer sales and $24 billion in business-to-business sales.

New technologies are changing catalog marketing. Today's catalogs can be updated quickly, providing consumers with the latest information and prices. CD-ROM catalogs allow marketers to display products in three-dimensional views and can include video sequences of product demonstrations.

Direct Selling

Chapter 13 discussed arrangements by some manufacturers that completely bypass retailers and wholesalers. Instead, they set up their own channels to sell their products directly to consumers. Companies that rely on direct selling include Avon, which sells cosmetics; Electrolux Corp., which sells

MARKETING DICTIONARY

off-price retailer Store that finds exceptional deals on well-known, brand-name clothing and resells it at low prices.

outlet mall Shopping center that houses only off-price merchandise retailers.

hypermarket Giant mass merchandiser of soft goods and groceries that operates on a low-price, self-service strategy.

supercenter Large store, though still smaller than a hypermarket, that combines groceries with discount store merchandise.

FIGURE 14.11 **Direct-Response Retailing**

vacuum cleaners; and the Fuller Brush Company, which markets household items.[32] Direct selling also includes the party plan selling methods of companies like Tupperware.

Direct-Response Retailing

Customers of a direct-response retailer can order merchandise by mail or telephone, by visiting a mail-order desk in a retail store, or by computer or fax machine. The retailer then ships the merchandise to the customer's home or to a local retail store for pickup. PR Nutrition is a direct-response retailer. As its ad in Figure 14.11 states, customers can purchase the retailer's energy bar only by telephone.

Many direct-response retailers rely on direct mail, such as catalogs, to create telephone and mail-order sales and to promote in-store purchases of products featured in the catalogs. Additionally, some firms, such as Lillian Vernon, make almost all of their sales through catalog orders. Mail-order sales have grown about 10 percent a year in recent years, about twice the rate of retail store sales.

Direct-response retailers are increasingly reaching buyers through the Internet and through unique catalogs. Lillian Vernon supplements its general merchandise catalogs with specialty catalogs of children's products and personalized gifts. Jackson and Perkins holiday season catalogs offer a variety of plants for gift giving. Signals advertises merchandise with tie-ins to Public Broadcasting Service programs.

Direct-response retailing also includes **home shopping,** which runs promotions on cable television networks to sell merchandise through telephone orders. One form of home shopping has existed for years—the late-night commercials that run for at least thirty minutes. Such products as K-Tel Records and Veg-O-Matic vegetable slicers have been featured on these commercials. More recently, TV networks like Home Shopping Network have successfully focused exclusively on providing shopping opportunities. Programming ranges from extended commercials to call-in shows to game-show formats. Shoppers call a toll-free number to buy featured products, and the retailer ships ordered goods directly to their homes.

Telemarketing

Telemarketing refers to direct marketing conducted entirely by telephone. It is the most frequently used form of direct marketing. It provides marketers with a high return on their expenditures, an immediate response, and the opportunity for personalized, two-way conversations. It is discussed in further detail in Chapter 17.

Internet Retailing

Conventional retailers are anxiously watching the rise of Internet-based retailers that sell directly to customers via the World Wide Web and online services such as Yahoo! and America Online. These retailers operate from *virtual storefronts*, usually maintaining little or no inventory, ordering directly from vendors to fill customer orders received via e-mail.

Consumer sales made via Internet retailers already total $8 billion a year and are predicted to reach $108 billion by 2003—an impressive annual growth rate of 69 percent. Chapter 4 discussed Internet retailing and other forms of e-commerce in detail.[33]

SOLVING AN ETHICAL CONTROVERSY

How Secure Is Shopping Online?

Just when you finally thought it was safe to venture onto the Internet for a bit of online shopping, stories of credit card fraud packed with the intrigue of a thriller novel may send you back to your local department store. Internet investigator Don Garlock's bank account was cleared out after he made some modest purchases from Amazon.com with a debit card; he traced the cybertrail to a ring of alleged hackers in Bangkok, Thailand. Larry Hountz discovered five strange charges on his credit card account, all to Amazon. Amazon paid refunds to both customers' accounts, but Paul Capelli, an Amazon spokesperson, claims, "Shopping at Amazon is 100 percent safe. We go above and beyond what you'll find at most sites." Although Hountz discovered that the only fraudulent charges were placed at Amazon, and Amazon itself has already recognized those charges as fraudulent, Capelli states, "We know whether or not a credit card number has been compromised at our site, and this one wasn't."

How widespread are security problems at online shopping sites? MSNBC decided to research this question and, with the help of a computer-savvy source, was able to view 2,500 credit card numbers stored by seven small Web sites. In each case, the list of customers, along with their personal information, was either not protected by password or the password itself was accessible from the site.

And in a case of Internet "kidnapping," a hacker calling himself Maxus broke into the database managed by online music retailer CD Universe and stole as many as 300,000 credit card numbers, then held them for ransom, demanding $100,000 for the return of the information. CD Universe declined, so Maxus and a partner posted the data for sale on their own Web site, where individuals interested in using credit card data for fraudulent purposes could purchase whatever they wanted.

Suspecting that e-commerce retailers might not be placing security high on their priority list, research firms Deloitte & Touche and GartnerGroup conducted separate studies to find out. In fact, they made two important findings: (1) most e-commerce organizations put security at a lower priority than profitability; and (2) it is easier than many people think for hackers to break into systems.

 Are e-commerce retailers ensuring the security of consumers' financial and personal data when they shop online?

Pro

1. An online retailer that collects financial and personal data from its consumers must be able to ensure security of that data; otherwise, e-commerce itself will be threatened.

2. Even though another firm might actually develop the security software, the retailer must ultimately hold itself responsible for its Web site's security, just as it does for traditional security measures.

3. An online retailer who can promise consumers a secure site will actually gain their trust and eventually their loyalty and repeat business.

Con

1. Using a credit card or debit card at any type of retail outlet is risky, and consumers assume that risk whenever they use their cards.

2. The company that develops the security software within the retailer's Web site should assume responsibility for the effectiveness of the software.

3. The consumer should take proper precautions when making online purchases, such as obtaining order numbers and keeping passwords to sites private.

Summary

As online retail business continues to grow, security becomes a bigger issue. No one doubts that there are flaws in the system, but even experts are cautious about assigning ultimate accountability. Scambusters, an online consumer advocacy organization, makes the point that it is safer for consumers to enter their credit card numbers on a secure online order form than it is to hand over a card to a waiter at a restaurant. For some, however, that argument sounds a little like the one that it is safer to fly than to drive, which is usually circulated right after a major plane crash. "There is definitely a problem and I think some people in the industry have known that it is a problem," comments Sheriff Michael Brown, who worked on Don Garlock's case. "It is not one that's going to be fixed easily. Consumers have just got to be careful."

SOURCES: Margaret Mannix, "News You Can Use," *U.S. News & World Report,* February 14, 2000, www.usnews.com; Sherman Fridman, "E-Businesses More Concerned With Profits Than Security," *Newsbytes* (Post-Newsweek Business Information), February 5, 2000; Robert Speigel, "Report: E-Commerce Sites Not Keeping Pace with Security Threats," *E-Commerce Times,* February 3, 2000, www.ecommercetimes.com; Bob Sullivan, "Stealing Cards Easy as Web Browsing," *MSNBC,* January 14, 2000, www.msnbc.com; Mike Brunker, "Web Site Offering Free Credit Cards Seen as Scheme to Sell Rest of Data," *MSNBC,* January 13, 2000, www.msnbc.com; Bob Sullivan and Mike Brunker, "Credit Card Victim Blames Amazon," *MSNBC,* January 3, 2000, www.msnbc.com; Molly Masland, "The Dark Side of Online Shopping," *MSNBC,* June 24, 1999, www.msnbc.com.

Automatic Merchandising

The world's first vending machines dispensed holy water for five-drachma coins in Egyptian temples around 215 B.C. This retailing method has grown

MARKETING   DICTIONARY

home shopping Method of retailing that uses television to sell merchandise through telephone orders for home delivery.

The H.J. Heinz Company is stepping up its global investment and leveraging its brand strength through expanding food-service channels. In downtown Oslo, Norway, consumers can buy its Ore-Ida brand french fries, crisp, and piping hot, from vending machines.

rapidly ever since; today about 4.7 million vending machines sell approximately $25 billion in convenience goods to Americans, ranging from soda and snack foods to lottery tickets.

The United States is not the only country where consumers like the convenience of automatic merchandising. Japan contains 6 million vending machines, approximately 1 for every twenty inhabitants. Japanese consumers can buy a wide variety of goods from vending machines, including sushi and underwear. Among the more unusual items offered in vending machines are large black horned beetles, called *kabutomushi*, which are popular with Japanese children as pets. The Mirai Seiko company has sold more than 1,300 beetles through its vending machines; the firm, which also sells fresh vegetables, had to adapt its technology to permit the automatic merchandising of live insects.[34]

ACHIEVEMENT CHECK SUMMARY

Read the learning objectives that follow, and consider the questions for each one. Answering these questions will reinforce your grasp of the most important concepts in the chapter and will allow you to check how well you have achieved these learning goals. Where a blank appears before a question, answer with *T* or *F* for true/false questions; for multiple-choice questions, choose the letter of the correct answer.

Objective 14.1: Identify the functions performed by wholesaling intermediaries.

1. _____ Wholesaling intermediaries improve channel efficiency.

2. _____ Wholesaling intermediaries can often perform marketing functions more efficiently than manufacturers.

3. _____ Wholesalers reduce costs by (a) offering wholesale prices to retailers; (b) reducing the number of contacts required between manufacturers and retailers; (c) taking over advertising for manufacturers.

Objective 14.2: Identify the major types of independent wholesaling intermediaries and the situations appropriate for each.

1. _____ A drop shipper (a) receives orders from customers and forwards these orders to producers; (b) ships directly to retailers who need new inventory; (c) takes goods to a central market for sale; (d) represents buyers to sellers.

2. _____ A merchant wholesaler can perform many marketing functions for manufacturers.

3. _____ A rack jobber (a) represents buyers to sellers; (b) makes sure merchandise is stocked in stores; (c) receives orders from customers and forwards these orders to producers; (d) takes goods to a central market for sale.

Objective 14.3: Explain how retailers select target markets.

1. _____ Retailing today shows a trend toward targeting broad customer segments rather than focusing on narrowly defined segments.

2. _____ Retailers seldom redefine their target markets.

3. _____ Target marketing encourages retailers to develop their marketing strategies before identifying their target market.

Objective 14.4: Show how the elements of the marketing mix apply to retailing strategy.

1. _____ Before a retailer can make decisions about pricing, product, or promotion, it must first determine its location strategy.

2. _____ The amount a retailer adds to a product's cost in determining the selling price is called (a) wholesale price; (b) markup; (c) retail price; or (d) markdown.

3. _____ Atmospherics do not influence (a) customer buying behavior; (b) promotion; (c) store image; (d) distribution.

Objective 14.5: Explain the concept of scrambled merchandising.

1. _____ Scrambled merchandising refers to (a) store layout; (b) retailers that carry dissimilar product lines; (c) pricing using UPC codes; (d) placing messages in a variety of promotional media.

2. _____ Scrambled merchandising has blurred distinctions between classifications of retailers.

Objective 14.6: Compare the basic types of direct marketing and non-store retailing.

1. _____ A Tupperware party is an example of (a) direct response selling; (b) direct selling; (c) automatic merchandising.

2. _____ A catalog from NM Direct is an example of discount merchandising.

3. _____ When you buy candy from a vending machine, you are using automatic merchandising.

Students: See the solutions section located on page S-2 to check your responses to the Achievement Check Summary.

Key Terms

wholesaler	manufacturers' agent
retailing	wheel of retailing
direct marketing	retail image
wholesaling intermediary	planogram
sales branch	category management
sales office	stockkeeping unit (SKU)
trade fair	slotting allowances
merchandise mart	markup
merchant wholesaler	markdown
rack jobber	planned shopping center
cash-and-carry wholesaler	selling up
truck wholesaler	suggestion selling
drop shipper	atmospherics
mail order wholesaler	chain store
agents and brokers	scrambled merchandising
commission merchant	specialty store
auction house	limited-line store
broker	category killer
selling agent	general merchandise retailer

variety store	outlet mall
department store	hypermarket
mass merchandiser	supercenter
discount house	home shopping
off-price retailer	

Review Questions

1. What is a wholesaling intermediary? Describe its function(s) in a marketing strategy.

2. Distinguish among the different types of manufacturer-owned wholesaling intermediaries. What conditions might suit each one?

3. A carpet store in Flint, Michigan, marks up merchandise 66.67 percent on cost. If the store were to convert to markup on retail, what would be the equivalent markup percentage?

4. How do retailers identify target markets? Explain the major strategies by which retailers reach their target markets.

5. An arts-and-crafts shop in the Black Hills of South Dakota purchases decorative wooden carvings for $10 each and then in turn sells them for $30 each. What are the shop's markup percentages on selling price and on cost?

6. What is the current status of shopping center development in the United States? Describe the major types of shopping centers.

7. Outline the five bases for categorizing retailers. Cite examples of each subclassification.

8. Identify the major types of general merchandise retailers. Cite examples of each type.

9. Define the term *scrambled merchandising*. Why has this practice become so common in retailing?

10. Differentiate between direct selling and direct-response retailing. Cite examples of both.

Questions for Critical Thinking

1. Match each industry with the most appropriate type of wholesaling intermediary.

   _____ hardware

   _____ perishable foods

   _____ lumber

   _____ wheat

   _____ used cars

   a. drop shipper

   b. truck wholesaler

   c. auction house

   d. full-function merchant wholesaler

   e. commission merchant

2. Research and then classify each of the following retailers:

   a. Circuit City

   b. Petite Sophisticates

   c. Limited

   d. Ethan Allen Galleries

   e. Bergdorf Goodman

3. Based on the fact that 80 percent of Americans can get to a Kmart in 15 minutes or less, the nation's third largest retailer has come up with a new "high frequency" planogram for its stores. The new emphasis is on frequently purchased items like milk, bread, and paper products arranged in the order in which people shop. For example, storage con-

tainers are now placed in the housewares section, not the hardware. Visit a nearby Kmart and look at how the merchandise is displayed. What do you think of the new Kmart strategy? Have other stores implemented a similar merchandising format?

4. The Gap is the leader in the so-called "graduating customers" strategy. The idea is to move your customer base along through different stores as they have more money to spend. The Gap's Old Navy stores merchandise is targeted at teenagers. The buyers are then graduated to regular Gap stores, which fall in the mid-price range. Finally, Gap hopes to graduate its customers into the more upscale Banana Republic. What do you think of Gap's "graduation" strategy? Where would Baby Gap and Gap Kids fit into this model? Discuss.

5. Develop a retailing strategy for an Internet retailer. Identify a target market and then suggest mix of merchandise, promotion, service, and pricing strategies that would help a retailer to reach that market via the Internet. What issues must Internet retailers address that do not affect traditional store retailers?

'net**W**ork

1. **Retailing Strategy.** Go to *www.mvp.com* and answer the following questions regarding the retailing strategy at this site: (a) Describe the target market. (b) Describe several elements that combine to establish MVP.com's retail image—such things as merchandise strategy, customer service standards, and "store atmosphere."

mvp.com

2. **Slotting Allowances.** Go to *www.ftc.gov* and conduct a search for information on slotting allowances. Read two or three articles, print out one article you found to be most insightful, and bring it to class so that you may contribute your findings in a classroom discussion on the topic.

ftc.gov

3. **Promotional Strategy.** Find a Web site such as *www.rsn.com* that provides a one-stop shopping and information location that promotes the kind of vacation you would like to take (cruise, camping trip, ski trip). For this assignment, assume your options are not limited by time or money. In other words, plan your dream vacation. The following directions may be used if you're planning a ski trip: Select a ski resort from the Resort Sports Network Web site at *www.rsn.com*, where you can find information on 2,000 resorts in 60 countries. Identify how the Resort Sports Network has provided a one-stop shopping Web site to promote skiing in general and the approximately 2,000 resorts in particular.

rsn.com

Video Case 14 on Wine.com begins on page VC-16.

Gateway Continuing Case Part 6 begins on page GC-10.

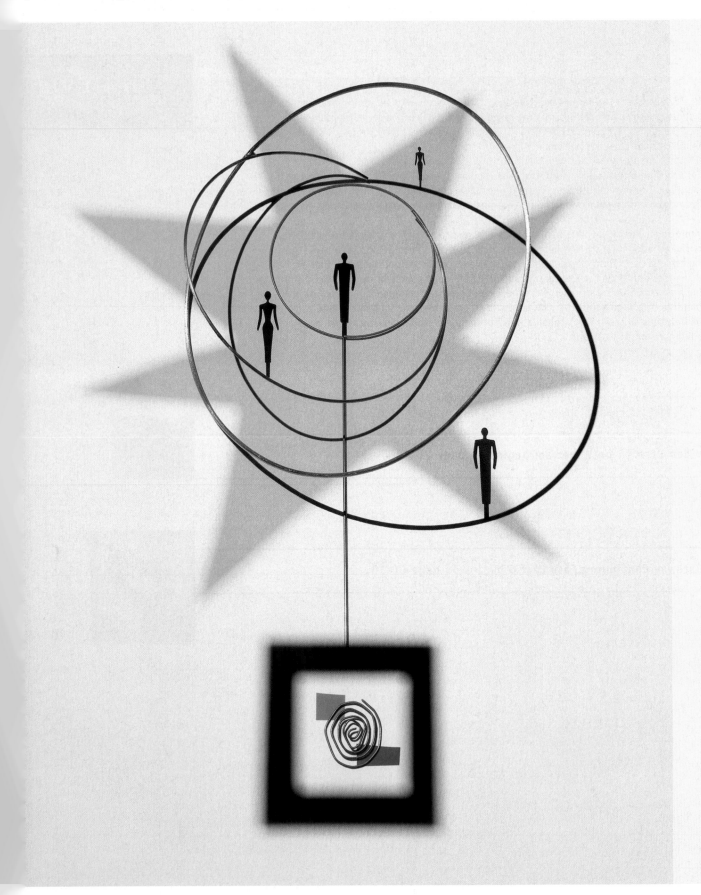

PART

7

PROMOTIONAL STRATEGY

CHAPTER 15   Integrated Marketing Communications

CHAPTER 16   Advertising, Sales Promotion, and Public Relations

CHAPTER 17   Personal Selling and Sales Management

451

Gateway Continuing Case Part 7 begins on page GC-11.

Integrated Marketing Communications

CHAPTER

15

newline.com

Oh Yeah! Baby, Austin Powers Is Hot

Dig it, baby. One of the coolest, hippest happenings in promotion today is Austin Powers—a sexy, psychedelic, time-warped pop star straight out of the 1960s. Who would have believed marketers would be scrambling to get a piece of the top pop retro-media action of the past five years? After all, Mike Myers, the star who brought Austin Powers to life, was scarcely known outside the circle of *Saturday Night Live* fans. But partnering with Austin Powers turned out to be one of the grooviest places a marketer could be.

The first film, *Austin Powers: International Man of Mystery,* was a modest box-office success for New Line Cinema. But viewers talked about it, and soon it seemed that everyone knew Austin Powers, the velvet-attired symbol of the 1960s culture whose words drip with sexual innuendo and whose reason for being is to party. And these new fans could hardly wait for the sequel.

The second film, *Austin Powers: The Spy Who Shagged Me,* proved a box-office sensation. It reintroduced the world to pop art, pop music, and pop styles, and moviegoers spent over $200 million to see it. New Line Cinema marketers knew early on that they had a film with high hit potential—if they could successfully develop an integrated marketing communications program that would put a trip to the movies on everyone's to-do list. This meant a coordinated blend of traditional advertising, cooperative promotions with other products, contests, giveaways, and even a direct-mail offer of Austin Powers Visa cards to college students. And, of course, the film's star was given his very own online pad—AustinPowers.com, with cross-advertising on Web sites of the film's promotional partners.

New Line's promotion was highly selective. Rather than partnering with every willing marketer, the studio deliberately sought out alliances with products likely to enhance the Powers' image. As New Line president Bob Friedman explains, "We went with an airline that had a personality, if you will, sort of like Austin, which was Virgin Atlantic Airways. We went with a beer, which was Heineken. We did not go with McDonald's or with Burger King but instead went with Bob's Big Boy. Everything from the partner that we chose to the message that we developed was one that was in line with the property."

A tie-in with America Online gave New Line marketers immediate access to nearly 20 million AOL subscribers. New Line sold tickets to advance screenings of *Austin Powers* exclusively to AOL members through its Moviefone ticket services. AOL support included banners and welcome screens, as well as appearances on AOL sites including Today, Entertainment, Feature Special, and Digital City Entertainment.

Another partnership linked Europe to the Austin Powers phenomenon. Virgin Atlantic entered the deal with some light advertising. "But then," says Sarah Buxton, the airline's marketing director, "I figured that this thing could be as big as we wanted to make it and given that the brand fit was so perfect it made sense to really blow it out on all levels." Virgin ended up sponsoring New Line's live Cannes Cybercast of the *Austin Powers* party, and gave away free airline tickets on AustinPowers.com.

New York–based Loews Cineplex Entertainment was also involved in *Austin Powers* promotional efforts. An online coupon promotion was conducted in 400 theaters nationwide. Visitors to the Loews' site received coupons for a free *Austin Powers*

453

mini-poster and *Launch* CD-ROM magazine. The site was also "Austin Powerized" to include colorful 1960s-style clips of *Austin* images to help persuade them to see the movie.

Marketers have become shag-happy about tie-ins with this groovy movie that bring millions of people to the "Click me, baby" icon and who are looking forward to seeing what Austin Powers has in the bag for the 21st century.[1]

CHAPTER OVERVIEW

Two of the four components of the marketing mix—product and distribution strategies—were discussed in previous chapters. The following three chapters in Part 7 analyze the third marketing mix variable—promotion. A good place to begin the discussion of promotion is with a definition of the term. **Promotion** is the function of informing, persuading, and influencing the consumer's purchase decision. Consider how this definition applies to New Line's various marketing techniques used to promote the *Austin Powers* movies. New Line informs one target market—moviegoers—of the new movie; it persuades AOL subscribers, another market segment, to see the movies; and through tie-ins with Virgin Airlines and Loews Theatres, it offers games, prizes, and discount coupons that involve consumers in the "shagadelic" experience created by seeing the movie.

This chapter introduces the concept of integrated marketing communications, briefly describes the elements of a firm's promotional mix—personal and nonpersonal selling—and explains the characteristics that determine the success of the mix. Next, the chapter identifies the objectives of promotion and describes the importance of developing promotional budgets and measuring the effectiveness of promotion. Finally, the chapter discusses the importance of the business, economic, and social aspects of promotion. Chapter 16 covers advertising, sales promotion, and the other nonpersonal selling elements of the promotional mix. Chapter 17 completes this section by focusing on personal selling.

Throughout the text, special emphasis has been given to new information that focuses on how technology is changing the way marketers approach *communication*, the transmission of a message from a sender to a receiver. Consumers receive **marketing communications**—messages that deal with buyer-seller relationships—from a variety of media, including television, magazines, and the Internet. Marketers can broadcast an ad on the Web to mass markets or design a customized appeal targeted to a small market segment. Each message the customer receives from any source represents the brand, company, or organization. Unless a company coordinates all these messages, the consumer can become confused and may entirely tune out the message.

To prevent this loss of attention, marketers are turning to **integrated marketing communications (IMC)**, which coordinate all promotional activities—media advertising, direct mail, personal selling, sales promotion, and public relations—to produce a unified, customer-focused promotional message. For example, *Austin Powers'* tag lines, "Shagadelic" and "Yeah, Baby," appear in print ads and carry through to Web promotions. IMC is a broader concept than marketing communications and promotional strategy. It uses database technology to refine the marketer's understanding of the target audience, segment this audience, and select the best type of media for each segment.

This chapter will show that IMC involves not only the marketer but also all other organizational units that interact with the consumer. Marketing managers set the goals and objectives of the firm's promotional strategy in accordance with overall organizational objectives and marketing goals. Based on these objectives, the various elements of the promotional strategy—personal selling, advertising, sales promotion, direct marketing, publicity, and public relations—are formulated into an integrated communications plan. This becomes a central part of the firm's total marketing strategy to reach its selected market segments. The feedback mechanism, including marketing research and field reports, completes the system by identifying any deviations from the plan and suggesting improvements. ■

INTEGRATED MARKETING COMMUNICATIONS

Successful marketers use the marketing concept and relationship marketing to develop customer-oriented marketing programs. The customer is also at the heart of integrated marketing communications. An IMC strategy begins not with the organization's goods and services but with consumer wants or needs and then works in reverse to the product, brand, or organization. It sends receiver-focused rather than product-focused messages. For example, advertising agency Saatchi & Saatchi won the Just for Feet account because it impressed the client with its understanding of the athletic shoe *buyer*, while competing agencies focused on the shoe *business.*

Rather than separating the parts of the promotional mix, IMC looks at these elements from the consumer's viewpoint: as information about the brand, company, or organization. Even though the messages come from different sources—TV, radio, newspaper, billboards, direct mail, coupons, public relations, the Internet, and online services—consumers may perceive them as "advertising." IMC broadens promotion to include all the ways a customer has contact with the organization, adding to traditional media and direct mail such sources as packaging, store displays, sales literature, and online and interactive media. Unless the organization takes an integrated approach to present a unified, consistent message, it may send conflicting information that confuses consumers.

Dr Pepper and Fox Television Network recently partnered in an IMC effort dubbed "Find Love on Wednesdays." The watch-to-win promotion ran during both *Beverly Hills 90210* and *Party of Five* and targeted 12- to 34-year-olds. Prizes included trips to Rome, San Francisco, and Rio de Janeiro; cash; CDs; T-shirts; and Sony Watchman TVs. The Fox tie-in drew a record 17.5 million callers during a one-hour episode.[2]

Another popular integrated marketing effort involves video game tie-ins. General Mills and Nintendo hooked up to leverage the equity of Nintendo's name, technology, and characters with General Mills' strong presence in its

1

Relate the concept of integrated marketing communications to the development of an optimal promotional mix.

MARKETING   DICTIONARY

promotion Function of informing, persuading, and influencing the consumer's purchase decision.

marketing communication Transmission from a sender to a receiver of a message dealing with the buyer-seller relationship.

integrated marketing communications (IMC) Coordination of *all* promotional activities—media advertising, direct mail, personal selling, sales promotion, and public relations—to produce a unified, customer-focused promotional message.

A game for Chevrolet Tracker drew 1.3 million entries online and another 100,000 offline.

gm.com

market. Nintendo video game tips were printed on 11 million packages of Betty Crocker Fruit Roll Ups. In another IMC effort with Sony, 20 million cereal boxes included $5 rebates on such video games as *Crash Bandicoot* and *Rugrats Search for Reptar.*[3]

Today's marketing environment is characterized by many diverse markets and media, creating both opportunities and challenges. Success of any IMC program depends critically on identifying the members of an audience and understanding what they want. Without good information about existing and potential customers, their purchase histories, needs, and wants, marketers may send the wrong message. But they cannot succeed simply by improving the quality of the messages or by sending more of them. IMC must not only deliver messages to intended audiences but also gather responses from them. Databases and interactive marketing are important IMC tools that help marketers collect information from customers and then segment markets according to resulting analysis of demographics and preferences. Marketers can then design specialized communications programs to meet the needs of particular segments.

Detroit-based General Motors (GM) has implemented a highly effective IMC program that allows dealers to respond directly to consumer questions and offer personalized service. Recognizing that many consumers dislike the high pressure sales tactics that characterize showroom floors, www.gm.com has streamlined the car-buying experience. Online shoppers contact a dealer electronically, select from a Chevrolet to a Cadillac to a Pontiac to a GMC, and then get a price quote. They are also eligible to enter contests by answering a short questionnaire. As Chevrolet-brand manager Margaret Brooks explains, "Our goal is simple. Attract customers, draw useful info from them, then reward them for it in a form that would prompt them to return."

Buick marketers, for example, created a sweepstakes that combined media inserts, print ads, and Web interaction. The inserts and ads generated thousands of visitors to the Web site. "Consumers are very busy," says Brooks. "You need a lot of different media to get to them. When you put together TV, print, direct mail, and Web promotion, and tell an integrated story, you maximize your opportunity to have them experience the brand in a memorable way."[4]

The increase in media options provides more ways to give consumers product information; however, it can also create information overload. Marketers have to spread available dollars across fragmented media markets and a wider range of promotional activities to achieve their communication goals. Mass media such as TV ads, while still useful, are no longer the mainstays of marketing campaigns. In 1960, a company could reach about 90 percent of U.S. consumers by advertising on the three major television networks. Today, these network ads reach less than 60 percent. Audiences are also more fragmented. Therefore, to reach desired groups, organizations are turning to niche marketing through special-interest magazines; by purchasing time on cable television channels to target consumers with sports, family, science, history, comedy, and women's interests; through reaching out through telecommunications like the Internet; and by sponsoring events and activities.

Without an IMC program, marketers frequently encounter problems within their own organizations because separate departments have authority and responsibility for planning and implementing specific promotional mix elements. A company's sales department plans and controls sales presentations; the advertising department works with the firm's advertising agency to create media promotions; and sales promotion and direct-marketing activities take place in still other departments. All too often, these disjointed efforts result in an uncoordinated overall promotional effort that fails to achieve the marketers' objectives. Personal selling efforts may not be directly linked with the themes stressed in advertising and sales promotion. Public relations activities may fail to support specific promotional objectives.

These aspects of the business environment, coupled with fragmented promotional efforts in many organizations, have prompted the move toward integrated marketing communications to coordinate all promotional activities. Such coordination frequently produces a competitive advantage based on synergy and interdependence among the various elements of the promotional mix. With an IMC strategy, marketers can create a unified personality for the product or brand by choosing the right elements from the promotional mix to send the message. At the same time, they can develop more narrowly focused plans to reach specific market segments and choose the best form of communication to send a particular message to a specific target audience. IMC provides a more effective way to reach and serve target markets than less well-coordinated strategies.

Importance of Teamwork

IMC requires a big-picture view of promotion planning, a total strategy including all marketing activities, not just promotion. Successful implementation of IMC requires that everyone involved in every aspect of promotion—public relations, advertising, personal selling, and sales promotion—function as a team. They must present a consistent, coordinated promotional effort at every point of customer contact with the organization. In this way, they avoid duplication of efforts, increasing marketing effectiveness and reducing costs.

Teamwork involves both in-house resources and outside vendors. It involves marketing personnel; members of the sales force who deal with wholesalers, retailers, and organizational buyers; and customer service representatives. A firm gains nothing from a terrific advertisement featuring a toll-free telephone number that has unhelpful, surly operators on the other end. The company must train its representatives to send a single, positive message to consumers and to also solicit information for the firm's customer database.

IMC also challenges the traditional role of the advertising agency. A single agency may no longer fulfill all of a client's communications requirements, including traditional advertising and sales promotions, interactive marketing, database development, direct marketing, and public relations. To best serve client needs, an agency must often assemble a team with members from other companies.

| FIGURE 15.2 | RadioShack: Using Database Information to Stock Retail Stores |

Role of Databases in Effective IMC Programs

With the growth of the Internet during the last decade, marketers have been given the power to gather more information faster and to organize it easier than ever before in history. By sharing this detailed knowledge appropriately among all relative parties, a company can lay the foundation for a successful IMC program.

The move from mass marketing to a customer-specific marketing strategy—a characteristic of online marketing—requires not only a means of identifying and communicating with the firm's target market, but also information regarding important characteristics of each prospective customer. Organizations can compile different kinds of data into complete databases with customer information, including names and addresses, demographic data, lifestyle considerations, brand preferences, and buying behavior. This information provides critical guidance in designing an effective IMC strategy that achieves organizational goals and finds new opportunities for increased sales and profits.

Radio Shack has implemented an IMC program based on a computerized database of customers. The nationally-known electronics chain started out in the 1940s as a catalog operation. In fact, as late as 1963, only 9 stores existed. Today, the company still maintains a strong catalog customer base but has also grown to include more than 7,000 retail stores and a newly established Web presence. The 300-plus-page catalog is an information source for both customers and sales personnel and a traffic builder for retail stores and the Web site.

Radio Shack customers are coded by categories of merchandise. For example, a "never E" is someone who has never bought an end product (like a telephone or flashlight), but only buys anchor items (parts and accessories). Anchor items represent 33 percent of Radio Shack's top merchandise line, 45 percent of gross sales, and 80 percent of traffic. Other items are not typically stocked in retail stores but can be ordered from the catalog or Web site. The chain's marketers analyze data on customer purchases and demographics in deciding which items will be stocked.[5]

snyder.com

Direct sampling is another method frequently used to quickly obtain customer opinions regarding a particular firm's goods and services. Snyder Communications, an Illinois-based direct sampler for consumer-products companies, uses a database to target its programs to Hispanic households with children aged 6 to 12. Similarly, Toronto-based ICOM Information and Communications sends out unique packages containing samples and coupons to over 9 million U.S. homes. ICOM targets consumers based on brand and category usage, loyalty, and key habits in addition to demographics. For example, ICOM knows that consumer X suffers from arthritis, drinks coffee, uses body wash, and regularly buys such brands as Advil, Yuban, and Oil of Olay. So consumer X's portfolio only gets stocked with samples of competitors' products like Tylenol, Folgers, and Dove.

During this first decade of the 21st century, the Information Age will come to maturity as marketers begin to not only learn more about consumers, but also learn new ways to apply that information. Direct sampling and coupons are no longer generic, mass-distribution practices. Consider the fact that more than a dozen newspapers in the United States have the ability to get a sample into a subscriber segment as small as 250 households, and with little or no increase in the costs passed on to marketers.[6]

THE COMMUNICATIONS PROCESS

2

Explain the relationship of promotional strategy to the process of communication.

The top portion of Table 15.1 shows a general model of the communications process and its application to promotional strategy. The *sender* acts as the source in the communications system as

TABLE 15.1   Relating Promotion to the Communications Process

| Marketing Manager | → Transmits messages such as sales presentations, ads, displays, direct mail, publicity releases | → Delivers message via salesperson, print and electronic advertising media, public relations | → Receiver or customer interprets message | → Receiver or customer makes decision | → Customer responses, market research, market share changes, field sales reports |

← NOISE →   ← NOISE →

TYPE OF PROMOTION	SENDER	ENCODING BY SENDER	CHANNEL	DECODING BY RECEIVER	RESPONSE	FEEDBACK
Personal selling	IBM e-solutions networking system	Sales presentation on new applications of system	IBM sales representative	Office manager and employees discuss sales presentation and those of competing suppliers.	Order placed for IBM e-solutions system installation.	Customer asks about a second system for subsidiary company.
Dollar-off coupon (sales promotion)	Kellogg's Special K cereal	Coupons prepared by Kellogg's marketing department and advertising agency	Coupon insert in Sunday newspaper	Newspaper reader sees coupon for Special K cereal and saves it.	Special K purchased by consumer using coupon.	Kellogg researchers see increase in market share.
Television advertising	Styx River Water World	Advertisement developed by Styx River's advertising agency featuring the new park rides	Network television ads during program with high percentages of viewers under 20 years old	Teens and young adults see ad and decide to try out the new park.	Water World tickets are purchased.	Customers purchase season ticket packages for Water World.

he or she seeks to convey a *message* (a communication of information, advice, or a request) to a *receiver.* An effective message accomplishes three tasks:

1. It gains the receiver's attention.
2. It achieves understanding by both receiver and sender.
3. It stimulates the receiver's needs and suggests an appropriate method of satisfying them.

The table also provides several examples of promotional messages. Although the types of promotion may vary from a highly personalized sales presentation to such nonpersonal promotions as television advertising and dollar-off coupons, each goes through every stage in the communications process.

The above three tasks are related to the **AIDA concept** (attention-interest-desire-action) proposed by E. K. Strong over 60 years ago as an explanation of the steps through which an individual reaches a purchase decision. First, the promotional message must gain the potential consumer's attention. It then seeks to arouse interest in the good or service. At the next stage, it stimulates desire by convincing the would-be buyer of the product's ability to satisfy his or her needs. Finally, the sales presentation, advertisement, or sales promotion technique attempts to produce action in the form of a purchase or a more favorable attitude that may lead to future purchases.

The message must be *encoded,* or translated into understandable terms, and transmitted through a communications channel. *Decoding* is the receiver's interpretation of the message. The receiver's response, known as *feedback,* completes the system. Throughout the process, *noise* can interfere with the transmission of the message and reduce its effectiveness.

The marketing manager is the sender in Table 15.1. He or she encodes the message in the form of sales presentations, advertising, displays, or publicity releases. The *channel* for delivering the message may be a salesperson, a public relations outlet, or an advertising medium. Decoding is often the most troublesome step in marketing communications because consumers do not always interpret promotional messages in the same way that senders do. Since receivers usually decode messages according to their own frames of reference or experiences, a sender must carefully encode a message in a way that matches the frame of reference of the target audience. Consumers today receive many sales messages through many media channels. This communications traffic can create confusion as noise in the channel increases. Consumers choose to process only a few messages each, and ignored messages waste communications budgets.

The AIDA concept is also vital to online marketers. It is not enough to say a Web site has effective content or high response rates. Marketers must know just how many "eyeballs" are looking at the site, how often they come to view a message, and what things they are examining. Most important, they must find out what consumers do besides just look. Bottom line, if nobody is responding to a Web site, it might as well not exist. Business writer and management professor Tom Davenport offers online marketers several tips that reinforce the AIDA concept:

1. To attract eyeballs, remember that humans find other people interesting. Web sites should present people in multiple forms—narrative, celebrity photos, and chat lines.
2. Eyeballs get bored easily and the price for new and interesting ideas is always being raised. Online marketers must continuously re-create Web sites by adding new content and new formats.

FIGURE 15.3   **Calvin Klein: Kiosks Provide Instant Feedback for Fragrance Marketers**

MARKETING   DICTIONARY

AIDA concept Acronym for attention-interest-desire-action; the traditional explanation of the steps an individual must take to complete the purchase decision.

PointCast Gets Pushed Out

BACKGROUND At what point does communication become noise? Too bad this question never occurred to the founders of Point-Cast, an Internet broadcaster of personalized news and information to business consumers. Instead of customers taking the traditional pull approach of searching out Web pages on their browsers, PointCast used push technology to deliver information directly to the users' computers. The service which featured Netscape, CNN, and *The New York Times* proved to be an immediate hit, attracting 250,000 new viewers a month at its peak.

THE PROBLEM Push technology proved to be a solution searching for a problem. As it turned out, the typical PointCast users found themselves receiving too much information too often. The messages dominating their computer screens amounted to a recurrent annoyance.

continued on next page

3. Eyeballs alone are not worth much. What actually matters is that someone actually clicks on a banner or button, visits an advertiser, and ultimately buys goods and services.[7]

Feedback, the receiver's response to the message, provides a way for marketers to evaluate the effectiveness of the message and tailor their responses accordingly. Feedback may take the form of attitude changes, purchases, or non-purchases. In some instances, organizations use promotion to create favorable attitudes toward their goods or services in the hope of future purchases. Other promotional communications have the objective of directly stimulating consumer purchases.

Repeat customers are the foundation of fragrance and cosmetics companies. Fragrance marketers' greatest challenge is to get consumers to try their colognes and perfumes. The majority of the time, consumers who like a particular fragrance will buy it more than once. For several years, consumers have been bombarded with the latest scents by scent-strips in magazines and automatic atomizers located at department store entrances and escalators. But new applications of scent technology allow less intrusive distribution methods to get consumer feedback on perfumes. Calvin Klein and L'Oréal now test their fragrances using kiosks set up in large department stores like Macy's and Bloomingdale's. Consumers step up to the computerized kiosks and press an on-screen icon for a squirt of their fragrance of choice. The direct-response kiosks allow marketers to tally data to determine what shoppers in that store like and compare the results against sales patterns. Based on this feedback, marketers can spot trends and preferences and determine the appropriate inventory mix.[8]

Even non-purchases may serve as feedback to the sender. Failure to purchase may result from ineffective communication in which the receivers do not believe or remember the message. Alternatively, the message may have failed to persuade the receiver that the firm's goods or services are superior to those of its competitors. Marketers frequently gather feedback through such techniques as marketing research studies and field sales reports.

Noise represents interference at some stage in the communications process. It may result from disruptions such as transmissions of competing promotional messages over the same communications channel, misinterpretation of a sales presentation or advertising message, receipt of the promotional message by the wrong person, or random events such as people conversing during a television commercial or leaving the room. Noise can also result from distractions within an advertising message itself.

Noise can be especially problematic in international communications. Disruption often results from too many competing messages. Italian television channels, for instance, broadcast all advertisements during a single half-hour slot each night. Noise might stem from differences in technology, such as a bad telephone connection, or from poor translations into other languages. Nonverbal cues, such as body language and tone of voice, are important parts of the communication process, and cultural differences may lead to noise and misunderstandings. For example, in the United States, the round *o* sign made with the thumb and first finger means "okay." However, in Mediterranean countries, it means "zero" or "the worst." A Tunisian interprets this same sign as "I'll kill you," and to a Japanese it means "money."

Perhaps the most misunderstood language for U.S. marketers is English. It is often said that the 74 English-speaking nations are separated by a common language. The following examples illustrate how easy it can be for marketers to make mistakes in English-language promotional messages:

- *Underpants*: pants (Britain), underdaks (Australia)
- *Police*: bobby (Britain), garda (Ireland), Mountie (Canada), police wallah (South Asia)
- *Porch*: stoep (South Africa), gallery (Caribbean)
- *Bar*: pub (Britain), hotel (Australia), boozer (Australia, Britain, New Zealand)
- *Bathroom*: loo (Britain), dunny (Australia), lav (Britain, South Africa)
- *Ghost or monster*: wendigo (Canada), duppy (Caribbean), taniwha (New Zealand)
- *Barbecue*: braai (South Africa), barbie (Australia)
- *Pickup truck*: bakkie (South Africa), ute (Australia), utility vehicle (New Zealand)[9]

Faulty communications can be especially risky on a global level, where noise can lead to some interesting misinterpretations. Here are three recent international examples:

■ *On a sign in a Bucharest hotel lobby:* The lift is being fixed for the next day. During that time, we regret that you will be unbearable.

■ *From a Japanese information booklet about using a hotel air conditioner:* Cooles and Heates: If you want just condition of warm in your room, please control yourself.

■ *In an Acapulco hotel:* The manager has personally passed all the water served here.

OBJECTIVES OF PROMOTION

What specific tasks should promotion accomplish? The answers to this question seem to vary as much as the sources one consults. Generally, however, marketers identify the following objectives for promotion:

1. Provide information to consumers and others.
2. Increase demand.
3. Differentiate a product.
4. Accentuate a product's value.
5. Stabilize sales.

Provide Information

The traditional function of promotion was to inform the market about the availability of a particular good or service. Indeed, marketers still direct large portions of current promotional efforts at providing product information for potential customers. For example, the typical newspaper advertisement for a university or college extension program emphasizes information such as the availability, times, and locations of different courses. Industrial salespeople inform buyers of new products and how they work. Retail advertisements, such as the one shown in Figure 15.4, announce the eight flavors of Häagen-Dazs sorbet as well as the ice-cream marketer's Web site.

In addition to traditional print and broadcast advertising, companies now distribute videocassettes as low-cost tools to give consumers product information. A ten-minute video costs about $1.50 to duplicate and send (not including production costs), compared to $8 or more for a full-color brochure. Consumers regard the video as a novelty that stands out from other promotions, so they are less likely to throw out the cassette. In fact, about 90 percent of recipients view them. In some cases, response rates are as high as 49 percent and returns on investment exceed 1,000 percent. These figures translate into substantial profits for companies involved in video promotions.

Mercedes-Benz built the largest and broadest marketing campaign in their company's history around a lead-generating, direct marketing video campaign. Walt Disney World promotes its resorts via video. Not-for-profit groups like the World Wildlife Fund solicit contributions through video marketing. NordicTrack practically built the company around video. McDonnell Douglas trains its employees with quarterly video magazines. St. Mary's College sends a video tour of their campus to prospective students. Video direct marketing helped Nintendo of America make *Donkey Kong Country* the fastest-selling game title in the history of the video game, selling a record-breaking 6.1 million games in the first 15 days of release.[10]

Increase Demand

Most promotions pursue the objective of increasing demand for a good or service. Some promotions are aimed at increasing *primary demand*, the desire for a general product category. When P&G first introduced Pampers disposable diapers in Hungary, most Hungarian parents used

MARKETING STRATEGY FAILURE

THE OUTCOME Success was fleeting for PointCast as the number of new viewers was offset by deserters. The company, which spurned a $450 million buy-out offer by Rupert Murdock's News Corp. in 1997, did not survive to see the 21st century. It joined a host of other online information service providers, including IFusion, Freeloader, BullsEye, and Headliner, that either shutdown or were bought out or closed in recent years. These firms all failed to recognize that consumers did not always want information the *second* it happened and they were upset with alerts and banners that popped up on their computer screens, interrupting work in progress.

LESSONS LEARNED Information providers must provide their services *when* consumers want it—not when vendors want to send it—and they only want the information that is relevant to them—not anything and everything that makes the news. While push technologies can perform important functions in e-commerce, they must be performed from a customer-oriented point of view.

@ **haagen-dazs.com**

3

List the objectives of promotion.

FIGURE 15.4

Häagen-Dazs: Providing
Information to Consumers

Here's to a long, hot summer.

Häagen-Dazs Sorbet. Loaded with refreshment and all the intense flavor you can handle. *It's just perfect.*"

nokia.com

mcphee.com

overpants with paper inserts to diaper their babies. Early P&G television commercials there focused on generating interest in the novel product by demonstrating its superiority.

More promotions, however, are aimed at increasing *selective demand*, the desire for a specific brand. For example, marketers for Nokia cellular phones developed an extensive print advertising campaign that appeared in such magazines as *GQ*, *Esquire*, *Sports Illustrated*, and *Fortune*. The effort was successful in targeting upscale businesspeople and in convincing them of Nokia's advantages over leading competitors Ericsson and Motorola.

Differentiate the Product

A frequent objective of the firm's promotional efforts is *product differentiation*. Homogeneous demand for many products results when consumers regard the firm's output as virtually identical to its competitors' products. In these cases, the individual firm has almost no control over marketing variables such as price. A differentiated demand schedule, in contrast, permits more flexibility in marketing strategy, such as price changes.

Recognizing that most consumers are not brand conscious when it comes to trinkets and novelties, Archie McPhee marketers have found a way to differentiate their party supplies to increase brand loyalty. In addition to its traditional catalog and Web site, the self-proclaimed "Outfitter of Popular Culture" recently opened a retail store in its hometown of Seattle. The grand opening was accompanied by 17,000 mailings that invited local residents to join its Passport Club, which offered a small, passport-sized booklet filled with free offers. Once a month, customers can bring it in to be stamped, thereby earning a free trinket (a skull magnet in one month, a pair of hatching cockroaches in another). Additional goodies, such as rabbi punching puppets, wind-up sparking Nunzillas, and happy squeak monks, are awarded based on graduated purchase amounts. The new store also features customer-friendly displays that tilt and rotate. All of McPhee's promotions are aimed at making the shopping experience so unique from any other venture that customers will not only remember the company but also come back for more party products.[11]

Accentuate the Product's Value

Promotion can explain the greater ownership utility of a product to buyers, thereby accentuating its value and justifying a higher price in the marketplace. This objective benefits both consumer and business products. A firm's promotional messages must build brand image and equity and at the same time, deliver a "call to action." Advertising typically offers reasons why a good or service fits into the consumer's lifestyle. Today, consumers everywhere value their time; the challenge for marketers is to demonstrate how their products will make their life better.[12]

The Coca-Cola Company's marketers in Spain were able to reach the illusive teenage market with a promotion that focused on the lifestyle benefits of drinking Coke. By sending in 15 bottle caps, Spanish teens could receive a free beeper. Seeing the offer as a great way to stay in touch with their friends, the target audience snapped up 300,000 beepers within 60 days.[13]

Stabilize Sales

For the typical firm, sales are not uniform throughout the year. Sales fluctuations may result from cyclical, seasonal, or irregular demand. Stabilizing these variations is often an objective of promotional strategy. Coffee sales, for example, follow a seasonal pattern, with purchases and consumption increasing during the winter months. To stimulate summer sales of Sanka brand decaffeinated coffee, General Foods created advertisements that included a recipe for instant iced coffee, promoting it as a refreshing, caffeine-free summer beverage. Hotels and motels often seek to supplement high occupancy during the week from business travelers by promoting special weekend packages at lower room rates. Some firms sponsor sales contests during slack periods that offer prizes to sales personnel who meet goals.

THE PROMOTIONAL MIX

Like the marketing mix, the **promotional mix** requires a proper blend of numerous variables to satisfy the needs of the firm's target market and achieve organizational objectives. In fact, the promotional mix is a subset of the marketing mix, with its product, pricing, promotion, and distribution elements. With the promotional mix, the marketing manager attempts to achieve the optimal blending of various elements to attain promotional objectives. The components of the promotional mix are personal selling and nonpersonal selling, including advertising, sales promotion, direct marketing, and public relations.

Personal selling, advertising, and sales promotion—the most significant elements—usually account for the bulk of a firm's promotional expenditures. However, direct marketing and public relations also contribute to efficient marketing communications. Later sections of this chapter examine direct marketing, and Chapters 16 and 17 present a detailed discussion of the other elements. This section will simply define the elements and discuss their advantages and disadvantages.

Novelty marketers for Archie McPhee differentiate their catalog offerings by providing superior, friendly customer service.

4

Explain the concept of the promotional mix and its relationship to the marketing mix.

Personal Selling

Personal selling, the original form of all promotion, may be defined as a seller's promotional presentation conducted on a person-to-person basis with the buyer. This direct form of promotion may be conducted face-to-face, over the telephone, through videoconferencing, or through interactive computer links between the buyer and seller. Today, about 14 million people in the United States are employed in personal selling, and the average sales call costs about $300.

Nonpersonal Selling

Nonpersonal selling includes advertising, sales promotion, direct marketing, and public relations. Advertising and sales promotion are usually regarded as the most important forms of nonpersonal selling. About one-third of marketing dollars pay for media advertising, and two-thirds fund trade and consumer sales promotions.

Advertising is any paid, nonpersonal communication through various media

MARKETING | DICTIONARY

promotional mix Blend of personal selling and nonpersonal selling (including advertising, sales promotion, direct marketing, and public relations) designed to achieve promotional objectives.

personal selling Interpersonal promotional process involving a seller's person-to-person presentation to a prospective buyer.

advertising Paid, nonpersonal communication through various media by a business firm, not-for-profit organization, or individual identified in the message with the hope of informing or persuading members of a particular audience.

FIGURE 15.5 | **A Joint Promotion Using Licensing**

about a business firm, not-for-profit organization, product, or idea by a sponsor identified in a message that is intended to inform or persuade members of a particular audience. It is a major promotional mix component for thousands of organizations. Mass consumption and geographically dispersed markets make advertising particularly appropriate for marketing goods and services using the same promotional messages to large audiences.

Advertising primarily involves the mass media, such as newspapers, television, radio, magazines, and billboards, but also includes electronic and computerized forms of promotion such as Web commercials, videotapes, and video screens in supermarkets. The rich potential of the Internet as an advertising channel to reach millions of people one at a time has attracted the attention of companies large and small, local and international.

Sales promotion consists of marketing activities other than personal selling, advertising, and public relations that stimulate consumer purchasing and dealer effectiveness. This broad category includes displays, trade shows, coupons, contests, samples, premiums, product demonstrations, and various nonrecurrent, irregular selling efforts. Sales promotion provides a short-term incentive, usually in combination with other forms of promotion, to emphasize, assist, supplement, or otherwise support the objectives of the promotional program.

General Mills marketers recently capitalized on the popularity of Pokémon trading cards with its new fruit snack treat shown in Figure 15.5. General Mills licensed the characters and offered free trading cards inside each package. The new product was introduced to coincide with the release of the first Pokémon movie.[14]

Sales promotion geared to marketing intermediaries is called **trade promotion.** Companies actually spend about as much on trade promotion as on advertising and consumer-oriented sales promotion combined. Trade promotion strategies include offering free merchandise, buy-back allowances, and merchandise allowances along with sponsorship of sales contests to encourage wholesalers and retailers to sell more of certain products or product lines.

Another element in a firm's integrated promotional mix is **direct marketing,** the use of direct communication to a consumer or business recipient designed to generate a response in the form of an order (direct order); a request for further information (lead generation); or a visit to a place of business to purchase specific goods or services (traffic generation). While many people equate direct marketing with direct mail, this promotional category also includes telephone marketing (telemarketing), direct-response advertising and infomercials on television and radio, direct-response print advertising, and electronic media.

Public relations refer to a firm's communications and relationships with its various publics. These publics include customers, suppliers, stockholders, employees, the government, the general public, and the society in which the organization operates. Public relation programs can conduct either formal or informal contacts. The critical point is that every organization, whether or not it has a formally organized program, must be concerned about its public relations.

Publicity is an important part of an effective public relations effort. It can be defined as nonpersonal stimulation of demand for a good, service, person, cause, or organization through unpaid placement of significant news about it in a published medium or through a favorable presentation of it through radio, television, or the stage. Compared to personal selling, advertising, and even sales promotion, expenditures for public relations are usually low in most firms. Since companies do not pay for publicity, they have less control over the publication by the press or electronic media of good or bad company news. For this reason, a consumer may find this type of news source more believable than if the information were disseminated directly by the company.

TABLE 15.2   Comparison of the Five Promotional Mix Elements

	PERSONAL SELLING	ADVERTISING	SALES PROMOTION	DIRECT MARKETING	PUBLIC RELATIONS
Advantages	Permits measurement of effectiveness Elicits an immediate response Tailors the message to fit the customer	Reaches a large group of potential consumers for a relatively low price per exposure Allows strict control over the final message Can be adapted to either mass audiences or specific audience segments	Produces an immediate consumer response Attracts attention and creates product awareness Allows easy measurement of results Provides short-term sales increases	Generates an immediate response Covers a wide audience with targeted advertising Allows complete, customized, personal message Produces measurable results	Creates a positive attitude toward a product or company Enhances credibility of a product or company
Disadvantages	Relies almost exclusively upon the ability of the salesperson Involves high cost per contact	Does not permit totally accurate measurement of results Usually cannot close sales	Is nonpersonal in nature Is difficult to differentiate from competitors' efforts	Suffers from image problem Involves a high cost per reader Depends on quality and accuracy of mailing lists May annoy consumers	May not permit accurate measurement of effect on sales Involves much effort directed toward non-marketing-oriented goals

As Table 15.2 indicates, each type of promotion has both advantages and shortcomings. Although personal selling entails a relatively high per-contact cost, it wastes less effort than do nonpersonal forms of promotion such as advertising. Personal selling often provides more flexible promotion than the other forms because the salesperson can tailor the sales message to meet the unique needs—or objections—of each potential customer.

The major advantages of advertising come from its ability to create instant awareness of a good, service, or idea; build brand equity; and deliver the marketer's message to mass audiences for a relatively low cost per contact. Major disadvantages of advertising include the difficulty in measuring its effectiveness and high media costs. Sales promotions, by contrast, can be more accurately monitored and measured than advertising, produce immediate consumer responses, and provide short-term sales increases. Direct marketing gives an action-oriented choice, permits narrow audience segmentation and customization of communications, and produces measurable results. Public relation efforts such as publicity frequently offer substantially higher credibility than other promotional techniques. The marketer must determine the appropriate blend of these promotional mix elements to effectively market the firm's goods and services.

5

Discuss the role of sponsorships and direct marketing in integrated marketing communications planning.

SPONSORSHIPS

Perhaps the hottest trend in promotion during the past ten years offers marketers the ability to integrate several elements of the promotional mix. Commercial sponsorships of an event or activity apply personal selling, advertising, sales promotion, and public relations in achieving specific promotional goals. These sponsorships link events with sponsors and with media ranging from

MARKETING   DICTIONARY

sales promotion Marketing activities other than personal selling, advertising, and publicity that stimulate consumer purchasing and dealer effectiveness (includes displays, trade shows, coupons, premiums, contests, product demonstrations, and various nonrecurrent selling efforts).

trade promotion Sales promotions aimed at marketing intermediaries rather than ultimate consumers.

direct marketing Direct communications other than personal sales contacts between buyer and seller, designed to generate sales, information requests, or store visits.

public relations Firm's communications and relationships with its various publics.

publicity Stimulation of demand for a good, service, place, idea, person, or organization by unpaid placement of commercially significant news or favorable media presentations.

FIGURE 15.6

Sponsorship Spending by North American Corporations*

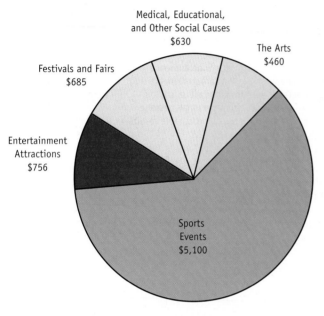

Data reported in Alan Baseden, "Up Front: The Big Picture," *Business Week,* February 8, 1999, p. 8.

 claritin.com

TV and radio to print and the Internet. They have become a $20 billion worldwide business.[15]

Sponsorship occurs when an organization provides cash or in-kind resources to an event or activity in exchange for a direct association with that event or activity. Essentially, the sponsor purchases two things: (1) the exposure potential with the activity's audience and (2) the image associated with the activity by its audience. The sponsorship arrangement typically involves advertising that includes direct mail, sales promotion, and personal selling at the event itself. It also introduces another form of relationship marketing, bringing together the event, its participants, and the sponsoring firms.

Sponsorship Spending

Global marketers have flocked to sponsorships as a means of reaching an increasingly segmented audience to leverage the equity of sports and entertainment properties. In addition, an army of e-commerce companies found sponsorships to be a quick way to enhance—and, in many cases, initiate—brand awareness. Sponsorships also provide a platform through which sports and entertainment properties can expand their programs and attract new partners. Even utilities and pharmaceutical firms that sell over-the-counter medication and prescription drugs are also increasing their activities. Claritin marketers were the first to include sponsorships as part of their promotional mix for prescription drugs. Part of the allergy medicine's $200 million annual promotion budget was spent on its title as the official antihistamine of Major League Baseball. As Figure 15.6 shows, two-thirds of the $7.6 billion spent annually by commercial sponsors in the U.S. and Canada goes to sporting events.[16]

A total of 61 companies spent more than $10 million to acquire sponsorships last year. Philip Morris, with its Kraft Foods and Miller Brewing Co. divisions, is the largest sponsor with over $145 million in sponsorship commitments. Anheuser-Busch placed second; General Motors, third; followed by The Coca-Cola Company and rival PepsiCo.

Marketers underwrite varying levels of sponsorships depending on the amount their companies wish to spend and the types of events. For example, a marketer might choose to be a *title sponsor* of an event. The title sponsor's name would be included in the event title and displayed in other places such as the hospitality tent, on-site signs, merchandise, and tickets. Examples of title sponsorships include the FedEx Orange Bowl football game and the Cadillac Seniors Professional Golf Association Tour. Total costs for a title sponsorship typically amount to $750,000 plus a commitment to purchase $1 million in TV advertising during the event's telecast.

Some marketers choose less expensive forms of sponsorship. A *presenting sponsor* receives the same benefits as the title sponsor (minus the use of the company name in the event title) for perhaps a $300,000 fee plus $500,000 in television advertising. As many as seven firms can be *associate sponsors*, which entitles them to on-site signs for fees ranging from $30,000 to $35,000. Many events also include official product sponsors. Infiniti was the title sponsor for the U.S. Men's Amateur Tennis Tournament, and Evian bottled water and adidas sports apparel were product sponsors. Banners with the sponsors' names and logos were displayed in local tennis clubs around the country.

Growth of Sponsorships

Commercial sponsorship of sporting and cultural events is not a new phenomenon. Aristocrats in ancient Rome sponsored gladiator competitions and chariot races featuring teams that were often supported financially by competing businesses. Over 2,000 years ago, wealthy Athenians underwrote drama, musical, and sporting festivals. Craft guilds in 14th-century England sponsored plays (occasionally insisting that the playwrights insert "plugs" for their lines of work in the scripts). In the United States during the 1880s, streetcar companies commonly sponsored local baseball teams.

Sponsorship as a promotional alternative has grown rapidly over the past three decades. During this period, corporate sponsorship spending has increased faster than promotional outlays for advertising and sales promotion. Several factors have influenced the growth of commercial sponsorships:

- Government restrictions on tobacco and alcohol advertising and the growing reluctance of newspaper and magazine publishers to accept print ads for alcoholic beverages and tobacco products have led marketers to seek out alternative promotional media.
- Escalating costs of traditional advertising media make commercial sponsorships cost-effective marketing tools.
- Additional opportunities resulting from diverse leisure activities, such as beach volleyball, in-line skating, and parasailing, as well as the increasing array of sporting events featured on television and in newspapers and magazines, allow marketers to target specific audiences.
- Greater media coverage of sponsored events allows sponsors to gain greater exposure for their money.
- Global marketers recognize sponsorship as an effective way to reach an international audience in a manner that is universally understood.
- The proven effectiveness of a sponsorship that is properly planned, linked to predetermined objectives, and aimed at specified target markets can buy highly effective marketing contacts. Moreover, sponsorships represent alternatives to the increased clutter associated with advertising and direct mail.

How Sponsorship Differs from Advertising

Even though sponsorship spending and traditional advertising spending represent forms of nonpersonal selling, they are more different from than similar to one another. Chief among these differences are the sponsor's degree of control versus that of advertising, the nature of the message, audience reaction, and measurements of effectiveness.

Marketers have considerable control over the quantity and quality of market coverage when they advertise. Sponsors, on the other hand, must rely on signs to present their messages. Also, they have little control of sponsored events beyond matching the audiences to profiles of their own target markets. In addition, sponsorship is a mute, nonverbal medium since the message is delivered in association with an activity possessing its own personality in the eyes of its audience. By contrast, a traditional advertisement allows the marketer to create an individual message containing an introduction, a theme, and a conclusion.

Audiences react differently to sponsorship as a communications medium than to other media. The sponsor's investment provides a recognizable benefit to the sponsored activity that the audience can appreciate. As a result, sponsorship is often viewed more positively than traditional advertising.

Assessing Sponsorship Results

To assess the results of sponsorships, marketers utilize some of the same techniques by which they measure advertising effectiveness. However, the differences between the two promotional alternatives often necessitate

MARKETING   DICTIONARY

sponsorship Provision of funds for a sporting or cultural event in exchange for a direct association with the event; in e-commerce, a long-term linkage between a Web site and a marketer.

some unique research techniques, as well. A few corporate sponsors attempt to link expenditures to sales. Kraft General Foods, for example, evaluates the effectiveness of its NASCAR sponsorship by comparing Country Time lemonade sales in the races' primary southeastern U.S. markets with sales in other markets. Other sponsors measure improved brand awareness and image as effectiveness indicators; they conduct traditional surveys before and after the events to secure this information. Still other sponsors measure the impact of their event marketing in public relations terms. Typically, a researcher will count press clippings featuring a sponsor's name or logo and then translate this number into equivalent advertising costs.

Despite the impressive visibility of special events like soccer's World Cup and football's Super Bowl, these events do not necessarily lead directly to increased sales. Marketers want their brands to be associated with characteristics of the sporting event such as speed, accuracy, precision, and teamwork. Since 1931, The Coca-Cola Company has been a sponsor of the Chattanooga Lookouts minor league baseball game. The world-famous, red-and-white logo was painted on a billboard at center field—a perfect place for signage. It is a great promotion for The Coca-Cola Company, but other sports promotions have not been as successful and have cost a lot more money. Jokes Steve Koonin, head of The Coca-Cola Company's 40-person U.S. sport and event marketing staff, "What's the difference between a sign in a stadium and a sign in a bus shelter? One million bucks." Today, The Coca-Cola Company marketers follow a precise six-step evaluation process before undertaking any sponsorship deal.[17]

Using Sponsorship in a Promotional Strategy

Despite sponsorships' limitations with regard to message control and delivery along with problems in measuring effectiveness, the number of firms using sponsorship as a component of the promotional mix continues to grow each year. Figure 15.7 illustrates the step-by-step approach of using sponsorships to accomplish specific marketing objectives.

DIRECT MARKETING

Few promotional mix elements are growing as fast as direct marketing. Overall media spending for direct marketing initiatives such as interactive electronic media, direct mail, telemarketing, infomercials, and direct-response advertising total more than $162 billion. Direct marketing accounts for 57 percent of total U.S. advertising expenditures—some $285 billion in 1998. As Figure 15.8 shows, nearly two-thirds of total direct marketing revenues are generated through telephone marketing and direct mail.[18]

Both consumers and business-to-business marketers rely on this promotional mix element to generate orders or sales leads (requests for more information) that may result in future orders. Direct marketing also helps to increase store traffic (visits to the store or office to evaluate and perhaps purchase the advertised goods or services).

Direct marketing opens new international markets of unprecedented size. Electronic marketing channels have become the focus of direct marketers, and as Chapter 4 pointed out, Web marketing is international marketing. Even direct mail and telemarketing will grow outside the United States as commerce becomes more global. Consumers in Europe and Japan are proving to be responsive to direct marketing. But most global marketing systems remain undeveloped, and many are almost dormant. The growth of international direct marketing is being spurred by marketing operations born in the United States.[19]

Direct marketing communications pursue goals beyond creating product awareness; marketers intend these forms of communication to generate actions such as placing an order, getting more information, or visiting a store by calling a toll-free number, sending back a form or coupon, responding to an e-mail message, or making some other type of response. This action orientation is a major reason for direct marketing's popularity. Other advantages include its interactive nature and the ability to narrowly target market segments and customize communications to them. Because direct marketing communications involve some type of response,

FIGURE 15.7   **Steps in the Sponsorship Process**

① The Product
El Capitan parkas and cold-resistant outerwear, high-priced, lightweight, waterproof winter sportswear in fashion colors that provide maximum protection against low temperatures and bitter winds.

② The Market
Most sales are during late fall and winter months. Consumers are typically teens and Generation Xers and active snow skiers. Performance, quality, and styling justify the premium price.

③ The Problem
El Capitan has low brand awareness due in part to the strong preference for well-established brands such as Gore-Tex.

④ The Solution
El Capitan marketers contact SportSearch, an international research firm that advises the firm to consider sponsoring a sporting event, snowboarding, which would appeal to the target market and coincides with the peak selling season.

⑤ The Decision
El Capitan decides to sponsor the "Snowboarding 2000" series of events at 11 eastern and western U.S. ski resorts since it is the nation's fastest growing sport, it appeals to participants and spectators who match the firm's target market, and it is quickly becoming an international sport. SportSearch is hired to conduct research to determine the right consumer psychographics. Fans will be interviewed to determine their levels of brand loyalty, their roles as opinion leaders, and how they feel about the event's sponsor.

⑧ The Commitment
SportSearch reports are positive. El Capitan marketers renew their sponsorship, add new events, and increase sport marketing spending, but decide to monitor the returns from its sponsorship program on a semiannual basis.

⑦ The Results
After the winter season, SportSearch conducts a general marketing study to determine the results of the sponsorship. Findings are compared to consumers with similar demographic and psychographic profiles.

⑥ The Cost
SportSearch estimates $400,000 would pay for sampling, an official sponsorship, on-site entertainment, and various promotional campaigns such as discounted event tickets, contests, and product coupons.

marketers can measure results more easily than with other forms of advertising and promotion. Also, companies can try different direct marketing packages and media combinations to see which gets the best response. Direct marketing is, therefore, a very powerful tool that helps organizations to win new customers and enhance relationships with existing ones.

The growth of direct marketing parallels the move toward integrated marketing communications in many ways. For example, both respond to fragmented media markets and audiences, growth in customized products, shrinking network broadcast audiences, and the increasing use of databases to target specific markets. Lifestyles also play a role because today's busy consumers want convenience and time savings.

Databases are an important part of direct marketing. Using the latest technology to create sophisticated databases, a company can select a narrow market segment and find good prospects within that segment based on desired characteristics. For example, New York-based Starwood Hotels & Resorts Worldwide used databases from airline and credit-card marketing partners it gained by buying the Westin and Sheraton hotel chains. Airline partners helped the chain identify high-potential targets,

FIGURE 15.8   **Direct Marketing Sales by Media Category**

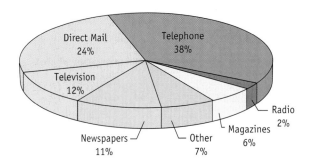

Direct Mail 24%
Telephone 38%
Television 12%
Newspapers 11%
Other 7%
Magazines 6%
Radio 2%

and the credit cards provided lists of people who spend a lot of money at the hotels. In addition to one million members already on file, Starwood marketers enrolled a million more.[20]

Marketers can cut costs and improve returns on dollars spent by identifying those customers who are most likely to respond to messages and by eliminating others from their lists who are not likely to respond. In fact, mining information about customers is a new trend boosted by the growth of e-commerce. Smart DNA software from Austin, Texas–based Smart Technologies can create profiles of customers, suppliers, and business partners by analyzing their movements on a Web site. Database products such as Smart DNA are being used by companies like Compaq, Motorola, and Internet Auction to get a better understanding of their customers.[21]

Direct Marketing Communications Channels

As Figure 15.8 shows, direct marketing uses many different media forms. Each works best for certain purposes, although marketers often combine two or more media in one direct marketing program. For example, a company can start with telemarketing to screen potential customers and then follow up by sending more material by direct mail to interested consumers.

Direct marketing is an important strategic tool for cable and broadcast networks such as NBC and the various A&E networks, which include Arts & Entertainment, Biography, and the History Channel. In addition to traditional direct marketing efforts, the Web also provides another channel for gathering information to use in program development decisions, building customer relationships, and integrating marketing efforts. For example, Biography has a TV program, a magazine, a toll-free telephone number, and an online presence. The magazine is promoted on the Web site, which is promoted in the magazine, and the TV program is promoted in both. A&E's customer database mirrors its viewing demographics: Buyers are more likely to be female, over the age of 35, upscale, and well-educated. Online customers are somewhat younger. The Web sites are visited for content more than commerce. Of the 15 million hits that A&E's sites get each month, only 10 percent result in sales. The online content is varied: On some sites, viewers can download a program quiz, buy a video, or get a sneak preview of a new show. In addition to the Web sites, A&E keeps in touch with its viewer-customers on average of once a month by e-mail by announcing new programs or new products and by using the Web to get viewers more involved with the programs.[22]

Direct Mail

As the amount of information about consumer lifestyles, buying habits, and wants continues to mount, direct mail has become a viable channel for identifying a firm's best prospects. Marketers gather information from internal and external databases, surveys, personalized coupons, and rebates that require responses. Direct mail is a critical tool in creating effective direct-marketing campaigns. It comes in many forms, ranging from sales letters, postcards, brochures, booklets, catalogs, and house organs (periodicals issued by organizations) to video and audio cassettes.

To promote a major Van Gogh exhibition scheduled for Detroit, Boston, and Philadelphia, museum marketers made use of virtually every promotional technique imaginable—advertising, public relations events, and sales presentations to agencies booking group tours. Funds provided by DaimlerChrysler and First Union National Bank were used for direct-mail messages to museum members and potential visitors. As Figure 15.9 illustrates, the informative and persuasive messages were intended to accentuate the value of the event, differentiate it from other offerings, and increase demand.

FIGURE 15.9 | **Targeted Direct Mail: Van Gogh Exhibition**

Direct mail offers advantages such as the ability to select a narrow target market, achieve intensive coverage, send messages quickly, choose from various formats, provide complete information, and personalize each mailing piece. Response rates are measurable and higher than other types of advertising. In addition, direct mailings stand alone and do not compete for attention with magazine articles and television programs. On the other hand, the per-reader cost of direct mail is high, effectiveness depends on the quality of the mailing list, and some consumers object strongly to what they consider "junk mail."

Catalogs

A highly popular form of direct mail is catalogs, with more than 10,000 different consumer, specialty, mail-order catalogs—and thousands more for business-to-business sales—finding their way into almost every mailbox in the United States. In a typical year, they generate over $57 billion in consumer sales and $36 billion in business-to-business sales. The selection includes general-merchandise catalogs, like Office Depot and Spiegel, and specialty catalogs like Williams-Sonoma for culinary goods and Ross-Simon for jewelry. Companies often develop several versions of their catalogs for different audiences and seasons. The Oriental Trading Co. sends catalogs that contain special holiday items from Valentine's and St. Patrick's Day novelties to Halloween and Thanksgiving items. In this way, catalogs provide an ideal format for customized marketing by allowing marketers to divide their products into narrow categories for specific segments and product lines. In 1983, Sears exchanged its all-inclusive catalog for more than 20 specialty catalogs that focus on segments such as women's clothing, tools, and home furnishings.

Many companies, such as Sears and Radio Shack, built their businesses and created a well-known image through their catalogs. In fact, for years, many companies depended on catalogs as their only or primary sales method—Spiegel, L. L. Bean, Lands' End, and Eddie Bauer, are some well-known examples. More recently, however, catalog companies have expanded into Web sites and some have even opened retail stores to increase sales and market share. Sophisticated electronic technologies are changing catalog marketing. Today's catalogs can be updated quickly, providing consumers with the latest information and prices. CD-ROM catalogs allow marketers to display products in three-dimensional views and include video sequences of product demonstrations.

Almost 45 percent of Americans still refuse to purchase from a catalog. Although many consumers like to receive direct mail, others object to unsolicited communications. Many catalog companies do not understand their customers' needs and wants but, instead, send loads of catalogs to millions of people whether or not they want them. The 21st-century consumer is time-pressed and overloaded with information. To help consumers escape the barrage of mail stuffed into their boxes, the Direct Marketing Association established its Mail Preference Service. This consumer service sends name removal forms to people who do not wish to receive direct-mail advertising. It also provides add-on forms for those consumers who enjoy receiving lots of mail.[23]

Telemarketing

Any person whose dinner has been interrupted by a sales call can attest that telemarketing is the most frequently used form of direct marketing. It provides marketers with a high return on their expenditures, an immediate response, and the opportunity for personalized, two-way conversations. **Telemarketing** refers to direct marketing conducted entirely by telephone. It can be classified as either outbound or inbound contacts. *Outbound telemarketing* involves a sales force that uses only the telephone to contact customers, reducing the cost of making personal visits. The customer initiates *inbound telemarketing*, which typically provides a toll-free number for customers to use at their convenience to obtain information and/or make

The Grateful Dead Is Still Alive!

BACKGROUND For over 30 years, the Grateful Dead has been a global rock-and-roll icon. With a unique but consistent music style and a carefully tended long-term relationship with its fans, the band was a case study in niche marketing. With the death of its lead singer and guitarist Jerry Garcia in 1995, the band passed away but a brand was born. Grateful Dead Productions (GDP), the band's long-time corporate entity, has pursued a marketing strategy that continues to appeal to loyal fans (called Deadheads) while attracting even more new fans.

THE CHALLENGE A truism in marketing is that the best brands are those that continually reinvent themselves. Despite Garcia's death, GDP marketers have strengthened the brand and increased sales of licensed products through a variety of promotional efforts. Their goal is to capitalize on the Grateful Dead's strong image and cult status.

continued on next page

 **oriental.com**

MARKETING DICTIONARY

telemarketing Promotional presentation involving the use of the telephone for outbound contacts by salespeople or inbound contacts initiated by customers who want to obtain information and place orders.

THE STRATEGY World headquarters of Grateful Dead Productions, the best-known, rock-music cataloger, is located in a 32,000-square-foot building in San Francisco. Over 15,000 people on its mailing list receive the combination magazine and catalog filled with over 500 items ranging from golf balls to CDs and from baby clothes to bracelets. Over 1,000 orders are filled each day from catalog shoppers and Web site customers. The highly-profitable, debt-free GDP is still operated by its founders with an overriding goal of catering to fans' devotion to the Grateful Dead's style of music.

THE OUTCOME Although the band has not performed since Garcia's death, its legions of followers refuse to let the memories fade. Licensing deals, record sales, and Grateful Dead novelties generate over $60 million in annual revenues. It may have been a long, strange trip, but for the original band members, who jointly own GDP, it has been a profitable one as well.

purchases. Like direct mail, telemarketing taps into databases to target calls based on customer characteristics like family income, number of children, and home ownership. For example, income is an important criterion for banks who use telemarketing to solicit new credit-card customers.

Telemarketing is gaining importance in the marketing strategies of many firms; revenues from phone sales, now at $600 billion annually, are expected to grow about 9 percent per year. New *predictive dialer* devices improve telemarketing's efficiency and reduce costs by automating the dialing process to skip busy signals and answering machines. When the dialer reaches a human voice, it instantaneously puts the call through to a salesperson. This technology is often combined with a print advertising campaign that features a toll-free number for inbound telemarketing. In Figure 15.10, Dillard's print ad explains its Bridal Registry program and invites brides-to-be to visit the company's Web site or to call the toll-free number. Electronic shoppers can also use the company's Web address.

Business-to-business telemarketing is on the rise as well. Marketers at Xerox and long-distance telephone companies use telemarketing to develop sales leads. Because recipients of both consumer and business-to-business telemarketing calls often find them annoying, the Federal Trade Commission passed a Telemarketing Sales Rule in 1996. The rule cracks down on abusive telemarketing practices by establishing allowed calling hours and regulating call content. Companies must clearly disclose details of any exchange policies, maintain lists of people who do not want to receive calls, and keep records of telemarketing scripts, prize winners, customers, and employees for two years. While designed to protect customers against fraud—with losses estimated in excess of $40 billion, almost 10 percent of telemarketing-generated revenues—the rule also helps improve the image of telemarketers. Consumers can cut down on undesirable sales calls by requesting that the DMA Telephone Preference Service put them on the "do not call" list.

FIGURE 15.10   **Offering Toll-Free Telephone Numbers to Catalog Shoppers**

 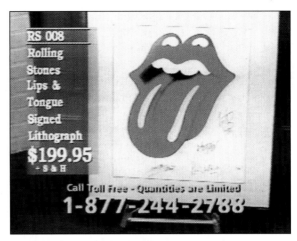

An $11 million infomercial campaign was used to market lithography, coinciding with the Rolling Stones' recent tour.

Direct Marketing via Broadcast Channels

Broadcast direct marketing can take three basic forms: brief direct-response ads on television or radio, home-shopping channels, and infomercials. Direct-response spots typically run 30, 60, or 90 seconds and include product descriptions and toll-free telephone numbers for ordering. Often shown on cable television and independent stations and tied to special-interest programs, broadcast direct marketing usually encourages viewers to respond immediately. Radio direct-response ads also provide product descriptions and addresses or phone numbers to contact the sellers. Radio proves expensive compared to other direct marketing media, and listeners may not pay close enough attention to catch the number or may not be able to write it down because they are driving a car, which accounts for a major portion of radio listening time.

Home shopping channels like Quality Value Channel (QVC) and Home Shopping Network (HSN) represent another type of television direct marketing. Broadcasting around the clock, these and similar channels offer consumers a variety of products from jewelry to toys to insurance. Customers place orders via toll-free telephone numbers and pay for their purchases by credit card. They work best for products in the $20 to $50 range.

Infomercials are 30-minute or longer product commercials that resemble regular television programs. Because of their length, infomercials do not get lost as easily as 30-second commercials can, and they permit marketers to present their products in more detail. Infomercials also provide toll-free telephone numbers so viewers can order products or request more information. Although infomercials incur higher production costs than prime-time, 30-second ads on national network TV, they generally air on less expensive cable channels and in late-night time slots on broadcast stations. However, these timing limitations may prevent marketers from reaching desired audiences. Another disadvantage of infomercials is their poor image.

Florida-based Reliant Interactive Media Corp. recently created an infomercial to sell licensed Rolling Stones merchandise, including signed lithographs and memorabilia, that coincided with the band's "No Security" tour. The $11 million promotional campaign, which ran on HSN, directs consumers to both a toll-free telephone number and a Web site. In addition, the infomercial was aired on independent local broadcast television channels in each planned concert city prior to the tour date, and print ads appeared in newspapers for local markets and even in *USA Today*. [24]

www.lifestylesmall.com

Electronic Direct Marketing Channels

Anyone who has ever logged onto the Web is abundantly aware of the growing number of commercial advertisements that now clutter their computer screen. Web advertising is a recurring theme throughout this text, alluding to its importance as a component of the promotional mix. In fact, Chapter 4 explained the growing role e-commerce is playing in contemporary marketing practices. Last year, Web companies sold $1 billion in advertising, and that number grows with each new application of electronic technology.

Web advertising, however, is only one component of electronic direct marketing. E-mail direct marketers have found that traditional practices used in print and broadcast media are easily adapted to electronic messaging. Experts agree that the basic rules for online direct marketing mirror those of traditional practices. Any successful offline direct marketing campaign can be applied to e-mail promotions.

Electronic media deliver data instantly to direct marketers and help them to track customer-buying cycles quickly. As a result, they can place customer-acquisition programs online for about 50 percent to 80 percent less than the cost of traditional programs. In the early years of the Internet, the most predominant products for direct marketers were books, music CDs, wine, and gourmet foods. Today, however, there seems to be no limit to the variety of goods and services available to online shoppers. In fact, consumer-to-consumer sales through auction sites are becoming the most popular avenue for direct online sales.

Other Direct Marketing Channels

Print media like newspapers and magazines do not support direct marketing as effectively as do Web marketing and telemarketing. However, print media and other traditional direct marketing channels are still critical to the success of all electronic media channels. For example, magazine ads with toll-free telephone numbers enhance inbound telemarketing campaigns. Companies can place ads in magazines or newspapers, include reader-response cards, or place special inserts targeted for certain market segments within the publications.

bhg.com

Kiosks provide another outlet for electronic sales. Price Costco's Quest buying service allows consumers to purchase a wide range of product offerings using computer terminals with touch-screen technology. *Better Homes & Gardens'* IMC program has added a high-tech kiosk to its annual tour that promotes home decor through displays in malls across America. Kiosks and sampling counters allow consumers to interact with elements of their dream house. They can shop for furniture online, see food prepared, and get information on products promoted in the tour and advertised in the magazine. The tour has a Kitchen Stage where chefs cook, a Kids' Corner with children's activities, and individual counters where sponsors' products are displayed. Many elements of the promotional mix tie the various activities together in this one event, including personal selling, advertising, sales promotions, and public relations.[25]

DEVELOPING AN OPTIMAL PROMOTIONAL MIX

6

Identify the primary determinants of a promotional mix.

By blending advertising, personal selling, sales promotion, and public relations to achieve marketing objectives, marketers create a promotional mix. Since they can refer to no quantitative measures to determine the effectiveness of each mix component in a given market segment, the choice of an effective mix of promotional elements presents one of marketers' most difficult tasks. Several factors influence the effectiveness of a promotional mix: (1) the nature of the market, (2) the nature of the product, (3) the stage in the product life cycle, (4) the price, and (5) the funds available for promotion.

Nature of the Market

The marketer's target audience has a major impact on the choice of a promotion method. When a market includes a limited number of buyers, personal selling may prove a highly effective technique. However, markets characterized by large numbers of potential customers scattered over sizable geographic areas may make the cost of contact by personal salespeople prohibitive. In such instances, extensive use of advertising may make sense. The type of customer also affects the promotional mix. Personal selling works better in a target market made up of industrial purchasers or retail and wholesale buyers than in a target market consisting of ultimate consumers. Similarly, pharmaceutical firms use large sales forces to sell prescription drugs directly to physicians and hospitals, but they advertise to promote over-the-counter drugs for the consumer market. When a prescription drug receives FDA approval to be sold over the counter, the drug firm must switch its promotional strategy from personal selling to consumer advertising.

Nestlé marketers have used IMC concepts to reintroduce the Nescafé brand to a growing youth market. Nescafé, the number one coffee brand everywhere but in the United States, is targeting the younger coffeehouse crowd. The new Nescafé includes seven trendy flavors of Frothé and eight whole-bean coffees. The $16 million advertising and promotional campaign is part of Nestlé's global strategy to build its brand worldwide.[26]

nescafe.com

Nature of the Product

A second important factor in determining an effective promotional mix is the product itself. Highly standardized products with minimal servicing requirements usually depend less on personal selling than do custom products with technically complex features and/or requirements for frequent maintenance. Consumer products are more likely to rely heavily on advertising than are business products.

Promotional mixes vary within each product category. For example, installations typically rely more heavily on personal selling than does the marketing of operating supplies. In contrast, the promotional mix for a convenience product is likely to involve more emphasis on manufacturer advertising and less on personal selling. On the other hand, personal selling plays an important role in the promotion of shopping products, and both personal and nonpersonal selling are important in the promotion of specialty goods. A personal-selling emphasis is also likely to prove more effective than other alternatives in promotions for products involving trade-ins.

Stage in the Product Life Cycle

The promotional mix must be tailored to the product's stage in the product life cycle. In the introductory stage, heavy emphasis on personal selling helps to inform the marketplace of the merits of the new good or service. Salespeople contact marketing intermediaries to secure interest in and commitment to handling the offering. Trade shows frequently inform and educate prospective dealers and ultimate consumers.

Marketers of new products may need to work closely with customers to answer questions and adjust promotional mixes as needed. Advertising and sales promotion at this stage create awareness and stimulate initial purchases. For example, marketers for digital versatile disk (DVD) systems have met resistance in the U.S. market. Americans have not rushed to trade in their perfectly good television sets and VCRs for the high cost of new technology. In an attempt to boost sales, manufacturers of DVD players, including Sony, Panasonic, Philips, Toshiba, RCA, Samsung, and Pioneer, teamed up with several leading movie studios in a promotional campaign that ran in leading news and entertainment magazines. As Figure 15.11 explains, with the purchase of any of the participating brands of DVD players, customers receive 5 free DVD movies and 13 free rentals on Blockbuster DVD movies.

As the good or service moves into the growth and maturity stages, advertising gains relative importance in persuading consumers to make purchases. Marketers continue to direct personal-selling efforts at marketing intermediaries in an attempt to expand distribution. As more competitors enter the marketplace, advertising begins to stress product differences to persuade consumers to purchase the firm's brand. In the maturity and early decline stages, firms frequently reduce advertising and sales promotion expenditures.

Mature products often require creative promotions to keep the product in the mind of the consumer. By the end of the 1990s, home video rental stores like Blockbuster, Hollywood Video,

FIGURE 15.11 DVD Players: Promotion for a New Product to Stimulate Demand

and Movie Gallery revamped their promotions and their prices to keep traffic in the stores. Special rental deals are frequently offered for special events and during holidays like Halloween and Christmas. Some campaigns offer free popcorn and sodas with the rental of a minimum number of movies. Many video-rental retailers offer quantity discounts, such as rent three and get one free.

Price

The price of the good or service is the fourth factor that affects the choice of a promotional mix. Advertising dominates the promotional mixes for low-unit-value products due to the high per-contact costs in personal selling. These costs make the sales call an unprofitable tool in promoting lower-value goods and services. Advertising, in contrast, permits a low promotional expenditure per sales unit because it reaches mass audiences. For low-value consumer goods, such as chewing gum, soft drinks, and snack foods, advertising is the most feasible means of promotion. On the other hand, consumers of high-priced items like luxury cars expect lots of well-presented information. High-tech direct marketing promotions like videocassettes, CD-ROMs, fancy brochures, and personal selling appeal to these potential customers.

Funds Available for Promotion

A real barrier in implementing any promotional strategy is the size of the promotional budget. A single, 30-second television commercial during the Super Bowl telecast costs an advertiser $2 million. While millions of viewers may see the commercial, making the cost-per-contact relatively low, such an expenditure exceeds the entire promotional budgets of thousands of firms.

Perhaps the biggest budget for any promotion during the 20th century was the "City of Millionaires" contest underwritten by the world's richest man, Bill Gates. The contest was an

TABLE 15.3	Factors Influencing Choice of Promotional Mix

	EMPHASIS	
	PERSONAL SELLING	**ADVERTISING**
Nature of the market		
Number of buyers	Limited number	Large number
Geographic concentration	Concentrated	Dispersed
Type of customer	Business purchaser	Ultimate consumer
Nature of the product		
Complexity	Custom-made, complex	Standardized
Service requirements	Considerable	Minimal
Type of good or service	Business	Consumer
Use of trade-ins	Trade-ins common	Trade-ins uncommon
Stage in the product life cycle	Often emphasized at every stage; heavy emphasis in the introductory and early growth stages in acquainting marketing inter-mediaries and potential consumers with the new good or service	Often emphasized at every stage; heavy emphasis in the latter part of the growth stage, as well as the maturity and early decline stages, to persuade consumers to select specific brands
Price	High unit value	Low unit value

elaborate effort to increase Microsoft Network subscribers in U.S. towns with populations under 100,000. The town that signed up the most households to the Microsoft Network won the grand prize: $1 million to each household in the city. Unfortunately, most companies do not have pockets this deep when it comes to promotion budgets.[27] Table 15.3 summarizes the factors that influence the determination of an appropriate promotional mix: nature of the market, nature of the product, stage in the product life cycle, and price.

PULLING AND PUSHING PROMOTIONAL STRATEGIES

Marketers may implement essentially two promotional alternatives: a pulling strategy and a pushing strategy. A **pulling strategy** is a promotional effort by the seller to stimulate final-user demand, which then exerts pressure on the distribution channel. When marketing intermediaries stock a large number of competing products and exhibit little interest in any one of them, a firm may have to implement a pulling strategy to motivate them to handle the product. In such instances, this strategy is implemented with the objective of building consumer demand so that consumers will request the product from retail stores.

Advertising and sales promotion often contribute to a company's pulling strategy. Home Depot's IMC strategy combines personal selling, sales promotion, and advertising. The home-improvement chain holds in-store seminars on product usage and project demonstrations and offers tips on various activities from plumbing to gardening. Sales personnel are trained to give superior one-to-one customer service. These live promotions are supported with print advertisements, such as the one shown in Figure 15.12, that inform consumers about the wide selection of brand-name tools found at Home Depot.

In contrast, a **pushing strategy** relies more heavily on personal selling. Here the objective is promoting the product to the members of the marketing channel rather than to final users. To achieve this goal, marketers employ cooperative advertising allowances, trade discounts,

7

Contrast the two major alternative promotional strategies.

MARKETING **DICTIONARY**

pulling strategy Promotional effort by a seller to stimulate demand among final users, who will then exert pressure on the distribution channel to carry the good or service, pulling it through the marketing channel.

pushing strategy Promotional effort by a seller to members of the marketing channel intended to stimulate personal selling of the good or service, thereby pushing it through the marketing channel.

FIGURE 15.12

Use of a Pulling Strategy by Home Depot

personal selling efforts by salespeople, and other dealer supports. Such a strategy is designed to gain marketing success for the firm's products by motivating representatives of wholesalers and/or retailers to spend extra time and effort promoting the products to customers. About half of manufacturers' promotional budgets—$30 million a year—pays for cash incentives to get retailers to stock their products.

While pulling and pushing strategies are presented here as alternative methods, few companies depend entirely on either one. Most firms combine the two methods. Pharmaceutical marketers have long pursued pushing strategies to promote prescription drugs to doctors and other health-care professionals. These strategies have included activities like advertising in trade journals, sponsoring professional meetings, funding research on the effects of various drugs, and providing free samples to health-care practitioners. Recently, drug manufacturers have also adopted pulling strategies by advertising directly to consumers. For example, Glaxo Wellcome advertises its Flonase, a prescription allergy medication, in consumer magazines.

Timing also affects the choice of promotional strategies. The relative importance of advertising and selling changes during the various phases of the purchase process. Prior to the actual sale, advertising usually is more important than personal selling. However, one of the primary advantages of a successful advertising program is the support it gives the salesperson who approaches the prospect for the first time. Selling activities are more important than advertising at the time of purchase. Personal selling provides the actual mechanism for closing most sales. In the post-purchase period, advertising regains primacy in the promotional effort. It affirms the customer's decision to buy a particular good or service and reminds him or her of the product's favorable qualities by reducing any cognitive dissonance that might occur.

The promotional strategies used by auto marketers illustrate this timing factor. Car makers spend heavily on consumer advertising to create awareness before consumers begin the purchase process. At the time of their purchase decisions, however, the personal-selling skills of dealer salespeople provide the most important tools for closing sales. Finally, advertising frequently maintains post-purchase satisfaction by citing awards such as *Motor Trend's* Car of the Year and results of J. D. Power's customer-satisfaction surveys to affirm buyers' decisions.

BUDGETING FOR PROMOTIONAL STRATEGY

8

Compare the primary methods of developing a promotional budget.

Promotional budgets may differ not only in amount but also in composition. Business-to-business marketers generally invest larger proportions of their budgets in personal selling than in advertising, while the reverse is usually true of most producers of consumer goods. Cannondale Associates, a leading U.S. sales and marketing consulting firm, conducts an annual survey of trade promotion spending in different industries. Figure 15.13 shows how different types of manufacturers typically allocate their promotional budgets.

Evidence suggests that sales initially lag behind promotional expenses for structural reasons—funds spent filling up retail shelves, boosting low initial production, and supplying buyer knowledge. This fact produces a threshold effect in which few sales may result from substantial initial investments in promotion. A second phase might produce sales proportionate to promotional expenditures—the most predictable range. Finally, promotion reaches the area of diminishing returns where an increase in promotional spending fails to produce a corresponding increase in sales.

| FIGURE 15.13 | Allocation of Promotional Budgets |

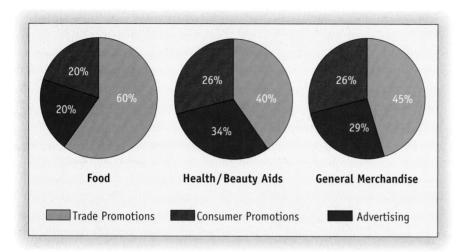

SOURCE: Data from "Trade Promotion Spending and Merchandising, 1999 Industry Study," Cannondale Associates, p. 40.

For example, an initial expenditure of $40,000 may result in sales of 100,000 product units for a consumer goods manufacturer. An additional $10,000 expenditure may generate sales of 30,000 more units, and another $10,000 may produce sales of an additional 35,000 units. The cumulative effect of the expenditures and repeat sales will have generated increasing returns from the promotional outlays. However, as the advertising budget moves from $60,000 to $70,000, the marginal productivity of the additional expenditure may fall to 28,000 units. At some later point, the return may actually become zero or negative as competition intensifies, markets become saturated, and marketers employ less expensive advertising media.

The ideal method of allocating promotional funds would increase the budget until the cost of each additional increment equals the additional incremental revenue received. In other words, the most effective allocation procedure increases promotional expenditures until each dollar of promotional expense is matched by an additional dollar of profit. This procedure—referred to as *marginal analysis*—maximizes the input's productivity. The difficulty arises in identifying the optimal point, which requires a precise balance between marginal expenses for promotion and the resulting marginal receipts. Traditional methods for creating a promotional budget include the percentage-of-sales and fixed-sum-per-unit methods, along with techniques for meeting the competition and achieving task objectives. Each method is briefly examined in Table 15.4.

The **percentage-of-sales method** is perhaps the most common way of establishing promotional budgets. The percentage can be based on sales either from some past period (such as the previous year) or forecasted for a future period (the current year). While this plan is appealing in its simplicity, it does not effectively support the achievement of basic promotional objectives. Arbitrary percentage allocations based on either historical or future sales figures fail to provide required flexibility. Further, the method employs circular reasoning in which the promotional allocation depends on sales rather than vice versa, as it should. For example, a decline in sales would force the marketer to further curtail the firm's promotional outlays, probably contributing to additional revenue losses.

The **fixed-sum-per-unit method** differs from budgeting based on a percentage of sales in only one respect: It allocates a predetermined amount to

MARKETING   DICTIONARY

percentage-of-sales method Allocating funds for promotion during a given time period based on a specified percentage of either past or forecasted sales.

fixed-sum-per-unit method Allocating promotional expenditures as a predetermined dollar amount for each sales or production unit.

TABLE 15.4	Promotional Budget Determination	

METHOD	DESCRIPTION	EXAMPLE
Percentage-of-sales method	Promotional budget is set as a specified percentage of either past or forecasted sales.	"Last year we spent $10,500 on promotion and had sales of $420,000. Next year we expect sales to grow to $480,000, and we are allocating $12,000 for promotion."
Fixed-sum-per-unit method	Promotional budget is set as a predetermined dollar amount for each unit sold or produced.	"Our forecast calls for sales of 14,000 units, and we allocate promotion at the rate of $65 per unit."
Meeting competition method	Promotional budget is set to match competitor's promotional outlays on either an absolute or relative basis.	"Promotional outlays average 4 percent of sales in our industry."
Task-objective method	Once marketers determine their specific, promotional objectives, the amount (and type) of promotional spending needed to achieve them is determined.	"By the end of next year, we want 75 percent of the area high-school students to be aware of our new, highly automated fast-food prototype outlet. How many promotional dollars will it take, and how should they be spent?"

each sales or production unit. This amount can also reflect either historical or forecasted figures. Producers of high-value, consumer durable goods, such as automobiles, often use this budgeting method.

Another traditional budgeting approach, **meeting competition,** simply matches competitors' outlays, either in absolute amounts or relative to the firms' market shares. However, this approach usually only preserves the status quo in which each company retains its percentage of total sales. Expenditures that meet a competitor's budget do not necessarily pertain to a firm's own promotional objectives. Therefore, this method seems inappropriate for most contemporary marketing programs.

The **task-objective method** develops a promotional budget based on a sound evaluation of the firm's promotional objectives. As a result, it attunes its allocation of funds to modern marketing practices. The method involves two sequential steps:

1. The firm's marketers must *define realistic communication goals* that they want the promotional mix to achieve. For example, a firm might specify a goal of a 25 percent increase in brand awareness or a 10 percent rise in the number of consumers who recognize certain specific, differentiating features in a product. This key step specifies in quantitative terms the objectives that promotion should attain. These objectives in turn become integral parts of the promotional plan.

2. Marketers must *determine the amount and type of promotional activity required for each objective* that they have set. Combined, these units become the firm's promotional budget.

A crucial assumption underlies the task-objective approach: Marketers can measure the productivity of each promotional dollar. That assumption explains why the objectives must be carefully chosen, quantified, and accomplished through promotional efforts. Generally, budgeters should avoid general marketing objectives such as "We want to achieve a 5 percent increase in sales." A sale is a culmination of the effects of *all* elements of the marketing mix. A more appropriate promotional objective might be "We want to achieve an 8 percent response rate from a targeted direct-mail advertisement."

Promotional budgeting always requires difficult decisions. Still, recent research studies and the spread of computer-based models have made it a more manageable problem than it used to be.

MEASURING THE EFFECTIVENESS OF PROMOTION

It is widely recognized that part of a firm's promotional effort is ineffective. John Wanamaker, a successful 19th-century retailer, observed the following: "I know half the money I spend on advertising is wasted, but I can never find out which half."

Evaluating the effectiveness of a promotion today is a far different exercise in marketing research than it was even a few decades ago. For years, marketers depended on store audits conducted by large organizations like A. C. Nielsen. Other research groups conducted warehouse withdrawal surveys. These research studies were designed to determine whether sales had risen as the direct result of a particular promotional campaign. In the 1980s, the introduction of scanners and automated checkout lanes completely changed marketing research. For the first time, retailers and manufacturers had a tool to obtain sales data quickly and efficiently. The problem was that the collected data was used for little else than determining how much of which product was bought at what price and at what time.

By the 1990s, marketing research entered another evolutionary period with the advent of the Internet. Now marketing researchers can delve into each customer's purchase behavior, lifestyle, preferences, opinions, and habits. All of this information can also be obtained in a matter of seconds. The next section explains the impact that electronic technologies have on measuring promotional effectiveness. However, marketers today still depend on two basic measurement tools: direct sales tests results and indirect evaluations.

Most marketers would prefer to use a *direct sales results* test to measure the effectiveness of promotion. Such an approach would reveal the specific impact on sales revenues for each dollar of promotional spending. This type of technique has always eluded marketers, however, due to their inability to control other variables operating in the marketplace. A firm may receive $20 million in additional sales orders following a new, $1.5 million advertising campaign, but the market success may really have resulted from price increases for competing products rather than from the advertising outlays.

Marketers often encounter difficulty isolating the effects of promotion from those of other market elements and outside environmental variables. *Indirect evaluation* helps researchers to concentrate on quantifiable indicators of effectiveness, such as *recall* (how much members of the target market remember about specific products or advertisements) and *readership* (size and composition of a message's audience). The basic problem with indirect measurement is the difficulty of relating these variables to sales. For example, does extensive ad readership lead to increased sales?

Marketers need to ask the right questions and understand what they are measuring. Promotion to build sales volume produces measurable results in the form of short-term returns; brand-building programs, however, and efforts to generate or enhance consumers' perceptions of value in a product, brand, or organization cannot be measured over the short term.

Measuring Online Promotions

The latest challenge facing marketers is how to measure the effectiveness of electronic media. As companies rush onto the Web, they are also moving quickly to develop techniques to measure the success of their promotions. Marketers agree that the Web helps traditional promotional efforts, but not all the "old ways" transfer to Web promotions. Early attempts at measuring online promotional effectiveness involved counting *hits* (user requests for a file) and *visits* (pages downloaded or read in one session). But, as Chapter 4 explained, it is not how many times a Web site is visited, but how many people actually buy something. Traditional numbers that work for other media forms

MARKETING   DICTIONARY

meeting competition Allocating promotional spending to match that of a competitor, either as an absolute amount or relative to the firms' market shares.

task-objective method Allocating promotional spending by defining goals and then determining the amount of promotional spending needed to achieve them.

SOLVING AN ETHICAL CONTROVERSY

Commercial Advertising versus Freedom of Speech

For the past quarter century, consumer advocates and social activists have been involved in a series of legal battles to control commercial advertising of so-called "sin products," which include cigarettes, liquor, and casino gambling.

In the 1970s, the tobacco industry began a defensive promotional struggle that continues today, although its efforts have been less than successful. Then, in the 1980s, beer and liquor marketers became the target, and inevitably, in the 1990s, casino gambling came under the gun. In 1998, the U.S. Supreme Court struck down a 1934 Federal Communications Commission law prohibiting private casinos from advertising on radio or television. While many cities, including Chicago, Cleveland, and Los Angeles, have attempted to ban outdoor billboards featuring alcohol ads and lobbyists have pushed to prevent radio and television casino ads, the Supreme Court ruled that the federal government could not make exceptions in advertising.

 Should the federal government regulate commercial advertising of alcohol, tobacco, and gambling?

Pro
1. The ability of advertising to increase consumption is well-known. Since underage drinking represents illegal behavior, advertising that uses youthful models or otherwise encourages illegal behavior should be prevented by law.
2. Without advertising regulation, compulsive gamblers and people with drinking problems would not only be fair game for alcohol, tobacco, and gambling marketers, but would actually be targeted as "loyal" and "preferred" customers.

Con
1. Tobacco, alcohol, and casino gambling are all products in a mature market. As one First Amendment legal expert explains, "The Supreme Court has not recognized what marketing experts have known for years; that in a mature market, advertising's primary effects are [not to increase consumption but] to encourage brand switching and maintain brand loyalty."
2. Consumers will be able to control advertising activities through their purchasing decisions.
3. Industry self-regulation creates a code of conduct for advertisers.

Summary
This controversy will be settled when the Supreme Court determines whether the First Amendment to the U.S. Constitution is being used or abused. The federal government has played an active role in controlling commercial advertising that, by some accounts, is harmful to society as a whole. On the other side of the argument, making exceptions in advertising laws for certain groups and not others is unfair and prohibits free speech.

SOURCES: Wendy Melillo, "Spirited Debate," *Adweek*, September 6, 1999, pp. 20-22; and Laurie Asseo, "Court Axes Federal Ban on Casino Gambling Ads," *Mobile Register*, June 15, 1999, p. 5A.

---

are not necessarily relevant indicators of effectiveness for a Web site. For one thing, the Web combines both advertising and direct marketing. Web pages effectively integrate advertising and other content, such as product information, that may be the page's main feature. For another consideration, consumers generally choose the advertisements they want to see on the Net, whereas traditional broadcast or print media automatically expose consumers to ads.

One-way marketers measure performance is by incorporating some form of direct response into their promotions. This technique also helps them to compare different promotions for effectiveness and rely on facts rather than opinions. Consumers may say they will try a product in response to a survey question yet not actually buy it. A firm may send out three different direct-mail offers in the same promotion and compare response rates. An offer to send for a sample may generate a 75 percent response rate; coupons might show a 50 percent redemption rate; and rebates might only appeal to 10 percent of the targeted group.

The two major techniques for setting Internet advertising rates are *cost per impression (CPM)* and *cost per response (click-throughs)*. CPM is a measurement technique that relates the cost of an ad to every thousand people who view it. In other words, anyone who sees the page containing the banner or other form of ad creates one impression. This measure assumes that the site's principal purpose is to display the advertising pitch. Cost per response is a direct marketing technique that relates the cost of an ad to the number of people who click on it. Measurement based on click-throughs assumes that those who actually click on an ad want more information and, therefore, consider the ad valuable. Both rating techniques have merit. Site publishers point out that click-through rates are influenced by the creativity of the ad's message. Advertisers, on the other hand, point out that the Web ad has value to those who click on it for additional information.

THE VALUE OF MARKETING COMMUNICATIONS

The nature of marketing communications is changing as new formats transform the traditional idea of an advertisement or sales promotion. Sales messages are now placed subtly, or not so subtly, in movies and television shows, blurring the lines between promotion and entertainment and changing the traditional definition of advertising. Messages show up on stadium turnstiles, buses, and even police cars.

9

Defend promotion against common public criticisms.

Despite new tactics by advertisers, promotion has often been the target of criticism. People complain that it offers nothing of value to society and simply wastes resources. Others criticize that promotion encourages consumers to buy unnecessary products that they cannot afford. Many ads seem to insult people's intelligence, and they criticize the ethics—or lack thereof— displayed by advertisers and salespeople. New forms of promotion are considered even more insidious because marketers make pitches that do not look like paid advertisements. Many of these complaints cite true problems. Some salespeople use unethical sales tactics. Some product advertising hides its promotional nature or targets consumer groups that can least afford the advertised goods or services. Many television commercials do, in fact, contribute to the growing problem of cultural pollution.

While promotion can certainly be criticized on many counts, it also plays a crucial role in modern society. This point is best understood by examining the social, business, and economic importance of promotion.

Social Importance

Criticisms of promotional messages as tasteless and lacking any contribution to society sometimes ignore the fact that our social framework provides no commonly accepted set of standards or priorities for these judgments. We live in a varied economy characterized by consumer segments with differing needs, wants, and aspirations. What one group finds tasteless may be quite appealing to another. This point was made abundantly clear recently when Casey Martin wanted to play in the PGA Tour with the aid of a golf cart rather than walking from hole to hole, as required by PGA rules, on his disabled right leg. PGA officials refused to make an exception to the no-cart rule, creating unfavorable publicity and causing many backers of the tour to reconsider their sponsorships. Then Nike's CEO Phil Knight stepped in, signing Martin to Nike's "Just do it" campaign, and the tables began to turn. Martin sued the PGA and won— the first time the Americans with Disabilities Act was invoked for competition in a major sport. As one writer for *Sports Illustrated* commented, "Anybody with a bus token for a heart knows Martin should get a cart."[28]

Promotional strategy faces an averaging problem that escapes many of its critics. The one generally accepted standard in a market society is freedom of choice for the consumer. Consumer buying decisions eventually determine acceptable practices in the marketplace.

Promotion has also become an important factor in campaigns aimed at achieving socially oriented objectives, such as stopping smoking, family planning, physical fitness, and elimination of drug abuse. Advertising agencies donate their expertise to creating public service announcements (PSAs) aimed at promoting these causes. Figure 15.14 uses humor to emphasize the importance of talking to kids about drugs.

FIGURE 15.14 Promotional Message Addressing a Universal Social Concern

Promotion performs an informative and educational task crucial to the functioning of modern society. As with everything else in life, what is important is *how* promotion is used rather than *whether* it is used. Chapter 16 will return to the subject of ethics in advertising.

Business Importance

Promotional strategy has become increasingly important to both large and small business enterprises. The well-documented, long-term increase in funds spent on promotion certainly attests to management's faith in the ability of promotional efforts to encourage attitude changes, brand loyalty, and additional sales. It is difficult to conceive of an enterprise that would not attempt to promote its good or service in some manner. Most modern institutions simply cannot survive in the long run without promotion. Business must communicate with its publics.

Nonbusiness enterprises also recognize the importance of promotional efforts. The U.S. government spends about $300 million a year on advertising and ranks 36th among all U.S. advertisers. The Canadian government is the leading advertiser in Canada, promoting many concepts and programs. Religious organizations have acknowledged the importance of promotional channels to make their viewpoints known to the public at large.

Economic Importance

Promotion has assumed a degree of economic importance, if for no other reason than because it provides employment for thousands of people. More importantly, however, effective promotion has allowed society to derive benefits not otherwise available. For example, the criticism that promotion costs too much isolates an individual expense item and fails to consider its possible beneficial effects on other categories of expenditures.

Promotional strategies increase the number of units sold and permit economies of scale in the production process, thereby lowering the production costs for each unit of output. Lower unit costs allow lower consumer prices, which, in turn, make products available to more people. Similarly, researchers have found that advertising subsidizes the information contents of newspapers and the broadcast media. In short, promotion pays for many of the enjoyable entertainment and educational opportunities in contemporary life as it lowers product costs.

STRATEGIC IMPLICATIONS

It is difficult to overstate the impact of the Internet on the promotional mix of 21st-century marketers. Small companies are on the Web; big businesses are there, as well. Even individual entrepreneurs have found a lucrative new launch pad for their enterprises. But even though cyberspace marketing has been effective in business-to-business transactions and, to a lesser extent, for some types of consumer purchases, a major source of Internet revenues is advertising. The Net has ads for almost every good or service imaginable. In fact, Web companies sell over $1 billion in advertising each year.

However, another aspect of the Web's pervasive presence in contemporary marketing is often overlooked: Online companies must also buy advertising. In addition to electronic advertising, they also depend on traditional, offline advertising and engage in many other promotional activities as well. Online marketers must perform many of the same tasks as their bricks-and-mortar counterparts—order fulfillment, customer service, logistics, and promotion. Net companies spend about as much as traditional ones do to get new consumers—on average, about $50 per customer. As the next chapter will describe in detail, newspapers and radio, two popular promotional media, are relatively inexpensive and finely segmented, allowing marketers to pinpoint certain age, income, and social groups. Billboards, many of which are now electrified and digitalized, are another inexpensive means for reaching mass audiences. And television industry experts have watched "dot com" ad revenues grow by nearly 300 percent.[29]

Integrated marketing communications will continue to play an important role as the Internet brings the global community closer together. The choice of language used online will continue to be English for some time to come, but as translation technologies evolve, communications will become simplified. Astute marketers recognize that even as the language barriers begin to crumble, cultures are likely to become even more segmented, making the selection of an appropriate promotional channel and message for a product or a brand even more critical.

ACHIEVEMENT CHECK SUMMARY

Read the learning objectives that follow, and consider the questions for each one. Answering these questions will reinforce your grasp of the most important concepts in the chapter and will allow you to check how well you have achieved these learning goals. Where a blank appears before a question, answer with *T* or *F* for true/false questions; for multiple-choice questions, choose the letter of the correct answer.

Objective 15.1: Relate the concept of integrated marketing communications to the development of an optimal promotional mix.

1. _____ In a company that practices integrated marketing communications, different departments often wield authority and responsibility for individual promotional elements.

2. _____ An integrated marketing communications (IMC) strategy begins with the product and works forward toward the consumer.

3. _____ Databases and interactive marketing are important IMC tools that help marketers to design mass-communications programs.

Objective 15.2: Explain the relationship of promotional strategy to the process of communication.

1. _____ The term *marketing communications* refers to advertisements appearing in print and broadcast media.

2. _____ The process by which promotional messages reach the consumer involves all of the following except: (a) decoding; (b) feedback; (c) noise; (d) differentiation.

3. _____ The newspaper that runs a press release about a new product represents the encoding of the message.

Objective 15.3: List the objectives of promotion.

1. _____ Vans uses promotions focused on primary demand to increase consumer demand in marketing its extreme-sports shoes.

2. _____ Radisson Seven Seas' ads explain that consumers should pay more for its cruises than for competing products because they offer better service, more activities, and other unique benefits. These ads are an example of promotion designed to (a) stabilize sales; (b) increase demand; (c) accentuate the product's value.

3. _____ Suppose that a toy manufacturer runs summer trade promotions to encourage retailers to stock up on its products. This promotion is intended to differentiate its products.

Objective 15.4: Explain the concept of the promotional mix and its relationship to the marketing mix.

1. _____ Public relations is a component of the personal selling element in the promotional mix.

2. _____ The promotional mix is a subset of the overall marketing mix.

3. _____ Promotional techniques geared toward distributors, retailers, and wholesalers are called (a) direct marketing; (b) trade promotion; (c) joint advertising; (d) public relations.

Objective 15.5: Discuss the role of sponsorships and direct marketing in integrated marketing communications planning.

1. _____ Organizations sponsor events in order to gain media exposure for their products and benefit from the images associated with the events.

2. _____ Commercial sponsorships cost more than traditional advertising media.

3. _____ Which of the following statements about direct marketing is not true?

(a) The Internet can be used for direct marketing. (b) Marketers can measure the results of direct marketing more easily than those of other forms of promotion. (c) Major companies are now using infomercials to describe the benefits of their products. (d) Direct mail represents the largest category of consumer direct marketing spending.

Objective 15.6: Identify the primary determinants of a promotional mix.

1. _____ A company that sells industrial products will typically spend most of its promotional budget on mass-market advertising.

2. _____ The stage in a product's life cycle is an important determinant of a firm's integrated marketing strategy.

3. _____ Promotion cost per sales unit is one reason for choosing advertising to promote low-priced items.

Objective 15.7: Contrast the two major alternative promotional strategies.

1. _____ A pulling strategy relies heavily on personal selling to the members of the marketing channel.

2. _____ An advertisement for Papa John's pizza that includes a two-for-one coupon would form part of a pulling strategy.

3. _____ Companies select either pulling or pushing strategies when promoting their products.

Objective 15.8: Compare the primary methods of developing a promotional budget.

1. _____ A gourmet caterer with sales of $150,000 spent $5,000 for promotion last year. Projected sales are expected to reach $180,000 next year, so it has budgeted $6,000 for promotion. Which method does the firm use to set its promotional budget?

(a) task-objective (b) meeting the competition (c) percentage-of-sales (d) fixed-sum-per-unit

2. _____ The task-objective approach allocates a predetermined amount for each sales or production unit; this amount can be based on either historical or forecasted costs.

3. _____ Marketers using the fixed-sum-per-unit method of promotional budgeting begin by setting reasonable promotional objectives, such as achieving 60 percent consumer awareness by the sixth month after introducing a new product.

Objective 15.9: Defend promotion against common public criticisms.

1. _____ Using product tie-ins in television shows and movies is an unethical promotional practice.

2. _____ Promotion helps to create demand for products and generates employment, an economic benefit to society.

3. _____ An ad describing how gasoline additives reduce air pollution makes a social contribution to society.

Students: See the solutions section located on page S-2 to check your responses to the Achievement Check Summary.

Key Terms

promotion	public relations
marketing communication	publicity
integrated marketing communications (IMC)	sponsorship
	telemarketing
AIDA concept	infomercial
promotional mix	pulling strategy
personal selling	pushing strategy
advertising	percentage-of-sales method
sales promotion	fixed-sum-per-unit method
trade promotion	meeting competition
direct marketing	task-objective method

Review Questions

1. Contrast integrated marketing communications (IMC) with the promotional mix concept. Explain the current emphasis on IMC by marketers.
2. Relate the steps in the communications process to promotional strategy and the AIDA concept. Explain the concept and causes of noise in marketing communications. How can marketers deal with noise?
3. Compare the five basic objectives of promotion. Cite specific examples for each.
4. Explain the concept of the promotional mix. What is its relationship to the marketing mix?
5. Discuss the reasons for the growth of direct marketing and briefly describe the key media that carry its messages.
6. Identify the major determinants of a promotional mix. Describe how they affect the selection of an appropriate blend of promotional techniques.
7. Under what circumstances should marketers adopt a pushing strategy for their promotions? When would a pulling strategy be effective?

8. Identify and briefly explain the alternative methods of developing a promotional budget. Which is the best approach?
9. How can a firm attempt to measure the effectiveness of its promotional efforts? Which techniques most effectively evaluate promotional success?
10. Identify the major public criticisms of promotion. Prepare a defense for each criticism.

Questions for Critical Thinking

1. "Perhaps the most critical promotional question facing the marketing manager concerns when to use each component of promotion." Comment on this statement. Relate your response to the product's classification, product value, marketing channels, price, and timing of the promotional effort.
2. What mix of promotional variables would you use for each of the following products? Why?
   a. WD-40 lubricant
   b. John Deere lawn tractor
   c. independent marketing research firm
   d. tower cranes for high-rise building construction
   e. personalized customer order forms
   f. children's school uniforms
3. Develop a hypothetical promotional budget for the following firms. State percentage allocations instead of dollar amounts for the various promotional variables (such as 30 percent of personal selling, 60 percent for advertising, and 10 percent for public relations).
   a. Titan motorcycles
   b. Harrah's casinos and resorts
   c. Phillips Petroleum Company
   d. Prudential Securities brokerage firm
4. Trace the history of advertising by physicians, dentists, and lawyers. How do these professionals currently promote their services? What restrictions apply to their promotional efforts?
5. Identify one or more firms and/or products associated with the following events or activities. Suggest methods for measuring the effectiveness of sponsorship spending on these events.
   a. LPGA golf tour
   b. Broadway show tour
   c. Boston Marathon
   d. science fair
   e. sailing regatta

1. **AIDA.** Go to an e-commerce Web site, such as *www.buy.com,* and explain how the site has applied the AIDA concept (attention-interest-desire-action).

2. **Sponsorships.** Go to *www.olympic.org* and access information on the Salt Lake Olympic Games of 2002 or the Athens Olympic Games of 2004. Identify the sponsor levels, what the sponsors do at each level, and the companies sponsoring at each level.

3. **Measuring Online Promotions.** Go to RealTIME Media's Web site at *www.realtimemedia.com.* Read 3 or 4 of the case studies explaining what RealTIME has done for some of its clients. Print out the case study you found most interesting and bring it to class to contribute during class discussion.

buy.com

olympic.org

realtimemedia.com

Video Case 15 on Polaroid begins on page VC-17.

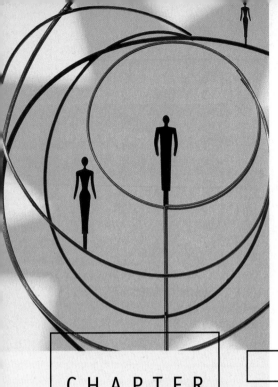

Advertising, Sales Promotion, and Public Relations

CHAPTER OBJECTIVES

1 Explain the current status of advertising, sales promotion, and public relations in today's promotional strategies, and identify two recent trends in advertising.

2 Identify the major types of advertising.

3 Describe the process of creating an advertisement.

4 List and compare the major advertising media.

5 Outline the organization of the advertising function and the role of an advertising agency.

6 Identify the principal methods of sales promotion.

7 Explain the roles of public relations, publicity, and cross promotions in an organization's promotional strategy.

8 Explain how marketers assess promotional effectiveness.

9 Discuss the importance of ethics in a firm's promotional activities.

Kodak: No Negatives Here

Technology is changing the world around us so rapidly that it resembles an automatic high-speed camera shutter. Fiction has turned to fact in every aspect of life. DNA and biotechnology discoveries, wireless communications, and e-commerce are all examples of fiction turned fact—snapshots at the beginning of a new century. And during the entire 20th century while all these events were taking place, Kodak was there capturing memories on film. The 112-year old, Rochester, New York–based company has not simply helped record history—it has made history.

With the slogan "You push the button, we do the rest," George Eastman put the first simple camera into the hands of a world of picture takers. Today, the company still focuses on providing convenience and quality to customers so they can experience photography by capturing and reliving their more cherished moments. From glass plates in 1888 to digital images in 2000, Kodak has made the transition to the Internet with the same ba-

sic idea: Kodak is not in the film business, it is in the picture business. Today, it sports a Web site with 30,000 pages that markets images to 16 countries. But the Web is more than just a brochure-type marketing tool. As Kodak's director of Internet initiatives, Terry Lund, explains, "It was clear that e-commerce was going to be a big deal and we did our initial e-commerce pilot in 1996. We started by selling NASCAR racing memorabilia—Kodak was a sponsor of NASCAR races, and it was a way to learn about e-commerce without having any of our own business units involved."

Kodak was one of the first major companies to take advantage of the Web's potential as a marketing tool. The Internet facilitated the firm's use of both pulling and pushing promotional strategies, described in the previous chapter. Pulling strategies connect Kodak customers with the newest innovations and offerings in digital photography, such as the Picture Playground Web site. In contrast, pushing strategies, such as providing information on the nearest outlets, direct customers to retail distributors for their traditional film and camera purchases. With each new offering, Kodak marketers use print ads, television and radio spots, and Web advertising to introduce the product to photographers around the world. In addition, publicity often helps customers learn about many of Kodak's new offerings through word-of-mouth. Says Internet marketing manager Thomas Hoehn, "In the summer of 1998, people heard there was a new camera coming out. Somehow word got out into the newsgroups, and we started to get flamed by people who wanted information about it. Two weeks before it came out, we had messages from about 3,000 people who wanted to buy it or learn about it, so we sent [mail-outs] saying here's where you can go. It was the kind of marketing that in print could have cost thousands of dollars."

Every day, Kodak's Web site receives some 325,000 page views, and each year, users pull more than 400,000 free software downloads from the site. While Kodak seldom releases information about its revenues, it does brag about the money it has saved. Corporate spokespeople say that the software downloads alone have saved the company more than $10 million, and much

489

more has been saved from the cost of buying and distributing paper documents, such as Kodak catalogs. Putting its Government Markets Catalogue online, for example, saves Kodak nearly $400,000 in printing costs alone.

Kodak has come a long way since it started in the industry in the 19th century. In 1999, Kodak PhotoNet launched a new section on its site called Kodak Picture Playground. The site allows customers who log on to alter their photos digitally. For example, users can "antique" pictures, turning color photos into sepia-toned images. In more humorous applications of the new technology, they can turn realistic images into cartoons or overlay a human face in a photograph on the image of an animal.[1]

CHAPTER OVERVIEW

As Chapter 15 pointed out, nonpersonal elements of promotion include advertising, sales promotion, and public relations—all of which Kodak marketers employ in creating successful business communications and in building strong customer relationships. Thousands of organizations rely on nonpersonal selling in developing their promotional mixes and integrated marketing communications strategies. While advertising is the most visible form of nonpersonal promotion, marketers spend three times as much on sales promotion, and they often use them together to create effective promotional campaigns. For example, Burger King spent $20 million on TV spots to support its tie-in promotions with the release of the Warner Bros. animated feature *Pokémon: The First Movie*. Sales promotion was also featured extensively. Over 100 million premiums were distributed, including trading cards and one of 57 different toys ranging from Pokémon key chains to bean bags.[2]

This chapter begins with a discussion of the types of advertising and explains how advertising is used to achieve a firm's objectives. It then considers alternative advertising strategies and the process of creating an advertisement. Next, the chapter gives a detailed look at various advertising media channels, from television and radio to print advertising and direct mail to outdoor and interactive media. Sales promotion, the second major type of nonpersonal advertising, is explained with detailed discussions of consumer-oriented sales promotions and trade promotions. The chapter then focuses on the importance of public relations, publicity, and cross promotions in e-commerce. Alternative methods of measuring the effectiveness of nonpersonal selling both online and offline are examined. The chapter concludes by exploring current ethical issues relating to nonpersonal selling. ■

1

Explain the current status of advertising, sales promotion, and public relations in today's promotional strategies, and identify two recent trends in advertising.

ADVERTISING

Advertising today is closely related to integrated marketing communications (IMC) in many respects. While IMC involves a message dealing with buyer-seller relationships, **advertising** involves paid, nonpersonal communication through various media with the purpose of informing or persuading members of a particular audience. Advertising is used by marketers to reach target markets such as business firms, not-for-profit organizations, or individuals identified in the message.

While the ability of the Internet to make every marketer a global marketer has become a truism, America remains the home to the world's leading advertisers. General Motors Corp., the global leader in advertising, spends about $3 billion annually—or about $8 million a day—on advertising. The runners-up are Procter & Gamble and Philip Morris Cos., each spending over $2 billion annually. Another 10 marketers spend at least $1 billion per year. Diageo of London, the parent company of Burger King, Guinness, and Pillsbury, is the only member of the top ten advertisers that has its headquarters outside the United States. Annual U.S. advertising expenditures total $200 billion, or approximately $725 for every man, woman, and child.

diageo.com

Advertising expenditures vary among industries and companies. Cosmetics producers are often cited as examples of firms that spend high percentages of their revenues on advertising and promotion. Marketers of fragrances like Ralph Lauren's Polo spend, on average, 10 percent of total sales revenues on advertising and promotion. But no industry surpasses the automakers in total advertising spending. Total auto ad spending amounts to almost $15 billion a year. By contrast, the aviation manufacturing industry, whose promotional budgets are concentrated on personal selling to major business customers like airline companies, spends a meager $48 million on advertising.

As previous chapters have discussed, the emergence of the marketing concept, with its emphasis on a company-wide consumer orientation, boosted the importance of integrated marketing communications. This change, in turn, expanded the role of advertising. Today, a typical consumer is exposed to hundreds of advertising messages each day. Advertising provides an efficient, inexpensive, and fast method of reaching the ever-elusive, increasingly segmented consumer market. Its current role rivals those of sales promotion and personal selling. Indeed, advertising has become a key ingredient in the effective implementation of the marketing concept.

Types of Advertising

Advertisements fall into two broad categories: product advertising and institutional advertising. **Product advertising** is nonpersonal selling of a particular good or service. This is the type of advertising the average person usually thinks of when talking about most promotional activities. **Institutional advertising,** in contrast, promotes a concept, an idea, a philosophy, or the goodwill of an industry, company, organization, person, geographic location, or government agency. This term has a broader meaning than *corporate advertising*, which is typically limited to nonproduct advertising sponsored by a specific profit-seeking firm.

2

Identify the major types of advertising.

Institutional advertising is often closely related to the public-relations function of the enterprise. The Healthy Choice ad in Figure 16.1, featuring a rich, creamy, low-fat bowl of ice cream, is an eye-catching example of product advertising aimed at increasing sales of the company's brand. The ad on the next page, showing a bowl of ice cream topped with slivered almonds, is an institutional ad designed to increase public awareness of almonds. The ultimate objective is to increase overall almond consumption rather than increase market share for a specific brand.

Objectives of Advertising

Marketers use advertising messages to accomplish three primary objectives: to inform, to persuade, and to remind. These objectives may be used individually or, more typically, in conjunction with each other. For example, an ad for a not-for-profit agency may inform the public of the existence of the organization and at the same time persuade the audience to take the intended action.

MARKETING   DICTIONARY

advertising Paid, nonpersonal communication through various media by business firms, not-for-profit organizations, and individuals who are identified in the advertising message and who hope to inform or persuade members of a particular audience.

product advertising Nonpersonal selling of a good or service.

institutional advertising Promoting a concept, an idea, a philosophy, or the goodwill of an industry, company, organization, place, person, or government agency.

FIGURE 16.1	Product and Institutional Advertising

Informative advertising seeks to develop initial demand for a good, service, organization, person, place, idea, or cause. The promotion of any new market entry tends to pursue this objective because marketing success at this stage often depends simply on announcing availability. Therefore, informative advertising is common in the introductory stage of the product life cycle.

Persuasive advertising attempts to increase demand for an existing good, service, organization, person, place, idea, or cause. It is a competitive type of promotion suited to the growth stage and the early part of the maturity stage of the product life cycle. Reminder advertising strives to reinforce previous promotional activity by keeping the name of a good, service, organization, person, place, idea, or cause before the public. It is common in the latter part of the maturity stage and throughout the decline stage of the product life cycle. Figure 16.2 indicates the relationship between advertising objectives and the stage in the product life cycle.

Traditionally, marketers stated their advertising objectives as direct sales goals. A more realistic standard, however, views advertising as a way to achieve communications objectives, including informing, persuading, and reminding potential customers of the product. Advertising attempts to condition consumers to adopt favorable viewpoints toward a promotional message. The goal of an ad is to improve the likelihood that a customer will buy a particular good or service. In this sense, advertising illustrates the close relationship between marketing communications and promotional strategy.

To get the best value for a firm's advertising investment, marketers must first determine what that firm's advertising objectives are. Effective advertising can enhance consumer perceptions of quality in a good or service, leading to gains in customer loyalty, repeat purchases, and protection against price wars. In addition, perceptions of superiority pay off in the firm's ability to raise prices without losing market share.

ADVERTISING STRATEGIES

If the primary function of marketing is to bring buyers and sellers together, then advertising is the means to an end. Effective advertising strategies accomplish at least one of three tasks: informing, persuading, or reminding consumers. The secret to success in choosing the best strategy is developing a message that best positions a firm's product in the audience's mind. Among the advertising strategies available for use by 21st century marketers are comparative advertising and celebrity advertising, as well as decisions about global and interactive ads. Channel-oriented decisions such as retail and cooperative advertising must also be devised.

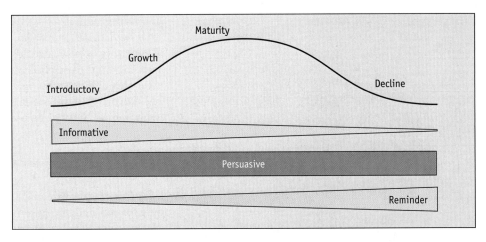

Marketers often combine several of these advertising strategies to ensure that the advertisement accomplishes set objectives. As markets become more segmented, the need for personalized advertising increases. The next sections describe strategies that contemporary marketers develop to reach their target markets.

Comparative Advertising

Firms whose goods and services are not the leaders in their markets often favor **comparative advertising,** an advertising strategy that emphasizes messages with direct or indirect promotional comparisons between competing brands. Many less dominant firms use this technique extensively, however.

Market leaders very seldom ever acknowledge in their advertising that competing products even exist, and when they do, they do not point out any benefit of the competing brand. In fact, when giant rivals do come face-to-face in the advertising ring, they generally fight about how data are presented and often demand proof to back up offending claims. Procter & Gamble (P&G) and General Foods, for example, traditionally have devoted little of their huge promotional budgets to comparative advertising. Recently, however, P&G marketers attracted the attention of the ad industry with full-page ads that compared their Crest MultiCare toothpaste to Colgate Total. The ads, which ran in 100 newspapers nationwide, showed a checklist of each brand's benefits: Both brands help fight cavities, both help fight tartar, both help with plaque removal, and both fight bad breath. But next to the category "Helps reduce and prevent gingivitis," P&G gives Colgate Total a check and leaves blank the box next to its own Crest MultiCare. The strategy is based on research that shows taste to be the most important factor in the decision to buy a particular brand of toothpaste. "For tens of millions of people who don't have gingivitis, MultiCare is a preferred product in that it provides better taste, as well as other important benefits," says a P&G spokesperson.[3]

Breakfast cereal marketers frequently point out the benefits of their cold

pg.com

FIGURE 16.3

Comparative Advertising: Kellogg's versus General Mills and Kraft Foods

cereal over competitors. The ad in Figure 16.3 compares Kellogg's Special K plus with General Mills' Cheerios, Total, and Basic 4, and Kraft Foods' Post Fruit & Fibre. Kellogg marketers explain that Special K plus provides twice as much calcium as any other national cereal brand *before* the milk is added.

The Federal Trade Commission encourages comparative advertising. Regulators believe such ads keep marketers competitive and inform consumers about their choices. Generally speaking, where there is competition through advertising, prices tend to go down because people can shop around. This has proved increasingly true for online consumers, who now use bots to help find the best prices on goods and services.

Celebrity Testimonials

Many marketers hire celebrity spokespeople to try to boost the effectiveness of their advertising messages. About 20 percent of all U.S. ads include celebrities. Celebrity advertising is also popular in foreign countries. In Japan, 80 percent of all ads use celebrities, both local and international stars. U.S. celebrities featured in Japanese ads include actors Harrison Ford for Kirin Beer, Brad Pitt for Honda, Jodie Foster for Keri Cosmetics and Latte Coffee, and Paul Newman for Evance watch stores. While Japanese celebrities appear more frequently, Japanese consumers view foreign stars differently. They view them as images more than people, which helps marketers to sell products. They also associate American stars with quality.

Both the number of celebrity ads and the dollars spent on those ads have increased in recent years. Professional athletes are among the highest-paid product endorsers. In a recent year, basketball player Michael Jordan earned $69 million just from product endorsements, German speedster Michael Schumacher signed with Ferrari for $38 million, and golf champion Tiger Woods garnered almost $27 million in product endorsements.[4] Figure 16.4 pairs tennis star Pete Sampras with Dannon yogurt. The ad copy explains that Sampras has been a Dannon man since he was a boy and that peach is his favorite flavor.

The primary advantage of associations with big-name personalities is improved product recognition in a promotional environment filled with hundreds of competing 15-second and 30-second commercials. Advertisers use the term *clutter* to describe this situation. As e-commerce continues to soar, one inevitable result has been the increase in advertising clutter as companies rush to sell their goods and services online. What marketers must remember is that an effective online site must have meaningful content and helpful service; otherwise, it remains clutter.[5]

A celebrity testimonial generally succeeds when the celebrity is a credible source of information for the product being promoted. The most effective ads of this type establish relevant links between the celebrities and the advertised goods or services. Several studies of consumer responses show that celebrities improve the product's believability, recall of the product, and brand recognition. Celebrity endorsements also create positive attitudes, leading to greater brand equity.

Another potential problem is that a celebrity who endorses numerous products may create marketplace confusion when customers remember the celebrity but relate the ad to a competing brand. Some advertisers try to avoid such problems by using cartoon characters as endorsers. Two highly popular animated comedies on Fox—*The Simpsons* and *King of the Hill*—are top contenders for celebrity advertising dollars. In fact, in addition to Bart Simpson pitching candy bars ("Nobody better lay a finger on my Butterfinger"), his whole TV family has appeared in a Japanese TV ad for a laundry detergent.[6] Cartoon characters are oftentimes preferred by advertisers because they never say anything negative about the product, they do exactly what the marketers

@ **mercedesbenz.com**

@ **dannon.com**

want them to do, and they cannot get involved in scandals. The only drawback is high licensing fees; popular animated characters can cost more than live celebrities.

Retail Advertising

Perhaps the advertising strategy that most consumers are confronted with on a daily basis is **retail advertising,** which includes all advertising by retail stores that sell goods or services directly to the consuming public. While this activity accounts for a sizable portion of total annual advertising expenditures, retail advertising varies widely in its effectiveness. One study showed that consumers often respond with suspicion to retail price advertisements. Source, message, and shopping experience seem to affect consumer attitudes toward these advertisements.

Too often, retail stores do not give advertising its due, but rather treat it as a secondary activity. Except for the retail giants, retailers rarely use independent advertising agencies. Instead, store managers usually accept responsibility for advertising in addition to their other duties. To correct this deficiency, management should assign one individual the sole responsibility and authority for developing an effective retail advertising program.

A retailer often shares advertising costs with a manufacturer or wholesaler in a technique called **cooperative advertising.** For example, an apparel marketer may pay a percentage of the cost of a retail store's newspaper advertisement featuring its product lines.

Cooperative advertising campaigns originated to take advantage of the media's practice of offering lower rates to local advertisers than to national ones. Later, cooperative advertising became part of programs to improve dealer relations. The retailer likes the chance to secure advertising that it could not run otherwise. Cooperative advertising can create vertical links, as when a manufacturer and retailer coordinate their resources. It can also involve firms at the same level of the supply chain. In a horizontal arrangement, a group of retailers—for example, all the Ford dealers in the northeastern United States—might pool their resources.

Interactive Advertising

Welcome to the world of interactive advertising! Advertising messages float across idle computer screens in offices around the country on a daily basis. Net surfers play games that are embedded with ads from the site sponsors. Companies offer free e-mail service to people willing to receive ads with their personal messages. Video screens on grocery carts display ads so shoppers can see these ads as they wheel down the aisles of grocery stores.

Since marketers realize that two-way communications provide more effective methods for achieving promotional objectives, they are interested in **interactive media.** Interactive media are communication channels that induce message recipients to participate actively in the promotional effort. Achieving this involvement is the big task facing contemporary marketers. Although interactive advertising has become nearly synonymous with e-commerce and the Web, it also

FIGURE 16.4   Effective Use of Celebrity Testimonials

Pete, age 8. Big serve. Big Dannon fan. Also, big hair.

World's Best Tennis Player   Pete Sampras

Even as a boy, he was a Dannon man. His big favorite? Peach. For him, it was always about the taste. Now, it's about that great *new* peach taste. But the real fruit, protein, those healthy active cultures—they were just *fringe benefits.* And a thousand or so aces later, he just happened to win a few grand slam tournaments.

Coincidence or Dannon?

MARKETING   DICTIONARY

retail advertising Nonpersonal selling by stores that offer goods or services directly to the consuming public.

cooperative advertising Sharing of advertising costs between the retailer and the manufacturer of the good or service.

interactive media Communication channels in which message recipients actively participate in the promotional effort.

Saks Fifth Avenue and Chanel use a cooperative strategy to draw traffic into the store and increase sales of Chanel N° 5, "the world's most luxurious bath collection."

includes kiosks in shopping malls. Multimedia technology, the Internet, and commercial online services are changing the nature of advertising from a one-way, passive communication technique to a more effective way to facilitate two-way marketing communications. Interactive advertising creates a dialogue, providing more materials as the user asks. The advertiser's challenge is to gain and hold consumers' interest in an environment where these consumers control what they want to see.

Interactive advertising changes the balance between marketers and consumers. Unlike the traditional role of advertising—providing brief, entertaining, attention-catching messages—interactive media provide information to help consumers throughout the purchase and consumption processes. As consumers choose among growing numbers of products in the course of their fast-paced lives, they want more information in less time to help them make necessary comparisons between available products. Today, online resources fill the gap between ads and personal selling, especially for higher-priced products like appliances and automobiles and for specialty goods such as consumer electronics and computer products. Advertising is moving from an emphasis on brief, one-way spots or single-page print ads to layered, interactive measures, where consumers choose to learn more about products and also provide information about themselves to the advertiser.

Successful interactive advertising adds value by offering the viewer more than just product-related information. An ad on the Web can do more than promote a brand; it can create a company store, customer service, and line and other content. As Chapter 4 described in detail, the Web has also given birth to cybercommunities—groups of Internet users who share some common interest.

Most companies deliver their interactive advertising messages through proprietary online services and through the Web. In fact, online ad spending has soared more than 533 percent in the last 3 years. The growth is coming from all over. In the past, only market leaders bought online advertising; now, companies that are infants in their industries are online. The computer and software, financial services, and direct-response industries are the top three online advertisers. Top high-tech Internet spenders include Microsoft, IBM, Excite, and Compaq. Of the eight largest Internet spenders not based in information technologies, four are auto firms—General Motors, Ford, Toyota, and Honda. The other four include CBS Sportsline, Disney, Visa, and Amazon.[7]

CREATING AN ADVERTISEMENT

3

Describe the process of creating an advertisement.

Marketers spend about $200 billion a year on advertising campaigns in the United States alone. With so much money at stake, they must create effective, memorable ads that increase sales and enhance their organizations' images. They cannot afford to waste resources on bad ads that may lead to consumer disdain for a product, boycotts, and even federal investigations. For example, in recent years, companies such as Nike and Wal-Mart have utilized portions of their advertising campaigns to fight off claims that their products were produced in foreign sweatshops.

Research helps marketers create better ads by pinpointing goals that an ad needs to accomplish, such as educating consumers about product features, enhancing brand loyalty, or improving consumer perception of the brand. These objectives should guide the design of the ad. Marketers can also discover what appeals to consumers and can test ads with potential buyers before committing funds for a campaign.

FIGURE 16.5   **Elements of the Advertising Planning Process**

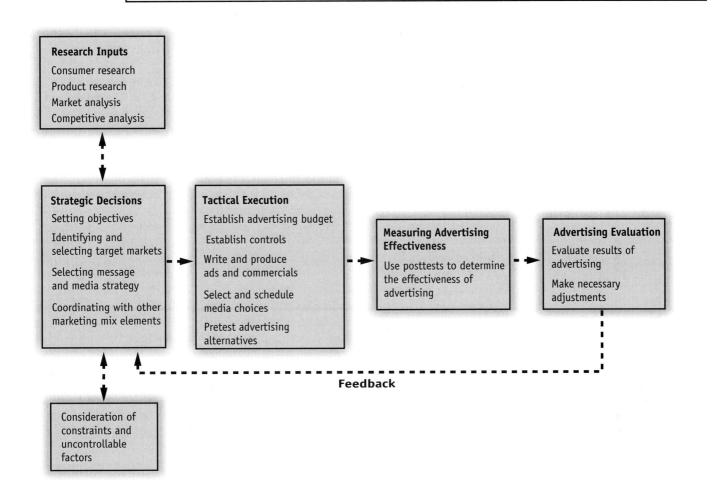

Translating Advertising Objectives into Advertising Plans

Once a company defines its objectives for an advertising campaign, it can develop its advertising plan. Market research assists managers in making strategic decisions that guide choices in technical areas such as budgeting, copyrighting, scheduling, and media selection. Posttests, which will be discussed in greater detail later in the chapter, measure the effectiveness of advertising and form the basis for feedback concerning possible adjustments. The elements of advertising planning are shown in Figure 16.5.

Marketers should carefully follow a sequential process in any advertising decision. Novice advertisers often focus too closely on the technical aspects of creating advertisements and ignore more basic steps, such as market analysis. The type of advertisement suited to a particular situation depends largely on the results of the planning phase of this process.

As Chapter 8 explained, positioning involves developing a marketing strategy that aims to achieve a desired position in a prospective buyer's mind. Marketers use a positioning strategy that distinguishes their good or service from those of competitors. Effective advertising then communicates the desired position by emphasizing certain product characteristics, such as performance attributes, price/quality, competitors' shortcomings, applications, user needs, and product classes.

Advertising Messages

The strategy for creating a message starts with the customer benefits a product offers and moves to the creative concept phase, in which marketers strive to bring an appropriate message to consumers using both visual and verbal components. Marketers work to create an ad with meaningful, believable, and distinctive appeals—one that stands out from the clutter and escapes "zapping" by the television remote control.

Usually, ads are not created in an isolated fashion but as part of specific campaigns. An *advertising campaign* is a series of different but related ads that use a single theme and appear in different media within a specified time period. The Ameritrade online brokerage ads featuring slacker-punk pitchman, Stuart intended to be a sharp, hilarious contrast to the suits around him, are part of a recent campaign built around the slogan, "Believe in yourself."[8]

In developing a creative strategy, advertisers must decide how to communicate their marketing message. They must balance message characteristics, like the tone of the appeal, the extent of information provided and the conclusion to which it leads the consumer, the side of the story the ad tells, and its emphasis on verbal or visual primary elements.

Should the tone of the advertisement focus on a practical appeal such as price, or should it evoke an emotional response of, say, fear, humor, or fantasy? In recent years, the use of fear appeals in advertising has escalated. Ads for insurance, cars, and automotive products like tires all carry messages that incorrect buying decisions may endanger the well-being of the environment, consumers, or children. Public service campaigns against smoking and substance abuse evoke fears of damage to health and social rejection with slogans like the following: "This is your brain. This is your brain on drugs" and "Friends don't let friends drink and drive." Fear appeals pursue a goal of encouraging consumers to do what is necessary to remove the identified threats, usually either by avoiding undesirable behavior or by purchasing the advertised products. Fear appeals do not work for all products. Viewers practice selective perception and tune out statements they perceive as too strong. These messages work best for products that solve problems and remove the indicated fears.

Humorous ads seek to create positive moods and catch viewer attention. Humor can improve audience awareness and recall and enhance the consumer's favorable image of the brand. But advertising professionals differ in their opinions of the effectiveness of humorous ads. Some believe that humor distracts attention from brand and product features; consumers remember the humor but not the product. Humorous ads, because they are so memorable, may lose their effectiveness sooner than ads with other kinds of appeals. To date, no one has offered conclusive proof that these kinds of ads help to persuade the consumer.

Although radio and television are considered the best media for humorous ads, Figure 16.6 shows that print ads can also use humor effectively. This ad for Velamints is a takeoff on rival Kraft Foods' award-winning Altoids ads. Another Velamint ad reads, "If you insist on breath mints that hurt, bite your lip first."[9]

@ **ameritrade.com**

FIGURE 16.6   **Using Humor in Advertising Messages**

Developing and Preparing Ads

The final step in the advertising process—the development and preparation of an advertisement—should flow logically from the promotional theme selected. This process should create an ad that becomes a complementary part of the marketing mix with a carefully determined role in the total marketing strategy. Preparation of an advertisement should emphasize features like its creativity, its continuity with past advertisements, and possibly its association with other company products.

What immediate tasks should an advertisement accomplish? Regardless of the chosen target, an advertisement should (1) gain attention and interest, (2) inform and/or persuade, and (3) eventually lead to a purchase or other desired action. It should gain attention in a productive way; that is, it should instill some recall of the good or service. Otherwise, it will not lead to buying action.

Gillette Company found this objective difficult to achieve with a commercial that showed a chimpanzee shaving a man's face. After testing the commercial in two cities, one Gillette spokesperson noted that lots of people remembered the chimp, but hardly anyone remembered the product. The ad stimulated fantastic interest in the ape but no payoff for Gillette.

An advertisement should also inform and persuade. For example, many insurance advertisements provide informative details about policy features. Many also include persuasive testimonials designed to appeal to prospective purchasers.

Stimulating buying action is often difficult because an advertisement cannot actually close a sale. Nevertheless, if an ad gains attention and informs or persuades, it probably represents a worthwhile investment of marketing resources. Too many advertisers fail to suggest—how audience members can purchase their products if they desire to do so. Creative design should eliminate this shortcoming.

The ad for Gentle Breeze Gain in Figure 16.7 combines a humorous headline with a breathtaking photo that reinforces the new product's appeal as an effective detergent with a refreshing scent. The figure also identifies the four major elements of a print advertisement: headline, illustration, body copy, and signature. *Headlines* and *illustrations* (photographs, drawings, or other artwork) should work together to generate interest and attention. *Body copy* serves to inform, persuade, and stimulate buying action. The *signature*, which may include the company name, address, phone number, slogan, trademark, or product photo, names the sponsoring organization. An ad may also have one or more *subheads*—headings subordinate to the main headline that either link the main headline to the body copy or subdivide sections of the body copy.

After advertisers conceive an idea for an ad that gains attention, informs and persuades, and stimulates purchases, their next step involves refining the thought sketch into a rough layout. Continued refinements of the rough layout eventually produce the final version of the advertisement design that is ready to be executed, printed, or recorded.

The creation of each advertisement in a campaign requires an evolutionary process that begins with an idea and ultimately results in a finished ad that is ready for distribution through print or electronic media. The idea itself must first be converted into a thought sketch, which is a tangible summary of the intended message.

Advances in technology allow advertisers to create novel, eye-catching advertisements. Innovative computer software packages now allow artists to merge multiple images to create a single image with a natural, seamless appearance. Computer-generated images appeal to younger, computer-literate consumers. For example, a computerized Reebok ad incorporated memorable special effects that featured Shaquille O'Neal playing basketball against eight images of himself, a Chevron ad includes giggling and squealing car characters, and a little boy who finds himself sucked into a Pepsi bottle as he desperately tries to get the last drop of his soda.

@ gillette.com

FIGURE 16.7 **Elements of a Typical Advertisement**

Illustration

Headline

Body Copy

Signature

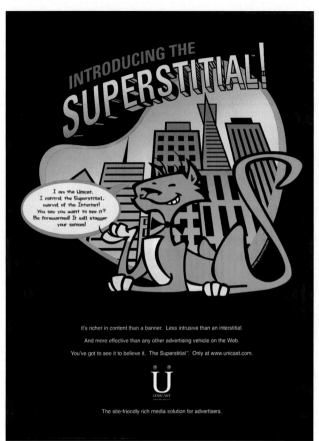

Internet marketers are continuously offered more efficient ways to deliver their online advertising messages. Unicast has fine-tuned interstitial advertising with its Superstitial, which provides more content than a banner ad but is less intrusive than the typical interstitial.

Creating Interactive Ads

Web surfers want engaging, lively content that takes advantage of the medium's capabilities and goes beyond what they find elsewhere. Advertisers and specialists who create Internet ads are still learning how to use the Web and other interactive media effectively. The Web does not yet match television's ability to provide high-quality moving pictures, sound, and passive entertainment or its ability to distinguish commercial breaks from programming on the site. Increasingly, however, Web ads compete with television ads by enhancing their content with video and audio clips. This orientation overlooks the Web's major advantages: speed, providing information, exchanging input through two-way communications, offering self-directed entertainment, and allowing personal choice.

A growing number of new ways to advertise on the Web attests to the rapidly changing environment marketers encounter on the Internet and in e-commerce in general. Web ads have grown from information-based home pages to innovative, interactive channels for transmitting messages to cyberaudiences, including banners, keyword ads, advertorials, and interstitials. In fact, many online ads now closely resemble television commercials.

Advertising banners were the trend setters in online advertising, allowing customers to quickly access a company's goods and services through other Web site links. **Banners,** advertisements on a Web page that link to an advertiser's site, are the most common type of advertising on the Web. They can be free of charge or cost in the thousands of dollars per month depending on the amount of hits the site receives. The Internet Advertising Bureau (IAB) set a standard size of 60 pixels by 468 pixels (about half an inch by 5 inches) for an ad banner. Autoweb, Shop-Now, eBay, Casino On Net, and Lowestfare are among the most viewed advertising banners.[10]

Online advertisers often describe their Internet ads in terms of "richness," referring to the degree to which new technologies—such as streaming video, 3-D animation, Java script, and interactive capabilities—are implemented in the banners. A recent study found that the click-through rate nearly doubles when an interactive element is added to a banner. Rich advertising creates innovative and interesting messages that appeal to banner-bombarded Web surfers.[11]

Banners have evolved into a more target-specific technique for Internet advertising with the advent of *missiles,* which are messages that appear on the screen at exactly the right moment. For example, when a customer visits the site of Company A's competitor, a missile can be programmed to appear on the customer's monitor that allows the customer to click-on a direct link to Company A's site. Internet marketers for NetZero also offer an Ad Missile Defense Shield to prevent competitors from doing the same thing. Capabilities like this make one-to-one advertising a reality.

Keyword ads are an outcropping of banner ads. Used in search engines, keyword ads appear on the results page of a search, specific to the term being searched. Advertisers pay search engines to target their ads and only display the banners when users search for relevant keywords, allowing marketers to target specific audiences. For example, if a user searched on the term "digital camera," keyword ads might appear for electronic boutiques or camera shops that sell digital cameras and film.

Banner designs that have also evolved into larger advertising squares, which are typically on the right and left sides of a Web page and that closely resemble advertisements in the telephone Yellow Pages, are called *advertorials.* An advertorial on the Forbes Web site costs about $25,000 a month. Advertisers quickly expanded on these advertorials with **interstitials**—ads that pop up between Web pages of related content. Meaning *in between,* interstitials appear in a separate browser window while the user waits for a Web page to download. One of the most frequent user complaints is that they are intrusive and unwanted. Interstitials are more likely to contain large graphics and streaming presentations than banner ads and, therefore, are more difficult to ignore than typical banner ads. In addition, some studies show that users are more likely to click on interstitials than banners.

Web advertisers are now moving beyond banners, advertorials, and interstitials and are devoting more of their marketing dollars to creating their own sites and to placing links on other sites. However, ads that remain on other sites offer limited flexibility and require frequent changes. They serve primarily as links to the sponsors' main content sites.

Web site developers can now add 3-D effects to their sites, a capability that provides new opportunities for advertisers. For example, graphics can show products in lifelike representations. Retailers can create 3-D stores where visitors can take a stroll through the virtual aisles viewing merchandise on display; Web sites need no longer provide their information in catalog-like formats.

@ unicast.com

MEDIA SELECTION

One of the most important decisions in developing an advertising strategy is the selection of appropriate media to carry the firm's message to its audience. A mistake at this point can waste literally millions of dollars on ineffective advertising. The media selected must be capable of accomplishing the communications objectives of informing, persuading, and reminding potential customers of the good, service, person, or idea being advertised.

Research should identify the ad's target market to determine its size and characteristics. Advertisers then match the target characteristics with the media best able to reach that particular audience. The objective of media selection is to achieve adequate media coverage without advertising beyond the identifiable limits of the potential market. Finally, cost comparisons between alternatives should determine the best possible media purchase.

Table 16.1 compares the major advertising media by noting their shares of overall advertising expenditures. It also compares the advantages and disadvantages of each media alternative. *Broadcast media* include television and radio. Newspapers, magazines, outdoor advertising, and direct mail represent the major types of print media.

The table reveals that newspaper and television are the leading advertising media, followed closely by direct mail. Radio, magazine, and outdoor advertising rank at the bottom. Since 1950, newspaper, radio, and magazines have all lost market share to television. While interactive advertising still accounts for well under 1 percent of total advertising expenditures, this category is expected to grow considerably over the next five years.

4

List and compare the major advertising media.

Television

Even though the broadcast media of television and radio account for only 30 cents of every advertising dollar spent, television offers so many characteristics favorable to effective advertising that it has grown to rival newspapers as the dominant advertising medium. The attractiveness of television advertising is that marketers can reach local and national markets. Whereas most newspaper advertising revenues come from local advertisers, the greatest share of television advertising revenues come from companies that advertise nationally. The newest trend in television advertising are virtual ads—banner-type logos and brief messages that are superimposed onto television coverage of sporting events so that they seem to be a part of the arena's signage, but cannot be seen by anyone attending the game. Many viewers are unaware of just how many virtual ads are showing up in TV sports, from baseball games to bullfights

MARKETING DICTIONARY

banner Web advertisement that links to an advertiser's site

keyword ad Web advertisement that appears on the results page of a search function and that is specific to the term being searched.

interstitials Web advertisements that pop up between Web pages of related content.

MARKETING STRATEGY FAILURE

Just for Feet Just Forgot

BACKGROUND Picture this: a Super Bowl audience of 127 million sports fans and an ad for retailer Just for Feet featuring Nike's newest athletic shoe. Sounds like an unbeatable team unless you saw the ad. A college student at Iowa State University who saw it described it this way: "Four white hunters track down a black man, drug him, tag him, and release him with a tag he tries to shake off but cannot." Not funny, not good.

THE MARKETING PROBLEM World-renowned ad agency Saatchi & Saatchi created the television ad for Just for Feet as part of a Super Bowl promotional campaign. But once the ad aired, everyone realized that it was a disaster. Calls immediately started coming in from outraged consumers. This was followed by a flurry of stinging reviews and editorials.

continued on next page

TABLE 16.1		**Comparison of Advertising Media Alternatives**	

MEDIA OUTLET	PERCENTAGE OF TOTAL[a]	ADVANTAGES	DISADVANTAGES
Broadcast			
Television	22	Mass coverage; repetition; flexibility; prestige	High cost; temporary message; public distrust; lack of selectivity
Radio	7	Immediacy; low cost; flexibility; targeted audience; mobility	Short life span; highly fragmented audience
Print			
Newspapers	26	Tailored to individual communities; ability to refer back to ads	Short life span
Direct mail	18	Selectivity; intense coverage; speed; flexibility; opportunity to convey complete information; personalization	High cost; consumer resistance; dependence on effective mailing list
Magazines	5	Selectivity; quality image reproduction; long life; prestige	Lack of flexibility
Outdoor	1	Quick, visual communication of simple ideas; link to local goods and services; repetition	Brief exposure; environmental concerns
Electronic/Print			
Interactive	<1	Two-way communications; flexibility; link to self-directed entertainment	Poor image reproduction; limited scheduling options; difficult to measure effectiveness

[a]An additional 25 percent is spent on a variety of miscellaneous media, including Yellow Pages listings, business papers, transit displays, point-of-purchase displays, cinema advertising, and regional farm papers.

to the Super Bowl. The technology includes state-of-the-art graphics and allows national brands, such as Coca-Cola, Miller Beer, and Chevrolet, to target ads regionally.[12]

Another trend in television advertising is the abbreviated spot—15- and 30-second spots—that cost less to make and buy and are too quick for most viewers to zap with their remote controls. Master Lock, a division of Wisconsin-based Fortune Brands, now holds the record for the shortest TV ad: a one-second blink ad that shows the most popular selling lock being hit by a bullet that shreds but does not open the lock.[13]

In the past decade, cable television's share of ad revenues has grown by more than 30 percent, while the networks' share is falling. Satellite television has contributed to increased cable penetration, which almost three-fourths of all Americans now have installed in their homes. In response to declining ratings and soaring costs, network television companies like NBC, CBS, ABC, Fox, and Warner Bros. (WB) are refocusing their advertising strategies with a heavy emphasis on moving onto the Net to capture younger audiences. NBC has stakes in Web portal Snap!; CBS has alliances with sports, business, and entertainment Web sites; and Fox has tied in with Yahoo! ABC and WB marketers, believing the future of network TV belongs to young viewers, air more programs aimed at this audience, including *Dawson's Creek* and *Buffy the Vampire Slayer*.[14]

As cable audiences grow, programming improves, and ratings rise, advertisers are compelled to earmark more of their advertising budgets to this medium. Cable advertising offers companies access to more narrowly defined target audiences than other broadcast media can provide. The great variety of special-interest channels devoted to subjects such as food, history, home and garden, health, ethnic issues, and golf attract specialized audiences and permit niche marketing.

Television advertising offers the advantages of powerful impact, mass coverage, repetition of messages, flexibility, and prestige. Its disadvantages include loss of control of the promotional message to the telecaster (which can influence its impact), high costs, high mortality rates for commercials, and some public distrust. Compared to other media, television can suffer from lack of selectivity since specific TV programs may not reach consumers in a precisely defined target market without a significant degree of wasted coverage. However, the growing specialization of cable TV channels should help to resolve that problem.

Radio

Radio advertising has always been a popular media choice for up-to-the-minute newscasts and for targeting advertising messages to local audiences. But in recent years, radio has become the fastest growing media alternative. As more and more people find they have less and less time, radio provides immediate information and entertainment at work, play, and in the car. In addition, as e-commerce continues to push the growth in global business, more people are traveling abroad to seek out new markets. For these travelers, radio, because of the fact that many radio stations are airing over the Internet, is a means of staying in touch with home—wherever that may be. Marketers frequently use radio advertising to reach local audiences. But in recent years, it plays an increasingly important role as a national and even global listening favorite. In the United States, public radio stations have aired many programs that are now weekly favorites, including Garrison Keillor's *Lake Woebegon*. Thousands of online listeners use the Internet to beam in on radio stations from almost every city—tuning in on an easy-listening station in London, a top forty Hong Kong broadcaster, or a chat show from Toronto.

Radio ad revenues in the United States are growing faster than revenues for all other media except cable television. Advertisers also like the chance to reach people while they drive. With an increase in commuters, this market is growing. Stations can adapt to local preferences by changing format—for example, going from country and western to an all-news or rock-and-talk radio. The variety of stations allows advertisers to easily target audiences and to tailor their messages to those listeners. Other benefits include low cost, flexibility, and mobility. Disadvantages include fragmentation, the temporary nature of messages, and a lack of research information as compared with television.

While most radio listening is done at home, in cars, or with headset-equipped portables, technology has given birth to Net radio. Web-cast radio allows customers to widen their listening times and choices through their computers. The potential for selling on this new channel is greater. A listener can simply "click here to purchase the song you're hearing." Other goods are easily adapted to click-and-sell possibilities. If Web-cast radio works today, Net-TV should soon be a reality as well.[15]

Newspapers

Newspaper advertising continues to dominate local markets. In addition to retail advertisements, classified advertising is an important part of newspaper revenues. The average daily newspaper generates 40 percent of its revenue from hundreds of tiny multicolumn ads placed by individuals selling their goods and services.[16] Four of the top five newspaper advertisers in the United States are department stores; the fifth is electronics and appliance retailer Circuit City. Each spends well above $200 million on newspaper advertising. In fact, Federated Department Stores' newspaper advertising expenditures total almost $500 million annually.[17]

Newspapers' primary advantages start with flexibility since advertising can vary from one locality to the next. Newspapers offer community prestige since readers recognize they have deep impacts on their communities. Newspapers allow intensive coverage for ads; in a typical location, a single newspaper reaches 90 percent of the homes. Readers control their exposure to the advertising message, unlike television or radio advertising messages, and can refer back to newspaper ads. Newspapers facilitate coordination between local and national advertising, they offer powerful merchandising services (such as promotional and research support), and they give

justforfeet.com

access to some special techniques such as single-sheet or multipage insert ads. Newspaper advertising also suffers from disadvantages: short life span, hasty reading (the typical reader spends about 40 minutes reading the newspaper), and relatively poor reproduction quality.

Automobile marketers often use newspaper ads to react quickly to market conditions and reach potential buyers. Research shows that auto buyers check newspapers diligently during the last week or two before a purchase. General Motors Corp. recently turned to newspaper advertising as part of its efforts to generate more floor traffic and improve market share.[18]

Magazines

Advertisers divide magazines into two broad categories: consumer magazines and business magazines. These categories are also subdivided into monthly and weekly publications. The four top magazines in the United States in order of their ad revenue ranking are *TV Guide*, *People*, *Sports Illustrated*, and *Time*. Of these four, only *TV Guide* is not owned by Time Warner. With over 37 million readers, the number one weekly magazine by paid circulation is *Parade*, which accompanies most of the nation's Sunday newspapers.[19]

The primary advantages of magazine advertising include the following: selectivity in reaching precise target markets, quality reproduction, long life, the prestige associated with some magazines, and the extra services that many publications offer. The primary disadvantage is that magazines lack the flexibility of newspapers, radio, and television.

Media buyers study circulation numbers and demographics information for various publications to choose placement opportunities and to negotiate rates. Advertising volume soared to over $64 billion annually for the top 100 advertisers in the United States, and for several years the same advertising categories have claimed the title for big spenders as well. Automotive, retail, and movies and media advertising have held their first, second, and third places respectively each year and have continued to show strong growth percentages.[20]

The magazines shown in Figure 16.8 are examples of how publishers such as Condé Nast develop magazines to attract readers with strong interests in food *(Bon Appétit* and *Gourmet)*, fitness

| **FIGURE 16.8** | **Targeting Different Consumer Interests through Magazine Advertising** |

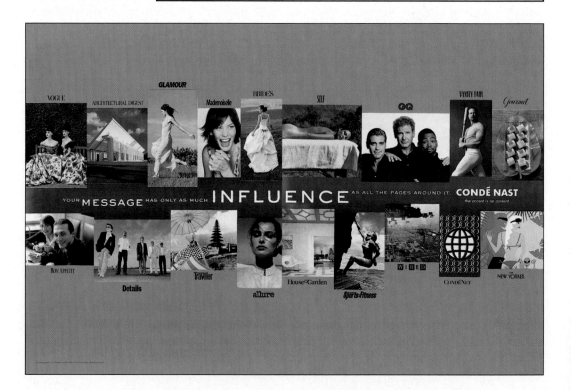

(Women's Sports & Fitness and *Self)*, computers *(Wired* and *CondéNet)*, homes *(Architectural Digest* and *House & Garden)*, travel *(Condé Nast Traveler)*, weddings *(Bride's)*, lifestyles and trends *(The New Yorker* and *Vanity Fair)*, and fashion *(GQ, Vogue, Glamour, Allure, Details,* and *Mademoiselle)*. Advertisers seeking to promote their products to these target markets can reach them by advertising in the appropriate magazines.

Direct Mail

As discussed in Chapter 15, forms of direct-mail advertising include sales letters, postcards, leaflets, folders, booklets, catalogs, and house organs (periodicals published by organizations to cover internal issues). The advantages of direct mail come from selectivity, intensive coverage, speed, formal flexibility, completeness of information, and personalization. Disadvantages of direct mail include high cost per reader, dependence on the quality of mailing lists, and some consumers' resistance to it.

The advantages of direct mail explain its widespread use. Each year, over 4.5 million tons of catalogs and other direct-mail offers fill U.S. mailboxes. Even though almost half of it is discarded immediately, Americans will spend about $200 billion annually on such promotions, including $50 billion for catalog merchandise. Not only are direct-mail lists easily available, they are segmented into categories to help the mailers in reaching the audiences they are seeking. Data are available on previous purchase patterns and preferred payment methods, as well as such household characteristics as the number of children and their ages. Not surprisingly, use of direct mail is expected to triple during this decade.[21]

Outdoor Advertising

Outdoor advertising, the oldest and simplest media business around, is growing at nearly 10 percent a year—faster than newspapers, magazines, and network TV. Only the Internet and cable television surpass its growth rate. Advertisers spend almost $5 billion annually on outdoor advertising, twice what they spent on online ads. Outdoor advertising takes the form of billboards, painted bulletins or displays (such as those that appear on the walls of buildings), and electric spectaculars (large, illuminated, and sometimes animated signs and displays). This form of advertising has the advantages of immediate communication of quick and simple ideas, repeated exposure to a message, and strong promotion for locally available products. Outdoor advertising is particularly effective along metropolitan streets and in other high-traffic areas.[22]

Its disadvantages include the brevity of exposure to its messages and public concern over aesthetics. The Highway Beautification Act of 1965, for example, regulates the placement of outdoor advertising near interstate highways. In addition, many cities have local ordinances that set regulations on size and placement of outdoor advertising messages. Critics have even labeled billboard advertising as "Pollution on a stick."

But in the last decade, billboards have taken on a new chic look, sporting ads for more than cigarettes and alcohol products. The entire Los Angeles Chamber Orchestra now appears all day and all night in an ad posted on the side of the city's performing arts building. Heavy users of outdoor ads include fashion apparel makers like Calvin Klein and Dockers, beauty products like Oil of Olay and Pantene, movie ads, automobiles, and even religious messages such as the one in Fort Lauderdale, Florida, that reads: "Let's meet at my house Sunday before the game. God."[23]

As outdoor ads set new highs for creativity, marketers have come to expect the unexpected. For instance, Dayton Hudson's downtown Minneapolis department store advertised Valentine's Day candy on a billboard that released a mint scent that traveled for blocks. Improved technology has also slashed costs. For example, the more than 400 billboard ads for the California Milk Board cost an estimated $5 to $6 per 1,000 viewers, about half what a newspaper ad would cost.[24]

New technologies are helping to revive outdoor advertising, offsetting the huge drop that resulted from limitations on ads for tobacco and alcohol products. Technology livens up the billboards themselves with animation, large sculptures, and laser images. Digital message signboards can display winning lottery numbers or other timely messages like weather and traffic reports. The best-known digital signboard in the United States is in New York's Times Square. Given the

MARKETING STRATEGY SUCCESS

The Blair Witch Project Conjures Up Guerrilla Advertising

BACKGROUND No sorcery was involved; no magic potion was served; no spells or incantations murmured. Instead, student filmmakers at the University of Central Florida used something called *guerrilla advertising* to entice moviegoers to buy tickets to *The Blair Witch Project*. The film, using a documentary style, focuses on a trio of filmmakers who investigate the legendary and mysterious witch but never return from their investigation to tell what they found. Although the total $50,000 production costs amounted to less than an Arnold Schwarzenegger extravaganza, box-office revenues boiled over. Ticket receipts passed $100 million the first month.

THE CHALLENGE The movie's filmmakers, while inexperienced, were confident about their cinematic abilities. They were much less secure about turning it into a marketing winner on their shoestring budget. After all, their summer release would be competing with a series of high-profile films, each produced with $50 million-plus production budgets and promoted with $50 million ad budgets and lucrative corporate tie-ins. In order to make the film stand out on the crowded release schedule, the film's marketers would have to devise a novel—and inexpensive—promotional strategy. And so they did.

THE STRATEGY Guerrilla advertising focuses on unusual,

continued on next page

unorthodox, and highly creative means of leveling the competitive playing field. To build word of mouth, Artisan Entertainment, the film's distributor, hired 100 college interns to distribute comic books featuring the Blair Witch folklore, T-shirts, and missing-person fliers with the actors' pictures to clubs, bookstores, trendy clothing retailers, and cybercafes around the nation. Also fanning the grassroots efforts to build prerelease interest was the Web site—a site so compelling that it lured over 200 million unsuspecting surfers into its domain. By the time the film was first shown at the Sundance Film Festival, it had already attracted a large community of Web surfers anxious for its debut on the neighborhood big screen.

THE OUTCOME The key to the success of *The Blair Witch Project* is less about production magic and more about promotion magic. Internet resources allow even undercapitalized advertisers to create a one-on-one, face-to-face, word-of-mouth campaign. It reaches out to the audience unlike any full-page magazine or newspaper ad can ever do by bringing Web site visitors together to talk about what is being advertised.

official task of counting down the last minutes of each year, a message on this outdoor billboard costs $50,000 to $150,000 to run for one month.[25]

Interactive Media

This relatively new advertising medium contains characteristics of both print and broadcast media. Interactive media enhance two-way communication and encourage audience participation. A high level of consumer involvement is inherent to any successful interactive advertisement. Although e-mail is considered a form of direct mail, it recently has taken on the characteristics of interactive media. While e-mail campaigns boast high viewer responses of 14 percent to 22 percent, banner ads have a low 1 percent click-on rate. Wine.com, formerly known as Virtual Vineyards, recently established an e-mail newsletter that allows subscribers to communicate online with company representatives. The online wine distributor asks subscribers to provide an optional profile so that the company can target messages more precisely and can create an effective interactive relationship with its customers.[26]

Companies use interactive advertising media like the Web and e-mail to supplement their messages over traditional media. Online and offline retailer The Sharper Image is embracing e-mail as an interactive marketing tool for its direct marketing campaigns. The office and personal accessory catalog company expanded its operations with the addition of a Web site. Information gathered online is then used to create e-mail messages that target each cybershopper. Says one promotion and marketing writer, "The cost of e-mail is a pittance by comparison to direct mail."[27]

Other Advertising Media

As consumers filter out appeals from traditional as well as Internet ads, marketers need new ways to catch their attention. In addition to the major media, firms use many other vehicles to communicate their messages. Transit advertising includes ads placed both inside and outside buses, subway trains and stations, and commuter trains. Some firms place ads on the roofs of taxicabs, on bus stop shelters and benches, on telephone booths, and even on parking meters. A growing but controversial form of advertising in the United States, cinema advertising, has been popular in European countries for many years. About half of the 23,000 U.S. movie theaters accept commercials. Movie-theater ads have proved especially effective for targeting young people aged 12- to 24-years old.

Ads also appear on T-shirts, inlaid in store flooring, in printed programs of live-theater productions, and as previews on movie videocassettes. Directory advertising includes the familiar Yellow Pages in telephone books along with thousands of business and industry directories. Some firms pay to have their advertising messages placed on hot-air balloons, blimps, banners behind airplanes, and on scoreboards at sporting events. Other companies have their own advertising vehicles, called mobile marketing squads. Nantucket Nectars, which generates about $50 million in annual revenue from sales of its fruity snack drinks, uses purple Winnebagos to supply beverages to outdoor events that target 18- to 35-year-old consumers.[28]

MEDIA SCHEDULING

Once advertisers have selected the media that best match their advertising objectives and promotional budget, attention shifts to **media scheduling**—setting the timing and sequence for a series of advertisements. A variety of factors influence this decision, as well. Sales patterns, repurchase cycles, and competitors' activities are the most important variables.

Seasonal sales patterns are common in many industries. For example, an airline might reduce advertising during peak travel periods and boost its media schedule during low travel months. (Refer back to the discussion of promotion as a variable for stabilizing sales in Chapter 15.)

Repurchase cycles may also play a role in media scheduling—products with shorter repurchase cycles will more likely require consistent media schedules throughout the year. Competitors' activities are still other influences on media scheduling. For instance, a small firm may elect to avoid advertising during periods of heavy advertising by its rivals.

Advertisers use the concepts of reach, frequency, and gross rating points to measure the effectiveness of media scheduling plans. *Reach* refers to the number of different people or households exposed to an advertisement at least once during a certain time period, typically four weeks. *Frequency* refers to the number of times an individual person is exposed to an advertisement during a certain time period. By multiplying reach times frequency, advertisers quantitatively describe the total weight of a media effort, which is called the campaign's *gross rating point.*

Recently, marketers have questioned the effectiveness of reach and frequency to measure ad success online. The theory behind frequency is that the average advertising viewer needs a minimum of three exposures to a message to get it. For Web surfers, the "wear-out" is much quicker, hence, the greater importance of building customer relationships through advertisements.[29]

Hypothetical Media Schedule

Figure 16.9 shows a hypothetical media schedule for advertising devoted to the introduction of a new automobile designed to appeal primarily to male buyers. The model is introduced in November with a direct-mail piece offering test drives to recipients. Extensive outdoor and transit advertising support the direct-mail blitz during a three-month introductory period, and the firm airs commercials during a Christmas television special early in December.

The car's manufacturer also advertises during selected network shows throughout the year, as well as on football and baseball telecasts. The manufacturer advertises extensively in magazines, as well. One publication carries ads for the model every month, and two national magazines carry ads in alternating issues: one for the first two weekly issues and the second for the last two weeks each month. Finally, newspapers run cooperative advertising for which the manufacturer and dealer share the costs.

ORGANIZATION OF THE ADVERTISING FUNCTION

Although the ultimate responsibility for advertising decision making often rests with top marketing management, organizational arrangements for the advertising function vary among companies. A producer of a technical industrial product may interact with one person within the company, who works primarily to write copy for submission to trade publications. A consumer goods company, on the other hand, may staff a large department with advertising specialists.

The advertising function is usually organized as a staff department reporting to the vice president (or director) of marketing. The director of advertising is an executive position with the responsibility for the functional activity of advertising. This position requires not only a skilled and experienced advertiser but also an individual who communicates effectively within the organization. The success of a firm's promotional strategy depends on the advertising director's willingness and ability to communicate both vertically and horizontally. The major tasks typically organized under advertising include advertising research, design, copyrighting, media analysis, and, in some cases, sales and trade promotion.

5

Outline the organization of the advertising function and the role of an advrtising agency.

Advertising Agencies

Many major advertisers hire independent **advertising agencies,** firms of marketing specialists who assist advertisers in planning and preparing advertisements. McCann-Erickson

MARKETING DICTIONARY

media scheduling Timing and sequencing of advertisements.

advertising agency Marketing specialist firm used to assist advertisers in planning and implementing advertising programs.

FIGURE 16.9   Hypothetical Media Schedule for a New Car Introduction

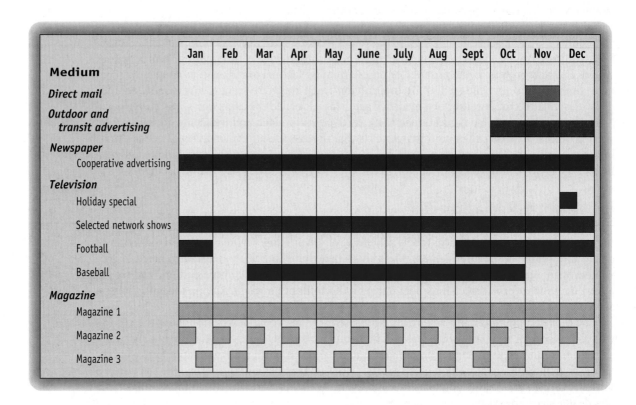

Worldwide, the largest advertising agency in the world, represents 58 clients in 1,248 different markets. DDB Worldwide and Grey Advertising rank second and third, respectively.[30]

Most large advertisers cite several reasons for relying on agencies for at least some portion of their advertising. Agencies typically employ highly qualified specialists who provide a degree of creativity and objectivity that is difficult to sustain in a corporate advertising department. Some also manage to reduce the cost of advertising by allowing the advertiser to avoid many of the fixed expenses associated with maintaining an internal advertising department.

Figure 16.10 shows a hypothetical organization chart for a large advertising agency. Although job titles may vary among agencies, the major functions may be classified as creative services; account services; marketing services, including media services, marketing research, and sales promotion; and finance and management.

SALES PROMOTION

6

Identify the principal methods of sales promotion.

Although marketers sometimes mistakenly relegate their overall promotional strategy to a secondary role, another type of nonpersonal selling actually commands double the promotional dollar outlays of advertising. **Sales promotion** may be defined as marketing activities other than personal selling, advertising, and publicity that enhance consumer purchasing and dealer effectiveness. Like advertising, these activities trace their roots to the far reaches of antiquity. Examples of both sales promotion and advertising have been found among the ruins of Pompei and Ephesus. In the United States, Adolphus Busch gave away samples of his beer and a pocket knife as a premium in 1880. Ten years later, Procter & Gamble exchanged watch-chain charms for Ivory soap wrappers. In 1895, Grape Nuts cereal marketers were the first to offer a coupon on the box (for a one-cent discount off the purchase price), and in 1914, Ford Motor Co. offered a

FIGURE 16.10 Advertising Agency Organization Chart

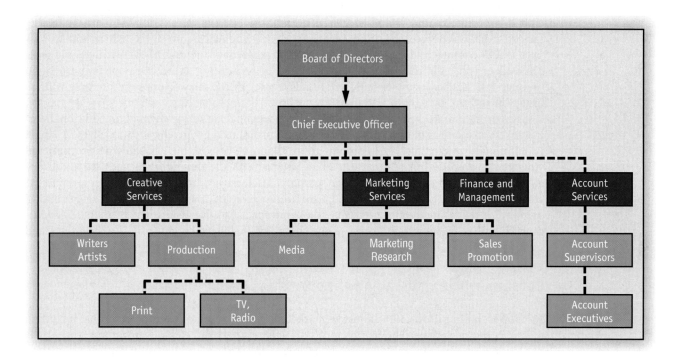

rebate of $50 for each $490 Model T. Marketers spend over $250 billion annually on such consumer and trade sales promotion activities as coupons, sampling, displays, trade shows and exhibitions, demonstrations, and various nonrecurrent promotional efforts. A breakdown of sales promotion budgets reveals that the typical large package-goods company spends 50 percent on trade promotion, 24 percent on consumer promotion, and 26 percent on media advertising.[31]

Sales promotion techniques were originally intended as short-term incentives aimed at producing immediate consumer buying responses. Traditionally, these techniques were viewed as supplements to other elements of the firm's promotional mix. Today, however, marketers recognize them as integral parts of many marketing plans, and the focus of sales promotion has shifted from short-term to long-term goals of building brand equity and maintaining continuing purchases. For example, a frequent-flyer program enables an airline to build a base of loyal customers where it had none before. American Airlines was one of the first to develop a loyalty marketing program when it introduced AAdvantage in 1981. Now it is also selling miles for pure revenue. Of the estimated $10 billion worth of miles awarded to travelers, 40 percent were earned on the ground. Infrequent flyers are earning tickets for family vacations, and occasional travelers are choosing credit cards and phone services based on mile giveaways.[32]

americanairlines.com

Both retailers and manufacturers use sales promotions to offer consumers extra incentives to buy. Rather than emphasizing product features to make consumers feel good about their purchases, these promotions are likely to stress price advantages. The general objectives of sales promotion are to speed up the sales process and increase sales volume. Through a consumer promotion, a marketer encourages consumers to try the product, use more of it, and buy it again. The firm also hopes to foster sales of complementary products and increase impulse purchases.

Sales promotion complements advertising, and marketers often produce their best results when they combine the two. Ads create awareness, while

MARKETING DICTIONARY

sales promotion Marketing activities other than personal selling, advertising, and publicity that stimulate consumer purchasing and dealer effectiveness; includes displays, trade shows and expositions, demonstrations, and various nonrecurrent selling efforts.

sales promotions lead to trial or purchase. Promotions encourage immediate action because they impose limited time frames. For example, cents-off coupons and rebates have expiration dates. In addition, sales promotions produce measurable results, making it relatively easy for marketers to evaluate their effectiveness.

It is important to understand what sales promotions can and cannot do. They can encourage interest from salespeople and consumers for both new and mature products, help introduce new products, encourage trial and repeat purchases, increase usage, neutralize competition, and reinforce advertising. On the other hand, sales promotions cannot overcome poor brand images, product deficiencies, or poor training for salespeople. While sales promotions increase volume in the short term, they often lead to lower profits.

Sales promotion techniques may serve all members of a marketing channel. In addition, manufacturers may use trade promotion methods to promote their products to resellers. A single promotional strategy may well combine more than one option, but probably no promotional strategy has ever used all of them in a single program. While the different types are not mutually exclusive, promotions generally are employed selectively. Sales promotion techniques include the following consumer-oriented promotions: samples, bonus packs, premiums, coupons, price-off deals, rebates, contests, sweepstakes, and specialty advertising. Trade-oriented promotions include trade allowances, point-of-purchase advertising, trade shows, dealer incentives, and training programs.

Consumer-Oriented Sales Promotions

In the $85 billion promotion industry, marketers use all types of sales promotions, including games, contests, sweepstakes, and coupons to persuade new and existing customers to try their products. Consumer-oriented sales promotions encourage repurchases by rewarding current users, boosting sales of complementary products, and increasing impulse purchases. These promotions also attract consumer attention in the midst of advertising clutter. Table 16.2 lists the most popular consumer promotion techniques for firms using this element of the promotional mix. If overused, however, sales promotions can damage brand equity because consumers begin to expect price discounts. The following sections briefly describe the various forms of consumer-oriented sales promotions.

Coupons and Refunds

Coupons, the most widely used form of sales promotion, offer discounts on the purchase price of a good or service. Consumers can redeem the coupons at retail outlets, which receive a handling fee from the manufacturer. Consumers using coupons save nearly $3.5 billion annually. Mail, magazine, newspaper, and package insertions are the standard methods of distributing coupons.

TABLE 16.2	Seven Most Popular Consumer Promotion Techniques

TECHNIQUE	PERCENTAGE OF MARKETERS WHO USE IT
Coupons in retail ads	90
In-store coupons	88
Refunds	85
Electronic in-store displays	83
Samples of established products	78
Premiums	75
Sweepstakes	70

Free-standing inserts (FSIs) in Sunday newspapers account for about 75 percent of all coupons distributed. The average household receives about 3,000 coupons a year at an overall annual cost of about $8 billion to marketers.[33]

Despite the popularity of coupons as a sales promotion method, marketers recognize their inefficiency. Of almost 300 billion coupons issued in a typical year, only 2 percent—less than 6 billion—are actually redeemed. Marketers are now experimenting with online couponing. Says one industry expert, "The key feature of Internet couponing is the ability to build a database and respond to personal preferences." Shoppers access and print out coupons from such Web sites as CoolSavings.com that link to a retailer's site or banner ad. A recent survey reported that 60 percent of respondents from online households would use coupons offering discounts on goods and services.[34]

 CoolSavings.com

Refunds offer cash back to consumers who send in proof of purchasing one or more products. Refunds help packaged-goods companies to increase purchase rates, promote multiple purchases, and reward product users. They can reinforce brand loyalty, but many consumers find the refund forms too bothersome to complete.

Samples, Bonus Packs, and Premiums

Marketers are increasingly adopting the "Try it, you'll like it" approach as an effective means of getting consumers to try and purchase their goods and services. Procter & Gamble marketers handed out more than 80 million samples last fall—it is the largest sampling program ever.[35] *Sampling* refers to the free distribution of a product in an attempt to obtain future sales. Samples may be distributed door-to-door, by mail, via demonstrations in stores or at events, or by including them in packages with other products.

Sampling produces a higher response rate than most other promotions. About three-quarters of the consumers who receive samples try them. In fact, a recent survey showed that 92 percent of consumers preferred receiving free samples rather than coupons. With sampling, marketers can target potential customers and be certain that the product reaches them. Sampling provides an especially useful way to promote new or unusual products because it gives the consumer a direct product experience.

One of the disadvantages of sampling is the high cost. Not only must the marketer give away small quantities of a product that might otherwise have generated revenues through regular sales, but also the market is, in effect, closed for the time it takes consumers to use up the samples. In addition, the marketer may encounter problems in distributing the samples. Hellman's marketers annoyed consumers instead of pleasing them when the firm distributed sample packets of Italian and French salad dressing in home-delivered copies of *The New York Times.* Many of the packets burst when the papers hit the driveways.

A *bonus pack* is a specially packaged item that gives the purchaser a larger quantity at the regular price. For instance, Camay soap offered three bars for the price of two, and Salon Selectives often increases the size of its shampoos and conditioners for the same price as regular sizes.

Premiums are items given free or at reduced cost with purchases of other products. For example, Pantene frequently attaches a purse-size bottle of hair spray to the sides of its other hair-care products. Premiums have proven effective in motivating consumers to try new products or different brands. A premium should have some relationship with the product or brand it accompanies, though. For example, a home-improvement center might offer free nail aprons to its customers.

Contests and Sweepstakes

Firms often sponsor contests and sweepstakes to introduce new goods and services and to attract additional customers. *Contests* require entrants to solve problems or write essays, or they may also require proofs of purchase. A recent contest by Irish brewer Guinness gave a pub in Ireland to the author of a winning essay. *Sweepstakes,* on the other hand, choose winners by chance, so no product purchase is necessary. They are more popular with consumers than contests because they do not take as much effort on the part of the consumer to enter. Marketers like them, too, because they are inexpensive to run and the number of winners is predetermined. With some

For an additional 99 cents, Taco Bell customers received a special premium—their own spine-tingling Monster Eye straw. The fast-food chain sold 8 million eerie eyes in two-and-a-half-weeks.

contests, the sponsors cannot predict the number of people who will correctly complete the puzzles or gather the right number of symbols from scratch-off cards.

Companies like WebStakes and NetStakes specialize in Web-based sweepstakes, designing and implementing customized sweepstakes for marketers who want to deliver their brand messages to targeted audiences; these sophisticated services use elaborate databases, and they also track entrant activity. With the recent rash of court rulings and legal restrictions, the use of contests requires careful administration. Any firm contemplating using this promotional technique should engage the services of an online promotion specialist.

Specialty Advertising

The origin of specialty advertising has been traced to the Middle Ages, when artisans gave wooden pegs bearing their names to prospects, who drove them into the walls at home to serve as convenient hangers for armor. In more modern times, corporations began putting their names on a variety of products in the late 1800s, as newspapers and print shops looked for ways to make more money from their presses.

Specialty advertising is a sales promotion technique that places the advertiser's name, address, and advertising message on useful articles that are then distributed to target consumers. Marketers give out more than $8 billion worth of specialty advertising items each year. Wearable products, including T-shirts, baseball caps, and jackets, are the most popular products, accounting for nearly a third of distributor sales. Writing instruments, glassware, and calendars are other popular forms of specialty advertising.[36]

Advertising specialties help to reinforce previous or future advertising and sales messages. Consumers like these giveaways, which generate stronger responses to direct mail, resulting in three times the dollar volume of sales as compared to direct mail alone. Companies use this form of promotion to highlight store openings and new products, motivate salespeople, increase visits to trade-show booths, and improve customer relationships.

Trade-Oriented Promotions

Sales promotion techniques can also contribute effectively to campaigns aimed at such channel members as retailers and wholesalers. **Trade promotion** is sales promotion that appeals to marketing intermediaries rather than to consumers. Marketers use trade promotion in push strategies by encouraging resellers to stock new products, continue to carry existing ones, and promote both effectively to consumers. As discussed earlier, the typical firm actually spends half of its promotional budget on trade promotion—as much money as it spends on advertising and consumer-oriented sales promotions combined. Successful trade promotions offer financial incentives. They require careful timing and attention to costs and are easy to implement by retailers. These promotions should bring quick results and improve retail sales.

Trade Allowances

Among the most common trade promotion methods are **trade allowances**—deals offered to wholesalers and retailers that purchase or promote specific products. These offers take various forms. A *buying allowance* gives retailers a discount on goods. These include *off-invoice allowances*, through which retailers deduct specified amounts from their invoices or receive free goods, such as one free case for every ten ordered, when they order certain quantities. When a manufacturer offers a *promotional allowance*, it agrees to pay the reseller a certain amount to cover the costs of special promotional displays or extensive advertising that features the manufacturer's product. The goal is to increase sales to consumers by encouraging resellers to promote effectively.

Campbell's marketers recently teamed up with Pathmark grocery chain in a successful sweepstakes promotion. With the purchase of any three Campbell's products, customers could win gift certificates for groceries ranging from $1 off their next shopping order to a grand prize of $7,500 worth of groceries.

Some retailers require vendors to pay a special *slotting allowance* before they agree to take on new products. These fees guarantee so-called *slots*, or shelf space, in the stores for new items. Retailers defend these fees as essential in covering the added costs of carrying the products, such as redesigning display space and shelves, setting up and administering control systems, managing inventory, and taking the risks inherent in stocking new products. These fees can be sizable, from several hundred dollars per store to many thousands of dollars for a retail chain and millions of dollars for nationally distributed products. The ability of stores to demand slotting allowances indicates how much power retailers hold today. Many marketers consider these fees as a form of blackmail or bribery that only increases retailer profits. The controversy has resulted in recent Congressional inquiries to determine whether they constitute unfair methods of competition.[37]

Point-of-Purchase Advertising

A display or other promotion located near the site of the actual buying decision is known as **point-of-purchase (POP) advertising.** This method of sales promotion capitalizes on the fact that buyers make many purchase decisions within the store, so it encourages retailers to improve on-site merchandising. They directly benefit the retailer by creating special displays designed to stimulate sales of the item being promoted.

MARKETING DICTIONARY

specialty advertising Sales promotion technique that involves the use of articles such as key rings, calendars, and ball-point pens that bear the advertiser's name, address, and advertising message.

trade promotion Sales promotion geared to marketing intermediaries rather than consumers.

trade allowances Deals offered to wholesalers and retailers for purchasing or promoting specific products.

point-of-purchase (POP) advertising Displays and other promotions located near the site of the actual buying decision.

FIGURE 16.11 | **POP Display for Children's Clothing**

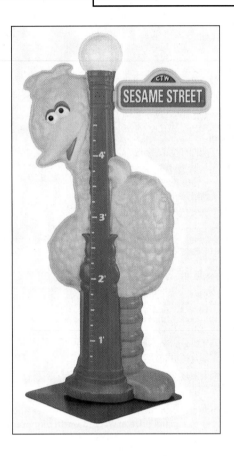

Free-standing POP promotions often appear at the ends of aisles, such as the Sesame Street display in Figure 16.11 featuring Big Bird in children's clothing departments. In-store promotions of consumer goods are common. Such displays may provide useful supplements for themes developed in other areas of the promotional strategy. A life-sized, in-store display of a celebrity who appears in television advertising can very effectively reinforce the broadcast message.

Trade Shows

To influence resellers and other members of the distribution channel, many marketers participate in trade shows. These shows are often organized by industry trade associations, perhaps as part of these associations' annual meetings or conventions. Vendors who serve the industries are invited to appear at the shows to display and demonstrate their products for members. Every year, over 4,300 different shows in the United States and Canada draw over 1.3 million exhibitors and 85 million attendees. The National Restaurant Association, for example, sponsors an annual trade show in Chicago each year. More than 100,000 members attend, gathering from all 50 U.S. states and 70 countries, along with almost 2,000 exhibitors.

Because of the expense involved in trade shows, a company must assess the value of such a show on several criteria, such as direct sales, any increase in product awareness, image building, and any contribution to the firm's marketing communications efforts. Trade shows give especially effective opportunities to introduce new products and to generate sales leads. Some types of shows reach ultimate consumers as well as channel members. Home, recreation, and automobile shows, for instance, allow businesses to display and demonstrate home improvement, recreation, and other consumer products to entire communities.

Dealer Incentives, Contests, and Training Programs

Manufacturers run dealer incentive programs and contests to induce retailers and their salespeople to increase sales and to promote products. These channel members receive incentives for performing promotion-related tasks and can win contests by reaching sales goals. Manufacturers may offer major prizes to resellers like trips to exotic places. *Push money* is another incentive that gives retail salespeople cash rewards for every unit of a product they sell. This benefit increases the likelihood that the salesperson will try to convince a customer to buy the product rather than a competing brand.

For more expensive and highly complex products, manufacturers often provide specialized training for retail salespeople. This background helps salespeople explain features, competitive advantages, and other information to consumers. Training can be provided in several ways: A manufacturer's sales representative can conduct training sessions during regular sales calls, or the firm can distribute sales literature and videocassettes.

PUBLIC RELATIONS

7

Explain the roles of public relations, publicity, and cross promotions in an organization's promotional strategy.

Chapter 15 defined **public relations** as the firm's communications and relationships with its various publics, including customers, employees, stockholders, suppliers, government agencies, and the society in which it operates. Organizational public relations efforts date back to 1889, when George Westinghouse hired two people to publicize the advantages of alternating-current electricity and to refute arguments for direct-current systems.

Public relations is an efficient, indirect communications channel through which a firm can promote products, although it serves broader objectives than those of other components of promotional strategy. It is concerned with the prestige and image of all parts of the organization. Today, public relations plays a larger role than ever within the promotional mix, and it may emphasize more marketing-oriented information. In addition to its traditional activities, such as surveying public attitudes and creating a good corporate image, PR also supports advertising in promoting the organization's goods and services.

Approximately 160,000 people work in public relations in both the not-for-profit and profit-oriented sectors. Some 1,800 public relations firms currently operate in the United States. In addition, thousands of smaller firms and one-person operations compete to offer these services.

Public relations is in a period of major growth as a result of increased public pressure on industries regarding corporate ethical conduct and environmental and international issues. International expenditures on public relations are growing more rapidly than those for advertising and sales promotion. Many top executives are becoming more involved in public relations as well. The public expects top managers to take greater responsibility for company actions than they have accepted in the past. Those who refuse are widely criticized.

The PR department is the link between the firm and the media. It provides press releases and holds news conferences to announce new products, formation of strategic alliances, management changes, financial results, or similar developments. The PR department may issue its own publications, as well, including newsletters, brochures, and reports.

A PR plan begins much like an advertising plan with research to define the role and scope of the firm's overall public relations and current challenges. Next come strategic decisions on short-term and long-term goals and markets, analysis of product features, and choices of messages and media channels—or other PR strategies such as speaking engagements or contests—for each market. Plan execution involves developing messages highlighting the benefits that the firm brings to each market. The final step is to measure results.

Marketing and Nonmarketing Public Relations

Nonmarketing public relations refer to a company's messages about general management issues. When a company makes a decision that affects any of its publics, input from public relations specialists can help to smooth its dealings with those publics. A company that decides to close a plant would need advice on how to deal with the local community. Other examples include a company's attempts to gain favorable public opinion during a long strike or an open letter to Congress published in a newspaper during congressional debates on a bill that would affect a particular industry. Although some companies organize their public relations departments separately from their marketing divisions, PR activities invariably affect promotional strategies.

In contrast, *marketing public relations (MPR)* refers to narrowly focused public relations activities that directly support marketing goals. MPR involves an organization's relationships with consumers or other groups about marketing concerns and can be either proactive or reactive.

With proactive MPR, the marketer takes the initiative and seeks out opportunities for promoting the firm's products, often including distribution of press releases and feature articles. For example, companies send press releases about new products to newspapers, television stations, and relevant consumer, business, and trade publications. It is a powerful marketing tool since it adds news coverage that reinforces direct promotion activities.

Reactive MPR responds to an external situation that has potential negative consequences for the organization. Examples of reactive MPR are responses to product tamperings, such as the deaths caused by cyanide in Tylenol (1982) and Sudafed (1991) capsules. Prompt corrective action and strong PR campaigns from Johnson & Johnson and Burroughs Wellcome, respectively, prevented these situations from becoming disasters. On the other hand, Coca-Cola failed in its

MARKETING DICTIONARY

public relations Firm's communications and relationships with its various publics.

Underwear marketer Joe Boxer Corp. publicizes its Web site by sewing its Web address into the waistband of each pair of shorts. Customer feedback is also encouraged, and site visitors can send messages that are then posted on the scrolling zipper of the firm's huge billboard in New York's Times Square.

reactive MPR efforts when contaminated water was found in its bottled soft drinks in several European countries, including France and Belgium. Company officials inappropriately held back any comment until days after deaths had occurred and several governments had banned sales of the soft drink.[38]

Publicity

The aspect of public relations that is most directly related to promoting a firm's products is **publicity,** nonpersonal stimulation of demand for a good, service, place, idea, person, or organization by unpaid placement of significant news regarding the product in a print or broadcast medium. It has been said that if advertising is the hammer, publicity is the nail. It creates credibility for the advertising to follow. Firms generate publicity by creating special events, holding press conferences, and preparing news releases and media kits. Many firms, such as the Body Shop, Starbucks, and Wal-Mart's Sam's Club, have built their brands with virtually no advertising. Pharmaceutical products including Viagra, Prozac, and Valium have become worldwide brands with relatively little advertising. In the toy field, Furby, Pokémon, and Tickle Me Elmo all became first-year hits with minimal advertising. On the Internet, Yahoo!, Amazon.com, and Excite became powerhouse brands with hardly any advertising.[39]

While publicity generates minimal costs compared to other forms of promotion, it does not deliver its message entirely free of cost. Publicity-related expenses include the costs of employing marketing personnel assigned to create and submit publicity releases, printing and mailing costs, and related expenses.

Firms often pursue some publicity to promote their images or viewpoints. Other publicity efforts involve organizational activities such as plant expansions, mergers and acquisitions, management changes, and research-and-development programs. A significant amount of publicity, however, provides information about goods and services, particularly new goods and services.

Because many consumers consider news stories to be more credible than advertisements as sources of information, publicity releases are often sent to media editors for possible inclusion in news stories. The media audiences perceive the news as coming from the communications media, not the sponsors. The information in a publicity release about a new good or service can provide valuable assistance for a television, newspaper, or magazine writer, leading to eventual broadcast or publication. Publicity releases sometimes fill voids in publications, and at other times they become part of regular features. In either case, they offer firms valuable supplements to paid advertising messages.

CROSS PROMOTION

In a recent trend, marketers have begun to combine their promotional efforts for related products using a technique called **cross promotion,** in which marketing partners share the cost of a promotional campaign that meets their mutual needs—an important benefit in an environment of rising media costs. Relationship marketing strategies like co-marketing and co-branding are forms of cross promotion. Marketers realize that these joint efforts between established brands provide greater benefits in return for both companies; investments of time and money on such promotions will become increasingly important to many partners' growth prospects.

The movie industry is one of the most prominent users of cross promotion. Movie studios frequently partner with fast-food chains. The movie studios, which spend an average of $54 million to produce and promote a film, find that cross promotions can bring effective ways in creating public awareness of their films. Children who open their fast-food meals and find movie character toys are likely to ask their parents to see the movies. Some of the more recent cross promotions include Burger King and Pokémon trading cards for Warner Bros.' *Pokémon: The First Movie*; McDonald's and Teenie Beanie Babies for Walt Disney's animated film *Tarzan*, and Domino's and Easter Seals for *SimCity 3000* video game.

San Diego–based Jack-in-the-Box made a hit with its latest cross promotion with PEZ Candy dispensers, featuring the chain's clown-faced personification. Jack-in-the-Box marketers knew it would be a success since the Jack Pez dispensers were selling for hundreds of bucks on the Web. At $1.99, the new versions were sure to spring out of the box.[40]

Procter & Gamble, the billion-dollar consumer products company, recently tied its line of Max Factor cosmetics to the video release of Academy-award winner *Shakespeare in Love*. P&G offered free movie rentals with each mascara purchase and supported the promotion with in-store POP displays and magazine print ads.[41]

@ **jackinthebox.com**

MEASURING PROMOTIONAL EFFECTIVENESS

Each element of the promotional mix represents a major expenditure for a firm. While promotional prices vary widely, advertisers typically pay a fee based on cost to deliver the message to viewers, listeners, or readers—the so-called cost per thousand (CPM). Billboards are the cheapest way to spend advertising dollars with an average CPM of $2, compared to $5 for drive-time radio, $9 for magazines, and $10 to $20 for newspapers or prime-time television.[42] So, while price is an important factor in media selection, it is by no means the only one—or all ads would appear on billboards!

Because promotion represents such a major expenditure for many firms, they need to determine whether their campaigns accomplish appropriate promotional objectives. Companies want their advertising agencies and in-house marketing personnel to demonstrate how promotional programs contribute to increased sales and profits. Marketers are well aware of the number of advertising messages and sales promotions that consumers encounter daily—and they know that these people practice selective perception and simply screen out the messages.

By measuring promotional effectiveness, organizations can evaluate different strategies, prevent mistakes before spending money on specific programs,

8

Explain how marketers assess promotional effectiveness.

MARKETING **DICTIONARY**

publicity Stimulation of demand for a good, service, place, idea, person, or organization by disseminating commercially significant news or obtaining favorable media presentations not paid for by the sponsor.

cross promotion Technique in which marketing partners share the cost of a promotional campaign that meets their mutual needs.

and improve their promotional programs. As the earlier discussion of promotional planning explained, any evaluation program starts with objectives and goals; otherwise, marketers have no yardstick against which to measure effectiveness. However, determining whether an advertising message has achieved its intended objective is one of the most difficult undertakings in marketing. Sales promotions and direct marketing are somewhat easier to evaluate because they evoke measurable consumer responses. Like advertising, public relations is also difficult to assess on purely objective terms.

Measuring Advertising Effectiveness

Measures to evaluate the effectiveness of advertising, while difficult and costly, are essential parts of any marketing plan. Without an assessment strategy, marketers will not know whether their advertising achieves the objectives of the marketing plan or if the dollars in the advertising budget are well spent. To answer these questions, marketers can conduct two types of research. *Media research* assesses how well a particular medium delivers the advertiser's message, where and when to place the advertisement, and the size of the audience. Buyers of broadcast time base their purchases on estimated Nielsen rating points, and the networks have to make good if ratings do not reach promised levels. Buyers of print advertising space pay fees based on circulation. Circulation figures are independently certified by specialized research firms.

The other major category, *message research*, tests consumer reactions to an advertisement's creative message. Pretesting and posttesting, the two methods for performing message research, are discussed in the following sections.

Pretesting

In order to assess an advertisement's likely effectiveness before it actually appears in the chosen medium, marketers often conduct **pretesting.** The obvious advantage of this technique is the opportunity to evaluate ads during the development stage. Marketers can conduct a number of different pretests, beginning during the concept phase in the campaign's earliest stages when they have only rough copy of the ad and continuing until the ad layout and design are almost completed.

Pretesting employs a variety of evaluation methods. Focus groups can discuss their reactions to mockups of ads using different themes, headlines, or illustrations. To test magazine advertisements, the Batten, Barton, Durstine & Osborn ad agency cuts ads out of advance copies of magazines and then inserts the ads it wants to test. Interviewers later check the impact of the advertisements on readers who receive free copies of the revised magazines.

mccann.com

Another ad agency, McCann-Erickson, uses a *sales conviction test* to evaluate magazine advertisements. Interviewers ask heavy users of a particular item to pick one of two alternative advertisements that would convince them to purchase it.

To screen potential radio and television advertisements, marketers often recruit consumers to sit in a studio and indicate their preferences by pressing two buttons, one for a positive reaction to the commercial and the other for a negative reaction. Sometimes, proposed ad copy is printed on a postcard that also offers a free product; the number of cards returned represents an indication of the copy's effectiveness. *Blind product tests* are also frequently used. In these tests, people are asked to select unidentified products on the basis of available advertising copy.

Mechanical devices offer yet another method of assessing how people read advertising copy. One mechanical test uses a hidden camera to photograph eye movements of readers. The results help advertisers to determine headline placement and copy length. Another mechanical approach measures the galvanic skin response—changes in the electrical resistance of the skin produced by emotional reactions.

Posttesting

Posttesting assesses advertising copy after it has appeared in the appropriate medium. Pretesting generally is a more desirable measurement method than posttesting because it can save the cost of placing ineffective ads. However, posttesting can be helpful in planning future advertisements and in adjusting current advertising programs.

In one of the most popular posttests, the *Starch Readership Report* interviews people who have read selected magazines to determine whether they observed various ads in them. A copy of the magazine is used as an interviewing aid, and each interviewer starts at a different point in the magazine. For larger ads, respondents are also asked about specifics, such as headlines and copy. Figure 16.12 shows an advertisement with the actual *Starch* scores. All such *readership*, or *recognition*, tests assume that future sales are related to advertising readership.

Unaided recall tests are another method of posttesting the effectiveness of advertisements. Respondents do not see copies of the magazine after their initial reading but must recall the ads from memory. Interviewers for the Gallup and Robinson marketing research firms require people to prove they have read a magazine by recalling one or more of its feature articles. The people who remember particular articles receive cards with the names of products advertised in the issue. They then list the ads they remember and explain what they can recall about those ads. Finally, the respondents answer questions about their potential purchases of the advertised products. Readership tests conclude Gallup and Robinson interviews. Burke Research Corp. conducts telephone interviews the day after a commercial has aired on television to test brand recognition and the advertisement's effectiveness. Another unaided recall test is adWatch, a joint project of *Advertising Age* magazine and the Gallup Organization. It measures ad awareness by telephone polling that asks each consumer to name the advertisement that first comes to mind of all the ads he or she has seen, heard, or read in the previous 30 days.

Inquiry tests are another popular form of posttest. Advertisements sometimes offer gifts—generally product samples—to people who respond to them. The number of inquiries relative to the advertisement's cost forms a measure of its effectiveness.

Split runs allow advertisers to test two or more ads at the same time. Although advertisers traditionally place different versions in newspapers and magazines, split runs on cable television systems frequently test the effectiveness of TV ads. With this method, advertisers divide the cable TV audience or a publication's subscribers in two: Half view advertisement A and the other half view advertisement B. The relative effectiveness of the alternatives is then determined through inquiries or recall and recognition tests.

Regardless of the exact method they choose, marketers must realize that pretesting and posttesting are expensive efforts. As a result, they must plan to use these techniques as effectively as possible.

| FIGURE 16.12 | Magazine Advertisement with *Starch* Scores |

Measuring Sales Promotion Effectiveness

Because many sales promotions, especially consumer-oriented techniques, result in direct consumer responses, marketers can relatively easily track their effectiveness. As with other elements in the promotional mix, marketers must weigh the cost of the promotion against the benefits. They can measure the redemption rate of cents-off coupons, for example, and coupons often carry printed codes indicating their sources to let manufacturers and retailers know which media provide the highest redemption rates. To evaluate sampling, one of the most popular

MARKETING   DICTIONARY

pretesting Assessment of an advertisement's effectiveness before it is actually used.

posttesting Assessment of an advertisement's effectiveness after it has been used.

types of consumer promotions, marketers want to know how effectively it induces consumers to actually buy the product once they try the sample. Sweepstakes and contest entries can also be tracked.

Studies have shown that sampling does promote trial purchases. As yet, however, marketers have found no definitive answers about whether sampling helps the rate of repurchase.

Some trade promotions—allowances, contests, and dealer incentives, for example—give easily measurable results like sales increases or heavier customer traffic. Other promotions, however, like trade shows and training programs, may require more subjective judgments of the first results, such as greater product awareness and knowledge, while sales gains will take longer to show up.

Measuring Public Relations Effectiveness

As with other forms of marketing communications, organizations must measure PR results based on their objectives both for the PR program as a whole and for specific activities. In the next step, marketers must decide what they want to measure. This choice includes determining whether the message was heard by the target audience and whether it had the desired influence on public opinions.

The simplest and least costly level of assessment involves outputs of the PR program: whether the target audience received, paid attention to, understood, and retained the messages directed to them. To make this judgment, the staff could count the number of media placements and gauge the extent of media coverage. They would count attendees at any press conference, evaluate the quality of brochures and other materials, and pursue similar activities. Formal techniques include tracking publicity placements, analyzing how favorably their contents portrayed the company, and conducting public opinion polls.

To analyze PR effectiveness more deeply, a firm could conduct focus groups, interviews with opinion leaders, and more detailed and extensive opinion polls. The highest level of effectiveness measurement looks at *outcomes*: Did the PR program change people's opinions, attitudes, and behavior? PR professionals measure these outcomes through before-and-after polls (similar to pretesting and posttesting) and more advanced techniques like psychographic analysis, cluster analysis, and communicants audits.

Evaluating Interactive Media

Marketers employ several methods to measure how many users view Web advertisements: *hits* (user requests for a file), *impressions* (the number of times a viewer sees an ad), and *click-throughs* (when the user clicks on the ad to get more information). However some of these measures can be misleading. Because each page, graphic, or multimedia file equals one hit, simple interactions can easily inflate the hit count. For example, a page design increases hits when it includes a lot of small graphics that the viewer clicks on to move to other pages. The same effect occurs when the design places small amounts of information on each page so that a viewer has to link to other pages to get the whole story. Software downloads at a site also count as hits. In these cases, tracking hits or impressions tells an advertiser little about the effectiveness of an ad. To increase effectiveness, advertisers must give viewers who do click through their site something good to see. Successful Web campaigns use demonstrations, promotions, coupons, and interactive features.

Internet marketers price ad banners based on cost per thousand (CPM). Web sites that sell advertising typically guarantee a certain number of impressions—the number of times an ad banner is downloaded and presumably seen by visitors. Marketers then set a rate based on that guarantee times the CPM rate. For example, a Web site that has a CPM rate of $25 and that guarantees advertisers 600,000 impressions will charge $15,000 for the ad banner. Other Web sites price ad banners based on cost per click (CPC)—an Internet marketing formula based on the number of clicks a specific ad banner gets. Cost usually ranges between $.10 and $.20 per click.

Although the Web does not yet have a standard measurement system, a number of companies like I/Pro, NetCount, and Interse offer different Web tracking and counting systems. At least two auditing services, Audit Bureau of Verification Services and BPA International, are currently in operation. Nielsen ratings for Internet sites are based on the number of different visitors.[43]

ETHICS IN NONPERSONAL SELLING

Chapter 2 introduced the topic of marketing ethics and noted that promotion is the element in the marketing mix that raises the most ethical questions. As Chapter 15 explained, people actively debate the question whether marketing communications contribute to better lives. The following section will now take a closer look at ethical concerns in advertising, sales promotion, and public relations.

9

Discuss the importance of ethics in a firm's promotional activities.

Advertising Ethics

Even though laws allow certain types of advertising, many promotions still may involve ethical issues. For example, many people believe in curtailing advertising to children, as discussed in the Solving an Ethical Controversy box on page 522. To woo younger consumers, especially teens and those in their twenties, advertisers make messages as different from advertisements as possible; they design ads that seem more like entertainment.

Liquor advertising on television is another controversial area. Beer marketers advertise heavily on television and spend far more on advertising in print and outdoor media than do marketers of hard-liquor brands. Some members of Congress want much stricter regulation of all forms of liquor advertising on television and other media. This change would restrict ads in magazines with a 15 percent or more youth readership to black-and-white text only. Critics decry advertisements with messages implying that drinking the right beer will improve one's personal life or help to win a sports contest. Many state and local authorities are considering more restrictive proposals on both alcohol and tobacco advertising.

Marketers must also carefully draw the line between advertising and entertainment. The History Channel, a part of some cable TV selections, had to withdraw a planned series of company profiles in the face of harsh criticism because the series featured documentaries about the channel's sponsors. Those firms had some control over the final series.

In cyberspace ads, it is often even more difficult to separate advertising from editorial content since many sites resemble magazine and newspaper ads or television infomercials. Another ethical issue surrounding advertising online is the use of **cookies,** small text files that are automatically downloaded to a user's computer whenever a site is visited. Each time the user returns to that site, the site's server accesses the cookie and gathers information: What site was visited last? How long did the user stay? What was the next site visited? What was done on that site? This device helps marketers determine who their customers are, what they are interested in, and what they do when they visit the company's site. Cookies are stored on the user's PC, not on the marketer's Web site. The problem is that cookies can and do collect personal information without the user's knowledge. Because the U.S. government has resisted Internet privacy regulation, companies must implement self regulation. Consumer privacy must be taken seriously by Internet marketers since trust is the key to building long-term relationships.[44]

Puffery and Deception

Puffery refers to exaggerated claims of a product's superiority or the use of subjective or vague statements that may not be literally true. For example, a company might advertise the "most advanced system" or the "ultimate in state-of-the-art machinery."

SOLVING AN ETHICAL CONTROVERSY

Ads In School: Teaching or Teasing Kids?

Ten years ago, a young entrepreneur named Chris Whittle came up with an idea. He would wire the nation's high schools to receive a daily 12-minute newscast (and a few commercials) from his Channel One programming. In return, schools would get free TV sets for every classroom and a free satellite hookup. Today, 8.3 million teenagers watch the newscast and commercials every day, and 30-second ads sell for up to $200,000, producing annual net revenues for Channel One of about $30 million. Advertised products range from acne medication and breakfast cereals to fast foods and athletic shoes.

Schools have become an increasingly popular channel for promotions and advertising. Last year, companies spent $2 billion on advertising to children—20 times more than a decade ago. In just one year, the average American child aged 6 to 12 spends only 64 hours reading at home but sees some 30,000 TV commercials. At 60 seconds per TV ad, that comes to 500 hours a year. What is alarming parents and child advocates is that companies are now advertising in schools as well.

Should children be exposed to commercial advertising during school hours?

Pro
1. Advertising in schools is acceptable as long as companies are also providing improvements in educational equipment or processes that schools cannot afford.
2. Children need access to critical communication technologies such as computers and software. There is nothing wrong with allowing these companies a few minutes to advertise their products in return for contribu-

tions to education, especially since they are already exposed to advertising in almost every other aspect of their lives.
3. Most students have acquired the ability to "tune out" commercials in the same way they ignore boring lectures and other stimuli that fail to engage them. Besides, even educational Web sites like GeoCities, AOL, and Hotbot are filled with overt, intrusive advertising.

Con
1. The school population is not only the nation's largest market segment, it is the only one where students are held as a captive audience for 6 hours a day. At school, they should be treated as learners—not consumers.
2. The Internet has no added value to education. It is inherently only a commercial channel that gathers information to create databases of children and their families.
3. Forcing children to watch commercials is like prayer in schools—it should be voluntary, not mandatory.

Summary
Controversy grows as to whether advertising in schools corrupts and contaminates education or enhances learning and prepares students for the future. One thing for sure, the market potential is enormous and unless critics can find new ways to get money for educational equipment, it will be hard for cash-strapped schools to just say no.

SOURCES: Peggy J. Farber, "Schools for Sale," *Advertising Age,* October 25, 1999, pp. 22–26; Rob Brooks, "Lions Among Lambs?" *Promo,* February 1999, pp. 46–51; and "Who Are These Kids?" *Promo,* July 1999, pp. 23–27.

---

channelone.com

Exaggeration in ads is not new. Consumers seem to accept a tendency of advertisers to stretch the truth in their efforts to distinguish their products and get consumers to buy. This inclination may provide one reason that advertising does not encourage purchase behavior as successfully as sales promotions do. A tendency toward puffery does raise some ethical questions, though: Where is the line between claims that attract attention and those that provide implied guarantees? To what degree do advertisers deliberately make misleading statements?

The Uniform Commercial Code standardizes sales and business practices throughout the United States. It makes a distinction between puffery and any specific or quantifiable statement about product quality or performance that constitutes an "express warranty," which obligates the company to stand behind its claim. General boasts of product superiority and vague claims are puffery, not warranties. They are considered so self-praising or exaggerated that the average consumer would not rely on them to make a buying decision.

A quantifiable statement, on the other hand, implies a certain level of performance. For example, tests can establish the validity of a claim that a brand of long-life light bulbs outlast three regular light bulbs.

Ethics in Sales Promotion and Public Relations

Both consumer and trade promotions can also raise ethical issues. Sales promotions provide opportunities for unscrupulous companies to take advantage of consumers. For example, companies may not fulfill rebate and premium offers or may mislead consumers by inaccurately stating the odds of winning sweepstakes or contests. Trade allowances, particularly slotting allowances, have been criticized for years as a form of bribery.

Several public relations issues open organizations to criticism. Various PR firms perform services for the tobacco industry; publicity campaigns defend unsafe products. Also, marketers must weigh ethics before they respond to negative publicity. For example, do firms admit to problems or product deficiencies or do they try to cover them up? It should be noted that PR practitioners violate the Public Relations Society of America's Code of Professional Standards if they promote products or causes widely known to be harmful to others.

STRATEGIC IMPLICATIONS OF ADVERTISING AND SALES PROMOTION

The future of promotion on the Web is expected to look surprisingly similar to traditional broadcast advertising. With a strong interactive capability, Web promotion also closely resembles personal selling—the topic of Chapter 17. More than 1,300 sites sell Web ads, and commissions run as high as 70 percent of each site's total revenue.[45]

Greater portions of corporate ad budgets will migrate to the Web in the near future. While Web promotions currently account for less than 1 percent of U.S. annual advertising spending, a massive 80 percent of all Web ad space goes unsold, even at Net giants like Yahoo! Only 25 Web firms currently sell more than 80 percent of their available ad space. As the Internet becomes more entwined in our daily lives, such as access through interactive television sets, Web ads will become a primary medium for more marketers. The first online ad ran in September 1994; since then, Web advertising has grown to several billion ads each month. Even today, however, fewer than 1 percent of all ads get a follow-up click. Today, still fewer than half of all Web ads let consumers respond by placing an order; most are static billboards that take you to more ads.[46]

In the rapidly changing Web world, businesses worry about upsetting their dealers and suppliers, consumers worry about the security of their credit cards, and media companies worry that selling goods online will reduce the dependence on other more traditional forms of advertising. However, it should not be forgotten that online companies depend heavily on offline advertising, sales promotion, and public relations as well.

One of the most formidable weapons in the online advertising revolution is **bandwidth,** the number of bytes that can be transmitted at a time. The greater the bandwidth, the greater the use of elaborate graphics, digital video, and multimedia for promotional purposes. These bandwidth capabilities allow for increased interactive promotional programs.[47] A recent survey conducted by @Home Network found that broadband ads increase brand recall, engage viewers longer, and offer lower CPM than narrowband ads. The study included ads from AT&T, Bank of America, First USA, Intel, Johnson & Johnson, Levi Strauss, and Toys "Я" Us. Recall percentages were as much as 34 percent higher, and consumers who clicked on the ads spent up to 5 minutes interacting with the ads. The study also found that 93 percent of respondents preferred the broadband ad to print and 72 percent preferred it to television.[48]

Promotion industry experts agree that e-commerce broadens marketers' job tasks, though many promotional objectives still remain the same. Today, advertisers need 75 different ways to market their products in 75 countries in the world and innumerable market segments. In years to come, advertisers also agree that channels will become more homogeneous while markets become more fragmented.[49] As Shelly Lazarus, CEO of New York–based ad agency Ogilvy & Mather Worldwide, explains, "In the past 10 years, we have witnessed the uncanny ability of commercial messages to adapt—to become new, attention-getting formulas in traditional media, to migrate into unexpected encounters in

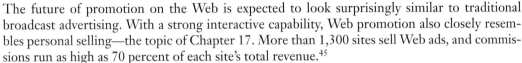

MARKETING   DICTIONARY

bandwidth Number of bytes that can be transmitted over the Internet at one time; enables use of elaborate interactive programs.

retail, sponsorship, mail, and to forge original paths across new media. In short, to find ways to be present wherever the consumer might be—from the Internet to interactive displays, to giant concert billboards, to postcard kiosks and personalized catalogs. More is on the way. Much more."[50]

ACHIEVEMENT CHECK SUMMARY

Read the learning objectives that follow, and consider the questions for each one. Answering these questions will reinforce your grasp of the most important concepts in the chapter and will allow you to check how well you have achieved these learning goals. Where a blank appears before a question, answer with T or F for true/false questions; for multiple-choice questions, choose the letter of the correct answer.

Objective 16.1: Explain the current status of advertising, sales promotion, and public relations in today's promotional strategies and identify two recent trends in advertising.

1. _____ The average U.S. business spends more on advertising than on sales promotion.

2. _____ Most U.S. advertisements can be used effectively in other countries by simply translating them into that country's native language.

3. _____ Interactive advertising allows consumers rather than advertisers to control how much information consumers receive.

Objective 16.2: Identify the major types of advertising.

1. _____ An advertisement for Fidelity Magellan mutual funds is an example of product advertising.

2. _____ Informative advertising is well-suited to the maturity stage of a product's life cycle.

3. _____ Consumers generally have positive attitudes toward products endorsed by celebrities.

Objective 16.3: Describe the process of creating an advertisement.

1. _____ Fear appeals influence consumers to take action to remove a perceived threat.

2. _____ A successful advertisement for a financial planning firm would be likely to provide a firm conclusion for the consumer.

3. _____ Which of the following is not a major objective when creating an advertisement? (a) gain attention; (b) use of interactive technology; (c) informing and persuading consumers; (d) encourage purchase behavior.

Objective 16.4: List and compare the major advertising media.

1. _____ Magazines are the most popular advertising media.

2. _____ Cable television's popularity is increasing because advertisers can target audiences more precisely than with network stations.

3. _____ The apparel industry spends the most on both television and magazine advertising.

Objective 16.5: Outline the organization of the advertising function and the role of an advertising agency.

1. _____ Today, most advertising agency revenue is based on a 15 percent commission on media placements.

2. _____ Indpendent ad agencies often supply technical expertise not present in the client's marketing department.

3. _____ Knowledge of interactive media is an important criterion when choosing an advertising agency.

Objective 16.6: Identify the principal methods of sales promotion.

1. _____ Consumer promotions account for the biggest percentage of a firm's communications budget.

2. _____ Sales promotions are a good way to raise interest in a mature product.

3. _____ Slotting allowances allow a retailer to take a discount on the invoice price of goods.

Objective 16.7: Explain the roles of public relations, publicity, and cross promotions in an organization's promotional strategy.

1. _____ Public relations efforts are usually targeted toward customers rather than investors, employees, or news media.

2. _____ Publicity involves paying a fee to obtain placement of company information in various news media.

3. _____ Paying the producer a fee for featuring the new BMW Z8 roadster in the James Bond movie, *The World is Not Enough*, is an example of cross promotion.

Objective 16.8: Explain how marketers assess promotional effectiveness.

1. _____ Marketers evaluate how well consumers react to advertising through message research.

2. _____ Cents-off coupons are the most popular consumer sales promotion technique.

3. _____ "Hits" are the best measure of an interactive advertisement's effectiveness.

Objective 16.9: Discuss the importance of ethics in a firm's promotional activities.

1. _____ The blurring of lines between advertising and entertainment has become a major ethical concern.

2. _____ "BMW: The ultimate driving machine" is an example of puffery.

3. _____ Puffery is illegal.

Students: See the solutions section located on pages S–2–S–3 to check your responses to the Achievement Check Summary.

Key Terms

advertising
product advertising
institutional advertising
informative advertising
persuasive advertising
reminder advertising
comparative advertising
retail advertising
cooperative advertising
interactive media
banner
keyword ad
interstitials
media scheduling
advertising agency

sales promotion
specialty advertising
trade promotion
trade allowances
point-of-purchase (POP)
   advertising
public relations
publicity
cross promotion
pretesting
posttesting
cookie
puffery
bandwidth

Review Questions

1. Explain the wide variation in advertising expenditures as a percentage of sales in the different industries mentioned in the chapter.
2. Describe the primary objectives of advertising. Offer a local example of an advertising campaign, and explain how the campaign seeks to accomplish specific objectives.
3. Identify the six basic types of advertising. Give a specific example of each.
4. Discuss the relationship between advertising and the product life cycle. What type of advertising matches up with specific product life cycle stages?
5. What are the major advantages and disadvantages associated with using each of the advertising media? Give examples of types of advertisers most likely to use each medium.
6. Discuss the organization of the advertising function. Consider all the major activities associated with advertising.
7. Under what circumstances are celebrity spokespersons in advertising likely to be effective? Give recent examples of effective and ineffective uses of spokespersons in advertisements.
8. Why is retail advertising so important today? Relate cooperative advertising to the discussion of alternative promotional strategies in Chapter 15.
9. Distinguish between advertising and sales promotion. Explain the principal methods of sales promotion, and give an example of each.
10. Describe the public relations components of a firm's promotional mix. Do you agree with the statement that publicity is free advertising?

Questions for Critical Thinking

1. Many states have government-operated lotteries. Suggest a promotional plan for marketing lottery tickets with a particular emphasis on the nonpersonal-selling aspects of the promotional mix.
2. Outline the primary methods used to assess the effectiveness of each major type of nonpersonal selling. Evaluate the currently used techniques for evaluating interactive media. Suggest ways to minimize the measurement problems described in the chapter.
3. Review the changes in the relative importance of the various advertising media during the past 40 years that are mentioned in the chapter. Suggest likely explanations for these changes.
4. Present an argument favoring the use of comparative advertising by a marketer who is currently preparing an advertising plan. Make any assumptions necessary.
5. Develop a sales promotion program for each of the following. Justify your choice of each sales promotion method employed.
   a. independent insurance agent
   b. retail carpet store
   c. local exterminator
   d. local AM radio station

1. **Advertising.** Go to Advertising Age's Web site at *www.adage.com/century* to access information on "The Advertising Century" issue with its analysis of advertising in the 20th century. Complete the following: (a) Go to the "Timeline" and find two interesting historical facts to contribute during class discussion. (b) List the top two in each of the Top 100 Campaigns, Top 10 Jingles, Top 10 Slogans, and Top 10 Ad Icons categories.

adage.com/century

2. **Celebrity Testimonials.** Go to *www.consumersunion.org*, select "Search," and key in "celebrity endorsements." Search results will return a link to "Captive Kids: A Report on Commercial Pressures on Kids at School." In the sidebar of the article, select the "Celebrity Endorsements" section of the article and summarize the key points being made in this section of the article.

consumersunion.org

3. **Outdoor Advertising.** Find the Web site for an outdoor advertising firm such as Lamar (*www.lamar.com*), identify the product categories of outdoor advertising the firm supplies, and print out a copy of your favorite ad featured at the site.

lamar.com

Video Case 16 on Pizza Hut begins on page VC-18.

Personal Selling and Sales Management

CHAPTER OBJECTIVES

1. Explain the conditions that determine the relative importance of personal selling in the promotional mix.

2. Contrast over-the-counter selling, field selling, telemarketing, and inside selling.

3. Describe each of the four major trends in personal selling.

4. Identify the three basic sales tasks.

5. Outline the steps in the sales process.

6. Describe the sales manager's boundary-spanning role.

7. List and discuss the functions of sales management.

8. Discuss the role of ethics in personal selling and sales management.

Reggie Jackson: New Pitch for an All-Star Hitter

Seeing sports celebrities featured in television and magazine ads for products is nothing unusual. And Reggie Jackson can play with the best of them. The 53-year-old Baseball Hall of Famer has a few credits under his cap: 573 home runs, three of which were hit in the 1977 World Series game that earned him the title "Mr. October." The Yankee slugger is now hitting home runs as a spokesperson for his own business ventures and for companies like Viking Components, a maker of computer memory upgrades. Jackson looks at it this way, "I'm an alliance guy, a relationship builder."

In 1987, Jackson hung up his Yankee uniform and went straight into business. First it was car dealerships. He owned three in northern California before they put him $5 million in debt. Another of Jackson's early deals was Reggie!, a candy bar manufactured by Standard Brands that carried his likeness on the wrapper. It was pulled off the shelves in 1980 after three years of steadily declining sales. He also served for a time on the board of directors for Upper Deck, a trading card company.

But Jackson's failures have not lowered his self-confidence or his ability to make his second career—personal selling—as successful as the years he spent on the baseball diamond. Today, he has built a net worth of around $20 million and claims nearly 20 sources of income, from real estate to classic cars to autographs. One friend describes Jackson as "a one-man conglomerate!" Jackson knows there is more to selling than a few handshakes. His batting line-up of business associates includes some power hitters, including New York Yankees owner George Steinbrenner, computer company founder Michael Dell, deal maker Michael Milkin, and telecommunications brothers John and Bruce McCaw.

So what is it that Jackson is doing right these days? California-based Viking, a computer components company and one of Jackson's primary current clients, keeps him on the payroll at least six days a month promoting the company's RAM upgrades to industry giants like Dell Computer. After trying repeatedly to become a Dell supplier, Viking was never able to ever reach first base. At least, not until Reggie stepped up to the plate. He cold-called Michael Dell twice; the second time, he was able to talk the secretary into putting his name on Dell's calendar. He followed up by sending a confirmation note written on a baseball (which Dell had on his desk during the meeting).

But meeting the Dell CEO did not guarantee any business for Viking. At Jackson's first meeting with the PC executive, Dell made it clear right off that he was not a sports fan and that he did not believe that Viking would be able to handle the computer maker's needs. But Jackson is a smooth salesman, and he quickly explained to Dell the following, "I struck out 2,597 times and you wouldn't want me back here another 2,500 times." (In fact, Jackson holds the record for strikeouts.) Dell accepted his proposal to bring Viking technicians in to demonstrate just what they had to offer. After 14 months, Viking got the account.

Jackson describes the Dell story as a good example of how past successes do not substitute for performance today. He says, "You need a real business story with *content*, that has added value. If you don't grab them in the first three minutes, then it's like, 'See you again at the next function.'"

Reggie Jackson is a 21st-century salesman, always on the move looking for tomorrow's connection and knowing that it's not *what* you sell but *how* you sell that makes a winning game plan. He is currently part of a syndicate trying to buy the Oakland A's baseball team. And he continues to build his roster of power hitters in case an opportunity presents itself. He e-mailed Bill Gates but received no response and continues to try to talk to Microsoft Corp. co-founder Paul Allen in an effort to expand his ties for future business ventures. But his dream is to meet billionaire investor George Soros. "I don't know him, but I have his phone number. I don't have a project that would be right for him yet, but George Soros is the type of guy I want to get in front of me."[1]

vikingcomponents.com

CHAPTER OVERVIEW

Reggie Jackson is the epitome of relationship selling; he never gives up and always keeps smiling. His success lies in his ability to cover all the bases and outplay the competition. Chapters 15 and 16 focused on the concept of promotion, the promotional mix, and the use of advertising and other nonpersonal promotion in achieving marketing objectives. This chapter discusses the challenges involved in personal selling and the professional qualities that managers look for in hiring effective salespeople. Perhaps the most important attribute for a salesperson is the ability to communicate effectively with people.

Personal selling, as defined in Chapter 15, is an interpersonal influence process. Specifically, it involves a seller's promotional presentations conducted on a person-to-person basis with the buyer. This activity is an inherent function of any enterprise. Accounting, engineering, human resource management, production, and other organizational activities produce no benefits unless a seller matches the needs of a client or customer. The 15 million people employed in sales occupations in the United States testify to the importance of selling. While the average firm's advertising expenses may represent from 1 to 3 percent of total sales, personal selling expenses are likely to equal 10 to 15 percent. In many firms, personal selling is the single largest marketing expense.

Personal selling is a primary component of a firm's promotional mix in certain, well-defined conditions:

1. Consumers are geographically concentrated.

2. Individual orders account for large amounts.

3. The firm markets goods and services that are expensive, technically complex, or require special handling.

4. Trade-ins are involved.

5. Products move through short channels.

6. The firm markets to relatively few potential customers.

TABLE 17.1	Factors Affecting the Importance of Personal Selling in the Promotional Mix

VARIABLE	CONDITIONS THAT FAVOR PERSONAL SELLING	CONDITIONS THAT FAVOR ADVERTISING
Consumer	Geographically concentrated	Geographically dispersed
	Relatively low numbers	Relatively high numbers
Product	Expensive	Inexpensive
	Technically complex	Simple to understand
	Custom made	Standardized
	Special handling requirements	No special handling requirements
	Transactions frequently involve trade-ins	Transactions seldom involve trade-ins
Price	Relatively high	Relatively low
Channels	Relatively short	Relatively long

Table 17.1 summarizes the factors that influence the importance of personal selling in the overall promotional mix based on four variables: consumer, product, price, and marketing channels. ■

THE EVOLUTION OF PERSONAL SELLING

Selling has been a standard business activity for thousands of years. The earliest peddlers sold goods in which they had some type of ownership interest after manufacturing or importing them. These people viewed selling as a secondary activity.

Selling later became a separate business function. During 18th-century America, peddlers sold directly to farmers and settlers of the vast territories to the west. In the 19th century, salespeople called *drummers* sold to both consumers and marketing intermediaries. These early sellers sometimes used questionable sales practices and techniques and earned undesirable reputations for themselves and their firms. Negative stereotypes persist today. To some people, the term *salesperson* conjures up unpleasant visions of Arthur Miller's antihero Willy Loman in *Death of a Salesman*:

> Willy is a salesman. . . . He don't put a bolt to a nut. He don't tell you the law or give you medicine. He's a man way out there in the blue, riding on a smile and a shoe shine. And when they start not smiling back—that's an earthquake.

But selling is far different from what it was in its early years. Far from the fast-talking, joke-telling, back-slapping caricatures in some novels and comic strips, today's salesperson is usually a highly-trained professional. Professors Thomas Ingram and Raymond LaForge define *sales professionalism* as "a customer-oriented approach that employs truthful, nonmanipulative tactics to satisfy the long-term needs of both the customer and the selling firm."[2] Professional salespeople are problem solvers who focus on satisfying the needs of customers before, during, and after the sales are made. Armed with knowledge about their firm's goods or services, those of competitors, and their customer's business needs, salespeople pursue a common goal of creating long-term relationships with customers.

Personal selling today is a vital, vibrant, dynamic process. As domestic

1
Explain the conditions that determine the relative importance of personal selling in the promotional mix.

MARKETING DICTIONARY

personal selling Interpersonal influence process involving a seller's promotional presentation conducted on a person-to-person basis with the buyer.

and foreign competition increases emphasis on productivity, personal selling is taking on a more prominent role in the corporate marketing mix. Salespeople must communicate the subtle advantages of their firms' goods and services over those of competitors. The salesperson's role has changed from persuader to consultant and problem solver. In addition, mergers and acquisitions along with a host of new products and promotions have expanded the scope and complexity of many selling jobs.

As discussed in Chapter 5, relationship marketing affects all aspects of an organization's marketing function, including personal selling and sales management. This transition involves marketers in both internal and external relationships and forces them to develop different sales skills. Instead of working alone, many salespeople now join their efforts in sales teams. The customer-focused firm wants its salespeople to form long-lasting relationships with buyers by providing high levels of customer service, rather than going for quick sales. Even the way salespeople perform their jobs is changing. Growing numbers of companies are integrating communications and computer technologies into the sales routine. These trends are covered in more detail later in the chapter.

Personal selling is an attractive career choice for today's college and university students. Approximately 60 percent of all marketing graduates choose sales jobs as their first marketing positions, in part because they see attractive salaries and career potentials. The Bureau of Labor Statistics projects that jobs in selling and marketing occupations requiring a college degree will show faster than average rates of growth as compared with all occupations during the next ten years. A sales background provides visibility for the individual and serves as an excellent route to the top of the corporate hierarchy. Many corporations are headed by executives who began their careers in sales.

THE FOUR SALES CHANNELS

2

Contrast over-the-counter selling, field selling, telemarketing, and inside selling.

When people think of personal selling, most imagine end users buying products directly from salespeople, such as when people buy cars or clothes for their personal use. These types of selling transactions are called *direct-to-customer sales*. However, many salespeople work at *business-to-business sales*, calling on wholesalers and retailers and selling to purchasing agents and committees in businesses, government agencies, and institutions such as schools and hospitals.

Personal selling occurs through several types of communication channels: over-the-counter selling, field selling, telemarketing, and inside selling. Each of these channels includes both business-to-business and direct-to-customer selling. Although telemarketing and online selling are lower-cost alternatives, their lack of personal interaction with prospective customers often makes them less effective than the personalized, one-to-one field selling and over-the-counter channels. In fact, many organizations use a number of different channels.

dell.com

Dell Computer uses its direct field sales force for large customer acquisitions and its telecommunication sales and Internet channels primarily for retention of those customers. For big system sales, the customer works directly with the field representative, but for smaller transactions such as product upgrades, the customer works with the telecommunication channel. The benefits of this approach is a striking increase in productivity. Sales revenues at Dell grew from $5 million per rep to $15 million over a three-year period.[3]

Over-the-Counter Selling

The most frequently used sales channel, **over-the-counter selling**, typically describes selling in retail and some wholesale locations. Most over-the-counter sales are direct-to-customer, although wholesalers serve business customers. Customers typically visit the seller's location on their own initiative to purchase desired items. Some visit their favorite stores because they enjoy shopping and consider it a type of leisure activity. Others come in response to many kinds of

True to the original.

Discover life's vibrant colors.
Capture delicate detail and rich shadow.
Printouts most like your original photos.
The new HP DeskJet 970C.
Just $399.* www.hp.com/go/original.

Although advertising aids Hewlett Packard's sales efforts by increasing buyer awareness of the firm and its high-quality color printers, the firm's promotional emphasis is on one-to-one continuing relationships between its highly-trained, professional sales force and office-products buyers around the world.

hp.com

invitations, including direct-mail appeals, personal letters of invitation from store personnel, and advertisements for sales, special events, and new-product introductions. From the electronics-products salesperson at Circuit City to the diamond purveyor at Tiffany's, this type of selling typically involves providing product information and arranging for completion of sales transactions.

A century ago, when customers entered the local drugstore or hard goods store, they typically would be greeted by the owner who not only knew their names but also knew their lifestyles and what they needed and preferred. During the 1950s, that customer-oriented sales method began to disappear as big chain retailers and discount stores began practicing product-oriented marketing to satisfy the mass market. Instead of being greeted at the door, most customers had to first find someone to ask for assistance in making their purchase. Today, this top-down thinking is being replaced with a back-to-the-future scenario, where one-to-one sales tactics are paying off. L. L. Bean telemarketers, for example, are armed with a sophisticated computer database that identifies the caller and any recent purchases he or she has made.[4] This customer recognition helps build strong relationships in over-the-counter sales as well. Starbucks is a successful model of how over-the-counter selling builds relationships by creating an enjoyable and satisfying experience for customers. As the company Web site shown in Figure 17.1 explains, Starbucks emphasizes "one customer, one partner, one cup at a time." Customers are willing to pay premium prices for Starbucks coffee because they are buying more than just coffee—it's the personal touch that keeps them coming back.[5]

While many marketers today are trying to re-create the personalized, one-to-one experience of over-the-counter selling on the Web, it still remains an elusive concept. More consumers demanding professional service in addition to quality products are forcing online marketers to provide answers and assistance over the Internet. Net Effect Systems, a California-based, real-time online customer service provider, allows online shoppers to virtually take a company's entire sales force with them wherever

MARKETING   DICTIONARY

over-the-counter selling Personal selling conducted in retail and some wholesale locations in which customers come to the seller's place of business.

FIGURE 17.1	Starbucks Offers Personalized Over-the-Counter Selling

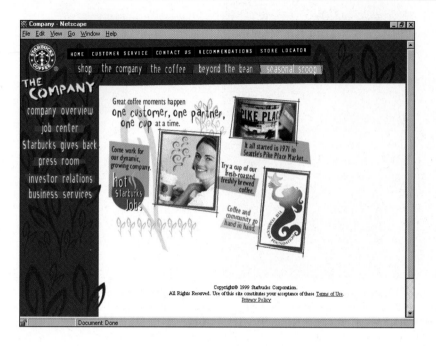

they browse. As Net Effect's CEO Julie Schoenfeld points out, "Most of us need guidance and comparative information from a knowledgeable salesperson before making many purchases." Unfortunately, most online shoppers never receive this kind of help. Only one in five online companies has a live agent ready to help customers make their purchases.[6]

Field Selling

Field selling involves making sales calls on prospective and existing customers at their businesses or homes. Some situations involve considerable creative effort, such as in-home sales of encyclopedias and insurance or industrial sales of major computer installations. Often the salesperson must convince customers first that they need the good or service and then that they need the particular brand the salesperson is selling. Field sales of large industrial installations also often require considerable technical expertise.

Cathy Metry has spent the last 10 years building her promotion and advertising company on face-to-face field selling. The 32-year-old CEO of AD XL Promotions develops promotional programs with local companies to generate traffic and sales in their stores. The companies offer certificates for goods and services, such as a $40 beauty treatment at a neighborhood salon or $20 for fresh flowers every month for a year. Metry and her team of 20 salespeople then sell those certificates in lobbies and lunchrooms of area businesses. AD XL (as in "ad—extra large") keeps the money from the promotions they sell to cover the cost of designing and printing the certificates and to earn a profit.[7]

In fairly routine field selling situations, such as calling on established customers in industries like food, textiles, or wholesaling, the salesperson may basically act as an order taker who processes regular customers' orders. Field selling may involve regular visits to local stores or businesses, or it may involve many days and nights of travel, by car or plane, every month. Salespeople who travel a great deal are frequently labeled *road warriors*. A recent study found that over half the salespeople surveyed spend more than $500 per month on travel, and a firm's average travel cost is $2,045 a month.

As technology seeps into every modern business transaction, marketers have adapted their personal selling techniques to take advantage of electronic communications channels, including voice mail, e-mail, and the Internet. Fuller Brush marketers recognize that two-career couples make it hard for independent sales reps to find anyone home to approach—that is, unless they went online. In addition, recruiting door-to-door sales reps is a never-ending challenge. As one Fuller spokesperson explains, "With the decline of the Fuller Brush people and the fact that Fuller-brand products are not available at Wal-Mart or Kmart, for us to again try to revitalize the brand over the Internet is a fantastic opportunity."[8]

fullerbrush.com

Telemarketing

The telephone is the basis for a third approach to personal selling, **telemarketing**, in which the selling process is conducted by telephone. Telemarketing serves two general purposes—sales and service—and two general markets—business-to-business and direct-to-customer. (Marketing research is not usually considered telemarketing.) As we noted in Chapter 15, telemarketing is a form of direct marketing that can be classified as either outbound or inbound.

Outbound telemarketing involves a sales force that relies on the telephone to contact customers. This approach is designed to reduce the substantial costs of personal visits to customers' homes or businesses. Telemarketers now have several methods of increasing their chances of reaching customers at home, including predictive dialers and autodialing. Predictive dialers weed out busy signals and answering machines, nearly doubling telemarketers' productivity. Instead of dialing 50 numbers an hour, an operator can dial twice that many. Autodialing is another sales call technique that dials numbers continually. When a customer answers the phone, he or she is automatically routed to a live sales agent. These systems cost about $3,000 per work station, but are much more sophisticated than the first autodialers. [9]

Most consumers have had the experience of being interrupted—and perhaps annoyed—by outbound telemarketers. Surveys indicate that up to 60 percent of consumers are so bothered by telemarketing that they will not listen to a telephone sales presentation. The technique has produced enough consumer complaints about unwanted calls to prompt action by regulatory agencies. The Telephone Consumer Protection Act of 1991 requires companies to keep a list of people who request not to receive such calls and gives consumers the right to sue telemarketers $500 for each violation. In addition, since 1996, the Federal Trade Commission's Telemarketing Sales Rules have granted certain protections to consumers, such as restricting calls to daytime and early evening hours (not after 9 P.M.). The requirements do not, however, apply to calls placed by charities and political organizations. In addition to federal regulations, telemarketers have also become the focus of state legislation. Alabama, Alaska, Florida, Louisiana, Tennessee, and Oregon are just a few of the states that have created no-call rules with high fines for violators. Last year, Georgia's consumer-affairs office fined TruGreen/Chemlawn $45,000 for repeated violations.[10]

trugreen.com

Why, then, is outbound telemarketing such a popular sales technique? Companies like it because it is cost-effective and it works. An average telemarketing call costs $5, while an average field sales call can cost up to $500. Despite the annoyance of receiving unsolicited calls, some people do respond. Outbound calling has a 6 percent to 8 percent positive response rate, compared to only 2 percent for a standard direct mail piece. Success of telemarketers can be evaluated on various bases: total calls made per work shift, calls per hour, revenue per sale or per hour, and profitability, among others. In general, outbound telemarketing calls geared toward men get the best responses between 7 P.M. and 9 P.M., whereas women tend to respond more favorably to telemarketers between 10 A.M. and 4 P.M.

The effectiveness of telemarketing as a sales technique is evidenced by the size of the industry. Over 900 telemarketing

MARKETING DICTIONARY

field selling Sales presentations made at prospective customers' homes or businesses on a face-to-face basis.

telemarketing Promotional presentation involving the use of the telephone on an outbound basis by salespeople or on an inbound basis by customers who initiate calls to obtain information and place orders.

agencies employing almost 5 million people are currently operating in the United States. The industry is a major employer of persons with special career needs: college students, people with disabilities, senior citizens, full-time homemakers, and people with second jobs.

Inbound telemarketing typically involves a toll-free number that customers can call to obtain information, make reservations, and purchase goods and services. When a customer calls in on a toll-free line, the caller can be identified and routed to the sales agents with whom they have done business before, creating a human touch not previously found before. This form of selling provides maximum convenience for customers who initiate the sales process. Many large catalog merchants, like The Sharper Image, Lillian Vernon, and Land's End, keep their inbound telemarketing lines open 24 hours a day, seven days a week. Indeed, one can even call L. L. Bean on Christmas Day to place an order! Other catalogs maintain reputations for superior customer service standards and marketing ideas. Williams-Sonoma, a kitchen and culinary cataloger, for instance, satisfies its customers by guaranteeing that any product defect will be corrected or repaired using genuine parts from the manufacturer or with a new product.[11]

@ **sharperimage.com**

Inside Selling

Telemarketing has evolved from a traditional selling method known as the **canned approach**, originally developed by John H. Patterson of National Cash Register Company during the late 1800s. The canned approach is a memorized sales talk used to ensure uniform coverage of the points management deems important. For example, the Learning Co., a division of Mattel Inc., developed personalized teleservices scripts and special sales offers for its telemarketers to use in their outbound calling strategies.[12]

The dinnertime telemarketing call is an example of a canned approach that follows a carefully planned script, although it may provide the salesperson with different options depending on answers to specific questions. Canned presentations are still used in such areas as door-to-door *cold canvassing*—unsolicited sales calls on a random group of people. However, most sales forces have long since abandoned them. Many customers resent canned presentations, and over half the buyers in such a situation, feeling their time has been wasted, react angrily and decide not to buy.

However, telemarketing has taken on a new dimension. In a recent survey of sales divisions at 165 companies, 62 percent have shifted responsibilities of their field sales reps to inside salespeople.[13] The role of many contemporary telemarketers involves a combination of field selling techniques applied through inbound and outbound telemarketing channels with a strong customer orientation, called **inside selling**. Inside sales reps perform two primary jobs: They turn opportunities into actual sales, and they support technicians and purchasers with current solutions. Today's inside sales reps are much more than unidentified callers reading a script to unwilling prospects. They perform a dynamic selling function that goes beyond taking orders to solving problems, providing customer service, and selling. As the call center manager for Healthier You, a Florida-based catalog company that sells nutritional supplements, points out, "Inside sales reps have to have a sales mentality." Healthier You telephone representatives now make outbound calls that involve promoting the product as well as the company's image.[14]

@ **ahealthieryou.net**

A successful inside sales force relies on close working relationships with field representatives to solidify customer relationships. Firstwave Technologies Inc., a $20 million sales force automation company headquartered in Atlanta, recently created an inside sales force team. After sales manager Dave Fisher realized he could not meet the company's quota through field sales alone, he began recruiting inside salespeople from both competitors and high-tech companies outside his industry. Fisher looks for people who work well in teams and who possess general selling skills. As he explains, "You're asking the inside rep *not* to take 100 percent ownership of the account. If they're too individual-centric, they're not going to work."[15]

@ **firstwave.net**

Integrating the Various Selling Channels

Figure 17.2 illustrates how firms are likely to blend the alternative sales channels—from over-the-counter selling and field selling to telemarketing and inside selling—to create a successful,

| FIGURE 17.2 | Alternative Sales Channels for Serving Customers |

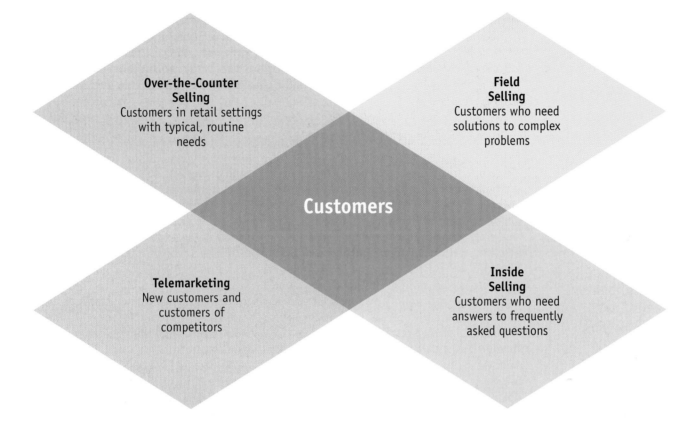

Over-the-Counter Selling
Customers in retail settings with typical, routine needs

Field Selling
Customers who need solutions to complex problems

Customers

Telemarketing
New customers and customers of competitors

Inside Selling
Customers who need answers to frequently asked questions

cost-effective sales organization. Existing customers whose business problems require complex solutions are likely to be best served by the traditional field sales force. Other current customers who need answers but not the same hand-holding as the first group can be served by inside sales reps who call on them as needed. Over-the-counter sales reps serve existing customers by supplying information and advice and completing sales transactions. Telemarketers are often used in contacting prospective customers and in attempting to win back previous clients who are currently purchasing from competitors. In some instances, telemarketers will attempt to complete the sale; in other, more complex selling situations, they will turn promising sales leads over to the field sales force for follow-up.

RECENT TRENDS IN PERSONAL SELLING

Personal selling today requires different strategies than salespeople practiced in the past. Although the traditional method of selling one-on-one is gaining in popularity, salespeople may need to sell to teams of corporate representatives called *decision-making units*. Especially in business-to-business sales situations involving technical products, customers expect salespeople to answer technical questions—or bring along someone who

3

Describe each of the four major trends in personal selling.

MARKETING   DICTIONARY

canned approach Memorized sales talk used to ensure uniform coverage of the points that management has deemed important.

inside selling Performing the functions of field selling but avoiding travel-related expenses by relying on phone, mail, and electronic commerce to provide sales and product service for customers on a continuing basis.

can. They also want representatives who understand technical jargon and can communicate using sophisticated technological tools. Patience is also a requirement for personal selling because the sales cycle, from initial contact to closing, may take years. The average industrial sale takes at least four sales calls to close, and the larger and more expensive the equipment, the longer it takes.

To address these concerns, companies are turning to relationship selling, consultative selling, team selling, and sales force automation—major personal selling trends that are changing the sales forces of companies of all sizes. This section will briefly explain these trends, which have taken root in recent years. The balance of the chapter will then examine their effects on personal selling activities.

Relationship Selling

As competitive pressures mount, more firms are emphasizing **relationship selling,** a technique for building a mutually beneficial relationship with a customer through regular contacts over an extended period. Such buyer-seller bonds become increasingly important as companies cut back on the number of suppliers and look for companies that provide high levels of customer service and satisfaction. Salespeople must also find ways to distinguish themselves and their products from competitors. To create strong, long-lasting relationships with customers, salespeople must meet buyers' expectations. Table 17.2 summarizes the results of several surveys that indicate what buyers expect of professional salespeople.

@ jeepunpaved.com

The success of tomorrow's marketers depends on the relationships they build today, in both the business-to-customer and business-to-business markets. For example, Jeep marketers focus on building strong customer relationships between the drivers and the brand. Forty years ago, Jeeps were seldom seen outside a military environment—on Army bases or negotiating remote trails. These days they are part of every urban landscape, taking kids to school, going to work, running errands, and sometimes venturing off the road. After marketers began sponsoring events for their owners across the country in the 1960s, Jeep catapulted from a small business-to-business market to take its place as one of the favored vehicles of the consumer market. By participating in what is now known as the Jeep Jamboree, owners such as those in Figure 17.3 take simulated driver training classes, navigate off-road courses, and engage in other outdoor activities that are part of the so-called Jeep lifestyle. Not only do these events boost sales, they also build long-term loyalty that goes beyond the vehicle itself. In 1996, Jeep sent ethnographic researchers to study attendees at the Jamboree to get a better understanding of Jeep owners and their relationships with their vehicles. As one researcher put it, "The Jeep becomes a key component of owners' lifestyles, which is a stronger form of loyalty than owning something because it's cool to have." Hosting these activities is expensive for Jeep, but the company believes the opportunity to meet thousands of customers face-to-face is worth it.[16]

TABLE 17.2	**What Buyers Expect from Salespeople**

Buyers prefer to do business with salespeople who:

■ Orchestrate events and bring to bear whatever resources are necessary to satisfy the customer

■ Provide counseling to the customer based on in-depth knowledge of the product, the market, and the customer's needs

■ Solve problems extremely proficiently to ensure satisfactory customer service over extended time periods

■ Demonstrate high ethical standards and communicate honestly at all times

■ Willingly advocate the customer's cause within the selling organization

■ Create imaginative arrangements to meet buyers' needs

■ Arrive well-prepared for sales calls

Relationship selling is equally important in business-to-business sales, as Jeffrey Sherick, senior vice president of ProSlide, will attest. Put simply, ProSlide Technology sells water rides to amusement parks, but a closer look reveals that their success is centered around the ability of ProSlide's sales force to customize each customer order. As Sherick explains, "We don't consider ourselves fiberglass manufacturers. Our mission is to design great rides." Canadian-based ProSlide generates almost $20 million in sales each year by asking customers what they want, designing and building a quality product, and keeping them satisfied. Over 70 percent of ProSlide's business comes from the same customers. But Sherick never depends on established relationships. Instead, relationships are shaped and reshaped with each individual order a customer places.[17]

Consultative Selling

The once-popular "good-old boy" sales style—getting chummy with customers, buying them a meal or a drink, giving the standard sales presentation, applying pressure, and expecting to get the sale on that basis—is rapidly going the way of the dinosaur. Field representatives and inside sales reps require sales methods that satisfy today's cost-conscious, knowledgeable buyers. One such method, **consultative selling**, involves meeting customer needs by listening to customers, understanding—and caring about—their problems, paying attention to details, and following through after the sale. It works hand-in-hand with relationship selling in building customer loyalty.

As rapid technological changes drive business at an unprecedented pace, selling has become a more complex activity, especially in the e-commerce environment. Companies are increasingly instituting consultative selling models that create long-term online customers. Currently, the majority of business online involves simple, shrink-wrapped products that can be easily shipped. For more complicated, high-priced products that require installation or specialized service, Web sellers must be able to communicate the benefits and features of their products to buyers online. They accomplish this through consultative selling. Take Furniture.com, for example. The Framingham, Massachusetts–based retailer has 15 design consultants who offer real-time assistance to shoppers. "We can monitor where people are on the site," says Lee Chaissan, vice president of engineering, "and if we think they're a hot prospect or they need assistance, we can send out a chat window." About 60 percent of shoppers participate in the online chat session to get answers to questions and suggestions on decorating. "Our business is high tech and high touch," explains CEO Andrew Brooks. "Our consultants can help customers navigate the Web site and the online purchase process, but they can also help them understand what things look and feel like and what fabrics integrate with their existing pieces." The design consultants seem to be working well for Furniture.com. Its average revenue per order is more than $1,000.[18]

Similar to consultative selling, *cross-selling* is another technique that capitalizes on a firm's strengths. Sprint Communications enrolls all of its 600 inside sales reps in a comprehensive cross-selling training program. Apparently, cross-selling has paid off for the Kansas City, Missouri–based telecommunications company: Sales have increased, and the company is retaining more of its customers, as well. In the past, Sprint's inside sales reps would simply take orders for whatever long-distance service a small business owner requested. Now they cross sell, asking questions to help

FIGURE 17.3 **Jeep Jamboree: Relationship Selling to Enhance Consumer Satisfaction**

@ **proslide.com**

@ **Furniture.com**

FIGURE 17.4 | **Team Selling at CDW Computer Centers**

customers choose the most appropriate service plan and proposing additional products as well. As Sprint's educational consultant Kevin Christensen explains, "Customers are staying with us longer, because we're able to find solutions to their problems."[19]

Team Selling

One of the latest developments in the evolution of personal selling is **team selling**, in which the salesperson joins with specialists from other functional areas of the firm to complete the selling process. Team selling has become important to an increasing number of firms.[20] Teams can be formal and ongoing or created for a specific, short-term selling situation. Some salespeople have hesitated to embrace the idea of team selling. Many still view personal selling as a "Lone Ranger" kind of profession, with a salesperson working pretty much alone, except for long-distance supervision and regular monitoring of sales results. However, in sales situations that call for detailed knowledge of new, complex, and ever-changing technologies, team selling has given many companies a competitive edge in meeting customers' needs. Many customers prefer the team approach, which makes them feel well served. Another advantage of team selling is the formation of relationships between companies rather than individuals.

CDW Computer Centers relies on team selling to serve its 600,000 consumer and business customers in the United States. Over the past 15 years, the Illinois-based firm has become the largest direct seller of Compaq, IBM, Microsoft, Toshiba, and other top-name computer brands. As Figure 17.4 explains, each customer is provided with an account manager who serves as the team leader of a group of specialists dedicated to finding solutions to buyers' needs. In a typical day, more than 700 systems will be custom configured for CDW customers. Customers can receive continuing lifetime technical support by visiting the CDW extranet or by calling a toll-free telephone number to speak with factory-trained technicians.

Sales Force Automation

oldediscount.com

A major trend in personal selling is **sales force automation (SFA)**—the application of new technologies to the sales process. Broadly used, the term refers to the use of everything from pagers and cellular phones, to voice and electronic mail, to laptop and notebook computers. More narrowly used, it refers to the use of computers by salespeople for activities beyond the use of word processors, spreadsheets, and connections to order-entry systems.

The benefits of SFA include improvements in the quality and effectiveness of sales calls due to improved access to information; low selling, printing, and training costs; improved product launches; and attentive customer service. For example, integrating telephony with the Internet helps companies to provide consultative selling on the Web. OLDE Discount Brokers enables its customers and brokers to exchange investment data and analyst reports while on the phone. Brokers can download financial information for the customer to work with while continuing their phone conversation, making recommendations, and completing the sales process.[21]

SFA usage differs sharply by industry: Food, beverage, and pharmaceutical industries are using sophisticated, third-generation systems, whereas many apparel companies have not yet moved to SFA. Software for sales force automation also falls into several categories depending on its intended use. Most salespeople use basic productivity and general purpose programs like word processors, e-mail, and spreadsheets. Some programs help to organize prospect lists and to remind salespeople to make follow-up calls. More expensive systems may integrate order processing and other types of information.

Sales-force automation tools such as Lotus Notes give mobile salespeople the ability to establish virtual offices in airports, hotel rooms, and other locations on the road. This technology provides a single point of access to e-mail, calendars, intranets, and Web sites.

With SFA tools, both large and small companies can increase their efficiency and spend more time on client acquisition and retention. Indeed, 31 percent of companies surveyed about rewards of SFA cited better customer service and satisfaction as the top benefit, while 24 percent emphasized productivity gains.[22] Cisco Systems, the world leader in Internet networking, depends on sales force automation to keep its sales force informed of prices and lead times, to help them configure customized systems for customers, to place orders and write up invoices, and to provide customer service. Similarly, other large corporations including IBM and Boeing use SFA to help their salespeople figure out which parts fit together and the total cost. Salespeople use the system to submit on-the-spot bids in the field, interacting remotely with back-end corporate systems.[23]

Perhaps the ultimate outcome of SFA is the *virtual office*, a workplace that exists in only electronic space. *Voice mail*, a computer-based, call-processing system that can handle both incoming and outgoing calls, is a key fixture of the virtual office. It enables sales reps to communicate with customers on a sort of electronic bulletin board. Information such as price changes, sales incentive programs, and meeting times can be transmitted by giving customers a digital code, eliminating the need to play "telephone tag" when salespeople are away from the phone.

SALES TASKS

Today's salesperson is more concerned with establishing long-term, buyer-seller relationships and with helping customers select the correct products for meeting their needs than with simply selling whatever is available. Where repeat purchases are common, the salesperson must be certain that the buyer's

---

4
Identify the three basic sales tasks.

MARKETING DICTIONARY

team selling Combination of salespeople with specialists from other functional areas to promote a product.

sales force automation (SFA) Applications of computer and other technologies to make the sales function more efficient and competitive.

THE STRATEGY Sebastiani implemented a sales force automation program with four objectives: (1) Enhance communication through the use of e-mail, file-sharing, intranet technology, and fax services; (2) provide multimedia presentation capabilities; (3) provide data analysis capabilities; and (4) ease the administrative burden. The program was supported with employee training. On day one of the three-day course, reps learn PC and networking basics, Windows 95, and e-mail. Day two covers such tasks as how to back up the data on their laptops and how to retrieve data from the company's mainframe. On day three, reps learn how to create custom reports and presentations. In addition, the company pays tuition for reps to attend a basic computer course directed by local Comp USA stores.

THE OUTCOME The move to sales force automation has cut the time spent on administrative tasks by 50 percent. With state-of-the-art equipment and intensive training, Sebastiani sales reps are pouring orders in from across the country.

purchases are in his or her best interest; otherwise, no future sales will be made. The seller's interests are tied to the buyer's in a symbiotic relationship.

Not all selling activities are alike. While all sales activities assist the customer in some manner, the exact tasks that are performed vary from one position to another. Three basic sales tasks can be identified: (1) order processing, (2) creative selling, and (3) missionary sales. These tasks form the basis for a sales classification system.

However, most sales personnel do not fall into a single category but often perform all three tasks to some extent. A sales engineer for a computer firm may be doing 50 percent missionary sales, 45 percent creative selling, and 5 percent order processing. Most selling jobs, however, are classified on the basis of the primary selling task performed.

A major consideration for most businesses is improving productivity throughout their operations, and sales force productivity is no exception. With the climbing costs of travel and compensation for experienced salespeople, each sales rep must spend time efficiently and effectively in order to raise productivity.

Order Processing

Order processing, which can involve both field selling and telemarketing, is most often typified by selling at the wholesale and retail levels. For instance, a Pepsi-Cola route salesperson who performs this task must take the following steps:

1. *Identify customer needs.* The route salesperson determines that a store has only 7 cases left in stock when it normally carries an inventory of 40 cases.
2. *Point out the need to the customer.* The route salesperson informs the store manager of the inventory situation.
3. *Complete (write up) the order.* The store manager acknowledges the need for more of the product. The driver unloads 33 cases, and the manager signs the delivery slip.

Order processing is part of most selling positions. It becomes the primary task in situations where needs can be readily identified and are acknowledged by the customer. Even in such instances, however, salespeople whose primary responsibility involves order processing will devote some time convincing their wholesale or retail customers to carry more complete inventories of their firms' products or to handle additional product lines. They also are likely to try to motivate purchasers to feature some of their firms' products, increase the amount of shelf space devoted to their products, and improve product location in the stores.

Sales force automation is easing order-processing tasks. In the past, salespeople would write up an order on the customer's premises but spend much time later, after the sales visit, completing the order and transmitting it to headquarters. Today, many companies have automated order processing. With portable computers and state-of-the-art software, the salesperson can place an order on the spot, directly to headquarters, thus freeing up valuable time and energy. Computers have even eliminated the need for some of the traditional face-to-face contacts for routine reorders.

Creative Selling

When a considerable amount of analytical decision making is involved in purchasing a good or service, the salesperson must use **creative selling** techniques to solicit an order. While the order processing task deals mainly with maintaining existing business, creative selling generally is used to develop new business either by adding new customers or by introducing new goods and services. New products often require a high degree of creative selling. The salesperson must first identify the customer's problems and needs and then propose a solution, in the form of the good or service being offered. Creative selling techniques are used in over-the-counter selling, field selling, telemarketing, and inside selling.

MARKETING
STRATEGY
FAILURE

FIGURE 17.5   **Use of Endorsements in a Creative Sales Strategy**

Lennox Lewis: WBC Heavyweight Champion Of The World

FUBU THE COLLECTION
www.fubu.com

Toys "Я" Us Is Not Fun Anymore

BACKGROUND Retailers all agree that a key to building customer relationships is creating a satisfying shopping experience. In fact, that is how Toys "Я" Us became America's number one toy store: The New Jersey–based chain had everything and anything a child could want at competitive prices.

THE PROBLEM Toys "Я" Us marketers knew they had a serious problem as they watched the toy market more than double in the past five years and their market share plummet 50 percent. The chain's 1,400 stores were crammed with inventory stacked to the ceiling and boxes of unpacked toys filling the aisles. Toys "Я" Us was a dead-ringer for a warehouse—not a retail store. But the real clincher was hard-to-reach toys and nonexistent sales help. Parents did not want to take their kids into the dirty, cramped stores with hardly any sales help. When Toys "Я" Us started, its competitors were

continued on next page

Creative selling may involve reorganizing a firm's entire approach to sales. When Daymond John and three other designer friends first started selling their own line of clothes, they were literally selling on the street to any New Yorker who walked by. Within a few years, the men had created a full-fledged enterprise, calling themselves FUBU (For Us, By Us), although still relatively unknown among their target market—31 million U.S. teenagers. The greatest challenge was finding a way to communicate to the $141 billion teen market—a demographic collage of urban culture and pop trends. Marketers generally agree that the way to gain street credibility among teens is to follow two basic steps: Identify who they are, and let them know that is who you are, too.

FUBU mailed free clothing samples to well-known personalities with whom urban teens would identify. Their big break came when hip-hop artist and entertainer L. L. Cool J, who grew up in the same Queens neighborhood as the company founder, appeared on MTV wearing FUBU clothes. When teenagers saw the popular singer wearing FUBU styles, they immediately spread the word: FUBU is cool. Others who helped build the brand include singers Mariah Carey, Boys II Men, Fugees, and Sean "Puffy" Combs, as well as such athletes as Tim Hardaway, Kevin Garnett, and Terrell Davis. Figure 17.5 shows another FUBU supporter—heavyweight boxing champion Lennox Lewis.[24]

fubu.com

MARKETING   DICTIONARY

order processing Selling, mostly at the wholesale and retail levels, that involves identifying customer needs, pointing them out to customers, and completing orders.

creative selling Personal selling involving situations in which a considerable degree of analytical decision making on the buyer's part results in the need for skillful proposals of solutions for the customer's needs.

limited to thousands of mom-and-pop toy shops. Now it competed with titans like Wal-Mart, Kmart, and Target, as well as start-ups like Zany Brainy and Noodle Kidoodle. Web retailers such as eToys also moved in to offer convenience, variety, and low prices.

THE OUTCOME Two years ago, Robert Nakasone took the reins of Toys "Я" Us. As a first step to recapturing lost market share, Nakasone reduced inventory and increased delivery times. Stores have been renovated with kid-friendly decor, low shelves, and wider aisles. Internal changes have also included a stronger in-store sales force trained to interact with parents. Although Toys "Я" Us is staying alive, it may never recover its lost kingdom.

LESSONS LEARNED Once the king of toy retailers, Toys "Я" Us is struggling to pull children back into its stores. Marketers will have to convince parents that Wal-Mart or eToys may be closer, but Toys "Я" Us is more fun for the kids.

toysrus.com

5

Outline the steps in the sales process.

Missionary Sales

Missionary sales are an indirect type of selling: Salespeople sell the firm's goodwill and provide their customers with information and technical or operational assistance. For example, a toiletries company salesperson may call on retailers to check on special promotions and overall stock movement, even though a wholesaler is used to take orders and deliver merchandise. A pharmaceuticals salesperson seeks to persuade doctors (the indirect customers) to specify the pharmaceutical company's product brand in prescriptions. However, the company actually completes ultimate sales through a wholesaler or directly to the pharmacists who fill prescriptions.

Missionary sales may involve both field selling and telemarketing. Many aspects of team selling can also be seen as missionary sales, as when technical support salespeople help design, install, and maintain equipment; when they train customers' employees; and when they provide information or operational assistance. For example, Harris InfoSource, a Cleveland-based corporate communications company, compiles and markets databases profiling U.S. manufacturers and their decision makers. Harris' salespeople gather leads from such sources as trade shows and field sales activities and follow up with missionary sales strategies. After each trade show, between two and three people from Harris' internal sales staff call on the leads, looking for customers who need accurate, in-depth sales lead information. The Harris selling approach begins at the trade show booth and continues with follow-up letters, phone calls, and sales calls.[25]

THE SALES PROCESS

After describing various selling channels and sales tasks, the chapter now considers how salespeople actually sell. If you have worked in a retail store or simply sold candy or wrapping paper to raise money for your band, swim team, or other organization, you will recognize some of these activities, although perhaps you did not know how they were formally classified.

What are the steps involved in selling? While the terminology may vary, most authorities agree on the following sequence: (1) prospecting and qualifying, (2) approach, (3) presentation, (4) demonstration, (5) handling objections, (6) closing, and (7) follow-up.

As Figure 17.6 indicates, the steps in the personal selling process follow the attention-interest-desire-action (AIDA) concept discussed in Chapter 15. Once a sales prospect has been qualified, an attempt is made to secure his or her attention. The presentation and demonstration steps are designed to generate interest and desire. Successful handling of buyer objections should arouse further desire. Action occurs at the close of the sale.

Salespeople modify the steps in this process to match their customers' buying processes. For instance, the Girl Scout whose Aunt Ada buys boxes and boxes of Girl Scout Thin Mint cookies every year probably needs no presentation. She could just call her aunt and tell her that cookies are on sale. She might also remind her aunt how grateful she is for her order each year and highlight the new cookies, in the hope that she will also order some of those. If every other house has a girl selling the cookies, the scout may need to join with other members of her troop to find new customers in different locations, such as the lobby of local grocery stores.

Prospecting and Qualifying

Prospecting, the process of identifying potential customers, is difficult work involving many hours of diligent effort. Leads about prospects may come from many sources: computerized databases, trade show exhibits, previous customers, friends and neighbors, other vendors, non-sales employees in the firm, suppliers, and social and professional contacts. A recent study found that 14 percent of a salesperson's time is spent prospecting.[26] While a firm may emphasize personal selling as the primary component of its overall promotional strategy, direct mail and advertising campaigns are also effective in identifying prospective customers.

New sales personnel may find prospecting frustrating because they usually receive no immediate payback. But selling is frequently a numbers game, and for many salespeople, sales num-

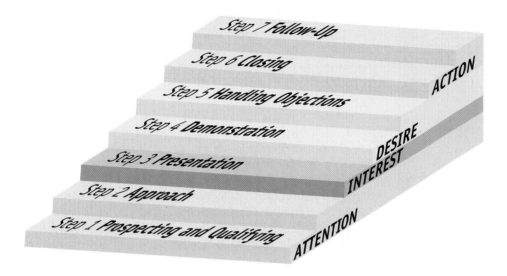

FIGURE 17.6   The AIDA Concept and the Personal Selling Process

bers start with prospecting.[27] Without successful prospecting, future sales growth is limited to current accounts. Prospecting is a continuous process because of the inevitable loss of some customers over time as well as the emergence of new potential customers or first-time prospects.

Recently, salespeople have turned to the Internet in their efforts to identify prospective customers. Few sectors of the economy have been more active in prospecting on the Web than the automobile industry. Auto marketers offer Internet car shoppers an array of promotional incentives, including coupons off the purchase price, gift certificates, savings bonds, sweepstakes, and games. Once consumers sign up for the incentives, they are often asked information about themselves and their preferences. Auto marketers use this information to track and communicate with customers in ways they could not do offline. In addition, respondents to Web giveaways become real customers at a higher rate than consumers targeted by other media. In addition to prospecting for potential car buyers, Honda Motor Co.'s U.S. sales division is using its Web site to cross sell other Honda products, such as lawn mowers and all-terrain vehicles.[28]

Qualifying—determining that the prospect really is a potential customer—is another important sales task. Not all prospects are qualified to make purchase decisions. A person with an annual income of $25,000 may wish to own a $200,000 house, but his or her ability to actually become a customer is questionable.

Qualifying can be a two-way street. The sales representative determines that the prospect has the authority and the resources to make the purchase decision. Likewise, prospects must agree that they are candidates for the goods or services being offered. If either of those conditions is not met, then further contact is not likely to lead to a sale and will be a waste of time for both salesperson and prospect. By one estimate, for every 36 sales prospects identified, 13 turn out to be qualified sales leads. These 13 sales leads can be expected to generate about five opportunities that reach closing (where the salesperson asks for the order) and, eventually, lead to a second order.[29]

The Internet is another way to generate and qualify leads. With demographic data available from and about Web site visitors, companies can identify the types of sites their target market

CNET GENERATES 130,000 QUALIFIED LEADS EVERY DAY.
NUMBER 9,109 HAS AN ANNUAL TECH BUDGET OF $14 MILLION.

They're not just faceless numbers to us. They're loyal CNET enthusiasts. Zealous devotees who come here to check out the news, reviews, and incredibly persuasive ads before unloading their overstuffed IS budgets. Who create 130,000 qualified leads every day. Who account for 8.3 million unique visitors a month. And who dropped a cool $80 million here in a single quarter. Sound good? Pick up an online media kit at CNET.com/media.

130,000 daily qualified leads generated to merchant partners during Q2, 1999.

The source for computers and technology.™ CNET.com

NEWS | INVESTING | REVIEWS | PRODUCT COMPARISONS | PRICES | TECH AUCTIONS | GADGETS | HELP | AND MORE

CNET advertisers can identify qualified prospects from among the 8 million monthly visitors to the firm's news and information Web sites.

visits. Placing ads and links at those sites can provide valuable leads as potential customers request product information, much like the prospecting efforts of Honda's online marketers discussed earlier.

Many firms engage in telemarketing as a cost-effective approach to prospecting and qualifying. Telemarketers and inside sales reps pass on qualified leads to field salespeople, who can concentrate on prospects most likely to buy.

Approach

Once the salesperson has identified a qualified prospect, he or she collects all available, relevant information and plans an **approach**—the salesperson's initial contact with the prospective customer. Information about the prospect can provide invaluable help to ease the initial contact for telemarketers, inside sales reps, and field salespeople. Salespeople can gather information from secondary sources (magazine or newspaper articles) or from the prospect's own published literature (annual reports, press releases, and even Internet sites). In collecting information, the salesperson must be sensitive to the issue of invading the prospect's privacy. A sales professional does not use unethical tactics to obtain personal information about a prospect.

Information-gathering makes **precall planning** possible. A salesperson who has gathered relevant information about a prospect can make an initial contact armed with knowledge about the prospect's purchasing habits; his or her attitudes, activities, and opinions; and common interests between the salesperson and the prospect. This kind of preparation often provides key help for winning an account. As David Green, a career-development systems manager for Dale Carnegie & Associates, explains, "All the hard work is in the preparation. If you've done that, the presentation will take care of itself."[30]

Retail salespeople usually cannot conduct precall planning, but they can compensate by asking leading questions to learn more about the purchase preferences of buyers. Business marketers have access to far more data than retail sellers, and they should review it before scheduling the first sales contact. Marketing research studies often provide invaluable information that serves as the basis of a sales approach. Answering the following questions can help salespeople complete effective precall planning:

- Who are the audience members and what jobs do they perform each day?
- What is their level of knowledge? Are they already informed about the idea you are going to present?
- What do they want to hear? Do they want detailed, technical jargon or general information?
- What do they need to hear? Do they need to know more about your company or more about the good or service your company provides? Do they need to know more about the availability and cost of your product or more about how your product actually works?[31]

Presentation

The salesperson gives the sales message to a prospective customer in a **presentation**. The seller describes the product's major features, points out its strengths, and concludes by citing illustrative successes. One popular form of presentation is a "features-benefits" framework, wherein the seller's objective is to talk about the good or service in terms that are meaningful to the buyer. The salesperson will relate product features to customer needs and explain benefits of those features, rather than relate technical specifications.

The presentation should be well organized, clear, and concise, and it should emphasize the positive. Printed sales support materials (charts, product literature, market research, product reviews), charts designed on a laptop computer, and audiovisual aids such as videotapes enhance the clarity and effectiveness of presentations. The level of preparation depends on the type of call. For a routine sales call, up-to-date product knowledge and information about the prospect may be sufficient. When the salesperson is competing with several other companies for an account, a major presentation requires in-depth preparation and rehearsals to ensure that everything goes perfectly. Flexible presentations are nearly always needed to match the unique circumstances of each purchase decision. Proper planning and sensitivity to the customer's reactions are an important part of tailoring a presentation to each prospective customer.

Increasingly, presentations are going high-tech. Computer-based multimedia presentations are considered the next wave in sales force automation. With a multimedia-ready laptop or a larger PC or LCD projection computer, salespeople can bring color, animation, video, audio, and interactivity—as well as the latest product and pricing information—to their presentations. *CNN Headline News* salespeople previously used ordinary PowerPoint presentations to sell ads to cable operators. But when the company recently decided to change the look and feel of the Atlanta-based, 24-hour cable news network, executives knew their sales force would need multimedia presentation materials that matched the network's more modern cutting-edge look. Presentations now include audio and video clips and high-tech graphics.[32]

Demonstration

One important advantage of personal selling over most advertising is the ability of salespeople to actually demonstrate the good or service to the potential buyer. As the advertisement in Figure 17.7 illustrates, creative print illustrations and television commercials sometimes simulate product demonstrations. This dramatic photograph shows the benefits of the Oldsmobile Intrigue's precision control braking system that can selectively apply any of the car's four brakes to counteract a front- or rear-end slide. The tire marks left as the auto swerves around the raccoon produces an image with which most drivers can relate.

But a static magazine advertisement or even a quasi-demonstration of a product in action on a television screen is a far cry from the real thing. A demonstration ride in a new automobile, for example, allows the prospect to become involved in the presentation. It awakens customer interest in a way that no amount of verbal presentation can.

More firms use new technologies to make their demonstrations more effective. Multimedia interactive demonstrations are now common. Sales representatives for magazines such as *Forbes* and *Newsweek*, for instance, use data stored on CD-ROM or interactive laser disks to demonstrate the magazine's demographics and circulation patterns. These presentations use full-color video and sound, along with animation, statistics, and text to demonstrate how a prospective client's ad will appear.

The key to a good demonstration— one that gains the customer's attention, keeps his or her interest, is convincing, and stays in the customer's memory—is planning. The salesperson should check and recheck all aspects of the demonstration prior to its delivery.

FIGURE 17.7   Demonstration—A Critical Step in Consumer Decision Making

INTRODUCING THE PRECISION CONTROL SYSTEM. CONTROL THE UNEXPECTED.

INTRIGUE

MARKETING   DICTIONARY

approach Salesperson's initial contact with a prospective customer.

precall planning Use of information collected during the prospecting and qualifying stages of the sales process and during previous contacts with the prospect to tailor the approach and presentation to match the customer's needs.

presentation Describing a product's major features and relating them to a customer's problems or needs.

Handling Objections

A vital part of selling involves handling objections. *Objections* are expressions of sales resistance by the prospect, and it is reasonable to expect them: "Well, I really should check with my spouse." "Perhaps I'll stop by next week." "I like everything except the color." Objections typically involve the product's features, its price, and services to be provided by the selling firm. A sales professional uses each objection as a cue for providing additional information for the prospect. In most cases, an objection such as "I don't like the color of the interior" is really the prospect's way of asking what other choices or product features are available. A customer's question reveals an interest in the product and gives the seller an opportunity to expand a presentation by supplying additional information. For instance, testimonials from satisfied customers may be effective in responding to product objections. Also, providing a copy of the warranty and the dealer's service contract may resolve the buyer's doubts about product service.

During this stage of the selling process, salespeople often are confronted with objections concerning competitors' products. Professional salespeople avoid criticizing the competition. Instead, they view objections as an opportunity to provide more information about the product or service. Often this requires conducting extra behind-the-scenes research. Sales force automation can help sales representatives handle certain objections by making certain information immediately available. In just a few moments, the salesperson can confirm for the customer that the amount and type of a certain product is in stock and can be quickly shipped, for example.

Overcoming objections in the marketplace starts with a "we can do it" attitude. When children's video producer EKA Productions, for example, began its efforts to get a major toy store chain to carry its product line, it sent a copy of its newest video detailing the product line and its features to the store buyer. Three months later, EKA Productions executive Jill Luedtke received a brief message from the buyer reporting that the chain would not carry their products. Luedtke immediately called the buyer to determine the reason for the rejection. As Luedtke recalls, "She admitted she had never watched it. So I told her no one who had actually seen the video had ever turned us down." Intrigued, the buyer watched the video, liked what she saw, and placed a sizable order with EKA.[33]

Closing

The moment of truth in selling is the **closing**—the point at which the salesperson asks the prospect for an order. If the sales representative has made an effective presentation based on applying the product to the customer's needs, the closing should be the natural conclusion. However, a surprising number of sales personnel find it difficult to actually ask for an order. Nearly 80 percent of salespeople fail to close when the buyer is ready, and many customers are ready to close much earlier than the salesperson is.

To be effective, salespeople must learn when and how to close a sale. Commonly used methods of closing a sale include the following:

1. The *"If I can show you . . ." technique* first identifies the prospect's major concern in purchasing the good or service and then offers convincing evidence of the offering's ability to resolve it. ("If I can show you how the new heating system will reduce your energy costs by 25 percent, would you be willing to let us install it?")
2. The *alternative-decision technique* poses choices for the prospect in which either alternative is favorable to the salesperson. ("Will you take this sweater or that one?")
3. The *SRO (standing-room-only) technique* warns the prospect that a sales agreement should be concluded now because the product may not be available later or an important feature, such as price, will soon be changed.
4. *Silence* can be used as a closing technique since a discontinuance of a sales presentation forces the prospect to take some type of action (either positive or negative).
5. An *extra-inducement close* offers special incentives designed to motivate a favorable buyer response. Extra inducements may include quantity discounts, special servicing arrangements, or layaway options.

FIGURE 17.8   **Number of Sales Calls Required to Make a Sale**

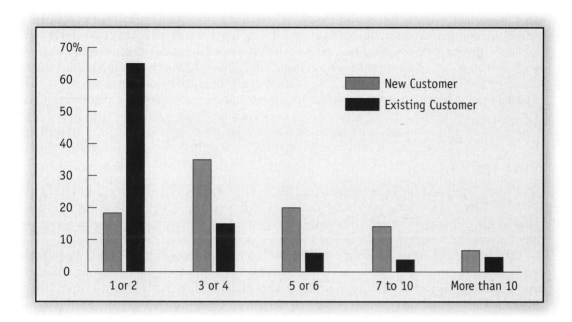

FIGURE 17.8   **Number of Sales Calls Required to Make a Sale**

Getting to a closing point may require selling efforts over a span of time. Figure 17.8 shows the typical number of sales calls it takes to make sales to new and existing customers.

Follow-up

The word *close* can be misleading since the point at which the prospect accepts the seller's offer is where much of the real work of selling begins. In today's increasingly competitive sales environment, the successful salesperson seeks to ensure that today's customers will be future purchasers. It is not enough to close the sale and move on. Relationship selling requires the salesperson to reinforce the customer's purchase decision and make sure that the company delivers high-quality goods or services on schedule. Salespeople must also ensure that customer service needs are met and that satisfaction results from all of a customer's dealings with the company. Otherwise, another company may get the next order.

These postsales activities, which often determine whether a person will become a repeat customer, constitute the sales **follow-up**. Whenever possible, the sales representative should contact customers to find out whether they are satisfied with their purchases. This step allows the salesperson to psychologically reinforce the customer's original decision to buy. It also gives the seller an opportunity to correct any sources of discontent with the purchase and to secure important market information and make additional sales, as well.

Follow-up helps to strengthen the bond salespeople try to build with customers in relationship selling. Automobile dealers, for example, often keep elaborate records of their previous customers so that they can promote new models to individuals who already have shown a willingness to buy from them. Some auto dealers assign representatives from their service departments to call several days after a customer's appointment to make sure the customer is satisfied with the work. Proper follow-up is a logical part of the selling sequence.

Chris Zane, owner of Zane's Cycles in Branford, Connecticut, uses

zanes.com

MARKETING   **DICTIONARY**

closing Stages of personal selling where the salesperson asks the customer to make a purchase decision.

follow-up Postsales activities that often determine whether an individual who has made a recent purchase will become a repeat customer.

follow-up techniques to increase sales and retain customers. "To us," he explains, "the lifetime value of a customer is $2,000." This makes it important for Zane to keep in touch with customers after they walk out of his store, letting them know he has not forgotten them and does not want them to forget Zane's Cycles. Zane uses a database to "remember" his customers and their purchases. For example, every March he searches for customers who bought baby seats three years earlier. He then sends them postcards entitling them to a discount on a child's bike. About 60 percent of those customers return to the store and buy a new bike. The database can also search for such customer-specific characteristics as people who have bought Nike biking shorts in size large. When the shop has an excess supply of size large biking shorts, Zane then sends these customers a postcard giving them a discount off the purchase of Nike shorts.[34]

MANAGING THE SALES EFFORT

6

Describe the sales manager's boundary-spanning role.

7

List and discuss the functions of sales management.

The overall direction and control of the personal-selling effort is in the hands of **sales management**, which is organized on a hierarchical basis. For example, in a typical geographical sales structure, a district or divisional sales manager might report to a regional or zone manager, and these people, in turn, may report to a national sales manager or vice president of sales.

Sales managers perform a **boundary-spanning role** in that they link the sales force to other elements of the internal and external environments. The internal organizational environment consists of top management, other functional areas in the firm, and other internal information sources. The external environment includes trade groups, competitors, customers, suppliers, and regulatory agencies.

The sales manager's job requires a unique blend of administrative and sales skills, depending on the specific level in the sales hierarchy. Sales skills are very important for first-level sales managers since these managers must train and directly lead the sales force. But as one rises in the sales management structure, more managerial skills and fewer sales skills are required for performing the job. Over 60 percent of a typical salesperson's time is devoted to prospecting, face-to-face selling, and travel. The typical time allocations for a salesperson are shown in Figure 17.9.

FIGURE 17.9   **How Salespeople and Sales Managers Spend Their Time**

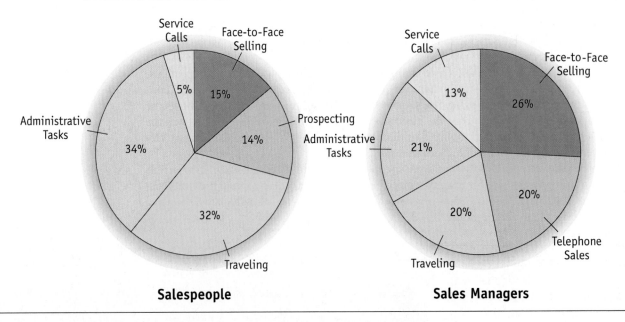

Salespeople   **Sales Managers**

Source: Salesperson time allocations reported in "How Salespeople Spend Their Time," *Sales & Marketing Management*, March 1998, p. 96.

As with other promotional activities, personal selling requires effective planning and strategic objectives. These include such strategies as selling existing products to new customers, selling new products, servicing customer accounts to enhance retention and satisfaction, and expanding customer relationships by selling more products to existing customers.

Sales management is the administrative channel for sales personnel; it links individual salespeople to general management. The sales manager performs seven basic managerial functions: (1) recruitment and selection, (2) training, (3) organization, (4) supervision, (5) motivation, (6) compensation, and (7) evaluation and control. Sales managers perform these tasks in a demanding and complex environment. They must manage an increasingly diverse sales force that includes more women and minorities. Women account for almost half of the nation's professional salespeople, and their numbers are growing at a faster rate than that for men. The fastest growth rate is among salespersons of Hispanic and Asian descent. However, only 26 percent of business-to-business salespeople are women. As the workforce composition continues to change, more people will be needed to fill a growing number of selling positions such as product specialists, sales consultants, telemarketers, and customer service and sales support representatives.

Recruitment and Selection

Recruiting and selecting successful salespeople is one of the sales manager's greatest challenges. The turnover rate of salespeople is the highest of all white-collar professions. Sources of new salespeople include colleges and universities, trade and business schools, sales and nonsales personnel in other firms, and the firm's current nonsales employees. A growing number of companies are offering bonuses and perks for employees who help find recruits. EarthLink Networks, a California-based Internet service provider, pays cash bonuses and gives trips to vacation resorts like Hawaii to workers who help fill positions.[35]

Not all of these methods are equally productive. One problem area involves the reluctance of some high-school guidance counselors and college instructors to promote the advantages of a selling career to students. But, in fact, a successful sales career offers satisfaction in all of the following five areas that a person generally considers when deciding on a profession:

1. *Opportunity for advancement.* Studies have shown that successful sales representatives advance rapidly in most companies. Advancement can come either from within the sales organization or laterally to a more responsible position in some other functional area of the firm.

2. *High earnings.* The earnings of successful salespeople compare favorably with those of successful people in other professions. The average top-level consumer goods salesperson can earn more than $75,000 per year.

3. *Personal satisfaction.* A salesperson derives satisfaction from achieving success in a competitive environment and from helping customers satisfy their wants and needs.

4. *Security.* Contrary to what many students believe, selling provides a high degree of job security. Experience has shown that economic downturns affect personnel in sales less than they do people in most other employment areas. In addition, there is a continuing need for good sales personnel.

5. *Independence and variety.* Salespeople most often operate as "independent" businesspeople or as managers of sales territories. Their work is quite varied and provides an opportunity for involvement in numerous business functions.

Careful selection of salespeople is important for two reasons. First, the selection process involves substantial

MARKETING **DICTIONARY**

sales management Activities of planning, organizing, staffing, motivating, compensating, and evaluating and controlling a sales force to ensure its effectiveness.

boundary-spanning role Role performed by a sales manager in linking the sales force to other elements of the organization's internal and external environments.

amounts of money and management time. Second, selection mistakes are detrimental to customer relations and sales-force performance and are costly to correct, as well.

A seven-step process typically is used in selecting sales personnel: application, screening interview, in-depth interview, testing, reference checks, physical examination, and analysis and hiring decision. An application screening is followed by an initial interview. If the applicant looks promising, an in-depth interview is conducted. During the interview, sales managers look for personal characteristics like enthusiasm, good organizational skills, ambition, persuasiveness, the ability to follow instructions, and sociability.

Next, the company may use testing in its selection procedure, including aptitude, intelligence, interest, knowledge, and personality tests. One testing approach gaining in popularity is the *assessment center*. This technique, which uses situational exercises, group discussions, and various job simulations, allows the sales manager to measure a candidate's skills, knowledge, and ability. Assessment centers enable managers to see what potential salespeople can do rather than what they say they can do. After testing, references are checked to ensure that job candidates have represented themselves accurately. A physical examination is usually included before the final analysis and hiring decision.

Training

To shape new sales recruits into an efficient sales organization, management must conduct an effective training program. The principal methods used in sales training are on-the-job training, individual instruction, in-house classes, and external seminars.

Popular training techniques include instructional videotapes, lectures, role-playing exercises, slides, films, and interactive computer programs. Simulations can help salespeople improve their selling techniques. Another key area for training is sales force automation (SFA). However, salespeople who are not very computer-literate can balk when presented with SFA tools.

Many firms supplement their training by enrolling salespeople in executive development programs at local colleges and by hiring specialists to teach customized training programs. In other instances, sales reps attend courses and workshops developed by outside companies. Figure 17.10 describes a buyer-focused, selling-skills course offered by office technology giant Xerox Corp.

Ongoing sales training is also important for veteran salespeople. Much of this type of training is conducted by sales managers in an informal manner. A standard format is for the sales manager to travel with a field sales representative periodically and then compose a critique of the person's work. Sales meetings, training tapes, classes, and seminars are other important forms of training for experienced personnel.

FIGURE 17.10	**Classroom Training for New and Experienced Salespeople**

Organization

Sales managers are responsible for the organization of the field sales force. General organizational alignments, which are usually made by top marketing management, may be based on geography, products, types of customers, or some combination of these factors. Figure 17.11 presents a simplified organizational chart illustrating each of these alignments.

A product sales organization should have specialized sales forces for each major category of the firm's products. This approach is common among industrial product companies that market large numbers of similar but separate products of a very technical or complex nature and that are sold through different marketing channels.

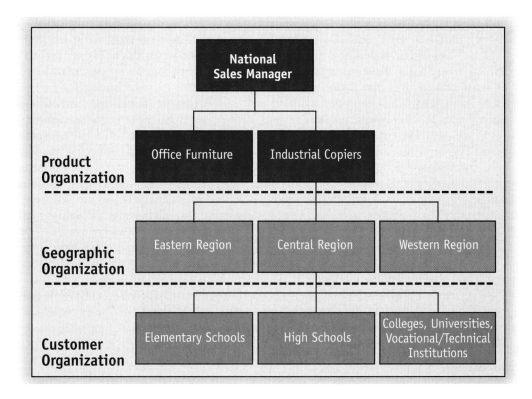

FIGURE 17.11   Basic Approaches to Organizing the Sales Force

Firms that market similar products throughout large territories often use *geographic specialization*. For example, multinational corporations may have different sales divisions in different continents. Geographic organization may be combined with one of the other organizational methods. However, companies are moving away from using territorial sales reps as they adopt customer-focused sales forces. When confronted with a sales territory problem, Stephen Wald, CEO of apparel manufacturer Naturally Knits, had to devise a plan that would settle a dispute between two of his salespeople. The problem arose when one sales rep lost a lucrative account when the territories in his district were reconfigured. Wald knew the importance of maintaining positive relationships between the salesperson and the customer—even though the customer was now located in another sales rep's territory. The company, therefore, added a "cherry-picking clause" that spells out exceptions to the home-territory rule. This reorganization saved two multimillion-dollar accounts that came to the company through relationships developed long-distance by reps outside their territories.[36]

Customer-oriented organizations use different sales force strategies for each major type of customer served. Some firms assign separate sales forces for their consumer and organizational customers. Others have sales forces for specific industries, such as financial services, educational, and automotive. Sales forces can also be organized by customer size, with a separate sales force assigned to large, medium, and small accounts.

A growing trend among firms using a customer-oriented organizational structure is the **national accounts organization**. This structure, designed to strengthen a firm's relationship with large and important customers, involves assigning senior sales managers or sales teams to major accounts in each market. Organizing by national accounts helps sales representatives arrange cooperations between departments in order to meet customer needs. The classic example of a national account selling situation is the relationship between Wal-Mart and its major vendors. Many companies, including Procter & Gamble, set up sales offices near Wal-Mart's Bentonville, Arkansas, headquarters. Doing so places dedicated sales resources close to this key account.

A decade ago, the Boise Cascade office products sales force was organized on a regional basis, and large customers were required to deal with a different sales representative in each region. The system was inefficient, resulting in additional selling expenses for Boise Cascade and complicating the purchasing process for buyers. "Our corporate customers were telling us that we were a very good provider on a regional basis, but they wanted us to meet their strategic needs," says Tom VanHootegem, director of national accounts for the Itasca, Illinois–based company. In response, Boise created a formal national account management program that today includes 23 national account managers who call on approximately 600 accounts worth $250,000 in annual revenues. This reorganization has boosted total revenues to over $1 billion in just six years.[37]

As companies expand their market coverage across national borders, they may use a variant of national account sales teams. These global account teams may be staffed by local sales representatives in the countries in which a company is operating. In other instances, the firm selects highly trained sales executives from its domestic operations. In both instances, training is critical to the success of a company's global sales force. As Mary Elliott, worldwide director of sales and training for Eastman Kodak, explains, "Each culture is so different. The Japanese, for example, want you to teach them." In other countries, people are more open to an interactive, learning-by-doing instructional style.[38]

The individual sales manager also has the task of organizing the sales territories within his or her area of responsibility. Factors such as sales potential, strengths and weaknesses of available personnel, and workloads are considered in territory allocation decisions.

bcop.com

Supervision

A source of constant debate among sales managers concerns the supervision of the sales force. It is impossible to pinpoint the exact amount of supervision that is correct in each situation since the individuals involved and the environments in which they operate vary. However, the concept of the *span of control* helps to reach some generalizations. The span of control refers to the number of sales representatives who report to the first level of sales management. The optimal span of control is affected by such factors as complexity of work activities being performed, ability of the individual sales manager, degree of interdependence among individual salespersons, and the extent of training each salesperson receives. Johnson, Kurtz, and Scheuing, authors of *Sales Management*, suggest a 6-to-1 ratio as the optimal span of control for first-level sales managers supervising technical or industrial salespeople. In contrast, they suggest a 10-to-1 ratio if the sales representatives are calling on wholesale and retail accounts.[39]

In many ways, supervision involves training. It is not uncommon for sales managers to accompany subordinates on sales calls to act as a mentor. For example, every new salesperson at Dublin, Ohio–based Ashland Chemical is assigned a mentor after they complete the company's training program. Mentors shadow new recruits for a week out in the field, but the relationships are ongoing. Says Ashland sales rep Brian Combs, "For the first four or five months, my mentor really put me at ease. . . . It's nice to have someone to go to who knows how things are done." In addition to being less expensive than outside training, mentor programs allow experienced performers to share important sales skills.[40]

ashchem.com

Motivation

The sales manager's responsibility for motivating the sales force cannot be taken lightly. Because the sales process is a problem-solving one, it often leads to considerable mental pressures and frustrations. Sales often result only after repeated calls on customers and may involve a long completion period, especially with new customers and complex technical products. Efforts to motivate salespeople usually take the form of debriefings, information sharing, and both psychological and financial encouragement. Appeals to emotional needs, such as ego needs, recognition, and peer acceptance, are examples of psychological encouragement. Monetary rewards and fringe benefits, such as club memberships and sales contest awards, are types of financial incentives.

However, not all incentive programs are effective in motivating employees. Poorly planned programs—for example, those that have targets set too high, are poorly publicized, allow only the top performers to participate, or feature trips that do not include spouses—can actually have an adverse effect. Companies should not expect these programs to solve all their sales problems. Travel awards are frequently used to reward superior sales performance. The successful sales incentive program offered by Delta Air Lines is described in Figure 17.12.

Sales managers can improve sales force productivity by understanding what motivates individual salespeople. They can gain insight into the subject of motivation by studying the various theories of motivation developed over the years. One theory that has been applied effectively to sales force motivation is the **expectancy theory** proposed by management author Victor Vroom. According to this theory, motivation depends on the expectations an individual has of his or her ability to perform the job and on how performance relates to attaining rewards that the individual values.

Sales managers can apply the expectancy theory of motivation by following a five-step process:

1. Let each salesperson know in detail what is expected in terms of selling goals, service standards, and other areas of performance. A Coopers & Lybrand study found that it is useful to set goals more frequently than just once a year. Companies that set only annual goals (about seven out of every ten companies) have the lowest rate of meeting or exceeding their sales goals; whereas those that set goals more frequently (monthly, quarterly, or semiannually), reported greater success in meeting sales goals.[41]

2. Make the work valuable by assessing the needs, values, and abilities of each salesperson and then assigning appropriate tasks.

3. Make the work achievable. As leaders, they must inspire self-confidence in their salespeople and offer training and coaching to reassure them.

4. Provide immediate and specific feedback, guiding those who need improvement and giving positive feedback to those doing well.

5. Offer rewards that reinforce the values of each salesperson. Managers at Cable & Wireless, a Virginia-based, long-distance provider for businesses, used a reward system to encourage use of their new SFA. When sales representatives turn on their computers, they immediately see their year-to-date sales commissions. Explains a Cable & Wireless salesperson, "The thing I'm concerned most with is making money. You can bet I'll use the system when I can immediately find out what my paycheck is going to say."[42]

FIGURE 17.12 Travel Awards Used as Sales Incentives

 cw-usa.net

Compensation

Because monetary rewards are an important factor in motivating subordinates, compensating sales personnel is a critical matter for managers. Basically, sales compensation can be based on a

MARKETING DICTIONARY

expectancy theory Theory that motivation depends on an individual's expectations of his or her ability to perform a job and how that performance relates to attaining a desired reward.

commission plan, a straight-salary plan, or some combination of these. Bonuses based on end-of-year results are another popular form of compensation.

A **commission** is a payment tied directly to the sales or profits that a salesperson achieves. For example, a salesperson might receive a 5 percent commission on all sales up to a specified quota and a 7 percent commission on sales beyond that point. This approach to sales compensation is growing in popularity. According to sales recruiter Russ Riendeau of Thomas Lyle & Co., 60 percent of his clients adjusted their compensation plans during the past two years to include more performance-based incentives.[43] While commissions reinforce selling incentives, they may cause some sales force members to shortchange nonselling activities, such as completing sales reports, delivering sales promotion materials, and performing normal account servicing.

A **salary** is a fixed payment made periodically to an employee. A firm that bases compensation on salaries rather than commissions might pay a salesperson a set amount every week. A company must balance benefits and disadvantages in paying predetermined salaries to compensate management and sales personnel. A straight salary plan gives management more control over how sales personnel allocate their efforts, but it reduces the incentive to expand sales. As a result, many firms develop compensation programs that combine features of both salary and commission plans.

Because good salespeople are both hard to find and expensive to train, sales managers want to do what they can to encourage productive workers to stay with their firms. Incentive plans that favor experienced sales representatives tend to provide fewer benefits for new representatives who are not yet fully productive. Some companies, therefore, have developed interim compensation plans for new recruits, such as a straight salary for a given period of time or a commitment that the salesperson will not earn less than a certain amount but can earn more during his or her training period.

The typical U.S. sales representative earns $50,000 in salary with an average bonus of $65,100. Figure 17.13 shows total sales compensation figures for various levels of sales personnel. Salary plus bonus is the most common sales pay plan: 44 percent of respondents in a recent compensation survey worked under such a plan, while fewer than 1 percent of all salespeople were paid by straight commissions.[44]

FIGURE 17.13	Annual Pay for Sales Representatives and Sales Managers

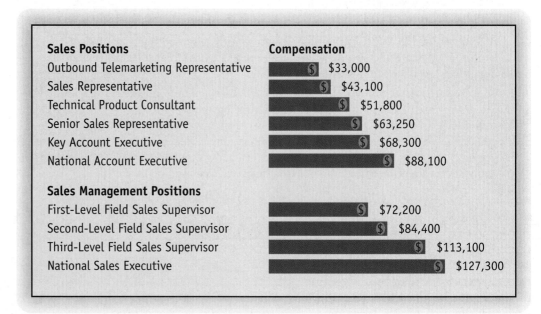

Sales Positions	Compensation
Outbound Telemarketing Representative	$33,000
Sales Representative	$43,100
Technical Product Consultant	$51,800
Senior Sales Representative	$63,250
Key Account Executive	$68,300
National Account Executive	$88,100
Sales Management Positions	
First-Level Field Sales Supervisor	$72,200
Second-Level Field Sales Supervisor	$84,400
Third-Level Field Sales Supervisor	$113,100
National Sales Executive	$127,300

Well-managed incentive programs can motivate salespeople and improve customer service. A recent survey by the Incentive Federation, a consortium of supplier associations in the incentive industry, revealed that companies spend more money per person motivating dealer salespeople than for any other group. The average per-person cost of dealer incentives is $2,317 for a travel program and $809 for a merchandise program. This is considerably higher than the per-person budget for programs aimed at corporate sales staffs, which average $1,981 for travel and $552 for merchandise. Most companies base their incentive programs on participant earnings and income level, and many others such as Volkswagen tie incentives to completion of training programs.[45]

However, commission programs can also backfire. Some retailers, like Sears and electronics chain Highland Superstores, modified their compensation systems after discovering that salespeople were being too aggressive or recommending unnecessary services.

Because of the increasing popularity of team selling, companies are setting up reward programs to recognize performance of business units and teams. Today, about one in four companies reward business-unit performance. About 13 percent of companies provide team performance rewards, compared to 5 percent in 1991.

Evaluation and Control

Perhaps the most difficult tasks required of sales managers are evaluation and control. Sales managers are responsible for setting standards and choosing the best methods for measuring sales performance. Sales volume, profitability, and investment return are the usual means of evaluating sales effectiveness. They typically involve the use of **sales quotas**—specified sales or profit targets that the firm expects salespeople to achieve. For example, a particular sales representative might be expected to sell $720,000 in territory 27 during a given year. In many cases, the quota is tied to the compensation system. SFA has greatly improved the ability of sales managers to monitor the effectiveness of their sales staffs. Databases enable sales managers to break out revenue by salesperson, by account, and by geographic area.

In addition to sales quotas, other measures such as customer satisfaction, profit contribution, share of product-category sales, and customer retention are also coming into play. The changes are the result of three factors:

- An increasingly long-term orientation that results from increasing use of total quality management and customer-relationship building efforts
- The realization that evaluations based on sales volume alone can lead to overselling and excessive inventory problems that work against customer relationship building
- The need to encourage sales representatives to develop new accounts, provide customer service, and emphasize new products. A concentration on sales quotas tends to focus salespeople's attention on short-term selling from which they can generate the most sales today.[46]

Regardless of the key elements in the evaluation program, the sales manager must follow a formal system of decision rules. Such a system supplies information to the sales manager for action. This input helps the sales manager to answer three general questions.

First, where does each salesperson's performance rank relative to the predetermined standards? This comparison should fully consider the effect of uncontrollable variables on sales performance. Preferably, each adjusted rank should be stated as a percentage of the standard. This system simplifies evaluation and facilitates converting various ranks into a single, composite index of performance.

The second evaluation question asks about the salesperson's strong points.

MARKETING DICTIONARY

commission Incentive compensation directly related to the sales or profits achieved by a salesperson.

salary Fixed compensation payments made periodically to an employee.

sales quota Level of expected sales for a territory, product, customer, or salesperson against which actual results are compared.

One way to answer this question is to list areas of the salesperson's performance in which he or she has surpassed the respective standard. Another way is to categorize a salesperson's strong points in three areas of the work environment:

1. *Task, or technical ability.* This strength appears in knowledge of the products (end uses), customers, and company, as well as selling skills.

2. *Process, or sequence of work flow.* This strength pertains to actual sales transactions—the salesperson's application of technical ability and interaction with customers. Managers frequently measure process performance based on personal observation. Other measures are sales calls and expense reports.

3. *Goal, or end results (output) of sales performance.* Sales managers usually state this aspect of the salesperson's work environment in terms of sales volume and profits.

The third evaluation question asks about the weaknesses or negatives in the salesperson's performance. The manager should categorize these faults as carefully as the salesperson's strong points. The sales manager should explain candidly, but kindly, the employee's weak areas. Because few people like to hear this part of an evaluation and consequently tend to listen with only "half-an-ear," the manager should make sure the employee understands any performance problems that he or she needs to correct and how the manager will measure progress. The manager and employee should then establish specific objectives for improvement and set a timetable for judging the employee's improvement.

In completing the evaluation summary, the sales manager should follow a set procedure:

1. Each aspect of sales performance for which a standard exists should be measured separately. This helps prevent the *halo effect*, in which the rating given on one factor influences those on other performance variables.

2. Each salesperson should be judged on the basis of actual sales performance rather than potential ability. This emphasizes the importance of rankings in the evaluation.

3. Sales managers should judge each salesperson on the basis of sales performance for the entire period under consideration rather than for the particular incidents. As an evaluator, the sales manager should avoid reliance on isolated examples of the salesperson's success or failure.

4. Each salesperson's evaluation should be reviewed for completeness and evidence of possible bias. Ideally this review would be made by the sales manager's immediate superior.

While evaluation includes both revision and correction, the sales manager must focus attention on correction. This priority translates into a drive to adjust actual performance to conform with predetermined standards. Corrective action, with its obviously negative connotations, typically poses a substantial challenge for the sales manager.

ETHICAL ISSUES IN SALES

8

Discuss the role of ethics in personal selling and sales management.

As the previous chapter discussed, promotional activities raise many ethical questions, and personal selling is no exception. The pervasiveness of personal selling in our daily lives and the vast differences in the training, experience, and professionalism of different types of salespeople combine to produce a negative image of the profession for many. Plays like *Death of a Salesman*, television shows, and movies reinforce this poor image.

Today's highly-paid, highly-professional salesperson knows that long-term success is based on building and maintaining mutually satisfying relationships with clients. Still, the stereotype lingers. A recent Gallup poll offered still more evidence of how much people dislike certain types of salespeople. Auto sales was considered the least ethical among 26 careers, and insurance sales fared only slightly better with a 23 ranking.

SOLVING AN ETHICAL CONTROVERSY

Campus Marketing: The Business of Education

While most of the publicity on advertising to students focuses on grades kindergarten through twelfth, another area of controversy is concerned with college students, many of whom represent captive targets on hundreds of U.S. campuses.

College students are often young and enthusiastic, and almost always need more money. So when marketers from Korea's Daewoo Motor Co. wanted to crack the U.S. market, they hired 2,000 "student advisors" from 400 colleges and universities to sell the economy car to their friends and classmates in return for sales commissions of $300 to $400. The advisors were sent to Korea to tour auto plants and dealerships and to be trained for 8 to 10 hour workweeks when they return to campus.

Critics, however, see a darker side to this Daewoo deal and other similar arrangements that lure inexperienced and often easily-influenced college students. Credit-card companies are the most highly criticized industry when it comes to targeting college students. One tangible result of aggressive soliciting on campus is an average unpaid credit balance of $1000 per card per student. This burden can often force a self-supporting student to drop out of school to get a job to pay overdue credit-card bills.

Are college students fair game for marketers?

Pro
1. Marketers who use students to sell their goods and services are giving college students an opportunity to learn basic business strategies such as personal selling, the sales process, and relationship selling.

2. Credit-card companies are simply encouraging college students to start building their credit histories early by issuing them credit cards. These cards typically set low credit lines, making it possible for students to make small purchases and learn how to budget their money and use credit wisely.

Con
1. College students are under too much pressure without listening to a sales presentation for a car or a credit card.
2. Students do not pay tuition to shop for a car or to get a credit card. Marketers should not take advantage of this captive audience by pushing products on campuses.

Summary
Some companies are responding to complaints of aggressive selling tactics that target college students. MasterCard ran a full-page ad with the word "NO" in all caps and with ad copy at the bottom that explained, "If you abuse your credit cards, get used to this answer when applying for car loans, apartments, or anything else that requires a check of your credit history." But critics continue to push for regulations on campus selling.

SOURCES: Marcy Gordon, "College Marketing Practices Send Some Students into Debt," *USA Today*, September 18, 1998, p. 6B; Larry Armstrong, "Big Car on Campus?" *Business Week*, August 31, 1998, p. 32; and Al Urbanski, "The Old College Try," *Promo*, July 1998, pp. 49–50.

Some people believe that ethical problems are inevitable due to the very nature of the sales function. They simply do not trust someone who by making the sale will personally benefit from the interaction.

Thousands of companies are working to overcome the stigma associated with sales careers and to educate the general public about the contributions of today's sales professionals. It is to their advantage to do so because salespeople generate the firm's revenue, link the company to the customer, and provide valuable product information to customers and members of the marketing channel as well as supplying feedback for the producer. By recruiting highly ethical, educated individuals and by training them in relationship selling techniques, companies develop sales forces able to win the customer's respect and trust. By stressing consultative selling techniques, sales professionals meet customer needs without resorting to unethical behavior. In addition, sales managers create an ethical sales environment by doing the following:

- Promoting ethical awareness during training programs, sales meetings, and sales calls
- Making sure that all employees—salespeople and other company personnel—know that the firm opposes unethical conduct
- Establishing control systems to monitor ethical conduct

Ethical Dilemmas

Despite management efforts to foster ethical behavior, from time to time salespeople may find themselves in situations with their employers, fellow employees, and customers that involve ethical dilemmas. Among the ethical breaches that occur between salespeople and their employers are improper use of company assets and cheating. Use of a company car for personal purposes is one such possibility; padding expense reports is another. A salesperson might resort to deception in an attempt to win a sales contest, such as holding on to orders until a contest begins or shipping unordered merchandise to customers, which will not be returned until after the contest ends.

Sexual harassment is another problem faced by many sales representatives. An Ohio State University study reported that about 30 percent of business-to-business saleswomen—and about 20 percent of salesmen—have experienced unwanted sexual advances from customers.

Another type of unethical conduct involves using bribes to secure a sale. While gifts such as pens and tickets to sporting events are accepted business practices, they can be misused. Since expensive gifts may be considered a form of bribery, many firms prohibit their employees from accepting any gift from a sales representative.

Customer demand for cash kickbacks represents another ethical dilemma. Suppose, for example, a copy-machine salesperson calls on an important business customer who is planning to order new copiers for most of his company's departments. The purchasing manager offers her the account if she will share half of her commission with him. Although she knows this is illegal and she has signed her company's strong code of ethical conduct, she also wants the sale.

In cases like this, possible options include going along with the unethical request, ignoring the request, confronting the person, or reporting the behavior. Experts recommend telling the purchasing manager that the representative wants to gain the buyer's business without resorting to such tactics. If the purchasing agent refuses to move forward on these terms, the salesperson should report the incident to a manager, who should then speak to the customer representative's supervisor. Company-wide codes of ethics should help guide salespeople with such situations and should aim to protect all parties.

STRATEGIC IMPLICATIONS OF PERSONAL SELLING

Today's sales forces are a new breed of businesspeople. Richly nourished in a tradition of sales, their roles are strengthened even further through technology. However, as many companies are discovering, nothing can replace the power of personal selling in generating sales and in building strong, loyal customer relationships.

Selling has experienced a series of evolutionary stages, each building on the strengths of previous ones. Whereas salespeople of the early 1900s were familiar with each customer's personal lifestyles as well as their occupational needs, the mid-1900s moved selling from a one-to-one environment to a process of providing goods and services to massive numbers of people who remained largely anonymous. In the past decade, however, the Internet has once again placed salespeople in positions of satisfying the needs of individual customers through teamwork and partnerships. Instead of eliminating many of the processes performed by a salesperson, electronic technologies enhance the ability to sell the right product to the right consumer at the right time.

Salespeople today are a critical link in developing relationships between the customer and the company. They communicate customer needs and wants to coworkers in various departments and divisions within an organization, enabling a cooperative, company-wide effort in improving product offerings and in better satisfying individuals within the target market. For salespeople, the greatest benefit of electronic technologies is the ability to share knowledge when it is needed with those who need to know, including customers, suppliers, and employees.

A number of environmental pressures have led to changes in personal selling and sales management:

- Buyers are more sophisticated, demanding more rapid, low-cost transactions.
- Customer and supplier data are linked via computerized data warehousing systems that identify optimal consumer characteristics.
- New technology makes alternative, low-cost distribution methods possible.
- Automatic inventory reorder processes reduce the need for face-to-face meetings with buyers.
- Computer databases, telecommunication sales, catalogs, and the Internet provide transaction mediums at much lower costs per transaction than the traditional field-selling channel.
- Product life cycles are accelerating, with products moving more rapidly into and out of the marketplace.
- Customers in some market segments are less loyal and more prone to switch suppliers.

These factors demand that traditional sales force responsibilities be developed and enlarged to reflect the 21st-century environment. Recognizing the long-term impact of keeping satisfied buyers (those who make repeat and cross-purchases and provide referrals) versus dissatisfied buyers (who generally tell about 11 other people of their dissatisfaction), organizations are increasingly training their sales forces to provide superior customer service. In fact, many companies evaluate and often reward their salespeople based on customer satisfaction.[47]

Professional salespeople of the 21st century will have a number of skills that distinguish them from their 20th-century counterparts. Where skills of the last century's salesperson were likely to include persuasion, selling ability, and product knowledge, the 21st-century sales professional is more likely to possess communication skills, problem-solving skills, and knowledge of products, customers, industries, and applications. Last century's salesperson tended to be self-driven; today's sales professional is more likely to be a team player as well as a customer advocate who serves his or her buyers by solving problems.

ACHIEVEMENT CHECK SUMMARY

Read the learning objectives that follow, and consider the questions for each one. Answering these questions will reinforce your grasp of the most important concepts in the chapter and will allow you to check how well you have achieved these learning goals. Where a blank appears before a question, answer with *T* or *F* for true/false questions; for multiple-choice questions, choose the letter of the correct answer.

Objective 17.1: Explain the conditions that determine the relative importance of personal selling in the promotional mix.
1. _____ Personal selling expenses represent a smaller outlay for most companies than advertising.
2. _____ Personal selling is likely to be relatively important when consumers are geographically concentrated and relatively few in number.
3. _____ Companies are likely to rely on personal selling when there are many intermediaries between the manufacturer and the final consumer.

Objective 17.2: Contrast over-the-counter selling, field selling, telemarketing, and inside selling.
1. _____ A salesperson who visits a farmer and demonstrates a new insect-repellent fertilizer is engaged in field selling.
2. _____ When a farmer buys an insect-repellent fertilizer on the Internet, he has made use of telemarketing.
3. _____ Inside selling takes place when a telemarketer discovers that a farmer who buys from them is not applying the insect-repellent fertilizer correctly and then refers the customer to a field salesperson to obtain more information.

Objective 17.3: Describe each of the four major trends in personal selling.
1. _____ Relationship selling involves establishing a sustained relationship, sometimes formalized and sometimes not, between buyer and seller.
2. _____ Relationship selling works because the buyer wants to improve the relationship by focusing on the seller's short-term sales goals.
3. _____ Team selling is often immediately popular with salespeople because they are naturally gregarious and they do not mind sharing sales responsibility.
4. _____ Though expensive, SFA pays off in all selling situations.

Objective 17.4: Identify the three basic sales tasks.
1. _____ The three basic sales tasks are order processing, creative selling, and closing the sale.
2. _____ Selling a new health-insurance program to a business customer is a good example of order processing.
3. _____ The most demanding of the three sales tasks is (a) order processing, (b) creative selling, or (c) missionary selling.
4. _____ An example of missionary selling is (a) a salesperson who visits a store's lingerie department to help organize the company's product displays; (b) the annual Butterball Turkey hotline that consumers can call at Thanksgiving with questions about cooking turkeys; or (c) the sale of religious products to foreign customers.

Objective 17.5: Outline the steps in the sales process.

1. _____ The first step in the sales process is (a) approach, (b) prospecting and qualifying, (c) presentation.

2. _____ Information gathered from secondary sources is of limited use in preparing a sales approach because it is information every other competing salesperson has access to.

3. _____ A customer's objections often reveal an underlying interest in the product, which gives the salesperson an opportunity to provide additional information.

4. _____ Most salespeople find closing a sale the easiest part of the sales process.

5. _____ Follow-up activities after a sale strengthen the bond between seller and buyer and allow the salesperson to reinforce the customer's decision to buy.

Objective 17.6: Describe the sales manager's boundary-spanning role.

1. _____ The sales manager's boundary-spanning role refers to his or her responsibility for overseeing salespeople in several geographic areas.

2. _____ The sales manager links the sales force to elements of the company's internal and external environments.

3. _____ The external environment to which the sales manager helps link the sales staff includes all of the following except: (a) trade groups, (b) competitors, (c) customers, (d) the department that approves travel and entertainment vouchers, (e) suppliers, (f) regulatory agencies.

Objective 17.7: List and discuss the functions of sales management.

1. _____ One of the greatest challenges among the sales management functions is (a) the general organizational alignment of the sales force, (b) recruiting and selecting successful salespeople, or (c) keeping travel costs down.

2. _____ According to the expectancy theory, motivation depends on (a) individuals' expectations of their ability to perform a job and be rewarded for that performance or (b) individuals' perceptions of how fairly they are compensated by their sales managers.

3. _____ Commission plans provide maximum selling incentives but sometimes backfire by causing salespeople to shortchange nonselling activities or focus on their own quotas rather than customers' needs.

Objective 17.8: Discuss the role of ethics in personal selling and sales management.

1. _____ Sales managers can reduce the occurrences of unethical behavior through training, supporting the company code of ethics, and monitoring ethical conduct.

2. _____ Sexual harassment is a problem faced only by female sales representatives.

3. _____ Giving gifts to customers is an example of unethical behavior.

Students: See the solutions section located on page S-3 to check your responses to the Achievement Check Summary.

Key Terms

personal selling	creative selling
over-the-counter selling	missionary sales
field selling	prospecting
telemarketing	qualifying
canned approach	approach
inside selling	precall planning
relationship selling	presentation
consultative selling	closing
team selling	follow-up
sales force automation (SFA)	sales management
order processing	boundary-spanning role

national accounts organization	salary
expectancy theory	sales quota
commission	

Review Questions

1. How does personal selling differ among the four major selling channels? Give examples of local firms that operate in each channel.
2. What is meant by *relationship selling?* Why is it becoming such a factor in personal selling?
3. What is meant by *team selling?* Why is it important?
4. Explain how sales force automation can improve the sales function in a company.
5. Cite two local examples of each of the three basic sales tasks.
6. Under what conditions is the canned approach to selling likely to be used? What are the major problems with this method?
7. Give an example of each function performed by sales managers in an organization.
8. Compare the alternative sales compensation plans. Point out the advantages and disadvantages of each.
9. Explain how a sales manager's problems and areas of emphasis might change in dealing with each of the following.
   a. telephone salespeople
   b. over-the-counter retail salespeople
   c. field sales representatives
   d. missionary salespeople
10. Give three examples of situations that present ethical dilemmas for salespeople.

Questions for Critical Thinking

1. Explain and offer examples of how the following factors affect the decision to emphasize personal selling or advertising.
   a. geographic market concentration
   b. length of marketing channels
   c. degree of product technical complexity
   d. price
   e. number of customers
   f. prevalence of trade-ins
2. What sales tasks are involved in selling the following products?
   a. Lexmark laser printers
   b. American Heart Association (to an employee group)
   c. used Honda Accord
   d. fast food from Broadway Bagels
   e. janitorial supplies for use in plant maintenance
3. How would you describe the job of each of the following salespersons?
   a. salesperson in a Blockbuster Video store
   b. Coldwell Banker real-estate sales representative
   c. route driver for Keebler snack foods (sells and delivers to local food retailers)
   d. sales engineer for Dell computers
4. As marketing vice president of a large paper company, you are asked to address a group of university students regarding selling as a career. List the five most important points you would make in your speech.
5. Suppose that you are the local sales manager for the telephone company's Yellow Pages and that you employ six representatives who call on local firms to solicit advertising space sales. What type of compensation system would you use? What types of sales force automation would be effective in presenting the benefits of advertising in the Yellow Pages? How would you suggest that your sales personnel be evaluated?

'net**W**ork

hotjobs.com

cathcart.com

crystalgraphics.com

1. **Job Opportunities in Sales.** Go to a job search site such as *www.hotjobs.com* and search for job opportunities in sales. Print out the job description for a job in the location and at a company that would appeal to you if you were looking for a job in sales.

2. **Relationship Selling.** Go to the Cathcart Institute Web site at *www.cathcart.com* to learn more about relationship selling. Jim Cathcart, author of Relationship Selling: The Key to Getting and Keeping Customers, provides several links to information about relationship selling at his Web site. For example, watch the 5-minute video clip on relationship selling and service and read the synopsis of his book on the topic. Write a 2- to 3-paragraph summary of what you learned at this Web site.

3. **Presentation.** As discussed in the chapter, salespeople at such organizations as CNN Headline News are finding that their ordinary PowerPoint presentations need to be replaced with more multimedia presentation materials that include high-tech graphics. PowerPoint add-in tools that work in conjunction with Microsoft's PowerPoint are available to try for free at *www.crystalgraphics.com*. Here you can download several options for adding high-tech graphics to your PowerPoint presentations. Select one to download and try out with your existing PowerPoint program. Be prepared to comment in class on which one you tried and what you liked or disliked about its ability to add high-tech graphics to your PowerPoint presentation.

Video Case 17 on Concept2 begins on page VC-19.

Gateway Continuing Case Part 7 begins on page GC-11.

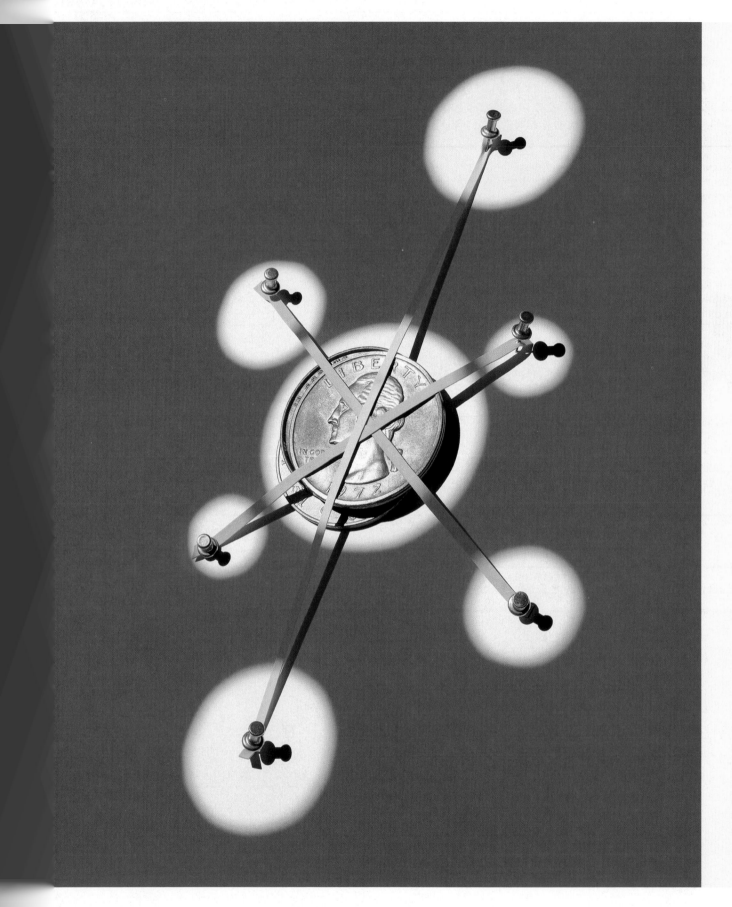

PART

8

PRICING
STRATEGY

CHAPTER 18 Price Determination

CHAPTER 19 Managing the Pricing
Function

563

Gateway Continuing Case Part 8 begins on page GC-13.

Price Determination

eBay Customers Name Their Own Price

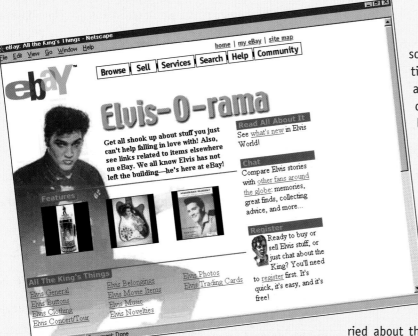

In one of the zaniest startup stories of the decade, Pierre Omidyar goes online to find Pez candy dispensers for his fiancée's collection and ends up an owner of a hot new online auction company—eBay. That was in 1995. Today, the Internet star has watched sales figures soar from just under $6 billion to nearly $50 billion in one recent year, and industry analysts predict this is only the beginning.

The number of online auctioneers is growing and now includes names such as Onsale, Buy.com, UBid, CitiAuction, icollector, and even the world's largest online bookseller, Amazon.com. However, eBay has remained the top auctioneer by building a community of buyers and sellers who have built common-interest relationships online. Says CEO Meg Whitman, "Our competitors are in anywhere between 10 and 50 other businesses. This is the only business we're in, and it's a full-time, 24-by-seven job to make person-to-person trading on the Internet fun, fast, entertaining, and easy to use."

eBay has been dubbed by some "the world's biggest flea market." It neither owns the merchandise nor sells it—eBay simply brings together ordinary people who share many of the same interests. An estimated 147 million online bidders are predicted to generate over $6.5 billion in sales of collectibles by 2003. Antiques, sports memorabilia, toys, coins, books, and artwork are some of the items that go up on eBay's virtual auction block. Despite the number of competing online auction sites, eBay is so dominant that 100 of its competitors recently agreed to share their auction listings, making an item on one site available for bidding on all the other sites. Included in this agreement are Microsoft Corp.'s MSN, Excite@Home Corp., and Lycos Inc.'s *The New York Times*. Another major new competitor is Amazon.com, which teamed up with the prestigious fine-art auction house, Sotheby's, to add name recognition and expertise to its new online auction site.

Since it now owns Butterfield & Butterfield of San Francisco, one of the largest and oldest auction houses in the world, eBay is not worried about the recent competition. Bidders on eBay can now compete for everything from Ren and Stempy toys to Rembrandt etchings. Whitman also points out that Amazon's 8 million book browsers cannot compare to eBay's 2 million dedicated buyers and sellers. After all, eBay has well over 2 million items for sale in over 1,500 categories. Amazon's approach, she explains, "is more retail. It has large dealers for the most part, selling new items. That's quite different from our community of individual and very small dealers who are selling unique items."

The family of buyers and sellers on eBay are entirely in charge of setting prices for their goods and services. The Internet auctioneer generates revenues by charging fees for its services. These fees are relatively low and structured on three levels. The first fee covers the cost of listing an item on the site. Feature fees allow an item to be placed in high-visibility areas on the site. Finally, value fees depend on the actual price paid. eBay doesn't take physical possession or title to inventory, so its operating costs are small. Starting with a very high gross margin gives eBay the flexibility to spend money where and when it is needed—mainly on advertising and promotion designed to expand its customer base of buyers and sellers even more. As one industry expert points out, "It benefits both the buyer and seller to be in the most active market." And eBay customers are in the most liquid market in the world today.

So how much is Liberace's seventh limousine worth? To a recent eBay bidder, $17,000.[1]

CHAPTER OVERVIEW

One of the first questions shoppers ask is, "How much does it cost?" Marketers understand the critical role the price of a good or service plays in the consumer's decision-making process. From lipstick and perfume to automobiles and gasoline to donuts and coffee, marketers must develop strategies that price products to achieve their firms' objectives.

As a starting point for examining pricing strategies, consider the meaning of the term *price*. A **price** is the exchange value of a good or service—in other words, what it can be exchanged for in the marketplace. Price does not necessarily involve money. In earlier times, the price of an acre of land might have been 20 bushels of wheat, three head of cattle, or one boat. This barter process still applies in some areas of the world. However, in a modern monetary system, *price* refers to the amount of funds required to purchase a product.

As eBay buyers and sellers recognize, the method of setting prices is a major component of a successful listing on the online auction site. Prices are both difficult to set and dynamic; they shift in response to a number of variables. A higher-than-average price can convey an image of prestige, while a lower-than-average price may connote good value. Price can also powerfully affect a company's overall profitability and market share.

This chapter discusses the process of determining a profitable but justifiable (fair) price. The chapter focuses on management of the pricing function and discusses pricing strategies, price-quality relationships, and pricing in both the industrial and public sectors. It also looks at the effects of various conditions on price determination, including legal constraints, competitive pressures, and changes in global and online markets. ■

LEGAL CONSTRAINTS ON PRICING

1

Outline the legal constraints on pricing.

Pricing decisions must be made with a variety of legal constraints imposed by both federal and state governments. The next time you pull up to a gas station, consider where each dollar goes: Almost 50 percent goes to federal, state, local, and excise taxes. Tariffs—taxes levied on the sale of imported goods and services—often permit firms to set prices on domestically produced goods well above world market levels. Restrictions on importing Mexican-grown Hass avocados mean that San Diego supermarket shoppers may pay $1.79 for the California-grown variety, while Vancouver purchasers can buy Mexican-grown produce for $.79 each. Similar restrictions result in higher prices for bananas in Europe than what Americans generally pay.[2]

If you are looking for an industry where the legal environment has had a major impact on prices, consider the handgun marketplace. Following a rash of public shootings and mass murders—often on school grounds and just as often at the hands of teenage gunmen—antigun activists pressured Congress to pass additional restrictions regulating ownership and sales. At the same time, survivors, families of victims, and even cities began filing lawsuits against handgun manufacturers. Proponents of civilian gun ownership, such as the National Rifle Association, countered that government could accomplish more by enforcing existing laws rather than simply passing additional legislation. The growing legal assault prompted handgun marketers to raise prices almost 10 percent. The industry justified the price increases citing additional legal expenses, but critics say another reason exists for the price hikes. Demand is soaring and manufacturers, wholesalers, and retailers are taking advantage of the market.[3]

Pricing is also regulated by the general constraints of U.S. antitrust legislation, as outlined in Chapter 2. The next few pages contain a discussion on some of the most important pricing laws for contemporary marketers.

Robinson-Patman Act

The **Robinson-Patman Act** (1936) typifies Depression-era legislation. Known in some circles as the *Anti-A&P Act*, it was inspired by price competition from the developing grocery store chains—in fact, the original draft was prepared by the United States Wholesale Grocers Association. Legislators saw the country in the midst of the Great Depression, and they intended the law primarily to save jobs. They perceived the developing chain stores as threats to traditional retailing and employment and established the act to reverse the trend.

The Robinson-Patman Act, which technically was an amendment to the Clayton Act, prohibits price discrimination in sales to wholesalers, retailers, and other producers; basically, differences in price must reflect cost differentials. The act also disallows selling at unreasonably low prices in order to drive competitors out of business. The Clayton Act had applied only to price discrimination between geographic areas, which injured local sellers. Supporters justified the Robinson-Patman legislation by arguing that the chain stores might secure volume discounts from suppliers, while small, independent stores would continue to pay regular prices.

The practice of price discrimination, where some customers pay more than others, goes back 3,000 years to the beginning of trade and commerce. Today, however, technology has added to the frequency and complexity of price discrimination. Many companies get around the law by inviting certain customers to become "preferred customers," entitling them to average discounts of 10 percent. As long as companies can justify their price discounts and promotional allowances without restricting competition, they will escape restrictions of the Robinson-Patman Act. Direct-mail marketers frequently send out catalogs of identical goods but with differing prices. Zip-code areas that traditionally consist of high spenders get the high-price catalogs, while price-sensitive zip-code customers get a low-price catalog. Victoria's Secret, Staples, and Simon & Schuster are among the hundreds of companies that employ legal price discrimination strategies.[4]

Firms accused of price discrimination often argue that they set price differentials to meet competitors' prices and that cost differences justify variations in prices. When a firm asserts that it maintains price differentials as good-faith methods of competing with rivals, a logical question arises: What constitutes good-faith pricing behavior? The answer depends on the particular situation.

A defense based on cost differentials works only if the price differences do not exceed the cost differences resulting from selling to various classes of buyers. Marketers must then justify the cost differences; indeed many authorities consider this provision one of the most confusing areas in the Robinson-Patman Act. The varying interpretations of the act certainly qualify it as one of the vaguest laws that affects marketing. Courts handle most charges brought under the act as individual cases. Therefore, domestic marketers must continually evaluate their pricing actions to avoid potential Robinson-Patman violations.

The Robinson-Patman Act does not cover export markets, though. U.S. law does not prohibit a domestic firm from

MARKETING | **DICTIONARY**

price Exchange value of a good or service.

Robinson-Patman Act Federal legislation prohibiting price discrimination that is not based on a cost differential; also prohibits selling at an unreasonably low price to eliminate competition.

selling a product to a foreign customer at a price significantly lower than the domestic wholesale price.

Unfair-Trade Laws

States supplement federal legislation with their own **unfair-trade laws**, which require sellers to maintain minimum prices for comparable merchandise. Enacted in the 1930s, these laws were intended to protect small specialty shops, such as dairy stores, from the *loss-leader pricing* tactics, in which chain stores might sell certain products below cost to attract customers. Typical state laws set retail price floors at cost plus some modest markup.

Although most unfair-trade laws have remained on the books for the past 70 years, marketers had all but forgotten them until recent years. Then in 1993, Wal-Mart, the nation's largest retailer, was found guilty of violating Arkansas' unfair-trade law for selling drugs and health-and-beauty aids below cost. The lawsuit filed by three independent drugstore owners accused the mass merchandiser of attempting to drive them out of business through predatory pricing practices. Wal-Mart appealed the decision and the decision was overturned, but similar lawsuits have been filed in several other states, all seeking to end the chain's low-price marketing strategy.

Fair-Trade Laws

The concept of fair trade has affected pricing decisions for decades. **Fair-trade laws** allow manufacturers to stipulate minimum retail prices for their products and to require dealers to sign contracts agreeing to abide by these prices.

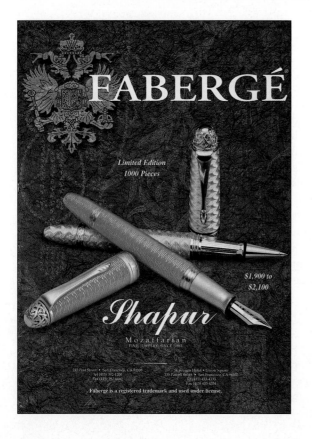

FIGURE 18.1 | Protecting Brand Image by Avoiding Price Discounting

The basic argument behind this legislation asserts that a product's image, determined in part by its price, is a property right of the manufacturer. Therefore, the producer should have the authority to protect its asset by requiring retailers to maintain a minimum price. The Fabergé name—internationally respected for its exquisite gold and jewel-encrusted eggs and jewelry designs—exudes images of royalty, nobility, and wealth. The name is also a registered trademark and used under license by companies such as Mozaffarian jewelers, an exclusive distributor for Fabergé fine writing instruments, such as the one shown in Figure 18.1. Enhanced with the Fabergé name, each limited-edition Shapur fountain pen retails for about $2,000. By severely restricting the number of retail stores that carry their writing instruments, Fabergé marketers can coordinate the prices charged by their retail partners and discourage price discounting, which might adversely affect the company's image.

The origins of fair-trade legislation trace back to lobbying efforts by organizations of independent retailers fearful of chain store growth. The economic mania of the Depression years was clearly reflected in these statutes. In 1931, California became the first state to enact fair-trade legislation. Most other states soon followed; only Missouri, the District of Columbia, Vermont, and Texas failed to adopt such laws.

A U.S. Supreme Court decision invalidated fair-trade contracts in interstate commerce, and Congress responded by passing the *Miller Tydings Resale Price Maintenance Act* (1937). This law exempted interstate fair-trade contracts from compliance with antitrust requirements, thus freeing states to keep these laws on their books if they so desired.

Over the years, fair-trade laws declined in importance as discounters emerged and price competition gained strength in marketing strategy. These laws became invalid with the passage of the *Consumer Goods Pricing Act* (1975), which halted all interstate enforcement of resale price maintenance provisions, an objective long sought by consumer groups.

THE ROLE OF PRICE IN THE MARKETING MIX

Ancient philosophers recognized the importance of price in an economic system. Some early written accounts refer to attempts to determine fair or just prices. Price continues to serve as a means of regulating economic activity. Employment of any or all of the four factors of production—natural resources, capital, human resources, and entrepreneurship—depends on the prices that those factors receive. An individual firm's prices and the resulting purchases by its customers determine how much revenue the company receives. Prices, therefore, influence a firm's profits as well as its employment of the factors of production.

PRICING OBJECTIVES

Just as price is a component of the total marketing mix, pricing objectives also represent components of the organization's overall objectives. As Chapter 6 explained, marketing objectives state the outcomes that executives hope to attain. They derive from and support the overall objectives of the organization. The objectives of the firm and its marketing organization guide development of pricing objectives, which in turn lead to development and implementation of more specific pricing policies and procedures.

A firm might set a major overall objective of becoming the dominant producer in its domestic market. It might then develop a marketing objective of achieving maximum sales penetration in each region, followed by a related pricing objective of setting prices at levels that maximize sales. These objectives might lead to the adoption of a low-price policy implemented by offering substantial price discounts to channel members.

Price affects and is affected by the other elements of the marketing mix. Product decisions, promotional plans, and distribution choices all impact the price of a good or service. For example, products distributed through complex channels involving several intermediaries must be priced high enough to cover the markups needed to compensate wholesalers and retailers for services they provide. Basic so-called "fighting brands" are intended to capture market share from higher-priced, options-laden competitors by offering relatively low prices to entice customers to give up some options in return for a cost savings.

While pricing objectives vary from firm to firm, they can be classified into four major groups: (1) profitability objectives, (2) volume objectives, (3) meeting competition objectives, and (4) prestige objectives. Profitability objectives include profit maximization and target-return goals. Volume objectives seek to either maximize sales or increase market share. Not-for-profit companies must also consider similar objectives in their pricing strategies. Table 18.1 outlines the pricing objectives marketers rely on to meet their organization's overall goals.

Profitability Objectives

Marketers at for-profit firms must set prices with profits in mind. Even not-for-profit organizations realize the importance of setting prices high enough to cover expenses and provide a financial cushion to cover unforeseen needs and expenses. But both groups of price setters are well aware of the Russian proverb, "There are two fools in every market: One asks too little, one asks too much." For consumers to pay these prices, they must be convinced they are receiving fair value for their money.

Classical economic theory is based on two major assumptions. First, it presumes that firms will behave rationally and, second, that this rational behavior will result in an effort to maximize

2

Identify the major categories of pricing objectives.

MARKETING   DICTIONARY

unfair-trade laws State laws requiring sellers to maintain minimum prices for comparable merchandise.

fair-trade laws Statutes enacted in most states that permitted manufacturers to stipulate a minimum retail price for their product.

THE OUTCOME Customers complained by the thousands that they expected to spend $10 to $40—not $50 plus—on their orders. They also missed their fat little catalogs and complained they could no longer find the traditional quality household goods that had made Lillian Vernon an industry leader.

LESSONS LEARNED Although it is difficult to secure a position in the minds of prospective customers, it is all too easy to give it away. As soon as the firm's marketers recognized the error of their ways, they quickly reverted to more and bigger catalogs filled with the products customers wanted and at the prices they had come to expect. While catalog preparation and mailing account for major direct-marketing expenses, changes in these features should be the result of careful research into likely sales impact—not a knee-jerk response to increased costs.

blissnet.com/~huckleberry/ index.htm

TABLE 18.1 **Pricing Objectives**

OBJECTIVE	PURPOSE	EXAMPLE
Profitability objectives	• Profit maximization • Target return	Low introductory interest rates on credit cards with high standard rates after 6 months
Volume objectives	• Sales maximization • Market share	Compaq's low-priced PCs increase market share and sales of services
Meeting competition objectives	• Value pricing	Price wars among major airlines
Prestige objectives	• Lifestyle • Image	High-priced luxury autos such as Ferrari and watches by Rolex
Not-for-profit objectives	• Profit maximization • Cost recovery • Market incentives • Market suppression	High prices for tobacco and alcohol to reduce consumption

gains and minimize losses. Some marketers use elaborate calculations based on predicted future sales; others estimate profits by looking at historical sales data. It has been said that setting prices is an art, not a science. The talent lies in a marketer's ability to strike a balance between desired profits and the customer's perception of a product's value.

Marketers should evaluate and adjust prices continually to accommodate changes in the environment. The technological environment, for example, forces Internet marketers to respond quickly to competitors' pricing strategies. New search capabilities performed by *bots*, (described in Chapter 4) allow customers to compare prices locally, nationally, and globally in a matter of seconds.

Marketers at Huckleberry Mountain Co., a Jackson Hole, Wyoming–based specialty manufacturer of candies and preserves, determine wholesale prices by multiplying ingredient costs by two then adding 20 percent. The doubling of ingredient costs covers labor and overhead, while the 20 percent addition covers distribution and sales commissions. But consumer demand cannot be ignored, and Huckleberry regularly compares their prices against those of leading competitors. Says Judy Johnson, co-owner with her husband, "We have to balance our ideal with what the market will pay. We attend about 40 trade shows a year and see what customers are paying. If we're 40 percent higher than the competition, then we'd better have something really special or drop our prices."[5]

Profits are a function of revenue and expenses:

$$\text{Profits} = \text{Revenue} - \text{Expenses}.$$

Revenue is determined by the product's selling price and number of units sold:

$$\text{Total Revenue} = \text{Price} \times \text{Quantity Sold}.$$

Therefore, a profit maximizing price rises to the point at which further increases will cause disproportionate decreases in the number of units sold. A 10 percent price increase that results in only an 8 percent cut in volume will add to the firm's revenue. However, a 10 percent price hike that results in an 11 percent sales decline will reduce revenue.

Economists refer to this approach as *marginal analysis*. They identify **profit maximization** as the point at which the addition to total revenue is just balanced by the increase in total cost. Marketers must resolve a basic problem of how to achieve this delicate balance when they set prices. Relatively few firms actually hit this elusive target. A significantly larger number prefer to direct their effort toward more achievable goals.

Consequently, marketers commonly set **target-return objectives**—short-run or long-run goals usually stated as percentages of sales or investment. The practice has become particularly popular among large firms in which other pressures interfere with profit-maximization objectives. Target-return objectives offer several benefits for marketers in addition to resolving pricing questions. For example, these objectives serve as tools for evaluating performance. They also satisfy desires to generate "fair" profits as judged by management, stockholders, and the public.

Volume Objectives

Many business executives argue that pricing behavior actually seeks to maximize *sales* within a given profit constraint. In other words, they set a minimum acceptable profit level and then seek to maximize sales (subject to this profit constraint) in the belief that the increased sales are more important than immediate high profits to the long-run competitive picture. Such a company continues to expand sales as long as its total profits do not drop below the minimum return acceptable to management.

Hawaiian hotel and resort marketers stay in heated competition to attract business travelers and vacationers. Price is a popular and effective tool in maximizing sales in this booming travel industry. To encourage guests to prolong their stay at one of Westin's Hawaiian resorts, such as the one shown in Figure 18.2, marketers created a "splash package." In addition to golf privileges, gourmet dining, and beachfront rooms, guests receive a $100 daily resort credit—stay 3 nights and get $300 in credit.

Sales maximization can also result from non-price factors such as service and quality. For example, marketers increased sales for Dr. Scholl's new shoe insert, Dynastep, by heavily advertising in magazines. The ads explained how the Dynastep insert would help relieve leg and back pain. Priced around $14 per insert—twice as much as comparable offerings—the Dynastep ran over its competitors to become number one in its category.

Another volume-related pricing objective is the *market-share objective*—the goal set for controlling a portion of the market for a firm's good or service. Dr. Scholl's was able to increase its market share to 29 percent by focusing on the benefits of Dynastep. The company's specific goal may be to maintain its present share of a particular market, or to increase its share, for instance, from 10 percent to 20 percent. Volume-related objectives such as sales maximization and market share play an important role in most firms' pricing decisions.

The PIMS Studies

Market-share objectives may prove critical to the achievement of other organizational objectives. High sales, for example, often mean more profits. The extensive **Profit Impact of Market Strategies (PIMS) project**, conducted by the Marketing Science Institute, analyzed more than 2,000 firms and revealed that two of the most important factors influencing profitability were product quality and market share. Advertisements like the one in Figure 18.3 help to enhance profitability for the Clorox Co. As the industry leader in bleach sales, Clorox marketers do not focus on low price but rather on product benefits such as the pleasing fragrance and high-quality performance of its bleach compared to lesser-known brands that attempt to compete with a lower price. Numerous studies confirm the link between market share and profitability.

MARKETING **DICTIONARY**

profit maximization Point at which the additional revenue gained by increasing the price of a product equals the increase in total costs.

target return objective Short-run or long-run pricing objectives of achieving a specified return on either sales or investment.

Profit Impact of Market Strategies (PIMS) project Research that discovered a strong positive relationship between a firm's market share and its return on investment.

Clorox: Increasing Profitability through Product Quality and Market Share

Rain Clean Clorox Bleach smells fresh as a spring rain.

No bargain bleach has a fragrance like it.

And no bargain bleach beats that unbeatable Clorox Bleach white. Don't be fooled by bargain bleaches. Get Rain Clean Clorox Bleach.

RAIN CLEAN

©1998 The Clorox Company

The relationship of market share and profitability is evident in PIMS data that reveal an average 32 percent return on investment (ROI) for firms with market shares over 40 percent. In contrast, average ROI decreases to 24 percent for firms whose market shares are between 20 and 40 percent. Firms with a minor market share (less than 10 percent) generate average pretax investment returns of approximately 13 percent.[6]

The relationship also applies to a firm's individual brands. The PIMS researchers compared the top four brands in each market segment they studied. Their data revealed that the leading brand typically generates after-tax ROI of 18 percent, considerably higher than the second-ranked brand. Weaker brands, on average, fail to earn adequate returns.

Marketers have developed an underlying explanation of the positive relationship between profitability and market share. Firms with large shares accumulate greater operating experience and lower overall costs relative to competitors with smaller market shares. Accordingly, segmentation strategies might focus on obtaining larger shares of smaller markets and on avoiding smaller shares of larger ones. A firm might achieve higher financial returns by becoming a major competitor in several smaller market segments than by remaining a relatively minor competitor in a larger market.

Meeting Competition Objectives

A third set of pricing objectives seeks simply to meet competitor's prices. In many lines of business, firms set their own prices to match those of established industry price leaders.

In 1999, Worldcom shook up the long-distance telephone market by advertising 5-cents-per-minute pricing for nights and weekends. AT&T countered with a 7-cents-per-minute rate all the time. Since both telecommunication firms offer a service most customers consider interchangeable, neither of these multinational giants could continue operations unless they came close to matching each other's prices. Also, any price reductions below the 5-cent level are likely to lead to flat-rate monthly service offers due to the cost of preparing and mailing itemized bills.[7]

Pricing objectives tied directly to meeting prices charged by major competitors de-emphasize the price element of the marketing mix and focus more strongly on non-price variables. Pricing is a highly visible component of a firm's marketing mix and an easy and effective tool for obtaining a differential advantage over competitors; still, other firms can easily duplicate a price reduction themselves. The airline price competition of recent years exemplifies the actions and reactions of competitors in this marketplace. Rather than emphasizing the lowest fares of any carrier, most airlines choose to compete by offering convenient arrival and departure times, an attractive frequent-flyer program, and customer-focused alliances with automobile rental, lodging, and other partners. Because price changes directly affect overall profitability in an industry, many firms attempt to promote stable prices by meeting competitors' prices and competing for market share by focusing on product strategies, promotional decisions, and distribution—the non-price elements of the marketing mix.

Ford Escort marketers focus on such non-price elements as the company's award-winning reputation for quality and the economy sedan's low price in the ad shown in Figure 18.4. In competition with Chrysler's Neon, the Kia Sephia, and Geo's Metro, the low price helps Ford to reach targeted young adults and college graduates who are just entering the workforce. Ford marketers point out that the Escort offers the standard features of economy cars in this price range but emphasize the extras, including a remote keyless entry system, safety cell construction, and a great sound system.

FIGURE 18.4 **Ford Escort: Meeting Competition Objectives in Pricing**

Value Pricing

When discounts become normal elements of a competitive marketplace, other marketing-mix elements gain importance in purchase decisions. In such instances, overall product value, not just price, determines product choice. In recent years, a new strategy—**value pricing**—has emerged that emphasizes the benefits a product provides in comparison to the price and quality levels of competing offerings. This strategy typically works best for relatively low-priced goods and services.

Laundry detergents are a good example of value pricing. The label on Dash detergent proclaims *Value Price*, While Arm & Hammer's label assures customers that it *Cleans Great—Value Price, Too!* Yes detergent announces *Great Value!*, while Ultra Rinso claims *Super Value*, and the back label on Ultra Trend boasts that it offers *hard-working performance at a reasonable price*. The label on another detergent, All, simply advises customers to *Compare & Save*.

Value-priced products generally cost less than premium brands, but marketers point out that *value* does not necessarily mean *inexpensive*. The challenge for those who compete on value is to convince customers that low-priced brands offer quality comparable to that of a higher-priced product. An increasing number of alternative products and private-label brands has increased competition among marketers in recent years. In the dry cereal market, sales industry-wide have plummeted 15 percent. Kellogg, the number one cereal maker in the United States, watched market share drop drastically before it

This Kellogg ad focuses on the role folic acid in Kellogg's Corn Flakes can play in helping reduce the risk of some birth defects.

began implementing strategies based on price-value. Kellogg now focuses on promoting the quality ingredients and nutritional benefits of its cereals.[8]

Value pricing is perhaps best seen in the personal-computer industry. In the past few years, PC prices have collapsed, reducing the effectiveness of traditional pricing strategies intended to meet competition. In fact, PCs priced at under $600 are now the fastest growing segment of the market. In one year, this category has grown 657 percent and now accounts for almost 20 percent of PCs sold in stores. Industry leaders like Dell, Compaq, and Gateway cannot continue to cut prices, so they are adding features such as increased memory and 3-D graphic accelerator cards that increase speed.[9]

Prestige Objectives

The final category of pricing objectives, unrelated to either profitability or sales volume, is prestige objectives. Prestige pricing establishes a relatively high price to develop and maintain an image of quality and exclusiveness that appeals to status-conscious consumers. Such objectives reflect marketers' recognition of the role of price in creating an overall image of the firm and its goods and services.

Prestige objectives affect the price tags of such products as Waterford crystal, Alpha Romeo sports cars, Omega watches, and Tiffany jewelry. When a perfume marketer sets a price of $135 or more per ounce, this choice reflects an emphasis on image far more than the cost of ingredients. Analyses have shown that ingredients account for less than 5 percent of a perfume's cost. Thus, advertisements for Joy that promote the fragrance as the "costliest perfume in the world" use price to promote product prestige.

In contrast to low-price strategies used by marketers of economy cars, ads for the Bentley Azure target wealthy clientele interested in the vehicle's classic design that conveys their lifestyle. The Azure is flaunted as a sophisticated, turbocharged, 150-mile-per-hour sports car with a leather interior and a hand-polished walnut dashboard. Appearing in upscale magazines such as *Conde Nast Traveler*, the ads state: "Bentley. You don't park it, you position it."

While ads for luxury products, such as the one shown in Figure 18.5 for Royal Secret perfume, may hint at high prices, few openly mention price. Marketers tell perfume shoppers to "Do it for love." Cosmetics companies, in general, seldom talk price in their advertisements. More recently, however, marketers of prestigious products have experimented with their own version of value pricing. Cosmetics manufacturer Clinique, for example, now includes product samples and retail prices in its advertisements.

In the corporate world, private jet ownership imparts an image of prestige, power, and high price tags—too high for most business travelers to even consider. Recognizing that cost is the primary factor that makes jet ownership prohibitive for business travel, marketers at Flight Options have created an alternative in the marketplace. This new target market is willing to buy, and has authority to buy, but cannot afford a new Citation, Beechjet, Hawker, or Challenger aircraft. In efforts to satisfy this untapped market, Flight Options broke the price barrier by advertising pre-owned aircraft at 35 percent less than a new model. In addition to affordability and value, customers are granted a 30-day walkaway guarantee of satisfaction.

FIGURE 18.5 Royal Secret Marketers Emphasize Prestige

flightoptions.com

Pricing Objectives of Not-for-Profit Organizations

Pricing typically is a very important element of the marketing mix for not-for-profit organizations. Pricing strategy can help these groups to achieve a variety of organizational goals:

1. **Profit maximization.** While not-for-profit organizations by definition do not cite profitability as a primary goal, there are numerous instances in which they do try to maximize their returns on single events or a series of events. A $1,000-a-plate political fund-raiser is a classic example.

2. **Cost recovery.** Some not-for-profit organizations attempt to recover only the actual cost of operating the unit. Mass transit, publicly supported colleges, and bridges are common examples. The amount of recovered costs is often dictated by tradition, competition, and/or public opinion.

3. **Providing market incentives.** Other not-for-profit groups follow a lower than average pricing policy or offer a free service to encourage increased usage of the good or service. Seattle's bus system offers free service in the downtown area in an attempt to reduce traffic congestion, encourage retail sales, and minimize the effort required to access downtown public services.

4. **Market suppression.** Price can also discourage consumption. High prices help to accomplish social objectives independent of the costs of providing goods or services. Illustrations include tobacco and alcohol taxes, parking fines, tolls, and gasoline excise taxes.

METHODS FOR DETERMINING PRICES

Marketers determine prices in two basic ways—by applying the theoretical concepts of supply and demand and by completing cost-oriented analyses. During the first part of the 20th century, most discussions for price determination emphasized the classical concepts of supply and demand. During the last half of the century, however, the emphasis shifted to a cost-oriented approach. Hindsight reveals certain flaws in both concepts.

Treatments of this subject often overlook another concept of price determination—one based on the impact of custom and tradition. **Customary prices** are retail prices that consumers expect as a result of traditional and social habit. Candy makers have attempted to maintain traditional price levels by considerably reducing product size. Similar practices have prevailed in the marketing of soft drinks as bottlers attempt to balance consumer expectations of customary prices with the realities of rising costs.

Wm. Wrigley Jr. Co., manufacturer of such chewing gum standards as Juicy Fruit, Doublemint, and Big Red, took advantage of the weakness in the industry's customary pricing strategy by introducing a smaller-quantity pack at a lower price. While competitors continued to offer only seven-piece packs for 35 cents, Wrigley priced its five-piece packs at 25 cents. To spur impulse buying, the company prominently displayed the price on the package. The strategy was so successful that within two years of its inception, Wrigley discontinued selling seven-stick gum packs.

With over 800 convenient locations across the United States, Motel 6 has carved out a comfortable share of the lodging market by offering the best prices of any national chain. Its popular tag line, "We'll leave the light on for you," earned Motel 6 a position in the top 100 advertising campaigns of the century. In fact, it was the only motel chain to be included in the top 100 awards given by *Advertising Age*. Building market share based on the company's strong reputation and position as the nation's leader in the budget segment of the travel hospitality industry, Motel 6 marketers recently began offering a new program for extended-stay travelers. The new Studio 6 properties, shown in Figure 18.6, offer full kitchens, coffeemakers, voice mail, alarm clock, and other amenities for one low weekly rate.[10]

At some point, however, someone has to set initial prices for products. In addition, competitive moves and cost changes necessitate periodic reviews of price structures. The remaining sections delve into the issue of price determination. This section also considers how marketers can most effectively integrate the concepts to develop realistic pricing systems.

FIGURE 18.6	Studio 6: Enhancing Value through Customary Prices

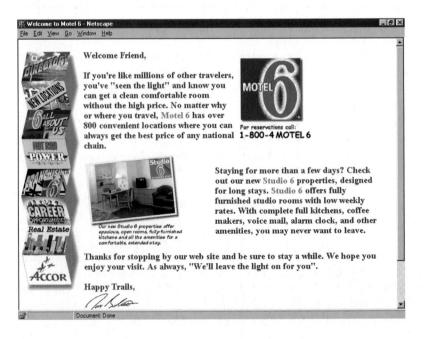

PRICE DETERMINATION IN ECONOMIC THEORY

Microeconomics suggests a way of determining prices that assumes a profit-maximization objective. This technique attempts to derive correct equilibrium prices in the marketplace by comparing supply and demand. It also requires more complete analysis than actual business firms typically conduct.

Demand refers to a schedule of the amounts of a firm's good or service that consumers will purchase at different prices during a specified period. **Supply** refers to a schedule of the amounts of a good or service that will be offered for sale at different prices during a specified time period. These schedules may vary for different types of market structures. Businesses operate and set prices in four types of market structures: pure competition, monopolistic competition, oligopoly, and monopoly.

Pure competition is a market structure with so many buyers and sellers that no single participant can significantly influence price. Pure competition presupposes other market conditions, as well: homogeneous products and ease of entry for sellers due to low start-up costs. While most of today's businesspeople encounter this market structure only in theory, the agricultural sector exhibits many characteristics of a purely competitive market, making it the closest actual example.

Monopolistic competition typifies most retailing and features large numbers of buyers and sellers. These diverse parties exchange heterogeneous, relatively well-differentiated products, giving marketers some control over prices.

Relatively few sellers compete in an **oligopoly**. Each seller may affect the market, but no single seller controls it. High start-up costs form significant barriers to entry for new competitors. Each firm's demand curve in an oligopolistic market displays a unique kink at the current market price. Because of the impact of a single competitor on total industry sales, competitors usually quickly match any attempt by one firm to generate additional sales by reducing prices. Price cutting throughout such an industry reduces total industry revenues. Oligopolies operate in the petroleum refining, automobile, and tobacco industries.

The availability of alternative air transportation in the form of such discount carriers as Southwest Airlines and Frontier Airlines forces established air carriers to maintain competitive airfares—or risk losing business to the upstarts. When these alternatives disappear, prices often rise. For example, before United Express began offering service to the Gulf Coast, the market had only one major airline—Delta. United Express was a welcome alternative for travelers who found prices two-thirds cheaper than the lowest competing fare.[11]

A **monopoly** is a market structure where only one seller of a product exists and for which there are no close substitutes. Antitrust legislation has nearly eliminated all but temporary monopolies, such as those created through patent protection and regulated monopolies, like utility companies. The government allows regulated monopolies in markets in which competition would lead to an uneconomical duplication of services. In return for such a license, government reserves the right to regulate the monopoly's rate of return.

Table 18.2 compares the four types of market structures on the following bases: number of competitors, ease of entry into the industry by new firms, similarity of competing products,

MARKETING | **DICTIONARY**

customary prices In pricing strategy, the traditional prices that customers expect to pay for certain goods and services.

demand Schedule of the amounts of a firm's product that consumers will purchase at different prices during a specified time period.

supply Schedule of the amounts of a good or service that firms will offer for sale at different prices during a specified time period.

pure competition Market structure characterized by homogeneous products in which there are so many buyers and sellers that none has a significant influence on price.

monopolistic competition Market structure involving a heterogeneous product and product differentiation among competing suppliers, allowing the marketer some degree of control over prices.

oligopoly Market structure involving relatively few sellers and barriers to new competitors due to high start-up costs.

monopoly Market structure involving only one seller of a good or service for which no close substitutes exist.

TABLE 18.2	Distinguishing Features of the Four Market Structures

TYPE OF MARKET STRUCTURE

CHARACTERISTICS	PURE COMPETITION	MONOPOLISTIC COMPETITION	OLIGOPOLY	MONOPOLY
Number of competitors	Many	Few to many	Few	No direct competitors
Ease of entry into industry by new firms	Easy	Somewhat difficult	Difficult	Regulated by government
Similarity of goods or services offered by competing firms	Similar	Different	Can be either similar or different	No directly competing goods or services
Control over prices by individual firms	None	Some	Some	Considerable
Demand curves facing individual firms	Totally elastic	Can be either elastic or inelastic	Kinked; inelastic below kink; more elastic above	Can be either elastic or inelastic
Examples	200-acre ranch	Gap stores	Texaco	Commonwealth Edison

degree of control over price by individual firms, and the elasticity or inelasticity of the demand curve facing the individual firm. Elasticity—the degree of consumer responsiveness to changes in price—is discussed in more detail in a later section.

Cost and Revenue Curves

Marketers must set a price for a product that generates sufficient revenue to cover the costs of producing and marketing it. A product's total cost is composed of total variable costs and total fixed costs. *Variable costs* change with the level of production (such as labor and raw materials costs), while *fixed costs* remain stable at any production level within a certain range (such as lease payments or insurance costs). *Average total costs* are calculated by dividing the sum of the variable and fixed costs by the number of units produced. Finally, *marginal cost* is the change in total cost that results from producing an additional unit of output.

The demand side of the pricing equation focuses on revenue curves. *Average revenue* is calculated by dividing total revenue by the quantity associated with these revenues. Average revenue is actually the demand curve facing the firm. *Marginal revenue* is the change in total revenue that results from selling an additional unit of output. Figure 18.7 shows the relationships of various cost and revenue measures; the firm maximizes its profits when marginal costs equal marginal revenues.

Table 18.3 illustrates why the intersection of the marginal cost and marginal revenue curves is the logical point at which to maximize revenue for the organization. Although the firm can earn a profit at several different prices, the price at which it earns maximum profits is $22. At a price of $24, $66 in profits are earned—$4 less than the $70 profit at the $22 price. If a price of $20 is set to attract additional sales, the marginal costs of the extra sales ($7) are greater than the marginal revenues received ($6), and total profits decline.

The Concept of Elasticity in Pricing Strategy

3

Explain price elasticity and its determinants.

Although the intersection of the marginal cost and marginal revenue curves determines the level of output, the impact of changes in price on sales varies greatly. In order to understand why it fluctuates, it is necessary to understand the concept of elasticity.

Elasticity is the measure of responsiveness of purchasers and suppliers to price changes. The price elasticity of demand (or elasticity of demand) is the percentage change in the quantity of a good or service demanded divided by the percentage change in its price. A 10 percent increase

FIGURE 18.7   Determining Price by Relating Marginal Revenue to Marginal Cost

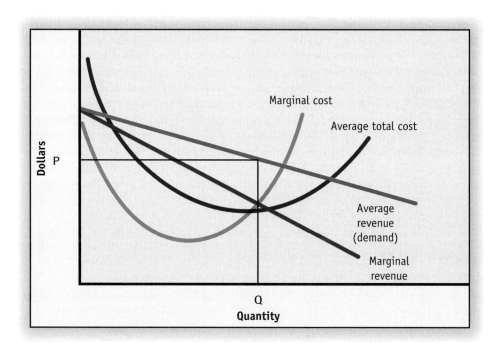

TABLE 18.3   Price Determination Using Marginal Analysis

PRICE	NUMBER SOLD	TOTAL REVENUE	MARGINAL REVENUE	TOTAL COSTS	MARGINAL COSTS	PROFITS (TOTAL REVENUE MINUS TOTAL COSTS)
—	—	—	—	—	—	($50)
$34	1	$34	$34	57	$7	(23)
32	2	64	30	62	5	2
30	3	90	26	66	4	24
28	4	112	22	69	3	43
26	5	130	18	73	4	57
24	6	144	14	78	5	66
22	7	154	10	84	6	70
20	8	160	6	91	7	69
18	9	162	2	100	9	62
16	10	160	(2)	110	11	50

in the price of eggs that results in a 5 percent decrease in the quantity of eggs demanded yields a price elasticity of demand for eggs of 0.5. The price elasticity of supply of a product is the percentage change in the quantity of a good or service supplied divided by the percentage change in its price. A 10 percent increase in the price

MARKETING   DICTIONARY

elasticity Measure of responsiveness of purchasers and suppliers to a change in price.

Estée Lauder

BACKGROUND This family-owned, cold-cream business has become a global cosmetics empire. Since its founding in 1946, Estée Lauder has captured over 45 percent of the cosmetics market in fine department stores throughout the United States. In fact, the four best-selling prestige perfumes in America come from the house of Estée Lauder.

THE CHALLENGE Renowned fragrance marketer Charles Revson explained his industry's challenge this way: "In our factory we make lipstick. In our advertising, we sell hope." For Estée Lauder marketers, the task is to convince their customers that lipstick is more than just lipstick—it will change their lives—and perfume can be a stairway to paradise. A glance at ads for Beautiful and Pleasures fragrances shows how this challenge is addressed by Estée marketers.

continued on next page

@ fourseasons.com

of shampoo that results in a 25 percent increase in the quantity supplied yields a price elasticity of supply for shampoo of 2.5.

Consider a case in which a 1 percent change in price causes more than a 1 percent change in the quantity supplied or demanded. Numerically, that means an elasticity greater than 1.0. When the elasticity of demand or supply is greater than 1.0, that demand or supply is said to be *elastic*. If a 1 percent change in price results in less than a 1 percent change in quantity, a product's elasticity of demand or supply will be less than 1.0. In that case, the demand or supply is called *inelastic*. For example, the demand for cigarettes is relatively inelastic; research studies have shown that a 10 percent increase in cigarette prices results in only a 4 percent sales decline.

In countries such as Argentina and Brazil, where the annual inflation rate has been known to top 100 percent, prices on almost all products have risen accordingly. These higher prices have led to elastic demand for some items, such as houses and cars; many of the cars on Argentina's roads are over 10 years old, and the nation's housing market is severely depressed. For other products, demand has been inelastic; families continue to buy food because, after all, they need to eat. However, even if they do not affect demand, inflationary prices can alter consumers' buying patterns. Lower income Brazilians, for instance, buy all the food they can afford when they get each paycheck.

Determinants of Elasticity

Why is the elasticity of supply or demand high for some products and low for others? What determines demand elasticity? One major factor influencing the elasticity of demand is the availability of substitutes or complements. If consumers can easily find close substitutes for a good or service, the product's demand tends to be elastic. During the late 1990s, an increase in the number of businesses and individuals using e-mail cut into U.S. Postal Service (USPS) revenues. Fearing another price increase would only drive profits down further, marketers tried to boost revenues by adding value to current service offerings. None of these efforts generated enough revenues to cover rising costs, though, and finally marketers were forced to increase postage rates. In 1999, a penny was added to first-class postage and other rates were either increased or revised. Surprisingly, this smallest price change in USPS history allowed the USPS to reach its $200 million net income plan.[12] In another example, the relatively inelastic demand for motor oil reflects its role as a complement to a more important product, gasoline.

As increasing numbers of buyers and sellers complete their business transactions online, the elasticity of a product's demand is drastically affected. Take large discounters, for example. Small businesses and individual do-it-yourselfers shop Home Depot for tools, such as wheelbarrows; parents look for Furbies at Toys "Я" Us; and homeowners can go to Circuit City for new refrigerators or stoves. Today, however, the Internet lets consumers contact product manufacturers and service providers directly, often giving them better selections and prices for their efforts. (The power struggle between brick-and-mortar retailers and Internet suppliers is the topic of the Solving an Ethical Controversy in Chapter 19.) In the case of an item such as the wheelbarrow, which once was sold at almost identical prices at a relatively small number of retail outlets (inelastic demand), today's shoppers can find the item in dozens of different locations—traditional hardware stores, home-improvement centers, discount stores, and even some department stores. The one-wheelbarrow-fits-all approach has been replaced with different sizes, colors, and materials to match the specific needs of different users. The availability of different models and different prices for each combine to create a market characterized by demand elasticity.[13]

Elasticity of demand also depends on whether a product is a necessity or a luxury. For example, the Four Seasons chain of luxury hotels and resorts enjoys such a strong reputation for service, comfort, and exclusiveness that it has become a favorite among affluent individual travelers and business professionals. The combination of personal service and exclusiveness, depicted in Figure 18.8, attracts a select group of upscale travelers, who consider reservations at Four Seasons hotels essential components of their trips to Atlanta or Tokyo. Because such a customer views Four Seasons' accommodations as a necessity, not a luxury, sales remain strong despite the high room rates. Most people regard high-fashion clothes, such as a $2,000 Armani suit, as luxuries. If prices for designer outfits increase, people can respond by purchasing lower-priced substitutes instead. In

| FIGURE 18.8 | Four Seasons Hotels: Inelastic Demand for a Service Viewed as a Necessity by Upscale Travelers |

THE STRATEGY Growth means continuing to create the dream for every woman by offering products that appeal to a wide range of customers—the young and the old, the hip and the so-phisticated, and ecologically sensitive customers as well. It means positioning products to satisfy self-esteem needs. In addition, different segments have varying degrees of disposable income and certain limits on prices they will pay. To reach masses of shoppers and still not damage the exclusive image of top-selling Estée Lauder brands, the firm acquired several smaller cosmetic lines and tailored them to shoppers in Kmart as well as Saks Fifth Avenue. New products include Bobbi Brooks lipstick, priced around $16 in department stores like Macy's, Jane by Sass-aby, priced at only $2.99 and sold at large discount stores like Target and at drugstores like Rite Aid.

THE OUTCOME Estée Lauder marketers have certainly created a paradise of prices. They not only hold the top four selling perfumes in the United States but market their cosmetics to customers in 118 countries around the world.

contrast, medical and dental care are considered necessities, so price changes have little effect on the frequency of medical or dental visits.

However, under the continuing influence of higher prices, some products once regarded as necessities may be dismissed as luxuries, leading to decreasing demand. For instance, German consumers have traditionally been eager buyers of brand-name consumer electronics goods. As prices and unemployment in Germany have risen, however, demand for these products has become highly elastic. As a result, retail outlets have encountered dramatically declining electronics sales.

Elasticity also depends on the portion of a person's budget that he or she spends on a good or service. People no longer really need matches, for example; they can easily find good substitutes. Nonetheless, the demand for matches remains very inelastic because people spend so little on them that they hardly notice a price change. In contrast, the demand for housing or transportation is not totally inelastic, even though these are necessities, because both consume large parts of a consumer's budget.

Elasticity of demand also responds to consumers' time perspectives. Demand often shows less elasticity in the short run than in the long run. Consider the demand for home air conditioning. In the short run, people pay rising energy prices because they find it difficult to cut back on the quantities they use. Accustomed to living with specific temperature settings, dressing in certain ways, and so forth, they prefer to pay more during a few months out of the year than to explore other possibilities. Over time, though, with global warming becoming a real and present danger, they may find ways to economize. They can better insulate their homes, plant shade trees, or even move to cooler climates.

Sometimes the usual patterns do not hold true, though. Alcohol and tobacco, which are not necessities but do occupy large shares of some personal budgets, are also subject to inelastic demand.

bart.org

Elasticity and Revenue

The elasticity of demand exerts an important influence on variations in total revenue as a result of changes in the price of a good or service. Assume, for example, that San Francisco's Bay Area Rapid Transit (BART) officials are considering alternative methods of raising more money for the city budget. One possible method for increasing revenues would be to change rail pass fares for BART commuters. But should the city raise or lower the price of a pass? The correct answer depends on the elasticity of demand for subway rides. A 10 percent decrease in fares should attract more riders, but unless it stimulates more than a 10 percent increase in riders, total revenue will fall. A 10 percent increase in fares will bring in more money per rider, but if more than 10 percent of the riders stop using the subway, total revenue will fall. A price cut will increase revenue only for a product with elastic demand, and a price increase will raise revenue only for a product with inelastic demand. BART officials seem to believe that the demand for rapid rail transit is inelastic; they raise fares when they need more money for the city budget.

Practical Problems of Price Theory

4

List the practical problems involved in applying price theory concepts to actual pricing decisions.

Marketers may thoroughly understand price theory concepts but still encounter difficulty applying them in practice. What practical limitations interfere with price setting?

First, many firms do not attempt to maximize profits. Economic analysis is subject to the same limitations as the assumptions on which it is based—for example, the proposition that all firms attempt to maximize profits. Second, it is difficult to estimate demand curves. Modern accounting procedures provide managers with a clear understanding of cost structures, so managers can readily comprehend the supply side of the pricing equation. But they find it difficult to estimate demand at various price levels. Demand curves must be based on marketing research estimates that often are less exact than cost figures. Although the demand element can be identified, it is often difficult to measure in real-world settings.

PRICE DETERMINATION IN PRACTICE

5

Explain the major cost-plus approaches to price setting.

The practical limitations inherent in price theory have forced practitioners to turn to other techniques. **Cost-plus pricing**, the most popular method, uses a base-cost figure per unit and adds a markup to cover unassigned costs and to provide a profit. The only real difference among the multitude of cost-plus techniques is the relative sophistication of the costing procedures employed. For example, a local apparel shop may set prices by adding a 45 percent markup to the invoice price charged by the supplier. The markup is expected to cover all other expenses and permit the owner to earn a reasonable return on the sale of clothes.

In contrast to this rather simple pricing mechanism, a large manufacturer may employ a complex pricing formula requiring computer calculations. However, this method merely adds a more complicated procedure to the simpler, traditional method for calculating costs. In the end, someone still must make a decision about the markup. The apparel shop and the large manufacturer may figure costs differently, but they are remarkably similar in completing the markup side of the equation.

Cost-plus pricing often works well for a business that keeps its costs low, allowing it to set its prices lower than those of competitors and still make a profit. American discounter Wal-Mart keeps costs low by buying directly from manufacturers rather than going through wholesalers and other intermediaries. This strategy has helped the company in its rise to become the world's largest discount retailer.

Alternative Pricing Procedures

The two most common cost-oriented pricing procedures are the full-cost method and the incremental-cost method. *Full-cost pricing* uses all relevant variable costs in setting a product's price. In addition, it allocates those fixed costs that cannot be directly attributed to the produc-

SOLVING AN ETHICAL CONTROVERSY

Politics, Patents, and the Price of Loratadine

The debate seems to be never ending between a company's right to make money versus the public's right to low-cost medicine. Schering-Plough pharmaceutical company recently came face to face with this controversy, having enjoyed great success with Claritin, its prescription drug, containing loratadine, that combats allergies. Millions of allergy sufferers have purchased the medication, generating $2.3 billion in sales for the firm. In spite of the high demand, prices have not fallen because Schering-Plough holds the patent on the drug.

Patents are intended to protect companies as they enter the market with a new invention or innovation from competitors. In effect, patents create a monopoly situation to reward members by giving them time to recoup their research-and-development costs. Schering-Plough and other drug companies not only obtain patents but frequently appeal for extensions. Recently, however, businesses have figured out how to use the political process for monopoly-price protection that critics claim goes far beyond what is legitimate. With soaring drug prices, low-cost generic drug makers spend millions of dollars lobbying members of Congress not to extend the patent on drugs. In one recent year, Schering-Plough had nine lobbying companies under contract and contributed more than $280,000 to the Democratic and Republican parties. Consumer advocate groups have joined the fight to stop patent extensions on drugs that typically cost 60 percent more than generic equivalents. Says one critic, "If they get away with it, it's a message to any company with a best-selling drug: 'You did it for Claritin, why not me?'"

 Should drug companies be allowed to extend patents?

Pro
1. Patents should be extended when companies need more time to recover their research and development costs associated with new medicines.

2. Drug prices do not always affect the consumer significantly since many HMOs and other group health programs cover many prescription drugs. Over half of Americans now receive discounted medicines through such managed-care programs.
3. Drug prices set by pharmaceutical companies are not aimed at hurting the consumer but helping the company continue research and development.

Con
1. Patent extensions are anticonsumer and encourage monopolistic market behavior.
2. Lobbying for patent extensions is an attempt to buy price protection for large pharmaceutical companies. The giant drug companies are simply profiting from the illnesses of their consumers, rather than trying to heal the sick.
3. Granting extensions undermines the primary purpose of a patent and may result in high prices that force the consumer to forego needed medications.

Summary
Patents have long served to protect the creators of new goods and services. However, in any industry, the costs of production are reflected in the prices charged. Since every product involves different cost levels, a simple time limit on patents may be unrealistic for all products in all industries.

Source: Bill Walsh, "Drugmaker Fights to Extend Patent on Best-Selling Claritin," *Mobile Register,* July 1, 1999, pp. A1, A4.

---

tion of the specific item being priced. Under the full-cost method, if job order 515 in a printing plant amounts to .000127 percent of the plant's total output, then .000127 percent of the firm's overhead expenses are charged to that job. This approach allows the marketer to recover all costs plus the amount added as a profit margin.

The full-cost approach has two basic deficiencies. First, there is no consideration of competition or demand for the item. Perhaps no one wants to pay the price the firm has calculated. Second, any method for allocating overhead (fixed expenses) is arbitrary and may be unrealistic. In manufacturing, overhead allocations often are tied to direct labor hours. In retailing, the square footage of each profit center is sometimes the factor used in computations. Regardless of the technique employed, it is difficult to show a cause-effect relationship between the allocated cost and most products.

One way to overcome the arbitrary allocation of fixed expenses is with *incremental-cost pricing*, which attempts

MARKETING   DICTIONARY

cost-plus pricing Practice of adding a percentage of specified dollar amount (markup) to the base cost of a product to cover unassigned costs and to provide a profit.

to use only those costs directly attributable to a specific output in setting prices. Consider a small-scale manufacturer with the following income statement:

Sales (10,000 units at $10)		$100,000
Expenses:		
Variable	$50,000	
Fixed	40,000	90,000
Net Profit		$10,000

Suppose the firm is offered a contract for an additional 5,000 units. Since the peak season is over, these items can be produced at the same average variable cost. Assume that the labor force would be idle otherwise. How low should the firm price its product in order to get the contract?

Under the full-cost approach, the lowest price would be $9 per unit. This figure is obtained by dividing the $90,000 in expenses by an output of 10,000 units. The incremental approach, on the other hand, could permit any price above $5, which would significantly increase the possibility of securing the additional contract. This price would be composed of the $5 variable cost associated with each unit of production plus a $.10-per-unit contribution to fixed expenses and overhead. With a $5.10 proposed price, the income statement now looks like this:

Sales (10,000 at $10; 5,000 at $5.10)		$125,500
Expenses:		
Variable	$75,000	
Fixed	40,000	115,000
Net Profit		$10,500

Profits thus are increased under the incremental approach.

Admittedly, the illustration is based on two assumptions: (1) the ability to isolate markets such that selling at the lower price will not affect the price received in other markets, and (2) the absence of legal restrictions on the firm. The example, however, does illustrate that profits can sometimes be enhanced by using the incremental approach.

6

List the major advantages and shortcomings of using breakeven analysis in pricing decisions.

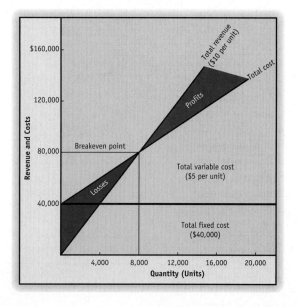

FIGURE 18.9   **Breakeven Chart**

Breakeven Analysis

Breakeven analysis is a means of determining the number of goods or services that must be sold at a given price in order to generate sufficient revenue to cover total costs. Figure 18.9 graphically depicts this process. The total cost curve includes both fixed and variable segments, and total fixed cost is represented by a horizontal line. Average variable cost is assumed to be constant per unit as it was in the example for incremental pricing.

The breakeven point is the point at which total revenue just equals total cost. In the example in Figure 18.9, a selling price of $10 and an average variable cost of $5 result in a per-unit contribution to fixed cost of $5. The breakeven point in terms of units is found by using the following formula, where the per-unit contribution equals the product's price less the variable cost per unit:

$$\text{Breakeven Point (in Units)} = \frac{\text{Total Fixed Cost}}{\text{Per-Unit Contribution to Fixed Cost}}$$

$$\text{Breakeven Point (in Units)} = \frac{\$40,000}{\$5} = 8,000 \text{ units}$$

The breakeven point is found with the following formula:

$$\text{Breakeven Point (in Dollars)} = \frac{\text{Total Fixed Cost}}{1 - \text{Variable Cost per Unit Price}}$$

$$\text{Breakeven Point (in Dollars)} = \frac{\$40,000}{1 - \dfrac{\$5}{\$10}} = \frac{\$40,000}{0.5} = \$80,000$$

Once the breakeven point has been reached, sufficient revenues will have been obtained from sales to cover all fixed costs. Any additional sales will generate per-unit profits equal to the difference between the product's selling price and the variable cost of each unit. As Figure 18.9 reveals, sales of 8,001 units (1 unit above the breakeven point) will produce net profits of $5 ($10 sales price less per-unit variable cost of $5). Once all fixed costs have been covered, the per-unit contribution will become the per-unit profit.

Thomas Lipsky knew enough about breakeven analysis to convince himself that he could start a record label—and make money. With limited financing and even less clout in the music business, the Raleigh, North Carolina–based concert promoter knew he would not be signing hot groups like the teenybopper Backstreet Boys, who can sell 1.2 million copies of a new album in a single week. So he signed the only acts he could afford: 1980s rock groups like Slaughter and Warrant that featured gaudy guitar solos and oversized stage theatrics. Even though Slaughter had sold 3 million albums in 1990, they quickly fell off the charts—and Lipsky had much more modest expectations for the Las Vegas–based group.

The way to make money was contained within the breakeven formula. Slaughter already owned a recording studio, so the $100,000 advance Lipsky shelled out went into the band members' pockets. Another $150,000 was spent on promotion, much of which went to retailers to persuade them to stock his product. Lipsky's record company makes a gross profit of $5 per disc, so he starts making money once an album sells more than 50,000 copies. Even though the advances are meager, the band goes along with it because (1) nobody else is beating down their doors to record them, and (2) the new albums make it easier to convince concert promoters to book them for tours. Lipsky is happy; the band rocks; and breakeven analysis shows how profits can be gleaned from modest sales by shrewd marketers who can control overhead.[14]

Target Returns

Although breakeven analysis indicates the sales level at which the firm will incur neither profits nor losses, most firms' managers include some target profit in their analyses. In some instances, management sets a desired dollar return when considering a proposed new product or other marketing action. A retailer may set a desired profit of $250,000 in considering whether to expand to a second location. In other instances, the target return may be expressed in percentages, such as a 15 percent return on sales. These target returns can be modified as follows:

$$\text{Breakeven Point (including specified dollar target return)} = \frac{\text{Total Fixed Cost} + \text{Profit Objective}}{\text{Per-Unit Contribution}}$$

$$= \frac{\$40,000 + \$15,000}{\$5} = 11,000 \text{ units}$$

If the target return is expressed as a percentage of sales, it can be included in the breakeven formula as a variable cost. Suppose the marketing manager in the above example seeks a 10 percent return on sales. The desired return is $1 for each product sold (the $10 per-unit selling price multiplied by the 10 percent return on sales). In this case, the basic breakeven formula will remain unchanged, although the variable cost

MARKETING **DICTIONARY**

breakeven analysis Pricing technique used to determine the number of products that must be sold at a specified price in order to generate enough revenue to cover total cost.

per unit will be increased to reflect the target return, and the per-unit contribution to fixed cost will be reduced to $4. As a result, the breakeven point will increase from 8,000 to 10,000 units:

$$\text{Breakeven Point} = \frac{\$40,000}{\$4} = 10,000 \text{ units.}$$

Evaluation of Breakeven Analysis

Breakeven analysis is an effective tool for marketers in assessing the sales required for covering costs and achieving specified profit levels. It is easily understood by both marketing and non-marketing executives and may help them decide whether required sales levels for a certain price are in fact realistic goals. However, it has its shortcomings.

First, the model assumes that costs can be divided into fixed and variable categories. Some costs, such as salaries and advertising outlays, may be either fixed or variable depending on the particular situation. In addition, the model assumes that per-unit variable costs do not change at different levels of operation. However, these may vary because of quantity discounts, more efficient utilization of the workforce, or other economies resulting from increased levels of production and sales. Finally, the basic breakeven model does not consider demand. It is a cost-based model and does not directly address the crucial question of whether consumers will actually purchase the product at the specified price and in the quantities required for breaking even or generating profits. The marketer's challenge is to modify the breakeven analysis and the other cost-oriented pricing approaches to incorporate demand analysis. Pricing must be examined from the buyer's perspective. Such decisions cannot be made in a management vacuum in which only cost factors are considered.

TOWARD REALISTIC PRICING

7

Explain the superiority of modified breakeven analysis over the basic breakeven model and the role of yield management in pricing decisions.

Traditional economic theory considers both costs and demand in determining an equilibrium price. The dual elements of supply and demand are balanced at the point of equilibrium. In actual practice, however, most pricing approaches are largely cost oriented. Since purely cost-oriented approaches to pricing violate the marketing concept, modifications that will add demand analysis to the pricing decision are required.

Consumer research on such issues as degree of price elasticity, consumer price expectations, existence and size of specific market segments, and buyer perceptions of strengths and weaknesses of substitute products is necessary for developing sales estimates at different prices. Because much of the resulting data involves perceptions, attitudes, and future expectations of present and potential customers, such estimates are likely to be less precise than cost estimates.

The Modified Breakeven Concept

The breakeven analysis method illustrated in Figure 18.10 assumes a constant $10 retail price regardless of quantity. But what happens at different retail prices? **Modified breakeven analysis** combines the traditional breakeven analysis model with an evaluation of consumer demand.

Table 18.4 summarizes both the cost and revenue aspects of a number of alternative retail prices. The $5 unit variable cost and the $40,000 total fixed cost are based on the costs utilized in the basic breakeven model. The expected unit sales for each specified retail price are obtained from marketing research. The table contains the information necessary for calculating the breakeven point for each of the five retail price alternatives. These points are shown in Part A of Figure 18.10.

The data shown in the first two columns of Table 18.4 represent a demand schedule that indicates the number of units consumers are expected to purchase at each of a series of retail prices. As Part B of Figure 18.10 shows, these data can be superimposed onto a breakeven chart to identify the range of feasible prices for the marketer to consider.

FIGURE 18.10

FIGURE 18.10   Modified Breakeven Chart: Parts A and B

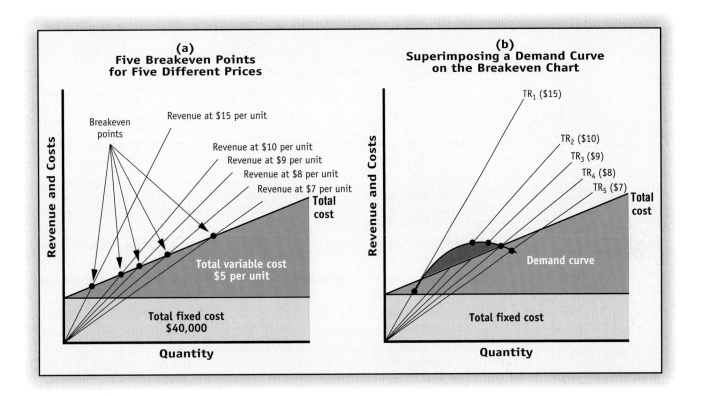

TABLE 18.4   Revenue and Cost Data for Modified Breakeven Analysis

	REVENUES			COSTS			
PRICE	QUANTITY DEMANDED	TOTAL REVENUE	TOTAL FIXED COST	TOTAL VARIABLE COST	TOTAL COST	BREAKEVEN POINT (NUMBER OF SALES REQUIRED TO BREAK EVEN)	TOTAL PROFIT (OR LOSS)
$15	2,500	$37,500	$40,000	$12,500	$52,500	4,000	$(15,000)
10	10,000	100,000	40,000	50,000	90,000	8,000	10,000
9	13,000	117,000	40,000	65,000	105,000	10,000	12,000
8	14,000	112,000	40,000	70,000	110,000	13,334	2,000
7	15,000	105,000	40,000	75,000	115,000	20,000	(10,000)

Figure 18.10 reveals that the range of profitable prices exists from a low of approximately $8 (TR$_4$) to a high of $10 (TR$_2$), with a price of $9 (TR$_3$) generating the greatest projected profits. Changing the retail price produces a new breakeven point. At a relatively

MARKETING   DICTIONARY

modified breakeven analysis Pricing technique used to evaluate consumer demand by comparing the number of products that must be sold at a variety of prices in order to cover total cost with estimates of expected sales at the various prices.

high $15 ($TR_1$) retail price, the breakeven point is 4,000 units; at a $10 retail price, it is 8,000 units; and at the lowest price considered, $7 ($TR_5$), it is 20,000 units.

The contribution of modified breakeven analysis is that it forces the marketer to consider whether the consumer is likely to purchase the number of units of a good or service required for achieving breakeven at a given price. It demonstrates that a large number of units sold does not necessarily produce added profits, since—other things equal—lower prices are necessary for stimulating additional sales. Consequently, it is important to consider both costs and consumer demand in determining the most appropriate price.

Yield Management

When most of a firm's costs are fixed over a wide range of outputs, the primary determinant of profitability will be the amount of revenue generated by sales. This situation is typical of such goods and services as the following:

- *theater tickets*—lower prices in the afternoons to offset low demand and higher prices in the evening when demand rises
- *lodging*—lower prices off season and higher prices during peak season periods; low-priced weekend rates
- *auto rental*—lower prices on weekends when business demand is low and higher prices during the week when business demand is higher
- *airfares*—low prices on nonrefundable tickets with travel restrictions such as advance-purchase and Saturday-night stay requirements and penalties for flight changes; high prices on refundable tickets that can be changed without penalty

The following example from the airline industry demonstrates how the strategy of **yield management** maximizes revenues in situations where costs are fixed.[15]

Airlines constantly monitor reservations on every flight. Beginning approximately 330 days before the flight, space is allocated between full-fare, discount-fare, and free tickets for frequent flyers who qualify for complimentary tickets. This allocation is monitored and adjusted at regular intervals until the actual departure.

Assume, for example, that Northwest Airlines has scheduled a 180-seat plane as Flight 1480 with an 8 A.M. departure from Memphis to Minneapolis on October 23. When Flight 1480 leaves its gate for departure, all costs associated with the flight (fuel, food, crew, and other operating expenses) are fixed. The pricing that maximizes revenues on this flight will also maximize profits. An examination of past sales indicates that Northwest could sell 40 to 60 round-trip, full-fare tickets at $600 per passenger and 100 to 150 round-trip restricted-fare tickets at $200 per passenger. Demand for frequent-flyer space should be at least 10 seats.

If Northwest reserves 60 seats for full-fare passengers and accepts reservations for 110 restricted-fare tickets but sells only 40 full-fare tickets (leaving 20 vacant seats), total revenues will be:

$$\text{Revenues} = (40 \times \$600) + (110 \times \$200)$$
$$= \$46,000$$

On the other hand, if Northwest's pricing decision makers want to reduce vacancies, they might decide to reduce the number of full-fare tickets to 20 and increase the restricted-fare tickets to 150. If the plane leaves the gate at full capacity, the flight will generate the following total revenues:

$$\text{Revenues} = (20 \times \$600) + (150 \times \$200)$$
$$= \$42,000$$

Instead of rigidly maintaining the allocations established nearly a year before the flight, Northwest will use yield management to maximize the revenue per flight. In this example, the airline initially holds 60 full-fare seats and accepts reservations for up to 110 restricted-fare seats. Thirty days before the October 23 departure, updated computer projections indicate that 40 full-fare seats are likely to be sold. The allocation is now revised to 40 full-fare and 130 restricted-fare tickets. A full flight leaves the gate and revenues are:

$$\text{Revenues} = (40 \times \$600) + (130 \times \$200)$$
$$= \$50,000$$

Applying yield management for the Memphis–Minneapolis flight increases revenues by at least $4,000 over the inflexible approach of making advance allocations and failing to adjust them based on passenger reservations and other data.

8

Identify the major pricing challenges facing online and international marketers.

GLOBAL ISSUES IN PRICE DETERMINATION

It is equally important for a firm engaging in global marketing to use a pricing strategy that reflects its overall marketing strategy. Prices must support the company's broader goals, including product development, advertising and sales, customer support, competitive plans, and financial objectives.

In general, there are five pricing objectives that firms can use to set prices in global marketing. Four of these are the same pricing objectives that we discussed earlier in the chapter: profitability, volume, meeting competition, and prestige. In addition, international marketers work to achieve a fifth objective: price stability.

In the global arena, marketers may choose profitability objectives if their company is a price leader that tends to establish international prices. Profitability objectives also make sense if a firm is a low-cost supplier that can make a good profit on sales.

Volume objectives become especially important in situations where nations lower their trade barriers to expose domestic markets to foreign competition. As the European Union lowered economic barriers between countries, for instance, competition for customers soared. A recent trend has been mergers of European firms to form larger companies that can achieve volume objectives. As one economist notes, "Merger activity [is] a way to get economies of scale." French grocery chain Carrefour, for example, recently acquired a former French competitor to become the world's second-largest retailer behind Wal-Mart.

Increased competition in Europe has also spurred firms to work toward the third pricing objective of meeting competitors' prices. Dutch corporation Philips Electronics offers U.S.-style coupons that give buyers 10 to 15 percent discounts off kitchen appliances. Aldi and Lidl, two German-owned food retailers, have opened discount outlets in France, forcing native French stores such as Carrefour to reduce prices. Automaker Fiat once boasted a 54 percent share of the Italian car market; its share has since dropped to 44 percent thanks to inroads from competitively-priced Ford of Europe, Inc. Fiat is fighting back by offering $1,600 rebates and zero-interest financing on certain models.

Prestige is a valid pricing objective in international marketing when products are associated with intangible benefits, such as high quality, exclusiveness, or attractive design. The greater a product's perceived benefits, the higher its price can be. Marketers must be aware, however, that cultural perceptions of quality can differ from one country to the next. Sometimes

The endorsement fees that sports apparel and other consumer-goods marketers have paid to teenage tennis phenomenons Serena and Venus Williams are expected to be recouped through increased sales as the sisters take them to new heights—both in the United States and at major international events in London, Paris, and Melbourne. U.S. Open champion Serena Williams became the first African-American since Arthur Ashe in 1975 to win a Grand Slam singles title and the first African-American woman to do so since Althea Gibson in 1958.

MARKETING   DICTIONARY

yield management Pricing strategies designed to maximize revenues in situations such as airfares, lodging, auto rentals, and theater tickets where costs are fixed.

items that command prestige prices in the U.S. are considered run-of-the-mill in other nations; sometimes products that are anything but prestigious in America seem exotic to overseas consumers. American patrons, for instance, view McDonald's restaurants as affordable fast-food eateries, but in China they are seen as fashionable and relatively expensive.

The fifth pricing objective, price stability, is desirable in international markets although it is difficult to achieve. Wars, terrorism, economic downturns, changing governments and political parties, and shifting trade policies can alter prices. An example is the computer industry. A few years ago, U.S. computer manufacturers sold their products in Europe for 30 to 50 percent more than U.S. prices. Today, greater competition within the European Union has forced computer prices down until they average only 10 percent higher than the U.S. prices, barely enough to cover manufacturers' costs in retooling machines for the local market. Falling prices have slashed profits for both American and European manufacturers, including IBM, Compaq, and Olivetti.

Price stability can be especially important for producers of commodities—goods and services that have easily accessible substitutes that other nations can supply quickly. Countries that export international commodities, such as wood, chemicals, and agricultural crops, suffer economically when their prices fluctuate. A nation such as Nicaragua, which exports sugar cane, can find that its balance of payments changes drastically when the international price for sugar shifts. This makes it vulnerable to stiff price competition from other sugar cane producers.

In contrast, countries that export value-oriented products, rather than commodities, tend to enjoy more stable prices. Prices of electronic equipment and automobiles tend to fluctuate far less than prices of sugar cane or bananas.

STRATEGIC IMPLICATIONS OF PRICING IN THE 21ST CENTURY

This chapter has focused on traditional pricing concepts and methods—principles that are critical to all marketing strategies, especially in e-commerce. Consumers can now compare prices quickly, heightening the already intense competitive pricing environment. The Web allows for prices to be negotiated on the spot and anything can be auctioned. From airline tickets to automobiles, the Web allows consumers to name their price. The Coca-Cola Company marketers are currently testing variable pricing for vending machine soft drinks, based on time of day, temperature, and the historical demand curve. On a cold, wintry day, a 12-ounce can may cost only a quarter; on a dry, hot summer day, the price may be as high as $3![16]

Consumers will reap the greatest rewards of competition created by online price cutters. A recent study of prices on the Web found that books and music CDs were 9 percent to 16 percent lower online than at conventional stores. One research analyst explains how deep discount sites are empowering consumers in the pricing environment, "If you're a consumer and you're thinking about any kind of researched purchase, you're leaving thousands of dollars on the table if you don't at least look online. It's a great time to be a consumer. You have more power than you could possibly imagine."[17] In the near future, online shoppers will use electronic wallets that send intelligent agents out on the Net to find the lowest prices or even facilitate auctions in which merchants will bid to become the lowest-cost supplier for the products a consumer wants.

Electronic delivery of music, books, and a thousand other goods and services will only lead to further price reductions. E-commerce has smoothed out the friction of time, which kept pricing relatively static. Microsoft cofounder Bill Gates recently gave a futuristic view of what he sees as a "friction-free economy." The current obsession with time and the ability to measure it will change perceptions and pricing of tangible goods. Goods and services are no longer made before they are ordered and their prices will no longer be fixed; instead, prices will shift up and down.

While consumers rejoice, retailers worry as they watch their profit margins disappearing. Says Buy.com founder and CEO Scott Blum, "Every company is vulnerable, every company is under attack." The Internet discounter lures Web shoppers with low prices on brand-name products. That seems to be the blueprint for success: Spend generously to win new customers, offer the lowest prices possible, and then give them superior customer services to keep them loyal.[18]

ACHIEVEMENT CHECK SUMMARY

Read the learning objectives that follow, and consider the questions for each one. Answering these questions will reinforce your grasp of the most important concepts in the chapter and will allow you to check how well you have achieved these learning goals. Where a blank appears before a question, answer with *T* or *F* for true/false questions; for multiple-choice questions, choose the letter of the correct answer.

Objective 18.1: Outline the legal constraints on pricing.

1. _____ Unfair-trade laws require sellers to maintain minimum retail prices for comparable products.

2. _____ Price discrimination is prohibited under the Consumer Goods Pricing Act.

3. _____ Interstate usage of fair-trade laws was banned under the Robinson-Patman Act.

Objective 18.2: Identify the major categories of pricing objectives.

1. _____ Pricing objectives include all of the following except: (a) profit maximization objectives; (b) meeting competition; (c) market-share objectives; (d) quality performance objectives; (e) prestige objectives.

2. _____ Profits are (a) the most important objective for a firm; (b) the result of supply and demand; (c) a function of revenue and expenses; (d) determined primarily by the quantity of a product sold.

Objective 18.3: Explain price elasticity and its determinants.

1. _____ Elasticity is the measure of the responsiveness of manufacturers and distributors to inventory being held.

2. _____ If a good or service has close substitutes, demand tends to be elastic.

3. _____ When the measurement of elasticity in demand or supply is greater than 1.0, it is said to be elastic.

Objective 18.4: List the practical problems involved in applying price theory concepts to actual pricing decisions.

1. _____ All firms try to maximize profits.

2. _____ It can be difficult to estimate demand at various price levels.

3. _____ Using computer software, managers can accurately forecast demand for a product and thereby determine the price.

Objective 18.5: Explain the major cost-plus approaches to price setting.

1. _____ Cost-plus pricing approaches include incremental-cost pricing and full-cost pricing.

2. _____ Full-cost pricing takes competition and demand for the item into consideration.

3. _____ Incremental-cost pricing helps to overcome the arbitrary allocation of fixed expenses by only using costs directly attributable to a specific output in setting prices.

Objective 18.6: List the major advantages and shortcomings of using breakeven analysis in pricing decisions.

1. _____ Breakeven analysis (a) is a means of setting prices to determine rates of production; (b) is used in determining the quantity that must be sold to cover total costs; (c) assumes that per-unit variable costs will change at different levels of operation; (d) indicates how much profit will be made by producing a specified quantity of a good or service.

2. _____ Breakeven analysis (a) cannot reflect target return objectives; (b) considers how much of the product consumers will purchase; (c) is used to set profitability objectives; (d) is frequently used in price determination.

Objective 18.7: Explain the superiority of modified breakeven analysis over the basic breakeven model and the role of yield management in pricing decisions.

1. _____ Modified breakeven analysis helps marketers determine price regardless of demand.

2. _____ A large number of units sold does not necessarily produce added profits.

3. _____ Costs and consumer demand are equally important in determining the best price for a product.

Objective 18.8: Identify the major pricing challenges facing online and international marketers.

1. _____ A firm's global pricing strategy reflects its global marketing strategy.

2. _____ In addition to the four major categories of pricing objectives, marketers must consider price stability in their international pricing strategies.

3. _____ Internet marketers use the same pricing techniques as traditional marketers to reach global and domestic markets.

4. _____ Competitive pricing strategies are especially important to Web marketers because consumers can quickly search online for the best price.

Students: See the solutions section located on page S-3 to check your responses to the Achievement Check Summary.

Key Terms

price	supply
Robinson-Patman Act	pure competition
unfair-trade laws	monopolistic competition
fair-trade laws	oligopoly
profit maximization	monopoly
target-return objective	elasticity
Profit Impact of Market	cost-plus pricing
Strategies (PIMS) project	breakeven analysis
value pricing	modified breakeven analysis
customary prices	yield management
demand	

Review Questions

1. Distinguish between fair-trade laws and unfair-trade laws. As a consumer, do you support such laws? Would your answer change if you were the owner of a small retail store?

2. Identify the major categories of pricing objectives. Give an example of each.

3. What are the major price implications of the PIMS studies? Suggest possible explanations for the relationships they reveal.

4. Explain the concept of elasticity. Identify each factor influencing elasticity and give a specific example of how it affects the degree of elasticity in a good or service.

5. Explain the advantages of using incremental-cost pricing rather than full-cost pricing. What potential drawbacks exist?

6. Why do many firms choose to de-emphasize pricing as a marketing tool and instead concentrate on the other marketing mix variables in seeking to achieve a competitive advantage?

7. How can locating the breakeven point assist in price determination? What are the primary dangers in relying solely on breakeven analysis in pricing decisions?

8. What is the breakeven point for a product with a selling price of $40, average variable cost of $24, and related fixed cost of $37,500? What impact would a $4-per-unit profit requirement have on the breakeven point?

9. Explain how yield management results in greater revenue than other strategies. Under what conditions is yield management a useful pricing strategy?

10. Identify the factors that can affect prices in international and on-line marketing.

Questions for Critical Thinking

1. Categorize each of the following as a specific type of pricing objective. Suggest a company or product likely to utilize each pricing objective.
   a. a 5 percent increase in profits over the previous year
   b. prices no more than 6 percent higher than prices quoted by independent dealers
   c. a 5 percent increase in market share
   d. a 25 percent return on investment (before taxes)
   e. following the price set by the most important competitor in each market segment
   f. setting the highest prices in the product category to maintain favorable brand image

2. Describe the market situations that exist for the following products. Defend your answers.
   a. local dry-cleaning service
   b. DVD players
   c. golf clubs
   d. platinum
   e. soybeans
   f. remote control car alarms
   g. razors
   h. personal watercraft

3. How are the following prices determined and what do they have in common?
   a. ticket to a museum exhibit
   b. your college tuition fee
   c. local sales tax rate
   d. printing of business cards

4. WebTech Development of Nashville, Tennessee, is considering the possible introduction of a new product proposed by its research-and-development staff. The firm's marketing director estimates that the product can be marketed at a price of $70. Total fixed cost is $278,000, and average variable cost is calculated at $48.
   a. What is the breakeven point in units for the proposed product?
   b. The firm's president has suggested a target profit return of $214,000 for the proposed product. How many units must be sold in order to both break even and achieve this target return?

5. The marketing research staff at Cleveland-based Cyber Novelties has developed the following sales estimates for a proposed new item designed to be marketed through direct mail sales:

PROPOSED SELLING PRICE	SALES ESTIMATE (UNITS)
$8	55,000
10	22,000
15	14,000
20	5,000
24	2,800

The new product has a total fixed cost of $60,000 and a $7 variable cost per unit.
   a. Which of the proposed selling prices would generate a profit for Cyber Novelties?
   b. Cyber Novelties' director of marketing also estimates that an additional $.50 per-unit allocation for extra promotion will produce the following increases in sales estimates: 60,000 units at an $8 unit selling price, 28,000 units at $10, 17,000 units at $15, 6,000 units at $20, and 3,500 units at $24. Indicate the feasible range of prices if this proposal is implemented and results in the predicted sales increases.
   c. Indicate the feasible price or prices if the $.50 per-unit additional promotion proposal is not implemented but management insists on a $25,000 target return.

1. **Unfair Trade Laws.** Use a search engine to find recent news on predatory pricing practices for two different industries. In your summary identify the company or companies involved in each industry and the basis for the predatory pricing charges.

2. **Yield Management.** The chapter discussion on yield management used theater tickets, lodging, auto rental, and airfares as examples to illustrate the concept of yield management. For this assignment, locate a specific pricing example of yield management in any area of interest to you. Bring your printout to class to use as an example during classroom discussion on the topic. A good site that you could use for this assignment comes from the Web site for the Phoenix Luxury Condominiums located on the Gulf of Mexico in Orange Beach, Alabama. At *www.brett-robinson.com,* you click on the photograph of the condominium for which you'd like rental rates. Included in the information that will appear is a breakdown of the seasons with dates, as well as the rates during each season.

3. **Strategic Implications of Pricing in the 21st Century.** Go to www.quicken.com/shopping and complete the following: (a) Download and install the Quicken Shopper program. (b) Go through the steps of pricing a recent bestseller at a site such as *www.amazon.com* or *www.barnesandnoble.com* (without actually making a purchase) or of pricing a DVD or CD at a site such as *www.cduniverse.com, www.valueamerica.com,* or *www.dvdwave.com.* (c) Once you've selected an item, launch the Quicken Shopper and print out the results to bring to class.

brett-robinson.com

amazon.com

barnesandnoble.com

valueamerica.com

dvdwave.com

Video Case 18 on Cybex International begins on page VC-20.

Managing the Pricing Function

C H A P T E R

19

CHAPTER OBJECTIVES

1   Compare the alternative pricing strategies and explain when each strategy is most appropriate.

2   Describe how prices are quoted.

3   Identify the various pricing policy decisions that marketers must make.

4   Relate price to consumer perceptions of quality.

5   Contrast competitive bidding and negotiated prices.

6   Explain the importance of transfer pricing.

7   Compare the three alternative global pricing strategies.

8   Relate the concepts of cannibalization, bundle pricing, and bots to online pricing strategies.

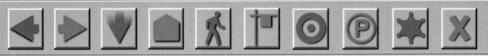

Priceline.com: Where the Right Price Is Your Price

> ## An empty hotel room is a crying shame.
>
> ## Just think about how lonely the mint on the pillow is.
>
> Name your own price on a quality, brand-name hotel room and save up to 20%, 40% or more.
>
> Why stay in an OK hotel when you can stay in a great hotel? With priceline.com you can take advantage of the fact that each night thousands of rooms, in the hotels you want to stay in, go unoccupied in every city in America. And each week, more than 15,000 of those rooms are bought by people who name their own price at priceline.com and get big savings on two-, three-, four- and five-star hotels. Log on today at www.priceline.com.
>
> ### priceline.com
> *Name your own price*

Many consumers were first introduced to Priceline.com by William Shatner—not as the famed Captain Kirk of the Starship Enterprise but as a spokesperson for the online air travel broker. In radio, television, and print ads, Shatner challenged audiences to "Name your own price" on airline tickets and hotel rooms—something travelers could not do anywhere else.

Priceline uses a novel Internet pricing system that lets people name their own price for goods and services they want to buy. Sellers are notified of the bids and can then fill as many of the orders as they wish at the bid price. Priceline focuses on four distinct product categories: a travel service that offers airline tickets and hotel rooms; a personal finance service offering home mortgages, refinancing, and home equity loans; an automotive service that allows car buyers to bid on buying or leasing a new car or truck; and a grocery service that lets Internet users bid on items ranging from pork chops and beer to diapers,

pay for these items by credit card, and pick up the items from participating food stores.

The proposition to customers is both simple and compelling—"Name your price." But what happens when someone takes the firm up on its offer? Each bid received is guaranteed by the bidder's credit card, and bids are forwarded to participating sellers. By requiring bidders to be flexible about sellers and minor product features, Priceline helps sellers generate incremental revenues without disrupting their merchandise inventory. By keeping the prices of successful bids secret, Priceline also does not create problems among the supplier's regular customers who pay regular prices.

During a typical week, 30,000 air travelers will get tickets through Priceline. In some cases, it simply passes the bids along to airline ticketing offices. However, it also negotiates private, discounted deals for hard-to-sell seats on certain flights for particular airlines. In instances where Priceline can respond to bids by offering its own inventory, it fills orders itself.

In addition to airline tickets, Priceline also represents hotels in over 1,100 cities. Naming your own price for a hotel room might even get you a better deal than the price you bid. So if you ask Priceline to look for a two-star hotel at a certain price, you may find yourself in a three-star or even a four-star hotel for the same rate.

Priceline also attempts to match bidders with mortgage lenders and auto dealers. Undeterred by industry giant eBay, the firm is also exploring the possibility of expanding into online auctions. While competition is intense, so are the growth trends in this sector. By 2002, the Internet auction market is expected to exceed $6.4 billion. Rather than getting directly involved in the auction business, Priceline is considering licensing its brand name and promotional tag-line to two new companies who would handle the business.

Groceries represent the firm's most recent name-your-price venture. Jay Walker, Priceline's founder, hopes to be able to offer customers deals comparable to those available in warehouse-style stores, without requiring people to buy in bulk. If the system works out, it will probably be expanded to include prescription drugs.

Part of Priceline's marketing strategy is to expand the name-your-price concept to other areas of e-commerce. That is where these consumer-to-consumer and retail merchandise ideas come in. One possible consumer-to-consumer business would allow buyers to make conditional purchase offers to acquire used goods, such as stereos, from other consumers. Presumably the stereo buyer could leaf through and select one of the offers collected by Priceline.

Although the firm's 43-year-old founder predicts that, in the future, "A significant amount of the global economy will be priced this way," Priceline has not earned a penny of profit so far. It also faces competition at every turn, including, among others, its own suppliers.

On the issue of price, Priceline seems both up-front and evasive. The evasiveness stems from its efforts to protect its ongoing relationships with its suppliers—major airlines, lending institutions, auto dealers, and hotels. But the firm is up-front in emphasizing its contributions in helping buyers get the best price they can find—and giving them the means of placing their offers in front of suppliers. "It's never that we've got the *best* price," says Walker. "It's just that it's *your* price." He adds that customers should shop around and grab a low fare if they can find one. If they cannot, they should come to Priceline. Either way, they are playing a big role in setting the prices they pay in the marketplace.[1]

CHAPTER OVERVIEW

As Priceline marketers will attest, setting prices is not a one-time decision nor is it a routine or standard practice. Pricing is a dynamic function of the marketing mix. Some even consider pricing as much an art as a calculated scientific process. One recent government study found that about half the surveyed companies changed prices once a year or less, and only one in ten makes a price change more than once a month. On the other hand, online companies face enormous price competition on the Web and, as a result, prices often are adjusted daily and other online firms even negotiate prices on the spot.

Companies translate pricing objectives into pricing decisions in two major steps. First, someone must accept responsibility for making pricing decisions and administering the resulting pricing structure. Second, someone must set the overall pricing structure—that is, basic prices and appropriate discounts for channel members, quantity purchases, and geographic and promotional considerations.

The decision to make price adjustments is directly related to demand. Most businesses slowly change the amounts they charge customers, even when they clearly recognize strong demand. Instead of raising prices, they may choose to scale down customer service or add fees to cover the added costs. They may also wait to raise prices until they see what their competitors will do. (Few businesses want the distinction of being the first to charge higher prices.) Since many businesses base their prices on manufacturing costs rather than consumer demand, they may wait for increases in their own costs before responding with price changes. These increases generally emerge more slowly than changes in consumer demand. Finally, since many business executives believe that steady prices will help to preserve long-term relationships with customers, they are reluctant to raise prices even when strong demand probably justifies the change.

Chapter 18 introduced the concept of price and its role in the economic system and marketing strategy. This chapter examines various pricing strategies and price structures, such as reductions from list prices and geographic considerations. It then looks at the primary pricing policies, including psychological pricing, price flexibility, product-line pricing, and promotional pricing, as well as price/quality relationships. Competitive and negotiated prices are discussed and one section focuses entirely on transfer pricing. Finally, the chapter concludes by describing important factors in pricing goods and services for online and export companies. ■

PRICING STRATEGIES

The specific strategies that firms use to price their goods and services grow out of the marketing strategies they formulate to accomplish overall organizational objectives. One firm's marketers may price products to attract customers across a wide range; another group of marketers may set prices to appeal to a small segment of a larger market; still another group may simply try to match competitors' price tags.

In general, firms can choose from three pricing strategies: skimming, penetration, and competitive pricing. The following sections look at these choices in more detail.

1

Compare the alternative pricing strategies and explain when each strategy is most appropriate.

Skimming Pricing Strategy

A **skimming pricing strategy** is sometimes called *market-plus pricing* because it intentionally sets a relatively high price compared to the prices of competing products. The name comes from the expression "skimming the cream."

A company may practice a skimming strategy in setting a market-entry price when it introduces a distinctive good or service with little or no competition. For example, in recent years the price of gold has fallen drastically, making bullion a bargain. But jewelry prices have remained steady. Raw materials account for only 28 percent of the price of a gold necklace. A custom jewelry designer such as Tiffany or Cartier may create a 14-karat gold necklace weighing 10 grams and sell it for $5,000. However, a replica necklace of the same karat and gram weight at a discount jeweler such as Service Merchandise will sell for only $200. Tiffany and Cartier marketers justify their prices by pointing out the exclusivity and craftsmanship of their creations.[2]

As another example, in recent years, the Weber brand name has become the ultimate in patio grills. The distinctive shape and superior performance of the grills attract lovers of char-broiled foods and outdoor cooking. The model shown in Figure 19.1 combines the convenience of gas grills with the best features of a charcoal grill. It is the first charcoal grill, in fact, to offer the ease of a gas start: no matches, no lighter fluid, no mess. Coals are lit evenly and efficiently the first time, every time. Weber marketers ignore price in their promotional strategies and instead focus on the benefits of cooking on a Weber grill.

@ **webergrills.com**

Skimming strategies are often used by marketers of high-end goods and services. German pen-maker Montblanc, for example, has built a strong reputation as a designer of superior quality writing instruments. Owners of Montblanc pens, who pay anywhere from $500 to $10,000 for the gold-and-gem encrusted fountain pens, are willing to pay extra for the company's exquisite designs. In addition to the prestige of owning one of these easily recognized fountain pens, Montblanc marketers have created a boutique-type shopping experience for the firm's customers. Its De-Acceleration Studio in New York City allows shoppers to relax in leather armchairs, read books or write letters, listen to music, take a nap, or buy a pen. As CEO Norbert Platt explains, "Handwriting in today's world means I take my own personal time for you and, subsequently, you are important to me."[3]

@ **mbpensonline.com**

Improvements in existing products may allow firms to change from other

MARKETING   DICTIONARY

skimming pricing strategy Pricing strategy involving the use of a high price relative to competitive offerings.

FIGURE 19.1   **Weber: Distinctive Grills Marketed through a Skimming Pricing Strategy**

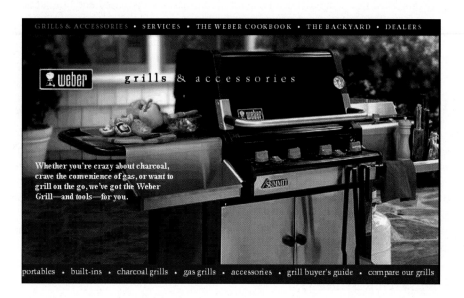

blackanddecker.com

pricing structures to skimming strategies. Consider the common scrub brush, which until recently sold for about $1—the cheaper the better. Then came the Black & Decker ScumBuster, a cordless scrubber that features battery-powered brushes for convenience and ease of use. The ScumBuster comes with its own carrying case and is available at major home improvement stores like Lowe's and Home Depot as well as drugstores and hardware stores for around a whopping $40.

A firm may maintain a skimming strategy throughout most stages of a product's life cycle. Sometimes this tactic works and sometimes it does not. Automobile manufacturers have kept prices for some models relatively high due to continued demand. During the last decade, Ford generated huge profits from three types of its vehicles: Ford trucks, sport utility vehicles, and specifically the Lincoln Town Car. The huge, plush, comfortable-riding Town Car proved to be a long-term favorite among older car buyers and continues to be marketed with only minimal changes for nearly 15 years. These extremely long production runs create eye-popping, per-car profits for Ford's Lincoln division.

Some added features were designed to justify the high prices being paid for the vehicles. Lincoln added Cartier trim to its Town Car sedan and rare African hardwood panels to its Blackwood utility vehicle. The Lincoln Navigator shown in Figure 19.2 offers three rows of leather-trimmed seats. Option packages for Jaguar's S-type models include voice-activated controls for sound, temperature, and navigation systems. GM's Oldsmobile Silhouette Premier minivan comes equipped with an entertainment center and accounts for 30 percent of Silhouette total sales.

A skimming strategy offers several benefits. For one, it allows a manufacturer to quickly recover its research-and-development (R&D) costs. Drugmakers cite this argument as one reason why new drugs cost so much, pointing out that no other industry invests as much in R&D—an average of 16 percent of sales, compared to 8 percent for computer makers and 4 percent in the aerospace industry. A skimming strategy also allows a firm to maximize revenue from a new product before competitors enter the field. In many industries, increasing competition eventually drives down initially high prices, as with VCRs and personal computers.

A skimming pricing strategy is a useful tool for segmenting a product's overall market on a price basis. For a new product that represents a significant innovation, a relatively high price conveys an image of distinction, helping the product to appeal to buyers with low sensitivity to

price. Americans began the 21st century with a booming economy, wealthy consumers with high discretionary incomes, and hundreds of premium products that carried premium prices. Marketers flooded retail shelves and showrooms with higher-priced versions of existing products from razor blades to luxury automobiles. In just one year, Procter & Gamble launched new higher-priced versions of Dawn dish soap, Head & Shoulders shampoo, Crest toothpaste, and Pampers diapers. P&G marketers expect these new versions to generate an additional 2 percent in annual revenues from price increases alone. Similarly, Williams-Sonoma, the gourmet cookware cataloger, sold more $369 Dualit toasters than any other item it carried in its catalog last year. As one marketing consultant explains, "People are just more willing to spend money now when they perceive the benefit is worth it."[4] Other examples of products introduced under skimming strategies include laser printers, VCRs, and camcorders.

A third advantage of a skimming strategy is that it permits marketers to control demand in the introductory stages of a product's life cycle and then adjust productive capacity to match demand. A low initial price for a new product risks problems if demand outstrips the firm's production capacity, resulting in consumer and retailer complaints and possibly permanent damage to the product's image. Excess demand occasionally leads to poor-quality products, as the firm strives to satisfy consumer desires for the product with inadequate production facilities.

During the late growth and early maturity stages of its life cycle, a product's price typically falls for two reasons: (1) the pressure of competition and (2) the desire to expand its market. Figure 19.3 shows that 10 percent of the market would buy Product X at $10.00, and another 20 percent would buy at a price of $8.75. Successive price declines expand the firm's market and meet challenges posed by new competitors.

A skimming strategy brings one chief disadvantage: It attracts competition. Potential competitors see innovative firms reaping large financial returns and decide to enter the market. This new supply forces the price of the original product even lower than its eventual level under a

williams-sonoma.com

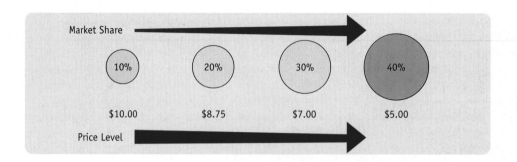

FIGURE 19.3 Price Reductions to Increase Market Share

sequential skimming procedure. However, if patent protection or some other unique proprietary ability allows a firm to exclude competitors from its market, it may continue a skimming strategy for a relatively long period. Gillette marketers have taken advantage of the 35 patents the company has on its new Mach3 shaving system. Some of the high-tech features include three blades with a new type edge (applied atom by atom with chip-making technology), an ergonomic handle, and a new, easier method of loading cartridges. Gillette's revolutionary new razor carries a price more than 50 percent higher than its own Sensor Excel brand, and blade cartridges cost $1.60 each. The aggressively high-priced Mach3 took seven years and $750 million to perfect, but within one year following its launch, Gillette's share of the $7 billion razor-and-blade market jumped to 72 percent.[5]

Penetration Pricing Strategy

A **penetration pricing strategy** sets a low price as a major marketing weapon. Marketers often price products noticeably lower than competing offerings when they enter new industries characterized by dozens of competing brands. Once the product achieves some market recognition through consumer trial purchases stimulated by a product's low price, marketers may increase the price to the level of competing products. Marketers of consumer products such as detergents often use this strategy. A penetration pricing strategy may also extend over several stages of the product life cycle as the firm seeks to maintain a reputation as a low-price competitor.

A penetration pricing strategy is sometimes called *market-minus pricing* when it implements the premise that a lower-than-market price will attract buyers and move a brand from an unknown newcomer to at least the brand-recognition stage or even to the brand-preference stage. Since many firms begin penetration pricing with the intention of increasing prices in the future, success depends on generating many trial purchases.

nwa.com

Marketers attempting to use a penetration strategy often discover that their competitors are simply matching their prices. When Northwest Airlines, the nation's fourth largest air carrier, recently announced fare reductions for the off-peak season, United Airlines, the nation's largest carrier, joined a host of others to match the lower prices. Northwest then used special offers to its ConnectFirst frequent-flyer members to attract added business. As Figure 19.4 describes, Northwest passengers who purchase full-fare coach tickets on selected flights receive an automatic upgrade to first class.[6]

The increased popularity of cell phones in the United States during the past 10 years heightened competition among service providers. As hundreds of new companies flooded the market, cell phone prices remained fairly stable while service providers lowered fees, increased time and geographic limits, and offered improved customer service.

Retailers may use penetration pricing to lure shoppers to new stores. These may take such forms as zero-interest charges for credit purchases at a new furniture store, two-for-one offers for dinner at a new restaurant, or offering first-day customers an extremely low price on a single product purchase to get them to come in and shop.

Penetration pricing works best when a good or service experiences highly elastic demand. Large numbers of highly price-sensitive consumers pay close attention to this kind of appeal. The strategy also suits situations in which large-scale operations and long production runs result in low production and marketing costs. Finally, penetration pricing may be appropriate in market situations in which introduction of a new product will likely attract strong competitors. Such a strategy may allow a new product to reach the mass market quickly and capture a large share prior to entry by competitors. Research shows that about 25 percent of companies frequently use penetration pricing strategies.

Everyday Low Pricing

Closely related to penetration pricing is **everyday low pricing (EDLP)**, a strategy devoted to continuous low prices as opposed to relying on short-term, price-cutting tactics such as cents-off coupons, rebates, and special sales. EDLP can take two forms. In one, retailers like Wal-Mart compete by offering low retail prices to consumers. For several years, Wal-Mart has featured an animated, yellow, smiling face as a spokesperson for their "falling prices" advertisements. Using the second method, manufacturers seek to set stable wholesale prices that undercut those that competitors offer to retailers, which often rise and fall due to trade promotion deals.

Many marketers reduce the list prices on a number of products while simultaneously reducing promotion allowances to retailers. These allowances permit retailers to fund in-store promotions such as shelf merchandising and end-aisle displays. During the 1990s, Procter & Gamble initiated a program that led to many dramatic price cuts on some of its products such as detergents, paper towels, and disposable diapers. This trend toward EDLP quickly spread to other industries. For example, in the telecommunications industry, Sprint and MCI Worldcom battled for consumers' nickels and dimes by offering low prices on off-peak, long-distance telephone calls.

Some retailers oppose everyday low pricing strategies. Grocery stores, for instance, operate on "high-low" strategies that set profitable regular prices that offset losses of frequent specials and promotions. Other retailers feel that EDLP will ultimately benefit both sellers and buyers. Supporters of EDLP in the grocery industry point out that it already succeeds at two of the biggest competitors, Wal-Mart and warehouse clubs. Marketing theorists express differing opinions about the prospects of EDLP emerging as a dominant pricing strategy.

One popular myth of pricing is that a low price is a sure sell. While low prices are an easy means of distinguishing the offerings of one marketer from other sellers, such moves are easy to counter by competitors. Unless overall demand is price-elastic, overall price cuts will mean less revenue for all firms in the industry. In addition, low prices may generate an image of questionable quality. As the 19th century critic John Ruskin put it, "There is hardly anything in the world that some men can't make a little worse and sell a little cheaper, and the people who consider price only are this man's lawful prey." The astute marketer should evaluate both the benefits derived from low-price strategies and the costs involved before launching an EDLP strategy.

FIGURE 19.4   Northwest Airlines: Succeeding with a Penetration Pricing Strategy

First Class for the price of Coach. If only my economics professor could see me now.

ConnectFirst fares. Move up to First Class for the price of Coach.

NORTHWEST AIRLINES
ConnectFirst
3-800-225-2525 / www.nwa.com

MARKETING   DICTIONARY

penetration pricing strategy Pricing strategy involving the use of a relatively low entry price as compared with competitive offerings; based on the theory that this initial low price will help secure market acceptance.

everyday low pricing (EDLP) Pricing strategy of continuously offering low prices rather than relying on such short-term price cuts as cents-off coupons, rebates, and special sales.

Competitive Pricing Strategy

Although many organizations rely heavily on price as a competitive weapon, even more implement **competitive pricing strategies**. These organizations try to reduce the emphasis on price competition by matching other firms' prices and concentrating their own marketing efforts on the product, distribution, and promotion elements of the marketing mix. As pointed out earlier, while price offers a dramatic means of achieving competitive advantage, it is also the easiest marketing variable for competitors to match. In fact, in industries with relatively homogeneous products, competitors must match each other's price reductions in order to maintain market share and remain competitive.

Retailers like Home Depot and Lowe's Home Improvement Centers use price-matching strategies, assuring consumers they will meet—and beat—competitor's prices. Grocery chains like Safeway, Winn-Dixie, and Raley's often compete with seasonal items: watermelons, soft drinks, and hot dogs in the summer; apples, hot chocolate, and turkeys in the winter. As soon as one store lowers the price per pound on turkeys, the rest follow suit.

Even when marketers sell relatively heterogeneous products, they analyze the prices of major competing offerings and ensure their own prices do not markedly differ. When IBM entered the personal computer market, its marketing efforts emphasized the versatility and power of its machines. However, the firm's marketers also quickly pointed out that each PC in the line carried a competitive price.

Under competitive pricing, a price reduction spreads financial effects throughout an industry as other firms match the drop. Unless the lower prices can attract new customers and expand the overall market enough to offset the loss of per-unit revenue, the price cut will leave all competitors with less revenue. Research shows that nearly two-thirds of all firms set prices at standard levels for comparable products as their primary pricing strategies.

Web marketing is typically associated with penetration pricing strategies due to the inroads that book, music, and air travel sales have made using low, negotiable prices with little or no profit margins. However, online marketers are discovering that such customer benefits as selection, quick order fulfillment, and easy returns are equally important, too. Customers drawn to a Web site with lots of perks and lavish customer service are likely to pay full price for more individualized, high-ticket items like brand-name apparel and accessories. Dressmart is one such online clothier that demonstrates that many customers will pay more to obtain superior products and avoid shopping in stores. The Stockholm-based firm, which sells expensive men's dress attire only, captured over $4 million in online sales last year, over 50 percent of the total online market in this segment.[7]

@ **dressmart.com**

By pricing products at the general levels of competitive offerings, marketers largely negate the price variable in their marketing strategies. They must then emphasize non-price variables to develop areas of distinctive competence and attract customers. More than a dozen firms compete with one another in the color-copier market. While many of them emphasize price as a primary component of their marketing mixes, Tektronix marketers focus on their firm's reputation for quality and state-of-the-art technology. The Tektronix ad shown in Figure 19.5 points out that the superior performance of its color copier has made it the preferred choice of graphic artists, scientists, and designers for over 15 years. Since the price is comparable to competing models, it is not emphasized in the advertisement.

PRICE QUOTATIONS

2

Describe how prices are quoted.

The choice of the best method for quoting prices depends on many industry conditions, including competitive trends, cost structures, and traditional practices, along with the policies of individual firms. This section examines the reasoning and methodology behind price quotation practices.

Most price structures are built around **list prices**—the rates normally quoted to potential buyers. Marketers usually determine list prices by one or a combination of the methods discussed

FIGURE 19.5 Tektronix: Meeting Competition with a Competitive Pricing Strategy

in Chapter 18. The sticker price on a new automobile is a good example: It shows the list price for the basic model and then adds the prices of options.

T-shirts offer another familiar example of list prices. About 1 billion of them are bought in the United States each year, generating sales revenues of $10 billion. Many of the most lucrative sales involved T-shirts sporting images of musical groups or sports stars and event dates. But where does the money go when you purchase a concert T-shirt at a list price of $25? Figure 19.6 supplies the answers.

Although 54 percent of the $25 list price goes for production costs, the $7.50 licensing fee paid to the recording artist accounts for nearly half of the total. The remaining 46 percent is paid to the retailer (the concert arena) and to concert vendors.

Reductions from List Price

The amount that a consumer pays for a product—its **market price**—may or may not equal the list price. Discounts and allowances sometimes reduce list prices. A list price often defines a starting point from which discounts set a lower market price. Marketers offer discounts in several classifications: cash, trade, and quantity discounts.

Cash Discounts

Consumers, industrial purchasers, or channel members sometimes receive reductions in price in exchange for prompt payment of bills; these price cuts are known as **cash discounts**. Discount terms usually specify exact time

MARKETING DICTIONARY

competitive pricing strategy Pricing strategy designed to de-emphasize price as a competitive variable by pricing a good or service at the general level of comparable offerings.

list price Established price normally quoted to potential buyers.

market price Price that a consumer or marketing intermediary actually pays for a product after subtracting any discounts, allowances, or rebates from the list price.

cash discount Price reduction offered to a consumer, industrial user, or marketing intermediary in return for prompt payment of a bill.

FIGURE 19.6 — The Take on a $25 T-Shirt

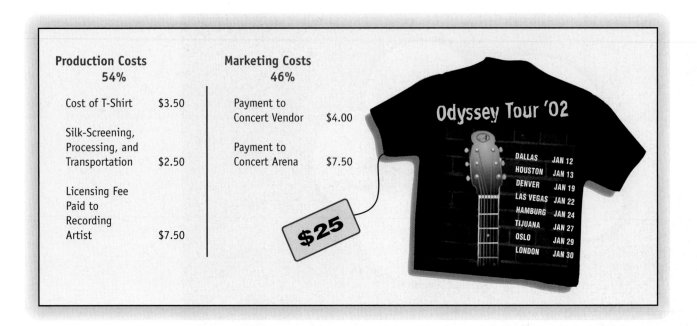

Production Costs
54%

Cost of T-Shirt	$3.50
Silk-Screening, Processing, and Transportation	$2.50
Licensing Fee Paid to Recording Artist	$7.50

Marketing Costs
46%

Payment to Concert Vendor	$4.00
Payment to Concert Arena	$7.50

Odyssey Tour '02

DALLAS JAN 12
HOUSTON JAN 13
DENVER JAN 19
LAS VEGAS JAN 22
HAMBURG JAN 24
TIJUANA JAN 27
OSLO JAN 29
LONDON JAN 30

$25

periods, such as 2/10, net 30. This notation means that the customer must pay within 30 days, but payment within 10 days entitles the customer to subtract 2 percent from the amount due.

Cash discounts represent a traditional pricing practice in many industries. They fulfill legal requirements provided that all customers can take the same reductions on the same terms. Sellers originally instituted such discount practices to improve their own liquidity positions, reduce their bad-debt losses, and cut collection expenses. Whether these advantages outweigh the relatively high cost of capital that sellers incur by offering cash discounts depends on the need for liquidity as well as alternative sources (and costs) of funds.

Trade Discounts

Payments to channel members for performing marketing functions are known as **trade discounts** or *functional discounts*. Earlier chapters discussed the services performed by various channel members and the related costs. A manufacturer's list price must incorporate the costs incurred by channel members in performing required marketing functions and expected profit margins for each member.

Trade discounts initially reflected the operating expenses of each category, but they have become more or less customary practices in some industries. The Robinson-Patman Act allows trade discounts as long as all buyers in the same category, such as all wholesalers or all retailers, receive the same discount privileges.

Figure 19.7 shows how a chain of trade discounts works. In the first instance, the trade discount is "40 percent, 10 percent off list price" for wholesalers. In other words, the 40 percent discount on the $40 product is the trade discount the retailer receives to cover operating expenses and earn a profit. The wholesaler receives 10 percent of the $24 price to retailers to cover expenses and earn a profit. The manufacturer receives $21.60 from the wholesaler for each order.

In the second example, the manufacturer and retailer decide to bypass the wholesaler. The producer offers a trade discount of 45 percent to the retailer. In this instance, the retailer receives $18 for each product sold at its list price and the manufacturer receives the remaining $22. Either the retailer or the manufacturer must assume responsibility for the services previously performed by the wholesaler, or they can share these duties between them.

FIGURE 19.7 | **Chain of Trade Discounts**

"40 PERCENT, 10 PERCENT OFF" TRADE DISCOUNT

List Price	–	Retail Trade Discount	–	Wholesale Trade Discount	=	Manufacturer Proceeds
$40	–	$16 ($40 × 40%)	–	$2.40 ($24 × 10%)	=	$21.60 ($40 – $16 – $2.40)

"45 PERCENT" TRADE DISCOUNT

List Price	–	Retail Trade Discount	=			Manufacturer Proceeds
$40	–	$18 ($40 × 45%)	=			$22 ($40 – $18)

Quantity Discounts

Price reductions granted for large-volume purchases are known as **quantity discounts**. Sellers justify these discounts on the grounds that large orders reduce selling expenses and may shift some costs for storage, transportation, and financing to buyers. The law allows quantity discounts provided they are applied on the same basis to all customers.

Quantity discounts may specify either cumulative or noncumulative terms. *Cumulative quantity discounts* reduce prices in amounts determined by purchases over stated time periods. Annual purchases of at least $25,000 might entitle a buyer to a 3 percent rebate, while purchases exceeding $50,000 would increase the refund to 5 percent. These reductions are really patronage discounts, since they tend to bind customers to a single supply source.

Noncumulative quantity discounts provide one-time reductions in the list price. For example, a firm might offer the following discount schedule for a product priced at $1,000 per unit:

1 unit	List: $1,000
2–5 units	List less 10 percent
6–10 units	List less 20 percent
Over 10 units	List less 25 percent

Many businesses have come to expect quantity discounts from suppliers. Ignoring these expectations can create competitive trouble for a firm. When United Parcel Service (UPS) balked at providing quantity discounts for large clients such as DuPont, it created an opportunity for competitors. One rival, Roadway Package System, lured several UPS customers by offering discounts to a wide range of organizational clients.

Marketers typically favor combinations of cash, trade, and volume discounts. For example, catalogers like Oriental Trading Co. that specializes in novelty products and Current, Inc. that specializes in stationery supplies offer their customers discounts according to how much they purchase. They typically place time limits on when such discounts are applicable for each catalog. In addition, Current includes free samples of seasonally-timed greeting cards for customers on their mailing list.

MARKETING DICTIONARY

trade discount Payment to a channel member or buyer for performing marketing functions; also known as a *functional discount*.

quantity discount Price reduction granted for a large-volume purchase.

FIGURE 19.8 | Promotional Pricing: A Competitive Pricing Tool for Automobile Dealers

Allowances

Allowances resemble discounts by specifying deductions from list price. The major categories of allowances are trade-ins and promotional allowances. **Trade-ins** are often used in sales of durable goods such as automobiles. The new product's basic list price remains unchanged, but the seller accepts less money from the customer along with a used product—usually the same kind of product as the buyer purchases.

Promotional allowances reduce prices as part of attempts to integrate promotional strategies within distribution channels. Manufacturers often return part of the prices that buyers pay in the form of advertising and sales-support allowances for channel members. Automobile manufacturers frequently offer allowances to retail dealers to induce those retailers to lower prices and stimulate sales. Dodge, for example, provides a program that allows dealers to pass savings on to car buyers. The Chevrolet Metro shown in Figure 19.8 offers car buyers one of the lowest priced sedans on the market. As the ad implies, consumers will pay higher monthly bills for food and shelter than for transportation when they choose this low-priced economy car. Frequently, dealers will offer even better deals with trade-ins, rebates, and various promotional allowances.

Rebates

In still another way to reduce a consumer's cost, marketers may offer a **rebate**—a refund of a portion of the purchase price. Rebates have appeared most prominently in automobile promotions by manufacturers eager to move models during periods of slow sales. However, firms have also offered rebates for sales in product categories ranging from appliances and sports equipment to grocery products and toiletries.

Bed manufacturer Sealy introduced its first rebate program to consumers with a promotion that sought to persuade buyers to focus on the upper end of the category. Rebate amounts

 sealy.com

ranged between $10 and $50 on super premium mattresses and between $15 and $75 on ultra premium mattresses. The rebate was a tool for retailers to move the consumer up the product line and an excellent incentive for the consumer to consider $799 and $899 bedding. The program reversed the trend of consumers buying less expensive mattresses.

Geographic Considerations

Rare is the 21st-century business whose operations are not affected by geographic considerations. In industries dominated by catalog and online marketers, these factors weigh heavily on the firm's ability to deliver orders in a cost-effective manner at the right time and place. In other instances, geographic factors affect the marketer's ability to receive additional inventory quickly in response to demand fluctuations. And while geographic considerations strongly influence prices when costs include shipping heavy, bulky, low-unit-value products, they can also impact lightweight, lower-cost products. Jerilyn Winstead discovered this when she attempted to market the BlanketStrap, a device she invented to give new mothers more privacy when nursing their babies in public places. The invention is a simple one: A strap wraps around the mother's neck and clips to the baby blanket. Winstead priced her products at a rock-bottom $4.99 and marketed it through baby-products catalogs. But practically no one ordered it. With the aid of a marketing researcher, she discovered the problem. Consumers were turned off by shipping and handling charges that were higher than the price she charged for the product.[8]

Buyers and sellers can handle transportation expenses in several ways: (1) The buyer pays all transportation charges; (2) the seller pays all transportation charges; or (3) the buyer and the seller share the charges. This choice has particularly important effects for a firm seeking to expand its geographic coverage to distant markets. How can a firm compete with local suppliers in distant markets who are able to avoid the considerable shipping costs that the firm must pay? The seller's pricing can implement several alternatives for handling transportation costs.

FOB (free on board) plant, or *FOB origin*, prices include no shipping charges. The buyer must pay all freight charges to transport the product from the manufacturer's dock. The seller pays only to load the merchandise aboard the carrier selected by the buyer. Legal title and responsibility pass to the buyer after the seller's employees load the purchase and accept a receipt from the representative of the common carrier.

Many marketing intermediaries, such as Virginia-based General Medical Corp., sell only on FOB plant terms to downstream channel members. These distributors believe that their customers have more clout than they do in dealing with long-distance carriers. They prefer to assign transportation costs to the channel members in the best positions to negotiate the most cost-effective shipping terms.

Sellers may also quote prices as *FOB origin-freight allowed*. These terms permit buyers to subtract transportation expenses from their bills. The amount such a seller receives for its product varies with the freight charged against the invoice. This alternative, also called **freight absorption**, is popular among firms with high fixed costs because it helps them to considerably expand their markets by quoting the same prices regardless of shipping expenses.

When a firm quotes the same price, including transportation expenses, to all buyers, it adopts a **uniform-delivered price** policy. Such a pricing structure is the exact opposite of FOB origin pricing. This system resembles the pricing structure for mail service, so it is sometimes called *postage-stamp pricing*. The price quote includes a transportation charge averaged over all of the firm's

MARKETING | **DICTIONARY**

trade-in Credit allowance given for a used item when a customer purchases a new item.

promotional allowance Advertising or sales promotion funds provided by a manufacturer to other channel members in an attempt to integrate promotional strategy within the channel.

rebate Refund for a portion of the purchase price, usually granted by the product's manufacturer.

FOB (free on board) plant Price quotation that does not include shipping charges; also called *FOB origin*.

freight absorption System for handling transportation costs under which the buyer may deduct shipping expenses from the cost of the goods.

uniform-delivered price System for handling transportation costs under which all buyers are quoted the same price, including transportation expenses.

Martin Guitars Play a New Tune

BACKGROUND Martin & Company began making all-wood guitars in 1833. Today the 6-generation family business is considered the Stradivarius of guitars. The rich tone of the fine musical instruments is the choice of the best guitar players in the world—Eric Clapton, Jimmy Buffett, and Elvis Costello all depend on their Martins to put music to their songs. At prices that begin at around $1,500 and rise above $15,000 for a custom guitar, it is no wonder Martin is considered the best brand money can buy.

THE CHALLENGE Christian Martin IV, the founder's great-great-great-grandson, recently decided that his firm must increase market share to remain competitive. Although most of his firm's $50 million annual sales come from higher-priced guitars, he is all too aware that two of every three new guitars sold carry a price tag well below $800.

continued on next page

usps.com

3

Identify the various pricing policy decisions that marketers must make.

---

customers, meaning that distant customers actually pay a smaller share of shipping costs while nearby customers pay what is known as *phantom freight* (the amount by which the average transportation charge exceeds the actual cost of shipping).

Zone pricing modifies a uniform delivered pricing system by dividing an overall market into different zones and establishing a single price within each zone. This pricing structure incorporates average transportation costs for shipments within each zone as part of the delivered price of goods sold there; by narrowing distances, it reduces but does not eliminate phantom freight. The primary advantage of zone pricing comes from easy administration methods that help a seller to compete in distant markets. The U.S. Postal Service's parcel rates depend on zone pricing.

In a **basing-point system**, the price of a product to a customer includes the list price at the factory plus freight charges from the basing-point city nearest the buyer. The basing point specifies a location from which to calculate freight charges—not necessarily the point from which the goods are shipped. In either case, the actual shipping point does not affect the price quotation. Such a system seeks to equalize competition between distant marketers since all competitors quote identical transportation rates. Few buyers would accept a basing-point system today, however.

The best-known basing-point system for many years was the Pittsburgh-plus pricing structure common in the steel industry. Steel buyers paid freight charges from Pittsburgh regardless of where the steel was produced. As the industry matured, manufacturing centers emerged in Chicago; Gary, Indiana; Cleveland; and Birmingham, Alabama. Still, Pittsburgh remained the basing point for steel pricing, forcing a buyer in Atlanta that purchased steel from a Birmingham mill to pay phantom freight from Pittsburgh.

PRICING POLICIES

Pricing policies contribute important information to buyers as they assess the firm's total image. A coherent policy provides an overall framework and consistency that guides day-to-day pricing decisions. Formally, a **pricing policy** is a general guideline that reflects marketing objectives and influences specific pricing decisions.

Decisions concerning price structure generally tend to focus on technical, detailed questions, while decisions concerning pricing policies cover broader issues. Price structure decisions take the firm's pricing policy as a given, from which they specify applicable discounts. Pricing policies have important strategic effects, particularly in guiding competitive efforts. They form the basis for more practical price-structure decisions.

Firms implement variations of four basic types of pricing policies: psychological pricing, price flexibility, product-line pricing, and promotional pricing. Specific policies deal effectively with various competitive situations; the final choice depends on the environment within which marketers must make their pricing decisions.

Psychological Pricing

Psychological pricing applies the belief that certain prices or price ranges make products more appealing to buyers than others. No research offers a consistent foundation for such thinking, however, and studies often report mixed findings. Nevertheless, marketers practice several forms of psychological pricing. Chapter 18 discussed one—prestige pricing. Two more psychological pricing techniques include odd pricing and unit pricing.

In **odd pricing**, marketers set prices at odd numbers just under round numbers. Many retailers assume that a price of $4.99 appeals more strongly to consumers than $5.00, supposedly because buyers interpret it as $4.00 plus change. Odd pricing originated as a way to force clerks to make change, thus serving as a cash-control device. Odd pricing remains a common feature of contemporary price quotations.

Some producers and retailers practice odd pricing but avoid prices ending in 5, 9, or 0. These marketers believe that customers view price tags of $5.95, $5.99, or $6.00 as regular retail prices, but they think of an amount like $5.97 as a discount price.

Unit pricing states prices in terms of some recognized unit of measurement (such as grams and liters) or a standard numerical count. Unit pricing arose to improve convenience when consumer advocates complained about the difficulty of comparing the true prices of products packaged in different sizes. These advocates felt that posting prices in terms of standard units would help shoppers make better-informed purchases. Some supermarket chains have come to regard unit pricing as a competitive tool, and they feature it extensively in advertising. However, unit pricing has not improved consumers' shopping habits as much as supporters originally envisioned that it would. Instead, research shows that standard price quotes most often affect purchases only by relatively well-educated consumers with high earnings.

Price Flexibility

Stradivarius Marketing executives must also set company policies for **price flexibility**—that is, the choice between just one price or variable prices. Generally, one-price policies suit mass-selling marketing programs, whereas variable pricing suits marketing programs based on individual bargaining. In a large department store, customers do not expect to haggle over prices with retail salespeople; instead, they expect to pay the amounts shown on the price tags. Generally, customers pay less only when the retailer replaces regular prices with sale prices.

Traditionally, car buyers have come to expect variable pricing policies from dealers. During the 1990s, however, when Saturn marketers chose to stray from the norm with a nonnegotiable pricing policy on its vehicles, many other automakers such as Ford and Honda were attracted to its success and followed suit. More recently, the trend toward fixed pricing is quickly moving back to flexible pricing policies as a result of the intense competition that accompanies e-commerce. Not only are car prices highly negotiable online, but they now frequently include special deals on everything from theater tickets to bank loans to camcorders. As Chapter 4 pointed out, e-commerce technologies allow sellers to collect detailed data about customers' buying habits, preferences, and spending limits that marketers can use to tailor their products and prices.[9]

The telecommunications industry, on the other hand, is now moving to flat-rate pricing strategies. Take cellular-phone service, for example. In the early 1990s, cell-phone customers paid different rates for different times of the day. Then AT&T introduced the one-rate nationwide plan. Combining long-distance with cell calls refined the entire industry's pricing strategies. AT&T marketers made it simpler and more affordable by offering one rate for the entire country, no matter when the call was made. Leading competitor Worldcom quickly followed suit by offering its own one-rate plan. Today, an increasing number of people use cell phones as their only phones.[10]

While variable pricing adds some flexibility to selling situations, it may conflict with provisions of the Robinson-Patman Act. It may also lead to retaliatory pricing by competitors, and it may stir complaints among customers who find that they paid higher prices than necessary.

Product-Line Pricing

Since most firms market multiple product lines, an effective pricing strategy

MARKETING STRATEGY SUCCESS

THE STRATEGY Martin centered his firm's growth strategy around adding a new, lower-priced guitar to its product line. The new DXM model held costs down by using layers of wood fiber and glue covered with decals of spruce and mahogany grains. While it did not contain the fine rosewood and spice hardwoods used in the more expensive models, it produced a high-quality sound—and it sold for around $450.

THE OUTCOME Even at this low price, the high-quality sound of the DXM did not harm the Martin image. The firm continues to offer its top-of-the-line, high-priced guitars, which account for 40 percent of annual revenues and 60 percent of profits. But, by 2001, one of every four Martin guitars sold will be the low-priced DXM model. The aggressive move in adding the new product line strengthened Martin's competitive position at the dawn of the 21st century.

MARKETING DICTIONARY

zone pricing System for handling transportation costs under which the market is divided into geographic regions and a different price is set in each region.

basing-point system System for handling transportation costs used in some industries during the early 20th century in which the buyer's costs included the factory price plus freight charges from the basing-point city nearest the buyer.

pricing policy General guidelines based on pricing objectives and intended for use in specific pricing decisions.

psychological pricing Pricing policy based on the belief that certain prices or price ranges make a good or service more appealing than others to buyers.

odd pricing Pricing policy based on the belief that a price ending with an odd number just under a round number is more appealing—for instance, $9.97 rather than $10.

unit pricing Pricing policy in which prices are stated in terms of a recognized unit of measurement or a standard numerical count.

price flexibility Pricing policy permitting variable prices for goods and services.

must consider the relationships among all of these products instead of viewing each in isolation. **Product-line pricing** is the practice of setting a limited number of prices for a selection of merchandise. For example, a clothier might offer three lines of men's suits—one priced at $375, a second at $525, and the most expensive at $695. These price points help the retailer define important product characteristics that differentiate the three product lines and contribute to customer choices to trade up and trade down.

Retailers practice extensive product-line pricing. In earlier days, five-and-dime variety stores exemplified this technique. It remains popular, however, because it offers advantages to both retailers and customers. Shoppers can choose desired price ranges and then concentrate on other product variables such as colors, styles, and materials. Retailers can purchase and offer specific lines in limited price categories instead of more general assortments with dozens of different prices.

Airlines have long divided their seating areas according to product-line pricing. Each flight offers a certain percentage of discount, business-class, first-class, and coach-price seats on each flight. On an overseas flight, for instance, the industry averages about 18 percent business-class seats. A round-trip, business-class ticket from Houston to Paris on Continental Airlines costs almost twice the regular coach fare and several times more than the discount fare.

Marketers must resolve one problem with product-line pricing, though. Once they decide on a limited number of prices to change as price lines, they may have difficulty making price changes on individual items. Rising costs, therefore, force sellers to either change the price lines, which results in confusion, or reduce costs through production adjustments. The second option opens the firm to customer complaints that its merchandise is not what it used to be.

Promotional Pricing

In **promotional pricing**, a lower-than-normal price is used as a temporary ingredient in a firm's selling strategy. Some promotional pricing arrangements form part of recurrent marketing initiatives, such as a shoe store's annual "buy one pair, get the second pair for one cent" sale. Another example would be "7 CDs for 1 cent." This artificially low price attracts customers who must then agree to purchase a set number of CDs within a specified time limit. Another firm may introduce a promotional model or brand with a special price to begin competing in a new market.

Leader Pricing and Loss Leaders

Retailers rely most heavily on promotional pricing. In one type of technique, stores offer **loss leaders**—goods priced below cost to attract customers who, the retailer hopes, will also buy other, regularly priced merchandise. Loss leaders can form part of an effective marketing program, but states with unfair-trade laws prohibit the practice, as discussed in Chapter 18.

Retailers frequently use a variant of loss-leader pricing called *leader pricing*. To avoid violating minimum-markup regulations and to earn some return on promotional sales, they offer so-called *leader merchandise* at prices slightly above cost. Among the most frequent practitioners of this combination pricing/promotion strategy are supermarkets and mass merchandisers such as Wal-Mart, Kmart, and Target. Retailers sometimes treat private-label products (like Sam's Choice colas at Wal-Mart stores) as leader merchandise since prices of the store brands average 5 percent to 60 percent less than those of comparable national brands. While store brand goods generate lower per-unit revenues than national brands would produce, higher sales volume will probably offset some of the difference, as will related sales of high-margin products like toiletries and cosmetics.

The personal-computer industry provides an excellent example of this trend in pricing. In the early 1990s, PCs cost approximately $3,000 to $5,000. By 1998, however, the industry was embroiled in a heated price war. Profit margins virtually disappeared, and many small manufacturers were shut down. In fact, there were no winners. IBM lost $1 billion on its PC business; Compaq, Hewlett-Packard, Apple Computer, and Dell also entered the sub-$1,000 market, and profits plummeted. So how are these companies surviving with PC prices as low as $399? They have realigned their operations to provide services they can bundle along with products. Many entrepreneurs, Internet-service providers, and telecommunications companies are handing out free hardware in hopes that services and accessory products will generate enough revenues to cover losses.[11]

Marketers should anticipate two potential pitfalls when making a promotional pricing decision:

1. Some consumers do not react strongly to promotional pricing.
2. By maintaining an artificially low price for a period of time, marketers may lead customers to expect it as a customary feature of the product. For example, grocers treated poultry as a loss leader during the 1930s and 1940s, and it has long suffered price pressure as a result. Airlines may suffer a similar fate. Pervasive ticket discounting has taught consumers to expect to pay prices below full fare. As a result, airlines are losing money because many travelers will fly only if they can get discounted fares.

Price-Quality Relationships

One of the most thoroughly researched aspects of pricing is its relationship to consumer perceptions of product quality. In the absence of other cues, price serves as an important indicator of a product's quality to prospective purchasers. Many buyers interpret high prices as signals of high-quality products.

The relationship between price and perceived quality provides a widely used tool for contemporary marketers. Ads for Maytag's Neptune washing machines equate its above-average price with above-average performance. As one company representative explains, "They are willing to pay a lot more to save time or obtain significant benefits." Even though the environmentally-friendly Neptune's price tag of $1,100 is more than twice the cost of a conventional washer, both its market-leading price and the benefits emphasized in its promotions enhance the image of quality. Promotional materials point out that each year the Neptune will use $100 less electricity and save 7,000 gallons of water over its competitors.[12]

The strong U.S. economy has also benefited marketers of upscale services. Consider Hands On, for example. The Los Angeles–based nail salon offers a basic manicure for $16. However, prices go up for enhanced nail treatments. Add exfoliation of the hands and forearms and a 5-minute massage on each arm, and the price doubles to $32, and for $99 the customer can receive the *creme de la creme* in pampering: a nail technician at each limb massaging, buffing, moisturizing, and polishing nails; a neck and shoulder massage; and a gift basket of personal-care items. Hands On founders Anthony Wootton and Michael Wolper reasoned that if they offered superior quality service, LA shoppers would be willing to pay premium prices. So far, success has been tremendous, and the salon expects to open new locations in southern California, New York, and Miami.[13]

Probably the best statement of the price-quality connection is the idea of *price limits*. Supporters of this idea argue that consumers define certain limits within which their product-quality perceptions vary directly with price. A potential buyer regards a price below the lower limit as too cheap, whereas a price above the higher limit seems too expensive. This perception holds true for both national brands and private-label products. U.S. commercial airlines have recently felt the pain of failing to recognize their customers' price limits. Last year, business travelers revolted against high-priced fares and began looking for alternative ways to save on travel,

Relate price to consumer perceptions of quality.

MARKETING | **DICTIONARY**

product-line pricing Practice of marketing different lines of merchandise at a limited number of prices.

promotional pricing Pricing policy in which a lower than normal price is used as a temporary ingredient in a firm's marketing strategy.

loss leader Product offered to consumers at less than cost to attract them to stores in the hope that they will buy other merchandise at regular prices.

SOLVING AN ETHICAL CONTROVERSY

PCs for Free

"Here's the deal, customer: We'll give you a house, but what we want is your utility bill, your Internet access, and your telephone service for the rest of your life and the rest of your children's lives," joked Gateway CEO Ted Waitt recently. He was referring to the recent trend in cybermarketing of offering a free personal computer in exchange for consumer information.

Recently, FreePC.com, an Internet-based market research company, announced it would distribute 10,000 new computers free to applicants willing to provide information such as age, income, and hobbies. If the program proved successful, FreePC would increase the size of the giveaway to as many as 1 million PCs. The concept is similar to one used by cell-phone companies that give away phones to attract subscribers to the service. Even though PC prices have fallen dramatically in recent months, the initial cost continues to be the primary barrier preventing more people from buying their own computer and getting Internet access.

Consumer advocates support the distribution of free PCs but worry that people who receive them may be unaware of the long-term effects of giving away personal information. Many of these offers do not specify how the information they gather will be used or protected. In addition to privacy issues, the free PCs are not top-of-the-line and often have little hard-drive capability left since so much space is taken up with all of the promotions and advertisements contained therein. As one consumer advocate quipped, "Free is good—but read the small print."

 Should the acquisition of personal information by marketers be more tightly regulated?

Pro
1. Some regulation is necessary to prevent information gatherers from taking advantage of consumers. Consumers should be informed about how the information will be used and whether it will be given to other parties without the owner's approval.

2. Without regulation, children may be targeted as information providers, letting strangers find out information about their families' behaviors and lifestyles.

3. Some people will sell anything for the right price. Without regulation it would be possible to sell false information, which may lead to misconceptions and poor decision making by the purchasers.

Con
1. People have total ownership of their personal information and can do what they like with it.

2. The United States was colonized by people who sold their labor and years of their lives in exchange for passage to the "free world." Selling personal information is an individual choice that should not be interfered with by regulations.

3. Regulating information gathering would severely hinder marketing research. The U.S. government already collects an enormous amount of personal information in its 10-year census.

Summary
Gathering personal information with offers of free computers can be beneficial to marketers who want to increase their knowledge about how the Internet is being used. To reach online consumers, marketers must first get them online; that is why they are giving the PCs away in the first place. At this point, the consumer still has the option of choosing whether to let companies monitor their behavior. As Beth Givens, director of the Privacy Rights Clearing House, points out, consumers must ask, "What guarantee is there that the data that's gathered, which could be significant, will not be used sometime in the future for law enforcement investigations, insurance purposes, employment, or decision making?"

SOURCES: Michael White, "Compaqs Exchanged for Consumer Information," *Marketing News*, March 15, 1999, p. 9; David P. Hamilton, "PCs for Under $600 Seize a Chunk of the Market," *Wall Street Journal*, March 26, 1999, pp. B1, B4; and Ann Grimes and Nicole Harris, "How Low Can You Go?" *Wall Street Journal*, July 1, 1999, p. B4.

@ **travelscape.com**

including using the Internet to find cheaper fares and chartering their own planes. In fact, General Motors and DaimlerChrysler are backing an upstart airline to keep prices competitive on flights in and out of Detroit. Meanwhile, airlines are continuing to board the same number of passengers but with less profit margin. The ad in Figure 19.9 for TravelScape.com promises travelers the lowest rates, or it will pay the difference. Not only does TravelScape guarantee discount travel fares, but it also offers convenience, selection, 24/7 customer care, and—most important—value.[14]

In some South American and Asian countries, hyperinflation has left little relationship in consumers' minds between price and quality. In Brazil during the mid 1990s, for example, a consumer could buy a deluxe ice-cream sundae or two kitchen blenders for 950 cruzados ($15). Moreover, prices for a single product also varied tremendously from store to store. Consequently, a consumer could end up paying anywhere from 2 cruzados ($.03) to 21 cruzados for a pencil eraser.

COMPETITIVE BIDDING AND NEGOTIATED PRICES

Many government and organizational procurement departments do not pay set prices for their purchases, particularly for large, nonrecurring purchases such as a weapons system for the Department of Defense. Instead, they determine prices through competitive bidding, a process in which they invite potential suppliers to quote prices on proposed purchases or contracts. Detailed specifications describe the good or service that the government or organization wishes to acquire. One of the most important tasks in purchasing management is to develop accurate descriptions of products that the organization seeks to buy. This process generally requires the assistance of the firm's technical personnel, such as engineers, designers, and chemists.

In some cases, business and government purchasers negotiate contracts with favored suppliers instead of inviting competitive bids from all interested parties. The terms of such a contract emerge through offers and counteroffers between the buyer and the seller.

Where only one supplier offers a desired product or where projects require extensive research and development, buyers and sellers often set purchase terms through negotiated contracts. In addition, some state and local governments permit their agencies to negotiate purchases under certain dollar limits—say $500 or $1,000. This policy seeks to eliminate economic waste that would result from obtaining and processing bids for relatively minor purchases.

Negotiating Prices Online

As the Priceline example featured at the beginning of the chapter describes, many people today see the 21st century cyberworld as one big auction site. Whether it is toys, art, or automobiles, there seems to be an online auction site to serve every person's needs—buyer and seller alike. Auctions are the purest form of negotiated pricing. As Figure 19.10 shows, buyers and sellers electronically communicate ask and bid prices until a mutually agreed upon price is set.

Ticket sales are an online auction favorite. Whether it is a Broadway show, a NASCAR race, a trip to the zoo, or an 'N Sync concert, you can find tickets online. Tickets.com catalogs the dates, times, and locations of everything from concerts to museum exhibits. It recently tied in with the Advantix ticketing system, opening up a sales site for sports venues. In addition, Tickets.com also functions as a reseller through its own online auctions. Super Bowl tickets in January were selling online for $1,500 each, and tickets to the *Lion King* on Broadway were bringing $110.[15]

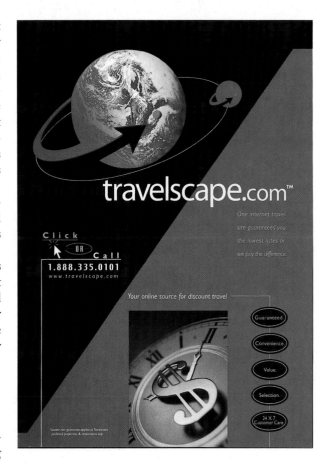

FIGURE 19.9 TravelScape.com: Guaranteed Low Prices

5 Contrast competitive bidding and negotiated prices.

THE TRANSFER PRICING DILEMMA

6 Explain the importance of transfer pricing.

A pricing problem peculiar to large-scale enterprises is the determination of an internal **transfer price**—the price for moving goods between **profit centers**, which are any part of the organization to which revenue and controllable costs can be assigned, such as a department. As companies expand, they tend to decentralize management and set up profit centers as a control device in the newly decentralized operation.

MARKETING DICTIONARY

transfer price Cost assessed when a product is moved from one profit center in a firm to another.

profit center Any part of an organization to which revenue and controllable costs can be assigned.

FIGURE 19.10	Online Auctions: Purest Form of Negotiated Pricing

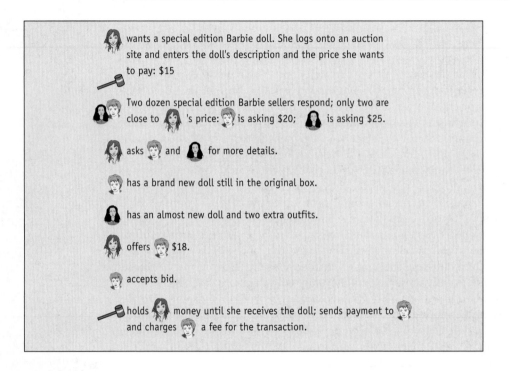

In a large company, profit centers might secure many needed resources from sellers within their own organization. The pricing problem thus poses several questions: What rate should profit center A (maintenance department) charge profit center B (sales department) for the cleansing compound used on B's floors. Should the price be the same as it would be if A did the work for an outside party? Should B receive a discount? The answers to these questions depend on the philosophy of the firm involved.

Transfer pricing can be a complicated process, especially for multinational organizations. The government closely monitors transfer pricing practices because these exchanges offer easy ways for companies to avoid paying taxes on profits. Figure 19.11 shows how this type of pricing manipulation might work. Suppose that a South Korean VCR manufacturer sells its machines to its U.S. subsidiary for distribution to dealers. Although each unit costs $50 to build, the manufacturer charges the distributor $150. In turn, the distributor sells the VCRs to retailers for $200 each. This arrangement gives the South Korean manufacturer a $100 profit on each machine, on which it pays taxes only in South Korea. Meanwhile, the American distributor writes off $50 for advertising and shipping costs, leaving it with no profits—and no tax liability.

Companies may run into legal trouble over transfer pricing, even if they intended no wrongdoing. A few years ago, the Internal Revenue Service (IRS) disputed Apple Computer's tax returns. The argument arose over transfer pricing on products that Apple bought from its Singapore manufacturing plant. The IRS slapped Apple with a bill for back taxes on $100 million that the IRS claimed constituted extra income.

GLOBAL CONSIDERATIONS AND ONLINE PRICING

7

Compare the three alternative global pricing strategies.

Throughout the text and especially in Chapter 4, we have seen the impact of the Internet on every component of the marketing mix. This chapter has touched on the outer edges of the Net's influence on pricing practices. Remember that every online marketer is inherently a global marketer who must understand the wide variety of internal and external conditions that affect global

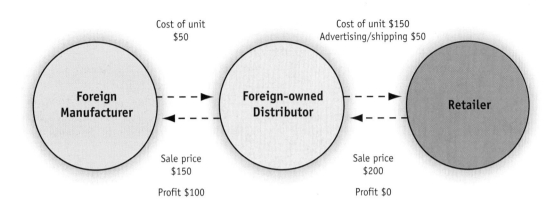

| FIGURE 19.11 | Transfer Pricing to Escape Taxation |

Cost of unit
$50

Cost of unit $150
Advertising/shipping $50

Foreign Manufacturer   **Foreign-owned Distributor**   **Retailer**

Sale price
$150

Sale price
$200

Profit $100

Profit $0

pricing strategies. Internal influences include the firm's goals and marketing strategies; the costs of developing, producing, and marketing its products; the nature of the products; and the firm's competitive strengths. External influences include general conditions in international markets, especially those in the firm's target markets; regulatory limitations; trade restrictions; competitors' actions; economic events; and the global status of the industry.

Traditional Global Pricing Strategies

In general, a company can implement one of three export pricing strategies: a standard worldwide price, dual pricing, or market-differentiated pricing. Exporters often set standard worldwide prices, regardless of their target markets. This strategy can succeed if foreign marketing costs remain low enough that they do not impact overall costs or if their prices reflect average unit costs. A company that implements a standard pricing program must monitor the international marketplace carefully, however, to make sure that domestic competitors do not undercut its prices.

The dual pricing strategy distinguishes prices for domestic and export sales. Some exporters practice cost-plus pricing to establish dual prices that fully allocate their true domestic and foreign costs to product sales in those markets. While these prices ensure that an exporter makes a profit on any product it sells, final prices may exceed those of competitors. Other companies opt for flexible cost-plus pricing schemes that allow marketers to grant discounts or change prices according to shifts in the competitive environment or fluctuations in the international exchange rate.

The third strategy, market-differentiated pricing, makes even more flexible arrangements to set prices according to local marketplace conditions. The dynamic global marketplace often requires frequent price changes by exporters who choose this approach. Effective market-differentiated pricing depends on access to quick, accurate market information.

Marketers for Glaxo Wellcome's AIDS drugs practice market-differentiated pricing in their global marketing strategies. While they cannot openly admit that they are levying a North American surcharge on the drug, marketers can set a high price on the treatment for wealthier patients in America while setting low prices in poverty-stricken and disease-ridden areas in Africa. Glaxo marketers refer to these lower prices as a humanitarian gesture by their firm.[16]

Characteristics of Online Pricing

In order to deal with the influences of the Net on pricing policies and practices, marketers are applying old strategies in new ways and companies are updating operations to compete with new electronic technologies.

MARKETING STRATEGY FAILURE

Buying College Textbooks Online— Not In Line

BACKGROUND For decades, the 3,100-member National Association of College Stores (NACS) has controlled the campus bookstore market with little or no competition. Although their traditional drawing card has been textbooks, in reality, texts are the least profitable part of college stores' inventory. They take up lots of space and are sold only about one week per term. Talk to the bookstore manager and you will quickly learn that the key to bookstore profits can be found in all of the college-logo merchandise, office and general supplies, music, gifts, and snacks. In fact, used books are much more profitable than the sale of new ones. Bookstores typically apply a 50 percent markup on the sale of used books, as compared with 33 percent on new-book sales.

THE MARKETING PROBLEM Online bookstores such as VarsityBooks and BigWords have crashed the $8.5 billion college textbook market, sending traditional campus stores in a spin. Promotion efforts to attract attention include campus newspaper, radio, and TV ads, as well as contests and discount coupons. In some

continued on next page

 8

Relate the concepts of cannibalization, bundle pricing, and bots to online pricing strategies.

MARKETING
STRATEGY
FAILURE

cases, Internet purchasing produces a small savings of 5 to 10 percent; in other instances, online and in-store prices are identical. The major advantage of Web purchasing is avoiding the hassle of fighting crowds at the bookstore.

THE OUTCOME Although the diversion of textbook sales has not taken huge profits from the college bookstores, the reductions in student traffic has many of them worried. Not only are book sales lagging, but other high-profit merchandise is not moving off the shelves. A growing number of traditional bookstores have responded by offering their own online options for students. These online "companion retailers" emphasize the benefits of having a bricks-and-mortar store on campus to handle customer-service issues such as book returns for dropped courses, wider selection of used books, and one-stop shopping (since most online sellers will not have access to customized classroom materials).

LESSONS LEARNED Even the most captive market will eventually leave when competitors find a way to provide lower prices and added convenience. Campus stores that view textbooks as necessary evils must attract shoppers or lose prospective purchasers of their higher-margin merchandise.

One new application of a traditional pricing practice is **cannibalization**. The new twist to an old tactic is that companies are self-inflicting price cuts by creating competition among their own products. By building new e-businesses designed to compete head-on with the mother company, marketers are hoping to survive the transition from bricks-and-mortar to electronic storefronts on the Web. e.Schwab cannibalized its parent company Charles Schwab when it offered online investors a flat $29.95 transaction fee. Traditional clients, who were still being charged $65 per trade, demanded and received the same flat fee.[17]

Books-A-Million, the nation's third largest bookstore chain, sells such top-20 best-sellers as the newest John Grisham legal thriller at 40 percent below list price. But click on the company Web site and you can buy the same book at a dazzling 55 percent discount. Why sell the book online at a lower price than you charge at the store? Books-A-Million's head of online marketing describes it as a purely defensive move—the company would rather have the business than lose it to Amazon.com.

As marketers have watched e-commerce weaken their control over prices, they have modified their use of the price variable in the marketing mix. Whenever possible, they have moved to an approach called **bundle pricing**, where customers acquire a host of goods and services in addition to the tangible products they purchase. In Dallas, SBC Communications' customers can purchase a full-service bundle for $137 a month. This entitles the household to two telephone lines; DirectTV satellite television; discounted local toll calling, wireless calling, and dial-up Internet services; inside wire maintenance on both lines; and 13 add-on features such as voice mail and caller ID. The personal computer industry has proven the feasibility of almost giving away products that require installation, hook-ups, and ongoing maintenance. In the face of intense price competition for PCs, these firms generate earnings by supplying software, Internet access, e-mail, and downloaded pay-per-view entertainment.[18]

Still another characteristic of online pricing is the use of search programs called *bots*—short for robots—that act as comparison shopping agents. As Chapter 5 explained, bots hunt the Web for a specific product, then print out a list of sites that offer the best prices. For Web-based marketers, bots force prices to be kept low. Marketing researchers, however, point out that 79 percent of all shoppers check out several sites before buying, and price is not the only variable that cybershoppers consider when making a purchase decision. For example, the quality of service and support information is a powerful motivator in the decision-making process. Also, while price is an important factor with products such as CDs and books, it is not as important with complex or highly differentiated products, such as real estate or investment banking. Customer service and brand image often outweigh price in these purchase decisions.[19]

STRATEGIC IMPLICATIONS

Over the years, price was, arguably, the marketing variable least likely to be used as a source of competitive advantage. Even in industries where the discounting phenomenon resulted in radical changes in customer service levels, marketers gradually moved away from this competitive weapon. In moves consistent with Chapter 14's discussion of the wheel of retailing theory, minimal-service, low-priced operations added services and prices began to creep up. Some retailers—including giants like Wal-Mart with annual sales that match the gross domestic product of Canada—continued to use price as a major (but not sole) feature. But firms who use price to attract and retain customers cannot be ignored, and the risk of dangerous, money-losing price wars in such industries is ever present. Not surprisingly, then, many marketers drift toward developing marketing mixes that feature non-price competition.

But technology has forever changed these markets. The traditional geographic monopolies that permitted inefficient marketers to continue in business are being destroyed by lower-priced, big-selection mass merchandisers whose rapid expansion now places them within a few miles of most shoppers. Category killers operate in fields as diverse as office supplies and pet food, sporting goods and books, and toys and pharmaceuticals.

In addition to the new breed of high-volume marketers featuring unsurpassed selections and major price savings, the Internet has delivered competition to the homes and offices of even the most geographically-isolated shoppers. For example, a customer in Kansas might want to purchase a walking stick from Kenya or an ornamental fan from Kyoto. Not a problem—the Web connects buyers and sellers around the globe. Similarly, the cost of shipping an overnight FedEx package from New York to California is no more than shipping it to a nearby city. Even groceries can be ordered and brought to the customer's doorstep for a minimal delivery charge.

Not only is it possible to escape the boundaries of time and space on the Internet, but price is no longer a constant in the marketing process. With the increasing number of auction sites and new search technologies like bots, customers now have more power to control the prices of goods and services. Not only can consumers find the lowest prices on the market, but they can also negotiate prices for many of the products they buy.

What marketers must continue to do to remain successful in the 21st century is offer value— good prices for quality goods and services—and superior customer service. These factors will be the critical success factors in marketing in the new millennium.

ACHIEVEMENT CHECK SUMMARY

Read the learning objectives that follow, and consider the questions for each one. Answering these questions will reinforce your grasp of the most important concepts in the chapter and will allow you to check how well you have achieved these learning goals. Where a blank appears before a question, answer with a *T* or *F* for true/false questions; for multiple-choice questions, choose the letter of the correct answer.

Objective 19.1: Compare the alternative pricing strategies and explain when each strategy is most appropriate.

1. _____ Marketers often practice penetration pricing in industries with few products and little competition.

2. _____ Most firms follow variations of the competitive pricing strategy.

3. _____ A skimming pricing strategy sets a high market-entry price for a product with little or no initial competition.

Objective 19.2: Describe how prices are quoted.

1. _____ Methods for quoting prices depend on all of the following variables except (a) cost structures; (b) traditional industry practices; (c) the quantity produced; (d) policies of individual firms.

2. _____ FOB plant pricing (a) sets price objectives; (b) allows a buyer to deduct transportation expenses from a bill; (c) includes no shipping charges; (d) sets a single price within each region.

3. _____ Price quotes involve all of the following elements except (a) list prices; (b) customer demand; (c) market prices; (d) trade discounts.

Objective 19.3: Identify the various pricing policy decisions that marketers must make.

1. _____ A pricing policy is a general guideline based on a firm's pricing objectives.

2. _____ Marketers follow pricing policies in making long-term competitive pricing decisions.

3. _____ Pricing policy choices include psychological pricing, unit pricing, price flexibility, product-line pricing, and promotional pricing.

Objective 19.4: Relate price to consumer perceptions of quality.

1. _____ In general, consumers perceive a high price as a symbol of high quality.

2. _____ Price limits are directly associated with supply and demand.

3. _____ The concept of price limits suggests that unusually low prices may indicate poor quality.

Objective 19.5: Contrast competitive bidding and negotiated prices.

1. _____ Buyers and sellers negotiate prices most often when (a) multiple suppliers compete for an order; (b) only one available supplier can fill an order; (c) contracts cover unchanging and routine purchases; (d) prices are set once and remain unchanged.

2. _____ Competitive bidding involves all of the following situations, except (a) price quotations from various suppliers on a proposed contract; (b) input from engineers, designers, and other technical personnel; (c) specifications that describe the project; (d) limits on the contract price.

Objective 19.6: Explain the importance of transfer pricing.

1. _____ A transfer price determines the cost of goods or services exchanged between departments or divisions within a larger organization.

2. _____ Transfer pricing assigns simple, clear-cut costs for exchanges between profit centers.

3. _____ Profit centers function as control devices in large, decentralized organizations.

Objective 19.7: Compare the three alternative global pricing strategies.

1. _____ Firms almost always implement the same pricing strategies for domestic and export sales.

2. _____ Firms can implement three alternative export pricing strategies: a standard worldwide price, dual pricing, or market-differentiated pricing.

3. _____ Market-differentiated pricing allows a firm to price its products according to local marketplace conditions.

Objective 19.8: Relate the concepts of cannibalization, bundle pricing, and bots to online pricing strategies.

MARKETING DICTIONARY

cannibalization Securing additional sales through lower prices that take sales away from the marketer's other products.

bundle pricing Offering two or more complementary products and selling them for a single price.

1. _____ Cannibalization is a pricing strategy used by international marketers when entering new markets.

2. _____ When companies have limited inventory, they often bundle assorted products together with low-price offers.

3. _____ Bots are search programs that help customers find the lowest prices for goods and services.

Students: See the solutions section located on page S-3 to check your responses to the Achievement Check Summary.

Key Terms

skimming pricing strategy	zone pricing
penetration pricing strategy	basing-point system
everyday low pricing (EDLP)	pricing policy
competitive pricing strategy	psychological pricing
list price	odd pricing
market price	unit pricing
cash discount	price flexibility
trade discount	product-line pricing
quantity discount	promotional pricing
trade-in	loss leader
promotional allowance	transfer price
rebate	profit center
FOB (free on board) plant	cannibalization
freight absorption	bundle pricing
uniform-delivered price	

Review Questions

1. What is a skimming pricing strategy? What benefits does it offer for a firm?

2. What is penetration pricing? Under what circumstances do marketers prefer penetration pricing?

3. What is everyday low pricing? Explain why it stirs controversy among marketers and retailers.

4. Contrast the freight absorption and uniform delivery pricing systems. Cite examples of each. How does a basing-point system incorporate transportation costs? Discuss Pittsburgh-plus pricing in the steel industry.

5. Define the term *pricing policy*. List and discuss the reasons for establishing pricing policies.

6. When does a price become a promotional price? What pitfalls does a firm risk in promotional pricing?

7. How does price relate to consumer perceptions of quality? Give examples of your perception of an acceptable price range for a common consumer good or service, such as toothpaste, a haircut, or mouthwash. How might a price outside this range affect your image of the product's quality?

8. What is a transfer price? How does it affect management of a large organization?

9. Describe three possible strategies that a company might follow to price exports.

10. Give examples of how marketers can benefit from using cannibalization, bundle pricing, and bots in their pricing strategies.

Questions for Critical Thinking

1. Skimming pricing, penetration pricing, and competitive pricing are the three alternative pricing strategies. Which of the three appears most appropriate for the following products? Defend your answers.
   a. Nintendo video game
   b. digital television
   c. fuel additive that substantially increases automobile mileage
   d. remote-control burglar, smoke, and fire alarm
   e. new brand of men's cologne

2. Frequent-flyer programs are discount schemes designed by airlines to secure and reward consumer loyalty. In what category of discount plans do these programs fit? Explain. What potential dangers may limit the effectiveness of such programs?

3. How do sellers quote prices for each of the following products?
   a. American Airlines ticket to Buenos Aires
   b. installation of a flashing sign by a local contractor
   c. scuba-diving suit from a sportswear retailer
   d. new Lincoln Navigator sport utility vehicle

4. Assume that a product sells for $100 per ton and that Pittsburgh is the basing-point city for calculating transportation charges. Shipping from Pittsburgh to a potential customer in Cincinnati costs $10 per ton. The actual shipping costs of suppliers in three other cities are $8 per ton for Supplier A, $11 per ton for Supplier B, and $10 per ton for Supplier C. Using this information, answer the following questions:
   a. What delivered price would a salesperson for Supplier A quote to the Cincinnati customer?
   b. What delivered price would a salesperson for Supplier B quote to the Cincinnati customer?
   c. What delivered price would a salesperson for Supplier C quote to the Cincinnati customer?
   d. How much would each supplier net (after subtracting actual shipping costs) per ton on the sale?

5. Use the campus library or the Internet to identify the major alliances, mergers, and acquisitions by AT&T or Worldcom during the past two years. Which of these combinations may have been influenced by bundle pricing? Explain.

1. **Rebates.** Assume you are going to purchase a new car and want to use the Internet to find out what rebates are currently available on certain cars. Use your search engine to find rebate information such as that found at *www.edmunds.com* and then select the best rebate offer—based on a car you might like to purchase and the attractiveness of the rebate.

edmunds.com

2. **Loss Leaders.** The following notice appeared in an April 2, 1999, E-Commerce News feature at *www.internetnews.com* titled "PriceGrabber.com Finds Loss-Leaders": "PriceGrabber.com allows consumers to use technology that automatically searches the Internet for products that are sold below cost, as "loss leaders." Go to *www.pricegrabber.com*, find a bargain, and bring a description of it, including pricing details, to use as an example during class discussion.

pricegrabber.com

3. **Negotiating Prices Online.** The Priceline example featured at the beginning of the chapter describes the four distinct product categories featured at the company's site. No doubt between the time this textbook went to press and the time you are reading this exercise, Priceline has made changes to its product categories. Visit *www.priceline.com* and update the textbook description of this Web site.

priceline.com

Video Case 19 on Learjet begins on page VC-21.

Gateway Continuing Case Part 8 begins on page GC-13.

VIDEO CASE CONTENTS

Neiman Marcus

You've probably never spent $3,000 for a suit, even if the label came from a designer and the quality was impeccable. But would you drive several hours to shop at a store that carried all the clothing brands and styles you loved? Maybe, if you were a diehard shopper and you felt a strong bond with the store. What if the store offered you a trip to Paris for your loyalty? It might happen if you're a Neiman Marcus shopper.

Neiman Marcus. The name tumbles across the tongue, conjuring up visions of affluence, high fashion, and an anxiously-awaited annual catalog featuring exotic—and expensive—holiday gifts for the recipient whose closets and carports are already filled with clothing and cars most of us would die for. The specialty retailer that traces its beginnings to Dallas, opened early during the last century and has gradually expanded nationally to 15 states and more than 30 locations from Boston to Southern California. Neiman Marcus is known around the world as a specialty retailer offering high-end fashion, jewelry, gifts, and home furnishings. Billy Payton, vice president of marketing and customer programs identifies Neiman's customers as consumers—mostly women—whose household income is $150,000 and above, who are between the ages of 35 and 55, and who like the one-to-one relationship that Neiman's tries to build with them. He says that the Neiman's customer "appreciates fashion and appreciates quality in merchandise and gifts and apparel." Burton Tanksy, president of the Neiman Marcus Group targets his customers this way: "Our customer wants designer clout. She wants something easily recognizable so that people will know she paid a lot for it." Payton further identifies two main categories of customer: long-term customers who have shopped with the store for years and occasional customers who visit the store for a specific need such as a wedding gift.

How does Neiman Marcus develop relationships with customers who could shop anywhere they want? First, by recognizing the very fact that these customers can afford to shop anywhere, then by looking for ways to create greater utilities for them. "Neiman Marcus is all about developing relationships with customers, through our sales associates, through our marketing efforts, through editing the selection of quality merchandise and fashion. So it's all about a one-one-one relationship," explains Payton. One important way of doing this is attracting customers to the InCircle Program, a frequent buyer program that was the first of its kind when it was launched in 1984. For every dollar a customer spends at Neiman Marcus, one point is added to the customer's InCircle account. Later, customers can redeem points for gifts and purchasing privileges—say, that trip to Paris. So a long drive to a

Neiman's store becomes worthwhile to many customers. Neiman's has also upgraded the old-fashioned gift certificate, replacing it with a plastic card that looks like a credit card. The new card has a new name: the NM Gift Card.

To increase personal service even more, Neiman's sales associates develop exclusive relationships with particular customers. Pat Ames, a sales associate, notes that she often drops off a purchase at a customer's home or workplace or selects appropriate gifts for customers when they are short on time or ideas. Finally, there's Neiman's famous "The Book," a large, glossy fashion publication that is more idea book than catalog; customers are encouraged to sift through its pages, glean fashion and gift ideas, then visit the stores themselves for personal service. Customers treasure their copies as if they were first editions.

Whereas Neiman's traditionally focused on developing long-term customer relationships, recently the company has broadened its marketing focus to include the occasional customer. Payton notes, "The new buzz term is CRM, continuous relationship management, meaning, are we serving the occasional customer—all of their needs? All of their shopping needs, or fashion needs, their gift needs, their accessory needs, their cosmetic needs? Are we maximizing the servicing and our selling opportunity to all of our customers?" The new NM Gift Card is a result of this thinking, and Payton notes that every holiday—or occasion—counts at Neiman's. In fact, he refers to the company's new focus on occasions as a "year-round business." Another new area of focus is "the whole culture of successful young Gen-Xers craving high fashion, high-quality merchandise who may not think of Neiman Marcus as a place for them," says Payton. The trick, he says, is to attract the younger shoppers without alienating the older ones.

Not willing to be left behind in the wake of Internet technology, Neiman Marcus has already launched its own online shopping site at www.neimanmarcus.com and has joined forces with other organizations on the Internet. Neiman's and several other retailers have signed up with a new wedding registry site called www.dellajames.com, which allows wedding guests to buy gifts directly online from the group of retailers. As for the company's regular Web site, Billy Payton notes, "We definitely recognize and know that the [W]eb will play a major part in our marketing in the future. . . . We're trying to reach a very sophisticated customer, who appreciates technology, who understands technology and responds to it." Will Neiman's be able to replicate its bricks-and-mortar presence and also become a leading upscale Internet retailer? If its sales associates can still offer the personal touch, if customers still believe they are getting the best of the best, and if occasional consumers like the idea of buying a wedding gift with the click of the mouse, the company could do very well online. Still, it is probably safe to predict that not a single Neiman's customer will give up that precious copy of "The Book."

Questions

1. In what ways does Neiman Marcus create time, place and ownership utilities for its customers? In what ways does Neiman Marcus avoid marketing myopia?

2. Describe the typical Neiman Marcus customer. How well do you think Neiman Marcus meets the needs of this market?

3. In what ways might technology affect Neiman's future marketing strategy?

4. Neiman's sales associates are known for providing excellent personal service for their customers. Describe how Neiman's Web site (www.neimanmarcus.com) has attempted to integrate a "personal touch" for their online customers.

SOURCES: Neiman Marcus company Web site, www.neimanmarcus.com and www.neimanmarcusgroup.com, accessed February 15, 2000; Bruce Horovitz, "Neiman Marcus Spins Own Webcast," *USA Today*, August 30, 1999, www.usatoday.com; "My Biggest Mistake: Stanley Marcus," inc.com, July 1, 1999, www.inc.com; Wendy Bounds, "Retailers Say "I Do" to Wedding Web Site," *Wall Street Journal*, June 9, 1999, p. B9.

VIDEO CASE 2

The Timberland Co.

Timberland makes boots—all kinds of boots, from work boots to hiking boots to mountain biking shoes. They come in all shapes, sizes, and colors. Timberland also churns out backpacks for school children, outerwear, and leather fashion boots for women. Most of these products come at a premium price—a pair of hiking boots can cost more than $100. But the economy has been good, and people are snapping up Timberland's products, which were in a slump a decade ago. Consumers like the image that Timberland products evoke—love of the outdoors, rugged individuality, health consciousness, and fashion.

But Timberland has taken its product image a step farther, integrating the company with socially responsible activities. Touting the virtues of volunteerism, Timberland encourages both its customers and its employees to give their time and effort to create a better world. "With your boots and your beliefs, you will be able to interact responsibly and comfortably within the natural and social environments that all human beings share," says the company's Web site. In other words, Timberland boots aren't just boots, they are vehicles for good works.

Timberland doesn't just talk the talk; the company walks the walk, in its own boots. Through their Path of Service Program, all full-time Timberland employees receive 40 hours of paid time a year to volunteer within their community. By the year 2000, employees had performed over 80,000 hours of service. Timberland employees have renovated day care facilities, cleared hiking trails, cleaned streets, worked at animal shelters, installed playgrounds, and even assisted in hurricane relief efforts. Timberland gives employees a wide range of volunteer options to suit their skills and interests; or they can participate in City Year, a nationwide program designed to get young people more involved in restoring inner-city communities. In addi-

tion, Timberland keeps in close contact with various United Way organizations, matching employee volunteers to organizations that need help.

Some Timberland employees take the volunteer mandate even further and head up individual activities. Glenn Myers of New Hampshire spearheaded a fundraising effort that collected $18,000 in relief for the people of war-torn Kosovo. Timberland matched his efforts so that a check for $36,000 was presented to the Red Cross. Then Myers offered to temporarily house a Kosovo refugee in his home. When two entire families arrived instead, he and several Timberland coworkers arranged for the families to occupy an apartment. When winter arrived, Myers conducted a clothing drive throughout the Timberland headquarters in Stratham, New Hampshire, and delivered 10 boxes of warm clothing to the Kosovo families. "Timberland believes in the power of the individual," notes the company's Web site. "That one voice can and must make a difference." Employees like Glenn Myers take this message to heart.

Timberland is well known for its corporate donations to socially responsible causes, ranging from local events such as a road race to benefit an elementary school parent-teachers organization to the expansion of a homeless shelter to its support of the City Year program, which has received over $10 million from Timberland.

What about Timberland's economic responsibilities? The company now earns over $800 million per year in revenues and continues to announce growth in revenues. Company president and CEO Jeffrey Swartz notes that the formula for social responsibility works just as well on the bottom line. "I am pleased to report Timberland's fourth consecutive year of record revenue and improved earnings," he stated in 2000. "Results in

1999 reflect Timberland's continued focus on developing a portfolio of businesses that are diversified by product, geography, and channel."

Timberland's careful balance between social responsibility and economic responsibility has earned the company a spot on *Fortune's* list of 100 best companies to work for. Timberland was number 30 in the January 2000 issue of the magazine. With roughly 4,000 employees worldwide, nearly 50 percent of whom are women and 25 percent of whom are minorities, the New Hampshire bootmaker needs to combine a cosmopolitan and local outlook in the way it presents itself to the public. In doing so, the company has managed to sell both its footwear and its social mission in one slogan: "Pull on your boots and make a difference."

Questions

1. How do Timberland's social responsibility activities fit the social-cultural marketing environment?

2. How does Timberland use social responsibility to promote its products? Is this ethical? Why or why not?

3. On the pyramid of social responsibility, how does Timberland balance its philanthropic actions with its economic responsibilities?

4. As stated in the chapter text, "Socially responsible marketing involves campaigns that encourage people to adopt socially beneficial behaviors." Explore Timberland's Web site (www.timberland.com). Does Timberland's site effectively work towards this goal? Explain your answer.

SOURCES: Timberland Web Site, www.timberland.com, accessed February 16, 2000; Kate Barbera, "Reaching Out to the Homeless," *Portsmouth Herald*, February 13, 2000, www.seacoastonline; "Timberland Announces Record Fourth Quarter and Full Year Revenue and Earnings," *Business Wire*, February 3, 2000; "100 Best Companies to Work For," *Fortune*, January 10, 2000, www.pathfinder.com/fortune/bestcompanies; "Here and Abroad, People Are Doing Wonders for Relief Effort," *Portsmouth Herald*, November 18, 1999, www.seacoastonline; Christine Gillette, "Agency Plans Center," *Portsmouth Herald*, June 28, 1999, www.seacoastonline.

VIDEO CASE 3

ESPN

I t began by mistake. Back in the late 1970s, Bill Rasmussen decided to launch a cable station to broadcast Connecticut-area sports. With the assistance of his partners, Rasmussen leased a building in Bristol from which to broadcast and then bought some satellite time. Only after signing the agreement did he learn that his satellite coverage was national—and his smale-scale plan of New England sports coverage began to grow. Their early name for the channel—Entertainment and Sports Programming Network—proved too much of a tongue twister and, in 1985, they settled on the ESPN acronym as the corporate name. The letters now stand for nothing—except a sports phenomenon.

Since those early days during which the network scrambled to televise whatever it could—from a men's pro, slow-pitch softball game to its first NHL game in 1979—the organization has grown dramatically, filling what Will Burkhardt of ESPN says is now a saturated market for televised sports in the United States and rapidly moving overseas. "We reach 150 to 155 million households around the world [excluding the United States]; that encompasses about 180 markets and territories," says Burkhardt. ESPN reaches all 7 continents, including one of the scientific stations located in Antarctica. The expansion has taken place over the last 15 years, beginning when ESPN provided groundbreaking coverage of the America's Cup inter-

national sailing race from Australia in 1987. That race seemed to be a turning point not only for ESPN, but for cable broadcasting itself. From there, ESPN purchased a majority interest in the European Sports Network (called Eurosport) and began service to 25 Middle Eastern and North African nations. In addition to its Eurosport market, ESPN's largest international markets have become China, India, and Argentina.

Burkhardt notes that ESPN entered the international marketplace because of a "desire to grow outside of the U.S. borders and to take what we had learned in the United States in terms of people's passion for sport . . . and bring that to the international marketplace." This was around the same time that cable and satellite television were expanding around the world, so ESPN's timing seemed perfect.

However, marketing around the world isn't easy. For instance, although India has a huge middle-class population, middle class in that country means that a family might earn about $1,800 per year, as opposed to an American middle-class family's earnings of $35,000 per year. Thus, attracting viewers to pay for television is more difficult in India. In addition, the infrastructure for cable television is very different from that of the United States, which requires more effort for ESPN marketers. India has tens of thousands of cable entrepreneurs serving approximately 100 customers each, instead of a giant like AOL-Time Warner, which serves 13 million. Still, ESPN thinks that serving India is worth the effort and tailors its programming to the single most-watched sport in the nation: cricket.

In the burgeoning South American markets, where sports fanatics thrive, viewers can watch all kinds of programming—Argentine rugby, Argentine polo, Brazilian basketball, and Brazilian tennis, to name a few. But Burkhardt emphasizes that ESPN starts with a regional marketing strategy, "building a bed of programming from which you then start to localize." Currently, most broadcasts are in English or the local language, but dealing with some countries' multiple local dialects is extremely difficult. In addition, consumers in smaller markets want to see broadcasters of their own nationality instead of ESPN's standard crew of broadcasters. "There is no question that people in Mexico would prefer all of our commentators to be Mexican instead of some which are Argentine," remarks Burkhardt. ESPN simply can't afford to provide this degree of customization yet.

Ultimately, ESPN's goal is to reach as many households worldwide as possible, despite any difficulties in penetrating new markets. For example, the company landed a huge deal that gave it distribution rights in Latin America for all four rounds of the Masters Golf Tournament. ESPN Latin America alone is now distributed in more than 11 million households in 41 countries and territories, broadcasting in English, Spanish, and Portuguese.

In spite of recent victories like the Masters, perhaps one of the greatest challenges to ESPN is that the company must, in large part, make its pitch to cable and satellite television operators before its programming ever reaches the consumers themselves. Those operators conduct business in different ways, they lack rating systems, and some even replace ESPN programming with home grown shows. Then there are political challenges, such as when ESPN was thrown off Chinese cable after the United States mistakenly bombed its embassy in Eastern Europe. And there are legal tangles in each country that need to be dealt with, as well. But sports are an international language that tries to provide entertainment without political ramifications, and people everywhere love to watch. "We're obviously not trying to promote any kind of political message through the showing of an American baseball game," says Burkhardt. And perhaps that is the key to ESPN's success—its ability to bring sport to everyone, everywhere, anytime.

Questions

1. What questions might ESPN marketers ask themselves as they try to develop business in Asia or South America?

2. Why is it important for ESPN to global? What might be some barriers to trade for ESPN?

3. How would you describe ESPN's global marketing strategy?

4. Search ESPN's Web site at www.espn.com and summarize what they are currently doing in international markets.

SOURCES: Telephone interview with Will Burkhardt of ESPN, January 2000; "TV Listings," February 8, 2000, ESPN.com; "ESPN International Lands Masters for Latin America," company press release, November 11, 1999, ESPN.com; Michael Hiestand, "Did You Know? ESPN Is 20 Today," *USA Today*, September 7, 1999, www.USAToday.com; "Looking Back, Back, Back . . . ," company press release, September 6, 1999, ESPN.com; Rudy Martzke, "ESPN at 20," *USA Today*, August 18, 1999, p. 2c.

VIDEO CASE 4

Tower Records

E-commerce has struck the music industry, and the echoes are still reverberating. Today, musicians can record high quality music online from their homes, *aficionados* can download their favorite tunes or soundtracks, and of course, consumers can order just about any tape or CD they can imagine with the click of a mouse. How does a company like Tower Records—the nationally known chain of music, book, and video stores—keep pace with the times?

Tower Records has survived in a tough industry where others have faltered. The company was founded in 1960 by Russ Solomon, who managed to coax his father, a drugstore owner, into a small loan. Today Tower operates 219 stores, including 39 franchise locations, and it has 7,400 employees worldwide. Although Tower offers books and videos at its stores, music still makes up 85 percent of the company's business. The company understands the need to establish a presence on the Internet, but Tower executives—including Russ Solomon himself—believe that they should do so cautiously. They have watched other companies jump headlong onto the Internet, sinking a lot of money into Web sites and ultimately losing millions because the move was made too quickly, without enough research. Indeed, Solomon says that he's not going to get caught up in the "hysteria about the Internet."

So Tower has taken its move to the Internet one step at a time, incorporating this effort with its overall marketing strategy, which includes developing more and larger stores, new markets, and a new product line—consumer electronics. Instead of concentrating solely on its Web site, Tower managers prefer to make the Internet part of an overall strategy so that the company doesn't lose "millions and millions," according to Michael Solomon, Russ Solomon's son and president and CEO of Tower. "We would like it to be profitable." Currently, Tower's online sales account for roughly 2 percent of the total, or "the equivalent of one of our good stores."

The Solomons believe that, although many consumers like to shop online, just as many like to visit Tower's stores. They also agree with experts who assert that online and traditional shopping can coexist peacefully, and even benefit each other. Jim Donio, spokesman for the National Association of Recording Merchandisers says, "For a lot of people there's nothing that can equate with the social experience" of visiting a store, talking with salespeople, picking up and handling the merchandise. So in addition to continually upgrading its Web site, Tower is building new, larger stores that will contain more inventory, more listening stations and all kinds of new electronic gadgets for consumers to play with.

What will you find on Tower's Web site? Consumers can log on and order music in six different languages, in 150 currencies, from 40 locations in Tower's global distribution network. In the United States, you can click on your favorite music, video/DVD titles, and books. You get store locators, chart lists—the works. If you log onto Tower Europe, you get great specials, a look at Tower's Music Magazine, a chance to play games, and a list of top chart titles in every category imaginable, from blues to movie soundtracks. Click over to the link for Japan, and you'll find much the same thing—presented in both English and Japanese. "Whether you are mad for Madonna in Mozambique or avid for ABBA in Alaska, Tower Record's range of over 600,000 entertainment titles . . . will be

available at the end of your fingertips," says the company in a press release about the unveiling of its site. "We're in a competitive business," notes Tower board member Bob Lorber. "All of a sudden, we have lots more competition." Tower has no intention of being left behind the online competition.

Some Internet music marketers worry about the problem of people illegally downloading music from the Internet, but Michael Solomon is philosophical about it. "You can get music for free now," he observes. Indeed, music buffs have been taping songs from the radio or each other's collections for decades. "You can do it [download] and some people do, but I don't think it's a threat."

So Tower Records continues to rock to its own beat. "We're comfortable and secure, but we're never satisfied and complacent," says Michael Solomon. "You've got to be on edge all the time," adds his father, who in his seventies still holds the position of chairman of the company. It looks like this music company will be heard from for a long time.

Questions

1. What are the benefits to Tower Records in offering online shopping?
2. In what ways might Tower customize or personalize its Web site and online services for individual customers?
3. In what ways might Tower combine its marketing strategies for its bricks-and-mortar stores and its e-commerce site?

SOURCES: Tower Europe Web site, www.towereurope.com, accessed February 18, 2000; Tower Japan Web site, www.towerrecords.co.jp, accessed February 18, 2000; Kelly Johnson, "Solomons Still Feel That Tower Power," *Sacramento Business Journal*, April 19, 1999, www.amcity.com/sacramento; "Tower Records to Launch Online Sales," *Sacramento Business Journal*, August 17, 1998, www.amcity.com/sacramento; "Tower Records Hangs Out Shingle on Internet," *Reuters News Service*, April 19, 1998.

VIDEO CASE 5

FedEx Corp.

If you've ever ordered anything by phone or over the Internet, chances are you've received a package delivered by a purple and orange FedEx truck. Millions of other customers, both consumers and businesses, received their packages on the same day. In fact, FedEx makes 3 to 4 million deliveries each day, in more than 200 countries, 24 to 48 hours after the shipping order was placed.

Shipping a package via FedEx costs more than shipping via UPS or Airborne. But FedEx maintains its competitive position

by offering security and reliability—in other words, FedEx relies on the trusting relationship it builds with customers. FedEx claims that more than 99 percent of its deliveries arrive on time. And when there's a mistake, the company offers a two-way, money-back guarantee: First, the customer is given a refund if the delivery is late; second, the customer receives a refund if there is any difficulty in obtaining tracking information.

Technology is the foundation of FedEx's ability to build complex, integrated relationships with its customers. FedEx maintains a database that details every aspect of each shipping transaction. With FedEx's database, both the company and customer know where the package is during every moment of the transaction; if there is ever a gap in this information, the customer gets a refund. But FedEx's service goes much farther than tracking packages. Major customers, such as L.L. Bean, Dell Computer, or any of the major American automakers, can download FedEx software solutions right into their own desktop computers to customize the way they want to use the information that FedEx can provide. For instance, FedEx Ship API software allows business customers to customize the application to their own shipping needs, from generating shipping labels to tracking packages in real time.

Jeff Wyne, marketing manager for FedEx, notes that one of his organization's goals is to help other businesses be successful. One way to do this is to help a customer manage its supply chain. For instance, FedEx not only handles shipping but also owns warehouses throughout the world, where it holds inventories for companies that don't want to manage their own. FedEx has also become involved in handling international logistics for its customers, through its recently formed subsidiary, FedEx Trade Networks Inc. "We listened to our customers, and that's what they wanted," says G. Edmond Clark, head of the new subsidiary.

If you order an anorak or a pair of hiking boots from L.L. Bean in Maine, the FedEx truck will be at your house in two days. FedEx is an integral part of L.L. Bean's entire business, from the order system on down to the customer service system, where a representative locates a product number, fulfills the request, and generates a FedEx shipping label. Shipping personnel attach a label to the box and scans it, then places the box on the truck. Being part of the entire logistics process helps FedEx build a long-term relationship with customers like L.L. Bean—a relationship in which each company helps the other grow.

FedEx has the reputation of pulling out all the stops to get a package delivered on time, no matter what. The company has even been known to rent commercial jets when its own planes have suffered mechanical failures. If a delivery doesn't make it, not only is the customer's money refunded, a FedEx manager will make a personal phone call or visit to apologize and try to find a solution to the problem. Then FedEx will study the situation to make sure it doesn't happen again. "We strive for 100-percent satisfaction guaranteed," says Jeff Wyne. And they'll do whatever it takes.

Questions

1. How does FedEx's use of technology help build relationships with its customers?

2. Go to FedEx's Web site at www.fedex.com, select "U.S." and then "eBusiness Tools." On that page, you'll see a link for "FedEx eCommerce Solutions" (currently found at www.fedex.com/us/software/ecommerce/). Choose one of the e-commerce options described, click on its link, and read more about it. Do you think the solution is easy for customers to use? Why or why not?

3. How do FedEx and L.L. Bean benefit from the reciprocity of their relationship?

4. How does FedEx strengthen a relationship after making a mistake?

SOURCES: Alan Gersten, "FedEx Creates New Unit for Logistics Focus," *Reuter's Limited*, February 17, 2000; "FedEx Trade Networks to Offer Full Range of Global Trade Services," *Business Wire*, February 17, 2000; Brian O'Reilly, "They've Got Mail!" *Fortune*, February 7, 2000, www.pathfinder.com/fortune; "FedEx eShipping Tools," FedEx Web site, www.fedex.com, accessed February 4, 2000; Scott Kirsner, "Digital Competition—Laurie A. Tucker," *Fast Company*, December 1999, p. 166.

VIDEO CASE 6

Furniture.com

"Decorating one's home is an extremely personal and information-intensive decision," says Andrew L. Brooks, president and CEO of Furniture.com. Decorating in general, and furniture shopping in particular, can be a frustrating, time-consuming, and intimidating experience for many people. Few people relish dragging spouses or kids from furniture store to furniture store to sit on sofas and order swatches. And many consumers are just plain afraid to make a decision—what if the color or style is "wrong"? What if the dining room table is too big for the room? Furniture.com is determined to change all that.

Unlike other Internet businesses, Furniture.com is not an online start-up company. The idea to sell furniture on the Web actually began with the owner of a brick-and-mortar furniture store called Empire Furniture Showroom in downtown Worcester, Massachusetts. Steven Rothschild and his partner, Misha Katz, launched the first version of the online company from the Worcester store in the late 1990s. Rothschild is now company chairman and Katz is vice president of new technology. Throughout the changes the company has undergone, however, it has maintained a clear mission, as articulated by Brooks: "to take a shopping experience in the traditional world, which is not particularly easy, to re-create it, and to make it fun, easy, and accessible to everybody."

Rothschild and Katz recognized an opportunity. "The traditional brick and mortar environment hasn't been very good to furniture consumers," explains Brooks. "The average consumer needs to go to five or six retail establishments. That potentially ruins five or six weekend days with kids in tow, trying to find the perfect place. That is often a frustrating exercise." With more and more consumers flocking to the Internet to do their shopping, Furniture.com took advantage of a strategic window to attract customers early and keep them coming back for more. The company offers over 50,000 items from 140 manufacturers through its site, and it provides free delivery and setup. Most brick-and mortar-stores offer only 4,000 to 10,000 items, and many charge for delivery beyond a few miles.

Connecting all these pieces of furniture with the right customers requires strategic and tactical planning. Perhaps the company's most important strategy is considering the impact every decision its managers make have on the consumer. "Examples of that include multiple ways to search," explains Brooks. "You can search on our site by room, by piece, and by very specific criteria. . . . What sets us apart is the extent to which we have identified real consumer needs. We then found technology that can provide solutions as opposed to technology for technology's sake." To that end, customers can build their own virtual showroom at the Web site, filled with their favorite pieces of furniture to see what the finished product will look like. The Room Planner, Style Guide, Furniture Finder, and Personal Shopper features of Furniture.com's site are all implementations of the overall strategy.

Furniture.com's strengths include the following:

- its huge selection—as already mentioned, the company offers over 50,000 items, much more than competitors

- its service—customer service is open around the clock, by phone, live Internet chat, or e-mail, and sales reps contact customers after delivery to make certain the right items arrived on time

- its freedom from having to hold inventory—most items are shipped directly from manufacturers.

Its one major weakness is the fact that currently the company does not offer cash refunds; instead, customers receive an exchange or store credit. Since furniture is a major purchase for most consumers, having $500 or $1,000 tied up in store credit could be a problem. However, Furniture.com does have a "no questions asked" return policy, and the company pays return shipping fees.

Looking toward future growth, Furniture.com has entered into several strategic alliances with other organizations. The company now has online advertising agreements with MSN Internet services, Yahoo!, and Lycos as part of a move to strengthen its position in the e-commerce marketplace. Indeed, Furniture.com's position is already at the head of its class. In review after review, the company receives high marks for selection and service. Entertainment Weekly calls the site "best of breed." *Access* rates the company with four stars, and *PC Magazine* reports, "The smartest furniture shoppers are heading to Furniture.com." That's a satisfying image for Furniture.com's founders: smart shoppers buying products from a smart company.

Questions

1. Do Furniture.com's strategic and tactical planning accurately reflect the company's overall mission? Why or why not?

2. Describe one or two strategies that Furniture.com might use to plan to expand into foreign countries.

3. Identify some potential threats to Furniture.com over the next few years?

4. Visit Furniture.com's Web site at www.furniture.com. What are the site's strengths? What are its weaknesses?

SOURCES: Furniture.com Web site, www.furniture.com, accessed March 23, 2000; Anne Stuart, "Furniture.com," *CIO Magazine*, January 15, 2000, www.cio.com; Karen Lake, "Creating an Internet Following," *Inc.com*, November 10, 1999, www.inc.com; Karen Lake, "Lead Your Industry to the Internet," *Inc.com*, November 10, 1999, www.inc.com; June Fletcher, "Internet Home Stores Grow, But Selection Stays Limited," *Wall Street Journal*, October 15, 1999, www.djreprints.com; "Furniture.com Announces Multimillion-Dollar Online Advertising Agreements with Lycos and MSN," press release, July 27, 1999, www.lycos.com; Timothy J. Mullaney and David Leonhardt, "A Hard Sell Online? Guess Again," *Businessweek.com*, July 12, 1999; Beth Cox, "Furniture.com Launches Multimillion-Dollar Brand Campaign," *InternetNews.com*, June 30, 1999, www.internetnews.com; "Furniture.com Offers Proactive, Live Online Assistance," *InternetNews.com*, April 30, 1999, www.internetnews.com; "Furniture.com and Amazon.com Team Up on Home Furnishing/Decorating 'Reading Room,'" press release, March 8, 1999.

VIDEO CASE 7

Fisher-Price

The toy business isn't child's play. It's a marketing environment in which competition is tough, consumers are fickle, and truly new ideas are hard to come by. Shelly Glick Gryfe, director of marketing research at Fisher-Price, knows all that, yet she still enjoys searching for that perfect product, the one that children and their parents will buy—and buy again—with fierce loyalty. Gryfe and her colleagues at Fisher-Price believe in the value of marketing research to bring a new toy to store shelves. But they don't conduct research indiscriminately; they carefully choose which types will be most useful and stick to the budget.

Through exploratory research, Fisher-Price marketers discovered that there was a gap in toys available for preschool and early elementary school boys. Little boys liked the idea of action figures that their older brothers and friends played with, but those toys were difficult for them to understand and handle. And their moms clearly did not want their young children playing with toys that had violent overtones. The research caused Fisher-Price to coin the term KAGOY—Kids Are Getting Older Younger—meaning that younger children want more grown-up toys. Yet those toys must be designed for little hands and young imaginations. "So we were then looking for something that might move away from the [traditional Fisher-Price playset] and be more specifically action figure, but in a way that was more appropriate for preschool boys on many dimensions," explains Gryfe.

Fisher-Price marketers combined the idea of action figures with an age-appropriate context, and the idea for a new group of figures—Rescue Heroes was born. Fisher-Price used a combination of in-house and outside researchers to obtain primary data on their concept, and later the toy itself. First, marketers conducted in-house focus groups they called "mom talks." Gryfe explains, "A mom talk is basically a focus group that we do in-house. It's done very early in the process to see if we're on the right track . . . . We do this before we spend lots of money on out-of-house focus groups and prototypes." During the mom talks, marketers interviewed mothers to find out what they wanted—and didn't want—in a new toy. They learned quickly that mothers liked the idea of imaginative play but didn't want their children playing with aggressive or violent toys. Gryfe admits that these in-house focus groups tend to be subject to sampling bias, because the people who participate are those who want to have an impact on products; they aren't necessarily representative of the general buying public. She also believes that participants may edit their responses when they are on site, whereas they may be more candid when they participate in focus groups located elsewhere. Once they got some answers, Fisher-Price marketers refined their research and took it on the road. They hired outside moderators to conduct focus groups, often in shopping malls.

Once they had prototype Rescue Heroes, Fisher-Price marketers invited children to the on-site "play lab" to test the figures, each of whom represents an occupation in which a hero rescues people in need—such as firefighters Billy Blazes and Wendy Waters, emergency medical assistant Perry Medic, alpine guide Cliff Hanger, and scuba diver Gil Gripper. In the play labs, boys played with Rescue Heroes and other toys while researchers observed them through a one-way mirror. During these sessions, marketers learned that the figures needed to have oversized feet to stand on their own and not topple over. Similar studies were conducted off the premises to refine the products, including one at Simon Fraser University in British Columbia, Canada, which involved 28 families with boys aged 3 to 6. Later, Fisher-Price actually sent the toys home with children to play with for a week and then interviewed the mothers about their boys' activities. Finally, marketers interviewed parents about whether they would buy the toys and whether they were comfortable with the price.

One nagging theme that emerged from all this research was, "Who are the rescuers? Whom do they rescue? Are there stories behind them?" Marketers realized that they needed to create a scenario for the figures, so little synopses about the characters were developed and printed on the backs of the packages. Then CBS decided that the Rescue Heroes would make a terrific basis for a new children's animated series, and the Saturday morning show of the same name was launched. With careful marketing research behind them, it looks like the Rescue Heroes are going to stand on their own two feet after all.

Questions

1. Why was it important for Fisher-Price marketers to define their problem through exploratory research?

2. Do you think that Fisher-Price's methods for collecting primary data are effective? Why or why not? Describe other techniques that might be effective.

3. In what ways might Fisher-Price use secondary data in its research?

4. Go to the Fisher-Price Web site (www.fisher-price.com) and see what Rescue Heroes information and/or activities are available. Describe what you found at the Web site. Does the site contain any elements that would allow it to collect further research on this product?

SOURCES: Fisher-Price Web site, www.fisher-price.com/us/rescueheroes/ products, accessed February 28, 2000; Karl Taro Greenfeld, "Mattel: Some (Re)Assembly Required," *Time Magazine*, October 25, 1999, www.time.com; "Rescue Hero Toys Offer Positive Influence," Simon Fraser University WEB site, May 31, 1999, www.sfu.ca.

Fresh Samantha

A decade ago, Douglas Levin decided he wanted to live the good life: He quit his high stress advertising job in New York and moved to Maine with his wife to help his in-laws run their alfalfa sprout farm. While he was delivering sprouts to various stores around the region, Levin kept encountering another local product, a blended carrot juice aptly named 24 Carrot. He tried some of the juice and loved it so much, he bought the business. Levin and his wife renamed the juice business Fresh Samantha after their 2-year-old daughter. As Levin began producing the juice, his wife Abby designed a logo for the product. Then Levin took Fresh Samantha on the road to small grocery stores around rural Maine. No one wanted the juice.

"That wasn't our consumer," Levin now says of his first efforts. People living in rural Maine were not enthusiastic about paying 2 to 3 dollars for a 16-ounce bottle of juice when they could buy private label or name brand apple juice for $1.30 a gallon. No one was willing to spend the extra money for the luxury of premium juice. Levin knew his product, but he hadn't targeted his market accurately. That first year, he lost $20,000 from his own pocket.

Then a friend suggested that Levin try a certain age group: college students. So he drove to Tufts University in Boston and handed the university's food buyer a bottle of his juice. The buyer liked the taste and agreed to stock it throughout Tufts's eateries. Fresh Samantha clicked with the college kids: they loved the taste, they loved the idea of fresh juice, they even loved the names of the different blends that Levin was now producing, like Desperately Seeking C and Mango Mama. With success at Tufts, Levin was able to convince some of the regional supermarkets around New England to begin stocking Fresh Samantha. "Reception was suspicious at first, because no one on the East Coast had heard of a super-premium refrigerated juice," recalls Betta Stothart of Fresh Samantha. "Today, we have gained widespread acceptance in health food stores, whole food markets, bagel and coffee shops, as well as grocery store chains."

With more and more people searching for healthful foods, Fresh Samantha took off around New England. College students continued to be strong supporters of the juice, but adult consumers bought the juice as well. With its higher price, Fresh Samantha had to differentiate itself from those gallons of apple juice or orange juice, and even from the single serving juices marketed by such companies as Veryfine. So, the health benefits that consumers would get from drinking its juices became Fresh Samantha's calling card. Consumers could learn as much as they wanted about the ingredients and health benefits of Fresh Samantha's products by visiting the company's Web site, which has everything from a definition of the word *calorie*

to a list of the natural ingredients in the juices and the way they work in the body, "to give your body the material it needs for energy and many nutrients essential to good health."

As consumers grew more sophisticated in their tastes, marketers had to refine further the position of Fresh Samantha products. So Levin and his colleagues developed more complex products, blending more fruits and adding nutraceuticals such as St. John's Wort into flavors like Oh Happy Day. By now, Fresh Samantha had its own refrigerator in many supermarkets, often placed near the health-food aisle.

Still, Fresh Samantha's target market included only consumers living in New England and down the eastern seaboard. It included college students and Generation Xers who were health conscious and who also had the income to spend on premium food products. Levin wanted more. "There's a place for this product in the mass market—I'm convinced of it," he noted. Several years after making that remark, Levin announced that Fresh Samantha would merge with Odwalla Inc., the leading brand of super-premium juice on the West Coast. "We are excited about bringing Fresh Samantha together with Odwalla," said Stephen Williamson, Odwalla's chairman and chief executive officer. "Since our respective inceptions, Odwalla and Fresh Samantha's spirit have been aligned in our visions of delivering great-tasting nourishment. Together, these two innovative brands have national leadership of this category."

Levin agreed. "We will go further in growing the super-premium refrigerated juice category together than by going at it alone." Odwalla and Fresh Samantha now hope to quench an entire nation's thirst for juice.

Questions

1. Based on what you've read, from which psychographic consumer segment(s) do you think Fresh Samantha drinkers come? Why?

2. Why was it so important for Fresh Samantha marketers to differentiate the product early on?

3. In what ways might the merger of Fresh Samantha and Odwalla change the positioning of each?

4. Find the Fresh Samantha Web site, does it reflect the target market accurately? Why or why not?

SOURCES: Fresh Samantha Web site, www.freshsamantha.com, accessed February 21, 2000; "Odwalla Announces Purchase Agreement and Merger with Fresh Samantha," *Business Wire*, February 2, 2000; KellyAnn LaCascia, "Chilling the Organic and Natural Beverage Market," *Organic & Natural News*, November 1999, www.organicandnaturalnews.com; Leigh Gallagher, "Mango Mama Anyone?" *Forbes Global*, April 6, 1998, www.global.forbes.com.

VIDEO CASE 9

Goya Foods, Inc.

Eighty years ago, Spanish immigrant Prudencio Unanue and his wife longed for the comfort foods of their home, so they started an import business to satisfy the need. However, a few years later, the Spanish Civil War broke out, and they could no longer obtain the foods they wanted for their business. So they began importing sardines from a cannery in Morocco. "He had to do something. He had four kids, and we had to eat," recalls his son, Joseph A. Unanue, now in his 70s. The elder Unanue bought the brand name, Goya, along with the sardines. The name cost an extra dollar. Throughout the years, Unanue added olive oil, olives, and other products the Hispanic community in America requested. During the 1960s, Goya began canning everything from beans to coconut juice. Today, Goya serves up entire menus of beans, rice, pasta, seasonings, beverages, and a variety of specialties.

On the surface, it might seem to be a simple matter to import and manufacture food products to serve what appears to be a niche community. But it isn't. First, the Hispanic population, including immigrants and descendants, now numbers more than 30 million in the United States. By 2050, Hispanics will make up about 25 percent of the population. Thus, Hispanic consumer tastes are becoming more and more a part of the mainstream, not to mention a huge segment of purchasing power. Second, there is no such thing as a single Hispanic population. Although Goya was founded originally to serve consumers of Spanish descent, American Hispanics come from a variety of countries, from Puerto Rico and Mexico to Nicaragua and Cuba. Their cultures, family structures, attitudes, and tastes in food are different. "Hispanics from different countries eat different foods," notes Andy Unanue, Joseph's son and likely successor as CEO. But Goya is ahead of other marketers in pinpointing the location of different populations. "Luckily, we have a big arm out in the field who act as the census. We know which Hispanics are moving into what regions before anybody else," says Andy. For instance, Andy's sister Mary Ann moved to Chicago to run the Goya business for that location and focused on the growing Mexican community there. "We started thinking like Mexicans, deciding what they would like."

Of course, Goya often ends up serving different groups of Hispanic consumers within the same geographical region. But its marketers know that Cubans prefer black beans, while Nicaraguans want small chili beans, and Mexicans will buy pintos. So they provide all three—and more.

Changing roles in Hispanic families have also reflected a change in purchasing habits, and Goya has adeptly kept up with the times, serving both the young and the old. Hispanic seniors still want to create their own meals from scratch; they don't want packaged or prepared foods. So Goya offers a full complement of ingredients for this market. But "the younger people are busy, they are used to the microwave, and they want to eat those things they grew up on that they don't have time to make or can't make as well as their mothers," explains Mary Ann. So Goya provides a wide range of rice and bean mixes and other foods that can be prepared quickly by working mothers or fathers. The company Web site offers even more help for this new generation: a section with favorite recipes that includes menus for holiday celebrations and other occasions.

By being first to the grocery shelves decades ago, Goya established itself as the premiere Hispanic food brand, and it has been discovered by more and more non-Hispanic consumers whose food tastes are changing. Moreover, Goya has managed to ward off attempts by larger companies to tread on its turf by simply producing higher quality, more authentic products. "We firmly believe that Hispanics like buying things they consider their own, that are authentic," remarks Andy Unanue. "And we are. We're Hispanic and we give them authenticity." Not only do Hispanic consumers prefer Goya's authenticity, but so do non-Hispanics. Thus, after failed attempts to introduce their own Hispanic food lines, giants like Campbell's Soup are trying to compete by purchasing genuine Hispanic food businesses. Goya is watching carefully.

Goya remains a privately owned business steeped in strong family tradition, with no plans to change the way it operates. Although Goya products generally represent low involvement purchase decisions, consumers relate strongly to the traditions that these products represent. When they fill their shopping carts with Goya rice, olives, and salsa, they feel like members of a community.

Questions

1. On Maslow's hierarchy, which needs do Goya products fulfill for its consumers? How does the company's Web site (www.goyafoods.com) appeal to those needs?

2. Why is it so important for Goya marketers to understand the different subgroups within the Hispanic community?

3. What might be some pros and cons of Goya's attracting more and more non-Hispanic consumers to its products?

SOURCES: Goya Foods Web site, www.goyafoods.com, accessed March 4, 2000; "Venezuela's Flood Victims Desperately Waiting for Aid," *PR Newswire*, January 3, 2000; Bill Saporito, "Food Fight," *Corporate Board Member*, Autumn 1999, www.boardmember.com; "Goya Foods," *Hispanic Online*, January/February 1999, www.hisp.com.

VIDEO CASE | 10

UPS

Nearly a century ago, United Parcel Service (UPS) drivers began delivering packages for Seattle department stores from Model T Fords and the backs of a few motorcycles. Today, UPS employees are easy to spot, in their crisp brown uniforms and lumbering brown trucks that have earned the company just one of its nicknames: the brown bear. Although everyone reading this has probably received a package delivered by UPS at one time or another, perhaps UPS's biggest impact is behind the scenes as it helps businesses and nonprofit organizations of all sizes get rolling.

UPS delivers about 12 million packages a day around the world for 2.5 million customers, using 225 jets and nearly 160,000 trucks. But UPS wants to do more for its business customers than just drop a box at the front desk. "We want to increase our global footprint across the entire supply chain," says CEO James Kelly. UPS has spent a whopping $11 billion on upgrading its technology in the last decade—on everything from mainframes, PCs, wireless communication devices, cellular networks, and 4,000 programmers and technicians. The reason? With this huge investment in technology, UPS is setting itself up to help its customers cope with different types of demand by assisting them manage inventory, offering warehouse services, and even helping repair products. For instance, UPS has set up an "end of runway" facility near its air hub in Louisville, Kentucky. Computers and other electronic devices in need of repair are trucked from the airport to the facility close by, where technicians repair them on site for customers like Hewlett Packard and then reship them quickly either to HP itself or to one its customers. In addition, UPS has revived the old-fashioned COD service for large customers such as Gateway, but it is doing so in high tech fashion. UPS drivers collect payments from customers and deposit the funds directly into Gateway's bank through electronic funds transfer. No other shipping company currently offers that type of service.

UPS intends to be a major player in e-commerce, where it already dominates shipping by Internet retailers. UPS stocks shoes and other clothing for Nike.com in its Louisville warehouse and fulfills orders every hour. A UPS call center in San Antonio actually handles customer orders from Nike.com. In this way, UPS grows its own business by handling more of Nike.com's operations, while Nike.com reduces its overhead and reaps the benefits of reliability and quick turnaround from UPS. Still, this isn't enough for UPS, which recently launched a new group, called UPS e-Ventures, to act as the research and development division of the company's e-commerce initiatives. The first project, among many to come, is e-Logistics, which will be designed to provide end-to-end business logistics solutions for small- and medium-sized Web businesses. "UPS recognizes the power the Internet has to impact business-to-business and business-to-consumer commerce," notes Mark Rhoney, president of UPS e-Ventures.

To assist its business customers, UPS must communicate with them to get them to think about logistics on a larger scale. One challenge faced by UPS as it develops these B2B efforts has been to increase customers' awareness of ways that UPS can make them more successful. But UPS must reach more people within an organization than just those who are directly involved in the company's transportation or shipping. "We need to work deeper in our customers' organizations," notes Ed Buckley, vice president of marketing, Europe. "There are people [within an organization] who don't see any connection to shipping; we try to get them to think differently." For instance, UPS now has a product called Document Exchange, which provides a secure venue for executives to transmit information.

One way the company raises its profile is to team up with very visible sports organizations such as the Olympic Games and NASCAR, both of whom are customers of UPS. UPS has been a worldwide partner of the Olympic Games since 1994 and the official express delivery sponsor of the NFL since 1993. Most recently, the company sealed an agreement with NASCAR that includes customer promotions, hospitality events, a souvenir program, and a specially designed UPS package delivery car. If nothing else, affiliations like these might get other potential customers to think about UPS as more than a big brown truck.

Questions

1. How might derived demand affect UPS's business?

2. Choose a company or nonprofit organization that interests you—say, Holiday Inn, Kentucky Fried Chicken, Old Navy clothing, Hard Candy cosmetics, Harley Davidson motorcycles, or the Red Cross. In what ways could UPS serve the organization you've chosen?

3. The UPS Web site (www.ups.com) includes links to click for tracking, shipping, transit time, pick up, drop off, and supplies. If you were an entrepreneur starting a small business, in what ways would these be helpful to you? Are there any categories you would add to make the site more useful?

SOURCES: UPS Web site, www.ups.com, accessed March 7, 2000; "UPS Takes to the Track as Official Express Delivery Company of NASCAR," *Business Wire*, February 17, 2000; Jennifer Couzin, "UPS Tests Its Peddle's Mettle," *Industry Standard*, February 7, 2000; Sandeep Junnarkar, "UPS Delivers e-Commerce Unit," *CNet News*, February 7, 2000, www.news.cnet.com; Kelly Barron, "Logistics in Brown," "At Ground Level," and "Addicting the Customer," *Forbes*, January 10, 2000, www.forbes.com; "Out of the Box at UPS," *Business Week Online*, January 10, 2000, www.businessweek.com; Scott Kirsner, "Venture Vérité: United Parcel Service," *Wired*, September 9, 1999, www.wired.com.

VIDEO CASE 11

Pfizer, Inc.

A few years ago, the most successful pharmaceutical product ever introduced to the marketplace was launched. In its first year, the drug had worldwide sales of over $1 billion. Was it a cure for the common cold? No. It was Pfizer's new product Viagra (*sildenafil*), approved for sale by the Food and Drug Administration (FDA) to relieve the male condition known as erectile dysfunction (ED).

Although Viagra may have appeared to be an overnight sensation, in reality the product had taken years just to reach the introductory stage in its life cycle. In general, pharmaceuticals require rigorous testing, clinical trials, and lengthy review procedures before being approved for sale by the FDA. A decade before Viagra hit the market, Pfizer researchers were researching potential drugs for heart patients. *Sildenafil* didn't work very well on heart symptoms, but during trials it became apparent that it worked on another problem. It was a relatively easy decision for Pfizer marketers and researchers to pursue a new direction: roughly 30 million American men suffer from erectile dysfunction, and only about 10 percent were being treated for the condition. Viagra was also easy to differentiate from treatments already on the market, which were invasive and sometimes difficult to use. Viagra was an easy pill to swallow that promised localized effects.

Despite its popularity, Viagra encountered technical difficulties during its introductory stage. Side effects included headaches, indigestion, and hazy vision. But the worst side effect received the most publicity: it could put some cardiac patients at risk for heart attack. In addition, says David Brinckley, director of marketing, Pfizer "had to contain misinformation about the condition [of erectile dysfunction] and the drug."

As Viagra entered the growth stage in its product life cycle, competing products began to arrive on the scene, including Uprima (from TAP Pharmaceuticals) and Vasomax (from Zonagen and Schering-Plough). Bayer and ICOS/Eli Lilly also had products in the works. It was clear that with these new competitors Pfizer needed to capitalize on its position as first in the marketplace. One way it did that was to be a force in raising awareness about the condition. David Brinckley describes former senator Bob Dole's awareness advertisements as a "natural" because Dole's image among older men—the greatest number of ED patients—is as someone with great courage. Brinckley calls Dole's advertisements "the second wave of the ED discus-

sion," in which the situation was made more human and less clinical. Of course, Pfizer's hope was that consumers would associate Bob Dole's courage with their product.

Brinckley notes that Viagra "is like a lot of other pharmaceutical products," in that, because it is sold only by prescription, its relationship to the services of physicians and pharmacists is important to its success. "Our biggest job as marketers is to get guys to talk to their doctors and get doctors to talk to them," he notes. Of course, if doctors and patients don't talk about sexuality, thousands of bottles of Viagra could sit on the shelves.

Brinckley says that Viagra has recently settled into a "more traditional life cycle process," during which Pfizer plans to do further development to refine the product and investigate the potential of related products, such as a faster acting Viagra wafer and a similar product for women. However, because of the nature of the pharmaceutical business, all of these developments will take time and millions of dollars. Still, Brinckley is optimistic. As new products are developed, he says, "the winner is really the patient."

Questions

1. As a product like Viagra reaches the maturity stage of the life cycle, what steps can Pfizer take to maintain its product's position in the marketplace?

2. In what ways is the connection between goods and services important to the future success of a product like Viagra?

3. Visit Pfizer's main Web site (www.pfizer.com) and choose the "Health, Medicines, & Lifestyle" and then the "Diseases and Conditions" links. Select a condition and then view the products that Pfizer offers. How does the Web site enhance Pfizer's product line?

SOURCES: Viagra Web site, www.viagra.com, and Pfizer Web site, www.pfizer.com, accessed March 3, 2000; Alexandra Alger, "Viagra Falls," *Forbes*, February 7, 2000, pp. 130, 132; Mindy Blodgett, "Prescription Strength," *CIO Magazine*, February 1, 2000, www.cio.com; "Move Over Viagra: Competition Is on the Way," *Health Central*, November 30, 1999, www.healthcentral.com; David Friedman, "A Real Growth Stock," *Salon News Real*, April 1998, www.salon.com.

Hasbro, Inc.

How many of these names do you recall from childhood—Play-Doh, Tonka toys, Nerf balls, G.I. Joe, Risk, Monopoly, Trivial Pursuit? Chances are, you played with at least one or two of these toys and games, along with plenty of other products from Hasbro, Inc. Hasbro is the second largest toy manufacturer in the United States, after Mattel. And its brands are well known around the world. Even with such strong brands, company revenues began to founder during the late 1990s as both children and adults began to turn away from traditional toys and games toward electronic and interactive choices. So Hasbro marketers looked for ways to strengthen existing brands as well as develop new products for these new media. According to the GartnerGroup, "Companies that have strong brand identities and popular time-tested products can leverage those corporate assets in cyberspace rather than fall over and die in the face of the threat presented by the new medium." Hasbro decided to trade on its strengths rather than fall over and die.

What came out of the crisis was a perfect blend of the old and the new: Monopoly for the new millennium. Since its introduction in 1935, the traditional Monopoly board game has sold more than 200 million copies, in 80 countries, translated into 26 languages. Monopoly has now been played by four generations of devoted fans, whether at camp on a rainy summer day or in formal tournaments. Although not everyone necessarily knows that the game was originally set in Atlantic City, almost everyone knows the streets Park Place and Boardwalk, not to mention the phrase "go directly to jail." All of these identifying features are part of Monopoly's brand recognition. So Hasbro marketers looked to its popular old standby to help attract a new generation of customers.

The company formed a subsidiary, Hasbro Interactive, to develop new interactive games and transform old favorites. In 1995, the division released its first Monopoly CD-ROM, which sold 1 million copies and became the fifth best-selling PC game of all time. Four years later an updated version hit the market. In the new version, players could customize the 3D board properties with streets and landmarks of their own choosing, even their own hometowns. They could choose from several game board options: 1930s Atlantic City, a custom-made town such as their own, or one of ten modern preprogrammed city boards, including Atlanta, New York, Boston, San Francisco, and Toronto. Still, the CD-ROM version wasn't all the company had in store. Hasbro decided to bring Monopoly and other favorite games to the Internet. "We're pioneering e-mail

as a new on-line game platform," explained Tom Dusenberry, president of Hasbro Interactive. "We don't see board games disappearing, but we do see that there needs to be an alternative means of delivering games to customers in today's marketplace. . . . We've been in the interactive game business for [several] years now. Our primary focus has been taking our games into the computer world. But, that being said, the number one reason why people are buying computers is so they can get on the Internet. And the number one reason why they get on the Internet is e-mail. So we came up with the concept of making e-mail a computing game platform."

How does e-mail Monopoly work? Consumers can purchase the game at Hasbro's Web site or even at a retail store. They load the game into their computer, then e-mail a friend, asking if the friend wants to play. "They can play and send a message back to you at the same time," explains Dusenberry. Thus, the game hasn't changed at all—just the medium over which it is played. Players still get rich, go broke, go to jail. They just don't have to be in the same room with each other.

Hasbro's ability to adapt one of its strongest brands to new media and new marketplaces speaks volumes about its capacity to survive and grow as a company. Being able to transfer a brand from one generation to the next is perhaps the best test of brand loyalty. Even expert analysts are impressed by Hasbro's most recent move. "I haven't heard of anybody else doing this kind of thing to date," says Jim Browning, senior analyst with GartnerGroup. "Hasbro is taking advantage of the ubiquitous nature of e-mail to make it easy and fun for people to play games. Millions of people have e-mail, and users can play at their convenience." That's just what Hasbro has in mind: millions of consumers having fun playing Hasbro games.

Questions

1. Think of your favorite Hasbro toy or game—or any toy you remember well from childhood. Jot down everything you can remember about it, from its name to what it looked like, to what the packaging looked and felt like. Now look back at this toy as a marketer; what features most effectively made it a strong brand in your mind?

2. Do you think that Hasbro's move to put some of its games on the Internet will increase or decrease its brands' equity? Why?

3. Browse through the Monopoly Web site at www.monop-oly.com. What are some characteristics you would use to describe the game's trade dress?

4. Again, go to the Monopoly Web site. What activities have Hasbro marketers been doing to strengthen its Mo-nopoly brand?

SOURCES: Monopoly Web site, www.monopoly.com, accessed March 7, 2000; "Hasbro, Inc.," *Hoover's Online*, www.hoovers.com, accessed March 7, 2000; "Hasbro Interactive's New Monopoly CD-ROM Lets You Play Your Way," press release, Hasbro Web site, November 15, 1999, www.hasbro.com; Gene Koprowski, "Park Place in Cyberspace," *Executive Edge*, April-May 1999, www.ee-online.com.

 VIDEO CASE **13**

RadioShack

"You've got questions? We've got answers." RadioShack's new slogan permeates its ads, its 7,000 stores, its new corporate culture. When Leonard Roberts took over as CEO of RadioShack (formerly Tandy), in the mid-1990s, RadioShack was suffering against competitors like Best Buy and Circuit City. RadioShack, then dubbed "the Technology Store," didn't have the selection or the low prices that the large discount stores offered. But Roberts discovered that RadioShack had something no one else did: answers to questions that consumers asked when they visited RadioShack's stores. So Roberts told his managers to tear up their job descriptions. "From now on, you have a new job description: either you serve our customers directly, or you serve someone who does." When Roberts was through reshaping RadioShack's mission and corporate culture, "We were no longer selling products, we were selling answers," he says.

Meanwhile, competition for all aspects of wireless communications was growing more and more intense. RadioShack had several suitors for partnerships in delivering communications goods and services, but it settled on Sprint. Roberts cites five reasons for doing so: (1) Within a few years, Sprint would have the largest wireless system in the United States. (2) The agreement would grant RadioShack exclusivity of the Sprint brand on its residential phone equipment. (3) 70 percent of RadioShack's customers were actually AT&T users, so Roberts saw great potential for converting customers. (4) The Sprint management team was stable and shared many of the values held by RadioShack managers. (5) Sprint was the most technologically innovative company that RadioShack was dealing with. Later, Roberts would cite number 4 as the most important reason for entering into a channel agreement with Sprint.

Sprint also benefited tremendously from the agreement. First, RadioShack literally has a store in every American neighborhood; most consumers have to drive no more than a few minutes to reach a RadioShack store. Second, Sprint gained access to RadioShack's 30,000 sales representatives. Third, RadioShack agreed not to sell competitors' goods and services. Fourth, RadioShack's ability to acquire customers for Sprint was tremendous.

RadioShack took the opportunity the agreement presented to remodel its outdated stores, constructing actual "Sprint stores" within all of its RadioShack stores. Customers now knew exactly where to go for Sprint products—and to get answers to questions concerning Sprint. The relationship has had some channel conflict, but for the most part it has worked well. The companies made a mutual agreement to advertise the Sprint stores, and Roberts laughs as he recalls the challenges of combining two different advertising agencies to get the job done. To help smooth over potential or actual conflicts, Sprint and RadioShack developed a joint steering committee, composed of three top executives below the rank of CEO from each company. The committee meets monthly on tactical and strategic issues.

Then Sprint and MCI merged. Did Roberts see this as a threat? No, he insisted, because the Sprint brand remained strong. Outside telecommunications industry analyst Dennis Telzrow predicted that "MCI-Sprint will give RadioShack the opportunity to leverage their marketing expertise with a much larger telecommunications entity." Meanwhile, Roberts intends to intensify RadioShack's presence in consumers' homes via Sprint's constantly connected Internet service (called ION) and a more recent agreement with Microsoft involving an e-commerce alliance. The ultimate goal? "We want to be known as the home connectivity store," says Roberts. In other words, Roberts wants RadioShack to deliver everything consumers need to integrate their Internet, cable or satellite TV, and local and long distance calling services. Delivering all this technology—and all these answers—to consumers' homes means actually dispatching fleets of service vans to neighborhoods to make installations and adjustments. Roberts has decided to franchise potentially half of this business to accomplish fast delivery of these services and to offset training costs with the franchise fees. This may mean that RadioShack loses some control over this part of the channel, but the company is willing to take that risk. Why? Because getting there first is critical to winning the market. "Everyone's building the big engines," notes Roberts, "but no one's building the tracks. We're building the tracks." That sounds like a good answer.

VC

Questions

1. How does Leonard Roberts's retooling of his managers* job descriptions relate to RadioShack's partnership with Sprint?

2. Between RadioShack and Sprint, whom would you designate channel captain? Why?

3. Is exclusivity important in the agreement between RadioShack and Sprint? Why or why not?

4. Visit the RadioShack Web site at www.radioshack.com. Does the site itself reflect the company's slogan "You've got questions,? We've got answers." Why or why not?

SOURCES: RadioShack Web site, www.radioshack.com, accessed March 2000; Edward C. Baig, "CEO of Tandy Tunes in on Fix for RadioShack," *USA Today,* January 18, 2000, p. 10B; Mike Ricciuti and Jim Hu, "Microsoft, RadioShack in Surprise Deal," *CNET News.com,* November 11, 1999, www.news.cnet.com; Andrea Ahels, "MCI-Sprint Merger Has Big Ties to Texas," *Fort Worth Star-Telegram,* October 5, 1999, www.star-telegram.com; Om Malik, "Going Digital," *Forbes,* April 5, 1999, www.forbes.com; "Cable, Phone, Internet: Just Call . . . RadioShack?" *BusinessWeek Online,* March 1, 1999, www.businessweek.com.

VIDEO CASE 14

Wine.com

"Wine.com is a direct marketing company," states Wine.com's Web site, under the section that describes the company's business model. "It sources directly from producers, markets directly to customers, and manages product delivery. This gives the company control over the execution of all aspects of the ordering process, thus ensuring quality." The description makes Wine.com sound like a traditional organization engaged in traditional direct marketing—but it isn't. Nor are many other companies that operate exclusively online. In fact, these companies are practically changing the definition of direct marketing because of their ability to, as Wine.com co-founder Peter Granoff puts it, "collapse geography." In other words, although Wine.com's target market may be fairly narrow in that it encompasses adults who are interested in wine, the market encompasses wine lovers everywhere, not just in California or New York.

If you're over 21 and want to order a bottle of wine—expensive or inexpensive—you can click on to Wine.com from anywhere and make your choice. If you're interested in good food or even the restaurant business, Wine.com's Web site can offer you helpful information to educate you about wine. That's Wine.com's major point—information. Yes, the company wants to sell eligible customers its wine products, but in doing so it wants to educate them about what they are buying. "Wine is the ideal product for the Internet," notes Granoff, because the Internet can overcome geographic obstacles and because of the amount of information that many consumers want about the products they are purchasing.

What does Wine.com offer consumers that their local wine shop doesn't? First, a larger selection of wines that have been selected by experts. "We do the selecting for you," says Granoff. But it doesn't stop there. Wine.com's site includes wine tasting charts and notes from tasters. If after making a purchase based on all this information a consumer isn't happy with a choice, Wine.com offers a money-back guarantee. Of course, says Granoff, if a consumer is looking for a bottle of wine to have for dinner that evening, the place to shop is the local bricks-and-mortar store. But for those who think ahead, want to stock up, or are planning for a special occasion, Wine.com offers the widest range of choices backed by the most information, and it emphasizes customer service every step of the way.

When you visit the site, you can browse through red, white, bubbly and rare wines; find out what's new; get suggestions for gifts; even e-mail questions to experts. Within the site, you can visit specialty shops such as the Rare Wine Shop. "We are dedicated to offering a quality selection of wines to meet the needs of a wide range of wine lovers, from novices to the more seasoned collectors," notes Bill Newlands, president and CEO of Wine.com. "The Rare Wine Shop at Wine.com offers us the opportunity to capitalize on the demand for world class, hard-to-find vintages." Your neighborhood wine store is unlikely to have much—if any—inventory of rare wines because they are so expensive to stock.

Selling wine over the Internet isn't necessarily complicated, but distributing it is, due to state laws regarding alcohol sales and distribution. So, although the company calls itself a direct marketer, and began as a direct shipper, Wine.com now functions within a network of in-state wholesalers and retailers to deliver wine shipments within the United States. The delivery systems must be customized to meet the regulations of each state. International shipments can be made directly to the consumer.

Recently, Wine.com has entered into a number of co-marketing and co-branding agreements with such diverse companies as United Airlines, the Bloomberg Business Report, America Online, Amazon.com, and Microsoft. Granoff comments that the marketing budget is huge—upwards of $10 million per year. This hefty budget is targeted to one goal: making consumers aware of the site. Co-branding and co-marketing alliances assist in boosting consumer awareness.

It's not surprising that Granoff sees Wine.com's ultimate market in global terms—beyond simply shipping bottles of wine from the United States to another country. "I see a global business in the future, with global sourcing and distribution," he predicts. Undoubtedly, many of his customers would be willing to drink to that.

Questions

1. Why is customer service so important to a company like Wine.com?

2. As a consumer, what do you see as the advantages to shopping for wine this way? Any disadvantages?

3. In addition to those mentioned, describe one or two other types of organizations that Wine.com might benefit from establishing co-marketing or co-branding agreements.

4. Browse through the Wine.com Web site at www.wine.com. Do you find it to be as information-rich as Peter Granoff claims it to be? Why or why not?

SOURCES: Wine.com Web site, www.wine.com, accessed March 2000; "Wine.com Pulls the Cork on Remarkable Rare Wines," company press release, February 24, 2000, www.wine.com; Paul M. Sherer, "Thomas H. Lee Leads an Investment of $50 Million in Retailer Wine.com, *Wall Street Journal*, November 10, 1999, www.djreprints.com; Sandeep Junnarker, "Growing Wine Rivals Pour It On," *CNet News.com*, September 27, 1999, www.news.cnet.com; "Wine.com Announces Next Phase of Wine Portal," September 24, 1999, company press release, www.wine.com; Julie Landry, "Virtual Vineyard.com goes Wine.com Tasting," *Redherring.com*, September 16, 1999, www.redherring.com; Sandeep Junnarker, "Virtual Vineyards Harvests Venture Cash," *Cnet News.com*, June 18, 1999, www.cnet.com.

VIDEO CASE 15

Polaroid

"Where will you stick it?" If you hear those words from a young teen brandishing a brightly-colored camera, relax. You aren't being attacked or insulted. To the contrary, your friend probably just wants to take your picture. "Where will you stick it?" is Polaroid's slogan for its new I-Zone pocket camera, the firm's new consumer-product introduction in more than 20 years. It's also a new target market for Polaroid product: teens. Polaroid, famous for its instantly-developing film, has come up with a new filmstrip with a sticky back that turns tiny photos into instant stickers. Kids can snap a photo, pull out the strip, wait a few seconds for the picture to develop, then peel it off the strip and stick it anywhere—on a notebook, on a jacket or hat, on a key chain, on a purse, or on a bicycle. Within months of its launch, the I-Zone became the No. 1-selling camera in the United States.

How did the I-Zone zoom to the top of the charts so quickly? Polaroid made a commitment to integrated marketing communications in researching the market, getting the product to the right consumers, and promoting it. First, they did the research, and discovered that teens now have more spending power than any other generation of teens before them. "Polaroid decided to enter the kids market because the kids market right now is the biggest it's ever been in history," says Mary Courville. Second, they divided the market further, into pre-teens—tweens—and older teenagers. Girls seem to be most interested in taking pictures, so the Polaroid team focused there. Third, they thought "outside the box" about different uses for a camera. For instance, the younger girls actually view the camera as a fashion accessory—so a sleek design in fashion bright colors was important. By thinking creatively, the team came up with whole new ways to use a camera. "It's not about taking pictures to put in a photo album," explains Courville. This is "a cool camera that allows kids to be creative and have fun. It's about play and doing what you want to do." The I-Zone's sticky film lets young photographers become artists. They can take their camera anywhere and stick their pictures anywhere.

Courville stresses that Polaroid couldn't have come up with either the product or the promotion that followed without integrated communications among the marketing, public relations, advertising, and promotion staff. "We're a very tight group," she says. "We're always together." They conducted focus groups and field tests together. They met with the advertising agency together. "We are just always talking to each other," she says. "Always, always, always." Not only does this increase the efficiency with which the product is launched it keeps the message to the consumer consistent. The consumer sees the same message through television commercials, magazine or Internet ads, and various promotions.

What exactly is the message? For Polaroid in general, says Courville, it's about instant gratification. "Only Polaroid can give you that photograph instantly. Only Polaroid can enliven your time, your party, right then. Polaroid is the only one that allows you to capture the moment instantly." I-Zone takes it a step farther by giving kids instant pictures that they can use to transform and personalize something else—a backpack, a belt buckle, a baseball cap.

In addition to advertising in traditional media as well as the Internet, Polaroid decided to hook up with the popular teen group the Backstreet Boys, becoming a sponsor of their "Into the Millennium" tour. "Sponsorship allowed us wonderful promotional opportunities," comments Courville. Since the group's biggest fans are girls age 14 to 17, the match was perfect. The Backstreet Boys actually used the I-Zone cameras during their concerts, and girls were invited on stage to have their pictures taken with band members, with I-Zone cameras, of course. Polaroid distributed cameras to fans at concerts so they could take pictures of each other and the band. Results were so positive that Polaroid decided to sponsor another pop singer, Britney Spears, the following year. "This sponsorship is the perfect combination of music, fun, and friendship—all key aspects of our target consumers' lifestyle. Polaroid is committed to giving teens and tweens exactly what they want." Even the stars themselves seem hooked on I-Zone. "I'm psyched to be working with Polaroid," says Spears. "The I-Zone is the coolest way for me and my fans to have fun taking pictures. We can stick them everywhere." That's just what Polaroid has in mind.

Questions

1. In what ways does Polaroid link its promotional strategy to the process of communication?

2. What steps might Polaroid's IMC group take to market I-Zone overseas? Would it be successful? Why or why not?

3. Did the I-Zone promotion with the Backstreet Boys succeed according to standard objectives? Why or why not?

4. Visit the Polaroid Web site (www.polaroid.com) to find out more about I-Zone. Imagine that you are part of the IMC group, and write a slogan for the site with suggestions for more ways to use the I-Zone and more places to stick the photos. Where else besides the Web would you advertise or conduct a promotion?

SOURCES: Polaroid Web site, www.polaroid.com, accessed March 10, 2000; "Polaroid and Britney Spears Will Drive You Crazy," *PR Newswire*, March 3, 2000; Cara Beardi, "Targeting Teens Pays Off for Polaroid" *Advertising Age*, March 6, 2000, p. 16. "Polaroid's New I-Zone Pocket Camera #1 Selling Camera in the United States," *PR Newswire*, December 2, 1999.

VIDEO CASE 16

Pizza Hut

Just about everyone loves pizza. And just about everyone has a favorite pizza joint, whether it's a local neighborhood spot or one of the big chains. If you're a pizza lover, maybe it's the cheese that makes your mouth water; or maybe it's the sauce, toppings, or crust. Whatever your favorite pizza is, Pizza Hut wants to serve it to you. Pizza Hut is the world's largest pizza chain, with more than 11,000 outlets in the United States and 85 countries around the world. Pizza Hut's Pan Pizza brand is its best selling pizza, but pizza lovers can get everything from its Stuffed Crust brand to a line of dessert pizzas with fruit and other sweet toppings at its popular lunch buffet. The latest blockbuster, though, is called the Big New Yorker.

The Pizza Hut marketing team doesn't care whether you live in New York or Wisconsin; they don't care whether you've ever even been to New York. But they are betting that if you love pizza, you'll love the Big New Yorker. Initial ads and press releases for the new pizza were informative. After all, most people would ask, what is a Big New Yorker? Consumers learned that the Big New Yorker is big: 16 inches instead of 14 inches. The crust is thicker without losing a bit of crustiness. It's also cut into eight slices instead of twelve, so people can fold a slice. Then there's more cheese and a sweeter sauce. Those are the

facts. But with all the pizzas out in the marketplace, Pizza Hut still needed to find a way to differentiate this specialty.

The company's marketers chose a series of celebrity testimonials, leading up to the Super Bowl—guys like Donald Trump and Spike Lee, whose images represent New York. "We picked larger-than-life celebrities because we wanted to make sure people understood that this pizza was huge," says Sean Gleason, director of advertising at Pizza Hut. "And it really doesn't get much more simple than that, quite honestly. We wanted to communicate the size and the value price of $9.99." Gleason points out that no other pizza chain uses celebrities the way the Big New Yorker ads did. "This is a statement that we are number one in pizza, and no one else could do this." Pizza Hut spent millions of dollars for the pre-game Super Bowl commercials, running one every twenty minutes in the hour leading up to the game. This made 200 million consumers aware of the new product.

The marketing team, including advertising, public relations, and promotion, chose television as the medium because they thought they could present the product in the best light—literally and figuratively. A television commercial showing a steaming hot pizza could send viewers to the phone quickly and more effectively than any other medium. It also reaches the most people.

In addition to the commercials, Pizza Hut mailed print coupons and other promotional materials to consumers. The public relations team also found a unique way to launch the actual product: a press conference attended by New York Mayor Rudolph Giulliani. Although the mayor couldn't endorse the pizza, he bit into a slice and said, "This pizza is great." The photo and caption ran nationally in ads. But one of the largest promotional programs Pizza Hut engaged in was a tie-in with Star Wars: Episode I. The Big New Yorker pizza is targeted at the same broad-based audience as Star Wars, including baby boomers and their children. The release of the new Star Wars movie was also a big media event. "Because of that kind of qualitative tie-in to our product of the Big New Yorker, we've really focused on size," explains Bill Ogle, director of promotions. "We felt there was some kind of neat intrinsic tie-in." Pizza Hut broadened the promotion even more, tying in the Big New Yorker and the movie with its sister brands, KFC and Taco Bell, with a game that consumers could play to win prizes. Subsequent tongue-in-cheek commercials focused on the size of outer space as it related to the size of the Big New Yorker.

To celebrate the Big New Yorker's huge success—70 million sold in its first year—Pizza Hut teamed up with CDNow in a promotion that offered consumers a free, custom CD with every order of a Big New Yorker. CDNow is an e-commerce company that offers music and entertainment products, including custom CDs and music downloads. "We wanted to thank

consumers in a big way," explained Randy Gier, chief marketing officer of Pizza Hut. "What better way to celebrate than by combining two of America's favorite tastes—pizza and music—with the same kind of value and variety that have made Pizza Hut famous." He's right: consumers are eating it up in a big way.

Questions

1. Do you think that comparative advertising would have worked better than celebrity testimonials in Pizza Hut's launching of the Big New Yorker? Why or why not?

2. Would the U.S. advertising campaign automatically work overseas? Why or why not? If not, what changes might the marketing team make?

3. Pizza Hut chose a tie-in with Star Wars: Episode I as a sales promotion. Can you think of another tie-in that might be equally effective?

4. Visit the Pizza Hut Web site at www.pizzahut.com. Is the site effective as an interactive ad for The Big New Yorker and other products? Why or why not?

SOURCES: Pizza Hut Web site, www.pizzahut.com, accessed February 15, 2000; "Pizza Hut," company capsule, *Hoover's Online*, www.hoovers.com, accessed February 15, 2000; "Pizza Hut Predicts Big Win with Pizza Hut Big Game Day Ad Strategy," *PR Newswire*, January 26, 2000; "The Big New Yorker from Pizza Hut Celebrates 1st Anniversary and Offers Consumers a Free, Customized CD from CDNow," *PR Newswire*, January 21, 2000.

VIDEO CASE 17

Concept2

Concept2 is the story of two brothers who turned their passion for a sport into a passion for a business, involving their wives, children, friends, and relatives. In 1976, Pete and Dick Dreissigacker, avid rowers, were training to make the final cut for the U.S. Olympic Team in rowing. During training, they started tinkering with a design for a new oar—Pete is a design engineer; Dick is a mechanical engineer. They didn't make the Olympic team, but they came up with an oar design that has since swept through the sport around the world. Made from synthetic materials instead of wood, the oars are stronger, lighter, and cheaper than their traditional counterparts, and rowers worldwide love them. Within a few years, the brothers, who had settled in Vermont, were kicking around ideas for an indoor rowing machine that would allow them to continue their beloved pastime during winter, when Vermont rivers and lakes were frozen. So they turned Pete's old bicycle upside down, nailed it to the floor, added a handle and seat that would slide, and presto—they had the first indoor rowing machine.

Twenty years later, the Concept2 Indoor Rower is still sold directly from the Dreissigacker's factory in Morrisville, Vermont. Customers can place orders via phone or the Web site, and although miles may separate Concept2 from its customers, the company has worked hard to develop relationship selling so that everyone who buys a Concept2 rower will feel like part of the Concept2 "family." Customer service is a top priority. "We aren't trying to sell a lot of machines," explains Judy Geer, wife of cofounder Dick Dreissigacker. "We're trying to have a lot of satisfied customers." Although the Web site has a section containing answers to most-asked questions, customers can contact someone at Concept2 for in-person answers anytime. Shawn Larose is a service technician who handles problems or warranty questions for customers who call: "When people call with what they think is a very serious problem and it turns out to be a 30-second answer, that's very rewarding."

Concept2 also has an on-staff "coach," Larry Gluckman, to help customers learn how to use the rower and improve their individual workouts. Concept2 publishes a semiannual newsletter called Ergo Update, with product and company news, rowing stories from customers, and letters the company receives. "We get letters [that describe how] we've changed someone's life, we've really improved their health, and that definitely makes it," notes Judy Geer. To make the sport of indoor rowing a bit more interesting—and to keep customers connected with each other and the company—Concept2 started a world ranking system, in which rowers from anywhere in the world can send in their best times achieved rowing a virtual distance on their rower. Ergo Update publishes the rankings once a year. Finally, anyone can take a tour of the Concept2 factory. They just need to call or show up. All of these approaches help build continuous relationships with customers by keeping them connected to Concept2 in personal ways, no matter where they live.

Concept2 makes ordering a rower easy, but the company had to find ways to provide demonstrations to potential buyers to sell their product. After all, at roughly $800 plus shipping, an indoor rower is not a small purchase for most individuals, no matter how passionate they are about the sport. Once the questions are answered, people still want to see how the equipment works before making a purchase. So Concept2 has a 22-minute promotional video that shows how the machine functions—how it's built, how to assemble it, and how to use it. Anyone who watches the short film—narrated by Dick and Judy's 8-year-old daughter, Hannah—will pull out a credit card in a single stroke.

Questions

1. Concept2 focuses on relationship selling. As the company grows, in what ways might the company use consultative selling and telemarketing? If you think either of these approaches would be a poor choice for the company, explain why.

2. In what ways might Concept2 practice creative selling?

3. Why is demonstration an important part of the Concept2 sales process? Do you think that Concept2 handles this well? Why or why not?

4. Visit the Concept2 Web site at www.concept2.com and browse through the site for ways that the company uses the site to develop its relationship with customers. Discuss your findings in class.

SOURCES: Concept2 Web site, www.concept2.com, accessed March 23, 2000; Concept2 video and promotional materials, 1999; Sean Thomas Langan, "The Big Blade," *Vermont Inc.*, February 2000, pp. 22-23, 59; David Churbuck, "Virtual Racing," *Forbes.com*, May 6, 1996, www.forbes.com.

VIDEO CASE | 18

Cybex International

"Fitness reaches into every motion and emotion in our daily lives, whether at work, at home, or at play. It electrifies our every action and thought, from the most mundane tasks to the most dramatic achievements. The pursuit of fitness is about nothing less than the quality of our lives." Cybex's vision statement elevates the pursuit of fitness far beyond pumping iron and doing sit-ups. In fact, it sounds more like the philosophy of ancient Greek athletes, whose fitness was virtually deified.

Cybex International manufactures premium fitness equipment—cardiovascular systems, strength systems, and personal systems. More than 80 percent of the company's products are sold to commercial markets, including health and fitness clubs, hotels, and schools, with nearly 20 percent going to consumers through independent retailers. Cybex emphasizes quality, technology, and prestige, from the way it builds and markets its products to the way it prices them. Thus, fitness buffs who know the brand names of equipment used at their clubs or schools recognize Cybex as a top-flight name. Some gyms even advertise that they have Cybex treadmills, cycles, steppers, and hikers, along with its resistance machines and weights. Yet Cybex is careful to balance the image of the workout fanatic with the one of the average athlete who wants to keep fit. "Life is about finding the perfect balance," says the company's Web site. "Whether you're a club owner, a weekend warrior or a soccer mom, deep down, you know this is true. It's our goal, too. To offer superior technology that produces maximum results. With plenty of enjoyment.20"

Cybex assumes that its customers are serious about the good life—including the best workout equipment. "At Cybex, we continue to examine trends within the industry to develop new products that help improve human performance and address the daily needs of users," says Peter Haines, CEO and President of Cybex International. So, getting fit on a Cybex machine does cost more than slapping on a pair of running shoes and heading out the door for a quick jog. If you want a Personal Climber 400s stepper, it will cost you around $2,395, plus shipping. Your own commercial-quality personal gym system will run you $4,195. Strength systems come in components that can run anywhere from $500 to $1,000 each. If you purchase options at the time you buy your system, they'll cost less than if you wait to purchase them later. Cybex products, particularly the commercial-quality items, are manufactured to take a beating—they are designed using the latest technology and constructed of the strongest materials. Because of the premium construction and durability, Cybex customers expect to pay more for their workouts than those who purchase other machines.

Prestige pricing requires Cybex to seek out partnerships and alliances with other organizations that have similar images and objectives. One such organization is FitCare.com, an online integrated health source that specializes in sports, health, and fitness lifestyles, giving credence both to traditional and alternative approaches to health. "The Web site represents the best that all related philosophies have to offer and uniquely packages these choices for consumers and professionals to make educated decisions," states one press release. Cybex and FitCare.com have planned a partnership that includes such elements as articles on new developments in human performance and exercise science by Cybex training expert Tracy Morgan. Cybex will also offer an advanced personal training certification program online at FitCare.com. Again, Cybex and FitCare.com assume that Web site customers—both consumer and commercial—are looking for the best in health and fitness training resources.

Finally, Cybex launched a new site called eCybex.com, which allows consumers and trade partners to log in to a secure account where they can shop online and track their orders. "This new site is what we're all about at Cybex—a passion for human performance," says Peter Haines. "We intend for eCybex.com to be an easy, educational and fun tool for everyone from our dealers to club owners to fitness beginners and world-class athletes." Cybex wants all of its customers to feel as though they belong to an elite, virtual Cybex health club. The company even wants them to "feel like millionaires." As part of the site launch, the company held an online contest, "Who

Wants to Feel Like a Millionaire," a takeoff on the popular television game show. For eight weeks, a new health and fitness question was posted on the site each week. Contestants submitted their answers, and each correct answer was entered into the grand prize drawing. What was the grand prize? A vacation at an elite spa, where any millionaire can afford to go.

Questions

1. Suppose the economy went into a recession and the demand for premium exercise equipment fell. Toward which of the other pricing objectives might Cybex marketers be forced to shift? Explain your choice.

2. How does Cybex's current choice of pricing objectives reflect the company's vision, and vice versa?

3. How and where do you exercise? Is cost a consideration in your choice? Did image—of the sport you participate in, the club you belong to, and so forth—play a part in your decision? Why or why not?

4. Visit the new Cybex site at www.ecybex.com and browse through it to look for ways that Cybex uses the idea of prestige to market its products. Then, come up with your own slogan for a single product line, or for all of Cybex's products in general, emphasizing prestige.

SOURCES: Cybex Web sites, www.cybexintl.com and www.ecybex.com, accessed April 5, 2000; "Cybex International," company capsule, *Hoover's Online*, April 5, 2000, www.hoovers.com; "Cybex Introduces Products to Improve Human Performance; New Cardiovascular and Strength Products Make Exercise Functional and Easier," *Business Wire*, March 23, 2000; "Cybex Announces Strategic Partnership with FitCare.com," *Business Wire*, March 20, 2000; "Cybex's Passion for Human Performance Goes On-Line, New Web site Launched with 'Who Wants to Feel Like a Millionaire' Contest," *Hoover's Online*, February 28, 2000, www.hoovers.com; "Cybex International, Inc. Launches eCybex.com for Online Shopping and Customer Support Services for Fitness Equipment," *Business Wire*, February 3, 2000.

VIDEO CASE 19

Learjet

Bombardier Aerospace would be happy to sell you a sleek little Learjet so you can hop from customer to customer over a wide geographic area with ease and style. If you don't have $10 million but can come up with $1 million, Bombardier can still accommodate you. Here's how.

There's a brisk demand for business aircraft during a good economy, and Bombardier has been building more than usual. In 1994, the company built about 60 jets; five years later, it turned out 183. And while there is now more demand for these aircraft, industry executives also claim that they are building

better planes, so that increased quality is also increasing demand. But Bombardier and other manufacturers have figured out a way to increase demand even further by spreading the price of a single plane among several owners. Called "fractional ownership," the pricing program works like this: A business customer buys a share of a Learjet; a share of the model 60 would be about $1.4 million, with $300,000 a year in operating costs. The share comes with a guaranteed 100 hours of annual flying time. Bombardier maintains a fleet of 82 Learjets ready at all times so that each customer has access to a plane within

10 hours of a request. Since the $10 million price tag for a jet and roughly $1 million annually in running costs is more than many small businesses can afford—not to mention the fact that they are paying for the plane's down time—fractional ownership is becoming increasingly popular. When the fractional ownership business began in 1993, the aircraft industry sold three planes for the purpose. In 1999, more than 90 planes were sold into fractional ownership programs. "There is no sign of it leveling off in the next few years," predicts John Lawson, sales president of Bombardier.

Bombardier is also looking at other ways to manage the pricing function of its Learjets by managing supply chain costs. Recently, the company signed a contract with Optum, Inc. for Optum's supply chain software to improve logistics at Learjet's manufacturing facility in Wichita, Kansas. Optum will work through consulting firm Arthur Andersen. Optum's warehouse management software (WMS) will help Learjet manage its aircraft inventory levels as well as improve its receiving and shipping processes. The distribution software is intended to help Learjet track shipping in real time as well as detail individual aircraft parts as they move from the warehouse stock room to the assembly floor. Better logistics efficiency should help the company reduce the time it takes to assemble or repair an aircraft, reduce the cost of mistakes, and increase customer satisfaction. "Bombardier is looking to leverage supply chain automation and real-time inventory visibility to improve our manufacturing and service operations, and work more quickly and profitably," explains Alan Young, director of work and material planning for Bombardier Aerospace in Wichita. If the company can build more planes, more quickly—and reduce turnaround time on repairs—then it has the freedom either to invest the savings elsewhere in the business or to reduce the price of the Learjet.

If you purchase a Learjet what benefits do your millions buy you? First, Learjet offers what it calls a "strong warranty," which includes five years on major parts like airframe and structure and two years on smaller parts like windshields and paint. Second, the company offers several maintenance programs and says that operating costs are predictable because of the reliability of the plane's parts. Finally, there is a guaranteed trade-in value program. Of course, availability of some of these programs vary between outright ownership and fractional ownership, but Bombardier remains committed to customer support for all of its Learjets. "Our mission is to provide the finest support in the industry by understanding and fulfilling customer needs," notes the company Web site. That's a lofty goal, at any price.

Questions

1. If Bombardier could reduce its manufacturing and distribution costs and thus reduce the price of a Learjet, do you think that more or fewer of the planes would sell? Why?

2. Can you think of another high-priced product that would benefit from a fractional ownership program (excluding time-share apartments)? Describe your idea.

3. Visit the Learjet Web site at www.bombardier-stagearea.com and browse through the sections on "Business Transportation" for some the Learjet models, including the "Ownership" link, which provides information on operating cost, maintenance programs, and warranties. Does Bombardier appear to be practicing product line pricing with its Learjets? Why or why not?

SOURCES: Bombardier Web site, www.bombardierstagearea.com, accessed March 16, 2000; "Learjet Flies High with Optum Supply Chain Software," *PR Newswire*, March 6, 2000; "Heady Days for Bizjet Makers," *Reuters Company News*, Reuters Limited, February 27, 2000; "Bombardier Aerospace Enjoys Record Growth in Asia-Pacific and Continues to Invest in Strategic Partnerships," *PR Newswire*, February 22, 2000; "Bombardier Provides an Update on Its Deliveries and Backlogs," *Business Wire*, February 16, 2000.

CONTENTS

PART 1

Growing by Building Relationships

GC

Outside North Sioux City, South Dakota, cows graze in pastures. Nearby, cardboard boxes with black-and-white Holstein cow spots printed on them were being packed with computers and shipped all over the country. What's the connection? It was the mid-1980s, and Theodore W. Waitt, a self-described high tech maverick, had decided to start a computer company. His would be different from powerhouses like IBM or Compaq. Instead of selling through a long marketing channel that involved distributors, wholesalers, and retailers, Waitt would build and ship computers directly to customers. He set up his company as far away from a large city or California's Silicon Valley, the acknowledged mecca of the computer industry, as he could. He decided to call his new venture Gateway 2000.

Nearly twenty years later, Gateway continues to grow its business by developing strong relationships directly with organizational buyers and consumers. The marketing environment has changed; strong competitors have emerged; the economy has ridden through a recession into a boom, especially for technology-based firms; consumers have discovered the Internet; and the government has begun to review possible regulations of online commerce. Consumers who now have more discretionary income are not only willing but eager to spend it on computers and related products. They also like the convenience of custom-built computers delivered to their door.

For those who prefer to touch what they are buying and receive in-person service, the company now offers Gateway Country retail stores, where experts help consumers customize their computer and its peripherals, allowing them to try out different configurations along the way. Small businesses like the convenience and support services that Gateway offers them. "Our serve-to-order focus drives everything we do and is intended to reduce our clients' total [information technology] costs," notes Nemo Azamian, vice-president of Gateway's client care group. For instance, Gateway now has a Mobile Access program that lets business customers pick up loaner laptops at nearby Gateway Country Stores while their machines are being serviced. Jeff Weitzen, president and chief operating officer, echoes the company's customer focus: "Knowing our clients and serving their needs is absolutely everything at Gateway." In fact, as part of a major retooling in 1998, Gateway's business model included the introduction of a new product called Your:) Ware, a software program designed to personalize Gateway's relationship with its customers by connecting them to the company's Web site, where they can obtain attention and special services. Instead of focusing on how its goods and services were marketed and sold, Gateway marketers began to "spend more and more time understanding individual clients needs and building business units specifically focused on those clients," states the company's annual report. That year, Ted Waitt finally sold a computer system to his dad.

As Gateway has grown, it has also embraced all levels of the social responsibility pyramid, including the philanthropic. Through the Gateway Foundation, whose primary focus is education, the company makes corporate gifts to hundreds of nonprofit organizations. The Gateway Foundation follows strict guidelines for giving, including the fact that it does not make gifts to individuals, and organizations requesting help must be headquartered in the cities where Gateway has manufacturing operations or call centers, including North Sioux City, San Diego, Kansas City, and Salt Lake City.

Making ethical decisions is also an important part of a marketer's job at Gateway. Several years ago, marketers gave away tiny foam-rubber cows—called Stress Cows—as part of a gift package when customers purchased Gateway computer systems. Stress Cows were designed to let people squeeze away tension and stress. But it soon became apparent that small children could bite off parts of the cow, creating a choking hazard. Gateway immediately advised consumers to discard the cows. For the small number of people who had actually purchased the cows at a Gateway Country store, the company offered an immediate exchange for another Gateway product.

Overseas marketing is a vital part of Gateway's growth. McCann-Erickson is Gateway's global ad agency, and the company now has an entire division devoted to global logistics and distribution, dealing with everything from transportation regulations to import and export trade compliance. Gateway is expanding conservatively—first to Canada, then to Mexico. "You're not going to see Gateway around the globe, but you're going to see us add four to five countries," observes John Todd, Gateway's chief financial officer. Gateway has also entered into an alliance with ComputaCenter in Europe to develop store within a store environments there. Within a year or two, the company expects to be making 25 percent of its revenue from outside the United States. "We want to build the 'beyond the box' business segment," notes Todd. "We want to build it in Europe, and we want to build it in Asia. We will add 100 plus stores worldwide. The only constraint is real estate."

As the new millennium approached, Gateway made two major changes; one involving its location and one involving its name. Waitt relocated his company from the pastures of North Sioux City to the beaches of San Diego. In addition, it became apparent that Gateway was going to succeed far beyond the year 2000, executives voted to drop "2000" from the name. But the company's mission remained the same: "to humanize the digital revolution" and to develop "great client relationships." In fact, the company stopped referring to its customers and began referring to its clients, because, according to the annual report, "A 'customer' completes a transaction with a business and then leaves. We don't want anyone to leave. A 'client,' on the other hand, establishes a long-lasting relationship with a business that includes the familiarity of a common history and the interdependence of a joined future."

Questions

1. Gateway, like Dell Computer, sells directly to customers. What are some advantages that Gateway marketers have by doing so?

2. Describe ways in which you think the social-cultural environment will be an important influence on Gateway's future growth.

3. Considering various marketing environment issues, do you think it is wise for Gateway to go slow when moving into global markets? Why or why not?

4. Visit Gateway's Web site at www.gateway.com and browse through it for examples in which Gateway strives to develop relationships with its customers. Discuss your findings in class.

SOURCES: Gateway Web site, www.gateway.com, accessed March 22, 2000; "Gateway Offers Windows 2000 across Servers, Desktops, and Notebooks for Business," *PR Newswire*, February 15, 2000; "Gateway Magazine Features Michael Bolanos," *Business Wire*, February 11, 2000; Michael Kanellos, "Gateway to Expand into Canada, Elsewhere," CNET News.com, February 4, 2000, www.news.cnet.com; Stephanie Milies, "Gateway to Broaden Small-Business Services," CNET News.com, October 19, 1999, www.news.cnet.com; Elizabeth Corcoran, "Gateway 2005," *Forbes Global*, March 8, 1999, www.forbes.com; Gateway, *Annual Report*, 1998.

GC

PART 2

Gateway

Humanizing the Digital Revolution

From the very first day those cow-spotted boxes were shipped to its customers, Gateway has maintained that its relationships with its customers—both businesses and consumers—are the most important part of its marketing effort. The company is not interested in transaction-based marketing; rather, Gateway wants its name to be synonymous with relationship-based marketing. "We've created a unique model," notes Ted Waitt, who is now a billionaire. "We have more direct relationships with our customers than anyone else." Compaq and HP still sell their products through intermediaries. So Gateway executives maintain that their company has the competitive edge because customers can go right to the source for information, service, and products.

Gateway manages its relationships in a variety of ways. Because each order is personalized to fit a customer's needs, Gateway obtains a large amount of information about its customers—everything from hardware and software preferences to their birthdays. Gateway is now automating the information so

GC

that its marketers can make more efficient use of database mining and personalization technologies. The idea behind these databases is to be able to personalize communication with clients the way Amazon.com does. For instance, Gateway marketers could recommend new products on the basis of previous purchases or suggest appropriate computer-related gifts for a child's upcoming birthday.

Gateway also seeks to bond with its clients by offering them a range of products and services to buy and different venues from which to purchase them. Marketers call this increasing "attach rates," or the number of items that customers purchase along with their PCs. When a client purchases a Gateway PC, the company also offers financing, Internet access, and a personalized portal that will guide the client to related online sites where Gateway has alliances with other firms. If the strategy works, Gateway has only spent marketing dollars once to acquire a customer instead of several times to attract the same customer to different venues or different products. Gateway has also begun to develop a long-term relationship with its customer. "It is a very competitive business, but we feel by focusing on the lifetime value of the customer, and by focusing on customer satisfaction and delivering complete computer solutions, we can have a very bright future," explains Waitt.

One way to deliver complete solutions to customers is to team up with other companies to create strategic alliances. Gateway has forged alliances with such companies as OfficeMax, Sun Microsystems, and America Online (AOL). Under its co-marketing agreement with OfficeMax, Gateway plans to install Gateway "stores-within-stores" in OfficeMax retail outlets around the country. Gateway and Sun Microsystems plan to offer customers "one-stop shopping for heterogeneous, interoperable computing solutions." Under this co-marketing agreement, Sun sales reps will market Gateway computers to appropriate customers, and Gateway will pre-load these PCs with Sun's Web application software, the Sun Portal Pack. Finally, there's the huge AOL deal, in which the two companies will be able to sell high-speed Internet access services from Gateway's retail stores; Gateway will promote AOL to its clients; and AOL will handle the operation of Gateway.net, the company's own Internet service provider.

With regard to the Internet, Gateway has already established a Net presence with its own Web site, ISP, and online selling and marketing. But the alliances just described—particularly the one with AOL—increase the company's commitment to e-commerce. For instance, the Gateway-AOL agreement to sell high-speed Internet access services is based on new digital subscriber line (DSL) technology, which allows existing phone lines to carry high-speed Internet data at the same time traditional voice traffic is being carried. Some experts believe that Gateway.net will be swallowed up by further agreements with AOL, but that won't reduce Gateway's Web presence. And the AOL-Time Warner merger could mean even more opportunities for Gateway with the new $40 billion corporation.

As Gateway broadens its Internet base, the company remains committed to issues of privacy and trust among clients—both consumers and the small businesses it serves. Gateway's Web site contains a formal online privacy statement and personal reassurance from Ted Waitt that the company will always respect the client's privacy. "You can be certain that Gateway will never sell, rent, or disclose in any manner personal information you give us to any other company for their use in selling their products and services. When we do contract with another company to market or to advertise products or services for us, we will require those companies to protect your information consistent with our stringent practices," writes Waitt. Thus, despite rapid changes in technology, Gateway extends a reassuring hand to all its clients, reinforcing the image of the company that wants to humanize the digital revolution.

Questions

1. Describe at least three ways that you think Gateway's presence on the Internet will enhance its marketing efforts.

2. Write a brief memo describing your idea for an affinity program for Gateway.

3. Do you think that strategic alliances with other companies will become more or less important for Gateway over the next five years? Why?

4. Visit Gateway's Web site at www.gateway.com and click on the "Interactive Gateway" link. In what ways might this section of the site benefit Gateway's relationships with its clients?

SOURCES: Gateway Web site, www.gateway.com, accessed March 22, 2000; "Gateway and eSoft Announce Strategic Alliance," *PR Newswire*, February 23, 2000; "OfficeMax and Gateway Computer Announce Major Long-Term, Multi-Channel Strategic Alliance," *PR Newswire*, February 23, 2000; "Sun Microsystems and Gateway Announce Strategic Alliance for Integrated, End-to-End Computing Solutions," *PR Newswire*, February 23, 2000; "Gateway Offers Windows 2000 across Servers, Desktops and Notebooks for Business," *PR Newswire*, February 15, 2000; John Borland, "AOL, Gateway Strike Deal for Retail DSL," CNET News.com, January 19, 2000, www.news.cnet.com; David

Simons, "What's the Deal: Gateway Milks AOL, Squeezes Yahoo," *The Standard*, November 14, 1999, www.thestandard.com; "AOL, Gateway in Strategic Partnership," AAP, October 21, 1999, www.news.ninemsn.com; Jim Davis, "Gateway's Earnings Jump," CNET News.com, October 20, 1999, www.news.cnet.com; "A Net Gain for Gateway?" *Business Week Online*, July 19, 1999, www.businessweek.com; Anna Driver, "Gateway to Expand into Net Market," *ZDNet News*, May 20, 1999, www.zdnet.com; Jason Krause, "Ted Waitt, Net Mogul?" *The Standard*, May 13, 1999, www.thestandard.net; Elizabeth Corcoran, "Gateway 2005," *Forbes Global*, March 8, 1999, www.forbes.com; Gateway, *Annual Report*, 1998.

PART 3

Gateway

Asking All the Right Questions— and Listening

Who buys Gateway computers? College students, homemakers, entrepreneurs? Gateway marketers are finding out and using a variety of strategies and tactics to target its marketing efforts and position its products. Gateway customers now include both consumers and small to medium-sized businesses, so Gateway learns as much as it can about each to provide the best goods and services for each market. Then it tries to position its products so that customers will remember them and come back for more.

"Only by exceeding our clients' expectations can we exceed our own dreams," says company chairman Ted Waitt. Exceeding clients' expectations requires planning—overall strategic planning as well as tactical planning. And a big part of planning well is gathering information to determine who Gateway's potential and current customers are, as well as to understand what they want and need. In some cases, it means actually helping customers predict or anticipate what their needs might be. One way to gather this information is to ask questions, which Gateway does every time a customer walks into a Gateway Country store or logs onto its Web site. Questions don't necessarily focus on computers. They include everything from queries about hobbies to how many children a customer has so that marketers can begin to segment the market according to demographics such as gender or age or psychographics such as lifestyle. Then Gateway adds the information to its database for later use. However, Gateway makes its policy on privacy absolutely clear the company does not "sell, rent, or disclose in any manner personal information" that consumers provide for marketing purposes. Because of this policy, Gateway can foster closer relationships with its clients.

Recently, Gateway began to focus attention—and some concentrated marketing effort—on college students by developing a product that uses MP3, a software file format that stores computer audio files such as the latest hit songs. Use of MP3 has

been popular among the college group for several years. Gateway wants to develop a special "MP3 ready" personal computer to sell directly to college students. In addition, the company has been investigating strategic and marketing alliances with two Web sites that have already been a hit with students: College-Club.com and Embark.com. Research throughout the computer industry shows that the only segment of the PC market that is still growing is small and medium-sized businesses, and Gateway is determined to capture as much of this market as it can.

But marketers discovered that small business owners don't really want to buy their computers by phone or online; they want to be able to test products, ask questions in person, and purchase a complete set of computer solutions tailored to their own business. "I don't feel comfortable unless I can sit down and see who I am talking to," explains Bruce Short, a small-business executive. So the Gateway Country retail stores, located in 44 states—everywhere except northern New England, Wyoming, Alaska, and Hawaii—have become technology consultants for entrepreneurs. Each Gateway store assigns a personal sales representative to a business buyer and offers training classes and other support. The result has been a significant shift in Gateway's market: 45 percent of Gateway's customers are now small businesses, as opposed to individual consumers. Computer products are costly to develop, so sometimes it makes sense to test one in the marketplace before engaging in a full-scale launch.

When AOL and Gateway teamed up to sell high-speed Internet access from Gateway Country stores, marketers decided to try it out in a couple of locations first—San Diego and Baltimore. "We want to see how it's working with customers first," explained AOL spokesperson Wendy Goldberg. "Then we'll look at expanding it." Test marketing also helps a company work out any bugs before the good or service goes nationwide.

Rapid changes in technology and the marketplace mean that Gateway needs to keep asking questions to gain a competitive edge over rivals like Dell Computer, which also sells customized computers. Listening carefully to the answers will help Gateway exceed its clients' expectations—and perhaps its own.

Questions

1. Conduct your own miniature SWOT analysis of Gateway: List one strength, one weakness, one opportunity, and one threat faced by the company.

2. Imagine that you are a marketer involved in Gateway's effort to reach college students as potential customers. List ten questions you think would be helpful to ask students in a survey that could become part of your marketing database.

3. Visit Gateway's Web site at www.gateway.com and browse through either some of its consumer products or its business products to learn what you can about their target markets.

4. Once you have browsed through the products of your choice, put yourself in the place of a Gateway marketer and position the products according to one of the following strategies: attributes, price/quality, competitors, application, product user, or product class. Then come up with a slogan that reflects your positioning choice. For example, Xerox positioned its products by application and calls itself "The Document Company."

SOURCES: Gateway Web site, www.gateway.com, accessed March 22, 2000; Steven V. Brull, "A Net Gain for Gateway?" *Businessweek Online*, July 19, 1999, www.businessweek.com; John Borland, "AOL, Gateway Strike Deal for Retail DSL," CNET News.com, January 19, 2000, www.news.cnet.com; Anna Driver, "Gateway to Expand into Net Market," *ZDNet News*, May 20, 1999, www.zdnet.com; Elizabeth Corcoran, "Gateway 2005, *Forbes Global*, March 8, 1999, www.forbes.com; Gateway, *Annual Report*, 1998.

PART **4**

Gateway

Going After Consumers and Business Customers

What brought Gateway's first customers through the company's virtual door? Was it those cow-spotted boxes? Was it the intrigue of ordering a computer from a warehouse in South Dakota? Or was it the idea that Gateway would customize or-

ders not only for small businesses but also for individual consumers? Every day, marketers strive to understand the behavior of their customers—consumers and businesses—to better anticipate and serve their needs.

67% of Gateway owners come back for more.*

Thanks to everyone who made us #1 in customer loyalty.™

In roughly a decade, consumer attitudes toward computers have changed dramatically. No longer do people view computers as the domain of nerds or useful solely for writing letters and balancing the household checkbook. Now consumers view the computer as a necessary tool for everything from doing taxes, to conducting research for the kids' homework, to booking airline and vacation reservations online. These days, many people click onto their e-mail rather than pick up the phone to communicate with family and friends. More than half of all households in the United States have PCs in the home, at least half of those households have CD-ROMs, and people are connecting to the Internet faster than surveys can account for. Forrester Research predicts that in the next year, consumers will spend $16.5 billion per year on Internet access and $15.8 billion on PCs. In other words, having a computer in the home is a new norm. Gateway marketers are responding to these shifts in consumer attitudes. For instance, in its effort to court college students—an important subculture—Gateway is focusing on ways to provide them with music and entertainment through their PCs. And if a consumer does have trouble accepting and working comfortably with a PC, Gateway Country store staff can let the customer try out a machine, and the stores even offer training classes in how to use a computer.

Looking ahead, Gateway is planning for a new consumer trend—the digital home of the future, in which all of a household's information appliances are linked together and can com-

municate and regulate their functions. Gateway is already marketing a hybrid computer-TV that it calls "Destination PC-TV," but it is developing even more sophisticated versions of this product to anticipate this new consumer trend.

Gateway has also focused much of its efforts on its small- to medium-sized business customers. For most businesses, a computer is considered a capital item, one that requires at least some form of formal purchasing decision by managers. Because many of these managers prefer to try out a computer before buying one, the Gateway Country stores are staffed with Gateway personnel trained to assist business managers in designing the best computer systems for their companies. In addition, both business customers and consumers can pay for their Gateway computers in installments. Finally, Gateway's alliances with other organizations—such as Sun Microsystems—actually help business customers with their purchasing decisions. The alliance with Sun, which is known for its computer networking expertise, offers business customers one-stop shopping for many different "computing solutions." Sun sales representatives now refer software customers to Gateway for certain hardware needs. In turn, Gateway can pre-load these PCs with the Sun Portal Pack, which is Sun's Webtop application software.

Gateway strives to provide its business customers with advantages that its competitors don't. "Understanding our clients' individual business needs allows us to personalize solutions by combining the right hardware, software and support to help them leverage technology for a competitive advantage," notes Ron Smith, vice president of marketing for Gateway Business. In other words, Gateway can tailor information systems and customer service to individual businesses' needs rather than try to sell everyone the same "box." Thus, Gateway offers a wide range of products and support services designed to strengthen the company's relationship with its customers. One such service is Gateway's expanded suite of training programs, which cover more than 175 of the currently popular business-to-business applications ranging from basic tools to enhance office productivity to building an Internet presence. "With today's rapid technology advancements, clearly there's a competitive advantage for businesses to have their employees adequately trained on emerging applications," says Nemo Azamiam, vice president of Gateway Client Care Services. "As a trusted technology guide, we're empowering our clients with critical skills required for success in today's business market."

Gateway pays equal attention to all its customers, businesses and consumers alike. "Gateway is committed to giving customers immediate access to the latest technology combined with the ability to customize a solution specifically for their requirements," notes Mike Stinson, director of product marketing for Gateway Business. "Whether they are building an IT [information technology] infrastructure for their business or purchasing a home system . . . customers rely on Gateway to deliver cutting-edge technology."

GC

Questions

1. In what ways does a person's culture—values, beliefs, and traditions—influence a consumer's decision to purchase a computer?

2. To market its products successfully to consumers in other countries, what kinds of information must Gateway marketers obtain about these consumers?

3. In what ways can Gateway marketers influence a business buying decision?

4. Look at the Gateway Web site at www.gateway.com. In what ways do the text and graphics of the site break through clutter?

SOURCES: Gateway Web site, www.gateway.com, accessed March 22, 2000; "Gateway Gives Clients Increased Computing Power," *PR Newswire*, March 21, 2000; "Internet Tourists," Forbes.com, March 16, 2000, www.forbes.com; "Gateway Continues Building Its Beyond-the-Box Initiatives with Expanded Suite of Training Solutions for Businesses," *PR Newswire*, March 7, 2000; "Gateway Breaks Performance Barrier with New 1GHz Desktop Computers," *PR Newswire*, March 6, 2000; "Sun Microsystems and Gateway Announce Strategic Alliance for Integrated, End-to-End Computing Solutions," *PR Newswire*, February 23, 2000; "Gateway Offers Windows 2000 across Servers, Desktops and Notebooks for Business," *PR Newswire*, February 15, 2000; Om Malik, "Gateway: A Company in Transition," Forbes.com, December 9, 1999, www.forbes.com; Om Malik, "Gateway Goes after College Crowd," Forbes.com, November 29, 1999, www.forbes.com; Steven V. Brull, "A Net Gain for Gateway?" *Businessweek Online*, July 19, 1999, www.businessweek.com; Gateway, *Annual Report*, 1998.

GC

Putting Its Spots on Everything

PART | **5**

Gateway

Think about it: If you saw a cardboard box covered with cow spots, what's the first thing that would come to your mind? Even if you hadn't been following this case, chances are you'd answer Gateway. That's because Gateway has been so successful with packaging its brand of computers and other products that the packaging has become part of the overall trade dress, and consumers recognize the Gateway brand immediately. The package certainly evokes the product's image as something of a maverick—a company that arose from a cow pasture in South Dakota rather than from the typical slick setting in California's Silicon Valley. By now, the package also communicates value because of Gateway's reputation for building good computers at reasonable prices and offering support services for its products. But marketing concepts aside, people just plain like the spotted boxes. They get the humor and like to be in on the joke.

What about the goods that are packed in those boxes and the services that support the goods? Gateway offers a variety of computers, from complete business systems to user-friendly systems designed for individual consumers. Gateway wants its brand to be thought of as the one that blends leading technology with a human touch. "Molding technology to fit human need requires intimate knowledge of both," says Peter Ashkin, senior vice president of Gateway products. So, in selecting the product mix, "Our rule is simple: if it doesn't hold current or

future benefits for our clients, it's not for us," states the company's annual report. Gateway marketers worked with clients in developing its product line of Solo portable computers that allow users maximum flexibility wherever they are located. "Gateway's built-to-order model puts more options within reach of our small- and medium-sized business customers," says Michael Stinson, director of portable and desktop product marketing. "This flexibility lets our customers choose the level of processing power most important to them, in the system that best meets their needs, all at a price that easily fits within their budget."

Gateway also offers a line of desktop computers containing an incredibly speedy 1 gigahertz (GHz) processor, including the Gateway Select 1000, aimed at both computer enthusiasts and small businesses. "The performance of the 1GHz processor opens the door for our consumer and small business clients to reach beyond today's preconceived limits of computing to positively impact the way they live, work, learn and play," says Peter Ashkin, chief technology officer.

Gateway knows that it can't sell computers without support services, which are an integral part of the company's overall product strategy. So the company has services to meet every need, from training to installation. In addition, Gateway relies on alliances with other companies, like American Online (AOL) and OfficeMax, in co-branding projects. For instance,

name. Customers can visit the company Web site to buy everything from cow-spotted golf bags and golf balls to sport watches, baseball caps, denim shirts, and baseball caps. They can even buy toys for kids—Floppy the Cow or Mootilda, for example. If they're really gung-ho on Gateway, they can buy a soft, cow-spotted "Beanie Box" replica of the real thing for the little ones. For the office, there's the Bio Moo-chanical Pencil, cow-spotted CD sleeves, and a mug that reads "Call, Click & Come In." Gateway definitely wants you to see its particular brand of spots wherever you go.

Questions

1. What steps might Gateway take to extend the life cycle of its products?

2. Would Gateway's cow-spotted packaging work as well overseas in countries like India or China? Why or why not?

3. According to the descriptions in Chapter 11, which type of consumer would have adopted a Gateway computer in 1985? In the year 2001–2003? Explain why.

4. Visit the Gateway Web site at www.gateway.com. Click on the "Gateway Gear" link and browse through several categories of products, such as men's or women's gear, kids' gear, and computer/office gear. Do you think the addition of these products to Gateway's product mix strengthens or weakens Gateway's brand equity? Explain your answer.

SOURCES: Gateway Web site, www.gateway.com, accessed March 22, 2000; "Gateway Gives Clients Increased Computing Power," *PR Newswire*, March 21, 2000; "Gateway Breaks Performance Barrier with New 1GHz Desktop Computers," *PR Newswire*, March 6, 2000; "Gateway and eSoft Announce Strategic Alliance," *PR Newswire*, February 23, 2000; "OfficeMax and Gateway Computer Announce Major Long-Term, Multi-Channel Alliance," *PR Newswire*, February 23, 2000; "Sun Microsystems and Gateway Announce Strategic Alliance for Integrated, End-to-End Computing Solutions," *PR Newswire*, February 23, 2000; "Gateway Offers Windows 2000 across Servers, Desktops and Notebooks for Business," *PR Newswire*, February 15, 2000; "Gateway Delivers Increased Flexibility with Widest Range of Processor Choices across Its Entire Line of Solo Portable Computers," *PR Newswire*, February 14, 2000; David Kirkpatrick, "New Home. New CEO. Gateway Is Moo and Improved," *Fortune* archives, December 20, 1999, www.library.northernlight.com; Gateway, *Annual Report*, 1998.

customers recognize both Gateway and AOL as strong brands, so the agreement between the companies to market and distribute each other's products should enhance both brands. "As the Internet fans out into the mainstream . . . people are looking for technology leaders like Gateway and AOL to drive out the complexity and simplify the Internet," notes Jeff Weitzen, Gateway president and CEO. "This exciting new relationship does just that."

Then there's a whole line of other products called Gateway Gear—low-tech products that bear the Gateway logo and

PART 6

Being Everywhere

Gateway

In 1985, Gateway's founder, Ted Waitt, had a unique idea: skip the intermediaries and sell custom-built computers directly to customers. Waitt had his doubters but has continued to prove them wrong. In fact, the business has grown to include not only PCs but also a wide range of software and Internet services, as well as hardware support services. Customers can order products by phone or on Gateway's Web site, and now they can walk into one of the company's Gateway Country retail stores.

Selling computers directly to customers seemed like risky business at first, both for buyer and seller. After all, how could customers be certain that they'd get the system they wanted from this little company stuck out in a pasture? Did the com-

pany really know anything about computers? Would there be customer support when something went wrong? Could it ship its products safely, quickly, and reasonably? In the end, buyer and seller answered each other's questions with a resounding yes.

Although the idea of building computers and sending them directly to customers sounds simple, it isn't. Gateway must manage its supply chain, logistics, and distribution efficiently; failures in any one of these areas can result in significant losses for the company. For instance, in 1999 the computer industry suffered a shortage of Intel microprocessors, the "brains" of many Gateway products. The shortage, although brief, resulted in revenue losses for Gateway of over $200 million. In the end, Gateway used the experience as a lesson in the importance of developing relationships with more than one supplier. Now Gateway's Supply Management group's objectives include "identification of potential suppliers, strategic sourcing, contract negotiation, cost management, and periodic business reviews," according to the Web page. Gateway believes that long-term alliances with supply chain members minimize total cost and "yield superior customer service and quality throughout the product life cycle."

Some PC companies, such as Compaq and Hewlett-Packard, sell through intermediaries. But through direct selling, Gateway—and its most direct competitor, Dell Computer—maintains a lower overhead because the company holds almost no inventory and incurs fewer distribution expenses. Industry expert David Kirkpatrick writes that "even more important is a business model that allows [Gateway and Dell] to interact directly with the customer, which gives them numerous ways to profitably extend and grow their business." Naturally, direct selling also provides Gateway with the opportunity to develop closer relationships with its customers, resulting in brand loyalty.

Just when the industry thought it had Gateway pegged, the company surprised everyone by opening Gateway Country retail stores. Experts feared that the retail outlets would simply be an unnecessary expense without much return. But sales in Gateway stores cost the company no more than its phone sales because sales conducted through online kiosks in the stores themselves eliminate the need for inventory. In fact, the retail stores have become Gateway's fastest source of growth, generating about 25 percent of the company's total revenue. Both individual consumers and small-business managers shop in the stores, now located in 44 states. And because they are so successful, Gateway plans to double the number of stores from 200 to 400 over the next few years.

Perhaps the biggest reason the stores are so successful is the "see it, touch it, try it" aspect of shopping that they offer, in addition to in-person advice and training sessions. People who are not yet comfortable with computers can try out a keyboard, learn how to operate a mouse, find out what type of system is best for them—and then receive training in how to use it. Gateway focuses on its small-business customers through its Gateway Business Solutions Centers located in the stores. "Our specially trained business sales representatives will analyze your business computer network, or set you up with one if you don't have one," explains the Web site "complete with all the build-to-order solutions your business needs." Anyone looking for a store can find the nearest one by clicking on the "store locator" at Gateway's Web site. And if there isn't one near you, there will be soon. Gateway will let you know by sending a VW Beetle painted like a spotted cow to cruise through the streets of your town.

Questions

1. Do you think that Gateway's decision to bypass intermediaries gives the company a competitive edge over other organizations that rely on them? Why or why not?

2. In what ways do Gateway's direct selling and retail outlets complement each other?

3. Would you prefer purchasing a computer through direct sales or at one of the Gateway Country stores? Why?

4. Visit Gateway's Web site at www.gateway.com. Is the site easy to make purchases from? Why or why not?

SOURCES: Gateway Web site, www.gateway.com, accessed March 22, 2000; Steve Lohr, "Gateway Says Earnings Will Fall Below Analysts' Expectations," *New York Times*, January 6, 2000, www.nytimes.com; "Gateway Shares Tumble on Profit Warning," *USA Today*, January 6, 2000, www.usatoday.com; David Kirkpatrick, "New Home. New CEO. Gateway Is Moo and Improved," *Fortune*, December 20, 1999, www.library.northernlight.com; Steven V. Brull, "A Net Gain for Gateway?" *Businessweek Online*, July 19, 1999, www.businessweek.com; Gateway, *Annual Report*, 1998.

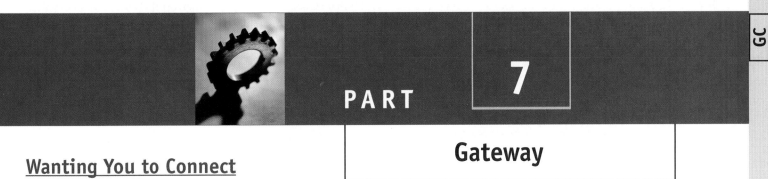

GC

PART 7

Wanting You to Connect

Gateway

"Connect with us." Gateway's slogan runs in a banner across the top of its Web pages. On the Web site itself, you can get "hot deals & cool rebates" on a variety of Gateway products. For instance, for a limited time, if you buy one of two PC models, you'll get a free Epson Stylus Color 440 printer, or choose a different printer and receive $49 off the price. If you buy a new consumer Gateway PC model and a $99 software bundle, you'll get a second bundle at half price—it's a bit like buying one pair of shoes and getting the second pair at half off. Gateway even has deals on kidstuff: Parents who purchase a Blue's Clues, Rugrats, or Gateway Astro PC get a free mousepad, monitor buddies, and CD carrying case. All of these offers are examples of sales promotions, which are valid for a designated period of time. And all are designed to generate additional sales of Gateway products.

Selecting a promotional mix for computers and related services can be complicated. Gateway has to appeal both to consumers and to businesses. The company has to reach customers who are new to computers as well as sophisticates looking to upgrade their systems and services. Some people want an entirely "digital" home; others just want to send and receive e-mails. Most businesses, no matter how small, now recognize the need for a Web presence. How can Gateway market to such a diverse collection of customers?

Sales promotions are part of the mix. During the late 1990s, with McCann-Erickson hired as its global advertising agency, Gateway also made a strong push through television advertising and increased its direct mail and online communication efforts. In one year, through these combined promotional efforts, the company raised consumer awareness of the Gateway brand from 78 percent to 92 percent. That same year, the company enjoyed some free publicity: U.S. president Bill Clinton and Ireland's prime minister Bertie Ahern met with Ted Waitt before they digitally signed a joint communique at Gateway

European headquarters in Dublin, Ireland. Gateway also sponsored a Y2K summit, placing it in the spotlight once again. Mixed publicity resulted from the company's decision to move the offices to San Diego. Events like these—some planned and paid for, others a lucky bit of publicity—help promote Gateway products.

In addition to mass media and promotions such as television commercials and free printers with purchase, Gateway has relied on personal selling, particularly at its Gateway Country stores, where customers come for in-person contact with Gateway salespeople and computers. Here, customers can ask as many questions as they want, sit down in front of any computer, and try their hand at a keyboard or mouse. They can receive personal instruction in how to use both hardware and software at all levels and choose whichever system suits them best. They don't take home their system in a spotted box, though. They place their orders at an interactive kiosk, then go home to wait for the arrival of their chosen purchase. Gateway has had tremendous success with this form of selling and plans to expand the number of stores and training courses available. For customers who can't or don't need to visit a store, the Gateway Web site offers a version of personal selling on its interactive Web site, where customers will find answers to most commonly asked questions and can receive online guidance in choosing a system, its installation, and technical support.

Not only does Gateway engage in its own promotional efforts, but its products enhance its customers' sales strategies, particularly portable models that sales representatives can travel with and use for presentations, order taking, and communication with their own or Gateway's offices.

Gateway executives view the company's "three main connections with clients—the phones, World Wide Web, and Gate-

way Country retail outlets—as complementing each other." Thus, marketers continually develop the company's complete promotional mix together. Whether you pick up the phone to order a PC, walk into a Gateway Store to ask a question, or log on to the Web site to buy Floppy the Cow, you are a customer with whom Gateway hopes to have a long and happy relationship.

Questions

1. Imagine that you were going to develop an advertising campaign for Gateway. Which strategies do you think would work best—comparative, celebrity testimonial, or cooperative? Explain your choice(s).

2. Imagine that you are a Gateway marketer and think of an idea for a sales promotion for one of Gateway's product lines, its retail stores, or the like. Outline or describe your idea in a brief memo.

3. Why is personal selling an important component of Gateway's promotional mix?

4. Visit the Gateway Web site at www.gateway.com. As you browse through various sections, what types of advertising and promotion do you see? Write them down to discuss your findings in class.

SOURCES: Gateway Web site, www.gateway.com, accessed March 22, 2000; "Gateway Offers Windows 2000 across Servers, Desktops and Notebooks for Business," *PR Newswire*, February 15, 2000; "Gateway Delivers Increased Flexibility with Widest Range of Processor Choices across Its Entire Line of Solo Portable Computers," *PR Newswire*, February 14, 2000; Om Malik, "Gateway Goes after College Crowd," Forbes.com, November 29, 1999, www.forbes.com; Gateway, *Annual Report*, 1998.

Putting a Smile in its Prices

Gateway

There's a price crunch in the computer industry: customers are demanding quality hardware, software, and services at the lowest price possible. As consumer attitudes toward computers change and more and more households view computers as a necessity, particularly for Internet access, the price of such a purchase becomes an important consideration. With PC prices hovering around $1,500, a computer is still a shopping or capital item for most families and small businesses. Gateway, with its direct-selling business model, already has a slight competitive advantage over its competitors that deal with intermediaries. Still, Gateway faces challenges that mean the company must be clear about its pricing objectives—whether it should focus on profitability, volume, or competitiveness.

Gateway practices product line pricing to help customers differentiate among its lines and to meet varied customer needs. Gateway desktops range in base price from $999 to $2,999. Portables cost more, with the Solo line ranging from $1,199 to $3,699. But that's just the beginning of Gateway's price options. For instance, if cost is an overriding concern, customers can purchase remanufactured Gateway computers for less: desktops start at $749, and Solos start at $949. All-in-one computers, popular choices for children, run from $799 to $898 for new models and start at $599 for remanufactured products.

If you visit the Gateway Web site, you'll find promotional pricing—maybe a free printer with a PC purchase, or half price on software bundles for a limited time. You'll even find a few rebates, all designed to get you to choose a Gateway PC. In addition, Gateway offers various warranties and technical support with its purchases. Customers who shop at Gateway Country stores can take training courses, including refresher courses, for $99.

To compete against such rivals as Compaq and Emachines, and to meet the demand for cheaper notebook computers, Gateway recently introduced its Solo 1100 for $1,200, aimed at the consumer market. However, to reach this lower price point, Gateway had to abandon its build-to-order practice for the cheaper notebook. Instead, the company will build its noncustom Solo 1100 notebooks in bulk and hold them in inventory. "This is not a build-to-order machine," emphasizes Andy Klopstad, Gateway Solo product marketing manager. It is important for Gateway to make this clear to customers, who might be expecting a customized notebook for the new low price, and convey to them the value that Gateway is presenting.

Gateway's most innovative pricing program is its Your:)Ware program, which not only helps customers select the system that meets their needs but also allows them to select among several pricing options. For instance, suppose you own a small business and you'd rather lease your computer system than purchase it outright. With Your:)Ware, Gateway can offer you a leasing program. Through this program, small businesses and K-12 schools get the systems they need immediately and pay for them through an installment lease that runs for three years. Businesses that want to purchase a system at the end of the lease have several options, including: (1) Fair market value, which involves a low monthly lease payment with flexible purchase options at the end of the lease; (2) $1 buyout, which gives the customer full ownership at the end of the lease; and (3) 10 percent buyout, which offers a lower payment than the $1 buyout and purchase option at the end. Other Your:)Ware options bundle together different services, including one that offers an allowance for a trade-in after two years if the system has become obsolete. Your:)Ware is a unique way to meet the pricing objectives of profitability and competition. Leases and monthly contracts are generally more profitable for a company than outright sales, and Gateway can meet the prices of its competitors. And the program is just as popular among consumers as it is among business customers: during one year, Gateway originated $1 billion in financing to help consumers purchase their PCs. That's more than milk money for a little company that started out in a cow pasture in South Dakota.

Questions

1. Some companies are offering free PCs in exchange for marketing information from customers. How might this type of promotion affect the pricing strategy of Gateway PCs?

2. Do you think that the strategy of odd pricing is as effective for a PC at, say, $1,199 as it is for a convenience item such as CD sleeves at $2.99? Why or why not?

3. As a consumer shopping for a PC, how important do you think strategies such as rebates and promotional pricing are? Would they affect your purchase decision? Why?

4. Visit the Gateway Web site at www.gateway.com and browse for information on the Your:)Ware program. Do you think that this pricing strategy creates value for customers? Why or why not?

SOURCES: Gateway Web site, www.gateway.com, accessed March 23, 2000; "Gateway Continues Building Its Beyond-the-Box Initiatives with Expanded Suite of Training Solutions for Businesses," *PR Newswire*, March 7, 2000; Joe Wilcox, "Gateway's New Approach on Cheap Notebook," CNET News.com, February 7, 2000, www.news.cnet.com; Steve Lohr, "Gateway Says Earnings Will Fall Below Analysts' Expectations, *New York Times*, January 6, 2000, www.nytimes.com; Om Malik, "Gateway Goes after College Crowd," Forbes.com, November 29, 1999, www.forbes.com; Jim Hu and Joe Wilcox, "AOL Partnership Calls Gateway ISP into Question," CNET News.com, November 16, 1999, www.news.cnet.com; Steven V. Brull, "A Net Gain for Gateway?" *Businessweek Online*, July 19, 1999, www.businessweek.com; Anna Driver, "Gateway to Expand into Net Market," Reuters Limited, accessed at *ZDNet News*, May 20, 1999, www.zdnet.com; Charles Dubow, "Gateway Gets Flexible," Forbes.com, April 29, 1999, www.forbes.com; Elizabeth Corcoran, "Gateway 2005," *Forbes Global*, March 8, 1999, www.forbes.com; Gateway, *Annual Report*, 1998.

Careers in Marketing

At this point, you should be congratulated on your decision to take this course. After all, marketing is a pervasive element in our lives. In one form or another, it reaches every person. As you begin this course, you should be aware of three important facts about marketing.

Marketing costs are a big component of your total spending. Approximately 50 percent of the total costs of products you buy are for marketing costs. In short, half of the $20 you pay for the chart-topping compact disc goes not for the plastic disc, protective sleeve, paper jacket, or the physical acts of burning the tracks onto the disk but for marketing costs.

Costs alone, however, do not indicate the value of marketing. The high living standard you enjoy in large part is a function of our nation's efficient marketing systems. When considered in this perspective, the costs of marketing seem more reasonable. For example, marketing expands sales, thereby spreading fixed production costs over more units of output and reducing total output costs.

Marketing provides an opportunity to contribute to society as well as to an individual company. Marketing decisions affect everyone's welfare. How much quality should be built into a product? Will people buy a safer product if it costs twice as much as the current version? Should every community adopt recycling programs? Because ethics and social responsibility are important topics to marketers, reading the Solving an Ethical Controversy Boxes in each chapter have hopefully allowed you to examine the not always black-and-white issues such as marketing tobacco products abroad, free personal computers (in exchange for personal information), fighting spam, and advertising in public schools.

Not only does marketing influence numerous facets of daily life, decisions regarding marketing activities affect everyone's welfare. Opportunities to advance to more responsible decision-making positions come sooner in marketing than in most occupations. This combination of challenges and opportunities to be involved in significant decisions at relatively early stages in your career has made marketing one of the most popular fields of academic study.

A recent survey by executive recruiter Korn/Ferry International revealed that the best route to the top of the corporate ladder begins in a company's marketing division: Three of every eight CEOs are chosen from a company's marketing division because the growing global economy demands proven market leaders in winning the fight to increase their firms' worldwide market shares. Finance, which had long dominated as the top career path for senior executives, fell to third place, and executives who had completed international assignments—many of the assignments being marketing related—came in second.

You may choose a career in marketing. Marketing-related occupations account for 25 to 30 percent of the jobs in the typical highly industrialized nations. History has shown that the demand for effective marketers is not affected by cyclical economic fluctuations.

YOUR QUEST FOR A CAREER IN MARKETING

The U.S. job market today is ripe for the picking. The demand for skilled workers far exceeds the supply, forcing employers to pay top prices in attracting talented employees. Nationwide, average top sales and marketing executive salaries increased 61 percent between 1997 and 2000. Since salaries are at optimum levels, job applicants frequently focus on additional benefits such as the opportunity for professional growth and family friendly organizations that offer high quality of life. While compensation is always an issue, employees want to feel recognized for their achievements, be assigned new responsibilities, and work in continuous-learning environments. In addition, many companies recognize the importance of loyalty and now offer employees an equity stake in the company.[1]

Of the many career paths chosen by business graduates, marketing is the single largest employment category in the U.S. labor force, and job growth in the field is expected to accelerate. The U.S. Bureau of Labor Statistics estimates that the number of jobs in marketing, advertising, and public relations management will grow much faster through 2008 than the average for all occupations. Every successful organization—profit-seeking or not-for-profit—recognizes the necessity of effective marketing for accomplishing its goals of providing customer satisfaction by hiring highly motivated, professionally educated marketing specialists to design and implement these customer-driven programs.

This career appendix provides students with a brief look at the trends and opportunities available for future marketers in an increasingly diversified professional field. It describes essential elements of an effective résumé and discusses the new trends in electronic job searches. Finally, it provides a listing of primary marketing information sources that contain answers to many of the questions typically asked by applicants.

Many of the marketing positions you read about throughout the text are described here. Specifically, the job summaries describe the job and the responsibilities and duties that are typically required as well as the usual career path and salary for each of the eight marketing-related positions.

Marketing your skills to a prospective employer is much the same as marketing a product to a consumer. Increasingly, job seekers are selling their skills online, eliminating the middleman and leveling the playing field between applicant and the company. The greatest challenge for online job seekers is learning how to market themselves. Online job searches can focus on positions in a specialized field or location, or these positions can be posted on meta-sites like Monster.com with few if any particular limitations on company of location. In either case, the key to getting the job you want is letting the market know who you are and what you can do.

As you begin a career in marketing, you will apply many of the principles and concepts discussed in the text, including how to do the following: target a market, capitalize on brand equity, position a product, and use marketing research techniques. Even in jobs that seem remote from the marketing discipline, this knowledge will help you stay focused on the most important aspect of business: the customer.

TRENDS AND OPPORTUNITIES IN MARKETING PROFESSIONS

With the wide array of job choices for a graduate with a marketing degree, it is helpful to consider the projected growth of employment in various marketing positions. Table 1 shows the expected growth of selected marketing occupations through 2008. Two categories—marketing managers and sales positions in the financial and service sectors—are expected to grow by 25 percent or more over this time period.

A second encouraging trend in marketing job choices is the increased diversity of the job market. Ethnic minorities and women of all races have increased their presence and will con-

TABLE 1	Employment Projections for Selected Marketing Positions through 2008	
OCCUPATION	**RECENT EMPLOYMENT**	**PROJECTED GROWTH THROUGH 2008**
Marketing, advertising, and public relations managers	122,000	24.6
Purchasing agents and managers	176,000	7.1
Real-estate agents, brokers, and appraisers	285,000	9.0
Sales Workers		
Insurance	387,000	2.2
Retail	4,056,000	13.9
Securities and financial services sales representatives	303,000	41.0
Service sales representatives	612,000	35.0
Wholesale and retail buyers	118,000	−0.4

Source: Data downloaded from Bureau of Labor Statistics at www.bls.gov/asp/oep, January 14, 2000.

TABLE 2	Female and Minority Employment in Selected Marketing Occupations	

	PERCENTAGE OF TOTAL EMPLOYEES		
OCCUPATION	**FEMALE**	**AFRICAN-AMERICAN**	**HISPANIC**
Purchasing managers	40.9%	6.4%	4.6%
Marketing, advertising, public relations managers	34.6	3.7	4.8
Sales occupations	50.2	8.1	7.6
Supervisors/proprietors	38.4	4.8	6.8
Sales representatives:			
Advertising sales	56.6	10.0	4.2
Insurance sales	42.8	7.7	4.7
Real estate sales	50.0	4.6	5.1
Retail/personal services	65.7	11.9	10.0
Securities/financial services	44.0	6.9	4.5

Source: U.S. Bureau of the Census, *Statistical Abstract of the United States,* 118 edition (Washington, D.C.: U.S. Government Printing Office, 1999), pp. 405–406.

tinue to do so. While Table 2 indicates that the battle for equality is not yet over, it does show considerable progress for women, African-Americans, and Hispanic Americans.

According to the Small Business Administration, women are starting small firms at twice the rate of males. Women-owned businesses in the United States employ more people than all of the Fortune 500 companies combined. However, employment of African-Americans and Hispanics in marketing is not proportionate with their shares of the total population.

ENHANCING YOUR PERSONAL WORTH

No matter what career path you choose, you must do those things that increase your value to the company, whether it is through hands-on work experience, continuing your education, participating in internships, and volunteering in organizations not affiliated with your employer such as charitable organizations. The decision to pursue a college degree is financially rewarding. Last year, the average full-time employee 18 or older with no high school diploma earned $16,124. Recent Census Bureau statistics reveal that the average employee with a bachelor's degree earns $40,478 annually—two and one-half times the pay of the high school dropout. [2]

Not everyone, however, will graduate with a bachelor's degree and immediately enter the job market. Students often choose to continue their studies by pursuing MBA degrees or by entering master's programs specially suited to their career goals. A student who wishes to extend formal education in a specialized degree program should seek advice on specific programs from instructors who teach in that area. For example, a marketing research professor is likely to have information on master's programs in that field at many particular institutions.

Other activities that enhance your personal worth are internships and volunteering. Internships have been described as a critical link in bridging the theory-practice educational gap. They help to carry students between the academic present and the professional future. They provide students with an opportunity for learning how classroom theory is applied in real world business environments.

An internship is a partnership between the student, the university, and the agency or internship site. All of these parties assume definite responsibilities, perform specific functions, and achieve benefits as the results of their involvement. In addition, internships can serve as critical networking and job hunting tools. In some instances, internships are precursors for specific employment opportunities, allowing students to demonstrate technical proficiency while providing cost-effective employee training for the company.

An excellent source of information about the nation's outstanding internships can be found at your local bookstore: One good source by Mark Oldman and Samer Hamadeh is *America's Top 100 Internships*, published annually by Villard Books in New York.

YOUR RÉSUMÉ

Writing a résumé is a task that every job seeker dislikes. However, the task is made less daunting with the help of your faculty advisor or career counselor, a growing number of books and articles on résumé writing, and many computer software packages that require little more than filling in the blanks.

A résumé is probably the most important document that a job seeker can provide to a potential employer since it often provides the only written record of credentials available on which an evaluation and selection of a job candidate can be made. It is a concise summary of academic, professional, and personal accomplishments that makes focused statements about a job applicant.

Résumé Blunders

The following list of errors appeared in job résumés, applications, and cover letters received by Robert Half, founder of Accountemps:

"I have worked in a fairy wide range of industries."

"Great eye for derail."

"I have incredibly entertaining hair."

"I am accustomed to being in the hot seat."

"Education: Some."

Three basic formats are used in preparing a résumé. *Chronological résumés* arrange information in reverse chronological order, emphasizing job titles and organizations and describing responsibilities held and duties performed. This format highlights continuity and career growth. *A functional résumé* accents accomplishments and strengths, placing less emphasis on job titles and work history and often omits job descriptions. Some applicants use a *combined résumé* format, which emphasizes skills first followed by employment history. This format highlights a candidate's potential and suits students who often have little experience directly related to their desired positions.

> ### Briefly Speaking
>
> **Put it to them briefly so they will read it, clearly, so they will appreciate it; picturesquely, so they will remember it—and, above all, accurately, so they will be guided by its light.**
>
> *Joseph Pulitzer*
> *(1847–1911)*
> *American journalist*

Most résumés include full names, mail and e-mail addresses, and telephone and fax numbers. Statements of career objectives typically follow. Academic information is provided next, followed by experience and work history. Applicants with limited work histories and no internship experiences typically focus on relevant personal activities and interests. Any and all preprofessional and extracurricular activities, as well as academic, work, and internship experiences, should be included on your résumé. Most résumés close with lists of references.

Whether yours is a traditional résumé on paper or posted on an Internet résumé listing, the important thing to remember in creating an effective résumé is to present the most relevant information in a clear, concise manner that emphasizes your best attributes.

Cover Letter

An employer is typically first introduced to a job applicant through a cover letter. Like wrapping on a present, a résumé should attract attention and interest about what is inside and should be addressed to a specific person. The cover letter must provide specifically targeted information, state the particular position you are applying for, where you learned about the position, and why you are interested in that position. It should also describe attributes of your personality, such as dependability, responsibility, energy level, and technical skills, without sounding arrogant.

Next, your cover letter should specifically state when you will follow up with a phone call or letter. Your cover letter then should close with an expression of appreciation for being considered for the position. Make certain that your cover letter is neat and grammatically correct since employers often use it to evaluate written communication skills. Finally, sign the letter in blue or black ink.

Mark your calendar and follow up your cover letter and résumé when you stated you would. If you indicated that you would call, then use this opportunity to ask any additional questions and set a possible date for an interview.

Letters of Recommendation

Letters of recommendation serve as testimonials to your performance in academic and work settings. The best references provide information relative to the desired industry or marketing specialty, as well opinions of your skills, abilities, and character. References may be obtained from former or current employers, supervisors from volunteer experiences, professors, and others who can attest to your academic and professional competencies.

An effective letter of recommendation typically contains the following elements:

1. Statement of the length and nature of the relationship between the writer and the job candidate.
2. Description of the candidate's academic and career growth and potential.
3. Review of important achievements.
4. Evaluation of personal character (what kind of colleague the candidate will make).
5. Summary of the candidate's outstanding strengths and abilities.

Because letters of recommendation take time and effort, it helps to provide a résumé and any other information relative to the recommendation, along with a stamped, addressed (typed) envelope. When requesting letters of recommendation, it is advised to allow ample time for your references to compose them—as long as a month is not unusual.

In addition to a cover letter, résumé, and letters of recommendation, candidates should include photocopies of transcripts, writing samples, or other examples of work completed. For example, if you are applying for a position in public relations, advertising, or sports marketing, you may want to include examples of professional writing, graphics, or audio/visual tapes to support written evidence of your credentials. Research and service projects that resulted in published or unpublished articles may also enhance your portfolio.

Electronic Résumés

During the past decade, millions of people have turned to the Web for information, entertainment, and communication. Today, not only are companies relying on electronic recruiting to fill specialized positions, but job seekers are also using the Internet to find jobs that fulfill their career goals.

With the aid of the Internet, companies can post job listings and job seekers can list their résumés online. Computers then search for key words in job titles, job descriptions, or résumés to narrow the search. In fact, *manager is* the number one word for which companies search.[3] Job hunting on the Internet now includes individuals ranging from high tech savvy employees to low tech service providers as well as teams looking to hire out as a group. No matter the position or the person, the key to an effective electronic résumé is to use exact words and phrases, emphasizing nouns rather than action verbs as in a typed résumé. For example, a company looking for a marketing account manager with experience in Lotus 1-2-3, WordPerfect, and Microsoft Excel programs, conducts computer searches for only those résumés that include the job title and the three software programs. Margaret Riley Dikel, coauthor of *The Guide to Internet Job Searching*, advises job seekers to "Turn your experience into keywords and maximize the number of them in your résumé."[4]

Over 3,500 Web sites currently carry job postings. Table 3 provides a description of the top Internet job sites and the services they offer job hunters. Each of these sites is designed to make it easier to identify job opportunities that best match your interests. If, for example, you decide to limit your job search to a single city such as Boston, you would simply type *Boston* into Online Career Center's QuickSearch screening system. Almost immediately you would get over 2,600 listings. You could then narrow your scope to sales positions, for instance, and the list would shrink to 203 Boston listings.

Most job search sites charge between $40 and $150 to list one job for a month.[5] That amount is minuscule compared to about $250 for a 1-square-inch classified ad that runs once in a major Sunday newspaper. While newspapers are excellent for local employment searches, Web sites are more general, spreading a net of job postings for all types of jobs worldwide.

Because the life span of an electronic résumé may extend indefinitely, applicants must maintain any information they give out to ensure it is current and correct. Privacy is a major concern with any online involvement, especially regarding résumés since they often contain personal information. Some job sites sell résumés to other databases; others have no limits on who can access their databases. The most secure way to job search online is to not post a résumé at all. Instead, job seekers can register with a job agent service (available on NationJob.com and CareerBuilder.com) that brings notification of job openings to your computer.[6]

MARKETING POSITIONS

The basic objective of any firm is to market its goods or services. Marketing responsibilities vary among organizations and

TABLE 3	Five Hot Internet Job Sites		
SITE	**DESCRIPTION**	**RÉSUMÉ ON FILE**	**PRIVACY**
Monster Board *monster.com*	Résumé City, the site's job bank, posts some 25,000 openings and more than 300,000 résumés.	One year; then Monster Board asks for an update.	Name and contact information hidden from employers.
America's Job Bank *ajb.dni.us*	Government site where state agencies post 5,000 new openings each day; companies post another 3,000.	Sixty days unless you update it.	No way to block your résumé from employers.
CareerPath *careerpath.com*	Classifieds from more than 65 newspapers.	Six months, but inactive résumés are stored indefinitely.	Site e-mails you for permission before relating résumé information
CareerMosaic *careermosaic.com*	More than 70,000 jobs, updated daily.	Stays in database until you remove it.	Résumés are accessible by anyone.
OnLine Career Center (OCC) *occ.com*	The Pioneer in online recruiting with more than 100,000 résumés.	One year unless you update your résumé.	OCC asks permission before releasing your résumé.

industries. In a small firm, the owner or president may assume marketing responsibilities. A large firm needs a staff of experienced marketing, advertising, and public relations managers to coordinate these activities. Some typical marketing-management positions are described in the following sections. (Please remember, however, that specific titles of positions may vary among firms.)

Marketing, Advertising, and Public Relations Managers

Marketing management spans a range of positions, including vice president of marketing, marketing manager, sales manager, product manager, advertising manager, promotion manager, and public relations manager. The vice president directs the firm's overall marketing policy, and all other marketers report through channels to this person. Sales managers direct the efforts of sales professionals by assigning territories, establishing goals, developing training programs, and supervising local sales managers and their personnel. Advertising managers oversee account services, creative services, and media services departments. Promotion managers direct promotional programs that combine advertising with purchase incentives in order to increase the sales of the firm's goods or services. Public relations managers conduct publicity programs and supervise the specialists who implement these programs.

Job Description

Top marketing-management positions often involve long hours and extensive travel. Work under pressure is also commonplace. For sales managers, job transfers between headquarters and regional offices may disrupt one's personal life. Approximately 460,000 marketing, advertising, and public relations managers are currently employed in the United States.

Career Path

For most marketing, sales, and promotion management positions, employers prefer degrees in business administration, preferably with concentrations in marketing. In highly technical industries, such as chemicals and electronics, employers prefer bachelor's degrees in science or engineering combined with master's degrees in business administration. Liberal arts students can also find many opportunities, especially if they have business minors. Most managers are promoted from positions such as sales representatives, product or brand specialists, and advertising specialists within their organizations. Skills or traits that are most desirable for these jobs include high motivation, maturity, creativity, resistance to stress, flexibility, and the ability to communicate persuasively.

Salary

The median annual salary for marketing, advertising, and public relations specialists ranges from $37,000 for a marketing specialist in the services sector to $138,380 for a marketing vice president in the manufacturing sector. The average incomes for specific positions in each field are shown in Table 4.

Sales Representatives

Millions of items are bought and sold every day. The people a firm hires to carry out this activity work under a variety of titles such as sales representative, account manager, manufacturer's representative, sales engineer, sales agent, retail salesperson, wholesale sales representative, and service sales representative. Most companies require that all marketing professionals spend some time in the field to experience the market firsthand and to understand the challenges faced by front-line marketing personnel.

TABLE 4	Average Compensation for Manufacturing and Service Marketers	
POSITION	**MANUFACTURING INDUSTRIES**	**SERVICE INDUSTRIES**
Vice president for marketing	$138,580	$105,000
Assistant marketing director	111,300	59,983
Brand manager	85,000	55,100
Marketing specialist	53,940	37,000
Marketing communication specialist	41,670	37,200
Marketing research analyst	48,392	48,000

Source: "Make It, and Make More," *Marketing News,* November 22, 1999, p. 11.

Job Description

All salespeople must fully understand and be able to competently discuss the products offered by the company. Salespeople usually develop prospective client lists, meet with current and prospective clients to describe the firm's products, and then follow up. In most cases, the salesperson must learn about each customer's business needs in order to identify products that best satisfy these needs. These professionals answer questions about the characteristics and costs of their offerings and try to persuade potential customers to purchase these offerings. After the sale, many representatives revisit their customers to ensure that the products are meeting their needs and to explore further business opportunities or referrals with these customers. Some sales of technical goods and services involve lengthy interactions. In these cases, a salesperson may work with several clients simultaneously over a large geographical area. Those responsible for large territories may spend most of their work days on the phone or on the sales floor.

Briefly Speaking

Ever since Moses came down from the mountain with the tablets, the world has been moved by salesmen. I'm a salesman.

David Mahoney
Chairman, Norton Simon, Inc.

Work as a sales representative can be rewarding for those who enjoy interacting with people, enjoy competition, and feel energized by the challenge of expanding sales in their territories. Successful sales professionals should be goal oriented, persuasive, self-motivated, and independent people. In addition, patience and perseverance are important qualities for a sales representative.

Career Path

The background needed for a sales position varies according to the product line and market. Most professional sales jobs require a college degree, and many companies run their own formal training programs that can last up to two years for sales representatives. This training may take place in a classroom, in the field with a mentor, or most often a combination of both methods.

Salary

Salaries for sales positions vary widely. In a recent year, annual earnings for senior sales representatives averaged $89,400; those selling technical services typically earn more than those selling nontechnical services. As Table 5 indicates, salaries increase substantially at higher levels of management.

Advertising Specialists

Advertising is one of the ten hottest career fields in the United States today. Many firms maintain small groups of advertising specialists who serve as liaisons between those companies and outside advertising agencies. The leader of this liaison function is sometimes called a *marketing communications manager.* Positions in an advertising agency include the categories of account services, creative services, and media services. Account services functions are performed by account executives, who work directly with clients. An agency's creative services department develops the themes and presentations of the advertisements. This department is supervised by the creative director, who oversees the copy chief, art director, and their staff members. The media services department is managed by the media director, who oversees the planning group that selects media outlets for ads.

TABLE 5	Average Total Compensation in Sales Professions
Senior sales representative	$ 89,400
National account representative	98,700
District sales manager	109,800
National account sales manager	152,000
Regional sales manager	136,400
Top sales executive	244,300

Source: Data downloaded from http:Hpublic.wsj.com/careers/resources/documents, January 14, 2000.

Job Description

Advertising can be one of the most glamorous and creative fields in marketing. Because the field combines the best of both worlds—that is, the tangible and scientific aspects of marketing along with creative artistry—advertising attracts people with a broad array of abilities

Career Path

Most new hires begin as assistants or associates for the positions they hope to acquire, such as copywriters, art directors, and media buyers. Often, a newly hired employee must receive two to four promotions before becoming manager of these functions. College degrees in liberal arts, graphic arts, journalism, psychology, or sociology, in addition to marketing training, are preferred for entry level positions in advertising.

Salary

In recent years, professionals in the advertising industry have enjoyed a considerable increase in average annual earnings. Table 6 lists the average base salaries for various positions in advertising agencies in the United States.

Public Relations Specialists

Specialists in public relations strive to build and maintain positive relationships with various publics. They may assist management in drafting speeches, arranging interviews, overseeing company archives, responding to information requests, and handling special events, such as sponsorships and trade shows, that provide promotional value to the firm.

Job Description

Public relations specialists normally work a standard 40-hour week, but sometimes they need to rearrange their normal schedules to meet deadlines or prepare for major events. Occasionally they are required to be on the job or on call around the clock to respond to an emergency or crisis. Over 109,000 public relations specialists are employed in the United States; two-thirds of them in service industries. Public relations positions tend to be concentrated in large cities near press services and communications facilities. However, that centralization is changing with the increased popularity of new communications technologies, such as the Internet, which allow more freedom of movement. Many public relations consulting firms are located in New York, Los Angeles, Chicago, and Washington, D.C.

Essential characteristics for a public relations specialist include creativity, initiative, good judgment, and the ability to express thoughts clearly and simply—both in writing and verbally. An outgoing personality, self-confidence, and enthusiasm are also recommended traits of public relations specialists.

Career Path

A college degree combined with public relations experience, usually gained through an internship, is considered excellent preparation for public relations. Many entry-level public relations specialists hold degrees with majors in advertising, marketing, public relations, or communications. New employees in larger organizations are likely to participate in formal training programs; those who begin their careers at smaller firms typically work under the guidance of experienced staff members. Entry level positions carry such titles as research assistant or account assistant. A potential career path includes a promotion to account executive, account supervisor, vice president, and eventually senior vice president.

Salary

According to a recent salary survey, the median salary for all public relations job titles was $50,804. Entry-level public relations specialists in corporate settings typically earn higher salaries than their counterparts in not-for-profit organizations. By contrast, senior public relations executives of not-for-profit organizations receive higher salaries, on average, than those in the business sector. The highest pay in public relations goes to those involved in investor relations and international and environmental affairs. Entry-level salaries average $54,700 for a publicity agent and $60,949 for an in-house publicist.

Purchasing Agents and Managers

The two key marketing functions of buying and selling are performed by trained specialists. Just as every organization is involved in selling its output to meet the needs of customers, so too must all companies make purchases of goods and services required to operate their businesses and turn out items for sale.

Modern technology has transformed the role of the purchasing agent. The transfer of routine tasks to the computer now allows contract specialists, or procurement officers, to focus on products, suppliers, and contract negotiations. The main function of this position is to purchase the goods, materials, supplies, and services required by the organization. These agents ensure that suppliers deliver quality and quantity levels that suit the firm's needs; they also secure these inputs at reasonable prices and make them available when needed.

TABLE 6	Average Salaries for Positions in Advertising
Advertising copywriter	$ 55,800
Art director	54,000
Account executive	45,600
Creative director	107,000

Source: R. Craig Endicott, "Salary Survey," *Advertising Age*, December 6, 1999, p. S1.

Purchasing agents must develop good working relationships both with colleagues in their own organizations and with suppliers. As the popularity of outsourcing has increased, the selection and management of suppliers have become critical functions of the purchasing department. In the government sector, this role is dominated by strict laws, statutes, and regulations that constantly change.

Job Description

Purchasing agents can expect a standard work week with some travel to suppliers' sites, seminars, and trade shows. Over 600,000 people work in purchasing jobs in the United States, most of them in manufacturing and government.

Career Path

Organizations prefer college-educated candidates for entry-level jobs in purchasing. Strong analytical and communication skills are required for any purchasing position. Often, new hires into the field enroll in extensive company training programs to learn procedures and operations; training may include a production planning assignment. In private and public industries, professional certification is becoming an essential criterion for advancement. A variety of associations serving the different categories of purchasing confer certifications on agents, including Certified Purchasing Manager, Professional Public Buyer, Certified Public Purchasing Officer, Certified Associate Contract Manager, and Certified Professional Contract Manager.

Salary

An entry-level purchasing agent can expect to earn on average $46,460 annually. The industry average is $58,080, and the typical salary for a firm's chief purchasing agent should approximate $69,690.

Wholesale and Retail Buyers and Merchandise Managers

Buyers working for wholesalers and retail businesses purchase goods for resale. Their goal is to find the best possible merchandise at the lowest prices. They also influence the distribution and marketing of this merchandise. Successful buyers must understand what appeals to consumers and what their establishments can sell. Bar codes on products and point-of-purchase terminals have allowed organizations to accurately track goods that are selling and those that are not; buyers frequently analyze this data to improve their understanding of consumer demand. Buyers also check competitors' prices and sales activities and watch general economic conditions to anticipate consumer buying patterns.

Job Description

Approximately 361,000 people are currently employed in the United States as wholesale and retail buyers and merchandise managers. These jobs often require substantial travel, as many orders are placed on buying trips to shows and exhibitions. Effective planning and decision-making skills are strong assets in this career. In addition, the job involves anticipating consumer preferences and ensuring that the firm keeps needed goods in stock. Therefore, the job requires resourcefulness, good judgment, and self-confidence.

Career Path

Most wholesale and retail buyers begin their careers as assistant buyers or trainees. Larger retailers seek college-educated candidates, and extensive training includes job experience in a variety of positions. Advancement often comes when buyers move to departments with larger volumes or become merchandise managers to coordinate or oversee the work of several buyers.

Salary

Median annual earnings of wholesale and retail buyers average $27,610. However, income depends on the amount and type of product purchased as well as seniority. Buyers often receive cash bonuses based on their performance.

Marketing Research Analysts

Marketing research analysts provide information that helps marketers to identify and define opportunities; they generate, refine, and evaluate marketing actions and minor marketing performance. Marketing research analysts devise methods and procedures for obtaining needed data. Once they compile data, analysts evaluate it and then make recommendations to management.

Job Description

Firms that specialize in marketing research and management consulting employ the majority of the nation's market research analysts. Positions are often concentrated in larger cities, such as New York, Los Angeles, and Chicago. Those who pursue careers in marketing research need to work accurately with detail, display patience and persistence, work effectively both independently and with others, and operate objectively and systematically. Significant computer skills are essential for success in this field.

Career Path

A bachelor's degree with an emphasis in marketing provides sufficient qualifications for many beginning jobs in marketing research. Because of the importance of quantitative skills, this education should include courses in calculus, linear algebra, statistics, sampling theory and survey design, computer science, and information systems. Students should try to develop experience in conducting interviews or surveys while still in college.

TABLE 7	Mean Compensation for Market Research Positions
Market analyst	$24,000–$ 50,000
Project director	45,000–70,000
Market research director	75,000–200,000

Source: Data downloaded from www.careers-in-marketing.com, January 14, 2000.

TABLE 8	Mean Compensation for Logistics Positions
Vice president/general manager	$104,722
Logistics manager	63,017
Private-fleet manager	56,122
Operations manager	55,934
Traffic manager	50,772
Purchasing manager	50,708
Warehouse manager	47,403
Assistant traffic manager	45,118

Source: Data downloaded from http:public.wsj.com/careers/resources/documents, January 14, 2000.

A master's degree in business administration or a related discipline is advised for improving opportunities for advancement.

Salary

As Table 7 indicates, compensation in this field ranges from $24,000 annually for marketing research analysts to over $137,500 annually for a typical director of marketing research. Compensation levels throughout the industry have shown larger percentage increases over the past ten years, and this trend will likely continue.

Logistics: Material Receiving, Scheduling, Dispatching, and Distributing Occupations

The area of logistics offers a myriad of career positions. Titles under the heading of logistics include material receiving, scheduling, dispatching, materials management executive, distribution operations coordinator, distribution center manager, and transportation manager. The logistics function includes responsibilities for production and inventory planning and control, distribution, and transportation.

Job Description

Approximately 3.8 million people are employed in logistics positions in the United States today, including material receiving, scheduling, dispatching, and distribution. These positions demand good communication skills and the ability to work well under pressure.

Career Path

Computer skills are highly valued in these jobs. Employers look for candidates with degrees in logistics and transportation. However, graduates in other business disciplines may succeed in this field.

Salary

Annual earnings for logistics management positions are reported in Table 8.

ADDITIONAL INFORMATION SOURCES

Marketing Careers: On the Boone and Kurtz Web Site

A wealth of helpful career information is continually updated for marketing students using *Contemporary Marketing* at the following Web site:

www.harcourtcollege.com/marketing/students/careers/htm.

The "Marketing Careers" section on the Web site enables students to learn more about marketing careers and to locate currently posted business job opportunities. The site provides a vast number of career resources such as links to job sites, career guidance sites, U.S. newspaper job ads, and company information and provides ways for researching cities you might

Job and Career Information Sites

Introduction

The sites in this section will help you learn more about management careers and locate currently posted business job opportunities. Also, many sites include extensive career information and guidance, such as interviewing techniques and resume-writing. For example, see our description of College View Careers.

like to move to. Also, many links include extensive career information and guidance, such as interviewing techniques and tips for résumé writing. The site is updated regularly.

Discovering Your Marketing Career—A Software Application

Each new copy of the tenth edition of *Contemporary Marketing* includes a CD-ROM with software to help you plan your career. Selecting a career ladder can be a daunting process. In today's competitive job market, the most desirable and highest-paying jobs will go to the most qualified candidates. Courses in marketing will prepare you for a number of entry-level positions. It is necessary for you to (1) recognize your own interests and abilities, (2) understand the general characteristics of the job you are seeking, and (3) know how your abilities can satisfy an employer's needs. You will notice that these three criteria resemble closely the elements leading to customer satisfaction in all business transactions

Discovering Your Marketing Career is a computer application that will help you determine which marketing careers most closely match your skills, experience, and interests. The software invites your input to questionnaires for each major career track in marketing to aid you in determining how well each job suits you. After you complete the questionnaire, the software generates an in-depth report assessing your compatibility with that track. The report also prints out a detailed profile of the career itself, its long-term opportunities, and its compensation levels. Once you have narrowed down your interests, you can begin engaging in the software's job search activities. These activities include guidelines for field research on careers, résumé preparation, letter writing, and preparation of telephone scripts. By matching your interests to the demands of a particular marketing career, you can then decide which elective courses will strengthen your marketability as a job candidate.

NOTES

Chapter 1

SOURCES FOR MARKETING STRATEGY SUCCESS: The Dusenberry quotation is from Kathy McCabe, "Hasbro Interactive Scores in Crowded Field," *Mobile Register,* June 6, 1999, p. 6F. See also Brian Palmer, "Hasbro's New Action Figure," *Fortune,* June 21, 1999, pp. 189–192.

SOURCES FOR MARKETING STRATEGY FAILURE: Nina Munk, "How Levi's Trashed a Great American Brand," *Fortune,* April 12, 1999, pp. 83–88; Dell Jones and Lorris Grant, "What Caused Levi's Blues?" *USA Today,* February 23, 1999, pp. B1–B2; and Rachel Beck, "Levi's to Close 11 Plants," *Mobile Register,* February 23, 1999, p. B9.

1. Janet Kornblum, "Idealab! Forecast: Branstormy," *USA Today,* June 8, 1999, pp. B1, B2; Larry Armstrong and Ronald Grover, "Bill Gross, Online Idea Factory," *Business Week,* June 29, 1998, pp. 100–102; Patricia Sellers, "Inside the First E-Christmas," *Fortune,* February 1, 1999, pp. 70–73; Joshua Macht, "Toy Seller Plays Internet Hardball," *Inc.,* October 1998, pp. 17–18; and Thom Weidlich, "Toys in the Bandwidth," *Direct,* October 1, 1998, p. 38.
2. Scott Davis, "All Wired Up and . . . Where to Go?" *Brandweek,* February 22, 1999, pp. 24–25.
3. Peter F. Drucker, *The Practice of Management* (New York: Harper & Row, 1954), p. 37.
4. Joseph P. Guiltinan and Gordon W. Paul, *Marketing Management,* 6th ed. (New York: McGraw-Hill, 1996), pp. 3–4.
5. Nikhil Deogun, "Burst Bubbles: Aggressive Push Abroad Dilutes Coke's Strength as Big Markets Stumble," *Wall Street Journal,* February 8, 1999, pp. A1, A8.
6. Brian Zajac, "Yankee Travelers," *Forbes,* July 27, 1998, pp. 162–163.
7. Zachary Schiller, "Make It Simple," *Business Week,* September 9, 1996, p. 102.
8. Paul A. Herbig, *Handbook of Cross-Cultural Marketing* (New York: The International Business Press, 1998), pp. 96–100.
9. Robert J. Keith, "The Marketing Revolution," *Journal of Marketing,* January 1960, p. 36.
10. Ibid., p. 38.
11. Theodore Levitt, *Innovations in Marketing* (New York: McGraw-Hill, 1962), p. 7.
12. General Electric Company, *Annual Report,* 1952, p. 21.
13. Andrew Kupfer, "Mike Armstrong's AT&T: Will the Pieces Come Together?" *Fortune,* April 26, 1999, pp. 82–89; and AT&T press release dated June 9, 1999, downloaded from www.att.com.
14. Roz Ayres-Williams, "The Changing Face of Nonprofits," *Black Enterprise,* May 1998, pp. 110–114.
15. Michael M. Phillips, "Taking Stock: Top Sports Pros Find a New Way to Score: Getting Equity Stakes," *Wall Street Journal,* April 18, 1997, pp. A1, A8.
16. Tyler Maroney, "Are Jimmy and Warren Buffett Related?" *Fortune,* June 21, 1999, pp. 41–43; and Eric Pooley, "Still Rockin' in Jimmy Buffett's Margaritaville," *Time,* August 17, 1998.
17. "Consumers Care About Causes," *Sales & Marketing Management,* June 1999, p. 74; and Linda I. Nowak, "Cause Marketing Alliances: Corporate Associations and Consumer Responses," *Proceedings of the Winter Educators Conference,* St. Petersburg, FL: American Marketing Association, February 1999.
18. Langdon Brockington, "NBC Reports Ad Sales Hitting Olympian Heights," *Sports-Business Journal,* June 13, 1999, pp. 1, 48; Ben Power, "The $6 Billion Olympic Bonanza," *The Age,* January 22, 1999; and *Sydney 2000 Economic Impact,* accessed at www.linkedsoftware.com, June 15, 1999.
19. Rebecca Blumenstein, "A Battle Rages Over the Humble Collect Call," *Wall Street Journal,* June 7, 1999, p. B1.
20. Salina Khan, "Aiming to Please Women," *USA Today,* June 10, 1999, pp. B1, B2.
21. Jonathan Boorstein, "Premium Blend," *Direct,* September 1, 1998, pp. 1, 35–36.
22. Karl Taro Greenfeld, "PC Makers Get Crunched," *Time,* April 5, 1999, pp. 50–51.
23. Emily Thornton, "Enviro-Cars: The Race Is On," *Business Week,* February 8, 1999, pp. 74–76.
24. Zajac, "Yankee Travelers."
25. Carol Hildebrand, "The New Realm of the Coin," *CIO Enterprise,* Section 2, April 15, 1999. pp. 54–64.
26. "There's No Stopping E Business," *Forbes,* April 19, 1999, pp. S1–S25.
27. Laura Bly, "Budget Car Rental Joins Online Name-Your-Price Fray," *USA Today,* June 4, 1999, p. A1; and M. M. Buechner, "Going, Going...Rented!", *Time,* June 14, 1999, p. 248.
28. "There's No Stopping E-Business," *Forbes,* April 19, 1999, pp. S12–S13; and Doug Levey and Steve Rosenbush, "Internet's Builders Rake in Biggest Bucks," *USA Today,* June 10, 1999, p. 3B.
29. Patricia B. Seybold, *Customers.Com* (New York: Random House, 1998), pp. 5–9.
30. Patricia Sellers, "Inside the First E Christmas," *Fortune,* February 1, 1999, p. 72.
31. "IDC Predicts Worldwide Internet Services Revenues Will Surge Past $78 Billion in 2003," PRNewswire, downloaded Jun 10, 1999 from www.netscorecard.com; and "Cyberspace's Predicted Economic Surge," downloaded from NetScorecard.com, June 10, 1999.
32. Dori Jones Yang, "The Empire Strikes Out," *U.S. News & World Report,* November 15, 1999, pp. 47–54.
33. "Shell Gives Students a Head Start," from a special report of the Shell Oil Company, *Fortune,* November 9, 1998, pp. S7–S8.

Chapter 2

SOURCES FOR MARKETING STRATEGY SUCCESS: The Griffin quotation is from Jennifer Bresnahan, "For Goodness Sake," *CIO Enterprise,* June 15, 1999, pp. 54–62. See also "Minority Suppliers Energize Growth and the Bottom Line," *Forbes,* April 20, 1998, p. 14.

SOURCES FOR MARKETING STRATEGY FAILURE: Edward O. Welles, "Ben's Big Flop," *Inc.,* September 1998, pp. 40–55.

1. Gwen Kinkead, "In the Future, People Like Me Will Go to Jail," *Fortune,* May 24, 1999, pp. 190–200; Warren Cohen, "Ray Anderson: Aspiring to Become the Greenest CEO in America," *U.S. News & World Report,* downloaded from www.usnews.com, June 29, 1999; and Charles Fishman, "Their 'Growth Agenda,'" *Fast Company,* April 1998, p. 139.
2. Peter Brimelow, "Creation and Destruction," *Forbes,* March 8, 1999, p. 62.
3. Paul Keegan, "Online Auctions: From Seedy Flea Markets to Big Business," *Upside,* July 1999, pp. 70–80; and Kip Cheng, "eBay: Best Virtual Marketing," *Adweek,* June 28, 1999, p.42.
4. "Love at First Site," *Art & Auction,* July/August 1999, p. 7.
5. "The Marketing 100," *Advertising Age,* June 28, 1999, p. 6.
6. Karen Lowry Miller and Joann Muller, "The Auto Baron," *Business Week,* November 16, 1998, pp. 83–90.
7. Alice Z. Cuneo, "Wal-Mart's Goal: to Reign Over Web," *Advertising Age,* July 5, 1999, pp. 1, 27.
8. Cherie Hicks, "Learning to Live with Wal-Mart," *Mobile Register,* July 4, 1999, pp. F1, F4.
9. Gerry Khermouch, "Heineken Tightens Lines Under Freshness Assault," *Brandweek,* June 21, 1999, p. 12.
10. Jack Neff, "Rivals Step Up Pace of Product Launches," *Advertising Age,* May 24, 1999, p. 26.
11. Rajiv Chandrasekaran, "Microsoft Executive Tells of Restrictions on Net Firms," *Washington Post,* February 9, 1999, p. E1; and Joseph Nocera, "Witnesses in Wonderland," *Fortune,* March 1, 1999, pp. 168–180.
12. "E-Crime Pays," *CIO Web Business,* April 1, 1999, p. 18; and "Virginia Can Spam," *Entrepreneur,* May 1999, p. 30.
13. "Bait and Switch," *Entrepreneur,* July 1999, p. 20.
14. James Heckman, "Today's Game Is Keep Away," *Marketing News,* July 5, 1999, pp. 1, 7; and John Simons, "New FTC Rules Aim to Protect Kid Web Privacy," *Wall Street Journal,* April 21, 1999, pp. B1, B4.
15. James Lardner, "I Know What You Did Last Summer—And Fall," *U.S. News & World Report,* April 19, 1999, pp. 55–56.
16. Rachel Beck, "Marketing Group Corrals Unwanted Solicitations," *Mobile Register,* July 7, 1999, p. 7B.
17. Michael J. Mandel, "The 21st Century Economy," *Business Week,* August 31, 1998, pp. 58–67.
18. Doug Donovan, "Captive Monster," *Forbes,* July 5, 1999, p. 126; and Jerry Useem, "For Sale Online: You," *Fortune,* July 5, 1999, pp. 67–78.
19. Douglas A. Blackmon, "Forget the Stereotype: America Is Becoming a Nation of Culture," *Wall Street Journal,* September 13, 1998, pp. A1, A8.
20. Brian Zajac, "Yankee Travelers" *Forbes,* July 27, 1998, p. 162.

21. "China OK's the Avon Lady," *Adweek,* October 29, 1998, p. 26; and Dexter Roberts and Kathleen Kerwin, "Ultimatum for the Avon Lady," *Business Week,* May 11, 1998, p. 33.

22. Eryn Brown, "VF Corp. Changes Its Underwear," *Fortune,* December 7, 1998, pp. 115–118.

23. Charles Gasparino and Rebecca Buckman, "Facing Internet Threat, Merrill to Offer Trading Online for Low Fees," *Wall Street Journal,* June 1, 1999, pp. A1, A10.

24. Dave Guilford, "Toyota, Honda Start to Push Hybrid Vehicles," *Advertising Age,* June 8, 1999, p. 20; and "Electric Vehicles Failing to Charge Up Consumers," *Advertising Age,* June 39, 1998, p. 45.

25. Hillary Chura, "Veggie-Burger Rivals Follow the Leader on Ads," *Advertising Age,* May 24, 1999, p. 65.

26. Jim Osterman, "Ford Talks en Español," *Adweek,* August 17, 1998, p. 3.

27. Andrew Serwer, "Ben & Jerry's Is Back: Ice Cream *and* a Hot Stock," *Fortune,* August 2, 1999, p. 267.

28. Barbara S. Peterson, "Contrarians at the Gate," *Conde Nast Traveler,* May 1999, pp. 47–54.

29. "Companies Can Advertise Health Benefits," downloaded July 7, 1999 from Yahoo! News, http://dailynews.yahoo.com.

30. Jennifer Bresnahan, "For Goodness Sake," *CIO Enterprise,* June 15, 1999, pp. 55–62.

31. Corinne Economaki, "Still Smokin' at the Track," *Brandweek,* March 22, 1999, pp. 20–22; Robert D. Deutsch, "A Eulogy for Joe Camel," *Brandweek,* May 3, 1999, pp. 29, 32; and Ira Teinowitz, "Tobacco Pact Creates Potential Print Windfall," *Advertising Age,* November 23, 1998, p. 4.

32. Megan Santosus, "The Price Is Right," *CIO Enterprise,* June 15, 1999, p. 24.

33. Carol Krol, "Consumers Reach the Boiling Point Over Privacy Issues," *Advertising Age,* March 29, 1999, p. 22.

34. "Enough Junk," *U.S. News & World Report,* May 25, 1999, p. 68.

35. Carol Krol, "Consumers Reach the Boiling Point."

36. Eilene Hu, "What That Seal of 'Approval' Really Means," *McCall's,* November 1998, p. 152.

37. Peter Carbonara, "Is That a Bomb in Your Dashboard?" *Money,* November 1998, pp. 131–138.

38. Ira Teinowitz, "Web Ad Disclosures Examined," *Advertising Age,* May 24, 1999, p. 48.

39. Joel Dreyfuss, "Planned Obsolescence Is Alive and Well," *Fortune,* February 15, 1999, p. 192.

40. John T. Maybury, "Your Wedding Band May Have Once Lived in a Computer," *Forbes ASAP,* February 22, 1999, p. 20.

41. "The Nation's CEOs Look to the Future," National Institute of Science and Technology, downloaded from www.quality.nist.gov, June 16, 1999.

42. Mandel, "The 21st Century Economy."

43. Don Tapscott, "In Networked Economy, Sectors Have New Roles," *USA Today,* November 16, 1998, p. 5E.

44. Lardner, "I Know What You Did Last Summer—And Fall."

Chapter 3

SOURCES FOR MARKETING STRATEGY SUCCESS: Craig S. Smith, "The Exotic Sound of Guam: 'Attention, Kmart Shoppers!'" *Wall Street Journal,* July 12, 1999, pp. A17, A20.

1. Rebecca A. Fannin and Louise Kramer, "As Taco Bell Enters Singapore, Gidget Avoids the Ad Limelight," *Ad Age International,* January 11, 1999, pp. 13–14.

2. Eric S. Hardy, "An Almost Perfect World," *Forbes,* July 26, 1999, pp. 160–161.

3. Michael Czinkota and Ilkka A. Ronkainen, *International Marketing,* Fifth Edition (Fort Worth, TX: Harcourt College Publishers, 1998), p. 7.

4. Rebecca Piirto Heath, "Think Globally," *Marketing Tools,* October 1996, downloaded from http://www.marketingtools.com on November 30, 1996; and Andrew Tanzer, "The Pacific Century," *Forbes,* July 15, 1996, pp. 109–113.

5. Andrew Kupfer, "Mike Armstrong's AT&T: Will the Pieces Come Together?" *Fortune,* April 26, 1999, pp. 82–89; and "AT&T/BT Global Venture Names Leadership Team and Principal Operating Locations," downloaded from www.att.com, June 10, 1999.

6. Bill Meyers, "Small Businesses Flock to Net," *USA Today,* August 3, 1999, p. 3B.

7. Claire Blackwell, "Tourism and Cultural Tourism: Some Basic Facts," *Preservation Issues,* vol. 7, no. 3, downloaded from www.umsl.edu, June 3, 1999; and Laurel Wents, "WTO: Tourists in 2020 Will Spend $2 Trillion," *Ad Age International,* November 9, 1998, pp. 29–32.

8. "IDC Predicts Worldwide Internet Services Revenues Will Surge Past $78 Billion in 2003," *NetScorecard,* downloaded from www.netscorecard.com, June 9, 1999.

9. "U.S. to Study Foreigners' Use of Financial Services," *Wall Street Journal,* July 12, 1999, p. A24; and Thomas K. Grose, "U.S. Shares Cross Borders Via Internet," *USA Today,* June 1, 1999, p. B1.

10. Louise Lee, "To Sell Movies in Asia, Sing a Local Tune," *Wall Street Journal,* September 22, 1998, pp. B1, B4.

11. "Arby's to Open 102 Restaurants in Britain," *Mobile Register,* July 11, 1999, p. 6B.

12. Larry Light, "Well, The Russians Like It," *Business Week,* September 28, 1998, p. 8.

13. Jack Neff, "Test It in Paris, France, Launch It in Paris, Texas," *Advertising Age,* May 31, 1999, p. 26; and Jack Neff, "P&G Marks First with U.S., Euro Test of Swiffer," *Advertising Age,* August 24, 1998, p. 32.

14. "World Population Profile: 1998-Highlights," U.S. Census Bureau, downloaded from www.census.gov, July 16, 1999.

15. Dawn Thorndike Pysarchik, Jae-Eun Chung, and Linda Fernandes Plank, "Indian Market Has Food for Thought," *Marketing News,* July 19, 1999. p. 12.

16. Peter Spiegel, "Foreign Fizz," *Forbes,* August 23, 1999, p. 41.

17. Richard C. Morais, "Sizzler," *Forbes,* March 22, 1999, pp. 96–98.

18. Mercedes M. Cardona, "J&J Readies U.S. Intro of Leading French Brand," *Advertising Age,* July 12, 1999, p. 57.

19. Ernest Beck and Rekha Balu, "Europe Is Deaf to Snap! Crackle! Pop!" *Wall Street Journal,* June 22, 1998, pp. B1, B2.

20. Miriam Jordan, "Marketing Gurus Say: In India, Think Cheap, Lose the Cold Cereal," *Wall Street Journal,* October 11, 1996, p. A7.

21. Andrew Tanzer, "China Goes Wireless," *Forbes,* July 26, 1999, pp. 60–63.

22. Christian Caryl, "They Love Our Money," *U.S. News & World Report,* April 27, 1998, pp. 28–29.

23. Daniel Tilles, "The French Exception," *Adweek,* April 20, 1998, pp. 24–27.

24. Richard H. Levey, "Home Market," *Direct,* June 1999, pp. 1, 39–40.

25. "The Web Is Truly Worldwide," *Global Insights,* June 1999, pp. 1–2.

26. Robert McGarvey, "Web Site," *Entrepreneur,* July 1999, p. 32.

27. Amy Bowdler and Emily Felt, "GMO's Exporters Should Follow the Debate," *Insight,* Summer 1999, pp. 1–2.

28. Anne Neville, "France's Shopping Frenzy: All's Well That Sells Well," *Mobile Register,* February 25, 1999, p. 3D.

29. Sarah Lorge, "Can ISO Certification Boost Sales?" *Sales & Marketing Management,* April 1998, p. 19.

30. Grace Cha, "U.S. Eases Sanctions on Cuba," *ChannelOne.com,* downloaded July 23, 1999; and "U.S. Chamber Says Clinton Administration Missed Opportunity on Cuba Sanctions," U.S. Chamber of Commerce press release dated April 28, 1999.

31. "Italy Files Trade Charges Against Coke," *CBS Marketwatch,* downloaded August 13, 1999.

32. Joyce-Ann Gatsoulis, "Czech Law Bans Foreign Sales Promo Contests," *Ad Age International,* November 9, 1998, pp. 34–35.

33. Miriam Jordan, "Debut of Rival Diet Colas in India Leaves a Bitter Taste," *Wall Street Journal,* July 21, 1999, pp. B1, B4.

34. Len A. Costa, "Who's Afraid of Japan, Brazil, and Russia?" *Fortune,* February 15, 1999, pp. 40, 45, 48.

35. James Cox, "Tariffs Shield Some U.S. Products," *USA Today,* May 6, 1999., pp. B1, B2.

36. Douglas A. Irwin, "Lamb Tariffs Fleece U.S. Consumers," *Wall Street Journal,* July 12, 1999, p. A28.

37. Gordon Fairclough and Darren McDermott, "Why Bananas, A Rotten Business, Set Off a Trade War," *Wall Street Journal,* August 9, 1999, pp. A1, A8; and Karl Taro Greenfeld, "Banana Wars," *Business Week,* June 21, 1999, pp. 37–38.

38. James Cox, "Tariffs," p. B2.

39. James Bennett, "To Clear Air with Europe, U.S. Waves Some Sanctions," *The New York Times,* May 19, 1998, downloaded from www.nytimes.com, July 27, 1999.

40. Martin Crutsinger, "U.S. Apple Growers File Trade Case Against China," *Mobile Register,* June 14, 1999, p. 7B.

41. James Cox, "Tariffs," p. B2.

42. "Export Issues: China," downloaded from www.exporthotline.com, July 16, 1999.

43. "USWA Challenging NAFTA Constitutionality in Lawsuit," Fair Trade Watch, downloaded from www.fairtradewatch.org, July 27, 1999; and David C. Datelle, "NAFTA's Effect on U.S. Jobs," Public Policy Institute, downloaded from www.dlcppi.org, July 28, 1999.

44. Charlotte Mulhern, "Going the Distance," *Entrepreneur,* May 1998, pp. 129–133.

45. Lambeth Hochwald, "Are You Smart Enough to Sell Globally?" *Sales & Marketing Management,* July 1998, pp. 53–55.

46. Jocelyn Noveck, "Vive Le Lance!" *Mobile Register,* July 26, 1999, pp. A1, A6; and Jim Litke, "Armstrong Inspiration to Cancer Survivors," *Mobile Register,* July 26, 1999, pp. C1, C6.

47. "New AIC Hilton Hotel to Open at Lagos Airport, Nigeria," Hilton Hotels Corp. press release dated July 22, 1999, downloaded from www.hilton.com, July 29, 1999.

48. Russell B. Scholl, "The International Investment Position of the United States at Yearend 1998," *Survey of Current Business,* U.S. Bureau of Economic Analysis, July 1999, pp. 4, 7.

49. David Jonas, "Delta, Air France Join Forces," *Business Travel News,* July 5, 1999, pp. 3–4.

50. Jeffery D. Zbar, "Esso Sells with Emotion," *Ad Age International,* July 1999, p. 9.

51. Melanie Wells, "Worldwide Ads Can Produce Global Gaffes," *USA Today,* June 25, 1998, p. 4B.

52. Juliana Koranteng, "SonicNet Tunes Into Youth Music Worldwide," *Ad Age International*, June 1999, p. 29.
53. John H. Christy, "A Bureaucrat with a Head for Oil," *Forbes*, July 26, 1999, pp. 112–115.
54. Laurie Freeman, "Teletubbies," *Advertising Age*, June 28, 1999, pp. 26–27.
55. Thomas G. Condon and Kurt Badenhausen, "Spending Spree," *Forbes*, July 26, 1999, pp. 208–220.

Chapter 4

SOURCES FOR MARKETING STRATEGY SUCCESS: Jaclyn Easton, *Striking It Rich.com* (New York: McGraw-Hill; 1999), pp. 89–101.
SOURCES FOR MARKETING STRATEGY FAILURE: Richard H. Levey, "Smarten Up!" *Direct*, March 15, 1999, pp. 1, 71–72.
1. Lorrie Grant, "Art and Soul Sell Online," *USA Today*, July 15, 1999, pp. B1, B2; Robert Goff, "Native Impressions," *Forbes*, May 31, 1999, p. 290; and "Testing the Web's Limits with Monet," *Inc.*, October 1998, p. 19.
2. Bernard Wysocki Jr., "The Outlook: Internet Is Opening Up a New Era of Pricing," *Wall Street Journal*, June 8, 1998, p. A1.
3. Robert Hof, Gary McWilliams, and Gabrielle Saveri, "The 'Click Here' Economy," *Business Week*, June 22, 1998, pp. 122–128.
4. Vladimir Zwass, "Electronic Commerce: Structures and Issues," *International Journal of Electronic Commerce*, Fall 1996, p. 3.
5. Kate Maddox, "E-Commerce Becoming Reality," *Advertising Age*, October 26, 1998, pp. S1, S2.
6. Alice Z. Cuneo, "Gap Boosts E-Commerce with Plans for New Sites," *Advertising Age*, September 21, 1998, p. 34; The Gap Web site accessed at www.gap.com.
7. George Anders, "Buying Frenzy," *Wall Street Journal*, July 12, 1999, pp. R6, R10.
8. Maricris G. Briones, "Wired Homes Opening Up More Avenues for Marketers," *Marketing News*, April 26, 1999, p. 3.
9. Andy Reinhardt, "Log On, Link Up, Save Big," *Business Week*, June 22, 1998, pp. 132–133.
10. Ibid.
11. Peter Coffee, "Workgroup Products That Work," *PC Week*, December 22–29, 1997, p. 49.
12. David Lieberman, "Net Hangs Out of Reach of Have-Nots," *USA Today*, July 9, 1999, p. 2A.
13. Ibid.
14. Kevin Maney, "The Networked Economy Changes Everything," *USA Today*, November 16, 1998, pp. 1E, 2E.
15. Marc Gunther, "The Newest Addiction," *Fortune*, August 2, 1999, pp. 122–124.
16. "Nordstrom Launches Online Shopping," *Marketing Online*, November 23, 1998.
17. Kevin Maney, "The Networked Economy Changes Everything."
18. Daniel Roth, "E*trade's Plan for World Domination," *Fortune*, August 2, 1999, pp. 95–98.
19. Andy Reinhardt, "Log On, Link Up, Save Big."
20. Catherine Yang, "America Online: Often Down, Never Out," *Business Week*, July 20, 1998, p. 16; and Marc Gunther, "The Internet Is Mr. Case's Neighborhood," *Fortune*, March 30, 1998, p. 76.
21. Elliot Zaret, "The Theory of Portal Evolution," downloaded from www.msnbc.com/news, August 23, 1999; and David Kirkpatrick, "The Portal of the Future? Your Boss Will Run It," *Fortune*, August 2, 1999, pp. 222–226.
22. Peter Coy, "You Ain't Seen Nothin' Yet," *Business Week*, June 22, 1998, p. 130.
23. Erika Brown, "Terminal Terminals," *Forbes*, July 27, 1998, p. 41; Richard H. Levey, "100 Voodoo Dolls to Palo Alto?" *Direct*, September 1, 1998, p. 19; Leigh Buchanan, "Shark Bytes," *Inc. Tech 1998*, No. 3, p. 30; and John A. Byrne, "The Corporation of the Future," *Business Week*, August 31, 1998, pp. 102–106.
24. Don Tapscott, "New Universe Forming as Business Between Businesses Explodes," *USA Today*, November 16, 1998, pp. 1E–2E.
25. George Anders, "Click and Buy," *Wall Street Journal*, December 7, 1998, p. R4.
26. Janice Maloney, "The E-Trade Stampede," *Time*, September 6, 1999.
27. Robert D. Hof, et al., "The 'Click Here' Economy," p. 124.
28. Andy Reinhardt, "Log On, Link Up, Save Big," p. 133.
29. Karen Southwick, "Found in the Crowd," p. 59.
30. Lorrie Grant, "Lands' End Tailors Internet Site for Sales," *USA Today*, October 13, 1998, p. 12B.
31. Robert D. Hof, "Now It's Your Web," *Business Week*, October 5, 1998, p. 164.
32. Ibid.
33. Maricris G. Briones, "Customer Service the Key to Online Relationships," *Marketing News*, November 23, 1998, p. 2.
34. Pam Black, "All the World's an Auction," *Business Week*, February 8, 1999, pp. 120–121.

35. Bruce Horovitz, "Web Site Helps Untangle Mess of E-Customer Service," *USA Today*, August 16, 1999, p. 7B.
36. Roger Crockett, "Invisible—and Loving It," *Business Week*, October 5, 1998, pp. 124-128.
37. Ibid.
38. Julie Schmit, "Asia's Culture Hampers Internet Commerce," *USA Today*, February 16, 1999, p. 6B.
39. William Echikson, "The Net: Europeans Aren't Buying," *Business Week*, September 6, 1999, p. 8.
40. W. Wossen Kassaye, "Global Advertising and the World Wide Web," *Marketing 99/00* Annual Edition (New York: Dushkin/McGraw-Hill, 1999), p. 200.
41. Steven Vonder Haar, "Web Crawling," *IQ*, January 18, 1999, p. 42.
42. Ibid.
43. David Lieberman, "Net Hangs Out of Reach of Have-Nots," *USA Today*, July 9, 1999, p. 2A.
44. Pam Black, "All the World's an Auction."
45. "Online Auctions Blasted," *Mobile Register*, February 24, 1999, p. 11B.
46. Kara Swisher, "Seller Beware," *Wall Street Journal*, December 7, 1998, p. R22.
47. Telephone conversation with Amazon.com customer service representative, August 30, 1999.
48. Pam Black, "All the World's an Auction."
49. Nick Wingfield, "A Marketer's Dream," *Wall Street Journal*, December 7, 1998, p. R20.
50. Maria Seminerio, "Kids' Online Privacy Issues Debated," *ZDNet News*, July 20, 1999.
51. Mary Mosquera, "FTC Seeks Children's Privacy Regulation," *Tech Web*, downloaded from www.techweb.com, June 4, 1998.
52. Rochelle Barner, "The E-Commerce Connection," *Sales & Marketing Management*, January 1999, pp. 40, 42.
53. Timothy Hanrahan, "Lessons Learned," *Wall Street Journal*, December 7, 1998, p. R16.
54. George Anders, "Discomfort Zone," *Wall Street Journal*, November 4, 1998, pp. A1, A14.
55. AnnMarie Harris, "E-Commerce Made Easy," *Sales & Marketing Management*, November 1998, p. 94.
56. Ellen Shapiro, "Web Retailers Are Racing to Sell Videotapes," *Wall Street Journal*, October 2, 1998, pp. B1, B4.
57. Larry Armstrong, "Anything You Can Sell, I Can Sell Cheaper," *Business Week*, December 14, 1998, pp. 130–132.
58. Bill Meyers, "Small Businesses Flock to Net," *USA Today*, August 3, 1999, p. 3B.
59. David Lieberman, "Net Hangs Out of Reach of Have-Nots."
60. Bradley Johnson, "ZDNet Hones Targeting to Link Marketers, Prospects," *Advertising Age*, May 31, 1999, p. 60.
61. Maricris G. Briones, "On Ramp," *Marketing News*, April 26, 1999, pp. 1, 13–14; and Thomas E. Weber, "Nothing to Sniff At," *Wall Street Journal*, December 7, 1998, p. R18.
62. Lorrie Grant, "Grocery Chore No More," *USA Today*, July 21, 1999, pp. 1B, 2B; Lorrie Grant, "Soon, Online Grocers Will Deliver the Goods to Your Door," *USA Today*, March 8, 1999, p. B1; Henry Goldblatt, "Cool Companies 1999," *Fortune*, July 5, 1999, pp. 93–106; and James Lardner, "Please Don't Squeeze the Tomatoes Online," *U.S. News & World Report*, November 9, 1998, p. 51.
63. Bernhard Warner, "Claritin Among Drugs Not Sneezing at Online Sponsorships," *Adweek*, August 10, 1998, p. 36.
64. Beth Snyder, "Sony Pursues Difficult-to-Reach College Students," *Advertising Age*, September 7, 1998, pp. 30–33.
65. D'Ann Weimer, "Can I Try (Click) That Blouse (Drag) in Blue?" *Business Week*, November 9, 1998, p. 86.
66. Jeff Rothfeder and Ann Graham, "Community Spirit," *Executive Edge*, August/September 1999, pp. 32–36.
67. Neil Gross, "Building Global Communities," *Business Week E.Biz*, March 22, 1999, pp. 42–43.
68. Lorrie Grant, "Let Your Fingers Do Shopping . . . In Store," *USA Today*, July 29, 1999, p. 3B.
69. Richard H. Levey, "Smarten Up!" *Direct*, March 15, 1999, pp. 1, 71–72.
70. Susan Kuchinskas, "Val Pak Goes Virtual: Coupon Company Launches Web Site," *Adweek*, November 2, 1998, p. 42.
71. David Vaczek, "Online Trial Tries to Click," *Promo*, September 1998, p. 40.
72. Lisa Chadderdon, "How Dell Sells on the Web," *Fast Company*, September 1998, p. 60.
73. Jeff Jensen, "Airwalk, Vans Web Sales Focus on Brand-Building," *Advertising Age*, September 18, 1998, p. 48.
74. Joel Dreyfuss, "Selling on the Internet Made Easy," *Fortune*, November 23, 1998, p. 278.

75. Robert D. Hof, "Amazon.com, The Wild World of E-Commerce," *Business Week*, December 14, 1998, pp. 106–110; and Lesley Hazleton, "Jeff Bezos," *Success*, July 1998, p. 60.

76. Perry Glasser, "Plugged In," *CIO Enterprise*, June 15, 1999, p. 12.

77. Melissa Campanelli, "Hot on the Trail," *Entrepreneur*, August 1999, p. 40–43.

78. Fred Vogelstein, "Rating Web Sites," *U.S. News & World Report,* April 5, 1999, p. 50.

79. Bob Wehling, "The Future of Marketing," *Marketing 99/00* Annual Edition (New York: Dushkin/McGraw-Hill, 1999), pp. 10–14.

80. Gary Hamel and Jeff Sampler, "The E-Corporation," *Fortune*, December 7, 1998, p. 82.

81. George Anders, "The View From the Top," *Wall Street Journal*, July 12, 1999. p. R52.

Chapter 5

SOURCES FOR MARKETING STRATEGY SUCCESS: "Garden.com Extends Its Virtual Warehousing Strategy with Launch of Fresh Stems Product Line," November 18, 1999, www.garden.com; "Garden.com Builds Brand, Extends Market Reach through an Exclusive Partnership with iVillage.com," www.garden.com, November 10, 1999; and Edward O. Welles, "The Perfect Internet Business," *Inc.*, August 1999, pp. 70–78.

SOURCES FOR MARKETING STRATEGY FAILURE: Mary Hillebrand, "RealNetworks Launches Privacy Initiative after Breach Fiasco," *E-Commerce Times,* www.EcommerceTimes.com, November 9, 1999; Chet Dembeck, "Is Real Networks' Privacy Violation the Tip of the Iceberg?," *E-Commerce Times, www.EcommerceTimes.com,* November 4, 1999; N. Michael Eskenazi, *"RealNetworks Says It's RealSorry,"* Time Daily, www.time.com, November 2, 1999; and Nathaniel Wice, "RealNetworks Caught Spying on Users," *Digital Daily,* www.timedigital.com, November 2, 1999.

1. "Calgary Firm's Web site Selected as One of the Twenty Best Small Businesses in North America," www.onair-canada.com/company/news, November 15, 1999; "Hear, Here," *Inc. Tech 1999*, no. 4, pp. 71–72; and "On Air Founder Named Young Entrepreneur of the Year by Profit Magazine," www.onair-canada.com/company/news, June 9, 1999.

2. Jonathan R. Copulshy and Michael J. Wolf, "Relationship Marketing: for the Future," *Journal of Business Strategy,* July/August 1990, pp. 16–20.

3. Jack Griffin and Marcie Lynn Avram, "Databases Identify Best Prospects," *Advertising Age*, October 12, 1998, pp. A-4, A-15.

4. Maria Stefanidu, "Reward Loyal Customers by Being Loyal to Them," *Marketing News*, February 15, 1999, p. 4.

5. Leyland F. Pitt and Susan K. Foreman, "Internal Marketing Role in Organizations: A Transaction Cost Perspective," *Journal of Business Research 44*, (1999), pp. 25–36.

6. "Charity Begins at Home: Nurture Your Current Customers," *Customer Service Review,* downloaded from www.csr.com June 16, 1999.

7. Andrea Petersen, "A Fine Line," *Wall Street Journal,* June 21, 1999.

8. Robert F. Lusch, Thomas Boyt, and Drue Schuler, "Employees as Customers: The Role of Social Controls and Employee Socialization in Developing Patronage," *Journal of Business Research,* vol. 35, 1996, pp. 179–187.

9. Martin Christopher, Andrian Payne, and David Ballantyne, *Relationship Marketing* (Oxford, UK: Butterworth-Heineman Ltd., 1993), p.4.

10. Thomas Brinckwirth and Stephan Butscher, "Germany's Most Popular Radio Station Creates Loyal Listeners," *Colloquy*, vol. 6, issue 3, 1998, p. 10.

11. Mary Jo Bitner, "Building Service Relationships: It's All About Promises ," *Journal of the Academy of Marketing Science,* Fall 1995, pp. 246–251.

12. James Lardner, "Your Every Command," *U.S. News & World Report*, July 5, 1999, pp. 44–46.

13. Michael B. Callaghan, Janelle McPhail, and Oliver H. M. Yau, "Dimensions of a Relationship Marketing Orientation," paper delivered at Seventh Biannual World Marketing Congress, Melbourne, Australia, July 1995.

14. Gabrielle Solomon, "Co-Branding Alliances: Arranged Marriages Made by Marketers," *Fortune*, October 12, 1998, p. 188-N.

15. Andy Cohen, "Six Ways to Make Your Dealers Love You," *Sales & Marketing Management*, April 1998, pp. 53–56.

16. Leonard L. Berry, "Relationship Marketing of Service-Growing Internet, Emerging Perspectives," *Journal of the Academy of Marketing Science,* Fall 1995, p. 240.

17. http://www.hog.com.

18. Cohen, "Six Ways to Make Your Dealers Love You," pp. 53–56.

19. Louis E. Boone, *Quotable Business* (New York: Random House, 1999), p. 138.

20. Stefanidu, "Reward Loyal Customers by Being Loyal to Them," p. 4.

21. Lardner, "Your Every Command," pp. 44–46.

22. Richard Levey, "Tracking May Avoid Customer Defections," *Direct*, September 1, 1998, p. 50.

23. "Marriott Maintains Its Lead among Frequent-Guest Programs," *Colloquy*, vol. 6, issue 3, 1998, pp. 7–9.

24. Richard Barlow, "Future Looks Bright for Frequency Marketing," Marketing News, July 5, 1999, p. 14.

25. Wayne D'Orio, "Looking for Loyalty in All the Right Places," *PROMO Magazine*, October 1998, pp. 57–60.

26. Griffin and Avram, "Databases Identify Best Prospects," pp. A-4, A-15.

27. Ibid.

28. http://www.metmuseum.org.

29. Stephan Butscher, "Loyalty Programs Can Work for B-to-B Customers, Too," *Marketing News,* June 22, 1998, p. 6.

30. Richard Sale, "We're Going to Disney World!" *PROMO Magazine*, October 1998, pp. 32–36.

31. Gabrielle Solomon, "Co-Branding Alliances: Arranged Marriages Made by Marketers," *Fortune*, October 12, 1998, p. 188-N.

32. Joanne Cleaver, "Subtle Net Pitch Works For Seniors," *Marketing News*, July 19, 1999, pp. 1, 7.

33. Henry Canaday, "Is Bigger Better?" *Selling Power*, April 1999, pp. 64–65.

34. Howard Millman, "Easy EDI for Everyone," *Infoworld*, August 17, 1998, pp. 38–39.

35. Lynne Cusack and Beth Enslow, "Mission Imprintable," *Executive Edge*, September 1998, pp. 20–22.

36. Ibid.

37. David Field, "Delta's Marketing Chief Aims to Please Passengers," *USA Today*, June 15, 1998, p. 6B.

38. Malcolm Fleschner, "What's in a Brand?" *Selling Power*, April 1999, pp. 60–63.

39. Stephan Butscher, p. 6.

Chapter 6

SOURCES FOR MARKETING STRATEGY SUCCESS: "Seasons Retailing," *Entrepreneur*, November 1999, p. 48; "Feed back the Feedback," *Inc.*, August 1999, p. 110; and Rebecca Berne, "Oop! Juice Aims for a National Appeal," *Herald Sphere*, www.theherald.org, November 16, 1998.

SOURCES FOR MARKETING STRATEGY FAILURE: Michael Hopkins, "Paradise Lost," *Inc.*, November 1999, pp. 67–79; George Gendron, "The News Today, Oh Boy," www.inc.com/articles, November 1, 1999; and Michael Hopkins, "The Antihero's Guide to the New Economy," www.inc.com/articles, January 1, 1998.

1. "MicroStrategy Partners with Sybase to Extend Customer Relationship Management Offering," *Hoover's Online,* www.hooovershb.newsalert.com, November 24, 1999; Tam Harbert, "Stars of the New Millennium," *Electronic Business*, www.eb-mag.com, January 1999; and Janet Novack, "Database Evangelist," *Forbes,* September 7, 1998, pp. 66–68.

2. Helen Jung, "Tyson Foods' Foray into Fishing Costly from Beginning," *The Morning News*, June 27, 1999, p. C8.

3. Russ Mitchell, "Microsoft's Parent Trap," *U.S. News & World Report*, August 9, 1999, pp. 36–38.

4. Corporate Overview, http://www.globalstar.com, March 8, 2000.

5. Ibid.

6. Ibid.

7. Eric Kriss, "Where Have All the PCs Gone?" *Inc.*, February 1999, p. 100; and Mitchell, "Microsoft's Parent Trap."

8. Darrell Rigby, "Smart Managing/Best Practices, Careers, and Ideas: What's Today's Special at the Consultants' Cafe?" *Fortune*, September 7, 1998, p. 162.

9. Kathleen Kerwin, "GM: It's Time to Face the Future," *Business Week*, July 27, 1998, p. 25.

10. Derek F. Abell, "Strategic Window," *Journal of Marketing*, July 1978, pp. 21–26; and John K. Ryans and William L. Shanklin, *Strategic Planning: Concepts and Implementation* (New York: Random House, 1985), p. 11.

11. Julie Schmit, "Firms Slipping the Grasp of Giants Intel, Microsoft," *USA Today,* June 11, 1998, pp. 1B–2B.

12. Daniel Kadlec, "How Blockbuster Changed the Rules," *Time*, August 3, 1998, pp. 48–49.

13. William Symonds, "Paddling Harder at L. L. Bean," *Business Week*, December 7, 1998, pp. 72–73.

14. Janice Maloney, "Mr. Surround-Sound," *Time*, August 3, 1998, p. 50.

15. Russell Garland, "Boston-Based Gillette's New Razor Sharpens Sales," *Knight-Ridder Tribune Business News: Providence Journal-Bulletin—Rhode Island*, May 5, 1999.

16. "Going Native," *Forbes*, August 9, 1999, p. 70.

17. John Bissell, "Top of Mind: No. 1 Means Little in Fast Times," *Brandweek*, March 22, 1999, p. 28.

18. A meta-analysis of 48 studies revealed a positive relationship between market share and profitability. See David M. Szymansky, Sundarwaj G. Bharadgaj, and P. Rajan Varadarajan, "An Analysis of the Market Share—Profitability Relationship," *Journal of Marketing*, July 1993, pp. 1–18.

19. Alex Taylor III, "Goodyear Wants to Be No. 1 Again," *Fortune*, April 27, 1998, pp. 130–134.
20. Susan Greco, "How to Benchmark Sales-and-Marketing Budgets," *Inc.*, February 1999, p. 99; and Thor Valdmanis, "Corporate Execs Examine Strategic Tool," *USA Today*, May 12, 1999, p. 5B.
21. Chandrani Ghosh, "Mint Juleps and One-Armed Bandits," *Forbes*, August 9, 1999, p. 53.

Chapter 6 Appendix

1. Corporate Purpose, http://www.unilever.com, March 8, 2000.
2. Ibid.
3. Eleena de Lisser, "The Front Lines: Start-Ups Are Tough, Even When Mozart Created the Product," *Wall Street Journal*, September 3, 1999, p. B1.
4. Anne Faircloth, "The Best Retailer You've Never Heard Of," *Fortune*, March 16, 1998, pp. 110–112.
5. Terril Jones, "Roadster Rage," *Forbes*, August 9, 1999, pp. 54–55.
6. Brands, http://www.unilever.com, March 8, 2000.

Chapter 7

SOURCES FOR MARKETING STRATEGY SUCCESS: Joseph Rydholm, "Forming a New Covenant," *Quirk's Marketing Research Review,* December 1998, pp. 20–21; Covenant Healthcare Web page, www.slha.com.
SOURCES FOR MARKETING STRATEGY FAILURE: Joseph Rydholm, "Are We Getting Ahead of Ourselves?" *Quirk's Marketing Research Review,* July 1999, pp. 19, 95–97; and John Eckberg, "Making Most of the Web," *The Cincinnati Enquirer,* www.enquirer.com, October 18, 1998.
1. "NCR More than Doubles Data Warehouse for World's Leading Retailer to Over 100 Terabytes," NCR press release, August 17, 1999, accessed at www.ncr.com; William J. Holstein, "Data-Crunching Santa," *U.S. News & World Report,* December 21, 1998, pp. 44–48; and "Wal-Mart Relies on NCR Data Warehouse to Help Manage Its Business," NCR press release, December 17, 1998, accessed at www.ncr.com.
2. Maricris Briones, "Up Next," *Marketing News*, June 8, 1998, p. H34.
3. Gilbert A. Churchill, Jr., *Basic Marketing Research,* Fourth Edition (Fort Worth, TX: Harcourt, Inc., 2001), pp. 12–13.
4. "Top 25 Global Research Organizations," *Marketing News*, August 17, 1998, p. H4; Maricris Briones, "Up Next," *Marketing News*, June 8, 1998, p. H34; and Maricris Briones, "Cheaper Desktops Will Help Net Researchers Corral Clients," *Marketing News*, November 9, 1998, pp. 1, 17.
5. Deborah Orr, "A Giant Reawakens," *Forbes*, January 25, 1999, pp. 52–54.
6. William Helmreich, "Louder Than Words: On-Site Observational Research," *Marketing News*, March 1, 1999, p. 16.
7. Eli Seggew, "A Role in Flux," *Marketing Management*, Winter 1995, p. 35.
8. "Spies Like Us," *Inc.*, August 1998, p. 45.
9. Ibid.
10. Joshua Macht, "The New Market Research," *Inc.*, July 1998, pp. 86–94.
11. Ibid.
12. Phillip Longman, "Down for the Count," *U.S. News & World Report*, September 7, 1998, p. 57.
13. U.S. Census Bureau Web site, www.census.gov/dmd/www/genfaq.htm, April 1999.
14. Kevin Murphy, "Opening the Gates," *Executive Edge*, February–March 1999, p. 13.
15. Rudy Nadilo, "On-line Research Taps Consumers Who Spend," *Marketing News*, June 8, 1998, p. 12.
16. Maricris Briones, "Cheaper Desktops Will Help Net Researchers Corral Clients," *Marketing News*, November 9, 1998, pp. 1, 17.
17. Phaedra Nise, "Getting Smart On-Line," *Inc. Technology*, March 19, 1996, pp. 59–65.
18. Michelle Fellman, "A SMART Move," *Marketing News*, September 14, 1998, pp. 1, 7, 43.
19. Melanie Wells, "New Ways to Get into Our Heads," *USA Today*, March 2, 1999, pp. 1B–2B.
20. Michael McCarthy, "Stalking the Elusive Teenage Trendsetter," *Wall Street Journal*, November 18, 1998, pp. B1, B10.
21. Mike Hofman, "Virtual Shopping," *Inc.*, July 1998, p. 88.
22. Staff reports, "Marketing Briefs: It Plays in Kansas," *Marketing News*, May 11, 1998, p. 2.
23. McCarthy, "Stalking the Elusive Teenage Trendsetter."
24. Norton Paley, "Getting in Focus," *Sales & Marketing Management,* March 1995, pp. 92–95.
25. Leslie M. Harris, "Expanding Horizons," *Marketing Research*, Summer 1996, p. 12.
26. Wells, "New Ways to Get into Our Heads," pp. 1B–2B.
27. Nadilo, "On-line Research Taps Consumers Who Spend," p. 12.
28. Kate Maddox, "Virtual Panels Add Real Insight for Marketers," *Advertising Age*, June 29, 1998, pp. 34, 40.
29. Nadilo, "On-line Research Taps Consumers Who Spend," p. 12.
30. George Anders, "The Race for 'Sticky' Web Sites," *Wall Street Journal*, February 11, 1999, p. B1.
31. Nick Wingfield, "A Marketer's Dream," *Wall Street Journal*, December 7, 1998, p. R20.
32. Heather Green, "Tracking Who Surfs Where," *Business Week*, April 27, 1998, p. 78.
33. Lambeth Hochwald, "Are You Smart Enough to Sell?" *Sales & Marketing Management,* July 1998, p. 53.
34. Ibid.
35. Orr, "A Giant Reawakens."
36. Skip Press, "Fool's Gold?" *Sales & Marketing Management,* June 1998, pp. 58–62.
37. Christopher Koch, "The Middle Ground," *CIO*, January 15, 1999, pp. 49–54.
38. Srikumar Rao, "Diaper-Beer Syndrome," *Forbes*, April 6, 1998, pp. 128–130.
39. Carol Krol, "Data Warehouse Generates Surprises, Leads for Camelot," *Advertising Age*, January 4, 1999, p. 20.
40. Rao, "Diaper-Beer Syndrome."
41. Ibid.
42. U.S. Census Bureau Web site, www.census.gov/dmd/www/genfaq.htm.
43. Hochwald, "Are You Smart Enough to Sell?"

Chapter 8

SOURCES FOR MARKETING STRATEGY SUCCESS: Mike Hofman, "Searching for the Mountain of Youth," *Inc.*, December 1999, pp. 33–38; "Vans, Inc. and Sony Computer Entertainment American Enter into Sponsorship and Licensing Partnership," *Hoover's Online*, November 29, 1999, www.hoovershbn.newsalert.com; and "Vans, Inc. Opens World's Biggest Skatepark and BMX Facility in Ontario, California," *Hoover's Online*, November 5, 1999, www.hoovershbn.newsalert.com.
SOURCES FOR MARKETING STRATEGY FAILURE: D. M. Osborne, "Fast-Paced Rivals Silence Talking-Beeper Service," *Inc.*, December 1999, p. 40; and Monica Alleven, "Conxus Disconnects," *Wireless*, August 30, 1999, www.wirelessweek.com.
1. Ross Anderson, "Used Booksellers Thrive in Online Market," *Seattle Times,* July 13, 1999, www.seattletimes.com; Michelle V. Rafter, "The Online Bookstore That Makes Money," *The Standard,* March 8, 1999, www.thestandard.com; and Powell's Web site, www.powells.com.
2. This story is told in Richard S. Tedlow, *New and Improved: The Story of Mass Marketing in America.* (New York: Basic Books, 1990), and elsewhere.
3. Kerry Dolan, "What the Doctor Ordered," *Forbes*, January 25, 1999, p. 74.
4. "AMA Membership Benefits Skyrocket with American Medical Association Partnership with MedBookStore.com," www.medsite.com, March 9, 2000.
5. Laura Shapiro, "A Glass Half Empty," *Newsweek*, October 5, 1998, pp. 74–76.
6. Joshua Macht, "Niche Bank Targets White-Collar Market," *Inc.*, March 1999, pp. 23–24.
7. "The 219 Cities with More than 100,000 People," *USA Today*, November 19, 1997, p. 20a.
8. U.S. Census Bureau Web site, www.census.gov/population/www/pop-profile/stproj.html, March 9, 2000.
9. Mark Hammond, "GIS Lands on the Map," *PC Week*, January 4, 1999, p. 1.
10. Howard Millman, "Mapping Your Business Strategy," *Computerworld*, January 18, 1999, p. 77.
11. Microsoft advertisement, *Fortune Tech Buyer's Guide*, Summer 1999, pp. 98–99.
12. Beth Brenner, "Plugging into Women," *Brandweek*, March 15, 1999, pp. 25–26.
13. Jonathan Boorstein, "Gender Vendors," *Direct*, January 1999, pp. 1, 41.
14. Ibid.
15. Geoffrey Meredith and Charles Schewe, "Market by Cohorts, Not Generations," *Marketing News*, February 1, 1999, p. 22.
16. Ellen Neuborne and Kathleen Kerwin, "Generation Y," *Business Week*, February 15, 1999, pp. 81–88; and Ellen Neuborne, "We Are Going to Own This Generation," *Business Week*, February 15, 1999, p. 88.
17. Meredith and Schewe, "Market by Cohorts, Not Generations," p. 22.
18. Tobi Elkin, "AT&T Augments Marketing Efforts against Students, Ethnic Consumers," *Brandweek*, August 10, 1998, p. 14.
19. Laura Tiffany, "Isn't It Grand?" *Entrepreneur*, May 1999, pp. 129–134.
20. Josh Chetwynd, "Hotter Than Movies' Teen Steam," *USA Today*, March 10, 1999, pp. D1–D2; and Andy Seiler, "Cocoon Bubble Bursts as More People Flock to Films," *USA Today*, March 10, 1999, p. D1.
21. Tiffany, "Isn't It Grand?"
22. Staff Reports, "Marketing Briefs: Graying Global Population," *Marketing News*, Oct. 26, 1998, p. 2.
23. "Census Bureau Says Median Age Oldest Yet," *The Morning News,* June 15, 1999, p. D6.

24. Phillip Longman, "The World Turns Gray," *U.S. News & World Report,* March 1, 1999, pp. 30–39; and "Marketing Briefs: Graying Global Population," p. 2.

25. Meredith and Schewe, "Market by Cohorts, Not Generations."

26. Ira Teinowitz, "Multicultural Marketing," *Advertising Age,* November 16, 1998, pp. s1, s22.

27. Jeffery Zbar, "With Right Touch, Marketers Can Hit Multiple Cultures," *Advertising Age,* November 16, 1998, pp. s24–s25.

28. Paul Campbell, "State Population Projections," U.S. Census Bureau, www.census.gov/population/www/pop-profile.stproj.html, March 9, 2000.

29. Ibid.

30. Wilfred Masumura, "Money Income," U.S. Census Bureau, www.census.gov/population/www/pop-profile.moninc.html, March 9, 2000.

31. Ira Teinowitz, "Multicultural Marketing," *Advertising Age,* November 16, 1998, pp. s1–s22.

32. "Marketwatch," *Women & Marketing,* June 1998, p. 4.

33. Longman, "The World Turns Gray."

34. "Marketwatch," *Women & Marketing.*

35. Rutt advertisement in *Architectural Digest,* April 1999, p. 207.

36. Andy Cohen, "Where the Money Is," *Sales & Marketing Management,* September 1997, p. 17.

37. "The 20 Hottest Cities for Selling in 1999," *Sales & Marketing Management* Web site, June 15, 1999, www.salesandmarketing.com/more/Selling99.htm.

38. "Marketing Briefs: Graying Global Population," p. 2.

39. http://future.sri.com/vals, March 9, 2000.

40. www.y-interactive.com/products/monitor/monitor.asp, March 9, 2000.

41. Tom Miller, "Global Segments from 'Strivers' to 'Creatives,'" *Marketing News,* July 20, 1998, p. 11.

42. Ibid.

43. Ibid.

44. Jim Steinberg, "Loyalty to the Power of One-to-One," *Brandweek,* May 3, 1999, pp. 32–34.

45. Jim Desrosier, "Now's the Time to Hitch Up to the EWagon," *Brandweek,* September 21, 1998, p. 16.

46. Steinberg, "Loyalty to the Power of One-to-One."

47. Tiffany, "Isn't It Grand?"

48. Lisa Bannon, "Little Big Spenders," *Wall Street Journal,* October 13, 1998, pp. A1, A6.

49. Ibid.

50. D. Allan Kerr, "Where There's Gray, There's Green," *Marketing News,* June 22, 1998, p. 2.

51. Michelle Fellman, "Destination: Culture," *Marketing News,* July 6, 1998, pp. 1, 15.

52. Ibid.

53. Jeff Rubin, "Businesses Gain a Foothold Through Niche Marketing," *Wall Street Journal,* June 25, 1998, p. B18.

54. Ibid.

55. Wendy Zellner, Ann Palmer, David Greising, and Andrew Osterland, "Little Banks Are Sprouting in the Shadow of Giants," *Business Week,* May 4, 1998, p. 44

56. Gordon Fairclough, "Campbell's Recipe for Higher Profit: Reheat Soup Sales," *Wall Street Journal,* May 19, 1999, p. B6.

57. Leslie Chang, "A Phoenix Rises in China," *Wall Street Journal,* May 26, 1999, pp. B1, B4.

58. "Census Bureau Says Median Age Oldest Yet," *The Morning News,* p. D6.

59. Ann M. Raider, "Programs Make Results Out of Research," *Marketing News,* June 21, 1999, p.14.

Chapter 9

SOURCES FOR MARKETING STRATEGY SUCCESS: Alessandra Bianchi, "What's Cooking On-Line?" *Inc.,* January 2000, pp. 23–25; "What Tavolo Offers," www.tavolo.com, accessed January 10, 2000; James Lardner, "World-Class Workaholics," *U.S. News & World Report,* December 20, 1999, pp. 42–53; Cynthia E. Griffin, Victoria Neal, Heather Page, Michelle Prather, and Laura Tiffany, "Time-Stressed Consumers," from "What's Hot," *Entrepreneur,* December 1999, p. 98.

SOURCES FOR MARKETING STRATEGY FAILURE: Elise Ackerman, "The Cigar Boom Goes Up in Smoke," *U.S. News & World Report,* November 29, 1999, p. 55; Sharon Gerrie, "Cigar Stores Still Lighting Up Despite Fading Stogie Fad," *Las Vegas Business Press,* www.lvbusinesspress.com, November 8, 1999; and "Tamboril Cigar Co. Quarterly Report," www.biz.yahoo.com, June 4, 1999.

1. "Lifestyles of the Online Shoppers"; "Women Taking the Internet Lead"; "Increase Seen in Internet Shopping"; "Computer, Internet Use Up Among Americans," all accessed December 1999 from www.cyberatlas.internet.com.

2. Jagdish N. Sheth, Banwari Mittal, and Bruce Newman: *Customer Behavior: Consumer Behavior and Beyond* (Fort Worth, TX: The Dryden Press, 1999), p. 5.

3. Melanie Wells, "Worldwide Ads Can Produce Global Gaffes," *USA Today,* June 25, 1998, p. 4B.

4. Stephanie Armour, "Personal Services No Longer a Luxury," *USA Today,* June 3, 1998, p. 1A.

5. Noreen O'Leary, "The Boom Tube," *Adweek,* May 18, 1998, pp. 45–52.

6. Fredreic Smoler, "Brown Stuff, Sticky Fingers," *Worth,* February 1999, pp. 79–80.

7. Eric Roston, "Will the U.S. Chicken Out on Russia?" *Fortune,* November 23, 1998, p.52.

8. Galina Espinoza, "Five U.S. Stocks with Latin Heat," *Money,* December 1997, pp. 140–148.

9. Carey Gillam, "New NationsBank Group to Court Black Community," *American Banker,* September 16, 1998, p. 5.

10. Jennifer Gore, "Ethnic Marketing May Become the Norm," *Bank Marketing,* September 1998, p. 12.

11. Leon Wynter, "Samplers and Getaways Help Push Black Books," *Wall Street Journal,* February 3, 1999, p. B1.

12. Gore, "Ethnic Marketing May Become the Norm," p. 12.

13. Tad Szule, "The Fastest Growing Minority in America," *Parade Magazine,* January 3, 1999, pp. 4–7; Christy Haubegger, "The Latin Beat," *Entrepreneur,* June 1998, p. 145.

14. Alice Cuneo and Jean Halliday, "Ford, Penney's Target California's Asian Populations," *Advertising Age,* January 4, 1999, p. 28.

15. Gore, "Ethnic Marketing May Become the Norm," p. 12.

16. Saul Gitlin, "Cars: Dealing with Asians," *Brandweek,* January 5, 1998, p. 15.

17. Shelly Reese, "Culture Shock," *Marketing 99/00 Annual Editions,* ed. John E. Richardson (Guilford, CT: Dushkin/McGraw-Hill, reprinted from *Marketing Tools,* May 1998), p. 44.

18. Henry Assael, *Consumer Behavior and Marketing Action,* Sixth Edition (Boston: Southwest-ITP, 1998), p. 416.

19. Michelle Wirth Fellman, "Merged Models Not Expected from Auto Marriages—Yet," *Marketing News,* June 22, 1998, p. 1.

20. Yumiko Ono, "Kitty-Mania Grips Grown-Ups in Japan," *Wall Street Journal,* December 15, 1998, p. B1.

21. Roger D Blackwell, Paul W. Miniard, and James F. Engel, *Consumer Behavior,* Eighth Edition (Fort Worth, TX: Dryden Press, 1998), pp. 747–750

22. Stacy Perman, "The Joy of Not Cooking," *Time,* June 1, 1998, p. 66.

23. Noreen O'Leary, "The Boom Tube," *Adweek,* May 18, 1998, pp. 45–52; and James McNeal, "Tapping the Three Kids' Markets," *Marketing 99/00 Annual Additions,* ed. John E. Richardson (Guilford, CT: Dushkin/McGraw-Hill, reprinted from *American Demographics,* April 1998), pp. 36–41.

24. *Smithsonian Study Tours* catalog, 1999, pp. 12, 34.

25. Beth Berselli, "Marketing and Advertising-with-Attitude Targets the 'Generation X' Market," *The Morning News,* March 29, 1998, p. D8.

26. "Carnival Puts 420 Mil. Into Autumnal Cruise Campaign," *Brandweek,* October 5, 1998, p. 12; and "Port of Call: Your Living Room," *Brandweek,* November 30, 1998, p. 1.

27. Chris Woodyard and Lorrie Grant, "E-tailers Dash to Wild, Wild, Web," *USA Today,* January 13, 1999, pp. 1B–2B.

28. This section is based on Michael L. Rothschild and William C. Gaidis, "Behavioral Learning Theory: Its Relevance to Marketing and Promotions," *Journal of Marketing,* Spring 1981, pp. 70–78.

29. Evan Ramstad, "Why Is It So Hard to Buy a TV?" *Wall Street Journal,* December 4, 1998, pp. W1, W18.

30. These categories were originally suggested in John A. Howard, *Marketing Management: Analysis and Planning* (Homewood, IL: Richard D. Irwin, 1963). This discussion is based on Donald R. Lehmann, William L. Moore, and Terry Elrod, "The Development of Distinct Choice Process Segments over Time: A Stochastic Modeling Approach," *Journal of Marketing,* spring 1982, pp. 48–50.

31. Tara Parker-Pope, "Makeup for Moppets: Lots of Glitter, Hot Sales," *Wall Street Journal,* December 4, 1998, pp. B1–B2.

Chapter 10

SOURCES FOR MARKETING STRATEGY SUCCESS: Fred Barbash, "The Business of Business Is Net's Future," *Washington Post,* January 2, 2000, www.washingtonpost.com; Len Boselovic, "FreeMarkets Investors Strike Gold," *Pittsburgh Post-Gazette,* December 11, 1999, www.post-gazette.com; "The Two Brains behind FreeMarkets," *Pittsburgh Post-Gazette,* December 11, 1999, www.post-gazette.com; Roger O. Crocketts, "Glen Meakom," *Business Week Online,* September 27, 1999, www.businessweek.com; "Seller Door," *Inc. Technology,* September 15, 1998, pp. 62–66.

SOURCES FOR MARKETING STRATEGY FAILURE: Joshua Macht, "Falling Phone Rates Squash Global Fax Service," *Inc.,* April 1999, p. 25; Ian Olgeirson, "Intergram Collapses, Sinks into Chapter 7," *The Denver Business Journal,* July 13, 1998, www.amcity.com; Emily Cohen, "Paperless Faxing," *PC Magazine Online,* April 21, 1998, www.zdnet.com.

1. "About Sight & Sound Software," Sight & Sound Web site, www.sight-n-sound.com, accessed January 12, 2000; Geoff Williams, "Crash Course," *Entrepreneur,* January 2000, p. 91; Warren Lutz, "Wal-Mart Launches Online Travel Site," WebTravel-News.com, January 3, 2000, www.webtravelnews.com; John Courtmanche, "Sight & Sound VP Tells Why Wal-Mart Chose BookSmart," WebTravelNews.com, November 3, 1999, www.webtravelnews.com; Jacqueline Love, "Fasten Your Seat Belts, It Could Be a Bumpy Ride," *The Oregonian,* July 5, 1999, www.oregonlive.com; and James E. Gaskin, "American Airlines Making Web Connections," *Interactive Week,* September 5, 1998, www.zdnet.com.

2. Edward Robinson, "The Pentagon Finally Learns How to Shop," *Fortune,* December 21, 1998, pp. 174–182.

3. Frederick E. Webster Jr. and Yoram Wind, "A General Model for Understanding Organizational Buying Behavior," *Marketing Management,* Winter/Spring 1996, pp. 52–57.

4. The market orientation of resellers is discussed in Thomas L. Baker, Penny M. Simpson, and Judy A. Siguaw, "The Impact of Suppliers' Perceptions of Reseller Market Orientation on Key Relationship Constructs," *Journal of the Academy of Marketing Science,* 27, Winter, 1999, pp. 50–57.

5. Dana James, "Hit the Bricks," *Marketing News,* September 13, 1999, p. 15.

6. Michael D. Hutt and Thomas W. Speh, *Business Marketing Management,* 6th Edition (Fort Worth, TX: The Dryden Press, 1998), pp. 164–166.

7. Stephan Butscher, "Loyalty Programs Can Work for B-to-B Customers, Too," *Marketing News,* June 22, 1998, p. 6.

8. www.census.gov/eped/www/naics; and www.census.gov/eped/naics, downloaded September 22, 1999.

9. Stannie Holt, "Back on the Supply-Chain Gang," *Infoworld,* November 9, 1998, pp. 78–83.

10. Robinson, "The Pentagon Finally Learns How to Shop," pp. 174–182.

11. Butscher, "Loyalty Programs Can Work for B-to-B Customers, Too," p. 6.

12. Larry Riggs, "Exploring the Far East," *BtoB Direct,* Fall 1998, pp. B1, B6.

13. Marq Ozanne and Michael Corbett, "Outsourcing '98: Winning in Today's Global Marketplace," *Fortune,* July 20, 1998, pp. S1–S32.

14. Doug Levy, "PC Prices Falling for Corporations," *USA Today,* June 16, 1998, p. B1.

15. David Raymond, "Embedded Bets," *Forbes ASAP,* June 1, 1998, pp. 63–64.

16. Kevin Murphy and Erik Keller, "Just in Time To Be Too Late?" *Executive Edge,* August/September 1999, pp. 45–48; and Holt, "Back on the Supply-Chain Gang."

17. Ozanne and Corbett, "Outsourcing '98: Winning in Today's Global Marketplace."

18. Ibid.

19. "Seller Door," *Inc. Tech* 1998, no. 3, pp. 62–66; and Sarah Lorge, "Online Bidding Keeps Suppliers in Line," *Sales & Marketing Management,* August 1998, p. 16.

20. Ozanne and Corbett, "Outsourcing '98: Winning in Today's Global Marketplace."

21. References for the organizational buying process incorporate several stages. Arthur Hughes, "Building Profits with Relationship Marketing," *Direct,* January 1999, pp. 49–52, reflects use in stages 1, 2, 3, 4.

22. Robinson, "The Pentagon Finally Learns How to Shop."

23. Sarah Lorge, "The Coke Advantage," *Sales & Marketing Management,* December 1998, p. 17.

24. Hughes, "Building Profits with Relationship Marketing."

25. Hutt and Speh, *Business Marketing Management,* pp. 164–166.

26. Richard Levey, "Keeping in Touch," *Direct,* February 1999, pp. 115–116.

27. Paulette Thomas, "Number Crunching," *Wall Street Journal,* July 26, 1999, pp. A1, A10.

28. Robinson, "The Pentagon Finally Learns How to Shop."

29. "Department of Commerce's Efforts to Advance Electronic Commerce Applications of the NII," http://nii.nist.gov/nii/applic/eleccom/elccom.html, March 14, 2000.

30. Robinson, "The Pentagon Finally Learns How to Shop," pp. 174–182.

31. Matt Forney, "Cultural Revolution: Taiwan Breaks Free of China Syndrome," *Wall Street Journal,* July 27, 1999, pp. A1, A12.

32. J. M. Smucker Web site, www.smucker.com, March 14, 2000.

Chapter 11

SOURCES FOR MARKETING STRATEGY SUCCESS: Paul A. Greenberg, "IBM Announces Two Major E-Commerce Initiatives," *E-Commerce Times,* January 19, 2000, www.EcommerceTimes.com; "Thompson Steers IBM's Software Strategy," *Infoworld,* January 17, 2000, p. 16; Rob Spiegel, "IBM and Sprint Join Forces on Wireless Business Applications," *E-Commerce Times,* December 1, 1999, www.Ecommerce-Times.com; Paul Krill, "IBM Commits to Service Providers," *Infoworld Electric,* October 27, 1999, www.infoworld.com.

SOURCES FOR MARKETING STRATEGY FAILURE: "Office Depot Promotes Rolf Van Kaldek-erken to Executive Vice President–Europe," *Hoover's Online,* January 17, 2000, www.hoovershbn.hoovers.com; David Rocks, "Why Office Depot Loves the Net," *Business Week Online,* September 27, 1999, www.businessweek.com; Troy Wolverton, "Office Depot Broadens Net Business," CNET News.com, June 29, 1999, www.news.cnet.com; Marc Ballon, "I Was Seduced by the New Economy," *Inc.,* February 1999, pp. 35–36.

1. Joshua Cooper Ramo, "Jeffrey Preston Bezos: 1999 Person of the Year," *Time,* December 27, 1999, pp. 54–55; Joshua Quittner, "An Eye on the Future," *Time,* December 27, 1999, pp. 57–66; Michael Krantz, "Cruising Inside Amazon," *Time,* December 27, 1999, pp. 69–73; James Lardner, "A Flea Market for Webheads," *U.S. News & World Report,* October 11, 1999, pp. 50–52; Clint Willis, "Does Amazon.com Really Matter?" *Forbes ASAP,* April 6, 1998, pp. 55–58.

2. The concept of a goods-services continuum is suggested in G. Lynn Shostack, "Breaking Free from Product Marketing," *Journal of Marketing,* April 1977, p. 77; and John M Rathmell, "What Is meant by Services?" *Journal of Marketing,* October 1980, pp. 32–36.

3. Samuel Fromartz, "The Face of an Emerging Industry," *Inc.,* September 1998, pp. 24–25.

4. U.S. Census Bureau, 1997 Economic Census: Advance Summary Statistics for the United States, www.census.gov/www/advanc1a.htm, July 14, 1999.

5. Scott Woolley, "Virtual Banker," *Forbes,* June 15, 1998, pp. 127–128.

6. Mary Walton, *The Deming Management Method* (New York: Putnam Publishing, 1986), p. 26.

7. Information on the 1999 Baldrige Award downloaded from www.nist.gov, June 16, 1999.

8. Del Jones, "Baldrige Winners Named," *USA Today,* November 24, 1999, p. 3B.

9. Richard Heller, "Gucci's $4 Billion Man," *Forbes,* February 8, 1999, pp. 108–109.

10. Michael D. Hutt and Thomas W. Speh, *Business Marketing Management,* Seventh Edition, (Fort Worth, TX: Harcourt, Inc., 2001), Chapter 1.

11. FedEx Web site, www.fedex.com, March 22, 2000.

12. Becky Ebenkamp, "L'eggs Goes Multicultural in Spring," *Brandweek,* February 16, 1998, p. 4.

13. Stephanie Thompson, "Pam Spray Jumps Out of Frying Pan," *Brandweek,* February 16, 1998, p. 4.

14. Stephen Manes, "Gutenberg Need Not Worry—Yet," *Forbes,* February 8, 1999, pp. 106–107.

15. Gary McWilliams, "PC Problems May Snag Compaq Crusade," *Wall Street Journal,* April 15, 1999, p. B7.

16. Gregory White and John Lippman, "Satellite Radio Gets a Lift from Ford and GM," *Wall Street Journal,* June 16, 1999, pp. B1, B6.

17. Nancy Rutter and Owen Edwards, "Ready to Ware: Software & Hardware, That Is," *Forbes ASAP,* April 5, 1999, pp. 30–32.

18. Ernest Beck, "Populist Perrier? Nestlé Pitches Bottled Water to World's Poor," *Wall Street Journal,* June 18, 1999, pp. B1, B4.

19. Arm & Hammer Natural Baking Soda package, 1999; and Dana James, "Rejuvenating Mature Brands Can Be a Stimulating Exercise," *Marketing News,* August 16, 1999, p. 16.

20. Miriam Jordan, "In India's Toothpaste War, an Oddly Familiar Smile," *Wall Street Journal,* April 15, 1999, pp. B1, B12.

21. Hotel Reservation Service, www.hrs.de, March 22, 2000.

22. Erick Schonfeld, "Schwab Puts It All Online," *Fortune,* December 7, 1998, pp. 94–100.

23. White and Lippman, "Satellite Radio Gets a Lift from Ford and GM."

Chapter 12

SOURCES FOR MARKETING STRATEGY SUCCESS: "The Gap, Inc.," *Hoover's Online,* accessed December 9, 1999, www.hoovers.com; Carol Emert, "Old Navy's Model Plan," *San Francisco Chronicle,* October 20, 1999, p. C1.

SOURCES FOR MARKETING STRATEGY FAILURE: "History of Fruit of the Loom," Fruit of the Loom Web site, accessed January 20, 2000, at www.fruit.com; Stephen Franklin, "Fruit of the Loom Ousts Farley," *Chicago Tribune,* January 11, 2000, pp. B1, B6; "Fruit of the Loom Files for Chapter 11 Reorganization," *PR Newswire,* December 29, 1999.

1. Warren Cohen, "Oysters, Scotch, and Hoops," *U.S. News & World Report,* November 15, 1999, pp. 92–93; Mindy Charski, "The NBA Jumps Into the Food Business," *U.S. News & World Report,* November 15, 1999, p. 93; NBA.com TV Announces Talent Lineup," November 1, 1999, www.nba.com; "NBA To Launch NBA.com TV," September 23, 1999, www.nba.com; Bernhard Warner, "NBA's Site Is Nothin' But Net," *The Standard,* June 28, 1999, www.thestandard.com.

2. Alex Taylor III, "Kellogg Cranks Up Its Idea Machine," *Fortune,* July 5, 1999, pp. 181–183.

3. Louise Kramer, "McDonald's Adds Bottled Water to the Menu," *Advertising Age,* August 10, 1998, p. 6.

4. Nick Pachetti, "Smart Shopper," *Worth,* September, 1999, p. 46.

5. Bill Bowden, "Wal-Mart on Target," *Northwest Arkansas Business Journal,* August 9, 1999, pp. 1, 10–11.

6. Betty Morris, "The Brand's the Thing." *Fortune,* March 4, 1996, pp. 72–86.

7. "What Is Brand Asset Valuator?" Brand Development Findings, www.yr.com/bav. March 22, 2000.

8. Jon Auerbach and Gary McWilliams, "How CMGI Plans to Make AltaVista Hot Again," *Wall Street Journal,* June 30, 1999, pp. B1, B4.

9. Maxine Lans Retsky, "Trade Secrets: The Things You'll Never Know," *Marketing News,* February 15, 1999, p. 5.

10. Tim Carvell, "Y2K Profiteering: Trademarking the Millennium," *Fortune,* August 3, 1998, p. 44.

11. Justin Hyde, "Cadillac Redesigns Traditional Logo in Hopes of Attracting Young Buyers," *The Morning News,* August 28, 1999, p. C5.

12. The concept of trade dress is examined in Michael Harvey, James T. Rothe, and Laurie A. Lucas, "The 'Trade Dress' Controversy: A Case of Strategic Cross-Brand Cannibalization"; *Journal of Marketing Theory and Practice,* 6, Spring 1998, pp. 1–15. The Kendall-Jackson–E&J Gallo case is discussed in "Jury Clears E&J Gallo-Winery in Lawsuit Over Bottle Design," *Wall Street Journal Interactive Edition,* April 7, 1997.

13. Charles Goldsmith, "French Filmmaker Pathé Makes Its Rooster a Little Less Cocky," *Wall Street Journal,* June 30, 1999, p. B1.

14. M. Dale Beckman, David L. Kurtz, and Louis E. Boone, *Foundations of Marketing,* Sixth Canadian Edition (Toronto: Harcourt Brace & Company, Canada, 1997), p. 221.

15. Joseph Pereira, "Hasbro Strikes Back," *Wall Street Journal,* April 15, 1999, pp. B1, B12.

16. Ibid.

17. Suein Hwang, "Light Brigades," *Wall Street Journal,* April 21, 1999, pp. A1, A6.

18. Susan Warren, "Souped-Up Shades," *Wall Street Journal,* June 14, 1999, pp. B1, B4.

19. "Flanker Movement," *Delaney Report,* March 8, 1999, p. 3.

20. Carl Quintanilla, "Forget Microwaves: 'Speed Cookers' Also Crisp and Brown," *Wall Street Journal,* June 30, 1999, pp. B1, B4.

21. Everett M. Rogers and F. Floyd Shoemaker, *Communication of Innovation* (New York: Free Press, 1971), pp. 135–157. Rogers later relabeled his model as an *innovation-decision process.* He called the five steps *Knowledge, persuasion, decision, implementation,* and *information.* See Everett M. Rogers, *Diffusion of Innovations,* 3rd ed. (New York: Free Press, 1983), pp. 164–165.

22. Robert Simison, "The Vroom-Vroom Toy of the Baby Boom—a Honda?" *Wall Street Journal,* July 14, 1999, pp. B1, B4.

23. Thomas Weber, "Coming Soon: The Internet, 24/7," *Wall Street Journal,* June 16, 1999, pp. B1, B6.

24. Quintanilla, "Forget Microwaves: 'Speed Cookers' Also Crisp and Brown."

25. Frank Gibney, Jr., and Belinda Luscombe, "The Redesign of America," *Time,* March 30, 2000, pp. 66–75.

26. Paul Judge, "Cell Phone Meets Laptop," *Business Week,* May 25, 1998, p. 86.

27. Ron Winslow, "For the Disabled, Upward Mobility," *Wall Street Journal,* July 1, 1999, pp. B1, B12.

28. Quintanilla, "Forget Microwaves: 'Speed Cookers' Also Crisp and Brown."

29. Simison, "The Vroom-Vroom Toy of the Baby Boom—a Honda?"

30. John Lippman, "Can Kubrick's 'Eyes' Open Wide?" *Wall Street Journal,* July 14, 1999, pp. B1, B4.

31. Winslow, "For the Disabled, Upward Mobility."

32. Frederic Biddle, "Drugs, Net Lead to Lean Times at Jenny Craig," *Wall Street Journal,* July 12, 1999, pp. A17, A20.

33. Tim Carvell, "Double-Tall, Skinny, Decaf Web Portal," *Fortune,* August 2, 1999, pp. 31–32.

Chapter 13

SOURCES FOR MARKETING STRATEGY SUCCESS: Bruce Upbin, "Profit in a Big Orange Box," *Forbes,* January 24, 2000, www.forbes.com; "The Handyman," *Business Week Online,* January 10, 2000, www.businessweek.com; "Home Depot Wants Its Suppliers Off the Net," *Bloomberg News,* July 28, 1999, www.news.cnet.com.

SOURCES FOR MARKETING STRATEGY FAILURE: Myra P. Saefong, "Hershey Sweetens on Fourth-Quarter Results," *CBSMarketWatch,* January 31, 2000, www.cbs.marketwatch.com; Edward Tobin, "Hershey Profits Off on Slow Holiday Sales," *Reuters Limited,* January 31, 2000; S. McVey, "Hershey's Halloween Nightmare All Too Common for Supply Chain Implementations," TechnologyEvaluation.com, November 1, 1999, www.technologyevaluation.com; George Strawley, "No Hershey's on Halloween a Nasty Trick," *The Salt Lake Tribune,* October 30, 1999, www.sltrib.com; Associated Press, "Computer Problem Foils Hershey Halloween Sales," *The Tribune News.com,* October 30, 1999, www.thetribunenews.com.

1. "Air Express International Corporation," *Hoover's Online,* www.hoovers.com, accessed February 3, 2000; "AEI's World," AEI Web site, www.aeilogistics.com, accessed January 31, 2000; Robert Selwitz, "Is Bigger Better?" *Global Business,* November 1999, pp. 48–52.

2. Harris Collingwood, "No, Really, We're a .Com," *Worth,* November 1999, pp. 55–58.

3. Amanda Spake, "Brownie Wise Had One Word for You: Plastics," *U.S. News & World Report,* October 18, 1999, p. 82; and Sarah Rose, "Tupperware Rolls Out a Fresh Sales Style," *Money,* September 1999, p. 44.

4. William Holstein, "No Place Like Home," *U.S. News & World Report,* September 27, 1999, pp. 44–45.

5. Ben Pappas, "Have a Coke When You Dial," *Forbes,* May 3, 1999, p. 45.

6. Josh McHugh, "Changing Channels—Sort Of," *Forbes,* June 14, 1999, p. 55.

7. Gary L. Frasier and Walfried M. Lassar, "Determinants of Distribution Intensity," *Journal of Marketing,* October, 1996, pp. 39–51.

8. Lauren Goldstein, "Could Signore Zegna Be the Next Signore Bezos?" *Fortune,* September 27, 1999, p. 56.

9. Joanne Gordon, "Rush," *Forbes,* February 22, 1999, pp. 84–86.

10. Jakki J. Mohr and Robert E. Speckman, "Protecting Partnerships," *Marketing Management,* Winter/Spring 1996, pp. 35–42.

11. Goldstein, "Could Signore Zegna Be the Next Signore Bezos?"

12. Mark Maremont and Robert Berner, "Store Markdowns," *Wall Street Journal,* March 31, 1999, pp. A1, A6.

13. Stuart Brown, "Wresting New Wealth from the Supply Chain," *Fortune,* November 9, 1998, pp. 204[C]–204[Z].

14. David A. Aaker, *Strategic Marketing Management* (New York: John Wiley & Sons, 1992), pp. 257–263.

15. Editor, "The Wonder Years," *Entrepreneur,* January 1999, pp. 180–184.

16. Libby Estell, "Unchained Profits," *Sales & Marketing Management,* February 1999, pp. 63–67.

17. Ibid.

18. Ibid.

19. Gene Bylinsky, "The Challengers Move In on ERP," *Fortune,* November 22, 1999, pp. 306 (C), 306 (D), 306 (H), 306 (I), 306 (L), 306 (P), 306 (Q), 306–T).

20. Peter Buxbaum, "Marketing and Logistics: Making the Marriage Work," *Inbound Logistics,* October 1998, pp. 44–52.

21. Maricris Briones, "What Technology Wrought: Distribution Channel in Flux," *Marketing News,* February 1, 1999, pp. 1, 15.

22. Andrew Tanzer, "Warehouses That Fly," *Forbes,* October 18, 1999, pp. 120–124.

23. Ibid.

24. Connie Gentry, "FedEx APIs Create Cinderella Success Stories," *Inbound Logistics,* October 1998, pp. 66–67.

25. Geoffrey Smith, "How Staples Is Taking the Right Tack," *Business Week,* December 7, 1998, p. 62.

26. Ibid.

27. Gentry, "FedEx APIs Create Cinderella Success Stories."

Chapter 14

SOURCES FOR MARKETING STRATEGY SUCCESS: Julie Vallone, "Going Once . . . Going Twice," *Entrepreneur,* February 2000, pp. 86–93; Dennis Tenney, "The Woodchuck and the Penguin," www.fwn.net, accessed February 8, 2000; "Amazon.com and Leading Collectibles Companies Team Up for the Holidays," company press release, November 5, 1999, www.biz.yahoo.com; Daisy Whitney, "His Goal: Put Every U.S. Comic Book on Web," *The Denver Post,* May 4, 1999, www.denverpost.com.

SOURCES FOR MARKETING STRATEGY FAILURE: Chuck Squatriglia, "El Cerrito Plaza to be Rescuscitated," *San Francisco Chronicle,* December 8, 1999, p. A21; Marci McDonald, "The Pall in the Mall," *U.S. News & World Report,* October 18, 1999, pp. 64–67; Eileen Barry, "The Mall Doctor," *Metropolis magazine,* May 1999, www.metropolismag.com.

1. Phil Harvey, "Who Will Buy Buy.com?" January 29, 2000, www.redherring.com; Joanna Glasner, "Buy.Com Wants to Sell.shares," *Wired,* October 27, 1999, www.wired.com; J. William Gurley, "Buy.com May Fail, But If It Succeeds, Retailing May Never be the Same," *Fortune,* January 11, 1999, pp. 150, 152; Mark Halper, "Zero Hero," no date, 1999, www.business2.com, accessed February 4, 2000.

2. SYSCO Corp. Web site, www.syscosmart.com. March 27, 2000.

3. Handleman Web site, www.handleman.com. March 27, 2000.

4. Bart Ziegler, "Personal Technology: As eBay Rivals Emerge, Some Tips on Bidding and Selling on the Web," *Wall Street Journal,* September 23, 1999, p. B1; and Suein Hwang, "I Was an Internet Bride," *Wall Street Journal,* September 24, 1999, pp. W1, W4.

5. Emily Nelson, "Logistics Whiz Rises at Wal-Mart," *Wall Street Journal,* March 11, 1999, pp. B1, B8.
6. Hwang, "I Was an Internet Bride."
7. Home Depot Web address, www.homedepot.com. March 27, 2000.
8. Lowe's Web address, www.lowes.com. March 27, 2000.
9. Penelope Ody, "A Transformation in Retailing," *Financial Times,* June 3, 1998, p. 4.
10. Mihir Somaiya and Siddharth Sood, "Hitch On to the Retail Bandwagon," *The Economic Times,* November 8, 1999.
11. Donna Fenn, "Niche Picking," *Inc.,* October 1999, pp. 97–98.
12. *Dierbergs School of Cooking Holiday Schedule,* November-December 1999.
13. Julie Creswell, "Toymakers 'R' Scared," *Fortune,* November 9, 1998, pp. 36–38.
14. Bruce Upbin, "Beyond Burgers," *Forbes,* November 1, 1999, pp. 218–223.
15. Marci McDonald, "The Pall in the Mall," *U.S. News & World Report,* October 18, 1999, pp. 64–67.
16. Ibid.
17. Keith Naughton, "Hitting the Bull's-Eye," *Newsweek,* October 11, 1999, p. 64.
18. Michelle Abrams, "Going Up, Down Under," *Bloomberg Personal Finance,* September 1999, p. 48.
19. Allya King, "The New Sound of Music," *Black Enterprise,* May 1999, p. 50.
20. Kelly Barron, "Wal-Mart's Ankle Biters," *Forbes,* October 18, 1999, pp. 86–92.
21. Kelly Barron, "The Prince of Peddlers," *Forbes,* October 18, 1999, p. 144.
22. Karen Roche and Bill O'Connell, "Dig a Wider Channel for Your Products," *Marketing News,* November 9, 1998, p. 10.
23. Allyson Stewart-Allen, "Europe Says 'That's Shoppertainment!'" *Marketing News,* August 16, 1999, p. 7.
24. Shelly Branch, "Inside the Cult of Costco," *Fortune,* September 6, 1999, pp. 184–190.
25. Stewart-Allen, "Europe Says 'That's Shoppertainment!'"
26. Judy Sutton, "East to East Coast: Tang Sells Fine China," *Marketing News,* March 2, 1998, p. 2.
27. Patricia Sellers, "Category Killers," *Fortune,* September 27, 1999, pp. 224–226.
28. Christopher Palmeri, "Filling Big Shoes," *Forbes,* November 15, 1999, pp. 170, 172.
29. Marci McDonald, "The Last Frontier of the American Mall," *U.S. News & World Report,* October 18, 1999, p. 67; and McDonald, "The Pall in the Mall."
30. Shelly Branch, "Inside the Cult of Costco," *Fortune,* September 6, 1999, pp. 184–190.
31. Lorrie Grant, "California Big-Box Stores Escape Limitations," *USA Today,* September 27, 1999, p. 10B.
32. Bethany McLean, "Not Your Mother's Avon," *Fortune,* May 24, 1999, pp. 44–46.
33. Joanne Cleaver, "Playtime's Over," *Marketing News,* April 26, 1999, pp. 25, 33.
34. Michael Fitzpatrick, "Connected: Bugs, Beer, Underwear—Please Insert Payment," *The Daily Telegraph,* September 16, 1999, p. 6.

CHAPTER 15

SOURCES FOR MARKETING STRATEGY SUCCESS: Sam Hill and Glenn Rifkin, "Listen to the Band," *Entrepreneur,* June 1999, pp. 132–141.
SOURCES FOR MARKETING STRATEGY FAILURE: Jesse Berst, "Company Failures Underline Blindness of Push Vendors," *AnchorDesk,* downloaded from ZDNet, September 15, 1999; and "How PointCast Lost Its Way—and $450 Million," *eMarketer,* downloaded on September 15, 1999.
1. Sloane Lucas, "Austin Online, Baby!" *Brandweek,* September 6, 1999, pp. 56–62; and T. L. Stanley, "Shag 'Em, Baby," *Brandweek,* September 6, 1999, p. 3.
2. Al Urbanski, "In Knots," *Promo,* November 1998, pp. 49–52.
3. Peter Breen, "Even Better Than the Real Thing," *Promo,* August 1999, pp. 103–106.
4. "General Motivation," *Promo,* September 1999, p. i8.
5. Jonathan Boorstein, "The Brand Plays On," *Direct,* May 15, 1999, pp. 1, 51–52.
6. Peter Breen, "Sophisticated Sampling," *Promo,* September 1999, pp. 63–68.
7. Tom Davenport, "The Eyes Have It," *CIO,* September 1, 1999, pp. 28–30.
8. Peter Breen, "Leading People By the Nose," *Promo,* September 1999, p. 66.
9. "Speaking in Tongues," *Time,* August 30, 1999, p. 25.
10. Steven M. Dworman, *Marketing with Video, DVD, and CD-ROM,* supplement to *Adweek,* Summer 1999, p. 9.
11. Richard H. Levey, "Hey Kids—Free Cockroaches!" *Direct,* May 15, 1999, p. 5.
12. Jonathan M. Kramer, "Marketers Need Fusion, Not Illusion," *Advertising Age,* September 6, 1999, p. 19.
13. Amie Smith and Al Urbanski, "Excellence × 16," *Promo,* December 1998, p. 32.
14. Stephanie Thompson, "Gen'l Mills Taps into Craze with Pokémon Rolls Treat," *Advertising Age,* October 4, 1999, p. 10.
15. "The Right Price," *Promo,* March 1998, p. 15.
16. "Specialty Media and Marketing Services," *Veronis, Suhler & Associates Communications Industry Transactions Report,* October 27, 1998.
17. Andy Bernstein, "Industry Getting Taste of a New Coke," *SportsBusiness,* January 18–24, 1999, pp. 26–28.
18. Data downloaded from the Direct Marketing Association, www.the-dma.org, September 22, 1999.
19. Alan K. Gorenstein, "Direct Marketing's Growth Will Be Global," *Marketing News,* December 7, 1998, p. 15.
20. David Vaczek, "Up Close and Personal," *Promo,* August 1999, pp. 80–82.
21. Gary McWilliams and Marcia Stepanek, "Taming of the Info Monster," *Business Week,* June 22, 1998, pp. 170–172.
22. Jonathan Boorstein, "Must-Sell TV," *Direct,* June 1999, pp. 1, 47–48.
23. Katie Muldoon, "Why Don't Consumers Buy from Catalogs?" *Direct,* September 15, 1999, p. 41.
24. Carol Krol, "Infomercial Tags Along with the Rolling Stones," *Advertising Age,* February 1, 1999, p.36.
25. Kate Fitzgerald, "Homing In on 2000," *Advertising Age,* September 6, 1999, p. 20.
26. Stephanie Thompson, "Nestlé Rejiggers the Java," *Brandweek,* June 14, 1999, pp. 1, 10.
27. Al Urbanski, "Sweep Surprises," *Promo,* August 1999, p. 172.
28. "Consultant Predicts Disaster in PGA Stance," *Marketing News,* March 2, 1998, p. 8; and "Martin Wins In a Walk," *CBS SportsLine,* downloaded from golfweb.com, September 28, 1999.
29. Joseph R. Garber, "Will the Web Kill TV Ads? Nope." *Forbes,* September 20, 1999, p. 207.

Chapter 16

SOURCES FOR MARKETING STRATEGY SUCCESS: T. L. Stanley, "High-Tech Throwback," *Brandweek,* September 27, 1999, pp. 36–40; and "The Legacy of 'Blair Witch,'" *USA Today,* August 17, 1999, pp. D1–D2.
SOURCES FOR MARKETING STRATEGY FAILURE: Carrick Mollenkamp and Kelly Greene, "How Just for Feet Wound a Path from Supremacy to Financial Peril," *Wall Street Journal,* November 3, 1999, pp. S1–S3; Debra Goldman, "Pay or Play," *Adweek,* June 14, 1999, p. 68; and John Eighmey, "Safety Net Failed in Super Bowl Flap," *Advertising Age,* February 15, 1999, p. 24.
1. Art Jahnke, "Still in the Picture," *CIO Web Business,* August 1, 1999, pp. 40–48; historical information downloaded from www.kodak.com, October 1, 1999.
2. Thomas Content, "Burger King Bets Big on Pokémon," *USA Today,* November 3, 1999, p. 12B; and Theresa Howard, "Burger King Looks to 'Trading Nights' to Foment Pokémon Frenzy at Units," *Brandweek,* October 18, 1999, p. 84.
3. Sally Beatty, "P&G's Comparisons Defend Toothpaste," *Wall Street Journal,* June 29, 1998, p. B6.
4. Peter Kafka, "Live Action Heroes," *Forbes,* March 22, 1999, pp. 216–226.
5. David Webster, "Will We Choke the Web with Ad Clutter?" *Advertising Age,* September 21, 1998, p. 26.
6. Michael McCarthy, "Bart Horrifies Y&R," *Adweek,* September 27, 1999, p. 90.
7. Greg Farrell, "Advertising on Internet Zooms," *USA Today,* May 10, 1999, p. 9B; and Roberta Bernstein, "The Media Is the Message," *Brandweek,* September 27, 1999, pp. 80–84.
8. Daniel Eisenberg, "The Net Loves Old Media," *Time,* November 1, 1999, p. 61.
9. "As Strong As Needed," *Advertising Age,* May 4, 1998, p. 26.
10. "Top Internet Banner Ads," *AdAge.com,* September 26, 1999.
11. Adrienne Mand, "There's Gold in Them Banners," *Brandweek,* April 27, 1998, pp. 38–40.
12. William Power, "The Virtual Ad: On TV You See It, at Games You Don't," *Wall Street Journal,* July 30, 1998, pp. B1, B10.
13. Alistair Christopher, "Blink of an Ad," *Time,* August 3, 1998, p. 51.
14. Kyle Pope, "Tuning Into Hard Truths," *Wall Street Journal,* April 19, 1999, pp. B1, B4; and Lynn Elber, "WB's Young Audience Is Where the Money Is, Network Chief Says," *Marketing News,* February 15, 1999, p. 2.
15. Alan Gottesman, "Station WWW," *Adweek,* May 31, 1999, p. 16.
16. Kelly Barron, "Bill Gates Wants Our Business," *Forbes,* April 6, 1998, pp. 46–47.
17. "Leading National Advertisers," *Advertising Age,* September 27, 1999, p. S28.
18. Jean Halliday, "GM Boosts Newspaper Ads to Drive Traffic, Win Share," *Advertising Age,* July 12, 1999, p. 20.
19. "Ad Age 300," *Advertising Age,* June 14, 1999, pp. S1–S14.
20. Ibid.
21. Susan Headden, "The Junk Mail Deluge," *U.S. News & World Report,* December 8, 1998, pp. 40–48.
22. Marc Gunther, "The Great Outdoors," *Fortune,* March 1, 1999, pp. 150–157.
23. Tim Nudd, "The Outer Limits," *Adweek,* June 28, 1999, pp. 25–26.
24. Ronald Grover, "Billboards Aren't Boring Anymore," *Business Week,* September 21, 1998, pp. 86–88.

25. Carol Krol, "Life After Tobacco," *Advertising Age,* April 19, 1999, pp. 1, 48, 50.

26. Debra Aho Williamson, "Virtual Vineyards Pumps Bottom Line with E-mail," *Advertising Age,* April 19, 1999, p. 71.

27. Susan Kuchinskas, "Sudden Impact: E-mail Firm Breaks Campaigns," *Adweek,* May 31, 1999, p. 38; and Richard Sale, "The Modem or the Mailbox?" *Promo,* May 1999, pp. 51–57.

28. Joel Kurtzman, "Advertising for All the Little Guys," *Fortune,* April 12, 1999, p. 162.

29. Kathy Sharpe, "Web Punctures the Idea That Advertising Works," *Advertising Age,* September 13, 1999, p. 44.

30. Joy Dietrich, "World Brands," *Ad Age International,* September 1999, pp. 29–44.

31. Richard Sale, "What's Hot and What's Not," *Promo,* October 1998, pp. 63–64, 176–180.

32. Betsy Spethmann, "500 Million Miles To Go," *Promo,* April 1999, pp. 32–37.

33. "Dollars Up, Redemption Down," *Promo 1999 Industry Report,* July 1999, pp. S17–S18.

34. Craig MacClaren, "Net Results," *Promo,* September 1998, p. 26.

35. "Something for Everyone," *Promo 1999 Industry Report,* July 1999, pp. S29–S31.

36. "The Big Get Bigger," *Promo 1999 Industry Report,* July 1999, p. S16.

37. "Slotting Fees Under Attack," *Advertising Age,* September 27, 1999, p. 50.

38. Tricia Campbell, "Crisis Management at Coke," *Sales & Marketing Management,* September 1999, p. 13; and Kathleen V. Schmidt, "Coke's Crisis," *Marketing News,* September 27, 1999, pp. 1, 11.

39. Al Ries and Laura Ries, "First Do Some Great Publicity," *Advertising Age,* February 8, 1999, p. 42.

40. David Vaczek, "Pay to Play," *Promo,* June 1999, pp. 101–110.

41. "Max Factor to Tie With 3 Others for Video Promo," *Advertising Age,* September 6, 1999, p. 42.

42. Marc Gunther, "The Great Outdoors," *Fortune,* March 1, 1999, pp. 149–155.

43. Fred Vogelstein, "Rating Web Sites," *U.S. News & World Report,* April 5, 1999, p. 50.

44. Ann B. Graham, "The Cookie Monster?" *Executive Edge,* June/July 1999, pp. 14–15.

45. Michael Krauss, "The Next Step for Internet Advertising," *Marketing News,* November 23, 1998, p. 10.

46. Luisa Kroll, Julie Pitta, and Daniel Lyons, "World Weary Web," *Forbes,* December 28, 1998, pp. 98–100.

47. Bill Bishop, *Strategic Marketing for the Digital Age* (Chicago: NTC Business Books, 1998), p. 239.

48. Adrienne Mand, "@Home Study Lays Down Broadband Mat," *Adweek,* March 1, 1999, p. 31.

49. "Future Forum," *Advertising Age: The Next Century,* 1999, pp. 32–44.

50. Raju Narisetti, "New and Improved," *Wall Street Journal,* November 16, 1998, p. R33.

Chapter 17

SOURCES FOR MARKETING STRATEGY SUCCESS: Jay Winchester, "Ripe for a Change," *Sales & Marketing Management,* August 1998, p. 81.

SOURCES FOR MARKETING STRATEGY FAILURE: Hillary Chura and Laura Petrecca, "Toys 'Я' Us Pitch: Kids Find Joy Shopping Here," *Advertising Age,* September 27, 1999, p. 91; Dolly Setton, "Toy Story," *Forbes,* June 14, 1999, p. 392; and Terry Colon, "Toy Story," *Brandweek,* February 1, 1999, pp. 48–52.

1. Caroline Waxler, "Mr. October Becomes Mr. Rainmaker," *Forbes,* September 20, 1999, pp. 126–130.

2. Thomas N. Ingram, Raymond W. LaForge, Charles H. Schwepker Jr., Ramaon A. Avila, Michael R. Williams, *Sales Management: Analysis and Decision Making,* 4th ed. (Fort Worth, TX: Harcourt, 2001).

3. Malcolm Campbell, "The New Sales Force," *Selling Power,* July/August 1999, pp. 49–50.

4. Arthur Middleton Hughes, "Service with a :-)," *Direct,* October 1999, pp. 57–59.

5. Greg Farrell, "Marketers Get Personal," *USA Today,* July 19, 1999, p. 9B.

6. "Live Help Now," *Fortune,* July 19, 1999, special advertising section.

7. Sarah Lorge, "Now That's One-to-One Marketing," *Sales & Marketing Management,* October 1999, p. 14.

8. Jack Neff, "Door-to-Door Sellers Join the Party Online," *Advertising Age,* September 27, 1999, pp. 62, 68.

9. Gene Koprowski, "Nonstop Numbers," *Entrepreneur,* August 1999, p. 24.

10. Julie Rawe, "More States Are Putting Telemarketers on Hold," *Time,* September 6, 1999, p. 55; and Karen L. Shaw, "States Hang Up on Telemarketers," *Marketing News,* March 1, 1999, p. 12.

11. Katie Muldoon, "Setting the Standard," *Direct,* July 1999, pp. 65–67.

12. Jim Emerson, "Sales Syllabus," *TeleDirect,* October 1999, pp. T4–T5.

13. Michele Marchetti, "Look Who's Calling," *Sales & Marketing Management,* May 1998, pp. 43–46.

14. Erika Rasmusson, "Can Inside Sales Be a Rep's True Calling?" *Sales & Marketing Management,* April 1999, p. 82.

15. Michele Marchetti, "Look Who's Calling," p. 45.

16. Daintry Duffy, "Drive Customer Loyalty," *CIO-100,* August 15, 1999, pp. 76–80.

17. Chad Kaydo, "Selling a Product That's All Wet," *Sales & Marketing Management,* June 1999, p. 18.

18. Scott Kirsner, "Complex Commerce," *CIO Web Business,* August 1, 1999, pp. 24–27; and Susan E. Fisher, "E-Business Strategy Boom," *Upside,* October 1999, pp. 52–56.

19. Melinda Ligos, "The Joys of Cross-Selling," *Sales & Marketing Management,* August 1998, p. 75.

20. Monica L. Perry and Craig L Pearce, "Who's Leading the Selling Team?" presented at the *Winter Marketing Educators Conference,* St. Petersburg, Florida, February 1999.

21. Karen Starr, "The Personal Touch Via the Web," *Selling Power,* July/August 1999, p. 86.

22. Thayer C. Taylor, "Sales Automation Cuts the Cord," *Sales & Marketing Management,* July 1995, p. 111.

23. Karen Starr, "Techaction," *Selling Power,* July/August, 1999, pp. 86–87.

24. Geoff Williams, "Keeping Your Cool," *Business Start-Ups,* September 1999, pp. 70–73.

25. Malcolm Campbell, "Trade Secrets," *Selling Power,* July/August 1999, pp. 94–98.

26. "How Salespeople Spend Their Time," *Sales & Marketing Management,* March 1998, p. 96.

27. John Alexander, "Good Prospects," *Selling Power,* June 1999, pp. 36–38.

28. Jess McCuan, "Auto Companies Head Online in Search of Sales Leads," *The Wall Street Journal,* July 6, 1999, p. A20.

29. Roger L. Fetterman and H. Richard Byrne, *Interactive Selling in the '90s* (San Diego, Calif.: Ellipsys International Publications, 1995), p. 16.

30. Jennifer Delahunty Britz, "You Can't Catch a Marlin with a Meatball," *Sales & Marketing Management,* October 1999, pp. A1–A22.

31. Ibid.

32. Ginger Conlon, "Multimedia Can Boost Business—News at 11," *Sales & Marketing Management,* September 1999, pp. 94–95.

33. Danielle Kennedy, "Objection Overruled," *Entrepreneur,* May 1998, pp. 99–101.

34. Chad Kaydo, "Planting the Seeds of Marketing Success," *Sales & Marketing Management,* August 1998, p. 73.

35. Susan Greco, "Hot Tips," *Inc.,* September 1999, p. 102.

36. Greco, "Hot Tips."

37. Tricia Campbell, "National Champions," *Sales & Marketing Management,* November 1998, pp. 58–69.

38. Erika Rasmusson, "A Whole New World of Training," *Sales & Marketing Management,* October 1999, p. 80.

39. Eugene M. Johnson, David L. Kurtz, and Eberhard Scheuing, *Sales Management* (New York: McGraw-Hill, 1994).

40. Erin Strout, "Your Sales Force's Best Teachers," *Sales & Marketing Management,* September 1999, p. 88.

41. "How Often Do You Set Sales Goals?" *Sales & Marketing Management,* July 1994, p. 34.

42. Andy Cohen, "Smooth Sailing," *Sales & Marketing Management,* March 1995, pp. 10–16.

43. Michele Marchetti, "No Commissions? Are You Crazy?" *Sales & Marketing Management,* May 1998, p. 83.

44. "What Salespeople Are Paid," *Sales & Marketing Management,* February 1995, p. 32.

45. Vincent Alonzo, "Showering Dealers with Incentives," *Sales & Marketing Management,* October 1999, pp. 24–25.

46. David W. Cravens, "The Changing Role of the Sales Force." *Marketing Management,* Fall 1995, p. 55.

47. G. David Hughes, Daryl McKee, and Charles H. Singer, *Sales Management A Career Path Approach* (Cincinnati, OH: South-Western College Publishing, 1999), pp. 5–9.

Chapter 18

SOURCES FOR MARKETING STRATEGY SUCCESS: Nina Munk, "Why Women Find Lauder Mesmerizing," *Fortune,* May 25, 1998, pp. 96–106.

SOURCES FOR MARKETING STRATEGY FAILURE: "My Biggest Mistake," *Inc.,* August 1999, p. 109.

1. Chuck Lenatti, "Auction Mania," *Upside,* July 1999, pp 84–92; Robin Campbell, "EBay Names Head of Authentication," *Art & Auction,* July/August 1999, p. 34; and "Internet Sites to Share Auction Listings," *CBS MarketWatch,* September 17,1999.

2. Ed Brown, "Where Your Gas Money Goes," *Fortune,* April 27, 1998, p 72.

3. Vanessa O'Connell, "Blaming Suits, Gun Industry Boosts Prices," *Wall Street Journal,* July 2, 1999, pp B1, B3.

4. Scott Woolley, "I Got It Cheaper Than You," *Forbes,* November 2, 1998, pp 82–84.

5. Jan Norman, "How To Set Prices," *Business Start-Ups*, December 1998, pp 42–45.

6. Robert D Buzzell and Frederick D. Wiersema, "Successful Share Building Strategies," *Harvard Business Review* (January–February 1981), pp. 135–144.

7. Steven V. Brull, "Why Talk Is So Cheap," *Business Week*, September 13, 1999, pp. 34–36.

8. Manju Bansal, "Wooing a Skeptical Consumer," *Brandweek*, December 14, 1998, pp 20–22.

9. Susan Gregory Thomas, "That Voodoo You Do So Well," *US. News & World Report*, April 12, 1999, p. 61; and David P. Hamilton, "PCs for Under $600 Seize a Chunk of the Market," *Wall Street Journal*, March 26, 1999, pp. B1, B4.

10. "Motel 6 Introduces Studio 6," Motel 6 press release dated April 12, 1999, downloaded August 5, 1999.

11. Jeff Amy, "United Express Plans Low Introductory Fares" *Mobile* Register, August 8, 1999, pp. 1B, 9B.

12. "Postal Service Finances Improve," press release dated July 13, 1999, downloaded from wwwusps.gov.

13. Katrina Brooker, "E-Rivals Seem to Have Home Depot Awfully Nervous," *Fortune*, August 16, 1999, pp 28–29.

14. Peter Kafka, "Rock On," *Forbes*, September 20, 1999, p 142.

15. See James L McKenney, *Stouffer Yield Management System*, Harvard Business School Case 9-190-193 (Boston: Harvard Business School, 1994); and Anirudh Dhebar and Adam Brandenburger, *American Airlines, Inc: Revenue Management*, Harvard Business School Case 9-190-029 (Boston: Harvard Business School, 1992).

16. Rich Karlgaard, "Digital Rules," *Forbes*, September 21, 1998, p 43.

17. David Bank, "A Site-Eat-Site World," *Wall Street Journal*, July 12, 1999, pp R8, R10.

18. Ibid.

Chapter 19

SOURCES FOR MARKETING STRATEGY SUCCESS: Stephane Fitch, "Stringing Them Along," *Forbes*, July 26, 1999, pp. 90–91.

SOURCES FOR MARKETING STRATEGY FAILURE: Laurie Freeman, "Battle of the (College) Books Gains Intensity," *Advertising Age*, August 23, 1999, pp. 16–18; David Carnoy, "Web Sales 101," *Success*, January 1999, p. 24; and Adrienne Mand, "Textbook Vendors to Chase Students Online," *Adweek*, January 4, 1999, p. 33.

1. Nick Wingfield, "New Battlefield for Priceline Is Diapers, Tuna," *Wall Street Journal*, September 22, 1999, pp. B1, B4; Peter Elkind, "The Hype Is Big, Really Big, At Priceline," *Fortune*, September 6, 1999, pp. 193–202; and "Priceline Eyes Consumer Auctions," *Internetnews.com*, downloaded from www.internetnews.com August 3, 1999.

2. Kim Clark, "A Slippery Standard for Gold Prices," *U.S. News & World Report*, November 16, 1998, pp. 84–86.

3. Suzanne Koudsi, "It's Been a Hard Day, So Sit Back, Relax, and Buy a $500 Pen," *Fortune*, August 16, 1999, p. 42.

4. Mercedes M. Cardona and Jack Neff, "Everything's At a Premium," *Advertising Age*, August 2, 1999, pp. 12, 15.

5. William C. Symonds, "Would You Spend $1.50 for a Razor Blade?" *Business Week*, April 27, 1998, p. 46; and Dave Califano, "Gillette Just Isn't Cutting It," *Worth*, September 1999, p.22.

6. "Major Airlines Cutting Fall Fares Systemwide," *Mobile Register*, August 3, 1999, p. 7B.

7. Kim Strassel, "Aiming High," *Wall Street Journal*, July 12, 1999, p. R48.

8. Don Debelak, "No Time? No Problem," *Business Start-Ups*, July 1999, p. 54.

9. Amy E. Cortese and Marcia Stepanek, "Good-Bye to Fixed Pricing?" *Business Week*, May 4, 1998, pp. 71–84.

10. Manju Bansal, "Wooing a Skeptical Consumer," *Brandweek*, December 14, 1998, pp. 20–22.

11. "Price Wars," *Technology Buyers Guide, Fortune*, Summer 1999, pp. 33–41.

12. William C. Symonds, "Build a Better Mousetrap Is No ClapTrap," *Business Week*, February 1, 1999, p. 47.

13. Leigh Gallagher, "Clip Joint," *Forbes*, August 23, 1999, p. 94.

14. David Leonhardt, "Revolt of the Executive Class," *Business Week*, February 1, 1999, pp. 68–71.

15. Bruce Orwall, "Ticket Scalpers Find a Home on the Web," *Wall Street Journal*, February 4, 1999, pp. B1, B10.

16. Scott Woolley, "I Got It Cheaper Than You," *Forbes*, November 2, 1998, pp. 82–84.

17. Jerry Useem, "Internet Defense Strategy: Cannibalize Yourself," *Fortune*, September 6, 1999, pp. 121–134.

18. Stephanie N. Mehta, "SBC Will Launch Service 'Bundles' In Two Markets," *Wall Street Journal*, August 24, 1999, p. B8.

19. Brent Pollock, "Calling All Cyber-Customers," *Success*, October 1998, p. 36; Michael Bernstein, "Window Shopping," *Executive Edge*, August/September 1999, p. 62; and Michael Krantz, "The Next E-volution," *Time*, July 12, 1999, p. 47.

Careers in Marketing Appendix

1. *Marketing News,* November 22, 1999, pp. 1, 11-12.

2. "Education and Pay," *USA Today,* January 6, 2000, p. Al.

3. Stephanie Armour, "Job Seeking on the Net Gets More Traditional," *USA Today,* January 14, 1999, p. B1.

4. Margaret Riley Dikel, "12 Tips for Rewriting Your Résumé," *Fast Company,* August 1999, pp. 194-195.

5. Margie Davis, "Post It!" *Business Start-Ups,* December 1999, pp. 100-101.

6. Jerry Useem, "Read This Before You Put a Résumé Online," *Fortune,* May 24, 1999, pp. 290-291.

GLOSSARY

SOLUTIONS FOR THE ACHIEVEMENT CHECK SUMMARY SECTIONS

Chapter 1

Objective 1.1
1. T
2. T
3. T

Objective 1.2
1. F
2. B
3. F

Objective 1.3
1. T
2. T
3. F

Objective 1.4
1. F
2. F
3. E

Objective 1.5
1. B
2. F
3. F

Objective 1.6
1. T
2. F
3. F

Objective 1.7
1. F
2. D
3. T

Objective 1.8
1. F
2. F

Chapter 2

Objective 2.1
1. B
2. T
3. F

Objective 2.2
1. B
2. T
3. T

Objective 2.3
1. F
2. T
3. F

Objective 2.4
1. F
2. F
3. T

Objective 2.5
1. F
2. T
3. T

Objective 2.6
1. T
2. T
3. C

Objective 2.7
1. T
2. T
3. F

Objective 2.8
1. F
2. T
3. T

Chapter 3

Objective 3.1
1. T
2. F
3. F

Objective 3.2
1. T
2. T
3. C

Objective 3.3
1. F
2. F
3. C

Objective 3.4
1. T
2. D
3. F

Objective 3.5
1. T
2. T
3. C

Objective 3.6
1. F
2. C
3. T

Objective 3.7
1. F
2. T
3. F

Chapter 4

Objective 4.1
1. F
2. T
3. C

Objective 4.2
1. T
2. F
3. T

Objective 4.3
1. T
2. T
3. F

Objective 4.4
1. F
2. F
3. T

Objective 4.5
1. F
2. B
3. T

Objective 4.6
1. F
2. F
3. T

Objective 4.7
1. T
2. D
3. T

Objective 4.8
1. T
2. T
3. T

Chapter 5

Objective 5.1
1. F
2. C
3. F

Objective 5.2
1. F
2. T
3. T

Objective 5.3
1. T
2. D
3. T

Objective 5.4
1. B
2. F
3. F

Objective 5.5
1. T
2. F
3. T
4. T

Objective 5.6
1. F
2. T

Objective 5.7
1. F
2. T
3. C

Objective 5.8
1. T
2. F
3. F

Objective 5.9
1. T
2. F
3. T

Objective 5.10
1. T
2. T
3. F

Objective 5.11
1. T
2. T
3. T

Chapter 6

Objective 6.1
1. B
2. T
3. F

Objective 6.2
1. F
2. T
3. F

Objective 6.3
1. D
2. B
3. T

Objective 6.4
1. F
2. C
3. T

Objective 6.5
1. T
2. B
3. T

Objective 6.6
1. A
2. T
3. F

Objective 6.7
1. T
2. T
3. F

Chapter 7

Objective 7.1
1. F
2. B
3. F

Objective 7.2
1. T
2. B
3. T
4. T

Objective 7.3
1. T
2. T
3. F

Objective 7.4
1. F
2. A
3. T

Objective 7.5
1. T
2. T
3. C

Objective 7.6
1. F
2. T
3. T

Objective 7.7
1. A
2. T
3. T

Chapter 8

Objective 8.1
1. T
2. F
3. T
4. B

Objective 8.2
1. F
2. T
3. F

Objective 8.3
1. T
2. T
3. F

Objective 8.4
1. T
2. B
3. B
4. T
5. T
Objective 8.5
1. F
2. T
3. F
Objective 8.6
1. T
2. A
3. A
4. B
Objective 8.7
1. B
2. C
3. F

Chapter 9
Objective 9.1
1. T
2. T
Objective 9.2
1. T
2. F
3. F
4. B
Objective 9.3
1. T
2. A
3. T
4. B
Objective 9.4
1. C
2. F
Objective 9.5
1. F
2. T
3. B
4. D
Objective 9.6
1. T
2. B
3. T

Chapter 10
Objective 10.1
1. F
2. F
3. F
Objective 10.2
1. T
2. F
3. C

Objective 10.3
1. F
2. D
3. F
Objective 10.4
1. F
2. T
Objective 10.5
1. F
2. F
3. F
Objective 10.6
1. T
2. F
3. F
Objective 10.7
1. F
2. B
3. T
Objective 10.8
1. F
2. F
3. F
Objective 10.9
1. T
2. T
3. D

Chapter 11
Objective 11.1
1. F
2. T
3. T
4. T
Objective 11.2
1. T
2. F
3. F
Objective 11.3
1. A
2. F
3. F
4. B
Objective 11.4
1. F
2. F
3. T
Objective 11.5
1. T
2. T
3. A
4. T
Objective 11.6
1. F
2. F
3. T
4. T

Objective 11.7
1. F
2. F
3. T
Objective 11.8
1. A
2. F
3. T
4. F
5. T
Objective 11.9
1. F
2. F
3. T
4. T
5. T
Objective 11.10
1. T
2. F
3. C

Chapter 12
Objective 12.1
1. T
2. C
3. F
Objective 12.2
1. F
2. B
3. F
Objective 12.3
1. B
2. T
3. T
Objective 12.4
1. T
2. B
3. B
4. T
5. T
Objective 12.5
1. B
2. C
3. T
4. F
Objective 12.6
1. F
2. T
3. T
Objective 12.7
1. F
2. A
3. F
4. T
5. F
Objective 12.8
1. T
2. T
3. F

Objective 12.9
1. F
2. T
3. F

Chapter 13
Objective 13.1
1. B
2. T
3. T
4. F
Objective 13.2
1. C
2. A
3. A
Objective 13.3
1. B
2. A
3. B
4. T
Objective 13.4
1. F
2. T
3. A
4. B
5. B
Objective 13.5
1. F
2. T
3. T
4. F
Objective 13.6
1. F
2. F
3. T
Objective 13.7
1. T
2. T
3. T
Objective 13.8
1. B
2. F
3. F
4. T
Objective 13.9
1. B
2. B

Chapter 14
Objective 14.1
1. T
2. T
3. B
Objective 14.2
1. A
2. T
3. B

Objective 14.3
1. F
2. F
3. F
Objective 14.4
1. F
2. B
3. D
Objective 14.5
1. B
2. F
3. T
Objective 14.6
1. B
2. T

Chapter 15
Objective 15.1
1. F
2. F
3. T
Objective 15.2
1. T
2. D
3. T
Objective 15.3
1. T
2. C
3. F
Objective 15.4
1. F
2. T
3. B
Objective 15.5
1. T
2. T
3. D
Objective 15.6
1. F
2. F
3. T
Objective 15.7
1. F
2. T
3. F
Objective 15.8
1. C
2. F
3. F
Objective 15.9
1. F
2. T
3. F

Chapter 16
Objective 16.1
1. F
2. F
3. T

Objective 16.2
1. T
2. F
3. T
Objective 16.3
1. T
2. T
3. B
Objective 16.4
1. F
2. T
3. F
Objective 16.5
1. F
2. T
3. T
Objective 16.6
1. F
2. T
3. F
Objective 16.7
1. F
2. F
3. T
Objective 16.8
1. T
2. F
3. F

Objective 16.9
1. T
2. T
3. F
Chapter 17
Objective 17.1
1. F
2. T
3. F
Objective 17.2
1. T
2. F
3. T
Objective 17.3
1. T
2. F
3. F
4. T
Objective 17.4
1. F
2. F
3. B
4. B
Objective 17.5
1. B
2. F
3. T
4. F
5. T

Objective 17.6
1. F
2. T
3. D
Objective 17.7
1. B
2. A
3. T
Objective 17.8
1. T
2. F
3. T
Chapter 18
Objective 18.1
1. T
2. F
3. F
Objective 18.2
1. D
2. C
Objective 18.3
1. F
2. T
3. T
Objective 18.4
1. F
2. T
3. F

Objective 18.5
1. T
2. F
3. T
Objective 18.6
1. B
2. D
Objective 18.7
1. F
2. T
3. T
Objective 18.8
1. T
2. T
3. T
4. T
Chapter 19
Objective 19.1
1. F
2. T
3. T
Objective 19.2
1. C
2. C
3. B

Objective 19.3
1. T
2. F
3. T
Objective 19.4
1. T
2. F
3. T
Objective 19.5
1. B
2. D
Objective 19.6
1. T
2. F
3. T
Objective 19.7
1. F
2. T
3. T
Objective 19.8
1. F
2. F
3. T

CREDITS

NAME AND COMPANY INDEX

SUBJECT INDEX

INTERNATIONAL INDEX

There is only one boss: the customer. And he can fire everybody in the company, from the chairman on down, simply by spending his money somewhere else.
—Sam Walton (1918–1992), Founder, Wal-Mart Stores

Don't sell the steak; sell the sizzle!
—Elmer Wheeler (1903–1968), American Advertiser

Before you build a better mousetrap, it helps to know if there are any mice out there.
—Mortimer B. Zuckerman (1937–), Chairman and Editor-in-Chief, *U.S. News & World Report*

Anything that won't sell, I don't want to invent.
Its sale is proof of utility and utility is success.
—Thomas A. Edison, American Inventor

The dollar bills the customer gets from the tellers in four banks are the same.
What is different are the tellers.
—Stanley Marcus, Chairman Emeritus, Neiman Marcus Department Stores

Kodak sells film, but they don't advertise film. They advertise memories.
—Theodore Leavitt (1925–), American Educator

The magic formula that successful businesses have discovered is to treat customers like guests and employees like people.
—Thomas J. Peters (1942–), American Business Writer

Free is good—but read the fine print.
—Anonymous

Marketing is the delivery of a standard of living.
—Paul Mazur, American Investment Banker

You'll never fail until you quit trying.
—Florence Griffith-Joyner, U.S. Olympic Gold Medalist

Segment. Concentrate. Dominate.
—Don Tyson, Chairman, Tyson Foods